PSYCHOLOGY

The Adaptive Mind

PSYCHOLOGY
The Adaptive Mind

James S. Nairne
Purdue University

Brooks/Cole Publishing Company

 An International Thomson Publishing Company

Pacific Grove • Albany • Belmont • Bonn • Boston • Cincinnati • Detroit • Johannesburg • London • Madrid
Melbourne • Mexico City • New York • Paris • Singapore • Tokyo • Toronto • Washington

Sponsoring Editor: *Jim Brace-Thompson*
Project Development Editor: *Joanne Tinsley*
Marketing Team: *Margaret Parks, Gay Meixel*
Marketing Representative: *Jay Honeck*
Editorial Assistant: *Terry Thomas*
Production Editor: *Marjorie Z. Sanders*
Design Coordinator: *E. Kelly Shoemaker*
Manuscript Editor: *Jackie Estrada*
Permissions Editor: *May Clark*
Art Developmental Editor: *Audre Newman*

Interior Design: *Jeanne Calabrese Design*
Interior Illustration: *Precision Graphics*
Cover Design: *E. Kelly Shoemaker*
Cover Photo: *Susan G. Drinker/The Stock Market*
Art Coordinator: *Kathy Joneson*
Photo Coordinator: *Larry Molmud*
Photo Editor: *Meyers Photo-Art*
Indexer: *James Minkin*
Typesetting: *GTS Graphics*
Printing and Binding: *Von Hoffman Press, Inc.*

For more information, contact:

BROOKS/COLE PUBLISHING COMPANY
511 Forest Lodge Road
Pacific Grove, CA 93950
USA

International Thomson Publishing Europe
Berkshire House 168-173
High Holborn
London WC1V 7AA
England

Thomas Nelson Australia
102 Dodds Street
South Melbourne, 3205
Victoria, Australia

Nelson Canada
1120 Birchmount Road
Scarborough, Ontario
Canada M1K 5G4

International Thomson Editores
Seneca 53, Col. Polanco
México, D. F., México
C. P. 11560

International Thomson Publishing GmbH
Königswinterer Strasse 418
53227 Bonn
Germany

International Thomson Publishing Asia
221 Henderson Road
#05-10 Henderson Building
Singapore 0315

International Thomson Publishing Japan
Hirakawacho Kyowa Building, 3F
2-2-1 Hirakawacho
Chiyoda-ku, Tokyo 102
Japan

Printed in the United States of America

10   9   8   7   6   5   4   3   2   1

Library of Congress Cataloging-in-Publication Data

Nairne, James S., [date]
     Psychology : the adaptive mind / James S. Nairne.
         p.   cm.
     Includes bibliographical references and index.
     ISBN 0-534-20682-4
     1. Psychology.   I. Title
BF121.N27 1996   96-28954
150—dc20   CIP

BARBIE® is a registered trademark of Mattell, Inc. PROZAC® is a registered trademark of Eli Lilly and Company. VALIUM® is a registered trademark owned by Roche Products Inc. XANAX® is a registered trademark owned by the Upjohn Company. Credits continue on page 661.

To Virginia and Stephanie

About the Author

James S. Nairne is currently Professor of Psychological Sciences at Purdue University in West Lafayette, Indiana. He received his undergraduate training at the University of California, Berkeley (B.A., 1977) and his Ph.D. in psychology from Yale University (1981). As a graduate student, he was recruited to provide demonstrations for all sections of introductory psychology at Yale, and he has been an enthusiastic teacher of introductory psychology ever since. He is an active researcher in cognitive psychology, specializing in human memory, and he's published dozens of articles in professional journals. He is currently a consulting editor for the journal *Memory,* and he sits on the editorial boards of *Journal of Memory and Language, Memory & Cognition,* and *Journal of Experimental Psychology: Learning, Memory, and Cognition.*

Brief Contents

Contents

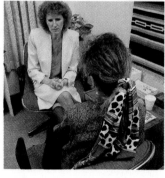

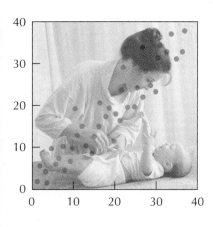

CHAPTER 3   Biological Processes   64

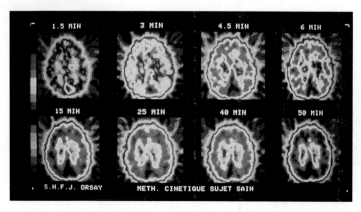

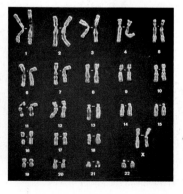

CHAPTER 4   Human Development   110

CHAPTER 5

Sensation and Perception   156

CHAPTER 6   Consciousness   202

CHAPTER 7   # Learning from Experience   238

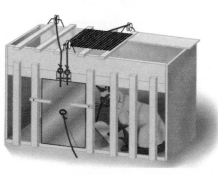

CHAPTER 8   Remembering and Forgetting   276

CHAPTER 9   # Thought and Language   314

CHAPTER 10 Intelligence 350

Rich soil

CHAPTER 11   Motivation and Emotion   382

CHAPTER 12   Personality   420

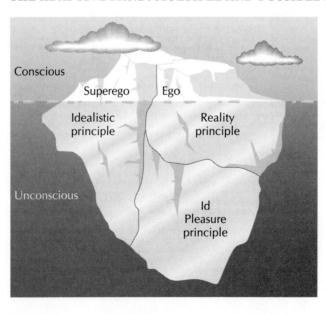

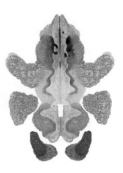

CHAPTER 13 Social Psychology 454

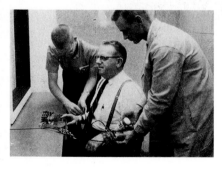

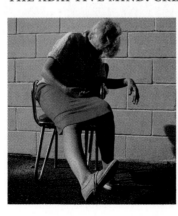

CHAPTER 15

Therapy   524

CHAPTER 16

Stress and Health   558

Preface

One of the first hurdles instructors face in an introductory psychology course is convincing students that psychology is more than just the study of abnormal behavior. Introduce yourself as a psychologist, or even as a student of psychology, and you're likely to get a response such as: "Don't analyze me," or, "I better watch what I say around you." It takes time for students to realize that psychology, as a subject matter, is much more than just the study of abnormal behavior—it's a vast, interdisciplinary field of study covering all aspects of normal and abnormal behavior and mind.

But our problem as instructors is more serious than just convincing people about psychology's breadth and scope. Even after exposure to the topics and subject matter of the course, students often remain mystified by the coverage they find. Most who open the learning chapter, for example, find a collection of topics that seems to bear little, if any, resemblance to the normal, everyday sense of what it means to "learn." The students find extended discussions of drooling dogs and key-pecking pigeons, but they see little discussion of the critical link between the topics of classical and instrumental conditioning and the kinds of learning problems that people face on a daily basis.

In *Psychology: The Adaptive Mind,* I've tried to write a textbook that emphasizes function first. Each of the chapters in the book is organized around a set of problems—either adaptive problems or conceptual/practical problems—that are designed to (1) focus the discussion on the relevance and function of the material, and (2) promote a theme, called "the adaptive mind," proposing that we act and think for adaptive reasons. For example, classical conditioning is introduced as a solution to an adaptive problem: How do people learn about the signaling properties of events? It does not simply occur in the learning chapter, for its own sake, as yet another "topic" to be studied and memorized. Electrochemical transmission in the nervous system is introduced as a "solution" to the adaptive problem of communicating internally; it's not simply one of the many topics discussed in the biology chapter. The experimental method is introduced as a "solution" to the conceptual problem of determining the causes of behavior; it's not just a psychological method that needs to be learned. Notice the shift in emphasis—rather than topic followed, perhaps, by function, it's function followed by topic.

I believe the adaptive problem-solving approach offers a number of advantages. First, the reader is given a reason for following the discussion. A paradigm such as classical conditioning was developed to provide insight into how people learn to associate things that often occur outside of their control. It is not simply the way that a Russian named Pavlov studied drooling in dogs. Second, because the discussion revolves around an adaptive or conceptual problem, the discussion naturally promotes critical thinking. Rather than just learning about conditioning, the reader is required to make the connection between that particular procedure and the adaptive problem of learning to associate events. Third, I believe the organizational structure provides an effective aid for study and chapter outlining. The student can group the various topics under the rubric of meaningful questions, as solutions to easily understood concrete problems. Fourth, and perhaps most important, the adaptive problem-solving framework provides the structure through which a common theme of understanding can be promoted across chapters. The discipline of psychology gains cohesion when behavior is viewed as the product of adaptive systems. The reader learns that behavior, as well as the methods of psychologists, are reactions to problems faced. Emphasizing adaptiveness helps to loosen people's egocentric view of the world and to increase their sensitivity to why behavior, both within and across species, is so diverse. Students need to appreciate individuality and diversity, but not without understanding why these differences are natural consequences of behaving organisms.

For an overview of how the adaptive problem-solving approach is actually implemented in the text, as well as the specific pedagogical features that the textbook employs, I invite you to take a look at "A Guide Through the Book," which follows the preface.

Teaching and Learning Aids for This Book

A number of useful ancillaries accompany the text. For more information about these materials, please contact your local representative. The complete teaching and learning package consists of:

Instructor's Resource Guide Charles R. Grah, Austin Peay State University, and Greg L. Robinson-Riegler, University of St. Thomas, have prepared a thorough and creative Instructor's Resource Guide. This extensive volume offers a wide array of teaching resources including demonstrations, lecture materials, and a critical thinking journal. Special emphasis is placed on issues of diversity, empirical research, and the integration of material across chapters. Available in both printed and electronic versions.

The Integrator: A Multimedia Introduction to Psychology CD-ROM Authored by Arthur J. and Wendy Kohn and a developmental team at Pacific University, this CD-ROM for Macintosh and Windows offers dramatic new ways for students to learn and instructors to teach. Students can reinforce their learning or explore independently by calling up interactive experiments, animations, homework assignments, video clips, transparencies, audio clips, dynamic images, demonstrations, study pages, and interactive surveys. All materials are directly keyed to the textbook. The CD-ROM also includes the "Multimedia Lecture-Maker," a program that allows professors to quickly and easily present professional multimedia lectures. This CD-ROM is available free to faculty on adoption of the text. It is available for sale to students and on a site-license basis to departments. For U.S. customers only, the book and *The Integrator* CD-ROM can be bundled together for a discount (ISBN: 0-534-85902-X).

Test Items Written by Shirley Hensch of the University of Wisconsin, Marshfield/Wood County, this text bank contains approximately 3,700 items, including multiple-choice questions, short-answer completion questions, and essay questions. Each multiple-choice and short-answer question is categorized on the basis of the type of knowledge that is being assessed: factual, definitional (text and applied), application (text and extended), and conceptual. Each question is keyed to a main concept found in the text and includes a page reference. We also offer a computerized testing system for DOS, Macintosh, and Windows.

Transparencies Two extensive sets of full-color transparencies are available free on adoption: approximately 125 text-specific transparencies selected by me, and a set of 95 introductory psychology transparencies.

Study Guide Janet D. Proctor of Purdue University prepared this extensive study guide, which offers a mixture of matching exercises, fill-in-the-blank items, and free-response questions, as well as a review of key ideas, and a self-test for each chapter of the text. For U.S. customers, the text and study guide can be bundled together for a discount (ISBN: 0-534-85911-9). The Study Guide is also available electronically for Windows and Macintosh. The electronic study guide provides questions and answers in an interactive format, reinforcing students for correct answers and providing helpful cues for incorrect answers.

Psychology/Careers for the Twenty-First Century Booklet This 30-page pamphlet, produced by the American Psychological Association, is exclusive to APA and Brooks/Cole. It describes the field of psychology, as well as the "how to" for career preparation in the many areas of psychology. Career options and resources are also discussed. This 30-page pamphlet can be shrink-wrapped with the text at no additional cost.

Psychology/Careers for the Twenty-First Century Video Brooks/Cole has an exclusive agreement to offer this dynamic, 13-minute video produced by the APA free to adopters of Brooks/Cole's introductory psychology texts. The video gives the viewer an overview of the emerging growth opportunities in the field of psychology and advice about how to choose a career path.

Brooks/Cole Film and Video Library for Introductory Psychology Adopters can choose from the video options below, based on size of adoption. Please contact Brooks/Cole Marketing for information (800-354-0092).

- **The Pennsylvania State University's PCR: Films and Videos in the Behavioral Sciences:** Adopters receive a set of three complimentary film/video rental vouchers and can choose from the world's largest collection of films and videos on human behavior.
- **"The Brain"** videotapes: 30 video modules and a faculty guide prepared by Frank Vattano of Colorado State University in conjunction with the Annenberg/CPB Project Video Collection.
- **"The Mind"** videotapes: 38 brief video modules offering examples of important concepts in introductory psychology, and a faculty guide prepared by Frank Vattano of Colorado State University in cooperation with WNET, New York.
- **"Seeing Beyond the Obvious: Understanding Perception in Everyday and Novel Environments":** A videotape that provides an introduction to basic concepts of visual perception, created by the NASA Ames Research Center in conjunction with the University of Virginia.
- **"Discovering Psychology"** videotapes: A series of 26 programs from the Annenberg/CPB Collection.
- **"Animations Plus!"** videodisk: Produced by Brooks/Cole, this videodisk includes a collection of animations with still-frame review and quizzing, diagrams, and video segments. The videodisk comes with an Instructor's Guide including bar codes for easy reference.

Complimentary Telephone Testing or "Tele-Testing" ITP Technology Services will construct a test for any instructors who have adopted a Brooks/Cole ITP text. Technology Services requests a minimum of 48 hours notice to construct these complimentary tests. For tele-testing call (800) 327-0325.

Psych Lab I and II Created by Roger Harnish of the Rochester Institute of Technology, these interactive software programs provide psychology demonstrations and simulations and are available for DOS and Macintosh.

Acknowledgments

Writing this textbook has been a unique experience for me. College professors live relatively solitary professional lives; we may interact daily with students and colleagues, but we're not usually part of a "team," especially one of the size required to produce a textbook such as *Psychology: The Adaptive Mind*. My publisher, Brooks/Cole, deserves enormous credit for organizing the team and for helping me to carry out my original plan for the book. Particular thanks are due to Bill Roberts, the president of Brooks/Cole, and to the editor-in-chief, Craig Barth, for demanding that the book have a "soul," as well as a distinctive author voice. I am also very grateful to Ken King and Jay Honeck for convincing me to write the book, and for helping to bring me to Brooks/Cole.

I've had the opportunity to work with a number of very talented individuals during the writing and production of this book. My sponsoring editor, Jim Brace-Thompson, was my main contact at Brooks/Cole; he did a spectacular job of shepherding the project from initial signing to final publication. Jim has great instincts and he influenced me in more ways than he probably realizes. My developmental editor, Joanne Tinsley, read every word of the manuscript, multiple times, and produced an endless stream of perceptive comments. My art developmental editor, Audre Newman, was the driving force behind the book's unique illustration program. The general "look" of the book was elegantly designed by Jeanne Calabrese and Kelly Shoemaker. Each of these individuals contributed greatly to the final product, and I thank them all.

On the production side, the captain of the team was Marjorie Sanders, a consummate professional, who held together the tight production schedule. Kathy Joneson coordinated the complicated illustration program and worked hard, along with Precision Graphics, to make certain that the final renderings fit the vision. The unique photographs in the text were researched and compiled by photo editor Joan Meyers Murie, based on rather sketchy input from me; Joan and I had a great time choosing every single shot. I'd also like to thank manuscript editor Jackie Estrada for improving the prose, proofreaders Chad Colburn and Louise Rixey for being meticulous, and indexer James Minkin for his fine work. Gay Meixel managed the marketing campaign with creativity, Faith Stoddard coordinated the supplements program, May Clark handled the permissions, and Margaret Parks wrote much of the glowing advertising copy.

Of course, I could never have written this book without the help and guidance I received from the outside reviewers listed on page XXIX. I hope the reviewers can see their mark on the book, because it's substantial. My colleagues at Purdue also played an important role in the final product. Many suffered through questions about one research area or another, especially Peter Urcuioli. Graduate student Fabian Novello helped me a great deal on many of the chapters and illustrations, and Alicia Knoedler, Georgia Panayiotou, and Esther Strahan read and commented on individual chapters; undergraduates Jennifer Bataille, Lauren Baker, and especially Kate Gapinski read portions of the manuscript and also provided valuable feedback. Julie Smith helped me in innumerable ways, including assistance with the references and glossary.

Finally, I want to thank my family. Everyone, including my parents, experienced the writing of this book in one way or another—and these experiences were not all pleasant. My wife, Virginia, and daughter, Stephanie, "lived" the book as I did, and I dedicate it to them with love.

James S. Nairne

Reviewers

Karin Ahlm
DePauw University

Mary Ann Baenninger
Trenton State College

Daniel R. Bellack
Trident Technical College

Ira Bernstein
University of Texas at Arlington

Kenneth Bordens
Indiana Univeristy–Purdue University at Fort Wayne

Nancy S. Breland
Trenton State College

James Calhoun
University of Georgia

D. Bruce Carter
Syracuse University

John L. Caruso
University of Massachusetts–Dartmouth

Regina Conti
Colgate University

Eric Cooley
Western Oregon State College

Randall Engle
University of South Carolina, Columbia

Roy Fontaine
Pennsylvania College of Technology

Nelson L. Freedman
Queen's University, Ontario, Canada

Richard Froman
John Brown University

Grace Galliano
Kennesaw State College

Eugene R. Gilden
Linfield College

Perilou Goddard
Northern Kentucky University

Tim Goldsmith
University of New Mexico

Joel Grace
Mansfield University

Charles R. Grah
Austin Peay State University

Terry R. Greene
Franklin & Marshall College

George Hampton
University of Houston–Downtown

Linda Heath
Loyola University of Chicago

Phyllis Heath
Central Michigan University

Shirley-Anne Hensch
University of Wisconsin Center–Marshfield/ Wood County

Michael Hillard
University of New Mexico

Vivian Jenkins
University of Southern Indiana

James J. Johnson
Illinois State University

Timothy Johnston
University of North Carolina at Greensboro

John Jung
California State University–Long Beach

Salvatore Macias III
University of South Carolina at Sumter

Carolyn Mangelsdorf
University of Washington

Edmund Martin
Georgia Tech

Michael McCall
Ithaca College

Laurence Miller
Western Washington University

Carol Pandey
Pierce College

Blaine F. Peden
University of Wisconsin–Eau Claire

William J. Pizzi
Northeastern Illinois University

Anne D. Simons
University of Oregon

Steven M. Smith
Texas A & M University

John E. Sparrow
University of New Hampshire–Manchester

Irene Staik
University of Montevallo

Robert Thompson
Shoreline Community College

Diane Tucker
University of Alabama–Birmingham

John Uhlarik
Kansas State University

Lori Van Wallendael
University of North Carolina at Charlotte

Fred Whitford
Montana State University

Carsh Wilturner
Green River Community College

Deborah Winters
New Mexico State University

We offer special thanks to the following professors and their students for conducting student reviews of the manuscript.

F. Samuel Bauer
Christopher Newport University

Gabriel P. Frommer
Indiana University

R. Martin Lobdell
Pierce College

Robert M. Stern
The Pennsylvania State University

The students of
Dominican College

A Guide Through the Book

What do you hope your students will remember about their introductory psychology course? If you are like most professors who responded to this question, you don't expect them to be able to remember dozens of specific studies or hundreds of isolated facts. Rather, you want to give them a new way of understanding and analyzing behavior that will be with them for the rest of their lives. Students frequently bring to the course questions about psychology, but they may quickly become so bogged down in memorizing details that they lose sight of the big picture.

To write a text that would answer students' questions in a meaningful way and to show them how psychological concepts can affect their everyday interactions, Purdue psychology professor James S. Nairne has conceived a novel way of presenting the traditional topics of the course. The result is the textbook you hold in your hands, **Psychology: The Adaptive Mind**, a book that takes an innovative "adaptive problem-solving" approach.

In this approach, Nairne "reframes" the subject matter of psychology by emphasizing how particular behaviors, cognitive processes, and emotions help people solve important adaptive problems—not just survival problems, but everyday problems. For example, he introduces the principles of classical conditioning as "solutions" to the problem of how people learn about signals in their environment and introduces neural transmission as a "solution" to the problems associated with communicating internally.

The response from the academic community to this new approach has been overwhelmingly positive. Many find the Nairne text the "book they've been waiting for!"

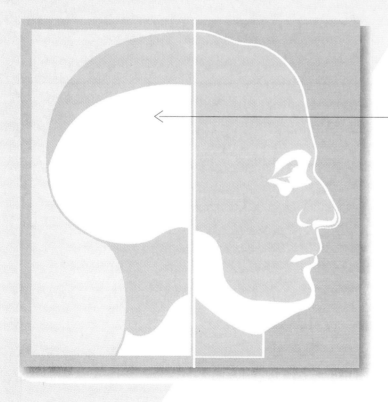

The pages that follow demonstrate how Jim Nairne's "adaptive problem-solving" approach provides a distinctive and cohesive viewpoint that effectively organizes and integrates the material, engages readers with the "why" of the study of each topic in psychology, and makes psychology fascinating and easy to learn.

Each chapter is organized around a set of adaptive, conceptual, or practical problems.

Nairne's adaptive mind framework is designed to help readers focus on the challenges or specific demands that we must resolve—either as humans attempting to survive or as psychologists seeking to understand behavior and mind. In every chapter, Nairne demonstrates how people use their minds to deal effectively with everyday challenges, adjusting actions to meet the needs of new conditions they encounter.

"What makes this book unique, and, in my opinion, preferable, is the emphasis on what the author refers to as 'the adaptive mind.' . . . This integrates the disparate areas in a way not commonly found in most textbooks. Connections are made between material presented in one chapter and the new information presented later. Students will find the prose interpretable, while the professor will likely find the kind of enthusiasm and clarity of writing that brought them to this field in the first place. My reaction to this work might best be summarized as 'This is what excited me about psychology so many years ago.'"

Michael McCall—*Ithaca College*

Adaptive problems

The table at right provides examples of how people use these adaptive "tools" to help solve the various obstacles and survival problems they face.

Conceptual and practical problems

In many chapters, Nairne focuses on conceptual and practical problems that psychologists tackle either to advance basic knowledge or to help troubled individuals in need. The lower half of the table provides examples of the types of conceptual and practical problems solved in the text.

TABLE 1.1
Examples of Adaptive, Conceptual, and Practical Problems

	Chapter	Problem to Be Solved	Example	Solution "Tools"
Adaptive problems	3	Communicating internally	A bicyclist weaves suddenly into the path of your car.	Electrochemical transmission in the nervous system
	7	Learning what events signal	You hear a rattling tail on a mountain path.	Interevent associations acquired through classical conditioning
	8	Remembering over the short term	You try to remember a telephone number as you cross the room.	Rehearsal in short-term memory
	13	Interpreting the behavior of others	A shadowy figure emerges suddenly from an alleyway.	Knowledge-based social "schemas" used to predict outcomes
Conceptual and practical problems	2	Determining the causes of behavior	Sally watches a violent TV program and becomes aggressive.	Experimental research
	10	Conceptualizing intelligence	Andy is excellent at fixing mechanical devices but is terrible at reading and math.	Psychometric tests designed to measure the mind
	14	Defining abnormality	Lucinda hears "voices" and thinks she's immortal.	*Diagnostic and Statistical Manual of Mental Disorders*
	15	Treating the mind	Ralph is mired in the depths of depression.	Psychoactive drug therapy or "insight" therapy

Note: The solution tools shown in the far-right column will be discussed in detail in the relevant chapters.

strike of a venomous snake—but what basic learning processes enabled you to acquire such pivotal information?

In other chapters, we'll focus on conceptual and practical problems that psychologists seek to solve, either to advance basic knowledge or to help troubled individuals in need. For example, what are the best tactics and strategies to use to under-

An easy-to-follow chapter structure

In these excerpts from Chapter 7, "Learning from Experience," notice how the author leads students through the problems to be solved. Every chapter follows a standard organization, making the book especially effective as a study tool. Nairne begins each chapter with an outline, an intriguing quote, and a narrative introduction, then provides a "Previewing the Adaptive Problems" section. Nairne then works through the problem "solutions" in the main body of the chapter and concludes with "Solving the Problems: A Summary." A "Terms to Remember" list with definitions appears at the end of each chapter.

"The problem-solving approach gives this text a unique presentation. The author accomplished what he set out to do—he provided an overview of the topic with thought-provoking questions. He then answered those questions in the chapters. This was SQ3R and critical thinking in a creative new approach."

Daniel Bellack—*Trident Technical College*

"I like the way each chapter opens with an extended discussion of key issues within a given area of psychology and closes with a focused discussion of how those issues have been addressed. . . . The short critical thinking exercises are integrated well with the material that is presented within each chapter and they do not appear to be 'tacked on' the way they are in some other introductory books. The author takes the time to develop an idea completely, and to show specific links between previous and subsequent material. This helps to convey the connectedness that exists within the field of psychology. The examples are well chosen and contemporary and should go a long way in helping the students relate the theoretical concepts to everyday situations they will encounter."

Shirley-Anne Hensch—*University of Wisconsin Center*

PREVIEWING THE ADAPTIVE PROBLEMS

Learning About Events: Noticing and Ignoring
Habituation and Sensitization
Short- and Long-Term Effects

Learning What Events Signal: Classical Conditioning
Acquiring the CS-US Connection
Conditioned Responding: Why Does It Develop?
Second-Order Conditioning
Stimulus Generalization
Stimulus Discrimination
Extinction: When CSs No Longer Signal the US
Conditioned Inhibition: Signaling the Absence of the US

Learning About the Consequences of Behavior: Instrumental Conditioning
The Law of Effect
The Discriminative Stimulus: Knowing When to Respond
The Nature of Reinforcement
Schedules of Reinforcement
Acquisition: Shaping the Desired Behavior
Punishment: Lowering the Likelihood of a Response

Learning from Others: Observational Learning
Modeling: Learning Through Example
Practical Considerations

SOLVING THE PROBLEMS: A SUMMARY

THE ADAPTIVE MIND:
ON THE GENERALITY OF LEARNING PRINCIPLES

Chapter opening outlines help students organize material and are an excellent way for them to make sure they've understood the chapter's "big picture."

A text that engages students first with the "why" of the topic

Nairne opens with a **quote** that immediately invites students to think about the material to come. Here, Mark Twain's humorous observation foreshadows future discussion of instrumental conditioning.

Each chapter's **narrative introduction** gives students a context for reading and understanding the topics that follow. In every chapter, Nairne refers back to material previously covered in other chapters to help students understand psychology as more than just a series of unrelated topics.

Important terms appear in boldface and are defined as they are presented. These terms also appear in the end-of-chapter "Terms to Remember" section.

Critical Thinking Exercises in the margins challenge students to think beyond the obvious and apply what they're learning.

We should be careful to get out of an experience only the wisdom that is in it—and stop there; lest we be like the cat that sits down on a hot stove-lid. She will never sit down on a hot stove-lid again—and that is well; but also she will never sit down on a cold one anymore.

Mark Twain

The way people think and act throughout their lives is influenced continuously by interactions with the environment. We may arrive into the world with a certain genetic potential, but experience plays a pivotal role in shaping how that potential is realized. The body (*nature*) and experiences (*nurture*) act in concert, and it can be difficult to isolate the influences of each when observing behavior. In this chapter, our discussion focuses primarily on the nurture part of the nature-nurture equation. Our topic is the psychological process that accounts for much of the remarkable flexibility of the adaptive mind—the ability to *learn from experience*.

What is learning? Most people think of learning as simply the process of acquiring knowledge. In essence, that's correct. But as we discussed in Chapter 2, psychologists like to define concepts in terms of how those concepts can be directly measured. At this point, it's not possible to measure the "knowledge" in people's heads directly or to track all the neural mechanisms involved in knowledge acquisition. For this reason, **learning** is typically defined as a relatively permanent change in behavior, or potential to respond, that results from experience. Notice that the emphasis is on changes in *behavior*. Unlike acquired knowledge, behavior is something we can directly observe. We make inferences about learning and the acquisition of knowledge by observing behavior and noting how behavior changes over time.

Of course, behavior can sometimes change as a result of experience in ways that we would not want to classify as learning. For example, your behavior might change because you forgot something, such as a telephone number you've recently dialed. Or suppose your neighbor Al loses an arm in an industrial accident. Getting injured imposes physical limitations on the body that will certainly change his behavior in many ways. But not all of these changes will result from the actions of a flexible learning process. The concept of learning is reserved for those cases where behavior changes in a way that reflects the experience—people change their behavior, either as a reaction to the experience or as a result of practice, to maximize adaptive behavior in the future.

One final point to note in the definition of learning is the phrase *potential to respond*. Sometimes people acquire knowledge but don't change their behavior in any way that reflects what they've learned. For example, you have now "learned" the textbook definition of *learning*. But is your behavior going to change? Not likely, unless you need to retrieve the information during an examination. You may also have learned a great deal about the location of fast-food restaurants in your community. But your behavior isn't going to reflect that knowledge unless you're hungry. Once again, it's important to keep in mind the relationship between learning and *performance*—to demonstrate that learning has occurred, it needs to be reflected in actual behavior.

Historically, researchers have studied learning in relatively simple kinds of situations, often with animal subjects such as rats, pigeons, or sea snails. The goal has been to uncover basic principles, or "laws of learning," that can be applied widely across species and situations. There are two principal reasons why animals are used as research subjects. First, more experimental control is available in animal studies, so experimenters are better able to identify the factors that actually cause learning to occur. Second, it's assumed that the learning process in animals is simpler and therefore easier to understand. Overall, this research strategy has

 Do you think it's ethical to use animals in basic research? Remember, we discussed this issue in some detail in Chapter 2.

The field of psychology presented in the context of "adaptive problem solving"

"Perhaps the greatest strength is the author's ability to present the field of psychology in the context of a distinctive and cohesive viewpoint. . . . The very choice of three or four 'problems to be solved' gives each chapter a manageable feel that should make the reader's job easier."

John L. Caruso—*University of Massachusetts–Dartmouth*

▶ PREVIEWING THE ADAPTIVE PROBLEMS

Regardless of how much animals and humans might differ, it's fair to assume that all species face common learning problems. For example, all species, sea snails as well as people, need to learn about the consequences of their behavior. It's also useful to learn about the signaling properties of stimuli, or events, in the environment. When does one event predict that a second event is likely to follow? In this chapter, we'll consider four general adaptive learning problems: How do people learn about events? How do they learn about the signaling properties of events? How do they learn about the consequences of their behavior? Finally, how do they learn from others?

▷ **LEARNING ABOUT EVENTS** Humans and other organisms need to recognize significant events when they occur and react to them appropriately. They must also learn to ignore events that occur repeatedly but have no immediate consequence. The shrill cry of an infant, the screech of automobile brakes—these sounds demand our attention and cause us to react. Humans and animals notice sudden changes in their environment; they notice those things that are new and potentially of interest. But our reactions to these novel events change with repeated experience, and these changes are among the most basic and important of all learning processes. In the first section of the chapter, we'll discuss two elementary processes that focus on how organisms learn about events: *habituation* and *sensitization*.

▷ **LEARNING WHAT EVENTS SIGNAL** Many events that occur in our world signal the presence of other events. For instance, you know that lightning precedes thunder and that the rattling of a tail can signal the bite of a venomous snake. Often, you can't *do* anything about the co-occurrence of such events, but if you recognize the relationship, you can respond accordingly. (You can take cover or move to avoid the snake.) Events can even signal the *absence* of other events, such as when you are greeted with a "Sold Out" sign in the concert ticket window. Psychologists have studied the signaling properties of events through a procedure called *classical conditioning*, which is one of the oldest and most widely used techniques in learning research.

▷ **LEARNING ABOUT THE CONSEQUENCES OF BEHAVIOR** Actions produce consequences. The child who flicks the tail of a cat once too often may receive an unwelcome surprise. The family dog learns that if he hangs around the dinner table, an occasional scrap of pork chop might very well come his way. Behaviors are instrumental in producing rewards and punishments; it is through the study of the aptly named *instrumental conditioning* procedure that psychologists have come to appreciate the influence that rewards and punishments in the environment exert over the behavioral repertoires of humans and other animals.

▷ **LEARNING FROM OTHERS** Often, our most important teachers are not our own actions and their consequences, but the actions of others. Humans learn by example, as does most of the animal kingdom. Observational learning has considerable adaptive significance: A teenager learns about the consequences of drunk driving, one hopes, not from direct experience but from observing others whose fate has already been sealed. A young monkey in the wild learns to be afraid of snakes not from a deadly personal encounter but from observing her mother's fear.

With the **"Previewing the Adaptive Problems"** sections, Nairne gets to the heart of the presentation. These sections introduce readers to three to five "problems to be solved" that will be explored in the chapter. Note how Nairne begins each discussion with common, everyday events to which students can readily relate.

"Inside the Problem" sections give students an "inside view" of psychological research.

"Inside the Problem" sections in every chapter take students behind the scenes to see how psychological research is used to explore questions and how the research then results in practical applications.

INSIDE THE PROBLEM: *Developing Taste Aversions*

On St. Thomas in the Virgin Islands, researchers Lowell Nicolaus and David Nellis encouraged captured mongooses to eat eggs laced with carbachol, a drug that produces temporary illness. After 5 days of eating eggs and getting sick, the still-hungry mongooses reduced their consumption of eggs to around 37% of their normal consumption level (Nicolaus & Nellis, 1987). In a very different context, in a research program designed to combat the negative effects of chemotherapy, young cancer patients were allowed a taste of some unusually flavored ice cream just before the onset of their normal chemotherapy—a treatment that typically produces nausea and vomiting. Several weeks later, when offered the ice cream, only 21% of the children were willing to taste it again (Bernstein, 1978).

Both of these situations represent naturalistic applications of classical conditioning. Can you identify the critical features of each? How do these two examples involve the learning of a relation between two events, a conditioned stimulus and an unconditioned stimulus, that largely occurs outside the organism's control? First, let's look for the unconditioned stimulus—the stimulus that unconditionally produces a response prior to training. In both of these cases, the unconditioned stimulus is the illness-producing event, either the drug carbachol or the cancer-fighting chemotherapy. The response that is automatically produced, unfortunately for the participants, is stomach distress. Children don't need to learn to vomit from chemotherapy; a mongoose doesn't need to be taught to be sick after receiving carbachol. These are inevitable consequences that require no prior conditioning.

Now, what is the conditioned stimulus—the event that provides information about the occurrence of the unconditioned stimulus? In these examples, it is the taste of the food, either the eggs or the ice cream, that signals the later onset of nausea. It's worth noting that the children were aware that their nausea was produced by the chemotherapy, not the ice cream, yet an association was still formed between the taste of the ice cream and a procedure that led to sickness. A condi-

tioned response, feelings of queasiness to the food, was produced whenever the opportunity to eat was presented. Taste aversions are easy to acquire. They often occur after a single pairing of a novel food and illness (see The Adaptive Mind at the end of this chapter).

It is extremely adaptive for people and mongooses to acquire taste aversions to potentially dangerous foods—it is in their interest to avoid those events that signal something potentially harmful. In the two studies we've just considered, the researchers investigated the aversions for a particular reason. Mongooses often eat the eggs of endangered species (such as marine turtles). By baiting the nests of mongoose prey with tainted eggs and establishing a taste aversion, scientists have been able to reduce the overall rate of egg predation. Similar techniques have also been used to prevent sheep from eating dangerous plants in the pasture (Zahorik, Houpt, & Swartzman-Andert, 1990).

In the case of chemotherapy, Illene Bernstein was interested in developing methods for *avoiding* the establishment of taste aversions: Cancer patients who are undergoing chemotherapy also need to eat, so it's critical to understand the conditions under which aversions are formed. Taste aversions often develop as a side effect of chemotherapy. Patients tend to avoid foods that they've consumed just before treatment, potentially leading to weight loss that impedes recovery. Researchers have found that associations are particularly likely to form between *unusual* tastes and nausea. Broberg and Bernstein (1987) found that giving children an unusual flavor of candy just before treatment reduced the likelihood of their forming aversions to their normal diet. These children formed a taste aversion to the candy rather than to their normal diet. Another helpful technique in preventing taste aversions from developing is to ask the patient to eat the same, preferably bland, foods before every treatment. Foods that do not have distinctive tastes and that people eat regularly (such as bread) are less likely to elicit taste aversions.

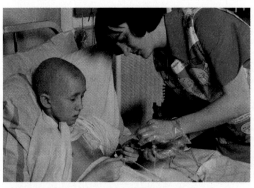

For children undergoing the rigors of chemotherapy, like this young boy suffering from leukemia, it's important to prevent taste aversions from developing as a negative side effect of the treatment. Broberg and Bernstein (1987) found that giving children an unusual flavor of candy just prior to treatment reduced the chances of a taste aversion forming to their normal diet.

An art program as superlative as the narrative

Nairne's vision for an introductory text extended beyond words and ideas to figures and illustrations that make concepts come alive for students. Nairne worked directly with artists, designers, and illustrators to develop an art program that is totally unique in the field. He personally reviewed every piece of art for the book with the following goal in mind: "If a student can't just look at this piece of art and immediately know what we're trying to convey, then we have to redo it."

food loses its reinforcing value because you've already reached your natural bliss point for eating.

Importantly, the response deprivation theory predicts that the presentation of *any* event or response, in principle, can serve as positive reinforcement (see also Premack, 1962). If you have been deprived of responding to an event for long enough (that is, you have fallen below your bliss point), the presentation of that event should be reinforcing. Most children, for example, would rather color than do math problems (presumably because the bliss point for coloring is naturally high). But it's been found that if children are deprived of doing math problems long enough to fall below their natural "math bliss point," the opportunity to do math can actually serve as positive reinforcement—even for a desirable response, such as coloring (see Konarski, 1985; Timberlake, 1980).

Negative Reinforcement. With **negative reinforcement**, the *removal* of an event after a response increases the likelihood of that response occurring again. In most cases, negative reinforcement occurs when a response allows an individual to eliminate, avoid, or escape from an *unpleasant* situation. For instance, you hang up the phone on someone who is criticizing you unfairly, shut off the blaring alarm clock in the morning, or walk out of a movie that is boring you to tears. These responses are more likely to occur again in the future, given the appropriate circumstance, because they lead to the removal of something negative—criticism, noise, or boredom. But, as you may have guessed, the event that is removed doesn't have to be "unpleasant"—it simply has to increase the likelihood of the "contingent" response (the response that led to the removal).

Researchers who study negative reinforcement in animals have historically used two kinds of learning procedures: escape conditioning and avoidance conditioning. In *escape conditioning*, the animal learns that a response will end some kind of unpleasant stimulus. For example, a rat might learn that jumping over a short barrier separating one part of the cage from another will eliminate a mild electric shock. The jumping response is reinforced because it allows the animal to escape from a negative situation (see the top row in Figure 7.12). In *avoidance con-*

FIGURE 7.12
Escape Versus Avoidance Conditioning. In escape conditioning (top row), a response is negatively reinforced because it ends an aversive event. The rat learns that jumping over a short barrier will terminate a mild electric shock. In avoidance conditioning (bottom row), the rat learns to make a response that prevents the aversive stimulus from occurring. Here, the rat learns to avoid the shock by jumping when the light comes on. Often, the animal will learn first to escape from, and then to avoid, an aversive event.

After intensive development, the art program is truly unparalleled in its clarity and pedagogical effectiveness. Note how the illustrations in Figure 7.12 effectively convey the procedures of escape versus avoidance conditioning without requiring written explanation. Nairne also provides a narrative explanation in the figure caption.

Superlative end-of-chapter pedagogy

"Solving the Problems: A Summary" sections capture—in just a few lines—the essence of the various "problems to be solved," each linked with key illustrations or photos.

SOLVING THE PROBLEMS: A SUMMARY

As organisms struggle to survive in their environments, their capacity to learn—that is, to change their behavior as a result of experience—represents one of their greatest strengths. Psychologists have long recognized the need for understanding how behavior changes with experience; historically, research on learning predates research on virtually all other topics, with the possible exception of basic sensory and perceptual processes.

Even today, the study of learning in one form or another is the cornerstone for much of psychology. In attempting to understand and treat mental disorders, clinical psychologists often seek their answers in an individual's prior experiences. To understand the dynamics of group behavior, social psychologists appeal increasingly to the effects of prior experience. Cognitive psychologists, as we'll see in the next two chapters, consider experience to be perhaps the most important determinant of the content and structure of thought and other mental processes. Indeed, it is difficult to find an area of psychology that does not consider learning to be fundamental to its enterprise.

LEARNING ABOUT EVENTS Individuals need to *recognize* events when they occur. Novel, or unusual, events cause organisms to produce an orienting response, which helps ensure that they will react quickly to sudden changes in their environment. The sound of screeching automobile brakes leads to an immediate reaction; you don't have to stop and think about it. At the same time, organisms cannot attend to all the stimuli that surround them, so they must learn to ignore events that are of little adaptive significance. Through the process of habituation, characterized by the decline in the tendency to respond to an event that has become familiar, individuals become selective about responding to events that occur repeatedly in their environment.

LEARNING WHAT EVENTS SIGNAL Individuals need to learn about what events *signal*—it's helpful to know, for example, that green traffic lights mean you can move your car forward freely and that red lights mean you should stop. Signals, or conditioned stimuli, are established through classical conditioning. Events that provide information about the occurrence or nonoccurrence of other significant events become conditioned stimuli. A conditioned stimulus elicits a conditioned response, which is a response appropriate for anticipating the event that will follow.

LEARNING ABOUT THE CONSEQUENCES OF BEHAVIOR Individuals need to learn about the *consequences* of their actions. They must learn that when they act a certain way, their behaviors produce outcomes that are sometimes pleasing and sometimes not. In instrumental conditioning, the presentation and removal of events after responding can either increase or decrease the likelihood of one responding in a similar way again. When a response is followed by reinforcement, either positive or negative, the tendency to respond in that way again is strengthened. When a response is followed by punishment, either positive or negative, subjects are less likely to behave that way again. It's also important to consider the schedule of reinforcement. Schedules affect not only how rapidly subjects will learn and respond, but also the pattern of responding and how likely they are to change their behavior if they no longer receive reinforcement.

LEARNING FROM OTHERS Through observational or social learning, individuals imitate and model the actions of other people, thereby learning from example rather than from direct experience. We study how other individuals behave and how their behavior is reinforced or punished, and we change our own behavior accordingly. Observational learning can have a number of effects, both positive and negative, on the individual and on society.

End-of-chapter "Terms to Remember"

Terms to Remember

learning A relatively permanent change in behavior, or potential to respond, that results from experience.

LEARNING ABOUT EVENTS: NOTICING AND IGNORING

orienting response An inborn tendency to shift one's focus of attention toward a novel or surprising event.

habituation The decline in the tendency to respond to an event that has become familiar through repeated exposure.

sensitization An increase in the tendency to respond to an event that has been repeated; sensitization is more likely when a repeated stimulus is intense.

LEARNING WHAT EVENTS SIGNAL: CLASSICAL CONDITIONING

classical conditioning A set of procedures, initially developed by Pavlov, used to investigate how organisms learn about the signaling properties of events. Classical conditioning leads to the learning of relations between events—conditioned and unconditioned stimuli—that occur outside of one's control.

unconditioned stimulus (US) A stimulus that automatically produces—or elicits—an observable response prior to any training.

unconditioned response (UR) The observable response that is produced automatically, prior to training, on presentation of an unconditioned stimulus.

conditioned response (CR) The acquired response that is produced to the conditioned stimulus in anticipation of the arrival of the unconditioned stimulus. Often, the conditioned response resembles the unconditioned response, although not always.

conditioned stimulus (CS) A neutral stimulus (one that does not produce the unconditioned response prior to training) that is paired with the unconditioned stimulus during classical conditioning.

second-order conditioning A procedure in which an established conditioned stimulus is used to condition a second neutral stimulus.

stimulus generalization Responding to a new stimulus in a way similar to the response produced by an established conditioned stimulus.

stimulus discrimination Responding differently to a new stimulus than one responds to an established conditioned stimulus.

extinction Presenting a conditioned stimulus repeatedly, after conditioning, without the unconditioned stimulus, resulting in a loss in responding.

spontaneous recovery The recovery of an extinguished conditioned response after a period of nonexposure to the conditioned stimulus.

conditioned inhibition Learning that an event signals the absence of the unconditioned stimulus.

LEARNING ABOUT THE CONSEQUENCES OF BEHAVIOR: INSTRUMENTAL CONDITIONING

instrumental conditioning A procedure for studying how organisms learn about the consequences of their own voluntary actions; they learn that their behaviors are instrumental in producing rewards and punishments. Also called **operant conditioning.**

law of effect The idea that if a response in a particular situation is followed by a satisfying or pleasant consequence, it will be strengthened; if a response in a particular situation is followed by an unsatisfying or unpleasant consequence, it will be weakened.

discriminative stimulus The stimulus situation that "sets the occasion" for a response to be followed by reinforcement or punishment.

reinforcement Response consequences that increase the likelihood of responding in a similar way again.

positive reinforcement An event that, when *presented* after a response, increases the likelihood of that response occurring again.

negative reinforcement An event that, when *removed* after a response, increases the likelihood of that response occurring again.

schedules of reinforcement A rule that an experimenter uses to determine when particular responses will be reinforced. Schedules may be fixed or variable, ratio or interval.

fixed-ratio schedule A schedule in which the number of responses required for reinforcement is fixed and does not change from trial to trial.

variable-ratio schedule A schedule in which a certain number of responses is required for reinforcement, but the number of required responses typically changes from trial to trial.

fixed-interval schedule A schedule in which the reinforcement is delivered for the first response that occurs following a fixed interval of time.

variable-interval schedule A schedule in which the allotted time before a response will yield reinforcement changes from trial to trial.

shaping A procedure in which reinforcement is delivered for successive approximations of the desired response.

"Terms to Remember" with definitions appear at the end of every chapter, organized by the main sections of the text.

"The Adaptive Mind"—an in-depth look at key topics

"I find that the 'Adaptive Mind' sections help hold the text together as a coherent book rather than as a set of independent chapters. The chapter summaries do an excellent job of giving the reader a true overview of the important content of each chapter. I also appreciate the way that in each chapter there are references to ideas or information that will be covered in more detail later in the text."

Eugene Gilden—*Linfield College*

"The Adaptive Mind" sections conclude each chapter and provide "optional" advanced material that takes a more in-depth look at current and often cutting-edge research or current controversies (such as neural network models, the repressed memory controversy, and rational memory theory).

THE ADAPTIVE MIND — On the Generality of Learning Principles

Consider the following scenario. At lunch today, you decide to be daring and order the fresh gooseberry pie for dessert instead of your usual slice of apple pie. Unbeknownst to you, an eccentric billionaire experimenter is sitting elsewhere in the restaurant and decides to reward you for choosing the gooseberry pie; he places an unmarked envelope in your car containing $100, which you happily discover 2 hours later. Now consider a different scenario: Same restaurant, same gooseberry pie, but instead of finding $100 you suffer severe nausea and gastric distress 2 hours later. In which of these two cases are you more likely to form an association between eating gooseberry pie and a particular contingent consequence?

In each case, there is an event, eating gooseberry pie, and a powerful consequence, receiving $100 or getting sick. Let's assume that the value of the two consequences, as potential reinforcers and punishers, is the same. Because of the 2-hour delay, it's possible that you would have a problem forming any kind of association under these conditions, but, in fact, the answer is relatively clear: You're likely to associate the pie with the illness and to make no connection between the pie and the $100. This finding is important because it *constrains* the generality of learning principles (that is, principles that can be applied to any and all learning situations). It suggests that not all events and consequences are created equal. Organisms may be predisposed to associate certain things, such as tastes and nausea; certain responses may "belong" with certain reinforcers or punishers.

The Relation of Cue to Consequence

The gooseberry pie scenario, first described by Revusky and Garcia (1970), illustrates a principle about the relation between cues and consequences that can be demonstrated directly in the laboratory. In 1966, Garcia and Koelling let thirsty rats drink water flavored with saccharin. The drinking was also accompanied by flashing lights and distinct clicking noises. (This stimulus complex is sometimes referred to by the colorful name "bright-noisy-sweet water.") After the rats drank the water, researchers punished the drinking response in one group of rats by administering a moderate foot shock, whereas they gave a second group a small dose of X-irradiation (which produces sickness). Learning was later tested by allowing the rats in each group to choose between drinking sweetened water alone and drinking unsweetened water in the presence of the flashing lights and the noisy clicking sounds.

The design and results of the experiment are shown in Figure 7.15. When irradiation was used as the punishing consequence, thus making the rats sick, the rats were reluctant to drink the water laced with saccharin, but they showed no evidence of avoidance of "bright and noisy" water and consumed near-normal amounts. The opposite finding was obtained with the rats that had received shock. Those that received a shock in the presence of the bright-noisy-sweet water learned to avoid the flashing and clicking unsweetened water but showed no resistance to the sweet water presented alone. These results indicate that certain cues *belong* with certain consequences; there appears to be a natural tendency to associate flavors with gastric distress (in this case, the sweet taste with nausea) and novel environmental events with shock (shock was readily associated with bright lights and noise).

Belongingness

The idea that natural predispositions, perhaps rooted in an organism's genetic code, might have to be factored into the learning equation was foreign to most learning researchers of the 1960s. Most believed that the principles of classical and instrumental conditioning were fixed and immutable and could be applied successfully in any environment. But the results of the Garcia and Koelling (1966) study showed that the amount of learning that results depends on the particular cues and consequences used. Actually, Thorndike, in his studies of cats in puzzle boxes, had introduced the concept of *belongingness* several years earlier, but his warnings were largely ignored. Thorndike had noted, for example, that it seemed impossible to increase the probability of yawning or of certain reflexive scratching responses in cats through the application of reinforcement.

Similar observations were reported later by animal trainers Keller and Marion Breland (1961). The Brelands, who were former students of Skinner, encountered some interesting difficulties while attempting to train a variety of species to make certain responses. In one case, they tried to train a pig to drop large wooden coins into a piggy bank (for a bank commercial). They followed the *shaping* procedure, in which successive approximations of the desired sequence are reinforced, but they could not get the pig to complete the response. The animal would pick up the coin and begin to lumber toward the bank but would stop midway and begin "rooting" the coins along the ground. Despite their using punishment and nonreinforcement of the rooting response, the Brelands could never completely eliminate the response. They encountered similar problems trying to teach a raccoon to put coins in a bank:

> We started out by reinforcing him for picking up a single coin. Then the metal container was introduced, with the requirement that he drop the coin into the container. Here we ran into the first bit of difficulty: he seemed to have a great deal of trouble letting go of the coin. He would rub it against the inside of the container, pull it back out, and clutch it firmly for several seconds. However, he would finally turn it loose and receive his food reinforcement. Then the final contingency: we

PSYCHOLOGY

The Adaptive Mind

1

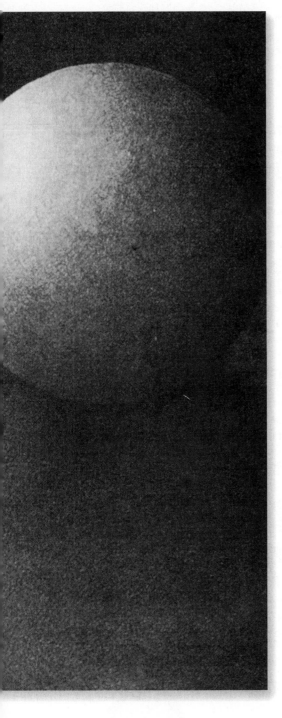

I have come to realise that I must not put overmuch confidence in the story teller who lives in my mind.

Sir Arthur Eddington

When I look into the mirror, I often see two very different people staring back, depending on my perspective. I see me, of course, the human being of everyday experience. This is the "me" who thinks, loves, feels, and dreams. But I also see another image reflected there—not as clearly defined perhaps, but an enduring presence nonetheless. It's the image I see when I look at myself from a scientific view, as a psychologist might: then I see an image constructed from the building blocks of my scientific knowledge. For reasons that you'll discover in this book, in many ways this image bears little resemblance to my more obvious physical self.

From my perspective as a scientist, I still see someone who thinks, loves, feels, and dreams. But I see these behaviors and feelings occurring only as a consequence of the activation of billions of brain cells operating in a complex communication network. I still see someone who behaves and who makes choices about how to act, but only as a consequence of sophisticated learning and motivational systems that mirror the environment and its demands. This other "me" still feels and expresses emotion, but only after interpreting physical changes in my body with brain structures that are deeply rooted in my evolutionary past.

My goal in this textbook is to introduce you to this other image—to teach you how to see yourself and others from the perspective of modern **psychology:** the scientific study of behavior and mind. In the coming chapters, we'll describe the essentials of behavior and mind—how people act, think, and feel—using the scientific method as our primary analytic tool. As your scientific perspective develops, you can expect several benefits. First, as we trace the scientific origins of behavior and mind, you will see how psychologists have acquired the ability to predict behavior in a variety of situations. Systematic observation and logical analysis have yielded insights into the cause and expression of many kinds of behavior. I'm hopeful you'll gain some understanding of your own actions, as well as of the actions of the people around you. Second, you will be exposed to techniques that can potentially help you control and improve your own behavior. Modern psychology has something to say about everything from the treatment of irrational fears (such as the fear of spiders) to the development of effective study skills to the design of the kitchen stove. Third, and perhaps most important, you will be exposed to a method of inquiry that will teach you how to think critically about yourself and about others. You will learn how researchers ask questions about behavior, how they draw conclusions about cause and effect, and how they

Most psychologists believe that human thoughts and emotions arise ultimately from complex activities in the brain.

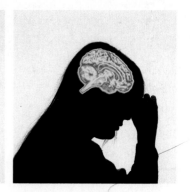

build theories and models that enable them to predict the circumstances in which particular behaviors will occur.

As your own scientific reflection begins to reveal itself, however, you may not easily recognize yourself in its image. You will learn things about the way you behave and think that may be difficult to reconcile with the more familiar image of everyday experience. You will learn, for example, that many of your personal memories may be figments of an active mind's imagination—rather than literally true, they may be elaborate "reconstructions" of the past created by sophisticated mechanisms in your brain. You will learn that many of the beliefs you hold about yourself—about how you would act and treat others—are not as principled and unchanging as you might think, but instead are easily changed in the face of a demanding environment. You may even start to question the amount of control you actually have over your own behavior. We'll consider the possibility (although with a critical eye) that people's actions are controlled by unconscious forces, biological drives, and external stimuli that are not under direct willful control.

So be forewarned: The content of this textbook may make you feel uncomfortable at times. But what you'll learn will likely change the way you view yourself, the world, and others around you. Although that may seem like a rather tall order at the moment, it's one I hope you'll find intriguing as you begin your journey into the adaptive mind.

▶ PREVIEWING THE CONCEPTUAL PROBLEMS

To help frame the subject matter of psychology, each of the chapters in this textbook is organized around a set of "problems" that we'll briefly preview at the beginning of each chapter. These problems are intended to focus our discussion and to help emphasize *why* people think and act the way they do. The word *problem* in this context is not meant to be interpreted in a negative sense, as in doubt, difficulty, or a failure to understand. Instead, you should think of our "problems" as challenges or specific demands that are in our interest to resolve—either as humans attempting to survive or as psychologists seeking to understand behavior and mind. To get a brief look ahead, take a look at Table 1.1 for some examples of the types of problems that we'll be discussing.

The decision to adopt a problem-solving approach to psychology reflects the commitment of this text, which is to the general theme of the adaptive mind. The term **adaptive mind** refers to the fact that people use their brains in purposive ways, adjusting their actions, often in a flexible and strategic fashion, to meet the needs of new conditions as they arise. People and animals come equipped with a kind of adaptive tool kit, acquired either from learning or naturally as a by-product of evolution, that helps them initiate, direct, and control behavior. For many of the topics that we'll encounter in coming chapters, you'll see how people use these adaptive "tools" to help solve the various obstacles and survival problems they face.

In most chapters, our discussion will revolve around three or four core problems that highlight the kinds of adaptive tools humans possess. For example, as listed in Table 1.1, in Chapter 3 (Biological Processes) we'll examine how organisms communicate information internally through a vast communication network called the nervous system. Internal communication is a crucial problem for your body to solve—if a wayward bicyclist weaves suddenly into the path of your car, the message needs to be communicated quickly and efficiently to the muscles controlling the foot-to-brake connection. We'll consider some of the internal mechanisms that enable you to accomplish this task. In Chapter 7 (Learning from Experience), we'll examine how people and animals learn about the signaling properties of events. You know that lightning precedes thunder and that the rattling of a tail can signal the

TABLE 1.1
Examples of Adaptive, Conceptual, and Practical Problems

	Chapter	Problem to Be Solved	Example	Solution "Tools"
Adaptive problems	3	Communicating internally	A bicyclist weaves suddenly into the path of your car.	Electrochemical transmission in the nervous system
	7	Learning what events signal	You hear a rattling tail on a mountain path.	Interevent associations acquired through classical conditioning
	8	Remembering over the short term	You try to remember a telephone number as you cross the room.	Rehearsal in short-term memory
	13	Interpreting the behavior of others	A shadowy figure emerges suddenly from an alleyway.	Knowledge-based social "schemas" used to predict outcomes
Conceptual and practical problems	2	Determining the causes of behavior	Sally watches a violent TV program and becomes aggressive.	Experimental research
	10	Conceptualizing intelligence	Andy is excellent at fixing mechanical devices but is terrible at reading and math.	Psychometric tests designed to measure the mind
	14	Defining abnormality	Lucinda hears "voices" and thinks she's immortal.	*Diagnostic and Statistical Manual of Mental Disorders*
	15	Treating the mind	Ralph is mired in the depths of depression.	Psychoactive drug therapy or "insight" therapy

Note: The solution tools shown in the far-right column will be discussed in detail in the relevant chapters.

strike of a venomous snake—but what basic learning processes enabled you to acquire such pivotal information?

In other chapters, we'll focus on conceptual and practical problems that psychologists seek to solve, either to advance basic knowledge or to help troubled individuals in need. For example, what are the best tactics and strategies to use to understand the causes of a behavior? We'll discuss how psychological research is conducted in Chapter 2. What are the best ways to conceptualize and then measure an abstract internal construct such as intelligence? Intelligence is not something that can be measured directly, like height or weight; it can only be inferred by measuring various aspects of behavior. In Chapter 10, we'll see how intelligence is currently conceptualized and measured. How can abnormal behavior be classified, and, once identified, how can it be treated (Chapters 14 and 15)? These are practical problems that psychologists attempt to solve. Understanding the "solutions," and how those solutions have been reached, will occupy a substantial portion of our time.

In this first chapter, we'll address three introductory conceptual problems that are designed to acquaint you with the science of psychology: (1) How should the profession of "psychology" best be defined and described? (2) How can we trace the evolution of psychological thought? (3) How can we best understand the focus of modern psychology? Let's begin with a brief synopsis of each.

▶ **DEFINING AND DESCRIBING PSYCHOLOGY** As a profession, psychology is probably not what you think it is. Most people identify psychology with the study of mental illness—"crazy" people, mental "breakdowns," or activities designed to put one in touch with things like the "inner child." But psychology is much more than the image depicted on afternoon talk shows, or even in the "self-help" books that line the shelves of your local bookstore. Psychology is an academic as well as a professional discipline that includes the study of normal as well as abnormal behavior. We'll discuss some of the challenges facing psychologists, and we'll see what psychologists actually do with their time.

▶ **TRACING THE EVOLUTION OF PSYCHOLOGICAL THOUGHT** It's often said that psychology is a science with a short history but a very long past. Indeed, the study of mind and behavior dates back thousands of years. But as an independent subject matter of science, psychology is a recent arrival on the scene, originating only a little over a century ago. We'll discuss how psychological thinking has evolved over the past hundred years—from early attempts to understand the "structure" of the mind by turning attention inward, to insights gained from the treatment and study of individuals in clinical settings, to the experimental analysis of behavior inside and outside of the laboratory.

▶ **UNDERSTANDING THE FOCUS OF MODERN PSYCHOLOGY** Finally, we'll end the chapter with a discussion of the focus of modern psychology. How does current thinking reflect the intellectual history of psychological thought? Are all psychologists of one mind as to how to approach the study of behavior and mind? We'll see early on that the answer is often "no." Modern psychologists tend to adopt an "eclectic" approach: They solve problems by borrowing freely from many sources. We'll also discuss the current popularity of *cognitive* approaches to psychology and of *biological* explanations of behavior. We'll conclude this section by returning briefly to the theme of this text: the adaptive mind.

Defining and Describing Psychology

As defined earlier, *psychology* is the scientific study of behavior and mind. The word *psychology* has its roots in the Greek words *psyche,* which translates as "soul" or "breath" but which Greek philosophers used in much the same way as we use the word *mind,* and *logos,* which signifies the study or investigation of something (as in bio*logy* or physio*logy*). The word *psychology* was not in common use before the 19th century, and psychology did not actually gain status as an independent subject matter of science until around the middle of the 19th century (Boring, 1950). Prior to that point, discussions about "the study of the mind," as psychology was widely known, were the main province of philosophers and, to some extent, those who were interested primarily in physiology.

Notice that today's definition of psychology is quite precise—it is not simply the study of the mind, but rather it is the *scientific* study of *behavior* and mind. The emphasis on science, and particularly the scientific method, helps distinguish psychology from the closely related field of philosophy. The essential characteristic of the scientific method, as we'll see in Chapter 2, is *observation*: Scientific insight is gained and validated by some kind of direct or indirect observation. Psychologists collect observations, look for regularities, and then generate predictions based on what they've observed.

By **mind,** psychologists usually mean the contents and processes of subjective experience: sensations, thoughts, and emotions. Behavior and mind are kept separate in the definition because only **behavior** can be directly measured by the scientific observer. Most psychologists interpret the term *behavior* in a quite general way. Besides referring to overt actions such as moving, talking, gesturing, and so on, many psychologists consider the activities of cells within the brain (measured through physiological recording devices) and the thoughts and feelings of individuals (revealed through oral and written expression) to be types of "behavior."

Do you think it's possible to study behavior independently of mind? Or does all behavior result from the actions of a willful mind? Cockroaches, snails, and starfish all behave, but do they have minds?

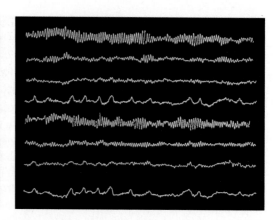

The term behavior *can mean many things to a psychologist—overt actions, thoughts and feelings as revealed through written reports, and even recordings of electrical activity in the brain.*

Studying the Mind: Unlocking Hidden Processes

Let's pause for a moment and think about how difficult it is to study something like the mind. Imagine that you accidentally unearth a small black box that is capable of responding to questions by displaying answers on a small screen. A quick examination reveals that the box acts intelligently. You ask it questions; it responds appropriately. What kind of strategy might you use to discover how this box works? In an important sense, your task is similar to the one facing the psychologist: There is an intelligent object—in the case of a psychologist, it's a human being—and the object responds to questions and appears to think intelligently. But it's not immediately obvious how or why that object works the way that it does. The internal mechanisms and processes are hidden, locked away within an external shell.

Because the box is intelligent, you might begin by asking it to *tell* you how it works (see Figure 1.1). Instruct the box to look inward, to reflect on the internal mechanisms responsible for its intelligence. This approach is likely to yield lots of useful and interesting data, but it entails a potentially serious problem: How can you tell whether the box's insights, once delivered, are really accurate? The box could be lying, or simply misinformed about its underlying operating mechanisms. What the box thinks is going on may not, in fact, be an accurate representation of reality. As we'll see later in this chapter, psychologists have faced similar problems in their efforts to understand the mind. People are often capable of providing detailed accounts of why they act the way they do. But the psychologist faces the difficult task of separating fantasy and fabrication from reality. It's difficult to rely entirely on self-reports, although they're often useful sources of data, unless an alternative way exists to verify the accuracy of the claims (Crutcher, 1994; Ericsson & Simon, 1993; Payne, 1994).

Another approach might be simply to pry the box open to see what you find inside. This is obviously something a psychologist cannot do, although examining the internal structure of the human brain is an active area of research in psychology (you'll find out how this is possible in Chapter 3). But here, too, potential problems loom. Suppose that you find billions of little objects with long threadlike tails that appear to be interconnected in a vast network. What do they mean? These bizarre internal objects will themselves require explanation, and even if you succeed in determining their function, you face further obstacles. For one thing, you run the risk of breaking the machine by prying it open and examining its working parts. Moreover, understanding any one of these objects doesn't necessarily tell you how the machine as a whole operates (although it might). The intelligent behavior of the box could be the result of many components working together, in ways that cannot be understood by studying the individual parts in isolation.

FIGURE 1.1
Studying the Mind. It is difficult to study the mind because mental events are not directly observable. Using the analogy of a "black box," these three panels depict some of the ways that one might attempt to "study the mind": Ask the box itself for insight (left panel), pry the box open to see what's inside (middle panel), or measure the box's behavior and look for regularities (right panel).

Leaving the box intact, you might try to understand how it works by looking for regularities in its behavior. You could measure things such as the time it takes the box to answer questions, the number of errors that it makes, how long it takes the box to forget previous responses, and so on. By measuring and describing the box's behavior—its limits and range of abilities—you could infer things, or at least start to devise theories, about how the box potentially operates. This last approach is closest to the way that most modern psychologists approach their subject matter. They observe behavior in a systematic way, looking for regularities, in order to develop ideas that can then be tested through more observations of behavior.

In general, to understand the mysteries of the mind—such as the origins of sensations, thoughts, and emotions—psychologists must first and foremost study how the body behaves. Most psychologists believe that this is the only reasonable scientific approach, because the mind itself cannot be observed directly. Psychologists observe behavior, along with the environmental conditions that induce changes in behavior, and use these observations to draw inferences about the structure and content of mental processes. In Chapter 2 we'll discuss some of the methods that psychologists use to accomplish these ends.

What Psychologists Do

According to our definition, a psychologist is someone who is engaged in the scientific study of behavior and mind. But what do psychologists actually do on a daily basis? How do they earn a living? Where do they work? As shown in Figure 1.2, we can divide the job description of "psychologist" into three main categories: *clinical psychologist, applied psychologist,* and *research psychologist.* These are not meant to be exclusive categories—for example, clinical psychologists often work in applied settings and conduct research—but they do represent a useful way of generally subdividing the profession.

Clinical Psychologists. To most people, a psychologist is someone who either diagnoses and treats psychological problems—such as depression, anxiety, phobias, or schizophrenia—or gives advice on such things as how to raise children or how to get along with one's boss. Professionals who deal with such problems are called **clinical psychologists,** and they typically work in clinics or in private practice delivering human services such as psychotherapy or counseling. Distinctions are sometimes made between clinical and "counseling" psychologists, although the dividing line between the two is not clear and firm. *Counseling psychologists* are

	Clinical psychologists	Applied psychologists	Research psychologists
	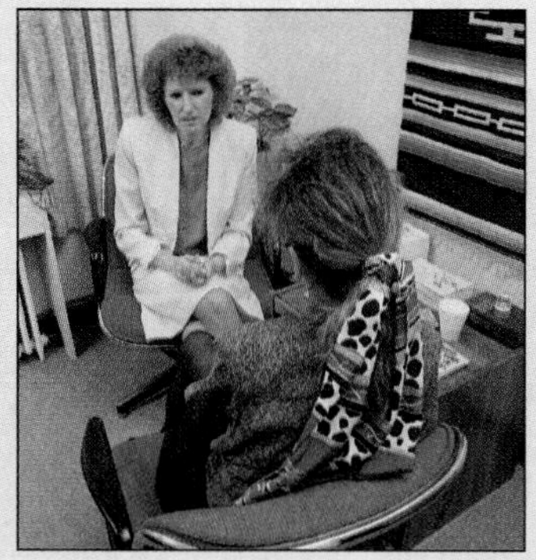	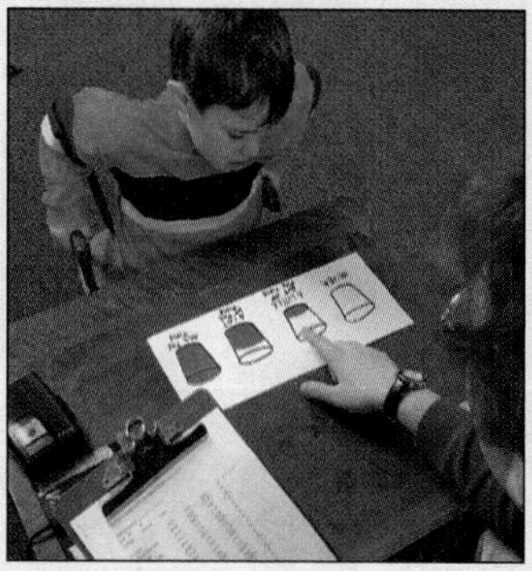	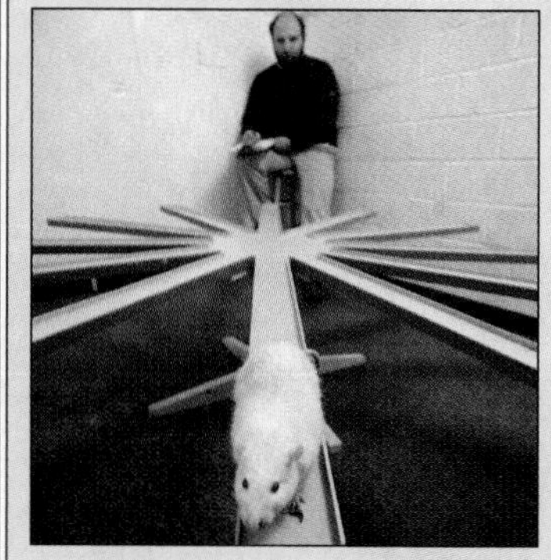
Guiding Focus:	The diagnosis and treatment of psychological problems	Extending psychological principles to practical problems in the world	Conducting experiments or collecting observations to discover the basic principles of behavior and mind
Primary Workplace:	Clinics Private practice Academic settings	Private industry Schools Academic settings	Academic settings Private industry

FIGURE 1.2

Types of Psychologists. Psychologists can be classified into three main overlapping categories: clinical, applied, and research. These are not meant to be exclusive categories but rather, represent a useful way of subdividing the profession.

more likely to deal with adjustment problems (marriage and family problems), whereas clinical psychologists tend to work with more severe psychological disorders. Together, clinical and counseling psychologists make up the majority of psychologists; over half of all professionals in the discipline are actively involved in the treatment of mental health (American Psychological Association, 1993).

Applied Psychologists. Not all psychologists are concerned with the understanding and treatment of abnormal behavior or with helping people adjust. Another category of professional psychologists tends to focus on average, "normal" people (we'll consider what it means to be normal or abnormal in Chapter 14). The goal of **applied psychologists** is to extend the principles of scientific psychology to practical, everyday problems in the real world. Applied psychologists are often distinguished on the basis of their particular problem area of interest. For example, a *school psychologist* might work with students in primary and secondary schools to help them perform well academically and socially; an *industrial/organizational psychologist* might be employed in industry to help improve employee morale, train new recruits, or help managers establish effective lines of communication with their employees. *Human factors psychologists* play a key role in the design and engineering of new products: Have you ever wondered why telephone numbers are seven digits long, grouped in three then four (e.g., 555-9378)? How about traffic lights—why red and green? Does it make a difference whether the word *delete, remove,* or *erase* is used in a word processing program? These are examples of practical problems that have occupied the attention of human factors psychologists (Proctor & Van Zandt, 1994).

Research Psychologists. At the university or college level, and to some extent in private laboratories and clinics, you are likely to find **research psychologists** who collect data on both basic and applied issues in psychology. Research psychologists conduct experiments or collect observations in an attempt to discover the basic principles of behavior and mind; they, too, are usually associated with a specialty. *Biopsychologists,* for instance, seek to understand how physical or genetic factors influence and determine behavior. *Personality psychologists* are concerned with the internal factors that lead people to act consistently across situations, as well as with the determinants of individual differences in behavior. *Cognitive psychologists* focus on higher mental processes such as memory, learning, and reasoning. *Developmental psychologists* study how behavior and internal mental processes change over the course of a lifetime. *Social psychologists* are interested in how people think about, influence, and relate to each other. As you work your way through the chapters of this text, you will be exposed to an even wider range of research and clinical interests.

Psychiatrists. Finally, you might be wondering about the differences between psychologists and **psychiatrists.** Psychiatrists are medical doctors who specialize in psychological problems. To become a psychiatrist you must graduate from medical school and then complete further specialized training in the subject matter of psychology. Like clinical psychologists, psychiatrists are involved in the treatment of mental disorders, but unlike psychologists, they are licensed to prescribe drugs. As you'll see in Chapter 15, drug therapy is often useful for treating the physical problems that sometimes induce or accompany problems of the mind. It is not unusual for psychologists and psychiatrists to work together. A clinical psychologist, for example, may refer a client to a psychiatrist if he or she suspects that a physical problem might be involved.

Tracing the Evolution of Psychological Thought

The emergence of psychology as a separate subject matter of science may be of relatively recent origin, but the search for an understanding of mind dates back thousands of years. The Greek philosopher Aristotle (384–322 B.C.) wrote extensively on such topics as memory, sleep, and sensation—topics that today are part of the subject matter of psychology. It was Aristotle who first conceived of the mind as a kind of *tabula rasa*—a blank tablet—upon which experiences are written to form the basis of knowledge. The idea that knowledge arises directly from experience, a philosophical position known as **empiricism,** continues to be a dominant theme in modern psychological thought.

The Mind-Body Connection

As mentioned earlier, the intellectual roots of modern psychology lie in the disciplines of both *philosophy* and *physiology.* In a sense, psychology has always occupied a kind of middle ground between these two areas (Bolles, 1993). Philosophers such as Aristotle, Plato, and others helped frame many of the fundamental questions that occupy the attention of psychologists today: Where does knowledge come from? What are the laws, if any, that govern sensation? What are the necessary conditions for the learning and remembering of associations?

Physiologists, on the other hand, through their attempts to explain the workings of the human body, generated data that could be used to develop a *scientific* understanding of behavior and mind. In 1833, for example, the German Johannes Müller published an enormously influential *Handbook of Human Physiology* that proposed clear links between the nervous system and psychological phenomena such as perception. By the 1860s, a number of researchers, including Paul Broca, had established connections between certain kinds of brain damage and the loss of specific functions, such as the ability to produce or comprehend spoken language. Advances in our knowledge about the physical operation of the brain continue to shape and constrain the kinds of theories that psychologists propose. We'll discuss these advances in Chapter 3, as well as later in this chapter.

Psychology is the scientific study of behavior and mind. Is it really surprising then that its intellectual roots lie in physiology and philosophy?

FIGURE 1.3
Descartes and the Reflex. René Descartes first introduced the concept of the reflex, which he described as an automatic, involuntary reaction of a mechanical body to an event in the world. He identified the mediating structure as the pineal gland, shown here as a tear-shaped object in the back of the head.

Questions about the fundamental relationship between the physical *body*, as studied by the physiologists, and the *mind*, as studied by philosophers, have been at the center of many debates. Are the mind and body separate and distinct, or are they one and the same? Do they interact in ways that we can decipher? Can we learn anything about one by studying the other? In the 17th century, the French philosopher René Descartes (1596–1650) proposed an *interactionist* position. He was convinced that the mind and body should be kept separate: The physical body, he claimed, cannot "think," nor can thinking be explained by appealing to physical matter. But he did allow for the possibility that one can importantly influence the other. The mind, he argued, initiates and controls the actions of a mechanical body through the pineal gland, a small structure at the base of the brain (see Figure 1.3).

Descartes helped frame the "mind-body problem" clearly, and his attempt to describe the human body in machinelike terms was to have an important influence on future generations of physiologists. His particular proposals about the body turned out to be largely incorrect—the pineal gland, for example, plays a role in producing hormones, not muscle movements—but he did make several lasting contributions. It was Descartes, for instance, who first introduced the concept of a *reflex*, which he described as an automatic, involuntary reaction of the mechanical body to events in the environment (we'll return to the concept of the reflex in Chapter 3). But his "solution" to the mind-body problem did little to advance the scientific study of mind. By depicting the mind as an entity separate from the material world and not subject to direct observation, he placed the subject matter of psychology outside the boundaries of the scientific method, which relies on observation. It is impossible to study something with the scientific method that cannot be observed in some way, especially if the object operates according to rules that are different from those in the physical world.

Modern psychologists approach the mind-body problem quite differently than Descartes did—they reject the separation of body from mind and assume they are one and the same. The mind, at least the mind that can be studied by scientific psychology, is thought to be the functional outcome of brain activity; put simply, the mind is what the brain does. Early proponents of this position, which is sometimes called **materialist identity theory,** include the English philosopher Thomas Hobbes (1588–1679). As we'll see throughout this text, there is an extremely close link between the operation of the brain and the initiation and expression of behavior. Many psychological disorders appear to arise directly from dysfunction in the physiology of the brain, and many of the symptoms can be treated effectively through biological intervention (usually the administration of drugs).

The Origins of Knowledge and Behavior

In addition to raising questions about the mind-body connection, psychologists along with philosophers have historically engaged in vigorous debates about the origins of knowledge. As noted earlier, Aristotle adopted an empiricist position—he believed that knowledge and ideas spring from everyday interactions. It is one's day-to-day experiences—the information gathered in through one's senses—that determines what one knows, and what is potentially knowable. This position was later developed extensively by a school of philosophy known as *British empiricism,* represented by the work of such 17th- and 18th-century British philosophers as John Locke, David Hume, and George Berkeley.

Empiricism can be contrasted with **nativism,** which holds that certain kinds of knowledge and ideas are innate. Nativists believe that humans arrive into the world knowing certain things, and these forms of knowledge, they argue, cannot be explained by appealing just to experience. Nativists do not believe that *all* knowledge is present at birth; rather, they adopt the position that only certain

INSIDE   THE PROBLEM: *Are We Born Knowing?*

In each chapter you will encounter special sections, such as this one, designed to bring you a bit more deeply "inside the problem" under discussion. The point of these sections is to expand the discussion in the text, perhaps by providing a demonstration or particularly relevant study, or simply to discuss things from a slightly different angle or perspective. Here we'll focus briefly on this issue of innate knowledge: Are we born knowing?

As you can probably guess, the question of whether humans are born knowing fundamental things about their world is extremely difficult to answer. For one thing, no one is really sure at what point "experience" begins. We could draw a line at birth, and say that any knowledge or abilities that exist at that very moment are "innate," but as you'll see in Chapter 4 the environment can exert tremendous influences on embryos as they develop in the womb. It's folly to think that we can ever eliminate experience completely—in

fact, the very act of assessing knowledge is itself a kind of experience. So we're always faced with the tricky problem of disentangling which portions of the knowledge that we observe are inborn and which are produced through experience.

One attack on the problem, proposed by a school known as *Gestalt psychology,* was to demonstrate that people use certain organizing principles of perception that cannot be altered by experience. Take a look at Figure 1.4. If I showed you (a) and then (b), do you think you could easily recognize that (a) is, in fact, embedded in (b)? It's not easy to see, is it? More important, it doesn't really matter how many times I show you (a). Even if I force you to look at (a) 100 times, it's always going to be difficult to find when you look at (b). The reason, according to the Gestalt psychologists, is that humans are born with a certain fixed way of viewing the world. The visual system, in this case, naturally organizes the sensory input in (b) in

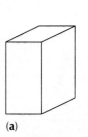
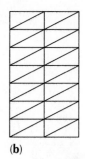

(a)   **(b)**

FIGURE 1.4
From Bolles, 1993.

such a way that (a) is masked. These organizing principles are innate, and experience cannot change them (Ellis, 1938).

We'll have more to say about organizing principles when we take up the topics of sensation and perception in Chapter 5. At that time, we'll return to this issue of experience and its effects on perception, and we'll see that experience can indeed affect basic perceptions in some interesting and surprising ways.

kinds of knowledge are innate. For example, the German philosopher Immanuel Kant (1724–1804) believed that humans are born with a certain mental "structure" that determines how they are capable of perceiving the world. People are born with a natural tendency, for instance, to see things in terms of cause and effect, and to interpret the world in terms of space and time (Bolles, 1993; Wertheimer, 1987). For a better understanding of the nativist position, take a look at the accompanying Inside the Problem.

Darwin's Theory of Evolution. By the last half of the 19th century, the writings of Charles Darwin (1809–1882) were increasingly influential in the debate about the origins of knowledge. Darwin's position was that all living things are essentially the end products of an extended period of evolution, guided by the principles of natural selection. Cats have fur, seals have thick skin, and babies cry because these physical and behavioral traits have been passed along, and selected for, during the evolutionary history of the species. By *natural selection,* Darwin was referring to the fact that, because of inherited characteristics, some individuals are better than others at overcoming obstacles and solving the problems present in their environment. Because animals compete for survival and for opportunities to reproduce, those inherited characteristics that enhance survival and reproduction will be the traits most likely to persist from generation to generation. If an inborn tendency to cry, for example, helps to communicate feelings about hunger effectively, then crying increases the likelihood that one will live long enough to pass this natural tendency on to offspring. Such tendencies are selected for naturally

Certain physical characteristics, such as effective camouflaging, are selected for in nature because they are adaptive—they improve the chances of an organism surviving.

because they are *adaptive*—they improve the chances for meeting the needs demanded by the environment (Darwin, 1859, 1871).

Notice the emphasis is on *inherited* tendencies. Darwin believed that the principles of natural selection apply to characteristics—not only physical traits but also behavioral and psychological ones—that pass from parents to their offspring. It was later learned that the principal vehicle for the transmission and expression of these inherited traits is the genetic material that resides inside the cells of the body. During development, the activity of the genes, together with other internal and external influences, gives rise to the physical structure of the brain and the rest of the body.

With his emphasis on the adaptive value of inherited characteristics, Darwin's ideas had an enormous impact on the thinking of psychologists. Once the role of natural selection in the evolution of mental abilities is accepted, the idea that humans might inherit certain adaptive ways of thinking or of viewing the world (the *nativist* position) becomes more plausible. Researchers now commonly argue, for example, that humans have an inherited predisposition to acquire language, much as birds have an inherited predisposition to fly.

Separated at birth, the Mallifert twins meet accidentally.

Nature Versus Nurture. As we'll see throughout this text, there is evidence that many psychological phenomena—intelligence, emotion, personality—are influenced, in part, by innate genetic factors. At the same time, there's no question that personal experience plays an equally profound role in thought, emotions, and behavior. How a genetic message is expressed depends on an interaction between the native message coded in the genes and environmental effects that occur during development. With respect to the origins of knowledge, recognition of this interaction has led virtually all psychologists to the following important compromise: The study of mind and behavior requires that one appeal to the effects of *nature* (innate factors) as well as *nurture* (experience) in the pursuit of understanding.

The Emergence of Psychology as a Science

The first psychological laboratory was established in 1879 at the University of Leipzig by a German professor named Wilhelm Wundt (1832–1920). Wundt was a medical doctor by training, and early in his career he worked with some of the great physiologists of the 19th century. But, fittingly, his laboratory was established during his tenure as a professor of *philosophy*. (Remember, the intellectual roots of psychology lie at the union of philosophy and physiology.) It is Wundt who is traditionally recognized as the founder of psychology, and 1879 is seen as the year that psychology finally emerged as a subject matter separate from philosophy and physiology. Prior to Wundt, there simply were no official psychology departments, nor official psychologists (Bolles, 1993).

It is noteworthy that the birth of psychology is identified with the establishment of an experimental laboratory. Wundt's background in physiological research convinced him that the proper approach to the study of mental events is through experimentation. He believed that systematic observations should be collected about the phenomena of mind in the same way that one might twitch frogs' legs in an effort to understand the principles of nerve conduction. Wundt did not believe that *all* mental processes could be studied in this way, but he was firmly convinced about the value of a scientific approach. Over the course of his lifetime, he wrote a remarkable number of articles demonstrating how experimentation could be used to investigate mental events.

Structuralism. Wundt (1896) believed that the proper focus for psychology should be the study of immediate conscious experience, by which he meant the things that people sense and perceive when they reflect inward on their own minds. Immediate experience to Wundt was best conceptualized in terms of *elements*—primarily, sensations and feelings—and it was the job of the psychologist to (1) identify these elements, and then (2) discover how they combine to produce meaningful wholes. This approach was later named **structuralism** by one of Wundt's students, Edward Titchener (1867–1927). (Titchener eventually emigrated to the United States, where he set up his own influential laboratory at Cornell University.) The structuralists believed that psychologists should seek to understand the *structure* of the mind by breaking it down into its basic constituent parts, much like a chemist might try to understand a chemical compound (Titchener, 1899).

One problem with structuralism, however, is that while one can directly observe and measure a chemical compound, one cannot directly observe the inter-

Wilhelm Wundt, shown in the center circa 1912, established the first psychological laboratory at the University of Leipzig in 1879.

William James, shown here in 1868, was convinced that to understand a mental process, it's important to consider its function—how does that mental process help the individual solve problems in his or her environment?

nal workings of the human mind. Mental events are subjective and personal, and they cannot be recorded in the same way that a wavelength of light or the frequency of a sound can be recorded. The structuralists' solution to this problem was to use a technique called **systematic introspection,** which required subjects to provide *rigorous* descriptions of their own subjective experiences. In principle, anyone can turn attention inward and observe his or her active mental life. Someone who is trained properly, the structuralists argued, can make systematic observations of that mental life. Wundt believed that self-reports from individuals trained in systematic introspection were best supplemented by objective measures, such as the time it takes to react to presented events, but he maintained that a systematic science of psychology could still be constructed primarily by the introspection technique.

Life in the laboratory for one of Wundt's or Titchener's trained subjects—who were called "introspectionists"—was no walk in the park. Imagine sitting in an armchair in a dark room day after day trying to decompose the fundamental visual elements found in a picture of an apple or a banana. The structuralists tended to restrict their domain of study to simple sensory events because these kinds of stimuli were presumed to be easier to decompose. One by-product of the effort was the amassing of volumes of data about elementary sensory experiences. Titchener's laboratory, for example, was one of the first to document that complex tastes can be broken down into combinations of four elementary tastes: salty, bitter, sour, and sweet (Webb, 1981).

Functionalism. Once psychology was legitimized by Wundt as an independent subject matter of science, psychology departments began to spring up rapidly throughout the world. This was particularly true in North America, where literally dozens of psychology laboratories were established in the last two decades of the 19th century (Hilgard, 1987). By 1890 the discipline already had a number of professional journals reporting the results of psychological research, as well as a number of highly influential textbooks of psychology (e.g., James, 1890). In 1892 the American Psychological Association was founded (with a grand total of some 31 members), and an American who had earlier trained under Wundt in Germany, G. Stanley Hall (1846–1924), was installed as its first president. By 1905 the Association had elected its first woman president, Mary Whiton Calkins (see photo).

Mary Whiton Calkins, the first woman president of the American Psychological Association, was denied admittance to Harvard University in the latter part of the 19th century; at the time, Harvard had a policy of refusing to admit women. She was eventually allowed to study with William James as a "guest" graduate student, and she passed the final examinations for the Ph.D. but never was awarded the degree. Still, despite these obstacles, she made substantial contributions to psychology for over three decades.

But North American psychology quickly took on a different flavor from that represented by the German-based structuralist approach. Whereas the structuralists tended to focus exclusively on the *content* of immediate experience, dissecting the mind into constituent parts, North American psychologists worried more about the *function* of immediate experience. What is the *purpose* of the mental operations that underlie immediate experience? How are the components of mind *used* to achieve this end? Because the emphasis was on function rather than content, this school of thought became known as **functionalism**—it is not the analysis of structure, but the analysis of function and purpose that is the proper guide to the study of mind (Angell, 1903; Dewey, 1896; James, 1890).

Functionalists such as William James (1842–1910) and James Rowland Angell (1869–1949) were convinced that it's not possible to understand a "whole" like the mind by simply looking at its parts—that's like trying to understand a house by analyzing the underlying bricks and mortar (James, 1884). It's necessary to first understand the goal—what specifically is trying to be achieved by the mental operation; then one can try to decipher how the individual components interact to help achieve that goal.

Darwin's ideas about evolution through natural selection were extremely influential in the development of this way of thinking. If we want to analyze the color markings on a butterfly's wings, a Darwinian theorist would argue, we need to ask how those markings help the butterfly to survive. Similarly, when analyzing the operations and processes of mind, a functionalist would argue, we need to focus first on the adaptive value of those operations—how they help people solve the problems they uniquely face.

Functionalism had a liberalizing effect on the development of psychology in North America. It greatly expanded the range of topics that were acceptable for the scientific discipline of psychology to cover. For example, it became important to study how an organism interacts with its environment, which led to an early emphasis on learning (Thorndike, 1898) and to the study of individual differences (how people differ). Later, some functionalists turned their attention to applied issues, such as how people solve practical problems in industry and in educational settings (e.g., Taylor, 1911). To a functionalist, just about any aspect of behavior or mind was considered fair game for study, and psychology in North America boomed.

James Mark Baldwin, shown here in 1928, established the first Canadian psychology laboratory in Toronto in 1889.

Behaviorism. The distinctive shape of psychology was destined to undergo an even more radical transformation in the first two decades of the 20th century. Although functionalism and structuralism differed in their fundamental emphasis, both schools of thought still agreed that the important problem in psychology was to understand immediate conscious experience. The great functionalist William James, in particular, is well known for his superb analysis of the content and purpose of *consciousness*, which he compared to a flowing and ever-changing stream (see Chapter 6). Circa 1900, the technique of introspection—looking inward to observe one's own mind—remained the dominant method of analysis in the tool kit of the experimental psychologist.

But not all psychologists were convinced that self-observation, even when systematic, could lead to consistent and valid scientific data. By definition, personal observations are "personal," so there is no way to confirm that the recorded observations accurately reflect the internal workings of the mind or are representative of all people (remember our earlier problem with the "black box"?). It was also recognized that introspection might change the mental operations being observed. If you're concentrating intently on documenting the elements of "banana," it seems likely that you are experiencing "banana" in an atypical way—not as something to eat, but rather as a complex collection of sensations that need to be decomposed. Introspection also limited the range of populations and topics that could be covered—it's difficult to ask a man with a severe mental disorder, for example, to introspect systematically on his condition (Marx & Cronan-Hillix, 1987).

For these and other reasons, psychologists began to shift their focus away from exclusive study of the "mind" toward more of an emphasis on *behavior*. The intellectual leader of this new movement was a young professor at Johns Hopkins University named John B. Watson (1878–1958). Watson believed that psychology should discard all references to consciousness or mental events. Such events cannot be publicly observed, he argued, and therefore fall outside of the proper domain of science. Observable behavior should be the proper subject matter of psychology; consequently, the task for the scientific researcher is to discover how changes in the environment can lead to changes in measurable behavior. Because of its emphasis entirely on overt behavior, Watson called this new way of thinking **behaviorism** (Watson, 1913, 1919).

John Watson, who rejected the study of the mind in favor of the study of observable behavior, is shown here at age 30.

Behaviorism had an enormous impact on the development of psychology, particularly in North America. Remember, the psychology of Wundt and James was the psychology of mind and immediate experience. Yet by the second and third decades of the 20th century, references to consciousness or immediate experience had largely vanished from psychology's vocabulary, as had the technique of sys-

TABLE 1.2
Early Scientific Schools in Psychology

School	Key Figures	Guiding Focus	Research Tool
Structuralism	Wilhelm Wundt Edward Titchener	Analysis of the "structure" of immediate conscious experience by breaking it down into constituent parts or elements	Systematic introspection
Functionalism	William James James Rowland Angell John Dewey	Analysis of the adaptive functions and purpose of immediate conscious experience	Introspection combined with the study of behavior and individual differences
Behaviorism	John Watson B. F. Skinner	Observation of overt behavior, not mental processes	Controlled observation of overt behavior and the cataloging of relations between environmental stimuli and responses

B. F. Skinner, shown here with one of his famous "Skinner boxes," championed the behaviorist approach and became one of the most influential psychologists of the 20th century.

tematic introspection. Researchers now concerned themselves with measuring behavior, especially in animals, and noting how carefully controlled laboratory experiences could change behavior. The language of psychology became the language of stimuli and responses, and most influential theories were those that specified in fine detail how connections between stimuli and responses could be formed and cataloged (e.g., Hull, 1943; Skinner, 1938). The dominion that the behaviorist approach soon held over psychology was to continue unabated for decades. But it was not to last forever, as we'll see later in this chapter. To help you put things in perspective, Table 1.2 summarizes the three main schools of psychology's early days.

The Influence of the Clinic: Freud and the Humanists

At roughly the same time psychology in America was undergoing its identity crisis, a medical doctor practicing in Vienna was mounting his own kind of psychological revolution. Although Sigmund Freud (1856–1939) had been trained as a neurologist (someone who studies the nervous system), his insights were to come not from the laboratory, but from his experiences as a practitioner, or clinician. Freud regularly encountered patients with physical problems that turned out to be psychological in origin. His efforts to develop effective methods of treatment for these disorders led him to an all-encompassing theory of mind that was to influence legions of future psychologists and psychiatrists (Freud, 1900, 1910, 1940).

Psychoanalysis. Freud called his theory of mind and system of therapy **psychoanalysis.** The term *psychoanalysis* is appropriate because Freud believed that the mind and its contents need to be analyzed extensively before effective treatments can be initiated. In his view, the solution for psychological problems lies in *insight*—understanding how memories and mental processes conspire to produce problem behaviors. Freud's most distinctive departure from the prevailing attitude of the time was his emphasis on *unconscious* determinants of behavior. Freud believed each person houses a kind of hidden reservoir in the mind, filled with memories, urges, and conflicts that guide and control his or her actions. By unconscious, he meant that these hidden conflicts and memories cannot be accessed directly through conscious introspection. If you accept Freud's reasoning, it follows that psychology cannot be based solely on the study of immediate experience, because conscious awareness can often be misleading. People's thoughts as well as their behaviors, Freud argued, are the by-products of unconscious forces that are well beyond current awareness.

Although Freud was not technically a psychologist—he was a medical doctor—if forced, would you classify him as a clinical, an applied, or a research psychologist?

Though Freud was basically working outside of mainstream developments in scientific psychology, he, too, would have rejected systematic introspection as a viable technique for the analysis of mind—but for different reasons than the behaviorists. Freud believed that recording immediate experience was of interest, but only as a way of deciphering hidden conflicts and desires. Freud relied instead on the analysis of dreams—which he believed were largely symbolic—and the occasional "slip of the tongue" as his primary investigative data. He would spend long hours listening to his patients relate their latest dreams or fantasies in the hope that he would discover some symbolic key that would unlock the contents of their unconscious minds. His complex analyses of the mind and its symbols led him to develop a theory of how the unconscious mind defends itself from those seeking to unlock its secrets. We'll consider this theory, as well as its applications for the treatment of psychological disorders, in more detail in Chapters 12 and 15.

In addition to stressing unconscious influences on behavior, Freud emphasized the role of childhood experiences in shaping adult behavior. He suggested that children go through stages of psychological development and that progression through the stages depends on a complex interplay between innate sexual urges and experience. He proposed, for example, that boys become erotically attached to their mothers during childhood and experience anxiety about potential castration by their father. These urges and anxieties are unconscious, of course, so the adult male is unlikely to have any recoverable memories of these conflicts. Freud's theory was considered shocking when it was first introduced (Freud lived during the highly moralistic Victorian era), and it continues to be criticized today. For example, Freud has been criticized for being biased against women (Lerman, 1986; Masson, 1984). But there is no denying the impact of psychoanalytic thought. Psychodynamic theories of human personality—those that stress unconscious forces in determining behavior—continue to be influential in modern psychology.

Sigmund Freud, developer of psychoanalysis, is shown here in the early 1920s.

The Humanistic Response. As noted, Freud's influence was substantial, especially among clinicians seeking to provide effective therapy for psychologically disturbed patients. The familiar image of the client lying on a couch talking about his or her childhood, while the therapist silently jots down notes, is a fairly accurate description of the way early psychoanalysis was performed. But not all psychologists were comfortable with this approach. Freudian psychology paints a dark and pessimistic view of human nature. It presents human actions as the product of unconscious animalistic urges related to sex and aggression. Moreover, it dismisses any awareness that people might have about why they act the way they do

Carl Rogers, shown dressed in shirt sleeves, helped develop the humanistic perspective, which focuses on people's unique capacity for self-awareness, responsibility, and growth.

as symbolic and misleading—people's actions are really motivated by deeply hidden conflicts of which they are unaware.

In the 1950s negative reactions to Freud's view of therapy and mind coalesced into a new movement known as **humanistic psychology.** Humanistic psychologists such as Carl Rogers (1905–1987) and Abraham Maslow (1908–1970) rejected the pessimism of Freud and focused instead on what they considered to be the human's unique capacity for self-awareness, choice, responsibility, and growth. People are not helpless unknowing animals, the humanists argued, controlled by unconscious forces—they are ultimately in control of their own destinies and can rise above whatever innate sexual or animalistic urges they possess. Humans are built for personal growth, to seek their fullest potential, to become all they are capable of being (Maslow, 1954; Rogers, 1951).

The optimistic message of the humanists was to play a significant role in theories of personality development, as well as in the treatment of psychological disorders. Carl Rogers, for example, promoted the idea of *client-centered therapy,* in which the therapist is seen not as an analyst or judge, but rather as a supporter and friend. Humanistic psychologists believe that all individuals have a considerable amount of untapped potential that must be nurtured by an empathetic therapist. This idea remains influential among modern psychological approaches to therapy (see Chapters 12 and 15).

Understanding the Focus of Modern Psychology

The subject matter of psychology has undergone substantial changes since Wundt established the first psychological laboratory in 1879. Vigorous arguments have ensued—often lasting for decades—about the proper focus for psychology (mind or behavior), and about how to conceive of human nature (e.g., is there free will?). The fact that there has been controversy is not surprising, however, given that the discipline is only a little over a century old. Psychology is still getting its theoretical feet wet, and dramatic shifts in approach and method are not unusual in a developing science.

As the 21st century approaches, the majority of psychologists have turned away from a strict adherence to one school of thought, such as behaviorism or psychoanalysis, and have adopted a more **eclectic approach.** The word *eclectic* in this context means that one selects or adopts information from many different sources, rather than relying entirely on one perspective or school of thought. Eclecticism is common among both clinicians working in the field and research psychologists locked away in the laboratory.

In the case of the clinical psychologist, the best technique or approach often depends on the preferences of the client and on the particular problem at hand. For instance, some kinds of phobias—irrational fears of things like heights or spiders—can be treated effectively by focusing on the fearful behavior itself and ignoring its ultimate origin. (We don't need to know why you're afraid of snakes; we can just try to deal with the fear itself.) Other kinds of problems may require the therapist to determine how factors in childhood contribute to and prolong maladaptive adult behavior. Modern clinical psychologists tend to pick and choose among perspectives in an effort to find the approach that works best for their clients.

Many research psychologists also take an eclectic approach. For example, depending on the circumstance, a researcher might seek to determine the genetic or biological origins of a behavior, or seek simply to describe the conditions under which the behavior occurs. Most researchers continue to believe that it's perfectly appropriate to study behavior for its own sake, which is the position advocated by the behaviorist school of thought. If it is possible to catalog when and under what environmental conditions a behavior occurs, the behavior can be modified in a number of positive ways. Influential psychologists such as B. F. Skinner (1904–1990) were able to provide repeated demonstrations of the practical value of a purely behavioral approach. Skinner discovered principles of behavior modification—how actions change with the application of reinforcement and nonreinforcement—that are now widely used in such settings as mental hospitals, schools, and the workplace (Skinner, 1969). We'll discuss these principles in some detail in Chapter 7.

Two additional trends or perspectives have become quite influential in recent years. Although modern psychologists remain eclectic, increasingly you'll find them appealing to *cognitive* and *biological* factors to explain behavior. Because of the special emphasis that these two approaches receive, we'll highlight them briefly in the following sections.

The Cognitive Revolution

By the middle to late 1950s, many psychologists had grown uncomfortable with the strict tenet of behaviorism that overt behavior is the *only* proper subject matter for psychology. Researchers began to show renewed interest in the fundamental problems of consciousness and internal mental processes (Miller, Galanter, & Pribram, 1960; Neisser, 1967). A general shift away from strict behaviorism began, and this movement, which is still going strong in the 1990s, has been labeled the **cognitive revolution** (*cognitive* refers to the process of knowing or perceiving).

There are a number of reasons that many psychologists returned to the study of internal mental phenomena such as consciousness. One factor was the development of research techniques that enabled investigators to infer the characteristics of mind directly from observable behavior. Recording such regularities in behavior as reaction times or forgetting rates can provide detailed information about internal mental processes, provided the experiments are conducted properly. We'll discuss some of the specific tactics of psychological research in Chapter 2, and in subsequent chapters we'll see how those techniques have been applied to the study of the mind as well as behavior.

Another important factor that helped fuel the cognitive revolution was the development of the computer, which became a model of sorts for the human mind. Computers function through an interplay between *hardware*—the fixed

Cognitive psychologists sometimes use the computer as a model of the human mind. Although this analogy is misleading in many respects, it is useful to conceive of behavior as reflecting the interplay between biological factors (the "hardware" of the body) and the strategies that people acquire from experience (the "software" of the mind).

structural features of the machine such as the internal chips and the disk drives—and *software*, or the programs that tell the hardware what to do. Although the human mind cannot be compared directly to a computer, it's useful to conceive of behavior as reflecting the interplay between biological (or genetic) factors—that is, the hardwired structures of the brain and nervous system—and the tactics and strategies (the software) that we learn from the environment. Cognitive psychologists tend to develop explanations of behavior based on appeals to *information processing systems*—internal structures in the brain that have developed to process or manipulate information from the environment in ways that help to solve problems (see Chapters 8 and 9).

As we'll see throughout this book, people's behavior is often influenced by their beliefs and by the manner in which they think. Everything from perceptions and memories to decisions about what foods to eat to choice of friends is critically influenced by prior knowledge and beliefs. Moreover, as we'll discuss in Chapters 14 and 15, many psychologists are convinced that the key to understanding certain psychological disorders, such as depression, lies in the analysis of an individual's thought patterns. Depressed individuals tend to think in rigid and inflexible ways, and some forms of therapy are directed specifically at challenging these entrenched thoughts and beliefs. You'll see references to thoughts and "cognitions" arise repeatedly as we investigate a range of psychological phenomena.

Developments in Biology

An equally important contributor to the focus of modern psychology has been the substantial developments in the understanding of the *biological* underpinnings of behavior. Over the years researchers have uncovered fascinating links between structures in the brain and the phenomena of behavior and mind (see Figure 1.5). It is now possible to record the activity of brain cells directly, and it's been discovered that individual brain cells often respond to particular kinds of events in the environment. For example, there are cells in the "visual" part of the brain that respond actively only when particular colors, or patterns of light and dark, are shown to the eye. Cells in other parts of the body and brain respond to inadequate supplies of nutrients by "motivating" one to seek food.

Moreover, technology is now allowing psychologists to take "snapshots" of mental life in action. As we'll see in Chapter 3, it is now possible to create images of how activities in the brain change as the mind processes different things in its environment. These "pictures" of the brain in action are helping researchers understand normal as well as abnormal brain activity, which potentially may help them find effective treatments for physical and psychological problems.

FIGURE 1.5
Specificity in the Brain.
Researchers have discovered that certain functions in the body appear to be controlled by specific areas of the brain. Developments in the biological sciences continue to have an enormous impact on the thinking of psychologists.

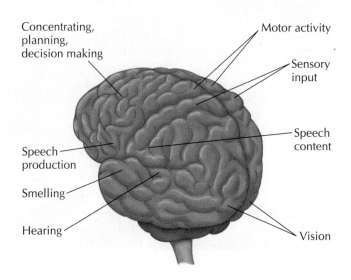

Finally, great strides have also been made in the understanding of brain chemistry—that is, of how natural drugs inside the brain control the range of behaviors people are capable of expressing. It turns out that certain psychological problems, such as depression and schizophrenia, may be related to imbalances among the chemical messengers in the brain. These developments, which we'll discuss in detail in Chapters 3, 14, and 15, are shaping the way psychological theories are constructed and how psychological problems are treated.

Solving Problems with the Adaptive Mind

As the scientific study of behavior and mind, psychology faces the difficult task of seeking regularity in the face of incredible diversity. Research psychologists are in the business of explaining behavior—discovering general principles—but the thoughts and actions of most people appear to be ever-changing. Pick any two people (or animals for that matter), put them in the same situation, and you may well see two different reactions. Take your closest friend—can you predict how he or she will react to a new experience with any kind of certainty? Or think about the number of times you have been surprised or even shocked by the reaction or moodiness of someone you thought you knew.

It's difficult to predict behavior because everyone's view of the world is highly personal and subjective. No two people have had exactly the same experiences, nor have they been born with the same physical or genetic attributes (even identical twins have *some* differences). Behavior is virtually always determined by multiple causes, so it's hard to gather the information needed to generate a reasonable prediction. At the same time, psychologists are convinced that people and animals do not act in haphazard ways; there are reasons why people react the way they do, and it is the job of the psychologist to try to ferret out exactly what those reasons might be. The cause of the behavior may lie completely in the environment—perhaps the individual has been rewarded or punished for acting that way in the past, and these experiences are continuing to control his or her behavior. Alternatively, the actions might arise from the operation of some internal biological system that motivates behavior to help the person survive.

Behavior can be difficult to predict but still be governed by understandable principles. Think about how hard it is to predict the weather, or even the movement of a ball rolling down an inclined plane. Would you claim that these activities are not controlled by principled "laws of nature"?

As we discussed at the beginning of the chapter, each of the chapters in this textbook is organized around a set of *problems*—either adaptive problems or conceptual/practical problems—that psychologists face in their efforts to understand behavior and mind. The problem-solving approach is designed to help promote our theme of the adaptive mind, which proposes that we act for adaptive reasons, but it is also designed to provide you with a direct link between the topic discussions and the real world. For instance, in Chapter 7 we'll discuss some technical laboratory procedures used in the study of learning. Why? Because these procedures have helped psychologists gain insight into how people and animals solve particular learning problems. For example, how do people learn about the signaling properties of events? How do they learn about the consequences of their behavior?

The problem-solving approach is also intended to promote *critical thinking* on your part. Rather than just learning about the details of a conditioning procedure, you should try to make the connection between that particular procedure and solving the learning problem. For example, how exactly does a procedure such as classical conditioning, which we'll learn about in Chapter 7, help us to understand how people learn about the signaling properties of events?

Finally, and perhaps most important, the problem-solving approach is designed to help promote a common theme of understanding across the chapters. The discipline of psychology gains cohesion when behavior is viewed as the product of an adaptive mind. You are encouraged to understand that behaviors, as well as the methods of psychologists, are reactions to problems faced. Emphasizing adaptiveness will increase your sensitivity to the diversity of behavior, both within and across species. Recognizing the diversity of human behavior, across cultures and gender, flows naturally from the perspective of the adaptive mind. Individuals respond and react to unique situations, use strategies that are culturally bound, and are influenced by their individual biological states.

◢ SOLVING THE PROBLEMS: A SUMMARY

At the end of every chapter, you'll find a section titled Solving the Problems. The purpose of this section is to summarize the main points of the chapter from the perspective of our "problems to be solved." This is a good point to stop and think about the facts and theories you've read about and to try to see how they relate to the particular problems that we've discussed. In this chapter, our primary goal was to introduce you to the science of psychology. We framed our discussion around three main problems.

▶ **DEFINING AND DESCRIBING PSYCHOLOGY** What exactly is the subject matter of psychology, and what do psychologists do? As we've seen, psychology is the scientific study of behavior and mind. Notice that this definition makes no specific reference to psychological problems or to any kind of abnormal behavior. Although many psychologists (especially clinical psychologists) do indeed work to promote mental health, applied psychologists and research psychologists tend to work primarily on normal populations of individuals. The goal of the scientific study of behavior and mind is to discover general principles that can be applied widely to help people adapt more successfully—in the workplace, in school, or at home.

▶ **TRACING THE EVOLUTION OF PSYCHOLOGICAL THOUGHT** Even though psychology has existed as a separate subject matter of science for little more than a century, thinkers have pondered the mysteries of behavior and mind for thousands of years. Psychological thought has its primary roots in the areas of philosophy and physiology. Thinkers in these fields addressed several fundamental psychological issues, such as the relation between the mind and the body, and the origins of knowledge. Most psychologists solve the mind-body problem by assuming that the two are essentially one and the same—thoughts, ideas, and emotions are considered to arise out of the biological processes of the brain. It is also common for psychologists to assume that many basic kinds of behaviors originate from natural ingrained tendencies (nature) as well as from lifetime experiences (nurture).

Once the discipline of psychology was established by Wundt in 1879, vigorous arguments ensued over the proper way to characterize and study the mind. Structuralists, such as Wundt and Titchener, believed the world of immediate experience could be broken down into elements, much like how a chemist seeks to understand a chemical compound. The functionalists argued instead that the proper focus should be on the function and purpose of behavior. The behaviorists, on the other hand, rejected the world of immediate experience in favor of the exclusive study of behavior. Added to the mix were the insights of Sigmund Freud, with his emphasis on the unconscious mind, and the arguments of the humanists, who strongly advocate free will and the power of personal choice.

▶ **UNDERSTANDING THE FOCUS OF MODERN PSYCHOLOGY** Each of the psychological perspectives that were influential in psychology's first century remain influential to a certain extent today. But most modern psychologists adopt an eclectic approach—they pick and choose from the perspectives based on the problem at hand. The study of behavior remains of primary importance, but the world of inner experience is also considered fair game for study, as evidenced by the cognitive revolution and by recent developments in the biological sciences.

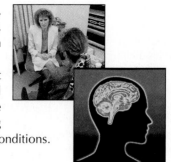

The problem-solving approach in this book is based on the concept of the adaptive mind: People, as well as other animals, use their mental machinery—rooted in the biological processes of the brain—to achieve certain fundamental ends. Individuals adjust their actions in a continuing effort to solve the problems that arise from ever-changing environmental conditions.

Terms to Remember

psychology The scientific study of behavior and mind.

adaptive mind A term referring to the fact that people use their brains in purposive ways, adjusting their actions, often in a flexible and strategic manner, to meet the needs of new conditions as they arise.

DEFINING AND DESCRIBING PSYCHOLOGY

mind The contents and processes of subjective experience: sensations, thoughts, and emotions.

behavior Overt actions such as moving, talking, gesturing, and so on; can also refer to the activities of cells, as measured through physiological recording devices, and to thoughts and feelings, as measured through oral and written expression.

clinical psychologists Professional psychologists who specialize in the diagnosis and treatment of psychological problems; clinical psychologists often work in clinics or private practice delivering human services such as psychotherapy or counseling.

applied psychologists Psychologists who attempt to extend the principles of scientific psychology to practical, everyday problems in the world. Applied psychologists might work in schools, helping students or teachers perform well, or in industry, helping to improve employee morale or training.

research psychologists Psychologists who conduct experiments or collect observations in an attempt to discover the basic principles of behavior and mind. Research psychologists often work in academic settings or in private laboratories to advance the understanding of both basic and applied issues in psychology.

psychiatrists Medical doctors who specialize in the diagnosis and treatment of psychological problems. Unlike psychologists, psychiatrists are licensed to prescribe drugs.

TRACING THE EVOLUTION OF PSYCHOLOGICAL THOUGHT

empiricism The idea that knowledge arises directly from experience.

materialist identity theory The philosophical position purporting that the mind arises entirely from the physical properties of the brain.

nativism The idea that certain kinds of knowledge and ideas are innate—present at birth.

structuralism An early school of psychology that argued for understanding the structure of immediate conscious experience by breaking it down into its basic constituent parts, much like a chemist might try to understand a chemical compound.

systematic introspection An investigative technique used to study the mind that required subjects to look inward and provide rigorous descriptions of their own subjective experiences.

functionalism An early school of psychology that suggested the proper route to understanding immediate conscious experience and behavior lies in analyzing their function and purpose.

behaviorism A school of psychology holding that the proper subject matter of psychology is overt behavior, and the situations that lead to changes in behavior, rather than immediate conscious experience.

psychoanalysis A term used by Freud to describe his theory of mind and system of therapy.

humanistic psychology A movement in psychology that emerged largely as a reaction against the pessimism of Freud. Humanistic psychologists focus on people's unique capacity for choice, responsibility, and growth.

UNDERSTANDING THE FOCUS OF MODERN PSYCHOLOGY

eclectic approach The position adopted by many psychologists that it's useful to select or adopt information from many sources—one need not rely entirely on any single perspective or school of thought.

cognitive revolution The shift away from strict behaviorism, begun in the 1950s, characterized by renewed interest in fundamental problems of consciousness and internal mental processes.

Wherever you're sitting right now, stop, look around, and list all the objects in your surroundings. There are a lot of them—more than you realize. There's probably a telephone, a lamp, possibly a computer, definitely a lot of books, and maybe even a coffeemaker. Each of these objects has a function, from the stapler on the desk to the light fixture to the watch wrapped around your wrist, and luckily, in most cases, that function is clear and unambiguous. Most of the time you use these objects automatically and without much thought, and your life is improved as a result. If you think about it, this is rather remarkable given that there are tens of thousands of such everyday objects in our world.

But still—are you among the many who find themselves engaged in an unrelenting battle with technology? Ask yourself: Do you really know how to get your VCR to tape that program next Wednesday at 3:00 A.M.? Do you know what every menu option means in your word processing program? Do you find yourself hopelessly lost on the Internet? Can you put telephone callers on hold and then transfer them to the appropriate person without cutting someone off (you, the caller, or a third party)? How quickly can you find the correct button to push when the alarm sounds on your clock radio in the morning? Do you merely

shrug your shoulders when the simple-looking gadget you just bought has an instruction booklet with chapters? When you encounter problems like these, your first instinct might be to think the trouble lies in your capabilities, or lack thereof—"I'm just not good at mechanical things." But if you ask most psychologists, they'll tell you the problem usually lies in the product, not in you.

Natural and Unnatural Mappings
Although you may not have thought about turning to a psychologist for help in solving such problems, psychologists actually have a great deal to contribute to proper product design. Between every object and its successful use sits a human user; it's this human "factor" that often dictates whether a product will be a winner or a disaster. A product can be brilliantly designed from a technical standpoint, but it will be of limited value if it's impossible to use. What determines whether a product will be psychologically "correct" or "incorrect"? Let's consider some examples that are very close to home: stoves and doors.

Does your stove look like the one depicted in the left panel of Figure 1.6? Mine does. There are four burners, arranged in a rectangle, and four control knobs that line up horizontally along the

front (or sometimes the back). Your job as a user is to learn the relationship, or what psychologists call the *mapping*, between the control knobs and the activation of each burner. In this case, for example, you need to learn that the far left knob controls the back burner on the left. Or is it the front burner on the left? If you have a stove like this, which is psychologically "incorrect," the odds are that you have trouble remembering which knob controls which burner. Many a time, I've placed a pot of water on one of the burners and turned a control knob, only to find moments later that I've turned on the wrong burner. The reason is simple: The stove has been designed with an unnatural mapping between its controls and the burners. (By the way, the stove came with the house.)

This idea of "mapping" becomes easier to understand when you look at a psychologically "correct" design, which is depicted in the middle panel of Figure 1.6. Notice in this case that the arrangement of the burners naturally aligns with the controls. The left-to-right display of the control knobs matches the left-to-right arrangement of the burners. There is no need to learn the mapping in this case—it's obvious at first sight which knob you need to turn to activate the appropriate burner. Alternatively, if you want to keep the rectangular

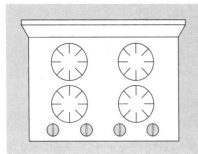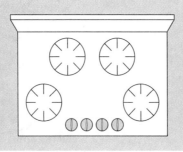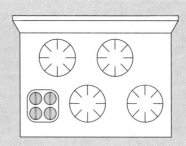

FIGURE 1.6
The Human Factors of Stove Design. The stove on the left does not provide a natural "mapping" between the control knobs and the burners and is therefore difficult to use. The stoves in the middle and on the right provide psychologically "correct" designs that reduce user errors.

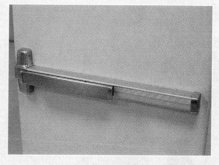

Examples of psychologically "incorrect" and "correct" door designs.

arrangement of the stove top, then simply arrange the control knobs in a rectangular manner that matches the burners, as shown in the far right panel. The point is that there are natural and unnatural ways to express the relationship between product control and product function. Taking advantage of the natural mapping requires that you consider the human factor—in this case, the fact that humans tend to rely on spatial similarity (left knob to left burner; right knob to right burner).

Doors provide additional excellent examples of psychologically correct and incorrect design. Take a look at the first door shown in the series of three door photos. I'm sure you've seen a door like this, with a single bar that needs to be pushed or pulled. But how many times have you slammed yourself into the wrong side of the bar, leaving yourself with an unopened door and a rapidly growing bruise? People do this all the time, even when the door in question is one they use (or misuse) on a regular basis. The middle door shows another example of bad design. In this instance, there is a large flat plate bearing the word PULL. This design is faulty because large flat plates naturally lead us to push, not pull. The fact that the door requires

the PULL sign in large letters is one indication of a rather significant design flaw. Want to see a psychologically correct door design? The door in the far right panel is unambiguous and easy to use: The flat plates naturally induce us to push, and the top plate on the left tells which side to hit. Simple enough—that is, if you take the human factor into account.

User-Centered Design

The two examples we've considered, stoves and doors, illustrate the need for what psychologist Donald Norman (1988) has called "user-centered" product design. Designing a product for easy use requires that the user's natural tendencies be taken into account. As we've stressed in this chapter, all humans interact with the world with a kind of adaptive tool kit—people use certain strategies and have certain natural tendencies that help them to adapt the ever-changing experiences of the world. People are naturally inclined to push on large flat things because this tendency is usually adaptive: If the object has a large flat side, you can use the entire weight of your body, through pushing, to produce movement. But if a product, like a door, works against this natural tendency, it

can become extremely difficult to use. It's critical therefore that people's natural behavioral tendencies be taken into account at some point during the design process.

Moreover, the need for proper user-centered design goes well beyond stoves and doors. The problem becomes much more serious when we consider potentially lethal technology, such as the heavy machinery regularly used in industry. Consider how important the human factor could be in the proper design of nuclear power plants, or sophisticated air traffic control systems. The tragic nuclear accidents of Chernobyl and Three Mile Island have been blamed, in part, on poor user-centered design. In each case, the accident occurred because users either misinterpreted or improperly reacted to ambiguous control features at the plant. Airline accidents as well are often blamed on user failure, either because the cockpit of the plane was badly designed or because the controller on the ground misread or miscommunicated the appropriate traffic information. Fortunately, it is becoming commonplace for industry to recognize the need for user-centered design. Virtually all major technology companies are attempting to deal with the problem, and the demand for professional psychologists who specialize in human factors is rising rapidly.

2

In Chapter 1, we encountered a small black box. Unearthed accidentally, it appeared to be intelligent. When asked questions, it would display answers on a small screen. To discover how the box works, which is a task comparable in many ways to that facing psychologists seeking to understand the mind, we considered three methods of investigation: (1) engaging the box in introspection—asking it to reflect on its own inner workings and describe what it finds; (2) prying it open and looking inside; (3) systematically recording how the box responds to questions—measuring errors, reaction times, and so on. Notice that each of these methods relies on *observation* as the primary knowledge-gathering tool. Knowledge derived from systematic observation is called *empirical knowledge.* Psychology, as a branch of science, is concerned first and foremost with empirical knowledge.

But there are other ways, rather than through observation, that we could have approached our task. For example, we might have gone to the nearest college or university and asked a professor in the psychology department for his or her opinion. We could accept the professor's response as truth, regardless of what the answer might be, simply because it came from someone who is an acknowledged "expert." In this case, we would be relying on *authority,* rather than on systematic observation, as our method of accumulating knowledge. Reliance on authority is actually a common way to solve problems. For example, you will probably rely heavily on your instructor (or this textbook) as a way of deciding what is important to understand about psychology. But appealing to authority is inappropriate as a general strategy in scientific research. Authority figures can be wrong, and the underlying rationale for their offered "truths" is usually hidden and unattainable.

Knowledge acquired through empirical methods has the important advantage of being *self-correcting:* One idea can be clearly shown to be better than another if it more closely fits the evidence collected from observation. If initial observations suggest that all children toilet-train by the age of 2, but subsequent observations reveal that large groups of toddlers are still dependent on their diapers at age 3, then we'll need to correct our initial conclusion. You'll see throughout this text that psychologists, like all scientists, are constantly rethinking and challenging existing conclusions based on the collection of additional empirical evidence. Empirical methods also have the advantage of being *public*—anyone who observes is capable of adding to the empirical knowledge database. We don't need to rely on the idiosyncratic methods of the authority figure.

Because observation is the supreme court of appeal in psychology, psychologists rely on the **scientific method** as their primary tool for answering questions. A full discussion of science and its methods is outside the scope of this text, but we can highlight some of the important steps in the process. The scientific method always begins, appropriately, with *observation.* In psychology, we choose the behavior of interest and begin recording its characteristics, as well as the conditions under which the behavior occurs. Second, the researcher looks for *regularities* in the observations, or data, that have been collected—are there certain consistent features that the behaviors show, or conditions under which the behaviors commonly appear? Third, the researcher generates a *hypothesis,* which is essentially a prediction, or general statement, about the characteristics of the behavior under study. Hypotheses are normally expressed in the form of testable "if-then" statements—if some set of conditions is present and observed, then a certain kind of behavior will occur. Finally, in the last step the predictions of the hypothesis are checked for accuracy—once again, through *observation.* If the new data that are collected are consistent with the prediction of the hypothesis, the hypothesis is

OBSERVE

Rat receives food for jumping through checkerboard panel on left

DETECT REGULARITIES

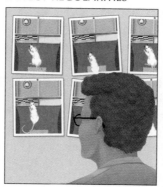

Over trials, rat consistently chooses to jump toward the checkerboard panel on left

GENERATE HYPOTHESIS

Rat has learned to associate checkerboard with food, so if checkerboard is moved to the right, then the rat will jump to the right

OBSERVE

Rat jumps to the left, suggesting rat has learned that jumping left produces food

supported. The four steps of the scientific method are demonstrated in Figure 2.1. We'll discuss some specific instances of how the scientific method can be applied in practice later in this chapter.

Notice that the scientific method is anchored on both ends by observation—observation always begins and finishes the scientific process. As a result, psychological terms, especially those contained in hypotheses or in more broadly based sets of statements called *theories,* must be defined in such a way that they can be observed. It is critical that any psychological explanation be specific about how the concepts involved can be directly measured. Otherwise, the explanation is untestable and falls outside the domain of psychological science. Psychologists therefore use **operational definitions,** in which concepts are defined specifically in terms of how they can be measured, as a way of ensuring testability (Levine & Parkinson, 1994; Stevens, 1939). For example, "intelligence" is typically defined in terms of performance on a psychological test, whereas "memory" may be defined as the number of words correctly recalled on a retention test.

▶ PREVIEWING THE CONCEPTUAL AND PRACTICAL PROBLEMS

As the scientific study of behavior and mind, psychology's primary goal is understanding. Psychologists want to know what causes behavior; they want to understand what mechanisms or processes in people or in the environment conspire to produce the remarkable diversity of human thought and action. But understanding is not always easy to achieve, nor is it the only acceptable goal of psychology. Sometimes it is sufficient merely to describe and predict. Consider television sets, refrigerators, or computers. Most of us have no idea how these things work, nor could we fix them if they broke, but we do know how to manipulate them in ways to enrich our lives. The same might be said of psychology; we may not always understand why people act the way they do, but if we can catalog *when* people will act in a particular way, we gain more effective control over our environment.

In this chapter we will consider the general tactics and strategies that underlie psychological research. The discussion focuses on four conceptual and practical problems that researchers investigating behavior and mind often attempt to solve: What are the proper techniques for observing and describing behavior? How can researchers predict behavior and use it for selection? How can researchers determine

FIGURE 2.1

Steps in the Scientific Method. The four major steps in the scientific method. The first step, shown in the first panel, is observation; here, the rat is observed jumping toward a checkerboard panel on the left. In step two, the researcher looks for regularities in behavior and notes that the rat, over repeated trials, consistently jumps to the checkerboard on the left. In step three, the researcher generates a hypothesis (If I move the checkerboard to the right, the rat will jump to the right), and in step four, the researcher tests the hypothesis. Here the hypothesis has turned out to be wrong. The rat is jumping left rather than following the checkerboard.

the causes of behavior? What procedures must be used to ensure that research participants are treated ethically? In each case, we'll examine the techniques considered to be "solutions" to these problems, and we'll pay particular attention to the pitfalls that can hinder the research process.

▶ **OBSERVING AND DESCRIBING BEHAVIOR** Among the most important steps in any psychological research project is to choose the behavior of interest and begin recording its characteristics. But observation in research is more than just casual looking or listening—the methods of observation must be systematic. But what does being systematic really entail? Should just one instance of the behavior be observed, or many? Should the target actions be recorded in a natural setting or in the laboratory? Should researchers make their presence known to the subject, or try to hide their role as observers? Moreover, once a set of systematic observations has been collected, how are those observations best summarized and described? How can a researcher tell whether any one instance of a behavior is truly representative of the way that individual normally acts? Psychologists have a number of observational and descriptive techniques at their disposal; we will consider some advantages and disadvantages of each.

▶ **PREDICTING AND SELECTING BEHAVIOR** Once a set of behavioral data has been collected and described, the researcher typically begins to think about the possibility of prediction and selection. Descriptive research yields facts about behavior. Based on what has been learned, can one anticipate when and how the behavior will occur in the future? Prediction allows more effective "control" of future environments. For example, researchers can *identify* and then *select* individuals who are likely to perform in a certain way in the future. Consider the manager of a company who is looking for a potential employee. If some test or other assessment technique can pinpoint those individuals who are likely to have the relevant job skills, the hiring process becomes more efficient. Psychologists often use *correlational research,* which is designed to determine whether a statistical relationship exists between two measures of behavior, as one way of generating predictions about behavior. Depending on the size of the statistical relationship, psychologists are able to predict behavior on one measure, such as job performance, given that they know how the subject performed on a second measure, such as an aptitude test. We'll discuss the logic behind correlational research and describe the advantages and limitations of the conclusions that can be drawn.

▶ **DETERMINING WHY BEHAVIOR OCCURS** Correlational research is useful for prediction, but it usually reveals little, if anything, about *why* behavior

Employers sometimes use psychological tests as a means for predicting and selecting behavior. They seek to identify and select individuals who are likely to perform in a particular way in the future.

occurs. The fact that two things are related statistically, such as grades in high school and grades in college, does not mean that one causes the other. To determine causality, it is necessary to conduct *experimental research*. Through experiments, the researcher systematically manipulates the environment in order to determine the effect of that manipulation on behavior. For example, if an experimenter wants to know whether forming mental pictures helps memory, he or she will need to compare conditions in which people form mental pictures and conditions in which they do not. If conducted properly, experiments allow the researcher to understand *why* behavior occurs or changes in a particular situation. We'll discuss how experimental research is conducted and how cause-and-effect conclusions are drawn.

▶ **TREATING RESEARCH PARTICIPANTS ETHICALLY** One of the most important challenges facing researchers is ensuring that the participants in psychological research receive the proper ethical treatment. Psychologists seek to understand, through observation, the behavior and minds of others. But observing others—be they people or animals—requires invading, to a certain extent, the environment of these subjects. Is it proper for the psychologist to lurk in the shadows, carefully recording your every move, in some grand attempt to advance scientific knowledge? Is it proper to experiment on animals—depriving them of food or water, or destroying portions of their brain—simply to learn about the mechanisms underlying behavior? These are not easy questions to answer for any branch of science. Psychology has a set of established safeguards and ethical standards that researchers use; we'll discuss these standards and see how they are generally applied in the conduct of psychological research.

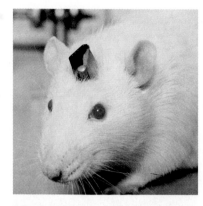

Many important insights in psychology have come from the study of animals, but using animals as laboratory subjects can raise serious ethical questions.

Observing and Describing Behavior: Descriptive Research Methods

Because observation is so pivotal to psychological research, it is appropriate that we begin with a discussion of **descriptive research,** which consists of the tactics and methods that underlie the direct observation and description of behavior. At face value, the act of observation appears to be simple enough—after all, most people can watch and record the behavior of themselves or others. But it's actually easy to be misled, even when the goal is simply to record behavior passively (Rosenthal & Rosnow, 1969; Rosnow & Rosenthal, 1993).

Let's suppose that you want to observe the behavior of preschoolers in the local day-care center. You arrive at the center with cameras and recording devices in hand and begin systematic observations of the children at play. After a few moments, you notice that the children distract easily—many seem uneasy and hesitant to engage in the activities suggested by the teacher. Several children show outward signs of fear and eventually withdraw, crying, to a corner of the room. Later, in describing your results, you conclude that children in day-care centers adjust badly, and some even show early signs of poor psychological health.

It shouldn't take much thought to recognize that your research strategy may suffer from a basic problem. Whenever you observe the actions of someone else, the very act of observing can affect the behavior being recorded. In the case of the day-care center, it's likely that your unexpected presence in the center (with cameras and the like) made the children feel uncomfortable and led them to act in ways that were not representative of their normal behavior. Psychologists refer to this condition as a problem of reactivity. **Reactivity** occurs whenever an individual's behavior is changed in some way by the process of being observed; the behavior recorded by the researcher becomes essentially a *reaction* to the obser-

Psychologists need to worry about the problem of reactivity: Are the behaviors being observed simply a reaction to the observation process? If the behavior of these children is changed as a result of the observer's presence, then the observations may not generalize well to other situations.

vation process (Orne, 1969; Webb, Campbell, Schwartz, Sechrist, & Grove, 1981). The children are probably not naturally hesitant and distracted—they were simply startled by you and your recording devices.

One of the negative consequences of reactivity is that the data are likely to lack external validity. **External validity** refers to how well the results of an observation generalize to other situations, or are representative of real life (Campbell & Stanley, 1966; Cook & Campbell, 1979). If the children's behavior is largely a reaction to your presence as an observer, it is clearly not representative of real life. More generally, even if these children are naturally fearful, your one set of observations cannot guarantee that your conclusions are representative of how children at other day-care centers will act. To enhance external validity, you would need to record the behavior of children at another day-care center, to see whether similar patterns of behavior emerge.

Naturalistic Observation: Focusing on Real Life

One way that researchers try to reduce the problem of reactivity and improve external validity is to observe behavior in natural settings using nonintrusive measures (Martin & Bateson, 1993; Timberlake & Silva, 1994). In **naturalistic observation,** the researcher records only naturally occurring behavior, as opposed to behavior produced in the laboratory, and makes a serious effort not to interfere with the behavior in any way. Because the recorded behavior is natural and has not been "manufactured" by the researcher, the observational data are generally considered to be representative of real life (of course, it is also necessary to repeat the observations in different settings to be sure the results generalize). Also, if the subjects being studied are unaware of being observed, their behavior cannot simply be a reaction to the observation process. Naturalistic observation has been used with great success by psychologists as well as by *ethologists,* biologists who study the behavior of animals in the wild (Goodall, 1990; Lorenz, 1958).

But how is it possible to observe behavior in a way that is truly unobtrusive? To observe natural behavior directly, researchers sometimes use a technique called *participant observation,* in which the observer attempts to become a part of the activities being studied. For example, in the 1950s a group of psychologists infiltrated a "doomsday" cult group by passing themselves off as "true believers." This particular cult preached the impending end of the United States, on a particular date, from a natural disaster. Once they were on the inside, the psychologists were able to record and study the reactions of the cultists when the inevitable day of doom failed to materialize (Festinger, Riecken, & Schachter, 1956). In another classic project that we will return to in Chapter 14, a group of researchers had themselves committed to local mental hospitals—they complained of "hearing voices"—in an effort to obtain an unobtrusive record of patient life inside an institution (Rosenhan, 1973). Participant observation could easily be used in our day-care center example: You could simply introduce yourself as a new teacher, rather than as a researcher, and hide your cameras or other recording equipment so that the children can't tell they're being recorded.

Do you see any ethical problems with the technique of participant observation? After all, isn't the researcher misleading people by assuming a false identity?

Another useful technique is to measure behavior indirectly, by looking at the *results* of a behavior rather than the behavior itself. For example, you might be able to learn something about the social habits of teenagers at the local mall by measuring the content and quality of the litter they leave behind. (You could probably tell, for instance, their shopping preferences and eating habits.) Administrators at museums have been able to determine the popularity of various exhibits by noting how quickly floor tiles in front of each wear out and need to be replaced (see Figure 2.2; Webb et al., 1981). Neither of these examples requires direct observations of behavior; it is the aftereffects—the products—of the behavior that provide the insightful clues.

FIGURE 2.2
Naturalistic Observation of Behavioral Results. In a study conducted at the Chicago Museum of Science and Industry, researchers gauged the popularity of exhibits by noting how quickly the vinyl tiles in front of each display needed to be replaced. The live chick hatching exhibit proved to be extremely popular.

Naturalistic observation is an effective technique for gaining a record of natural behavior, but it can also be used to verify the results of laboratory experiments (Miller, 1977; Timberlake & Silva, 1994). To gain control over a behavior, and to understand what causes an action to be performed, researchers usually need to manipulate the behavior directly through an experiment. Because it is difficult to conduct experimental research in natural settings, laboratory studies usually generate concerns about external validity. For instance, most studies of human memory have been conducted in the laboratory by having subjects learn artificial lists of words (Bruce, 1985; Neisser, 1978). But to what extent are the psychological principles gleaned from such studies relevant to learning and remembering in natural settings? To answer this question, psychologists also record natural instances of remembering and forgetting, such as eyewitness accounts of naturally occurring events, to determine whether the patterns of remembering and forgetting resemble those obtained in the lab (e.g., Conway and associates, 1994). For reasons that will become clear later in this chapter, naturalistic observation, by itself, is a poor vehicle for determining causality. But it can be used effectively to gather basic information about a phenomenon and, in conjunction with laboratory research, to establish the generality of psychological principles.

Case Studies: Focusing on the Individual

Another widely used descriptive research technique is the case study. In a **case study,** the research effort is focused on a single case, usually an individual, in an effort to accumulate a great deal of relevant information about a psychological issue (Bromley, 1986; Elmes, Kantowitz, & Roediger, 1995; Heiman, 1995). Because lots of information is collected about the background and behavior of one person, case studies often give the researcher a historical perspective that can aid in forming hypotheses about a behavior's origin. The psychology sections of your local bookstore are undoubtedly littered with popularized versions of case studies. There's the famous case of Chris Sizemore, popularized in the movie *The Three Faces of Eve,* who coped with emotional distress by shifting among three distinct and quite different personalities (Thigpen & Cleckley, 1957). *Sybil,* depicted in a television miniseries of the same name, was the subject of another famous case study of multiple personality disorder. One of the most influential psychological theories of the 20th century, the psychoanalytic theory of Sigmund Freud, was based primarily on descriptive data derived from case studies.

But like naturalistic observation, the case study methodology suffers from some limitations. By focusing on a single case, researchers essentially place all of their theoretical eggs in one basket. This situation raises questions about external validity: Are the experiences of the subject truly representative of others (Liebert & Liebert, 1995)? Sybil's frightening descent into multiple personality disorder (now known as dissociative identity disorder) may or may not be representative of how psychological disorders normally develop. Another problem with case studies is difficulty in verifying the claims of the individual under study. If the observations of the single subject are somehow tainted with inaccuracies—if the subject is lying, for example—the entire study must be viewed with suspicion. Once again, as with naturalistic observation, case studies are excellent vehicles for generating hypotheses but are generally ineffective for determining cause-and-effect relationships.

Survey Research: Focusing on the Group

Whereas a case study focuses on a single individual, psychologists use a **survey** to sample reported behavior broadly, usually by gathering responses from many people. Most surveys are administered in the form of a questionnaire—individuals, or groups of individuals, are asked to answer a series of questions about some personal behavior or psychological characteristic. You are of course familiar with opinion surveys, which are conducted by political campaigns or by the news media to capture the current attitudes of voters. But surveys can be used purely for research purposes, to gain valuable descriptive information about behavior and mind. For example, researchers can use a survey to determine the widespread psychological aftereffects of a significant environmental disaster (Dooley, Catalano, Mishra, & Sexner, 1992), or to determine whether problems such as depression are more likely in elderly people who suffer financial hardships (Krause & Liang, 1993).

In naturalistic observation, the researcher records only naturally occurring behavior, as opposed to behavior produced in the laboratory, and a concerted effort is made not to interfere with the behavior in any way.

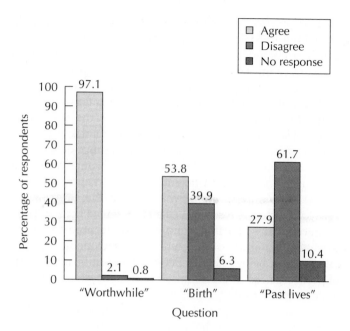

FIGURE 2.3
Opinions About Hypnosis.
Selected results from the Yapko
(1994) survey of psychotherapists.
The bars show the percentage of
respondents who agreed, disagreed,
or gave no response to following
statements: "Hypnosis is a worthwhile
psychotherapy tool," "Hypnosis can
be used to recover memories of actual
events as far back as birth," and
"Hypnosis can be used to recover
accurate memories of past lives."

Figure 2.3 shows results of a survey conducted to assess some current beliefs of practicing psychotherapists. Michael Yapko (1994) asked 869 psychotherapists with differing degrees of academic training to respond to questions about the use of hypnosis as a technique for recovering forgotten or "repressed" memories of prior events. As you may know, hypnosis is sometimes used by therapists as a memory "aid" to help troubled clients recover forgotten instances of trauma. Ninety-seven percent of Yapko's (1994) survey respondents agreed that hypnosis is a worthwhile tool in psychotherapy, and nearly 54% were convinced that hypnosis can be used to recover memories of actual events as far back as birth. More than one in four of the respondents actually believed that hypnosis can be used to recover accurate memories of past lives.

Surveys can be significant, if conducted properly, because they provide researchers with valuable insight into what people believe. In this case, Yapko's data are alarming because they reveal how widespread misinformed views can be, even among professional psychotherapists. As you'll find in Chapters 6, 8, and 12, there is little, if any, scientific evidence to support the belief that memories recovered through hypnosis are especially accurate, nor is there any scientific evidence to support the existence of past lives (remembered or otherwise)! These survey findings point to the need for improved education and training, at least for this group of respondents. But, as we'll see shortly, before survey results like these can be accepted as truly representative of a target group, such as practicing psychotherapists, the researchers must ensure that the participants in the survey have been sampled randomly.

Sampling from a Population. The point of a survey is to gather lots of observations, from many people, to determine the characteristics of a larger group or population. If the population of interest is extremely large, such as everyone between 18 and 25 in the United States, researchers must decide how to select a representative subset of individuals to measure. A subset of individuals from a target population is referred to as a *sample.*

A researcher needs to consider a number of technical details when sampling from a population. For example, it is easy to end up with an unrepresentative, or *biased,* sample unless the proper precautions are taken (Weisberg, Krosnick, & Bowen, 1989). Let's imagine that a researcher named Bob wants to know how often

People who volunteer to participate in research studies may not always be representative of the population. In order to achieve an unbiased sample, researchers need to sample randomly from the population of interest.

college-aged adults practice "safe sex." He puts an ad in selected college newspapers, containing a toll-free telephone number. He hopes that students will call the number and answer questions about their sexual practices. But not every college-aged student in the country will choose to participate, so Bob will certainly end up with only a subset, or sample, of his population of interest. Do you think that the data collected from his subset will be truly representative of college students?

In this case, the answer is clearly "no" because the method of sampling depends on people *choosing* to participate. Volunteers tend to produce biased samples, because such individuals usually have strong feelings or opinions about the study (Rosenthal & Rosnow, 1975). Think about it—would you call in and tell a researcher that you regularly fail to practice safe sex? Representative samples are produced through **random sampling,** which means that everyone in the target population has an equal likelihood of being selected for the survey. In principle, for Bob to achieve a truly unbiased sample he would need to sample randomly from the entire population of college students—everyone in the group needs to have an equal chance of being selected. Because this is difficult to achieve in practice, Bob will probably need to limit himself to sampling randomly from the population of students going to his particular college.

Now let's return to the Yapko's (1994) survey, in which 869 practicing psychotherapists gave their views on the use of hypnosis as an effective memory aid. The results showed that some psychotherapists erroneously believe that memories recovered through hypnosis are accurate. Unfortunately, however, Yapko did not use a random sample of psychotherapists in his study—he simply asked therapists who attended certain conventions and workshops for their opinions. His data may therefore suffer from a "volunteer problem" that limit their generalizability. Only psychotherapists with strong opinions about hypnosis may have chosen to participate. To claim his results are truly representative of psychotherapists as a whole, he would need to use random sampling.

Even if a proper sample of the population has been selected, however, surveys can suffer from additional problems (Weisberg et al., 1989). Because large numbers of people need to be assessed, it is not usually possible to gain in-depth information about the behavior or opinion of interest. For example, researchers who use surveys are typically unable to obtain detailed historical information of the sort that can be collected in a case study. The basic data in a survey also consist of self-reports, and subjects cannot always be counted on to provide accurate observations. Some subjects lie or engage in wishful thinking, while others answer questions in ways they think might please the researcher. Researchers can write surveys in ways that minimize these risks—for example, questions can be asked several times with slightly different wording to check on the consistency of the participant's responses—but inaccuracies in responding are always a concern and difficult to eliminate.

If conducted properly, surveys can be great vehicles for obtaining general information from a target population. If the sample is truly random, concerns about external validity are reduced. But as with the other descriptive research methods that we've discussed, surveys rarely provide definitive information about behavior and mind. They are best used in conjunction with other techniques, such as case studies or naturalistic observation, in a multifaceted research effort.

Psychological Tests: Assessing Individual Differences

A major area of descriptive research in psychology is psychological testing. Psychological tests, which come in a variety of forms, are designed primarily to measure individual differences among people. For example, *achievement tests* measure a person's current level of knowledge or competence in a particular subject (such as mathematics or psychology) compared to others; *aptitude tests* are designed to measure a person's potential for success in a given profession or area of study. Researchers also use various kinds of intelligence and personality tests to classify ability or to characterize a person's tendencies to act in consistent ways.

Psychological tests have enormous practical value, as well as value in helping to advance basic research (Anastasi, 1985). Intelligence tests can be used to identify children who might need extra help in school or who are "gifted" and can benefit from an enriched curriculum; for adults, intelligence test scores are sometimes used to predict future performance on the job (Ree & Earles, 1992). Moreover, psychologists have used analysis of test performance as one method for trying to decipher the fundamental components of the mind. Data collected from psychological tests have been used to address such questions as, are people saddled with a fixed amount of intelligence, present at birth, or do they have multiple kinds of intelligence that rise and fall with experience? Do people have consistent personality traits, such as honesty or pleasantness, or do their behaviors change haphazardly across situations? We'll return to these specific questions, and address several others, when we treat psychological tests in more detail in Chapters 10 and 12.

Statistics: Summarizing and Interpreting the Data

At the end of most research projects, no matter what research method is used, the researcher is typically faced with lots of information to analyze. The next step is to organize and summarize the data in a form that allows for interpretation. The ultimate goal is to find regularities in the observations, so that effective hypotheses can be formulated and tested. When observing children in a day-care center, for instance, an investigator would normally collect information from many children, along with repeated observations of the same child, in an effort to ensure that the results can be generalized. It would be inappropriate simply to pick and choose from the results, based on what looks interesting, because selective analyses of data can introduce systematic biases into the interpretation (Barber, 1976; Rosenthal, 1994).

If the collected observations can be expressed in the form of some kind of number, it is possible to calculate *statistics,* or values derived from mathematical manipulations of the data, to summarize and interpret the results. For any set of numerical observations, such as how often day-care providers wash their hands during a fixed period of diaper changing, it is useful to begin with a measure of *central tendency,* which is the value around which scores tend to cluster. You are probably familiar with the **mean,** which is the arithmetic average of a set of scores. To calculate a mean, you simply add up the numbers representing each observation and divide the total by the number of observations. So, if Jack washed his

Psychologists use psychological tests to predict and select as well as to help decipher the fundamental components of mind.

hands 4 times, Sally 9 times, Kim 4 times, Jessica 5 times, and Rowena 8 times, the mean of these scores would be 6 (4 + 9 + 4 + 5 + 8 = 30; 30 ÷ 5 = 6). The mean summarizes the observations into a single representative number: On average, day-care providers in your study washed their hands 6 times while changing diapers. Notice that in this case none of the workers actually washed his or her hands exactly 6 times. The mean provides only an estimate of central tendency; it does not indicate anything about particular scores.

Other measures of central tendency include the **mode,** which is the most frequently occurring score (in the handwashing example the mode is 4), and the **median,** which is the middle point in the set of scores. The mode has the advantage that it always represents a real score—someone actually washed his or her hands 4 times—and it is easy to calculate. Calculating the median takes a bit more work. First, order the scores from smallest to largest (4, 4, 5, 8, 9), then look for the middle score. With the handwashers, half the scores fall below 5, and half fall above, so 5 is the median. If the number of scores is even, with no single middle score (e.g., 4, 4, 5, 6, 8, 9), the median is often calculated by taking the midpoint of the two middle scores (the midpoint between 5 and 6 is 5.5).

Researchers usually like to compute several measures of central tendency for a set of scores. The mean is an excellent summary of the average score, but it can sometimes be misleading. Suppose, for example, that Sally is replaced at the day-care center by Anthony, who suffers from an abnormal compulsion to wash his hands. Anthony washes his hands 29 times during the recording period. If we replace Sally with Anthony, we now have the following set of scores: 4, 4, 5, 8, 29. The arithmetic average, or mean, will shift rather dramatically, from 6 to 10, but neither the mode nor the median will change at all (see Figure 2.4). Because of

FIGURE 2.4
Comparing the Mean, the Median, and the Mode. The top row shows the differences between the *mean* (arithmetic average), the *median* (middle point in a set of scores), and the *mode* (most frequently occurring score), for handwashing behavior at a day-care center. The bottom row shows how the mean can be affected by an extreme score, someone who washes his hands 29 times. Notice that the extreme score has no effect on the median or mode.

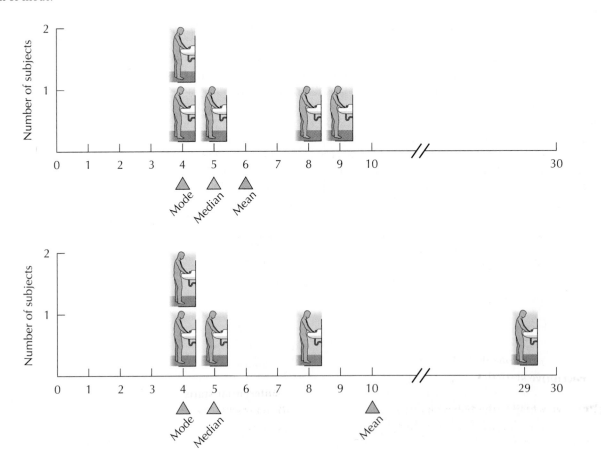

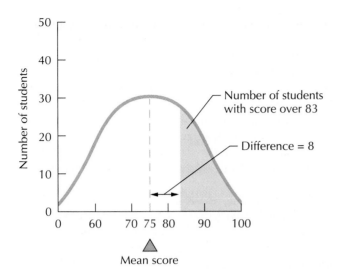

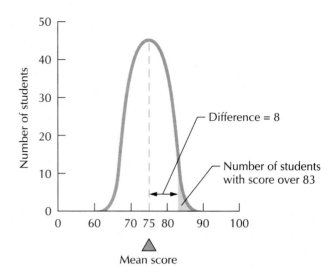

FIGURE 2.5
Variability. Researchers are often interested in variability, or the extent to which scores in a set differ from one another. Each of these two distributions has the same average, or mean, but the distribution on the left has more variability. Notice that the difference between the mean and a particular score, such as 83, is the same in the two cases. But scoring 8 points above the mean is highly unusual in the distribution on the right, while more common in the distribution on the left. If you received a score of 83, which class would you rather be in?

the way they are calculated, means are very sensitive to extreme scores—the value shifts in the direction of the deviant score. On the other hand, the mode and the median are unaffected. In our example, the median or the mode is probably a better summary of the behavior than the mean.

In addition to calculating measures of central tendency, researchers are also quite interested in summarizing **variability,** or how much the scores in a set differ from one another. The mean indicates the average, but it provides no information about how far apart the individual scores are from each other. To see why variability is important, think about your last exam score. Let's assume that you received an 83 and the average score was 75. What can you conclude about your performance? Your best guess is that you did about average because your score was relatively close to the mean. But perhaps not. If the scores were all bunched toward the middle, your performance might have been spectacular—in fact, an 83 could have been the highest grade in the class. Thus, researchers need to know more than the average of a set of scores—they also need to know something about variability (see Figure 2.5).

Several measures of variability are available to researchers. A simple one is the **range,** which measures the difference between the largest and smallest scores in the distribution. If the highest score in the class was a 90 and the lowest score a 50, the range would be 90 − 50 = 40. A more widely used index is the **standard deviation,** which provides an indication of how much individual scores vary from the mean score. It's calculated by (1) finding the difference (or deviation) of each score from the mean, (2) squaring those deviations, (3) finding the average, or mean, of the squared deviations, and then finally, (4) calculating the square root of this average. We'll return to the concept of standard deviation later in the text, particularly in Chapter 10, because psychologists often define psychological characteristics, such as intelligence, in terms of how far away a measured score "sits" from the mean in a distribution of scores.

Inferential Statistics. Statistics such as the mean and the standard deviation help researchers *describe* their data; as such, they form a part of what is generally called **descriptive statistics.** But it is also possible to use statistics to draw inferences from data—to help *interpret* the results. Researchers use **inferential statistics** to decide whether the behaviors recorded in a sample are representative of some larger population or about whether the differences among observations can be attributed to chance.

Grade point average is typically calculated using the mean. Suppose the mean was replaced with a grade point "mode" or a grade point "median." What would be the advantages and disadvantages of calculating grade point in this way?

Inferential statistics are based on the laws of probability. Researchers always assume that the results of an observation, or group of observations, might be attributable to unknown chance factors. For example, suppose that you find that male day-care providers wash their hands 5.8 times a day on average, whereas female providers wash 6.2 times a day (a difference of 0.40). Is there really a gender difference in handwashing behavior? It could be that your recorded gender difference is accidental, and unrepresentative of a true difference. Maybe if you had recorded handwashing behavior on a different day, you would have found that male day-care providers wash their hands more often. It is in your interest, then, to determine how representative your handwashing data are of "true" handwashing behavior.

Through the use of inferential statistics, researchers attempt to determine the likelihood, or probability, that the collected pattern of data might have occurred by chance. More specifically, you need to ask: If there is really no true gender difference in handwashing behavior, how often would you expect to find, if handwashing behavior was sampled on any particular day, that females would wash their hands 0.40 times more than males? The details of the procedures are beyond the scope of this text, but if you find that the probability of the recorded observations being due to chance is extremely low, then your findings can be treated as *statistically significant*. In most psychological studies, the probability that an outcome is due to chance must be lower than .05 (5%) for the outcome to be accepted as statistically significant. This means you can treat a female handwashing advantage of 0.40 as significant only if that difference occurs less than five times out of a hundred by chance factors alone.

Predicting and Selecting Behavior: Correlational Research Methods

Facts are the important by-product of descriptive research—researchers collect observations systematically and then describe them in ways that yield useful summaries of natural or laboratory behavior. But psychologists are rarely satisfied with simply describing behavior; they like to use what they've learned to make predictions about behavior in the future. For example, after observing and describing the academic performance of someone in high school, a psychologist might want to predict how well that individual will perform in college. As we discussed earlier, prediction allows one to determine which individuals are likely to perform in a certain way in the future. Thus, the manager of a company can select the best potential employee based on present performance; the school administrator can manage a student's curriculum to maximize future performance.

Correlational Research

One way to predict future performance is to determine whether a *relationship* exists between two measures of behavior: the one recorded in the present, and the one expected in the future. Psychologists often use a statistical measure called a *correlation* to help make this determination. A **correlation** assesses whether two *variables*, or measures that can take on more than one value (such as a test score), vary together in a systematic way. Correlations are computed by gathering observations on both measures of interest from a single set of individuals, then computing a quantitative index called a *correlation coefficient*. This statistic, once computed, gives the researcher a feel for how well the value of one behavioral variable, such as job success, can be predicted if the value of the second behavioral variable, such as an achievement test score, is known.

This building skills of the young girl on the left may or may not be predictive of a professional career in architecture.

When a correlation exists between two measures of behavior, those behaviors tend to vary together in some way. In the day-care example, there is probably a strong correlation between the number of diapers changed during the day and the number of times the caretakers wash their hands. The two measures vary together—the more diapers changed, the more frequently hands are washed. In this particular case, we have a *positive correlation,* which means that the two measures vary in the same direction—the more of one, the more of the other. A *negative correlation* exists when the two measures still vary together but in opposite directions. For example, there is an inverse relationship between the number of hours that Beverly practices on the piano and the number of errors she makes during her recital performance. The more she practices, the fewer errors she is likely to make. A relationship still exists between the two measures—we can predict one when we know the other—but the correlation is negative.

Calculating a correlation coefficient requires that you collect observations from a relatively large number of individuals. Moreover, you need to collect data initially on *both* behavioral measures. The details of the calculation are beyond the scope of this text, but *variability* among the collected observations is an important ingredient of the calculation. If calculated properly, correlation coefficients always range between -1.00 and $+1.00$. The absolute value of the coefficient (the range between 0 and 1 without the sign) indicates the *strength* of the correlation. The closer the value is to 1.00 (either positive or negative), the greater the relationship between the two measures, and the more likely you are to predict correctly. The sign of the coefficient indicates whether the correlation is positive or negative. Positive correlations fall within the range from 0 to $+1.00$; negative correlations fall within the range from 0 to -1.00. Figure 2.6 gives some examples of positive and negative correlations, displayed in the form of a *scatter plot.*

When a correlation coefficient is not statistically different from zero, the two behavioral measures are said to be *uncorrelated.* Technically, this means that knowing the value of one measure does not allow one to predict the value of the second measure with an accuracy greater than chance. It's important not to confuse the concept of a zero correlation with negative correlation. If the correlation

FIGURE 2.6
Positive and Negative Correlation. Two examples of "scatter plots." Each point shows an individual's scores on each of the two variables. (a) In a strong positive correlation, the values for both variables move in the *same* direction; that is, as more diapers are changed, more hands are washed. (b) In a negative correlation, the values for the two variables move in *opposite* directions; that is, as more time is spent practicing, fewer errors are made during the recital.

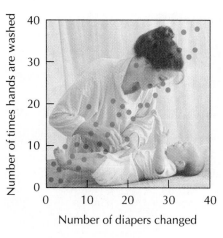

(**a**) Strong positive correlation

(**b**) Strong negative correlation

between two variables is zero, no statistical relationship is present—a value on one behavioral measures reveals nothing about the other behavioral measure. In a negative correlation, a clear relationship exists, it's just that the values move in opposite directions.

Behavioral measures rarely correlate perfectly—most correlations are only moderate. This means that when researchers make predictions about behavior based on correlations, the accuracy of their predictions will usually be limited. For example, the correlation between scores on the Scholastic Assessment Test and the grade point average of college freshmen is only +0.40, not 1.0 (Donlon, 1984). Researchers can use SAT scores to predict college performance at greater than chance levels, but the test's predictive abilities are far from perfect. Similarly, the correlation between height and weight is only about +0.60; on average, taller people do tend to weigh more, but there are obviously exceptions to this general rule. Correlation coefficients give researchers some important predictive ability, but they do not completely capture the variability that is out there in the world.

Correlations and Causality

Determining that a relationship exists between two measures of behavior is important because it helps people to anticipate what to expect from their environment. It is useful to know that if an individual exhibits a certain psychological characteristic at time 1, he or she is likely to exhibit another characteristic at time 2. Suppose, for example, that psychologists could demonstrate a meaningful correlation between the amount of violence that a child watches on television and how aggressive that child will act later in life. Knowing about such a relationship would probably influence the behavior of parents and might even lead to a social outcry for the monitoring of televised violence.

Correlations are useful devices for helping psychologists describe *how* behaviors co-occur in our world, but they are of only limited value when it comes to understanding *why* behaviors occur and co-occur. The presence of a correlation between two behaviors may help psychologists predict and select, but correlations do not allow them to determine causality. A finding of a correlation between watching violence on television and later aggression does not mean that television violence *causes* aggression, even if the correlation is perfect. Why not? Because other factors, of which we are unaware, can contribute to the relationship that the correlation describes (Cook & Campbell, 1979). One possibility is that aggressive children simply have a natural inclination to watch violent programs on televi-

Pat doesn't make any decisions in her life without consulting a psychic. She's convinced that most of what the psychic tells her about her future comes true. Given what you know about correlations and causality, how might you convince her otherwise?

INSIDE THE PROBLEM: *Predicting the Future*

Do you believe in *precognition,* commonly defined as the ability to predict the future? Do you believe that some individuals have knowledge about the future that they've obtained through extrasensory means? There is certainly plenty of anecdotal evidence. Jennifer, who dreams vividly about the death of her grandmother, awakens to a phone call announcing grandma's demise. Bradley, who senses a terrible plane crash on the drive home from work, is surprised to learn about an actual crash on the evening news.

But let's think about such occurrences from the perspective of what we've learned about correlations. In a sense, when psychologists conduct correlational research they are attempting to predict the future (although not through "extrasensory" means). They want to know whether the value on one variable, such as SAT scores, "predicts" how people will perform in the future on a second variable, such as college GPA. For the sake of argument, let's suppose that we track the performance of a "psychic" named Eleanor, who claims her dreams predict the future. We measure her performance over the course of many years on two variables: one variable corresponds to the number of times she dreams about a plane crashing in a given year; the other measures the number of planes that actually crash in that year. If you believe in precognition, you would expect to find a positive correlation between these two variables. That is, as the number of Eleanor's dream predictions about plane crashes goes up, so should the number of actual crashes.

But what if there is really no relationship between these two variables? What if the likelihood of Eleanor dreaming about a plane crash is uncorrelated with the probability of an actual crash? Under these conditions, the "relationship" between the two variables might look like the scatter plot depicted in Figure 2.7. Remember, when a correlation is near 0, there is no way consistently to predict the value of one variable when given the other. Sometimes a high value on one of the variables will be associated with a high value on the other variable; other times it will be associated with a low value. If no relationship exists between the two variables, then we shouldn't be able to estimate the number of plane crashes based solely on our knowledge of Eleanor's dreams.

But let's think more carefully about what a zero correlation means in this context: It means that in some years, when Eleanor has lots of dreams about planes crashing, there will also be lots of planes that crash. Notice that the scatter plot shows several instances where a high value on the dreaming variable is associated with a high value on the plane crashing variable (marked in red). Does this mean that in these selected years Eleanor possessed an uncanny ability to predict the future? Not necessarily, because these points could have occurred by chance. To get a true feeling for Eleanor's predictive ability, you need to look at the entire plot. As you can see, there are also years in which Eleanor "predicted" that lots of planes would crash and not very many planes crashed, and other years where many planes crashed but few dreams were reported.

The point to remember is that when two variables are unrelated, we cannot predict what will happen—sometimes

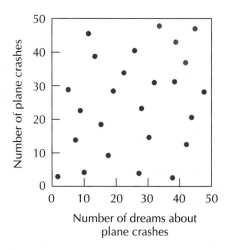

FIGURE 2.7
Zero Correlation. This scatter plot shows a zero correlation between variables measuring dreaming about plane crashes and planes actually crashing. Notice that overall it is not possible to predict the value on one of the variables by knowing a value on the other, although sometimes high values on each variable occur together (marked in red).

dreams will be associated with plane crashes and sometimes they won't. The mistake many people make is to look *only* at the cases where the two variables appear to be related. Remember, if there is no such thing as precognition—if the correlation is truly zero—then by chance we should expect to find situations where dreaming about plane crashes really is connected with unfortunate airline disasters! To read about more instances of faulty statistical thinking, see the Adaptive Mind section that closes this chapter.

---

sion. Thus, it is not the violence on TV that is causing the aggression, it is the child's aggressive tendencies that are leading to the choice of programs. Still other factors could be involved—perhaps children who are allowed to watch violence on television tend to be raised in households where aggression or lashing out is the normal way of dealing with the problems of life. Correlations describe relationships, but they typically provide no insight into cause and effect. To determine causality, as we'll see shortly, researchers cannot simply describe and predict behavior; they need to manipulate it.

Determining Why Behavior Occurs: Experimental Research Methods

If the ultimate goal of most psychologists is to establish the causes of behavior, what research strategy will allow them to do so? Suppose that researchers wanted to determine whether, in fact, watching violent programs really does cause later aggression. What specific steps should they take? They need to be certain that if aggressive behavior increases after violent television has been watched, then it is indeed the television violence that is responsible for the change. Alternative possibilities need to be eliminated, or at least accounted for, before researchers can confidently conclude that things are causally related. As we've just seen, the mere description of a relationship is not sufficient—correlation does not imply causation. Establishing causality requires *control*, which is one of the important functions of an experiment.

In **experimental research,** the investigator actively manipulates or alters some aspect of the environment in order to observe the effect of that manipulation on behavior. By the term *environment*, psychologists can mean just about anything. For instance, they might manipulate the external setting (room temperature, lighting, time of day), a person's internal state (hunger, mood, motivation to perform), or social factors (presence or absence of an authority figure or popular peer group). The particular manipulation is determined by the researcher's hypothesis. As mentioned earlier, hypotheses in psychology are usually expressed in the form of "if-then" statements about behavior: If some set of conditions is present and observed, then a certain kind of behavior will occur. The purpose of the experiment is to set up the proposed conditions and see what happens.

To examine the role of television violence on aggressive behavior, the experimenter would need to directly manipulate the amount of violence the person watches. Perhaps one group of children would be asked to watch a violent superhero cartoon while a second group would watch the playful antics of a lovable purple dinosaur. The experimenter would then carefully measure the effect of the

Do children model what they see on television? Many psychologists believe they do.

	Observational method	Correlational method	Experimental method
		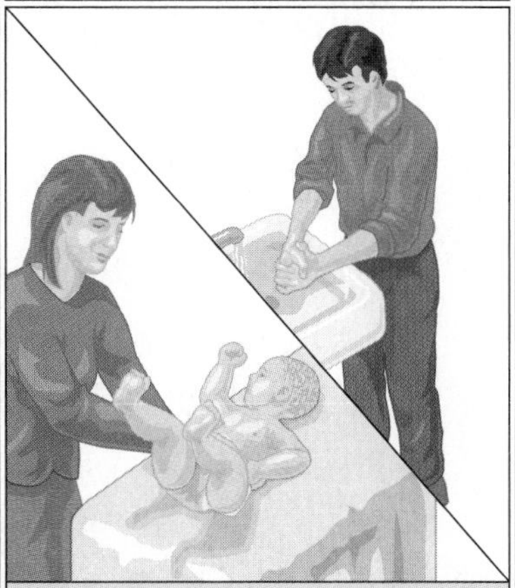	
Purpose:	Observing and describing behavior	Predicting and selecting behavior	Determining why behavior occurs: Establishing cause and effect
Research tactics:	Naturalistic observation Case studies Survey research Psychological tests	Statistical correlations based on two or more variables	Experiments manipulating the independent variable to note effects on the dependent variable

FIGURE 2.8
Summary of Major Research Methods. The chart summarizes the purpose and research tactics for the three major research methods: observational research, correlational research, and experimental research.

manipulation on the behavior of interest, aggression. This strategy of directly *manipulating* the viewing habits, rather than simply observing them, is the essential feature of the experimental approach. Notice the difference from correlational research, in which the investigator would simply record the viewing habits of lots of children and then measure later aggressive acts. It is only through a direct manipulation by the experimenter, as we shall see shortly, that control over the environment can be exercised and causality determined. Figure 2.8 compares experimental research to the other two approaches we've discussed, observational and correlational.

Independent and Dependent Variables

The aspect of the environment that is manipulated in an experiment is called the **independent variable.** Because it is a *variable* (that is, something that can take on more than one value), any experimental manipulation must consist of at least two different conditions. In our example, the independent variable is the amount of television violence observed by the children, and the two conditions are (1) watching a violent program, and (2) watching a nonviolent program. The aspect that is manipulated is called an *independent* variable because the experimenter produces the change, independently of the subject's wishes or desires.

The behavior that is measured or observed in an experiment is called the **dependent variable.** In our example, the dependent variable is the amount of aggressive behavior displayed following exposure to the violent or nonviolent program. The experimenter manipulates the independent variable, the level of TV violence, in order to observe whether the behavior measured by the dependent variable, aggression, changes. Notice that the experimenter is interested in whether the dependent variable *depends* on the experimental manipulation (hence the name, *dependent* variable).

FIGURE 2.9
The Major Components of an Experiment. The hypothesis is tested by manipulating the independent variable and then assessing its effects on the dependent variable. If the only thing changing systematically in the experiment is the independent variable, the experimenter can assume that changes in the independent variable are *causing* the changes measured by the dependent variable.

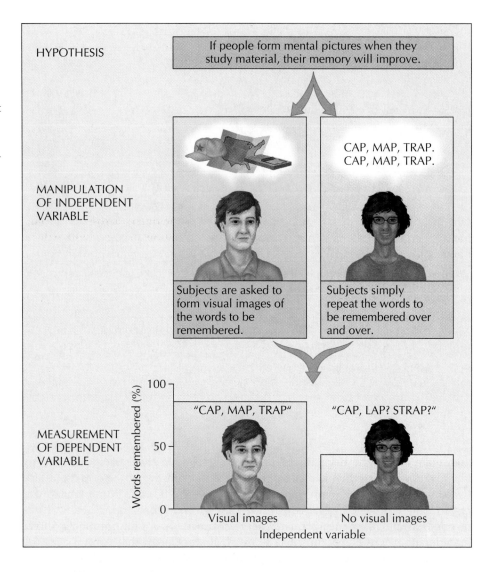

Let's consider another example. Suppose a researcher generates the following hypothesis: If people form mental pictures when they study material, their memory for the material will improve (see Figure 2.9). To test this prediction, the researcher gives two groups of subjects a list of common objects to memorize. One group is told to form a mental picture of each object during study; the other group is given no special instructions. Later, after the list is removed, everyone is asked to recall all of the objects from the list. What is the independent variable in this experiment? To answer this question, look for the aspect of the environment that is being manipulated: The independent variable is the type of instructions given to the subjects (half of the subjects are told to form mental pictures and half are not). What is the dependent variable? In this case, the researcher wants to know whether memory depends on imagery instructions, so the dependent variable is the amount of information recalled in the two groups. (As we'll see in Chapter 8, there's evidence to support the imagery hypothesis: Forming a visual image of to-be-remembered material really does help later recall [e.g., Paivio, 1971].)

Experimental Control

To conclude that changes in the dependent variable are really *caused* by the independent variable, researchers need to be certain that the independent variable is the only thing changing systematically in the experiment. This is the main reason why at least two conditions are needed in an experiment—researchers need to compare subjects who get the change, called the *experimental group,* with those who do not, called the *control group.* In the memory experiment, the experimental group consisted of the subjects receiving instructions to create mental pictures, whereas the control group consisted of those given the list of words without the imagery instructions. If recall differs between these two groups, and researchers know that the only difference between them was the instructions, they can conclude that forming mental pictures does indeed cause a change in memory.

The determination of cause and effect, then, hinges on the ability to be certain that the experimental and control groups are identical in all respects, except for the critical independent variable manipulation. But how can researchers be certain that this is indeed the case? If some other factor differs across the groups besides the independent variable, then any interpretation of the results will be hopelessly compromised (Levine & Parkinson, 1994; Rosenthal & Rosnow, 1991). Uncontrolled variables that vary systematically with the independent variable are called **confounding variables** (the word *confound* means to throw into confusion or dismay). Suppose, for example, that researchers allow the subjects in the memory experiment to choose whether they want to be in the experimental or the control group. This would introduce a confounding variable because the two groups might consist of different kinds of subjects. People who are terrible at remembering things, for instance, might volunteer to be in the experimental group in the hope that they will learn some magic technique for improving memory. But changes in the dependent variable could not then be attributed uniquely to the manipulation of instructions; differences in recall might be due to subject differences instead.

One solution to the problem of confounding variables is to try to equate the groups by holding constant all of the factors that might vary along with the experimental manipulation. The researchers can give everyone the same materials to learn, for instance, and conduct the experimental session at the same time of day for both groups. In addition, the researchers would want to ensure that subjects in both groups be given the same amount of time to study the materials and the same length of time for recall. Any factor that might affect remembering, other than the independent variable manipulation, should be controlled—held constant—across the different groups. When potential confounding variables are effectively controlled, allowing for the determination of cause and effect, the experiment is said to have **internal validity.**

Knowing what factors to worry about comes, in part, from experience. The more that researchers know about the phenomenon under study, the more likely they are to identify and control variables that might lead to confounding. Years of memory research have shown, for example, that it's essential to give the same to-be-remembered materials to everyone in the experimental and control conditions; some materials are just naturally easier to remember than others (Crowder, 1976; Greene, 1992). But other variables, such as the length of the participants' hair or their eye color, have no effect on remembering and need not be controlled for.

Random Assignment. But there is still the problem of subject differences—how can experimenters ever be certain that their two groups of subjects are equivalent? People differ in many ways: intelligence, memory ability, motivation to perform, and so on. Researchers cannot hold all of these factors constant. Just think about the task of finding two or more groups of subjects with exactly the same amount of intelligence, memory ability, motivation to perform, and so on—it would be impossible. The solution to the problem of intrinsic subject differences lies in the concept of random assignment, which is similar to the random sampling used for survey research. In **random assignment,** the experimenter ensures

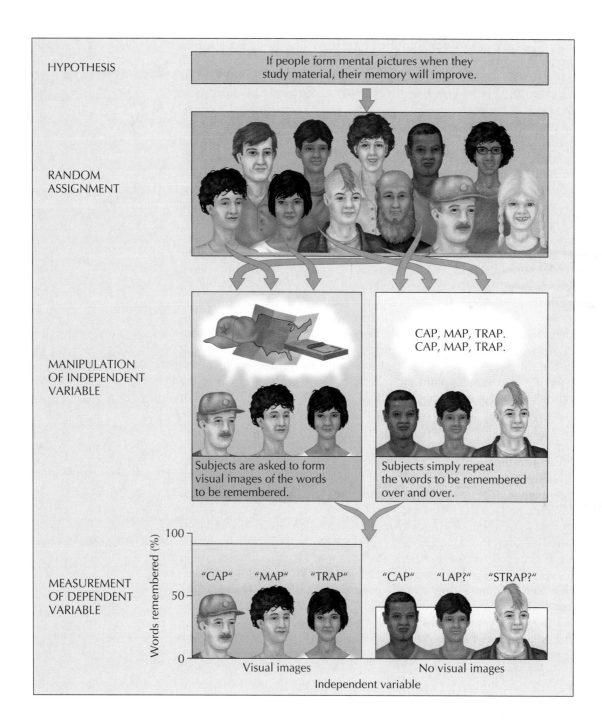

FIGURE 2.10

Random Assignment. In random assignment, the experimenter ensures that each participant has an equal likelihood of being assigned to any of the groups or conditions in the experiment. Here, people are randomly assigned to the two levels of the independent variable. Random assignment increases the chances that unique subject characteristics will be represented equally in each condition.

that each participant in the experiment has an equal chance of being assigned to any of the groups or conditions in the experiment. At the outset, each subject is assigned randomly to a group. Neither the subject nor the experimenter voluntarily chooses which group is assigned; the assignment is governed by chance.

Random assignment does not eliminate differences among people—some subjects will still be more intelligent than others, and some will be able to remember better than others. Random assignment simply increases the likelihood that these differences will be equally represented in each of the groups (see Figure 2.10). As a result, the researcher knows that group differences on the dependent variable cannot easily be attributed to some special characteristic of the individual subjects.

Expectancies and Biases in Experimental Research

Individuals who arrive ready to participate in a psychology experiment are almost certain to have expectations about what will happen. People are rarely passive participants in research—some active minds are almost certainly at work attempting to surmise the true purpose of the project. These expectations can sometimes affect a subject's behavior in ways that cloud interpretation of the results (Barber, 1976; Rosenthal & Rosnow, 1969). Let's suppose that on the first day of class, your teacher randomly selects half of the students, including you, to participate in a special "enrichment" program. You are to receive instruction in a special room, with carefully controlled lighting and temperature, to see whether your learning will improve. The rest of the students, forming the control group, are left in the original classroom. The end of the semester arrives and, sure enough, the enrichment group has consistently performed better than the control group. What can you conclude from these results?

Technically, this seems to be a well-designed experiment. It includes an experimental and a control group, the subjects were randomly assigned to groups, and we can assume that all other known potentially confounding variables were carefully controlled. But there is still a problem. The subjects in the enrichment group *expected* to perform better, based on their knowledge about the experiment—after all, they were selected to be in an "enrichment" group. Consequently, these students may have simply tried harder, or studied more, in an effort to live up to the expectations of the researcher (or at least to what they *perceived* the expectations of the researcher to be). At the same time, subjects in the control group were aware that they were failing to get special instruction—knowledge that might have lowered their motivation to perform, leading to poorer performance. The fact that the groups differed in what they learned, therefore, does not necessarily mean that the enrichment program itself is responsible.

There are two main ways that researchers can try to control for these kinds of *expectancy effects.* First, the investigator can be somewhat misleading in his or her initial description of the study. Subjects can be deceived, or misled, in a way that disguises the true purpose of the experiment. This approach raises obvious ethical questions. But it is sometimes possible simply to omit telling the subjects some critical feature of the study without severely violating ethical standards. We'll return to the issue of ethics in research later in the chapter.

Subjects who participate in research studies usually have expectations about the research. They expect certain things to happen, and these expectations can potentially influence the results.

Second, the investigator can try to equate expectations for both the experimental and control groups. For example, the researchers can lead the control group to believe that they, too, are receiving an experimental treatment. This technique is often used in drug studies. Participants in both the experimental and control groups receive a "pill" or an "injection," but the drug is actually present only in the medication given to the experimental group. The control subjects are given a **placebo**—an inactive, or inert, substance (a "sugar pill") that looks just like the true drug (Shapiro, 1960; White, Tursky, & Schwartz, 1985).

This kind of experimental procedure is typically used in what is called a **single-blind study.** That is, the subjects are kept "blind" about the particular group in which they have been placed (experimental or control). Single-blind studies effectively control for subject expectancies because the subjects don't know which group they are in. Researchers thus increase the probability that any expectations that subjects may have about the experiment will be equally represented in both groups. It is even possible to inform the subjects that some of them will be given a placebo—the inactive pill or injection—as long as no one knows who is in which group. Notice that the single-blind technique does not eliminate subject expectancies; it simply reduces the likelihood that expectancies will contribute differentially to the experimental and control groups.

The subjects participating in the experiment aren't the only ones who expect certain things to happen—the experimenter does, too (Rosenthal, 1966). Remember, it is the experimenter who formulated the hypothesis—the prediction about how behavior will change with manipulation of the independent variable. Experimenters are often convinced that behavior will change in a certain way, and these expectations can importantly influence the results. Imagine, for example, that a researcher has developed a drug designed to cure all forms of influenza. The researcher has worked hard on its development but still needs convincing scientific evidence to show that it is effective. So the researcher designs a single-blind experiment composed of two groups of flu-suffering subjects. One group receives the drug and the other a placebo. Later, after analyzing the results, the researcher is satisfied to report that indeed people in the experimental group recovered more quickly than those in the control group.

There are two ways that the experimenter's expectations might influence these results. First, there is always the possibility that the overzealous investigator has

Researchers who conduct experiments often expect the results to come out in a certain way. Their expectations can potentially influence the results unless certain precautions are taken in the design of the study.

deliberately manufactured results consistent with his or her hypothesis. Such intentional "errors" on the part of researchers are probably rare, but they have been documented on occasion in most branches of scientific research (for a discussion, see Barber, 1976; Broad & Wade, 1982). A second, and more likely, possibility is that the experimenter has unknowingly influenced the results in subtle ways. Perhaps, for example, he or she gave slightly more attention to the flu-stricken people in the experimental group; the researcher expected these people to get well and so was more responsive to changes in their medical condition. Alternatively, the researcher might simply have been more encouraging to the people who actually received the drug, leading them to adopt a more positive outlook on their chances for a quick recovery. Such biases are not necessarily deliberate on the part of the researcher. Nevertheless, these unintentional effects can cloud a meaningful interpretation of the results.

The solution to experimenter expectancy effects is similar to that for controlling subject expectancies—simply keep the researcher "blind" about the assignment of subjects to groups. If those administering the study do not know which subjects are receiving the experimental treatment, they are unlikely to treat members of each group differently. Obviously, someone needs to know the group assignments, but the information can be coded in such a way that the person doing the direct observations remains blind about the condition. To control for both experimenter and subject expectancies in the same context, a **double-blind study** is conducted, in which neither the subject nor the observer is aware of who is in the experimental and control conditions. Double-blind studies, often used in drug research, are considered to be an effective way of reducing bias effects.

Generalizing Experimental Conclusions

Properly designed experiments enable an investigator to determine the causes of behavior. The determination of causality is possible whenever the experimenter has sufficient control over the situation to eliminate factors other than the experimental manipulation as contributors to a change in behavior. But experimental control is not always gained without a cost. Sometimes in the search for appropriate controls, the researcher creates an environment that is sterile or artificial and is thus unrepresentative of situations in which the subject normally behaves. The results of the experimental research then cannot easily be generalized to real-world situations. As we discussed previously, researchers use the term *external validity* to refer to how well results generalize across subjects and situations.

Consider again the issue of television violence and aggression: does one really cause the other? A number of experimental studies have been conducted to explore this question (Friedrich-Cofer & Huston, 1986), but most have been conducted in the laboratory under controlled conditions. Subjects are randomly assigned to groups who watch violent programs or neutral programs, and their behavior is then observed for aggressive tendencies, again under controlled conditions. In one recent study, preschool children were exposed to neutral or aggressive cartoons and then were given the opportunity to play with aggressive toys (such as guns); more aggressive acts were recorded for the children who watched the violent cartoon (Sanson & di-Muccio, 1993). These results clearly demonstrate that witnessed violence can increase the likelihood of aggressiveness. But this does not necessarily mean that these children would act similarly in their homes, or that the effects of the brief exposure to violence will be long-lasting. In short, the experiment may lack external validity. Concerns about generalizability should not, however, be taken as a devastating critique of the experimental method—results demonstrated in the laboratory often do generalize to real-world environments. But it's legitimate to raise questions about how widely the results apply. As you might expect, we'll return to the problem of external validity in later chapters.

Experiments are sometimes criticized because they are considered artificial. Many psychology experiments use college students in introductory psychology courses as participants. Do you feel there is a problem in generalizing the findings from these studies to the whole population?

Researchers typically choose to investigate basic psychological principles in the laboratory because they can exercise more control over the phenomenon of interest. Establishing cause and effect requires that the environment be manipulated systematically—potential confounding variables need to be controlled for. But herein lies a dilemma: By investigating behavior in the laboratory and exercising rigorous control, are researchers discovering things about behavior and mind that are specific to the laboratory and unrepresentative of real life?

Fortunately, it is possible to conduct well-controlled experiments in real-world settings. Such experiments, where feasible, provide useful information about behavior in natural settings and allow researchers to help establish the generalizability of laboratory findings. Let's take a look at a study in which researchers attempted to extend laboratory principles about memory to a practical setting: the ability of scuba divers to remember safety information while under water (Martin & Aggleton, 1993).

As you'll learn in Chapter 8, laboratory research has established that people often remember things better if they're tested in conditions that resemble those present during original learning. Dozens of studies have been conducted examining so-called "context effects," in which the conditions present during learning and later remembering are either matched or mismatched. But the vast majority of these studies have been conducted in laboratory settings using artificial word lists (Davies & Thomson, 1988). Martin and Aggleton wanted to see whether similar principles applied in the real-life environment of the scuba diver.

One of the hazards that any scuba diver must face is *decompression;* as the diver moves from deep water to shallow water, the changes in water pressure can have potentially damaging effects on the body. It is essential that divers understand and remember basic information about pressure and depth, such as the data published in standardized decompression tables.

Martin and Aggleton (1993) asked 40 scuba divers to memorize and then remember data from standard decom-

pression tables. But they manipulated the conditions of initial learning and testing by randomly assigning each of the divers to one of four groups: (1) those who learned the decompression data on dry land and then had their memory tested in the same context, on dry land; (2) those who learned the data under water while diving and were tested later on dry land; (3) those who learned the data on dry land but were tested under water; and (4) those who both learned and remembered the data while diving under water.

What was the *independent variable* in this experiment? It was the manipulation of the match between the initial learning conditions and the testing environment (dry land or under water). Groups 1 and 4 studied the materials and were then tested in the same environments, whereas groups 2 and 3 had mismatched learning and testing environments. The *dependent variable* in this experiment— the divers' memory for the decompression data—was measured by recording how often they answered questions about the data correctly. (All of the participants, regardless of whether

Treating Research Participants Ethically: Human and Animal Guidelines

As we've seen, knowledge in psychology arises from observation, but observing others requires that psychologists invade, to a certain extent, the personal environment of the research participants. Earlier we considered the problem of *reactivity:* the fact that the use of observational techniques can importantly change the way that the subject behaves. Although psychologists have developed techniques for reducing reactivity—designing unobtrusive measures, keeping subjects "blind" about their actual role in the study, fooling subjects into thinking the observer is really a part of the environment—each method raises some significant ethical questions. Is it appropriate to deceive subjects into thinking they are not really being recorded? Is it appropriate to withhold treatment from some participants, through the use of placebos, in the interest of achieving proper experimental control? To deal with such issues, formal organizations such as the American Psychological Association (APA) develop and publish ethical guidelines and "codes of conduct" that members are expected to follow (American Psychological Association, 1992).

"wet" or "dry," wrote their answers on waterproof plastic sheets). The results of the experiment are shown in Figure 2.11, which presents the mean number of correct responses for each of the four groups.

According to standard laboratory findings, when conditions are matched between original learning and testing, people should remember things better. This is exactly what happened in the Martin and Aggleton study: The divers remembered the critical decompression data better when they learned and were tested in the same kind of environment (dry or wet). As you can see, the divers in groups 1 and 4 answered more questions correctly than the divers in groups 2 and 3. Thus, the experiment was successful in extending laboratory findings to a natural environment. But even more important, something of great practical value was learned: If divers want to remember vital safety information while under water, it's best for them to learn that information while they're diving, not on dry land.

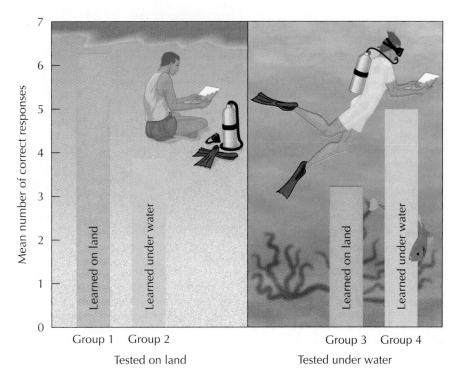

FIGURE 2.11
Context Effects in Remembering. This graph summarizes the results of the Martin and Aggleton (1993) underwater memory study. When testing occurred on land, decompression tables learned on land were remembered better than those learned under water; when testing was done under water, it was better to have learned the tables under water.

All psychologists have a professional responsibility to respect the rights and dignity of other people. This responsibility goes beyond research activities; the code of conduct applies to all psychologists' activities, from administering therapy to working in the field to giving testimony in the courtroom. First and foremost, respecting the rights of others means showing concern for their health, safety, and welfare; no diabolical mind-altering treatments that may permanently affect the participants are allowed, even "in the name and pursuit of science." Psychologists are expected to act responsibly in how they advertise their services, how they represent themselves in the media, and in how they charge and collect their fees.

Informed Consent

The cornerstone of the code of ethical conduct is the principle of **informed consent.** Participants in any form of research or therapy must be informed, in easy-to-understand language, of any significant factors that could affect their willingness to participate (Mann, 1994; Meisel & Roth, 1983). Physical and emotional risks should be explained, as well as the general nature of the research project or of the therapeutic procedures that will be used. Once informed, participants must then willingly give their written consent agreeing to participate in the research.

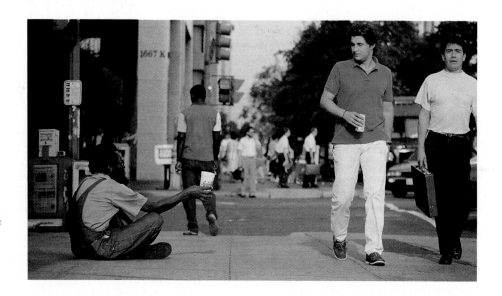

To study the behavior of people in natural settings, such as the willingness of bystanders to help others in need, sometimes requires that the researcher mislead or withhold information from the people being observed.

They should understand as well that if they choose not to participate, for whatever reason, they will suffer no negative consequences for withdrawal.

But informed consent can raise a significant problem for the researcher. Individuals cannot give truly informed consent unless they understand the details of the project, yet full disclosure could critically affect their behavior in the study. We've seen that it is often necessary to keep subjects "blind" about group assignments so that their expectations won't affect the outcome of the study. Imagine that you were interested in studying how readily the bystanders at an accident will come to the aid of a victim. To gain experimental control, you might stage a mock accident in the laboratory, in front of waiting research subjects, to see how they react. Conducting the study in the laboratory would enable you to investigate the likelihood of intervention under a variety of conditions (such as whether the subject is alone in the room when the accident occurs or others are around). But subjects in this situation would need to be misled—you certainly could not fully inform them about the procedure by telling them that the accident is not real.

The psychological research community recognizes that it is sometimes necessary to use some form of deception as part of a research procedure. Not all psychologists agree with this position (Baumrind, 1985), but it represents the majority opinion. According to the APA's code of ethics, deception in research is justified only if the prospective scientific, educational, or applied value of the study is clear, and there is no way to answer the research questions adequately without deceiving the subjects in some way. It is agreed as well that whatever deception might be involved, it should not be of a type that could cause subjects physical harm or affect their willingness to participate in the study. Experimenters have a responsibility, once again, to respect the rights and dignity of research participants at all times. Most universities and colleges ensure that subjects' rights are protected by requiring investigators to submit detailed descriptions of their studies to oversight review committees before any human or animal subjects can be tested. If a study fails to protect the subjects adequately, permission to conduct the study is denied.

Debriefing and Confidentiality

Two other key ingredients of the psychologist's code of ethical conduct are the process of *debriefing* and the maintenance of *confidentiality*. Psychologists are expected to "debrief" subjects fully at the end of the experimental session, meaning that everyone involved is to be informed about the general purpose of the study. **Debriefing** is intended to clear up any misunderstandings that the subject might have about the research and to explain in detail why certain procedures were used (Gurman, 1994; Holmes, 1976). Certainly if deception was a part of the study, the full nature of the deception should be disclosed during the debriefing process. Debriefing gives the researcher an opportunity to counteract any anxieties that the subject might have developed as a result of the research. If the subject had failed to intervene and help the victim of the staged accident, for example, the experimenter could explain that bystander passivity is a characteristic of most people (Darley & Latané, 1968).

Finally, once the participation is completed, the subject's right to privacy continues. Psychologists are obligated to respect the privacy of the individual by maintaining **confidentiality**—the researcher or therapist is not to discuss or report confidential information obtained in research or in therapy without the permission of the individual. Confidentiality makes sense for more than just ethical reasons. Research subjects, as well as people seeking help for psychological problems, are likely to feel more comfortable with the process, and to act more naturally, if they are convinced that their right to privacy will be respected.

The Ethics of Animal Research

In laboratories all over the world, animal subjects are actively participating in basic research. They're pressing metal bars for food, receiving small doses of electrical stimulation in the brain, and being raised in "enriched" environments designed to improve their ability to learn. Although animal subjects are probably used in less than 10% of all current psychological research studies, the famous "laboratory rat," along with numerous other types of nonhuman species, has been an incredibly important source of basic data in the discipline for decades (Coile & Miller, 1984). As you'll see in later chapters, many of the most significant psychological principles were originally discovered through the study of animal behavior (Domjan & Purdy, 1995).

Why use animal subjects? The most often cited reason is for experimental control. It is possible to raise and house nonhuman subjects in relatively "ideal" environments. Researchers can control diet, experience, and genetic background and

Using animals as subjects in research experiments raises many legitimate ethical questions. But psychologists point to the fact that animal studies have led to significant breakthroughs in the understanding of behavior and its disorders. Moreover, research with animals is subject to strict ethical guidelines.

thereby eliminate many of the potentially confounding variables that plague research with human subjects. Researchers can also study phenomena such as life-span development in ways that cannot be accomplished with human subjects. Studies that would take 70 or 80 years with humans take only a few years with rats. Nonhuman subjects are sometimes used because they are thought to contain simple, rather than complex, internal structures and systems. The basic biological machinery that underlies learning, for example, has been studied extensively with sea slugs; the number of neural connections in a sea slug is minuscule compared with the billions of connections residing in a human brain. Research with non-human subjects often serves as a vehicle for developing hypotheses that can later be tested, when feasible, with humans.

But is research with animal subjects ethical? There can be no informed consent in animal research, as animal rights activists point out. Does sufficient justi-fication exist for the invasive procedures sometimes used in animal research—for example, permanently destroying a region of brain in a cat in order to learn about how localized brain structures control behavior? Obviously, the use of animals in research is a highly controversial subject. Many millions of dollars are spent every year by animal rights groups, some of which oppose any sort of animal research (see Hubbel, 1990). Other critics question the intrinsic value of animal studies, arguing that an understanding of animals reveals little about human functioning and may even mislead researchers into drawing inappropriate conclusions (see Ulrich, 1991). In one recent survey of animal rights activists, 85% advocated the complete elimination of all animal research (Plous, 1991).

Can you think of any circum-stances in which it might be ethical to conduct research with animals even though the results won't generalize to humans?

Despite the claims of these critics, the majority of psychologists believe that animal research has enormous value. They base their belief on the fact that ani-mal studies have repeatedly led to significant breakthroughs in the understanding of behavior and of psychological disorders, as well as in medical and biological research (see Miller, 1985, 1991). To cite one instance, animal research in psy-chology over the past two decades has led to a reformulation of the root causes of depression, as well as to the development and testing of drugs that lessen the symptoms of this disorder (see Chapters 14 and 15). Similarly, through the study of monkeys' natural fear of snakes in the wild, psychologists have gained insight into how phobias (such as the fear of heights or the fear of being locked in small places) might be learned by imitating the behavior of one's parents, rather than through a traumatic experience (see Chapter 7). In virtually every chapter in this textbook, you will be exposed to psychological principles that have been gained from research with nonhuman subjects.

Moreover, it is important to understand that the American Psychological Association enforces strict guidelines with regard to the ethical treatment of non-human subjects. Psychologists who conduct research using animals are expected to treat their subjects *humanely*. They are responsible for ensuring the animal's proper care, and any treatments that cause discomfort, pain, or illness must be avoided unless absolutely necessary. When surgical procedures are performed, the animals must be given the appropriate anesthesia, and proper medical procedures must be followed to eliminate infections and minimize pain. Failure to adhere to these standards can result in censure or termination of membership by the gov-erning body of the association.

The issue of animal research is controversial, in part, because of misinforma-tion. Experiments that inflict pain and suffering on animals are extremely rare and do not fairly characterize the majority of animal studies (see Coile & Miller, 1984). It is also probably true that psychologists have failed to promote the intrinsic value of animal research adequately (Johnson & Morris, 1987). At the same time, researchers must continually recognize that the ends do not justify the means in the pursuit of knowledge and that the nature of the research subject can be an important determinant of the results. Findings established from research with nonhuman subjects may in fact not always apply to humans—because some animals may have evolved to solve different problems than humans—although clearly the critics of animal research have often overstated their case (see Miller, 1991).

SOLVING THE PROBLEMS: A SUMMARY

To reach the goal of understanding behavior and mind, psychologists rely on a set of established research tools. The facts and theories that make up the discipline of psychology have arisen from the systematic application of these tools. Understanding research methodology is important because the conclusions reached in research studies are inevitably influenced by the methods that have been used. Whether the recorded behavior of children in a day-care center will accurately represent "real life," for example, depends on how invasive the methods of observation have been. In addition, the extent to which an experiment has the capacity to determine whether television violence causes aggression depends on the experimenter's use of the proper controls and selection of subjects that are representative of the population of interest. In this chapter we divided our discussion of the methods of psychological research into four main problem areas.

OBSERVING AND DESCRIBING BEHAVIOR Descriptive research consists of the methodologies that underlie the observation and description of behavior. In *naturalistic observation,* the researcher observes behavior in natural settings, rather than in a laboratory environment. Naturalistic observation is a useful technique for generating research ideas and for verifying whether conclusions reached in the lab generalize to more realistic settings. In *case studies,* the focus is on a single instance of a behavior or psychological phenomenon. This technique allows the researcher to obtain lots of background information on the individual being studied, but the results may not always generalize to wider populations. In *survey research,* behavior is sampled broadly, usually by gathering responses from many people in the form of a questionnaire. Surveys typically provide information that is representative of the group being examined, but the amount of information that can be gathered is usually limited. Finally, through *psychological tests,* individual differences among individuals can be quantified.

Once the observational data have been collected, they are summarized through the application of *statistics.* Such statistics include measures of central tendency— the mean, median, and mode—and measures of variability, or how far apart individual scores are from each other in a set of scores. Researchers also use *inferential statistics,* based on the laws of probability, to test hypotheses. Inferential statistics can help the researcher decide whether a difference between an experimental and a control group, for example, is likely to have occurred by chance.

PREDICTING AND SELECTING BEHAVIOR In *correlational research,* the researcher seeks to determine whether a relationship exists between two measures of behavior. For instance, does high school grade point average predict college performance? Correlation coefficients, which provide an index of how well one measure predicts another, are statistics that vary between -1.00 and $+1.00$. Correlations are useful primarily because they enable the researcher to predict and select. If employers know, for example, that there is a correlation between achievement test scores and job performance, they can use someone's score on an achievement test to predict that person's success on the job. Correlations are useful tools for predicting and selecting, but they do not allow the researcher to infer causality.

▶ **DETERMINING WHY BEHAVIOR OCCURS** If researchers want to know whether an activity, such as watching violence on television, *causes* a change in behavior, they must conduct an *experiment.* In doing so, the researcher manipulates the environment in a systematic way and then observes the effect of that manipulation on behavior. The aspect of the environment that is manipulated is called the *independent variable;* the measured behavior of interest is called the *dependent variable.* To determine that the independent variable is really responsible for the changes in behavior, the researcher must exert experimental control—the only thing that must be changing systematically is the experimenter's manipulation of the independent variable. Researchers conducting experiments encounter a variety of potential pitfalls, including subject and experimenter expectancies, that need to be controlled. Control strategies include the use of random assignment and "blind" research designs.

▶ **TREATING RESEARCH PARTICIPANTS ETHICALLY** Scientific psychology is based on observation, and observing others requires that researchers invade, to a certain extent, the personal environment of their subjects. As a result, it is important that all researchers adhere to a strict code of ethical conduct. An important safeguard is informed consent, which is designed to guarantee that participants will be informed of any significant factors that could influence their willingness to participate. Other ethical standards govern proper debriefing and the maintenance of confidentiality. All researchers, regardless of the nature of the research, have a professional responsibility to respect the rights and dignities of their research subjects. This applies not only to human participants but also to animals whenever they are used as part of the research process.

Terms to Remember

scientific method An investigative method that generates empirical knowledge—that is, knowledge derived from systematic observations of the world. It involves generating a hypothesis on the basis of observed regularities, then testing the hypothesis with further observations.

operational definition Defining concepts in terms of how those concepts are measured.

OBSERVING AND DESCRIBING BEHAVIOR

descriptive research The tactics and methods that underlie the direct observation and description of behavior.

reactivity The extent to which an individual's behavior is changed as a consequence of being observed; the behavior becomes essentially a reaction to the process of being observed.

external validity The extent to which the results of an observation generalize to other situations, or are representative of real life.

naturalistic observation A research technique that involves recording only naturally occurring behavior, as opposed to behavior produced in the laboratory.

case study A descriptive research technique in which the research effort is focused on a single case, usually an individual.

survey A descriptive research technique designed to gather limited amounts of information from many people, usually by administering some kind of questionnaire.

random sampling A procedure for selecting a representative subset of a target population; the procedure guarantees that everyone in the population has an equal likelihood of being selected for the sample.

mean The arithmetic average of a set of scores.

mode The most frequently occurring score in a set or distribution of scores.

median The middle point in an ordered set of scores; half of the scores fall at or below the median score, and half fall at or above the median score.

variability A measure of how much the scores in a distribution of scores differ from one another.

range The difference between the largest and smallest scores in a distribution.

standard deviation An indication of how much individual scores differ or vary from the mean in a set of scores.

descriptive statistics Mathematical techniques that help researchers describe their data.

inferential statistics Mathematical techniques that help researchers decide whether recorded behaviors are representative of a population or whether differences among observations can be attributed to chance.

PREDICTING AND SELECTING BEHAVIOR

correlation A statistic that indicates whether two variables are related, or vary together in a systematic way; correlation coefficients vary from -1.00 to $+1.00$.

DETERMINING WHY BEHAVIOR OCCURS

experimental research A technique in which the investigator actively manipulates or alters some aspect of the environment (defined broadly) in order to observe the effect of the manipulation on behavior.

independent variable The aspect of the environment that is manipulated in an experiment. It must consist of at least two conditions.

dependent variable The behavior that is measured or observed in an experiment.

confounding variable An uncontrolled variable that varies systematically with the independent variable.

internal validity The extent to which an experiment has effectively controlled for confounding variables; internally valid experiments allow for the determination of causality.

random assignment A technique ensuring that each participant in an experiment has an equal chance of being assigned to any of the conditions in the experiment.

placebo An inactive, or inert, substance that resembles an experimental substance.

single-blind study An experimental design in which the participants do not know which of the conditions to which they have been assigned (e.g., experimental versus control); it's used to control for subject expectancies.

double-blind study An experimental design in which neither the participants nor the research observers are aware of who has been assigned to the experimental and control groups; it's used to control for both subject and experimenter expectancies.

TREATING RESEARCH PARTICIPANTS ETHICALLY

informed consent The principle that before consenting to participate in research, people should be fully informed about any significant factors that could affect their willingness to participate.

debriefing At the conclusion of an experimental session, informing the participants about the general purpose of the experiment, including any deception that was involved.

confidentiality The principle that all personal information obtained from a participant in research or therapy should not be revealed without the individual's permission.

As we've seen in this chapter, one important tool that the research psychologist uses to decipher the complexities of behavior and mind is statistics, which represent mathematical ways of summarizing and interpreting data. Psychologists calculate measures of central tendency and variability to summarize information, and they use inferential statistics to determine whether behaviors are representative of populations. But in a way, all people are intuitive statisticians, whether they recognize it or not. For example, when you meet someone new, you no doubt try to determine which of his or her actions represent the "real" person and which are only momentary quirks. You spend time trying to determine the collective beliefs of your friends, and you worry about how your beliefs might differ from theirs. It's natural and reasonable to act in this way, because everyday statistical intuitions help you describe and summarize your environment.

Errors in Statistical Reasoning

But there is evidence to suggest that from time to time people are simply not very good everyday statisticians. Their statistical intuitions are often wrong, and they draw statistically incorrect conclusions. Let's consider an example taken from a study by Fong, Krantz, and Nisbett (1986) involving a statistical principle called the *law of large numbers*. Imagine that you've just visited a new restaurant and had a spectacular meal. You confidently recommend the place to all your friends and decide to visit there as a group. But this time, the meal is a disaster—the food is overcooked and the service is bad. What conclusion would

you draw? If you're like most people, you will give a "deterministic" answer, which means that you will come up with some reason or excuse to explain the new experience. You might surmise, for example, that the chef has changed, or that the group's expectations were simply too high.

Let's consider another example that demonstrates the same point. You're a rabid baseball fan who has been following the career of the home team's new shortstop. The kid had a spectacular first year and won Rookie of the Year honors. He was awarded a new contract worth millions in the off-season, and expectations are high when the new season rolls around. But his second year turns out to be disappointing; his average drops 30 points and his home run production is down. What would you conclude? Is he slacking off? Is he living off his press clippings? Perhaps, but once again, from a statistical perspective, if you conclude these things your reasoning is faulty.

In both cases, your statistical error lies in your assumption that the original small sample of behavior provided a reliable indication of "true" characteristics. You have failed to recognize that variability is virtually always a significant part of data collection, whether you're talking about the behavior of a restaurant or the behavior of a person. Statistically, small samples of behavior—such as one meal in a restaurant or one year in the big leagues—cannot be expected to provide reliable indications of "true" quality or average ability. To achieve an accurate representation, you need to collect lots of observations. This is essentially the *law of large numbers:* The larger the sample size, the more likely

the conclusions will accurately represent the population of interest (see Figure 2.12).

Learning to Think Statistically

There are reasons to believe that people can learn to avoid errors in statistical reasoning of the type that we've just described. For example, if you ask Ph.D.-level scientists with training in statistics to comment on the restaurant or rookie examples, they will tend to give statistical rather than deterministic answers. They will point to the concept of variability and say things like "There are probably more instances of restaurants that serve an occasional excellent meal than ones that serve only excellent meals," or "You hit it lucky at an inconsistent restaurant" (Fong & Nisbett, 1991).

In a study by Fong and Nisbett (1991), undergraduate students were given statistical training on the law of large numbers. They were told that small samples of behavior often provide poor indices of true ability. For example, it was pointed out that "after the first two weeks of the major league baseball season the leading hitter typically has a batting average of .450, yet no batter has ever had an average that high over the entire season." It was stressed that two weeks is simply too small a sample of a batter's ability to draw firm conclusions. Following the training, everyone was given new problems to analyze. The results revealed a significant increase in the amount of correct statistical reasoning for students who received the training compared to a control group of students who had received no training.

Thus, there's hope for us all, as long as we listen to our statistics teachers.

But the errors of everyday statistical reasoning raise some important questions about our theme of the adaptive mind. How can it be adaptive to make these mistakes in reasoning? In what ways do such sometimes misguided statistical intuitions help people adapt to ever-changing environmental demands? We'll return to these questions in detail in Chapter 9 when we discuss the topics of thought and language. For the moment, though, you should recognize that simply because people make errors some of the time does not mean that human thought processes are generally unadaptive. A kind of thinking that leads to errors in one context might be very effective in another. For example, it might make a great deal of sense for someone to react quickly and decisively to the behavior of a novel intruder, even though a small sample of the intruder's behavior may provide statistically unreliable information about its "true" characteristics. In such a case, the reasoning may be deterministic rather than statistical, but it's probably better to be safe than sorry.

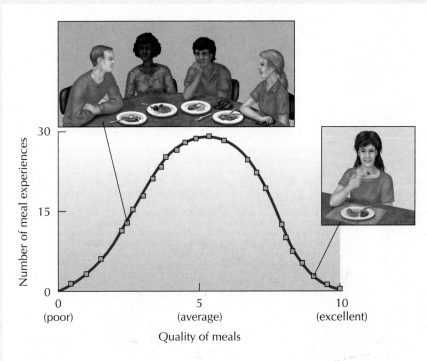

FIGURE 2.12

The Law of Large Numbers. The larger the sample size, the more likely it is that the sample will accurately represent the "true" average of the population. Any single small sample may or may not reflect the average. If you have a great meal one time at a restaurant, that doesn't mean it represents the "average" meal at the restaurant. Further sampling may yield results closer to the average.

3

Biological Processes

Embedded within the confines of a protective layer of bone floats a 3- to 4-pound mass of tissue called the brain. Fueled by simple blood sugar and amino acids, the brain's billions of cells are engaged in a continuous, frenetic dance of activity. At the moment, the rhythms and movements of this dance are not well understood, but a "whole" is somehow created that is collectively greater than the sum of the individual parts. From sporadic, seemingly chaotic patterns of cellular activity arise the intricacies of human behavior, thought, emotion, and creativity.

Throughout this book, and this chapter in particular, we'll assume that all behavior arises from the activities of this brain—not just mundane things like breathing, maintaining a beating heart, and walking, but also people's intimate thoughts and deepest feelings. Each behavior, thought, and feeling can be traced ultimately to the biological processes carried out by an active brain. At the same time, disorders of the mind, such as schizophrenia or clinical depression, are products of the brain as well—but they are by-products, perhaps, of what might be considered a "broken" brain. Those who study the link between the brain and behavior, in the field known generally as **neuroscience,** have made great strides in establishing the physical basis of behavior; many of their insights are translating into effective treatments for psychological problems resulting from "broken" brains.

The human brain is a remarkably sophisticated biological structure. It contains over 100 billion cells (perhaps a conservative estimate), which is roughly comparable to the number of stars in the Milky Way galaxy. But it is not the number, or the size of the mass, that really matters; it is the activities of the cells, operating in global patterns and in specialized regions, that underlie adaptive behavior and produce self-awareness. As we'll see, brain cells interact continuously; they produce a communication network that is unlike anything else that exists in the body. Neuroscientist Gerald Fischbach (1992) put it in these words: "the liver probably contains 100 million cells, but 1000 livers do not add up to a rich inner life" (p. 49).

Understanding the biological determinants of behavior requires more than reading a simple treatise on the brain. The brain is only a part of a broader system that includes the spinal cord and the connections that the brain makes to muscles, sensory organs, and other internal structures in the body. The brain and spinal cord make up what is called the **central nervous system** (see Figure 3.1). An additional network of nerves, the **peripheral nervous system,** acts as the communication link between the central nervous system and the rest of the body. A person may decide in the brain to move a leg, but somehow that decision needs to be communicated to the muscles that actually do the moving. It's the job of the peripheral nervous system to relay messages from the central nervous system to the muscles that produce overt behavioral responses. Later in this chapter, we'll expand on these basic divisions of the nervous system and outline their various functions in greater detail.

FIGURE 3.1
The Central Nervous System.
The central nervous system consists of the brain and the spinal cord.

Brain

Spinal cord

PREVIEWING THE ADAPTIVE PROBLEMS

To facilitate an understanding of the link between the body and the mind, our discussion of biological processes is divided into four central problems of adaptation: How does internal communication occur so rapidly and efficiently? How does the brain initiate and coordinate behavior? How are growth and other internal functions of the body regulated? How does the body store and transmit the genetic code that ensures perpetuation of the species? These are challenges that must be met by biological systems if organisms hope to survive and adapt successfully to their environment. As you'll soon see, the biological "solutions" provide important insight into the workings of the adaptive mind.

COMMUNICATING INTERNALLY Human behavior is adaptive because people are able to monitor their environment continuously and produce quick responses that best fit the needs of the situations they face. If your hand accidentally rests on the active burner on a stove, you react immediately by pulling your hand away. If a child trying to catch a bouncing ball runs suddenly into the path of your car, you step quickly on the brake and the child is saved. These nearly instantaneous world-to-behavior links are possible because of a communication network that exists between the outside world and the brain. Peripheral "receptor" cells in the body are stimulated by the environment; they relay a message inward toward the spinal cord and the brain; in the brain, the message is processed, and coordinated muscle movements are initiated.

There is a vast communication network in the body that helps people monitor the environment and produce quick adaptive responses when they're needed.

The nervous system, unlike other biological systems in the human body, is an active marketplace of information; information flows continuously between cells and is processed in a variety of ways. The basic units of the system, cells called *neurons,* communicate internally in a language that we'll see is part electrical and part chemical. We'll consider both the anatomy and the communication capabilities of neurons, and we'll discuss in some detail how these units act to pass information throughout the body. It is in the dynamics of the communication system that many interesting psychological phenomena arise, ranging from the altered states induced by drugs to the ravages of Alzheimer's disease.

▶ **INITIATING AND COORDINATING BEHAVIOR** Information is the primary commodity of the nervous system, but information per se does not translate into hand movements, quick reactions, or artistic creativity. Somehow the body must assign meaning to received information and coordinate the appropriate responses. To resolve this problem, discrete regions of cells inside the brain perform specialized functions; a person initiates and controls behavior through the actions of these parts of the brain. For example, one area of the brain is designed to process visual events, such as lines at certain angles, or patterns of light and dark. Other areas are specialized to comprehend or produce spoken language or to monitor emotional reactions. Humans even appear to have a remarkable division of mental processes between the left and right sides, or hemispheres, of the brain.

The idea that particular psychological and behavioral functions are controlled by localized regions of brain tissue is known as *localization of function.* Over the years this idea has evoked controversy, in part because complex behaviors tend to use many different regions of the brain (often at the same time). It can thus be difficult to pinpoint the brain areas that are actually involved in a thought or action. In recent years sophisticated brain-imaging techniques have been developed that are allowing neuroscientists a better look at localized regions in action. We'll discuss some of these techniques, along with clinical evidence on brain damage, in an effort to map out the hidden architecture of the brain.

▶ **REGULATING GROWTH AND INTERNAL FUNCTIONS** Besides relying on the rapid transmission of information from neuron to neuron in the form of electrochemical activity, body systems have widespread and long-term internal communication needs. To resolve these needs, structures in the body control the release of chemicals called *hormones* into the bloodstream. These chemical messengers serve important regulatory functions, influencing growth and development, sexual behavior, the desire to eat or drink, and even emotional expression. We'll discuss the brain systems that release these chemicals and describe some of their more important effects on behavior. We'll even consider how hormone production, especially during development, can create gender-based differences in the brain. We'll find that there's some truth to the idea that men and women "think" differently, and these differences might be accounted for, at least in part, by the idiosyncrasies of male and female brains.

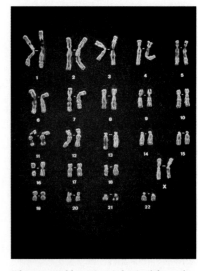

The genetic blueprint, inherited from the mother and father, importantly shapes a person's ultimate physical and even psychological characteristics.

▶ **STORING AND TRANSMITTING THE GENETIC CODE** If behavior reflects the activity of the brain, then heredity—the genetic blueprint that individuals inherit from their parents—must bear ultimate responsibility for much of what the individual is. Molecules that carry the genetic code influence more than simply eye color, height, or hair color. Intelligence, personality, and even susceptibility to mental disorders have at least some genetic basis. In this section of the chapter, we'll consider how the body transmits genetic material to its offspring, thereby helping to ensure survival of the species. We'll consider how the material is stored and how the genetic code, in combination with environmental influences, ultimately influences behavior. Psychologists have shown particular interest in the investigation of identical twins, who have essentially the same genetic code, because behavioral differences between members can be attributed uniquely to the influence of environmental factors. As we discussed in Chapter 1, the nature-nurture question is a central issue in psychology, and we'll see how twin studies help resolve important aspects of the controversy.

Communicating Internally: Connecting World and Brain

Strike a match and hold it an inch or so away from the tip of your index finger. Now move it a bit closer. Closer. Closer still. Let the flame approach and momentarily touch the flesh of your finger. You can do this experiment in your mind, if you prefer. Experience has probably already given you a pretty good idea of the consequences of finger-flame combinations. Flame touches flesh, and you withdraw your finger quickly, automatically, and efficiently. Let's consider the nervous system mechanisms that underlie this kind of reaction, because it represents one of the simplest and purest kinds of world-to-brain communications.

The main components of the nervous system are individual cells, called **neurons,** that come in three major types: *sensory neurons, interneurons,* and *motor neurons.* These neuron types differ physically from one another, and they serve quite different functions. **Sensory neurons** make the initial contact with the environment and are responsible for carrying the message inward toward the spinal cord and brain. The heat of the flame excites receptor regions in the sensory neurons in your fingertip, which then pass the message along to the spinal cord. **Interneurons,** which are the most plentiful type of neurons, make no direct contact with the world but rather convey information from one internal processing site to another. Interneurons in the spinal cord receive the message from the sensory neurons, then pass it on to the **motor neurons.** The motor neurons carry the messages and commands away from the central nervous system to the muscles and glands that directly produce the behavioral response. In the match example, which is depicted in Figure 3.2, the motor neurons contact the muscles of the finger, leading to a quick and efficient finger withdrawal.

FIGURE 3.2

A Simple Reflex Pathway. As flame touches flesh, the information travels via a sensory neuron to the spinal cord, where it's passed to an interneuron and then on to a motor neuron. The motor neuron then contacts the muscles of the finger, causing a quick and efficient finger withdrawal. The information is also passed upward to the brain, where the experience of pain occurs.

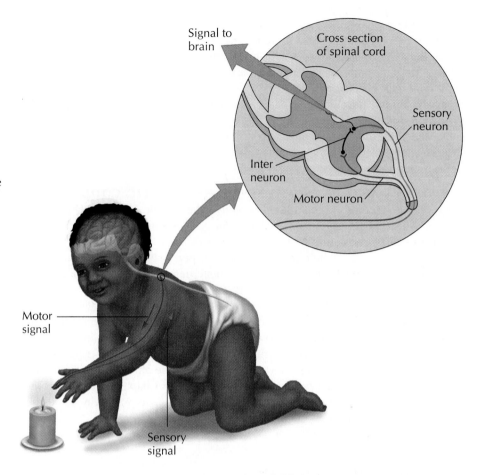

The nervous system also contains **glial cells,** which greatly outnumber neurons (by a factor of about ten to one) but do not directly communicate messages on their own. The details are beyond the scope of our discussion, but glial cells perform a variety of important functions in the nervous system, such as removing waste, filling in empty space, and helping neurons to communicate efficiently (see Kimelberg & Norenberg, 1989). Some types of glial cells wrap around portions of neurons, acting as a kind of insulation. This insulation, called the *myelin sheath*, protects the neuron and helps speed up neural transmission.

You may have noticed that so far the brain hasn't figured into our discussion of fingers and flames. Actually, the message is also passed upward to the brain, through the activity of more interneurons, and it is in the brain that you consciously experience the heat of the flame. But in situations requiring a quick response, as in the case of a flame touching your finger, the nervous system is capable of producing a collection of largely automatic reactions. These reactions, called **reflexes,** are controlled primarily by spinal cord pathways. A reflex requires no input from the brain. If your spinal cord were to be severed, blocking communication between most of the body and brain, you wouldn't feel the pain or react with a facial grimace, but your finger would still twitch. Reflex pathways allow the body to respond quickly to environmental events in a relatively simple and direct way. People don't think or feel with their spinal cords, but reflex pathways are an important part of the ability to adapt successfully to the world.

A reflex is a type of adaptive "behavior" that does not arise directly from activity of the brain. If you were building a body from scratch, what types of reflexes would you build in, and why?

The Anatomy of Neurons

Before we can understand how information passes from one neuron to another—how the message actually gets from world to brain—we need to consider the basic anatomical hardware of these cells. As shown in Figure 3.3, neurons typically have

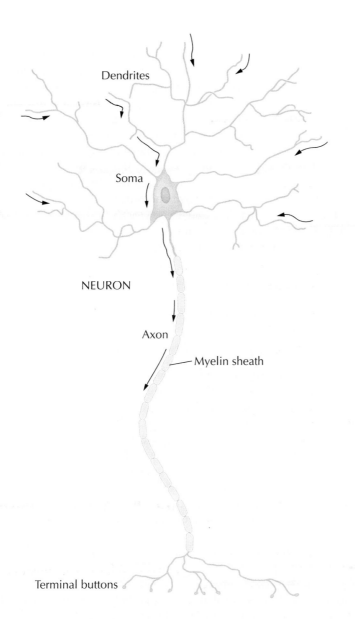

Dendrites

Soma

NEURON

Axon

Myelin sheath

Terminal buttons

FIGURE 3.3
The Components of a Neuron.
Shown here are the major anatomical components of a neuron. The *dendrites* are the primary information receivers, the *soma* is the cell body, and the *axon* is the cell's transmitter device. The myelin sheath that surrounds the axon plays a role in speeding up neural transmission. At the end of the axon are the *terminal buttons,* which contain the chemical messengers.

four major structural components: dendrites, a soma, an axon, and terminal buttons. For any communication system to work properly, it must have a way to receive information, a way to process any messages that are received, and a means for sending any appropriate response on its way. The four major structural components of the neuron interact to play these distinct roles in the communication chain.

The **dendrites,** which look like tree branches extending outward from the main body of the cell (*dendrite* is Greek for "tree"), are the primary information receivers. A sensory neuron, for example, passes information about a burning flame along to an interneuron by interacting with the interneuron's dendrites. A particular neuron may have thousands of these dendritic branches, allowing the cell to receive input from many different sources. Once received, the message is processed in the **soma,** the main body of the cell (*soma* is Greek for "body"). The soma is also the cell's metabolic center, and it's the place where the cell's genetic material is stored.

The **axon** (from the Greek for "axle") is the cell's transmitter device. When a neuron transmits a message, it sends an electrical signal called the *action potential* down its axon en route toward other neurons. Axons essentially play the role of biological "transmission cables," although the action potential in a neuron is considerably slower and qualitatively different from the electrical currents that operate in your house's wiring. Axons can vary dramatically in size and shape; in some cases, they can be several feet in length. Near its end, the axon branches out in preparation to make contact with other cells. At the tip of each branch are tiny swellings called **terminal buttons.** Chemicals released by these buttons play an important part in passing the message on to the next neuron.

Finally, although it's not really a part of the anatomy of a neuron, at the point of contact between neurons is a junction called the **synapse** (*synapse* is Greek for "junction"). Neurons don't actually touch; rather, the synapse is a small gap between cells, typically between the terminal buttons of one neuron and the dendrite or cell body of another. It is into this gap that the chemicals released by the terminal buttons flow. The synapse and the chemicals released into it are critical factors in the body's communication network, as we'll see next.

Neural Transmission: The Electrochemical Message

Neurons may differ in size and shape, but the manner and direction of information flow is predictable and consistent:

Dendrites → Soma → Axon → Terminal buttons

Information usually arrives at a neuron's dendrites from multiple sources—many thousands of contacts might be made—and is passed along to the soma. Here all the messages that have been received sum together; if sufficient energy is present, an action potential is generated. The action potential travels down the axon toward the terminal buttons, where it causes the release of chemicals into the synapse. These chemicals move the message from the end of the axon to the dendrites of the next neuron, starting the process all over again. That's the general sequence of information flow: Messages travel electrically from one point to another within a neuron, but the message is transmitted chemically between neurons. Now let's consider each of these processes in more detail.

The Resting Potential.   Neurons possess electrical properties even when they are neither receiving nor transmitting messages. Specifically, a tiny electrical charge, called the **resting potential,** exists between the inside and outside of the cell. This resting potential is created by the presence of electrically charged atoms and molecules, called *ions,* that are distributed unevenly between the inside and outside of the cell. The main ones of concern in neural transmission are positively charged *sodium* and *potassium* ions and negatively charged *chloride* ions.

Normally, ions will distribute themselves evenly in an environment, through a process called diffusion. But they are unable to do so around a resting neuron because free movement is blocked by the neuron's cell wall, or *membrane.* The membrane of a neuron is *selectively permeable,* which means that only certain ions are allowed to pass in and out through special ion "channels." As shown in Figure 3.4, when the neuron is resting, the sodium and chloride ions are concentrated outside of the cell and the potassium ions are largely contained inside. These unequal concentrations are maintained, in part, by a sodium-potassium "pump" that actively moves those ions into and out of the cell. If you were to measure the electrical potential of the neuron with an electrode at this point, you would find that the fluid inside of the cell is *negative* with respect to the outside (between −60 and −70 millivolts). This negative charge defines the *resting potential* for the cell. Most of the negative charge comes from large protein molecules inside the cell, which are too big to pass through ion channels.

Why is it adaptive for neurons to have a resting potential? It's likely that the resting potential helps the cell respond quickly when it is contacted by other neu-

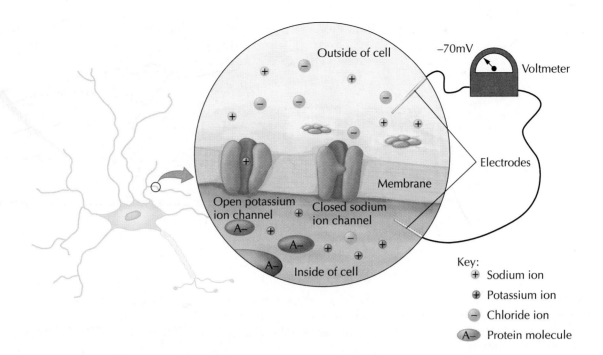

Key:
- ⊕ Sodium ion
- ⊕ Potassium ion
- ⊖ Chloride ion
- Ⓐ Protein molecule

FIGURE 3.4
The Resting Potential. Neurons possess electrical properties even when they are neither receiving nor transmitting messages. The resting potential is a tiny negative electrical charge across the inside and outside of the resting cell, created by an uneven distribution of ions across the cell membrane. Ion movement occurs through special "channels" in the membrane.

rons. When one neuron communicates with another, it releases chemicals that change the permeability of the contacted neuron's membrane. Ions that are normally outside of the cell rush in quickly through now-open channels. This changes the electrical potential inside the cell, which, as we'll see shortly, is a necessary prerequisite for the production of an action potential.

Generating an Action Potential. For a neuron to stop resting and generate its own message—the **action potential**—the electrical potential inside the cell needs to become less negative with respect to the outside. Changes in internal potential occur as a result of contact from other neurons. Two types of messages can be passed from one neuron to the next: excitatory messages and inhibitory messages. If the message is *excitatory,* sodium channels in the contacted region open, allowing sodium ions to flow inward. The movement of positive ions into the cell sends the electrical potential from negative toward zero, increasing the likelihood that an action potential will be generated. This process is called **depolarization,** because the size of the potential is being reduced. When the message is *inhibitory,* the opposite happens: The cell membrane changes in such a way as to either push more positive ions out of the cell or to allow negative chloride ions to move in. The result is **hyperpolarization:** the electrical potential of the cell becomes more negative, and the chances of generating an action potential decrease (see Figure 3.5b).

It's important to remember that any given neuron in the nervous system is in "contact" with many other neurons. Consequently, many local changes in potential are likely to be occurring all over the input regions of the neuron, as individual messages are received (see Figure 3.5a). Near the point where the axon leaves the cell body, in a special trigger zone called the *axon hillock,* all of the excitatory and inhibitory potentials combine together. If enough excitatory messages have been received, an action potential will be initiated. If not, the resting potential of the axon will be maintained. Action potentials are generated in an *all-or-none* fashion; that is, they will not begin until sufficient excitatory input has been received, but once the firing "threshold" is reached, they always travel completely down the length of the axon to its end. The process is somewhat analogous to the firing of a gun. Once sufficient pressure is delivered to the trigger, a bullet will fire and

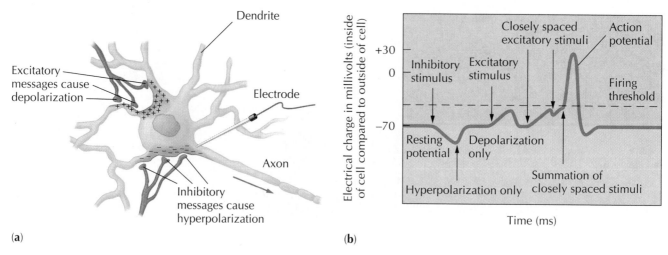

Dendrite

Excitatory
messages cause
depolarization

Electrode

Axon

Inhibitory
messages cause
hyperpolarization

(a)

Electrical charge in millivolts (inside of cell compared to outside of cell)

+30

0

−70

Inhibitory
stimulus

Excitatory
stimulus

Closely spaced
excitatory stimuli

Action
potential

Firing
threshold

Resting
potential

Depolarization
only

Hyperpolarization only

Summation of
closely spaced stimuli

Time (ms)

(b)

FIGURE 3.5
Summing Excitatory and Inhibitory Messages. Neurons are in "contact" with many other neurons. Some of these contacts initiate excitatory messages (depolarization), while others initiate inhibitory messages (hyperpolarization). A neuron will generate its own action potential only if the summed messages produce sufficient depolarization (the negative potential moves enough toward zero). The insert to the right shows how the potential of a cell might change over time, as excitatory and inhibitory messages are received. Notice that only when the potential inside the cell crosses the "firing threshold" will the all-or-none action potential be generated.

The speed of neural transmission is quite slow, at least relative to the speed of processing in a computer chip. How do you think it's possible, then, for people to make quick, seemingly instant, decisions? Could large groups of neurons acting together be involved?

move down the barrel in a characteristic way. Action potentials, like bullets, also travel forward in a way that is independent of the intensity of the messages that caused the firing. Bullets don't travel farther or faster if you pull the trigger harder.

Action potentials travel down the axon in a stereotypical fashion. It really doesn't matter whether the neuron is carrying a message about pain or pleasure, the characteristics of the signal won't vary from one neuron to the next, or from one point on the axon to the next. Ion channels in the membrane of the axon membrane open, allowing positively charged sodium ions to rush in, and a kind of chain reaction is created. Adjacent spots on the axon quickly become depolarized, creating an electrical impulse that moves rapidly forward. The overall speed, however, depends on the size and shape of the axon; in general, the thicker the axon, the faster the message will travel. Impulse speed varies among neuron types in a range from about 2 to 200 miles per hour (which is still significantly slower than the speed of electricity through a wire or printed circuit).

One feature that increases the speed of transmission in many neurons is the myelin sheath, which, as mentioned earlier, is built from a type of glial cell. Myelin provides an insulating wrap for the axon, like the plastic around copper wiring in your house. At regular points, gaps in the insulation allow the action potential effectively to "jump" down the axon rather than traveling from point to point. The myelin sheath speeds transmission and also protects the message from interference from other neural signals.

Neurotransmitters: The Chemical Messengers. When the action potential reaches the end of the axon, it triggers the release of chemical messengers from small vesicles in the terminal buttons (see Figure 3.6). These chemical molecules, called **neurotransmitters**, spill out into the synapse and interact chemically with the cell membrane of the next neuron (called the *postsynaptic membrane*). Depending on the particular characteristics of this membrane, the neurotransmitter will transfer either an excitatory or an inhibitory message.

The released neurotransmitter molecule acts as a kind of key in search of the appropriate lock. The substance diffuses quickly across the synapse—it takes only about 1/10,000 of a second—and activates receptor molecules that reside in the postsynaptic membrane. Depending on the particular type of receptor molecule that is present, the neurotransmitter will either increase or decrease the electrical potential of the receiving cell. When the message is excitatory, the neurotransmitter causes channels in the postsynaptic membrane to open, allowing positive sodium ions to flow into the receiving cell. When the message is inhibitory, negative chloride ions are allowed to enter the cell and positive potassium ions are

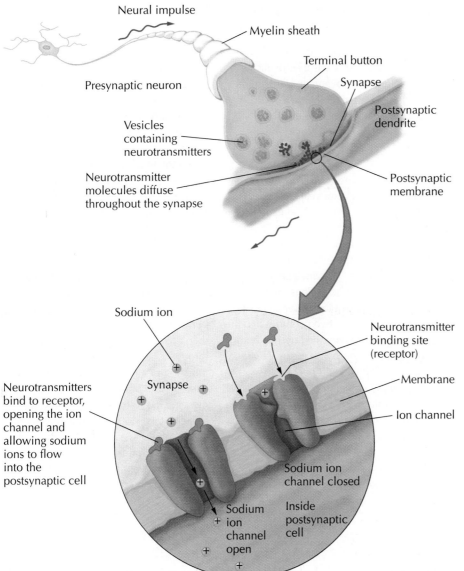

Neural impulse

Myelin sheath

Terminal button

Presynaptic neuron

Synapse

Postsynaptic dendrite

Vesicles containing neurotransmitters

Neurotransmitter molecules diffuse throughout the synapse

Postsynaptic membrane

Sodium ion

Neurotransmitter binding site (receptor)

Neurotransmitters bind to receptor, opening the ion channel and allowing sodium ions to flow into the postsynaptic cell

Synapse

Membrane

Ion channel

Sodium ion channel closed

Inside postsynaptic cell

Sodium ion channel open

FIGURE 3.6
Releasing the Chemical Messengers. When the action potential reaches the end of the axon, it causes the release of chemical messengers—neurotransmitters—into the synapse. The neurotransmitters interact with the postsynaptic membrane of the next neuron, opening or closing its ion channels. Here, the neurotransmitter is opening sodium channels, which should increase the chances of the receiving cell initiating its own action potential.

allowed to leave. It's worth emphasizing that neurotransmitters, by themselves, are neither excitatory nor inhibitory. It is really the nature of the receptor molecule that determines whether a particular neurotransmitter will produce an excitatory or inhibitory effect; the same neurotransmitter can produce quite different effects at different sites in the nervous system.

Dozens of neurotransmitters have been identified in the brain, along with their various functions. The neurotransmitter **acetylcholine** is a major messenger in both the central and peripheral nervous systems; it acts, for example, as the primary transmitter between motor neurons and muscles in the body. When released into the synapse between motor neurons and muscle cells, acetylcholine tends to create excitatory messages that lead to muscle contraction. The neurotransmitter **dopamine** produces largely inhibitory effects that help dampen and stabilize communications in the brain and elsewhere. Inhibitory neurotransmitters help keep the brain on an even keel and allow people to do things like produce smooth voluntary muscle movements, sleep without physically acting out their dreams, and maintain posture. If neurotransmitters had only excitatory effects, there would be an endless chain of communication, producing a blooming, buzzing ball of confusion in the brain.

INSIDE THE PROBLEM: *"Animal Electricity" and the Neural Impulse*

Mary Wollstonecraft Shelley, in her classic novel *Frankenstein,* used an electrical storm to infuse life into her monstrous creation. Even in her time, the early 19th century, people recognized that the neural impulse had a powerful electric component. In fact, the formal linking of electricity to the initiation of behavior in the nervous system dates back to the work of an Italian named Luigi Galvani in the last two decades of the 18th century. Galvani noticed that when the severed legs of frogs were hung from brass hooks connected to iron rods, they would sometimes twitch in the presence of electric storms, or when static electricity was discharged nearby.

This rather odd discovery led Galvani to begin experimenting with the relationship between electrical activity and muscle movement. He eventually learned that he could control and initiate the twitching movements by touching one end of a frog leg with a metal rod, touching the other end with a rod of a different metal, and then touching the free ends of the two rods together. We now know Galvani had formed a

rudimentary kind of "wet battery" with this procedure and was electrically stimulating the movement, but he didn't recognize this fact at the time. Galvani assumed that the leg was naturally generating "animal electricity," which he tried to capture by piling up frog legs in various ways. (You don't need frog legs to generate electricity, as Alessandro Volta showed several years later with the development of the first "inorganic" battery in 1800.)

Galvani's discovery eventually led to the development of practical batteries, but it also helped convince people that the behavior of living things might be governed by understandable forces of nature. Remember, two centuries ago the relationship between the physical body and behavior was by no means clearly established. It was still popular to attribute the initiation of behavior to spiritual forces. Galvani's work suggested that behavior might be studied and controlled in the laboratory, in the same way that forces of nature could be studied and controlled. For example, if the initiation of motor movements is

governed by a physical force such as electricity, perhaps there might be a way to measure something like the speed of internal "messages" in the body. A preliminary solution to this problem was worked out in 1849 by Hermann von Helmholtz.

By the time of Helmholtz, mental processes had become associated with activity of the brain. But the idea that the brain "decides" on an action and then carries it out by delivering a message to the muscles was still undeveloped. Then, as today, the initiation of movement seemed to be instantaneous with the "willful" decision. Think about it: There is certainly no personal sense of a delay between deciding to lift your hand and then lifting it. But Helmholtz showed, through a clever experiment, that the initiation of a movement does indeed occur in real time—the farther a message has to travel in the body, the longer it takes to initiate the movement.

Helmholtz's experiment was straightforward. He trained a volunteer to press a key whenever the subject felt touched on the body (see Figure 3.7). The

For much of recorded human history, psychological disorders were attributed to possession by evil spirits. Today, psychologists recognize that some psychological disorders arise from malfunctioning brains.

Psychologists have been particularly interested in dopamine because it is thought to play a role in schizophrenia, a serious psychological disorder that disrupts thought processes and produces delusions and hallucinations. When patients suffering from schizophrenia take drugs that inhibit the action of dopamine, their hallucinations and delusions are sometimes reduced or even eliminated. It has been speculated that perhaps an excess supply of dopamine is partly responsible for the disorder (Gershon & Reider, 1992; Sigmundson, 1994; Snyder, 1976). Further support linking dopamine and schizophrenia has come from the study of Parkinson's disease. This movement disorder apparently results from the underproduction of dopamine. Parkinson's patients are often given the drug L-dopa, which increases the levels of dopamine in the brain, to reduce the tremors and other movement problems that result from the disease. For some patients, however, one of the side effects of L-dopa can be a mimicking of the thought disorders characteristic of schizophrenia (Braff & Huey, 1988).

Neurotransmitters in the brain fundamentally affect people's thoughts and actions, but the particular mechanisms involved are not well understood. We know, for example, that people with Alzheimer's disease have suffered destruction of cells that play a role in producing acetylcholine (Mash, Flynn, & Potter, 1985; Quirion, 1993). This suggests that a connection may exist between acetylcholine and certain kinds of memory functioning, particularly memory loss (a common subject's "reaction time" to press the key was the measure of interest and formed the dependent variable in the experiment. The experimental manipulation, or independent variable, was where on the body the touch occurred. Helmholtz began the experiment by touching the subject on the toe and measuring the reaction time to press the key; next, he moved the point of contact higher up, near the thigh, and again measured the subject's speed in pressing the key. He found that it took the subject less time to press the key when touched on the thigh than when touched on the toe. To calculate the speed of the neural message, Helmholtz simply divided the distance between the two points of stimulation by the difference in reaction times, and he arrived at a remarkably accurate measure of the speed of neural transmission. More important, his estimate of neural speed, which he deduced was between 100 and 200 miles per hour, proved that the initiation of movement is not instantaneous in the body but rather is relatively "slow." The fact that messages travel at a rate well

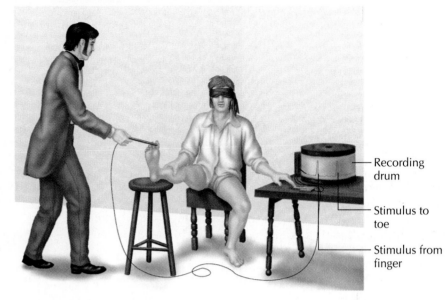

— Recording drum

— Stimulus to toe

— Stimulus from finger

FIGURE 3.7

Measuring the Speed of Neural Transmission. Helmholtz trained volunteers to press a response button whenever they felt a touch on the body. By comparing reaction times for touches on various parts of the body, Helmholtz was able to obtain a reasonably accurate measure of the speed of neural transmission.

below the speed of electricity confounded researchers of the time but provided a further indication that "willful" actions are importantly limited by the characteristics of the physical body.

---

problem for Alzheimer patients). We know that the neurotransmitter **serotonin**, another primarily inhibitory substance, affects sleep, dreaming, and general arousal and may also be involved in such psychological disorders as depression, schizophrenia, and obsessive-compulsive disorder (Potter & Manji, 1993; Thomsen, 1994). But in each of these cases, researchers still face the arduous task of mapping out the specific neural pathways and mechanisms involved. At this point, much of the link is correlational rather than causal. We simply know that as the levels of particular neurotransmitters vary in the body, so, too, do the symptoms of various disorders.

Drugs and the Brain. Because the transmission of messages *between* neurons is chemical, ingesting chemicals into the body can significantly affect the communication networks in the brain. Of particular concern are naturally occurring or artificial *drugs*. Some drugs mimic the action of neurotransmitters (they're called *agonists* from the Greek word for "contest"). For example, the nicotine in cigarette smoke can act like the neurotransmitter acetylcholine. Nicotine has a general stimulatory effect in the body, such as increasing the heart rate, because it produces excitatory messages in much the same way as acetylcholine.

Other drugs act as *antagonists*, which means that they oppose or block the action of neurotransmitters. The lethal drug curare, which South American natives

There may be a connection between the neurotransmitter acetylcholine and certain kinds of memory functioning, particularly memory loss of the type seen in Alzheimer's disease.

Some people rely on external drugs, such as the caffeine in coffee and the nicotine in cigarette smoke, to produce a general stimulatory effect in the body.

sometimes use on the tips of hunting arrows and blowdarts, is antagonistic to acetylcholine. Curare blocks the receptor systems involved in muscle movements, including those muscles that move the diaphragm during breathing. The result is paralysis and likely death from suffocation. The deadly toxin *botulin,* which sometimes is associated with the improper canning of food, acts in a similar fashion—it interferes with the action of acetylcholine, thereby producing paralysis.

In the early 1970s membrane receptor systems were discovered in the brain that bind directly with *morphine,* a pain-killing and highly addictive drug derived from the opium plant (Pert & Snyder, 1973). Further study revealed that humans have receptor systems that bind with morphine because the brain produces its own morphinelike substances called endorphins. **Endorphins** serve as a kind of natural painkiller in the body. They are thought to act as *neuromodulators,* or chemicals that modulate (increase or decrease) the effectiveness of neurotransmitters. Apparently, the brain has evolved systems for releasing endorphins under conditions of stress or exertion to reduce pain and possibly to provide pleasurable reinforcement (Schedlowski et al., 1995). We'll return to the study of drugs, particularly their effects on conscious awareness, in Chapter 6.

The Communication Network

We've tapped briefly into the electrochemical language of the nervous system. We've seen how information is transmitted electrically within a neuron, through the flow of charged ions, and how one neuron signals another through the release of chemical messengers. But understanding the dynamics of neuron-to-neuron communication is only part of the story.

Most brain researchers agree that if we are ever to unravel the complex relationship between the brain and mind, we must understand how neurons work together. A vast communication network permeates the brain, involving the operation of thousands of neurons, and the manner in which these cells interact is of critical importance. Behaviors, thoughts, feelings, ideas—they don't arise from the activation of single neurons; instead, it is the *pattern of activation* produced by groups of neurons operating at the same time that underlies both conscious experiences and complex behaviors. It is therefore necessary to pay attention to the

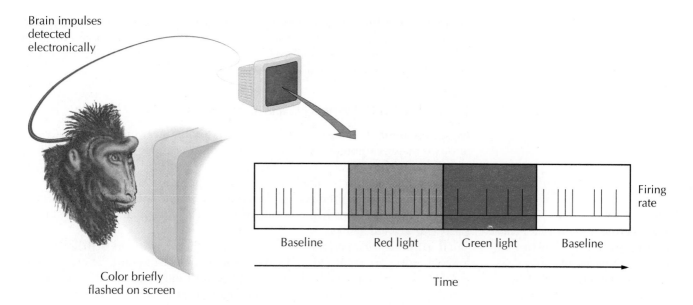

Brain impulses detected electronically

Color briefly flashed on screen

Baseline   Red light   Green light   Baseline

Firing rate

Time

FIGURE 3.8
Changes in Firing Rates. Information is partly communicated in the nervous system through changes in the firing rates of neurons. Here, neurons in the monkey's brain increase their firing rate, relative to baseline, when a red stimulus appears, and decrease their firing rate, relative to baseline, when a green stimulus appears.

specific ways in which neurons are connected and the means through which those connections can be modified by experience (Kandel, 1991).

Information is also communicated in the nervous system through the rate at which neurons generate action potentials. The *firing rate* of a neuron is defined by the number of action potentials it generates per unit of time. The firing rate is subject to some natural limitations. For instance, a **refractory period** follows the generation of an action potential, during which more action potentials cannot be generated. But neurons are still able to fire off a steady stream of messages in response to environmental stimulation. Many neurons even appear to have "spontaneous" firing rates, which means that they generate a steady stream of action potentials even with little or no apparent input from the environment. A continuously active cell is adaptive for the nervous system because information can be communicated partly by either increasing or decreasing the spontaneous firing rates of its neurons. The color red, for example, might be experienced when particular cells in the brain increase their pattern and frequency of firing, whereas "green" can arise from a decrease in the generation of action potentials (see Figure 3.8). In this way, more information is effectively coded into the system. Changes in firing rate, along with the global patterns of activation among large groups of cells, lie at the roots of understanding most complex psychological phenomena. (For more on this topic, see The Adaptive Mind section at the end of this chapter.)

Initiating and Coordinating Behavior: A Division of Labor

As a whole, the nervous system has a tremendously complicated set of problems to solve through its communication network of neurons. Beyond the generation of physical behaviors and of mental processes such as thinking and feeling, the brain needs to keep constant track of more mundane things, such as maintaining a beating heart, controlling breathing, and signaling the body that it's time to eat. If the body is deprived of food or water, or if its constant internal temperature is compromised, something needs to motivate the individual to seek food, water, or the appropriate shelter. Moreover, although you may not have thought about it too much, even the simplest of everyday activities—producing spoken language, walking, perceiving a complex visual scene—require a great deal of coordination among the muscles and sensory organs of the body. To accomplish such diverse functions, the nervous system divides its labor.

The Central and Peripheral Nervous Systems

As we discussed at the beginning of the chapter, the nervous system is divided into two major components: the central nervous system and the peripheral nervous system. The *central nervous system,* consisting of the brain and spinal cord, is the central executive of the body. Decisions are made here, and messages are then communicated to the rest of the body via bundles of axons called **nerves.** The collection of nerves lying outside of the brain and spinal cord make up the *peripheral nervous system.*

It is through the peripheral nervous system that muscles are actually moved, internal organs are regulated, and sensory input is moved toward the brain. Information travels toward the brain and spinal cord through *afferent* (sensory) nerve pathways; *efferent* (motor) nerve pathways carry central nervous system messages outward to the muscles and glands. As you can see in Figure 3.9, the peripheral

FIGURE 3.9
The Nervous System. The human nervous system can be broken down into the central nervous system, which contains the brain and the spinal cord, and the peripheral nervous system, which contains various subsystems. (Based on Kalat, 1996)

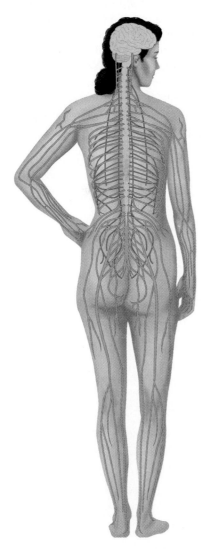

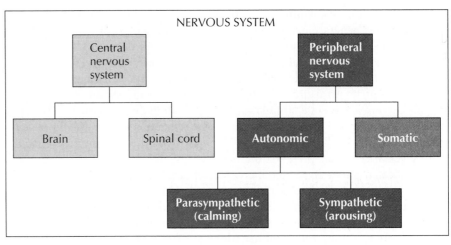

nervous system is further subdivided into the somatic and autonomic systems. The **somatic system** consists of the nerves that transmit sensory information toward the brain, as well as the nerves that connect to the skeletal muscles to initiate movement. The **autonomic system** controls the more automatic needs of the body, such as heart rate, digestion, blood pressure, and the activities of internal glands. These two systems work together to ensure that information about the world is communicated to the brain for interpretation, that movements are carried out, and that the life-sustaining activities of the body are continued.

One critical function of the autonomic system, besides performing the automatic "housekeeping" activities that keep the body alive, is to affect the body's readiness to handle and recover from emergency situations. The *sympathetic division* of the autonomic system prepares the body for emergencies by triggering the release of chemicals that put it in a state of readiness (such as by increasing heart rate, blood pressure, and breathing rate). After the emergency has passed, the *parasympathetic division* calms the body down by slowing heart rate and lowering blood pressure. Parasympathetic activity also helps increase the body's supply of stored energy that may have been reduced as a result of dealing with an emergency situation.

Research Techniques for Determining Brain Function

Before we embark on a detailed examination of the structure and function of the brain, it's useful to consider the techniques that researchers use to map out the divisions of labor contained within. The anatomical features of the nervous system as a whole—the various nerve tracts and so on—can be studied through dissection of the body. But the dissection of brain tissue, which contains billions of neurons, tells only a limited story. To determine the architecture of the brain, researchers need to rely on a broader set of tools. We'll briefly consider three general techniques: (1) the study of brain damage from injury or disease, (2) methods that allow the researcher to activate (or "talk" to) the brain directly, and (3) methods that allow researchers to "listen" to or eavesdrop on the brain in action.

Brain Damage and Lesion. The study of brain damage is one of the oldest available methods for isolating brain function. A patient arrives with some specific, localized region of damage—such as a blow to the right side of the head—

This patient, who may be suffering from a form of brain damage, is having his memory assessed at a memory disorders clinic.

and complains of a particular problem, such as trouble moving the left side of his or her body. In this way, a rudimentary link can be established between a brain area and a behavior or function. As early as the middle of the 19th century, for example, it was known that damage to isolated areas on the left side of the brain creates distinct patterns of speech difficulties. Destruction of *Wernicke's area* (named after its discoverer) results in a patient who cannot easily understand spoken language (Wernicke, 1874); damage to *Broca's area* results in a patient who can understand but not produce spoken language (Broca, 1861). Such cases lend support to the idea that different psychological and behavioral functions are controlled by specific areas of the brain.

Unfortunately, relying on instances of brain injury alone (through case studies) has its limitations. For one thing, researchers must wait around until the specific injury of interest presents itself for their inspection. To make matters worse, the patient usually needs to die before any precise mapping of injury to function can be established. The exact nature of the injury can typically only be established through autopsy. In addition, most instances of brain damage, either from an accident or from a tumor or a stroke, produce very general and widespread damage. So it is difficult to ascertain exactly which portion of the damaged brain is responsible for the behavioral or psychological problem. As we discussed in Chapter 2, case studies can be rich sources of information, but the researcher typically lacks important controls.

To establish a true structure-function relationship, it is necessary to observe the effects of systematic and localized removal of tissue in a controlled way. Researchers have taken advantage of the fact that brain tissue contains no pain receptors to explore brain function in lower animals, particularly rats. It's possible to destroy, or *lesion,* particular regions of an animal's brain by administering an electric current, injecting chemicals, or cutting tissue. Even here it is difficult to pinpoint the damage exactly (because everything in the brain tends to be interconnected), but lesioning techniques have become increasingly more accurate in recent years. There are chemicals, for example, that can selectively damage neurons in the brain without damaging neighboring nerve pathways (Jarrad, 1993). The lesioning procedure is then followed by controlled examination of the animal's behavior to see how it is affected.

Talking to the Brain. It is also possible to "talk" to the brain directly by capitalizing on the electrochemical nature of the communication network. Essentially, messages can be created where none would have normally occurred. Researchers can inject chemicals that serve to excite, rather than destroy, the neurons in a particular area of the brain. Alternatively, researchers can insert small wire electrodes into brain tissue, allowing an area's cells to be stimulated electrically. The researcher initiates a message externally, then observes any changes in behavior.

Electrical stimulation techniques have been used primarily with animals. It's possible to implant an electrode in such a way as to allow an animal to still move freely about in its environment (see Figure 3.10). A small pulse of current can then be delivered to various brain regions whenever the researcher desires. Studies have shown that electrical brain stimulation can induce animals to suddenly start eating, drinking, engaging in sexual behavior, or preparing for an attack. Using electrical stimulation, researchers have found that certain areas in the brain act as "pleasure centers" in rats, leading them to engage repeatedly in whatever behavior led to the stimulation (Olds, 1958; Simmons & Gallistel, 1994). For example, if rats are taught that pressing a metal bar leads to electrical stimulation of a reward area, they will press the bar thousands of times an hour. (The natural inference, of course, is that the stimulation is "pleasurable," although we really have no way to tell what a concept like "pleasure" means to a rat.)

Does it bother you that researchers often try to generalize the results of "rat" studies to humans? If so, does it also bother you that some of the basic principles of genetics were derived from the study of pea plants?

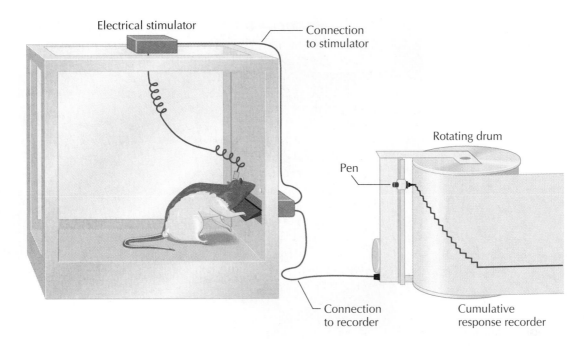

The electrical stimulation technique is often used by researchers to link the initiation and control of behavior to patterns of activity in localized areas in the brain. For example, a behavior that is produced by stimulation of brain region A but not by stimulation of brain region B suggests that region A plays at least some role in the overall production of the behavior. But the precise mapping of behaviors to brain locations still remains a difficult task. It is always possible to argue, for example, that a stimulated area is required to produce a particular behavior but that it does not act alone—it might serve only as a communication link, or relay connection, to some other brain region that actually initiates the behavior.

Under some circumstances, it has been possible to stimulate cells in the human brain and note the behavioral effects. During certain kinds of brain surgery (such as surgery to reduce the seizures produced by epilepsy), patients are kept awake and their brain is stimulated from time to time with an electrode. Because there are no pain receptors in the brain, patients typically receive only a local anesthetic (along with some drugs for relaxation) prior to the surgery. Keeping the patient awake is necessary because the surgeon can stimulate an abnormal area, prior to removal, to make sure that vital capabilities such as speech or movement will not be affected. Electrical stimulation under these conditions has induced patients to produce involuntary movement, hear buzzing noises, and even experience what the patients report as memories (Penfield & Perot, 1963).

Listening to the Brain. Brain lesioning and electrical stimulation are popular and effective research tools, but they are *invasive* in the sense that they require making contact with (or even destroying) actual brain tissue. Researchers have at their disposal other techniques, which can be applied more readily to the study of humans, that essentially eavesdrop on the brain without any penetration of the skull. The **electroencephalograph (EEG)** is a device that simply monitors the gross electrical activity of the brain.

FIGURE 3.10
Electrical Stimulation. A rat is shown here pressing a bar in order to receive a small pulse of electric current delivered to the brain. Stimulation of certain brain areas appears quite rewarding to the rat, leading the rat to press the bar at a very rapid rate.

An electroencephalogram is a record of the gross electrical activity in different regions of the brain. Red and violet colors in these photos show electrical activity usually associated with relaxation; blue indicates the total absence of such activity. In the upper row the subject's eyes were closed; in the bottom row, the subject's eyes were open.

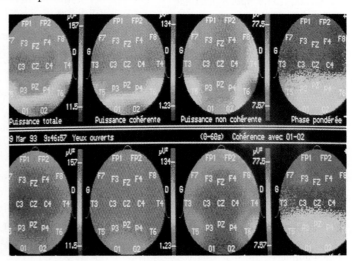

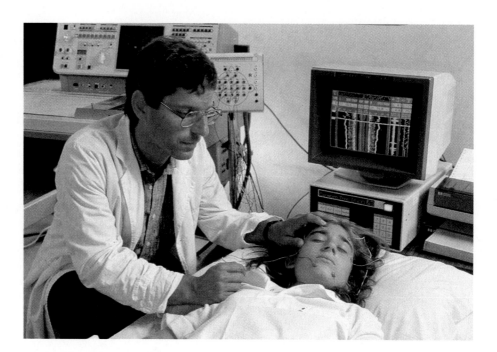

Researchers can eavesdrop on the electrical activity of a person's brain through the EEG device, shown here.

Recording electrodes attached to the scalp measure global changes in the electrical potentials of thousands of brain cells in the form of line tracings, or brain waves. The EEG is useful not only as a research tool but also for diagnostic purposes. Brain disorders, including psychological disorders, can sometimes be detected through abnormalities in brain waves (John et al., 1988; Sponheim et al., 1994).

An actual picture of the brain's anatomical structures, including abnormalities in brain tissue, can be obtained through a **computerized tomography scan** (or CT scan). CT scanners use computers to detect how highly focused beams of X rays change as they are passed through the body at various angles and orientations. The X-ray beams are absorbed differentially, depending on the type of structure they pass through; the computer analyzes the emission pattern mathematically and reconstructs a detailed anatomical map. CT scanners are most often used by physicians to detect tumors or injuries to the brain, but they can also be used to determine whether there is a physical basis for some chronic behavioral or psychological disorder.

Other imaging devices are designed to obtain a snapshot of the *active* brain at work. These techniques help the researcher determine how various tasks, such as reading a book, affect individual parts of the brain. In **positron emission tomography (PET),** the patient ingests a harmless radioactive substance, which is then absorbed into the cells of brain regions that are metabolically active. When the subject is performing a specific kind of task, such as speaking or reading, the active areas of the brain absorb more of the ingested radioactive material. The PET scanner then develops a pictorial blueprint that reveals how the radioactive substance has distributed itself over time. It is assumed that those parts of the brain that end up with concentrated traces of radioactive material probably play a significant role in initiating or controlling the task that the subject is performing.

A series of eight PET scans is displayed, demonstrating how a harmless radioactive substance is absorbed over time into the cells of brain regions that are active.

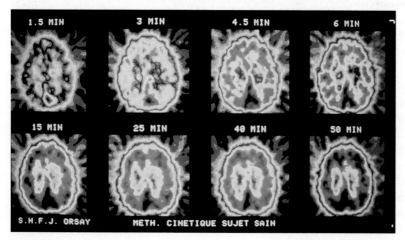

In recent applications of this technique, a kind of radioactive water is injected into the body that allows the PET scanning device to measure blood flow in the brain. Images of how blood flow changes when regions of the brain are active and inactive is believed to be a reliable indicator of how activity in the brain changes from moment to moment (Raichle, 1994).

Another technique that can be used to isolate both structure and function in the brain is **magnetic resonance imaging (MRI).** MRI has two main advantages over PET scanning: It doesn't require the participant to ingest any kind of chemicals, and it's capable of producing extremely detailed, three-dimensional images of the brain. MRI technology capitalizes on the fact that atoms behave in systematic ways in the presence of magnetic fields and radio-wave pulses (the details are rather complex). Although expensive to build and use, MRIs have proven to be excellent diagnostic tools for spotting brain damage, tumor growth, and other abnormalities. More recent applications of what is called "functional MRI" use the MRI technology to map changes in blood oxygen use as a function of task activity. Functional MRI, like PET scanning, is currently being used to help isolate structure-function relationships in the brain (Binder et al., 1994; Engel et al., 1994).

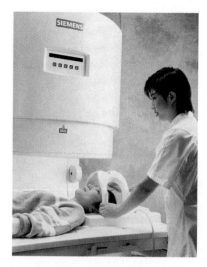

The magnetic resonance imaging device (MRI) is capable of isolating both structure and some function in the brain.

Brain Structures and Their Functions

Having discussed some of the research tools that scientists use to map out brain structure and function, we can now turn our attention to the brain itself. Remember, it is within the brain that mental processes are presumed to be represented, through the simultaneous activities of billions of individual neurons. Particular regions in the brain are thought to contribute unique features to an experience, helping to create a psychological "whole." Thus, your perception of a cat is not controlled by a single cell, or even by a single group of cells, but rather by different brain areas that detect the color of the fur, recognize a characteristic meow, or even generate the expectation that the cat will saunter into the room because you just put down the food dish. The contributions of specific brain regions are underscored by the study of brain-damaged patients, which shows that people can lose specific kinds of mental abilities. For instance, someone might lose knowledge about living things but not about inanimate things (Kandel, 1991), or a person might lose the ability to see moving objects but not objects that are stationary (Zeki, 1992).

We'll divide our discussion of the brain into sections that correspond to the brain's three major anatomical regions: the *hindbrain,* the *midbrain,* and the *forebrain.*

The Hindbrain: Basic Life Support. The **hindbrain,** which is the most primitive part of the brain, sits at the juncture point where the spinal cord and brain merge (see Figure 3.11). "Primitive" is an appropriate term for two reasons. First, structures in the hindbrain act as the basic life-support system for the body—no creative thoughts or complex emotions originate here. Second, from the standpoint of evolution, the hindbrain is the "oldest" part of the brain. Similar structures, with similar functions, can be found throughout the animal kingdom. You can think of the hindbrain as a kind of base camp, with higher structures that are situated further up into the brain controlling increasingly more complex mental processes. Not surprisingly, damage to these lower regions of the brain does not bode well for survival of the organism.

As you can see in Figure 3.11, the hindbrain contains several important anatomical substructures. The *medulla* and the *pons* are associated with the control of heart rate, breathing, blood pressure, and certain reflexes, such as vomiting, sneezing, and coughing. Both areas serve as conduction pathways for neural

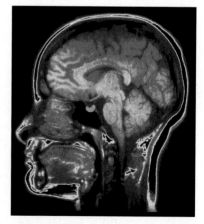

MRIs produce extremely detailed images of the brain and are thereby excellent diagnostic tools for spotting brain damage, tumor growth, and other physical abnormalities in the brain.

FIGURE 3.11
The Hindbrain. Shown here are the various structures of the human hindbrain. The hindbrain acts as the basic life-support system for the body, controlling such things as heart rate, blood pressure, and respiration.

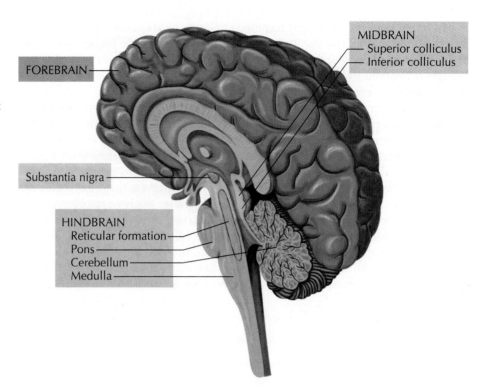

impulses traveling to and from the spinal cord (the word *pons* means "bridge"). These areas are particularly sensitive to the lethal effects of drugs such as alcohol, barbiturates, and cocaine. Drug death in the case of college basketball star Len Bias, for example, was due to effects of cocaine on blood pressure. Alcoholics can drown in their own vomit, and barbiturate users who overdose often suffocate because of drug action on neurological structures in the hindbrain.

The hindbrain also contains the *reticular formation,* a network of nerves linked to the control of general arousal, sleep, and possibly specific movements of the head (Siegel, 1983). Damage to the reticular formation can lead to the loss of consciousness. Finally, at the base of the brain sits a structure that in general appearance resembles a smaller version of the brain. This is the **cerebellum** (which means "little brain"), a structure involved in the planning and coordination of complex motor skills such as hitting a golf ball, playing the piano, or writing. When the cerebellum is damaged, the person can still initiate movements, but those movements tend to lack coordination and smoothness.

The Midbrain: Neural Relay Stations. The **midbrain,** which lies deep within the brain atop the hindbrain, is enveloped by other structures that make up the forebrain. Perhaps because of its central position, the midbrain and its accompanying structures receive input from multiple sources, including the sense organs. The *tectum* and its component structures, the *superior colliculus* and *inferior colliculus,* serve as important relay stations for visual and auditory information and help coordinate reactions to sensory events in the environment (such as moving the head to a sudden sound).

The midbrain also contains a dark-looking group of neurons, collectively called the *substantia nigra* (Latin for "black substance"), which release the neurotransmitter dopamine from their terminal buttons. As we saw earlier in the chapter, dopamine acts as a critical inhibitory neurotransmitter in the body, and it seems to be involved in a number of physical and psychological disorders. For example, the rigidity of movement or continuous muscle twitches and tremors

This patient, who is suffering from Parkinson's disease, may have lost the ability to produce sufficient amounts of the neurotransmitter dopamine in the brain.

that characterize Parkinson's disease apparently result from decreased levels of dopamine in the brain. Indeed, the death of neurons in the substantia nigra is believed to be the cause of the disorder (Jenner, 1990). Exactly why this portion of the midbrain degenerates is not known, although environmental toxins may be contributors (Snyder & D'Amato, 1986).

A number of important developments in the understanding and treatment of Parkinson-like disorders have resulted from investigating the substantia nigra. For example, in 1982 a group of young adults, in search of a heroin high, opted to inject themselves with a "designer drug" that was supposed to simulate the effects of heroin. The lab work was sloppy, however, and the amateur chemist produced a substance that permanently redesigned the users' brains. A chemical component of the drug, known as MPTP, destroyed the substantia nigra region of their midbrains. The result was severe Parkinson-like symptoms—the users became essentially "frozen" in their bodies, lacking the ability to communicate or to move about freely (Ballard, Tetrud, & Langston, 1985).

Ironically, this tragic accident proved to be of great value to researchers of Parkinson's disease. By studying these individuals, along with the component MPTP, researchers were able to confirm the link between the production of dopamine in the substantia nigra and the rigidity of movement that characterizes Parkinson's disease. It has even been possible to mimic the disorder in animals through the administration of MPTP (Schneider, Sun, & Roeltgen, 1994; Snyder & D'Amato, 1986).

More recently, some of the "frozen" users have volunteered to participate in a controversial transplant procedure involving brain tissue from aborted fetuses. There is some evidence that injecting portions of the substantia nigra from such fetuses into damaged adult brains can reverse Parkinson-like symptoms, although the results are by no means clearcut (see Lindvall et al., 1989). This research raises some serious ethical questions. Many people, for example, object to fetal tissue research of any kind. Proponents of transplant studies counter that this research is quite likely to lead to breakthroughs in the restoration of damaged or lost brain function in suffering human beings.

FIGURE 3.12

The Forebrain. Shown here are the various structures of the forebrain, including the limbic system and the cerebral cortex. Structures in the limbic system are thought to be involved in motivation, emotion, and memory. The cerebral cortex is the seat of higher mental processes.

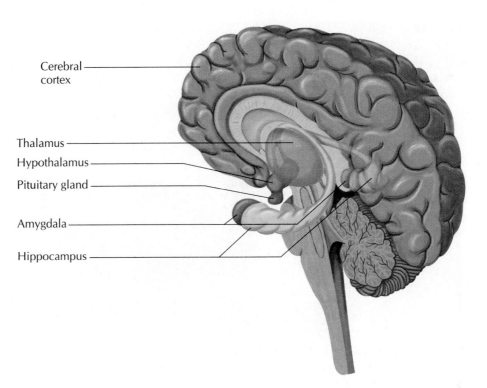

Cerebral cortex

Thalamus

Hypothalamus

Pituitary gland

Amygdala

Hippocampus

The Forebrain: Higher Mental Functioning. Moving up past the midbrain we encounter the **forebrain,** which, like the other brain areas we've discussed, is actually composed of several parts (see Figure 3.12). The most recognizable feature of the forebrain is the **cerebral cortex,** the grayish matter full of fissures, folds, and crevices that covers the outside of the brain (*cortex* is the Latin word for "bark"). The cortex is quite large in humans, accounting for approximately 80% of the total volume of the human brain (Kolb & Whishaw, 1990). We will look at the cerebral cortex in depth after we review the other structures of the forebrain.

Beneath the cerebral cortex are "subcortical" structures, including the thalamus, the hypothalamus, and the limbic system. The **thalamus** is positioned close to the midbrain and, like some of the midbrain structures, is an important gathering point for input from the senses. Indeed, the thalamus is thought to be the main processing center for sensory input before that information is parceled out to areas in the upper regions of the cortex. Besides simply being relayed upward, information from the various senses is probably combined in some way here.

The **hypothalamus,** which lies just below the thalamus, plays an important role in the regulation of eating, drinking, body temperature, and sexual behavior. In experiments on lower animals, administering electric current to different regions of the hypothalamus initiates a variety of behaviors. For example, male and female rats will show characteristic sexual responses when one portion of the hypothalamus is stimulated (Marson & McKenna, 1994; Pfaff & Sakuma, 1979), whereas damage to another region of the hypothalamus can seriously affect regular eating behavior (Sclafani, 1994). (We will have more to say about the neural basis of hunger in Chapter 11.) The hypothalamus also plays a key role in the release of hormones by the pituitary gland; we'll consider the actions of hormones later when we discuss the endocrine system.

The **limbic system** is composed of several interrelated brain structures, including the amygdala and the hippocampus. The *amygdala* is a small, almond-shaped piece of brain (*amygdala* means "almond") that has been linked to a variety of motivational and emotional behaviors, including aggression and defensive

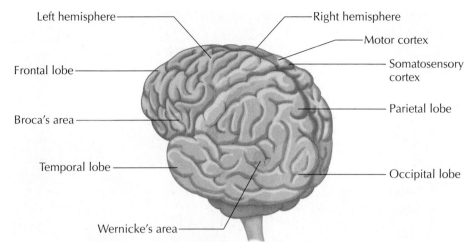

Left hemisphere

Right hemisphere

Motor cortex

Frontal lobe

Somatosensory cortex

Parietal lobe

Broca's area

Temporal lobe

Occipital lobe

Wernicke's area

FIGURE 3.13
The Cerebral Cortex. The cerebral cortex is divided into two hemispheres, left and right, and each hemisphere can be divided further into four parts, or lobes. The lobes appear specialized to control particular functions, such as visual processing in the occipital lobe and language processing by the frontal and temporal lobes.

behaviors (Aggleton, 1993). Destruction of portions of the amygdala in lower animals, through brain lesioning, can produce an extremely passive animal—one that will do nothing in response to provocation. The *hippocampus* (Greek for "seahorse," which it resembles anatomically) is thought to be critically involved in the formation of memories (Eichenbaum, Otto, & Cohen, 1994). People with severe damage to the hippocampus sometimes live in a kind of perpetual present—they are aware of the world around them, they recognize people and things known to them prior to the damage, but they remember almost nothing new. These patients act as if they are continually awakening from a dream; experiences slip away, and they recall nothing from only moments before. We'll return to disturbances of this type, and memory loss in general, in Chapter 8.

The Cerebral Cortex. On reaching the cerebral cortex, we finally encounter what is considered to be the seat of the higher mental processes. Thoughts, the sense of self, the ability to reason and solve problems—each is a manifestation of groups of neurons firing in synchronous patterns somewhere in specialized regions of the cerebral cortex. The cortex is divided into two *hemispheres,* left and right. The left hemisphere controls the sensory and motor functions for the right side of the body, and the right hemisphere controls these functions for the left side of the body. A structure called the *corpus callosum,* which we'll discuss later, serves as a communication bridge between the two hemispheres.

Anatomists further divide each hemisphere into four parts, or *lobes:* the *frontal, temporal, parietal,* and *occipital* (see Figure 3.13). These lobes (or at least parts of them) appear to control particular body functions, such as visual processing by the occipital lobe and language processing by the frontal and temporal lobes. An important caveat is in order here, however: Although research has found evidence for localization of function in particular brain structures, there is almost certainly considerable overlap of function.

How can we possibly assign something like a "sense of self" to a localized area of the cerebral cortex? Once again, the evidence is primarily correlational—some portion of the cortex is damaged, or stimulated electrically, and behavioral changes are noted. We know, for example, that damage to the frontal lobe of the cortex can induce dramatic changes in an individual's personality. In 1850 a railroad foreman named Phineas Gage was packing some black powder into a blasting hole when, accidentally, the powder discharged, driving a thick iron rod through the left side of his head. The result was a 3″ hole in his skull and a complete shredding of a large portion of the left frontal lobe of his brain. Remarkably, Gage recovered, and with the exception of the loss of vision in his left eye and some slight

Do you think it's possible that "personality" is completely localized in one portion of the brain? If so, how could you explain the fact that someone's personality can seem to change depending on the situation?

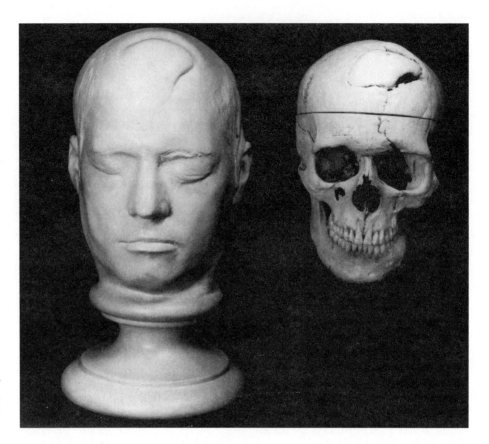

After a blasting accident produced substantial damage in the frontal lobe of Phineas Gage's brain, illustrated here, he was "no longer Gage" in the minds of his friends and acquaintances.

facial paralysis, he was able to move about freely and perform a variety of tasks. But he was "no longer Gage" in the minds of his friends and acquaintances—his personality had completely changed. Whereas prior to his injury he was known to all as someone with "a well-balanced mind" and "a shrewd businessman," after the meeting of brain and iron rod he became "fitful, irreverent, indulging at times in the grossest profanity (which was not previously his custom)" (Bigelow, 1850).

The **frontal lobes** contain the *motor cortex,* which controls the initiation of voluntary muscle movements, as well as areas involved in language production and, possibly, higher-level thought processes (Butler and associates, 1993). Broca's area, which is implicated in speech production, is located in a portion of the left frontal lobe in most people. The motor cortex is positioned at the rear of the frontal lobe in both hemispheres; axons from the motor cortex project down to motor neurons in the spinal cord and elsewhere. If neurons in this area of the brain are stimulated electrically, muscle contractions—the twitch of a finger or the jerking of a foot—can occur. Even more interesting, researchers have systematically mapped the relation of body parts to regions of the motor cortex, revealing a *topographic* organization scheme. That is, adjacent areas of the body, such as the hand and the wrist, are activated by neurons that sit in adjacent areas of the motor cortex.

Topographic organizational schemes are actually found in many regions of the cerebral cortex and represent a fundamental attribute of cortical organization. For example, the **parietal lobe** contains the topographically organized *somatosensory cortex,* through which people experience the sensations of touch, temperature, and pain. Thus, the brush of a lover's kiss on the cheek excites neurons that lie in close proximity to neurons that would be excited by the same kiss to the lips. In addition, as Figure 3.14 demonstrates, there is a relationship between sensitivity to touch (or the ability to control a movement) and size of the representation in the

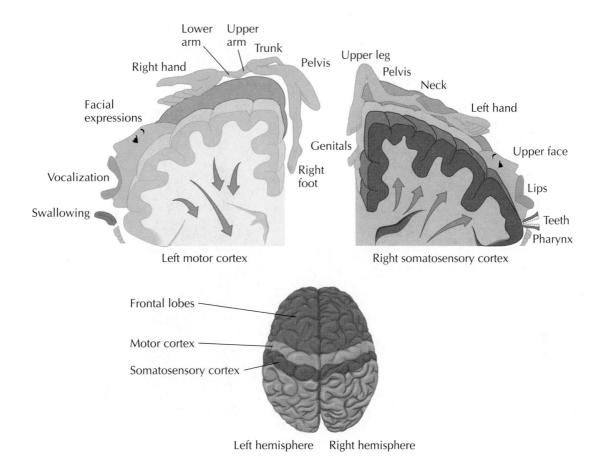

Left motor cortex

Right somatosensory cortex

Frontal lobes

Motor cortex

Somatosensory cortex

Left hemisphere   Right hemisphere

cortex. Those areas of the body that show particular sensitivity and fine motor control (such as the face, lips, and fingers) map onto relatively large areas of space in the cortex.

The **temporal lobes,** which lie on either side of the cortex, are involved in the processing of auditory information received from the left and right ears. As we will see in Chapter 5, there is a systematic relationship between the activities of particular neurons in the temporal lobe and the perception of certain frequencies of sound. As we noted earlier, one region of the temporal lobe, Wernicke's area, appears to control language comprehension (the ability to understand what someone is saying). A person with damage to Wernicke's area of the temporal lobe might be able to repeat a spoken sentence aloud with perfect diction and control yet not understand a word of it. For most people, the speech area is localized in the temporal lobe of the *left* cerebral hemisphere.

Finally, at the far back of the brain, we encounter the **occipital lobes,** where most visual processing occurs. We'll consider the organization of this part of the brain in more detail in Chapter 5; for now, recognize that it is here, in the far back of the brain, that the information received from receptor cells in the eyes is analyzed and turned into visual images. The brain paints an image of the external world through a remarkable division of labor—there appear to be separate processing stations in the occipital lobe designed to process color, motion, and form independently (Shapley, 1990). Damage to the occipital lobe, not surprisingly, tends to produce highly specific visual deficits—the person might lose the ability to recognize a face, a contour moving in a particular direction, or a color (Zeki, 1992).

The Divided Brain

Nowhere is the division of labor in the brain more evident than in the study of the two separate halves, or hemispheres, that make up the cerebral cortex.

FIGURE 3.14
Specialization in the Motor and Somatosensory Cortex. The motor cortex is located at the rear of the frontal lobes in each cerebral hemisphere. As you can see, a systematic body-to-brain relationship exists, such that adjacent parts of the body are activated by neurons that sit in adjacent areas of the cortex. The somatosensory cortex, which controls the sense of touch, is located in the parietal lobes of each hemisphere; again, there is a systematic mapping arrangement. Notice that for each type of cortex, the size or amount of the representation relates to degree of sensitivity.

FIGURE 3.15
Visual Processing in the Two Hemispheres. Images originating in the left visual field typically fall on the inside half of the left eye and the outside half of the right eye and are then projected to the right hemisphere. Information appearing in the right visual field, in contrast, projects to the left hemisphere. Because most language processing occurs in the left hemisphere, split-brain patients can only vocally report stimuli that are shown in the right visual field. In this case, the subject can only say "port" because that is the word available for processing in the left hemisphere.

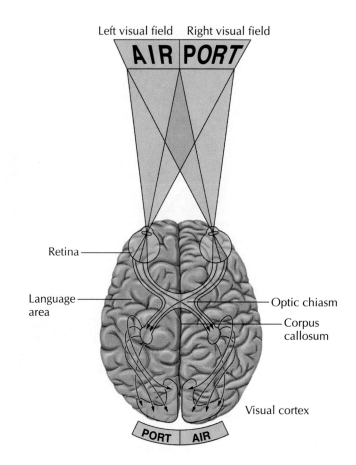

Although the brain is designed to operate as a functional "whole," the hemispheres are *lateralized,* in the sense that each side is responsible for performing some unique and independent functions (Hellige, 1990). As we've seen, the right hemisphere of the brain receives sensory input pertinent to the left half of the body and controls the movements of the left side of the body, whereas the left hemisphere handles the body's right side. This means that stimulating a region of the motor cortex in the left cerebral hemisphere would cause a muscle on the right side of the body to twitch. Similarly, if cells in the occipital lobe of the right cerebral hemisphere are damaged or destroyed, a blind spot develops in the left portion of the visual world. Lateralization undoubtedly serves some adaptive functions. For example, it may allow the brain to divide its labor in ways that produce more efficient processing.

Figure 3.15 shows how information received through the eyes travels to one side of the brain or the other. If you are looking straight ahead, an image originating from the left side of your body (the left visual field) falls on the inside half of the left eye and the outside half of the right eye; receptor cells in these locations transmit their images to the back of the *right* cerebral hemisphere. Both eyes project information directly to each hemisphere, as the figure shows, but information from the left visual field goes to right hemisphere and vice versa. By capitalizing on the nature of these neural pathways, as we'll see in a moment, researchers can present information initially to one side of the brain or the other.

Under normal circumstances, if an object, such as a car, approaches you from your left side, the information eventually arrives on both sides of your brain. There are two reasons why this is the case. First, if you turn your head or eyes to look at the object—from left to right—its image is likely to fall on both the inside and the outside halves of each eye over time. It might start off represented only on the inside half of the left eye, but as your eyes turn, the outside half will soon receive the message. Second, as we noted earlier, a major communication bridge—the **corpus callosum**—connects the two brain halves. Information arriving at the right hemisphere, for example, is transported to the left hemisphere via the corpus callosum in just a few thousandths of a second (Saron & Davidson, 1989). This transfer process occurs automatically and requires no head or eye turning.

Splitting the Brain. If you think about it, it's important that both sides of the brain receive pertinent information about objects in the environment. To see why, imagine what visual perception would be like for someone without a corpus callosum—someone with a sort of "split brain." Suppose an object appears suddenly, with great velocity, in the person's left visual field. There's no time to move the head or eyes, only time for a kind of reflexive response. Our patient, the one with the split brain, would be incapable of a coordinated response since the image would be registered only in the right hemisphere. Because the right side of the brain contains the machinery to control only the left side of the body, a fully coordinated body response could not be initiated. Moreover, the split-brain patient would be unable to name the menacing object, because the language comprehension and production centers are located, typically, on the left side of the brain.

Let's consider another experiment for our hypothetical patient. Suppose that we flash the word AIRPORT on a screen, very quickly, but arrange the presentation so that the first part of the word, AIR, appears in the left visual field and the second part, PORT, appears in the right visual field. What do you think the patient will report seeing? The answer is the word PORT, because that's the image received by the left hemisphere—the place where the language centers are located. The language part of the brain wouldn't even know that AIR had been presented, because the image would remain locked in the visual centers of the right hemisphere.

Actually, our hypothetical patient, as well as a version of the study that was just described, is *real* (Gazzaniga, 1970). There are a number of individuals who have "split brains." Some were born without a corpus callosum (Sanders, 1989); others had their communication gateway severed, on purpose, by surgeons seeking to reduce the spread of epileptic seizures (Springer & Deutsch, 1989). Epilepsy is a kind of electrical "fire storm" in the brain that tends to spread across the cortex, producing convulsions and loss of consciousness. Cutting the communication

It's adaptive for both sides of the brain to process information from the environment; otherwise, this person would probably have difficulty developing a coordinated response to this rapidly arriving ball.

gateway from one hemisphere to another creates a kind of "fire break" that limits epileptic seizures to one half of the brain. Severing the corpus callosum is a rarely used procedure because modern antiepileptic drugs are able to control seizures for most patients. But it has proven effective in some instances for patients who fail to respond to medication.

The two hemispheres of split-brain patients are not broken or damaged by the operation; information simply cannot easily pass from one side of the brain to the other. In fact, the behavior of split-brain patients, in general, appears to be remarkably normal. It's extremely unlikely that you would be able to identify one of them in a crowd. Their behavior appears normal because most input from the environment still reaches both sides of their brain. These patients can turn their heads and eyes freely as they interact with the environment, allowing information to fall on receptor regions that transmit to both hemispheres. The abnormal nature of their brain becomes apparent only under manufactured conditions like those encountered by our hypothetical patient and through the personal anecdotes that these patients sometimes report.

Much of the work on split-brain individuals has been conducted by the late Nobel Prize–winning neuroscientist Roger Sperry and his colleagues. In one classic study by Gazzaniga, Bogen, & Sperry (1965), a variety of objects (pictures, words, or symbols) were presented visually to either the left or right visual fields of split-brain subjects. As with our hypothetical patient, when an object was shown to the right visual field, it was easily named because the image could be processed by the language centers of the left hemisphere. For left visual field presentations, the patients remained perplexed and silent. It was later learned, however, that their silence did not mean that the brain failed to process the object. If split-brain patients were asked to *point* to a picture of the object just shown, they could do so, but only with the *left* hand (e.g., Gazzaniga & LeDoux, 1978). The brain had received the input but could not respond verbally.

Although split-brain patients behave relatively normally after surgery, they do report that sometimes their right and left hands act as if they have "minds of their own." These reports are anecdotal, of course, so they need to be viewed with some caution. Patients have claimed that it is difficult to read something, such as a newspaper or a book, unless it is held by the right hand; the left hand, which maps to the nonverbal right hemisphere, apparently has no interest in reading as a leisure activity (Preilowski, 1975). It has been claimed that the two hemispheres occasionally compete, sometimes over bizarre things like what clothes to wear. One patient reported buttoning a blouse with one hand while, at the same time, unbuttoning the blouse with the other. Again, it's difficult to know what to make of these claims, or to know how accurately they have been reported, but it does seem likely that independent processing activities can go on simultaneously in the two hemispheres of the brain. Some researchers have even suggested that each side may have its own kind of separate consciousness (Kandel, 1991).

Besides as a treatment for epilepsy, can you think of any situations in which having a "split brain" might actually be beneficial compared to having a "unified" brain?

Hemispheric Specialization. The available evidence strongly indicates that the two hemispheres of the cerebral cortex are specialized to perform certain kinds of tasks. The right hemisphere, for example, appears to play a more significant role in spatial tasks, such as fitting together the pieces of a puzzle or orienting oneself spatially in an environment. Patients with damage to the right hemisphere characteristically have trouble with spatial tasks, as do split-brain patients who must assemble a puzzle with their right hand (Kalat, 1992). The left hemisphere—perhaps in part because of the lateralized language centers—clearly contributes more to verbal tasks such as reading and writing.

Still, you should understand that a great deal of cooperation and collaboration goes on between the hemispheres. The two hemispheres interact continuously, and most mental processes, even language to a certain extent, depend on activity

The Brain Balancer!

Studies have shown that each side of the brain has different strengths. For instance—creativity lies in the right side of the brain. Further studies have shown that people are dominant in one side of their brain. It is also a known fact that only 10% of the brain is generally used. Think of all that brain power going to waste!

This needn't be you! With this kit, you will discover which side of your brain is dominant. Next, you will find out how to strengthen your less dominant half. Once your brain is equally balanced, there is no stopping!

Inner equilibrium brings outer equilibrium! With your brain's halves working together, you will increase your self-confidence, creativity, and ability to solve problems. **This will positively affect your life!**

With less of life's little annoyances to worry about, you can then concentrate on developing the 90% of the brain that is unused. It is believed that this is where motivation, intuition, and other such powers lie. The possibilities for personal, intellectual, and occupational growth are endless!

So, call and order your **BRAIN BALANCER** kit today! With a 30-day money-back guarantee, you have nothing to lose and everything to gain! The kit includes the **BRAIN BALANCER** booklet, workbook, and tape.

There is little, if any, scientific evidence to support claims of the type made in this advertisement. (From Kalat, 1996)

that arises in both sides of the brain. Specialization in the brain exists because it is sometimes adaptive for the two hemispheres to work independently—much in the same way that it is beneficial for members of a group to divide components of a difficult task, rather than trying to cooperate on every small activity (Hellige, 1993). You think and behave with a "whole" brain, not a fragmented one.

Over the last two decades or so, there has been an explosion of interest—often by people operating at the fringe of scientific psychology—in promoting a lateralized locus for an extraordinary variety of psychological phenomena. It has been suggested, for example, that the right side of the brain is "holistic" rather than analytic and underlies such varied activities as fantasy, dance, and music appreciation. The left side of the brain is argued to be the "rational mind," controlling not only language but also mathematical and scientific abilities. I once encountered a man who, after offering his left hand in greeting, claimed: "I'm trying to develop my right hemisphere"—he apparently felt that shaking with his right hand promoted too much "left brain" thinking. Companies have even started marketing packages designed to teach people to become more "right brained" or "left brained" in their approach to the world, or to develop ways to "synchronize" the two sides of the brain (see Druckman & Swets, 1988).

At present there is little, if any, scientific evidence to support such claims. It's extremely unlikely that people can learn to develop a particular side of the brain, or that individuals will ever be properly classified as "right brained" or "left brained." There is also no scientific rationale for proposing that a particular thinking style can be attributed to one hemisphere and not to the other (Hellige, 1990). Adding to the confusion is the fact that the proper experimental studies are rarely, if ever, conducted. Far too often the striking and newsworthy claims are based on anecdotal reports or poorly designed studies. For example, students who listened to tapes designed to stimulate "synchronization" of the hemispheres were found to perform better on a variety of tasks than students who weren't exposed to the

INSIDE   THE PROBLEM: *Studying Lateralization in Intact Brains*

The study of split-brain patients has produced a number of compelling findings supporting lateralization in the brain. But we don't need a split-brain patient to study hemispheric specialization. Techniques are available that work well with normal individuals and that don't require multimillion-dollar imaging equipment. All we need is a willing subject and some carefully calibrated equipment to record the time it takes to perform certain kinds of tasks. Let's work through the experimental logic that underlies one such procedure: the *concurrent activities paradigm.*

In the concurrent activities paradigm, volunteers are asked to perform two tasks concurrently, and their performance on each task is timed. As you know from personal experience, it's often difficult to do two things at once— it usually takes longer to perform each task and your accuracy goes down. Performance is slow and less accurate under these conditions because the brain has limited resources. When two tasks need to be performed, processing in the brain needs to be divided, or shared, across two activities. The concurrent activities paradigm also assumes that if two tasks draw on resources from the *same* side of the brain, performance will be slower than if the tasks are controlled

by different sides of the brain (or the tasks are controlled equally by both sides of the brain). Thus, by varying the types of tasks and measuring how much one task slows down performance on the other, researchers can infer how activities are specialized in a particular hemisphere.

To see how this process works in practice, imagine that we ask a subject to tap a telegraph key, as quickly as possible, with either the right or left index finger. Because of the way that things are wired in the brain, we know that tapping the right index finger should be controlled primarily by the left side of the brain, whereas left-hand tapping should be controlled by the right side. We now ask the subject to perform a second task, such as reading words aloud from a screen, at the same time as the rapid-fire finger tapping. If the new task slows down the tapping more for the right hand than for the left hand, we can assume that the new task is controlled primarily by the left hemisphere. The idea once again is that if one hemisphere needs to control both tasks at the same time, the tapping will slow down more (See Figure 3.16).

In fact, the concurrent activities procedure has produced results that are consistent with the findings gathered

from the study of brain-damaged patients and from the results of imaging techniques like the PET scan. Corina, Vaid, and Bellugi (1992) found that repeating presented English words aloud slowed the rate of finger tapping more for the right hand than for the left hand, but copying symbolic gestures (such as the "thumbs up" signal) showed no differential effect. This is exactly the result we would predict if speech and language processing is located primarily in the left hemisphere. Tapping with the right hand and repeating English words aloud both draw on resources from the same (left) hemisphere, so performance on both tasks is slowed. However, copying symbolic gestures does not require the use of specialized language centers and may not be lateralized, so performance is not differentially affected.

But be warned: we should not accept results like these uncritically. To draw conclusions about hemispheric specialization from such results requires blind acceptance of a number of assumptions that have not been tested directly. For example, in the Corina, Vaid, and Bellugi (1992) study no measure of brain activation was reported, so we have no way of telling whether the resources of the brain were actually being taxed by these two tasks or whether, in fact, the

tapes. But the students who participated were fully informed about the potential benefits of the tapes, so their task improvements could easily be attributed to a placebo effect (for further discussion, see Druckman & Swets, 1988).

Regulating Growth and Internal Functions: Widespread and Long-Term Communication

The human body actually has two communication systems. The first, the connective network of the nervous system, underlies the initiation and control of most behaviors—thoughts, certainly voluntary movements, and sensations and perceptions of the external world. Electrical activity in the form of the neural impulse moves rapidly down myelinated axons, like sparks traversing the fuses of firecrackers tied in series, forcing the release of neurotransmitters that complete the two tasks were really competing for the limited resources. What makes findings like these compelling is that they fit well into an overall pattern of results. When the results of Corina and his colleagues are interpreted in light of what we know from the study of split-brain patients and from imaging studies like the PET procedure, a strong case can be made for lateralized language centers. In short, making a convincing case in psychological research often requires a multipronged attack.

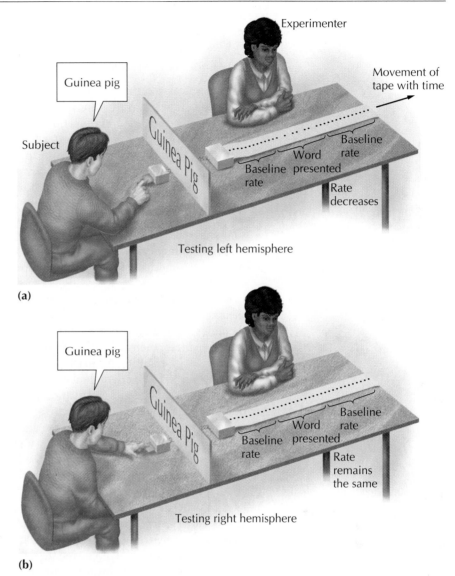

(a)

FIGURE 3.16
The Concurrent Activities Paradigm.
Repeating English words aloud slows the rate of finger tapping more for the right hand than for the left hand. This may occur because right-hand movement and speech processing are controlled by the same hemisphere, and therefore each task must compete for the same limited brain resources.

(b)

communication chain. But the body also has long-term communication needs. For example, the body must initiate and control growth and provide long-term regulation of numerous internal biological systems. Consequently, a second communication system has developed: a network of glands called the **endocrine system,** which uses the bloodstream, rather than neurons, as its main information courier. Chemicals called **hormones** are released into the blood by the various endocrine glands in an effort to control a variety of internal functions.

The word *hormone* comes aptly from the Greek word *hormon,* which means "to set into motion." Hormones play a role in many basic, life-sustaining activities in the body. Hunger, thirst, sexual behavior, and the "fight-or-flight" response are all regulated in part by an interplay between the nervous system and hormones released by the endocrine glands. Again, the fact that the body has two communication systems rather than one makes sense from an adaptive standpoint. One system, communication among neurons, governs transmissions that are quick and detailed; the other, the endocrine system, initiates the slower but more widespread and longer-lasting effects. In the section that follows, we'll consider the endocrine system in more detail, and then we'll consider how hormones influence some fundamental differences between men and women.

The Endocrine System

The chemical communication system of the endocrine glands differs in some important ways from the rapid-fire electrochemical activities of the nervous system. For one thing, communication in the nervous system tends to be *localized*, which means that a given neurotransmitter usually affects only cells in a small area. Conversely, hormones have widespread effects. Because they are carried by the blood, they travel throughout the body and interact with numerous target sites. Also in contrast to neurotransmitters, hormones have long-lasting effects. Whereas neural communication operates in time scales bordering on the blink of an eye, the endocrine system can produce effects lasting minutes, hours, or even days. In some animals, for example, it is circulating hormones that prepare the organism for seasonal migration or for hibernation. Thus, the endocrine system provides the body with a mechanism for both widespread and long-term communication that cannot be produced by interactions among neurons.

Although the endocrine and nervous systems communicate in different ways, their activities are closely coordinated. Structures in the brain (especially the hypothalamus) stimulate or inhibit the release of hormones by the glands; once released, these chemicals then feed back and affect the firing rates of neural impulses. The resulting feedback loop balances and controls the regulatory activities of the body. The hypothalamus is of particular importance because it controls the pituitary gland. The **pituitary gland** is a kind of "master gland" that controls the secretion of hormones in response to signals from the hypothalamus; these hormones, in turn, regulate the activity of many of the other vital glands in the endocrine system. It is the pituitary gland, for example, that signals the testes in males to produce *testosterone* and the ovaries in females to produce *estrogen*—both of critical importance in sexual behavior and reproduction.

Let's consider one example of the endocrine system at work. You leave a party late, convinced that you can walk the 2 plus miles home without incident. The streets, quiet without the noise of midday traffic, exert a calming influence as you pass the flashing traffic lights and the parked cars. But suddenly, across the street, two shadowy-looking figures emerge from an alleyway and move in your direction. You draw in your breath, your stomach tightens, and your rapidly beating heart seems ready to explode from your chest. These whole-body reactions, critical in preparing you for "fight or flight," are created by signals from the brain that lead to increased activity of the endocrine glands. The hypothalamus, acting via the pituitary gland, signals the *adrenal glands* (located above the kidneys) to begin secreting such hormones as *norepinephrine* and *epinephrine* into the blood. These hormones produce energizing effects on the body, increasing the heart rate, constricting the blood supply to the stomach and intestines, and increasing the amount of glucose (sugar) in the blood. The body is now prepared for action, enhancing the likelihood of survival (see Figure 3.17).

Gender Effects

Prior to birth, hormones released by the pituitary gland establish an individual's sexual identity. For instance, hormones determine whether a child ends up with male or female sex organs. At puberty, an increase in sex hormones (testosterone and estrogen) leads males to develop facial hair and deep speaking voices and females to develop breasts and to begin menstruation. It is now suspected that

> Initiation of the "flight-or-fight" response clearly has adaptive value. But can you think of any circumstances in which this response might actually *lower* the likelihood of adaptive behavior?

Fight-or-Flight Response
Hypothalamus Stimulates pituitary gland
Pituitary Gland Secretes hormone that stimulates the adrenal glands
Adrenal Glands Secrete norepinephrine and epinephrine into bloodstream
Norepinephrine and Epinephrine Cause surge of energy; heart rate increases; blood is shunted to areas that require it, away from the stomach and intestine; glucose is made available to the muscles

FIGURE 3.17
The Fight or Flight Response. In potentially dangerous situations the endocrine system generates a "fight-or-flight" response. Hormones are released that produce energizing effects on the body, increasing its chances of survival.

hormones released during development may even affect the basic wiring patterns of men's and women's brains. Evidence suggests that men and women may "think differently" as the result of gender-specific activities of the endocrine system.

Psychologists Doreen Kimura and Elizabeth Hampson (1994) report, for example, that the performance of women and men on certain tasks changes significantly as the level of sex hormones increase or decrease in the body. Women traditionally perform better than men on some tests of verbal ability, and their performance on these tasks improves with high levels of estrogen in their body. Similarly, men show slightly better performance on some kinds of spatial tasks (such as imagining that three-dimensional objects are rotating), and their performance seems to be related somewhat to their testosterone levels. The evidence is correlational, which means that we cannot be sure that it is the hormones that are causing the performance changes, but the data are suggestive of endocrine-based gender differences in thought.

It's also the case that girls who have been exposed to an excess of male hormones during the initial stages of prenatal development, either because of a genetic disorder or from chemicals ingested by the mother during pregnancy, tend to act particularly "tomboyish" during development (e.g, Resnick et al., 1986). They prefer to engage in play activities that are more traditionally associated with boys. In one study reported by Kimura (1992), researchers at UCLA compared the choice of toys by girls who either had or had not been exposed to excess male hormones during early development. The girls who had been exposed to the male hormones tended to prefer the typical masculine activities—smashing trucks and cars together, for example—more than the control girls did.

It's been known for some time that male and female brains may differ anatomically, although such differences have often been exaggerated historically (Shields, 1975). Animal studies have confirmed that male and female *rat* brains differ anatomically; moreover, these differences in rat brains are clearly attributable, in part, to the early influence of hormones (see Hines, 1982, for a review). For humans, the data are less clear and far more controversial. It's been reported that the right cortex of males tends to be slightly thicker than the right cortex of females (see Kimura, 1992), but whether this anatomical difference accounts, even in part, for the superiority that males show in performing certain spatial tasks is unclear. Other studies have reported that sections of the corpus callosum are more

There may indeed be gender differences in brain anatomy and functioning, but the decision of these two girls to play with Barbie dolls has almost certainly been influenced strongly by their environment as well.

elaborate in women, suggesting that the two hemispheres communicate more effectively in females (de Lacoste-Utamsing & Holloway, 1982). However, subsequent studies have had a difficult time replicating this particular result (see Witelson, 1992).

The evidence supporting gender-based differences in brain anatomy and mental functioning is provocative and needs to be investigated further. Hormones released by the endocrine system are known to produce permanent changes early in human development, and it's certainly possible that actions later in life are somehow influenced by these changes. But at this point no direct causal link has been established between anatomical differences and the variations in intellectual functioning that are sometimes found between men and women. Moreover, the performance differences that women and men show on certain laboratory tasks aren't large and don't reflect general ability. Many of the studies report that gender-based differences are extremely small (see Hyde & Linn, 1988). To repeat a theme that we brought up in Chapter 1, it is extremely difficult to separate the effects of biology (*nature*) from the ongoing influences of the environment (*nurture*). Men and women are faced with different environmental demands and cultural expectations during their lifetimes. Without question, these demands help determine the actions they take, thereby helping promote behavioral differences between the sexes. We will return to gender issues often in later chapters of this text.

Storing and Transmitting the Genetic Code: Genetic Influences on Behavior

At face value, our acceptance of the "central tenet" of modern brain science—namely, that all behavior is a reflection of the working brain—presents something of a philosophical puzzle. The mechanics of the mind, represented as the biological processes described in this chapter, seem understandable and predictable. PET scans of people engaging in a visual task reveal reliable activity in the occipital lobe of the cortex. Sudden paralysis to the right side of the body allows the physi-

More and more women are excelling at intellectual tasks traditionally associated with men. The idea that gender-based differences in brain functioning preclude women from certain intellectual pursuits is simply a myth.

cian to predict, usually successfully, that the stroke occurred in the left cerebral hemisphere. But behavior is the main interest of psychology, and it remains remarkably difficult to predict. People typically react differently to the same environmental situation—even if they are siblings raised in the same household. How do we explain the remarkable diversity of behavior, given that everyone carries around the same, understandable, 3- to 4-pound mass of tissue inside his or her head?

One answer, of course, is that no two brains are exactly alike. The patterns of neural activity that underlie people's behaviors (and thoughts) are uniquely determined by their individual experiences and by the genetic structure they inherit from their parents. Most of us have no trouble accepting that experience is a critical determinant of individual differences in behavior; but what about genetics? Sure, hair color, eye color, and blood type may be expressions of fixed genetic influences, but how could genetics govern intelligence, personality, or emotionality? Recognizing that heredity has a role in such characteristics is a given to the psychologist. As you'll see, we'll appeal to genetic principles repeatedly throughout our discussions of the adaptive mind. But it's also important to remember that the genetic code serves two adaptive functions for the human species. First, genes provide individuals with a kind of flexible blueprint for their physical and psychological development. Second, genes provide a means through which people are able to pass on some of their physical and psychological characteristics to their offspring, thereby helping to ensure continuation of the species.

Genetic Principles

Let's briefly review some of the important principles of genetics. How is the genetic code stored, and what are the factors that produce genetic variability? The genetic message resides within *chromosomes,* which are thin, threadlike strips of DNA. Human cells, with the exception of sperm cells and the to-be-fertilized egg cell, contain a total of 46 chromosomes, arranged in 23 pairs. Half of each chromosome pair is contributed originally by the mother, through the egg, and the other half arrives in the father's sperm. **Genes** are segments of chromosome that contain instructions for influencing and creating particular hereditary characteristics. For example, each person has a piece of chromosome, or gene, that helps determine height or hair color and another piece that may determine susceptibility to disorders such as muscular dystrophy or even Alzheimer's disease.

Because humans have 23 *pairs* of chromosomes, they end up with two genes for most developmental characteristics, or traits. People have two genes, for example, for hair color, blood type, and whether or not they will develop facial dimples. If both genes are the same, which means they are designed to produce the same trait (such as nearsightedness), the person is said to be *homozygous* for that genetic attribute. If the two genes differ—for example, the father passes along the gene for nearsightedness, but mother's gene is for normal distance vision—the person is *heterozygous* for that particular genetic attribute. What happens when the genes differ, producing conflicting instructions? Under these conditions, the trait that will be expressed is determined by the *dominant gene;* in the case of vision, the "normal" gene will dominate and mask or override the *recessive gene* for nearsightedness.

The fact that a dominant gene will mask the effects of a recessive gene means that everybody has genetic material that is not actually expressed in physical and/or psychological characteristics. A person may see perfectly clearly but still carry around the recessive gene for faulty distance vision. This is the reason why parents with normal vision can produce a nearsighted child, or two brown-haired parents can produce a child with blond hair—it depends on the particular

FIGURE 3.18
Genetic Transmission. Half of each chromosome pair is contributed by the mother, through the egg, and the other half is contributed by the father, through the sperm. If the genetic information relevant to a particular trait, such as hair color, is the same on both chromosomes, the offspring is said to be *homozygous* for that trait. But if the mother contributes one kind of gene, red hair, and the father contributes a different kind of gene, brown hair, the offspring is *heterozygous* for that trait. For heterozygous genotypes, the dominant gene determines the expression of the trait (the phenotype).

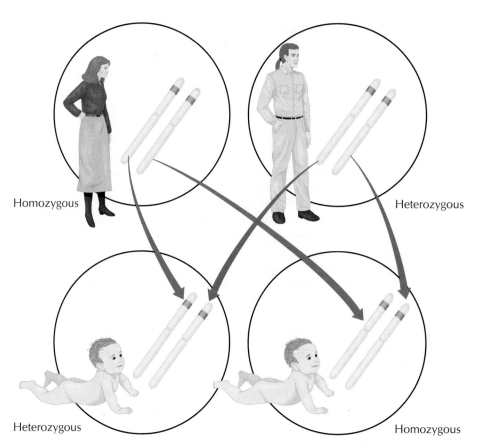

Homozygous

Heterozygous

Heterozygous

Homozygous

combinations of gene types that have been inherited by the child (see Figure 3.18). It's also worth noting that very few traits are governed by just one gene; most traits, even eye and hair color, are influenced by more than one gene.

Another important distinction is between the **genotype,** which is the actual genetic message, and the **phenotype,** which is a person's observable characteristics. The phenotype, such as clear distance vision or brown hair, is controlled mainly by the genotype, but it can also be influenced by the environment. A person's height and weight, for example, are shaped largely by the genotype, but environmental factors such as diet and physical health will contribute significantly to the final phenotype. This is an important point to remember: Genetic blueprints provide the materials from which characteristics develop, but the environment often shapes the final product. Exactly how a genotype is expressed into a phenotype defines the "nature-nurture" issue in its purest form.

Across individuals, variations in the genetic message arise because there are trillions of different ways that the genetic information from each parent can be combined at fertilization. Each egg or sperm cell contains a random half of each of the parent's 23 chromosome pairs. According to the laws of probability, this means that there are some 8 million different combinations of chromosome "halves" that can reside in either an egg cell or a sperm cell (2^{23}). The particular meeting of egg and sperm is also a matter of chance, which means that there are some 64 trillion ways that the genetic material from both parents can be combined at fertilization—and this is from the same set of parents!

Genes and Behavior

But we still haven't established the link between genetics and psychology—what is the connection between genotypes, phenotypes, and behavior? Any behavior, if it is indeed influenced by genetic factors, is likely to be the product of lots of genetic information interacting in complex ways. But as we'll see throughout the remainder of this book, there are instances where it is possible to predict, at least on average, things about the psychology of an individual by knowing something about his or her genetic record. Susceptibility to the psychological disorder *schizophrenia* is a case in point. Natural children of schizophrenic parents (where either one or both parents have the disorder) have a greater chance of becoming schizophrenic themselves, when compared to the children of nonschizophrenic parents. This is the case even if these children have been adopted at birth and never raised in an abnormal environment (Gottesman, 1991). Thus, genetic similarity probably plays some role in the increased tendency to become schizophrenic. We'll return to this issue in more detail in Chapter 14.

Psychologists often try to disentangle the relative influences of genes and the environment by conducting *twin studies.* In twin studies, researchers compare behavioral traits between *identical* twins, who share essentially the same genetic material, and *fraternal* twins, who were born at the same time but whose genetic overlap is only roughly 50% (fraternal twins can even be of different sexes). In studies of intelligence, for example, identical twins tend to have much more similar intelligence scores than fraternal twins, even when environmental factors are taken into account (Bouchard et al., 1990). Identical twins make ideal research subjects because researchers can control, at least in principle, for genetic factors. Because these twins essentially have the same genetic makeup, any physical or psychological differences that emerge during development must be attributable to environmental factors. Similarly, if identical twins are raised in different environments but still show similar traits, it's a strong indication that genetic factors are involved in expression of the trait.

We've provided only a brief sample of the study of genes and behavior in this section, because we'll be returning to the interplay between heredity and environment throughout many of the later chapters. For now, recognize that the adaptive mind is indeed influenced by the code that is stored in the body's chromosomes. Through the random processes that underlie genetic combinations at fertilization, nature secures diversity within the species—everyone receives a unique genetic blueprint that helps, in combination with environmental factors, determine brain structure as well as human psychology. From an evolutionary standpoint, diversity is of great importance because it increases the likelihood that at least some members of a species will have the necessary tools to deal successfully with the problems of survival.

In what ways are the environmental experiences of identical twins more similar than those for fraternal twins? Would this still be true if both sets of twins are raised apart from birth?

◤ SOLVING THE PROBLEMS: A SUMMARY

To account for the complexities and regularities of the behaving human, modern psychology accepts as given that human thoughts, feelings, and actions are by-products of active biological systems. The human brain, as well as the rest of the nervous system, is viewed as a biological solution to problems produced by constantly changing, and sometimes hostile, outside environments. Fortunately, out of these biological "solutions" arise those attributes that make up the human mind, including human intellect, emotion, and artistic creativity. In this chapter we've considered four central problems of adaptation that the human organism faces and effectively solves through its biological systems.

▸ **COMMUNICATING INTERNALLY** Networks of individual cells, called neurons, establish a marketplace of information called the nervous system. To communicate internally, the nervous system has developed an electrochemical language. Messages travel electrically within a neuron, usually from dendrite to soma to axon to terminal button, and then chemically from one neuron to the next. Combining electrical and chemical components creates a quick, efficient, and extremely versatile communication system. Neurotransmitters regulate the rate at which neurons fire, by producing excitatory or inhibitory messages, and the resulting global patterns of activation underlie the behaviors and thought processes that humans are capable of producing.

▶ **INITIATING AND COORDINATING BEHAVIOR** To accomplish the remarkable variety of functions that it controls, the nervous system divides its labor. Through the use of sophisticated techniques, including brain-imaging devices, researchers have begun to map out the localized regions of brain tissue that support particular psychological and life-sustaining functions. At the base of the brain, in the hindbrain region, structures control such basic processes as respiration, heart rate, and the coordination of muscle movements. Higher up are regions that control motivational processes such as eating, drinking, and sexual behavior. Finally, in the cerebral cortex more complex mental processes—such as thought, sensations, and language—are represented. Some functions in the brain appear to be lateralized, which means that they are controlled primarily by one cerebral hemisphere or the other. Through the development of specialized regions of cells, the human brain has become capable of increasingly more adaptive reactions to its changing environment.

▶ **REGULATING GROWTH AND INTERNAL FUNCTIONS** To solve its widespread and long-term communication needs, the body uses the endocrine system to release chemicals called hormones into the bloodstream. These chemical messengers serve a variety of regulatory functions, influencing growth and development, hunger, thirst, and sexual behavior, in addition to helping the body prepare for action. Hormones released early in development and on into adulthood may underlie some of the behavioral differences that are found between men and women.

▶ **STORING AND TRANSMITTING THE GENETIC CODE** Physical and behavioral characteristics are influenced by portions of chromosomes called genes. The particular combinations of genes that are inherited from the parents, along with influences from the environment, dictate the characteristics that an individual will actually display. Psychologists often try to disentangle the relative contributions of genes and the environment by conducting twin studies, comparing the behaviors and abilities of identical and fraternal twins under conditions where the twins have been raised in similar or dissimilar environments. When twins show similar behavioral characteristics, even though they have been raised in quite different environments, psychologists assume that the underlying genetic code may be playing an influential role.

Terms to Remember

neuroscience An interdisciplinary field of study directed at understanding the brain and its relation to behavior.

central nervous system The brain and the spinal cord.

peripheral nervous system The network of nerves that link the central nervous system with the rest of the body.

COMMUNICATING INTERNALLY

neurons The cells in the nervous system that receive and transmit information by generating an electrochemical signal; neurons are the basic building blocks of the nervous system.

sensory neurons Neurons that make initial contact with the environment and carry the message inward toward the spinal cord and brain.

interneurons Neurons that make no direct contact with the world but rather convey information from one neuron or processing site to another.

motor neurons Neurons that carry information away from the central nervous system to the muscles and glands that directly produce behavioral responses.

glial cells Cells in the nervous system that do not transmit or receive information but that perform a variety of functions, such as removing waste, filling in empty space, or helping neurons to communicate efficiently.

reflexes Largely automatic body reactions—such as the knee jerk—that are controlled primarily by spinal cord pathways.

dendrites The branchlike fibers that extend outward from a neuron and receive information from other neurons.

soma The cell body of a neuron.

axon The long tail-like part of a neuron that serves as the cell's transmitter device.

terminal buttons The tiny swellings at the end of a neuron's axon that contain chemicals important to neural transmission.

synapse The junction, or small gap, between neurons, typically between the terminal buttons of one neuron and the dendrite or cell body of another neuron.

resting potential The tiny electrical charge in place between the inside and outside of the resting neuron.

action potential The "all-or-none" electrical signal that travels down a neuron's axon.

depolarization The change in a neuron's electrical potential from negative toward zero; depolarization usually occurs when positive ions flow into the cell as a result of neural communication.

hyperpolarization An increase in the negative electrical potential of a neuron, reducing the chances of the cell generating an action potential.

neurotransmitters Chemical messengers that relay information from one neuron to the next. They are released from the terminal buttons into the synapse, where they interact chemically with the cell membrane of the next neuron; the result is either an excitatory or an inhibitory message.

acetylcholine A neurotransmitter that plays several roles in the central and peripheral nervous systems, including the excitation of muscle contractions.

dopamine A neurotransmitter that often leads to inhibitory effects; decreased levels have been linked to Parkinson's disease and increased levels have been linked to schizophrenia.

serotonin A neurotransmitter that has been linked to sleep, dreaming, and general arousal and may also be involved in some psychological disorders such as depression and schizophrenia.

endorphins Morphine-like chemicals that act as the brain's natural painkillers.

refractory period The period of time following an action potential during which more action potentials cannot be generated.

INITIATING AND COORDINATING BEHAVIOR

nerves Bundles of axons that make up neural "transmission cables."

somatic system The collection of nerves that transmits information toward the brain and connects to the skeletal muscles in order to initiate movement; part of the peripheral nervous system.

autonomic system The collection of nerves that controls the more automatic needs of the body, such as heart rate, digestion, blood pressure, and so on; part of the peripheral nervous system.

electroencephalograph (EEG) A device used to monitor the gross electrical activity of the brain.

computerized tomography scan (CT scan) The use of highly focused beams of X rays to construct detailed anatomical maps of the living brain.

positron emission tomography (PET) A method for measuring how radioactive substances are absorbed in the brain; it can be used to detect how different tasks activate different areas of the living brain.

magnetic resonance imaging (MRI) A device that uses magnetic fields and radio-wave pulses to construct detailed, three-dimensional images of the brain; "functional" MRIs can be used to map changes in blood oxygen use as a function of task activity.

hindbrain A "primitive" part of the brain that sits at the juncture point where the brain and spinal cord merge. Structures in the hindbrain, including the medulla, pons, and reticular formation, act as the basic life-support system for the body.

cerebellum A hindbrain structure at the base of the brain that is involved in the coordination of complex motor skills.

midbrain The middle portion of the brain, containing such structures as the tectum, superior colliculus, and inferior colliculus; midbrain structures serve as neural relay stations and may help coordinate reactions to sensory events.

forebrain The outer portion of the brain, including the cerebral cortex and the structures of the limbic system.

cerebral cortex The outer layer of the brain, considered to be the seat of higher mental processes.

thalamus A relay station in the forebrain thought to be an important gathering point for input from the senses.

hypothalamus A forebrain structure thought to play a role in the regulation of various motivational activities, including eating, drinking, and sexual behavior.

limbic system A system of structures thought to be involved in motivational and emotional behaviors (the amygdala) and memory (the hippocampus).

frontal lobe One of four anatomical regions of each hemisphere of the cerebral cortex, located on the top front of the brain; it contains the motor cortex and may be involved in higher-level thought processes.

parietal lobe One of four anatomical regions of each hemisphere of the cerebral cortex, located roughly on the top middle portion of the brain; it contains the somatosensory cortex, which controls the sense of touch.

temporal lobe One of four anatomical regions of each hemisphere of the cerebral cortex, located roughly on the sides of the brain; it's involved in certain aspects of speech and language perception.

occipital lobe One of four anatomical regions of each hemisphere of the cerebral cortex, located at the back of the brain; visual processing is controlled here.

corpus callosum The collection of nerve fibers that connects the two cerebral hemispheres and allows information to pass from one side to the other.

REGULATING GROWTH AND INTERNAL FUNCTIONS

endocrine system A network of glands that uses the bloodstream, rather than neurons, to send chemical messages that regulate growth and other internal functions.

hormones Chemicals released into the blood by the various endocrine glands to help control a variety of internal regulatory functions.

pituitary gland A kind of "master gland" in the body that controls the release of hormones in response to signals from the hypothalamus.

STORING AND TRANSMITTING THE GENETIC CODE

genes Segments of chromosomes that contain instructions for influencing and creating particular hereditary characteristics.

genotype The actual genetic information inherited from one's parents.

phenotype A person's observable characteristics, such as red hair. The phenotype is controlled mainly by the genotype, but it can also be influenced by the environment.

Open up the brain, peer inside, and all you're going to find are grayish cell bodies, white myelin-coated axons, and billions of glial cells helping to hold everything in place. There's no central executive in there, no little "being" pulling levers or pushing buttons to initiate and control behavior. As we've seen, scientists can measure the activities of neurons, particularly the firing rates of individual action potentials, but there's no special pattern of activity labeled "behavior," "thought," "idea," or "emotion." The challenge for the researcher is to decipher how the activities of individual neurons, operating in groups and in specialized regions of the brain, work together to create the intricacies of human psychology.

Because the brain contains roughly 100 billion neurons, it's quite impractical to try to map out the individual neural connections in it. So how can we ever hope to discover how everything works together to produce behavior? One solution is to study neural patterns in lower organisms, whose circuits of neurons are simpler and more easily mapped. Another option is to try to simulate activities of the mind—such as simple learning and memory processes—by creating *artificial* networks of neurons on computers. By programming in certain operating rules for these computerized neurons, based at least in part on what they know about real neurons, researchers might build artificial "brains" that show many of the important properties of the adaptive mind. At this point, no one has come close to achieving this goal, but simple computerized *neural networks* have been developed that show some "brainlike" properties: For example, neural networks can recognize objects when given incomplete information and can perform reasonably well in the face of damage.

Network Fundamentals

Computerized neural networks have been created in a variety of shapes and sizes (Caudill & Butler, 1990), but all share some fundamental properties. For example, all neural networks are built from individual processing *units,* roughly representing model neurons, that become "active" when information is received. Rules exist for determining how unit activations originate and change with time; an excellent summary of these rules can be found in the writings of David Rumelhart and Jay McClelland (1986), two of the leaders in the development of artificial networks. You can think about the activation of a unit in a neural network as comparable to the firing rate of an action potential in a real neuron.

As in the human nervous system, in artificial neural networks the individual processing units do not act alone. Meaningful concepts are usually represented not by the activity of single units but rather by groups of units. A mental representation, such as the image of a friend named Paul, is *distributed* as a pattern of activity across several processing units. For example, the blue circles on the right in Figure 3.19a represent the letters P, A, U, and L, which collectively form the name PAUL; the red circles on the left stand for some of the components of Paul's image—such as his wire glasses, his red hair, his mustache, and his round nose. Notice that each unit plays a specific role within a general pattern that represents your friend and his name. Your concept of Paul is represented by the activity pattern across the units as a whole, not by the activity of any single unit.

Units in a neural network are *connected,* such that the activation of one unit will affect the activation of other units. The particular pattern of connections among units is important because it determines how the network as a whole will operate. In the real nervous system, the network of neuron-to-neuron connections is also critical, of course, because it determines which brain regions are activated by information received from the environment. In Figure 3.19a, each of the input (red) units on the left is connected to each of the output (blue) units on the right. This means that activation of the first unit on the left will affect the activation of *all* of the units on the right.

Properties of Associative Networks

The neural network shown in Figure 3.19 is called a pattern associator. *Pattern associators* are designed to represent how the brain might "remember" one thing (such as a name) when given something else as a cue (such as an image of a person). The connections among units, or model neurons, are presumed to have been established through experience. For example, it is common to assume that two units will become connected if both units are active at the same time (Hebb, 1949). In this case, you learn to connect the physical features of a human, such as red hair, with the letters corresponding to the name Paul. Each unit is connected to many other things as well (the "red hair unit," for instance, is probably connected to the names of other people with red hair), but we'll ignore these other connections for the sake of keeping things simple.

When you see Paul on the street, his various physical features activate the red units on the left. Remember, Paul's appearance is represented by the activities of a *pattern* of units rather than by simply one. The input units then activate the output units on the right, corresponding to his name. The amount of activation that the output units will receive from the input will depend on the strength, or *weight,* of the connections that exist in the network. If you've just seen Paul once before in your life, for instance, we would expect the weights of the input-to-output connections to be relatively weak. But as long as the weights are sufficiently strong, the input units, activated by the appearance of Paul, will activate the output units (because of the connections), and you'll remember that it is "Paul" that you are seeing.

This pattern associator may seem incredibly simple, but it's not trivial. It reveals several important properties that

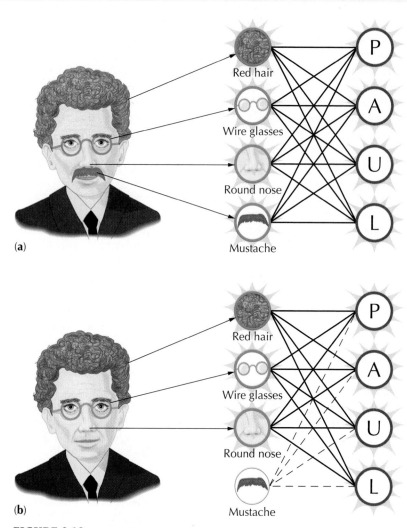

(a)

(b)

FIGURE 3.19
A Simple Neural Network. Neural networks are built from simple processing units that are connected in a network. In our example, the various features of Paul's face are connected with processing units corresponding to the letters of his name. Notice that each of the facial units is connected with all of the letters in his name. This means that if Paul shaves off his mustache (b), you will still be able to recognize his name through activation of the remaining features.

are believed to be characteristic of neural circuits in the brain. First, as noted earlier, information is *distributed* in the network—concepts, such as Paul, are represented through the activities of more than one unit. Second, in pattern associators the correct output is readily *reproducible* even if the original input has somehow changed. For example, imagine that Paul shaved off his mustache. As Figure 3.19b shows, the

network would still recognize him, even without the mustache, because each of his other features is connected to all of the relevant output units. Red hair, wire glasses, and a round nose all connect to each of the relevant letters of Paul. In the words of Caudill and Butler (1990), any good associative memory system "should be able to retrieve information even when the input stimulus is incomplete, approximate, or garbled" (p. 39).

Third, *generalization* is possible in pattern associators; that is, appropriate "memories" can be activated by inputs that are similar but not identical to inputs learned previously. Suppose, for example, that a child learns to run away from a four-legged brown dog foaming at the mouth. In the future, if she encounters another dog that is foaming at the mouth, she is likely to run even though that particular dog may not be brown. Because the associated output pattern can be reproduced from only a subset of relevant input, the foaming mouth and the fearsome-looking teeth should be sufficient to produce the response of running away. Remember, each input unit is connected to each output unit, so the activation of only a single input unit is capable, in principle, of activating the entire output pattern.

Finally, for many of the same reasons we've described, these simple pattern associators are quite *robust,* which means that they are resistant to damage or injury. If a subset of input units is turned off, perhaps mimicking damage to the brain, activation of the remaining units should still be sufficient to reproduce the correct output response. This is an adaptive characteristic of both neural circuits in the brain and neural networks. Each is able to sustain damage, or lesion, and still produce the correct needed responses.

Computerized neural networks are being developed to mimic increasingly more sophisticated psychological phenomena. Networks have been developed to model language development (McClelland & Elman, 1986), visual perception (Grossberg & Rudd, 1992), and even psychological disorders such as schizophrenia (Cohen & Servan-Schreiber, 1992). Most of these applications are quite a bit more complex than the simple pattern associator we've described, which has only two layers: input units and output units. It turns out that it is often necessary to develop networks with many layers: input units feed forward to inner (what are called "hidden") layers of

units, which then connect to the final output layer that represents a thought or a behavior.

Researchers have also spent a lot of time figuring out how these networks *learn*; that is, what determines when connections among units will form, and what are the appropriate rules for determining connection strengths? Neural network researchers still face a number of unresolved questions. For instance, why is it that neural networks are especially prone to "forgetting" old information when new information is learned (McCloskey & Cohen, 1989; Ratcliff, 1990)? But attempts are underway to resolve such issues.

As we mentioned at the opening of this chapter, somehow from the sporadic, seemingly chaotic patterns of cellular activity arise the mysteries of human behavior, thought, emotion, and creativity. The mechanisms that underlie these phenomena are not well understood at the moment, but the study of these artificial neural networks is providing some intriguing clues.

Human Development

4

From the moment that an individual's internal genetic code begins to express itself, to the moment of his or her final breath, life is characterized by continuous change. Over a lifetime, the body ages, intellectual abilities mature, and the ability to get along with others fluctuates. To the psychologist seeking to understand behavior and mind, the processes of **development,** as revealed through the age-related changes that occur over time, are vital ingredients of the human psychological equation. To understand why people act the way they do, it's important to begin with a discussion of our biological, intellectual, and social origins.

As we discussed in Chapter 1, philosophers and scientists have debated for centuries about the origins of knowledge and behavior. Do people's actions arise from ingrained biological tendencies that influence them from birth, or are people simply the product of their environment? Is Catherine a precocious child, delightfully alert and bright, because she was born with the "right" kind of genes, or is she simply reflecting the child-rearing strategies of her parents? By now, you should recognize that most psychologists believe that there is no single solution to the so-called *nature versus nurture* debate. The origins of behavior and mind lie exclusively in neither nature nor nurture, but most often in *both*. Behavior results from the interactions that occur between biological forces (of the type that we discussed in Chapter 3) and learning processes of the sort that we'll be discussing throughout the book.

▶ PREVIEWING THE ADAPTIVE PROBLEMS

Most modern *developmental psychologists*—those who study the developmental process—place a special emphasis on the concept of *interaction*. They argue that to understand the origins of any developmental change, it's necessary to view the developing human from the perspective of combined social, cultural, and biological forces (Sigelman & Shaffer, 1995; Zigler & Stevenson, 1993). As we saw in Chapter 3, unique genetic messages may compel the body to change over time, but the environment importantly shapes how those messages are realized. This means that it isn't possible to understand development by attending to any single factor in isolation, be it biological or environmental. Instead, development is better seen as a series of adjustments that the mind and body make to multiple factors. Moreover, these adjustments occur throughout the life span: From conception to death, the developmental process continues (Baltes, 1987; Baltes, Reese, & Lipsitt, 1980).

Why do humans need to develop? There is one very straightforward reason: There's no room for a full-sized adult in the mother's womb. Nature is forced to start small. But more important, extending the process of development over time enables humans to fine-tune their physical, intellectual, and social capabilities to better meet the needs of the environments they face. Nature has built a certain amount of flexibility, or *plasticity,* into the developmental process that allows the environment to modify the course of development. This flexibility has given humans, as individuals and as a species, an exceptional degree of adaptability to environmental influences (Corballis, 1991; Greenough, Black, & Wallace, 1987). You should keep the adaptive significance of development in mind as we consider the three main developmental problems that humans face: How do individuals move from fertilized eggs to fully functioning adults, capable of producing their own offspring? How do people develop the intellectual tools needed to solve survival problems?

| Developing physically | Developing intellectually | Developing socially and personally |

FIGURE 4.1
Adaptive Problems of Development. Humans face three main developmental problems: developing physically, intellectually, and socially/personally.

How do people form the social relationships they need for personal protection, nourishment, and continuation of the species? Figure 4.1 provides an overview of these three issues.

▶ **DEVELOPING PHYSICALLY** Individuals begin as fertilized eggs and over the course of years grow to become fully functioning adults, capable of reproduction and self-survival. As we've discussed, it takes time to develop physically partly because an organism must remain small to get through the birth canal, but also because development allows the environment to play an important modifying role. The environment helps shape the physical process of growth, or *maturation,* even though most physical changes turn out to be surprisingly consistent and predictable. Most children become physically capable of crawling, sitting up, and walking at roughly the same age. There is also a relatively predictable time period, although it differs for boys and girls, during which individuals enter puberty and reach sexual maturity. In general, the timing of development is a product of evolutionary history and reflects the problems of survival that the human species has been required to solve. In the first section of the chapter, we'll trace the major milestones of physical development, from the point of conception to the final years of life.

▶ **DEVELOPING INTELLECTUALLY** To psychologists interested in behavior and mind, the developmental changes that occur in how people think—what is called cognitive development—are of major importance. Intellectually, the newborn is hardly a miniature adult. There are good reasons to believe that infants see and think about the world somewhat differently than adults do. We'll begin this section with a brief discussion of perceptual development—particularly how children learn to interpret the visual world around them—and then we'll move forward to a discussion of how thought processes change as children grow. The thought processes of infants and children change over time partly because they learn from experience but also because they're faced with their own unique kinds of problems to solve. For example, newborns need desperately to acquire adequate nourishment, but they lack the necessary physical equipment to obtain nourishment on their own. In some ways, the way that a newborn "thinks" is directly related to solving the problem of maintaining proper nourishment. Finally, we'll tackle moral development in this section—how children acquire a sense of ethics and their own principles about what is right and wrong.

Part of the process of developing socially and personally is the development of personal identity. Here, Ellen demonstrates an awareness of herself as she discovers her nose in the mirror's reflection.

▶ **DEVELOPING SOCIALLY AND PERSONALLY** Humans are social animals. They are continually interacting with each other, and these relationships help people adapt successfully to their environments. Establishing a strong bond between the parent and child, for instance, helps ensure that the child will be protected and nourished in the proper way. But relationships with others also help each person to develop a sense of identity as an individual and as a member of a particular gender group. We'll consider the milestones of social development in this section, beginning with the formation of attachments to parents and caregivers, and ending with a discussion of how relationships change in middle and late adulthood.

Developing Physically

To a child, it seems to take forever to grow up. In fact, humans do take a relatively long time to reach full physical maturity, compared to other species. At birth, for example, the brain of a chimpanzee is at about 60% of its final weight, whereas the brain of a human newborn is only at about 25% of its ultimate weight (Corballis, 1991; Lenneberg, 1967). Humans do a lot of developing outside of the womb. Still, the main components of the body—the nervous system, the networks of glands, and so on—develop astonishingly rapidly from the point of conception. Guided by the genetic code, and influenced by the release of hormones by the endocrine system, individuals in the early years change physically at rates that will never again be matched in their lifetimes. To place the growth rate in some perspective, it's been estimated that if children continued to develop at their rate of progress in the first two years of life, adults would end up over 12 feet tall and weighing several tons! Fortunately, things slow down considerably after the first few years of life; but they never completely stop—people continue to change physically until the very moment of death.

Prenatal Development

The human developmental process begins with the union of egg and sperm at conception. Within the fertilized egg, or **zygote,** the 23 chromosomes from the father and the 23 chromosomes from the mother pair up to form the master genetic blueprint. Over the next approximately 266 days (9 months), the organism undergoes a steady and quite remarkable transformation. It begins as a single cell and ends as an approximately 7-pound newborn composed of literally billions of cells.

The period of development that occurs *prior* to birth is called prenatal development, and it's divided into three main stages: *germinal, embryonic,* and *fetal.*

It takes about two weeks after conception for the zygote, which rapidly begins to divide into more cells, to migrate down from the mother's fallopian tubes (where the sperm and egg meet) and implant itself in the wall of the uterus (often called the womb). The period from conception to implantation, called the **germinal period,** is characteristically fraught with difficulties. In fact, most fertilized eggs fail to complete the process—well over half fail to achieve successful implantation, perhaps because of abnormalities or because the implantation site is inadequate to sustain proper nutrition (Roberts & Lowe, 1975; Sigelman & Shafer, 1995).

If successful implantation occurs, the **embryonic period** begins. During the next six weeks, the human develops from an unrecognizable mass of cells to a somewhat familiar creature with arms, legs, fingers, toes, and a distinctly beating heart. Near the end of the embryonic period—in the seventh and eighth weeks after fertilization—sexual differentiation begins. Depending on whether the father has contributed an X or a Y chromosome (the mother always contributes an X), the embryo starts to develop the sexual characteristics of either a male or a female (see Figure 4.2). If the developing embryo has inherited a Y chromosome, it begins

FIGURE 4.2
Genetic Determinants of Gender.
Depending on whether the father has contributed an X or a Y chromosome, the child will develop the sexual characteristics of a female or a male.

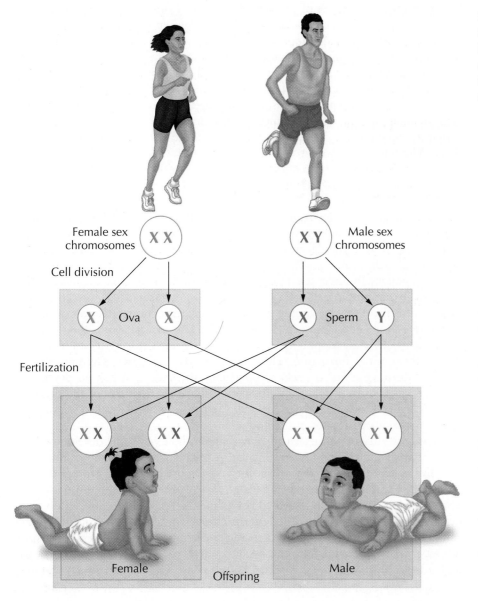

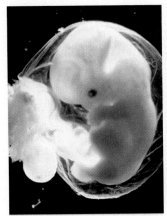

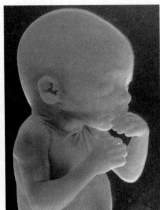
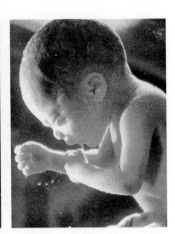

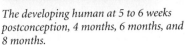

The developing human at 5 to 6 weeks postconception, 4 months, 6 months, and 8 months.

to secrete the sex hormone *testosterone,* which leads to the establishment of a male sexual reproductive system. In the absence of testosterone, the natural course of development is to become female.

After the eighth week of prenatal development, the **fetal period** begins and continues until birth. Early in the period, the bones and muscles of what is now called the *fetus* start to develop; by the end of the third month, the skeletal and muscular systems are intact enough to allow for extensive movement—even somersaults—although the fetus at this point is still only about 3 inches long (Apgar & Beck, 1974). By the end of the sixth month, the fetus has grown to over a foot long, weighs in at about 2 pounds, and may even be capable of survival if delivered prematurely. The last three months of prenatal development are marked by extremely rapid growth, both in body size and in the size and complexity of brain tissue. The fetus also develops a layer of fat under the skin during this period, which acts as protective insulation, and the lungs mature in preparation for the baby's first gasping breath of air.

Hazards from the Environment. Although the developing human is snugly tucked away within the confines of its mother's womb, it is by no means completely isolated from the effects of the environment. The mother's physical health and diet, as well as any possible exposure she might have to toxins in the environment, potentially affect the developing child. Mother and child are linked physically, so if the mother gets sick, smokes, drinks, or takes drugs, the effects can transfer directly to the developing fetus or embryo. Environmental agents that can do damage to the developing child are called **teratogens.** As a rule, the structures and systems of the developing fetus or embryo are most susceptible to teratogens during their initial formation. Thus, if the mother contracts German measles (rubella) during the first 6 weeks of pregnancy, the child is at risk for developing heart defects because it is during this period that the structures of the heart are formed. Figure 4.3 shows the periods of greatest susceptibility—called *critical periods*—for various structures in the body.

The powerful influence that the environment holds over the developing fetus or embryo should not be underestimated. A pregnant woman who drinks heavily—five or more drinks a day—is at least 30% more likely than a nondrinker to give birth to a child suffering from *fetal alcohol syndrome,* a condition marked by physical deformities and an increased risk of mental retardation (Streissguth, Randels, & Smith, 1991). Negative long-term effects can also result from drug consumption—even of over-the-counter and prescription drugs—as well as from improper nutrition, smoking, and possibly even drinking too much coffee (Day & Richardson, 1994; Sussman & Levitt, 1989). It's hard to predict with any certainty

This child on the left is one of thousands who are born each year afflicted with fetal alcohol syndrome. The age of the mother is also a risk factor in pregnancy, but the majority of women over the age of 35, such as the woman on the right, can expect to deliver normal, healthy babies.

what effect an environmental agent will have on development, because susceptibility is largely a matter of timing of exposure and the intricacies of the master genetic plan. Some mothers can abuse themselves terribly and still produce normal children; others who drink only moderately, perhaps as few as seven drinks a week, may produce a child with significant disabilities (Abel, 1981; Jacobson & Jacobson, 1994). Because the effects of maternal activities are impossible to pre-

FIGURE 4.3
Critical Periods of Susceptibility During Prenatal Development.
Specific organs and body parts are at greatest risk from teratogens during certain critical periods of prenatal development. The light part of each bar signifies the period of greatest susceptibility. (Adapted from Sigelman & Shaffer, 1995.)

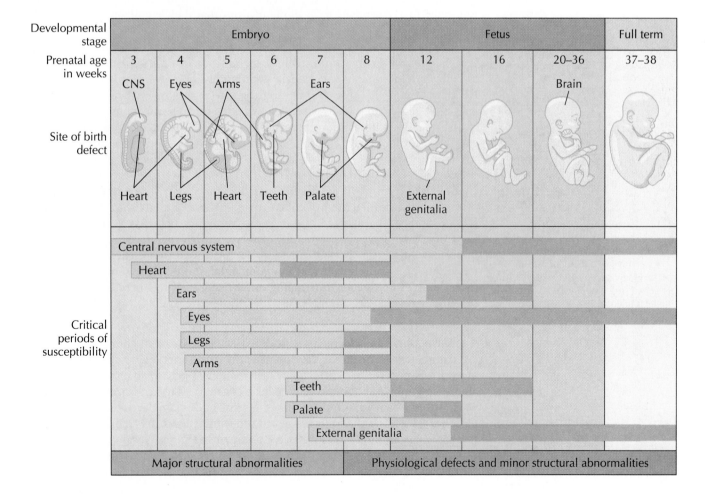

dict in any particular case, most doctors recommend against playing Russian roulette with the developing fetus or embryo; they suggest staying sober, well fed, and under a doctor's care throughout pregnancy.

Infancy and Childhood

Although we've stressed the negative impact of the environment on the developing human—how environmental agents consumed by the mother and maternal illness can limit or prevent expression of the normal genetic plan—in the vast majority of cases, the environment has a nurturing effect on the developing organism. The internal conditions of the mother's uterus are perfectly tuned for physical development. The temperature is right, the fetus floats cushioned in a protective fluid, and regular nourishment is provided through the umbilical cord and placenta. More often than not, the result is a healthy baby, with normal physical systems, who is ready to take on the world.

The average newborn weighs in at about 7 pounds and is roughly 20 inches in length. Over the next two years, as the child grows from baby to toddler, this weight will quadruple and the child will reach about half of his or her final adult height. Along with the rest of the body, the brain continues its dramatic growth spurt during this period. As mentioned earlier, a newborn enters the world with a brain that is only 25% of its final weight; but by birthday number 2, the percentage is up to 75%. Remarkably, this increase in brain size is not apparently due to the formation of new neurons, as most of the cells that make up the cerebral cortex are in place well before birth (Nowakowski, 1987; Rakic, 1991). Instead, the cells grow in size and complexity, and a number of supporting glial cells are added. But individuals essentially have all the neurons that they're going to possess at the moment they are born.

The fact that substantial numbers of neurons are intact at birth does not mean that the brain of the newborn infant is *mature*—far from it. The brain still needs to build and fine-tune its vast internal communication network, and it needs experience to accomplish this task. During the final stages of prenatal development, and especially during the first year or two after birth, tremendous changes occur in the neural circuitry. More branches (dendrites) sprout off from the existing cells, in order to receive information from other cells, and the number of connections, or synapses, greatly increases. There is even a kind of neural "pruning process" in which neurons that are not used simply atrophy or die. The key principle at work is *plasticity*: the genetic code does not rigidly fix the internal circuitry of the brain; instead, a kind of rough wiring pattern is established during prenatal development that is filled in during the important first few years of life. Studies with animals have shown that the quality of early experience may be extremely important during this period. For example, rats raised in enriched environments (with lots of social contact and environmental stimulation) show significantly more complex and better functioning brain tissue than rats raised in sterile, barren environments (Greenough et al., 1987; Rosenzweig, 1984).

Given that the environment plays such an important role in shaping brain development, what advice would you give new parents to maximize "enriched" development of their baby's intellectual capabilities?

Early Motor Development. Associated with the maturing brain and muscles are the milestones in motor development that thrill every wide-eyed parent. Ask any parent to describe the highlights of the baby's first year or two, and you'll almost certainly hear about when the baby began to sit up, crawl, stand alone, and walk. Before a baby can do these things, however, adequate development must take place within the brain and in the neuron-to-muscle links that radiate throughout the body. For example, the insulated coating of the axons (*myelin sheath*), which

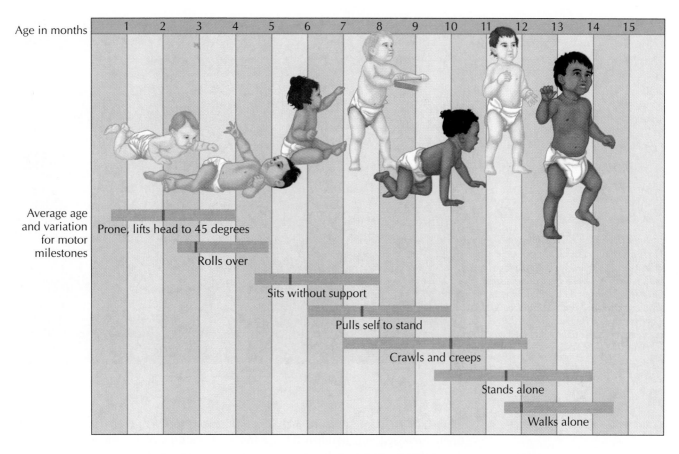

Age in months

Average age and variation for motor milestones

Prone, lifts head to 45 degrees

Rolls over

Sits without support

Pulls self to stand

Crawls and creeps

Stands alone

Walks alone

helps speed up neural transmission, needs to develop. Generally, the nervous system matures in an essentially "down and out" fashion—that is, from the head down and from the center out toward the extremities (Shirley, 1933). Infants can lift their heads before they can roll over because the neuron-to-muscle connections in the upper part of the body mature before those in the lower part of the body. Babies crawl before they walk because they are able to control their arms efficiently before their legs.

Although psychologists don't like to tie developmental milestones directly to age—because not all children develop at the same rate—most children learn to crawl, then stand alone, and then walk at about the same time. Figure 4.4 shows the major stages of an infant's motor development. The sequence of development, from lifting the head to walking alone, is stable, orderly, and predictable. As noted earlier, the baby sits before it stands and crawls before it walks partly because of the way that the nervous system develops. In addition, you can see that associated with each stage is a range of ages, although the range is not large. Roughly 90% of all babies can roll over by 5 months, sit without support by 8 months, and then walk alone by 15 months. But, whereas one baby might stand alone consistently by 9 months, another might not accomplish the same feat until nearly 14 months of age.

What accounts for these differences? The answer is impossible to pinpoint for most individual cases, but both nature and nurture contribute. Each individual has a genetic blueprint that uniquely determines when he or she will develop physically, but environmental experiences can speed up or slow down the process to a certain extent. Some cultures place higher value on early motor development than

FIGURE 4.4
Major Stages of Motor Development. Approximate time periods are given for the major points in motor development. Although psychologists are reluctant to tie developmental "milestones" to age, most children learn to crawl, stand alone, and walk at about the same age.

Why do you think learning plays such a limited role in certain aspects of motor development, such as walking? Would it be more advantageous for the species if all parents had to teach their children to walk?

 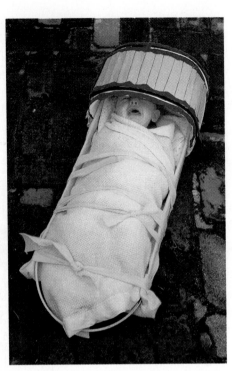

There are many cultural differences in child-rearing practices. The Shesone Indian baby shown on the left, unlike the Caucasian baby on the right, calmly accepts being swaddled to a cradleboard. However, even with the cultural differences, both of these babies should begin crawling and walking at roughly the same time.

others and therefore nurture such development in their children. If a baby is routinely exercised and handled during the early months of life, there is some evidence that he or she will progress through the landmark stages of motor development more quickly (Hopkins, 1991; Zelazo, Zelazo, & Kolb, 1972). But these differences are usually small, and they play little, if any, role in determining final motor development. Hopi babies are traditionally swaddled and bound to cradleboards for much of the first year of life, yet these babies begin walking at roughly the same time as babies who are not bound in this manner (Dennis & Dennis, 1940). To learn to walk at a reasonable age, the infant simply needs to be given the opportunity to move around at some point—to "test the waters" and explore things on his or her own (Bertenthal, Campos, & Kermoian, 1994). Hopi babies are bound to cradleboards for only their first nine or ten months; afterward, they are given several months to explore their motor capabilities before they begin to walk (Shaffer, 1993).

Grace and coordination in motor movements take time to develop. This 2-year-old will probably have little trouble bouncing a basketball successfully by the time he enters elementary school.

The Growing Child. From the onset of toddlerhood through puberty, the growth rate continues, but at a less rapid pace. The average child grows several inches in a year and puts on roughly 6 to 7 pounds annually. Even though these changes are significant, it's often hard for parents to detect them because they represent only a small fraction of the child's current size (adding 2 inches to a 20-inch baby is far easier to spot than adding 2 inches to someone who is 40 inches tall). More noticeable are the changes that occur in hand-to-eye coordination as the child matures. Three-year-olds lack the grace and coordination in their movements that are so obvious in a 6-year-old. The brain also continues to mature, although again at a pace far slower than that seen during prenatal development or during the first two years of life. There is also good evidence to suggest that general processing speed—how quickly people can think and react to sudden changes in their environment—increases consistently throughout childhood (Kail, 1991; Kail & Salthouse, 1994).

Not all children undergo their adolescent growth spurt at the same age. Boys typically lag behind girls by as much as two years.

From Adolescence to Adulthood

Between the end of childhood and the beginning of young adulthood lies the important physical and psychological transition period called *adolescence.* Physically, the two most dramatic changes that occur during this time are the adolescent *growth spurt* and the onset of **puberty,** or sexual maturity (the word *puberty* is from the Latin for "to grow hairy"). As with crawling and walking, it's not possible to pinpoint the timing of these changes exactly, particularly for a specific individual, but changes usually start occuring for girls at around age 11 and for boys at about 13. Hormones released by the endocrine system rock them out of childhood by triggering a rapid increase in height and weight accompanied by the enlargement and maturation of internal and external sexual organs.

 Sexual Maturation. Puberty is the developmental period during which individuals mature sexually and acquire the ability to reproduce. For the adolescent female, high levels of *estrogen* in the body lead to external changes, such as breast development and broadening hips, and eventually to the beginning of *menarche* (the first menstrual flow) at around age 12 or 13. For boys, hormones called *androgens* are released, leading to the appearance of facial hair, a lower voice, and the ability to ejaculate (release semen) at around age 13 or 14. Neither the initial appearance of menarche nor the first ejaculation necessarily means that the adolescent is ready to reproduce—ovulation and sperm production may not occur until months later—but psychologically these "firsts" tend to be highly memorable and emotional events (Golub, 1992).

 The onset of puberty is another classic instance of how the master genetic plan interacts with the nurturing effects of the environment. Did you know that the average onset age for menarche has dropped from about 16 in the 1880s to the current 12–13? Physically, people are maturing earlier than in past generations, and it's almost certainly not due to genetics. Instead, better nutrition, better living conditions, and improved medical care are responsible for the trend (Tanner, 1990). Even today, in parts of the world where living conditions are more stressful, the average age of menarche is later than in industrialized countries such as the United States (Chumlea, 1982). Although the environment does not cause sexual maturation—that's controlled by the genetic code—the environment modu-

Strenuous daily exercise programs, such as those practiced by Olympic athletes, can play a role in delaying the onset of puberty.

lates the expression of the code, either accelerating or delaying the point when changes start to occur.

Reaching Adulthood. The adolescent years are marked by dramatic changes in appearance and strength. Motor skills, including hand-to-eye coordination, improve to adult levels during the teenage years. As you're undoubtedly aware, there are world-class swimmers and tennis players who are barely into their teens. The brain reaches adult weight by about age 16, although the myelination of the neurons—so critical in early motor development—continues throughout the adolescent years (Benes, 1989). The continued maturation of the brain can also be seen in the gradual quickening of reaction times that occurs throughout adolescence (Kail, 1991).

When do individuals actually cross the threshold to adulthood? That's a difficult question to answer, because becoming an adult is, in some sense, a state of mind. There are differences in how the transition from adolescent to adult is defined across the world. Some cultures have specific "rites of passage" and others do not. And, as you know, not all adolescents are willing to accept the socially defined responsibilities of adulthood at the "appropriate" time. But by the time people reach their twenties, they are physically mature and at the height of their physical prowess.

Adulthood and Aging

It's barely noticeable at the time, but most people begin slowly and steadily to decline physically, at least with respect to their peak levels of strength and agility, at some point during their twenties. Unfortunately, the loss tends to be across the board, which means that it applies to virtually all physical functions, from strength to respiration rate to the heart's pumping capacity (Whitbourne, 1985). Individual differences occur in the rate of decline, of course, depending on such factors as exercise, illness, and heredity (I'm sure you can think of a 40-year-old who is in better physical shape than a 25-year-old). But wrinkles, age spots, sagging flesh, and loss of muscle tone are all reliable and expected parts of the aging process.

By about age 50, the average woman begins **menopause,** the period during which the menstrual cycle slows down and finally stops. Ovulation also stops, so women at this point lose the ability to bear children. These events are caused by hormonal changes, in particular by a decline in the level of female hormones in the body. Despite what you might have heard, menopause need not be particularly disruptive, either physically or psychologically (McKinlay, Brambilla, & Posner, 1992). The main physical symptoms, such as "hot flashes," can be controlled by hormone replacement therapy, and the idea that the majority of women undergo a sustained period of depression or crankiness is simply a myth (Matthews, 1992). Men do not experience "male menopause" because they never menstruate, although some men do lose the ability to father children in their later years because of a decline in the production or activity of their sperm. The loss in reproductive capacity, expressed by the term *climacteric* (meaning "critical time"), does not occur in all men.

With age, the brain also undergoes significant physical changes. Some individuals suffer brain degeneration—the loss of brain cells—which can lead to senility and, in some cases, to a disabling condition called Alzheimer's disease. But the good news is that the majority of older people never experience these problems; fewer than 1% of people at age 65 are afflicted with **dementia,** which is the technical name for physically based loss in mental functioning. Although that percentage may rise to as much as 20% for individuals over age 80 (Cavanaugh, 1993), significant losses in mental functioning or mental health are still the exception

Can you think of any adaptive reasons for aging? If not for the individual, what about for the species as a whole?

FIGURE 4.5
Age and Reaction Time. This figure shows how average reaction time changes from age 20 to age 80 for a cognitive task requiring subjects to match numbers with symbols on a computer screen. Although there is a gradual quickening of reaction time from childhood through adolescence, after age 20 reaction time gradually slows. (Based on Salthouse, 1994)

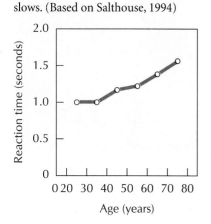

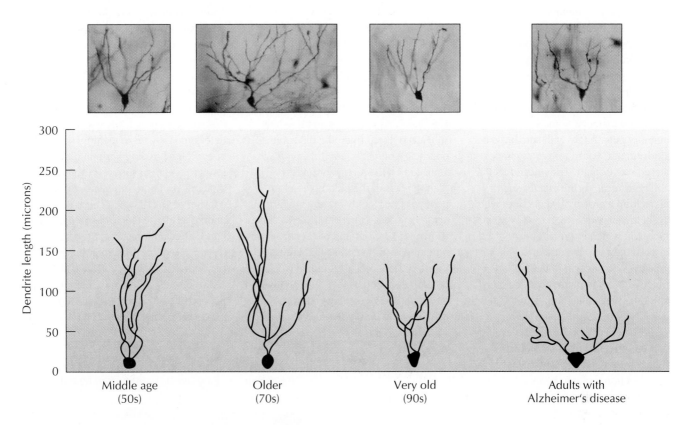

Dendrite length (microns)

300
250
200
150
100
50
0

Middle age
(50s)

Older
(70s)

Very old
(90s)

Adults with
Alzheimer's disease

FIGURE 4.6
Aging Neurons. Samples of hippocampal neurons taken from people in their fifties, seventies, nineties, and from adults afflicted with Alzheimer's disease. Notice that the dendrites of the samples actually increase in length and complexity from the fifties to seventies, declining only in late old age or in Alzheimer's disease.

rather than the rule. The bad news is that everyone loses brain cells with age—the extent of the loss depends on the particular site in the brain (Selkoe, 1992)—and associated declines occur in certain kinds of memory, sensory abilities, and reaction time, as shown in Figure 4.5 (Cavanaugh, 1993; Salthouse, 1994). For a closer look at how memory changes in the older years, see the next Inside the Problem section.

But the physical changes that occur in the aging brain may not be all bad. Neurons are lost, and the loss is apparently permanent, but the remaining neurons may in some instances increase in complexity. In a famous autopsy study by Buell and Coleman (1979), it was found that dendrites were significantly longer and more complex in samples of normal brain tissue taken from elderly adults when compared to those of middle-aged adults (see Figure 4.6). It would appear then that the brain may compensate for the losses that it experiences by making better use of the structures that remain intact. Some researchers have even argued that sustained mental "activity" in later years may help promote neural growth, thereby counteracting some of the normal decline in mental skills (Coleman & Flood, 1987; Black, Isaacs, & Greenough, 1991). This conclusion is still somewhat speculative at this point, but there does seem to be general agreement that adaptive changes in the brain can occur even in the later stages of the aging process.

Developing Intellectually

Throughout a person's lifetime, the connections among neurons in the brain are continually changing. New pathways are formed and others are abandoned in response to environmental experiences. The fact that the brain exhibits such *plasticity* (the ability to change and adjust its connections) is extremely adaptive,

What happens to memory as people get older? Is there an inevitable decline in the ability to remember? Although it's quite common for the elderly to report memory problems, such as increased forgetfulness, there is no simple or straightforward relationship between aging and memory. Some kinds of memory falter badly with age, but other kinds do not. For example, psychologists are now reasonably convinced that the ability to *recall* recent events, such as items from a grocery list, declines with age. However, in certain tests of *recognition,* in which information is re-presented and the task is to tell whether one has seen it before, little or no differences in memory ability are found between the young and the elderly (see Kausler, 1994; Parkin, 1993).

Researchers who study the developmental process typically conduct research using either *longitudinal* or *cross-sectional* research designs. In a **longitudinal design,** the same individuals are tested repeatedly over time, at various points in childhood or even on through adulthood. In a **cross-sectional design,** which is conducted over a limited span of time, researchers directly compare performance on some task among *different* people of different ages. For example, Craik and McDowd (1987) used a cross-sectional design to compare recall and recognition performance for two age groups: a "young" group of college students, with an average age of 20.7 years, and an "old" group, volunteers from a senior citizen center, with an average age of 72.8 years. All of the participants were asked to learn memory lists that consisted of short phrases ("a body of water") presented together with associated target words ("pond"). The lists were followed by either (1) an immediate recall test in which the short phrase was given and the subject needed to recall the target word, or (2) a delayed recognition test that required the subjects to decide whether a presented word had or had not been presented in one of the earlier lists.

In an experiment like this, attempts are made to match the participants on as many variables as possible—such as educational level and verbal ability—so

that the only difference between the groups is *age.* Any performance differences can then be attributed uniquely to the independent variable (age) and not to some other confounding factor (see Chapter 2). The results of the Craik and McDowd (1987) study are shown in Figure 4.7. As you can see, the young subjects outperformed the old subjects on the test of recall, but the advantage vanished on the recognition test. Memory loss in the elderly therefore depends importantly on how memory is actually tested. Other studies have shown that performance depends as well on the types of materials that are tested. When older subjects are asked to remember materials that fit naturally into their rich knowledge base, they may even perform better than their younger

counterparts (Zacks & Hasher, 1994).

Although most people past age 60 or 70 are able to perform well on certain kinds of memory tests, it is still the case that older people perform quite poorly on some kinds of memory tasks, especially those that require recall. Researchers are actively trying to determine why these memory deficits occur. One possibility is that older adults lose the ability to suppress irrelevant thoughts or ignore irrelevant stimuli (Hasher et al., 1991). Because they are unable to focus selectively on the task at hand, they fail to process the to-be-remembered information in ways that are conducive to later recall (Craik, 1994). As we'll see in Chapter 8, memory depends heavily on the kinds of mental processing that go on during initial study.

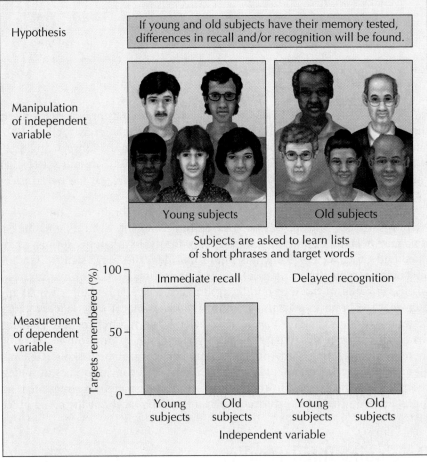

FIGURE 4.7

Memory and Aging. In the study by Craik and McDowd (1987), two groups, one with an average age of 20.7 years and one with an average age of 72.8 years, were asked to learn and then recall or recognize target words. Although the "young" subjects recalled more targets than the "old" group, the advantage disappeared for recognition.

especially during the early years of development. Because there is no way for the master genetic plan to predict the environments that an individual will encounter after birth, it builds in an intrinsic capacity to change.

As the brain changes physically in response to the environment, so, too, do the characteristics of the mind that are of main interest to psychologists. Infants are not born seeing and thinking about the world like adults do. Cognitive processes—how individuals think and perceive—develop over time. As with motor development, intellectual development depends on adequate physical maturation within the brain, as well as on exposure to the right kinds of experiences. In this section of the chapter, we'll consider three aspects of intellectual development: How do children learn to perceive and remember the world? How do thought processes change with age? How do individuals develop a sense of right and wrong?

Perceiving and Remembering

What does the world look like to a newborn child? Is it a complex three-dimensional world, full of depth, color, and texture? Or is it a "blooming, buzzing confusion," as claimed by the early psychologist William James? Let's stop for a moment and think about how a psychologist might answer a question like this. Deciphering the perceptual capabilities of an infant is not a simple matter. Babies can't tell us what they see, nor can they move around in ways that would easily allow us to infer what they see (that is, by avoiding some things and knocking into others).

The Tools of Investigation. Because infants don't communicate as adults do, the analysis of perceptual development requires a significant amount of methodological creativity on the part of the researcher. It's necessary to devise a way to infer perceptual capabilities from what is essentially an immobile, largely uncommunicative infant. Fortunately, young infants possess several characteristics that make the job a little easier: (1) they show *preferences,* which means they prefer some stimuli over others; (2) they notice *novelty,* which means they notice new or different things in their environment; and (3) they can *learn* to repeat activities that produce some kind of reward. As we'll see shortly, researchers have developed techniques that capitalize on these tendencies.

In the "preference method" developed by Robert Fantz (1961), an infant is presented with two visual displays simultaneously and the investigator simply records how long the infant looks at each (see Figure 4.8). Suppose that one of the displays shows a male face, the other a female face, and the baby "chooses" to look at the female face for a significantly longer period of time. By choosing to look longer at the female face, the infant has shown a "preference." By itself, this preference indicates very little. To infer things about what the baby can really see,

If you were designing a "blueprint" for a living thing, why do you think it would be important to build-in natural preferences?

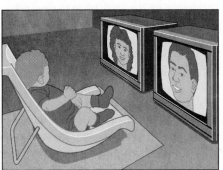

FIGURE 4.8
The Preference Method. Babies prefer to look at some visual stimuli over others. In this case, a preverbal infant is demonstrating a "preference" for a female face by tracking its location across trials. The preference can be determined by simply recording how long the baby looks at each face.

it's necessary to present the same two displays a number of times, switching their relative positions from trial to trial. If the baby continues to look longer at the female face even though it appears on the left on some trials and on the right on other trials, we can infer that the baby has the visual capability to tell the difference between the two displays. The infant "tells" us that he or she can detect differences by exclusively tracking the female face. Notice that we didn't need to ask the baby anything—we simply inferred things about his or her visual system by measuring overt behavior.

One of the preferences that babies consistently show is for novelty—they like to look at new things. But they tend to ignore events that occur repeatedly in their environment without consequence. For instance, if you show newborns a blue-colored card and track how their eyes move (or how their heart rate changes), you'll find that they spend a lot of time looking at the card when it first appears—it's something new. But if you present the same card over and over again, their interest wanes, and they'll begin to look at something else. This decline in responsiveness to repeated stimulation, called **habituation,** provides an effective tool for researchers seeking to map out the infant's perceptual world (Bornstein, 1992; Flavel, Miller, & Miller, 1993). By acting bored, which is defined operationally in terms of how long they look at the card, babies reveal that they remember the stimulus from its previous presentation and recognize that it hasn't changed. It's as if the baby is saying, "Oh, it's that blue card again."

Habituation can be used to discover specific information about how babies perceive and remember their worlds (Granrud, 1993). For example, suppose we wanted to discover whether newborns have the capacity to perceive color. We could show the blue card for a while, then suddenly switch to a green card that is matched on all other visual dimensions (such as size and brightness). If the infant shows renewed interest in the card—treating the stimulus as if it was novel—we can infer that the baby can discriminate, or tell the difference between, blue and green. If, on the other hand, the baby continues to ignore the new green card, that would suggest that perhaps the baby lacks color vision at this stage in development. We can also study memory by varying the time that elapses between presentations of the card. If the baby continues to act bored to the blue card even though we insert long pauses between successive presentations, we know that he or she is "remembering" the card over those particular time intervals.

A researcher can also gain insight into what a baby sees, knows, and remembers by *rewarding* a simple motor movement, such as kicking a leg or sucking on an artificial nipple, in the presence of particular kinds of events (Siqueland & DeLucia, 1969). For example, in research by Carolyn Rovee-Collier (1993) 2- and 3-month-old infants were taught that kicking their legs could produce movement of a crib mobile hanging overhead. A moving mobile is quite rewarding to babies at this age, and they'll double or triple their rate of leg kicking in a matter of minutes if it leads to movement. We can then study cognitive abilities such as memory by taking the mobile away, waiting for some period of time, and then replacing the mobile. If the baby begins leg kicking again at rates comparable to those produced at the end of training, we can infer that the baby has "remembered" what he or she has learned. We can also change the characteristics of the mobile after training and learn things about a baby's perceptual abilities. For example, if we train an infant with a blue mobile and then switch to a green one, any differences in leg kicking should help to tell us whether the baby can discriminate between green and blue.

Perceptual Development. Based on the use of such techniques, researchers have discovered that babies greet the world with sensory systems that function reasonably well. Although none of these systems is operating at peak efficiency, because their biological equipment is still maturing, babies still see a world of color

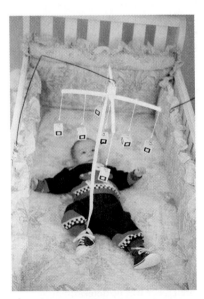

In research by Carolyn Rovee-Collier, infants learn that leg kicking can produce movement of a mobile hanging overhead.

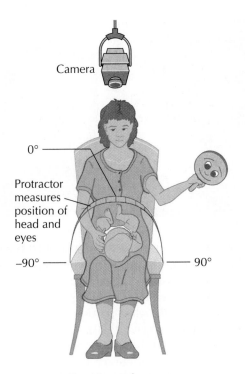

Camera

0°

Protractor
measures
position of
head and
eyes

−90°   90°

Experimental setup

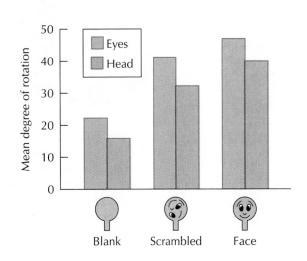

Blank   Scrambled   Face

FIGURE 4.9
Infant Preferences. In the experiment by Johnson and colleagues (1991), babies were shown either a blank stimulus, a stimulus with scrambled facial features, or a face. Each stimulus was positioned over the baby's head and then moved from side to side. The dependent variable measured the extent to which the baby "tracked" each stimulus by turning his or her head and eyes. As the results show, the babies tracked the face stimulus more than the others. (Graph adapted from Johnson et al., 1991.)

and shape (Banks & Shannon, 1993). They even arrive with built-in preferences for some colors and shapes. One-day-old babies, for example, respond more to patterned stimuli than to unpatterned ones; as shown in Figure 4.9, they even prefer to look at correctly drawn faces than "scrambled" faces with features placed in incorrect positions (Johnson et al., 1991; see also Walton & Bower, 1993). Learning, or experience, may play a role in some of these preferences, but it's clear that reasonably sophisticated perceptual processing can occur rapidly after birth.

Newborns also hear reasonably well, and they seem to recognize their mother's voice within a day or two after birth (DeCasper & Fifer, 1980). Remarkably, there's evidence to suggest that newborns can even hear and remember things that happen *prior* to birth. By the 28th week, fetuses will close their eyes in response to loud noises presented near the mother's abdomen (Parmelee & Sigman, 1983). Infants will also choose to suck on an artificial nipple that produces a recording of a story that was read aloud to them repeatedly before birth (DeCasper & Spence, 1986). If you think about it, you'll realize that this is an adaptive quality for the newborn to possess. Remember, the newborn needs nourishment and is dependent on others for survival. Babies who are born into the world with a visual system that can detect shapes and forms and an auditory system tuned to the human voice increase their likelihood of survival.

In addition to sights and sounds, babies are quite sensitive to touch, smell, pain, and taste. Place a drop of lemon juice in the mouth of a newborn and you'll see a distinctive grimacing reaction. Place a small amount of sugar in the baby's mouth, and the baby will smack his or her lips. These distinctive reactions are present at birth and are found even before the infant has had a single taste of food (Steiner, 1977). A baby's sense of smell is developed well enough that the newborn quickly learns to recognize the odor of its mother's breast (Porter et al., 1992). As for pain and touch, babies will reject a milkbottle that is too hot, and, as every parent knows, the right kind of pat on the baby's back is pleasurable enough to soothe the newborn into sleep.

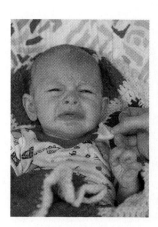

Distinctive reactions to a variety of tastes—such as the ones shown here to a taste of lemon, sugar, and salt—have been found to be present in infants immediately after birth.

Babies even seem to perceive a world that is three-dimensional. When placed on a "visual cliff," such as the one shown in the accompanying photo, at roughly 6 months of age babies are reluctant to cross over the apparent dropoff, or cliff, to reach a parent (Gibson & Walk, 1960). Even babies as young as 2 months show heart rate changes when they're placed on the glass portion covering the "deep" side of the visual cliff (Campos, Langer, & Krowitz, 1970).

But still, these are infant perceptions, and the infant's world is not the same as the one viewed by an adult. Newborn babies cannot see as well as adults. They're not very good at discriminating fine detail in visual patterns: Compared with the ideal "acuity" level of 20/20, babies see a blurry world that is more on the order of 20/600, meaning that what newborns see at 20 feet is like what adults with ideal vision see at 600 feet (Banks & Salapatek, 1983). In addition, newborns probably cannot perceive shapes and forms in the same way as adults do (Bornstein, 1992), nor can they hear as well as adults. For example, infants seem to have some trouble listening selectively for certain kinds of sounds, and sounds need to be louder for infants than for adults before they can be detected (Bargones & Werner, 1994). Infants' perceptual systems improve markedly during the first few months, partly because of continued physical maturation but also because experience plays an important role in "fine-tuning" of sensory abilities. Research with nonhuman subjects, such as cats or chimpanzees, has shown that if animals are deprived of visual stimulation during the early weeks or months of life, permanent visual impairments can result (Gandelman, 1992). Thus, perceptual development relies on experience as well as on physically mature sensory equipment.

By the time individuals leave infancy, their perceptual systems are reasonably intact. Most of the changes that occur during childhood and adolescence deal with the ability to *use* the equipment that they've got. For example, as children grow older their attention span improves, and they are better able to attend selectively to pertinent information. Memory improves throughout childhood, partly because kids learn strategies for organizing and maintaining information in memory. Moreover, as we'll see in Chapters 5 and 8, the way individuals perceive and remember the world depends on the knowledge they have about the way the world works. Individuals use their general knowledge about people and events to help them interpret ambiguous stimuli and to remember things that happen in their lives. Perception and memory are influenced by the knowledge gained from experience, which is one of the reasons why perceptual development is really a lifelong process.

In the visual cliff apparatus, there is a plate of glass that covers the apparent drop-off or "cliff." Beginning at roughly 6 months of age, babies are reluctant to cross over to reach a beckoning parent.

Cognitive Development: Piaget and the Development of Thought

The intimate connection between what an individual sees and what he or she knows explains why it's difficult for researchers to get a good grasp on how infants

Jean Piaget is shown here interacting with a group of children in a classroom.

truly perceive the world. It might be possible for a researcher to demonstrate that a newborn distinguishes between a purring kitten and a block of wood, but does this mean that the infant is really seeing what we think of as a *cat*? Babies might coo and smile to the rhythmic sound of music on the radio, but is their internal experience anything close to that of an adult? These may be more philosophical questions than scientific ones, but it's important to recognize that we can't easily talk about a baby's ability to perceive or remember without knowing something about how a baby thinks.

Much of what we know about how thought processes develop during childhood comes from the collective works of a Swiss scholar named Jean Piaget (1929, 1952, 1970). It was Piaget who first convinced psychologists that children think quite differently than adults. Children are not "little adults," he argued, who simply lack knowledge and experience; instead, they view the world in a unique and idiosyncratic way. Piaget believed that everyone is born with a natural tendency to organize the world meaningfully. People construct mental models of the world—called **schemata**—and use these schemata to guide and interpret their experiences. But these schemata are not very adultlike early in development—in fact, they tend not to reflect the true world accurately—so much of early intellectual development is spent changing and fine-tuning one's developing worldviews. One of Piaget's main contributions was to demonstrate that children's reasoning errors can provide a window into how the schema construction process is proceeding.

For example, consider the two tilted cups shown here. If young children are asked to draw a line indicating how the water level in the cup might look, they tend to draw a line that is parallel to the top and bottom of the cup, as shown in the cup on the left, rather than parallel to the ground, as shown in the cup on the right. This kind of "error" is important, Piaget argued, because children can't have learned such a thing directly from experience (water never tilts that way in real life). Instead, the error reflects a fundamental misconception of how the world is structured. Young children simply have an internal view, or model, of the world that is inaccurate.

As their brains and bodies mature, children are able to use experience to build more sophisticated and correct mental models of the world. Piaget suggested that

Some people might have trouble assimilating these objects into their existing schema for objects in a room.

this process of cognitive development is guided by two adaptive psychological processes: *assimilation* and *accommodation.* **Assimilation** is the process through which people fit—or assimilate—new experiences into their existing schemata. For example, suppose a small child who has been raised in a household full of cats mistakenly concludes that the neighbor's new rabbit is simply a new kind of "kitty." The new experience—the rabbit—has been assimilated into the child's existing view of the world—small furry things are *cats.* The second function, **accommodation,** is the process through which people change or modify existing schemata to accommodate new experiences when they occur. When the child learns that the new "kitty" hops rather than walks and seems reluctant to purr, he or she will need to modify and revise the existing concept of small furry things; the child is forced to change the existing scheme to "accommodate" the new information. Notice that the child plays an active role in constructing schemata by interacting directly with the world (Piaget, 1929).

Piaget believed that children develop an adult worldview by proceeding systematically through a series of four stages or developmental periods: *sensorimotor, preoperational, concrete operational,* and *formal operational* (see Table 4.1). Each of these periods is tied roughly to a particular age range—for example, the preoperational period usually lasts from age 2 to about age 7—but individual differences may occur in how quickly children progress from one period to the next. Although the timing may vary from child to child, Piaget believed that the *order* in which individuals progress through the stages is invariant—it remains the same for everyone. Let's consider these cognitive developmental periods in more detail.

The Sensorimotor Period. From birth to about age 2, schemata about the world revolve primarily around the infant's sensory and motor abilities (hence the name **sensorimotor period**). Babies initially interact with the world through a collection of "survival reflexes." For example, they'll start sucking when an object is placed in their mouth (called the *sucking reflex*), and they'll automatically turn their head in the direction of a touch or brush on the cheek (called the *rooting reflex*). In an important sense, this means that when an object comes into a newborn's view, that object is "interpreted" in terms of how it can be sucked. Of course, this behavior is far different from an adult's but it's *adaptive* for a newborn. Such reflexes increase the likelihood that adequate nourishment will follow, and attaining adequate nourishment is a significant problem that the newborn needs to solve.

TABLE 4.1
Piaget's Stages of Cognitive Development

Age Range	Stage	Characteristics
Birth to 2 years	Sensorimotor period	Schemata revolve around sensory and motor abilities; object permanence develops
2 to 6 years	Preoperational period	Symbolic thought begins; child fails to understand mental operations such as conservation
7 to 11 years	Concrete operational period	Child acquires ability to perform mental operations such as conservation, but operations are tied to concrete objects in the world
11 to adulthood	Formal operational period	Mastery is gained over abstract thinking and strategic problem solving

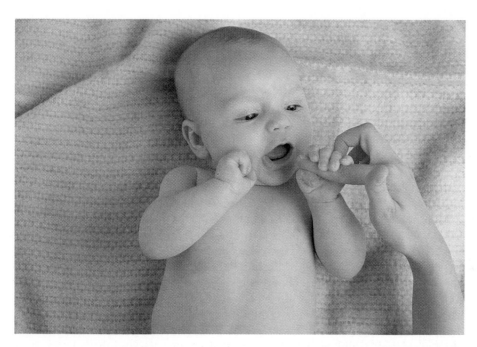

The rooting reflex is adaptive because it helps guarantee that the newborn will receive needed sustenance.

As infants develop intellectually over the first year, they begin to use their maturing motor skills to help them understand how they can voluntarily interact with the world. Babies start to vocalize to gain attention; they learn that they can kick their legs to make sounds; they acquire the ability to reach with their arms to touch or grasp objects. The initial stirrings of symbolic thought also begin during the sensorimotor period. The infant gradually develops the ability to represent things internally in terms of mental images or symbols. Early in the first year, for example, babies lack **object permanence,** which means that they fail to recognize that objects exist when they're no longer in sight. The adjacent photos illustrate how psychologists have measured object permanence. Notice that the baby loses interest when the toy is covered, suggesting that the baby is only capable of thinking about objects that are directly in view. Babies at this point are unable to represent objects symbolically—out of sight equals out of mind. But by the end of the first year, Piaget argued, the child has a different reaction to the disappearance of a favored toy; as object permanence develops, the child will begin to search actively for the lost toy.

According to Piaget, until object permanence develops, babies fail to understand that objects still exist when they're no longer in view. Notice how this boy loses interest when he can no longer see his favorite toy.

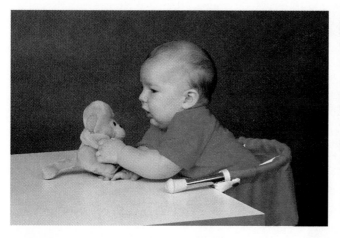

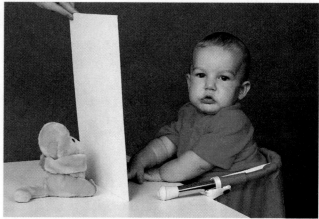

The Preoperational Period. From ages 2 through 7, the child's schemata continue to grow in sophistication. Children in the **preoperational period** no longer have problems thinking about absent objects, and they can use one sort of object to stand for another. A 4-year-old, for example, can effortlessly use a stick to represent a soaring airplane, or a cardboard box to stand for a stove. The child realizes that these are not the real objects, but he or she can imagine them to be real for the purposes of play. But as Piaget demonstrated in a number of clever ways, the child still thinks about the world quite differently than an adult. As we'll see momentarily, the child lacks the ability to perform certain basic mental *operations*—hence Piaget used the term *preoperational* to describe a child's mental abilities during this period.

Something that children at the preoperational stage often fail to understand is the principle of **conservation.** To understand conservation, one needs to be able to recognize that the physical properties of an object can remain the same despite superficial changes in its appearance (see Figure 4.10). If 4- or 5-year-old children are shown two playdough balls of exactly the same size and we ask them which object contains more playdough, most of the children will say that the two balls contain the same amount. But if one of the balls is then rolled into a long sausage-like shape, the children are now likely to think that the two quantities of playdough are no longer the same, saying that either the sausage or the ball now has more playdough. Children at this age simply do not understand that a basic property of an object, in this case its mass, doesn't change as the object changes its shape.

Typically, preoperational children will fail to conserve a basic quantity even if they directly *observe* the change in appearance taking place. Suppose that we ask 5-year-old Sam to pour a cup of water into each of two identical glasses. Sam performs the task and accepts that the two glasses now contain the same amount of water. We then instruct him to pour the water from one of the glasses into another glass that is tall and thin. Do the glasses now contain the same amount of water? "No," Sam explains, "now the tall one has more water." Sam is not showing any evidence of conservation—he does not yet recognize that how the water looks in the glass has no effect on its volume.

The reason children in the preoperational period make these kinds of errors, Piaget argued, is that they still lack the capacity to think in truly adultlike ways. For example, preoperational children suffer from *centration*—they tend to focus their attention on one particular aspect of a situation and to ignore other aspects. Sam is convinced that the tall glass has more water because he cannot simultane-

Can you think of any ways that a child's failure to show conservation might actually improve his or her chances of survival?

FIGURE 4.10
Examples of Conservation Problems. Understanding conservation means recognizing that the physical properties of objects remain the same even though the objects may superficially change their appearance. Preoperational children often fail conservation problems—they fail to detect, for example, that the objects to the right of the arrows still retain the same volume or number.

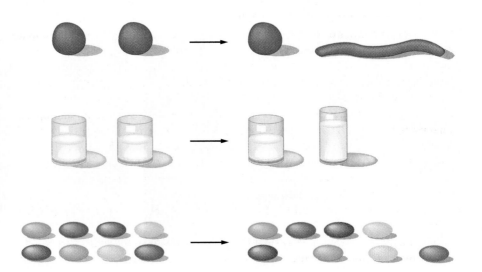

ously consider both the height and width of the glass; he focuses only on the height and therefore is convinced that the taller glass must contain more water. In addition, children at this age have a tough time understanding *reversibility*—they don't understand that one kind of operation can produce change and that another kind of operation can undo that change. For example, Sam is unlikely to consider what will happen if the water from the tall glass is poured back into the original glass. The capacity to understand that operations are reversible doesn't develop until the next stage.

The Concrete Operational Period. Between the ages of 7 and about 11, children enter the **concrete operational period** and gain the capacity for true mental *operations.* By mental operations, Piaget meant the ability to perform mental actions on objects—to verbalize, visualize, and mentally manipulate objects. A child of 8 can consider the consequences of rolling a long strip of playdough into a ball before the action is actually performed. The result is that children in the concrete operational period have fewer difficulties with conservation problems because they are capable of reversing operations on objects—they can mentally consider the effects of both doing and undoing an action.

Concrete operational children also show the initial stirrings of logical thought, which means that they can now mentally order and compare objects and can perform more sophisticated classifications. These children can do simple math problems and solve problems that require elementary reasoning. Consider a problem such as the following: Martin is faster than Jose; Jose is faster than Conrad. Is Martin faster or slower than Conrad? Children of 9 or 10 have little trouble with this problem because they can keep track of ordered relations in their heads. Younger preoperational children will probably insist on actually seeing Martin and Conrad race—they cannot easily solve the problem in their heads.

Although concrete operational children possess a growing array of mental operations, Piaget believed that they are still limited intellectually in an important way. The mental operations that they can perform remain *concrete,* or tied directly to actual objects in the real world. Children at this age have great difficulty with problems that do not flow directly from everyday experience. Ask an 8-year-old to solve a problem involving four-armed people and barking cats and you're likely to see a blank look on his or her face. Basically, if something can't be seen, heard, touched, tasted, or smelled, it's not going to be something that concrete operational children can easily consider in their heads. The ability to think abstractly doesn't develop until the final stage of cognitive development.

The Formal Operational Period. Piaget repeatedly stressed the idea that children tend to think differently than adults. Children's schemata, or mental models of the world, are limited because they lack the proper amounts of biological maturation and experience. These limitations in turn lead to errors in reasoning or judgment, although the child's view of the world can be adaptive for solving the particular problems that children face (as when a baby's viewing an object in terms of how it can be sucked increases the likelihood of obtaining nourishment). But by the time children reach their teenage years, most will be in the **formal operational period,** during which their thought processes become increasingly more like those of an adult. Neither teenagers nor adults have problems thinking about imaginary or artificial concepts; they can consider hypothetical outcomes, or make logical deductions about places they've never visited or that might not even exist. Teenagers as well as adults can develop systematic strategies for solving problems—such as using trial and error—that are beyond the capability of most preteens.

The formal operational period is the stage in which individuals start to gain mastery over *abstract* thinking. Ask a concrete operational child about the mean-

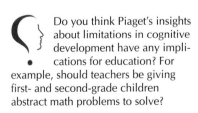

Do you think Piaget's insights about limitations in cognitive development have any implications for education? For example, should teachers be giving first- and second-grade children abstract math problems to solve?

The formal operational period, which most people reach by their teenage years, is the period in which mastery over abstract thinking is gained.

ing of education, and you'll be likely to hear about teachers and grades. But the formal operational adolescent is able to answer the question in a general and abstract way, perhaps describing education as a system organized by parents and the government to foster the acquisition of useful knowledge in young people. Piaget believed that the transition from concrete operational thinking to formal operational thinking probably occurs gradually, over several years, and may not be achieved by everyone (Piaget, 1970). But once it is reached, the adolescent is no longer tied to concrete real-world constructs and can invent and experiment with the possible rather than just with the here and now.

Challenging Piaget's Theory. As we discussed earlier, Piaget's contributions to the understanding of cognitive development have been substantial. He successfully convinced the psychological community that children have unique internal schemata, and he provided convincing demonstrations that those schemata, once formed, tend to change systematically over time. But not all of Piaget's ideas have withstood the rigors of experimental scrutiny. Many specifics of his theory are now commonly challenged, primarily his assumptions about what children really know and when they know it.

It now seems clear that Piaget was simply wrong in some of his conclusions about the young child's mental capabilities. Children and young infants are considerably more sophisticated in their "models of the world" than Piaget believed (Flavel et al., 1993; Kuhn, 1992; Spelke, 1991). For example, Piaget was convinced that object permanence doesn't develop until late in the child's first year. Although it's true that children will not search for a hidden toy in the first few months of life, more sensitive tests have revealed that even 1- to 4-month-old infants are capable of recognizing that vanished objects still exist. In research by child psychologist T. G. R. Bower (1982), for example, very young infants watched as a screen was moved in front of a toy, blocking it from view (see Figure 4.11). Moments later, when the screen was removed, the infants acted surprised if the toy was no longer there (it had been secretly removed by the experimenter). If the object no longer existed for the infant once it had been removed from view, he or she should not have been surprised by its sudden absence (see also Baillargeon, 1994). Other researchers have demonstrated that small infants can show symbolic thought—they understand, for instance, that objects move along continuous paths

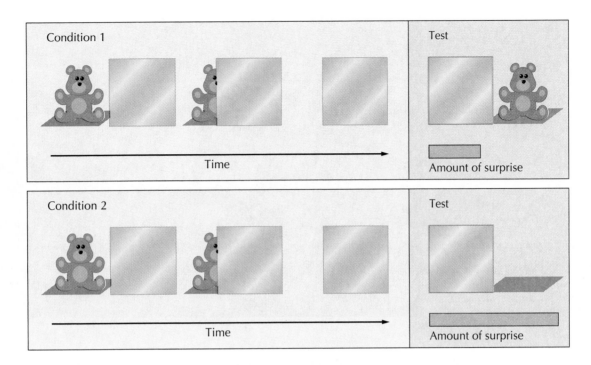

FIGURE 4.11
Reevaluating Object Permanence.
In this experiment by T. G. R. Bower, young infants watched as a screen was moved in front of a toy, blocking it from view. Moments later, the screen was removed and the baby's level of "surprise," defined as a change in heart rate, was measured. In one condition, the toy appeared behind the screen; in a second condition, the toy had vanished. Despite their young age, the babies showed more surprise when the toy was absent, suggesting that object permanence may develop earlier than Piaget suspected.

and do not jump around—and they gain this understanding at points in development far earlier than Piaget imagined (see Mandler, 1992; Spelke et al., 1992).

Piaget has also been criticized for his adherence to the notion of sharp *stages*, or periods of development (Flavel et al., 1993). Piaget recognized that not all children develop cognitively at the same rate, but he remained convinced that a child's thought processes are best described as undergoing sharp transitions from one qualitative stage to the next. Most modern developmental psychologists believe that cognitive development is better viewed as a process of continual change and adaptation. If we adopted a stage view, as Piaget did, we should expect that once the child undergoes a stage transition—say, from the preoperational stage to the concrete operational stage—the child should relatively quickly show the capacity to perform a variety of new tasks. But this is not usually the case. Children's thought processes do not seem to undergo rapid transitions; in fact, they often change slowly over long periods of time (Flavel, 1971). For example, it is not uncommon to find a 5-year-old who understands conservation of number but has no idea about conservation of mass or volume. So, a given child might show mental schemata that are characteristic of more than one stage.

Piaget was also rather fuzzy about the mechanisms that produce cognitive change. His demonstrations that infants, toddlers, and school-age children think in fundamentally different ways were brilliant, but he never clearly accounted for the psychological processes that produce those changes (Siegler, 1994). He also tended to ignore the importance of social context in explaining individual differences in cognitive ability. Cross-cultural research has demonstrated that children across the world develop cognitively in similar ways, but significant cultural differences occur in the rate of development (Matsumoto, 1994). For example, children raised in nomadic societies, which move frequently from place to place, seem to acquire spatial skills (the ability to orient themselves in their environment) earlier and better than children raised in single, fixed locales. Schooling may also be a factor: Ample cross-cultural evidence indicates that people who never attend school may have a difficult time reaching the formal operational stage of thinking, at least as measured through the use of traditional Piagetian tasks (Cole, 1992; Segall et al., 1990).

Children who are raised in nomadic societies, which move frequently from place to place, may be able to orient themselves in an environment faster and more efficiently than children raised in fixed locales.

The idea that we cannot fully understand the development of mental processes without considering social and cultural influences was actually pushed hard by a Russian psychologist, Lev Vygotsky, around the same time that Piaget was developing and fine-tuning his theoretical ideas. Vygotsky died in 1934, after only a decade of work in psychology, but his ideas continue to exert a powerful influence on modern developmental psychologists (Wertsch & Tulviste, 1992). Vygotsky argued that cognitive abilities emerge *directly* out of individuals' social interactions with others. He proposed, for example, that inner speech, which people use to think and plan activities, is simply a natural extension of the outer speech that people use to communicate with others. Vygotsky was convinced that intellectual development is tied to social interaction—it grows out of each person's attempts to master social situations. This means that we cannot understand development by considering the individual alone—we must always consider the individual in his or her social context (Vygotsky, 1978).

Beyond Formal Operational Thought. Another active area of controversy that surrounds Piaget's theory concerns the issue of adult cognitive development. Does intellectual development really end with the acquisition of formal operational thinking at some point during adolescence, as claimed by Piaget? A number of researchers believe that mastery over abstract thought, which is the hallmark of the formal operational period, is only one part of a much more extensive process of adult cognitive development (Cavanaugh, 1993; Commons et al., 1989; Riegel, 1976). There are probably fundamental differences between adolescent and adult thought processes that cannot be explained without the introduction of new, *postformal* stages of cognitive development.

According to Vygotsky, cognitive abilities arise directly out of the social and verbal interactions that children have with other people, including their friends and relatives.

Currently, there is no general consensus about exactly what these postformal kinds of thought represent. One popular idea is that postformal cognitive development is characterized by *relativistic thinking*. Adults tend to think about "truth" in a much more relative way than teenagers do; adults recognize, for instance, that the "correct" answer to a moral dilemma might vary from one situation to the next. Adults are also more tolerant of ambiguity in their thinking than teenagers are (although too much ambiguity in thought is obviously a problem). Adolescent thinking is typically rigid and absolute in the sense that teenagers tend to rely on fixed rules of right and wrong and show little intellectual flexibility (Labouvie-Vief, Hakim-Larson, & Hobart, 1987; Perry, 1970).

Other researchers have argued that adolescents are also less capable of thinking about *systems* of ideas. Teenagers who have reached the formal operational stage might be able to deal with abstract ideas, but they will have trouble dealing with higher-order systems of ideas of the type found in a scientific theory (Richards & Commons, 1990). Systematic comparisons among ideas, as in the analysis of the similarities and differences among theories, requires postformal thought processes. Ironically, many modern developmental psychologists would argue that Piaget himself must have been operating at a level of cognitive development beyond the formal operational stage when he developed his own theory.

Moral Development: Learning Right from Wrong

Developing intellectually means more than just learning to think logically and form correct internal "models of the world." As children mature intellectually, they also need to develop *character*. They need to acquire a sense of **morality,** which provides them with a way to distinguish among appropriate and inappropriate thoughts and actions. Piaget had strong opinions on this topic, arguing that the sense of morality is closely tied to one's stage of cognitive development and to one's social experiences with peers. For example, from Piaget's perspective children in the concrete operational stage would not be expected to show sophisticated moral reasoning skills, because morality is basically an abstract concept—something that cannot be handled until the formal operational stage of development. Partly for this reason, most of the research on moral development has tended to be conducted on adolescents and adults.

Kohlberg's Stage Theory. The most influential theory of moral development over the past several decades has been the stage theory proposed by Lawrence Kohlberg. Strongly influenced by the writings of Piaget, Kohlberg framed his theory around the idea that individuals progress through an orderly series of stages of moral development (Kohlberg, 1963, 1986). His investigative technique was to give people of various ages a hypothetical moral "dilemma" and use their "solutions" to identify their current state of moral development. Let's consider an example, based on Kohlberg (1969).

A woman is stricken with a rare and deadly form of cancer. There is a drug that can save her, a form of radium that was recently discovered by a druggist in the town. But the druggist is charging $2000 for the medicine, ten times what the drug cost him to make. The sick woman's husband, Heinz, tries desperately to raise the money but can raise only half of the needed amount. He pleads with the druggist to sell him the drug at a reduced cost, or at least to allow him to pay for the drug over time, but the druggist refuses. "No," the druggist says, "I discovered the drug and I'm going to make money from it." Frantic to save his wife, Heinz considers breaking into the druggist's office to steal the drug. What do you think? Should the husband steal the drug? Why or why not?

You probably have your own answer to this dilemma. But your "Yes, he should steal the drug" or "No, that would be wrong" answer is not the main interest to

Children need to develop a sense of morality, which helps them tell the difference between appropriate and inappropriate actions.

FIGURE 4.12
Kohlberg's Stages of Moral Development. Psychologist Lawrence Kohlberg proposed that individuals move through three main levels of moral development.

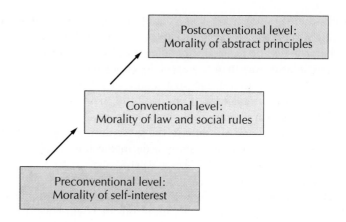

psychologists. Rather, it is the reasoning behind your answer, the kind of intellectual justification that you give for it, that fuels the interest of the psychologist. Kohlberg believed that people can be classified into stages of moral development based on the quality of their reasoning about such moral problems. Although Kohlberg's theory actually proposes as many as six stages of moral development, we'll just focus on his three main levels: the *preconventional*, the *conventional*, and the *postconventional* (see Figure 4.12).

At the lowest level of moral development—the **preconventional level**—decisions about right and wrong are made primarily in terms of external consequences. Young children will typically interpret the "morality" of a behavior in terms of its immediate individual consequences—that is, whether the act will lead directly to a reward or to a punishment: "Heinz shouldn't steal the drug because he might get caught and punished" or "Heinz should steal the drug because people will get mad at him if his wife dies." Notice that the rationale is based on the immediate consequences of the action rather than on some abstract moral principle.

Once the **conventional level** of moral reasoning is reached, individuals begin to justify their actions based on internalized rules. Now an action is "right" or "wrong" because it maintains or disrupts the *social order*. Someone reaching this level might argue that Heinz shouldn't steal the drug because stealing is against the law, or that Heinz should steal the drug because husbands have an obligation to protect their wives. Notice here that the moral reasoning has moved away from immediate individual consequences to societal consequences. Moral behavior is that which conforms to the rules and conventions of society. In general, individuals at the conventional level of moral reasoning tend to consider the appropriateness of their actions from the perspective of the resident authority figures in the culture.

At the final level of moral development, the **postconventional level,** the morality of actions is based on abstract principles that may even conflict with accepted standards. The individual adopts a moral standard not to seek approval from others or an authority figure but to follow some universal ethical principle. "An individual human life is more important than society's dictum against stealing," someone at this level might argue. In this case, moral actions are driven by personal codes of ethics that are general and abstract and that may not agree with societal norms.

Evaluating Kohlberg's Theory. The idea that individuals progress through periods of moral development, from an early focus on immediate individual consequences toward a final principled code of ethics, remains popular among many developmental psychologists (see Damon & Hart, 1992). A number of observational studies have confirmed aspects of Kohlberg's views. For example, people do seem to move through the various types of moral reasoning in the sequence that Kohlberg suggested (Walker, 1989). Furthermore, the link that both Piaget and

Based on what you've learned about moral development, what advice would you give parents who are trying to teach their children about right and wrong?

Kohlberg made between moral reasoning and level of cognitive development has clear merit. But Kolhberg's critics argue that his views lack generality because he ties the concept of morality too closely to an abstract code of *justice*—that is, to the idea that moral acts are those that ensure fairness to the individual (Damon & Hart, 1992).

For example, suppose that your sense of morality is not based exclusively on "fairness" but rather on concern for the feelings of others. You might believe that the appropriate action is always one that doesn't hurt anyone and that takes into account the happiness of the affected individual. Under these conditions, as analyzed by Kohlberg, your moral code is likely to lack abstract generality. Your behavior will appear to be driven more by an individual situation than by a consistent code of justice. Psychologist Carol Gilligan (1982) has argued that women in our culture often adopt such a view (a moral code based on "caring"), whereas men tend to make moral decisions based on an abstract sense of justice. According to Kohlberg's theory, however, this means that women will tend to be classified at a lower level of moral development than men. Gilligan sees this as an unfair and unjustified gender bias.

It now appears that Gilligan may have overstated the case for sex differences in moral reasoning. Men and women often think in much the same way about the types of moral dilemmas studied by Kohlberg (Walker, 1989). At the same time, other evidence indicates that important cross-cultural differences occur in moral thinking that are not captured well by Kohlberg's classification system. For example, studies of moral decision making in India reveal striking differences from those typically found in Western cultures. Richard Shweder and his colleagues (1990) found that both Hindu children and adults are likely to find it morally acceptable for a husband to beat a disobedient wife—in fact, keeping disobedient family members in line is considered to be the moral obligation of the head of the family. In the United States, such actions would be widely condemned. Western cultures also tend to place more value on individualism and to stress individual goals more than Eastern cultures, where the emphasis is on collective goals. These kinds of cultural values and teachings will need to be factored into any complete theory of moral development.

Developing Socially and Personally

Human beings do not develop in isolation. Humans are social animals, and their social and emotional relationships critically affect how they act and view themselves. For infants, relationships with caregivers—usually their parents—guarantee them adequate nourishment and a safe and secure environment. For children, the social task is to become part of a social group and thereby learn what it means to get along with peers and to follow the rules and norms of society. For adults, whose social bonds become increasingly intimate, the task is to learn to accept responsibility for the care and support of others. As with most aspects of development that we've considered, social and personal development is a continuous process that is shaped by innate biological forces as well as by learned experiences.

Attachment: Forming Bonds with Others

Think again about the problems faced by the newborn infant: limited motor skills, somewhat fuzzy vision, yet a powerful sustained need for food, water, and warmth. As we've noted, to gain the sustenance needed for survival, as well as protection from danger, the newborn relies on interactions with others—usually the mother—to stay alive. The newborn forms what psychologists call **attachments,** which are strong emotional ties to one or more intimate companions. The need

When a mother nurses her newborn child, she is providing more than just the food needed for survival. Her physical "contact comfort" helps to ensure that the attachment bond she forms with her child will be a secure one.

If forced to choose between two surrogate mothers, baby monkeys prefer a soft and cuddly "cloth" mother to a "wire" mother, even when it is the wire mother that provides the food.

for early attachments is so critical that many researchers believe that innate, biologically driven behavioral systems may be involved in their formation (Bowlby, 1969, 1988).

According to the influential child psychiatrist John Bowlby, both caregiver and infant are preprogrammed from birth to respond to certain environmental signals with attachment behavior. The newborn typically cries, coos, and smiles, and these behaviors lead naturally to attention and responsive support from the caregiver. It's no accident that adults like to hear babies coo, or watch them smile—these preferences may be built directly into the genetic code (Bowlby, 1969; Sigelman & Shaffer, 1995). At the same time, the baby arrives into the world with a genetic predisposition to respond to care and particularly comfort from the caregiver. Notice that both the infant and the caregiver are active participants in a reciprocal relationship—the attachment is formed because both parties are prepared to respond with bonding to the right kind of environmental events. The bond usually is formed initially between baby and mother because it is the mother who provides most of the early care (Lamb, Ketterlinus, & Fracasso, 1992).

Determinants of Attachment. The idea that humans are predisposed genetically to form strong emotional attachments makes sense from an adaptive standpoint because it helps ensure survival. But what determines the strength or quality of the attachment? Differences clearly exist in the quality of the bond that forms between infant and caregiver—some infants are securely attached to their caregivers, others are not. Research with animal subjects suggests that what may matter most is the amount of actual *contact comfort*—the degree of warm physical contact—that the caregiver provides.

In some classic research on early attachment, psychologist Harry Harlow noticed that newborn rhesus monkeys that had been separated from their mothers at birth tended to become attached to soft cuddly things, such as baby blankets, that were left in their cages. Removal of a blanket for laundering produced agitation in an otherwise isolated animal, who seemed to cling to the soft and cuddly blanket for support. Intrigued, Harlow began a series of experiments in which he isolated newborn monkeys and raised them in cages with artificial caregiver

Children housed in a Romanian hospital dubbed "the children's Auschwitz."

surrogates (Harlow & Zimmerman, 1959). In one experimental condition, baby monkeys were raised with two artificial "mothers" in the cage: one consisting simply of wire mesh fitted with an artificial nipple that delivered food, the other a nippleless "cloth" mother made of the same wire mesh but wrapped in a soft terrycloth and a padding of foam rubber.

The idea behind the experiment was to see which of the two surrogate mothers the monkeys preferred. If early attachments are formed primarily to caregivers who provide nourishment—that is, infants love the one who feeds them—we would expect the monkeys to prefer and cling to the wire mother, since it provides the food. But in the vast majority of cases, the monkeys actually preferred the cloth mother. If startled in some way, perhaps by the introduction of a foreign object into the cage, the monkeys ran immediately to the cloth mother, hung on tight, and showed no interest in the wire mother that provided the food. Harlow and his colleagues concluded that *contact comfort*—the warmth and softness provided by the terrycloth—was the primary motivator of attachment (Harlow, Harlow, & Meyer, 1971).

For obvious reasons, similar experiments have never been conducted with human babies. But we have every reason to believe that human infants are like rhesus infants in their desire and need for contact comfort. Many studies have examined how children fare in institutional settings that provide relatively low levels of contact comfort (Hodges & Tizard, 1989; Provence & Lipton, 1962; Spitz, 1945). Children reared in orphanages with poor infant-to-caregiver ratios (e.g., one caregiver for every 10–20 infants), on average show many more developmental problems than children reared in less deprived environments (Shaffer, 1993). In the country of Romania, for example, many orphaned children in recent years have been literally "warehoused with minimal food, clothing, heat, or caregivers" (Kaler & Freeman, 1994). When the social and intellectual functioning of these orphans is compared with that of children who have not been institutionalized, the orphans show significant and sometimes severe deficits (Kaler & Freeman, 1994).

Clearly, the emotional and physical responsiveness of parents to their infants is an important predictor of the quality of the parent-child attachment (Ainsworth et al., 1978; Cox et al., 1992). The quality of the attachment, in turn, can either enhance or hinder the normal developmental process. Securely attached infants tend to have warm and responsive caregivers who react promptly to the infant's needs. Insecurely attached infants tend to have unresponsive or avoidant caregivers. The baby's temperament can be a contributing factor—difficult or fussy babies tend to elicit less comforting and less responsive reactions, and the quality of the attachment between parent and child suffers as a result (Thomas & Chess, 1977).

Types of Attachment. To gain systematic insight into the various patterns and types of parent-child bonding, psychologists often use a technique called the **strange situation test.** This test can be used to classify 10- to 24-month-old children into three main attachment groups (e.g., Ainsworth & Wittig, 1969; Ainsworth et al., 1978). The idea behind the test is to subject the child gradually to a stressful situation and note how his or her behavior toward the parent changes. After arrival in the lab, the parent and child are ushered into a waiting room filled with toys; the child is encouraged to play with the toys. Various levels of infant "stress" are then introduced. A stranger might enter the room, or the parent might be asked to step out for a few moments leaving the child alone. Of main interest to the psychologist are several dependent measures of stress or discomfort: Initially, how willing is the child to move away from the parent and play with the toys? How much crying or distress does the child show when the parent leaves the room? How does the child react to the parent when the parent comes back into the room—does the child greet and cling to the parent, or does he or she move away?

Most infants—approximately 70%—react to the strange situation test with what psychologist Mary Ainsworth calls *secure attachment.* With the parent present, even if the situation is new and strange, these children play happily and are likely to explore the room looking for interesting toys or magazines to shred. But as the level of stress increases, they become increasingly uneasy and clingy. If the mother leaves the room, the child will probably start to cry but will calm down rapidly if the mother returns.

About 10% of children show a pattern called *resistant attachment;* these children react to stress in an ambiguous way, which may indicate a lack of trust for the parent. Resistant children will act wary in a strange situation, refusing to leave their mother's side and explore the room, and they do not react well to the sudden appearance of strangers. If the mother leaves the room, they cry, yet they are unlikely to greet the mother with affection on her return. Instead, these children act ambivalent, scorning their mother by temporarily resisting her affection.

The final group of children—about 20%—show a pattern of *avoidant attachment.* These children demonstrate no strong attachment to the mother in any aspect of the strange situation test. They are not particularly bothered by the appearance of strangers in the room, nor do they show much concern when the mother leaves the room or much interest when she returns. Ainsworth discovered that the parents of these children tend, on average, to be unresponsive and impatient when it comes to the child's needs and may even actively reject the child on a regular basis (Ainsworth, 1979). Why? It's difficult to tell because the parent-child relationship depends on particular personality characteristics of the parent, the temperament of the child, and on the child-rearing practices of the culture (see the Adaptive Mind section at the end of this chapter).

Long-Term Consequences. Given that infants can be easily divided into these attachment groups by around age 1, it's reasonable to wonder about the long-term consequences. For instance, are the avoidant children doomed to a life of insecurity and failed relationships? There is evidence to suggest that children with an early *secure* attachment do indeed have some social and intellectual advantages, at least throughout middle and later childhood. For example, it's been reported that

Why do you think it's important to measure attachment behavior in a "strange" situation? How might the findings change if similar tests were done in the child's home?

How children react when they are in a strange situation provides insight into the type of attachment they've formed with their parent or caregiver.

teachers rate these children as more curious and self-directed in school (Waters, Wippman, & Sroufe, 1979). By age 10 or 11, securely attached children also tend to have more close and mature relationships with their peers than children who were classified as insecurely attached (Elicker, Englund, & Sroufe, 1992).

But early patterns of attachment are not perfect predictors of later behavior. One problem is that early attachment patterns are not necessarily stable. Sometimes a child who appears to be insecurely attached at 12 months can act quite differently in the strange situation test a few months later (Lamb et al., 1992). In addition, a child who has a particular kind of attachment to Mom may show quite a different attachment pattern to Dad. Finally, it's also important to remember that when psychologists talk about predicting later behavior based on early attachment patterns, they are referring mainly to correlational studies. As we discussed in Chapter 2, it's not possible to draw firm conclusions about causality from simple correlational analyses. The fact that later behavior can be predicted based on early attachment patterns does not mean that early bonding necessarily causes the later behavior patterns—other factors might be responsible. For instance, children who form secure attachments in infancy typically have caregivers who remain warm and responsive throughout childhood, adolescence, and adulthood. So it could be that securely attached infants tend to have successful and meaningful relationships later in life because they live most of their lives in supportive environments.

Clearly, early attachments are important. But the relationships formed *after* infancy, especially during later childhood and adolescence, also significantly affect people's social behavior. There are good reasons to believe that individuals can "make up" or counteract negative experiences during infancy or childhood. As we discussed earlier, children who are neglected early in life are more likely to suffer problems later in life; but if these children are removed from their abusive environments, their chances of having long-term adjustment problems are significantly reduced (Lamb et al., 1992). For a discussion of how attachment might be affected by leaving a child in day care, see the accompanying Inside the Problem.

Forming a Personal Identity: Erik Erikson and the Crises of Development

One of the most important aspects of social development is the formation of **personal identity**—a sense of self, of who one is as an individual and how well one stacks up against peers. Many psychologists are convinced that people use social interactions—primarily the ones with parents during childhood and with peers later in life—to help them come to grips with who they are as individuals. One of the most influential theories of how this process of identity formation proceeds is the stage theory of Erik Erikson. Erikson (1963, 1968, 1982) postulated that personal identity is shaped by a series of personal *crises* that each person must confront at a characteristic stage in development (see Figure 4.13).

Erik Erikson.

Infancy and Childhood. For the first few years of life, infants are largely at the mercy of others for their survival. We've discussed this point repeatedly, but according to Erikson, this overwhelming dependency leads infants in the first year of life to their first psychosocial crisis: *trust versus mistrust.* Psychologically and practically, infants have an important problem to solve: Are there people out there in the world who will meet my survival needs? Resolution of this crisis leads to the formation of an initial sense of either trust or mistrust, and the infant begins to develop some rudimentary knowledge about how people differ. Some people can be trusted and some cannot. It is through the quality of social interactions that the newborn resolves the crisis and learns how to deal more effectively with his or her environment.

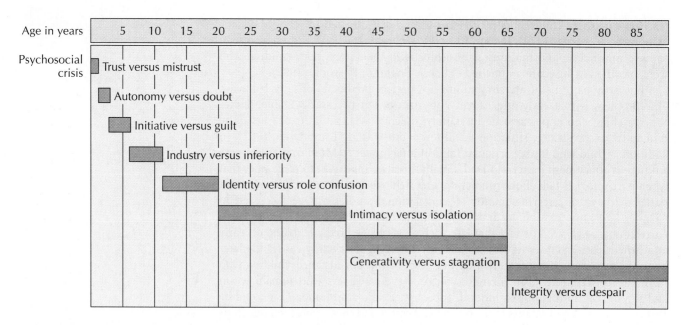

FIGURE 4.13
Erikson's Crises of Personal Development. Erik Erikson proposed that the process of forming a personal identity is shaped by a series of personal crises faced at various points in development. The age ranges are approximate.

Erik Erikson would probably argue that this young man is concerned with testing roles and with finding his true "identity."

As the child progresses through toddlerhood and on into later childhood, other fundamental conflicts need to be resolved. During the "terrible twos," the child struggles with breaking his or her dependence on parents. The crisis at this point, according to Erikson, is *autonomy versus shame or doubt:* Am I capable of independent self-control of my actions, or am I generally inadequate? Between the ages of 3 and 6, the crisis becomes one of *initiative versus guilt:* Can I plan things on my own, with my own initiative, or should I feel guilty for trying to carry out my own bold plans for action? In late childhood, beginning around age 6 and ending at around age 12, the struggle is for a basic sense of *industry versus inferiority:* Can I learn and master new skills, can I be industrious and complete required tasks, or do I lack fundamental competence?

Again, what's important in determining how these crises will be resolved is the quality of the child's interactions with parents, peers, and other significant role models. If 5-year-old Roberta's parents repeatedly scold her for taking the initiative and trying to get her own drink of milk, she may develop strong feelings of guilt for trying to become independent. According to Erikson, children with highly critical parents or teachers can acquire a self-defeating attitude toward themselves that carries over later in life. Children who resolve these crises positively learn to trust themselves and their abilities and acquire a strong positive sense of personal identity.

Adolescence and Young Adulthood. By the time individuals reach adolescence, their intellectual development has proceeded to the point where they naturally begin to consider personal qualities that are general and abstract. In particular, Erikson argued, adolescents face the fundamental crisis of *identity versus role confusion.* They become concerned with testing roles and with finding their true identity: Who am I? What kind of person do I really represent? In a very real sense, the teenager acts as a kind of personality theorist, attempting to integrate various self-perceptions about abilities and limitations into a single unified concept of self. Erikson (1968) coined the term *identity crisis* to describe this transition period, which he believed is often fraught with turmoil.

Empirical studies of how adolescents actually come to grips with the identity crisis reveal many individual differences (Offer & Schonert-Reichl, 1992; Peterson, 1988). Not all teenagers become paralyzed with identity "angst" and anxiety—

INSIDE THE PROBLEM: *Day Care*

Most parents of preschool children face a fundamental question about child care: Do I stay at home and provide full-time care for my child, or do I work outside the home and place my child in day care? In contemporary American society, *day care* often turns out to be the answer, although it is not always a choice made voluntarily by the parent. For many, day care has simply become an economic necessity. The last several decades have seen a steady rise in the number of mothers employed outside of the home. In 1960, for example, 16.5% of mothers with children under 3 worked outside of the home; by the middle 1980s, the percentage had risen to over 50%, where it remains today (Lamb & Sternberg, 1990).

What are the psychological consequences of day care? Does leaving children in the hands of nonparental caretakers, often for many hours a day, have dire consequences on their social and mental development? Fortunately, the answer turns out to be "no" for most children, and day care may even have positive effects on social and cognitive development. It's been reported that preschoolers who spend time in quality day-care centers adjust better in school—they are more sociable and popular among their classmates—than children who have received full-time care at home (Andersson, 1992). The day-care experience may also help speed up intellectual development,

Day care has simply become an economic necessity for many parents.

at least for some children. Recently, Caughy and colleagues (1994) found that day-care participation during the first three years of life was positively associated with improved reading and math skills, although the results applied only to children who lived in home environments classified as low in emotional support and intellectual stimulation.

In the mid-1980s it was widely reported that children in day care were

more likely to form insecure attachments (avoidant or resistant) than children who receive full-time home care (e.g., Belsky, 1988). More recent studies have failed to replicate these findings (Roggman et al., 1994) or have found the differences to be quite small (Clarke-Stewart, 1989). But still, psychologists acknowledge that day care can have detrimental effects under some circumstances. It's important to recognize that "day care" is a multi-faceted concept—the term can mean anything from occasional babysitting by a neighbor for a few hours a week, to care by nonparental relatives, to extended care by licensed professionals in for-profit day-care centers. Consequently, it's difficult to draw general conclusions about day care that will be of much use. Wide variations also exist in the *quality* of the service provided during day-care hours and in the quality of care that the child receives at home. Factors such as how early in life the child enters a program and whether the child attends regularly or intermittently may be important (Lamb & Sternberg, 1990). As with most environmental effects, the role that day care plays in the life of a child will depend on many factors interacting together, including the individual characteristics of the child, the parents, the home environment, and the quality and quantity of the service provided.

---

most, in fact, show no more anxiety during this transition period than they do at other points in their life. Individual differences also occur in how young people commit to a particular view of themselves (Marcia, 1966). Some adolescents choose an identity by modeling others: "I'm honest, open, and cooperative because that's the way I was brought up by my parents." Others develop a personal identity through a soul-searching evaluation of their feelings and abilities. Finally, some adolescents reject the crisis altogether, choosing instead not to commit to any particular view of themselves. The specific course or path that an individual takes depends on many factors, including his or her level of cognitive development, the quality of the parent-child relationship, and outside experiences (Compas, Hinden, & Gerhardt, 1995).

Entrance into young adulthood is marked by the crisis of *intimacy versus isolation*. Resolution of the identity crisis causes individuals to question the meaning of their relationships with others: Am I willing or able to form an intimate, committed relationship with another person? Or will my insecurities and fears about losing independence lead to a lifetime of isolation and loneliness? People who lack an integrated conception of themselves, Erikson argued, cannot commit themselves to a shared identity with someone else. Some have argued that this particular conclusion may be more applicable to men than women (Gilligan, 1982). Historically, women have been forced by societal pressures to deal with intimate commitments—raising a family and running a home—either at the same time as, or before, the process of searching for a stable personal identity. This trend may well be changing, however, because more women are giving priority to establishing a professional career prior to marriage.

Adulthood, Middle Age, and Beyond. With the establishment of career and family arrives the crisis of *generativity versus stagnation*. The focus at this point shifts from resolving intimacy to concern about children and future generations: Am I contributing successfully to the community at large? Am I doing enough to assure the survival and productivity of future generations? Failure to resolve this crisis can lead to a sense of meaninglessness in middle life and beyond—a condition Erikson calls *stagnation*.

For some people, especially men in their 40s, this point in psychosocial development is marked by soul-searching questions about personal identity reminiscent of those faced in adolescence (Gould, 1978; Levinson et al., 1978). According to psychologists such as Gould and Levinson, the so-called "midlife crisis" arises as people begin to confront their own mortality—the inevitability of death—and as they come to grips with the fact that they may never achieve their lifelong dreams and goals. There is no doubt that this can be an emotionally turbulent period, but recent evidence suggests that the midlife crisis is a relatively rare phenomenon. It gets a lot of attention in the popular press, and it's certainly consuming for those affected, but probably fewer than 5% of people in middle age undergo anything resembling a turbulent midlife crisis point (McCrae & Costa, 1990).

Is this man going through a turbulent "midlife crisis" as he begins to confront his own mortality?

The final stage in the process of psychosocial development, which occurs from late adulthood to the point of death, is the crisis of *integrity versus despair*. It is at this stage in people's lives, Erikson argued, that they strive to accept themselves and their past—both failures and successes. Older people undergo a kind of "life review" in an effort to resolve conflicts in their past and to find ultimate meaning in what they've done and accomplished. If successful in this objective search for meaning, they acquire wisdom; if unsuccessful, they wallow in despair and bitterness. An important part of the process is the preparation for death and dying, which we'll discuss in more detail later in the chapter.

Evaluating Erikson's Theory. Erikson's stage theory of psychosocial "crises" has been enormously influential in shaping how psychologists view identity development. Among its most important contributions is the recognition that personal development is a lifelong process. Individuals don't simply establish a rigid personal identity around the time they reach Piaget's formal operational stage; the way that people view themselves and their relationships changes continually throughout their lives. Erikson's theory is also noteworthy for its emphasis on the role of social and cultural interactions in shaping human psychology. Human beings do not grow up in a kind of psychological "vacuum"—the way people think and act is critically influenced by their interactions with others, and Erikson's theory fully acknowledges this fact.

Nevertheless, Erikson's theory suffers from the same kinds of problems as any stage theory. Although there may be an orderly sequence of psychosocial crises that people confront, overlap and "leakage" occur across the stages (Whitbourne et al., 1992). As we noted earlier, the search for identity is not confined to one turbulent period in adolescence—it is likely to continue throughout a lifetime. Furthermore, like Piaget, Erikson never clearly articulated *how* a person actually moves from one crisis stage to the next: What are the psychological mechanisms that allow for conflict resolution, and what determines when and how they will operate (Achenbach, 1992)? Finally, Erikson's theory of identity development, although useful as a general organizing framework, lacks sufficient scientific rigor. His concepts are vague enough to make scientific testing difficult.

> How well do you think Erikson's ideas describe the development of your own personal identity? Are you going through any fundamental "crisis" at the moment, or are you aware of having solved one in the past?

Gender-Role Development

In our discussion of Erikson's theory, we touched briefly on the role of *gender* in establishing personal identity. It's been argued that women are sometimes required to struggle with questions about intimacy and relationships before addressing the "identity crisis," as the burden of establishing a home and rearing children typically falls on their shoulders. But gender is itself a kind of identity; children gain a sense of themselves as male or female quite early in life, and this *gender identity* has a longlasting effect on how individuals behave and on how others behave toward them.

The available evidence suggests that the rudimentary foundations of gender identity are already in place by the age of 2 or 3. Children at this age recognize that they are either a boy or a girl (Thompson, 1975), and they sometimes even give stereotyped responses about gender when asked. For example, when shown a picture of an infant labeled as either a boy or a girl, 3-year-olds are more likely to identify the infant "boy" as the one who is strong, big, or hard and the infant "girl" as the one who is weak, small, and soft (Cowan & Hoffman, 1986). But children at this age have not developed sufficiently to recognize gender as a general and abstract characteristic of individuals. They might believe, for instance, that a boy can become a girl by changing hairstyle or clothing (Marcus & Overton, 1978). To understand that gender is a stable and unchanging condition requires some ability to conserve—to recognize that the qualities of objects remain the same despite superficial changes in appearance.

Children are often rewarded for acting in ways that are "gender-appropriate."

By the time children are firmly entrenched in elementary school, gender is seen as a permanent condition—"I'm a boy (or a girl) and I always will be." At this point, children tend to act in accordance with reasonably well-established **gender roles**—specific patterns of behavior that are consistent with how society dictates males and females should act. Children at this age have strong opinions about how boys and girls should behave, what occupations they should have when they grow up, and how they should look. Can you imagine the reaction that a 7-year-old boy might receive if he walked into his second-grade class wearing a dress, or with his fingernails polished a bright shade of pink?

Nature or Nurture? How do these firm ideas about gender roles develop? Are they the inevitable by-product of biological differences between male and female brains, or do they grow out of experience? We encountered this issue in Chapter 3, where we considered the evidence supporting gender-based differences in brain anatomy and functioning. Although data suggest that hormones released by the

Not all children will adopt rigid gender roles.

endocrine system early in development may account for some gender differences in behavior and thought (Kimura, 1992), psychologists are just as likely to appeal to the environment to explain gender-role development.

According to *social learning* accounts of gender-role development, children learn to act in a "masculine" or "feminine" manner because they grow up in environments that reward them for acting that way. Parents across the world quickly set up what Sigelman and Shaffer (1995) call "gender-role curriculums" to reinforce particular types of behavior from their male and female children. The socialization process begins the moment the new parents learn the answer to their question, "Is it a boy or a girl?" Parents become preoccupied with dressing Adorable Ginnie in pink bows and Active Glenn in blue. Television and movies continue the process: Children are exposed to hour after hour of stereotypical children acting in gender-appropriate ways (Hansen, 1989; Lovdal, 1989). Studies have indicated, for example, that children who watch a lot of television are more likely to prefer toys that are "gender appropriate" than children who watch little television (McGhee & Frueh, 1980).

One of the by-products of growing up under the gender-role curriculum is the establishment of **gender schemas** (Bem, 1981). A gender schema is an organized set of beliefs and perceptions held about men and women. Once established, these schemas guide and direct how individuals view others, as well as their own behavior. For example, as a male, my gender schema might direct me to judge my own behavior as well as the behavior of other men in terms of such general concepts as "strength," "aggression," and "masculinity." We encountered the concept of schemas (or schemata) earlier in the chapter when we talked about Piaget, and we'll have more to say in later chapters about schemas and the role they play in directing behavior. For the moment, you can think of schemas as little knowledge packages that people carry around inside their heads. Gender schemas are acquired through learning, they set guidelines for people's behavior, and they underlie the expectations that people hold about the appropriateness of actions.

Do you think that we, as a society, should work hard to eliminate specific gender roles? Do you think we should structure our society so that males and females are always treated the same?

Death and Dying

As we close our discussion of the developmental process, it's fitting that we turn our attention to the final stage of life: death and dying. It's common to hear people say that death is a part of living, but it's a part of living that most people would choose to avoid. It's the ethereal part of death that troubles people the most—the unpredictability, the uncertainty of the process, the failure to understand what the end will be like. There are many psychological aspects to death, and to the dying process, including how people come to grips with their own mortality, as well as how they grieve and accept the loss of others. One of the most influential approaches to the dying process is the stage theory of Elisabeth Kübler-Ross (1969, 1974).

Kübler-Ross proposed that people progress through five distinct psychological stages as they face death. She based her theory on a set of extensive interviews conducted with hundreds of terminally ill patients. Her fundamental insight was that people appear to

The shape and form of the final dying "trajectory" will depend on the particular illness, as well as on the personality of the individual.

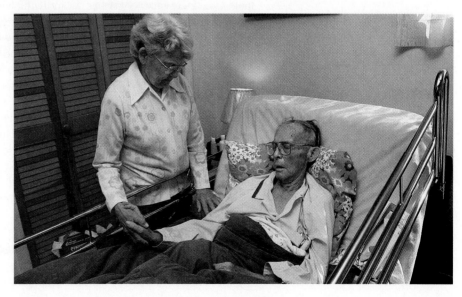

react to their own impending death in a characteristic sequence: (1) *denial*—"There must be some terrible mistake"; (2) *anger*—"Why is this happening to me?"; (3) *bargaining*—"What can I do to stop this terrible thing?"; (4) *depression*—"Blot out the sun because all is lost"; and (5) *acceptance*—"I am ready to die." As a stage theorist, Kübler-Ross essentially implied that people move through each of these five stages, from denial to acceptance, as a normal part of their emotional acceptance of death.

Kübler-Ross's views on the dying process have been highly influential, both in psychological and medical circles, in part because she was one of the first people to treat the topic of dying thoroughly and systematically. She sensitized legions of physicians to the idea that denial, anger, and depression are normal reactions to dying and that they should be treated with respect rather than dismissed out of hand. But currently, most developmental psychologists reject the idea that people progress through a fixed set of orderly stages in the way Kübler-Ross described. There are simply too many individual differences to support the theory. Not all dying people move through distinct emotional stages, and, even if they do, the stages do not seem to follow any particular set order. Stages might be skipped, might be experienced out of order, or might alternate, with the person being angry one day and accepting the next. In sum, there is no firm evidence to support a stage approach to the process of dying.

Many psychologists find it more appropriate to talk about *dying trajectories*. A dying trajectory is simply the psychological path that people travel as they face their impending death. Different people show different trajectories, and the shape and form of the path depends on the particular illness as well as on the personality of the patient (Bortz, 1990; Glaser & Strauss, 1968). Trajectories are preferred to stages because stages imply that all people react to impending death in fixed and characteristic ways. But there is no "right" or "wrong" way to deal with dying—some people may react with anger and denial, others with calm acceptance. The best that witnesses to the dying process can do is offer support and allow the individual to follow his or her own unique path.

▶ SOLVING THE PROBLEMS: A SUMMARY

As humans move from infancy through childhood and on to adulthood, they experience fundamental changes in physical, intellectual, and social functioning. For the most part, these developmental changes can be viewed as *adaptive* reactions to the facts that environments change as individuals grow and that people need to learn from experience. It's adaptive that humans are born with a genetic blueprint flexible enough to allow them to change how they think and behave in the most appropriate way. Humans are not born as biological machines, predestined to develop according to a fixed and inflexible plan. Instead, they are better viewed as individuals born with genetic potential that is realized, or not, based on experiences with the environment.

In many ways, this chapter on human development acts as a *précis*—or concise summary—of the topics that we'll encounter in the rest of the book. Understanding human development requires that we take into account all aspects of the psychology of the individual—how people change physically; learn to perceive, think, and remember; and develop as social animals. Thus, you can think about the "adaptive problems" in this chapter as opening acts for the remaining chapters in the book.

▶ **DEVELOPING PHYSICALLY** Individuals begin life as a fertilized egg, or zygote, which contains genetic material packed into chromosomes received from the mother and father. Prenatal development—which is divided into the germinal, embryonic, and fetal stages—takes place between conception and birth. The body develops rapidly during this time and is especially susceptible to both positive and negative influences from the environment. Infancy and childhood are marked by rapid growth in height and weight and by a further maturing of the nervous system. One of the by-products of nerve cell maturation is motor development. The major milestones in motor development—crawling, standing alone, walking—occur at similar times for most individuals, in part because of the systematic manner in which the nervous system develops.

As people move through adolescence and into early adulthood, their physical systems continue to change. Puberty is the developmental period in which individuals mature sexually, and it's marked by dramatic changes in physical appearance driven primarily by the release of gender-specific hormones. Once people reach their twenties, their bodies become physically mature, and most begin a gradual across-the-board decline in physical ability. Some declines occur in mental ability over time, especially in old age, although significant losses in mental functioning or mental health are still the exception rather than the rule. There is evidence to suggest that losses in the number of brain neurons may be counteracted by increases in the complexity of the remaining nerve cells. In general, there are individual differences in how the aging process proceeds; both the positive and negative consequences of aging are affected by one's genetic blueprint as well as by lifestyle choices (for instance, how much one exercises).

DEVELOPING INTELLECTUALLY Psychologists use the term *cognitive development* to refer to the changes in intellectual functioning that accompany physical maturation. Several innovative techniques have been used to map out the internal perceptual world of infants. Newborns have remarkably well-developed tools for investigating the world around them—they can see, hear, smell, feel, and taste, although not at the same level as they will later in childhood. Individuals leave infancy with well-developed perceptual systems and use the experiences of childhood to help fine-tune and use their sensory equipment.

Much of what we know about how thought processes develop during infancy and childhood comes from the work of Jean Piaget. Piaget's theory of cognitive development proposes that children use mental models of the world—called schemata—to guide and interpret ongoing experience. Central to the theory is the idea that as children grow physically, and acquire new experiences, their mental models of the world change systematically. Piaget argued that children pass through a series of cognitive stages (sensorimotor, preoperational, concrete operational, and formal operational) characterized by unique ways of thinking. Piaget's theory has been criticized for a number of reasons, but the idea that children do not function as "little adults" continues to be widely accepted among developmental psychologists. Piaget's theory is complemented by Lawrence Kohlberg's theory of moral development. Like Piaget, Kohlberg proposed a stage theory, suggesting that individuals pass through qualitatively different levels of moral development, which differ in the extent to which moral actions are seen as driven by immediate external consequences or by general abstract principles.

DEVELOPING SOCIALLY AND PERSONALLY Humans use relationships with others to help them solve the problems that arise throughout development. Infants, burdened with limited motor skills and immature perceptual systems, form attachments with others to gain the sustenance they need for survival. Both the infant and the caregiver are active participants in the attachment process and are prepared to respond, given the right kinds of environmental events, with mutual bonding. Ainsworth identified three main categories of attachment—secure, resistant, and avoidant—that may have long-term consequences. In general, the responsiveness of the parent early in life is a significant but not inevitable influence on the relationships formed later in life.

Another aspect of social development is the formation of personal identity—a sense of who one is as an individual. Erik Erikson argued that personal identity is shaped by a series of "psychosocial" crises that individuals confront over the life span. During infancy and childhood, individuals address questions about their basic abilities and independence and learn to trust or mistrust others. During adolescence and adulthood, individuals deal with the identity crisis and come to grips with their roles as participants in intimate relationships. In the later years, individuals struggle with questions of accomplishment, concern for future generations, and meaning. A final aspect of social development is the learning of gender roles—how each person learns to think and act as a member of a gender group. Individuals develop a gender identity that determines how they act toward others and how others act toward them.

Terms to Remember

development The age-related physical, intellectual, social, and personal changes that occur throughout an individual's lifetime.

DEVELOPING PHYSICALLY

zygote The fertilized human egg, containing 23 chromosomes from the father and 23 chromosomes from the mother, which pair up to form the master genetic blueprint.

germinal period The period in prenatal development from conception to implantation of the fertilized egg in the wall of the uterus.

embryonic period The period of prenatal development lasting from implantation to the end of the eighth week; during this period the human develops from an unrecognizable mass of cells to a somewhat familiar creature.

fetal period The period of prenatal development lasting from the ninth week until birth, during which the fetus develops functioning organ systems and increases are seen in body size and in the size and complexity of brain tissue.

teratogens Environmental agents—such as disease organisms or drugs—that can potentially damage the developing embryo or fetus.

puberty The period during which a person reaches sexual maturity and is potentially capable of producing offspring.

menopause The period during which a woman's menstrual cycle slows down and finally stops.

dementia Physically based losses in mental functioning.

longitudinal design A research design in which the same people are studied or tested repeatedly over time.

cross-sectional design A research design in which people of different ages are compared at the same time.

DEVELOPING INTELLECTUALLY

habituation The decline in responsiveness to repeated stimulation; habituation has been used as an effective tool to map out the perceptual capabilities of infants.

schemata Mental models of the world that people use to guide and interpret their experiences.

assimilation The process through which people fit—or assimilate—new experiences into existing schemata.

accommodation The process through which people change or modify existing schemata to "accommodate" new experiences when they occur.

sensorimotor period Piaget's first stage of cognitive development, lasting from birth to about 2 years of age; schemata revolve around sensory and motor abilities.

object permanence The ability to recognize that objects still exist when they're no longer in sight.

preoperational period Piaget's second stage of cognitive development, lasting from ages 2 to about 7; children begin to think symbolically but often lack the ability to perform mental operations like conservation.

conservation The ability to recognize that the physical properties of an object remain the same despite superficial changes in the object's appearance.

concrete operational period Piaget's third stage of cognitive development, lasting from ages 7 to 11. Children acquire the capacity to perform a number of mental operations, but still lack the ability for abstract reasoning.

formal operational period Piaget's last stage of cognitive development; thought processes become adult-like, and people gain mastery over abstract thinking.

morality The ability to distinguish between appropriate and inappropriate actions; a child's sense of morality may be tied to his or her level of cognitive development.

preconventional level In Kohlberg's theory, the lowest level of moral development, in which decisions about right and wrong are made primarily in terms of external consequences.

conventional level In Kohlberg's theory of moral development, the stage in which actions are judged to be right or wrong based on whether they maintain or disrupt the social order.

postconventional level Kohlberg's highest level of moral development, in which moral actions are judged on the basis of personal codes of ethics that are general and abstract and that may not agree with societal norms.

DEVELOPING SOCIALLY AND PERSONALLY

attachments Strong emotional ties formed to one or more intimate companions.

strange situation test Gradually subjecting a child to a stressful situation and observing his or her behavior toward the parent or caregiver. This test is used to classify children according to type of attachment—e.g., secure, resistant, or avoidant.

personal identity A sense of who one is as an individual and how well one stacks up against peers. Erik Erikson's theory postulates that personal identity is shaped by a series of personal crises that each person confronts at characteristic stages of development.

gender roles Specific patterns of behavior that are consistent with how society dictates males and females should act.

gender schemas The organized sets of beliefs and perceptions held about men and women.

As we've seen in this chapter, the process of human development results from a complex interplay between natural biological forces and environmental demands. Humans enter a world that is ever-changing, and they use the machinery of the adaptive mind to help solve the problems that they face. All human beings are faced with common survival problems, but to understand human development fully requires that we also consider the forces that act on the individual. Among the most powerful and pervasive of these influences are the socialization practices instilled in the individual by his or her culture. In recent years, developmental psychologists have turned increasingly to the study of culture to help explain how individuals develop.

Adopting a cultural perspective is beneficial because it helps psychologists understand developmental differences among individuals as well as groups. For example, did you know that, on average, it's more difficult to get a child raised in a Western industrialized country such as the United States to go to bed at night than it is for a child raised in Guatemala? A child from the United States is also more likely to demand and cling to a favored toy, such as a blanket or a teddy bear. Why? The answer lies partly in the fact that parents in the United States typically require their children to sleep alone, or at least in a separate room. In the United States, sleeping in the same room or bed with parents is thought to foster dependency, which is seen as an undesirable personality trait in children. But in most other countries of the world, including Guatemala, isolating children at bedtime is considered inappropriate and even shocking (Morelli et al.,1992). In Guatemala, Mayan mothers sleep in the same bed with their children at least until the infants reach toddlerhood. Perhaps not surprisingly, Mayan infants go to bed easily and do not require complex bedtime rituals of the type seen in most U.S. homes.

It's also been found that mothers in the United States tend to hold and touch their babies less often the mothers do, than mothers in some other cultures do. In one study, the parenting styles of middle-class Boston mothers were directly compared with those of Gusii mothers in the African country of Kenya. For both cultures, the type of contact that the mothers displayed toward their babies was observed and carefully recorded (Richman, Miller, & LeVine, 1992). It turned out that the Boston mothers were far more likely to leave their kids to their own devices for playtime and infant care. The Gusii mothers, in contrast, chose to hold and cuddle with their babies much of the time. On the other hand, the researchers also discovered that the Gusii mothers only made direct eye contact with their children and talked to them far less than their U.S. counterparts.

The Origins of Cultural Differences
What accounts for these differences? Why do American mothers touch their babies less but talk to them more? The

Some cultures encourage children to sleep in the same room or even the same bed as their parents; other cultures do not.

answer lies partly in the particular beliefs that parents have about their children and partly in the customs of the cultures. For example, it's widely believed among Gusii mothers that their babies are incapable of understanding speech until age 2. As a result, idle conversations with the infant are thought to be wasteful and of little value. It's also considered inappropriate—a kind of cultural taboo—in Gusii society to look directly into someone's eyes during a conversation. This probably explains why Gusii mothers rarely make direct eye contact with their infants. Mothers in the United States have a quite different set of cultural beliefs; they are confident that their babies respond to language very early in development, and they believe that sustained eye contact is an excellent and appropriate way to communicate. The U.S. culture also places high value on independence and self-reliance. Depositing the baby or toddler in a playpen is not considered a heartless act by most U.S. mothers—it's a way to break dependence and encourage independence.

Many researchers believe that an emphasis on instilling independence early in life, which is a common practice in the United States and other Western industrialized countries, affects the kinds of attachment bonds that are formed during childhood. Earlier in the chapter we discussed a technique called the strange situation test, in which the behavior of infants in a new situation is recorded under various levels of stress (ranging from the entrance of a stranger to the parent leaving the child alone). This test has been administered to children in many different cultures of the world, and some interesting cross-cultural differences in childhood behavior have been recorded. For example, it's been found that both U.S. and German children are far more likely to show avoidant attachment than children raised in Japan (Cole, 1992; van Ijzendoorn & Kroonenberg, 1988). Remember, avoidant children show little or no strong attachments; they are not bothered by the appearance of strangers in the room, nor do they seem distressed when their mother leaves the room. Some researchers believe that these cultural differences in attachment result from the fact that parents in the United States and Germany spend less time with their children, choosing instead to foster independence and autonomy. Children in Japan, on the other hand, spend very little time away from their mother during the first year or so of life.

It's important to understand that this decision of whether or not to stress independence can be more than simply a matter of cultural choice. Many of the child-rearing strategies that occur throughout the world are driven by the special problems that are faced by the society. For instance, middle-class mothers in the United States, Germany, and Japan do not face immediate survival problems. The child left momentarily unattended in the playpen is not likely to be attacked by a predator. But in some societies of the world, particularly nomadic societies, the infant's survival is a constant and pressing concern. Child-rearing practices are also affected by how the society has historically framed its economy. In agricultural societies, children are encouraged early in life to work in teams and to think of themselves as dependent on the actions of the group. In hunting societies or in nomadic societies that are constantly on the move, self-reliance and permissiveness are more likely to be stressed because parents often need to travel great distances alone in search of food. The unique problems faced by the culture drive the way that parents rear their children and, consequently, importantly shape how the children learn to behave.

5

[A]ll of the environment of which we are directly aware is quite literally plastered upon our body surface, for within this surface are located the specialized receptors that react to various forms of energy abounding in the physical world. Without these specialized receptors, we should be like insensate blocks of wood—no environment would exist for us.

Charles E. Osgood

You bolt upright, breathing heavily, startled awake by an uncertain sound. The rumbling of distant thunder rolls overhead; the rain, gentle now, creates a soft and steady patter on the roof. Awake, in the silence of mid-night, you listen. Myriad sounds beckon your interpretation: the hum of the fish tank filter, the irregular ticking of what must be the gas heater cooling, the creak of a settling floorboard. Normal sounds, you tell yourself, on a normal, slightly stormy night. Sinking back into the warmth of your bed, you shut your eyes and try to clear your mind. It's nothing, you convince yourself, you're okay—but the "silence" continues to tell its story.

Each of us is constantly bombarded by messages from the environment. Some messages come in the form of light energy, bouncing in all directions off objects in the "real" world; others, like strange "bumps in the night," arrive as regular changes in the pressure of a medium such as air. Some of these messages get translated into the electrochemical language of the nervous system for delivery deep within the brain. The products of this translation process, and their subsequent interpretation, serve as our focus in this chapter. We turn now to the important psychological processes of sensation and perception.

To help understand the difference between the psychological terms *sensation* and *perception,* consider the image shown in Figure 5.1. Although it's a geometric figure, a cube, it exists at another level of description as well. It consists of lines, angles, patterns of light and dark, colors, and so on. These elementary features— the building blocks of the meaningful image—are processed by the visual system, through reasonably well understood physiological systems, and the products are called **sensations.** Psychologists have historically thought of sensations—such as a pattern of light and dark, a bitter taste, a change in temperature—as the fundamental, elementary components of an experience. **Perception** is the collection of processes used to arrive at a meaningful "interpretation" of these sensations. The simple components are usually organized by higher-order processes (which are less well understood) into a recognizable form—in this case you perceive a *cube.*

Now, let's think more closely about what "interpretation" means in this context. Look closely at the cube once again. Stare at it for a while. The lines, the angles, and the colors remain fixed, but the cube itself appears to shift its shape from moment to moment. For a time, the shaded surface of the image is the front of the cube; then, in the next instance, it forms the back of the cube. First you see it from one perspective, and then from another. How is this possible? Certainly the image on the page remains fixed; the reflected light is not changing systematically with time. The answer lies in the *interpretation* of the sensory image. In this case, the message delivered to the brain is ambiguous. Because more than one interpretation of the physical image is possible, the brain engages in a perceptual dance, shifting from one interpretation to the other. As we'll see later when we discuss each of the sensory systems in detail, sometimes the brain gets it wrong altogether; in those cases, perceptual "illusions" may be produced.

FIGURE 5.1
The Necker Cube.

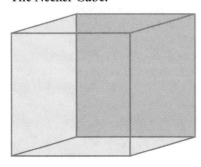

◢ PREVIEWING THE ADAPTIVE PROBLEMS

Our goal in this chapter is to understand how the brain senses and perceives the physical environment. Most psychologists are reluctant to maintain too rigid a distinction between the processes of sensation and perception because interpretation of the external message can occur at all points during processing. Even sensing a line, an angle, or a color involves a relatively complex set of systems that act together to determine what is seen. As we'll discuss later, people's expectations about what they believe to be "out there" strongly influence the processing and interpretation of the message the external environment delivers.

Because human survival depends on making reasonably *correct* interpretations about objects in the real world, people have developed multiple sensory systems to monitor their environment. The visual sense tells individuals what obstacles they are about to face and the pathways they can take to ensure their survival. Sounds, processed through the auditory system, signal the approach of significant events and allow individuals to communicate with others. The sense of touch or pain enables people to respond adaptively to stimuli that in all other respects might appear harmless. Smells, tastes, even the sense of balance secure knowledge about a person's position in the environment and act, in collaboration with the other senses, as significant windows to the world.

To appreciate how the brain builds its internal representation of the outside world, we'll discuss each sensory system from the perspective of three fundamental adaptive problems: How does the external message from the environment get translated into the language of the nervous system? How do the elementary components—the sensations—get extracted from the message? And finally, how does the brain build a stable and long-lasting interpretation of these components once they've been extracted? These three questions are depicted in Figure 5.2. We'll not be able to answer these questions satisfactorily in all cases, because there is still a great deal to be learned about how sensory systems operate. But you can assume these are three important "problems" that need to be resolved by each of the senses that we'll discuss.

FIGURE 5.2
Adaptive Problems of Sensation and Perception. To build its internal representation of the outside world, the brain needs to solve three fundamental adaptive problems for each of its sensory systems: (1) translating the message from the environment into the language of the nervous system; (2) extracting the elementary components of the message, such as colors, sounds, simple forms, and patterns of light and dark; and (3) building a stable interpretation of those components once they've been extracted.

Translating the message	Extracting the message components	Producing stable interpretations

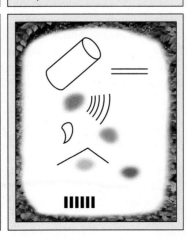 

▶ **TRANSLATING THE MESSAGE** It is first necessary to translate the external message coming from the environment into the internal language of the brain; this translation process is called **transduction,** which literally means "leading across." As we discussed in Chapter 3, communication in the nervous system is fundamentally an electrochemical process. When the outside world begins to "talk" to the brain, the message arrives in a variety of forms that are not electrochemical. For example, you see by means of reflected light, which arrives in the form of electromagnetic energy; you hear by interpreting sound "vibrations," or repetitive changes in air pressure. It's like trying to listen to someone who speaks a language you don't understand. The brain needs an interpreter—a process through which the incoming message can be changed into an understandable form. The brain's interpreters take the form of *receptor cells,* embedded in the various sense organs, that solve the translation problem for particular kinds of environmental stimulation.

▶ **EXTRACTING THE MESSAGE COMPONENTS** Once the environmental message has been successfully translated—appearing now in the form of neural impulses—the important message components need to be extracted or pulled out of the complex sensory array. In order to accomplish this feat, the newly formed sensory code is delivered from the translation sites to processing stations deep within the brain. Along each route or pathway, which differs for each of the sensory systems, are localized regions specialized to perform unique sensory functions. The cortex of the brain, for example, contains specialized *feature detectors* that respond selectively to lines of particular orientation, to individual colors, and even to dots that move in different directions across the visual field. As a result, damage, or lesion, to distinct regions of the visual cortex can create bizarre patterns of blindness—patients might retain the ability to see only one kind of attribute in the world, such as form, color, or motion. The neural processing stations in the brain often operate in parallel (at the same time), to combine and extract components of the message en route to its final interpretation.

▶ **PRODUCING STABLE INTERPRETATIONS** Although the sensory pathways may successfully break down the environmental message into a series of much simpler components, a significant problem remains. How do these extracted features, represented as the activities of many thousands of neurons, combine to produce perceptual experiences? You see objects, not patterns of colored light and dark; you hear melodies, not sequences of irregularly timed sounds. To appreciate the difficulty of the problem, consider that you need not only recognize the object but also understand that it remains fundamentally the same despite rather dramatic changes in the physical message presented to your brain. The pattern of light reflected from a moving object changes continuously with time, yet you still recognize a dancer gliding effortlessly across the stage. The biological bases of perception—the processes that produce the interpretation—are still poorly understood, but we'll see that the brain uses certain principles of organization that may well cut across all of the senses.

Vision: Building a World of Color and Form

We begin our discussion of sensation and perception with vision: the sense of sight. Vision is arguably the most important human sense, although each of the senses plays a key role in helping people adapt to their environment. To appreciate how the brain builds the visual world, we first need to discuss how the physical message—light—is translated into the language of the brain. Next, we'll trace

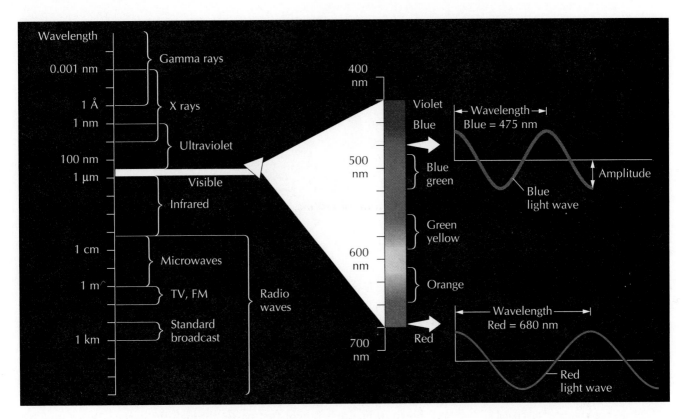

FIGURE 5.3
Light and the Electromagnetic Spectrum. Visible light is actually only a small part of the electromagnetic spectrum, which includes other energy forms such as X rays and radio and TV waves. Changes in the wavelength of light, from about 400 nanometers to 700 nanometers, are experienced as changes in color; short wavelengths are seen as violets and blues; medium wavelengths as yellows and greens; and long wavelengths as reds.

some of the pathways in the brain that are used to extract the basic components of the visual message. Finally, we'll tackle the topic of visual perception: how the brain creates its stable interpretation of the light information it receives.

Translating the Message: Visual Transduction

The physical message delivered to visual receptors, **light,** is a form of electromagnetic energy. What humans think of as visible light is actually only a small part of an electromagnetic "spectrum" that includes other energy forms, such as X rays, ultraviolet rays, and even radio and television waves (see Figure 5.3).

Light is typically classified by two main physical properties. The first is *wavelength,* which corresponds to the physical distance from one energy cycle to the next. Changes in the wavelength of light are generally experienced, psychologically, as changes in color, or **hue.** If you look at Figure 5.3, you'll discover that humans "see" wavelengths ranging from only about 400 to 700 nanometers (billionths of a meter). Psychologically, these wavelengths are experienced as colors ranging roughly from violet to red. The second physical property of light is its *intensity,* which corresponds to the amount of light falling on an object. Changes in intensity are generally experienced as increases or decreases in **brightness.**

Light originates from a source such as the sun or a light bulb. It arrives at visual receptors either directly from the source or after bouncing off objects in its path. What we think of as "white light" is actually a mixture of many different wavelengths. As white light hits an object, some of its wavelengths are absorbed— which ones depends on the physical properties of the object—and the remaining wavelengths reflect outward, where they potentially enter the eyes. It is here, in the eyes, that the important translation process occurs.

FIGURE 5.4

The Human Eye. Light enters the eye through the cornea, pupil, and lens. The lens changes shape, depending on the distance of the object, so that the reflected light will be focused at the back of the eye; there, in the retina, translation of the visual message begins.

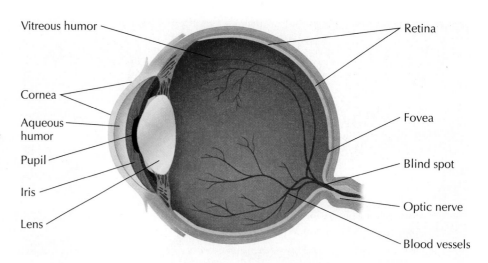

It's been reported that pupil size increases with interest or level of emotional involvement. What do you think the adaptive value of this kind of change might be?

One of the functions of the pupil is to regulate the amount of light entering the eye. In bright light, the pupil gets smaller, allowing less light to enter; in dim light, the pupil gets larger, allowing more light to enter.

Entering the Eye. The first step in the translation process, and the main function of the front portion of the eye, is to bring the incoming light energy to the light-sensitive receptor cells that sit at the back of each eye. When light bounces off a real-world object, the reflected wavelengths are scattered about; they need to be brought back together—or focused—for a clear image to be processed. In the human eye, these optical adjustments are accomplished by the **cornea,** the protective outer layer of the eye, and the **lens,** a flexible piece of tissue capable of changing its shape.

As shown in Figure 5.4, light first passes through the cornea, then through a watery material known as the *aqueous humor,* and finally the **pupil.** The pupil appears as a black spot of variable size, but it's actually a hole in a ring of colored tissue called the **iris.** The iris gives the eye its distinctive color (a person with green eyes has green irises), but eye color plays no role in vision. Relaxing or tightening the muscles around the iris changes the size of the pupil, thereby regulating the amount of light that enters the eye. In dim light, the pupil gets larger, which allows more light to get in; in bright light, the pupil gets smaller, allowing less light to enter. As light passes through the pupil, it is also restricted to the central portions of the lens, where there are fewer optical distortions (Thibos and others, 1990).

The lens focuses the light on the sensory receptors, much like the lens in a camera focuses light on film. But whereas in a camera focusing involves changing the distance between the lens and the film, in the human eye focusing is accomplished by changing the shape of the lens itself. This process, known as **accommodation,** is influenced by the distance between the lens and the object being viewed. For faraway objects, muscles in the eye stretch the lens into a long, thin shape; for close objects, the lens thickens. As people age, the lens loses some of its flexibility, making the accommodation process far less efficient (Fukuda, Kanada,

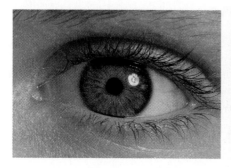
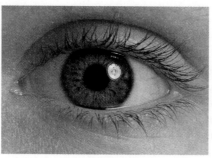
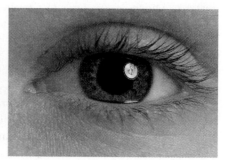

When light levels are low, such as at night, people see primarily with their rods. Rods play little, if any, role in color vision, so visual scenes at night often seem to lack color.

& Saito, 1990). This is one of the reasons that people sometimes require reading glasses or bifocals when they reach middle age. The corrective lenses in the glasses support the accommodation process, which the eyes can no longer successfully perform on their own.

Transduction in the Retina. After the light passes through the lens, it travels through another fluid called the *vitreous humor,* a jellylike material that maintains the shape of the eyeball. The light finally reaches a thin layer of tissue called the **retina** (Latin for "net" or "cobweb tunic"), which covers the back of the eye. It is here that the light energy gets translated into the inner language of the brain. Embedded in the retina of each eye are about 126 million light-sensitive receptor cells that *transduce,* or change, the light energy into the electrochemical impulses that characterize neural processing.

Of the approximately 126 million receptor cells in each eye, there are about 120 million **rods** and roughly 6 million **cones.** Each receptor type is named for its visual appearance—rods are generally long and thin, whereas cones are short, thick, and tapered to a point—but each plays a different role in visual processing. Rods are useful at night and in any situation in which the overall level of illumination is low. Rods are the more sensitive visual receptors; they can generate visual signals when very small amounts of light strike their surface. They tend to be concentrated along the periphery, or sides, of the retina. This is one reason that dim images can sometimes be seen better out of the corners of your eyes.

Cones are concentrated in the very center of the retina, bunched in a small central pit called the **fovea** (which means "central pit"). Unlike rods, cones need relatively high levels of illumination to operate efficiently, as the accompanying Inside the Problem section discusses. But they are responsible for several critical visual functions. Cones, for example, are used for processing fine detail, an ability called **visual acuity.** Cones also play an extremely important role in the early processing of color, as we'll discuss later. Rods, on the other hand, play little, if any, role in color vision.

The translation process for both rods and cones is chemically based. Each of the receptor cells contains a substance, known as a *photopigment,* that reacts to light. The resulting chemical reac-

Each human retina contains two types of photoreceptor cells: rods and cones. As shown in this color-enhanced photo, the rods are rod-shaped in appearance and the cones are cone-shaped.

FIGURE 5.5
Rods, Cones, and Receptive Fields. The signals generated by the rods and cones are passed along to other cells in the retina, particularly bipolar cells and ganglion cells. Each ganglion cell has a "receptive field," which is defined by the number of receptor cells that it receives input from. Ganglion cells in the fovea, which receive input from cones, tend to have smaller receptive fields than ganglion cells in the eye's periphery, which receive input from rods. This fact helps account for why the fovea provides better detail, and why the sides of the eyes are more sensitive to low levels of light.

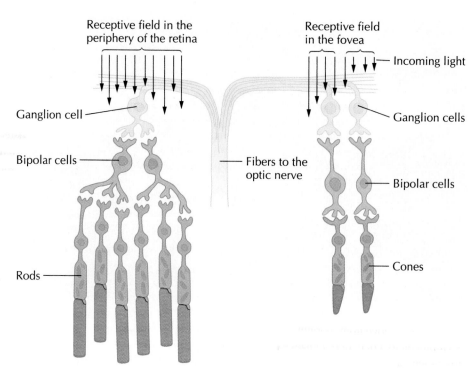

tion causes the receptor cell to generate a neural impulse. The electrical signal is then passed along to other cells in the retina, particularly *bipolar cells* and *ganglion cells,* where further processing occurs (see Figure 5.5). It's worth noting that even at this early stage in visual processing, cells in the retina are already interpreting the incoming visual message. The ganglion cells, for example, have **receptive fields,** which means they receive input from a group of receptor cells and respond only when particular patterns of light shine across the retina (Shapley, 1990; Shapley & Kaplan, 1989).

The visual signals eventually leave the retina, en route to the deeper processing stations of the brain, through a collection of nerve fibers called the *optic nerve.* The optic nerve consists of roughly 1 million axons (from the ganglion cells) that wrap together to form a sort of visual transmission cable. Because of its size, at the point where the optic nerve leaves each retina there is no room for visual receptor cells. This creates a biological **blind spot,** although people normally experience no "holes" in their visual field. As part of its interpretation process, the visual system fills in the gaps to create a continuous visual scene (Ramachandran, 1992). You can locate your blind spot by following the exercise described in Figure 5.6.

FIGURE 5.6
The Blind Spot. To demonstrate your blind spot, simply close your left eye and focus with your right eye on the guilty boy's face. Now, start with the book only a few inches from your face and slowly move it away. Find the point where the pie mysteriously disappears. Notice that your brain "fills in" the spot—complete with the checkerboard pattern.

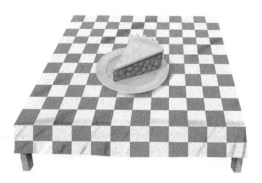

You arrive at the movie theater early, as usual, and settle into your seat. You've picked your spot with care—midway up, clean floor, nobody in the row directly in front of you. The lights dim, the movie begins, and you start to relax. A short time later, the door swings open and an awkward-looking fellow wanders in late, looking for a seat. He appears to bounce from side to side down the aisle, occasionally stopping to peer into a row with a confused look on his face. You can see him fine; he, on the other hand, appears to be nearly blind. The reason, of course, is that your eyes have adjusted to the dark, whereas his have not.

When you move from a brightly lit environment to a dark one, it takes about 20–25 minutes for your eyes to adjust, a process known as **dark adaptation.** Why does the adjustment process take so long? To discover the answer, we need to turn our attention once more to the rods and cones. As mentioned earlier, visual transduction occurs when light reacts chemically with photopigments in the receptor cells. In bright light, many of these photopigments break down, or become "bleached," and are no longer useful for generating a neural impulse. When you enter a dark movie theater from a bright environment, your receptor cells simply don't have enough of the depleted photopigments to detect the low levels of illumination. The photopigments need to be regenerated by the cells, a process that takes time. As long as there is enough light around, you won't have much of a problem because your eyes never completely run out of photopigment; difficulties arise only in dark environments, where your receptor cells need to operate at peak efficiency.

The timing of the adaptation process is shown in Figure 5.7. This dark adaptation "curve" is produced by measuring the smallest amount of light that people can reliably see, plotted as a function of time spent in the dark. Over 20–25 minutes, smaller and smaller amounts of light are needed to achieve accurate detection. Sensitivity increases,

once again, because the visual receptor cells are recovering from their earlier interactions with bright light, which broke down the visual pigments, requiring them to be regenerated.

Notice that a break, or point of discontinuity, occurs at about the 8-minute mark in the dark adaptation curve. To help understand its cause, think about the following two empirical facts: (1) If the light source used to measure sensitivity is of a particular color (such as green), then after the break point in the curve the color will seem to disappear and become gray. (2) If the light source used to measure sensitivity is presented only to the fovea, the dark adaptation curve will level off at about the 8-minute mark, and no further increases in sensitivity will be found. Based on what you already know about the visual system, can you deduce why the curve "breaks" in this fashion?

The explanation lies in the fact that the rods and the cones adapt to the dark

at different rates. Early in the dark adaptation function, the cones show the most sensitivity, but they achieve their maximum responsiveness rather quickly. After about 7 or 8 minutes in the dark, the rods, which can detect quite low levels of illumination, begin to take over. Since cones are needed to detect color, a green light source presented at a low level of illumination will appear colorless. In addition, if the light source is presented only to the fovea, where there are no rods, the dark adaptation curve will cease to improve beyond the point of maximum cone sensitivity.

To psychologists, the dark adaptation curve provides more than just a measurement of how the eyes "adjust" to the dark. It provides strong support for the contention that the human visual system relies on two types of receptor systems, each with quite different properties and each operating most efficiently under different conditions of illumination.

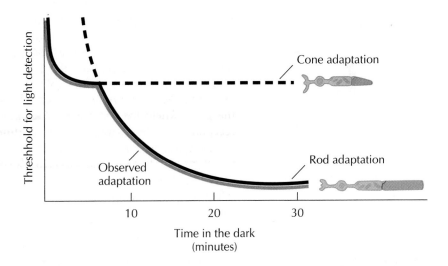

FIGURE 5.7
The Dark Adaptation Curve. As you spend time in the dark, your eyes "adjust" and become more sensitive. Sensitivity in this case means that you are able to detect lights at increasingly low levels of intensity. The rods and cones adapt at different rates and reach different final levels of sensitivity. The overall dark adaptation curve, marked in red, reflects the combined adaptation of the two receptor types. Notice that at about the eight-minute mark, there is a point of discontinuity; this is the point where further increases in sensitivity are due to functioning of the rods.

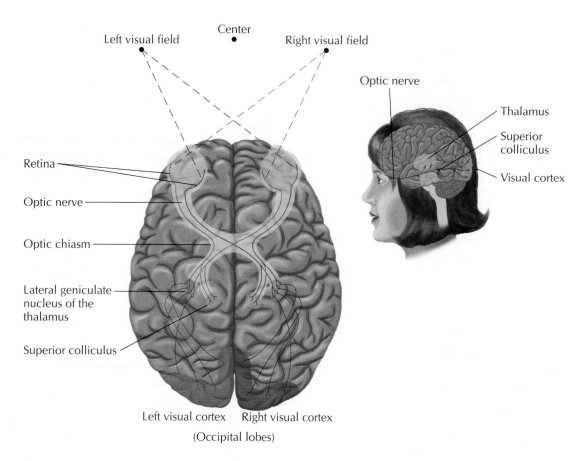

Center

Left visual field   Right visual field

Optic nerve

Thalamus

Superior colliculus

Visual cortex

Retina

Optic nerve

Optic chiasm

Lateral geniculate nucleus of the thalamus

Superior colliculus

Left visual cortex   Right visual cortex

(Occipital lobes)

FIGURE 5.8

The Visual Pathways. Input from the left visual field falls on the inside half of the left eye and the outside half of the right eye and projects to the right hemisphere of the brain; input from the right visual field projects to the left hemisphere. Visual processing occurs at several places along the pathway, including the lateral geniculate nucleus and the superior colliculus, ending in the visual cortex, where highly specialized processing takes place.

Extracting the Message Components: Visual Pathways

After leaving the retina, the patterns of neural activation flow along each optic nerve until they reach the *optic chiasm* (from the Greek word meaning "cross"), where the information splits into different tracts leading to the separate hemispheres of the brain (see Figure 5.8). Information that has been detected on the right half of each retina (from the left visual field) is sent to the right hemisphere, and information falling on the left half of each retina (from the right visual field) projects to the left hemisphere. About 80% of the visual signals move directly toward a major relay station in the *thalamus* called the *lateral geniculate nucleus;* the remaining 20% detour into a midbrain structure called the *superior colliculus.*

Significant early extraction and interpretation of the visual message occurs along these pathways. For example, it's currently believed that there are two primary visual pathways from the retina through the lateral geniculate nucleus. One, called the *parvocellular system,* is specialized to continue the processing of detail and color; the other, called the *magnocellular system,* is responsible for extracting and processing brightness, movement, and depth (Livingstone & Hubel, 1988; Shapley, 1990). At the same time, processing in the superior colliculus, a somewhat more primitive structure, controls the ability to localize objects in space by moving the head and eyes (Sparks, 1988). One of the hallmarks of the visual pathway is that all these quite different functions are carried out simultaneously, through specialized brain regions that operate concurrently.

Feature Detection in the Cortex. From the lateral geniculate nucleus, the visual message moves toward the back of the brain, primarily to portions of the occipital lobe. Here, in the "visual cortex," further highly specialized processing occurs. Experiments with animals have shown that cortical cells have well-defined

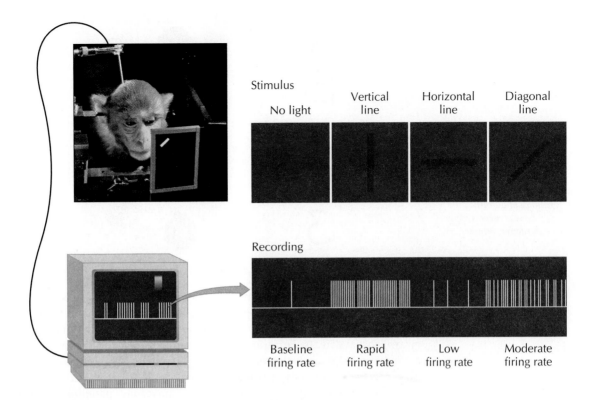

Stimulus

No light | Vertical line | Horizontal line | Diagonal line

Recording

Baseline firing rate | Rapid firing rate | Low firing rate | Moderate firing rate

FIGURE 5.9
Feature Detectors in the Visual Cortex. Hubel and Wiesel discovered feature detectors in the brains of cats and monkeys that increase their firing rates to specific bars of light presented at particular orientations.

visual functions. For example, David Hubel and Torsten Wiesel (1962, 1979) discovered **feature detectors**—single cells that respond best to very specific visual events—in the visual cortex of cats and monkeys. One type of feature detector, which Hubel and Wiesel called a *simple cell,* shows little or no response to general illumination but responds actively when barlike patterns of light or dark are shown in particular regions of the retina. These cells are also orientation specific, which means that the visual bar needs to be presented at a particular angle in order for the cell to respond. The properties of these cells were discovered by measuring neural impulses in individual cells, using implanted recording electrodes, while showing visual events to the eyes of monkey and cat subjects (see Figure 5.9).

Hubel and Wiesel also discovered that feature detectors are not randomly organized in the visual cortex—rather, there is a detailed organizational scheme, or "architecture," in the brain. Cells that respond to stimuli shown to the retina at a particular orientation, say 20 degrees, tend to be aligned together in the same "columns" of brain tissue. If a recording electrode is moved across neighboring columns, cells show regular shifts in their orientation specificity. So, if cells in a particular column A respond to bars at an angle of 20 degrees, then cells in a physically adjacent column B might respond actively only to bars presented at a 30-degree angle.

Clearly, this must mean that cells in the visual cortex are designed to break down the visual message into a number of basic component parts. But the brain is sensitive to more than just bars, or orientation-specific patterns of light and dark. Hubel and Wiesel also discovered cells that respond selectively to more complex patterns—for example, corners, edges, bars that move through the visual field, and bars that display a certain characteristic length. Other researchers have found cells—once again in monkey brains—that respond most actively to *faces.* Moreover, to get the most active response, the face needs to look realistically like a monkey—if the face is distorted or cartoonish, the cells do not respond as actively (Perrett & Mistlin, 1987).

Can you think of any reason why it might be adaptive for the brain to first break the visual pattern down into basic features—such as a bar or a pattern of light and dark—before recombining those features together into a unified whole such as a face?

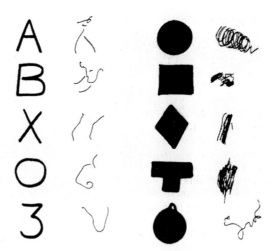

The right-hand side of each column shows the performance of a brain-damaged patient who was asked simply to copy the particular letter, number, or shape.

In humans, researchers have collected evidence of visual specificity in the brain by studying brain-damaged patients. When certain parts of the human brain are damaged because of stroke or injury, the result is often very selective, even bizarre, visual deficits. For example, one kind of damage in the brain can produce a condition called *akinetopsia,* in which patients possess normal vision only for objects at rest; if the object is placed in motion, it seems to vanish, only to reappear if it becomes stationary once more. Conversely, patients with a lesion in another cortical location might show the most sensitivity to objects that move rather than stay stationary (Zeki, 1992).

Additional evidence for specialization in visual processing in the human brain has come from studies using PET scanning procedures. In this procedure, the subject ingests a harmless radioactive substance that is then absorbed into the cells of brain regions that are metabolically active. A visual event of some kind is presented, and the researcher can observe which areas of the brain are activated. Using this technique, researchers have discovered that certain areas of the brain respond selectively to patterns of dots that *move* across the visual field (Dupont and others, 1994). Other areas respond selectively to object tasks, such as matching faces, but not to spatial tasks, such as finding dots in an array (McIntosh and others, 1994). Still other areas of the brain may be selectively involved in the processing

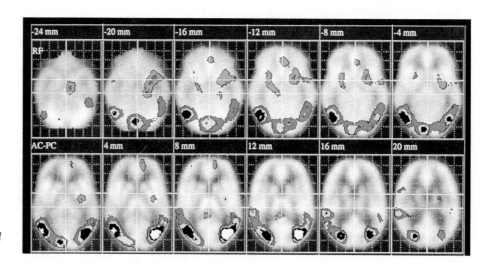

Many areas in the human brain appear to respond selectively to visual motion. The highlighted regions, derived from PET scanning, show areas of the human brain that react more to a moving visual stimulus than to a stationary one.

of mental *images,* such as mentally visualizing a letter in upper- or lowercase (Kosslyn and others, 1993). Results like these indicate that the human brain, like the monkey brain, divides its labor. Certain regions of the cortex are specifically designed to process particular parts of the visual message.

Chemical pigments in the fabric of this woman's clothes absorb some wavelengths and reject others. The colors we see come from the rejected wavelengths, which are the ones processed by the visual system.

Color Vision. One of the most significant components that the brain is able to "extract" out of the visual message is color. It turns out that color information is processed along the entire visual pathway: Retina → lateral geniculate nucleus → visual cortex. In the retina, as we'll see shortly, early color information is extracted by comparing the relative activations of different types of cone receptors; higher up in the brain, messages encounter cells that are "tuned" to respond only to particular colors.

Earlier we noted that color is determined primarily by the wavelength of light reflected back into the eye. In general, short wavelengths (around 450 nanometers) produce blues, medium wavelengths (circa 530 nanometers) produce greens, and long wavelengths (approximately 670 nanometers) produce reds. We also discussed the fact that white light, which most would classify as colorless, is actually a combination of all of the wavelengths of the visible spectrum. The reason why your neighbor's shirt looks red is that chemical pigments in the fabric of the shirt absorb all but the long wavelengths of light; the long wavelengths are reflected back into the eyes, and you see the shirt as red. But in a sense, the object itself, the shirt, is truly colorless; you perceive the object as red only because the shirt has "rejected," by reflecting outward, those forms of electromagnetic energy that your visual system will shortly classify as red.

When reflected wavelengths reach the retina, they cause cones in the fovea to become active. Physiological analysis of the human eye has revealed *three* types of cone receptors: One type generates neural impulses primarily to *short* wavelengths (420 nanometers), another type responds most energetically to *medium* wavelengths (530 nanometers), and a final type responds most to *long* wavelengths (560 nanometers) of light. The sensitivity of a particular cone type actually spreads across a relatively broad range of individual wavelengths and is determined by the photopigment that the receptor contains (Bowmaker & Dartnall, 1980; Schnapf & Baylor, 1987). Figure 5.10 shows the sensitivities for each of the cones, as well as for the rods.

The **trichromatic** ("three-color") **theory** of color vision proposes that color information is extracted through the activations of these three types of cones. An early version of the trichromatic theory was proposed in the 19th century by Thomas Young and Hermann von Helmholtz—long before modern techniques

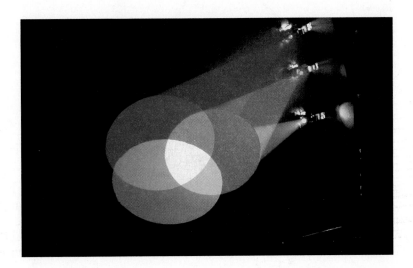

Additive mixing of lights with different wavelengths can create a variety of perceived colors—even white.

FIGURE 5.10
Receptor Sensitivity Curves. The three cone receptors respond best to different wavelengths of light. Blue-sensitive cones are most likely to respond to short wavelengths of light; green-sensitive cones respond best to medium wavelengths; red-sensitive cones respond best to long wavelengths. Also shown is the sensitivity curve for rods; notice that rods are not sensitive to long wavelengths of light. (Based on Jones & Childers, 1993.)

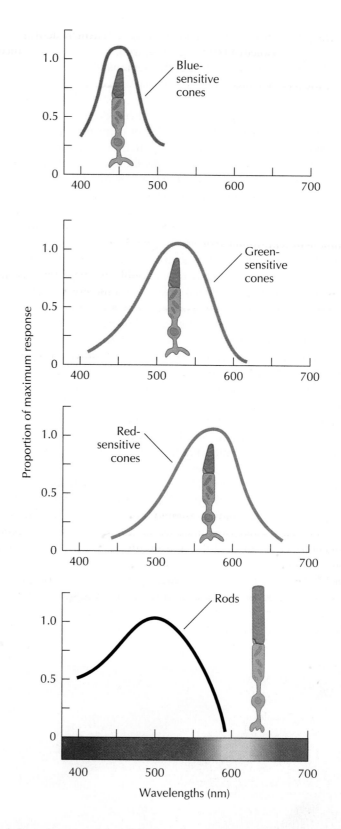

had verified the existence of the different cone types. As the basis for their theory Young and Helmholtz used the fact that most colors can be matched by mixing three basic, or *primary,* colors. They suggested that the brain must deduce the color of an object by comparing the relative activation levels of three primary receptors. When just one receptor type is strongly activated, you see one of the primary colors. For example, when a short wavelength cone is strongly activated, you might see something in the violet to blue region of the spectrum; when a medium cone is active, you would see something resembling green. For long wavelengths, which activate the third type of cone, you sense the color red. The rest of the colors, such as a pumpkin orange, are sensed when more than one of the receptor types is activated. Most "colors" correspond to a mixture of wavelengths and are sensed by comparing the activations of the three receptors.

The trichromatic theory explains a number of interesting aspects of color vision. For example, it explains certain kinds of color blindness. At times, nature makes a "mistake" and fills someone's red cones with green photopigment or the green cones with red photopigment (Boynton, 1979). Under these rare conditions, which affect more males than females, individuals are left with two rather than three operational cone receptors. The trichromatic theory predicts that *dichromats*—people with two rather than three cone types—should lose their ability to discriminate successfully among certain colors. Indeed, people who lack either the red or green cone type have a great deal of trouble distinguishing red from green. Other types of cone loss can produce trouble with blue-green discriminations. The particular type of color deficiency depends on the particular type of receptor that is lost.

The physiological evidence, combined with the color mixing and color blindness patterns, provides strong support for the trichromatic theory. But the theory fails as a complete account of color vision. For one thing, the trichromatic theory has a problem with *yellow*. Human observers seem convinced that yellow is every bit as "pure" a color as red, green, and blue; even 4-month old infants prefer dividing the color spectrum into four color categories rather than three (Bornstein, Kessen, & Weiskopf, 1976). Human observers also have no problem reporting a yellowish red or a bluish green but almost never report seeing anything resembling a yellowish blue or, for that matter, a greenish red. Why?

In fact, certain colors turn out to be specially linked, such as blue to yellow and red to green. To demonstrate, stop for a moment and take a look at Figure 5.11. You'll find that if you stare at a vivid color like red for a prolonged period of time and then switch over to a blank white space, you will see an *afterimage* of its *complementary* color. Exposure to red produces an afterimage of green; exposure to blue results in an afterimage of yellow. Also, when you mix complementary colored lights, you get white, or at least various shades of gray. The special status of yellow, in conjunction with the linking of complementary colors, is difficult for the trichromatic theory to explain.

The difficulties with the trichromatic view were recognized in the 19th century by the German physiologist Ewald Hering. Hering proposed the **opponent-process theory** of color vision, in which increased activation of one type of color

FIGURE 5.11
Color Afterimages. Stare closely at the middle of this face for about a minute. Then shift your gaze to the black dot on the right. What do you see now?

cell (such as red) creates decreased activation in another color cell (such as green). Instead of three primary colors, Hering proposed six: *blue,* which is linked to *yellow* (therefore solving the problem with yellow), *green,* which is linked to *red,* and finally, *white* linked to *black.* According to the opponent-process view, people have difficulty perceiving a yellowish blue because activation of, say, the blue cell inhibits or prevents the concurrent activation of the yellow cell. But a yellowish red would not present a problem because yellow and red are not linked in an opponent fashion.

Like Young and Helmholtz, Hering was operating in a kind of physiological vacuum—there was no solid physiological evidence for either a three-receptor system or for specially linked opponent-process cells. We know now that such evidence does exist. For example, in addition to the discovery of the different cone photopigments, researchers have found that cells in the lateral geniculate nucleus, as well as in the visual cortex, do indeed code color information in an opponent-process fashion (see DeValois & DeValois, 1980). The rate at which neural impulses are generated by these cells increases to one type of color (for example, red) and decreases to another (green).

So which theory of color vision is correct—the trichromatic view or the opponent-process view? The answer is that *both* are correct: The visual system extracts color information by relying on multiple processing stations. Color information is extracted first at the retinal level through the activations of different cones; further up in the brain, opponent-process cells fine-tune and further process the message. Although the specific pathways and combination rules have yet to be fully worked out, some sort of merging of the trichromatic and opponent-process views best characterizes our current knowledge about color extraction.

Producing Stable Interpretations: Visual Perception

Let's return, for a moment, to the cube in Figure 5.1. You have seen how the electromagnetic energy bouncing off the page gets translated into an electrochemical signal, and how specialized regions of the visual pathway break the message down—the brain extracts lines, edges, colors, even angles of orientation from the visual scene. But your fundamental perception is still of a cube—an object with form, not some complex combination of elementary particles.

To understand how the human brain can perceive "wholes" with visual machinery that seems destined to analyze "parts," it helps to remember that perception is only partly determined by what comes in through the eyes. People also rely a great deal on their knowledge and their expectations to "construct" what they see. Let's consider an example: Take a look at the two images depicted in Figure 5.12. At first glance, these appear to be rather meaningless collections of complex black shapes. But panel (b) soon comes into line—you see the word SKY, in white, against a solid black background. Panel (a) also depicts the word SKY, but written in Chinese calligraphy. People who can read English, but not Chinese, have

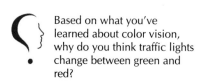

Based on what you've learned about color vision, why do you think traffic lights change between green and red?

FIGURE 5.12
Prior Knowledge and Perception.
Can you detect meaningful images in panels (a) and (b)? The answer probably depends on how much prior knowledge you bring to the perceptual "interpretation" process. (From Coren, Ward, & Enns, 1994.)

(a)

(b)

no problem interpreting and perceiving panel (b) as a meaningful image, but panel (a) remains a mystery (Coren, Porac, & Theodor, 1987). Thus, prior knowledge plays a critical role in helping people "interpret" what they see.

People also typically use one part of a visual display to help interpret other parts. Exactly the same visual event is shown in positions 2 and 4 of the following two lines

A 13 C D E F G
10 11 12 13 14 15 16

but you "see" the letter B or the number 13 depending on the surrounding events. The surrounding letters and digits act as *context* and generate expectations about what appropriate "whole" is likely to be present in positions 2 and 4. In some cases, the contextual elements in a visual display can even cause people to see things that aren't really there. Is there a white triangle embedded in the middle of Figure 5.13? Perhaps, but the perception in this case is really an illusion—there is no physical stimulus, no reflected pattern of electromagnetic energy on the retina, that corresponds to the triangular form. Yet, you interpret the pattern as a triangle.

Psychologists have recognized for some time that there is more to perception than what "meets the eye." Our perceptual world is constructed through a combination of *bottom-up processing*—the sensory analysis of the actual environmental message—and *top-down processing*—the influence of beliefs and expectations about how the world is organized. To help matters, people appear to possess certain innate rules or principles of organization that influence, and sometimes determine, their perception of figures and wholes.

Principles of Organization. You may remember that in Chapter 1 we briefly discussed the possibility that people are born with certain organizing principles of perception that cannot be altered by experience. This point of view was championed by a group of researchers known as *Gestalt psychologists* (the word *Gestalt* translates from the German as "configuration" or "pattern"). According to the Gestalt psychologists, people see objects as well-structured and organized wholes because they are born with tendencies to *group* the incoming visual message in sensible ways. For example, people have a natural, automatic tendency to divide any visual scene into a discernible *figure* and *ground*—they see the wine glass as separate from the table, the printed word as separate from the page. The rules governing the separation of figure and ground are complex, but as you can see from Figure 5.14, the task is easy or hard depending on whether strong or weak cues are available to guide the interpretation.

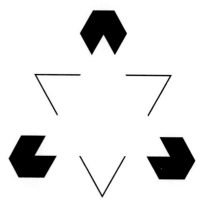

FIGURE 5.13
Illusory Contours. Can you see the white triangle embedded in this figure? There is no physical stimulus that corresponds to the triangular form. Nonetheless, people interpret the pattern as a triangle.

FIGURE 5.14
Separating Figure from Ground. People have a natural tendency to divide any visual scene into a discernible "figure" and "ground." The task can be difficult, as illustrated in the painting in (b), or it can be easy but ambiguous, as in panel (a): Which do you see, a vase or a pair of faces?

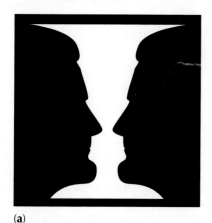

(a)

(b)

The Gestalt psychologists outlined a number of compelling and systematic rules, known generally as the **Gestalt principles of organization,** that govern how people organize what they see:

1. *The law of proximity.* If the elements of a display are close to each other—that is, they lie in close spatial proximity—they tend to be grouped together as part of the same object. Here, for example, you see three groups of dots, rather than a single collection.

Proximity

2. *The law of similarity.* Items that share physical properties—that physically resemble each other—are placed into the same set. Thus, here you see rows of X's and rows of O's rather than mixed-object columns.

Similarity

3. *The law of closure.* Even if a figure has a gap, or a small amount of its border is missing, people tend to perceive the object as complete.

Closure

4. *The law of good continuation.* If lines cross or are interrupted, people tend to see continuous lines that flow in a continuous direction. Here, you have no trouble perceiving the snake as a whole object, even though part of it is blocked from view.

Continuation

5. *The law of common fate.* If things appear to be moving in the same direction, people tend to group them together. Here, the moving dots are classified together, as a group with some fate in common.

Common fate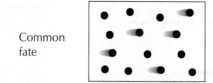

By imposing organization on the visual scene, these natural grouping rules simplify the problem of recognizing objects. For example, Irving Biederman (1987, 1990) has suggested that the Gestalt principles of organization help the visual system break down complex visual messages into components called *geons* (short for "geometric icons"). Geons are simple geometrical forms, such as blocks, cylinders, wedges, and cones. From a collection of no more than 36 geons, Biederman argues, more than 150 million possible complex and meaningful objects can be created—far more than people would ever need to capture the richness of their perceptual world. This means that once the brain is familiar with the basic geons, it acquires the capability to recognize the basic components of any perceptual experience. Rather like the 26 letters of the alphabet form the basis for an incredible variety of words, geons are the alphabet for building any object that a person might see.

One of the attractive features of Biederman's theory, which he calls **recognition by components,** is its ability to explain how people can successfully identify degraded or incomplete objects. Nature rarely provides all the identifying characteristics of a physical object; cars are usually partially hidden behind other cars; a hurried glimpse of a child's face in a crowd might be all the information that reaches the eye. Yet the viewer has no trouble recognizing the car or the child. According to Biederman (1987), only two or three geons can be sufficient for the rapid identification of most objects.

To illustrate, Biederman asked subjects to identify objects such as the ones shown in the left panel of Figure 5.15. In some cases, the items were presented intact; in other conditions, the images were degraded by removing bits of information that either maintained (the middle column) or disrupted (the right column) the component geons. Not surprisingly, people had no problem recognizing the objects in the middle column but had considerably more trouble when the geons were obscured. In fact, Biederman found that identification of the right-column objects was almost impossible—most subjects in this condition failed to identify any of the objects correctly.

The Perception of Depth. The ability to recognize objects and forms, perhaps as a product of inborn principles of organization, is only part of the story of perception. In addition to recognizing figures as separate from backgrounds, people also see those figures in depth. In fact, the ability to perceive depth is one of the most amazing capabilities of the visual system. Think about it: The visual message that arrives for processing at the retina is essentially two-dimensional. Yet, somehow, people are able to extract a rich three-dimensional world from the "flat" image plastered on the retina. How is this possible? Moreover, as we discussed in Chapter 4, the ability to perceive depth develops relatively early in life. Infants as young as a few months can clearly tell the differences between the shallow and deep sides of a visual "cliff" (Campos, Langer, & Krowitz 1970; Gibson & Walk, 1960).

The ability to extract depth from the visual message results from a combination of bottom-up and top-down processing. People use their knowledge about objects, in combination with the actual visual message, to create a three-dimensional world. For example, the brain knows and adjusts for the fact that distant objects produce smaller reflections on the retina. Thus, if you see two people that you *know* to be of comparable height, but the retinal images they produce are of different sizes, your brain deduces that one person must be standing closer than the other. Experience has also demonstrated that closer objects tend to block the image of objects that are farther away: If your view of a TV screen is blocked by a human form, you can be reasonably certain that your friend is standing in *front* of the television.

Another cue for distance, one that artists often use to convey depth in paintings, is *linear perspective.* As shown in the accompanying photo, parallel lines that recede into the distance tend to converge toward a single point. Generally, the farther away two lines are, the closer together those lines will appear to be. The relative *shading* of objects in a scene can provide important clues as well: If one object casts a shadow on another, you can often tell which of the two is farther away. Objects that are far away also tend to look blurry and slightly bluish. If you look

FIGURE 5.15
Recognition by Components.
Biederman proposed that people recognize visual forms, in part, by extracting simple geometric forms, called geons, from the visual message. Two degraded versions of the objects on the left are shown in the middle and right columns. People have no trouble recognizing the objects in the middle column but cannot identify the objects shown in the right column. The reason is that the important components of the message—the geons—are degraded in the right column but not in the middle column. (From Biederman, 1990.)

Can you identify the types of cues present in these "flat" pictures that allow people to perceive depth?

Have you ever seen those random-dot stereograms that contain 3-D images "hidden" in meaningless patterns? They work because they've been designed to present similar yet slightly different visual information to each eye.

at a realistic painting of a mountain scene, you'll see that the distant hills lack fine detail and are painted with a tinge of blue.

The depth cues that we've been considering are called *monocular cues,* which means they require input from only one eye. A person can close one eye and still see a world full of depth, based on the use of monocular cues. But the brain also uses *binocular cues* to perceive depth; these are cues produced by the fact that humans have two eyes and that each eye has a slightly different view of the world. Hold your index finger up about an inch or so in front of your eyes. Now quickly close and open each eye in alternation. You should see your finger jumping back and forth as you switch from one open eye to the other. The finger appears to move because each eye has a slightly different angle of view on the world, producing different images in each retina.

The differences between the images in the two eyes is called **binocular disparity.** It's a useful binocular cue for depth because the amount of disparity changes with distance. When an object is far away, there is less binocular disparity than when an object is closer. Move your finger farther away from your nose and repeat the exercise of rapidly closing one eye and then the other. You should see the finger shifting less as you move it farther from your face. The brain derives depth information, in part, by calculating the amount of disparity between the image in the left eye and the image in the right eye. The brain can also use the degree that the two eyes turn inward, called *convergence,* to derive information about depth. The closer an object is to the face, the more the two eyes need to turn inward, or converge, in order to see the object properly.

Perceptual Constancies. Another rather remarkable feature of the human visual system is its capacity to recognize that an object remains the same even though the reflected image in the retina might be constantly changing. To consider a case in point, in the previous section we discussed how the size of an object's retinal image decreases with distance. As you walk away from a parked car, for instance, the size of its retinal image can become so small that it eventually resembles the image that might be reflected from a toy car held at arm's distance. Do you ever wonder why your car has mysteriously been transformed into a toy? You don't, of course, because your visual system maintains a stable interpretation of the image, as a car, despite the changes in retinal size.

When you perceive the properties of an object to remain the same even though the physical properties of the message are changing, you are showing what is called a **perceptual constancy.** In the case of the car, it is *size constancy*—the perceived size of the car remains constant even though the distance of the object from your eyes changes. Figure 5.16 provides an example of *shape constancy.* Consider how many changes occur in the reflected image of a door as it slowly moves from closed to open. Yet you still recognize it as a door, not as some bizarre shape that evolves unpredictably over time. Size and shape constancies turn out to be related—both result, at least in part, from the visual system's use of cues to determine distance. Both are also extremely adaptive characteristics. In most instances, the object does, in fact, remain constant—only its reflected image changes.

To see what kind of cues might be used to produce constancy, take a look at Figure 5.17. Take particular note of the rectangular shapes on the ground marked as A, B, and C. You see these planters as the same size and shape, in part, because of the texture patterns covering the ground. Each of the open boxes covers three texture tiles in length and an additional three in width. The actual retinal image, however, differs markedly for each of the shapes (take a ruler and measure the physical size of each shape). You interpret and see them as the same because your experiences in the world have taught you that size and distance are related in systematic ways (but see the section on The Adaptive Mind that closes the chapter).

FIGURE 5.17
Constancy Cues. You see these three planters, marked A, B, and C, as similar in size and shape partly because of depth cues in the environment. Each covers three texture tiles in length and three in width.

People show perceptual constancies for a variety of object dimensions. In addition to size and shape constancy, the brightness and color of an object can appear to remain constant, even though the intensity and wavelength of the light changes. Once again, these characteristics help people maintain a stable and orderly interpretation of a constantly changing world. Think about how chaotic the world would appear if you "saw" a new and different object every time the physical properties of its reflected image changed. For example, instead of seeing the same dancer gliding across the floor, you might be forced to see a string of dancers each engaged in some unique and idiosyncratic pose.

Perceptual Illusions. Of course, the perception of constancy is not gained without a cost. In its effort to maintain stability in image interpretation, the visual system can be tricked—**perceptual illusions,** or inappropriate interpretations of physical reality, can be created. Take a look at the two people sitting in the room depicted in Figure 5.18. The girl sitting on the right appears much taller than the girl sitting on the left. In reality, these two are approximately the same size. You're tricked because your brain uses cues in the environment—combined with the belief that rooms are vertically and horizontally rectangular—to interpret the "size" of the inhabitants. Actually, as the rest of the figure shows, it is the room, not the difference in size of the girls, that is unusual.

FIGURE 5.18

The Ames Room. The person sitting on the right appears much taller than the person sitting on the left. But this is really an illusion induced by the belief that the room is rectangular. As you can see, the room itself is deviant—the sloping ceiling and floors simply provide misleading depth cues. To the viewer looking through the peephole the room appears perfectly normal. This famous illusion is called the Ames Room, after its designer, Adelbert Ames.

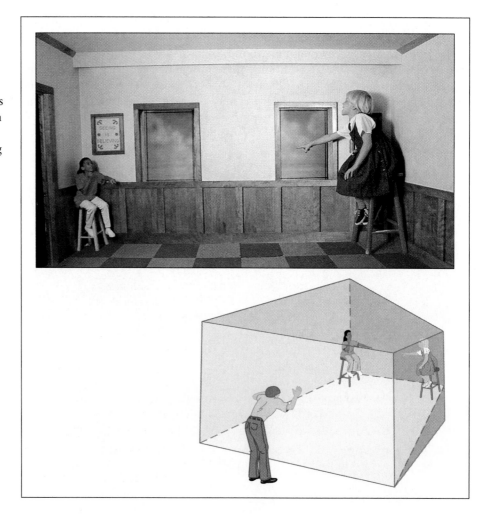

FIGURE 5.19
Illusions of Depth. These two figures illustrate how depth cues can lead to perceptual illusions. Each is based on the Ponzo illusion. In (a) the horizontal lines are actually the same size, as are the monsters in (b). (From Shepard, 1990.)

(a)   (b)

Based partly on your expectations about the shape of rooms, and partly on the unique construction of the room, as you look through the peephole you "think" you're looking at two people who are the same distance away from your eyes. But the person on the left is actually farther away, so a smaller image is projected onto the retina. Because the brain "assumes" the two are the same distance away, it compensates for the differences in retinal size by making the person on the right appear larger.

The Ponzo illusion, shown in Figure 5.19a, operates in a similar way. You see two lines that are exactly the same size as quite different because the linear perspective cue—the converging parallel lines—tricks the brain into thinking that the horizontal line near the top of the display is farther away. Because it has the same size retinal image as the bottom line (remember, the two are physically the same size) the brain compensates for the distance by making the top line "appear" larger. Figure 5.19b shows a similar illusion: The monsters are really the same, but the one on the top certainly appears larger!

Similar principles underlie perception of the Müller-Lyer illusion, which is shown in Figure 5.20 (see page 180). The vertical line with the wings turned up (a) appears longer than the line with the wings turned down (b), even though each line is identical in length. As (c) shows, this particular illusion has a real-life analog—the interior and exterior "corners" of a room or building. Notice that for the outside corner of this building, the "wings" are really perspective cues signaling that the front edge is thrusting forward and the walls are sloping away. For the inside corner, the perspective cues signal the opposite—the inside edge is farther away. In the Müller-Lyer illusion the two lines produce the same retinal image, but your visual system assumes that (a), which mimics the interior corner, is likely to be farther away, and consequently must be larger in size.

Interestingly, if the Müller-Lyer illusion is based on people's experiences with rooms and buildings, we can speculate about what it would be like to be raised in an environment with few rectangular corners. We can predict that a person who has limited experience with rectangular corners might actually be less susceptible to the illusion because he or she will be unlikely to interpret the "wings" as cues for depth. Indeed, when a group of Navajos who had been raised in traditional circular homes, called hogans, were tested for the illusion, they were more likely to consider the lines as equal in length (Leibowitz, 1971; Pedersen & Wheeler, 1983).

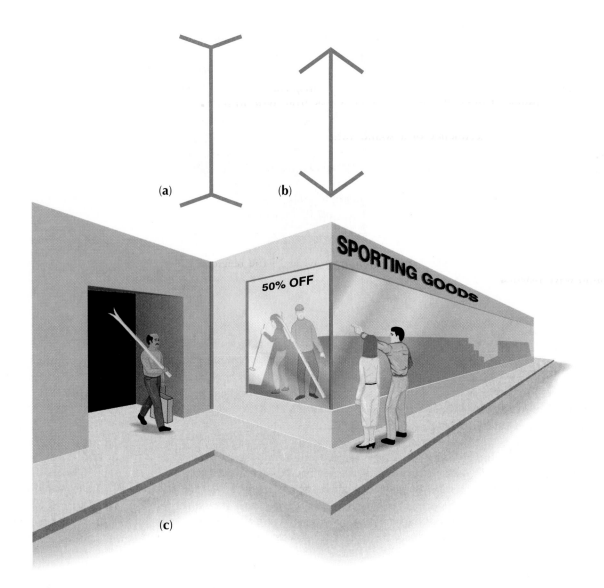

FIGURE 5.20
The Müller-Lyer Illusion. The vertical line with the wings turned up (a) appears longer than the line with the wings turned down (b). This particular illusion may be influenced by experiences with the interior and exterior corners of buildings, as (c) shows.

Hearing: Identifying and Localizing Sounds

The sense of sight builds one kind of representation of the outside world—a visual world that is driven by complex patterns of light and dark that lie across the retina. Hearing creates a different kind of world, but one that is just as adaptive as the world created by sight. Sounds help people identify and locate objects in their path. It is through sound that people are able to produce and comprehend the spoken word, thus nurturing their ability to socialize and interact with others. Even our most private sense of self—the world inside our heads—appears in the form of an inner voice, or an ongoing speech-based monologue (see Chapter 8).

Translating the Message: Auditory Transduction

The physical message delivered to the auditory system, **sound,** is a form of energy, like light, that travels as a wave. But sound, unlike light, is mechanical energy and requires a *medium* (such as air or water) in order to move. Sound begins with a vibrating stimulus, such as the movement of vocal cords, the plucking of a tight string, or the pounding diaphragm of a stereo speaker. The vibration pushes air molecules out into space, where they collide with other air molecules, and a kind of traveling chain reaction begins.

The rate of the vibrating stimulus determines the *frequency* of the sound, defined as the number of times the pressure wave moves from peak to peak per second (measured in units called *hertz*, where 1 Hz = 1 cycle (repetition)/second). Psychologically, when the frequency of a sound varies, people hear changes in **pitch**; for example, middle C on a piano has a frequency of 262 Hz, whereas the highest note on a piano corresponds to about 4000 Hz. Humans are potentially sensitive to frequencies from roughly 20 to 20,000 Hz, but we are most sensitive to frequencies in the 1000 to 5000 Hz range (Gulick, Gescheider, & Frisina, 1989; Sivian & White, 1933). Many important sounds fall into this range of maximum sensitivity, including most of the sounds that make up speech (Matlin & Foley, 1992).

The other major dimension of sound is *amplitude,* which is the height that the sound wave reaches. Psychologically, changes in amplitude are experienced as changes in *loudness.* As the wave increases in amplitude, it generally seems louder to the ear. The amplitude of a wave is typically measured in units called *decibels* (dB). To give you some perspective, a normal conversation measures around 60 dB, whereas an incredibly loud rock band can produce sounds over 100 dB. (Just for your information, prolonged exposure to sounds at around 90 decibels can produce permanent hearing loss.)

Entering the Ear. Let's follow a sound as it enters the auditory pathway (see Figure 5.21). We saw that in the visual system, an optical pathway focuses the light energy onto the visual receptors. In the auditory system, sounds travel toward the auditory receptor cells through the ears. The external flap of tissue usually referred to as the "ear" is known technically as the **pinna**; it helps capture the sound, which then funnels down the auditory canal toward the *eardrum,* or **tympanic membrane.**

The tympanic membrane responds to the incoming sound wave by vibrating. The particular vibration pattern, which differs for different sound frequencies, is

FIGURE 5.21
The Structures of the Human Ear.
Sound enters the auditory canal and causes the tympanic membrane to vibrate. The vibration pattern is then transmitted through three small bones in the middle ear to the oval window. Vibration of the oval window causes fluid inside the cochlea to be displaced, moving the basilar membrane. Also shown in the figure are the semicircular canals, which play a role in the sense of balance.

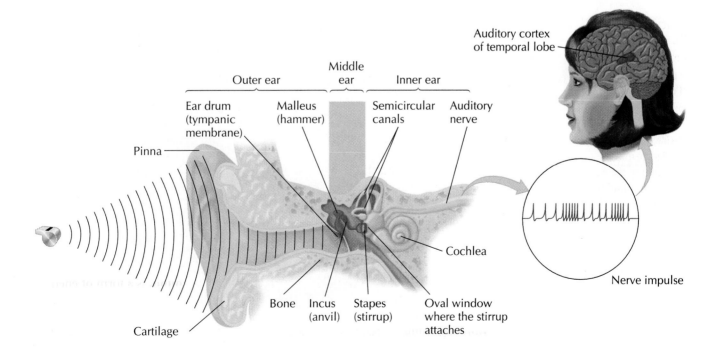

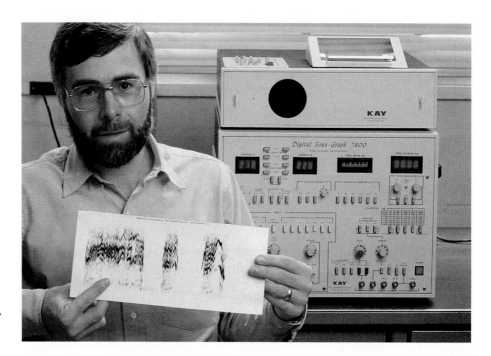

This researcher is holding a spectrogram, which records how the intensity and frequencies of sounds change over time.

then transmitted through three small bones in the **middle ear:** the *malleus* (or hammer), the *incus* (or anvil), and the *stapes* (or stirrup). These bones help intensify the vibration pattern and prepare it for passage into the fluid-filled "inner ear." Within the inner ear lies a bony, snail-shaped sound processor called the **cochlea** ("snail"); here, the sound energy gets its initial translation into the internal language of the nervous system.

Transduction in the Cochlea. The third bone in the middle ear, the stapes, is connected to an opening in the cochlea called the *oval window.* As the stapes vibrates, it causes fluid inside the cochlea to displace a flexible membrane, called the **basilar membrane,** that runs throughout the cochlear shell. Transduction takes place through the activation of tiny auditory receptor cells, called *hair cells,* that sit in close contact with the basilar membrane. As the membrane starts to ripple— like a cat moving under a bedsheet—tiny hairs, called *cilia,* that extend outward from the hair cells are displaced. The bending of these hairs causes the auditory

FIGURE 5.22

The Basilar Membrane. This figure shows an open slice of the cochlea. Sound vibrations cause fluid inside the cochlea to displace the basilar membrane that runs throughout the cochlear shell. Different sound frequencies trigger different movement patterns along the membrane. Transduction takes place through the bending of hair cells that sit in close contact with the membrane. Those hair cells nearest the point of maximum displacement will be stimulated the most, which helps the brain code information about pitch.

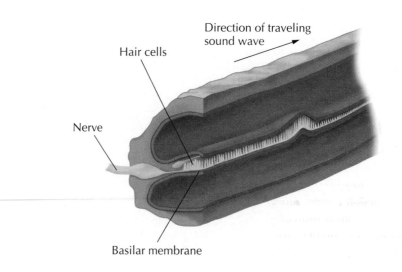

receptor cells to fire, creating a neural impulse that travels up the auditory pathways to the brain (see Figure 5.22).

Different sound frequencies trigger different movement patterns along the basilar membrane. Higher frequencies of sound cause the membrane to be displaced the most near the oval window; low frequencies produce a traveling wave that activates the entire membrane but reaches its peak deep inside the spiraling cochlea. As we'll discuss shortly, the particular receptor cells that are activated help the brain extract information about pitch. If hair cells near the oval window are responding the most, the incoming sound is perceived as high in pitch. If many cells along the membrane are active, and the most active ones are far away from the oval window, the incoming sound is perceived as low in pitch.

Extracting the Message Components: Auditory Pathways

Less is known about the auditory pathways than about the visual route toward the cortex, although there are some general similarities worth noting. The neural impulses generated from the hair cells leave the cochlea in each ear along the *auditory nerve.* Messages that have been received in the right ear travel mainly along pathways leading to the left hemisphere of the brain; left-ear messages go primarily to the right hemisphere. Analogous to processes in the visual system, auditory nerve fibers appear "tuned" to transmit a specific kind of message. In the visual system, the ganglion cells transmit information about regions of light and dark on the retina. In the auditory system, fibers in the auditory nerve pass on rough *frequency* information. Electrophysiological measurements of individual auditory nerve fibers show "tuning" curves—for example, a fiber might respond best to an input stimulus of around 2000 Hz and less well to others.

Extracting Pitch. Just as a complex visual pattern is built from simpler patterns of light and dark, complex sounds—such as speech patterns—are built from combinations of simpler sound frequencies. The auditory system extracts information about these simple frequencies, which correspond to different "pitches," through several mechanisms. Pitch information is clearly coded, in part, by the particular place on the basilar membrane that is active; for example, as we discussed earlier, activation of hair cells near the oval window leads to the perception of a high-pitched sound. The idea that pitch is perceived as a consequence of individual hair cell activation is called the **place theory** of pitch perception (Békésy, 1960). "Place" in this instance refers to the location of the activated hair cell along the basilar membrane.

Place theory helps explain certain kinds of hearing loss. For example, as people grow older they typically have great difficulty discriminating the higher frequencies of sound (such as those

Prolonged exposure to intense noise can create hearing loss.

in whispered speech). Why might this be so? Most sounds that enter the auditory system activate, to at least some extent, those hair cells nearest the oval window. Cells in the interior portions of the cochlea respond actively only when low-frequency sounds are present. Thus, if receptor cells "wear out" from years of prolonged activity, those nearest the oval window should be among the first to do so. Place theory thus explains, in part, why older people have difficulty hearing high-pitched sounds.

Despite its successes, place theory does not offer a complete account of pitch perception. One problem with place theory is that hair cells do not act independently—often, many are activated in unison. As a result, it is thought that pitch perception must also rely on the *rate* at which cells fire their neural impulses. According to the **frequency principle,** the pitch of a sound is determined partly by the frequency of neural impulses traveling up the auditory pathway: the higher the rate of firing, the higher the perceived pitch. High-frequency sounds produce more wave "peaks," providing more opportunities for the receptor cells to become activated. Moreover, because individual neurons can fire only at limited intervals (each has a "refractory period" during which neural impulses cannot be generated), it is also believed that groups of neurons, firing in particular relation to one another, are important elements in pitch discrimination. When groups of cells generate neural impulses rapidly in succession, they create *volleys* of impulses that provide additional clues about the pitch of the incoming message (Wever, 1949).

The Auditory Cortex. The auditory message eventually reaches the auditory cortex, which is located mainly in the temporal lobes of the brain. Cells in the auditory cortex appear to respond best to complex combinations of sounds rather than to individual sound frequencies. For example, a cell in the auditory cortex might respond only to a sequence of tones that moves from one frequency to another, or to a burst of noise (Pickles, 1988). It's been demonstrated in some animals that certain cortical cells respond only to sounds that exist in the animal's natural vocabulary—that is, to a particular "shriek," "cackle," or "trill" that is part of the animal's normal vocalization pattern (Wollberg & Newman, 1972).

Producing Stable Interpretations: Auditory Perception

Say the phrase "kiss the sky," then repeat it aloud in rapid succession. Now do the same thing with the word "stress" or "life." You'll notice that your perception of what you're saying undergoes some interesting changes. "Kiss the sky" begins to sound like "kiss this guy"; "stress" will probably turn into "dress" and "life" into "fly."

Organizing the Auditory Message. As with the ever-changing Necker cube, a one-to-one mapping does not always exist between the physical and the psychological interpretation of a sound event. The brain is often faced with auditory ambiguity—it seeks meaning where it can, usually by relying on established organizational rules (Bregman, 1990). As with vision, the brain separates the incoming auditory stream into figure and ground; it tends to group auditory events that are similar and that occur close together in time. Sound frequency, for example, can be used as a grouping cue to distinguish among voices. Females generally speak at higher frequencies than males. As a result, it is easier to tell the difference between a male and a female talking than it is to discriminate between two speakers of the same gender (Matlin & Foley, 1992).

The fact that the brain organizes and imposes structure on incoming sound messages should not come as much of a surprise. Think about how easily you can listen to a band or orchestra, filled with many different instruments, and pick out the trumpet, violin, or piano. Think about how easily you can focus on the intriguing voice of your date, to the exclusion of other voices, while in the midst of a

Think about how easily you can listen to an orchestra with many different instrument sounds and pick out the sound of the trumpet, violin, or piano.

noisy party. Moreover, the ability to identify and organize sounds increases with experience. People use their knowledge and expectations, through *top-down processing,* to interpret the incoming auditory sequence. Car mechanics, after years of experience, can identify an engine problem simply by listening to the particular "knocking" that the engine makes; cardiologists, as a result of experience, can use the intricacies of the heartbeat to diagnose the health of a cardiovascular system.

Prior knowledge not only influences how people perceive sounds, it also influences how they produce sequences of sounds. Try saying the following aloud, and listen closely to the sounds:

> Marzi doats n doze edoats n lidul lamzey divey.

Recognize anything familiar? Well, actually this is a well-phrased lesson in the dietary habits of familiar barnyard animals; it's taken from a popular 1940s song (Sekular & Blake, 1990). (Here's a hint: Mares eat oats and . . .) With a little knowledge, and a generated set of expectations about the content of the message, you should eventually arrive at an agreeable interpretation of the lyric. Notice how once you've arrived at that interpretation, the same groupings of letters produce quite a different reading aloud.

Can you think of any songs that you like now but didn't like when you first heard them? One possibility is that you've "learned" to organize the music in a way that makes it more appealing.

Localizing Sound. Another adaptive characteristic of the auditory sense is the ability to use incoming sounds to discern location. For example, if you're driving down the street fiddling with your car radio and hear a sudden screech of brakes, you're able to determine the source of the sound rapidly and efficiently. How do you accomplish this feat? Just as comparisons between the retinal locations of images in the two eyes provide information about visual depth, message comparisons between the ears help people *localize* objects in space. Let's assume that the braking car is approaching yours from the left side. Because your left ear is closer to the source of the sound, it will receive the relevant sound vibrations slightly sooner than your right ear; moreover, the sounds arriving first will also be somewhat more *intense.* Your brain can calculate the differences in arrival times between the two ears, plus any differences in intensity (or loudness), and use this information to localize the source (Giguere & Abel, 1993).

The Skin Senses: Touch, Temperature, and Pain

People's perceptual experiences might appear to be driven primarily by what comes in through their eyes and ears. People communicate through the spoken word; they usually identify objects in their path through vision. But consider the psychological significance of a world devoid of physical contact. It is through a lingering kiss, or the brush of a hand against a cheek, that experiences often gain meaning. Skin contact builds its own perceptual world: You can detect the location of a light switch in the dark, feel the warmth of a fire, or experience the pain of an accidental cut.

It's relatively easy to appreciate the adaptive significance of the skin senses. You need to be able to detect the presence of a spider crawling up your leg; if a blowing ember from the fireplace happens to land on your forearm, it is certainly adaptive for you to respond quickly. The human skin contains a variety of receptor cells that differ in shape, size, and presumably, function. We'll briefly consider three skin senses in this section—the senses of *touch, temperature,* and *pain.* In each case, as in our earlier discussions, the environmental message needs to be translated, transmitted to the brain, and interpreted in a meaningful fashion.

Touch

In the case of touch or pressure, the physical message delivered to the skin is mechanical. An object makes contact with the body—perhaps the fingers actively reach out and initiate the contact—and receptor cells embedded in the skin are disturbed. The mechanical pressure on the cell (it is literally deformed) produces a neural impulse, and the message is then transmitted to the spinal cord and up into the brain.

At this point, there doesn't appear to be a simple one-to-one mapping between receptor type and perceptual experience. Although certain cells, called **Pacinian corpuscles,** seem to respond most actively to pressure, other receptors in the skin respond to several kinds of stimulation, including touch, temperature, and pain. As with vision and hearing, touch information is transmitted up the neural pathway through distinct channels to processing stations in the brain, where the inputs

Humans use the sense of touch to acquire information about shape, firmness, texture, and weight.

received from various points on the body are combined (Bolanowski, 1989). One kind of nerve fiber might carry information about touch location; other fibers might transmit information about whether the touch has been brief or sustained.

At the level of the *somatosensory cortex,* located in the parietal lobe of the brain, a close connection is found among regions of skin and cortical representation (Prud'homme, Cohen, & Kalaska, 1994). As we discussed in Chapter 3, the cortex contains multiple "body maps," where adjacent cortical cells have areas of sensitivity that correspond to adjacent areas on the skin. Moreover, as in the visual cortex, some areas are represented more extensively than others. For example, a relatively large amount of cortical tissue is devoted to the hands and lips, whereas the middle portion of the back, despite its size, receives little representation in the cortex.

Virtually everyone has the ability to recognize complex objects exclusively through touch. When blindfolded, people show near-perfect identification of common objects (such as toothbrushes and paperclips) after examining them by touch (Klatzky, Lederman, & Metzger, 1985). Active skin contact with an object produces not only shape information but information about firmness, texture, and weight. Moreover, as with seeing and hearing, a person's final interpretation of an object depends on a mixture of what the person feels and what he or she expects to feel. For instance, if you expect to be touched by an object on a particular finger, you are more likely to identify the object correctly (Craig, 1985).

> Can you tell the difference between the touch of a loved one and the touch of a stranger? Do you think you can learn to "interpret" a touch differently with experience?

Temperature

At present, researchers have only a limited idea of how the body records and processes the temperature of an object. Electrophysiological research has detected the presence of **cold fibers** that respond to a cooling of the skin by increasing the production of neural impulses, as well as **warm fibers** that respond vigorously when the temperature of the skin increases. But the behavior of these temperature-sensitive receptor systems is not particularly well understood (Zotterman, 1959).

We do know, however, that the perception of warm and cold is only indirectly related to the actual temperature of the real-world object. To demonstrate, try plunging one hand into a bowl of cold water and the other hand into a bowl of hot water. Now place both hands into a third bowl containing water sitting at room temperature. The hand that was in the cold water will sense the water as warm; the other hand will experience it as cold. Same water, same temperature, but two different perceptual experiences. The secret behind this perceptual "enigma" lies in understanding that it is the temperature *change* that determines your perception. When your cold hand touches warmer water, your skin begins to warm; it is the increase in skin temperature that you actually perceive.

At times, these perceptual processes can lead to temperature "illusions." For instance, metal seems cooler than wood even when both are at the same physical temperature. Why? Because metal is a better conductor of heat than wood, so it absorbs more warmth from the skin; the brain thereby perceives the loss of heat as a cooler physical temperature.

Pain

Pain is a unique kind of sensory experience. It is not a characteristic of the external world that the brain seeks to interpret, such as an object or an energy source.

The fact that these people can take a "snow bath" in the middle of winter demonstrates how the perception of temperature can be influenced by psychological factors.

Rather, **pain** is an adaptive reaction that the body generates in response to any stimulus that is intense enough to cause tissue damage. The stimulus can be just about anything. It can come from outside or inside the body; it doesn't even need to be particularly intense (consider the effect of salt on an open wound).

If forced to identify a particular pain receptor system, most researchers would choose cells called *free nerve endings,* which apparently transmit signals to those areas of the brain that perceive pain. Pain is a complex psychological experience, however, often relying on much more than just the physical stimulus. There are well-documented examples of soldiers who report little or no pain after receiving serious injuries in battle; the same is true of many individuals entering an emergency room. In addition, certain non-Western cultures use rituals that should, from a Western perspective, inflict great pain but apparently do not (Melzak, 1973).

The interplay between the physical and the psychological in pain perception forms the basis for the widely accepted **gate-control theory** of pain (Melzak & Wall, 1965, 1982). The basic idea is that the neural impulses generated by pain receptors can be blocked, or gated, in the spinal cord by signals produced in the brain. If you've just sliced your finger cutting carrots on the kitchen counter, you would normally feel pain. But if a pan on the stove suddenly starts to smoke, the pain seems to evaporate while you try to prevent your house from burning down. According to the gate-control theory, the brain can block the critical pain signals from reaching higher neural centers when it is appropriate to do so.

How is the gating action actually carried out? Once again, the details of the mechanisms are unclear, but there appear to be two types of nerve fibers that are responsible for opening and closing the gate. So-called "large" fibers, when stimulated, produce nervous system activity that closes the gate; other, "small" fibers, when stimulated, inhibit those neural processes and effectively open the gate. External activities, such as rubbing or placing ice on a wound, also apparently stimulate the large fibers, which close the gate preventing further passage of the pain message toward the brain.

In addition to gating the pain signals, as we discussed in Chapter 3, the brain can also control the experience of pain through the release of chemicals called *endorphins,* which produce pain-killing effects like those obtained through morphine. The release of endorphins is thought to underlie those instances in which pain "should" be experienced, but is not. For example, sometimes swallowing a sugar pill can dramatically reduce pain even though there is no physical reason why sugar should be effective (a "placebo" effect). The locus of such effects, and other analgesic procedures such as acupuncture, might lie in the brain's internal production of its own antipain medication.

The Body Senses: Movement and Balance

Human sensory systems have developed not only to detect the presence of objects in the environment but also to provide accurate information about the body itself. We have just considered pain as an example of "body-monitoring"; we now briefly consider two additional systems that help people detect and control the movement and position of their body.

The Kinesthetic Sense

The word **kinesthesia** literally means "movement"; when used in connection with sensation, the term refers to the ability to sense the position and movement of one's body parts. For example, as you reach toward a blossoming flower, feedback

The vestibular sense helps people maintain balance by monitoring the position of the body in space.

from your skin, tendons, muscles, and especially joints helps you maintain the correct line toward the target. The kinesthetic sense shares many properties with the sense of touch—a variety of receptor types in the muscles that surround the joints react to the physical forces produced by moving the limbs or by forming complex body positions (Gandevia, McCloskey, & Burke, 1992).

The nerve impulses generated by the kinesthetic receptors travel, as in touch, to the somatosensory cortex. It is presumed that at the level of the cortex, there are increasingly complex cells that respond only when body parts, such as the arms, are placed in certain positions (Gardner & Costanzo, 1981). But, the psychological experience of movement is most likely influenced by multiple factors, as with other kinds of perception (Jones, 1988). The visual system, for example, provides additional feedback about current position, as does the sense of touch.

The Vestibular Sense

Humans have another complex receptor system, attached to the cochlea of the inner ear, that responds not only to movement but also to acceleration and to changes in upright posture. Each ear contains three small fluid-filled **semicircu-**

Continual disturbance of the semicircular canals or the vestibular sacs can produce dizziness, nausea, and motion sickness.

lar canals that are lined with hair cells similar to those found in the cochlea. If you quickly turn your head toward some object, these hair cells are displaced and nerve impulses signaling acceleration are transmitted throughout the brain. Some of the nerve fibers project to the cortex; others send messages to the eye muscles, so you can accurately adjust your eyes as your head is turning.

The vestibular system is also responsible for the sense of balance. If you tilt your head, or encounter a 360-degree loop on a roller coaster, receptor cells located in other inner ear organs, called **vestibular sacs,** quickly transmit the appropriate orientation information to the brain. Continual disturbance of the semicircular canals or the vestibular sacs can produce dizziness, nausea, and motion sickness (Lackner & DiZio, 1991).

The Chemical Senses: Smell and Taste

We end our review of the individual sensory systems with the chemical senses, *smell* and *taste*. Among the vast variety of messages received from the environment, few carry as much emotional impact as chemically based input. You can appreciate the touch from a loving caress, or the visual beauty of a sunset, but consider your reaction to the smell of decaying meat, or to the distinctive taste of milk left a bit too long in the sun! Smells and tastes are enormously adaptive because they possess powerful signaling properties; like other animals, humans learn to avoid the off-odor or the bitter taste.

The perception of both smell and taste is initiated by the activity of receptor cells, called **chemoreceptors,** that react to invisible molecules scattered about in the air or dissolved in liquids. These receptors solve the translation problem and project the newly formed neural impulses toward the brain. Psychologically, the two senses are related: Anyone who has ever had a cold knows that things "just don't taste right" with a plugged nose. You can demonstrate this phenomenon for yourself by holding your nose and trying to taste the difference between an apple and a piece of raw potato. In fact, people can identify a taste far more efficiently if they are also allowed a brief sniff (Mozell and others, 1969). Let's consider each of these chemical senses in a bit more detail.

A taster's ability to identify the smell, or "bouquet," of a fine wine depends on the constellation of airborne chemicals produced by the wine, as well as on the experience of the taster.

Smell

The technical name for the sense of smell is **olfaction,** which comes from the Latin word *olfacere* meaning "to smell." Airborne molecules enter through the nose or the back of the throat and interact with receptor cells embedded in the upper region of the nasal cavity (Lancet and others, 1993). Like the receptor systems that are used to hear and detect motion, the olfactory receptor cells contain tiny hairs, or *cilia*. The airborne molecules are thought to bind with the cilia, causing the generation of a neural impulse. The receptor fibers then move the message forward to the *olfactory bulb,* located at the bottom front region of the brain. From here, the information is parceled out to several areas in the brain.

Recent studies have indicated that people probably have up to a thousand or more unique kinds of olfactory receptor cells (Buck & Axel, 1991). Although it might seem reasonable to propose that the activation of a particular receptor maps onto the perception of a particular odor, there's no concrete evidence to support such a view. One reason may be that most odors are complex psychological experiences (Carrasco & Ridout, 1993; Kauer, 1987). People have no problem recognizing the smell of frying bacon, or the aroma of fresh coffee, but a chemical analysis of these events fails to reveal the presence of any single defining molecule. Clearly, the ability to apply the label "frying bacon" to a constellation of airborne chemicals arises from complex perceptual processes. The complexity of odor perception is further reinforced by the finding that it is possible to produce smell illusions—if you are led to expect that a particular odor is present, even though it is not, you are likely to report detecting its presence (O'Mahony, 1978).

The neural pathway for smell is unusual, compared with the other sensory systems that we've described, because connections are made with forebrain structures such as the amygdala, hippocampus, and the hypothalamus. As we learned in Chapter 3, these areas have been linked with the regulation of feeding, drinking, sexual behavior, and even memory. It's speculation, but part of the emotional power of olfactory cues might be related to the involvement of this motivational pathway. Certainly in lower animals, whose behavior is often dominated by odor cues, brain structures such as the hypothalamus and the amygdala seem likely to play a major role in the animal's reaction to odors in its environment.

Many animals release chemicals, called *pheromones,* that cause highly specific reactions when detected by other members of the species. Often pheromones induce sexual behavior or characteristic patterns of aggression, but a variety of reactions can be produced. Ants, for example, react to the smell of a dead member of the colony by carrying the decaying corpse outside the nest (Wilson, 1963). So far, much to the chagrin of the perfume industry, no solid support has been found for "human pheromones"; at least, no scents have been discovered that reliably induce sexual interest.

Taste

Smell's companion sense, taste, is known by the technical term **gustation,** which comes from the Latin *gustare* meaning "to taste." Unlike odors, which are difficult to classify, there appear to be four basic tastes: sweet, bitter, salty, and sour. When

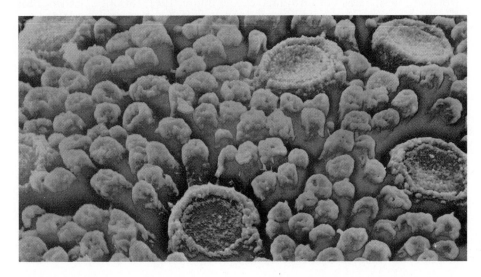

Taste buds, which contain the receptor cells for taste, are embedded within the folds of the papillae (shown here as the large, circular objects).

The flavors of a fine meal are influenced by taste, smell, and visual appearance, in addition to the expectations of the diners.

psychologists use the term *taste,* they are referring to the sensations produced by contact with the taste receptors; they are not referring to overall richness of the psychological experience that accompanies eating. Typically, the term **flavor** is used to describe the meal experience. Flavor is influenced by taste, smell, and the visual appearance of the food, as well as by expectations about the quality of the meal.

Taste receptors are distributed throughout the mouth, but mainly occur across the tongue. If you coat your tongue with a mouthful of milk and glance in a mirror, you'll see that your tongue is covered with tiny bumps called *papillae.* The **taste buds,** which contain the actual receptor cells, are embedded within the folds of the papillae. Currently, researchers are unsure exactly how the transduction process for taste actually occurs. One possibility is that taste stimuli directly penetrate the membrane of the receptor cell, causing the cell to fire; another idea is that taste stimuli simply alter the chemical structure of the cell membrane (Teeter & Brand, 1987). In any case, the neural impulse is generated and passed up toward the brain.

The neural pathway for taste takes a more traditional route than the one for smell: Information is passed toward the thalamus and then up to the somatosensory area of the cortex. Little work has been done on how cortical taste cells react, although taste-sensitive cells have been discovered (Scott, Plata-Salamn, & Smith-Swintosky, 1994; Yamamoto, Yuyama, & Kawamura, 1981). Stronger evidence for taste "tuning" has been found in analysis of the receptor fibers, but, as with many of the other senses, a given receptor cell seems to react to a broad range of gustatory stimuli. The neural code for taste is probably determined to some extent by the particular fiber that happens to react, and also by the relative patterns of activity across large groups of fibers.

The brain can produce stable interpretations of taste stimuli, but the identification process is complex. For one thing, prior exposure to one kind of taste often changes the perception of another. Anyone who has ever tried to drink orange juice after brushing his or her teeth understands how tastes interact. To some extent, the interaction process depends on the similarity of successive tastes. For example, a taste of a sour pickle, but not a salty cracker, will reduce the "sourness" of lemon juice. There are even natural substances that can completely change the normal perception of taste. One substance extracted from berries, called "miracle fruit," turns extremely sour tastes (such as from raw lemons) sweet. Another substance, taken from the leaves of a plant found in India and Africa, temporarily eliminates the sweet taste of sugar.

Some smells and tastes are truly disgusting, and lead to characteristic reactions. If you want to look ahead and learn more about the experience of "disgust," turn to the Adaptive Mind section at the end of Chapter 11.

From the Physical to the Psychological

Throughout this chapter, we've stressed the transition from the physical to the psychological. Messages may originate in the physical world, but conscious experiences—*interpretations*—of those messages are often driven by expectations and beliefs about how the world is organized. In the field of **psychophysics,** researchers search for ways to map the transition from the physical to the psychological in the form of mathematical laws. By quantifying the relationship between the physical properties of a stimulus and its subjective experience, researchers hope to develop *general* laws that cut across all kinds of sensory input. Let's consider some examples of how such laws are established.

Stimulus Detection

Psychophysics is actually one of the oldest research areas in psychology; it dates back to the work of Wilhelm Wundt, Gustav Fechner, and others in the 19th century. One of the first questions these early researchers asked was: What is the minimum amount of stimulus energy needed to produce a sensation? Suppose I present you with a very faint pure tone—one that you cannot hear—and gradually make it louder. At some point you will hear the tone and respond accordingly. This point is known as the **absolute threshold** for the stimulus; it represents the level of intensity that lifts the stimulus over the threshold of conscious awareness. One of the early insights of psychophysicists such as Fechner was the realization that absolute thresholds, on average, are really not absolute—that is, there is no single point in an intensity curve at which detection reliably begins. For a given intensity level, sometimes people will hear the tone, other times not. For this reason, absolute thresholds were redefined as the intensity level at which people can detect the presence of a stimulus 50% of the time (see Figure 5.23).

It might seem strange that a person's detection abilities change from moment to moment. Part of the reason for the variability is that trial-to-trial observations, for a number of reasons, are likely to be "noisy." It is virtually impossible for a researcher to control all the variables that potentially affect someone's performance. For example, a subject might have a momentary lapse in attention that causes him or her to miss a presented stimulus on a given trial. Some random activity in the nervous system might even create brief changes in the sensitivity of the receptor systems. Experimenters try to take these factors into account by presenting the subject with many detection opportunities and averaging performance over trials to determine the threshold point.

Psychologists have also tried to develop reasonably sophisticated statistical techniques to pull the "truth" out of noisy data. Human observers often have built-in biases that influence how they respond in a detection environment. For exam-

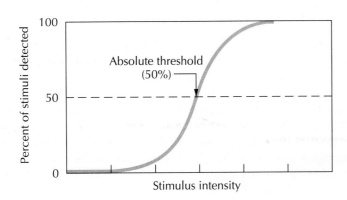

FIGURE 5.23
Absolute Threshold. This graph shows typical results for stimulus detection. As the intensity of the stimulus increases, so does the likelihood that it will be detected. The absolute threshold for detection is defined as the intensity level at which people can detect the presence of the stimulus 50% of the time.

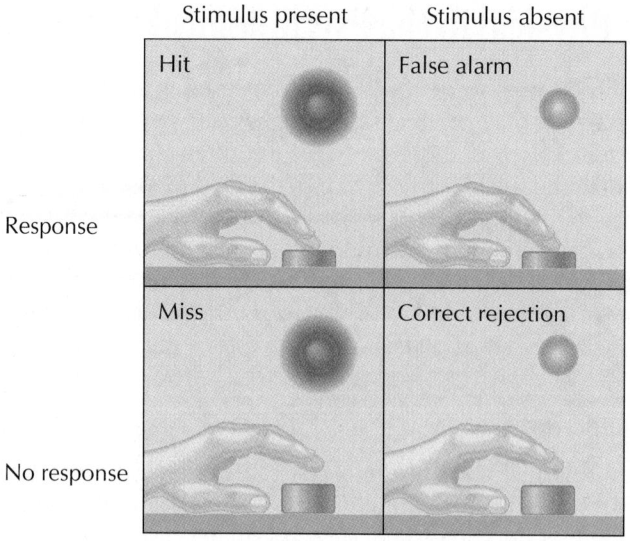

FIGURE 5.24
Signal Detection Outcomes.
This matrix shows the four possible outcomes in a signal detection experiment. If the stimulus is present and correctly detected, it's called a *hit;* if the stimulus is absent but the observer claims it's present, it's called a *false alarm*. A *miss* occurs when the stimulus is present but not detected, and a *correct rejection* occurs when the observer correctly recognizes that the stimulus was not presented.

Can you think of any occupations requiring detection— such as air traffic controller—for which it might be advantageous to be "biased" toward saying "Yes," that a stimulus has occurred?

ple, people will sometimes report the presence of a stimulus even though none has actually been presented. Why? Sometimes the observer is simply worried about missing a presented stimulus, so he or she says "Yes" on every trial. To control for these tendencies, researchers use a technique called **signal detection** that mathematically compares *hits*—in which a stimulus is correctly detected—to *false alarms*—in which the observer claims a stimulus was presented when it actually was not.

Four types of outcomes can occur in a detection situation. Besides hits and false alarms, the subject can also fail to detect a stimulus when it was actually presented—called a *miss*—or correctly recognize that a stimulus was, in fact, not presented on that trial—called a *correct rejection*. These four outcomes are shown in Figure 5.24. Researchers compare these outcomes over trials in an attempt to infer a subject's "true" detection ability.

To see why it's important to compare different outcomes, imagine that Lois is participating in a simple detection experiment and that her strategy is to say "Yes, a stimulus occurred" on every trial (even when no stimulus was actually presented). If the researcher pays attention only to hits, it will appear as if Lois has perfect detection ability—she always correctly identifies a stimulus when it occurs. But saying "Yes" on every trial will also lead to false alarms—she will say "Yes" on trials when no stimulus was actually presented. By comparing hits and false alarms, the researcher is able to determine whether her high number of "hits" is really due to detection ability or whether it's due to some other strategic bias on her part. If Lois can truly detect the stimulus when it occurs, she should show lots of hits and very few false alarms.

Difference Thresholds

Researchers in psychophysics have also been concerned with the detection of **difference thresholds**: the smallest difference in the magnitude of two stimuli that an observer can detect. Suppose I present you with two tones, each equally loud. I then gradually increase the intensity of one of the tones until you notice it as being louder than the other (called the *standard*). How much of a change in magnitude do I need to make for you to detect the difference? As with absolute thresholds, the required amount changes a bit from one moment to the next, but an important general principle emerges.

The addition of a single candle to a brightly lit room has little effect on perceived brightness (left photo); but when a candle is added to a dimly lit room (right photo), the increase in brightness will be quite noticeable.

It turns out that detection of a *just noticeable difference* (or *jnd*) in magnitude depends on how intense the standard was in the first place. If you have your stereo cranked up, small changes in the volume will not be noticed; but if the volume starts out low, the same changes are likely to produce a very noticeable difference. We can state this relationship more formally as follows: The jnd for stimulus magnitude is a constant proportion of the size of the standard stimulus. In other words, the louder the standard stimulus (the stereo), the more volume will need to be added before a difference in loudness will be detected. This general relationship, called **Weber's law,** doesn't work just for loudness—it applies across all the sensory systems. If the lights in your house go off, two candles will make the room a lot brighter than one; if the lights are on, the addition of one or two candles will lead to little, if any, noticeable increase in brightness (see the accompanying photos). Weber's law demonstrates once again that the relationship between the physical and the psychological is not always direct—increases in the magnitude of a physical stimulus will not always map directly onto the psychological experience.

Sensory Adaptation

There is one other feature of all sensory systems that was stressed by the early researchers in psychophysics. Sensory systems are more sensitive to a message when it first arrives than to its continued presence. Through **sensory adaptation,** the body quickly adapts, by reducing sensitivity, to a message that remains constant—such as the feel of a shirt sleeve on your forearm, your hand resting on your knee, or the hum of computers in the background. Think about what the world would be like without sensory adaptation. The water in the pool would never warm up; the smell of garlic from last night's dinner would remain a pervasive force; you would constantly be reminded of the texture of your sock pressing against your foot.

Adaptation is a feature of each of the sensory systems that we've described. Images that remain stable on the retina will vanish; this doesn't normally occur because the eyes are constantly moving and refreshing the retinal image. If you are presented with a continuous tone, your perception of its loudness decreases over time (Evans, 1982). If auditory adaptation didn't occur, no one would ever be able to work in a noisy environment. Human sensory systems are designed to detect *changes* in the incoming message; sensitivity is reduced to those aspects of the message that remain the same.

▶ SOLVING THE PROBLEMS: A SUMMARY

To navigate successfully in the world, people rely on multiple sensory systems. As we've seen, the external world itself is not very user-friendly—it bombards the body with energy-based messages, but none arrives in a form appropriate for the language of the brain. Moreover, the messages that sensory systems receive are complex and ever-changing. Thus, the body faces three fundamental problems of adaptation: How can the external message be translated into the internal language of the nervous system? How do the elementary components get extracted from the message? Finally, how does the brain build a stable and long-lasting interpretation of the message components once they've been extracted?

TRANSLATING THE MESSAGE To solve the translation problem, the body relies on the activation of specialized receptor cells that respond, appropriately enough, by generating neural impulses in the presence of particular energy sources. In the visual system, receptor cells—rods and cones—react to light; in the auditory system, sound energy leads to movement of the basilar membrane, which in turn causes tiny hair cells to generate a neural impulse. The body also has specialized receptors that react to pressure on the skin, free-floating chemicals in the air, and the relative position or movement of muscles. Each of these receptor systems acts as a kind of "translator," changing the messages delivered by the external world into the electrochemical language of the nervous system.

EXTRACTING THE MESSAGE COMPONENTS Once translated, the sensory message receives further processing in the brain to extract the message components. A variety of neural pathways seem specialized to look for particular kinds of sensory information. For example, opponent-process cells in the lateral geniculate region of the brain are specialized to process color—they signal the presence of one kind of color by increasing the rate that they generate neural impulses, and another kind of color by decreasing their firing rate. Similarly, highly specialized cells in the visual cortex respond only to particular patterns of light and dark that appear in the eye. One kind of cell might respond only to a bar of light presented at a particular orientation; another cell might respond only to a pattern of light that moves in a particular direction across the retina.

In the auditory cortex, the brain is adept at extracting information about the frequencies of sound in an auditory message. Psychologically, changes in frequency correspond to changes in perceived pitch. The brain extracts frequency information by noting the particular place on the basilar membrane where hair cells are stimulated and by noting the rate at which neural impulses are generated over time. It's not unusual for the brain to rely on multiple kinds of processing to extract a particular message component. The perception of color, for instance, relies not only on opponent-process cells but also on the relative activations of three different cone types that reside in the retina.

▶ **PRODUCING STABLE INTERPRETATIONS** To establish a coherent, stable interpretation of the sensory message, people use a combination of "bottom-up" and "top-down" processing—beliefs and expectations work with the actual sensory input to build perceptions of the external world. The fact that people are able to maintain a constant and stable interpretation of events in the world is really a quite remarkable accomplishment. As we noted at the beginning of the chapter, the pattern of light reflected from a continuously moving object changes continuously with time, yet you have no trouble recognizing a dancer moving effortlessly across the stage. You also have no trouble recognizing the voice of a friend in a crowded room, even though the actual auditory message reaching your ears may be filled with frequency information from lots of different voices.

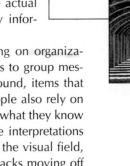

The brain solves the problems of perception, in part, by relying on organizational "rules." For example, people are born with built-in tendencies to group message components in particular ways. Figures are separated from ground, items that share physical properties are perceived together, and so on. But people also rely on prior knowledge to help them in the interpretation process. They use what they know about how cues are related in the environment to arrive at sensible interpretations of ambiguous objects. For instance, if two parallel lines converge in the visual field, the brain "assumes" that the lines are moving away—like railroad tracks moving off in the distance. Such top-down processing is usually extremely adaptive—it helps people maintain a stable interpretation—although in some cases, perceptual "illusions" can be produced.

Terms to Remember

sensations The elementary features, or building blocks, of an experience, such as a pattern of light and dark, a bitter taste, or a change in temperature.

perception The collection of processes used to arrive at a meaningful "interpretation" of sensations; through perception, the simple components of an experience are organized into a recognizable form.

transduction The process by which external messages are translated into the internal language of the brain.

VISION: BUILDING A WORLD OF COLOR AND FORM

light The small part of the electromagnetic spectrum that is processed by the visual system. Light is typically classified in terms of *wavelength* (the physical distance from one energy cycle to the next) and *intensity* (the amount of light falling on an object).

hue The dimension of light that produces color; hue is typically determined by the wavelength of light reflecting from an object.

brightness The aspect of the visual experience that changes with light intensity; in general, as the intensity of light increases, so does its perceived brightness.

cornea The transparent and protective outer covering of the eye.

lens A flexible piece of tissue that helps focus light toward the back of the eye.

pupil The "hole" in the center of the eye that allows light to enter; the size of the pupil changes with light intensity.

iris The ring of colored tissue surrounding the pupil.

accommodation In vision, the process through which the lens changes its shape temporarily in order to help focus light on the retina.

retina The thin layer of tissue that covers the back of the eye and that contains the light-sensitive receptor cells for vision.

rods Receptor cells in the retina, located mainly around the sides of the retina, that transduce light energy into neural messages; these visual receptors are highly sensitive and are active in dim light.

cones Receptor cells in the central portion of the retina that transduce light energy into neural messages; they operate best when light levels are high, and they are primarily responsible for the ability to sense color.

fovea The "central pit" area in the retina where the cone receptors are located.

visual acuity The ability to process fine detail in vision.

receptive field For a given neuron in the visual system, that portion of the retina that, when stimulated, causes the activity of the neuron to change.

blind spot The point where the optic nerve leaves the back of the eye.

dark adaptation The process through which the eyes adjust to dim light.

feature detectors Cells in the visual cortex that respond to very specific visual events, such as bars of light at particular orientations.

trichromatic theory A theory of color vision proposing that color information is extracted by comparing the relative activations of three different types of cone receptors.

opponent-process theory A theory of color vision proposing that cells in the visual pathway increase their activation levels to one color and decrease their activation levels to another color—for example, increasing to red and decreasing to green.

Gestalt principles of organization The organizing principles of perception proposed by the Gestalt psychologists. These principles include the laws of proximity, similarity, closure, continuation, and common fate.

recognition by components The idea proposed by Biederman that people recognize objects perceptually via smaller components called *geons.*

binocular disparity The spatial differences between the images in the two eyes; it's thought to provide an important cue for depth perception.

perceptual constancy Perceiving the properties of an object to remain the same even though the physical properties of the sensory message are changing.

perceptual illusions Inappropriate interpretations of physical reality. Perceptual illusions often occur as a result of the brain's using otherwise adaptive organizing principles.

HEARING: IDENTIFYING AND LOCALIZING SOUNDS

sound The physical message delivered to the auditory system; its mechanical energy that requires a medium such as air or water in order to move.

pitch The psychological experience that results from the auditory processing of a particular frequency of sound.

pinna The external flap of tissue normally referred to as the "ear"; it helps capture sounds.

tympanic membrane The "eardrum," which responds to incoming sound waves by vibrating.

middle ear The portion between the eardrum and the cochlea containing three small bones (the malleus, incus, and stapes) that help to intensify and prepare the sound vibrations for passage into the inner ear.

cochlea The bony, snail-shaped sound processor in the inner ear, where sounds get translated into nerve impulses.

basilar membrane A flexible membrane running through the cochlea that, through its movement, displaces the auditory receptor cells, called hair cells.

place theory The idea that the location of auditory receptor cells activated by movement of the basilar membrane underlies the perception of pitch.

frequency principle The idea that pitch perception is determined partly by the frequency of neural impulses traveling up the auditory pathway.

THE SKIN SENSES: TOUCH, TEMPERATURE, AND PAIN

Pacinian corpuscles A type of sensory receptor in the skin that responds most actively to pressure.

cold fibers Neurons that respond to a cooling of the skin by increasing the production of neural impulses.

warm fibers Neurons that respond vigorously when the temperature of the skin increases.

pain An adaptive response by the body to any stimulus that is intense enough to cause tissue damage.

gate-control theory The idea that neural impulses generated by pain receptors can be blocked, or gated, in the spinal cord by signals produced in the brain.

THE BODY SENSES: MOVEMENT AND BALANCE

kinesthesia In perception, the ability to sense the position and movement of one's body parts.

semicircular canals A receptor system attached to the inner ear that responds to movement and acceleration and to changes in upright posture.

vestibular sacs Contain receptors thought to be primarily responsible for the sense of balance.

THE CHEMICAL SENSES: SMELL AND TASTE

chemoreceptors Receptor cells that react to invisible molecules scattered about in the air or dissolved in liquids, leading to the senses of smell and taste.

olfaction The sense of smell.

gustation The sense of taste.

flavor A psychological term used to describe the gustatory experience. Flavor is influenced by taste, smell, the visual appearance of food, as well as by expectations about the food's quality.

taste buds The receptor cells on the tongue involved in taste.

FROM THE PHYSICAL TO THE PSYCHOLOGICAL

psychophysics A field of psychology in which researchers search for ways to map the transition from the physical stimulus to the psychological experience of that stimulus.

absolute threshold The level of intensity that lifts a stimulus over the threshold of conscious awareness; it's usually defined as the intensity level at which people can detect the presence of the stimulus 50% of the time.

signal detection A technique that can be used to determine the ability of someone to detect the presence of a stimulus.

difference threshold The smallest difference in the magnitude of two stimuli that an observer can detect.

Weber's law The principle stating that the ability to notice a difference in the magnitude of two stimuli is a constant proportion of the size of the standard stimulus. Psychologically, the more intense a stimulus is to begin with, the more intense it will need to become for one to notice a change.

sensory adaptation The tendency of sensory systems to reduce sensitivity to a stimulus source that remains constant.

Imagine, for a moment, that you're a fly buzzing about a room. Like humans, you're faced with some fundamental perceptual problems: (a) you need to detect the point at which air ends and the wall begins; (b) you need to find places to land and things to consume; and (c) you must avoid square, netlike objects that swing suddenly into your path.

According to the view of perception outlined in this chapter, you rely on incoming stimulus energy, such as reflected light, and your built-in knowledge about how rooms are structured to accomplish these tasks. You construct your world, and the objects in it, by piecing together multiple sources of input and making "guesses" about the structures you encounter. Sounds a little sophisticated for a fly, doesn't it?

There is a movement afoot, rooted in the writings of the late psychologist James J. Gibson (1904–1979), that rejects this view of perception in favor of a simpler, more stimulus-driven approach. According to the Gibsonians—proponents of *direct perception*—it is not necessary for flies or humans to *construct* a perceptual world, based on a sophisticated knowledge base, because all the necessary information is contained in the world itself. The stimulus array that reaches the eyes and ears provides everything an organism needs to know about the structure of the environment, even how to act in a meaningful way.

Invariants

The key to understanding how the world tells its story lies in the concept of *stimulus invariance.* An invariant is a property of the environment that doesn't change as the observer moves around, or as time passes. For Gibson (1966, 1979), the sensory message is full of invariants, both simple and complex. To illustrate, consider the checkerboard pattern in Figure 5.25. Because of the black and white squares on the board—which form a texture gradient—you can always tell the distance from square (1) to square

(2), regardless of where you happen to be positioned on the board. No matter where you move, or even the angle at which you view the board, the number of squares separating (1) and (2) will remain constant, or *invariant.*

What makes the Gibsonian approach so radically different from conventional approaches to perception, which rely on top-down and bottom-up processing, is that Gibson believed that these invariants could be *directly* perceived. Rather than "inferring" something such as distance from multiple cues, Gibson argued that human sensory systems have evolved to respond directly to things such as texture gradients. The objects in

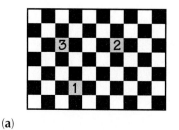

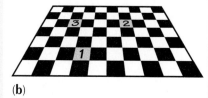

FIGURE 5.25
Stimulus Invariance: Distance.
Because of texture invariants, an observer can always tell the distance from Square 1 to Square 2, no matter from what angle the board is viewed.

Figure 5.26 appear to remain constant in size because in relation to the textured ground the objects remain constant—both cover the same number of bricks on the ground. People move around in the world, picking up on the invariants, without needing any complex "top-down" processing in the form of hypothesis testing or guessing.

The idea of direct perception makes sense if we view the world from an adaptive perspective. The traditional approach to perception assumes that the brain engages in sophisticated, time-consuming "interpretations" of the environment. But to avoid predators and other forms of danger, organisms usually need split-second, error-free perceptions; these requirements seem better served by direct, rather than indirect, perception. It may also be unreasonable to assume that all organisms have developed the complex knowledge structures needed to provide sophisticated "calculations" of the environment. Consider how many moment-to-moment computations would be required for a fly to navigate successfully across a room filled with objects.

Affordances

Another important ingredient of the direct perception movement is the idea that perceptual systems have evolved to detect information that organisms can *use.* The environment contains more than just objects—it offers organisms opportunities to engage in actions. The fact that you see a chair means that you can sit down; the fact that the chair is not connected to the ground means that you can pick it up and throw it at an unwelcome visitor. The table, as perceived by the fly, is an opportunity for landing, or possibly as a location for food. Gibson (1979) referred to these environmental opportunities as *affordances;* he believed that affordances, like the rest of the environment, are directly perceived.

The introduction of affordances complicates things. For instance, affordances are not fixed properties of the environment, as a chair would be in the

FIGURE 5.26
Stimulus Invariance: Size Constancy. The objects appear to remain constant in size because of invariants in the texture—both soda cans cover the same number of bricks on the ground.

traditional view; they are properties of organisms interacting with environments. Whether a tree stump *affords* sitting depends on the organism doing the perceiving; to an insect, the tree stump might provide the opportunity for a fine home. To understand perception, therefore, one is required to consider not only the information provided by the environment, but also the organism receiving the message. Because it stresses animals interacting with environments, the Gibsonian approach is also sometimes referred to as the *ecological approach* to perception.

The Gibsonian approach is not without its critics. Many have criticized Gibson for his lack of clarity about what constitutes a "direct" perception (e.g., Fodor & Pylyshyn, 1981). Others take issue with the idea of affordances: It's easy to see how a chair might provide the opportunity for sitting, but it's not so easy to see how a written note naturally "affords" the opportunity to contact a forgotten loved one. Most would argue

that the value of the Gibsonian approach lies in its broad redefining of the stimulus message. There is probably a great deal more information present in the environmental message than has been traditionally recognized.

6

Consciousness

Imagine for a moment that you could grab hold of conscious thought and take it for a ride. Forget about its contents—ideas, images, sounds—or even about what "it" is; concentrate only on the movements from thought-to-thought-to-thought-to-thought. Notice the transitions, the ways that ideas and feelings emerge, only to disappear a moment later. Would you call the movements bumpy? Smooth? The great American psychologist William James was convinced that consciousness should be described as a personal, always changing, sensibly continuous *flow* of thoughts and ideas. Consciousness isn't something that can be chopped up in bits, he argued: "words such as 'chain' or 'train' do not describe it fitly . . . a 'river' or 'stream' are the metaphors by which it is most naturally described" (James, 1890, p. 233).

Studying the characteristics of **consciousness,** which we'll define as the subjective awareness of internal and external events, was fundamental to psychologists of the 19th century. In fact, if you had taken a psychology course at the turn of the century, the subject matter would likely have been defined as "the science which describes and explains the phenomena of consciousness" (Ladd, 1896, p. 1). But as behaviorism began to assert its influence in the early part of the 20th century, psychologists shifted their focus away from the study of internal subjective experience. The shift originated, in part, from a growing dissatisfaction with the general technique of introspection, which required subjects to look inward and comment on their ongoing experience. As we discussed in Chapter 1, introspectionists of the 19th century were essentially trained to stand on the "banks" of the mind and watch the stream of consciousness flow by. The study of an elementary sensation like a light or a tone was analogous to throwing a stick into the stream and carefully recording how it bobbed and weaved with the current

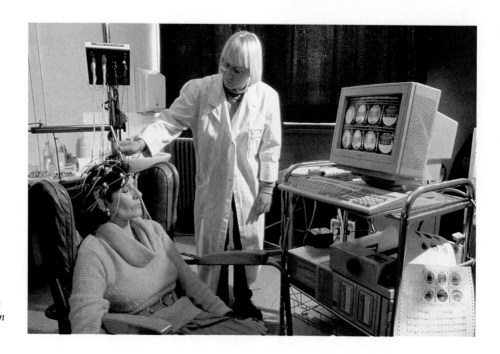

The development of technologies such as the EEG, shown here, are providing psychologists with a "window" through which the internal activities of the brain can be observed.

until passing out of sight. But observations of this sort proved to be difficult, if not impossible, to confirm objectively, so the behaviorists argued forcefully that "psychology must discard all reference to consciousness" (Watson, 1913, p. 163).

Even today, it's relatively easy to understand why the behaviorists were dissatisfied with the concept of subjective experience. Turning inward and asking questions about the contents of consciousness is "like asking a flashlight in a dark room to search around for something that doesn't have any light shining upon it. The flashlight, since there is light in whatever direction it turns, would have to conclude that there is light everywhere" (Jaynes, 1976, p. 23). It's tough to study the properties of an object when your only tool of discovery is the object itself. Consciousness by its very nature is a subjective, personal experience. It's not something that can be easily measured like a knee jerk or the speed of a rat running through a maze for food.

In recent years, however, there has been a resurgence of interest in the topic. In fact, it's fair to say that the study of consciousness has emerged from an intellectual "dark age" and has regained a measure of respectability (Milner & Rugg, 1992). One contributing factor has been the development of such technologies as the electroencephalograph (EEG) and positron emission tomography (PET). As we've discussed previously, these devices provide a clear window into the activities of the brain. It's become possible, as a result, to "listen" objectively to the brain and to measure how internal activity changes over time without needing to rely exclusively on unreliable verbal reports. Many neuroscientists are convinced that consciousness can ultimately be linked directly to patterns of neural activity in the brain, although no biological "seat" of consciousness has yet been discovered (Horgan, 1994). Clearly, as our tools of discovery have broadened, so too has our willingness to explore the workings of the inner world of the mind.

 Are you comfortable with the idea that consciousness originates entirely from brain activity?

◀ PREVIEWING THE ADAPTIVE PROBLEMS

We have defined *consciousness* as the subjective *awareness* of internal and external events. Intuitively, everyone has a reasonably good idea of what it means to be aware. It can mean anything from experiencing the "here and now," to the reawak-

Consciousness has a number of adaptive properties, including the fact that it allows people to imagine the outcomes of mental operations.

| Setting priorities for mental functioning | Sleeping and dreaming | Altering awareness: Psychoactive drugs | Altering awareness: Induced states |

FIGURE 6.1
Adaptive Problems of Consciousness. Consciousness serves a variety of adaptive functions. Summarized here are the four adaptive problems that we'll be considering in this chapter.

ening of past memories, to your general guiding "view of the world" (Klatzky, 1984). Awareness has the additional property that it can be focused: You can choose to attend to that bug walking up the page of your text, to the beautiful sunset outside your window, or to the voice of your roommate telling you to turn out the light. As an adaptive tool, conscious thought allows us to develop strategies for behavior internally; we can think about what we want to do and imagine the outcomes of those strategies without actually performing the behaviors. We can also use conscious thought to imagine the content of "other" minds—to predict the behavior of other people and to understand their motivation (Weiskrantz, 1992).

The concept of consciousness becomes a little easier to understand when we accept that the contents of conscious "awareness" are not the sole determinants of behaviors. Many actions are controlled by processes that operate *below* levels of awareness. To take an extreme case, you're not "aware" of the processes controlling your heartbeat or respiration, yet these functions are carried on like clockwork in your body. Your "awareness" also takes on different properties when you sleep, when you're hypnotized, or when you ingest certain types of drugs.

We'll focus on some of these properties of consciousness in this chapter, and we'll discuss how altering awareness helps humans solve certain adaptive problems. How do people set priorities for mental functioning? What are the characteristics and adaptive functions of sleep and dreaming? What processes underlie the alterations in awareness that accompany the ingestion of certain chemicals? Finally, what are the characteristics of hypnosis, and what does it tell us about the properties of the adaptive mind? These basic problems are summarized in Figure 6.1.

▶ **SETTING PRIORITIES FOR MENTAL FUNCTIONING** Whatever conscious awareness might be, it's pretty clear that there's often not enough of it to go around. There are limits to the number of things that a person can think about at the same time, or to the number of tasks that anyone can perform concurrently. Have you ever tried to solve a difficult thought problem while someone talks incessantly nearby? Obviously, it's critical for people to be selective about what they choose to focus on. Psychologists use the term *attention* to signify the psychological processes that are used to focus on certain aspects of the environment while ignoring others. We'll discuss some of the important properties of attention, and we'll see how the brain develops ways to keep track of several different things at the same time.

▶ **SLEEPING AND DREAMING** Despite what you might think, sleep is not a loss of consciousness, it's an *altered* state of consciousness. The electrical activity in the brain changes rhythmically throughout the night, in alternating cycles, and sleep states can be characterized by significant mental and physical activity. As an altered state of consciousness, sleep may serve a variety of adaptive functions for the human organism. Some researchers believe that humans sleep in order to give the brain a chance to rest and restore itself from the day's activities. Others believe that people sleep in order to protect themselves during periods when sensory equipment is unlikely to function well (such as at night). Even dreaming, with its sometimes bizarre imagery, may help individuals work out conflicts of which they may not be aware. We'll review the physiological characteristics of sleep and discuss the biological and psychological origins of dreaming.

▶ **ALTERING AWARENESS: PSYCHOACTIVE DRUGS** You may have heard about the mind-bending alterations of consciousness that are produced through the ingestion of psychoactive drugs, such as LSD or mescaline. What you may not know, however, is that the biological processes that underlie these alterations are natural and important ingredients of the adaptive mind. Although consuming psychoactive drugs can have harmful and long-lasting consequences, it's important to understand that artificial drugs operate, in part, by tapping natural adaptive systems that help people solve basic survival problems. Consider, for example, that during times of stress the brain releases its own mind-altering "drugs" that produce pleasurable effects, reducing and delaying the onset of pain. These pleasurable effects can reward adaptive behaviors that reduce stress, and the momentary delay of pain can allow an injured organism to escape from threatening situations. We'll discuss the biological and psychological effects of drugs, both natural and artificial.

▶ **ALTERING AWARENESS: INDUCED STATES** In the final part of the chapter, we'll consider some techniques that are specifically designed to alter conscious awareness. We'll consider the phenomenon of *hypnosis,* for instance, which is a procedure that induces a heightened state of suggestibility in a willing participant. Through the use of hypnosis, it's possible to break bad habits (such as smoking), drastically reduce the experience of pain, and eliminate nausea in a patient undergoing chemotherapy. Many of the psychological factors underlying hypnosis are not well understood, although a great deal of research has been conducted on its effectiveness; we'll look at some of that research in this chapter. We'll also briefly consider the techniques of *meditation,* which have also proven to be effective in the treatment of stress and psychological disorders. Hypnosis and meditation are used by humans in deliberate attempts to alter awareness in ways that serve adaptive functions.

Setting Priorities for Mental Functioning: Attention

As we saw in Chapter 5, the world is a continuous smorgasbord of sensory information. At each and every moment of your life, nature delivers an astonishing variety of sights, sounds, and smells. You don't experience every sight and sound, of course; you sample selectively from the table based on your current needs. If you're searching desperately for a child lost in a shopping mall, you key in on the familiar sound of the child's voice or the color of his or her shirt. If you're trying to determine what's for dinner tonight, you sniff the air for the smell of cooking pot roast or simmering spaghetti sauce. You notice those things that are relevant to the task at hand—you shift through, block out, and focus on those messages that are needed for solving the particular problem that you face.

Psychologists use the term **attention** to refer to the internal processes that are used to set priorities for mental functioning. For adaptive reasons, the brain uses the processes of attention to focus selectively on certain aspects of the environ-

Can you think of any circumstances in which the brain attends to things of which the person is not aware?

When searching for someone in a crowd, people use the processes of attention to key in on selected features, such as height or the color of a shirt.

ment while ignoring others. Obviously, the concepts of attention and consciousness are closely linked; you are conscious of only those things that receive a measure of attention. But why is awareness selective? There is probably more than one reason. First, the resources of the brain and nervous system are limited. The brain has only so many neurons, and there are limits to the speed and efficiency with which these neurons can communicate. These limitations in the resources of the system require people to make choices about which aspects of the environment to process (Broadbent, 1958; Kahneman, 1973).

Second, even if the resources were unlimited, it would still be in people's interest to make choices about the things relevant to their goals. In a mystery novel, certain events are relevant clues for solving the murder and others are "red herrings"—irrelevant points that lead the reader in the wrong direction and delay solving the crime. The trick is to be selective in deciding which components enter into the equation. A first-rate detective knows not only what to look for, but also what information to avoid. The same is true for even the simplest kind of action, such as walking across the room or reaching for a cup. The visual and motor systems need to focus on the objects in the person's *path,* not every single object in the room. If people looked at and thought about everything, they might suffer interference from irrelevant input. Prioritizing mental functioning is an important part of the coordination and control of human actions (Allport, 1989).

Experiments on Attention: Dichotic Listening

Experimental control over the phenomenon of attention began in the 1950s with the development of the **dichotic listening** technique (Broadbent, 1952; Cherry, 1953). As shown in Figure 6.2, in a typical experiment subjects are asked to listen to spoken messages presented individually to each ear through headphones. To promote selective attention, the subject's task is to *shadow,* or repeat aloud, one of the two messages while essentially ignoring the other. This kind of listening is called *dichotic,* meaning "divided into two," because two messages are involved, delivered separately and simultaneously into each of the two ears.

A dichotic listening experiment requires one to listen to two voices at the same time. Have you ever tried to watch television while someone next to you is filling you in on the details of his or her latest escapade? Not an easy task. In fact, in all likelihood you had to either ignore one of the two, or switch back and forth from one message to the other. This is essentially what happens in a dichotic listening experiment. By being forced to repeat one of the messages aloud, subjects appear

FIGURE 6.2
The Dichotic Listening Technique. In dichotic listening, a subject is asked to listen to spoken messages presented individually and concurrently to each ear. The task is to shadow, or repeat aloud, one of the messages while essentially ignoring the other. Because the subject is required to focus on one of two competing messages, the task is considered to tap the ability to *attend* selectively.

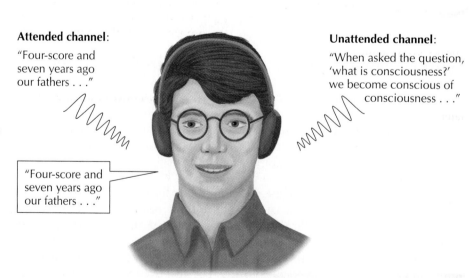

Attended channel:
"Four-score and seven years ago our fathers . . ."

Unattended channel:
"When asked the question, 'what is consciousness?' we become conscious of consciousness . . ."

"Four-score and seven years ago our fathers . . ."

The cocktail party effect. By using the processes of attention, it's possible to filter out competing conversations in a noisy environment. But if someone from across the room suddenly speaks your name, you'll probably notice it.

to process the other message poorly. For example, if at the end of the experiment subjects are given a surprise test for the unattended message, they can usually remember very little, if anything, about its content. They might pick up on the fact that one speaker was male and the other female, but they remember virtually nothing else about the second message (Cherry, 1953; Moray, 1959).

But people don't just shut off the part of the world that is not bathed in the spotlight of attention. If they did, their actions wouldn't be very adaptive, because the world is constantly changing. Some new, possibly critical, situation could suddenly arise. Instead, the brain appears to monitor many things at the same time, although the monitoring may be minimal and beyond one's current awareness.

A case in point is a phenomenon known as the **cocktail party effect.** Imagine you're at a large party, filled with noisy conversation, and you're focusing intently on what your date is saying. In all likelihood, you won't be consciously aware of the conversations around you; if I were to interrupt you and ask you to repeat what the couple standing next to you had been discussing, you probably couldn't do it. By using the processes of attention, you've successfully filtered out these competing messages. Now suppose that someone across the room suddenly speaks your name. The odds are that you'll turn your head immediately in response. Participants in dichotic listening experiments have shown the same effect: They appear to ignore the contents of the unattended message, but if their name is suddenly spoken in the unattended channel, they notice and remember it later.

Another compelling example of how people can monitor many things at the same time comes from an experiment by Treisman (1960), again using the dichotic listening technique. Participants were presented with compound sentences such as "Against the advice of his broker, the naive investor panicked" in one ear and "Released from his cage, the little lamb bounded into the field" in the other (see Figure 6.3). Subjects were asked to attend to the message in just one of the ears by repeating it aloud, but in the middle of some of the sentences Treisman switched things around—the second half of each sentence moved to the opposite ear. Thus, in the "attended" ear the subject heard something like "Against the advice of his broker, the little lamb bounded into the field," whereas in the "unattended"

FIGURE 6.3

Treisman's "Ear-Switching" Experiment. In a dichotic listening experiment by Treisman, subjects were asked to shadow a message presented to one ear and ignore a message presented simultaneously to the other ear. But at one point in the experiment, unknown to the participant, the to-be-shadowed message was suddenly switched to the "unattended" channel. The interesting finding was that subjects often continued to repeat portions of the meaningful sentence even though it was now presented in the "unattended" ear.

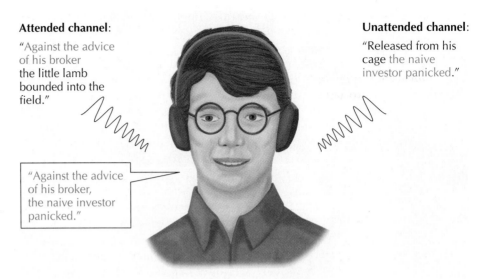

Attended channel:
"Against the advice of his broker the little lamb bounded into the field."

Unattended channel:
"Released from his cage the naive investor panicked."

"Against the advice of his broker, the naive investor panicked."

ear the message became "Released from his cage, the naive investor panicked." The interesting finding was that subjects often continued to repeat the meaningful sentence ("Against the advice of his broker, the naive investor panicked") even though the message had switched midway from the attended to the unattended ear. Moreover, many of the subjects reported being unaware that the message had switched.

Evidence such as the cocktail party effect and the findings of Treisman's ear-switching experiment indicate that the brain does not simply ignore what goes on in the unattended message. It focuses the spotlight of attention on things relevant to the task at hand, but it carries on "unconscious" monitoring of the rest of the environment as well. If something else is deemed important enough, the brain shifts the spotlight of attention and allows the new element to enter conscious awareness. In Treisman's experiment, the brain must have been following the meaning of the messages in both ears, against the overt instructions, even though the subjects were only aware of monitoring one thing. Exactly how all this works has been the subject of considerable debate over the last several decades (Cowan, 1995; Pashler, 1992), but the process itself is clearly adaptive. Humans wouldn't live for long in a world where they processed only those things in the realm of immediate awareness.

Processing Without Attention: Automaticity

The idea that the brain and body are doing things beyond current awareness may seem strange at first, but not if you think about it. After all, when's the last time you thought about breathing, or keeping your heart beating, or walking, or even forming words from your repertoire of spoken sounds? You can drive a car and carry on a conversation at the same time—you don't need to focus an attentional spotlight on every turn of the wheel or pressing of the brake. These things occur automatically. In the case of driving, people have developed a skill that demands less and less attention with practice.

Psychologists use the term **automaticity** to refer to fast and effortless processing that requires little or no focused attention (Logan, 1991). When you practice a task, such as playing Mozart on the piano or rolling cigars from tobacco leaves, overall speed steadily improves. You may even reach a point where performing the task seems automatic—Mozart rolls off your fingertips with such ease that you're not even consciously aware of finger movement. Automatic processes, once acquired, no longer require conscious control. The mind is free to consider other things, while the task itself is performed without a hitch. Many of the activities that people take for granted, such as reading, talking, and walking, are essentially automatic processes.

It's possible to measure the development of automaticity through what is called a *divided attention task* (Logan, 1988). In a typical experiment, subjects are asked to perform two tasks at the same time, such as playing a piece by Mozart on the piano while simultaneously trying to remember a short list of unrelated words. Automaticity is demonstrated when one task, the automatic one, fails to interfere with performance on the other task (Hasher & Zacks, 1979; Shiffrin & Schneider, 1977). Clearly, if you've just learned to play the Mozart piece, your mind will need to focus on every note, and you'll have enough trouble just getting through it without error, let alone recalling a list of words. But if you're an accomplished pianist—if your Mozart performance has become automatic—you can let your fingers do the playing and your mind can concentrate on remembering the word list.

Notice the relationship between automaticity and awareness, because it indicates something important about the function of consciousness. The better people become at performing a task—the more automatic the task has become—the less likely they are to be "aware" of what they're doing. This is a vital characteristic of the adaptive mind if we assume that the resources of the brain and nervous system are limited. Environmental conditions can change at any moment, and people need the resources of conscious thought to develop new and creative strategies for behavior. Thus, humans use consciousness as a kind of work space for handling the new and demanding, and they rely on the steady and effortless processes of automaticity to ensure continuity in their behavior and to free up the needed resources.

If you practice a task for extended periods, such as playing a particular piece on the piano, your performance may become automatic. Automatic processes, once acquired, no longer require much conscious control.

Disorders of Attention

We've stressed the link between attention and consciousness because, in many respects, attention is the "gateway to consciousness" (Ellis & Hunt, 1993). That is, before you can be conscious of something, you must first focus your attention on it. If the systems in the brain that control attention were to be damaged in some way, we would expect a corresponding loss or impairment in conscious awareness. Brain researchers have used clinical cases of brain damage to examine this possibility, and they are in the process of mapping out what appear to be attention-related areas of the brain (Posner & Rothbart, 1992). Let's briefly consider two examples of attentional disorders that may be related to brain dysfunction: *visual neglect* and *attention deficit disorder*.

Visual Neglect. It's been known for some time that damage to the right parietal lobe of the cerebral cortex can produce an odd and complex disorder of attention called **visual neglect.** People suffering from visual neglect show a tendency to ignore things that appear toward the left side of the body (remember from earlier chapters that the right side of the brain tends to be involved in processing things on the left side of the body). These people often read only from the right side of pages and copy only the right side of pictures. They may even dress, shave, or apply makeup to only the right side of the body (Bisiach & Rusconi, 1990). It's as if an entire side of their visual field has vanished from awareness. The condition sometimes recovers with time, and it's often associated with other kinds of processing deficits in the brain (Kerkhoff, Munssinger, & Meier, 1994; Mesulam, 1987). Visual neglect can also arise from damage to the left side of the brain, which then creates problems in the right visual field, although it occurs more frequently with right-brain damage (Posner, 1993).

 In what ways are the symptoms of visual neglect similar to the symptoms of the split-brain patients discussed in Chapter 3?

Patients suffering from visual neglect might consciously detect little, if any, differences between these two houses. But they would probably choose to live in the house without the flames.

In one study, a patient suffering from visual neglect caused by right-hemisphere damage was shown drawings of two houses. One house was normal in appearance; the other was normal on the right side but had bright red flames and smoke billowing out from a window on its left side. The patient was asked to choose which of the two houses she would prefer to live in. "The houses look the same to me," she reported, presumably because she was attending only to the right side of each picture. Nevertheless, she consistently chose to live in the house without the flames (Marshall & Halligan, 1988). This suggests that even though the brain mechanisms underlying conscious *awareness* had been damaged, her brain was still able to use the available information to help determine the appropriate behavior (Bisiach, 1992).

Attention Deficit Disorder. The right hemisphere of the brain may also be involved in **attention deficit disorder,** a psychological condition characterized by difficulties in concentrating. Individuals with attention deficit disorder have trouble sustaining attention for extended periods—they're easily distracted and often cannot finish tasks that they begin. It's one of the most common psychological problems in school-aged children, although it affects only about 3% of all children (Barkley, 1981). In addition to having attention problems, which hurt schoolwork, children with attention deficit disorder are commonly hyperactive and impulsive—they squirm and fidget continuously and regularly blurt out answers to questions before the questions have even been completely asked.

There is some evidence that attention deficit disorder might be caused by mild damage, or malfunctioning, of the right hemisphere of the brain. For example, in one study researchers measured the amount of time that it took children to turn their eyes to the left to see an unexpected visual stimulus. It was found that children with attention deficit disorder showed a different pattern of eye-movement times than children without the disorder (Rothlind, Posner, & Schaughency, 1991). Because leftward eye movements are controlled by the right hemisphere of the brain, these findings were interpreted to mean that the problem relates to a specific deficit in right-hemisphere brain functioning.

But the brain mechanisms involved in attention deficit disorder are still being debated. PET scan studies, for instance, have indicated that various regions of the brain, including the frontal lobes, may be selectively involved (Zemetkin and others, 1990). It's unlikely that any single brain location is responsible, because the disorder is quite complex and can manifest itself in a variety of ways. There are even ongoing debates about the disorder's proper definition (Shaywitz, Fletcher, & Shaywitz, 1994). Consequently, it may take some time before a complete neurological understanding of attention deficit disorder can be obtained.

Sleeping and Dreaming

In setting priorities for mental functioning, people focus attention selectively in an effort to resolve the demands of particular environments and tasks. For example, if you're trying to read a book, you focus on the visual features of the page and try to block out distracting sounds. If you're listening intently to music, you may close your eyes to appreciate fully the rhythms and harmonies of the sound patterns. But the redirection of attention does not necessarily imply a fundamental change in the processes of consciousness; instead, you may simply be altering the *content* of conscious awareness. In the case of sleep, however, the change is more fundamental—you are no longer consciously aware of the external world, as you are in a waking state, yet your mind is still actively processing in a strange, poorly understood inner world. For this reason, sleep is sometimes referred to as a different "state" of consciousness.

Biological Rhythms

The regular daily transition from a state of waking awareness to sleep is one example of an internal cycle in the body called a *biological rhythm.* Actually, many physiological functions work in cycles, which is something that humans share with all other members of the animal kingdom. Sleep and waking vary daily, along with body temperature, hormone secretions, blood pressure, and other processes (for a review, see Aschoff & Wever, 1981). Activities that rise and fall in accordance with a 24-hour cycle are known as **circadian rhythms** (*circa* means "about," and *dies* means "day"). Other biological activities may follow cycles that are either shorter or longer. The female menstrual cycle operates on an approximately 28-day cycle, for example, whereas changes in appetite and the ability to perform certain tasks may change several times throughout the day.

What controls these internal rhythms? Certainly cyclical changes in blood pressure or internal body temperature are not mediated by conscious control. You don't consciously alert the endocrine system that it's time to secrete hormones, or actively instruct some portion of your brain that your body temperature needs to start rising. These functions are controlled automatically by structures in the brain, called **biological clocks,** that trigger the needed rhythmic variations at the appropriate time. These clocks schedule the internal functions of the body and make sure that everything is performing as it should at the opportune time. Animal research has determined that a particular area of the hypothalamus, called the *suprachiasmatic nucleus,* may play a key role in regulating the clock that controls circadian rhythms (Ralph and others, 1990). But it's thought that the human brain probably has several clocks, each controlling its own function such as body temperature or activity level (Johnson & Hastings, 1986).

Researchers have also determined that the environment plays a critical role in helping the brain synchronize its internal biological clocks. Light is a particularly important controller, or *zeitgeber* (meaning "time giver"), of the pacing of internal clocks (Czeisler and others, 1989). If you were suddenly forced to live in a continuously dark or light environment, you would still sleep regularly (although your

FIGURE 6.4

Pacing the Internal Clock. Light is an important controller of internal biological "clocks." If you were suddenly forced to live in a continuously light environment, as depicted in this figure, you would still sleep your normal 8 hours (shown by the length of the bar). But sleep onset times would be likely to "drift" over days. Rather than falling asleep at 11:00 P.M. and waking at 7:00 A.M., after a while you might find yourself becoming sleepy at 2:00 A.M. and rising at 10:00 A.M.

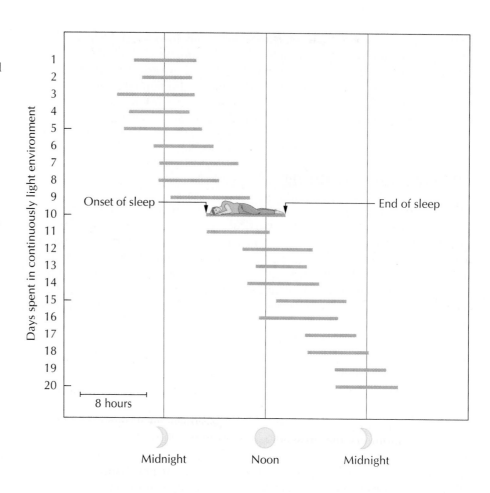

Speculate about how "jet lag" might be caused by disruption in the timing of internal clocks. Remember, people use the rising and setting of the sun as an important controller of biological clocks. Do you think workers who are frequently asked to change shifts might also have problems?

sleep activities may be disrupted somewhat). But the timing of the sleeping and waking cycles would "drift" and lose their connection with night and day (see Figure 6.4). Rather than falling asleep at your usual 11:00 P.M. and waking at 7:00 A.M., after a while you might find yourself becoming sleepy at 2:00 A.M. and rising at 10:00 A.M. People use light during the day, as well as the absence of light at night, as a way of "setting" their internal clocks.

The fact that the environment is so important in maintaining internal body rhythms makes considerable adaptive sense. Remember, the environment also operates in synchrony with universal cycles. The sun rises and sets every 12 hours. There are daily changes in air pressure and temperature induced, in part, by the continuous rotation of the earth about its axis. It's perfectly reasonable to assume that animals, including humans, have adapted to remain in harmony with these cycles. As the cold of winter approaches, birds fly south for the warmer temperatures and the more abundant food supplies; other animals stay put and prepare for hibernation. These changes in behavior are sensible adaptations to changes in the environment that are fixed and not under the animal's direct control.

The Characteristics of Sleep

As noted earlier, the transition from waking to sleep is sometimes described as an alteration in one's *state* or level of consciousness. Rather than being "death's counterfeit" (as Shakespeare once described it), sleep does involve some awareness, although the focus of that awareness no longer connects directly to events in the external world. The sticky problem facing researchers, of course, is that they cannot directly measure the subjective experience (because the subject is unrespon-

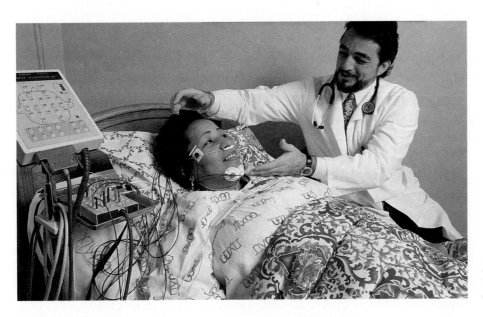

In sleep disorders clinics, the changes in the gross electrical activity of the brain are monitored throughout the night.

sive). What researchers *can* do is eavesdrop on the gross electrical activity of the brain, through EEG recordings, and infer things about changes in the sleeper's state of consciousness by documenting how the pattern of brain activity changes over time.

As you may recall from Chapter 3, the *electroencephalograph,* or EEG, is a device that monitors the gross electrical activity of the brain. Electrodes are attached to the scalp, and changes in the electrical potentials of large numbers of brain cells are recorded in the form of line tracings, or brain waves. It's possible to record EEG-based brain waves at any time, including when someone is asleep. The initial application of the EEG to sleep research was pioneered in the 1950s, when it was quickly recognized that sleep is by no means a passive process. EEG tracings revealed that sleep is characterized by cyclic changes in brain activity and that at certain points the gross electrical activity of the "sleeping" brain bears a striking similarity to the brain activity of a person who is wide awake (Aserinsky & Kleitman, 1955; Dement & Kleitman, 1957).

Figure 6.5 presents typical EEG recordings made during waking and sleep states. The main things to notice are (1) the *height,* or amplitude, of the brain waves; (2) the *frequency,* or number of cycles per second (usually described in Hertz); and (3) the *regularity,* or smoothness, of the pattern. Regular high-amplitude waves of low frequency reflect *neural synchrony,* meaning that large numbers of neurons are working together in synchronized fashion. In the first row of tracings, measured when a subject was awake, you'll see no evidence of neural synchrony—the EEG pattern is fast and irregular, and the waves are of low amplitude. Presumably, when people are awake and focusing their attention on some task, the brain is busy dividing its labor; lots of cells are working on specialized individual tasks, so the combined brain activity tends to look irregular. In contrast, when the brain is in a "relaxed" state, it produces **alpha waves,** which have a higher amplitude and cycle in a slower, more regular manner.

Sleep Stages. As you settle down for the night and prepare for sleep, the irregular wave pattern of the waking state diminishes and is replaced by slower, more synchronized alpha waves. The onset of sleep itself—what is called *stage 1* sleep—is signaled by a return to waves that are lower in amplitude and more irregular. The dominant wave patterns of stage 1 sleep, called **theta waves,** are easily distinguished from the patterns found in the waking state. Yet people often report that

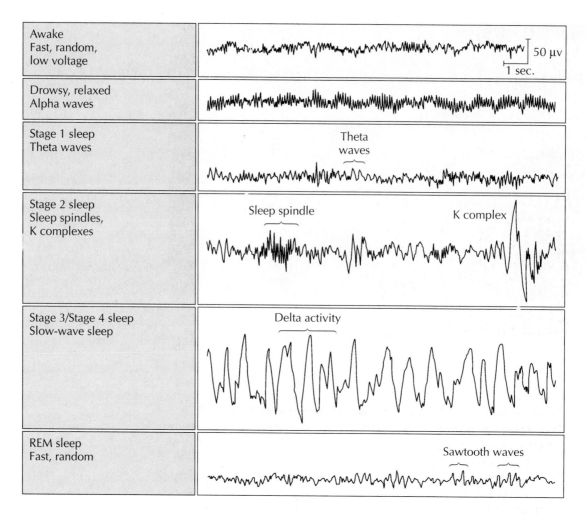

Awake Fast, random, low voltage	*(EEG waveform)* 50 μv / 1 sec.
Drowsy, relaxed Alpha waves	*(EEG waveform)*
Stage 1 sleep Theta waves	Theta waves *(EEG waveform)*
Stage 2 sleep Sleep spindles, K complexes	Sleep spindle K complex *(EEG waveform)*
Stage 3/Stage 4 sleep Slow-wave sleep	Delta activity *(EEG waveform)*
REM sleep Fast, random	Sawtooth waves *(EEG waveform)*

FIGURE 6.5

EEG Patterns Associated with Sleeping and Wakefulness. As a person moves from a waking state into sleep, characteristic changes occur in the electrical activity of the brain. Generally, as the person becomes drowsy and moves through the four stages of sleep, brain waves become slower, show more amplitude, and become more regular. But during REM sleep, when the sleeper is presumed to be dreaming, the EEG shows a pattern more closely resembling the waking state. (From Hauri, 1982)

they're not really asleep at this point; instead, they might report that their thoughts are simply "drifting." When the theta activity starts to be interrupted sporadically by short bursts of activity called *sleep spindles* and occasional sudden, sharp waveforms called *K complexes*, you have entered *stage 2* sleep. You're definitely asleep at this point, although the brain still shows sensitivity to events in the external world. Loud noises, for example, tend to be reflected immediately in the EEG pattern by the triggering of a K complex (Bastien & Campbell, 1992). *Stage 3* and *stage 4* are progressively deeper states and show more synchronized slow-wave brain patterns called **delta activity**; for this reason, these stages are sometimes called delta or **slow-wave sleep.**

It's fair to characterize the transition from stage 1 through to stage 4 as moving from a light to a deep sleep. It's very easy to arouse someone from stage 1 sleep, but it's tougher to do so in stage 4 (Kelly, 1991). Moreover, other physiological indices of arousal, such as breathing rate, heart rate, and blood pressure, decline regularly as one progresses through the stages. But about 70–90 minutes

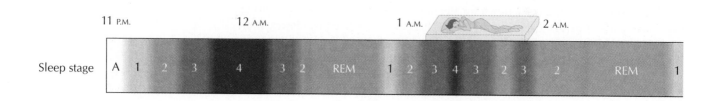

	11 P.M.			12 A.M.				1 A.M.		2 A.M.
Sleep stage	A 1	2 3	4	3 2	REM	1 2 3 4 3	2 3	2	REM	1

into the sleep cycle, something very interesting happens—abrupt changes appear in the entire physiological pattern. Heart rate increases rapidly and becomes more irregular; twitching movements might begin in the hands, feet, and face; in males, the penis becomes erect, and in females vaginal lubrication begins; the eyes begin to move rapidly and irregularly, darting back and forth or up and down behind the eyelids. The EEG pattern loses its synchrony and takes on low-amplitude, irregular patterns that resemble those of the waking state. But the person is not awake. The person has entered *paradoxical,* or **REM** (rapid eye movement) sleep.

REM sleep is called "paradoxical" for an obvious reason: The electrical activity of the brain resembles that found when people are awake, yet they're actually deeply asleep. Their muscle tone is extremely relaxed, and they're relatively difficult to arouse. But as the EEG indicates, the brain is extremely active during this period—if the person is jostled awake from REM sleep, he or she will seem instantly alert. This contrasts sharply with the reaction of people awakened from the early stages of sleep, when they're likely to act confused or even deny they've been asleep. Most important, people who awaken from REM sleep are likely to report an emotional and storylike *dream.* In fact, REM-based dreaming is reported well over 80% of the time, even in people who have previously denied that they dream (Goodenough, 1991; Snyder, 1967).

Over the course of an average night, most adults will cycle through the various stages of sleep, including REM sleep, about four or five times (see Figure 6.6). The entire sleep cycle takes about 90 minutes, but the amount of time spent in each stage changes as morning approaches. During the first cycle of sleep, the majority of time is spent in stages 3 and 4 (slow-wave sleep), but REM sleep tends to dominate the later cycles. The total amount of time spent in REM sleep, presumably dreaming, grows longer with the passage of time, and the interval between successive REM states becomes shorter (Ellman and others, 1991). Many dreams occur toward the end of the sleep period, and these are the dreams you're most likely to remember. We'll return to dreaming momentarily (to consider its adaptive function), but first we need to discuss the adaptive significance of sleep as a whole.

The Function of Sleep

If you sleep 8 hours a night and you live to the ripe old age of 75, you'll have spent a quarter century with your eyes closed, your limbs lying useless at your sides, and your outstretched body seemingly open to attack. Doesn't this seem a bit strange? Think about it. What could be the adaptive value, beyond the exercising of neurons during REM sleep, of redirecting the focus of awareness inward, away from the potential threats of predators lurking about in a constantly changing, often hostile environment?

Researchers aren't exactly sure why people sleep, but a number of plausible hypotheses have been offered. Most intuitive is the suggestion that sleep functions to *restore or repair* the body and mind. The daily activities of waking life presumably produce some wear and tear on the body, and some mind/brain "down time" may be needed to put things back in order. There are clearly some periods, especially during the slow-wave sleep of stage 4, when the metabolic activity of the

Can you think of any adaptive reasons why sleep occurs in stages? What might be the advantage to starting off in a "light" sleep and progressing to a "deeper" sleep?

FIGURE 6.6
Sleep Cycles. Over the course of the average night, most adults move through the various stages of sleep, including REM sleep, about four or five times. A complete cycle usually takes about 90 minutes. Moreover, as the figure shows, people tend to spend more time in REM sleep, presumably dreaming, as morning approaches. (Based on Kalat, 1996)

| 3 A.M. | 4 A.M. | 5 A.M. | 6 A.M. | 7 A.M. |

| 2 | 3 | 2 | REM | 1 | 2 | 3 | 2 | A | 1 | REM | A | 1 | A | 2 | REM |

Why do people sleep? It could be to restore or repair depleted resources, but research suggests that vigorous activity during the day does not necessarily change one's sleeping patterns.

brain is dramatically lowered (Sakai and others, 1979). Moreover, if people are deprived of sleep for any extended period of time, their ability to perform complex tasks, especially those requiring problem solving, deteriorates (Linde & Bergstrom, 1992).

But is the brain really working overtime during sleep—repairing disorganized circuits or restoring depleted resources? In general, there isn't strong empirical support for this idea (Horne, 1988). Although it's true that many restorative activities go on during sleep, these activities are not confined just to sleep. They occur regularly throughout the day, so sleep does not appear to be special in this regard. Neither does there appear to be a strong correlation between the amount of activity in a day and the depth and length of the sleep period that follows. Sleep researchers have tried to tire people during the day by having them engage in vigorous exercise or spend a long day at a shopping center or amusement park, but no great changes in the ensuing sleep patterns have been observed (Horne & Minard, 1985). Rest and restoration may be one of the important by-products of a good night's sleep, but that's clearly not the whole story.

Alternatively, many sleep researchers have stressed the adaptive significance of prolonged "down time" irrespective of any potential biological or psychological side benefits. It's possible to consider sleep as nothing more than an adaptive response to changing environmental conditions, a form of behavior that is useful because it increases the likelihood that humans will survive. Consider, for example, how much people rely on their visual systems. As a result, they aren't very efficient outside at night. Our ancestors could have moved about at night looking for food, trying to avoid being eaten or killed by some lurking predator, but it was probably a better idea for them to stay put in a cave somewhere until dawn. Sleep thus became adaptive—particularly sleeping at night—because it stopped people from venturing forth into a hostile environment.

We can find evidence in support of the idea that sleep developed primarily as an adaptive response to hostile environments by looking closely at the sleeping patterns of animal species in the wild. For example, if sleep is an adaptive reaction to light-dark cycles and susceptibility to predators, we should expect animals that rely on senses other than vision to be active primarily at night, when vision-based predators would be at a hunting disadvantage. This is indeed the case for mice, rats, and other rodents. Second, large animals that must eat continuously and can't easily find places to hide should sleep very little. And, indeed, grazing animals such as sheep, goats, horses, and cattle, which are vulnerable to surprise

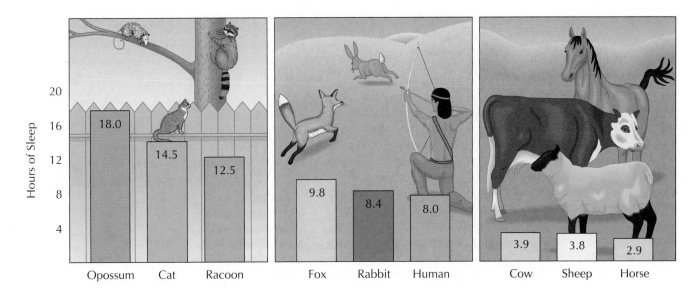

attack by predators, sleep only a few hours a day (see Figure 6.7). In one study, researchers found that body weight and susceptibility to attack could explain over half of all the variability found among the sleeping patterns of different species (Allison & Chichetti, 1976).

The Function of Dreaming

It's easy to see how sleep itself might have developed as an adaptive response, whether to repair, restore, or protect the organism struggling to survive. But why are there stages of sleep? Why, if people want to protect or rest the body, do they spend a significant amount of time in such an internally active state as REM sleep? Since REM sleep is strongly correlated with the recall of vivid dreams, does dreaming serve some unique biological or psychological function? Unfortunately, at this point we have no clear-cut answers to these questions.

It's not even clear whether REM sleep, like sleep in general, is even a necessary component of normal functioning. It's possible to deprive both people and animals selectively of REM sleep. One technique used with people involves carefully monitoring the EEG and then waking the subject whenever characteristic REM patterns appear in the recordings. Surprisingly, the effects of REM sleep deprivation in humans are not usually dramatic. Subjects may show a bit more irritability (compared to controls who are shaken awake during non-REM periods), and their performance on tasks requiring logical reasoning and problem solving is hurt, but the level of impairment is not large (Ellman and others, 1991). Some forms of severe depression even appear to be helped by REM sleep deprivation, and some effective antidepressant drugs suppress REM sleep as a side effect (Vogel and others, 1990).

On the other hand, some intriguing changes in the *patterns* of sleep occur after periods of REM deprivation. Sleep researchers have noticed that on the second or third night of REM deprivation, it is necessary to awaken the subject with much greater frequency. When people lose sleep, particularly REM sleep, their bodies attempt to make up for the loss during the next sleep period by increasing the total proportion of time spent in the REM stage. The more REM sleep lost, the more the body tries to make it up the next night. This tendency, known as **REM rebound,** is one reason that many researchers remain convinced that REM sleep serves some unspecified but extremely important function in the adaptive mind.

Of course, to the psychologist, at least historically, REM-based dreaming has

FIGURE 6.7
Sleep Times for Various Species.
Not all animals spend the same amount of time sleeping. Large grazing animals, such as cows and horses, eat frequently and are quite vulnerable to surprise attacks from predators. As the figure shows, such animals tend to sleep very little. Small, quick animals, such as cats and rodents, are less vulnerable to attack and sleep a great deal.

always been viewed as an important psychological phenomenon. Sigmund Freud believed that dreams, once interpreted, serve as a "royal road to the unconscious." Dreaming, he argued, is a psychological mechanism for *wish fulfillment,* a way to gratify forbidden wishes and desires (especially sexual ones) that are too disturbing to be allowed to come to consciousness directly. He believed that the often bizarre nature of dreams results from the fact that even in people's dreams their desires are hidden in the form of symbolism. To Freud, for example, a gun (in fact, any elongated object) might represent a phallic symbol, whereas a tunnel (or any entryway) would stand for a vagina. To establish the true meaning of a dream, Freud believed that it is necessary to distinguish between the dream's **manifest content**—the actual symbols of the dream—and its **latent content,** which are those hidden desires that are too disturbing to be expressed directly.

Since the time of Freud, psychologists have been more reluctant to search for hidden meaning in dreams. Although certain kinds of dream events cut across people and cultures (most people dream of flying or falling, for example), and most people have the unsettling experience of recurring dreams, critics have argued that interpretation is often in the eye of the beholder. Whether a cigar is a phallic symbol or just a cigar isn't the easiest or most clear-cut decision to make. Moreover, just because you repeatedly dream about being chased by a poodle that looks remarkably like your brother Ed doesn't mean that the dream is significant psychologically. A troubling dream, for example, might simply lead you to awaken suddenly and think about what has just occurred. As a result, the dream becomes firmly ingrained in memory and thus more likely to occur again (or at least be remembered) in the future (see Chapter 8).

Some sleep researchers reject the psychological significance of dreaming altogether, claiming that dream interpretation is of limited value scientifically. According to the **activation-synthesis hypothesis** of Hobson and McCarley (1977; Hobson, 1988), dreaming is really nothing more than the product of a reality-based brain trying to make sense of spontaneous brain activity. During REM sleep, for reasons that are not particularly clear, activities among cells in the hindbrain tend to activate the higher centers of the brain. This activity could arise simply to exercise the brain circuitry (Edelman, 1987), or it could be a consequence of random events in the room. Whatever the reason, the higher brain centers have evolved to interpret lower brain signals in meaningful ways. Thus, the brain creates a story, often bizarre, to try to make some sense out of the signals that it's receiving. The brain is simply doing the things that it would normally do when awake, as it receives signals from the environment. But in the activation-synthesis view, there's little of psychological significance here: Dreams typically represent only a "random synthesis of neurological activity" (Weinstein, Schwartz, & Arkin, 1991).

This is not to suggest that all psychologists reject the idea that dream content is meaningful. Many still feel that it is significant, but perhaps more in relation to events and troubles in everyday life than to deep-seated and forbidden desires. You may dream to focus your attention on particularly troubling current problems in order to work toward possible solutions (Cartwright, 1991; Fiss, 1991). Moreover, although the biological mechanisms that generate the REM state may not be psychologically driven, the bizarre *interpretations* of those purely physiological activities may tell us something important about the psychological functioning of the mind. The bottom line is that researchers really don't know at this point why there is a REM stage to sleep, or whether its correlated activity, dreaming, is of any psychological significance. Figure 6.8 summarizes some of the most popular theories of why people dream.

It is of interest to note that REM activity is commonplace in numerous organisms other than humans (Durie, 1981). Virtually all mammals show REM, as do birds, and even turtles. Moreover, human infants spend a remarkable amount of time in REM sleep; even human fetuses show REM patterns in the womb. If we

The activation-synthesis hypothesis proposes that dreams arise from the interpretation of random neural activity. Yet many people dream of flying, falling, or being unprepared for a test. How can you reconcile the fact that people have the same types of dreams with the idea that dreams arise from random neural activity?

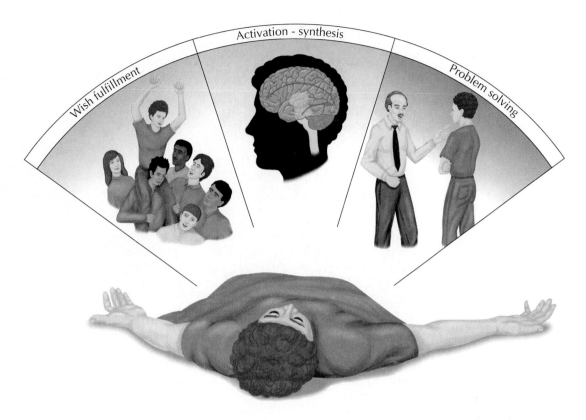

accept the questionable assumption that the fetus is dreaming, does it make sense to propose that the fetus is working out some hidden sexual conflict in some bizarre symbolic form? It's safe to assume that REM sleep and dreaming reflect some important property of the adaptive mind, but at the moment its identity remains a mystery. For some further information on REM and its possible role in learning, read the accompanying Inside the Problem.

Disorders of Sleep

We end our treatment of sleep and dreaming with a brief discussion of sleep disorders. Psychologists and other mental health professionals divide sleep disorders into two main diagnostic categories: (1) *dyssomnias,* which are problems associated with the amount, timing, and quality of sleep; and (2) *parasomnias,* which are abnormal disturbances that occur during sleep. Let's consider some prominent examples of each type.

The most common type of dyssomnia is **insomnia,** a condition marked by difficulties in initiating or maintaining sleep. Everyone has trouble getting to sleep from time to time, and everyone has awakened in the middle of the night and been unable to get back to sleep. But for the clinical diagnosis of insomnia, these difficulties need to be chronic—lasting for at least a month. It's been estimated that perhaps 30% of the population suffers from some degree of insomnia, although the number of truly severe sufferers is thought to be closer to 15% (Bootzin and others, 1993; Gillin, 1993). There are many potential causes for the condition, including stress, emotional problems, alcohol and other drug use, and medical conditions. Some kinds of insomnia may even be learned—for example, children who regularly fall asleep in the presence of their parents often have trouble getting back to sleep if they wake up later alone in their room (Adair and others, 1991). It's presumed that these children have learned to associate going to sleep with the presence of a parent and consequently cannot return to sleep without the parent present.

FIGURE 6.8
Theories of Dreaming. Psychologists are not sure why people dream. One theory, proposed by Freud, postulates that dreams are a psychological mechanism for wish fulfillment. The activation-synthesis hypothesis asserts that dreaming results from the brain's attempt to make sense of spontaneous brain activity. Others have proposed that dreams help solve particularly troubling problems in people's lives.

One common type of sleep disorder is insomnia, a condition marked by chronic difficulties in initiating or maintaining sleep.

Whereas insomnia is characterized by an inability to sleep, in **hypersomnia** the problem is *too much* sleep. People who are diagnosed with hypersomnia show excessive sleepiness—they're often caught catnapping during the day, and they complain about being tired all the time. The cause of this condition is unknown, although it has been suggested that genetic factors might be involved (Parkes & Block, 1989). Excessive sleepiness can also be caused by infectious diseases, such as mononucleosis or chronic fatigue syndrome, and by a sleep disorder called *sleep apnea.* Sleep apnea is a relatively rare condition in which the sleeper repeatedly stops breathing throughout the night, usually for short periods lasting up to a minute or so. The episodes typically end with the person waking up gasping for breath. Because these episodes occur frequently throughout the night, the affected person feels tired during the day. Significant sleep apnea problems are found in perhaps 1%–2% of the population, although a higher percentage of individuals may experience occasional episodes (Kales & Kales, 1984).

The second category of sleep disorders, parasomnias, includes such abnormal sleep disturbances as nightmares, night terrors, and sleepwalking. **Nightmares** are frightening and anxiety-arousing dreams that occur primarily during the REM stage of sleep. They inevitably cause the sleeper to awaken; if they recur frequently, they can lead to the symptoms of insomnia. What causes nightmares? No one is certain at this point, although frequent nightmares may indicate the presence of a psychological disorder.

Night terrors, which occur mainly in children, are terrifying experiences in which the sleeper awakens suddenly in an extreme state of panic—the child may sit in bed screaming and will show little responsiveness to others who are present. Night terrors are not considered to be serious indicators of psychological or medical problems, and they tend to go away with age. Finally, **sleepwalking** occurs when the sleeper rises during sleep and wanders about. Sleepwalking happens mainly in childhood, tends to vanish as the child reaches adolescence, and is not thought to result from a serious psychological or medical problem. It's interesting to note that both night terrors and sleepwalking occur during periods of non-REM sleep, which means that neither is probably related to dreaming.

INSIDE THE PROBLEM: *Does REM Sleep Help People Learn?*

For decades, sleep researchers have considered the possibility that activities during sleep may help strengthen, or *consolidate,* certain kinds of memories. As we'll discuss in Chapter 8, people who learn a list of words just before going to sleep remember those words better than people who learn the same words just prior to the start of a busy day. But the fact that sleeping after learning leads to better memory does not mean that sleep is responsible for the improvement. It could be that sleeping improves memory only because the activities of a busy day *interfere* with new learning. It's not that sleeping strengthens memory; rather, remaining active leads to the establishment of new memories that interfere with old ones.

However, a group of researchers in Israel has shown that a particular stage of sleep, REM, may at least play a role in promoting certain kinds of learning (Karni et al., 1994). Karni and colleagues asked subjects to solve a perceptual puzzle task that required detecting a small target pattern in a complex visual array. In earlier research it had been found that performance on this task improved with practice and, more important, that most of the improvement seemed to occur 8 to 10 hours after a practice session. This finding encouraged Karni and his colleagues to investigate (1) whether performance would also improve if subjects spent the 8 to 10 hours asleep, and (2) whether certain stages of sleep might be more important than others in promoting the learning consolidation process.

So a group of subjects was asked to practice this perceptual task just before going to sleep. Three experimental conditions were then investigated. In one condition, the subjects were allowed a normal night's sleep, without interruption. In a second condition, the subjects were awakened by a ringing bell every time their brain waves, as measured by EEG, revealed that they had entered a REM stage. In a third condition, sleep was again disrupted, but only when the EEG signaled a period of

slow-wave sleep (stages 3 and 4). In the morning, everyone was asked to perform the perceptual task again.

The results of this experiment are shown in Figure 6.9. The data show how much performance on the perceptual detection task improved from night to morning across the three conditions. The main finding of interest was that performance on the task did indeed improve after sleeping, but only if the subjects had been allowed normal levels of REM sleep. The subjects who had been REM deprived showed essentially no improvement in the task; in other words, they failed to learn from the practice session. Moreover, it wasn't just the fact that they were repeatedly awakened during that night that impaired learning; subjects in the slow-wave interruption condition were awakened just as often, on average, yet still showed considerable

improvement in performance.

These results suggest that activities during REM sleep are needed to consolidate some forms of learning overnight. But what are these activities? It's unclear at this point, but Karni and his colleagues speculate that the neurotransmitter *acetylcholine* (ACh) may be involved. Studies with animals have shown that ACh increases in the brain during REM sleep. This important neurotransmitter is thought to play a role in storing memories. As we mentioned in Chapter 3, memory problems are common in patients suffering from Alzheimer's disease, and it's known that neurons in the brain that produce ACh often degenerate during the disease. Thus, ACh may be needed to consolidate the storage of experience, explaining why REM activity is important in the consolidation process.

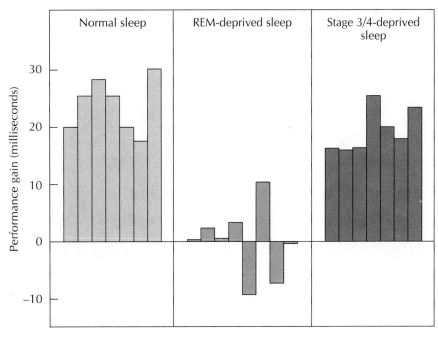

FIGURE 6.9
Performance Gains After Deprived and Nondeprived Sleep. This figure shows the performance results that occurred when subjects were allowed normal sleep or had either their REM sleep or slow-wave (stages 3 and 4) sleep deprived. Each bar shows the gain or loss on the morning perceptual task for an individual subject in the experiment. Notice that in the middle panel (the REM-deprived condition), subjects showed little or no performance gain. (Data from Karni et al., 1994)

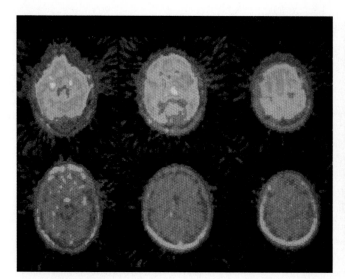

This series of PET scans shows how administration of an opium-like drug affects general activity in the brain. The first PET scan in the top row shows a normal active brain; the last PET scan in the bottom row shows diminished activity after the drug has taken full effect.

Altering Awareness: Psychoactive Drugs

The rhythmic cycles of sleep represent a classic instance of how conscious awareness shifts in dramatic ways as the gross electrical activity of the brain changes. We haven't talked much about the neurological determinants of these brain alterations, but it shouldn't surprise you to learn that the brain's chemical messengers, the neurotransmitters, are primarily responsible. The onset of REM sleep, for example, appears to be controlled by neurons in the hindbrain, particularly the *pons,* that secrete acetylcholine. In studies with animals, it has been found that levels of ACh in the cortex are highest during REM and waking states and drop to lower levels during the stages of slow-wave sleep (Jasper & Tessier, 1969). The initiation and duration of sleep may be affected by the actions of the inhibitory neurotransmitter *serotonin*; wakefulness and general arousal have been linked to *norepinephrine* and *dopamine.*

The brain is a kind of biochemical factory, altering moods and shifting awareness in response to the environment by enhancing or inhibiting the actions of its various neurotransmitters. As we've discussed previously, the brain sometimes reacts to stress or exertion by releasing brain chemicals called *endorphins,* which reduce pain and serve to generally elevate mood. Altering awareness chemically in such a fashion is highly adaptive, because the delay of pain can allow an organism to escape from a life-threatening situation.

Allowing some external agent, such as a drug, to enter the body can radically change the delicate biochemical balance that controls awareness and other mental processes. Conscious awareness can be altered artificially through the ingestion of drugs, often in ways that produce either pleasurable or unpleasurable consequences. Drugs can have tremendously beneficial effects, especially in the treatment of psychological and medical disorders (see Chapter 15). But drug *abuse,* particularly of alcohol and tobacco, is directly or indirectly responsible for hundreds of thousands of deaths annually in the United States (Coleman, 1993). In this section, we'll consider the actions of drugs labeled **psychoactive**—those that affect behavior and mental processes through alterations of conscious awareness.

Drug Actions and Effects

Psychologists are interested in the effects of psychoactive drugs for two main reasons. First, these drugs produce powerful effects on behavior and mental processes.

Second, they can help us understand more about the neural mechanisms underlying behavior. Psychoactive drugs, like most natural drugs produced by the brain, exert their effects primarily by changing the normal communication channels of neurons. It's possible to affect neuron-to-neuron communication in a variety of ways. Some drugs, such as *nicotine,* duplicate the action of neurotransmitters by actually attaching themselves to the receptor sites of postsynaptic membranes; this "mimicking" action allows the drug to produce the same effect as the brain's natural chemical messenger. Other drugs depress or block the action of neurotransmitters; some sleeping pills, for instance, decrease norepinephrine or dopamine stimulation. The psychoactive drug *fluoxetine* (known commercially as Prozac®) has been used successfully to treat depression; it acts by slowing the process through which the neurotransmitter serotonin is broken down and taken back up into the transmitting cell (Kramer, 1993).

Repeated use of a drug can cause changes in the way the body reacts. For example, a person can develop **tolerance,** which means that increasing amounts of the drug are needed to produce the same physical and behavioral effects. Tolerance represents a kind of adaptation that the body makes to compensate for the effects of the drug. Sometimes associated with the development of tolerance is **drug dependency,** which is manifested as either a physical or a psychological *need* for continued use. With physical dependency, the person can experience **withdrawal** symptoms when he or she stops taking the drug. These are clear, measurable physical reactions such as sweating, vomiting, changes in heart rate, or tremors. Drug dependency is the primary cause of substance abuse, although the mechanisms that lead to dependency are still a matter of some debate. At this point, it's not certain whether dependency develops as a consequence of "urgings" produced by biological withdrawal, or whether people essentially learn to become dependent on the drug with repeated use (Tiffany, 1990).

Categories of Psychoactive Drugs

It's useful to classify psychoactive drugs into one of four categories—depressants, stimulants, opiates, and hallucinogens—based on their specific mind-altering characteristics. We'll briefly examine each type and then conclude with a discussion of some psychological factors involved in drug use.

Depressants. In general, drugs classified as **depressants** slow, or depress, the ongoing activity of the central nervous system. *Ethyl alcohol,* which is present in beer, wine, and distilled drinks, is a well-known example of a depressant. Biochemically, alcohol appears to lead to an increase in either the secretion or general effectiveness of the neurotransmitters GABA and dopamine. Both are primarily inhibitory messengers in the brain, so neurons in a number of vital brain centers become less likely to fire (Suzdak and others, 1986). Drinkers feel "high" after consumption in part because the drug produces a calming effect on the body, which leads to a reduction in anxiety. Animals find the effects of alcohol quite reinforcing, which means that they will perform tasks that yield small amounts of alcohol as a reward (Wise & Bozarth, 1987).

As the consumption of alcohol increases, more complex psychological effects emerge as a result of increased inhibition of those brain centers that control judgment. It's often the case that people will start behaving in ways that counteract their normal behavioral tendencies (Steele & Josephs, 1990). Thus, the normally demure become loud and aggressive; the sexually inhibited become flirtatious and provocative. These behavioral changes are aided by the fact that alcohol reduces self-awareness. Drinkers are less likely to monitor their behaviors and actions closely, and they tend to forget about any problems that are currently bothersome (Hull & Bond, 1986). These carefree moments are stolen at a cost, of course,

Do you believe that psychoactive drugs should be legally available for "recreational" use? If not, how can you justify the legal availability of alcohol, nicotine, and caffeine?

The alcohol present in beer, wine, and distilled drinks depresses central nervous system activity and contributes annually to hundreds of thousands of deaths worldwide.

because the body eventually reacts to the drug in a more negative way. Fatigue, nausea, and depression are likely consequences of overconsumption.

Barbiturates and *tranquilizers* are also classified as depressant drugs. Both are widely prescribed for the treatment of anxiety and insomnia, and they produce effects in the brain similar to those induced by alcohol (the neurotransmitter GABA is again involved). Like alcohol, at low doses tranquilizing agents tend to produce pleasurable feelings of relaxation. But at higher doses one's concentration is weakened, memory is impaired, and speech becomes slurred. Barbiturate use also commonly leads to tolerance and dependency. With continued use, one's metabolism is changed, so that larger and larger doses of the drug are required to obtain the same effect, and the user becomes physically and psychologically dependent on the drug. Tranquilizers (such as the widely prescribed Valium® and Xanax®) are less habit forming than barbiturates and for this reason are more likely to be prescribed.

Stimulants. A **stimulant** is a drug that increases central nervous system activity, enhancing neural transmission. Examples of stimulants include *caffeine, nicotine, amphetamines,* and *cocaine.* These agents generally increase alertness and can affect mood by inducing feelings of pleasure. The morning cup of coffee is an excellent example of how a stimulant in low doses—caffeine—can improve one's mood significantly and even increase concentration and attention. Other effects of stimulants include dilated pupils, increased heart and respiration rate, and decreased appetite. In large doses, stimulants can produce extreme anxiety and even convulsions and death.

Both amphetamines and cocaine produce their stimulating effects by increasing the effectiveness of the neurotransmitters norepinephrine and dopamine. Dopamine is apparently primarily responsible for the positive, reinforcing qualities of these drugs (Wise & Rompre, 1989). Research has shown that animals will work hard to administer themselves drugs that increase the activity of dopamine-based synapses. In the case of cocaine, which is derived from the leaves of the coca plant, the drug blocks the reabsorption of both norepinephrine and dopamine. When reabsorption is blocked, these transmitter substances are able to exert their effects for a longer period of time. Cocaine produces intense feelings of euphoria, although the effects of the drug wear off relatively quickly. A half hour or so after the drug enters the body, the user "crashes," in part because the drug has temporarily depleted the user's internal supply of norepinephrine and dopamine. Regular use of cocaine has been found to produce a number of harmful side effects, including intense episodes of paranoia and even hallucinations and delusions.

Opiates. Drugs classified as **opiates** (also sometimes called *narcotics*) tend to depress nervous system activity, thereby reducing anxiety, elevating mood, and lowering sensitivity to pain. Well-known examples of opiates include opium, heroin, and morphine. As mentioned previously, morphine, derived originally from the flowering opium plant, binds directly with existing membrane receptor sites in the nervous system. Its pain-killing effects and pleasurable mood shifts (it's named after Morpheus, the Greek god of dreams) apparently arise from the fact that it mimics the brain's own chemicals (endorphins) that are involved in reducing pain. Opiates, however, typically produce strong physical and psychological dependence. The body is changed with continued use; once usage is stopped, the body rebels with intense and prolonged withdrawal symptoms.

Hallucinogens. In the case of hallucinogenic drugs, or *psychedelics,* the term "psychoactive" is particularly apt. **Hallucinogens** can play havoc with a person's normal internal construction of reality. Perception itself is fractured, and the world becomes awash in fantastic colors, sounds, and tactile sensations. Two of the best known examples of these drugs, *mescaline* and *psilocybin,* occur naturally in the environment. Mescaline comes from a certain kind of cactus, while psilocybin is a form of mushroom. Both of these drugs have been ingested by various civilizations for centuries, primarily in the context of religious rituals and ceremonies. Since the 1960s, they have served as potentially dangerous recreational drugs for those seeking "alternative realities."

Lysergic acid diethylamide (LSD) is a synthetic version of a psychedelic drug. LSD is thought to mimic the action of the neurotransmitter serotonin (Strassman, 1992); the drug binds to specific serotonin-based receptor sites in the brain, producing stimulation. For reasons that are not particularly clear, variations in sensation and perception are produced. A typical LSD experience, which can last for up to 16 hours, consists of profound changes in perception. Some users report a phenomenon called *synesthesia,* which is a blending of sensory experiences—colors may actually feel warm or cold, and rough textures may begin to sing. Also for unknown reasons, a user's experience can turn sharply wrong. Bad "trips" can induce extreme panic or depression in the user, increasing the likelihood of accidents and personal harm. Users also sometimes report the occurrence of "flashbacks," in which the sensations of the drug are reexperienced long after the drug has presumably left the body.

Marijuana, which comes from the naturally occurring hemp plant *Cannabis,* is also often classified as a hallucinogenic drug. It is unusual to see profound distortions of perceptual reality with this drug, however, unless large amounts are ingested. Marijuana is usually smoked or swallowed, and its effects last around 4 hours. Users typically report a melting away of anxiety, a general sense of well-being, and heightened sensory awareness. Changes in the perception of time and its passage are sometimes reported, along with increased appetite. The pleasant effects of the drug are usually followed by fatigue and sometimes sleep.

As with other hallucinogenic drugs, marijuana does not always produce a pleasant experience. Some users report anxiety, extreme fearfulness, and panic (Fackelmann, 1993). A number of studies have indicated that marijuana use impairs concentration, motor coordination, and the ability to track things visually (Moskowitz, 1985), which contributes to the likelihood of traffic accidents when used by drivers. Less is known about the long-term effects of regular use, but there's some evidence that marijuana may adversely affect the formation of memories (Hooker & Jones, 1987; Miller & Branconnier, 1983; Millsaps, Azrin, & Mittenberg, 1994).

Psychological Factors

One of the more interesting characteristics of psychoactive drugs, especially to psychologists, is the variability typically seen in the effects of these drugs. Two people can ingest the same drug, in exactly the same quantity, but experience completely different mind-altering effects. A small amount of LSD consumed by Phil produces a euphoric "religious experience"; the same amount for Jane produces a frightening descent into a whirlpool of terror and fear. Why? Shouldn't the pharmacological effects on the neurotransmitters in the brain produce similar or at least consistent psychological effects?

The answer is that the psychological effects are determined by interactions among numerous factors. The environmental setting in which a drug is taken, for example, is known to affect the experience. Smoking marijuana for the first time in a car speeding 75 miles per hour might seriously curtail the anxiety-reducing effects of the drug. Many users report that familiarity with the drug's effects is also important—users claim one needs to "learn" to smoke marijuana or take LSD before the innermost "secrets" of the drug are revealed. In fact, experienced users of marijuana have been found to experience a "high" after smoking a cigarette they only *thought* was marijuana; similar effects did not occur for novice users (Jones, 1971). Both familiarity and the environment affect the user's *mental set*—his or her expectations about the drug's harmful and beneficial consequences. Finally, the user's physical state is critical. Some people develop resistance or tolerance to a drug faster than others do. The experience of a drug may even depend on such mundane things as whether the person has eaten or is well rested.

Altering Awareness: Induced States

The setting is Paris, late in the year 1783. Dressed in a lilac silk robe, German-born physician Franz Anton Mesmer works to restore the delicate balance of universal fluids in his small collection of patients. With large magnets attached to the people's sides—the better to affect their "animal magnetism"—Mesmer rhythmically passes an iron rod, in large wavelike motions, over their outstretched bodies. His subjects quickly fall into a trancelike state; they can still talk and move their limbs on command, but each appears to have entered an alternative form of consciousness from which all forms of voluntary control have been lost. Upon later awakening, many feel better, apparently "cured" of their various physical and psychological maladies.

Magnetic "cures." In the latter part of the 18th century, Anton Mesmer helped to promote the belief that physical and psychological problems could be "cured" by passing magnets over the body.

Although Mesmer himself eventually fell into disrepute, rejected by the scientific community of his time, the phenomenon of "mesmerizing" did not. Today, of course, we recognize that the artificial "state" of awareness he induced in his patients had nothing to do with magnets or the balancing of universal fluids. Modern psychologists would explain the bizarre behavior of Mesmer's patients as an example of hypnosis. **Hypnosis** can be defined generally as any form of social interaction that produces a *heightened state of suggestibility* in a willing participant. It is of interest to psychologists, like the related topic of meditation, because it's a technique specifically designed to alter conscious awareness. As we'll see shortly, hypnosis has some highly adaptive properties.

Under what circumstances do you think it might be *adaptive* for someone to enter a heightened state of suggestibility?

The Phenomena of Hypnosis

It's worth noting at the outset that despite some two centuries of work on the topic, our understanding of hypnosis remains incomplete. For example, researchers are not even sure at this point whether hypnosis is truly an altered state of awareness or simply a kind of social "play acting" engaged in to please the hypnotist. But we do know a few things about what hypnosis is not. For one thing, even though hypnotized people seem at times to be asleep—in fact, the word *hypnosis* comes from the Greek *hypnos* meaning "to sleep"—hypnosis bears little physiological relation to sleep. The EEG patterns of a hypnotized subject, along with other physiological indices, more closely resemble those of someone who is relaxed rather than deeply asleep (Graffen, Ray, & Lundy, 1995). In addition, certain reflexes that are commonly absent during sleep, such as the knee jerk, are still present under hypnosis (Pratt, Wood, & Alman, 1988). Neither is it true that only weak-willed people are susceptible. Everyone appears to be susceptible to a degree, in the sense that all show heightened suggestibility—although hypnotic suggestibility scales indicate that only about 20% of the population are highly hypnotizable (Hilgard, 1965).

A variety of methods can be used to induce the hypnotic state. The most popular technique is one in which the hypnotist, acting as an authority figure, suggests to the client that he or she is growing increasingly more relaxed and sleepy with time: "Your eyes are getting heavier and heavier, you can barely keep your lids open," and so on. Often the client is asked to fixate on something, perhaps a spot on the wall or a swinging pendulum. The logic here is that eye fixation leads to muscle fatigue, which helps convince clients that they are indeed becoming increasingly relaxed. Other approaches to induction rely more on subtle suggestions (Erickson, 1964), but in general no one method is necessarily better than any other. In the words of one researcher, "The art of hypnosis relies on not providing the client with grounds for resisting" (Araoz, 1982, p. 106).

Once hypnotized, the subject becomes highly suggestible, responding to commands from the hypnotist in ways that seem automatic and involuntary. The trained practitioner can then use his or her power of suggestion to achieve such adaptive ends as helping people kick unwanted habits, such as persistent smoking or overeating. Anesthetic effects are also possible at certain deep stages of hypnosis. Hypnotized patients report less pain during childbirth (Harmon, Hynan, & Tyre, 1990) and typically suffer less during dental work (Houle and others, 1988). It has even been possible to perform major surgeries (such as appendectomies) using hypnosis as the primary anesthesia (Kihlstrom, 1985). Research is ongoing to determine the biological basis for these striking analgesic effects. It was once thought, for example, that the release of endorphins by the brain might be responsible, although this possibility has recently been ruled out (Moret and others, 1991).

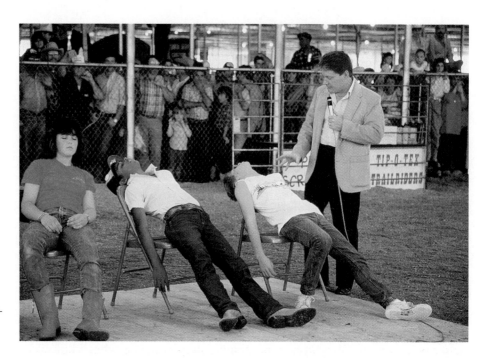

Although hypnosis is often used for entertainment purposes in stage shows, it can have considerable clinical value.

A visit to a stage hypnotist is likely to reveal an astonishing variety of hypnotically induced behaviors. For example, most audiences are impressed with a demonstration of **catalepsy**: The hypnotist places one of the subject's limbs in some unusual position (perhaps raising a leg or an arm in the air), and the subject then retains this position rigidly for long periods of time, without any signs of tiring. Perceptual effects are also common. The volunteer, acting as a kind of automaton, appears to "see" or "hear" things that are not really there; perhaps the subject carries on conversations with imaginary people or ignores loud noises that would normally cause someone to jump. Perceptual changes of this sort have sometimes been reported in the laboratory. In a number of these studies, researchers have looked for hypnotically based changes in vision. Susceptibility to perceptual illusions, for instance, can sometimes be reduced under hypnosis, although the data overall are not especially clear-cut (Kihlstrom, 1985). There has also been work demonstrating that perception of time can be altered under hypnosis, leading to underestimation of the hypnotic period (St.-Jean and others, 1994).

Memory Enhancement. One frequent claim is that hypnosis can have an enhancing effect on *memory,* a phenomenon called **hypnotic hypermnesia.** Perhaps you've heard of criminal cases in which hypnotized witnesses suddenly and miraculously recalled minute details of a horrific crime. In one famous kidnapping case from the 1970s, a bus driver was buried 6 feet underground along with 26 children inside a tractor trailer. Later, under hypnosis, he was able to reconstruct details of the kidnapper's license plate—digit by digit. There is a long-standing belief among many psychotherapists that hypnosis is an excellent tool for uncovering hidden memories of abuse or other forms of psychological trauma (Pratt et al., 1988). There have even been a number of well-publicized examples of *age regression* under hypnosis, in which the subject mentally traveled backward to some earlier place (such as his or her second-grade classroom) and was able to recall numerous details.

Unfortunately, there is little hard evidence to support these phenomena scientifically. A patient's memory may indeed improve after a hypnotic session, but this fact does not allow us to conclude that the hypnotic state was responsible for the improvement. One possibility is that hypnotic induction procedures (the relaxation techniques) simply create effective and supportive environments in which to remember (Geiselman and others, 1985). Controlled experiments in the laboratory have been unable to find any evidence for the alleged memory-enhancing properties of hypnosis (Dinges and others, 1992; Steblay & Bothwell, 1994). Another problem is that it's often difficult to judge whether what appear to be hidden memories are, in fact, accurate representations of what occurred. You may "remember" a particularly unfortunate experience from the second-grade classroom, but can you be sure that this traumatic episode indeed occurred as you remember? As we'll see in a moment, hypnotized subjects often adopt roles designed to please the practitioner. What appear to be memories, then, are sometimes *fabrications*—stories that the subject unintentionally "makes up" to please the hypnotist. For this reason, many states have banned the use of hypnotic testimony in criminal court cases.

Can you think of any situations in which memories accessed via hypnosis should be admitted as evidence in court? Why or why not?

Hypnotic Dissociations. Although a hypnotized subject is almost certainly mired in some kind of altered form of consciousness, there is considerable debate about exactly how this so-called "state" should be characterized. As noted earlier, the EEG patterns of someone in a hypnotic "deep sleep" resemble the patterns of someone in a relaxed waking state; in fact, there do not appear to be any reliable physiological indices that can be used to define the hypnotized condition biologically. Some prominent researchers have argued that **hypnotic dissociations** are induced in the subject. Such dissociations represent a kind of splitting of consciousness during which multiple forms of awareness coexist (Hilgard, 1986, 1992). Hilgard (1986) has argued, for example, that conscious awareness in a hypnotized subject is actually divided into separate components. One stream of consciousness follows the commands of the hypnotist, perhaps feeling no effects of painful stimulation, while another stream, the "hidden observer," is painfully aware of the true stimulation.

Hilgard has supported his position with experiments in which subjects are hypnotized and asked to submerge one arm into a bucket of extremely cold ice water (a common procedure to test for the analgesic effects of hypnosis). "You'll be aware of no pain," the subject is told, "but that other part of you, the hidden part that is aware of everything going on, can signal any true pain by pressing this key." A button is made available which the subject is allowed to press, at will, with the nonsubmerged hand. It turns out that the subjects not only press the key, but the key presses become much more frequent the longer the arm is kept submerged. During hypnosis, as well as afterward, the subjects claim to have no knowledge of what the nonsubmerged hand is doing. There is a hidden part of consciousness, Hilgard claims, that maintains realistic contact with what's going on; it is the other, "hypnotized" stream of awareness that feels no pain.

This idea that conscious awareness is divided or split during hypnosis may seem mystical, strange, and worthy of skepticism. But as we've made clear many times, the brain often divides its labor to arrive at adaptive solutions more effectively. You walk and talk at the same time, and you certainly don't consciously think about picking up one leg and putting down the other while making a point in the conversation. The idea that consciousness is regularly dissociated, or divided, is not really an issue to most psychologists; it's accepted as a given, as a normal attribute of psychological functioning. But whether it is correct to characterize *hypnosis* as a true dissociation of consciousness is still a matter of debate.

Social Role Playing. Skepticism about hypnosis representing a truly dissociated "state" of awareness, perhaps with its own operating laws, comes from the fact that hypnotized subjects often seem eager to please the hypnotist by acting in accordance with a kind of hypnotized "role." The behavior of the hypnotized subject is easily modified by expectations and by small changes in the suggestions of the hypnotist. It often appears as if subjects are trying desperately to "do whatever they can to achieve the suggested effects" (Kihlstrom & McConkey, 1990). For example, if subjects are told prior to the hypnotic session that a rigid right arm is a prominent feature of the hypnotized state, then rigid right arms are likely to be reported after induction even though no such specific suggestion is made during the induction process (Orne, 1959).

A number of researchers have suggested that hypnotic behavior may, in fact, simply be a kind of social role playing. Everyone has some idea of what hypnotized behavior looks like—to be hypnotized, one must fall into a "trance" state and act slavishly in compliance with the all-powerful hypnotist. So when people agree to be hypnotized, they implicitly agree to act out this "role" (Barber, Spanos, & Chaves, 1974; Sarbin & Coe, 1972; Spanos, 1982). The subjects have not actually lost voluntary control over their behavior; rather, they follow the lead of the hypnotist and obey his or her "every command" because they think, perhaps unconsciously, that involuntary compliance is an important part of what it means to be hypnotized (Lynn, Rhue, & Weekes, 1990). Once again, subjects may not make this decision consciously; it's better to characterize the process as "creative role engagement, where subjects generate the sensations, subjective experiences, and mental representations scripted by the hypnotic context" (Lynn and others, 1990, p. 172).

Quite a bit of evidence exists to support this role playing interpretation of the hypnotic state. One compelling finding is that essentially all hypnotic phenomena can be reproduced with *simulated subjects*—people who are never actually hypnotized but who are told to *act* as if they are hypnotized as part of an experiment (Spanos, 1986). Moreover, many of the classic phenomena—such as posthypnotic suggestions—turn out to be controlled mainly by subject expectations rather than by the whims of the hypnotist. For example, if subjects are told to respond to some cue, such as tugging on their ear every time they hear the word *psychology*, they will often do so after hypnosis. But posthypnotic suggestions of this kind turn out to be effective only if the subjects believe they are still participating in the experiment; if the experimenter leaves the room, or if the subjects believe the experiment is over, they stop responding appropriately to the cue (see Lynn and others, 1990, for a review).

Meditation

Hypnosis is an induction procedure that produces an altered state of awareness—heightened suggestibility—after interactions have taken place between a willing subject and someone trained in the appropriate hypnotic induction techniques. In **meditation,** it is the participant alone who seeks to manipulate awareness. Most meditation techniques require performance of some time-honored mental "exercise," such as concentrating on repeating a particular string of words or sounds called a *mantra*.

The variations in awareness achieved through meditation, as with hypnosis, are often described in mystical or spiritual ways. Meditators report, for example, that they are able to obtain an expanded state of awareness, one that is characterized by a "pure" form of thought unburdened by self-awareness. There are many forms of meditation, and numerous induction procedures; most trace their roots back thousands of years to the practices of a variety of Eastern religions.

Daily sessions of meditation have been prescribed for every sort of physical and psychological malady. As with hypnosis, the induction procedure usually begins with relaxation, but the mind is kept "alert" through focused concentration on breathing, internal repetition of the mantra, or efforts to clear the mind. The general idea is to step back from the ongoing stream of mental activity and set the mind adrift in the oneness of the universe. Great insights, improved physical health, and release from desire are some of the attributed benefits.

Scientifically, it's clear that meditation *can* produce significant changes in physiological functions. Arousal is lowered, so heart rate, respiration rate, and blood pressure tend to decline. EEG recordings of brain activity during meditation have revealed what appears to be a "relaxed" mind—specifically, there is a significant increase in alpha wave activity (Benson, 1975). Such changes are, of course, to be expected during any kind of relaxed state and do not necessarily signify anything special about a state of consciousness. Indeed, there appear to be no significant differences between the physiological patterns of accomplished meditators and those of nonmeditators who are simply relaxing (Holmes, 1987). At this point, researchers have little to say about the subjective aspects of the meditative experience—whether, in fact, the meditator has indeed merged with the oneness of the universe—but most researchers would agree that inducing a relaxed state once or twice a day has beneficial effects. Daily meditation sessions have apparently helped people deal effectively with chronic anxiety and other psychological disorders (Eppley, Abrams, & Shear, 1989).

▶ SOLVING THE PROBLEMS: A SUMMARY

Studying consciousness awareness is not the easiest of tasks for the psychologist. Consciousness is by its very nature a subjective, personal experience. It is a difficult concept to define objectively, and appealing to the scribblings of an EEG pattern or to a pretty picture from a PET scanning device may, in the minds of many, fail to capture the complexities of the topic adequately. Is consciousness some classifiable "thing" that can change its state, like water can as it freezes, boils, or evaporates? For the moment, psychologists are working with a set of rather loose ideas about the topic, although conscious awareness is agreed to have many adaptive properties. We considered four adaptive characteristics of consciousness in this chapter; each reveals ways that the adaptive mind adjusts in order to solve problems faced in the environment.

▶ **SETTING PRIORITIES FOR MENTAL FUNCTIONING** The processes of attention allow the mind to *prioritize* its functioning. Faced with limited resources, the brain needs to be selective about the enormous amount of information it receives. Through attention, people can focus on certain aspects of the environment while ignoring others; through attention, people can adapt their thinking in ways that allow for more selective and deliberate movement toward a problem solution. Attentional processes enable the brain to *divide* its processing. People don't always need to be consciously aware of the tasks they perform; automatic processes allow one to perform multiple tasks— such as driving a car and following a conversation—at the same time. Certain disorders of attention, including visual neglect and attention deficit disorder, provide some insights into attention processes. In both of these cases, which may be caused by malfunctioning in the brain, the person's ability to adapt to the environment is compromised.

▶ **SLEEPING AND DREAMING** Sleep is one part of a daily (circadian) rhythm that includes wakefulness, but sleep itself turns out to be composed of regularly changing cycles of brain activity. Studies using the EEG reveal that people move through several distinct stages during sleep, some of which are characterized by intense mental activity. Sleeping may allow the brain a chance to rest and restore itself from its daily workout, or it may simply be adaptive as a period of time out. Lying relatively motionless in the dark recesses of some shelter may have protected

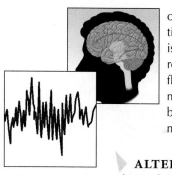

our ancestors at night when their sensory equipment was unlikely to function well. Whether dreaming, which occurs during the REM period of sleep, is an effective solution to some pressing problem faced by the organism remains unclear. Some psychologists believe that dreaming may reveal conflicts that are normally hidden to conscious awareness, or that dreaming may be one way to work out currently troubling problems. A third possibility is that dreaming is simply a manifestation of the brain's attempt to make sense of spontaneous neural activity.

▶ **ALTERING AWARENESS: PSYCHOACTIVE DRUGS** Psychoactive drugs alter behavior and awareness by tapping into natural brain systems that have evolved for adaptive reasons. The brain, as a biochemical factory, is capable of reacting to stress or injury by releasing chemicals (neurotransmitters) that help reduce pain or that shift mood in a positive direction. Many of the drugs that are abused regularly in our society activate these natural systems. As a result, the study of psychoactive drugs has enabled researchers to learn more about communication systems in the brain. There are four main categories of psychoactive drugs.[1] *Depressants,* such as alcohol and barbiturates, lower the ongoing activity of the central nervous system.[2] *Stimulants,* such as caffeine, nicotine, and cocaine, increase central nervous system activity by enhancing the likelihood that neural transmissions will occur.[3] *Opiates,* such as opium, morphine, and heroin, depress nervous system activity by mimicking the chemicals involved in the brain's own pain control system. Finally,[4] *hallucinogens,* such as LSD, play havoc with the user's normal internal construction of reality. Although the mechanisms involved are not known, it's believed that LSD mimics the actions of the neurotransmitter serotonin.

▶ **ALTERING AWARENESS: INDUCED STATES** Two techniques have been designed specifically to alter conscious awareness: hypnosis and meditation. Hypnosis is a form of social interaction that induces a heightened state of suggestibility in people. Hypnotic techniques usually promote relaxation, although, once achieved, brain activity under hypnosis more closely resembles the waking rather than the sleeping state. In meditation, it is the participant alone who manipulates awareness, often by mentally repeating a particular word or string of words. The biological mechanisms of both hypnosis and meditation are poorly understood at present, but each has some positive consequences. Pain and discomfort can be significantly reduced through hypnotic suggestion, whereas the continued use of meditation has been linked to the reduction of stress and anxiety.

Terms to Remember

consciousness The subjective awareness of internal and external events.

SETTING PRIORITIES FOR MENTAL FUNCTIONING: ATTENTION

attention The internal processes that people use to set priorities for mental functioning.

dichotic listening A technique in which different auditory messages are presented separately and simultaneously to each ear. Usually the subject's task is to shadow, or repeat aloud, one of the messages while ignoring the other.

cocktail party effect The ability to focus on one auditory message, such as a friend's conversation at a party, and ignore others; the term also refers to the tendency to notice when one's name suddenly appears in a message that one has been actively ignoring.

automaticity Fast and effortless processing that requires little or no focused attention.

visual neglect A complex disorder of attention characterized by a tendency to ignore things that appear on one side of the body, usually the left side.

attention deficit disorder A psychological condition, occurring most often in children, marked by difficulties in concentrating or in sustaining attention for extended periods.

SLEEPING AND DREAMING

circadian rhythms Biological activities that rise and fall in accordance with a 24-hour cycle.

biological clocks Brain structures that schedule rhythmic variations in bodily functions by triggering them at the appropriate times.

alpha waves The pattern of brain activity observed in someone who is in a relaxed state.

theta waves The pattern of brain activity observed in stage 1 sleep.

delta activity The pattern of brain activity observed in stage 3 and stage 4 sleep; it's characterized by synchronized slow waves. Also called **slow-wave sleep.**

REM A stage of sleep characterized by rapid eye movements and low-amplitude, irregular EEG patterns similar to those found in the waking brain. REM is typically associated with dreaming.

REM rebound The tendency to increase the proportion of time spent in REM sleep after a period of REM deprivation.

manifest content According to Freud, the actual symbols and events experienced in a dream.

latent content According to Freud, the true psychological meaning of dream symbols, which represent hidden wishes and desires that are too disturbing to be expressed directly.

activation-synthesis hypothesis The idea that dreams represent the brain's attempt to make sense out of the random patterns of neural activity generated during sleep.

insomnia A chronic condition marked by difficulties in initiating or maintaining sleep, lasting for a period of at least one month.

hypersomnia A chronic condition marked by excessive sleepiness.

nightmares Frightening and anxiety-arousing dreams that occur primarily during the REM stage of sleep.

night terrors A condition in which the sleeper, usually a child, awakens suddenly in an extreme state of panic; not thought to be associated with dreaming.

sleepwalking A condition in which the sleeper rises during sleep and wanders about; not thought to be associated with dreaming.

ALTERING AWARENESS: PSYCHOACTIVE DRUGS

psychoactive drugs Drugs that affect behavior and mental processes through alterations of conscious awareness.

tolerance An adaptation that the body makes to compensate for the continued use of a drug such that increasing amounts of the drug are needed to produce the same physical and behavioral effects.

drug dependency A condition in which an individual experiences a physical or a psychological need for continued use of a drug.

withdrawal Clear and measurable physical reactions, such as sweating, vomiting, changes in heart rate, or tremors, that occur when a person stops taking certain drugs after continued use.

depressants A class of drugs that slow or depress the ongoing activity of the central nervous system.

stimulants A class of drugs that increase central nervous system activity, enhancing neural transmission.

opiates A class of drugs that reduce anxiety, lower sensitivity to pain, and elevate mood; opiates often act to depress nervous system activity.

hallucinogens A class of drugs that tend to disrupt normal mental and emotional functioning, including distorting perception and altering reality.

ALTERING AWARENESS: INDUCED STATES

hypnosis A form of social interaction that produces a heightened state of suggestibility in a willing participant.

catalepsy A hypnotically induced behavior characterized by an ability to hold one or more limbs of the body in a rigid position for long periods without tiring.

hypnotic hypermnesia The supposed enhancement in memory that occurs under hypnosis; there is little, if any, evidence to support the existence of this effect.

hypnotic dissociation A hypnotically induced "splitting" of consciousness during which multiple forms of awareness coexist.

meditation A technique for self-induced manipulation of awareness, often used for the purpose of relaxation and self-reflection.

Robert didn't notice them in the ad, of course—the naked ladies, images slightly distorted, locked within ice cubes floating in a half-filled glass of Scotch. Not usually a drinker, Robert surprised himself later when he purchased a bottle of the Scotch. Just looked good, he thought, but he didn't bother himself much about it again. . . .

Todd leaned backed on his bed, headphones firmly in place, and cranked up the sound. He couldn't hear the song within the song, moving backward at a slightly altered speed, heralding the arrival of the Antichrist. He noticed nothing at all in particular, in fact, but he didn't feel much like going to church on Sunday either. . . .

Louise was slightly bored with the sound—crashing waves, the occasional cries of a gull—repeating continuously for hours from the speakers she had laced together throughout her house. "A minor inconvenience," she muttered; "after all, tomorrow I'll have lost another two pounds. . . ."

To some, our world is full of secret manipulation. Many people believe that messages abound, hidden from the naked eye by devious advertisers and dark-natured rock stars, which are generating persuasive communications at levels too dim to be noticed by conscious awareness. These so-called *subliminal stimuli* (*subliminal* means "below threshold") are claimed to be responsible for many of society's ills, such as people's sudden buying urges or especially deviant thoughts (Key, 1973).

We've seen how the mind prioritizes mental functioning through the process of attention; automatic processes can also develop that lead to fast and effortless behaviors that require little or no conscious thought. Is it possible that people are regularly influenced by covert messages that bypass awareness? Are they secretly controlled by subliminal stimuli hidden in advertisements or on the tracks of recordings? Can they change their behavior simply by listening to self-help tapes with embedded messages?

Americans are exposed to dozens, perhaps hundreds, of advertisements daily, and many thousands annually. If advertisers are able to enhance the effectiveness of their message through bypassing conscious awareness, then the general public has good reason to be alarmed. Actually, the public is already alarmed—legislation is regularly introduced in state capitals demanding that advertisements with subliminal messages either be outlawed or at least that the public be informed of their content.

From the perspective of the adaptive mind, it's reasonable to assume that people can be influenced by things that bypass conscious awareness. "Awareness" of external and internal events, as we've seen in this chapter, is one way that the brain prioritizes mental functioning. But consciousness is not necessarily the only gateway through which environmental input is received. When confronting the topic of subliminal influence, we really have two issues to consider. First, are these messages really out there? Do advertisers, rock stars, and marketers of self-help tapes actually embed subliminal messages in their final products? Second, assuming that the messages are really there, do they work? What's the evidence that covert messages can change attitudes and behaviors in the way desired or promised? We'll consider each of these issues in turn.

Are They There?

To argue that secret, covert messages (sometimes called "embeds") are affecting people's behavior requires, of course, that these messages actually be present in advertising and on recordings. Believe it or not, despite the public outcry about (and belief in) the dangers of this subliminal "conspiracy," there is virtually no solid evidence to support the widespread existence of embeds. Perhaps the most famous example of willful embedding occurred at a New Jersey movie theater in 1957 when unwitting viewers of the movie *Picnic*

PEOPLE HAVE BEEN TRYING TO FIND THE BREASTS IN THESE ICE CUBES SINCE 1957.

With a little imagination, people can "find" subliminal messages almost anywhere. However, research indicates that subliminal messages have only limited effects on behavior.

were exposed to subliminal presentations of the phrase "Eat Popcorn and Drink Coke." According to advertising expert James Vicary, consumption of popcorn and Coke increased dramatically, as robotlike consumers lined up at the refreshment stand. What most people don't know is that this study turned out to be a hoax devised by Vicary to increase sales at his advertising firm (Weir, 1984).

When it comes to the self-help tapes claimed to contain subliminal messages, critics question whether the embeds are actually present. In one study by Merikle (1988), samples from self-help tapes were subjected to spectrographic analysis to detect the presence of hidden speech. A spectrograph produces a kind of "voice print" that allows the researcher to analyze the various components of the auditory message; no evidence of any hidden speech was found in any of his samples. In a follow-up, Merikle presented people with two tapes, one alleged to contain hidden speech and another without, and asked his subjects to pick out the one with the covert message. It couldn't be done. In Merikle's own words, "The empirical results lead to the inescapable conclusion that the widely marketed subliminal cassettes do not contain any embedded messages that could conceivably influence behavior" (1988, p. 370).

Do They Work?

Of course, it's not possible to determine to what extent advertisers actually try to influence people subliminally (the advertisers are not talking), or whether all subliminal tapes lack the promised embedded messages. It is possible, however, to conduct controlled experiments in which messages are purposely embedded in advertisements or on tapes and their effects on behavior noted. Dozens of such studies have been conducted (Druckman & Bjork, 1991; Merikle, 1988; Rosen & Singh, 1992); the general consensus seems to be that the effects of subliminal influence are mild or nonexistent.

For example, it is sometimes claimed that subliminal messages lead to enhanced memory. In a study by Vokey and Read (1985), three or four instances of the word *sex* were inserted into vacation slides; the words were placed into the pictures in such a way that they were not directly noticeable but could be detected easily if pointed out by the experimenters. Immediately after viewing the slides, or after a delay, subjects were given a memory test for the slides. Even though we know in this instance that the message was actually there and could be detected, the subjects showed no improvement in the recognition of the slides relative to the proper control groups.

In a study by Rosen and Singh (1992), the embedded messages were of three types: (1) the word *sex,* (2) a picture of a naked woman and several phallic symbols, or (3) the word *death* combined with pictures of skulls. The "embeds" were placed in black-and-white print ads for liquor or cologne, and subjects were asked to view each ad as part of an experiment on advertising effectiveness. No direct mention was made of the embeds, which were present in some of the ads but not in others. This study is noteworthy because it used a variety of measures of advertising effectiveness to assess the effects of the subliminal messages. In none of these measures, which included a number of attentional, attitudinal, and behavioral indices, was any significant "influence" exerted by the covert information.

With regard to self-help tapes, again the data are clear. Greenwald and others (1991) recruited subjects to help evaluate the effectiveness of tapes designed to improve either memory or self-esteem. Unknown to the subjects, however, the labels on some of the tapes had been switched, and those who thought they were listening to a self-esteem tape were actually given a memory tape, and vice versa. After regular listening, people seemed to improve on posttests of self-esteem or memory, but it didn't matter which tape the subject had actually been given. A weight loss study by Merikle and Skanes (1992) produced similar results. Subjects improved as a result of participating in the study (in this case, they lost weight), but it didn't matter whether the tape actually contained the subliminal message, or even if the subjects had listened to a tape at all!

Why the improvement? Certainly, one would think, people would stop buying these tapes if they were completely ineffective. From a psychological perspective, though, it's important to remember that those who buy such tapes are *motivated* to improve. Thus, the people who volunteer for a weight loss study may simply be more conscious of their weight during the course of the experiment (Merikle & Skanes, 1992). Alternatively, a tape may act as a kind of *placebo,* leading to improvement because the listener believes in its magical powers. If subliminal "self-help" is placebo-related, we would expect the subject to improve regardless of whether the message was, in fact, actually embedded in the background. All that's necessary is that subjects *think* they are receiving something that will work.

So what can we conclude about subliminal messages? Is it possible to alter behavior without awareness? Perhaps. Most psychologists believe that a person's behavior can be affected under conditions in which no subjective conscious awareness is present (Greenwald, Schuh, & Klinger, 1995). As we'll see in Chapter 8, people often "remember" without awareness, and everyone regularly performs tasks (such as walking or talking) without thinking about it. But it's a bad idea to waste a lot of time worrying about subliminal conspiracies. There's little evidence that these messages are actually there, and even if they are, their influence is minimal at best.

7

The way people think and act throughout their lives is influenced continuously by interactions with the environment. We may arrive into the world with a certain genetic potential, but experience plays a pivotal role in shaping how that potential is realized. The body (*nature*) and experiences (*nurture*) act in concert, and it can be difficult to isolate the influences of each when observing behavior. In this chapter, our discussion focuses primarily on the nurture part of the nature-nurture equation. Our topic is the psychological process that accounts for much of the remarkable flexibility of the adaptive mind—the ability to *learn from experience*.

What is learning? Most people think of learning as simply the process of acquiring knowledge. In essence, that's correct. But as we discussed in Chapter 2, psychologists like to define concepts in terms of how those concepts can be directly measured. At this point, it's not possible to measure the "knowledge" in people's heads directly or to track all the neural mechanisms involved in knowledge acquisition. For this reason, **learning** is typically defined as a relatively permanent change in behavior, or potential to respond, that results from experience. Notice that the emphasis is on changes in *behavior*. Unlike acquired knowledge, behavior is something we can directly observe. We make inferences about learning and the acquisition of knowledge by observing behavior and noting how behavior changes over time.

Of course, behavior can sometimes change as a result of experience in ways that we would not want to classify as learning. For example, your behavior might change because you forgot something, such as a telephone number you've recently dialed. Or suppose your neighbor Al loses an arm in an industrial accident. Getting injured imposes physical limitations on the body that will certainly change his behavior in many ways. But not all of these changes will result from the actions of a flexible learning process. The concept of learning is reserved for those cases where behavior changes in a way that reflects the experience—people change their behavior, either as a reaction to the experience or as a result of practice, to maximize adaptive behavior in the future.

One final point to note in the definition of learning is the phrase *potential to respond*. Sometimes people acquire knowledge but don't change their behavior in any way that reflects what they've learned. For example, you have now "learned" the textbook definition of *learning*. But is your behavior going to change? Not likely, unless you need to retrieve the information during an examination. You may also have learned a great deal about the location of fast-food restaurants in your community. But your behavior isn't going to reflect that knowledge unless you're hungry. Once again, it's important to keep in mind the relationship between learning and *performance*—to demonstrate that learning has occurred, it needs to be reflected in actual behavior.

Historically, researchers have studied learning in relatively simple kinds of situations, often with animal subjects such as rats, pigeons, or sea snails. The goal has been to uncover basic principles, or "laws of learning," that can be applied widely across species and situations. There are two principal reasons why animals are used as research subjects. First, more experimental control is available in animal studies, so experimenters are better able to identify the factors that actually cause learning to occur. Second, it's assumed that the learning process in animals is simpler and therefore easier to understand. Overall, this research strategy has

 Do you think it's ethical to use animals in basic research? Remember, we discussed this issue in some detail in Chapter 2.

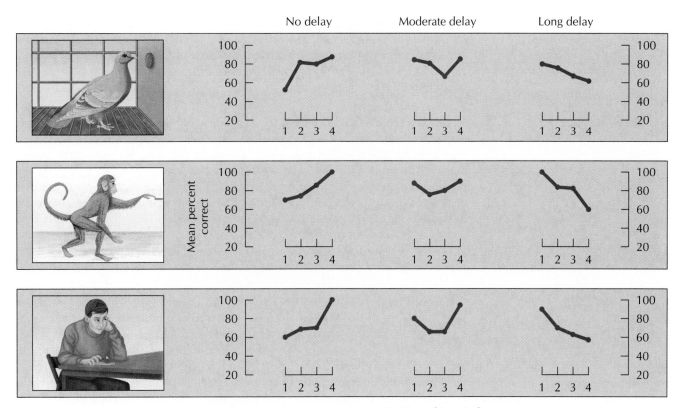

Position of item in list

helped researchers discover how the building blocks of more complex behaviors are acquired. Using animals as models to understand human psychology makes sense when we consider that all species—even sea snails—must learn in order to survive.

In fact, it's common for researchers to argue that all animal species, including humans, share a "library" of similar learning mechanisms (Roitblat & von Ferson, 1992). Let's consider an experiment by Anthony Wright and his co-workers (1985), who compared the learning and memory abilities of pigeons, monkeys, and humans. Every subject was required to learn short sequences of items, from briefly presented lists, and then to "remember" those items a short time later. (Pigeons identified items by pecking lighted disks; monkeys and human subjects pressed levers.) The details of the experiment and the specifics of the results aren't important for us here. What is important are the similarities in performance across species (see Figure 7.1). Notice how regular the changes are across the various conditions. For example, all types of subjects remembered items that occurred near the end of a list best when test delays were short, but they remembered items at the beginning of the list best when delays were long. For this task, at least, it doesn't really matter whether you are a pigeon, a monkey, or a human. As Wright (1990) concludes, the animal-human gap is probably narrower than we think; striking similarities in learning and performance cut across species.

FIGURE 7.1
Learning in Pigeons, Monkeys, and People. It's possible that most animal species, including humans, share basic learning mechanisms. In this experiment by Anthony Wright and his co-workers, pigeons, monkeys, and people were required to learn lists of four visual items, then remember them after various delays. Notice that it doesn't really matter whether the subject is a monkey, a pigeon, or a human—each remembers items at the end of the list best after no delay, items at the beginning and end of the list equally well at the moderate delay, and items first in the list best at the long delay. (Graphs from Wright et al., 1985)

▶ PREVIEWING THE ADAPTIVE PROBLEMS

Regardless of how much animals and humans might differ, it's fair to assume that all species face common learning problems. For example, all species, sea snails as well as people, need to learn about the consequences of their behavior. It's also useful to learn about the signaling properties of stimuli, or events, in the environment. When does one event predict that a second event is likely to follow? In this chapter, we'll consider four general adaptive learning problems: How do people learn about events? How do they learn about the signaling properties of events? How do they learn about the consequences of their behavior? Finally, how do they learn from others?

▶ **LEARNING ABOUT EVENTS** Humans and other organisms need to recognize significant events when they occur and react to them appropriately. They must also learn to ignore events that occur repeatedly but have no immediate consequence. The shrill cry of an infant, the screech of automobile brakes—these sounds demand our attention and cause us to react. Humans and animals notice sudden changes in their environment; they notice those things that are new and potentially of interest. But our reactions to these novel events change with repeated experience, and these changes are among the most basic and important of all learning processes. In the first section of the chapter, we'll discuss two elementary processes that focus on how organisms learn about events: *habituation* and *sensitization*.

▶ **LEARNING WHAT EVENTS SIGNAL** Many events that occur in our world signal the presence of other events. For instance, you know that lightning precedes thunder and that the rattling of a tail can signal the bite of a venomous snake. Often, you can't *do* anything about the co-occurrence of such events, but if you recognize the relationship, you can respond accordingly. (You can take cover or move to avoid the snake.) Events can even signal the *absence* of other events, such as when you are greeted with a "Sold Out" sign in the concert ticket window. Psychologists have studied the signaling properties of events through a procedure called *classical conditioning*, which is one of the oldest and most widely used techniques in learning research.

▶ **LEARNING ABOUT THE CONSEQUENCES OF BEHAVIOR** Actions produce consequences. The child who flicks the tail of a cat once too often may receive an unwelcome surprise. The family dog learns that if he hangs around the dinner table, an occasional scrap of pork chop might very well come his way. Behaviors are instrumental in producing rewards and punishments; it is through the study of the aptly named *instrumental conditioning* procedure that psychologists have come to appreciate the influence that rewards and punishments in the environment exert over the behavioral repertoires of humans and other animals.

▶ **LEARNING FROM OTHERS** Often, our most important teachers are not our own actions and their consequences, but the actions of others. Humans learn by example, as does most of the animal kingdom. Observational learning has considerable adaptive significance: A teenager learns about the consequences of drunk driving, one hopes, not from direct experience but from observing others whose fate has already been sealed. A young monkey in the wild learns to be afraid of snakes not from a deadly personal encounter but from observing her mother's fear.

Learning About Events: Noticing and Ignoring

Let's begin with the first problem: How do people learn about the events that occur and recur in their world? We're constantly surrounded by sights, sounds, and sensations—from the sound of traffic outside the window, to the color of the paint on the wall, to the feel of denim jeans against our legs. As we discussed in Chapter 6, it is impossible to attend to all of these stimuli. Instead, we must prioritize our mental functioning because the human nervous system has limited resources.

The bright colors and screeching sirens of a fire engine are designed to draw our attention, and to signal the need for us to get out of the way.

It's clearly adaptive to learn about the signaling properties of events. A distinctive rattle on a mountain trail signals the potential strike of the western diamondback rattlesnake.

This family dog has no problem learning about the consequences of hanging around the dinner table. She's learned that her begging behavior is instrumental in producing a tasty reward of yogurt.

And this is not just a human problem. Animals, too, have limited resources, yet they need to distinguish constantly among the important and the unimportant events in their surroundings. Not surprisingly, there are basic psychological processes that help humans and animals determine which events should continue to receive a measure of attention and which should not.

Habituation and Sensitization

As you learned in Chapter 4, humans are programmed from birth to notice *novelty;* when something new or different happens, we pay close attention. Suppose you hear a funny ticking noise in your car engine when you press the gas pedal. When you first notice the sound, it occupies your attention. You produce an **orienting response,** a kind of automatic shift of attention toward the novel event. Perhaps you lean forward and listen; you may even repeatedly press the gas pedal to establish the link between acceleration and ticking. But after driving with the problem for a while, your behavior changes—the ticking becomes less bothersome, and you may even stop reacting to it altogether. Your behavior in the presence of the event changes with repeated experience, which is the hallmark of learning.

The decline in the tendency to respond to an event that has become familiar through repeated exposure is called **habituation.** Birds will startle and become agitated when a hawklike silhouette passes overhead, but their level of alarm will rapidly decline when the object is presented repeatedly with no subsequent attack (Tinbergen, 1951). It makes sense for organisms to produce an initial orienting response to a sudden change in the environment. If the bird fails to attend rapidly to the shape of a potential predator, it's not likely to survive. Through the process of habituation, organisms learn to be *selective* about the things they orient toward. They attend initially to the novel and unusual but subsequently ignore events that occur repeatedly without significant consequence.

In other cases, we show **sensitization**—our responsiveness to an event *increases* with repeated exposure. Sensitization, like habituation, is a general learning phenomenon that cuts across the animal kingdom. Researchers currently believe that both habituation and sensitization are natural responses to repeated

It's adaptive for all living things to notice sudden changes in the environment. In this case, the unexpected appearance of a red-tailed hawk elicits distinctive orienting reactions from an opossum family.

events, and that each is probably controlled by different mechanisms in the nervous system. Whether organisms will increase or decrease responsiveness in any specific situation will depend on the relative strengths of the habituation and sensitization processes (Groves & Thompson, 1970). Generally, increases in responsiveness—sensitization—are more likely when the repeated stimulus is intense. For example, if you are exposed to repetitions of a very loud noise, you become "sensitized" to the noise—your reactions become more intense and prolonged with repeated exposure. But if the noise is relatively modest in intensity, repeated exposure may lead to decreases in responsiveness.

Short- and Long-Term Effects

Although habituation and sensitization are both examples of learning—primarily because they produce changes in behavior as a function of experience—researchers have tended to focus more on habituation. The effects of sensitization generally tend to be short-lived (Domjan, 1993), whereas habituation leads to either short-term or long-term effects. Researchers use the term *short-term habituation* to refer to those instances in which the loss in responsiveness produced by habituation is only temporary. The sea snail of the genus *Aplysia,* for example, produces a distinctive defensive reaction (gill retraction) when a particular portion of its body, the mantle shelf, is touched. Repeated tapping of the mantle shelf produces habituation of the gill response, but the effect is short-lived. After a short rest period, if the mantle shelf is tapped again, the sea snail's habituated response returns to its original level of reaction (Kandel & Schwartz, 1982).

In *long-term habituation,* the effects persist over an extended period. For example, when placed in a new environment, cats are often skittish when they eat. The slightest sound or movement is likely to send them scurrying under the nearest piece of furniture. With time the animal learns, and the adjustment is typically long-lasting (see Figure 7.2). Drug tolerance, which we discussed in Chapter 6, is

| Day 1 | Day 2 | Day 3 | Day 4 | Day 5 |

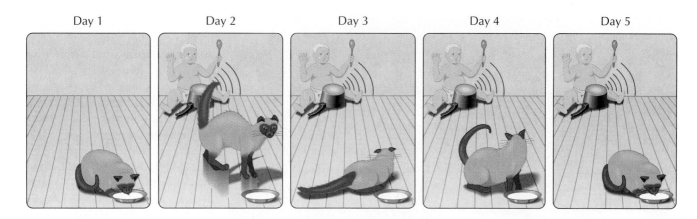

often classified as an example of long-term habituation. In humans, an initial dose of 100 to 200 milligrams of morphine produces profound sedation or even death, but morphine-tolerant subjects are capable of receiving over 100 times that amount without negative effects (Baker & Tiffany, 1985). The body's response to the drug changes after repeated use—that is, the body *habituates* to the drug. The exact nature of the learning that occurs as tolerance develops is still a matter of some debate (Siegel, 1983, 1989), but tolerance clearly shows how responsiveness to an event can change as a consequence of repeated exposure.

Because it is a general kind of learning process that occurs throughout the animal world, habituation is often used as a psychological model for understanding how behaviors change with experience. Some learning theorists, for example, have used short- and long-term habituation as the basis for proposing sweeping theories about the structure of basic learning and memory systems (Wagner, 1981). A number of neuroscientists have used habituation as a tool for mapping out the fundamental neural mechanisms of learning (Groves & Thompson, 1970). Moreover, as we discussed in Chapter 4, psychologists who are interested in development have used habituation as an experimental technique for discovering the content of an infant's mind (Bornstein, 1992).

As adaptive organisms, humans rely on simple learning processes such as habituation to help conserve their limited resources. The world is full of events to be noticed, far more than anyone can ever hope to monitor. Orienting responses guarantee that people will notice the new and unusual, but through habituation we learn to ignore those things that are repeated but are of no significant consequence. People are thereby able to solve a very important problem—how to be selective about the events that occur and recur in the world. But there is more to learning than just noticing and ignoring events; it is equally important to learn about relationships between events, as we'll see in the next section.

Learning What Events Signal: Classical Conditioning

Through habituation and sensitization, organisms learn that events occur and repeat over time. We next consider how individuals learn that some events signal the presence of other events. Everyone knows that a flash of lightning cutting across the sky means that a clap of thunder is likely to follow; experience has taught people to *associate* lightning with thunder. Individuals form associations between events, such as sights and sounds, when the events bear a meaningful relation to each other. Often, the meaningful relation is that one event closely follows the other in time. In this section, we'll consider how simple associations like these are learned and reflected in performance.

FIGURE 7.2
Long-Term Habituation.
Organisms notice sudden changes in their environment, but they can learn to ignore those changes if they occur repeatedly. To a cat eating dinner a novel sound leads initially to panic and escape, but if the sound repeats over days, the cat habituates and continues eating without the slightest reaction.

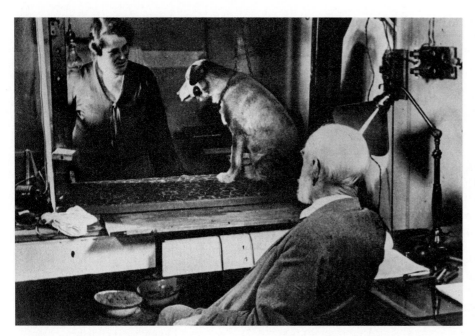

In the summer of 1934, the Russian physiologist Ivan Pavlov watched one of his experiments on "psychic" secretions in dogs. Notice the dog's cheek, which is fitted with a device for measuring salivation.

The scientific study of elementary associations was begun around the turn of the century by the Russian physiologist Ivan P. Pavlov (1849–1936). Pavlov and his co-workers developed a set of procedures—known collectively as **classical conditioning**—that remain in use today nearly 100 years after their initial development. Over the course of several decades, Pavlov and his colleagues conducted hundreds of experiments exploring how hungry dogs learn to associate signals with food. As you'll see shortly, these experiments led to a number of general learning principles that can be applied across many situations.

According to most accounts, Pavlov became interested in the study of learning in an incidental way. His main interest was in digestion, which included the study of how dogs salivate in the presence of a variety of foods. Humans produce saliva when food is placed in their mouths, as do dogs, because saliva contains certain chemicals that help in the initial stages of digestion. But to his annoyance, Pavlov found that his dogs often began to drool much too soon—before food was actually placed in their mouths. Pavlov referred to these premature droolings as "psychic" secretions and began to study why they occurred, partly to avoid future contamination of his experiments.

Pavlov recognized immediately that "psychic" secretions developed as a result of experience. But he was also keenly aware that drooling in response to food is *not* a learned response. He recognized that the presentation of some kinds of stimuli, which he called **unconditioned stimuli** (**US**s), automatically lead to observable responses, called **unconditioned responses** (**UR**s). For example, food is an unconditioned stimulus that automatically elicits salivation as an unconditioned response. Neither dogs nor humans need to be taught to drool when food is placed in their mouths; rather, this response is a reflex similar to the jerking of your leg when the doctor taps you just below the knee. The occurrence of an unconditioned response (salivation) in the presence of an unconditioned stimulus (food in the mouth) is *unconditioned*—that is, no learning, or conditioning, is required.

 Can you think of any reason why it might be adaptive to begin the digestion process *before* food is actually placed in the mouth?

The problem that Pavlov faced was that his dogs began to drool merely at the *sight* of the food dish or even at the sound of a food-bearing assistant entering the room. Food dishes and the footsteps of arriving assistants are not unconditioned stimuli that automatically elicit salivation in a dog. Drooling in response to such stimuli is learned; it is *conditioned*, or acquired as a result of experience. For this reason, Pavlov began referring to the "psychic secretions" as **conditioned responses** (**CR**s) and to the stimuli that produce them as **conditioned stimuli** (**CS**s). (Actually, it is thought that Pavlov meant to use the phrases *conditional stimuli* and *conditional responses,* to stress the role of experience, but the word *conditional* was translated incorrectly from the Russian as "conditioned.")

Let's take footsteps as an example. The sound of an approaching feeder leads to drooling because the dog has learned that the sound *signals* the appearance of the food. Footsteps and food bear a special relation to each other in time: When the footsteps are heard, the food is soon to arrive. To use Pavlov's terminology, the footsteps acted as a conditioned stimulus that produced salivation, a conditioned response, in anticipation of the food. Conditioned stimuli usually acquire the ability to produce conditioned responses because the conditioned stimulus and the unconditioned stimulus have been *paired* in time—the footsteps (the CS) reliably occur just before presentation of the food (the US). However, as we'll see shortly, simply pairing two events does not always lead to the formation of this kind of association.

Acquiring the CS-US Connection

What are the necessary conditions for establishing a connection between a conditioned stimulus and an unconditioned stimulus? It helps to remember the following general rule: A conditioned stimulus will acquire signaling properties, leading to the production of a conditioned response, whenever it provides *information* about the occurrence of the unconditioned stimulus (Rescorla, 1992). If a bell (CS) is struck just before the delivery of food (US), and the bell-food pairings are continued over time, the dog will begin to salivate (CR) whenever the bell (CS) is struck (see Figure 7.3). An association is established in this case because the bell provides information about the delivery of the food. This "informational" rule helps us interpret a wide variety of experimental findings:

1. For an effective association to be formed, the conditioned stimulus usually needs to be presented *before* the unconditioned stimulus. If the two are presented at the same time (*simultaneous conditioning*), or if the conditioned stimulus is presented *after* the unconditioned stimulus (*backward conditioning*), little evidence for learning is usually found. In both of these cases, the conditioned stimulus pro-

FIGURE 7.3
Classical Conditioning. Through classical conditioning, organisms learn about the signaling properties of events. Some kinds of events, such as the presentation of an unconditioned stimulus (US), lead to automatic unconditioned responses (URs) prior to training. In the classical conditioning procedure, a neutral stimulus (one that does not produce a relevant response before conditioning) is paired closely in time with a US. Eventually, the animal learns that this conditioned stimulus (CS) predicts the occurrence of the US and begins to show a conditioned response (CR), on presentation of the CS, that is appropriate for the expected arrival of the US. Although here the CR and the UR are the same, they needn't be.

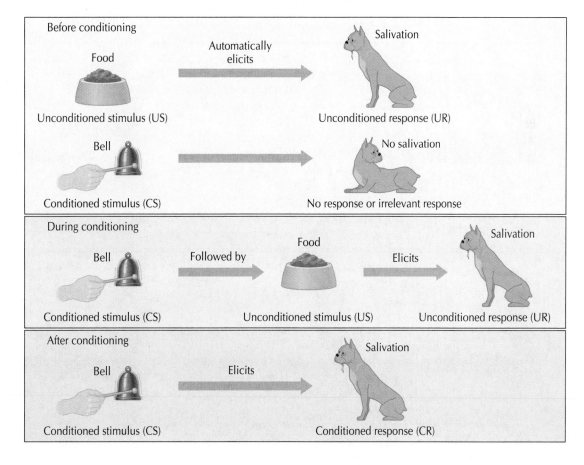

vides no information about when the unconditioned stimulus will appear, so conditioned responding does not develop. (For some exceptions to this general rule, see Matzel, Held, & Miller, 1988.)

2.   Under most circumstances, the unconditioned stimulus needs to follow the conditioned stimulus *closely in time.* For example, if there is a long delay between when the bell (CS) is struck and when the food (US) is delivered, the connection between the bell and the food is not easily established. As the gap between presentation of the conditioned stimulus and presentation of the unconditioned stimulus increases, one becomes a less efficient signal for the arrival of the other—that is, the conditioned stimulus provides less reliable information about the appearance of the unconditioned stimulus. (For an exception to this rule, read the Adaptive Mind section that closes this chapter.)

3.   If the unconditioned stimulus reliably follows the conditioned stimulus but also occurs when the conditioned stimulus is not present, little evidence of conditioned responding will be found. For example, Rescorla (1968) presented a tone (CS) to rats, followed by a mild electric shock (US). Shock is an unconditioned stimulus that causes animals to jump (UR) prior to any conditioning. In one group, the shock was administered only after the tone; these rats quickly began displaying a fear response, freezing (the CR), when they heard the tone. In a second group, the shock was presented both after the tone and also during times when the tone was not turned on. These rats showed little, if any, freezing to the tone (see Figure 7.4). In this second group, notice that the tone did not clearly indicate when shock would occur in the session, because shock also occurred when the tone was absent. The tone did not provide sufficient information about the occurrence of the shock, so it failed to acquire the appropriate signaling properties.

4.   Suppose we establish the tone as a reliable signal for the shock. Now, after the rats have learned to freeze to the tone, we start turning on a light at the same time

FIGURE 7.4
Informational Rules in Classical Conditioning. For a CR to develop to a CS, the CS needs to provide information about the occurrence of the US. In an experiment by Rescorla (1968), every time an auditory CS sounded for rats in Group 1, a shock US followed closely (left panel). These animals quickly learned to freeze in anticipation of the shock (right panel). For rats in Group 2, the shock was presented after the sound (left panel), but also during times when the sound was not turned on (middle panel). These animals showed no evidence of freezing to the sound (right panel), presumably because it did not provide sufficient information about the US occurrence.

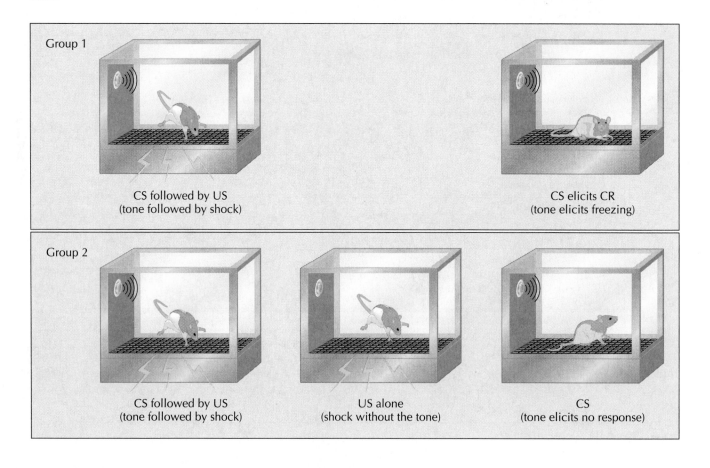

Group 1

CS followed by US
(tone followed by shock)

CS elicits CR
(tone elicits freezing)

Group 2

CS followed by US
(tone followed by shock)

US alone
(shock without the tone)

CS
(tone elicits no response)

as the tone. Both the light and the tone are then followed by the shock. Will the rats freeze to the *light* if it is later presented alone? Usually, rats will show little, if any, freezing to the light under these conditions (e.g., Kamin, 1968). This result, known as *blocking,* demonstrates that the regular pairing of a conditioned stimulus and an unconditioned stimulus is not sufficient to produce evidence of learning. Even though the light is always presented just before the shock, no conditioning occurs. Why? Because a conditioned stimulus needs to provide *new* information about the occurrence of the unconditioned stimulus for it to acquire signaling properties.

These four examples illustrate why learning researchers have adopted what is sometimes called a "cognitive" view of classical conditioning. Organisms learn that one event signals another event when the first event uniquely predicts, or provides information about, the second event. Individuals do not acquire associations between conditioned stimuli and unconditioned stimuli in a *passive* way, through the simple pairing of the events in time. Rather, they process their environment actively—they seek to establish when events predict, or even cause, the occurrence of other events.

Conditioned Responding: Why Does It Develop?

The learning of an association between the conditioned stimulus and the unconditioned stimulus—that is, that one signals the onset of the other—does not really explain the appearance of conditioned responding. Why should dogs drool to a bell that signals food, or rats freeze to a tone that predicts shock? In other words, why is the appearance of the conditioned response an appropriate way to express the learning that has occurred? One possibility is that conditioned responses prepare the organism for events that are expected to follow. Drooling readies the dog to receive food in its mouth, and "freezing" decreases the likelihood that any predators, who may be associated with a fearful event, will detect a rat's presence. Because the conditioned stimulus informs individuals that a significant event is about to occur, they respond in a way that is appropriate for the upcoming event.

Thinking about conditioned responding in this way forces us to adopt a rather broad view of how learning is expressed during and after classical conditioning. Before the cognitive view of classical conditioning gained wide acceptance, many researchers believed that the pairing of the conditioned stimulus and the unconditioned stimulus simply produced a shift or transfer of the unconditioned response to the conditioned stimulus. Pavlov believed, for example, that the conditioned stimulus acts as a kind of "substitute" for the unconditioned stimulus—organisms respond to the conditioned stimulus as if it were essentially identical to the unconditioned stimulus.

But this view makes the unique prediction that organisms should always produce a conditioned response that is identical, or at least highly similar, to the unconditioned response. Dogs should always *drool* to a stimulus that predicts the arrival of food; rats should always *jump* to a stimulus that predicts shock. But as we've seen, rats will freeze rather than jump to a signal predicting shock. Over the last several decades, a number of experimental findings have shown that the traditional "stimulus substitution" view of classical conditioning is incorrect:

1.   The response to the conditioned stimulus depends not only on the unconditioned stimulus, but also on the properties of the conditioned stimulus itself (Holland, 1977; Rescorla, 1988). As we noted earlier, a tone that signals shock causes freezing in rats, but rats will try to bury or cover up a more localized stimulus that predicts shock. For example, as shown in Figure 7.5, if rats learn that touching a bar in the cage means they will get shocked, they will try to cover the bar

FIGURE 7.5
Form of the Conditioned Response. In classical conditioning, the form of the CR depends not only on the expected US but also on the CS itself. In an experiment by Pinel and Treit (1979), rats attempted to bury an electric prod that produced shock on contact. Here, the CR—the response that is produced in anticipation of the US—is burying (right panel), which is a quite different response from the UR, withdrawal, that is automatically produced to the shock US (left panel).

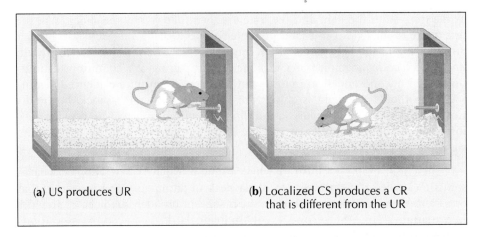

(a) US produces UR

(b) Localized CS produces a CR that is different from the UR

with material from the bottom of the cage (Pinel & Treit, 1979). Pigeons will peck a lighted disk that signals food but will show little or no change in behavior to a tone that predicts food (Nairne & Rescorla, 1981). In both of these cases, the conditioned response that is present after training shows little resemblance to the unconditioned response.

2.   In some cases, a conditioned response will appear that is actually *opposite* in direction to the unconditioned response. For example, when injection of the drug *epinephrine* is used as an unconditioned stimulus, it produces a decrease in the secretion of stomach acids as an unconditioned response. A stimulus that signals the impending injection of this drug, however, leads to an *increase* in secretions as a conditioned response. When a conditioned response acts in the opposite direction from an unconditioned response, it is called a *compensatory response.* Some researchers have argued that compensatory responses help offset a drug's effects, perhaps playing a role in the development of drug tolerance (Siegel, 1983). (As we discussed earlier, drug tolerance can also be viewed as an example of habituation; it is not yet clear whether tolerance develops from the learning processes involved in classical conditioning, from habituation, or from both.)

3.   The occurrence of a conditioned response after learning also depends on how the subject feels about the unconditioned stimulus. If you've learned that a bell signals the delivery of food, your response to the bell will depend on how you feel about the food. Experiments of this type have been conducted by Rescorla and his colleagues, using rats and pigeons as subjects. Hungry rats were taught that a light signaled the delivery of food. After conditioning, the animals were given unlimited access to the food or were spun around on a phonograph turntable after eating to produce temporary discomfort. In both cases, the animals stopped responding to the conditioned stimulus even though its signaling properties remained intact (Holland & Rescorla, 1975). The rats stopped responding, presumably, because they either felt sick or were no longer interested in the food. (Don't worry, the effects of the spinning were temporary, and the rats' appetites quickly returned to normal.)

Consequently, the form of the conditioned response depends on many things. As a rule, the idea that classical conditioning turns the conditioned stimulus into a literal substitute for the unconditioned stimulus—or that organisms simply learn to respond to the conditioned stimulus in the same way that they automatically respond to the unconditioned stimulus—cannot account for the complexities in responding just described. Robert Rescorla (1988) put it this way: "Pavlovian conditioning is not the shifting of a response from one stimulus to another. Instead, conditioning involves the learning of relations among events that are complexly represented, a learning that can be exhibited in various ways" (p. 158).

On St. Thomas in the Virgin Islands, researchers Lowell Nicolaus and David Nellis encouraged captured mongooses to eat eggs laced with carbachol, a drug that produces temporary illness. After 5 days of eating eggs and getting sick, the still-hungry mongooses reduced their consumption of eggs to around 37% of their normal consumption level (Nicolaus & Nellis, 1987). In a very different context, in a research program designed to combat the negative effects of chemotherapy, young cancer patients were allowed a taste of some unusually flavored ice cream just before the onset of their normal chemotherapy—a treatment that typically produces nausea and vomiting. Several weeks later, when offered the ice cream, only 21% of the children were willing to taste it again (Bernstein, 1978).

Both of these situations represent naturalistic applications of classical conditioning. Can you identify the critical features of each? How do these two examples involve the learning of a relation between two events, a conditioned stimulus and an unconditioned stimulus, that largely occurs outside the

organism's control? First, let's look for the unconditioned stimulus—the stimulus that unconditionally produces a response prior to training. In both of these cases, the unconditioned stimulus is the illness-producing event, either the drug carbachol or the cancer-fighting chemotherapy. The response that is automatically produced, unfortunately for the participants, is stomach distress. Children don't need to learn to vomit from chemotherapy; a mongoose doesn't need to be taught to be sick after receiving carbachol. These are inevitable consequences that require no prior conditioning.

Now, what is the conditioned stimulus—the event that provides information about the occurrence of the unconditioned stimulus? In these examples, it is the taste of the food, either the eggs or the ice cream, that signals the later onset of nausea. It's worth noting that the children were aware that their nausea was produced by the chemotherapy, not the ice cream, yet an association was still formed between the taste of the ice cream and a procedure that led to sickness. A condi-

tioned response, feelings of queasiness to the food, was produced whenever the opportunity to eat was presented. Taste aversions are easy to acquire. They often occur after a single pairing of a novel food and illness (see The Adaptive Mind at the end of this chapter).

It is extremely adaptive for people and mongooses to acquire taste aversions to potentially dangerous foods—it is in their interest to avoid those events that signal something potentially harmful. In the two studies we've just considered, the researchers investigated the aversions for a particular reason. Mongooses often eat the eggs of endangered species (such as marine turtles). By baiting the nests of mongoose prey with tainted eggs and establishing a taste aversion, scientists have been able to reduce the overall rate of egg predation. Similar techniques have also been used to prevent sheep from eating dangerous plants in the pasture (Zahorik, Houpt, & Swartzman-Andert, 1990).

In the case of chemotherapy, Illene Bernstein was interested in developing methods for *avoiding* the establishment of taste aversions: Cancer patients who are undergoing chemotherapy also need to eat, so it's critical to understand the conditions under which aversions are formed. Taste aversions often develop as a side effect of chemotherapy. Patients tend to avoid foods that they've consumed just before treatment, potentially leading to weight loss that impedes recovery. Researchers have found that associations are particularly likely to form between *unusual* tastes and nausea. Broberg and Bernstein (1987) found that giving children an unusual flavor of candy just before treatment reduced the likelihood of their forming aversions to their normal diet. These children formed a taste aversion to the candy rather than to their normal diet. Another helpful technique in preventing taste aversions from developing is to ask the patient to eat the same, preferably bland, foods before every treatment. Foods that do not have distinctive tastes and that people eat regularly (such as bread) are less likely to elicit taste aversions.

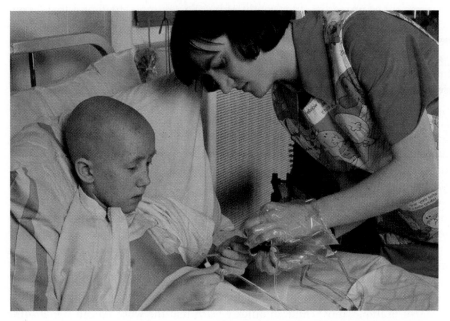

For children undergoing the rigors of chemotherapy, like this young boy suffering from leukemia, it's important to prevent taste aversions from developing as a negative side effect of the treatment. Broberg and Bernstein (1987) found that giving children an unusual flavor of candy just prior to treatment reduced the chances of a taste aversion forming to their normal diet.

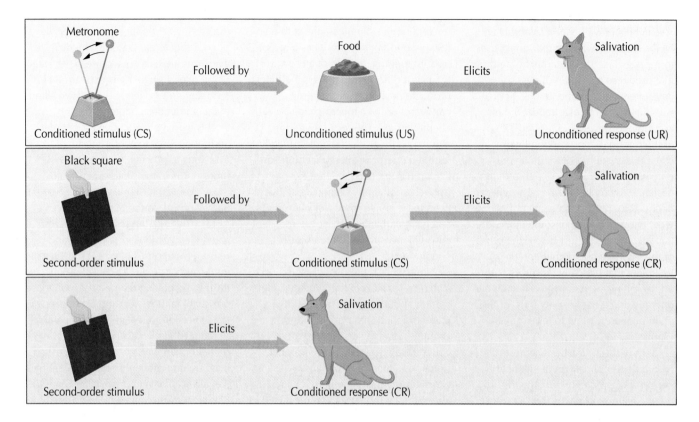

FIGURE 7.6
Second-Order Conditioning. In second-order conditioning, an established CS is used in place of a US to condition a second signal. In Dr. Frolov's experiment, a ticking metronome was first paired with food; after repeated pairings, the ticking elicited salivation as a CR. Next, a black square—which did not produce salivation initially—was paired with the ticking (no US was presented). After repeated pairings, the black square began to produce salivation.

When advertisers use images of sex and glamour in their ads, they are often relying on second-order conditioning. Can you see how?

Second-Order Conditioning

Another of Pavlov's contributions was his discovery that conditioned stimuli possess a variety of properties after conditioning. For example, he found that a conditioned stimulus can be used to condition a second signal. In **second-order conditioning,** an established conditioned stimulus, such as a tone that predicts food, is presented immediately following a new event, such as a light; the unconditioned stimulus itself is never actually presented. In such a case, the pairing of the tone with the light can be sufficient to produce conditioned responding to the light.

An example from Pavlov's laboratory will help illustrate the procedure. One of Pavlov's associates, a Dr. Frolov, first taught a dog that the sound of a ticking metronome signaled the application of meat powder in the mouth. The dog quickly started to drool in the presence of the ticking. A black square was then presented, followed closely by the ticking. After a number of these black square–metronome pairings, even though the ticking was never followed by food powder on these trials, the dog began to drool in the presence of the black square. The dog drooled in response to the square because it signaled the ticking, which the dog had previously learned signaled the food (see Figure 7.6).

The fact that conditioned stimuli can be used to condition other events is important because it greatly expands the number of situations in which classical conditioning applies. It is not necessary for an unconditioned stimulus to be present in a situation in order for individuals to learn something about its occurrence. For example, most children quickly learn that the word *no* can signal some very unpleasant consequences (e.g., being forced to stand alone in a corner); but, luckily for parents, the word *no* can then be paired with many other events without the need to actually deliver the unpleasant consequence. Thus, the parent can simply point to a container of ant poison and say "No," and the child will get the picture.

Stimulus Generalization

Pavlov also noticed that a response produced to the conditioned stimulus tended to generalize to other, related events. If a tone of a particular pitch was conditioned as a signal for food, other tones that sounded similar also produced salivation—even though they had never actually been presented. When a new stimulus produces a response similar to the one produced by the conditioned stimulus, **stimulus generalization** has occurred.

A well-known example of stimulus generalization was reported in a study of classical conditioning conducted around 1920 by John Watson and Rosalie Rayner. They presented Albert, an 11-month-old infant, with a white rat (the conditioned stimulus), which he liked, followed by a very loud noise (the unconditioned stimulus), which he did not like. (A steel bar was struck with a hammer just behind him.) Not surprisingly, this unconditioned stimulus produced a strong, automatic fear reaction: Albert cried (the unconditioned response). After several pairings of the rat with the loud noise, little Albert began to pucker his face, whimper, and try to withdraw his body (all conditioned responses) immediately at the sight of the rat. (It's worth noting that many psychologists question the ethics of this experiment.)

But crying when the rat appeared was not Albert's only response. His crying generalized to other stimuli, such as a rabbit, a fur coat, a package of cotton, a dog, and even a Santa Claus mask. These stimuli had been presented to Albert before the conditioning session had begun, and none had caused him to start crying. It was concluded, therefore, that Albert cried at the sight of them now because of his experience with the rat; he generalized his crying response from the white rat to the other stimuli.

As a rule, stimulus generalization occurs when a new stimulus is *similar* to the conditioned stimulus (see Figure 7.7). If you get sick after eating clams, there's a good chance you'll avoid eating oysters; if you've had a bad experience in the dentist's chair, the sound of the neighbor's high-speed drill may make you uncomfortable. Generalization makes adaptive sense: Things that look, sound, or feel the same often share significant properties. It really doesn't matter whether it's a tiger, a lion, or a panther leaping at you—you should run all the same.

Stimulus Discrimination

Watson and Rayner did find that Albert showed *no* tendency to cry when he was presented with a block of wood. He perceived a difference between white furry or fluffy things and things that were not white and fluffy. This is called **stimulus discrimination;** it occurs when organisms respond to a new stimulus in a way that is different from their response to the original conditioned stimulus. Through

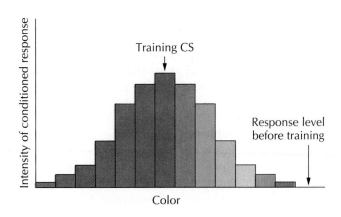

FIGURE 7.7
Stimulus Generalization. After conditioned responding to a CS is established, similar events will often produce conditioned responding, too, through stimulus generalization. For example, if a red light is trained as a CS, then similar colors that were not explicitly trained will also produce responding if tested. Notice that the less similar the test stimulus is to the training CS, the less generalization occurs.

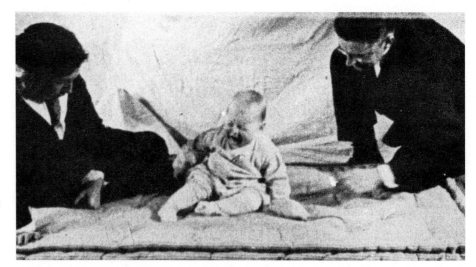

This photo, taken from a 1920 film, shows Little Albert reacting with dismay to a white rat. As described in the text, this rat had previously been paired with a very unpleasant noise. On the right is the famous behavioral psychologist John Watson; to the left of Albert is Watson's colleague, Rosalie Rayner.

stimulus discrimination, individuals reveal that they can distinguish among stimuli, even when those stimuli share properties.

When stimuli *do* share properties—for example, two tones of a similar pitch—people often need experience to teach them to discriminate. The natural tendency is to generalize—that is, to treat similar things in the same way. Albert certainly had the perceptual ability to tell the difference between rats, rabbits, and Santa Claus masks; what he needed to learn was which of those white, furry things signaled the unfortunate noise. In many cases, the development of stimulus discrimination requires that one directly experience whether or not the unconditioned stimulus will follow a particular event. If event A is followed by the unconditioned stimulus but event B is not, then one learns to discriminate between these two events and respond accordingly.

Extinction: When CSs No Longer Signal the US

Remember our general rule: A conditioned stimulus acquires signaling properties when it provides *information* about the occurrence of the unconditioned stimulus. So what happens when the conditioned stimulus stops predicting the appearance of an unconditioned stimulus? In the procedure of **extinction,** the conditioned stimulus is presented repeatedly, after conditioning, but is no longer followed by presentation of the unconditioned stimulus. Under these conditions, the conditioned stimulus loses its signaling properties, because it stops predicting the appearance of the unconditioned stimulus. Not surprisingly, conditioned responding gradually diminishes as a result. For example, if we continued to place the white rat in little Albert's crib but no longer followed the rat's appearance by the noise, we would be carrying out the procedure of extinction. After a while, it's likely that Albert would no longer cry when he saw the rat.

Notice the similarity between the procedure of extinction and the concept of habituation. Both involve the repeated presentation of an event accompanied by a gradual loss in responsiveness. The difference between them is that extinction involves a loss in responding that has been acquired as a result of conditioning—individuals change their behavior because the conditioned stimulus no longer signals the presence of another significant event. In habituation, no prior learning or conditioning is required to produce the changes in behavior that result from repeated exposure. Organisms naturally orient toward sudden changes in their environment—no learning is required—but they will learn to ignore those events that repeatedly occur without significant consequence.

No one knows what finally happened to little Albert in real life. But can you understand why psychologists believe that some psychological problems, like the specific fears called *phobias,* might originate primarily from learning experiences?

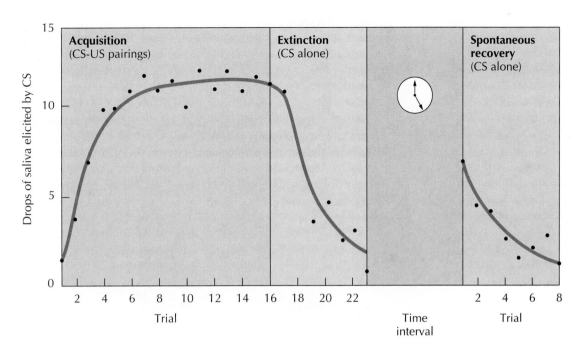

Spontaneous Recovery. Sometimes conditioned responding that has disappeared as a result of extinction will recover spontaneously with the passage of time. **Spontaneous recovery** is defined as the recovery of an extinguished response after a period of nonexposure to the conditioned stimulus (see the far right panel in Figure 7.8). In Pavlov's case, his dogs stopped drooling if a bell signaling food was repeatedly presented alone, but when the bell was rung again the day after extinction the conditioned response reappeared. Spontaneous recovery is another example of why it is important to distinguish between learning and performance. At the end of extinction, the conditioned stimulus can seem to have lost its signaling properties, but when it is tested after a delay, we see that at least some of the learning remained intact (see also Bouton, 1991).

Conditioned Inhibition: Signaling the Absence of the US

During extinction, organisms learn that a conditioned stimulus no longer signals the appearance of the unconditioned stimulus. As a result, they stop responding to a stimulus that once elicited a response, because they no longer anticipate that the unconditioned stimulus will follow. They have not forgotten about the unconditioned stimulus; instead, they have learned something new: A conditioned stimulus that used to signal the unconditioned stimulus no longer does.

In **conditioned inhibition,** one learns that an event signals the *absence* of the unconditioned stimulus, but the signal is not typically a previously conditioned stimulus. To create an inhibitory conditioned stimulus, we take a neutral stimulus, one that has no signaling properties, and arrange for it to be a reliable signal for the absence of the unconditioned stimulus. There are a variety of ways to do so, but common to all is the presentation of the new event under conditions where the unconditioned stimulus is normally expected but is not delivered (Williams, Overmier, & LoLordo, 1992). For example, if dogs are currently drooling to a bell that predicts food, then putting the bell together with a light and then following this compound (bell + light) with no food will establish the light as a conditioned inhibitor for food. The animal learns that when the light is turned on, food does not follow the bell.

What change in behavior is produced by a conditioned stimulus that predicts the absence of something? Inhibitory learning can be expressed in various ways,

FIGURE 7.8
Training, Extinction, and Spontaneous Recovery. During training, Pavlov found that the amount of salivation produced to the CS initially increased and then leveled off as a function of the number of CS-US pairings. During extinction, the CS is repeatedly presented without the US, and conditioned responding gradually diminishes. If no testing of the CS occurs for a rest interval following extinction, spontaneous recovery of the CR will often occur if the CS is presented again.

Keylight signaling food

Food
hopper

Keylight signaling no food

FIGURE 7.9
Conditioned Inhibition. In conditioned inhibition, the CS provides information about the absence of the US. Pigeons will approach and peck at a keylight CS that signals the appearance of food (upper panel), but they will withdraw from a keylight CS signaling no food (lower panel). Notice that the withdrawal response is an indication that the red light has become a conditioned inhibitor—a CS that predicts the absence of food.

but as a rule, the inhibitory conditioned stimulus will produce a reaction that is in some way the *opposite* of that produced by a signal that predicts the appearance of the unconditioned stimulus. For example, if a conditioned stimulus signaling food produces an increase in responding, then an inhibitory conditioned stimulus will lead to a decrease in the normal amount of responding. Several experiments have shown that pigeons and dogs will approach a signal predicting food but will withdraw from a conditioned stimulus signaling the absence of food (see Figure 7.9) (Hearst & Franklin, 1977; Jenkins et al., 1978).

The conditions needed for establishing the presence of conditioned inhibition are complex and need not concern us here, but it is important to appreciate the intrinsic value of an inhibitory signal. It's just as adaptive to know that a significant event will *not* occur as it is to know that the event will occur. For example, you understand that when your traffic light is green, it is unlikely that a car will travel directly into your path. Therefore, the green light signals to you that it's safe to go forward. Inhibitory stimuli often act as "safety signals," telling people when potentially dangerous events are likely to be absent or when dangerous conditions are no longer present.

Learning About the Consequences of Behavior: Instrumental Conditioning

Classical conditioning answers an important survival question: How do organisms learn that certain events signal the presence or the absence of other events? Through the processes tapped by classical conditioning, organisms produce responses in anticipation of the appearance or absence of other events. But these responses have little effect on the relation between the signal and the unconditioned stimulus. Usually, occurrences of the conditioned stimulus and the unconditioned stimulus are outside of the individual's control. For example, you can't change the fact that thunder will follow lightning; all you can do is prepare for an event (thunder) when a prior event (lightning) tells you it's coming.

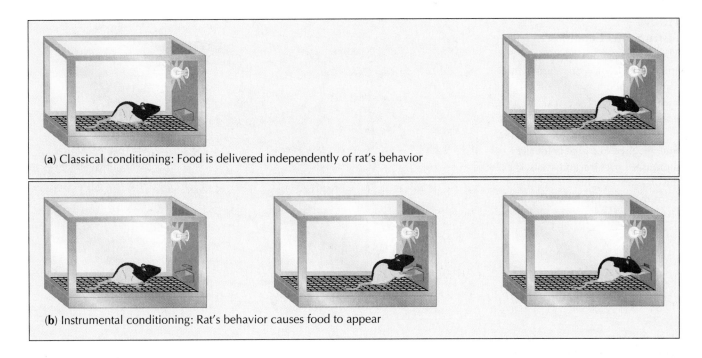

(a) Classical conditioning: Food is delivered independently of rat's behavior

(b) Instrumental conditioning: Rat's behavior causes food to appear

In another type of learning, studied through a procedure called **instrumental** or **operant conditioning,** individuals learn that their own *actions,* rather than conditioned stimuli, produce outcomes. If a child is allowed to watch an hour of television as a reward for cleaning her room, she learns that her behavior is *instrumental* in producing rewards; by *operating* on her environment, she produces a pleasing consequence. Some technical differences exist between instrumental and operant learning situations, but for our purposes, it is sufficient simply to remember that both involve learning about the consequences of behavior. Notice, though, how classical conditioning differs from instrumental conditioning: In the former, individuals learn that events signal outcomes; in the latter, the individual's own instrumental behaviors signal outcomes (see Figure 7.10).

The Law of Effect

The study of instrumental conditioning actually predates Pavlov's historic work by several years. In 1895, Harvard graduate student Edward Lee Thorndike (1874–1949), working in the cellar of his mentor, William James, began a series of experiments on "animal intelligence" with cats as his primary subjects. He built a puzzle box, which resembled a kind of tiny prison, and systematically recorded the time it took for his animals to escape. The boxes were designed so that escape was possible only through an unusual response, such as tilting a pole, pulling a string, or pressing a lever (see Figure 7.11). On release, the cats received a small amount of food as a reward.

Thorndike specifically selected escape responses that were unlikely to occur when the animals were first placed in the box. In this way, he could observe how the cats learned to escape over time. Through trial and error, the cats eventually learned to make the appropriate response, but the learning process was gradual. Thorndike also found that the time it took for an animal to escape on any particular trial depended on the number of prior successful escapes.

The relationship between escape time and the number of prior successful escapes led Thorndike to formulate the **law of effect:** If a response in a particular situation is followed by a satisfying or pleasant consequence, it will be strength-

FIGURE 7.10
Classical Versus Instrumental Conditioning. In classical conditioning (top row), food is delivered independently of the rat's behavior. The light CS signals the automatic arrival of the food US. In instrumental conditioning (bottom row), the rat must press the bar in the presence of the light in order to get the food. The light serves as a discriminative stimulus telling the rat that pressing the bar will now produce the food.

FIGURE 7.11
Instrumental Conditioning. In Thorndike's famous experiments on animal intelligence, cats learned that some kind of unusual response—such as pressing a lever or tilting a pole—allowed them to escape from a puzzle box. The graph shows that the time required to escape gradually diminished over learning trials. Here the cat is learning that its behavior is instrumental in producing escape. (Based on Weiten, 1995)

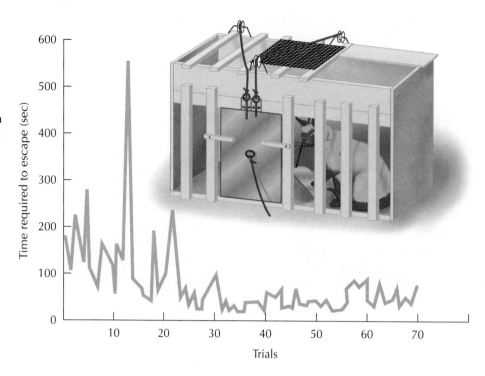

ened; if a response in a particular situation is followed by an unsatisfying or unpleasant consequence, it will be weakened. According to this law, all organisms learn to make certain responses in certain situations; the responses that regularly occur are those that have produced positive consequences in the past. If a response tends to occur initially (for example, scratching at the walls of the cage) but is not followed by something good (such as freedom from the box), the likelihood of that response occurring again in the situation goes down.

The Discriminative Stimulus: Knowing When to Respond

It is important to understand that the law of effect applies only to responses that are rewarded in particular situations. If you are praised for raising your hand in class and asking an intelligent question, you're not likely to begin walking down the street repeatedly raising your hand. You understand that raising your hand is rewarded only in a particular situation, namely, the classroom lecture. What you really learn is something like the following: If some stimulus situation is present (the classroom), and a certain response is produced (raising your hand), then some consequence will follow (praise).

B. F. Skinner (1938) referred to the stimulus situation as the **discriminative stimulus.** He suggested that a discriminative stimulus "sets the occasion" for a response to be rewarded. In some ways, the discriminative stimulus shares properties with conditioned stimuli of the type studied by Pavlov. For example, we can find *stimulus generalization* of an instrumental response: If a pigeon is trained to peck a key in the presence of a red light, the bird will later peck the key whenever a light of a similar color is turned on. If you're rewarded for asking questions in psychology, you might naturally generalize your response to another course, such as economics, and raise your hand there. Conversely, *stimulus discrimination* can also be established, usually after experiencing reward in one context but not in another. You may learn, for instance, that raising your hand in your psychology class leads to positive consequences, but a similar behavior in your economics class is frowned on by the professor. In such a case, one setting (psychology) acts as an effective discriminative stimulus for a certain instrumental response, but another setting (economics) does not.

Over the years, learning researchers have argued about exactly what subjects learn about the discriminative stimulus in instrumental conditioning, especially in studies with animal subjects. For example, if a rat is taught to press a lever to receive food, does the rat learn simply to press the lever whenever it is there? Does the reward merely "stamp in" an association between a discriminative stimulus (the lever) and a response (pressing)? For many years, this was the traditional view in psychology: Instrumental conditioning leads to the formation of associations between stimuli and responses. But in recent years, psychologists have recognized that more is learned in instrumental conditioning than connections between discriminative stimuli and responses. For example, as in classical conditioning, responding in the presence of the discriminative stimulus depends on how the animal feels about the reward—if a rat is taught to press a lever for a reward, and then the value of the reward is somehow changed, the rat will change its behavior accordingly (Colwill & Rescorla, 1986). Thus, the animal learns not only about the discriminative stimulus and the response but also about the specific reward that follows the response.

The Nature of Reinforcement

The law of effect states that responses will be strengthened if they are followed by a pleasant or satisfying consequence. By "strengthened," Thorndike meant that a response was more likely to occur in the future in that particular situation. But, what defines a pleasant or satisfying consequence? This is a tricky problem because the concept of a "pleasant" or "satisfying" event is highly subjective—what's pleasant for me might not be pleasant for you. Moreover, something that's pleasing at one time might not be pleasing at another. Food, for example, is "positive at the beginning of Thanksgiving dinner, indifferent halfway through, and negative at the end of it" (Kimble, 1993).

For these reasons, psychologists use the technical term **reinforcement** to describe consequences that *increase* the likelihood of responding. As we'll see, it's popular to distinguish between two major types of reinforcement: *positive* and *negative.*

Positive Reinforcement. When the *presentation* of an event after a response increases the likelihood of that response occurring again, **positive reinforcement** has occurred. Usually, the presented event is an *appetitive stimulus*—something the organism likes, needs, or has an "appetite" for. According to Thorndike (1911), an appetitive stimulus would be "one which the animal does nothing to avoid, often doing such things as to attain or preserve it"(p. 245). Food and water are obvious examples, but responses can be reinforcing, too (such as sexual activity or painting a picture). Remember, though, it's not the "subjective" qualities of the consequence that matter—what matters is whether the consequence increases the likelihood of the response occurring again.

Psychologists have discovered that it's often possible to predict whether the presentation of an event will be reinforcing by appealing to the concept of a behavioral *bliss point.* By bliss points, psychologists mean baseline tendencies to respond to events. Everyone has a certain desire to eat, drink, listen to music, play volleyball, study for school, and so on. These baseline levels of "satisfaction," which presumably differ from one person to the next, are called bliss points. According to the *response deprivation theory* of reinforcement, an event will be reinforcing as long as presenting it allows one to move toward his or her natural bliss point for that event (Allison, 1989; Timberlake, 1980). If you have been deprived of eating for a while, you have fallen below your natural bliss point for eating and therefore will find the presentation of food to be positively reinforcing. Once you've eaten,

Can you think of a case in which the presentation of an "unpleasant" event might actually increase the likelihood of the response that produced it?

food loses its reinforcing value because you've already reached your natural bliss point for eating.

Importantly, the response deprivation theory predicts that the presentation of *any* event or response, in principle, can serve as positive reinforcement (see also Premack, 1962). If you have been deprived of responding to an event for long enough (that is, you have fallen below your bliss point), the presentation of that event should be reinforcing. Most children, for example, would rather color than do math problems (presumably because the bliss point for coloring is naturally high). But it's been found that if children are deprived of doing math problems long enough to fall below their natural "math bliss point," the opportunity to do math can actually serve as positive reinforcement—even for a desirable response, such as coloring (see Konarski, 1985; Timberlake, 1980).

Negative Reinforcement. With **negative reinforcement,** the *removal* of an event after a response increases the likelihood of that response occurring again. In most cases, negative reinforcement occurs when a response allows an individual to eliminate, avoid, or escape from an *unpleasant* situation. For instance, you hang up the phone on someone who is criticizing you unfairly, shut off the blaring alarm clock in the morning, or walk out of a movie that is boring you to tears. These responses are more likely to occur again in the future, given the appropriate circumstance, because they lead to the removal of something negative—criticism, noise, or boredom. But, as you may have guessed, the event that is removed doesn't have to be "unpleasant"—it simply has to increase the likelihood of the "contingent" response (the response that led to the removal).

Researchers who study negative reinforcement in animals have historically used two kinds of learning procedures: escape conditioning and avoidance conditioning. In *escape conditioning,* the animal learns that a response will end some kind of unpleasant stimulus. For example, a rat might learn that jumping over a short barrier separating one part of the cage from another will eliminate a mild electric shock. The jumping response is reinforced because it allows the animal to escape from a negative situation (see the top row in Figure 7.12). In *avoidance con-*

FIGURE 7.12
Escape Versus Avoidance Conditioning. In escape conditioning (top row), a response is negatively reinforced because it ends an aversive event. The rat learns that jumping over a short barrier will terminate a mild electric shock. In avoidance conditioning (bottom row), the rat learns to make a response that prevents the aversive stimulus from occurring. Here, the rat learns to avoid the shock by jumping when the light comes on. Often, the animal will learn first to escape from, and then to avoid, an aversive event.

Escape

Avoidance

ditioning, the response that the animal learns *prevents* the negative situation from occurring. For example, if the mild electric shock is signaled by the appearance of a light, the rat might learn to jump over the barrier as soon as the light appears, thus *avoiding* exposure to the shock. Once again, the avoidance response is reinforced by the elimination of something negative (see the bottom row in Figure 7.12).

Students are often confused by the term *negative reinforcement* because they think negative reinforcement is a bad thing. Actually, whenever psychologists use the term *reinforcement,* both positive and negative, they are referring to outcomes that increase the probability of responding. The terms *positive* and *negative* simply refer to whether the response ends with the presentation of something or the removal of something. In both cases, the result is a rewarding aftereffect, and we can expect the reinforcement-producing response to occur again in that situation.

Conditioned Reinforcers. Sometimes an event or stimulus can act like a reinforcer even though it seems to have no intrinsic value. For example, money will serve as a satisfying consequence even though it's only a well-made piece of paper marked with interesting engravings. However, possession of money predicts something of intrinsic value, and this predictive relationship gives it its reinforcing value. In the same way, if a stimulus or event predicts the absence or removal of something negative, then its presentation is also likely to be reinforcing. Stimuli of this type are called "conditioned" reinforcers because their reinforcing properties are acquired through learning (they are also sometimes called "secondary" reinforcers to distinguish them from more "primary" reinforcers such as food or water). These stimuli are reinforcing because they signal the presence or absence of other events.

Schedules of Reinforcement

The law of effect implies that behaviors are more likely to be repeated if they are *followed* by positive or negative reinforcement. As in classical conditioning, however, the development of an instrumental response depends greatly on how often, and when, the reinforcements are actually delivered. It is necessary to teach someone that his or her behavior uniquely predicts the reward—if we deliver the reward in a haphazard way, or when the behavior in question has not occurred, learning can be slow or nonexistent (Dickinson & Charnock, 1985).

Most of the research that has been done on the acquisition of instrumental responding has been concerned with the scheduling of reinforcements. A **schedule of reinforcement** is simply a rule that the experimenter uses to determine when particular responses will be reinforced (Ferster & Skinner, 1957). If a response is followed rapidly by reinforcement every time it occurs, the reinforcement is said to be on a *continuous* schedule. If reinforcement is delivered only some of the time after the response has occurred, a *partial* schedule is in effect. There are four major types of partial reinforcement schedules to consider: fixed-ratio, variable-ratio, fixed-interval, and variable-interval. Each produces a distinctive pattern of responding (see Figure 7.13).

Fixed-Ratio Schedules. *Ratio* schedules of reinforcement require the subject to produce a certain *number* of responses before receiving reinforcement. In a **fixed-ratio schedule,** the number of required responses is fixed and doesn't change from one trial to the next. Suppose you are paid a dollar for every 100 envelopes you stuff for a local marketing firm. This schedule of reinforcement is referred to as an "FR 100" (fixed-ratio 100) because it requires 100 responses (envelopes stuffed) before the reinforcement is delivered (a dollar). You can stuff the envelopes as quickly as you like, but you must produce 100 responses before you get the reward.

When you study for an examination, or try generally to do well in school, are you seeking positive reinforcement or negative reinforcement?

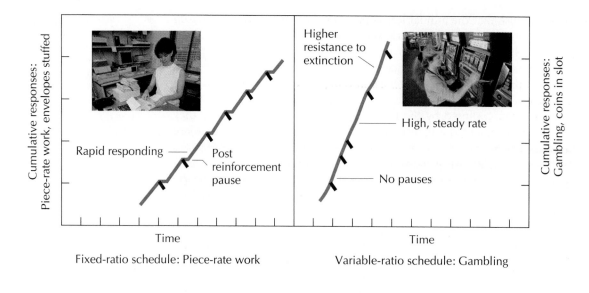

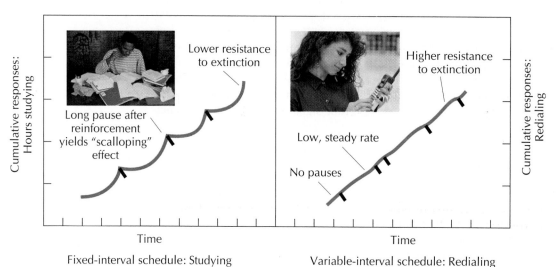

FIGURE 7.13
Schedules of Reinforcement.

Schedules of reinforcement are rules that the experimenter uses to determine when responses will be reinforced. Ratio schedules tend to produce rapid rates of responding because reinforcement depends on the number of responses. Interval schedules tend to produce lower rates of responding because reinforcement is delivered only for the first response after a specified time interval. In the cumulative response functions plotted here, the total number of responses is plotted over time.

Fixed-ratio schedules typically produce steady, consistent responding because the relationship between the instrumental response and the reinforcement is clear and predictable. For this reason, assembly-line work in factories is often reinforced on a fixed-ratio schedule. The only behavioral quirk occurs when the number of required responses is relatively large. For example, if you have to pick 10 bushels of grapes for each monetary reward, you are likely to pause a bit in your responding immediately after the 10th bushel. This delay in responding after reinforcement is called the *postreinforcement pause*. Pausing after reinforcement is easy to understand in this context—after all, you have to do a lot of work before you receive the next reward. But it can be an important factor to consider when choosing the most appropriate schedule for a given work environment.

If we stop delivering the reinforcement after the fixed number of responses has occurred, we can expect the individual to change his or her behavior accordingly. Eventually, the individual will simply stop responding. Similar to what happens in classical conditioning, the introduction of nonreinforcement following a period of training is known as *extinction*. How quickly subjects stop responding, or extinguish their behavior, when reinforcements are no longer delivered is determined partly by the reinforcement schedule in effect. Fixed-ratio schedules typically produce rapid rates of extinction because it quickly becomes clear to the organism that something about the schedule has changed—the reinforcement no longer occurs after the required number of responses has been produced.

What's another name for an FR 1 schedule—that is, a schedule in which every response leads to reinforcement?

Variable-Ratio Schedules. A **variable-ratio schedule** also requires that a certain *number* of responses be made before a reward is given. (This is the defining feature of a ratio schedule.) However, with a variable-ratio schedule, a different number of responses may be required on each trial. Reinforcement may be delivered after the first response on trial 1, after the seventh response on trial 2, after the third response on trial 3, and so on. It's called a variable-ratio (VR) schedule because the responder never knows how many responses are needed to obtain the reward (that is, the number of responses *varies,* often in a random fashion).

Variable-ratio schedules differ from fixed-ratio schedules in that subjects can never predict which response will get them the reward. As a result, these schedules typically produce high rates of responding, and the postreinforcement pause, seen in fixed-ratio schedules, is usually eliminated (after all, the next response might get you the reward again). Gambling is an excellent example of a variable-ratio schedule; because of chance factors, a gambler wins some bets and loses others, but the gambler never knows what to expect on a given bet.

The unpredictability of reward during a variable-ratio schedule makes it difficult to eliminate a response trained on this schedule when the response is no longer reinforced. Consider the typical compulsive slot machine player: Dollar after dollar goes into the machine; sometimes there's a payoff, more often not. Even if the machine breaks and further payments are never delivered (thus placing the responder on extinction), many gamblers would probably continue playing long into the night. On a variable-ratio schedule, it's hard to see that extinction is in effect because one has no particular expectation of when reinforcement will occur.

Fixed-Interval Schedules. In an *interval* schedule of reinforcement, the reward is delivered for the first response that occurs following a specified interval of time; if a **fixed-interval schedule** (FI) is in effect, the time period remains constant from one trial to the next. Suppose we reward a pigeon with food when it pecks a lighted response key after 2 minutes have elapsed. In this case, we would be using an "FI 2 min." schedule. Note that the pigeon must still produce the response to receive the reward. (Otherwise the learning procedure would not be instrumental conditioning.) Pecking just doesn't do any good until at least 2 minutes have elapsed.

You shouldn't be surprised to learn that fixed-interval schedules typically produce low rates of responding. Because no direct association exists between how much individuals respond and the delivery of reinforcement—they are rewarded only when they respond after the interval has passed—it doesn't make sense to respond all the time. Another characteristic of fixed-interval schedules is that responding slows down after reinforcement and gradually increases as the end of the interval approaches. If the total number of responses is plotted over time in a cumulative response record, the net effect is a *scalloping* pattern of the type shown in Figure 7.13.

To appreciate scalloping, consider how people generally study in school. Because "reinforcement" occurs only on fixed test days, students often wait until the week (or night) before the test to start studying the material. Studying behavior increases gradually throughout the test-to-test interval and peaks on the night before the exam. (Actually, studying is not reinforced on a true fixed-interval schedule, because you must take the test on a specific day; in a "true" fixed-interval schedule, you can respond anytime after the fixed interval has elapsed and still get reinforcement.)

Variable-Interval Schedules. When a **variable-interval schedule (VI)** is in effect, the allotted time before a response will yield reinforcement changes from trial to trial. For example, we may deliver reinforcement for a response occurring after 2 minutes on trial 1, after 10 minutes on trial 2, after 30 seconds on trial 3, and so on. Variable-interval schedules are common in everyday life. Suppose you are trying to reach someone on the telephone, but every time you dial you hear a busy signal. To be rewarded, you know that you have to dial the number and that a certain amount of time has to elapse, but you're not sure exactly how long you need to wait.

Like variable-ratio schedules, variable-interval schedules help eliminate the pause in responding that usually occurs after reinforcement. The rate of extinction also tends to be slower in a variable-interval schedule because of the uncertainty created about when the next reinforcement will be delivered. From the responder's point of view, the next response could very well produce the desired reward, so it makes sense to continue steady responding. For responding to cease, the individual needs to recognize that the relationship between responding and reinforcement has changed.

There are actually many different types of reinforcement schedules. The four partial schedules we have considered here are representative and demonstrate the remarkable consistency in behavior that scheduled reinforcements can produce. Moreover, as Skinner (1956) has argued, these principled behaviors are universal—the postreinforcement pause, for example, occurs regardless of the specific response, the nature of the reinforcement, or the species receiving the training. Reward, and the pattern with which it is delivered, exerts a powerful influence on everyday actions.

Acquisition: Shaping the Desired Behavior

In principle, you should be able to gain control over any behavior, such as getting your dog to sit or shake hands, by reinforcing the appropriate response according to a specified schedule. For example, if you use a variable-ratio schedule to train

Do you think fishing is reinforced on a variable-interval schedule of reinforcement or a variable-ratio schedule of reinforcement? How might the answer depend on the skill of the person doing the fishing?

Through shaping—in which reinforcements are delivered for successive approximations of a desired behavior—it is possible to produce some unusual behaviors in animals. These rabbits are shown in the early stages of training for an advertisement that featured them popping out of top hats (circa 1952).

INSIDE ▸ THE PROBLEM: *Superstitious Behavior*

Have you ever noticed the odd behavior of a professional baseball player as he approaches the batter's box? He kicks the dirt (a fixed number of times), adjusts his helmet, hitches up his trousers, grimaces, swings toward the pitcher a few times, and adopts a characteristic crouch. Basketball players, as they prepare to make a free throw, endlessly caress the ball with their hands, bounce it a certain number of times, crouch, pause, and release. Such regular patterns are a player's signature—you can identify who's in the batter's box or up at the line by watching these ritualistic preparation patterns.

Let's analyze these behaviors from the perspective of instrumental conditioning. According to the law of effect, these odd patterns of behavior must have been reinforced—they occurred, perhaps by chance, and were followed by a reward (a hit or a successful free throw). But because the pairing of the behavior with its consequence was really accidental, psychologists refer to this kind of reinforcement as *accidental* or *adventitious reinforcement*. In the player's mind, however, a cause-and-effect link has been formed, and he acts in a similar fashion again. Once the player starts to perform the behavior on a regular basis, it's likely that the behavior will continue to be accidentally reinforced, although on a partial schedule of reinforcement. (Can you identify the particular schedule?) The result is called a "superstitious" act, and because of the partial

schedule (a variable-ratio one), it is difficult to eliminate.

In 1948, B. F. Skinner developed an experimental procedure to mimic and gain control over the development of superstitious acts. He placed hungry pigeons in a chamber and delivered bits of food every 15 seconds, irrespective of what the bird happened to be doing at the time. In his own words:

> In six out of eight cases the resulting responses were so clearly defined that two observers could agree perfectly in counting instances. One bird was conditioned to turn counterclockwise about the cage, making two or three turns between reinforcements. Another repeatedly thrust its head into one of the upper corners of the cage. A third developed a "tossing" response, as if placing its head beneath an invisible bar and lifting it repeatedly. (Skinner, 1948, p. 168)

Remember, from the experimenter's point of view, no cause-and-effect relationship existed between these quirky behaviors and the delivery of food. Researchers since Skinner have replicated his results, but with some added caveats (Staddon & Simmelhag, 1971). For example, many of the behaviors that Skinner noted are characteristic responses that birds make in preparation for food; therefore, some of the "strange" behaviors Skinner observed might have been natural pigeon reactions to the expectation of being fed rather than learned responses. Never-

Many professional athletes perform odd rituals on a regular basis. This professional baseball player feels the need to brush his teeth vigorously before every time up at the plate. A learning theorist might argue that the player's bizarre behavior was somehow accidentally reinforced in the past, forming a superstitious cause-and-effect link between teeth brushing and successful performance.

theless, the point Skinner made is important to remember: From the responder's point of view, illusory connections can form between behaviors and outcomes. Once these connections have been made, if the behaviors recur, they might continue to be accidentally reinforced and thus serve as the basis for the familiar forms of "superstitious" acts.

---

your dog to sit, and you use food as a reward, then your dog should continue to sit on command even when food is not available as a reward. In this case, the dog knows that sitting is reinforced only some of the time, so failure to receive a reward doesn't necessarily weaken the response.

In practice, however, it can be difficult to train a behavior if the behavior is not likely to occur initially. How do you reward your dog for sitting if the dog never sits on command in the first place? Most people train a dog by yelling "Sit," pushing the dog's bottom down, and stuffing a food reward in its mouth. Under these conditions, however, they are not really establishing the proper instrumental relationship between the dog's own behavior and the delivery of a reward. They have actually set up a kind of classical conditioning procedure—the dog is taught that having his bottom pushed downward is a *signal* for an inviting food unconditioned stimulus. This might work, but it does not teach the animal that its own behavior is instrumental in producing the outcome. What you want your dog to learn is that the word *sit* is a discriminative stimulus that signals that a behavior (sitting) is instrumental in producing some kind of reward.

To solve this problem, Skinner (1938) developed a procedure called **shaping,** in which reinforcement is delivered for successive *approximations* to the desired response. Instead of waiting for the complete response—here, sitting to the command "Sit"—to occur, you reinforce some part of the response that is likely to occur initially. For instance, you might reward your dog for simply approaching you when you say, "Sit." As each part of the response is acquired, you become more strict in your criteria for what constitutes a successful response sequence. Skinner and others have shown that incredibly complex sequences of behavior can be acquired using the successive-approximation technique of shaping.

Shaping has also been used effectively as a technique for modifying behavior in people. In Chapter 15, we'll see that shaping is often applied in therapy to modify maladaptive thoughts, lessen fears, and help individuals handle stressful situations. Disturbed children who can't communicate have been taught to speak by reinforcing verbal sequences with candy or cereal. Whereas the child might be reinforced initially for any kind of verbal utterance, gradually the reward is withheld until the child produces a more natural flow of sounds. Shaping is also commonly used to teach sports activities. To teach someone an effective golf swing, it's best to begin by rewarding simple contact between the club and the ball. Later, the teacher can fine-tune the person's swing by offering praise only when the mechanics of the swing are more technically correct.

Punishment: Lowering the Likelihood of a Response

Up to now, we have considered how the likelihood of a response increases, in the presence of a discriminative stimulus, when it produces reinforcement. If an individual's behavior is instrumental in producing an appetitive event (positive reinforcement) or in removing something unpleasant (negative reinforcement), he or she is likely to behave in a similar fashion in the future. But the law of effect has another side: Thorndike claimed that if a response is followed by an unsatisfying or unpleasant consequence, it will be weakened. The term **punishment** is used to refer to consequences that decrease the likelihood of responding. Like reinforcement, punishment comes in two forms: positive and negative (see Figure 7.14).

Positive Punishment. When a response leads to the *presentation* of an event that lowers the likelihood of that response occurring again, this is **positive punishment.** Notice, as with reinforcement, the concept is defined in terms of its effect on behavior—lowering the likelihood of responding—rather than on its "subjective" qualities. But usually, positive punishment occurs when a response leads directly to the presentation of an *aversive* outcome. If you try to fix your broken doorbell and receive an electrical shock in the process, you probably will not dabble in electrical repair for some time to come. Provided the aversive event is intense enough, the instrumental response that produced this outcome will tend to disappear rapidly or become *suppressed.*

Negative Punishment. When the *removal* of an event after responding lowers the likelihood of that response occurring again, **negative punishment** has occurred. For example, if a response leads to the *removal* of a positive outcome,

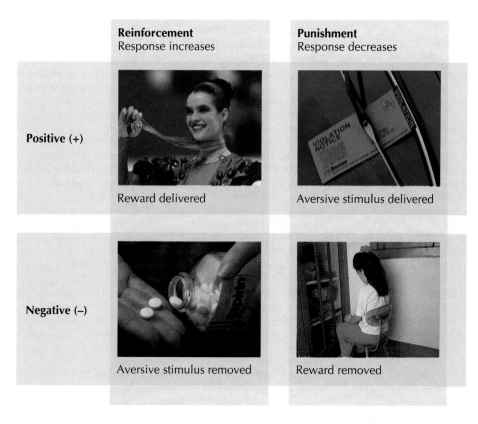

	Reinforcement Response increases	**Punishment** Response decreases
Positive (+)	Reward delivered	Aversive stimulus delivered
Negative (−)	Aversive stimulus removed	Reward removed

FIGURE 7.14
Reinforcement Versus Punishment. Psychologists use the term *reinforcement* to describe response consequences that increase the likelihood of responding. The term *punishment* is used to describe response consequences that decrease the likelihood of responding. *Positive* and *negative* refer to whether the consequence involves the presentation of some event (positive) or the removal of some event (negative).

you are unlikely to respond in that way again. If you perform poorly in your job and are fired as a result, your punishment is the removal of something you desire (your job and income). If you withhold a child's weekly allowance because his or her room is messy, you are punishing the child by removing something good—money. As with positive punishment, negative punishment is recognized as an effective training procedure for rapidly suppressing an undesirable response.

What accounts for the rapid suppression of the response that is punished? It seems likely that people simply learn the associative relationship between their behavior and the particular outcome. Individuals learn about the consequences of their actions—that a particular kind of behavior will lead to a relatively unpleasant consequence. In this sense, we don't really need two different explanations to account for the behavior changes produced by reinforcement and punishment; the only major difference is that behavior increases in one situation and declines in the other. In both cases, individuals simply use their knowledge about a behavior and its consequences to maximize gain and minimize loss in a particular situation.

Practical Considerations. In principle, although punishment is quite effective for suppressing an undesirable response, difficulties can arise in everyday practice. For example, with positive punishment it is often hard to gauge the appropriate strength of the aversive event. If a child feels ignored, yelling at him or her can actually be reinforcing because of the attention it provides. Children who spend a lot of time in the principal's office may be causing trouble partly because of the attention that the punishment produces.

It is also important to remember that punishment *suppresses* a behavior; it does not teach an individual how to act appropriately. For instance, spanking your child for lying might reduce the lying behavior, but it will not teach the child how to deal more effectively with the social situation that led to the initial lie. To teach the child about more appropriate forms of behavior, you would have to provide an alternative response followed by reinforcement.

Punishment can also produce undesirable side effects, including attempted escape, resentment, and aggression. Laboratory studies have documented numerous instances of aggressive behavior that have been produced as a consequence of punishment procedures. Animals that are shocked together in the same experimental context will often attack one another throughout the shock duration (Domjan, 1993). Parents who punish their children regularly invite future resentment and a potential decline in the quality of the parent-child relationship.

Learning from Others: Observational Learning

The world would be a very unpleasant place if people could learn about the consequences of their behavior only from the simple trial-and-error rules of the law of effect. Individuals could learn to avoid certain foods through positive punishment, but only after eating them and experiencing an unpleasant consequence. Through escape and avoidance conditioning, our children might learn not to play in the street, provided that they leap away from the oncoming traffic in time. Learning is a behavioral change produced as a result of experience, but sometimes it's advantageous to learn in a way that doesn't actually require one to undergo the experience.

In the wild, rhesus monkeys show an adaptive fear response in the presence of snakes. Because snakes are natural predators of monkeys, it makes sense for monkeys to avoid them whenever possible. But consider how that fear is originally acquired. According to a strict interpretation of the law of effect, the animal must acquire its fear and the accompanying avoidance response through some kind of direct reinforcement or punishment of an approach response. The monkey approaches the snake, is bitten, and thereby learns to fear the snake; unfortunately, this single learning experience is likely to be fatal.

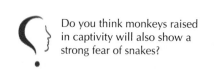
Do you think monkeys raised in captivity will also show a strong fear of snakes?

In fact, animals, including humans, acquire much of what they learn through observing the experiences of *others*. Individuals can learn by example, and this kind of **observational** or **social learning** has considerable adaptive value. In the wild, newly weaned rats acquire food habits by eating what the older rats eat (Galef, 1985); red-winged blackbirds will refuse to eat a certain food if they have observed another bird getting sick after it has consumed the food (Mason & Reidinger, 1982). Rhesus monkeys, it turns out, acquire their fear of snakes partly through social learning rather than through direct experience (Mineka, 1987). They watch other monkeys in their environment showing fear in the presence of a snake and thereby acquire the tendency to show fear themselves.

Modeling: Learning Through Example

What conditions produce effective observational learning? One important factor is the presence of a significant role model. Humans naturally tend to imitate, or **model,** the behavior of significant others, as do most members of the animal kingdom. Moreover, people model others' behavior even when no observable reinforcement is produced as a consequence. In one classic study, Albert Bandura and his colleagues showed nursery-school children a film that portrayed an adult striking, punching, and kicking a large, inflatable, upright "Bobo" doll. Afterward, when placed in a room with Bobo, many of these children imitated the adult and violently attacked the doll (Bandura, Ross, & Ross, 1963).

This modeling or imitative behavior is even more likely to occur if the model is rewarded for a particular action. Bandura observed that when the adult was praised ("You're the champion," for example) for attacking Bobo, children were more likely to kick the doll themselves. Bandura (1986) has claimed that the responses acquired through observational learning are especially strengthened through *vicarious reinforcement,* which occurs when the model is reinforced for an action, or weakened through *vicarious punishment,* in which the model is punished for an action. A clear parallel therefore exists between the law of effect and observational learning; the difference, of course, is that the behavior of others is being reinforced or punished rather than one's own.

Practical Considerations

It's easy to see how the techniques of observational learning might be used to improve or change unwanted behaviors. Many studies have shown that observation of a model performing some desirable behavior can lower maladaptive behavior. Children have been able to reduce their fear of dental visits (Craig, 1978) or impending surgery (Melamed & Siegel, 1975) by observing films of other children effectively handling their dental or surgical anxieties. Clinical psychologists now use observational learning as a technique to deal with specific fears and as a method for promoting cooperative behavior among preschoolers (Granvold, 1994).

We naturally tend to imitate, or model, the behavior of significant others. Modeling is adaptive because it allows us to learn things without always directly experiencing consequences.

Unfortunately, observational or social learning is often a powerful influence beyond our immediate control. It has been estimated that children now witness thousands of reinforced acts of violence just by watching Saturday morning cartoons. Although the causal connection between TV violence and personal aggression has not been firmly established (Freedman, 1988), the consensus among psychologists seems to support the link (Hearold, 1986). In addition, it can be difficult for a society to overcome unproductive stereotypes if they are repeatedly portrayed through the behavior of others. Many gender-related stereotypes, such as submissive or helpless behavior in females, continue to be represented in TV programs and movies. By the age of 6 or 7, children have already begun to shy away from activities that are identified with members of the opposite sex. Although it's unlikely that television is entirely responsible for this trend, it's widely believed that television plays an important role (Ruble, Balaban, & Cooper, 1981).

Even if people don't directly imitate or model a particular violent act, it's still likely that the observation itself influences the way they think. For instance, wit-

 Given the data on modeling, do you favor the passage of laws that will control the amount of violence shown on television?

Observational learning has powerful consequences that are not always what we intend. Children model the behavior of significant role models, even when the model acts in a way that lacks adaptive value.

nessing repeated examples of fictional violence distorts people's estimates of realistic violence—they are likely to believe, for example, that more people die a violent death than is actually the case. This can lead individuals to show irrational fear and to avoid situations that are in all likelihood safe. People who watch a lot of television tend to view the world in a fashion that mirrors what they see on the screen. They tend to think, for example, that a large proportion of the population are professionals (such as doctors or lawyers) and that few people in society are actually old (Gerbner & Gross, 1976). It's not just the imitation of particular acts that we need to worry about: Television and other vehicles of observational learning can literally change or determine people's everyday view of the world (Bandura, 1986).

◤ SOLVING THE PROBLEMS: A SUMMARY

As organisms struggle to survive in their environments, their capacity to learn—that is, to change their behavior as a result of experience—represents one of their greatest strengths. Psychologists have long recognized the need for understanding how behavior changes with experience; historically, research on learning predates research on virtually all other topics, with the possible exception of basic sensory and perceptual processes.

Even today, the study of learning in one form or another is the cornerstone for much of psychology. In attempting to understand and treat mental disorders, clinical psychologists often seek their answers in an individual's prior experiences. To understand the dynamics of group behavior, social psychologists appeal increasingly to the effects of prior experience. Cognitive psychologists, as we'll see in the next two chapters, consider experience to be perhaps the most important determinant of the content and structure of thought and other mental processes. Indeed, it is difficult to find an area of psychology that does not consider learning to be fundamental to its enterprise.

In this chapter, we've concentrated on relatively basic learning processes. To meet the needs of changing environments, all organisms must solve certain types of learning problems, and the principles of behavior that we've described apply generally across animal species.

▶ **LEARNING ABOUT EVENTS** Individuals need to *recognize* events when they occur. Novel, or unusual, events cause organisms to produce an orienting response, which helps ensure that they will react quickly to sudden changes in their environment. The sound of screeching automobile brakes leads to an immediate reaction; you don't have to stop and think about it. At the same time, organisms cannot attend to all the stimuli that surround them, so they must learn to ignore events that are of little adaptive significance. Through the process of habituation, characterized by the decline in the tendency to respond to an event that has become familiar, individuals become selective about responding to events that occur repeatedly in their environment.

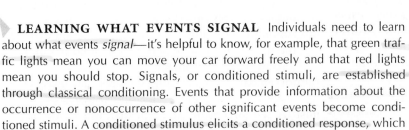

▶ **LEARNING WHAT EVENTS SIGNAL** Individuals need to learn about what events *signal*—it's helpful to know, for example, that green traffic lights mean you can move your car forward freely and that red lights mean you should stop. Signals, or conditioned stimuli, are established through classical conditioning. Events that provide information about the occurrence or nonoccurrence of other significant events become conditioned stimuli. A conditioned stimulus elicits a conditioned response, which is a response appropriate for anticipating the event that will follow.

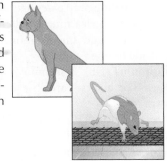

▶ **LEARNING ABOUT THE CONSEQUENCES OF BEHAVIOR** Individuals need to learn about the *consequences* of their actions. They must learn that when they act a certain way, their behaviors produce outcomes that are sometimes pleasing and sometimes not. In instrumental conditioning, the presentation and removal of events after responding can either increase or decrease the likelihood of one responding in a similar way again. When a response is followed by reinforcement, either positive or negative, the tendency to respond in that way again is strengthened. When a response is followed by punishment, either positive or negative, subjects are less likely to behave that way again. It's also important to consider the schedule of reinforcement. Schedules affect not only how rapidly subjects will learn and respond, but also the pattern of responding and how likely they are to change their behavior if they no longer receive reinforcement.

▶ **LEARNING FROM OTHERS** Through observational or social learning, individuals imitate and model the actions of other people, thereby learning from example rather than from direct experience. We study how other individuals behave and how their behavior is reinforced or punished, and we change our own behavior accordingly. Observational learning can have a number of effects, both positive and negative, on the individual and on society.

Terms to Remember

learning A relatively permanent change in behavior, or potential to respond, that results from experience.

LEARNING ABOUT EVENTS: NOTICING AND IGNORING

orienting response An inborn tendency to shift one's focus of attention toward a novel or surprising event.

habituation The decline in the tendency to respond to an event that has become familiar through repeated exposure.

sensitization An increase in the tendency to respond to an event that has been repeated; sensitization is more likely when a repeated stimulus is intense.

LEARNING WHAT EVENTS SIGNAL: CLASSICAL CONDITIONING

classical conditioning A set of procedures, initially developed by Pavlov, used to investigate how organisms learn about the signaling properties of events. Classical conditioning leads to the learning of relations between events—conditioned and unconditioned stimuli—that occur outside of one's control.

unconditioned stimulus (US) A stimulus that automatically produces—or elicits—an observable response prior to any training.

unconditioned response (UR) The observable response that is produced automatically, prior to training, on presentation of an unconditioned stimulus.

conditioned response (CR) The acquired response that is produced to the conditioned stimulus in anticipation of the arrival of the unconditioned stimulus. Often, the conditioned response resembles the unconditioned response, although not always.

conditioned stimulus (CS) A neutral stimulus (one that does not produce the unconditioned response prior to training) that is paired with the unconditioned stimulus during classical conditioning.

second-order conditioning A procedure in which an established conditioned stimulus is used to condition a second neutral stimulus.

stimulus generalization Responding to a new stimulus in a way similar to the response produced by an established conditioned stimulus.

stimulus discrimination Responding differently to a new stimulus than one responds to an established conditioned stimulus.

extinction Presenting a conditioned stimulus repeatedly, after conditioning, without the unconditioned stimulus, resulting in a loss in responding.

spontaneous recovery The recovery of an extinguished conditioned response after a period of nonexposure to the conditioned stimulus.

conditioned inhibition Learning that an event signals the absence of the unconditioned stimulus.

LEARNING ABOUT THE CONSEQUENCES OF BEHAVIOR: INSTRUMENTAL CONDITIONING

instrumental conditioning A procedure for studying how organisms learn about the consequences of their own voluntary actions; they learn that their behaviors are instrumental in producing rewards and punishments. Also called **operant conditioning.**

law of effect The idea that if a response in a particular situation is followed by a satisfying or pleasant consequence, it will be strengthened; if a response in a particular situation is followed by an unsatisfying or unpleasant consequence, it will be weakened.

discriminative stimulus The stimulus situation that "sets the occasion" for a response to be followed by reinforcement or punishment.

reinforcement Response consequences that increase the likelihood of responding in a similar way again.

positive reinforcement An event that, when *presented* after a response, increases the likelihood of that response occurring again.

negative reinforcement An event that, when *removed* after a response, increases the likelihood of that response occurring again.

schedules of reinforcement A rule that an experimenter uses to determine when particular responses will be reinforced. Schedules may be fixed or variable, ratio or interval.

fixed-ratio schedule A schedule in which the number of responses required for reinforcement is fixed and does not change from trial to trial.

variable-ratio schedule A schedule in which a certain number of responses is required for reinforcement, but the number of required responses typically changes from trial to trial.

fixed-interval schedule A schedule in which the reinforcement is delivered for the first response that occurs following a fixed interval of time.

variable-interval schedule A schedule in which the allotted time before a response will yield reinforcement changes from trial to trial.

shaping A procedure in which reinforcement is delivered for successive approximations of the desired response.

punishment Consequences that decrease the likelihood of responding in a similar way again.

positive punishment An event that, when *presented* after a response, lowers the likelihood of that response occurring again.

negative punishment An event that, when *removed* after a response, lowers the likelihood of that response occurring again.

LEARNING FROM OTHERS: OBSERVATIONAL LEARNING

observational learning Learning that occurs as a result of observing the experiences of others. Also called **social learning.**

modeling The natural tendency to imitate the behavior of significant others in one's surroundings.

Consider the following scenario. At lunch today, you decide to be daring and order the fresh gooseberry pie for dessert instead of your usual slice of apple pie. Unbeknownst to you, an eccentric billionaire experimenter is sitting elsewhere in the restaurant and decides to reward you for choosing the gooseberry pie; he places an unmarked envelope in your car containing $100, which you happily discover 2 hours later. Now consider a different scenario: Same restaurant, same gooseberry pie, but instead of finding $100 you suffer severe nausea and gastric distress 2 hours later. In which of these two cases are you more likely to form an association between eating gooseberry pie and a particular contingent consequence?

In each case, there is an event, eating gooseberry pie, and a powerful consequence, receiving $100 or getting sick. Let's assume that the value of the two consequences, as potential reinforcers and punishers, is the same. Because of the 2-hour delay, it's possible that you would have a problem forming any kind of association under these conditions, but, in fact, the answer is relatively clear: You're likely to associate the pie with the illness and to make no connection between the pie and the $100. This finding is important because it *constrains* the generality of learning principles (that is, principles that can be applied to any and all learning situations). It suggests that not all events and consequences are created equal. Organisms may be predisposed to associate certain things, such as tastes and nausea; certain responses may "belong" with certain reinforcers or punishers.

The Relation of Cue to Consequence

The gooseberry pie scenario, first described by Revusky and Garcia (1970), illustrates a principle about the relation between cues and consequences that can be demonstrated directly in the laboratory. In 1966, Garcia and Koelling let thirsty rats drink water flavored with saccharin. The drinking was also accompanied by flashing lights and distinct clicking noises. (This stimulus complex is sometimes referred to by the colorful name "bright-noisy-sweet water.") After the rats drank the water, researchers punished the drinking response in one group of rats by administering a moderate foot shock, whereas they gave a second group a small dose of X-irradiation (which produces sickness). Learning was later tested by allowing the rats in each group to choose between drinking sweetened water alone and drinking unsweetened water in the presence of the flashing lights and the noisy clicking sounds.

The design and results of the experiment are shown in Figure 7.15. When irradiation was used as the punishing consequence, thus making the rats sick, the rats were reluctant to drink the water laced with saccharin, but they showed no evidence of avoidance of "bright and noisy" water and consumed near-normal amounts. The opposite finding was obtained with the rats that had received shock. Those that received a shock in the presence of the bright-noisy-sweet water learned to avoid the flashing and clicking unsweetened water but showed no resistance to the sweet water presented alone. These results indicate that certain cues *belong* with certain consequences; there appears to be a natural tendency to associate flavors with gastric distress (in this case, the sweet taste with nausea) and novel environmental events with shock (shock was readily associated with bright lights and noise).

Belongingness

The idea that natural predispositions, perhaps rooted in an organism's genetic code, might have to be factored into the learning equation was foreign to most learning researchers of the 1960s. Most believed that the principles of classical and instrumental conditioning were fixed and immutable and could be applied successfully in any environment. But the results of the Garcia and Koelling (1966) study showed that the amount of learning that results depends on the particular cues and consequences used. Actually, Thorndike, in his studies of cats in puzzle boxes, had introduced the concept of *belongingness* several years earlier, but his warnings were largely ignored. Thorndike had noted, for example, that it seemed impossible to increase the probability of yawning or of certain reflexive scratching responses in cats through the application of reinforcement.

Similar observations were reported later by animal trainers Keller and Marion Breland (1961). The Brelands, who were former students of Skinner, encountered some interesting difficulties while attempting to train a variety of species to make certain responses. In one case, they tried to train a pig to drop large wooden coins into a piggy bank (for a bank commercial). They followed the *shaping* procedure, in which successive approximations of the desired sequence are reinforced, but they could not get the pig to complete the response. The animal would pick up the coin and begin to lumber toward the bank but would stop midway and begin "rooting" the coins along the ground. Despite their using punishment and nonreinforcement of the rooting response, the Brelands could never completely eliminate the response. They encountered similar problems trying to teach a raccoon to put coins in a bank:

> We started out by reinforcing him for picking up a single coin. Then the metal container was introduced, with the requirement that he drop the coin into the container. Here we ran into the first bit of difficulty: he seemed to have a great deal of trouble letting go of the coin. He would rub it against the inside of the container, pull it back out, and clutch it firmly for several seconds. However, he would finally turn it loose and receive his food reinforcement. Then the final contingency: we

[required] that he pick up [two] coins and put them in the container.

Now the raccoon really had problems (and so did we). Not only could he not let go of the coins, but he spent seconds, even minutes, rubbing them together (in a most miserly fashion) and dipping them into the container. He carried on this behavior to such an extent that the practical application that we had in mind—a display featuring a raccoon putting money into a piggy bank—simply was not feasible. The rubbing behavior became worse and worse as time went on, in spite of nonreinforcement. (Breland & Breland, 1961, p. 682)

In the cases of the pig and the raccoon, biological tendencies connected with feeding and food reinforcement interfered with the learning of certain response sequences. Pigs root in connection with feeding, and raccoons rub and dunk objects related to food (Domjan, 1993). These natural biological tendencies are adaptive responses for the animals—at least with respect to feeding—but they limit what the animals can be taught. As a consequence, learning psychologists must heed the following, now-familiar caveat: As behaving organisms, humans struggle to meet the needs of their environment and solve a number of fundamental learning problems; but the behaviors they produce are often more than simple adaptations from experience. People's behaviors are a joint product of their biology (nature) and their experiences (nurture), and it can be difficult, if not impossible, to isolate the influences of each in an observed behavior.

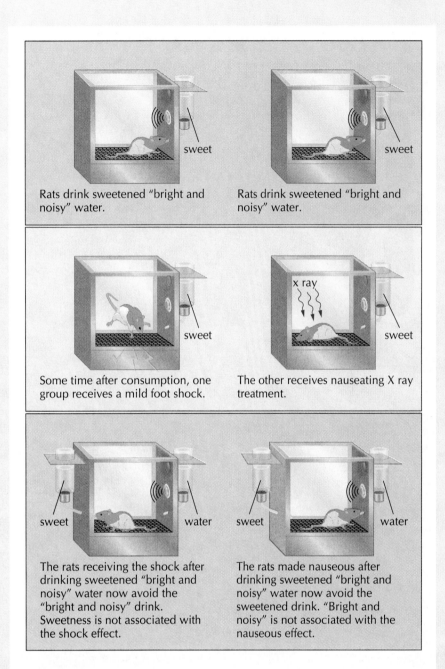

FIGURE 7.15
The Relation of Cue to Consequence. In the experiment by Garcia and Koelling (1966), rats demonstrate that certain cues "belong" with certain consequences. Rats have a natural tendency to associate flavors with nausea and novel environmental events with shock.

8

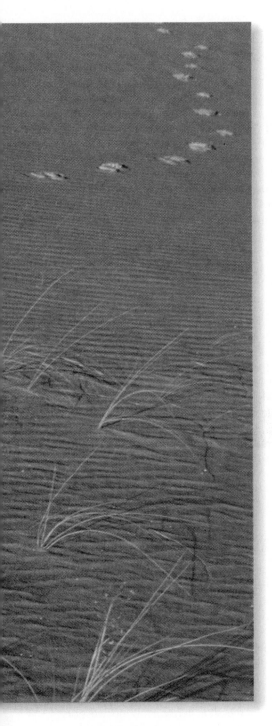

It's a poor sort of memory that only works backwards.

Lewis Carroll

What if the flow of time suddenly fractured and you were forced to relive the same 10 minutes, over and over again, in an endless cycle? You might be driving your car, or reading a book; it wouldn't matter—at the end of the interval you'd begin again, back at the same fork in the road, or the same location on the page. Think about how this might affect you. You wouldn't age, but would you be able to endure?

The answer, I suspect, depends on your capacity to remember and forget. If your memories remained intact from one cycle to the next, if you were aware of the repetition, life would soon become unbearable. But, if your memories were swept clean with each new interval, you'd lack awareness of your hopeless plight; life, albeit in an abbreviated form, would continue as usual. It is through **memory**—broadly defined as the capacity to preserve and recover information—that concepts like the past and the present gain meaning in our lives.

Researchers have discovered that certain brain injuries, or neurological disorders, actually seem to mimic some of the conditions just described. Individuals suffering from *anterograde amnesia* appear normal at first sight—their social skills and language abilities are intact—but they are forever locked in the past. They recognize no one new, not even the professionals who have been treating them for extended periods. They can't remember what they ate for breakfast or the year in which they are living. Each morning begins like the previous one, devoid of any sense of recent personal history. They read the same magazines; they experience the same grief over the death of a loved one (Ogden & Corkin, 1991).

But even these amnesics preserve some components of memory functioning. They retain the ability to communicate, which requires remembering the meaning of words and the rules for how to string words together. They retain a basic understanding of the world and the objects in it. They even remember personal experiences, as long as those experiences predate the point of serious brain dysfunction. A world truly without memory would be devoid of thought and reason. People would never learn; they would never produce spoken language or understand the words of others; their sense of personal history would be lost, and thereby much or all of their personal identity.

 If all components of memory functioning were lost, do you think it would be possible to still have conscious awareness—to still perceive, for example, the beauty of a rose?

▶ PREVIEWING THE ADAPTIVE PROBLEMS

Like learning, memory is not something that can be directly observed. It is an *inferred* capacity, one that psychologists assume must be operating in situations in which people act on the basis of information that is no longer physically present. To understand how memory works, we need to consider how memories are formed (**encoding**), how memories are maintained once they are encoded (**storage**), and how the stored information is recovered and translated into performance (**retrieval**). Each of these psychological processes is depicted visually in Figure 8.1; we'll examine them in more detail as we work through some adaptive problems that memory systems help solve: How do we remember over the short term? How do we store information for the long term? How is stored information recovered at the right place and time? Finally, how do we update memories and keep them current?

▶ **REMEMBERING OVER THE SHORT TERM** Psychologists generally agree that people need some kind of internal machinery for maintaining information over the short term. Consider the interpretation of spoken language. Because speech unfolds one word at a time, it is necessary to remember the early part of a

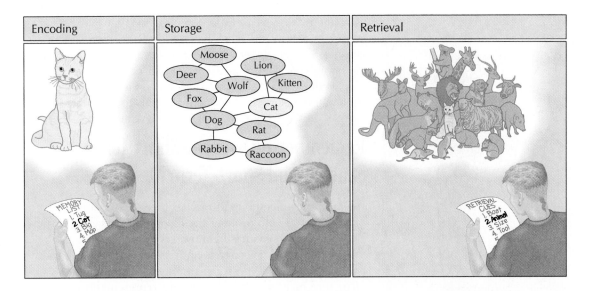

Encoding	Storage	Retrieval

FIGURE 8.1

Basic Memory Processes. Human memory consists of three principal processes: *encoding*, which determines and controls how memories are initially acquired; *storage*, which determines how memories are represented and maintained over time; and *retrieval*, which controls how memories are recovered and translated into performance. In panel 1, how the subject thinks about the word CAT will affect how that word is "encoded" into memory. Panel 2 shows how CAT might be "stored" in long-term memory through the activation of existing knowledge structures. In panel 3, the subject uses the cue ANIMAL to help "retrieve" the memory of CAT.

sentence, after it has receded into the past, in order to comprehend the meaning of the sentence as a whole. Likewise, in the performance of most mental tasks, such as solving math problems, certain bits of information need to be retained during the ongoing solution process. Try adding 28 + 35 in your head without remembering to carry the 1 (or subtract 2 if you round the 28 up to 30). The establishment of short-term memories helps people prolong the incoming message, giving them more time to interpret it properly or to choose the most adaptive response.

STORING INFORMATION FOR THE LONG TERM   Once information leaves the immediate present, it needs to be represented internally in a form that allows for quick recovery in the appropriate context. To establish effective long-term memories, people can process, or think about, information in ways that will aid encoding and promote long-term storage. For example, forming a visual image of a to-be-remembered item increases its durability in memory. It also helps to think about the meaning of the item or to relate the item to other material that has already been stored. We'll consider these techniques in some detail, as well as provide some tips that can help you improve your own ability to remember.

RECOVERING INFORMATION FROM CUES   Interactions with the world require people to recover images of the immediate and distant past continuously. But what initiates an act of remembering? What causes you to remember your appointment with the doctor this afternoon, or what you had for breakfast this morning, or a fleeting encounter with a stranger yesterday? Most researchers believe that the retrieval of stored memories is triggered by other events, or cues, encountered in the environment. As we'll see, cue-driven remembering does not always require conscious effort or intent—more often than not, people remember without really trying, or without an awareness that they are being "cued." Individuals also *interpret* their past by using cues that come from their general knowledge; memory is partly a reconstruction of the past, based on what people think must have happened. You'll see that this sort of reconstruction process can lead to inaccuracies in what people remember.

UPDATING MEMORY   It's upsetting to forget, but forgetting turns out to have considerable adaptive properties—it keeps people current and prevents them from acting in ways that are more appropriate for yesterday than for today. It's the study

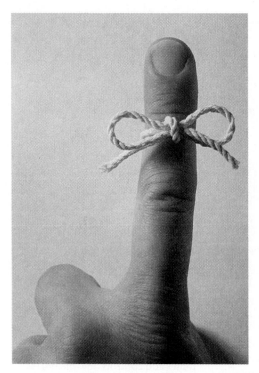

The retrieval of stored memories is often triggered by "cues" in the environment.

assignment that you need to complete *today* that is critical, not the one from yesterday or the week before. It is your *current* phone number that you need to remember, not the one from a previous apartment, or from the home you lived in as a child. We'll consider the major determinants of forgetting, both the normal kinds that underlie the ability to update, and abnormal forgetting of the type that characterizes amnesia.

Remembering over the Short Term: Sensory and Short-Term Memory

When environmental input reaches the senses, people rely on two memory systems to help prolong the incoming message over the short term. The first, called **sensory memory,** keeps the message in a relatively pure, unanalyzed form. Sensory memories are like fleeting snapshots of the world. The external message is represented in accurate detail—as a kind of picture or echo—but the sensory representation usually lasts only a few seconds or less. The second system, **short-term memory,** is a limited-capacity "working memory" that people use to hold information, after it has been analyzed, for periods lasting on the order of a minute or two. Short-term memories are also rapidly forgotten, but they can be maintained for extended periods through internal repetition, or **rehearsal.** We'll take a look at each of these systems and consider some of their important properties.

Sensory Memory: Icons and Echos

When you watch a movie or a television program, you experience a continuous flow of movement across the screen. As you probably know, the film does not actually contain moving images; it is composed of separate still pictures, separated by periods of darkness, that are presented rapidly in sequence. People perceive a continuous world, some researchers believe, because the nervous system activity left by one picture lingers for a brief period prior to presentation of the next. This extended nervous system activity creates sensory "memories" that help to fill the gap and provide a sense of continuity to visual perception.

Do you consider the lingering afterimage left by the "flash" of a camera to be a type of memory?

Iconic Memory. In visual processing, the lingering sensory memory trace is called an *icon* and the sensory memory system that produces and stores icons is known generally as **iconic memory** (Neisser, 1967). It's relatively easy to demonstrate an icon: Simply twirl a flashlight about in a darkened room and you will see a trailing edge. You can obtain a similar effect on a dark night by writing your name in the air with a sparkler or a match. These "trails" of light are not really present in the night air; they arise from the rapidly fading images of iconic memory, which act as "still photographs" of the perceptual scene. These images allow the visual sensations to be extended in time so that the brain can more efficiently process the physical message it receives.

Over 30 years ago psychology graduate student George Sperling (1960; also see Averbach & Coriell, 1961) developed a clever set of procedures for studying the properties of iconic memory. Using an apparatus called a *tachistoscope*, which presents visual displays for carefully controlled durations, Sperling showed people arrays of 12 letters arranged in rows. For example:

X L W F

J B O V

K C Z R

The trails of light created by a whirling sparkler are caused by visual sensory memories, which act as "still photographs" of the perceptual scene.

The subject's task was a simple one: Look at the display and then report the letters. But presentation time was extremely brief—the display was shown for only about 50 milliseconds (1/20 of a second). Across several experiments, Sperling found that people could report only about 4 or 5 letters correctly in this kind of task. But more important, they claimed to see an image—an iconic memory—of the *entire* display for a brief period after it was removed from view.

Sperling considered these results puzzling: If all 12 letters get registered in this short-lived memory system, as the subjects claimed, why could they only report 4 or 5 letters correctly? He reasoned that there were two possibilities: First, despite what the subjects believe, recall might be limited because only 4 or 5 letters can actually be read from the display in such a short presentation time. Second, the entire display might be read and stored accurately, but its memory fades before subjects have time to report everything they've seen. Again, it was the second alternative that corresponded to what the subjects reported: People who participated in the task were convinced that they saw an image of the entire display but claimed that it faded before everything could be recovered for recall.

To test between these alternatives, Sperling devised a way to sample selectively from the icon. Rather than asking subjects to recall everything from the display, he asked them to report only the letters shown in a particular row. After the display was turned off, subjects heard a tone. If the pitch of the tone was high, medium, or low, the task was to report the top, middle, or bottom row of the display, respectively (see Figure 8.2). Sperling called this new condition *partial report* because only a portion of the display needed to be reported. Results from partial report trials were then compared to those from the original *whole report* condition, which required the recall of all 12 letters. As Sperling anticipated, performance improved dramatically in the new condition—subjects reliably reported almost all of the row letters correctly.

To appreciate Sperling's experiment, it's important to remember that subjects always heard the tone *after* the display had been turned off. There was no way to predict which of the three rows would be cued on a particular trial, so the entire display *must* have been available in memory after the letters were removed. Otherwise, people would have been correct on only one-third of the trials—those in which the cue tapped the row that they happened to be reading. Requiring recall

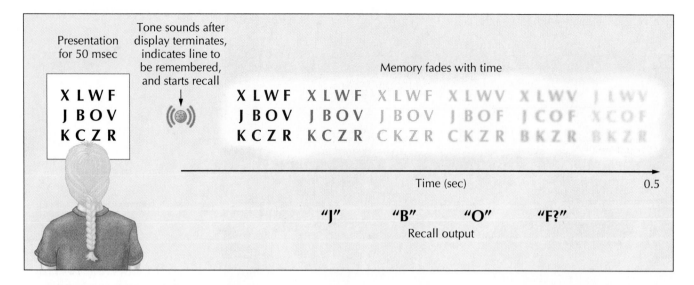

FIGURE 8.2

The Partial Report Technique. In the partial report technique, a tone sounds after presentation of the display, indicating which row of letters is to be recalled. As the subject attempts her recall, the visual "iconic memory" fades and becomes increasingly less accurate. But when recall of only part of the display is required, rather than the entire display, most of the relevant information can be reported before the image has been completely lost.

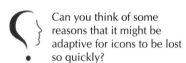 Can you think of some reasons that it might be adaptive for icons to be lost so quickly?

of only a portion of the display, rather than the entire display, improved performance because it was possible for subjects to report the relevant information before the iconic image had completely faded. In further experiments, by delaying presentation of the tone, Sperling was able to measure how quickly the sensory memory was actually lost. He discovered that the fleeting image—the iconic memory—was indeed short-lived; it disappeared in about a half-second.

In the years since Sperling first developed his "partial report" technique, psychologists have discovered that performance in this task is more complex than Sperling first thought. Considerable debate has centered on exactly what subjects "forget" from iconic memory after the half-second or so delay. Current evidence indicates that people may perform poorly after a delay because they become confused about *where* items were presented in the display (Yeomans & Irwin, 1985). Thus, information is not "lost" from iconic memory in the way that a television picture is lost after the set is turned off; instead, the image becomes more inexact—subjects may simply forget the item's spatial location (its row) rather than the item itself (Greene, 1992).

Echoic Memory. Psychologists assume that separate sensory memory systems exist for each of the sensory modalities. In the auditory system, for example, there is a lingering *echo,* or **echoic memory.** Pure sounds can be maintained for brief intervals to enhance auditory perception. In Chapter 5, we described how the brain can calculate the differences in arrival times between the two ears and use this information to help localize the sound. But in order to compare arrival times, the first sound needs to be retained until the second one arrives; echoic memory may help fill the gap. Echoic memory also probably plays a key role in language processing, perhaps to help retain exact replicas of sounds during sentence and word processing (Crowder, 1976; Nairne, 1990). Although echoic memory is also short-lived, it is believed to last quite a bit longer than iconic memory. Whereas icons last for only a half-second or so, in the absence of interference from other sounds echos may last for as long as 5–10 seconds (Cowan, Lichty, & Grove, 1990).

Short-Term Memory: The Inner Voice

The function of sensory memory is to maintain a relatively exact replica of the environmental message, for a short period, as an aid to perceptual processing. But sensory memory plays little role in the conscious *experience* of the immediate present; instead, internal thoughts and feelings are represented as short-term memories. Short-term memory is the system we use to temporarily store, think about, and reason with information. The term "working memory" is sometimes used because this temporary storage system often acts as a kind of mental scratchpad, allowing us to store the components of a problem as we work toward a solution (Baddeley, 1992; Nairne, 1996).

Unlike sensory memories, short-term memories are not brief replicas of the environmental message. They consist instead of the by-products, or end results, of perceptual analyses. Consider the letters M O N E Y. In this case, the environmental message is visual. Electromagnetic energy bounces off the page, enters through the eyes, and is processed visually. But internal thoughts are not about curves, straight lines, or letters. Our thoughts are likely to be about what the message stands for—in this case, a word that has meaning. Notice as well that components of the internal experience tend to resemble a kind of inner *voice*. You can repeat the word MONEY silently to yourself, either quickly or slowly, and if you desire, you can even insert internal pauses after each repetition. There is nothing visual about this repetition process—you have *recoded*, or translated, the visual message into another form—a kind of "inner voice."

The notion that people often use an inner voice to store information over the short term is supported by the types of errors that people make during short term recall. When recollecting from short-term memory, subjects invariably make errors that are acoustically based. Mistakes tend to *sound* like correct items even when the stimulus materials have never actually been presented aloud (Conrad, 1964; Hanson, 1990). For example, suppose that you're given five letters to remember— B X R C L—but you make a mistake and misremember the fourth letter. Researchers have found that in a case like this, your error will probably be a letter that sounds like the correct one, so you may incorrectly remember something like T or P. Notice that C and T and P all sound alike, but they *look* nothing alike. It is believed that errors tend to be acoustic because people recode the original visual input into an inner voice rather than an inner "eye" (see Figure 8.3).

Short-term memories are typically stored via this inner voice, but people are capable of representing information internally in a variety of ways. For example, information is sometimes stored over the short term in the form of visual

Short-term memories help people maintain information, such as telephone numbers, over relatively brief time intervals.

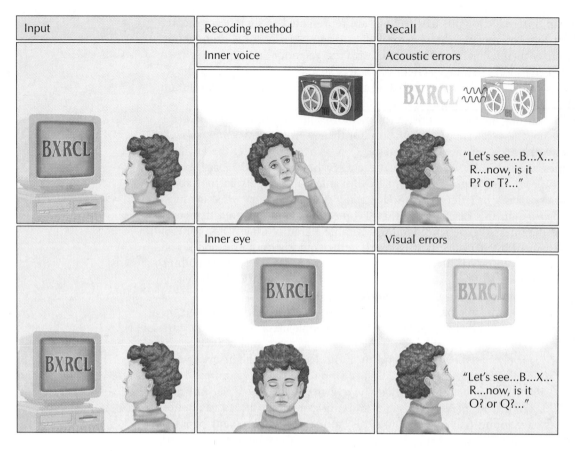

FIGURE 8.3
Recoding and Memory Errors.
Short-term memories consist of the by-products, or results, of perceptual analyses. People recode, or translate, the environmental message into other forms. The top row presents the normal case, in which the subject recodes the visually presented message into an "inner voice." Notice that recall "errors" are likely to sound like the letters that were actually presented. Alternatively, if to-be-remembered information is recoded into an "inner eye," shown in the bottom row, we would expect recall errors to be similar visually to the original message.

images (Baddeley, 1992). To illustrate, stop for a moment, close your eyes, and count the number of windows in your house or apartment. People usually perform this task by visualizing the rooms, one by one, and counting the number of windows that they "see." Nevertheless, psychologists believe that people tend to rely more on an inner voice, rather than an inner "eye," to remember things over the short term because they are often called on to interpret and produce spoken language. It makes sense to "think" in a way that is compatible with the way we communicate. Psychologists have also accumulated evidence indicating that it may be easier to store information about the temporal order of occurrence—which is also essential in language processing—when information is stored acoustically rather than visually (Glenberg & Fernandez, 1989; Hanson, 1990; Penney, 1989).

Short-Term Forgetting. It is possible to prolong short-term memories indefinitely by engaging in rehearsal, which is the process of internal repetition. (Think about the word *rehearsal* as re-*hear*-sal, as if listening to the inner voice.) Through rehearsal, the short-term memory system becomes an excellent tool for storing information, such as a telephone number you need to remember as you walk toward the phone. But to store things effectively, it's essential that you rehearse; in the absence of rehearsal, short-term memories are quickly lost (Atkinson & Shiffrin, 1968).

In a classic study, Lloyd and Margaret Peterson (1959) asked students to recall short lists of three letters (such as CLX) after delays that ranged from 3 to 18 seconds. The task sounds easy—remembering three letters for less than half a minute—but the experiment had an unusual feature: No one was allowed to

Input	Distraction interval, counting backward	Recall
Trial 1 — CLX	" . . . 391-388"	"C-L-X"
Trial 2 — FVR	" . . . 476-473-470"	"F-V-R"
Trial 3 — ZOW	" . . . 582-579-576-573"	"Z-W-O ?"
Trial 4 — LBC	" . . . 267-264-261-258-255"	"L-B- ?"
Trial 5 — KJX	" . . . 941-938-935-932-929-926"	"K- ? - ?"
Trial 6 — MDW	" . . . 747-744-741-739-736-733-730"	"? - ? - ?"

```
        0    3    6    9   12   15   18
                  Time (sec)
```

FIGURE 8.4
The Petersons' Distractor Task.
On each trial, subjects were asked to recall three letters, in correct order, after counting backward aloud for a period lasting from 3 to 18 seconds. The longer the subjects counted, the less likely they were to recall the letters correctly.

rehearse, or think about, the letters during the delay interval. To prevent rehearsal, the participants were required to count backward by threes aloud until a recall signal appeared. Under these conditions, the students forgot the letters very quickly; they were reduced to guessing after about 10 to 15 seconds of counting backward (see Figure 8.4).

More recent evidence suggests that the Petersons' task actually underestimates how quickly information is forgotten from short-term memory. When subjects are trying to remember material, as in the Petersons' experiment, they are sometimes able to "cheat" by rehearsing and counting backward at the same time (although it's difficult to do). If the task is redesigned so that everyone is induced to believe that the contents of short-term memory will *not* be tested but then a surprise test is given, information is forgotten after only a second or two (Muter, 1980; Sebrechts, Marsh, & Seamon, 1989).

Why is information forgotten so rapidly in the absence of rehearsal? This is a rather difficult question to answer, and psychologists have proposed a number of different hypotheses. Some researchers believe that short-term memories are lost spontaneously with the passage of time, through a process called *decay,* unless those memories are kept active through rehearsal (Baddeley, 1992; Cowan, 1995). Other researchers believe that short-term forgetting is caused by *interference* from new information, or because people confuse current memories with past memories (Crowder & Neath, 1991; Keppel & Underwood, 1962; Nairne, 1990, 1996). A third possibility is that both decay and interference operate together to produce information loss. We'll return to the general question of what causes forgetting at a later point in the chapter.

Short-Term Memory Capacity. The fact that short-term memories are quickly forgotten has implications for the *capacity* (or size) of the short-term memory system. How much information can actually be stored over the short term? Short-term **memory span**—which is defined as the number of items that a person can recall in the exact order of presentation on half of the tested memory trials—is typically about seven plus or minus two items; that is, short-term memory span ranges between five and nine incoming items (Miller, 1956). It's easy to remember a list of four items, but quite difficult to remember a list of eight or nine items (which is one of the reasons why telephone numbers are seven digits long).

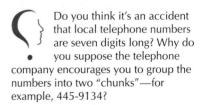

Do you think it's an accident that local telephone numbers are seven digits long? Why do you suppose the telephone company encourages you to group the numbers into two "chunks"—for example, 445-9134?

Some psychologists believe that the capacity of short-term memory is limited because it takes time to execute the process of rehearsal. To illustrate, imagine that you're asked to remember a relatively long list of letters arranged this way:

CA   TFL   YBU   G

First, try reading this list aloud, from C to G. You should find that several seconds elapse from start to finish. Now, imagine cycling through the list with your inner voice, as you prepare for short-term recall. It turns out that the C to G cycling takes a similar amount of time inside your head (Landauer, 1962).

Unfortunately, however, items stored in short-term memory are forgotten in a second or two, so the first part of the list tends to be forgotten during execution of the last. By the time you're finished with the last letter and return to the beginning of the list, the early items have already been dropped from memory. You can think about this relationship between forgetting and rehearsal as roughly analogous to an activity like juggling (see Figure 8.5). To juggle successfully, you need to win a battle against the unrelenting downward forces of gravity. You throw the dinner plates up, and gravity pushes them down. To prevent a plate from crashing, it's necessary to catch and toss it back up in the air before gravity runs it into the ground. Similarly, you need to return to the rapidly fading short-term memory trace and reactivate it through rehearsal before the "forces" of forgetting render the memory unobtainable. It's a race between two opposing forces—rehearsal and forgetting.

This means that there should be a close link between the rate of rehearsal (or internal speech) and the size of the memory span. The sooner the rehearsal cycle is completed and begun again, the less opportunity there will be for information loss. This relationship is supported by a number of experimental findings. For example, over the short term, it's more difficult to remember lists of long words (such as *conversation, rhinoceros*) than it is to remember lists of short words (such as *top, bat, sit*). It takes longer to cycle through a list of long words using the inner voice, so more of these items are likely to be forgotten (Baddeley, Thomson, & Buchanan, 1975; Schweickert, Guentert, & Hersberger, 1990). It also takes longer to count to ten in Arabic than it does in English. Consequently, people who speak

FIGURE 8.5
The Capacity of Short-Term Memory. The amount of information that can be stored in short-term memory depends on the process of rehearsal, which you can think of as roughly analogous to juggling. You need to return to each rapidly fading short-term memory trace, and reactivate it through rehearsal, before it is permanently lost or forgotten. Forming "chunks" from the to-be-remembered material makes it easier to rehearse and therefore increases the amount of information that can be retained.

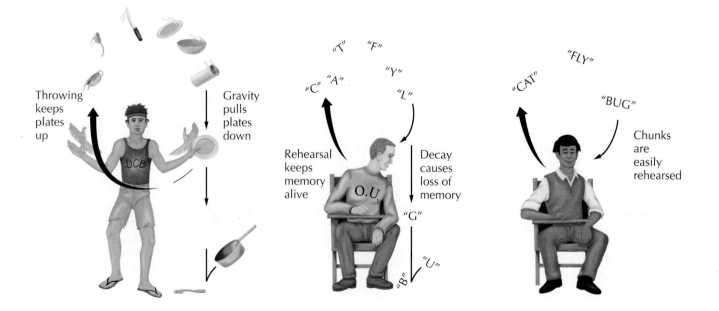

English can remember longer lists of digits over the short term than those who speak Arabic (Naveh-Benjamin & Ayres, 1986). Finally, children's ability to remember information over the short term improves with language development; as they learn to speak more fluently, their rate of rehearsal improves, which leads to an improved ability to recall information from short-term memory (Hitch & Halliday, 1983).

Chunking. As a general rule, memory span is roughly equal to the amount of material that can be internally rehearsed in about 2 seconds. To remember effectively over the short term, therefore, it's best to figure out a way to rehearse a lot of information in a short amount of time. One technique that can be used is **chunking,** which involves rearranging the incoming information into meaningful or familiar patterns called *chunks*. Remember that long list of letters presented earlier (CA TFL YBU G)? Perhaps you saw that the same list could be slightly rearranged:

CAT FLY BUG

Forming the letters into words drastically reduces the time it takes to repeat the list internally (try saying CAT FLY BUG over and over internally). Moreover, once you remember a word, prior knowledge allows you to recall the letters easily. The word becomes an extremely effective storage device for remembering the sequence of letters. Of course, the trick lies in finding meaningful chunks in what can appear to be a meaningless jumble of information.

The ability to create meaningful chunks, thereby improving memory span, often depends on how much you know about the material that needs to be remembered. Expert chess players can re-create most of the positions on a chessboard after only a brief glance—as long as a meaningful game is in session (Chase & Simon, 1973). They recognize familiar attack or defense patterns in the game, thereby creating easy-to-rehearse chunks of position information. Similar results are found when electronics experts are asked to remember complex circuit board diagrams (Egan & Schwartz, 1979). In both cases, if the materials are arranged in a more or less random fashion (for example, the chess pieces are simply scattered about the board), the skilled retention vanishes, and memory reverts to normal levels.

Expert chess players recognize familiar configurations in a chess game and can recreate them easily from memory (left); however, when chess pieces are arranged randomly on a board (right), which precludes the chunking of familiar patterns, experts show memory similar to novices.

Storing Information for the Long Term

Many of the processes used to store information over the short term also play a key role in the storage of information for the long term. Once material drops from short-term memory—the seat of conscious awareness—it becomes part of **long-term memory,** the system used to maintain information for extended periods. Exactly what enters long-term memory, as well as the durability of the information that is stored, depends on the processing activities used to encode the information for storage. To promote effective long-term storage, or at least to make stored material easy to recover, information must be encoded in certain ways during its initial presentation. In this section, we'll consider the kinds of encoding activities that lead to effective storage of information over the long term, but first we'll broadly look at the general kinds of information that are stored.

What Is Stored in Long-Term Memory?

When you take a test in one of your college courses, is the test tapping primarily episodic, semantic, or procedural memory?

Stop for a moment and think about your first kiss. The recollection (assuming you can remember your first kiss) is probably tinged with a measure of warmth, intimacy, and perhaps embarrassment. Do you remember the person's name, the situation, the year? Memories of this type, in which people recall some personal moment from their past, are known to psychologists as **episodic memories**—they are composed of particular events, or episodes, that happened to one personally. Most experimental research on remembering actually taps episodic memory. Participants are required to reproduce information that has occurred at some earlier point in the experimental session. The task is to remember an *event,* such as a word list, that forms a part of the personal history of the participant.

Now, think of a city in Europe that is famous for its fashion and fine wine. The correct response is *Paris,* but did you "remember" or "know" the answer? What about the square root of nine, or the capital city of the United States? These are certainly memories, in the sense that you have preserved and recovered the information from the past, but "remembering" these answers feels vastly different from remembering your first kiss. When you tap your meaningful knowledge about the world but make no reference whatsoever to particular episodes from your past, you are using what psychologists call **semantic memory** (*semantic* refers to "meaning"). It is through semantic memory that people record facts and remember the rules they need to adapt effectively in the world.

It's difficult to teach skills associated with procedural memory, like golf, because procedural memories tend to be inaccessible to conscious awareness.

Finally, try to remember how to tie your shoes, drive a car, or ride a bike. The knowledge about how to *do* things, to perform certain tasks, is called **procedural memory.** Most skills, including athletic prowess, rely on the establishment of procedural memories. Procedural memories differ from episodic and semantic memories in a fundamental way: They rarely produce any conscious experience of "remembering." Most people have a difficult time consciously reporting how to tie their shoes or ride a bike. Everyone can do these things, but people find it extremely

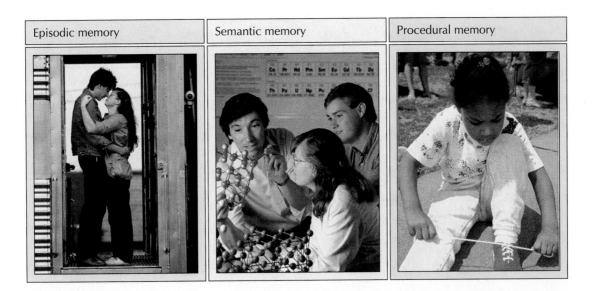

| Episodic memory | Semantic memory | Procedural memory |

FIGURE 8.6
Episodic, Semantic, and Procedural Memories. Psychologists generally distinguish among three types of long-term memories. *Episodic* memories are records of particular events, or episodes, that happen to one personally. *Semantic* memories reflect a person's general knowledge about the world, irrespective of his or her personal experiences. *Procedural* memories consist of knowledge about how to do things, such as tying shoelaces.

difficult to put the knowledge that they have into words. Procedural memories are among the simplest of all memories to recover, but, ironically, they are among the most difficult for psychologists to study—they seem inaccessible to conscious awareness (Tulving, 1983). For a summary of these memory types—episodic, semantic, and procedural—see Figure 8.6.

Elaboration: Connecting Material with Existing Knowledge

As a general rule, if you want to remember something over the long term, it helps to relate the material to your existing knowledge. Everyone houses an incredibly rich collection of information in long-term memory, stored as episodic, semantic, and procedural memories. This existing knowledge can be used to enrich, or elaborate, the material that you're trying to remember. Through **elaboration,** the process of relating input to other things, meaningful connections can be established that ease later recovery of the stored material.

In its simplest form, elaboration can involve just thinking about the *meaning* of information that you want to remember. In an experiment by Craik and Tulving (1975), people were asked questions about single words such as MOUSE. In one condition, the task required everyone to make judgments about the sound of the word (Does the word rhyme with HOUSE?); in another condition, the questions required thinking about the meaning of the word (Is a MOUSE a type of animal?). Substantially better memory was obtained in this second condition. Presumably, thinking about meaning, rather than sound, induces people to form more connections between presented events and other things in memory. The deeper and more elaborative the processing, the more likely that memory will improve (Craik & Lockhart, 1972).

You can also use your "mental database" to establish connections among the actual materials that need to be remembered, to organize what you need to learn. Suppose you were asked to remember the following list of words:

NOTES PENCIL BOOK NEWSPAPER MUSIC COFFEE

If you think about what the words mean and look for properties that the words have in common—perhaps things that you would take to a study session or a lecture—you are producing what psychologists call *relational processing*. Relational processing is a kind of elaboration, and it turns out to be an extremely effective strategy for promoting long-term retention (Hunt & Einstein, 1981).

Nonrelational processing	Relational processing

FIGURE 8.7

Relational Versus Nonrelational Processing. People often remember things better if they engage in relational processing, which means they relate to-be-remembered items together in some way, as in the panel on the right. The items on the memory list are placed into a rich and elaborate scene depicting a morning lecture. Relational processing can be contrasted with nonrelational processing, in which memory items are simply repeated or rehearsed individually (as on the left). Nonrelational processing usually leads to poor long-term memory.

Elaboration works because you are embellishing, or adding to, the stimulus input. If you're trying to remember the word PENCIL and you relate the word to an involved sequence of events depicting a morning lecture, you have created a richer and more elaborate memory record (see Figure 8.7). Later, when you try to remember this particular word, there are likely to be lots of cues that will help remind you of the correct response. Thinking about music, newspapers, drinking coffee—any of these can lead to the correct recall of PENCIL. You will also be better able to discriminate the correct memory record, when you think of it, from other things in memory that can interfere with the retrieval process.

Psychologists use the term **distinctiveness** to refer to how well the initial encoding processes have differentiated the event that needs to be remembered from other things in memory. If you simply encode the fact that PENCIL is a writing implement, you might incorrectly recall things like PEN, CHALK, or even CRAYON when tested. But if you specify the event's occurrence in some detail—we are talking about a yellow, Number 2 pencil, not some crayon—the memory record becomes *unique,* and thus easier to distinguish from other related, but not appropriate, material in memory. One of the common by-products of elaboration is a distinctive, and therefore easy-to-remember, memory record (Craik & Jacoby, 1979; Hunt & McDaniel, 1993).

Imagery: Remembering Through Visualization

Another way to produce an elaborative and distinctive memory record is to form a visual image of the material during its initial presentation. If you're trying to remember COFFEE, try forming a mental picture of a steaming hot, freshly brewed full mug. **Visual imagery** is the process used to construct an internal image, perhaps using the same brain mechanisms that are used to perceive events in the physical world (Farah, 1988). Forming mental pictures is an effective memory strategy because it naturally leads to elaborate, rich encodings. Mental pictures require people to think about the details of the material, and these details create a distinctive memory record.

If people think primarily in terms of an "inner voice," then why is visual imagery such an excellent tool for improving long-term memory storage?

Mnemonic Devices. Let's consider some encoding techniques, called *mnemonic devices,* that specifically make use of visual imagery and elaboration to

Although we've concentrated on how to use elaboration strategically, distinctive memory records are sometimes created automatically, even when no conscious attempt has been made to remember. **Flashbulb memories** are rich records of the circumstances surrounding emotionally significant and surprising events (Brown & Kulick, 1977). Flashbulb memories have been reported for such events as the assassination of John F. Kennedy, the attempted assassination of Ronald Reagan, the Space Shuttle *Challenger* disaster, and the start of the Gulf War. People who experience flashbulb memories are convinced they can remember exactly what they were doing when they first heard the shocking or surprising news. Playing in school, watching television, talking on the phone—whatever the circumstance, people report vivid details about the events surrounding their first exposure to the news. Do you remember what you were doing when you first heard the verdict in the O. J. Simpson trial? How about the tragic bombing of the Federal Building in Oklahoma City?

Some psychologists speculate that the high arousal levels produced by events of this type lead people to encode the surrounding events in a highly distinctive and elaborative manner. It's as if a giant "flash" goes off, burning the details surrounding the episode into people's brains. From an adaptive standpoint, it makes sense to propose that the brain is designed to remember significant events that might affect one's future ability to survive. Not all events are created equal from a survival perspective, and it is certainly in an individual's interest to remember the details that surround events that are of great personal significance.

Surprisingly, however, a number of reports have questioned the accuracy of this kind of memory. Neisser and Harsch (1992) asked college students one day after the Space Shuttle *Challenger* exploded to describe exactly how they first heard the news. The details were recorded, then three years later the same students were asked to recollect their experiences. Everyone

Do you remember what you were doing when you first heard about the tragic bombing of the Federal Building in Oklahoma City?

tended to be highly confident about their recollections, yet there was not much agreement between the original and the delayed memories. The students thought they were remembering things accurately, but the data proved otherwise. The fact that the memories were poor suggests that the psychological experience of flashbulb memories—that is, the strong conviction that one's memories are accurate—may be related more to the emotionality of the original experience than to the presence of a rich and elaborative memory record.

One factor that apparently needs to be considered is the *importance* of the event to the person doing the remembering. A study by Martin Conway and his colleagues (1994) looked at how well people could remember hearing about the resignation of the British Prime Minister Margaret Thatcher, which occurred in October of 1991. Within 14 days of the resignation, hundreds of participants around the world were asked by Conway and his research team to record the details of how and when they first heard the news. Only people who claimed to remember these details were allowed to participate. Two years later, everyone was tested again, and

the researchers discovered dramatic forgetting—but the forgetting occurred primarily for people who lived outside Great Britain. The British subjects remembered personal details about the event far more accurately than did subjects who lived in other countries. The resignation of the prime minister was clearly a more emotionally significant event to the British people; this factor may help to explain why the accuracy of their flashbulb memories was greater.

In many ways, the inaccuracies that have been found in recalling flashbulb memories are as interesting to memory researchers as the accuracies. As we'll see later in this chapter, people often misremember prior events yet think they're remembering things well. The reason is that an important part of remembering is based on *reconstruction* of prior events rather than literal reproduction. People tend not to store literal records of events in their brain; instead, they use their general knowledge to help them decide what must have occurred in a particular situation. This strategy is adaptive because it saves people from having to store minor details, but it can lead to inaccuracies in what they remember.

aid long-term remembering. **Mnemonic devices** (*mnemonic* means "pertaining to memory") are special mental tricks that help people think about material in ways that lead to effective everyday remembering. These devices were originally developed by the Greeks (Yates, 1966), so they've been around for a long time. As we describe each strategy in detail, look for ways to apply what you learn to your own practical memory problems.

One of the oldest mnemonic devices is the *method of loci* (*loci* is Latin for "places"). According to legend, the technique traces back to an ancient Greek named Simonides, who used it to identify the participants in a large banquet that had ended abruptly in tragedy. Simonides had apparently delivered a lecture at the banquet but was called away just before a portion of the building collapsed, killing many of the diners. To identify the bodies, Simonides formed a visual image of the room and used the seating assignments to reconstruct the guest list.

The method of loci, like most mnemonic devices, relies on visual imagery as its major encoding vehicle. The technique begins with the choice of some real-world pathway that is easy to remember, such as moving through the rooms in your house or along some familiar route to work or school. The to-be-remembered material—suppose that you wanted to remember a list of errands—is then systematically placed, in your mind, at various locations along the path. It's important to form a visual image of each memory item and to link the image to a specific location along the chosen route. So, if you wanted to remember to pay the gas bill, you might form a mental picture of a large check made out to the gas company and place it in the first location on your path (such as the entry hall in your house).

Depending on the size of your pathway, you can store a relatively large amount of material using this method. At the end of encoding you might have 15 different errands stored. Overdue library books might be linked to the living room sofa, clean shirts encased in plastic might be draped across the kitchen counter, or big bags of dog chow might be associated with a dog on the television screen (see Figure 8.8). To recover the material later, all you need to do is walk along the pathway in your mind, "looking" in the different locations for the objects that you've stored (Higbee, 1988). The method of loci is an effective memory aid because it forces you to use imagery—creating an elaborative and distinctive record—and the stored records are easy to recover because the storage locations are easy to access.

FIGURE 8.8
The Method of Loci. In the method of loci, to-be-remembered items are mentally placed in various locations along a familiar path. Here, the items have been placed along a pathway through a house. These items should be easy to remember because the use of visual imagery promotes an elaborate memory trace and because the stored locations are easy to access.

Number	Peg target	Interactive image
  "One is a bun"	"Return books"	
  "Two is a shoe"	"Buy dog food"	
  "Three is a tree"	"Pick up shirts"	

FIGURE 8.9
The Peg-Word Technique. In the peg-word technique, images of to-be-remembered material are linked visually to the images of specific rhyme cues, or pegs. Here, an image of a bun from the rhyme "one is a bun" is linked to an image of overdue library books, an image of a shoe is linked to an image of dog chow, and shirts are imagined to be hanging from a tree. The interactive visual image produces an elaborative memory trace, and the peg "cues" are easy to access.

The *peg-word method* is similar to the method of loci in that it requires you to link the to-be-remembered material to specific memory *cues,* but the cues are usually based on rhymes rather than specific mental pathways. Figure 8.9 shows one popular set of rhyme cues, or *pegs,* that can be used with this technique. The strategy, once again, is to link an image of the to-be-remembered material with an image of the peg. You might picture your overdue library books inside a hamburger bun, a bag of dog chow sitting inside a shoe, or some clean shirts hanging from a tree. To recover the memory records, you simply start counting, and the easily accessed peg word should lead you to the image of the to-be-remembered errand. One is a bun—return books; two is a shoe—buy dog chow; three is a tree—pick up shirts.

An alternative version of the peg-word method, called the *linkword system,* has been used successfully to assist in learning foreign language vocabulary (Gruneberg, Sykes, & Gillett, 1994). Suppose you wanted to remember the French word for rabbit (*lapin*). While studying, you should try to think of an English word that sounds like the French word; perhaps simply the word *lap* would do for *lapin.* Next, think about the meaning of the French word, and try to form a visual image of the result linked to the English rhyme. For example, you could imagine a white furry rabbit sitting in someone's lap. If you then see the word *lapin* later on a test, try thinking of the English rhyme, which should then act as a cue for bringing forth a remembered image of the rabbit (*lap* acts as a kind of peg word for rabbit). This method has been shown to produce nearly a doubling of the rate of learning for vocabulary words (Raugh & Atkinson, 1975).

FIGURE 8.10

Can You Recognize a Penny? Even though most people claim they can form an accurate mental image of a penny, they often have difficulty picking a "true" penny from a group of alternatives. Can you find the real penny in this display taken from the Nickerson and Adams (1979) experiment?

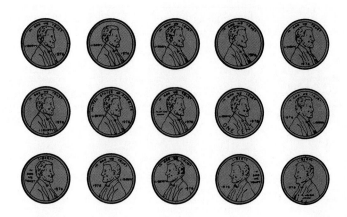

Are Visual Images Visual? Visual imagery helps memory, but are these mental "pictures" really visual? In other words, are the images produced through *remembering* similar to the images produced from *perception* (where the brain actually processes a message from the environment)? Over the past several decades, a substantial amount of research has been conducted trying to answer this question, primarily through an exploration of the psychological and neurological characteristics of mental images (Kosslyn & Koenig, 1992). Researchers have attacked the problem by focusing on questions such as the following: Do remembered images follow the same laws as images produced directly through perception? Do remembered and perceived images activate the same neural mechanisms and pathways in the brain? As you'll see, examination of these questions has produced some intriguing results.

Without looking, try forming a visual image of a penny or a quarter. You use coins daily, so this should be a fairly easy task. If you're like most people, you're probably convinced that you can form an accurate representation from memory of such an object. Now, try to reproduce the image on paper—simply draw the president depicted on the coin, which direction he is facing, and so on. Despite the apparent vividness of the image, it's likely that your performance will turn out to be mediocre at best. People are simply unable to reproduce the main features of the coin very accurately, despite the belief that they can "see" an accurate representation in their head. Even more surprisingly, it is difficult for people even to recognize the correct coin when it is presented along with incorrect versions of the coin. For a display like the one shown in Figure 8.10, fewer than half of the subjects are likely to pick out the right penny (Nickerson & Adams, 1979; for a British version of the experiment, see Jones & Martin, 1992). Certainly if you were looking at a coin, you would be able to trace the features accurately, so people's images—if they are, in fact, visual—are only fuzzy, relatively inaccurate representations of physical reality.

At the same time, there is a sense in which mental pictures do indeed "act visual." For example, try forming a visual image of a rabbit standing next to rat. Now ask yourself, does the rabbit in your image have whiskers? If I measure your reaction time, it turns out that you will answer a question like this more quickly if you imagine the rabbit standing next to a rat instead of an elephant (Kosslyn, 1983). This is exactly the kind of result we'd expect if you were looking at an actual picture—the larger the object is represented in the picture, the easier it is to "see." In another experiment by Stephen Kosslyn and his colleagues, people were asked to form a visual image of a map like the one depicted in Figure 8.11. Notice that there are certain landmarks in this map, including a lighthouse and a collection of huts. Once the image was formed, subjects were asked to focus on one of the

Once again, try counting the number of windows in your house. Is there any way you can perform this task without forming a visual image in your mind?

FIGURE 8.11
Scanning a Mental Image.
Kosslyn and his colleagues asked subjects to form an image of a map and then "scan" the image from one landmark to another. The time it took to complete the mental scan depended on the physical distances between landmarks on the actual map. The results suggested that people represent mental images "visually."

landmarks (such as the lighthouse) and then mentally "scan" to a second landmark (such as the huts) as quickly as possible. Kosslyn and his colleagues found that the time it took subjects to complete the scan depended on the physical distance between the landmarks on the map. The greater the distance between the locations, the longer it took subjects to complete the scan (Kosslyn, Ball, & Reiser, 1978). This suggests that subjects represented the spatial relations among the landmarks in their image in a way that mirrored the spatial relations on the map.

Additional data show that the same neurological mechanisms may actually be involved in both mental imagery and normal visual perception (Farah, 1988). For example, techniques that map the activity of brain regions have shown that imagery and perception activate the same regions of the occipital lobe (Kosslyn & Koenig, 1992). Other studies have indicated that people have trouble storing a visual image in their head while they are also performing a visually based tracking task, such as finding locations on a map (Baddeley & Lieberman, 1980). There are even brain-damaged patients who appear to have corresponding impairments in both imagery and visual perception (Levine, Warach, & Farah, 1985). For example, some patients whose brain damage has caused them to lose their color vision also have difficulty forming a colorful visual image. Data like these indicate that there may indeed be an important link between the brain systems involved in perception and those involved in mental imagery.

Factors of Presentation

The ability to remember information over the long term also depends on how the to-be-remembered events are actually presented over time. For example, if I give you a long list of items to remember, such as ten errands to complete, you will tend to remember the items from the beginning and the end of the list best, irrespective of whether you've used any of the mnemonic strategies that we've been discussing. This pattern is shown in Figure 8.12, which depicts how well each item is recalled as a function of its temporal, or serial, position in the list (this graph is often called a *serial position curve*). The improved memory for items at the start of the list is called the **primacy effect**; the end-of-the-list advantage is called the **recency effect.** Memory researchers believe that primacy and recency effects arise

FIGURE 8.12

The Serial Position Curve. When people are asked to recall a list of items, their performance often depends on the temporal, or "serial," position of the items in the list. Items at the beginning of the list are remembered relatively well—the primacy effect—and so are items at the end of the list—the recency effect.

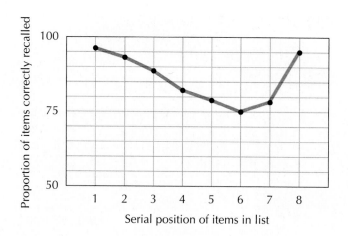

because items that occur at the beginnings and ends of a sequence are more naturally distinctive in memory and are therefore easier to recall (Murdock, 1960; Neath, 1993).

Another aspect of presentation that critically affects long-term retention is *repetition*: If information is presented more than one time, it will tend to be remembered better. The fact that repetition improves memory is not very surprising, but it might surprise you to learn that how you space those repetitions is extremely important. For instance, if you distribute the repetitions over time—a technique called **distributed practice**—you will remember the information better than if you mass all the repetitions together (*massed practice*). Practically, this means that all-night cram sessions in which you read the same chapter over and over again are not very effective study procedures. It's better to study a little psychology, do something else, and then return to your psychology. To the extent that you can engage in distributed practice, in which you put other activities between the repetitions of the material, your ability to remember the material over the long term will improve.

Given what you've learned about repetition and memory, do you think it's a good idea to have children learn arithmetic tables by rote repetition of the materials aloud?

Recovering Information from Cues

Can you still remember the memory list from a few pages back? You know, the one based on things that you might take to a morning lecture class? If you remembered the items, such as PENCIL, NOTES, and COFFEE, it's probably because you were able to use the common theme—things at a lecture—as a kind of *cue* to promote remembering. Most psychologists believe that *retrieval,* which is the process of recovering previously stored memories, is guided by the presence of cues, called *retrieval cues,* which are either generated internally (thinking of the lecture scene helps you remember PENCIL) or are physically present in the environment (a string tied around your finger).

Cue-Dependent Forgetting

A classic study conducted by Tulving and Pearlstone (1966) illustrates the critical role that retrieval cues play in remembering. Subjects were given lists to remember that contained words from a variety of meaningful categories (types of animals, birds, vegetables, and so on). Later, the participants were asked to remember the words either with or without the aid of retrieval cues. Half of the subjects were asked to recall the words without cues (a condition known as **free recall**); the other half were given the category names to help them remember (a condi-

Can you name all of your classmates from the fifth grade? Probably not, but your memory is sure to improve if you're given a retrieval cue in the form of a class photo.

tion known as **cued recall**). Subjects in the cued-recall condition recalled nearly twice as many words, presumably because the category names helped them gain access to the previously stored material.

Although these results may not seem surprising, they have important implications for how we need to think about remembering. Consider performance in the free-recall condition. Because these subjects performed so poorly, it's tempting to conclude that either they never learned or they forgot most of the items from the list. But the performance of the subjects who were cued shows that the poor memory resulted from a failure to *access* the relevant stored material. With the right retrieval cues, material that seems to have been lost, or never learned, can appear with striking clarity. For this reason, many memory researchers believe that most, if not all, instances of forgetting are really **cue-dependent forgetting.** The information, once encoded, is available somewhere in the brain; one simply needs the right kind of retrieval cues to gain access.

The Encoding-Retrieval Match

What conditions make retrieval cues effective? Psychologists believe that the effectiveness of a retrieval cue depends, in large part, on how well the cue *matches* the memory that was encoded. If you think about the sound of a word during its original presentation, rather than its appearance, then a cue that leads you to think about the stored sound will be more effective than a visual cue (some kind of rhyme might work). Similarly, if you think about the meaning of a word during study, then an effective cue will induce you to attend to an appropriate meaning during retrieval.

Let's consider an example. Suppose you were asked to remember the two words BANK and WAGON. You know about the effectiveness of elab-

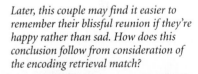

Later, this couple may find it easier to remember their blissful reunion if they're happy rather than sad. How does this conclusion follow from consideration of the encoding retrieval match?

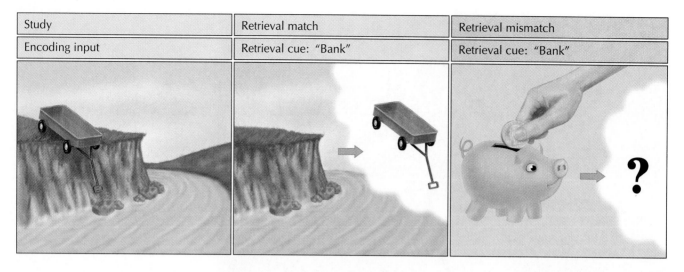

Study	Retrieval match	Retrieval mismatch
Encoding input	Retrieval cue: "Bank"	Retrieval cue: "Bank"

FIGURE 8.13

The Encoding-Retrieval Match. Memory often depends on how well retrieval cues *match* the way information was originally studied, or encoded. Suppose you're asked to remember the word pair BANK—WAGON; during study, you form a visual image of a wagon teetering on the edge of a river bank. When presented later with the retrieval cue BANK, you're more likely to remember WAGON if you interpret the cue as something bordering a river than as a place to keep money.

It's often difficult to remember the words of a song, or the events of a story, if you start in the middle. Given what you know about retrieval cues, why do you think it's best to always begin your recall from the beginning?

orate encodings, so you form a visual image of a WAGON perched precipitously on the BANK of a river (see Figure 8.13). Later, BANK is provided as a retrieval cue. Will it help you remember WAGON? Probably, but only if you interpret the retrieval cue BANK to mean a slope immediately bordering a river. If for some reason you think about the BANK as an attractive place to keep money, you probably will not recover WAGON successfully. A retrieval cue will be effective only if it you interpret it in the proper way. By "proper," psychologists mean that the cue needs to be interpreted in a way that matches the original encoding.

But it takes more than just a proper interpretation of the retrieval cue for it to be effective. According to the **encoding specificity principle,** a specific connection must also be formed between the cue and the to-be-remembered material at the time the material is studied (Tulving, 1983). For example, let's assume that you're asked to memorize the word NURSE. Later, you are given the word DOCTOR as a retrieval cue. DOCTOR and NURSE are naturally related, so you might think that presenting one would automatically help you remember the other. But presenting DOCTOR as a retrieval cue turns out to be effective for remembering NURSE only if the two words were encoded together during the original learning. If, for whatever reason, you fail to process DOCTOR while you are studying NURSE, DOCTOR will turn out to be a poor memory aid (Tulving & Thomson, 1973).

Transfer-Appropriate Processing

The encoding specificity principle asserts that for retrieval cues to be effective, they need to be encoded along with the to-be-remembered material. This means that if you want to remember something at a certain place and time, you need to pay close attention to the conditions that are likely to be present when you need to remember. You must engage in what psychologists call **transfer-appropriate processing;** that is, you need to study the material using the same kind of mental processes that will be required during retrieval. In other words, performance on a memory test will always depend on the match between the mental processes used during studying and the mental processes required by the test (Ellis & Hunt, 1993).

To illustrate, we've noted at various points in this chapter that elaboration—in which to-be-remembered material is related to other things—is a generally effective strategy for remembering. But the effectiveness of *any* encoding manipulation will depend on what kind of information is required by the memory test. Let's assume that you're asked to remember the word TUG (see Figure 8.14). If you form a visual image of a tugboat and you are then specifically asked about a tugboat on the memory test, you will probably perform well. But suppose you are

asked instead to remember whether the word TUG was printed in upper- or lower-case letters in the study materials. All of the elaboration in the world isn't going to help you unless you have specifically encoded the way the letters were shaped ("TUG," not "tug") during presentation. The lesson of transfer-appropriate processing is that you need to consider the nature of the testing environment before you can decide how to study most effectively.

On a practical level, then, this means that you should think about the characteristics of an exam *before* you sit down to study. An essay exam, for example, is a kind of *cued-recall* test—you are given a cue in the form of a test question, and you are required to recall the most appropriate answer. To study for such a test, it is best to practice cued recall: Make up questions that are relevant to the material, and practice recalling the appropriate answer with only the test question as a cue. For a multiple-choice test, which is a kind of *recognition test,* it is necessary to discriminate a correct answer from a group of incorrect answers (called *distractors*). The best way to study for a multiple-choice test is to practice with multiple-choice questions; either make up your own, or use the questions that are often available in study guides.

Do you ever say things to yourself like, "I'll just read the chapter one more time before I go to bed, and I'll ace the exam tomorrow"? Think about this reasoning from the perspective of transfer-appropriate processing—what exactly does the typical exam ask you to do? Exams don't measure the speed or fluency with which the chapter can be *read.* Most exams require you to recall or reproduce material in the presence of cues. Learn the material by reading the chapter, but prepare for the exam by doing the kind of thing that is required by the test. Practice reproducing the material by answering questions from memory, or practice discriminating correct from incorrect answers by responding to a variety of multiple-choice questions (Herrmann, Raybeck, & Gutman, 1993).

Reconstructive Remembering

Retrieval cues drive the memory process in much the same way that an incoming physical message drives the processes of perception. As you may recall from Chapter 5, what people perceive really depends on both the incoming environmental message and the expectations they hold about what's "out there." In a similar way, remembering depends on more than what is present in the physical environment (the retrieval cue)—beliefs and expectations can color an act of remembering just as they can color what people see and hear. Stop for a moment and try to remem-

FIGURE 8.14

Transfer-Appropriate Processing. It's useful to study material using the same type of mental processes that you'll be required to use when tested. Suppose you form a visual image of a to-be-remembered word during study (panel 1). If the test requires you to recognize an image of the word, you should do well (panel 2). But if the test asks how the word sounds (panel 3) or whether the word was presented originally in upper- or lower-case letters (panel 4), you're likely to perform poorly. You need to study in a way that is "appropriate" for the test.

According to the idea of transfer-appropriate processing, you should study for an exam using the same kind of mental processes required during the test.

ber what you had for breakfast two weeks ago. Maybe you skipped breakfast, or gulped down a quick bowl of cereal. It turns out, though, that what you "remember" is just as likely to correspond to habit as to actual fact. If you regularly eat a bowl of cereal in the morning, then eating cereal is what you are likely to recall, even if you broke the routine on that particular day and had a bagel.

Schemas. To understand why memory acts this way, you need to understand that long-term memory stores not only facts, but also relationships among facts. You know, for example, that houses contain rooms with walls, require insurance protection, and are susceptible to burning down if you're not careful. You know that 2-year-old children drool a lot, fall down, and put things into their mouths. These large clusters of related facts are organized into knowledge structures called **schemas.** A schema can be based on just about anything—a person, a place, or a thing. Schemas can even be about routines or systematic activities, such as going to a restaurant, visiting the local urgent care center, or following daily eating habits. When you remember, you use these organized knowledge packages to help reconstruct the past. For example, if it's unclear what you ate two weeks ago, it must have been cereal because cereal is what you usually eat for breakfast.

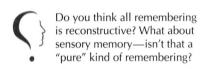
Do you think all remembering is reconstructive? What about sensory memory—isn't that a "pure" kind of remembering?

One interesting feature of schema-based remembering is that people are not usually aware that schematic information is influencing what they remember. Memories can be completely wrong, yet individuals will remain convinced that their memories are accurate (remember our earlier discussion of flashbulb memories?). In a well-known experiment conducted over 60 years ago, Sir Frederick Bartlett asked English undergraduates to read an unfamiliar North American Indian folk tale about tribe members who traveled up a river to engage in battle with some warrior "ghosts" (the story's title was "The War of the Ghosts"). In recalling the story some time later, the students tended to distort facts, omit details, and fill in information not included in the original version. For example, familiar things were substituted for unfamiliar things—the word *boat* was substituted for *canoe;* "hunting seals" was replaced with "hunting beavers." Because these things were not actually in the story, Bartlett's subjects must have used their prior knowledge to influence what they remembered—even though they were convinced they were remembering the material accurately (Bartlett, 1932).

In a study demonstrating the same point, Loftus and Palmer (1974) showed undergraduates a short film depicting an automobile accident. Later, when questioned about the film, the students were asked to estimate the speed of the cars just prior to the accident. What varied across the experimental groups was the nature of the question asked. Some students were asked to estimate how fast the cars were going when they *smashed* into each other; others were asked how fast the cars were going when they *contacted* each other. Notice the difference between the words *smashed* and *contacted*—the schema for *smashed* implies that the cars were traveling at a high rate of speed, whereas *contacted* suggests that the cars were moving slowly. As shown in Figure 8.15, subjects who heard the word *smashed* in the query estimated that the cars were traveling about 42 miles per hour; subjects in the *contacted* group gave an estimate about 10 miles per hour slower.

These results indicate that memories are importantly influenced by *top-down processing.* Expectations, which are driven by prior knowledge, strongly influence a person's memory for the actual event. Thus, everyone in the Loftus and Palmer experiment saw the same film, but different recollections were produced by manipulating the subjects' expectations in the testing phase. In addition to giving estimates of speed, some subjects were asked whether any broken glass was present in the accident scene. When *smashed* was used in the speed question, subjects were much more likely to incorrectly remember seeing broken glass, even though there wasn't any in the original film. By asking the right kinds of questions during testing, it is possible to make people think they experienced things that did not occur. As Loftus (1979, 1991) has emphasized, these findings have important implica-

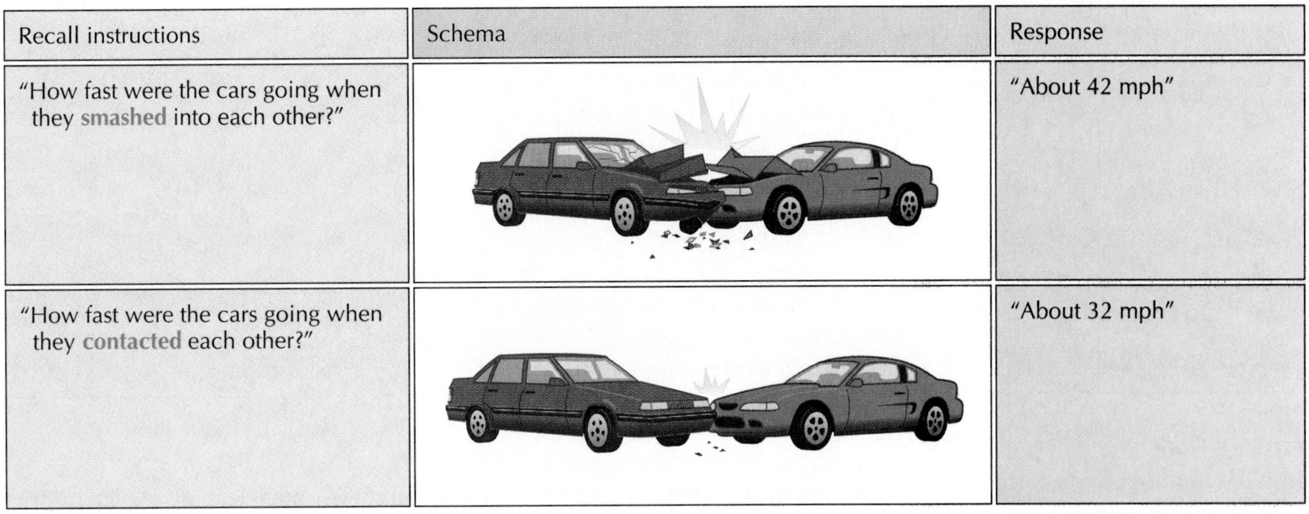

Recall instructions	Schema	Response
"How fast were the cars going when they smashed into each other?"		"About 42 mph"
"How fast were the cars going when they contacted each other?"		"About 32 mph"

FIGURE 8.15
Schema-Based Remembering.
Loftus and Palmer (1974) found that students would "remember" cars traveling at a faster rate of speed when retrieval instructions used the word *smashed* instead of *contacted*. All subjects had seen the same film, but their different schemas for the words *smashed* and *contacted* presumably caused them to reconstruct their memories differently.

tions for eyewitness testimony. Caution must be exercised in interpreting the testimony of any eyewitness—reconstructive factors can always be involved.

Overall, though, there is clearly adaptive value to schema-based reconstructive remembering. By relying on preexisting knowledge to "fill in the gaps," or to help interpret fuzzy recollections, people increase the chances that their responses in new environments will be appropriate—after all, the past is usually the best predictor of the future. People can also use their schematic knowledge to "correct" for any minor details they may have missed during the original exposure. If you already have a pretty good idea of what goes on during a visit to a fast-food restaurant, your mind doesn't need to expend a great deal of effort attending to details the next time you enter a McDonald's. You can rely on your prior knowledge to capture the "gist" of the experience, even though, on the down side, you may recollect a few things that didn't actually happen.

Remembering Without Awareness: Implicit Memory

Up to this point, we've concentrated on conscious, willful acts of remembering; that is, we've only considered instances in which someone is trying to remember something—such as what they ate for breakfast or the words from a memory list. But people often remember things without conscious intent or awareness. They produce spoken language, walk to work, recognize someone they know—all things that require memory, but not situations in which people are usually explicitly trying to remember anything.

Psychologists use the term **implicit memory** to refer to this kind of remembering (Graf & Schacter, 1985; Roediger & McDermott, 1993). It turns out that implicit memory—remembering without awareness—acts quite similarly to **explicit memory,** the name researchers use to describe conscious, willful remembering. Both implicit and explicit memory are critically influenced by retrieval cues in the environment. For instance, memory researchers have used the ability to solve word or picture fragment problems, such as the ones shown in Figure 8.16, as one way of testing implicit memory. The ability to complete these fragments is improved, or "primed," if individuals have encountered the solution word recently during reading (for example, the word fragment E_E__AN_ was easier to solve if the word ELEPHANT had been encountered in the prior 24 hours). But subjects didn't need to remember seeing the word. The improvement in performance was observed even if the prior exposure had never crossed their mind, which makes the remembering implicit rather than explicit. However, when solving a word fragment problem, if the earlier encounter was in the form of a picture instead of a

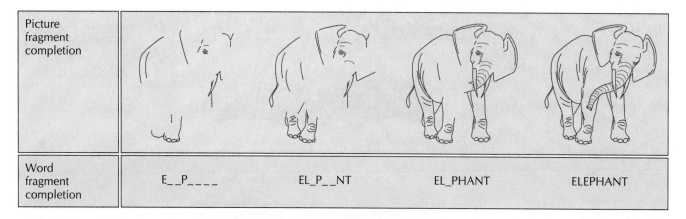

Picture fragment completion				

| Word fragment completion | E _ _ P _ _ _ _ | EL _ P _ _ NT | EL _ PHANT | ELEPHANT |

FIGURE 8.16

Implicit Memory Tests. Here are two examples of implicit memory tests. The subject's task in each case is to complete the picture or word fragment so as to identify the object shown on the far right. The fragments on the far left are meant to show cases in which the completion process would be difficult.

word—such as seeing a picture of an elephant—much less of a benefit was obtained (McDermott & Roediger, 1994; Weldon & Roediger, 1987). Once again, the conditions during testing needed to match the conditions present during the original exposure.

There are situations in which implicit memory appears to act somewhat differently from explicit memory. For example, processing strategies that typically improve conscious, willful remembering often have little or no effect on implicit memory (Roediger, Weldon, Stadler, & Riegler, 1992). If you elaborate material by thinking about its meaning, your ability to recall that information will improve on most explicit tests of memory, such as recall or recognition. But no similar improvements are usually found when memory is tested using an implicit test, such as solving word fragment problems (Graf, Mandler, & Haden, 1982). All that seems to matter is that the material be presented in a physically similar way during study and testing.

Memory Illusions. One of the more interesting features of implicit remembering is that prior experiences, when they affect behavior but are not consciously remembered, can lead to certain kinds of "memory illusions." *Déjà vu,* in which people feel a sense of familiarity about a location they've never before visited, is one example of such an illusion. The person may have encountered a similar location once before, producing a kind of automatic sense of familiarity, but he or she is unable to pinpoint the particular time and place consciously (see Jacoby & Witherspoon, 1982). A prior experience influences the person's behavior—producing a feeling of déjà vu—but the memory itself is beyond awareness.

In another kind of illusion based on implicit remembering, Larry Jacoby and his colleagues (1989) were able to induce people to think certain names were those of famous people when, in fact, the names were not. In step 1 of the experiment, subjects were shown a list of nonfamous names (such as Adrian Marr), which they were asked to remember. In step 2 of the experiment, a longer list was presented that contained three types of items: (a) slightly famous names (such as Minnie Pearl), (b) nonfamous names that were presented on the initial memory list, and (c) nonfamous names that were new to the experiment. For this second list, the task was simply to make a judgment about whether each name was famous. The researchers found that subjects were more likely to think a nonfamous name, such as Adrian Marr, was famous if the name had been part of the earlier memory list. But this "false fame effect" occurred only if the participants failed to recognize the name as having been presented in step 1. The first exposure "tricked" the subjects into thinking the name was famous—probably because the name now seemed "familiar"—but the trick worked only if the subjects could not explicitly remember having seen the name before in the experiment.

Can you think of any ways that advertising agencies might be able to use "memory illusions" to improve the image of a product?

A prior experience can influence a person's behavior, producing a feeling of déjà vu, even though the memory of that prior experience is beyond awareness.

The false fame effect illustrates how prior experience can affect people in ways that escape awareness. Prior experience can make something seem familiar, but if people cannot remember the specific time or place they encountered the person or object, they can draw erroneous conclusions. Such a process might well account for instances of *cryptomnesia,* or unintentional plagiarism (Brown & Murphy, 1989; Taylor, 1965). Have you ever discovered that one of your "great ideas" was actually suggested to you some time previously by one of your friends? Or perhaps that you had read the idea in a magazine or a book? These are instances in which you have been affected by a prior experience in ways that you cannot consciously remember. The stored memory is affecting your behavior, but the "remembering" is occurring without conscious awareness.

Updating Memory

Like other storage devices, the mind is susceptible to clutter. Effective remembering often hinges on whether you can successfully discriminate one occurrence from another—you need to remember where you parked your car *today,* not yesterday. You need to remember a current phone number, not some previous one. What if you felt the urge to buy two dozen paper cups every time you entered the grocery store because one time last year you needed paper cups for a party? **Forgetting,** the loss in accessibility of previously stored material, thus becomes one of the most important and adaptive attributes of the human memory system.

If you need further convincing that forgetting is adaptive, consider the strange case of a Russian journalist, known as S., who possessed an extraordinary ability to remember. It seems that S., through a fluke of nature, reacted automatically to stimuli in a way that formed unusual and distinctive encodings. When presented with a tone pitched at 500 hertz, for example, S. reported seeing "a dense orange color which made him feel as though a needle had been thrust into his spine" (Luria, 1968, p. 24). For a 3000 Hz tone, S. claimed that it "looks something like a firework tinged with a pink-red hue. The strip of color feels rough and unpleasant, and it has an ugly taste—rather like that of a briny pickle" (p. 24).

S. had a remarkable memory—he could remember grids of numbers perfectly after 15 years—but he suffered a near fatal flaw: He simply could not forget. He had trouble reading books because words or phrases so flooded his mind with previous associations that he had great difficulty concentrating. He would note, for example, small errors in the text: If a character entered the story wearing a cap

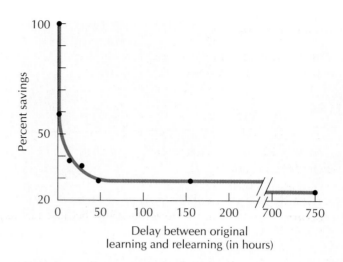

FIGURE 8.17

The Ebbinghaus Forgetting Curve. The German philosopher Hermann Ebbinghaus learned lists of nonsense syllables and then measured how long it would take to relearn the same material after various delays. Shown here are the percent "savings" found after the delays. (50% savings means it took half as long to relearn the list as it did to learn the list originally; 0% savings means that it took as long to relearn the list as it did to learn the list originally.)

and in later pages was described without a cap, S. would become greatly disturbed and disappointed in the author. He had trouble holding a job, or even a sustained conversation. For S., the failure to forget produced a truly cluttered mind.

The Time Course of Forgetting

For most people, once an item has left the immediate present, it is forgotten in a regular and systematic way. How quickly an item is forgotten depends on several factors: how the item was initially encoded, whether it was encountered again at some later time, and the kinds of retrieval cues that are present at the point of remembering. But in general, forgetting usually proceeds in a fashion that resembles the curve depicted in Figure 8.17. Most of the forgetting occurs early, but the person continues to forget gradually for a long period following the initial exposure (Wixted & Ebbesen, 1991).

The forgetting curve shown in Figure 8.17 is taken from some classic work by the German philosopher Hermann Ebbinghaus, who was one of the first researchers to investigate memory and forgetting systematically (Ebbinghaus, 1885/1964). Isolated in his study, he forced himself to learn lists of nonsense syllables (such as ZOK) and then measured how long it took to relearn the same material after various delays (his technique is called the *savings method*). As the graph shows, the longer the delay after original learning, the greater effort Ebbinghaus had to spend relearning the list. The systematic characteristics of the Ebbinghaus forgetting function—a rapid loss followed by a more gradual decline—are typical of forgetting in general. Similar forgetting functions are obtained for a variety of materials, and even for complex skills such as flying an airplane (Fleishman & Parker, 1962) or performing cardiopulmonary resuscitation (McKenna & Glendon, 1985).

A number of investigators have verified that even memories for everyday things, such as the names of high school classmates or the educational material learned in school, are forgotten in regular and systematic ways. In one study, Bahrick (1984) examined the retention of a foreign language (Spanish) over intervals that ranged from about 1 to 50 years. In another study, Bahrick and Hall (1991) examined the retention of high school mathematics over 50 years. In both cases, there was evidence for the rapid loss of recently learned material, followed by more gradual loss, but a considerable amount of knowledge was retained indefinitely. What's surprising about these studies is that a fair amount of the knowledge remained, even though the participants claim to have not rehearsed or thought about the material in over half a century.

Hermann Ebbinghaus (1859–1909).

The Mechanisms of Forgetting

We can agree that it is adaptive to forget, and we can measure the rate at which information becomes unavailable over time, but what are the main psychological mechanisms that produce the information loss? As we discussed earlier, most current memory researchers believe that forgetting is cue dependent—individuals fail to remember a prior event because they don't have access to the right retrieval cues. But for many years, psychologists were convinced that memories simply fade with the passage of time, in accordance with a "law of use" (Thorndike, 1914). If people fail to practice a learned habit, such as playing the piano, the habit fades, or *decays,* spontaneously with time.

As the analysis of memory gained sophistication, however, psychologists recognized that **decay**—the idea that memories fade just because of the passage of time—cannot explain most forms of forgetting. For one thing, as we've seen, memories that appear to have been lost can reappear under the right retrieval conditions. In addition, people often remember trivial things (such as a joke) for years but forget important things that once received a great deal of practice (such as elementary geometry). Even more significant, psychologists realized that just because memories are lost with time doesn't mean that *time* alone is causing the forgetting. A nail left outside becomes rusty with time, but it is not the passage of time that creates the rust—processes other than time (oxidation, in the case of the rusty nail) actually produce the changes.

Interference. In forgetting, the "other processes"—which are correlated with the passage of time but are not created by time—seem to depend on the establishment of other memories. After learning, a person learns new things, and these new memories compete, or *interfere,* with recovery of the original material. When you get a new apartment, you strive to associate your telephone with a new phone number. But after you succeed, it becomes more difficult to retrieve your old number, even if you actively try to remember. The retrieval cue "telephone number" has now become associated to something new; as a result, it loses its capacity to elicit the old number. Psychologists use the term **retroactive interference** to refer to cases in which the formation of new information hurts the retention of previously acquired material.

In a classic study of retroactive interference, Jenkins and Dallenbach (1924) asked two students from Cornell University to live in a laboratory for several weeks and learn lists of nonsense syllables either just before bed or early in the morning. The students were tested 1, 2, 4, or 8 hours after learning. The results, which are shown in Figure 8.18, were clear: When the students slept during the delay

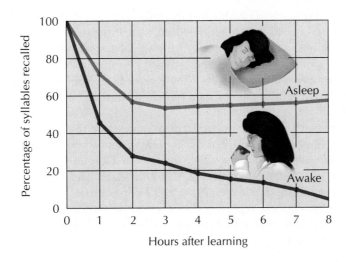

FIGURE 8.18
Interference and Memory. The activities that occur after learning affect how well information is remembered. In this study by Jenkins and Dallenbach (1924), the students showed better memory if they slept during the retention interval than if they remained awake. Presumably, the waking activities *interfered* with the learning.

interval, they remembered more than when they remained awake. Note that a constant amount of time passed in both conditions, so a decay theory would predict no differences between the conditions. The findings suggest that it was the activities that occurred during the students' waking hours that produced the information loss. When awake, the students formed new memories, which interfered with recovery of the old material.

But it is not just the learning of new information that produces forgetting. Previously learned information can also produce interference. **Proactive interference** occurs when old memories interfere with the establishment and recovery of new memories. If I try to teach you to remember the word DEATH every time you see the word HAPPY, you can see how prior associations might interfere with the learning process. Seeing the word HAPPY causes you to think of many things that are inconsistent with DEATH. To consider another example, suppose as part of an experiment you're asked to think of PENCIL as a potential weapon to be used in combat. You might be able to think about the word in this way for the experiment, but as time passes you will almost certainly revert back to thinking about PENCIL in the usual way. You might find it difficult to remember PENCIL as a weapon because the word has been used in a different way so many times before. Prior knowledge interferes with the learning and retention of the new material.

Most memory researchers believe that "interference" is the main cause of forgetting, although it's conceivable that "decay" might operate in certain situations, such as when people remember over the very short term—that is, in sensory memory and short-term memory (Cowan, 1995). It's also possible that when people learn new material, older memories are "overwritten" and permanently lost (Loftus & Loftus, 1980). But generally, people don't *lose* material with time; the material simply becomes harder to access because other things compete and interfere with the retrieval process. As new memories are encoded, old retrieval cues become less effective because those cues are now associated with new things. New experiences can also affect how people interpret retrieval cues that are available, rendering those cues less effective. Successful retention depends on retrieval cues that help discriminate one kind of memory from another. If a particular cue is associated with many things, that cue will not "guide" the rememberer uniquely to the relevant stored material. Once again, you can see why elaboration is an effective strategy for remembering. If the original event is encoded in an elaborative and distinctive way, the memory record is less likely to be subject to competition from other remembered events.

Motivated Forgetting

In our earlier discussion of flashbulb memories, we suggested that highly unusual or emotional events might sometimes lead to distinctive, and therefore easy to remember, memory records. The adaptive value of a system that "stamps in" significant events is easy to understand—remembering such events could increase the ability to survive. But what about those cases in which it is adaptive to *forget* something, such as a traumatic instance of child abuse or the witnessing of a violent crime?

The idea that the mind might actively repress, or inhibit, certain memory records is an important ingredient of Sigmund Freud's psychoanalytic theory, as you'll see when we discuss personality theories in Chapter 12. Freud introduced **repression** as one "defense mechanism" that individuals use, unknowingly, to push certain threatening thoughts, memories, and feelings out of conscious awareness. According to Freud, these repressed memories retain the capacity to affect behavior at an unconscious level but cannot be "remembered" in the conventional sense. The result to the behaving human is a reduction in the experience of anxiety.

Do you think it's possible that one of the reasons most adults can't remember things from early childhood is that they think about the objects in the world differently, thereby reducing the effectiveness of these objects as retrieval cues?

People recall more pleasant than unpleasant experiences, perhaps because they're reluctant to think about and rehearse unpleasant experiences.

Modern researchers acknowledge the occurrence of retrieval failure, but they remain undecided about the scientific validity of repression. On the one hand, it's clear that people typically recall more pleasant than unpleasant events (Linton, 1975; Wagenaar, 1986). Painful experiences, such as the pain associated with childbirth, also seem to be recollected less well with the passage of time (Robinson and others, 1980). There are also countless instances, reported mainly in clinical settings, of what appears to be the repression of traumatic experiences. But at this point, it's unclear whether these memory failures require us to appeal to the action of an unconscious psychological process such as repression.

For example, it's possible that people remember more positive events because these are the types of events that they rehearse and relate to others. Moreover, the fact that people forget painful experiences with the passage of time does not mean that repression is involved—many things are forgotten with the passage of time, especially those things that are unlikely to be rehearsed. It's also important to remember that recall processes are reconstructive. There is considerable evidence suggesting that people like to cast themselves in a positive light—individuals often remember donating more to charity than they actually did, or that they raised more-intelligent children (Cannell & Kahn, 1968; Myers & Ridl, 1979). Many instances of apparent retrieval failure, then, might be attributed to the reconstructive "recasting" of prior experiences rather than to the active repression of intact memories (see Loftus, 1993). We'll return to the issue of repression when we discuss the treatment of psychological disorders in Chapter 15.

Physically Based Forgetting

To explain the instances of forgetting that we've encountered up to this point, we've appealed largely to the actions of normal, adaptive psychological processes. But forgetting can also be caused by physical problems in the brain, such as those induced by injury or illness. Psychologists typically use the term **amnesia** to refer to forgetting that is caused by some kind of physical problem. (There is another type of amnesia that is psychological in origin—it arises from something called a dissociative disorder—but we'll delay our discussion of this kind of forgetting until Chapter 14.)

Types of Amnesia. There are two major kinds of physically based amnesia: retrograde and anterograde. *Retrograde amnesia* is defined as memory loss for events that happened *prior* to the point of injury (you can think of *retro* as meaning backward in time). People who are in automobile accidents, or who receive a sharp blow to the head, often have trouble remembering the events leading directly up to the accident. The memory loss can apply to events that happened only moments before the accident, or the loss can be quite severe; in some cases, patients lose their ability to recall personal experiences that occurred years before the accident. In most cases, fortunately, these memory losses are not permanent and recover slowly over time (Cermak, 1982).

Anterograde amnesia is defined as memory loss for events that happen *after* the point of physical damage. People who suffer from anterograde amnesia, as we noted at the beginning of this chapter, live in a kind of perpetual present—they are incapable of forming memories for new experiences. The disorder develops as a result of brain damage, which can occur from the persistent use of alcohol (a condition called *Korsakoff's syndrome*), from brain infections (such as viral encephalitis), or, in some cases, as a by-product of brain surgery. One of the most thoroughly studied amnesic patients, known to researchers as H. M., developed the disorder after surgery was performed to remove large portions of his temporal lobes. The purpose of the operation was to reduce the severity of H. M.'s epileptic seizures; the surgery was successful—his seizures *were* dramatically reduced—but anterograde amnesia developed as an unexpected side effect.

Over the past 25 years, considerable research has been directed at the problem of anterograde amnesia. Patients such as H. M. have been studied in great detail (Milner, 1966), and certain fundamental changes in our conceptions of amnesia have emerged. For example, it was originally believed that patients like H. M. fail to acquire new memories because some basic encoding (or acquisition) mechanisms have been destroyed. It is now clear, however, that these patients can, in fact, learn a great deal but must be tested in particular ways. If a patient like H. M. is tested indirectly, on a task that does not require *conscious* remembering, performance can approach or even match normal levels.

In one study, Jacoby and Witherspoon (1982) asked Korsakoff's patients with anterograde amnesia to learn auditorily presented homophones for a later memory test. Homophones are words that sound alike but have different meanings and spellings, such as READ and REED. To "bias" a particular interpretation for a given homophone, it was presented as part of a word pair, such as BOOK—READ or, in another condition, SAXOPHONE—REED. (Because the words were presented aloud, the only way to distinguish between the homophones READ and REED was through the accompanying context word BOOK or SAXOPHONE.) Later, the amnesics were asked to recognize the words but were unable to do so—they seemed to have acquired none of the presented information. But in a second test, the homophones were simply read aloud by the experimenter and the subjects' task was to provide the spelling. Surprisingly, if the amnesics had earlier received the pair BOOK—READ, they spelled the test homophone READ, but if the homophone had been paired with SAXOPHONE, they spelled it REED.

These results suggest that the presented homophones were "learned" by the amnesic patients. The way the subjects spelled the homophone during the test depended on the prior experience. Other experiments have revealed similar findings. For example, amnesics are more likely to complete a word fragment (such as E_E__AN_) correctly if they have seen the word before, but if asked to recall the word, their performance falls apart (Graf & Schacter, 1985). Patients who suffer from anterograde amnesia fail to retrieve past experiences whenever they must *consciously* recollect the experience; when the past is assessed indirectly, through a task that does not require conscious remembering, these amnesics often perform at normal levels.

Where Are Memories Stored? The study of brain-damaged individuals, such as Korsakoff's patients, has also encouraged researchers to draw tentative conclusions about how and where memories might be stored in the brain. We touched on this issue in Chapter 3, when we considered biological processes. At that point we paid special attention to a structure called the *hippocampus*, which most brain researchers believe is critically involved in the formation and storage of memories (Squire, 1992). Damage to the hippocampus, as well as to surrounding structures in the brain, leads to memory problems in a wide variety of species, including humans, monkeys, and rats. Areas surrounding the hippocampus also "light up" in a PET scan when subjects are asked to recall specific material (Raichle, 1994; Squire and others, 1992).

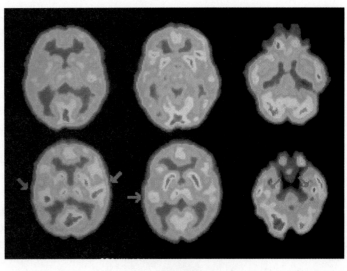

This PET scan shows regions of brain activity during auditory stimulation. The arrows are pointing to areas inside the temporal lobes that become active after words are heard; these same areas are thought to be associated with some kinds of memory.

But it is unlikely that any single brain structure, or group of structures, is exclusively responsible for all instances of remembering and forgetting. Things are vastly interconnected in the brain, and the activities of one part of the brain often depend on activities in other parts. For example, certain kinds of memory loss, such as those found in Alzheimer's disease, have been linked to inadequate supplies of neurotransmitters in the brain (Albert & Moss, 1992). Damage to a part of the brain that is involved in the production of a neurotransmitter could lead to inadequate functioning in another part of the brain that depends on that neurotransmitter. In sum, we still have a long way to go before we can draw anything but tentative conclusions about the physical basis of learning and remembering.

◢ SOLVING THE PROBLEMS: A SUMMARY

Time flows continuously, so experiences quickly leave the present and recede backward into the past. To understand the human capacity to preserve and recover this past, we considered some of the fundamental problems that memory systems help people solve.

▸ **REMEMBERING OVER THE SHORT TERM** First, to improve perception and aid ongoing comprehension, psychologists assume that people have internal processes that help them maintain information over the short term. In the case of sensory memory, people retain a relatively pure snapshot of the world, or replica of the environmental message. Sensory memories accurately represent the world as recorded by the sensory equipment, but they tend to be short-lived, lasting on the order of a few seconds or less. Short-term memory, in contrast, is the system used to store, think about, and reason with the message once it has undergone perceptual analysis. Items are typically maintained in short-term memory in the form of an "inner voice," and they are forgotten rapidly in the absence of rehearsal. The capacity, or size, of the short-term memory system is determined by a trade-off between the factors that lead to forgetting over the short term (either decay or interference) and the time-limited process of rehearsal.

▸ **STORING INFORMATION FOR THE LONG TERM** To promote the effective storage of information over the long term, the brain can actively process the environmental message in a number of ways to produce elaborate and distinctive memory records. Focusing on the meaning of the input, relating to-be-

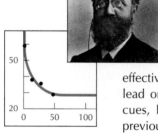

remembered information to other things in memory, and forming visual images of the input all lead to distinctive memory records that are easily discriminated from other things. Forming a visual image is particularly effective, and many memory aids, or mnemonic devices, are based on the use of imagery. In the peg-word method, for example, the idea is to form a visual image linking the to-be-remembered material to a set of specific memory cues; in the method of loci, the information is linked visually to a particular location or pathway. Long-term memory also depends on how information is actually presented: Items presented near the beginning and end of a sequence are remembered well, as are items that have been repeated. Spaced or distributed repetition turns out to be more effective than massed practice.

▶ **RECOVERING INFORMATION FROM CUES** Most memory researchers believe that successful remembering depends on having the right kinds of retrieval cues. Most forms of forgetting are probably cue dependent, which means that stored information is not really "lost," it simply is inaccessible because the appropriate retrieval cues are not present. Effective retrieval cues are those that *match* the conditions that were present during original learning. According to the encoding specificity principle, effective retrieval cues also need to be specifically encoded along with the to-be-remembered material. But when people recover information from cues, they also rely on their general knowledge. The past is often reconstructed, and we have seen how this reconstruction process can lead to adaptive, but sometimes inaccurate, recollections of the past.

▶ **UPDATING MEMORY** Forgetting is an adaptive process. If people did not constantly change and update their knowledge about the world, their minds would be cluttered with useless facts, such as where the car was parked last Wednesday. Although the psychological mechanisms of forgetting are still being investigated, it seems unlikely that long-term memories fade as a simple by-product of time. Rather, as people learn new things, previously learned material becomes harder to access because new memories compete and interfere with recovery of the old. Retrieval cues become less effective because they are associated with new things or because new experiences lead one to interpret retrieval cues in inappropriate ways. With the right kinds of cues, however—cues that discriminate one kind of occurrence from another—previously forgotten material becomes refreshed and available for use once again.

Terms to Remember

memory The capacity to preserve and recover information.

encoding The processes that determine and control the acquisition of memories.

storage The processes that determine and control how memories are stored and maintained over time.

retrieval The processes that determine and control how memories are recovered and translated into performance.

sensory memory The capacity to preserve and recover sensory information in a relatively pure, unanalyzed form; sensory memories are usually accurate representations of externally presented information and last on the order of seconds.

short-term memory A limited-capacity "working memory" system that people use to hold information, after it has been analyzed, for periods usually lasting less than a minute or two. Short-term memory is the system people use to temporarily store, think about, and reason with information.

rehearsal A strategic process that helps to maintain short-term memories indefinitely through the use of internal repetition.

iconic memory The system that produces and stores visual sensory memories.

echoic memory The system that produces and stores auditory sensory memories.

memory span The number of items that can be recalled from short-term memory in their proper presentation order on half of the tested memory trials.

chunking A short-term memory strategy that involves rearranging incoming information into meaningful or familiar patterns.

STORING INFORMATION FOR THE LONG TERM

long-term memory The system used to maintain information for extended periods of time.

episodic memory A memory for a particular event, or episode, that happened to one personally, such as remembering what one ate for breakfast this morning, or where one went on vacation last year.

semantic memory Knowledge about the world, stored as facts that make little or no reference to one's personal experiences.

procedural memory Knowledge about how to do things, such as riding a bike or swinging a golf club.

elaboration An encoding process that involves the formation of connections between to-be-remembered input and other information in memory.

distinctiveness A term used to refer to how well initial encoding processes have differentiated the to-be-remembered information from other things in memory.

flashbulb memories Rich memory records of the circumstances surrounding emotionally significant and surprising events.

visual imagery The processes used to construct an internal visual image, perhaps using the same brain mechanisms used to perceive events in the physical world.

mnemonic devices Special mental tricks that help people think about material in ways that improve later memory. Most mnemonic devices require the use of visual imagery.

primacy effect The better memory seen for items near the beginning of a memorized list.

recency effect The better memory seen for items near the end of a memorized list.

distributed practice Spacing the repetitions of to-be-remembered information over time.

RECOVERING INFORMATION FROM CUES

free recall A testing condition in which a person is asked to remember information without explicit retrieval cues.

cued recall A testing condition in which subjects are given an explicit retrieval cue to help them remember.

cue-dependent forgetting The idea that forgetting is caused by a failure to access the appropriate retrieval cue.

encoding specificity principle The idea that specific encoding processes determine which retrieval cues will be effective in aiding later memory.

transfer-appropriate processing The idea that the likelihood of correct retrieval is increased if a person uses the same kind of mental processes during testing that he or she used during encoding.

schema An organized knowledge structure in long-term memory.

implicit memory Remembering that occurs in the absence of conscious awareness or willful intent.

explicit memory Conscious, willful remembering.

UPDATING MEMORY

forgetting The loss in accessibility of previously stored material.

decay The proposal that memories are forgotten or lost spontaneously with the passage of time.

retroactive interference A process in which the formation of new memories hurts the recovery of old memories.

proactive interference A process in which old memories interfere with the establishment and recovery of new memories.

repression A defense mechanism that individuals use, unknowingly, to push threatening thoughts, memories, and feelings out of conscious awareness.

amnesia Forgetting that is caused by physical problems in the brain, such as those induced by injury or disease.

As psychologists continue to seek insight into the fundamental mechanisms of the mind, they're discovering, more and more, that effective answers often lie in nature itself, in the physical world that the human mind has evolved to understand. The adaptive mind is tuned to its environment—people think, react, and remember in ways that mirror, or reflect, the physical world in which they live. According to one recent perspective (Anderson, 1990; Anderson & Schooler, 1991), even basic memory processes, such as the ones that we've described in this chapter, may essentially be adaptive reactions to the way events occur and recur in everyday life. You are less likely to remember an experience with time because there is, in fact, a lower probability that you will *need* to remember

that experience with time. On the other hand, you may remember more recent events because it is important for your survival that you do so.

The Retention Function
In a provocative article, Anderson and Schooler (1991) provide some concrete examples of how people remember in ways that accurately reflect how events normally occur in the world. Remember the shape of the forgetting curve described earlier in this chapter? It's reproduced in the far-left panel of Figure 8.19. Notice that most of the forgetting occurs early after learning, but that forgetting proceeds for a long time after the original exposure. The middle panel of Figure 8.19 presents another curve, which looks strikingly similar to the

forgetting curve, but it is simply a record of how often particular words—such as the word *American*—appear in the headlines of the *New York Times* over time! To gather these data, Anderson and Schooler simply chose a set of words and then carefully recorded how often they appeared in the newspaper over a 100-day period. The middle panel presents the odds that any one of those words appeared in the headline on a particular day, day 101, as a function of how long it had been since the last occurrence of the word.

For instance, if the word *American* last appeared on day 80 and we look to see if the same word occurred again on day 101, there is only a small probability (about 0.03) that we're going to find it. But if the word appeared on day 100, the

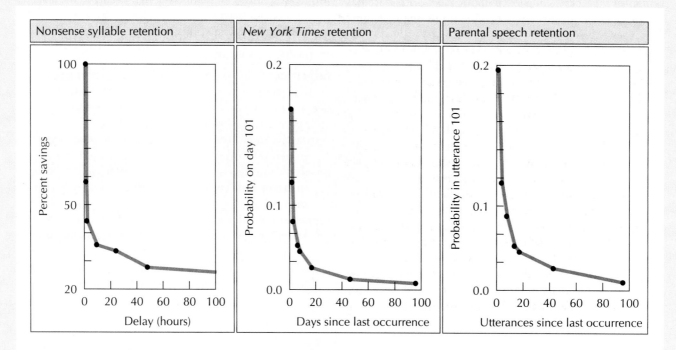

FIGURE 8.19
Reflecting the World. The graph on the far left shows the Ebbinghaus forgetting curve. The middle graph shows the likelihood that a particular word appeared in the headlines of the *New York Times* on day 101 as a function of how long it had been since the word previously occurred. The graph at the right shows the probability that a parent spoke a particular word in his or her 101st utterance to a child as a function of the last time the same word was used.

day before the test, the likelihood of it appearing again on day 101 shoots up dramatically. Anderson and Schooler found a similar pattern when they looked at how often parents use certain words when speaking with their young children. For example, imagine that a parent uses his or her child's name, "Kathy," one time in a series of 100 utterances. What's the probability that "Kathy" will then occur as the parent's 101st utterance? The far right panel in Figure 8.19 shows these probabilities as a function of where the critical word occurred in the initial sequence of 100 utterances. The data show that if the parent spoke the critical word as utterance 20, for example, it was

unlikely to occur again as the 101st utterance; but if the word had just been used, say as utterance 99, there was a high likelihood that it would occur again as utterance 101.

Adaptive Implications

What do these results mean? The data suggest that the human memory system may have evolved to respond optimally to the way events naturally occur and recur in the world. People remember recent events better than events from long ago because recent events are more likely to occur again in the immediate future. As time passes, there is less of a *need* to remember an event because the event is unlikely to occur again. The

human memory system is simply reflecting the way events are naturally distributed in the environment.

The Anderson and Schooler analysis becomes quite interesting when you consider that psychologists have spent a great deal of time and effort trying to understand the behavior of memory systems. What strange and complex internal machinery produces the regular shape of the forgetting curve? Part of the answer, it appears, can be found not by looking inward at the mind and brain, but rather by looking outward at the world. The human memory system, like the adaptive mind in general, reflects the world and behaves in a fashion that mirrors the behavior of the world itself.

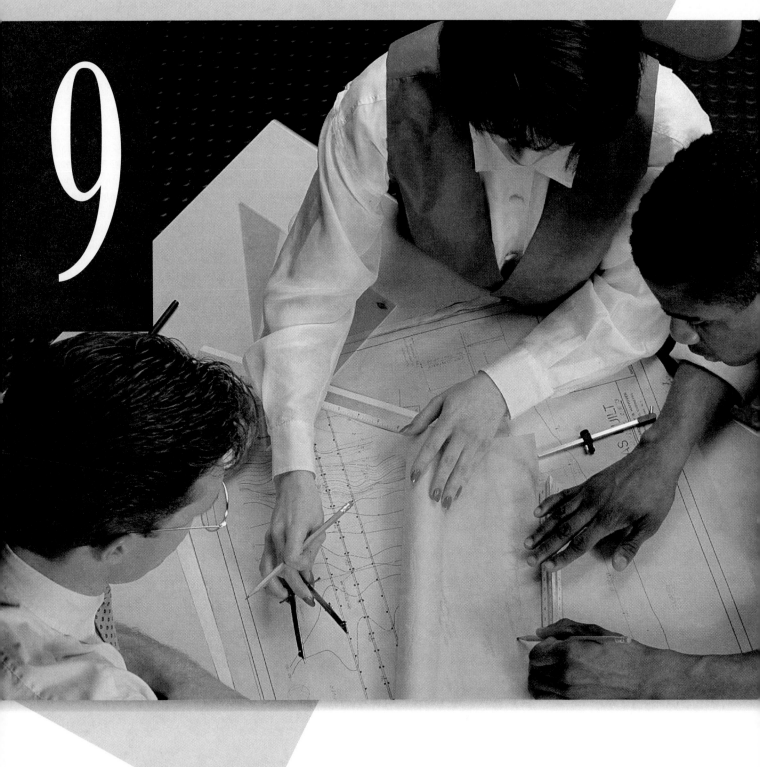

Thought and Language

9

Wayne Inges, a nefarious soul, chuckles silently to himself as he completes the deal. "That's right," he says, "center court, floor level—$100 for the pair." Having paid only $50 for the ticket pair himself, Wayne pockets a tidy little profit. But there are more fools in the world, so he decides to buy the tickets back for $150. With game time approaching, and desperation setting in, this time the pair goes for $200. Can you figure out Wayne's total profit for the evening?

To find the answer, your mind begins an internal, goal-directed activity called **thinking.** In its simplest description, thinking, or *cognition,* involves the processes used to mentally manipulate knowledge and ideas. Through thought, human beings act on their knowledge, in a directed and purposeful way, to solve problems, to reason and make decisions, and to understand and communicate with others. As with most other internally based psychological phenomena, we cannot measure the processes of thinking directly, but we can detect their presence as we observe the thinker moving steadily forward in pursuit of a solution.

Let's see, Wayne made $50 on the first transaction but spent $150 to buy the tickets back, so he lost the original $50. He finally sold the pair for $200, so his total profit for the evening must be $50, right? Easy enough. We've used our knowledge about the world, about mathematics in particular, to work systematically toward our goal. It's easy to see the adaptive value of the process. Thinking increases the ability to survive because people can act on their knowledge in precise, systematic, and purposeful ways.

But, as you may have guessed, our reasoning in this case was completely wrong. We arrived at an incorrect answer, as do many others who try this task. Using a slight variation of the same problem, Maier and Burke (1967) found that people produce the correct answer less than 40% of the time. The correct answer is $100—Wayne paid out a total of $200 ($50 for the first transaction and $150 for the second) and received $300 back from the buyers. Simple subtraction yields the correct answer of $100. What lies behind the error? The problem arises from thinking about Wayne's sales as one continuous transaction rather than as two separate and distinct transactions. This becomes clearer if we frame the problem slightly differently: Wayne bought tickets for Friday night's game for $50 and sold them for $100, then he bought tickets for Saturday's game for $150 and sold them for $200. Under these conditions, people rarely, if ever, make an error. One of the challenges of the modern study of thinking, and problem solving in particular, is to understand why human thought processes are so commonly led astray. How can thought processes that seem so illogical fit snugly into the mold of an adaptive mind?

PREVIEWING THE ADAPTIVE PROBLEMS

The topics of thought and language actually require us to consider a variety of psychological activities. To think, you need to be aware and possess the capacity to learn. To manipulate the knowledge in your head, you need first to remember. When you solve problems or make decisions, you establish criteria for what represents an acceptable solution. To express things symbolically in the form of language, you use rules for classifying objects and guidelines for transforming meaning into strings of sounds or symbols.

Since antiquity, philosophers have struggled to understand the components that make up the "higher mental processes" of thought and language. More recently, these processes have become the focus of *cognitive science,* a diverse field that

Communicating with others	Classifying and categorizing	Solving problems	Making decisions

FIGURE 9.1
The Adaptive Problems. Thought and language serve a variety of adaptive functions. Summarized here are the four adaptive problems that we'll be considering in this chapter.

draws on the work of professionals from a wide variety of disciplines, including psychology, linguistics, philosophy, biology, and even engineering and computer science. Once again, we'll discuss the insights of psychologists and cognitive scientists by considering a set of adaptive problems that regularly confront people in their efforts to survive. How do individuals communicate with others? How do they classify and categorize objects and events in their world? How do people solve problems like the one posed at the beginning of the chapter? How do individuals make decisions that require them to choose from among a set of alternatives? For a visual summary of these four adaptive problems, see Figure 9.1.

COMMUNICATING WITH OTHERS The ability to communicate, especially through written and spoken language, may well be humanity's greatest success story. No other species on the planet can claim the knack for transmitting knowledge through speech and writing. In fact, the use of language may be the "most pervasive and uniquely human characteristic of the species" (Wasow, 1989). Through language production, people transmit thoughts, feelings, and needs to others; through language comprehension, people learn and understand. It may be that language even forms the basis for thought itself—remember that little voice inside your head? We'll look at the structure of language, consider some basic principles of language development and comprehension, and include a look at the intriguing relation between language and thought. Finally, we'll touch briefly on language ability in other species, particularly apes.

CLASSIFYING AND CATEGORIZING To make sense of the world, especially the objects in it, people carve it into meaningful chunks called categories. Can you imagine a world in which every encounter was new and unique—a world where no two things shared features in common, where each encounter with a cat, or a bird, or a snake was a new and mysterious experience? Think about how doctors might deal with illness if they had no diagnostic categories for disease. They would fail to see or establish connections—no two people would ever suffer from the same disorder, no treatment would be seen as applicable from one patient to the next. The ability to see the resemblance among things, to classify objects and events into meaningful categories, allows people to simplify their environment. Through categorization, individuals can predict, based on prior experience, what the best or most appropriate response will be in a given situation. Clearly, this ability is adaptive in view of the multitude of experiences that people encounter each day. We'll consider the structure of categories and describe some of the fundamental psychological processes that may underlie their formation.

▶ **SOLVING PROBLEMS**   When psychologists talk about problem solving, they refer to situations in which someone wants to reach a goal, such as solving a math problem or hooking up the new VCR, but it is not immediately obvious how to get from here to there. Think about the dozens of practical problems that you face, and solve, each and every day. Did you have trouble finding your keys this morning? Have a difficult time choosing what to wear, or what to watch on TV? The adaptive value of problem solving should be relatively obvious—if humans couldn't solve the problem of where to find food and water, or how to woo and win the appropriate mate, *homo sapiens* would quickly take the path followed by the dinosaurs or the dodo bird. It turns out that effective problem solving requires more than just persistence, or even trial and error; individuals are often required literally to "see" the problem in the appropriate way before they can hope for a solution.

▶ **MAKING DECISIONS**   Whereas problem solving requires people to move forward toward an unknown solution (which may not even exist), *decision making* requires people to make a choice from among a set of alternatives. For example, should I buy the tickets for $100, use the money to help pay this month's rent, or gamble the money on the outcome of tonight's game? Note that an important ingredient of decision making is *risk*—choices have consequences, and an incorrect decision can lead to unpleasant and unadaptive outcomes. Decision making, like problem solving, is one area in which people are very often fooled. But, as with perceptual illusions, don't be misled into thinking that just because humans make mistakes, their minds are not well adapted to handle a wide variety of problems and choices in everyday life.

Communicating with Others

We begin our discussion of thinking, curiously enough, with an extended discussion of language. It might seem funny to lump language and thought together, but the two are closely linked: Language, through the use of words, importantly influ-

Words often carry significant gender connotations. When you hear the words "doctor" and "secretary," are you likely to picture the doctor as a man and the secretary as a woman?

ences the way people think about and view their world. Remember from Chapter 8 how the word *smashed* rather than *contacted* led people to infer and remember things about the meeting of two cars that they would not have otherwise? Think about the words *doctor* and *secretary*—are you likely to picture a man and a woman, respectively? Do you think twice about a sentence like "The secretary hates his boss"? Words, as the tools of thought, continue to carry significant gender connotations for many. If used inappropriately, words can become weapons, leading people to expect and draw conclusions about things that are misleading or wrong (Henley, 1989; Mackay, 1983).

Linguistic Relativity

How strong is the connection between language and thought? The **linguistic relativity hypothesis** asserts that language *determines* thought (Whorf, 1956). Without a word or a phrase to describe an experience, the experience can only reside, quite literally, "out of mind." To consider this hypothesis, researchers have often turned to nature's laboratory to see how the idiosyncrasies of language affect the way people think in different cultures. In the Philippines, for example, the Hanunoo people have some 92 different names to describe varieties of rice (Anderson, 1990). Deep in the mountainous terrain of the Andes lives a tribe of people called the Quechua who have no word in their language for "flat." Directions are given in terms of body images—such as the foot, belly, or head of a mountain—rather than in terms like north or south (Hunt & Agnoli, 1991).

The Quecha, who live in mountainous regions, have no word in their language for "flat." According to the linguistic relativity hypothesis, one might expect them to have a difficult time orienting themselves spatially in a flat environment.

According to the linguistic relativity hypothesis, these language particulars shape and constrain perception and thought. For example, we might expect the Hanunoo people to see curious things in rice that other cultures, with a more limited "rice" vocabulary, do not. If we took the Quechua out of their familiar environment and put them in a flat terrain, such as a Midwestern cornfield, how might they react? According to the linguistic relativity hypothesis, we might expect that individuals who speak only of sharp-angled inclines and precipitous drops would have a difficult time orienting themselves spatially in a flat environment.

To test the linguistic relativity hypothesis, Eleanor Rosch (published under her former name of Heider) studied the perceptual abilities of a tribe in New Guinea known as the Dani. The Dani's language, for reasons unique to their environment, contains only two basic color terms: *mola* for bright, warm hues, and *mili* for the darker, colder hues. If words completely shape thought, Rosch reasoned, the Dani should have trouble perceiving and remembering colors that lack Dani color names. But Rosch discovered that volunteers from the tribe had no trouble remembering novel colors that had been presented to them only moments before; moreover, the Dani seemed especially able to learn and remember things about focal colors—red, green, and blue—a result that is also commonly found for English speakers. Rosch interpreted her results to mean that English speakers and speakers of the Dani language probably perceive the world, at least with respect to color, in very similar ways. Color perception appears to be universal, depending more on the physiology of the visual system than on the particular vocabulary adopted by the perceiver (Heider, 1972).

Most psychologists believe that the linguistic relativity hypothesis, taken literally, simply cannot be true. Members of the Hanunoo might be more proficient

 Do you think the study of color perception is a fair way to test the linguistic relativity hypothesis?

than their Western counterparts at describing rice, but it's unlikely that rice "looks" any different to these people. Instead of tottering in the Midwestern cornfield, the Quechua will be able to orient themselves just fine, although they might have difficulty describing their flat environment. All humans share certain fundamental cognitive abilities, and these abilities remain intact even when they're not regularly tapped by the speaker's language and environment.

At the same time, there is little question that language *influences* thought. Both perception and memory depend on prior knowledge, and people often use words as tools to generate expectations that influence cognitive processing. As we learned in Chapter 8, memory for an event depends importantly on how individuals describe the event to themselves when it originally occurs. The richer the description, or encoding, the more likely they are to remember the event later. If a person's language abilities are impoverished, and he or she is unable to encode the event in an elaborate manner, then the ability to remember will suffer. Language may not be the sole determinant of thought, but it clearly shapes thought in some significant ways.

Defining Language and Its Structure

We now turn our attention to language itself. What is language, and how should it be properly defined? If you think about it, birds communicate effectively through the production of auditory sequences (songs). Bees can convey information about the exact location of honey through a tail-wagging dance (von Frisch, 1967). Even your dog barks incessantly at outdoor noises in what appears to be an effort to communicate. But to qualify as a true language, the communication system must have rules, known collectively as **grammar,** that allow the communicator to combine arbitrary symbols to convey meaning.

A grammar provides rules about which combinations of sounds and words are permissible and which are not. Grammar has three aspects: (1) **phonology,** the rules for combining sounds to make words; (2) **syntax,** the rules for combining words to make sentences; and (3) **semantics,** the rules used to communicate meaning. In English, for example, we would never say something like "The cautious the barked nasty at man poodle." This particular combination of words violates a number of rules of syntax, such as the rule that articles (*the*) and adjectives (*nasty*) come before nouns (*man*). We would also never generate a sentence like "Colorless green ideas sleep furiously." Although this is a well-structured sentence, it suffers from a violation of semantics—it has no meaning. Individuals use their knowledge about semantics to pick the appropriate words (perhaps "people" can sleep furiously, but "ideas" cannot) and to infer connections between words and other things in memory (cautious poodles bark at rather than bite nasty people).

The Units of Language. All human languages possess basic hierarchical structure, which ranges from the fundamental sounds of speech to the more complex levels of spoken conversation. At the base of the spoken language hierarchy are **phonemes,** which are the smallest significant sound units in speech. These speech sounds are produced through a complex coordination of the vocal cords, lungs, lips, tongue, and even the teeth. Table 9.1 lists some examples of phonemes in the English language. Notice that there isn't a simple one-to-one mapping between a given letter of the

Bees do a characteristic "waggle dance" to communicate information about the location of honey. But would you say bees have really developed language?

TABLE 9.1
Some Examples of English Phonemes

Symbol	Examples	Symbol	Examples
b	**b**urger, ru**bb**le	ng	sti**ng**, ri**ng**er
ē	**e**asy, zomb**ie**	oy	c**oi**l, empl**oy**
ĕ	**e**nter, m**e**tric	r	**r**at, c**r**ust
f	**f**ungus, **ph**one	s	**s**todgy, be**s**t
ĭ	**i**cky, w**i**g	t	**t**ramp, miss**ed**
ī	**i**ce, sh**y**	th	**th**at, o**th**er
k	**k**itty, a**ch**e	ŭ	**u**gly, b**u**tter
n	**n**ewt, a**nn**oy		

alphabet and a phoneme. The letter *e*, for example, maps onto one kind of speech sound in the word *head* and a different kind in the word *heat*.

Babies greet the world with the capacity to produce a large number of fundamental speech sounds, but they quickly restrict the number to a much smaller set. English speakers use only about 40–45 phonemes; other languages may use considerably more or fewer. Japanese speakers, for example, do not differentiate between the phonemes *r* and *l* in their native tongue (which makes it tough for a native Japanese speaker to hear the difference between *race* and *lace*). English speakers do not meaningfully distinguish the *p* sound in *pause* from the *p* sound in *camp*. In Thai or Hindi, these same sound units carry unique and different meanings. Part of the trick in acquiring a foreign language thus lies in mastering the basic phonemes of that language.

At the next level in the hierarchy are **morphemes**—the smallest units of language that carry meaning. Morphemes usually consist of single words, such as *cool* or *hip*, but they can also be prefixes and suffixes. For instance, the word *cool* contains a single morpheme, whereas *uncool* contains two—the root word *cool* and the prefix *un*. The grammar of a language dictates the acceptable order of morphemes within a word—*uncool* has definite meaning in our language, *coolun* does not. The morpheme *s* when placed at the end of a word (*oars*) designates plural. But the phoneme *s* when placed at the beginning of a word (*soar*) means something entirely different. All told, the average speaker of English knows and uses somewhere between 50,000 and 80,000 morphemes.

At the higher levels of the language hierarchy are *words*, *phrases*, and *sentences*. Words combine to form phrases; phrases, in conjunction with other phrases, form sentences. To illustrate, the sentence "Stephanie kissed the crying boy" contains a noun (*Stephanie*) and a verb phrase (*kissed the crying boy*). The verb phrase contains a verb (*kissed*) and a noun phrase (*the crying boy*). Perhaps you can remember diagramming sentences in this way in your high school English class (see Figure 9.2). Breaking sentences into phrases turns out to have psychological meaning—people actually use a kind of phrase structure when they generate a spoken sentence. For example, if I were to accurately time you speaking, I would find that you pause for a moment at the boundaries between major phrases (Boomer, 1965).

Language researchers have spent decades trying to decipher the rules of syntax that people use to combine words into phrases and phrases into sentences. It was once thought that a set of rules might be discovered that would effectively capture all of the nuances of sentence generation. Just apply the rules appropriately to words and you've got language. But as the linguist Noam Chomsky pointed

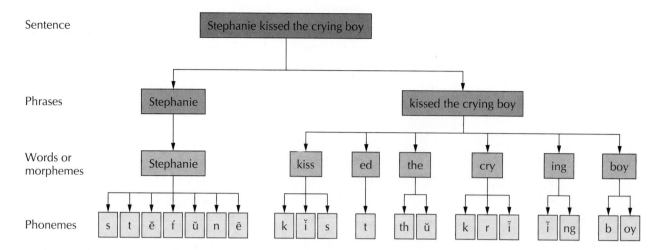

Sentence

Phrases

Words or morphemes

Phonemes

FIGURE 9.2

The Units of Language. Languages have a basic hierarchical structure, which ranges from the fundamental sounds of speech to the more complex levels of spoken conversation. Complex rules exist for how words are combined into phrases and sentences and for how fundamental speech sounds (phonemes) are combined to create the smallest units of meaning (morphemes) and words.

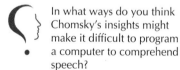

In what ways do you think Chomsky's insights might make it difficult to program a computer to comprehend speech?

out, it's unlikely that such a set of rules exists. To bolster his argument, Chomsky came up with sentences like "Visiting relatives can be a nuisance." It's easy to break this sentence down into its appropriate phrase structure, Chomsky argued, but the phrase structure tells us nothing about what the sentence actually means: Are we annoyed that the relatives are visiting, or is it a nuisance to visit relatives? Both meanings map onto the same phrase structure: Visiting relatives—pause—can be a nuisance. Thus, we cannot capture why or how sentences are generated during a meaningful conversation by appealing simply to the phrase structure.

Surface Versus Deep Structure. According to Chomsky (1957), to understand how language really works, we first need to accept that there is a difference between the "surface" structure of a sentence and its accompanying, more abstract, "deep" structure. The **surface structure** of a sentence corresponds to its superficial appearance (the literal ordering of words), whereas **deep structure** taps the underlying representation of meaning. Thus, two sentences can have the same surface structure but two different deep structures (the "visiting relatives" example). Or, two different surface structures can arise from the same deep structure ("Stephanie kissed the crying boy"—"The crying boy was kissed by Stephanie"). According to Chomsky, language production involves the transformation of deep structure into an acceptable surface structure (see Figure 9.3). Although most language researchers agree with the basic ideas of Chomsky's analysis, they do not necessarily agree on how this transformation process actually works (see Wasow, 1989, for a review).

Language Comprehension

In addition to understanding the structure and rules of grammar, psychologists who study language are also quite interested in the processes underlying language *comprehension*. For example, how do people use their practical knowledge about the world, and the general context of the conversation, to help them decide what information a speaker is trying to communicate?

Effective communication virtually always relies a great deal on *mutual knowledge* among the speakers. People do not simply process the physical energy arriving at their ears into words, phrase structures, and sentences—they guess as to what the speaker is trying to communicate, and they use this knowledge to interpret the sounds they hear. Thus, in an important sense, the comprehension of language shares properties with perception: both rely on a combination of *top-down*

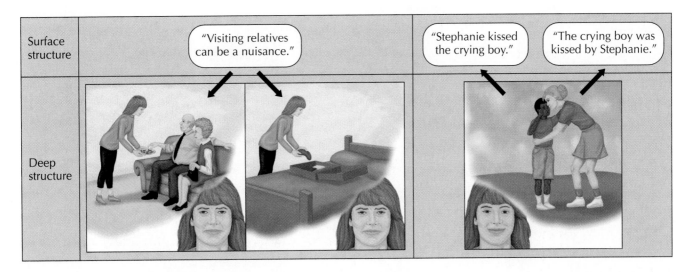

Surface structure	"Visiting relatives can be a nuisance."	"Stephanie kissed the crying boy." "The crying boy was kissed by Stephanie."
Deep structure		

FIGURE 9.3

Surface Structure and Deep Structure. The surface structure of a sentence refers to its "surface" appearance, the literal orderings of words. Deep structure refers to the underlying meaning of the sentence. This figure shows how the same surface structure—"Visiting relatives can be a nuisance"—can reflect two quite different deep structures. Similarly, a single deep structure can be transformed into two or more acceptable surface structures.

and *bottom-up* processing (McClelland & Elman, 1986). The term **pragmatics** is often used to describe the practical knowledge people use both to comprehend the intentions of speakers and to produce an effective response.

Consider your response to an *indirect* request like "Could you close the window?" If you process the request directly—that is, if you take its literal interpretation—you might respond, "Yes, I'm capable of putting enough steady pressure on the window to produce closure." You have answered the question, but clearly you have violated some important pragmatic rules. The speaker was making a request, not asking you about your ability to perform the task. In fact, if you had answered the question in this way, the speaker would have probably inferred that you were using *irony* or *sarcasm* in your reply (Gibbs, 1979).

The pragmatics of language make language comprehension processes a challenge to study. How you interpret someone else's words—be they babblings or profound commentary on the hypocrisy of our times—will depend on the shared context of the conversation, as well as on any prior expectations and beliefs that you bring to the exchange. To facilitate effective communication, there are certain pragmatic guidelines, or "maxims," that all good speakers follow (Grice, 1975). First, good speakers try to be informative and succinct (the maxim of *quantity*). Second, they try to tell the truth (the maxim of *quality*). Third, speakers attempt to be relevant in their statements (the maxim of *relation*). Finally, they try to be clear and avoid ambiguity (the maxim of *manner*). By following these simple rules, and by assuming the same for your conversational partner, you can enhance the ease and flow of the conversational process.

Language Development

How does language develop? Are humans born with a genetic "blueprint" that directs and shapes their communication skills? Or do people acquire language exclusively as a product of experience? Not all people of the world speak the same language, so experience must certainly play an important role. But the majority of language researchers are convinced that babies arrive into the world prepared to learn language, much like they arrive into the world prepared to learn to walk. There is a universal regularity to language development, as there is to the development of motor skills, that is difficult to explain by appealing simply to the environment (Chomsky, 1986).

The universality of language is apparent even at birth. Most babies cry in sim-

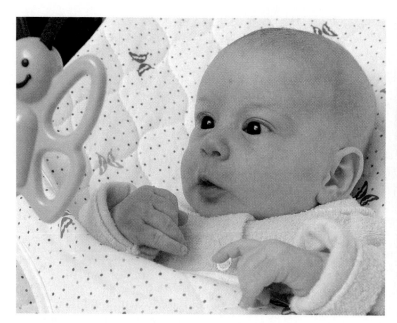

Infants and small children develop rather sophisticated ways to communicate meaningfully (cooing, kicking, pointing, and so on), even though their overt language skills may be limited.

ilar ways, and they move quickly through vocalization "milestones" that precede formal language development. By 3 to 5 weeks of age, *cooing*—repeating vowel sounds like "ooooh" and "aaaaah"—has been added to the baby's vocalization patterns. *Babbling*—repeating consonant/vowel combinations such as "kaka" or "baba"—begins in virtually all babies between the 4th and 6th months. Once again, it doesn't matter where you look in the world, this same sequence—crying then cooing then babbling—is found; even babies who are born unable to hear will cry, coo, and babble in characteristic ways during the first 6 months of life (Oller & Eilers, 1988).

Between the ages of 6 and 18 months, experience begins to play a role, shaping and fine-tuning the baby's babblings into language-specific utterings. Babies begin to restrict their vocalizations to the phonemes in the language that they hear every day from their parents or guardians; they even acquire a kind of language-specific "accent" by around 8 months of age (de Boysson-Bardies, Sagat, & Durand, 1984). Simple words—*mama, dada,* and so on—appear by the end of the first year, and by 24 months, most babies have developed a vocabulary of nearly 200 words (Nelson, 1973). Language comprehension also develops rapidly during this period—in fact, infants develop the ability to understand the words and commands of language *faster* than they actually learn to produce language.

As every parent knows, infants and young children develop rather sophisticated ways to communicate meaningfully, even though their overt language production skills may be limited. An 18-month-old child can point to the bear-shaped jar on the counter and say "ookie" and Mom or Dad immediately knows what their hungry child has in mind. An enormous amount of information can be packed into a single word, even if that word is spoken incorrectly, if its utterance is combined with a gesture, or if the utterance occurs in the right context.

As the child approaches the end of his or her second year of life, a phase of *telegraphic speech* begins. Telegraphic speech involves combining two words into simple sentences, such as "Daddy bad" or "Give cookie." It's called telegraphic speech because, like in a telegram, the child characteristically omits articles (*the*) and prepositions (*at, in*) from communications. But a 2-year-old's first sentences reflect a rudimentary knowledge of syntax: words are almost always spoken in the proper *order*. For example, a child will reliably say "Want cookie" instead of

In a normal conversation, how much meaning do you think is typically communicated through nonverbal means, such as frowning or the folding of arms?

"Cookie want." During the rest of the child's preschool years, up to around age 5 or 6, sentences become increasingly more complex, to the point at which the average child of kindergarten age can produce and comprehend sentences that reveal most of the important features of adult syntax.

It's of enormous interest to psychologists that children develop such sophisticated language skills during their preschool years. After all, few parents sit down with their children and teach them the rules of grammar (such as the differences between present and past tense). Moreover, as we discussed in Chapter 4, children at this age lack the ability to understand most abstract concepts, so they couldn't consciously understand grammatical rules even if parents took the time to try. Children pick up their language skills implicitly; they automatically learn rules for language production.

The rules that children learn during their preschool years are revealed partly by the errors that they commit. For example, at some point preschoolers acquire the rule "Add *ed* to the ends of verbs to make them past tense." But children sometimes *overgeneralize* the rule—they will say things like "goed" or "falled," which are incorrect in English but represent a correct application of the rule. Notice that *goed* is not something that the child could have learned to use directly from experience. No parent rewards a child for saying *goed,* nor does a child hear the word being used by his or her parents. Rather, the child appears to be naturally "tuned" to pick up communication rules and apply them generally—even if a rule sometimes leads to an incorrect utterance. The natural tendency to learn and apply rules is then shaped by experience; an adult or peer teaches the child that *goed* is incorrect.

Language development continues throughout the school years, as children fine-tune their articulation skills and knowledge about grammar. Vocabulary expands, as does the child's ability to communicate abstract concepts. But the sophistication of any child's language ability will depend partly on his or her degree of cognitive development. Children think differently as they age, and their increasingly sophisticated cognitive abilities are reflected in the conversations they are capable of generating. You should keep this fact in mind as we turn our attention to language abilities in nonhuman species.

Language in Nonhuman Species

Psychologists have recognized for decades that nonhuman animals communicate. Anyone who has ever seen a cat indicate that it would rather be inside the house than outside knows this to be true. The question is whether such forms of communication can be characterized as language. We know that animals sometimes express things symbolically, and there's little doubt that an animal's actions can convey meaning. But to qualify as a true *language* the animals would need to possess at least a rudimentary form of grammar—that is, a set of rules for deciding how arbitrary symbols can be combined to convey meaning.

Early attempts to foster language development in chimpanzees, in a form resembling human speech, were not very successful. Chimps were raised in homes, like surrogate children, in an effort to provide the ideal environment for language development. In one case, a chimp named Gua was raised along with the researchers' son, Donald (Kellogg & Kellogg, 1933). Donald and Gua were exposed to the same experiences, and careful attention was paid to rewarding the appropriate vocalizations. But in the end, the Kelloggs had merely produced a fine-speaking son and an effectively mute chimp. Later efforts to teach chimps to speak yielded the same discouraging results (Hayes & Hayes, 1951).

But these early attempts were misguided, in a way, because chimps lack the necessary vocal equipment to produce the sounds required for human speech

Chimpanzees lack the vocal equipment needed to produce the sounds of human speech. But chimps can be taught to communicate in relatively sophisticated ways using American Sign Language (left) or by learning to press keys on a board that represent objects such as food or toys (right).

(Hayes, 1952). It's kind of like a bird trying to teach a human to fly by raising a boy in a nest. Without wings, the boy just isn't going to fly. For these reasons, later researchers turned to visual communication mediums. Allen and Beatrice Gardner tried to teach a simplified form of American Sign Language to a chimp named Washoe (Gardner & Gardner, 1969; Gardner, Gardner, & Van Cantfort, 1989). By the age of 4, Washoe was capable of producing about 160 appropriate signs, and apparently she understood a great deal more. Even more impressive was her ability to produce word combinations, such as "more fruit" or "gimme tickle." In California, a chimp named Sarah was taught to manipulate plastic shapes that symbolized words (Premack, 1976); in Georgia, chimps learned to communicate by pressing keys that represented objects such as foods or toys (Rumbaugh, 1977; Savage-Rumbaugh et al., 1986).

All of these efforts were successful to a point. The animals learned to communicate through direct use of the visual medium. Washoe, for example, learned to respond to environmental events by producing novel (or new) signs. On seeing a duck, for instance, she reportedly signed "water bird." Sarah was able to communicate complex things, even information about cause-and-effect relationships in her environment. It has also been shown that some chimps can acquire such skills through observing other chimps, without being trained directly (Savage-Rumbaugh et al., 1986).

But despite the impressive learning, have these chimps really acquired *language*? The jury is still out on this issue. For one thing, much of the evidence (such as Washoe's "water bird") comes from trainer anecdotes rather than from systematic data collection, so there is room for multiple interpretations. In addition, the simple communication skills of these chimpanzees are not acquired easily. It takes protracted training, sometimes lasting years, to produce even the simplest of word combinations. Their vocabularies remain limited, and their utterances are usually far below the level of a normal preschool child. In the words of one researcher, "If any of our children learned or used language the way Washoe or Sarah does, we would be terror-stricken and rush them to the nearest neurologist" (Gleitman, 1996, p. 289).

Before you judge these chimps too harshly, however, it's important to remember that chimpanzees have not evolved to understand or produce human language. Chimps have evolved to solve their own problems—problems that arise from their own unique environments. We need to be careful to avoid adopting too egocentric a view of the world. The human mind has evolved to solve human problems, and those problems may or may not overlap with the domains of other members of the animal kingdom.

Classifying and Categorizing

We now turn our attention to another highly adaptive quality of the mind—the ability to classify and categorize objects. By carving the world, and the objects in it, into meaningful chunks, people create a world that is manageable, predictable, and sensible. If I tell you I ran into a "redneck" today, you will probably get from my communication a rich supply of unspoken knowledge about my experience— knowledge that goes far beyond the simple words I speak. You will bring to my mention of "redneck" all that you know about the term. You will probably "see" a male; you may well predict what kind of clothes he would wear and his general manner of speech; you could presumably imagine his reaction to a provocative commentary on the burning of the American flag. You might even form some sort of impression about me, depending on your views about whether being a redneck is a positive or negative characteristic. What you are doing is enhancing my communication by applying your knowledge about the category "redneck" to it.

A **category** is a class of objects (people, places, or things) that most people agree belong together (Smith, 1989). "Vegetables" is a category that contains such things as peas, carrots, and Brussels sprouts; "psychologists" is a category that includes researchers, clinicians, and applied persons working in the field. Categories allow people to *infer* invisible properties about objects. For example, a kite and a doll share important properties as children's toys, even though the two objects bear little physical similarity to each other. Once you have successfully categorized something, you can make *predictions* about the future. You know, for example, that if you bring your child an object from the category "toy," she is likely to be happy and smother you with a hug.

We'll divide our discussion of classifying and categorizing into three main topics: First, how do people decide whether an object is an appropriate member of a particular category? Second, in making decisions about category membership, do people rely on abstract representations called prototypes? Finally, we'll end the section with a brief discussion of the hierarchical structure of categories—when people categorize an object, do they do so in a general or a highly specific manner?

Defining Category Membership

Researchers have spent a lot of time trying to discover the criteria that people use to define category membership. What is it about a sparrow that allows people to classify it so effortlessly as a bird? How do people learn that a trout is a member of the category "fish" and not something to be used in the garden?

One possibility is that people easily and quickly classify a sparrow as a "bird" because it has certain features that all members of that category share. For example, to be a member of the category "bird," it might be assumed that a creature needs to have feathers and be able to do things like sing, fly, and build nests— these are necessary or **defining features** of the category "bird." If the object in question has all these things—the defining attributes or features—it must be an

People automatically classify objects, even other people, into well-defined categories. How would you categorize this individual, and what "invisible" properties would you infer about him? Can you predict how he might act in a social situation?

Properties	Generic bird	Robin	Sandpiper	Vulture	Chicken	Penguin
Flies regularly	+	+	+	+	–	–
Sings	+	+	+	–	–	–
Lays eggs	+	+	+	+	+	+
Is small	+	+	+	–	–	–
Nests in trees	+	+	–	+	–	–

FIGURE 9.4

Defining Features of a Category.
One way to define category membership is in terms of defining features. For example, members of the generic category "bird" might be expected to fly regularly, sing, lay eggs, be small, and nest in trees. Unfortunately, people have a tough time identifying and agreeing on the "defining features" for most natural categories. All of the objects shown here are "birds," but they don't necessarily share the same properties. (Based on Smith, 1989)

acceptable member of the category; if the object lacks one or more of these qualities, it must be something else (Medin, 1989). From this standpoint, category learning is simply a matter of acquiring the relevant set of defining features for the objects in a class (see Figure 9.4).

But the idea that category membership can be defined simply by appealing to a fixed set of defining features has certain difficulties. It works fine for mathematical categories such as "square" or "triangle," but it breaks down for natural objects. Take the category "vehicle," for example. What are the defining features of a vehicle—something that moves along the ground, has wheels, and can transport people? That applies well to things like cars and trucks, but what about a surfboard, or a monorail train? Surfboards move through water; monorail trains don't have wheels. What about an elevator, which doesn't have wheels and doesn't move along the ground? Research on natural categories such as birds, vehicles, furniture, and so on demonstrates that people have a tough time identifying and agreeing on just what constitutes the acceptable "defining features" of a category (Malt & Smith, 1984; Rosch & Mervis, 1975).

Most natural categories turn out to have uncertain or *fuzzy boundaries.* For example, in Figure 9.5 you can see a series of objects that collectively tap the fuzzy boundary of the category "cup." In an experiment by Labov (1973), people were presented with a selected set of these objects, such as shown in series 1 through

Does this monorail train fit snugly into your category for "vehicle"? If so, what "defining features" does it share with other members of the category?

FIGURE 9.5
Fuzzy Category Boundaries. Are all of these objects members of the category "cup"? Labov (1973) discovered that as the width of the object increased, people were more likely to label it as a "bowl." But the cup category boundary was fuzzy rather than firm; a significant number of people remained convinced that the fourth object was indeed a cup. (From Goldstein, 1994)

4, and were required to name each object as it was presented. Labov discovered that as the ratio of cup width to cup depth increased (as the object appeared wider), subjects were increasingly likely to dismiss the "cup" label and characterize the object as a "bowl." But the crossover point was gradual rather than fixed. Even for the object labeled 4, a significant number of people remained convinced that the object was indeed a cup. Results like these suggest that category members have *typical features* that are *characteristic* rather than defining attributes of the category.

Family Resemblance. Another way to think about the idea of typical or characteristic features is in terms of what Rosch and Mervis (1975) have called **family resemblance.** Category members share certain core features, and a given member may have some but not necessarily all of the critical attributes. Within an extended family, for instance, there may be a characteristic aquiline nose, close-set beady eyes, and a prominent, clefted chin. A particular member of the family may lack the cleft, or might not have such beady eyes, but a "family resemblance" for the character remains. Outsiders, for example, would probably have little difficulty fitting the individual into the appropriate family. For the category "vehicle," people know that a monorail train doesn't have wheels, and it's not shaped anything like a car, but it moves people along the ground and thus fits the category label for most people.

Family resemblance is determined by the particular set of critical features that an object possesses. Members of the same category will have many of these family features, but it's unlikely that any single member will have them all. If a given

Members of the same family often share physical features, creating a family resemblance, but it's unlikely that any single member of the family will share them all.

object has most of the family features, it will be seen as a "good" member of the category; if an object has only a few, it will be seen as a "poor" member of the category. A car, for example, has most of the basic features that people think of when they think of the category "vehicle"; an elevator does not. A robin has most of the features of "bird"; an ostrich or a flamingo has few. Through the notion of family resemblance, we can begin to see how natural categories achieve their "fuzzy" status. There is no absolute set of criteria for what constitutes a "vehicle" or a "bird," there are only good and poor examples of a class of objects that share features (Rosch and others, 1976).

Do People Store Category Prototypes?

When we talk about things like family resemblance and "good" and "poor" members of a category, we are led naturally to the concept of a *prototype*. **Prototypes** are defined as the best or most representative members of a category. For example, a robin is probably close to the prototype for the category "bird." Some psychologists have suggested that people store prototypes for categories in long-term memory and use these prototypes to help decide category membership. When trying to decide whether an object is a member of a specific category, individuals compare the object to the stored prototype. If the object and the prototype are similar enough, the person decides that the object may, in fact, be a member of the prototype's category (Homa, 1984). Prototype theories can explain some interesting kinds of data. For example, if people are shown examples of an artificial category but never the "best" example or prototype, they will sometimes think they've seen the prototype before, even though it was never actually presented (Posner & Keele, 1970). Results like these suggest that people use their individual experiences to form more abstract representations like prototypes.

Other researchers reject the idea that people store prototypes inside their heads. Instead, they argue that people simply store all of the examples (or **category exemplars**) of the category that they've encountered. To decide whether a new object is a member of the category, individuals compare the object's features to all of these stored exemplars and make a decision based on a measure of summed similarity (see Figure 9.6).

Whether prototypes or exemplars are used in categorization is currently unknown, although most cognitive psychologists seem to be leaning toward the exemplar position (Hintzman, 1986; Medin & Shaffer, 1978; Nosofsky, 1992). The

FIGURE 9.6
Prototypes Versus Exemplars. How do people decide whether an object is a member of a particular category? According to prototype theory, they compare the to-be-categorized object to the abstract "best" example of the category (a generic bird). If the new object is similar to the prototype, it is assigned to the prototype's category. Exemplar theories of categorization propose that no prototypes are formed; instead, people compare the new object to all the individual examples of the category that have been stored in memory. Category membership is decided based on the summed similarity between the new object and the exemplars.

reason is that people seem to know a lot more about the members of a category than the prototype theories allow. Prototypes are abstract representations, reflecting the average properties of category membership, yet people seem sensitive to the details of category membership. For example, people seem to know about what features go together—for example, that small birds are more likely to sing than large birds—and this kind of result is better handled by theories that propose the storage of exemplars rather than of prototypes.

The Hierarchical Structure of Categories

It turns out that most objects fit nicely into more than one natural category. The reason, in part, is that virtually all categories have a built-in hierarchical structure—there are categories within categories within categories. Consider the class of "living things." Under the umbrella of "living things," we find the category "animals"; under "animals" there are "cats"; under "cats" there are "Siamese cats"; and so on. Most of the time an object, once it's categorized, can easily be subsumed into another, more general, level of abstraction. A cat is an animal, a living thing, an object found on the planet Earth, and so on. These levels differ from one another in terms of their degree of inclusion. The more general the level, the more inclusive it becomes—there are more examples of living things than animals and more cats than Siamese cats.

What's interesting about the hierarchical structure of natural categories is that some levels appear to have special properties—they are, in a sense, "psychologically privileged." When people refer to an object during a normal conversation, they tend to use what is called its *basic-level* category descriptor. **Basic-level categories** turn out to be the ones that generate the most useful and predictive information. When a furry feline saunters by, you call it a cat, not a living thing, or an object found on the planet Earth. The category "cat" provides just the right amount of relevant information. People know you're talking about a four-legged object with fur (rather than the nondescript "animal"), but you haven't burdened the conversation with a needless amount of detail ("There's an 18-year-old seal-point Siamese that prefers salmon for dinner").

Basic-level categories tend to be at the intermediate levels of the category hierarchy (see Figure 9.7). The top-level categories, or *superordinates,* are simply not

If you wanted to decide whether your friend Bob could fit into the category "furniture," do you think you would compare him to a prototype (such as a couch or a table), or would you think about all the objects that you've used as a "seat" in your lifetime?

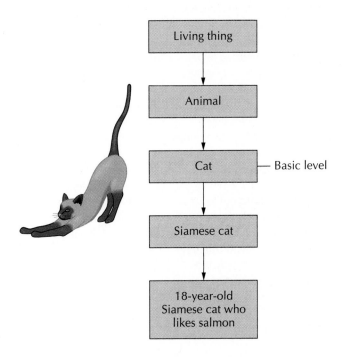

FIGURE 9.7
Category Hierarchies. Virtually all categories have a built-in hierarchical structure—there are categories within categories within categories. Most objects, such as the object shown to the left, fit nicely into several of these natural category levels. But when people refer to an object during normal conversation, they tend to use its intermediate, or *basic-level,* category label. They call this object a cat rather than a living thing, an animal, or an 18-year-old Siamese cat who likes salmon.

INSIDE THE PROBLEM: *Similarity and Categorization*

Once upon a time there was an animal, with typical birdlike properties, who sauntered into the wrong place at the wrong time. There was a peculiar experiment going on, you see, and the animal was transformed, by accident, into the shape of an insect. Instead of feathers, its body became encrusted in a hardened shell; instead of two legs with pointed feet, it had six legs that looked like sticks. Surprisingly, it went on to live a normal life, and even produced a flock of offspring that looked like birds. If forced to choose, would you call this animal a bird or an insect? Most people still think it's a bird, even though it looks like a bug (after Rips, 1989).

In a study by Gelman and Markman (1986), 4-year-old children were shown two pictures, one of a tropical fish, the other of a dolphin. The children were told that the tropical fish stays underwater to breathe, whereas the dolphin pops above water to breathe. They were then shown a picture of a shark, which was perceptually similar to the dolphin, and were asked: "See this fish? Does it breathe underwater or does it pop above water to breathe?" Nearly 70% of the 4-year-olds were convinced that the shark breathes underwater even though

it looked nothing like a tropical fish (Gelman & Markman, 1986).

Results like these are significant because they violate one of the main tenets of many theories of categorization—classification by similarity. The creature is more similar to an insect in the first case, and a shark certainly looks more like a dolphin than a tropical fish, but people's answers don't reflect the similarity; they choose the category with the least amount of shared features. If natural objects are assigned to categories based on their similarity to a prototype, or to other exemplars, then how can we explain the answers in these two examples?

Recently, researchers have started shifting away from using similarity as the "supreme court of appeal" for determining category membership. Two things can look very different, or share very few features, yet still be accepted as members of a category. Indeed, the whole concept of "similarity" turns out to be a little fuzzy. For example, is a zebra more similar to a horse or to a barber pole? The answer, of course, depends on the context. If we're trying to classify the world into "things with stripes" then zebras and barber poles are more similar.

It's more useful to think of similarity as a kind of guideline for establishing category membership. Things that are physically similar will usually belong in the same category, but appeals to similarity alone probably will not be sufficient to explain the richness of people's ability to categorize (Medin, Goldstone, & Gentner, 1993).

In many ways, the ability to place objects effortlessly into categories simply mirrors people's knowledge about the world. People know that objects can change their appearance yet remain fundamentally the same. Children know that two living things from the same category are likely to breathe in the same way, even if those particular examples look nothing alike. Rather than passively comparing features, individuals classify based on an inference process—does the object in question have properties that fit with their world view of how things in a particular category should act? The organization of categories appears to be "knowledge-based (rather than similarity-based) and driven by intuitive theories about the world" (Medin & Ross, 1992, p. 378).

very descriptive. When subjects were asked to list the distinguishing features of top-level categories (such as "living things"), Rosch and her colleagues found that only a few features were actually generated (try it yourself: list the properties that characterize "living things"). At the basic level, more properties were generated, and the generated properties tended to be ones that most members of the category share (Rosch and others, 1976). It is of interest to note that basic-level categories are also the category levels that children first learn to use. Through basic-level categorization, it appears, the adaptive mind cuts the world into its most useful and informative slices.

Solving Problems

We've spent a great deal of time in this text discussing various adaptive and conceptual problems—either problems that human beings regularly face in their efforts to survive or problems that psychologists confront as they try to advance knowledge or help people in need. In general, associated with any kind of problem—be it adaptive, conceptual, or practical—is a *goal*, along with a certain amount of *uncertainty* about how to reach that goal. In this section of the chapter, we'll discuss some of the thought processes that people use when they consciously seek to solve problems. Here is an example of the type of problem that has been studied:

> It's early morning, still dark, and you're trying to get dressed. Your 2-month-old baby, snuggled in her crib at the foot of the bed, sleeps peacefully after a night of sustained wailing. You can't turn on the light—she'll wake up for sure—but the black socks and the blue socks are mixed up in the drawer. Let's see, you recall, I have 5 pairs of black socks and 4 pairs of blue socks. How many socks do I need to take out of the drawer in order to guarantee myself a pair of matching colors?

Notice that there is a goal (selecting a pair of matching socks), and it's not immediately obvious how to get from the problem to the solution. Psychologists would call this a **well-defined problem** (even though you may have no idea how to solve it) because there is a well-stated goal, a clear starting point, and a rela-

Certain kinds of problems are well defined, such as trying to find the correct route on a map. Other problems are ill defined and may not even have a solution. Can you decipher the true meaning of the painting on the left?

Specifically, how might you break down an ill-defined problem such as "the pursuit of happiness" into a set of more manageable well-defined problems?

tively easy way to tell when a solution has been obtained. Other kinds of problems, called **ill-defined problems,** do not have well-stated goals, clear starting points, or effective mechanisms for evaluating progress. In fact, many ill-defined problems may not even have solutions. Many real-life problems are ill-defined. Ever wonder about the secret of happiness? Maybe you can agree on the starting point (I'm not happy enough), but the goal (happiness) is pretty tough to define, and it's not at all clear how to reach that goal or measure progress.

Most of the research that has been done on the thought processes involved in problem solving has been conducted using well-defined problems, such as our sock problem or those involving math or logic. We'll mainly consider these types of problems in this section, but ill-defined problems can be tackled with some of the same strategies. It's also the case that ill-defined problems can sometimes be broken down into smaller, more manageable, well-defined problems. So we can assume that similar psychological processes apply in most types of problem-solving situations.

The IDEAL Problem Solver

To provide an overview for what many cognitive scientists consider to be the way in which the ideal problem solver operates, we'll start by considering a set of problem-solving guidelines. These particular guidelines, which are based on psychological principles, are recommended by psychologists John Bransford and Barry Stein in their book *The Ideal Problem Solver* (1993). Bransford and Stein use the letters of the acronym IDEAL to stand for the five major steps that underlie effective problem solving. These steps are briefly described here and are summarized in Figure 9.8.

Step 1. **I**dentify the problem. Obviously, before you can solve a problem, you need to recognize that there is, in fact, a problem that needs solving. Strange knocking sounds, little spots of oil, and uneven acceleration are signs of car problems, but they need to be recognized as symptoms before the necessary diagnosis and repairs will be initiated.

Step 2. **D**efine, or represent, the problem information in the most efficient way. Not only is it important to define the goal—What exactly are you trying to solve?—it's also important to interpret correctly the problem components that you have to work with. As we discussed previously, the ticket scalping problem that opened the chapter is difficult because most people fail to see that Wayne actually made two *separate* ticket transactions. They tend to think about just *one* pair of tickets, so the cost of the second transaction is applied incorrectly to the first.

FIGURE 9.8
The IDEAL Problem Solver. John Bransford and Barry Stein have identified a set of useful problem-solving guidelines.

Identify the problem

Define the problem efficiently

Explore a variety of strategies

Act on the problem strategy

Look back and evaluate the problem strategy

Step 3. **E**xplore a variety of problem strategies. Once you have identified the problem, defined the goal, and developed some understanding of the information that you have to work with, it's time to try to move forward toward a possible solution. To do this, you need to decide on a strategy. Most solution strategies amount to "rules of thumb." They don't guarantee a solution, but they can speed up the problem-solving process or at least move you closer to your goal.

Step 4. **A**ct on the problem strategy that you've chosen in step 3. Work through the solution strategy, and as part of the process try to anticipate any dead ends or obstacles that might prevent you from reaching the goal.

Step 5. **L**ook back and evaluate the effectiveness of your selected strategy. Have you in fact solved the problem? Solutions can be achieved through strategies such as trial and error, but it's necessary to recognize whether an error has in fact occurred before you can try something new.

If you follow these five problem-solving guidelines, you have approximated the IDEAL problem solver (Bransford & Stein, 1993). Now let's consider some of the processes involved in somewhat greater detail.

Identifying and Defining: Problem Representation

To identify and define a problem correctly, it's essential to represent the problem information in the correct way. By problem representation, psychologists mean that people need to understand exactly what information is given and how that information can potentially be used. Solving a problem is like building a house. If you can't find the right tools, if you don't know which tools to use, or if you don't understand how to use those tools once you've found them, you're unlikely to ever complete the house or solve the problem.

Take the sock problem, for example. The correct answer is three. There are only two colors, so with three samples, you will get two that match. If you're like most people, you let the math get in your way. Did you start worrying about the four to five ratio of blue to black? Did you briefly consider calculating some sort of probability? To solve this problem, you must pay attention to the right problem components—you need to "see" the problem in the right way. Most people simply fail to detect which information is relevant and which is not. They get hung up with ratios and probabilities and the like. Let's consider another example:

> Dr. Adams is interrupted from his daily rounds by the arrival of a new patient, a child, who has been injured in a fall. "My god!" Adams cries, "It's my son!" Moments later, Dr. Henderson arrives with the same sense of panic and grief. "My son, my dear son," Henderson moans in despair. Is it a tragic mix-up?

You probably solved this one almost immediately, but it demonstrates the point. The two doctors are the mother and the father, which makes it easy to see why both are panicked about their injured son. But the word *doctor*, with its powerful gender connotations, can create an obstacle to correct problem representation. If you initially identify and define the doctors as men, the solution becomes more involved. Seeing the problem in the right way is even more difficult because the doctors have different last names.

Functional Fixedness. The two-doctor problem illustrates a common obstacle to correct problem representation. People allow their preconceptions, even their prejudices, to lock them into an incorrect view of the problem information. Con-

Think back to the linguistic relativity hypothesis that we discussed earlier. Do you think the doctor problem is an example of how language determines thought, or of how it merely influences thought?

FIGURE 9.9
The Maier Two-String Problem.
Can you figure out a way to tie these two strings together? Notice that there's a pair of pliers sitting on the table.

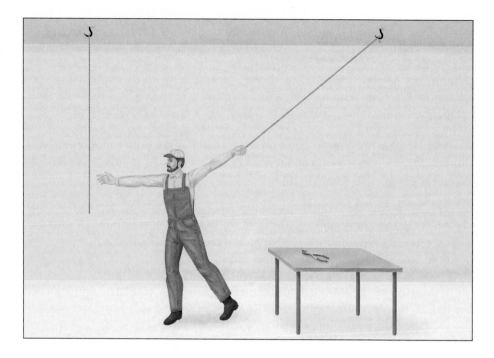

sider another example, illustrated in Figure 9.9, called the Maier two-string problem (after Maier, 1931). Imagine you are standing in a room with two lightweight strings hanging from the ceiling. The strings are hung such a distance apart that, when holding one of the strings, you cannot reach the other. Using only a pair of pliers, which happens to be sitting on a table in the room, can you tie the strings together?

This is a reasonably difficult problem because most people have a certain set, or fixed, way of viewing the function of pliers. The solution is to tie the pliers to one of the strings and swing it, like a pendulum, while you hold onto the other string. The correct solution, however, requires you to *restructure* the way that you normally think about pliers. Pliers are good for grabbing and holding, but in this case they can serve as pendulum weights, too.

Psychologists use the term **functional fixedness** to refer to the tendency to see objects, and their functions, in certain fixed and typical ways. Doctors are men, pliers are for grabbing, and so on. Functional fixedness during initial problem representation can be an obstacle to problem solving because it prevents people from recognizing the problem-solving "tools" that are present in the situation. Try solving the problem illustrated in Figure 9.10. You enter a room where a candle, a box of tacks, some matches, and a hammer lie on a table. You are told to mount the candle on the wall so it will still burn properly, using only the objects on the table. Work on the problem for a while; we'll return to its solution shortly.

First, let's stop for a moment and think about the adaptive significance of a concept such as functional fixedness. How can such a tendency possibly be characteristic of an adaptive mind? Wouldn't it be better to build an adaptive mind that always considers all possible object uses, a mind that never relies on regular past experiences to determine use? In fact, the kinds of problems we've been considering are quite artificial. They are set up by psychologists to lead the mind astray, in order to provide insight into normal problem-solving methods. Most of the time, if people view objects in fixed ways, or use fixed strategies that have worked well in the past, they are likely to be successful. After all, pliers usually do solve problems having to do with holding and grabbing, don't they? So the fact that people rely on **mental sets,** or well-established habits of perception and thought, is probably an effective adaptive strategy overall.

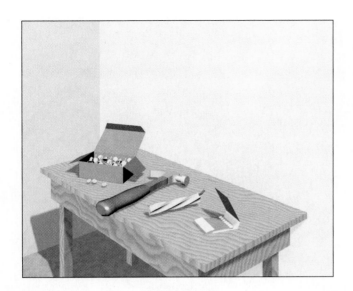

FIGURE 9.10
The Duncker Candle Problem.
Using only the materials shown, figure out a way to mount the candle on the wall.

Were you able to solve the candle-mounting problem? The correct solution is to dump the tacks out of the box, mount the box on the wall with one of the tacks, and then put the candle in the box (Duncker, 1945). The problem is difficult because most people see the box only as a device for holding the tacks, not as a potential problem-solving tool. They become *fixed* in their views about the *functions* of objects, and thereby fail to identify and define all of the available problem tools correctly.

Exploring and Acting: Problem Strategies

Although it's important to represent the problem correctly, as well as its accompanying solution "tools," problem representation alone cannot guarantee a solution. People also need an arsenal of problem *strategies*—techniques that allow us to move systematically toward a problem solution. Two classes of problem strategies can be used to solve problems: *algorithms* and *heuristics*.

Algorithms. For some kinds of well-defined problems, people can use **algorithms,** which are step-by-step rules or procedures that *guarantee* a solution. Everyone uses algorithms to solve math problems, for example. There are fixed rules for addition, subtraction, and so on; as long as people use the rules properly, they will always arrive at the correct solution. Solving anagrams, such as MBLOPRE, is another case in point. There are seven letters in the word, which means there are 5040 possible combinations of the letters. If you systematically work out each of the possible sequences, one will eventually provide a solution to the PROBLEM. But it could take a long time.

Computers are often programmed to use algorithms because computers are capable of examining lots of information very quickly. But algorithms are not always practical strategies for problem solution, even for computers. Consider chess, for example. In principle, it would be possible to use algorithms to play chess—the computer would simply need to consider all of the possible consequences of a particular move. But practically, computers cannot examine all the possible outcomes in a chess game; they can examine only some of them. Consider that there are some 10^{40} possible game sequences, so even if a computer could calculate a game in under one-millionth of one-thousandth of a second, it would still require 10^{21} centuries to examine all the game possibilities (Best, 1989). It could do so; it would just take a very long time. Another problem with algo-

People use heuristics—"rules of thumb"—when they play chess because the human mind simply cannot examine all the possible moves and their consequences during a game.

rithms is that they work for only certain kinds of well-defined problems—there is no algorithm, for example, for deciding how to be happy, or for deciding on an appropriate career.

Heuristics. In cases in which it's not feasible to use an algorithm, or in cases in which one is not readily available, it's possible to use **heuristics,** which are essentially problem-solving "rules of thumb." To solve an anagram, especially one with seven letters, it's hardly expedient to use an algorithmic approach, examining all 5040 possible letter sequences. Instead, you can turn to heuristics. You know that English words don't usually begin with MB, or end with BL, so you can avoid checking out those possibilities. You can use your knowledge about English words to make guesses about the most likely solution possibilities. Heuristics are extremely adaptive problem-solving tools because they often open the door to a quick and accurate solution. In natural environments, quick solutions can mean the difference between life and death. An organism cannot spend its time wrapped in thought, systematically working through a long list of solution possibilities. Instead, it's adaptive for the organism to guess, as long as the guess is based on some kind of logic.

Let's consider some of the more common heuristics that people use to solve problems. In **means-ends analysis,** people attack problems by devising *means,* or actions, that are designed to reduce the gap between the current starting point and the desired goal, or *ends* (Newell & Simon, 1972). Usually, this strategy requires breaking down the problem into a series of simpler subgoals, in which the appropriate means to an end are more immediately visible. Let's assume that Peter, a normally nonachieving undergraduate, wants to start a relationship with Jill, the brightest student in his psychology class. Obviously, asking Jill out immediately is unlikely to succeed, so Peter breaks the problem down into more manageable components.

First, he reasons, he'll impress her in class by making an insightful comment during the lecture. He now has a new goal, acting intelligent in class, for which there is relatively straightforward means—he needs to study hard so he can master the material. Assuming he is successful (everyone now thinks he is an amazingly insightful young man), he devises a new subgoal: making some kind of sus-

Consider a surgical problem. If your life were on the line, would you want a doctor who "goes by the book" or one who experiments with new techniques that might or might not produce a medical solution?

INSIDE THE PROBLEM: *Transferring Strategies Across Problems*

Solving problems through analogy is one of the most valuable heuristics you can use. But it requires that you see the connection between the problems that you've solved before and the current task at hand. Unfortunately, making the connection turns out to be quite difficult, even if the previous and current problems share many problem features. Consider the following problem, taken from Gick & McGarry (1992):

> One Saturday night, at a local country dance, 40 people, 20 men and 20 women, showed up to dance. The dance was a "contra dance," in which men and women face each other in lines. From 8 to 10 P.M., there were 20 heterosexual couples (consisting of one man and one woman each; i.e., two men or women cannot dance together) dancing on the floor. At 10 P.M., however, two women left, leaving 38 people to dance. Could the dance caller make arrangements so that the remaining people could all dance together at the same time in 19 heterosexual couples? (p. 638)

This problem is actually quite easy for most people to solve. They recognize that 20 men and 18 women cannot be divided into 19 mixed-sex couples, so the answer is "no" (this is sometimes called a "parity" problem). Now take a look at the checkerboard pattern shown in Figure 9.11:

> You are given a checkerboard and 32 dominoes. Each domino covers exactly two adjacent squares on the board. Thus, the 32 dominoes can cover all 64 squares of the checkerboard. Now suppose two squares are cut off at

diagonally opposite corners of the board. If possible, show how you would place 31 dominoes on the board so that all of the 62 remaining squares are covered. If you think it is impossible, give a proof of why. (Gick & McGarry, 1992, p. 625)

This problem turns out to be much more difficult to solve, even though it's actually very similar to the dance problem (it's also a "parity" problem). Just substitute the word "man" for black and the word "woman" for white, and think of the domino as the pairing of a mixed-sex couple. The first problem should serve as an effective *analogy* for solving the second. But most people fail to see the connection. In the study by

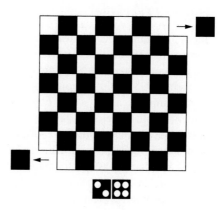

FIGURE 9.11
The Mutilated Checkerboard. The diagonally opposite corners of this checkerboard have been cut off. How would you place 31 dominoes on the board so that all of the 62 remaining squares are covered?

Gick & McGarry (1992), people were first shown how to solve the dance-partner problem and were then asked to solve the checkerboard problem. Very few solved the second problem correctly even though they understood the solution to the first.

What kinds of factors promote successful transfer from one problem-solving situation to another? For one thing, people who have a great deal of experience in a particular area seem better able to draw connections across situations relevant to their expertise than do nonexperts. Experts are able to see what amounts to the "deep structure" of a problem (its true meaning representation), and they can therefore map one kind of problem to another by noting how the problems are similar (Novick, 1988). Cognitive scientists who are familiar with parity problems, for example, might have little trouble recognizing the common link between the dance and checkerboard problems.

It also helps if problem-solving hints are provided. In our checkerboard problem, if subjects are told to try using the dance-partner solution as a way of solving the checkerboard problem, performance improves significantly. Finally, it may even help transfer somewhat if your initial attempts at solving the first problem *fail*. If you get stuck while you're solving one kind of problem and then find yourself stuck in a similar way during a later problem, you tend to use your earlier failure as a way of "reminding" yourself how you solved the first (Gick & McGarry, 1992).

---

tained contact with Jill. Forming a small study group would be a good means to that end, he surmises, so he approaches the recently impressed Jill with the idea. Notice the key ingredients of the problem-solving strategy: Establish where you are, figure out where you want to be, and then devise a means for effectively getting you from here to there. Often, as in Peter's case, means-ends analysis is made more effective by working systematically through subgoals.

Another heuristic that can be effective is **working backward**—starting at the goal state and trying to move back toward the starting point. Suppose someone asked you to generate a set of anagrams. How would you proceed? Would you try to generate sets of randomly arranged letters and then see whether a particular sequence forms a word? Of course not. You would start with the solution, the word, and work backward by mixing up the known sequence.

Let's consider another example: You're working on a biology project tracking the growth of bacteria in a petri dish. You know that this particular strain of bacteria doubles every 2 hours. After starting the experiment, you discover that the petri dish is exactly full after 12 hours. After how many hours was the petri dish exactly half full? To solve this one, it's better to work backward. If the dish is full after 12 hours, and it takes 2 hours for the bacteria to double, what did the dish look like after 10 hours? This turns out to be the answer, which is arrived at rather simply if the problem is attacked in reverse.

Finally, another useful heuristic for problem solving is **searching for analogies.** If you can see a resemblance between the current problem and some task that you have solved in the past, you can quickly obtain an acceptable solution. Imagine that a man buys a horse for $60 and sells it for $70. Later, he buys the same horse back for $80 and sells it again for $90. How much money did the man make in the horse-trading business? The attentive reader will not miss this one. It's a different version of the ticket scalping problem that opened this chapter. If you see the relationship between the two problems, you're unlikely to suffer the same problem-solving pitfalls you encountered before (see Inside the Problem on page 339).

Looking and Learning

The ideal problem solver identifies and defines the problem, seeks the best problem representation, and explores and acts on problem strategies. But the whole process is incomplete unless you also *look and learn* from your experience (Bransford & Stein, 1993). Think about a student who tries to use the principles of psychology to improve a test score. The goal is clear—an improved test score—and the student could develop a variety of possible study strategies to enhance performance. But the ideal problem solver doesn't stop at the final score; the ideal problem solver "debugs" performance in an effort to maximize the information gained. By analyzing your performance in detail, noting where you made mistakes as well as correct answers, you can determine whether your strategy helped solve one kind of problem, but not another. Through an after-the-fact analysis, you can gain insight into *why* a particular heuristic failed or succeeded. Look and learn from your experience so that the next time, you can do better still.

Making Decisions

In what ways does the topic of decision making differ from the topic of problem solving? Do you think decision making is a part of problem solving, or is problem solving a part of decision making?

We turn our attention now to the topic of **decision making,** which investigates the thought processes involved in evaluating and choosing from among a set of alternatives. Obviously, decision making and problem solving are closely aligned. When people make decisions, they are confronted with a set of alternatives and are required to make a choice. The choice is almost always accompanied by *risk*, so it's in an individual's interest to evaluate and select among the alternatives with care. Think about the military strategist on the brink of conflict, who must determine whether to attack with vigor or pull back in retreat. Or consider the physician who must choose between a risky treatment that may kill or save a patient with some unsettling probabilities.

As in problem solving, decision making is influenced by how people "see" or represent the alternatives in their minds, and by their choice of decision-making strategies. Let's examine how each of these processes affects the choices that people make.

The "Framing" of Decision Alternatives

It turns out that the manner in which the alternatives are structured, called **framing,** exerts a dramatic influence on the decision-making process. For example, in a study by McNeil and others (1982), practicing hospital physicians were asked to choose between two forms of treatment for a patient with lung cancer: either a surgical operation on the lungs, or a six-week treatment with radiation. Half of the physicians received the following information prior to making the choice:

> Of 100 people having surgery, 10 will die during treatment, 32 will have died by one year, and 66 will have died by five years. Of 100 people having radiation therapy, none will die during treatment, 23 will have died by one year, and 78 will have died by five years.

Put yourself in the doctor's shoes—which would you choose? The other half of the physicians were given the following:

> Of 100 people having surgery, 90 will be alive immediately after the treatment, 68 will be alive after one year, and 34 will be alive after five years. Of 100 people having radiation therapy, all will be alive immediately after treatment, 77 will be alive after one year, and 22 will be alive after five years.

Do you want to change your mind? Actually, exactly the same information is given in each of the choice scenarios. The only difference is that in the first description the treatment outcomes are "framed," or structured, in terms of who will die, whereas the second description emphasizes who is likely to survive. The treatment consequences, once again, are exactly the same in each case. Yet practicing physicians are more than twice as likely to choose radiation when the choices are "death based" than when the choices are framed around survival. Why? The reason probably has to do with the fact that death is abhorrent to physicians. The surgery alternative in the first example clearly states that people will die during the treatment, so it is to be avoided. Interestingly, doctors are even more susceptible to these framing effects than patients who are given the same choices!

This example reinforces the point that human decision making is a complex and not always "rational" process (at least from an "objective" perspective). Peo-

People are willing to take substantial risks when the outcome is uncertain, at least under some circumstances.

ple are prone to inconsistency in their judgments, in part because our minds weigh information differently in different situations (Kahneman, Slovic, & Tversky, 1982). Let's consider another example: Suppose you were given the choice of winning $40 with a probability of 0.40 or winning $30 with a probability of 0.50. Which would you choose? From a statistical perspective, there is a "rational" choice based on the *expected value* of each alternative. An "expected" value is simply the value that you would expect to gain, on average, by choosing one particular alternative many times. Winning $40 with a probability of 0.40 leads to an expected average gain of $16 ($40 × 0.40); winning $30 with a probability of 0.50 leads to an expected value of $15 ($30 × .50). The "rational" choice, then, is to pick the first alternative, which is what most people do.

But suppose you were given a choice of winning $40 with a probability of 0.80 or winning $30 with a probability of 1.00. Again, the rational choice is pick the first alternative (expected values of $32 versus $30), but people tend to act differently in this context. They go for a sure thing. How people weigh the decision-making alternatives depends on the particular situation. In general, when people are confronted with situations in which they think they can gain something (such as winning money), they tend to avoid taking risks—they choose certainty. But if the outcomes potentially lead to a loss of some kind (such as someone dying), people are much more likely to take a risk that will limit or avoid the loss.

Another factor that needs to be considered is the decision maker's interpretation of the problem. In the medical example, the doctors seemed to be acting irrationally, switching choices depending on how the same information was "framed." But the treatment problem might have been interpreted quite differently by the doctors in the two situations. For example, when the alternatives were "death based," perhaps the doctors readily connected the deaths to the treatment (surgery will kill 10 people and radiation none). In contrast, when the alternatives were framed around who was "living," they might have focused on long-term survival and not thought too much about the hazards of treatment (34 people who receive surgery will be alive after five years, but only 22 radiation patients will survive this long). Thus, you cannot assume that the problem information was identical in the two framings—you need to take into account how the problem was actually represented in the mind of the decision maker (Berkeley & Humphreys, 1982; Einhorn & Hogarth, 1981; Jou, Shanteau, & Harris, 1996).

Decision-Making Heuristics

When people are forced to choose from among a set of alternatives, most rely on heuristics, or "rules of thumb," just as they do when solving problems. These strategies simplify the decision-making process and often lead to correct judgments, but they can sometimes lead people astray.

Representativeness. In cases in which people are asked to judge the probability of an object or event occurring in some class A or B, they often rely on a rule of thumb called **representativeness.** They arrive at their decision by comparing the similarity of the object or event in question to the average, or prototypical, member of each class. It's easiest to demonstrate with an example. Let's assume that your friends, the Renfields, have six children. If B denotes boy and G denotes girl, which of the following two birth order sequences do you think is more likely?

1. B B B G G G
2. B G G B G B

If you said the second alternative, you're like most people. Actually, according to the rules of probability, the two outcomes are equally likely. People favor the second alternative because the first sequence clashes with their "worldview" of randomness; the first sequence just doesn't look like the outcome of a random process. What if you flipped a coin six times and you got six heads? You'd probably think it was a crooked coin. A sequence of six heads isn't similar to, or "representative" of, what you think of as a random sequence. You have taken the outcome and compared it to some standard and made your decision accordingly. People probably use representativeness often to make decisions in real-world settings. For example, there's evidence that clerks in stores use the type of products that a shopper buys as a way of judging age. If someone loads his or her shopping cart with products normally thought to be representative of an older consumer, the clerk's estimate of the shopper's age increases (McCall, 1994).

Using a heuristic such as representativeness is adaptive and beneficial most of the time, but it can lead to irrational decision making. Imagine that you're leafing through a stack of questionnaires that have been filled out by some adult men. One of the respondents lists his height as 6 feet 5 inches, but his answers are so sloppily written that you can't make out his circled profession—it's either bank president or basketball player (NBA). You need to make a choice: Which is he? Most people tend to choose NBA player because the applicant's tall and apparently not interested in careful writing (Beyth-Marom & Lichtenstein, 1984). But this is actually an illogical choice, because the chance of someone in the sample being a professional basketball player is extremely low—bank presidents outnumber NBA players by a wide margin (probably at least 50 to 1). In choosing basketball player, people have ignored the *base rate*, or the proportion of times that an object or event is likely to occur in the population being sampled.

The representativeness heuristic also dupes people into committing what is called the *conjunction error*. Consider the following: Linda is 31 years old, single, outspoken, and very bright. She majored in philosophy. As a student she was deeply concerned with issues of discrimination and social justice and participated in antinuclear demonstrations. Which of the following alternatives is more likely?

1. Linda is a bank teller.
2. Linda is a bank teller and active in the feminist movement.

In a study conducted by Tversky and Kahneman (1983), 85% of the participants judged alternative 2 to be the more likely. Why? Because Linda's description is more "representative" of someone active in the feminist movement than it is of a bank teller. But think about it—how can the odds of two things happening together be lower than the likelihood of any one of those events happening alone? Notice that the second alternative is actually a subset of the first alternative and therefore cannot be more likely. Those who choose alternative 2 have acted illogically, at least from the standpoint of the rational decision maker.

Availability. At other times, when people are asked to estimate the odds of some event occurring, they rely on their memories to influence their judgments. The **availability heuristic** induces people to base their estimates on the ease with which examples of the event come to mind. Imagine that you're asked to estimate the likelihood that you will forget to turn off your alarm clock on Friday night. If you can easily remember lots of instances in which your Saturday morning sleep was interrupted by a blasting alarm, your estimate of forgetting is likely to be high. You have relied on your previous experiences—particularly those experiences that easily come to mind—as a basis for judging probability.

Once again, the availability heuristic is likely to be an adaptive strategy much of the time. But, as with the representativeness heuristic, researchers can arrange situations in which these decision-making rules of thumb lead people astray. Which do you think is more likely, an English word that begins with the letter K or an English word with K in the third position? By now you're probably skeptical

Do you think people decide on the "representativeness" of an alternative by comparing it to a prototype or to a set of stored exemplars in long-term memory?

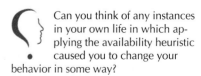

Can you think of any instances in your own life in which applying the availability heuristic caused you to change your behavior in some way?

People are much more likely to worry when they fly if a recently publicized airline disaster is fresh and "available" in their minds.

about your first choice, but most people think that English words that begin with K are more likely (Tversky & Kahneman, 1973). In fact, English words that have K in the third position are much more common (the ratio is about 3:1). Which do you think is more likely, someone dying from any kind of accident or someone dying from a stroke? Accidents, right? It's not even close. Over twice as many people are likely to die from stroke than from any kind of accident (Slovic, Fischoff, & Lichtenstein, 1982). People make the error because examples of the incorrect alternative are more likely to come to mind. It's easier to think of an English word with K in the first position, and accidental deaths get much more publicity than deaths due to stroke.

Anchoring and Adjustment. Judgments are also influenced by starting points—that is, by any initial estimates that one might be given. For example, Tversky and Kahneman (1974) asked people to estimate the number of African countries belonging to the United Nations. Prior to answering, subjects were given a number (between 0 and 100) and were asked to pick the number of countries by moving up or down from this starting point. So, you might be given the number 10 and asked to estimate the number of countries using 10 as a base. For groups that received 10 and 65 as the initial starting points, the estimated number of African countries was 25 and 45, respectively. The judgments were apparently adjusted based on initial estimates, or *anchors,* in a direction that stayed close to the starting point. The smaller the base, the fewer the countries that were estimated.

In another experiment described by Tversky and Kahneman (1974), one group of subjects was asked to estimate the product of the following numbers:

$$1 \times 2 \times 3 \times 4 \times 5 \times 6 \times 7 \times 8$$

whereas a second group was asked to estimate the product of the same numbers presented in reverse order:

$$8 \times 7 \times 6 \times 5 \times 4 \times 3 \times 2 \times 1$$

The correct answer in both cases is 40,320. But the first group gave an estimate, on the average, of 512, whereas the second group's estimate averaged 2250. Quite a difference, given that it's the same problem in both cases. In this example, the early numbers in the sequence serve as the anchors leading to either low or more moderate estimates.

The Value of Heuristics

What are we to make of such an imperfect decision maker? As psychologist Reid Hastie (1991) has noted, the heuristic tool user described by Kahneman and Tversky is "an image of a decision maker of 'small brain' attempting to make do with a limited set of useful, imperfect, and not-too-demanding cognitive subroutines" (p. 136).

However, imperfect as heuristics may be, there are several points worth making in their favor. First, the use of heuristics may lead to systematic errors under some circumstances, but, as Tversky and Kahneman (1974) have argued, they are usually surprisingly effective. Second, heuristics are *economical.* Optimal, or rational, decision making can be a complex, time-consuming activity. Strategies that lead to quick decisions with little cost are adaptive even if they sometimes lead to error. Third, to act optimally, in the sense of rational probability theory, people must possess all the information needed to calculate a choice; unfortunately, they often don't have all this information. In these cases, heuristics become useful tools for pointing people in the right direction.

Moreover, as we discussed in the section on framing effects, the fact that people make "errors" in artificial laboratory situations is somewhat misleading. We can define what the "rational" decision might be, based on objective information, but people do not always interpret the decision alternatives in the way the researcher intends. People bring background knowledge and expectations to any situation that affect how they think and behave. In addition, it's important to recognize that just because people make decision errors does not mean they're using maladaptive processes. Think back to Chapter 5 and our discussion of perceptual illusions. It's easy to arrange situations in which people see or hear things that aren't really there, but there is still wide agreement that human perceptual systems are highly adaptive.

◤ SOLVING THE PROBLEMS: A SUMMARY

In this chapter, we've discussed how people use their "higher mental processes" to communicate, categorize, find solutions to problems, and decide among alternatives. Each of the adaptive problems under consideration effectively illustrates how the mind samples from its adaptive "tool kit" to coexist successfully with its environment.

COMMUNICATING WITH OTHERS To communicate effectively, humans have developed rules (grammar) for combining arbitrary symbols in meaningful ways to express thoughts, feelings, and needs to others. A proper grammar consists of rules for combining sounds (phonology), rules for constructing sentences from words (syntax), and rules for meaning (semantics). In order to understand how language works, language researchers believe it is important to distinguish between the surface structure of a sentence—the literal ordering of words—and its deep structure, which taps the underlying representation of meaning. To comprehend the communications of others, people rely on mutual knowledge, or pragmatics, to interpret statements or requests that may be riddled with ambiguity.

Are humans born with a natural "blueprint" for language, or does language develop exclusively as a product of experience? The sequence of language development turns out to be quite universal—it doesn't matter where you look in the world, babies show similar "milestones" in language development. This finding has led many researchers to the conclusion that people are born "ready" to learn language in the same way they are born "ready" to learn to walk. The ability to produce written and spoken language allows people to gather and transmit knowledge in ways that seem to be one of the truly unique characteristics of the human species.

CLASSIFYING AND CATEGORIZING When people categorize, or put objects into meaningful groups, they create a world that is more sensible and predictable. Categorization skills enable people to infer invisible properties about objects—if X is a member of category Y, then X will have at least some of the properties of category Y members. As a result, people can make accurate predictions about the things they encounter. How do people define category membership? The evidence suggests that they often rely on "family resemblance" to make the categorization judgment. Members of the same category tend to share certain basic or core features. At the same time, categories are remarkably flexible; their boundaries are "fuzzy," which enables people to classify things adaptively even when those objects may not share all the typical features of the category members. Categories also have structures that are hierarchical—there are categories within categories within categories. An object that fits the category "Siamese cat" also fits the category "animal" or "living thing." Research indicates that people most commonly assign objects to "basic-level" categories, which tend to be at intermediate levels of the hierarchy.

SOLVING PROBLEMS When people are faced with a problem in their environment, there is a goal, which may or may not be well defined, and it's not immediately obvious how to get from the problem to the solution. What are the thought processes involved in finding an appropriate solution? Using the model of the IDEAL problem solver, good problem solving involves five main steps: (1) identify the problem; (2) define, or represent, the problem; (3) explore strategies for solution; (4) act on those problem strategies; and (5) look and learn from the experience. To identify and define a problem correctly, it's important that people "see" the problem in the right way. One of the common pitfalls with problem solving is that people allow their preconceptions to influence how they represent problem information. For example, most people fall prey to "functional fixedness," or the tendency to see objects and their functions in certain fixed ways.

People use a variety of problem-solving strategies. Algorithms are procedures that guarantee a solution, but they're often time-consuming and cannot always be applied. Heuristics are problem-solving "rules of thumb" that can be applied quickly but do not always lead to the correct solution. Examples of problem-solving heuristics include means-end analysis, working backward, and solving through analogies.

MAKING DECISIONS Decision making involves the thought processes used in evaluating and choosing from among a set of alternatives. When people make decisions, they are confronted with a set of alternatives and are required to make a choice. Choice in decision making is almost always accompanied by risk, so it's adaptive to evaluate and select among the alternatives with care. As with problem solving, decision making is influenced by how the alternatives are viewed or represented. For example, the "framing" or structuring of the alternatives can affect the decision that is made. People commonly use a variety of decision heuristics, including representativeness, availability, and anchoring and adjustment. Again, although these strategies may not always cause people to make the right decision, they allow people to move quickly and efficiently and to use their past experience as they strive to reach their goal.

Terms to Remember

thinking The processes that underlie the mental manipulation of knowledge, usually in an attempt to reach a goal or solve a problem.

COMMUNICATING WITH OTHERS

linguistic relativity hypothesis The proposal that language determines the characteristics and content of thought.

grammar The rules of language that allow the communicator to combine arbitrary symbols to convey meaning; grammar includes the rules of phonology, syntax, and semantics.

phonology Rules governing how sounds should be combined to make words in a language.

syntax Rules governing how words should be combined to form sentences.

semantics The rules used in language to communicate meaning.

phonemes The smallest significant sound units in speech.

morphemes The smallest units in a language that carry meaning.

surface structure The literal ordering of words in a sentence.

deep structure The underlying representation of meaning in a sentence.

pragmatics The practical knowledge used to comprehend the intentions of a speaker and to produce an effective response.

CLASSIFYING AND CATEGORIZING

category A class of objects (people, places, or things) that most people agree belong together.

defining features The set of features that are necessary to make objects acceptable members of a category (for example, to be a "bird" the object must have wings and feathers, must fly, and so on).

family resemblance The core features that category members share; a given member of the category may have some but not necessarily all of these features.

prototypes The best or most representative member of a category (such as robin for the category "bird").

category exemplars Specific examples of category members that are stored in long-term memory.

basic-level categories The level in a category hierarchy that provides the most useful and predictive information; the "basic level" usually resides at an intermediate level in a category hierarchy.

SOLVING PROBLEMS

well-defined problem A problem with a well-stated goal, a clear starting point, and a relatively easy way to tell when a solution has been obtained.

ill-defined problem A problem, such as the search for "happiness," that has no well-stated goal, no clear starting point, or no mechanism for evaluating progress.

functional fixedness The tendency to see objects, and their functions, in certain fixed and typical ways.

mental sets The tendency to rely on well-established habits of perception and thought when attempting to solve problems.

algorithms Step-by-step rules or procedures that, if applied correctly, guarantee a problem solution.

heuristics "Rules of thumb" that people use to solve problems; heuristics can usually be applied quickly, but they do not guarantee that a solution will be found.

means-ends analysis A problem-solving heuristic that involves devising actions, or means, that reduce the distance between the current starting point and the desired end (the goal state).

working backward A problem-solving heuristic that involves starting at the goal state and moving backward toward the starting point in order to see how the goal state can be reached.

searching for analogies A problem-solving heuristic that involves trying to find a connection between the current problem and some previous problem one has solved successfully.

MAKING DECISIONS

decision making The thought processes involved in evaluating and choosing from among a set of alternatives; it usually involves some kind of risk.

framing The way in which the alternatives in a decision-making situation are structured.

representativeness heuristic The tendency to make decisions based on an alternative's similarity, or representativeness, in relation to an ideal. For example, people decide whether a sequence is "random" based on how irregular the sequence looks.

availability heuristic The tendency to base estimates on the ease with which examples come to mind. For example, if you've just heard about a plane crash, your estimates of the likelihood of plane crashes increases because "plane crashes" easily come to mind.

We've seen how psychologists analyze the various components of mind. They break an internal activity such as thinking into "parts" and then, based on research, speculate as to how those parts are organized into a coherent "whole." Problem solving becomes a series of component stages, such as problem identification and definition, strategy exploration, evaluation of results, and so on. Decisions are made by applying heuristics, such as availability or representativeness, that themselves are based on more fundamental processes involving learning, memory, and perception.

But what about the average person on the street—a nonpsychologist, someone who has never heard of encoding processes, prototypes, heuristics, or deep structure? Does the average person have a theory of mind? Do people maintain a coherent set of beliefs about the way that mental activities are organized and about what mental activities represent? Of course they do. Everyone has a commonsense theory of mind, and these intuitive "folk" psychologies importantly affect how people behave.

An Adult's View of Mind

Recently, cognitive scientists have begun to examine systematically how people believe mental activities are organized. For example, when you think about "thinking," where do things like remembering, dreaming, emotions, or reasoning fit in? Is remembering a part of reasoning or of conceptualizing? Is planning a kind of deciding or is deciding a kind of planning? Commonsense ideas about the inner workings of the mind are worth examining because these ideas affect the explanations that people give for their own behaviors, as well as the behaviors of others. How individuals interpret a lie, for instance, depends on whether they believe the speaker intends to deceive them and whether he or she understands that the statement offered is false (Coleman & Kay, 1981).

Rips and Conrad (1989) analyzed nonpsychologists' beliefs about mental activities by asking whether one kind of psychological activity is *a kind of* or *a part of* another mental activity. It turns out that when people classify things, it is often in terms of *is-a-kind-of* and *is-a-part-of* relations. It's natural, for example, for people to say that reading is a kind of activity or that a wheel is a part of a car. As a first step, undergraduates (who were not psychology majors) were asked to make a list of common mental activities (thinking, reasoning, and so on). Next, two new groups of subjects were asked to evaluate these activities in terms of the *is-a-part-of* or *is-a-kind-of* relations.

Specifically, each group was shown pairs of mental activities in the form "X is a kind of Y" or "X is a part of Y." They were told to answer "yes" to an *is-a-kind-of* pair "only if every instance of one activity was among the instances of another." An example would be: "Conceptualizing is a kind of thinking— yes or no?" For the *is-a-part-of* relations, subjects were told to answer affirmatively "only if every instance of the one activity had an instance of the other as a part." For example, "Is imagining a part of dreaming?" All of the data were then configured into diagrams that showed relationships that were agreed on by the majority of the subjects.

Figure 9.12 shows examples of these diagrams, for activities such as thinking and planning. The left diagram maps onto the *is-a-part-of* relations; the arrows point from one mental activity that is considered to be a part of another mental activity. So, thinking is considered to be a part of conceptualizing, which is a part of remembering, which is a part of reasoning. The right diagram shows the *is-a-kind-of* relations. Here, the arrows point from one mental activity that is thought to be a kind of another mental activity. Planning is a kind of deciding, which is a kind of reasoning.

One interesting property of some of the diagram pairs is the expression of a reciprocal relationship: People tend to think, for example, that planning is a kind of thinking but also that thinking is a part of planning. How could this be? People don't tend to think about classes of real-world objects in this way. You might say that a hammer is a kind of tool, but you wouldn't say that a tool is a part of a hammer. You might say that an elephant is a kind of mammal, but you would never say that a mammal is a part of an elephant. According to Rips and Conrad (1989), internal ideas about mental activities tend to be more ambiguous and vague than conceptions of physical objects. As a result, people's decision rules about the classification of mental acts tend to be different, and perhaps more flexible, than their rules for classifying objects in the real world.

A Child's View of Mind

What about children—do they have a well-developed theory of mind? Children, it turns out, show evidence of thinking about things abstractly—that is, they can represent objects inside their heads—as early as 18 months. Children under age 2 understand that some kinds of objects don't exist and that goals or desires may not be realized (Gopnik, 1982). By the age of 3, children are able to distinguish among dreams, thoughts, and real objects (Wellman & Estes, 1986). By the age of 5, children not only think about objects in terms of representations in their heads, they also show some ability to make inferences about the psychological states of others.

For example, in one experiment (Perner, Leekam, & Wimmer, 1987) 3-year-old children were shown a candy box that was actually filled with pencils. After peering into the box and expressing some surprise, the children were then asked what someone else, such as another child, would think is inside the box. "Pencils," the children tended to respond, "Pencils will be inside the box." A 5- or 6-year-old won't say "Pencils"; instead, he or she is more likely to say "Candy." Older children understand that other people have different views of the world than they do; other people can have more or less knowledge, and different beliefs (Gopnik,

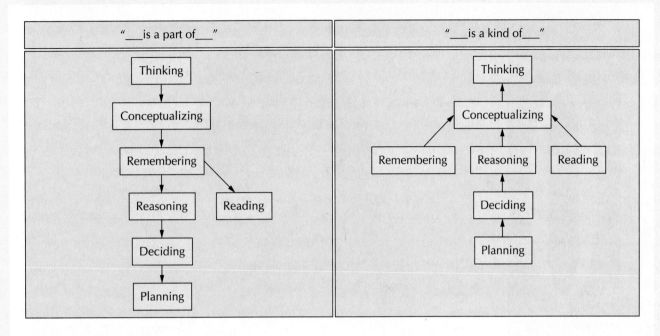

FIGURE 9.12

Diagramming Mental Activities. These examples of *is-a-part-of* and *is-a-kind-of* diagrams are derived from the research of Rips and Conrad (1989). The arrows in the diagram on the left indicate where one mental activity is considered to be a *part* of another mental activity (thinking is a part of conceptualizing, which is a part of remembering, and so on). The arrows in the diagram on the right indicate where one mental activity is considered to be a *kind* of another mental activity (planning is a kind of deciding, which is a kind of reasoning).

1993). By age 5 or 6, children have already begun developing an intuitive concept of the mind, both their own and others'.

In conclusion, now that you've worked your way through Chapter 9 and you understand some of the ways that psychologists tackle the inner workings of the mind, you might consider going back and thinking about these topics from your own perspective. How do you think about problem solving? How do you think people carve the world into meaningful chunks? Does the analysis of language and thought described in this chapter agree with your own sense of "inner space"? Sometimes, common-sense ideas about these things reveal great insight into what should be the correct scientific approach. It is with this idea in mind that current cognitive scientists have approached the study of "folk" psychology.

On a Saturday morning in October, Jefferson Tarpy drops down his yellow #2 pencil and glances about the room with a cocky grin. Around him, working feverishly, sit dozens of others, similar in age and general appearance, but with pencils raised and sweat collecting on furrowed brows. Jefferson has finished early, as is his custom, and he's just aced the most important standardized test of his life. Next stop: medical school, a top residency, a lifetime of security and bliss. . . .

Meanwhile, outside in a park across the street, Larry Steinway has also dropped his yellow pencil. But he doesn't notice. He will need to rely on his attendant to recover it. Although he is physically 22, Larry Steinway's mind drifts in a world occupied by a 4-year-old's thoughts and a 4-year-old's impulses. He uses language only haltingly; his hopes for an elementary school education are limited. Still, he responds quickly when his attendant asks him to calculate the number of seconds elapsing in 65 years, 14 days, and 15 hours. His correct answer includes the requisite number of leap years and arrives in slightly under a minute and a half. . . .

Overhead, oblivious to the exploits of Larry Steinway, flies a single nutcracker in search of a place to deposit his recently harvested supply of pine seeds. On this particular trip, one of many over the past few months, the bird will store its 25,000th seed. Across miles of terrain lie thousands of secret caches, all attributable to this one bird, scattered among the equally numerous storage locations of countless other nutcrackers. Over the coming winter months, this single bird will successfully revisit its own hiding places, ignoring others, and recover some 80% of the hidden seeds. . . .

These three short sketches each demonstrates behavior that *might* be characterized as intelligent. What do you think? Certainly we can agree that Jefferson Tarpy fits the description of intelligence—ace performer on standardized tests, self-assured; he probably gets all A's and is good at tennis. But what about Larry Steinway—someone who is poor at language, who operates at a mental level far below his physical age? Definitely not intelligent, you say; but then how do we explain his extraordinary calculating skills? Wouldn't you characterize "lightning calculation" as an odd but nevertheless intelligent behavior? Finally, consider the nutcracker. It can't do geometry or calculus, but could you remember where you put 25,000 seeds scattered across miles of confusing terrain? Don't you think this remarkable ability to adapt to the harshness of winter should be considered a prime example of intelligent behavior?

It probably won't surprise you to learn that psychologists, too, have had difficulty agreeing on a definition of intelligence. As we've seen, the term can have a variety of meanings. Practically, when psychologists use the term **intelligence,** it is usually in reference to individual differences—specifically, the differences that people show in their ability to perform tasks. People clearly differ in ability, and the measurement of these differences is used to infer the capacity called "intelligence." If you think about it, you'll realize that if everyone had the same ability to solve math problems, or devise novel and creative ideas, the label "intelligent" would lose its meaning. Psychologists who study intelligence attempt to measure individual differences and to study how and why those differences occur. One of the important goals is to use the measurement of individual differences to predict such things as job performance and success in school.

But "intelligence" is also a term psychologists use to characterize one's capacity to adapt. By studying intelligence, psychologists hope to uncover the mental activities that underlie the "purposive adaptation to, and selection and shaping of,

Most people would have no trouble accepting that Balamurati Krishna Ambati is "intelligent"—after all, at age 12 he was a third-year pre-med student at New York University.

Ten-year-old "savant" Eddie Bonafe was born with severe physical and mental handicaps. But he could reproduce every hymn he heard sung in church on the piano before he had learned to walk. Would you call Eddie "intelligent"?

This little bird, Clark's Nutcracker, can remember the locations of thousands of seeds scattered across miles of confusing terrain. Wouldn't you call that "intelligent" behavior?

real-world environments relevant to one's life" (Sternberg, 1985). What underlies the remarkable human ability to handle rapidly shifting environments? Is it the ability to think abstractly? Is it the ability to develop strategies for solving problems, or to acquire knowledge efficiently? Psychologists are fascinated at the prospect of measuring these capacities because they believe that therein lies the key to understanding the adaptive mind.

PREVIEWING THE CONCEPTUAL AND PRACTICAL PROBLEMS

Our focus in this chapter will be on how psychologists have attempted to resolve the conceptual and practical problems that are central to the study of intelligence. We'll consider intelligence as a capacity to be understood by the science of psychology: How should intelligence be conceptualized? How can we actually measure the individual differences that people show in their performance? What are the sources of intelligence—that is, does intelligent behavior arise primarily from one's genetic background or from one's life experiences? In each of the chapter sections, we'll see that the concept of intelligence has evolved over time—both in terms of fundamental conception and in terms of the techniques used to assess its presence.

CONCEPTUALIZING INTELLIGENCE It's normal for people to talk about intelligence as if it's some "thing" that is possessed by a person, such as blue eyes, long fingers, or a slightly crooked gait. But we cannot see intelligence, nor measure it directly with a stick. Intelligence may not even be best viewed as a single capacity. It may be better seen as a collection of separate abilities. You may be good at math but bad at reading maps; Jerry may be good at fixing mechanical things but terrible at reading. We'll discuss the logic that researchers have used to solve this problem of how to conceptualize intelligence, and we'll look at some of the "solutions" that particular psychologists have suggested. As we'll see, it may be necessary to distinguish between what might be called academic intelligence—the kind of thing measured by a typical intelligence test—and practical, everyday intelligence of the sort that allows people to scrape their way out of tight situations.

▶ **MEASURING INDIVIDUAL DIFFERENCES** Regardless of how we may choose to conceptualize "intelligence," there is still the practical problem of measuring how individuals differ. For any particular kind of task, such as performing well in school, there will be a distribution of abilities. Some people will perform extremely well; others will struggle. If these abilities can be measured accurately, through the use of psychological tests, then early intervention is possible. You can be advised not to enter cartography school if your spatial abilities are weak, or you can be steered toward a career as a mechanic if your mechanical skills are strong. We'll discuss the scientific foundations of intelligence tests and identify the characteristics of good and poor tests. We'll also consider the potential negative side effects of abilities testing, such as the effects of diagnostic labeling on the realization of human potential. But our main focus in this section will be on the famous concept of IQ, or intelligence quotient. We'll explain why it was developed and how IQ is used today.

▶ **DISCOVERING THE SOURCES OF INTELLIGENCE** The study of intelligence is also, in part, an investigation into the plasticity of the human mind. Granted that humans differ in ability, we can ask whether these differences are due to permanent genetic factors or simply to peculiarities in one's environmental history. Is poor map reading a permanent affliction, resulting from a lack of the right kind of genetic blueprint, or can a superior ability to read maps be taught? Because of the wiring in my brain, am I doomed to always have trouble fixing that leaky faucet in my kitchen, or can I be taught mechanical skill? These are important questions, but ones that have been steeped in controversy over the years. The idea that abilities might be genetically "hard-wired" is difficult to accept, because it suggests permanent limits to what education can achieve; it might also be used to discriminate among people, or groups of people, in ways that are potentially destructive to societal harmony. In the final section of this chapter we will discuss evidence that is pertinent to such nature-nurture interpretations of intellectual ability.

Conceptualizing Intelligence

From the perspective of the adaptive mind, it's natural for us to discuss intelligence in terms of the ability of the organism to adapt, or more specifically, to solve the particular problems that it faces. Indeed, this is a fairly common way to think about intelligence (Hilgard, 1987). Adaptive accounts of intelligence are commonplace because they present many advantages. For one thing, focusing our conception of intelligence on adaptation helps prevent us from adopting an anthropocentric bias—that is, from thinking that human thoughts and actions are the only proper measuring sticks for intelligent behavior. The fact that nutcrackers can efficiently hide and relocate thousands of seeds is certainly "intelligent" from the standpoint of adapting to the harshness of winter (Kamil & Balda, 1990). Understanding that different species (and people) have different survival problems to solve virtually guarantees that we will need to establish a wide range of criteria for what characterizes intelligence.

But conceptualizing intelligence simply in terms of adaptability does not tell us much about what produces individual differences. People (and nutcrackers) differ in their ability to fit successfully into their environments, even when they're faced with similar problems. We need to understand the factors that account for individual differences. In this section of the chapter, we'll consider four general ways to accomplish this end: (1) the *psychometric* approach, (2) the *cognitive* approach, (3) the theory of *multiple intelligences*, and (4) the *triarchic* theory. Each is designed to provide a general framework for conceptualizing intelligence, with

Based on this discussion, how reasonable do you think it is to compare "intelligence" among the different peoples and cultures of the world?

the expressed goal of explaining why people differ in mental ability. Why are there four different approaches? One reason is that intelligence has proven to be a difficult concept for psychologists to understand. There is no general agreement about the best way to treat the concept. But as we'll see, each of these approaches offers some interesting insights into the behavior and function of the adaptive mind.

Psychometrics: Measuring the Mind

We begin with the *psychometric approach*, which proposes that intelligence is a mental capacity that can be measured by analyzing performance on mental tests. The word **psychometric** literally means "to measure the mind." Intelligence is determined by giving individuals a variety of tests that assess specific mental skills, such as verbal comprehension, memory, or spatial ability. The collected data are then analyzed with various statistical techniques in an effort to discover any underlying mental "capacity" that can explain test performance.

One of the first systematic attempts to treat intelligence in this way was undertaken in the 19th century by Englishman Sir Francis Galton (1822–1911). Galton was a half-cousin of Charles Darwin, and, like his famous relative, he was deeply committed to the idea of "survival of the fittest." He believed that individual differences in adaptive ability had their basis in heredity and could be measured through a series of tests of sensory discrimination and reaction time. For a small fee, visitors to Galton's laboratory were given a variety of psychological and physical tests, measuring such things as visual acuity, grip strength, and reaction time to sounds. At the end of the test session they were handed a card with a detailed record of their scores (Hilgard, 1987; Johnson and others, 1985).

Galton believed that he was measuring the intelligence of his participants through their performance on his battery of tests. He based his belief partly on the fact that there sometimes appeared to be relationships among the various scores received by a particular individual. If an individual tended to score highly on a certain test, such as sensory acuity, he or she tended to score highly on other measures as well. This pattern suggested to Galton that each of the separate tests, even though they appeared to be measuring quite different things, might be tapping into some general ability—a general intelligence that contributed in part to each of the different measured skills. For an apt analogy, think about the star ath-

Sir Francis Galton (1822–1911) and his "anthropometric" laboratory, which he used to measure intellectual ability.

Deion Sanders, shown here, was able to perform at the highest levels in both professional football and professional baseball. Could Deion's skills be used to support the existence of a factor tapping "general athletic ability"?

How does the notion of general intelligence apply to your performance in school? If you're good in one subject, does that predict how well you do in your other classes?

lete who runs fast, jumps high, and moves well—isn't it natural to assume that this individual has general athletic ability that is simply revealing itself in a number of ways?

As it turned out, Galton's laboratory investigations into the measurement of intelligence were largely unsuccessful. His measurements were crude, and his tests were later revealed to be poor predictors of actual intellectual performance, such as academic success (Wissler, 1901). For these and other reasons, his contributions are of interest primarily for historical rather than scientific reasons. But his general approach captured the attention of other researchers, who went on to develop the psychometric approach in a more rigorous way. Among the more influential of those who carried on the Galton tradition was a mathematically inclined psychologist named Charles Spearman.

Factor Analysis. Spearman's principal contribution was the development of a mathematical technique called **factor analysis** that enabled researchers to analyze the relationships, or correlations, among test scores in a more sophisticated manner. The purpose of factor analysis is to discover, by analyzing statistical correlations among various tests, whether it is in fact possible to account for test performance by appealing to a single underlying ability or whether multiple abilities (or "factors") are needed.

To see how factor analysis works, let's return momentarily to the example of the athlete. If you're convinced that people possess general athletic ability, then you would expect to find correlations among various tests of athletic skill; that is, you should be able to predict how well someone will perform on one measure of skill, given that you know how well he or she performs on another. Good athletes, for example, should run fast, jump high, and have quick reflexes. The correlations exist because there is an underlying ability, athletic skill, that is tapped by each of the individual performance measures. Similar logic applies to intelligence: Someone who is high (or low) in intelligence should perform well (or poorly) on many different kinds of ability tests. Researchers should be able to predict performance on one type of test (such as math) if they know how well the person performs on other tests (such as verbal comprehension or spatial ability). But is this kind of reasoning justified by the data?

*Factors **g** and **s**.* Spearman's application of factor analysis to the testing of mental ability revealed that in order to predict mental test performance, it was necessary to consider *two* factors: (1) a common factor, called **g** for *general intelligence,* that applies to all kinds of test performance, and (2) a *specific* factor, **s,** that is unique to the particular kind of test being administered. The general intelligence factor *g* helps predict performance on a *variety* of tests, presumably because it reflects some general across-the-board ability. (Factor *g* corresponds roughly to what most people think of when they think of intelligence.) But Spearman (1904) discovered that it was not possible to explain individual test scores entirely by appealing to *g*. The correlations among the test scores were high, but not perfect. He found, for example, that someone who performed extremely well on a test of verbal comprehension did not necessarily excel to the same degree on a test of spatial ability. He argued, therefore, that it is necessary to take certain abilities into account, reflected in *s,* that are specific to each individual test (see Figure 10.1). So, to predict performance on a test of verbal comprehension, we would need a measure of ability that is specific to verbal comprehension, in addition to *g*.

Spearman's two-factor theory exerted considerable influence, both in its own time and in the modern analysis of intelligence. But over the years some researchers have challenged Spearman's conclusions, especially his overarching concept of *g*. Psychologist L. L. Thurstone, for example, applied a somewhat different version of factor analysis, as well as a more extensive battery of tests, and

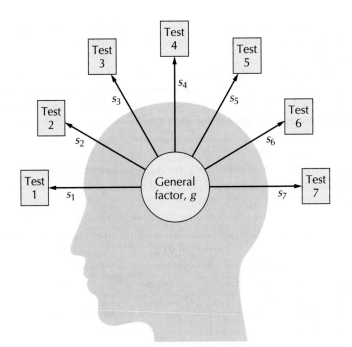

FIGURE 10.1
Spearman's General and Specific Factors. Spearman discovered that to explain performance on a variety of mental tests, it was necessary to consider (1) a common factor, called *g* for general intelligence, that contributes to performance on all of the tests, and (2) specific factors—labeled here as s_1 through s_7—that are "specific" to the particular tests.

discovered evidence for seven "primary mental abilities": verbal comprehension, verbal fluency, numerical ability, spatial ability, memory, perceptual speed, and reasoning (Thurstone, 1938). Thurstone rejected Spearman's notion of a single general intelligence, *g*, because his analysis indicated that these seven primary abilities are largely independent—just because someone is good at verbal reasoning, for example, doesn't mean that he or she will be good at memory or perceptual speed. If performance on one type of test tells us little or nothing about performance on a second test, it's unlikely that the two tests are tapping the same general underlying ability.

Hierarchical Models. Psychologists have argued for decades about (a) the proper way to apply factor analysis, (b) the particular kinds of ability tests that should be used, and (c) whether single or multiple factors are needed to explain the data (Jensen & Weng, 1994). But the evidence for a central *g* turns out to be hard to dismiss completely. For this reason, most modern psychometric theories of intelligence propose a hierarchical approach, as shown in Figure 10.2. General

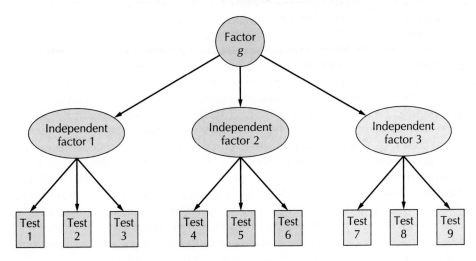

FIGURE 10.2
Hierarchical Models. Many psychologists now propose hierarchical models of intelligence, which include elements found in the theories of both Spearman and Thurstone. Like Thurstone, hierarchical models propose separate factors that contribute independently to certain types of tests (for example, factor 1 contributes to tests 1–3, but not to tests 4–9). But, like Spearman, these models also assume that each of the separate factors is influenced by an overall *g*.

intelligence, *g*, occupies a position at the top of the hierarchy, and various sub-factors that may or may not operate independently from one another sit at the lower levels.

For example, Raymond Cattell (1963) and John Horn (1985; Horn & Cattell, 1966) believe in the notion of general intelligence but contend that it should be broken down into two primary dimensions: *fluid* intelligence and *crystallized* intelligence. **Fluid intelligence** measures one's ability to solve problems, reason, and remember in ways that are relatively uninfluenced by experience. It's the type of intelligence that is probably determined primarily by biological or genetic factors and shouldn't change much as people grow. **Crystallized intelligence,** on the other hand, taps *acquired* knowledge and ability. People learn things about the world, such as how to solve arithmetic problems, and develop abilities that depend on level of schooling and other cultural influences. We'll return to this distinction later in the chapter when we talk specifically about how intelligence changes over time.

> Which do you think contributes the most to performance on an essay exam: crystallized or fluid intelligence?

The Cognitive Approach

Psychologists who use a psychometric approach to the study of intelligence might argue as to the number and types of mental "factors," but all agree that intelligence is ultimately discoverable through detailed analyses of test battery performance. In their view, it is test performance, and test performance alone, that determines how the concept of intelligence is defined and measured. Proponents of the cognitive approach argue instead that intelligence, or at least individual test performance, needs to be understood by analyzing internal mental processes—the information processing routines that underlie intelligent thought (Sternberg, 1985).

Some cognitive psychologists have suggested that performance on mental tests can be predicted by looking primarily at the *speed* of mental processing or by analyzing some measure of how well attention can be allocated across different tasks (see Hunt, 1985; Jensen, 1993; Vernon, 1983). Arthur Jensen (1993) has argued, for example, that intelligence reflects, in part, the speed of transmission among the neural pathways of the brain. The faster the brain communicates internally, the higher the individual's intelligence. The reason that communication speed might be important is that the brain has limited resources and must quickly allocate, or divide, its processing in order to perform efficiently (see Chapter 6). In support of this position, Jensen and his colleagues typically find a significant correlation between measures of neural communication speed and performance on mental tests of intelligence (Reed & Jensen, 1992; Vernon & Mori, 1992). For more on the relation between the speed of neural processing and intelligence, see the accompanying Inside the Problem.

In addition to analyzing the speed of mental processing, cognitive theorists have also attempted to identify the specific mental processes that contribute to superior test performance. Robert Sternberg (1977) developed a procedure called *componential analysis* that uses subjects' reaction times, as well as their error rates, to isolate the mental operations that are tapped by traditional intelligence tests. For example, to isolate the ability to detect relationships among concepts, laboratory subjects might be asked to solve analogies of the following form as quickly as possible: LAWYER is to CLIENT as DOCTOR is to ____? Sternberg argues that intelligent performers are able to infer the relation between the first two components of the analogy quickly (Sternberg & Gardner, 1983). They note, for example, that a LAWYER is typically hired by and works for the CLIENT, and they're able to then map and apply this perceived relation to generate the correct answer (PATIENT). Sternberg believes that intelligent subjects can generate effective overall plans for attacking problems—they represent problems well and then generate and monitor global strategies for problem solution (see Chapter 9).

One of the central tenets of the scientific study of behavior and mind is that all mental activity can be traced ultimately to neural activity in the brain—thoughts, emotions, ideas, and presumably, intelligence. Currently, researchers have no idea where the seat of "intelligence" lies in the brain, and it probably doesn't make sense to look for a single location, or even a group of locations. But researchers have sought to determine whether there are general biological processes that correlate with mental ability. One plausible candidate is the speed of transmission across neural pathways. The faster the brain communicates internally, the better its ability to quickly allocate, or divide, its processing in order to perform efficiently. But how is it possible to measure something like the speed of neural processing?

As we discussed in Chapter 3, recording the gross electrical activity of the brain is relatively easy. The procedure is noninvasive, requiring only that several electrodes be attached temporarily to locations on the scalp. Depending on the placement of the electrodes, electrical activity from different parts of the brain can then be recorded. To obtain a measure of the speed of neural processing, Reed and Jensen (1992) attached electrodes to scalp locations that are sensitive to the appearance of visual events. Subjects were seated in a dark room and were presented with a black-and-white checkerboard pattern on a video monitor. Approximately 100 milliseconds after presentation of the stimulus, the brain generates an electrical signal, known as P100, that can be measured in scalp areas over the primary visual cortex.

Reed and Jensen (1992) were not simply interested in the appearance of the P100 signal but rather in the *latency,* or time of appearance, of the signal. People differ in the amount of time that it takes for this signal to appear; this latency was assumed by Reed and Jensen to provide an indirect measure of the speed of information processing in the brain. They assumed that short latencies reflected fast processing in the brain and long latencies relatively slower pro-

cessing. The main question of interest was whether P100 latency could then be used to predict performance on an intelligence test.

P100 signal times were measured for 147 college students, and each individual's average latency was then compared with his or her score on an independent test of mental ability. Figure 10.3 shows how the intelligence scores varied with P100 latencies. The P100 values are divided into student quintiles, which means that the first bar on the left shows the intelligence scores for the 20% of students with the longest latency values, and the last bar on the right shows the 20% of students with the shortest average P100 latencies. As the data indicate, a relationship appears to exist between latency and performance on the intelligence test. The shorter the latency—that is, the faster the processing in the brain—the higher the intelligence score.

Does this mean that smarter brains are faster brains, as the data might imply? Not necessarily. It's important to remember that conclusions about cause

and effect cannot be drawn from correlational studies like the one conducted by Reed and Jensen. We may be able to predict intelligence scores to some extent by measuring neural processing speed, but that doesn't mean that processing speed is the underlying cause of intelligence. Moreover, the predictive ability of the P100 latencies was far from perfect; they explained only a small proportion of the subject differences that were found in intelligence scores.

Finally, knowledge about the electrical activity of various brain regions is still relatively meager. Researchers are not sure at this point just what the latency of the P100 signal is actually measuring in the brain. It's not a direct measure of the speed of neural impulses—at best, it is an indirect measure that may eventually indicate something about the conduction properties of neurons. Thus, although the Reed and Jensen data are provocative, they cannot tell us with any certainty what neurological processes actually underlie the capacity of intelligence.

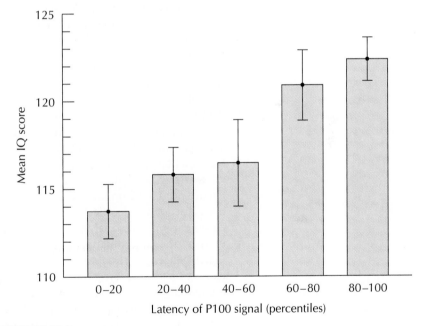

FIGURE 10.3

Signal Latency and IQ. This figure shows how latency, or time of appearance, of the P100 signal relates to the average IQ score. The first bar on the left shows the average IQ score for the 20% of students with the longest latencies; the last bar on the right shows the 20% of students with the shortest latencies. Notice that the higher IQ scores are associated with the students who showed the fastest P100 onset times. (Adapted from Reed & Jensen, 1992)

Like the psychometric theorists, cognitive theorists hope that once they identify the fundamental components of intelligence, those components can be used to predict and explain individual differences in task performance. If we can obtain a measure of someone's ability to analyze analogies, for instance, we might be able to predict how well that person will perform on a wide variety of tests of mental ability. Some cognitive theorists have been interested in developing computer software programs that mimic human intelligence, or at least expert thinking in more narrow domains. So the intent might be to develop a program that can successfully diagnose medical conditions, or solve physics or engineering problems (Simon, 1969, 1992). By conceptualizing intelligence in terms of underlying mental processes and then implementing those processes via computer programs, cognitive theorists hope to go beyond just measuring intelligent behavior to understanding and explaining its causes.

Multiple Intelligences

Before we turn to another way of conceptualizing intelligence—the multiple-intelligences approach—let's pause momentarily and return to Larry Steinway, that fictional lightning calculator we met in the opening to the chapter. After reading the previous sections, what do you think psychologists with a psychometric or cognitive bent would have to say about Larry's intelligence? How would someone with a highly specialized skill—lightning calculation—but with otherwise impaired mental abilities fit into these conceptualizations of intelligence? In some respects Larry has a "fast" brain, but it's highly doubtful that he could solve an analogy problem efficiently, or generate and monitor sophisticated global problem-solving strategies. We can also be sure that Larry will not perform well on a standardized battery of tests, which means that his assigned value of g will be far lower than average.

Consider the gifted athlete as well, who soars high above the basketball rim but has trouble reading his daughter's nursery rhymes. Or the respected mathematical wizard, full professor at a major university, who has trouble matching her shoes, let alone her socks, in the morning. The point to be made about Larry Steinway, or the athlete or the professor, is that people sometimes show specialized skills or abilities that stand alone, that are not representative of a general ability that cuts across all kinds of behavior. Spectacular skill can be shown in one area accompanied by profound deficits in another. Perhaps more important, these selective skills are often in areas that are *not* traditionally covered by the verbal and analytical battery of commonly used intelligence tests.

Howard Gardner (1983, 1993) argues that the traditional conceptions of intelligence need to be broadened to include special abilities or talents of the type we've been discussing. He rejects the idea that intelligence can be adequately conceptualized through the analysis of test performance or artificial laboratory tasks (as used by the psychometric and cognitive approaches). Rather than searching for "intelligence," we should understand that human behavior is rich in selective talents and abilities—we need a theory of **multiple intelligences,** not a method for discovering a single underlying g. An *intelligence* (rather than "the" intelligence) is defined as "an ability or set of abilities that permits an individual to solve problems or fashion products that are of consequence in a particular cultural setting" (Walters & Gardner, 1986). (Note that Gardner's treatment of intelligence has an adaptive flavor and fits snugly into our general conception of the adaptive mind.) Although Gardner believes that each of these separate intelligences may be rooted in the biology of the brain, each can manifest itself in a variety of ways, depending on one's culture.

Rather than studying intelligent behavior in the laboratory, Gardner uses a case study approach. He studies reports of particular individuals with special abil-

Do you think the average person on the street thinks that superior athletic or artistic ability is the same thing as intelligence?

Howard Gardner, who believes in multiple intelligences, would probably argue that the dancers on the left possess high levels of bodily-kinesthetic intelligence; similarly, successful politicians tend to display high levels of interpersonal intelligence—they can infer the intentions and motivations of others.

ities or talents, such as superior musicians, poets, scientists, and *savants* like Larry Steinway. He has also looked extensively at the effects of damage to the brain. He has noted, for example, instances in which brain damage can affect one kind of ability, such as reasoning and problem solving, yet leave other abilities, such as musical skill, intact. Based on his research, Gardner has identified what he believes to be seven kinds of intelligence:

1. *Musical intelligence:* the type of ability displayed by gifted musicians or child prodigies
2. *Bodily-kinesthetic intelligence:* the type of ability shown by gifted athletes, dancers, or surgeons, who have great control over body movements
3. *Logical-mathematical intelligence:* the type of ability displayed by superior scientists and logical problem solvers
4. *Linguistic intelligence:* the type of ability shown by great writers or poets who can express themselves verbally
5. *Spatial intelligence:* the type of ability shown by those with superior navigation skills or an ability to visualize spatial scenes
6. *Interpersonal intelligence:* the type of ability shown by those who can easily infer other people's moods, temperaments, or intentions and motivations
7. *Intrapersonal intelligence*: the ability shown by someone who has great insight into his or her own feelings and emotions

Notice that some forms of intelligence, as described by Gardner, are covered well by conventional tests of mental ability. The psychometric and cognitive approaches focus extensively on logical-mathematical intelligence and to some extent on linguistic and spatial intelligence. Some researchers who use the psychometric approach, including L. L. Thurstone, have also argued for the need to distinguish among distinct and independent types of intelligence. But researchers who conceptualize intelligence in terms of the psychometric and cognitive approaches rarely, if ever, concentrate on "intelligences" such as musical ability or great athletic skill. As a result, the multiple-intelligences approach considerably broadens the conceptualization of intelligence.

Triarchic Theory

It's fair to say that over the last decade or so, intelligence researchers have reached consensus about the need for a multipronged attack on intelligence. Not everyone agrees with Howard Gardner's treatment of intelligence. Some say that he's really talking about multiple "talents" rather than intelligences, and his theory remains primarily descriptive without much hard scientific evidence. But most psychologists agree with Gardner that intelligence should be broadly conceived—it's not simply performance on a battery of primarily verbal-linguistic or sensory tests.

Robert Sternberg's **triarchic theory** of intelligence is a good example of a recent "eclectic" approach (meaning it's made up of different elements). Sternberg was trained as a cognitive psychologist, and his theory contains important elements of the cognitive approach. He's convinced that it's important to try to understand the information processing routines involved in the planning and execution of specialized tasks. But he also believes that any complete conceptualization of intelligence must address behavior outside of the laboratory. For example, what is the form of "intelligence" that enables people to *apply* their mental processes creatively to problems that arise in the external environment? Furthermore, how does "intelligence" relate to the practical experience of the individual? Consequently, he accepts the idea that there may be multiple kinds of intelligence. The term *triarchic* means roughly "ruled by threes" so, not surprisingly, Sternberg's conceptualization of intelligence is divided into three major parts (Sternberg, 1985, 1988).

Sternberg proposes that any complete conceptualization of intelligence must refer in some way to basic analytic skills. Some people have internal cognitive processes that are particularly efficient at processing information. People with high degrees of what might be called *analytical intelligence* are likely to perform well on conventional tests that tap reasoning and logical-mathematical ability (such as the Scholastic Assessment Test). Because most psychometric tests of intelligence require these kinds of abilities, people who are high in analytic intelligence tend to be assigned a high *g*, for general intelligence.

But being efficient analytic processors of information does not guarantee that people will be able to apply their skills to the everyday world. For this reason, Sternberg proposes that people also differ in their amount of *creative intelligence*. Someone with a high degree of creative intelligence copes well with new or novel tasks. A good example might be a child who quickly and effortlessly learns to read after acquiring the rudiments of language (Sternberg, 1985).

Finally, people differ in their amount of *practical intelligence,* which indicates how well they fit into their environments. People with lots of practical intelligence solve the problems that are uniquely posed by their cultural surroundings. They mold themselves well into existing settings, and they can select new environments, if required, that provide a better fit or niche for their talents. In a nutshell, these individuals have "street smarts"—they size up situations well and act accordingly.

Sternberg's triarchic theory fits the current trend toward a broadening of the conceptualization of intelligence. Like Howard Gardner's approach, his theory deals with behaviors and skills that are not normally covered by the psychometric and purely cognitive approaches. At the same time, breadth is not gained without some cost—concepts such as practical and creative intelligence are not defined with ringing precision and, consequently, can be somewhat difficult to measure and test. Moreover, even if it is desirable to broaden our conceptualization of intelligence, that does not mean the cognitive or psychometric approaches to intelligence have no value. As we'll see in the next section, psychometric tests are often quite useful in predicting future performance, even though they may be measuring only narrow dimensions of intelligence.

Measuring Individual Differences

We've now discussed some of the ways to conceptualize intelligence theoretically. But we have yet to discuss in detail how individual differences are actually measured. People differ. Pick just about any attribute—height, weight, friendliness, intelligence—and you're going to find a scattering, or distribution, of individual values. Some people are tall, some are short; some people are friendly, some are not. As we discussed in the previous section, the study of individual differences is important because it can be used to infer fundamental attributes of mind. Important psychological concepts such as intelligence and personality are often defined and measured in terms of individual differences.

Moreover, if we can get a measure of how you compare to others on some psychological dimension, it becomes possible to assess your current and future capabilities. **Achievement tests,** for example, measure a person's current level of knowledge or competence in a particular subject (such as math or reading). Researchers or teachers can use the results of an achievement test to assess the effectiveness of a learning procedure or a curriculum in a school. It is also possible to use individual differences to make predictions about the future—how well you can be expected to do in your chosen profession or whether you are likely to succeed in college. **Aptitude tests** measure the ability to learn in a particular area, to acquire the knowledge needed for success in a given domain. Aptitude test results can be used to help choose a career path or even to decide whether to take up something such as car mechanics or the violin as a hobby.

The Components of a Good Test

We'll begin by discussing the qualities or characteristics of a "good" test—that is, a test that can be expected to provide a good measure of individual differences. Given that we recognize the need to measure these differences, it's crucial that the measurement device yield information that is scientifically useful. Researchers generally agree on three characteristics that are needed for a good test: *reliability, validity,* and *standardization.* Please note that these are characteristics of the *test*, not the person taking the test.

Reliability. The first test characteristic, **reliability,** is a measure of the *consistency* of the test results. Reliable tests produce similar scores or indices from one administration to the next. Suppose we want to measure creativity and we design a test that produces a score from 0 to 100 on a creativity scale. We measure Al and he gets a score of 13; we measure Cynthia and she tops out at 96. Clearly, we conclude, Cynthia is more creative than Al. But is she really? To be sure about the results, we administer the test again and find that the scores reverse. Sadly, our creativity test lacks reliability—it does not produce consistent scores from one administration to the next.

It's important for a test to be reliable because otherwise we cannot draw firm conclusions from the data. Cynthia might be more creative than Al, but the difference in scores could also be just an artifact or failing of the test. On this particular administration Cynthia scored higher, but that's no guarantee that tomorrow's results will yield the same conclusion. One way to measure a test's reliability is to give it to the same group of individuals on two separate occasions. *Test-retest reliability* is then calculated by comparing the scores across the repeated administrations. Often, a correlation coefficient is computed that indicates how well performance on the second test can be predicted from performance on the first. The closer the test-retest correlation comes to a perfect +1.00, the higher the reliability of the test.

Pick one of your classes in school. Do you think the tests you've taken so far are valid? What specific kind of validity are you using as a basis for your answer?

Validity. The second test characteristic, **validity,** refers to how well a test measures what it is supposed to measure. A test can yield reliable data—consistent results across repeated administrations—yet not truly measure the psychological attribute of interest. If a test of creativity actually measures shoe size, then the data are likely to be quite reliable but not very valid. Shoe size isn't going to change much from one measurement to the next, but it has little to do with creativity.

Actually, there are several different forms of validity: *Content validity* measures the degree to which the content of a test samples broadly across the domain of interest. If you're trying to get a *general* measure of creativity, your test should not be limited to one kind of creativity, such as artistic creativity. For the test to have a high degree of content validity, it should probably measure artistic, verbal, mechanical, mathematical, and other kinds of creativity.

Sometimes psychologists are interested in designing a test that predicts some future criterion outcome, such as job performance or success in school. For a test to have *predictive validity,* it needs in part to "predict" this outcome adequately. The Scholastic Assessment Test (SAT) is a well-known case in point. The SAT is designed to predict success in college. So to assess its predictive validity, we need to ask whether the SAT predicts college performance as expressed through a measure such as college grade point average. Various studies have shown that the correlation between the SAT scores and grade point averages of college freshmen is somewhere between +0.40 and +0.50 (Donlon, 1984; Willingham and others, 1990). Statistically, this means that we can predict college performance with the SAT at greater than chance levels, although our predictive abilities are not perfect.

There is still another kind of validity, *construct validity,* that measures how well a test taps into a particular theoretical scheme or construct. Suppose we have a theory of creativity that is developed well enough to generate a wide variety of predictions—how creative people act, the kinds of books that creative people are interested in, the susceptibility of creative people to mental disorders, and so on. To have high construct validity, our test would need to predict performance on each of these separate indices of creativity, rather than on just one. If a test has high construct validity, its scores tend to vary in ways that are predicted by the theory. So if the theory predicts that creative people are more likely to suffer from depression, then people who score highly on the creativity test should have a greater likelihood of being depressed.

Standardization. The third characteristic of a good test of individual differences is **standardization.** When you take a test such as the SAT, or any national aptitude or achievement test, you quickly learn that the testing procedures are extremely rigid. You can break the test seal only at a certain time, the instructions are parroted in monotone by an unsmiling administrator, and your yellow #2 pencil must be put down coincident with an exact tick of the clock. These tests are *standardized,* which means that the testing, scoring, and interpretation procedures are kept similar across all administrations of the test. Rigid adherence to standardization is important because it assures that all test takers will be treated the same.

In fact, the proper interpretation of a test score absolutely demands standardization. Remember, we're concerned with individual differences—it doesn't make much sense to compare two or more scores if different instructions or scoring procedures have been used across the test sessions. A person's score on a test of individual differences can be understood only with respect to a reference group, often called a *norm group,* and everyone within the group must receive the same test and administration procedures. We'll return to this concept of a norm reference group momentarily, as we consider the development and current status of the concept of IQ.

Throughout the school years, children regularly take standardized tests that are designed to measure aptitude or achievement.

IQ: The Intelligence Quotient

The most famous index of intelligence is the **IQ, or intelligence quotient.** It's a single number, derived from performance on a test, and it could well be the most widely applied psychological measure in the world. But how can a single number be used to measure intelligence? This might strike you as odd given our earlier discussion about multiple intelligences and the need to establish a wide variety of criteria for what it means to be intelligent. The key to appreciating the IQ, and to understanding why it is so widely applied, lies in the concept of *validity:* What is the IQ designed to measure, and how successfully does it achieve its goal? As we'll see momentarily, it turns out that IQ does a reasonably good job of predicting what it was designed to predict.

Binet and Simon. The historical roots of IQ trace back about a hundred years, to the work of the French psychologist Alfred Binet and his associate Théopile Simon. Binet and Simon were commissioned by the French government in 1904 to develop a test that would identify children who were considered "dull"—specifically, children who would have a difficult time grasping concepts in school. It was the French government's intention to help these children, once they were identified, through some kind of remedial schooling. Thus, the mission of the test was primarily practical, not theoretical: the charge was to develop a test that would accurately assess individual differences in future academic performance.

Not surprisingly, Binet and Simon designed their test to measure the kinds of skills that are needed in school—such as memory, reasoning, and verbal comprehension. The goal was to determine the **mental age**—or what Binet and Simon called the *mental level*—of the child, which was defined as the chronological age that best fit the child's current level of intellectual performance. Mental age is typically calculated by comparing a child's test score with the average scores for different age groups. For example, let's suppose that an average 8-year-old is able to compare two objects from memory, recognize parts of a picture that are missing, count backward from 20 to 0, and give the correct day and time. An average 12-year-old might be able to define abstract words, name 60 words in 3 minutes, and discover the meaning of a scrambled sentence. If Jenny, who is 8, is able to solve

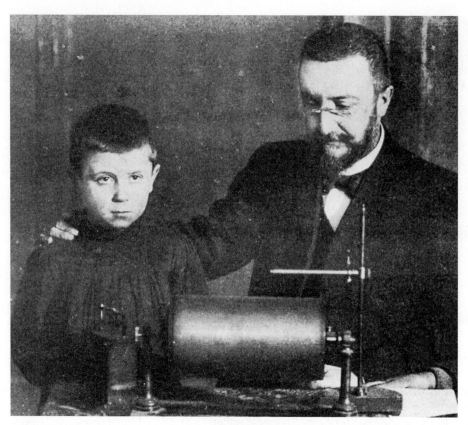

Alfred Binet, shown here with an uniden-tified child, was commissioned by the French government to develop a test that would help teachers identify students who might have a difficult time grasping concepts in school.

the problems of the typical 12-year-old, she would be assigned a mental age of 12.

Notice that mental age and chronological age do not have to be the same, although they will be on the average (an average 8-year-old should solve problems at the average 8-year-old level). Because intelligence tests are given to lots of children, it's possible to determine average performance for a given age group and then to determine the appropriate mental age for a particular child. By using mental age, Binet and Simon (1916) were able to pinpoint the slow and quick learners and recommend appropriate curriculum adjustments.

In the first two decades of the 20th century, Binet and Simon's intelligence test was revised several times and was ultimately translated into English for use in North America. The most popular American version was developed by psychologist Lewis Terman at Stanford University; this test later became known as the *Stanford-Binet* test of intelligence. It was also Terman who popularized the actual intelligence quotient (based on an idea originally proposed by German psychologist William Stern), which is defined as follows:

$$\text{Intelligence quotient (IQ)} = \frac{\text{Mental age}}{\text{Chronological age}} \times 100$$

The IQ is a useful measure because it establishes an easy-to-understand baseline for "average" intelligence—people of average intelligence will have an IQ of 100 because their mental age will always be equal to their chronological age. People with IQs greater than 100 will be above average in intelligence; those below 100 will be below average in intelligence.

Interpreting the IQ. Defining IQ simply in terms of the *ratio* of mental age to chronological age has some problems. For one thing, it's hard to compare the meaning of the ratio across different ages. If a 5-year-old performed at a level comparable to a 7-year-old, she would be given an IQ of 140 ($7/5 \times 100 = 140$). But if a 10-year-old scored at the level of a 12-year-old, his IQ would be only 120 ($12/10 \times 100 = 120$). Both are performing at levels two years above their chronological age, but they receive very different IQs. Moreover, how much sense does it make to argue that a 30-year-old who performs comparably to a 60-year-old should be given a vastly higher IQ ($60/30 \times 100 = 200$)?

To overcome this problem, most modern intelligence tests retain the term IQ but define it in terms of a *deviation,* or difference, rather than as a ratio. A **deviation IQ** still uses 100 as a baseline average, but a 100 IQ is redefined as the average score in the distribution of scores for people of a certain age. A particular individual's IQ is then calculated by determining where his or her test score "sits," relative to the average score, in the overall distribution of scores. (Note that *age* is

Do you see any similarities between the way that deviation IQ is interpreted and the way you normally interpret your exam scores in a class?

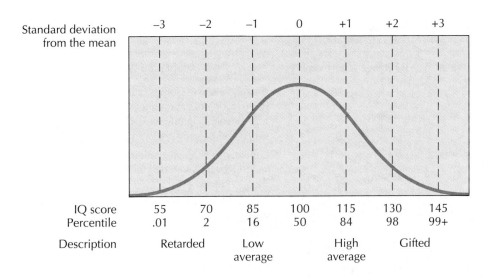

Standard deviation from the mean

| | | | | | | |
| −3 | −2 | −1 | 0 | +1 | +2 | +3 |

IQ score	55	70	85	100	115	130	145
Percentile	.01	2	16	50	84	98	99+

| Description | Retarded | Low average | High average | Gifted |

FIGURE 10.4
The Distribution of IQ Scores.
IQ scores for a given age group will typically be distributed in a bell-shaped, or "normal," curve. The average and most frequently occurring IQ score is defined as 100. Roughly 68% of the test takers in this age group receive IQ scores between 115 and 85, which includes everyone scoring between one *standard deviation* above and below the mean. People labeled as "gifted" (an IQ of 130 and above) or retarded (an IQ of 70 or below) occur infrequently in the population.

the "norm group" used for defining the concept of intelligence.) Figure 10.4 shows a frequency distribution of scores that might result from administering a test such as the Stanford-Binet to large groups of people. The average of the distribution is 100, and approximately half of the test takers will produce scores above 100 and the other half, below.

One of the characteristics of modern intelligence tests is that they tend to produce very regular and smooth distributions of scores. With most intelligence tests, for example, not only will the most common score be 100 (by definition), but roughly 68% of the people who take the test will receive an IQ score between 85 and 115. With a distribution such as the one shown in Figure 10.4, we can easily calculate the percentage of the population apt to receive a particular IQ score. You will find, for example, that approximately 98% of the people who take the test will receive a score at or below 130. Notice once again that IQ in this case is defined in terms of the relative location of a person's score in a frequency distribution of scores gathered from people in the same chronological age group.

Tests such as the Stanford-Binet or the related Wechsler Adult Intelligence Scale have been given to thousands and thousands of people. Consequently, we know a great deal about how IQ scores tend to be distributed in the population. Most people fall within a normal or average range, which covers scores from about 70 to about 130. Individuals who fall above or below this range represent *extremes* in intelligence. Someone who scores below 70 on a standard IQ test, for example, is likely to be given a diagnosis of **mental retardation,** although other factors (such as daily living skills) are equally important in determining the diagnosis. No single test score, by itself, is sufficient to arrive at a diagnosis of mental retardation. A four-level classification scheme has been developed by the American Association on Mental Deficiency. Table 10.1 shows how each category level for retardation is defined—in terms of IQ—and lists some of the adaptation skills that can be expected, on average, for individuals who meet the diagnostic criteria.

At the other end of the IQ scale are individuals considered to be **gifted,** with IQs at or above approximately 130. Numerous studies have tracked the intellectual and social accomplishments of gifted children, partly as a means of assessing the validity of the IQ measure. One of the most famous studies was initiated in the 1920s by Lewis Terman (1925; Terman & Ogden, 1947). Terman was interested in whether children who were identified early in life as "gifted" would be likely to achieve success throughout their lives. Generally, this turned out to be the case— Terman's gifted subjects earned more college degrees than average, made more money, wrote more books, generated more successful patents, and so on.

TABLE 10.1
Types of Mental Retardation

Type	IQ Range (approximate)	Adaptation Potential
Mild	50–70	May develop academic skills comparable to a sixth-grade educational level; with assistance, may develop significant social and vocational skills, and be self-supporting
Moderate	35–50	Unlikely to achieve academic skills over the second-grade level; may become semi-independent
Severe	20–35	Speech skills will be limited, but communication possible; may learn to perform simple tasks in highly structured environments
Profound	Below 20	Little or no speech is possible; requires constant care and supervision

Interestingly, these kids also turned out to be both stable emotionally and generally socially adept, which is surprising given the "bookworm" stereotype that most people have of highly intelligent people. Many had successful marriages, and the divorce rate was lower for them than for the general population (Terman, 1954). A more recent study examining gifted children who skipped high school and moved directly to college also found evidence for excellent social adjustment (Nobel, Robinson, & Gunderson, 1993). One problem with these data, however, is that the connection between IQ and success is correlational, and there are many potentially confounding factors. High-IQ children, for example, tend to come from economically privileged households, which might help account for later success and emotional stability (Tomlinson-Keasey & Little, 1990).

The Validity of Intelligence Testing

Do tests that measure intelligence provide a valid measure of intellectual ability? Does IQ, for example, truly tap some hidden but powerful attribute of mind that accounts for individual differences? Do intelligence tests adequately measure the ability to adapt and solve the problems of survival? Remember, the term *validity* has a technical meaning to the psychologist: How well does the test measure the thing that it is supposed to measure? To assess the validity of the IQ, then, we need to ask: How well do the tests that produce IQ scores predict their criterion of interest?

The most widely applied intelligence tests today are the Stanford-Binet, the Wechsler Adult Intelligence Scale (WAIS), and the Wechsler Intelligence Scale for Children (WISC, 3rd edition). These are not the only tests, of course; in fact, if we combine "intelligence" tests with measures of scholastic aptitude, at least 120 different tests are currently in use (Jensen, 1992). Their most common application, driven by the same concerns that originally motivated Binet and Simon, is to predict some kind of academic performance, usually grades in high school or college. From this standpoint, IQ as measured by Stanford-Binet or the Wechsler tests passes the validity test with flying colors: IQ typically correlates about $+0.50$ or higher with school grades (Ceci, 1991; Kline, 1991). Notice that the correlation is not perfect, but it is reasonably high when you consider all of the uncontrolled factors that can affect grades in school (motivation, home environment, participation in extracurricular activities, teacher bias, and so on). IQ is also thought to be a reasonable predictor of real-world job performance, although its success in

Wechsler Adult Intelligence Scale (WAIS)		
Test	**Description**	**Example**
Verbal scale		
Information	Taps general range of information	On what continent is France?
Comprehension	Tests understanding of social conventions and ability to evaluate past experience	Why are children required to go to school?
Arithmetic	Tests arithmetic reasoning through verbal problems	How many hours will it take to drive 150 miles at 50 miles per hour?
Performance scale		
Block design	Tests ability to perceive and analyze patterns by presenting designs that must be copied with blocks	Assemble blocks to match this design:
Picture arrangement	Tests understanding of social situations through a series of comic-strip-type pictures that must be arranged in the right sequence to tell a story	Put the pictures in the right order:
Object assembly	Tests ability to deal with part/whole relationships by presenting puzzle pieces that must be assembled to form a complete object	Assemble the pieces into a complete object:

this domain is more modest (Ree & Earles, 1992; Sternberg & Wagner, 1993) (see also the Adaptive Mind section that closes this chapter).

Most arguments against the validity of IQ scores make the case that these scores fail to provide a broad index of intelligence. As we discussed before, it's proper to define intelligence broadly—there are many ways that people can fit successfully into their environments—and it's certain that not all forms of multiple intelligence are tapped by traditional paper-and-pencil IQ tests. This criticism has been recognized for years by the community of intelligence test researchers, and efforts have been made to develop tests that tap a variety of abilities. The influential tests of David Wechsler, for example, were developed in part to try to measure *nonverbal* aspects of intellectual ability. The Wechsler tests include not only verbal-mathematical questions of the type traditionally found on the Stanford-Binet test but also nonverbal questions requiring things like the completion or rearrangement of pictures (see Figure 10.5). Performance is then broken down into a verbal IQ, a nonverbal (or "performance") IQ, and an overall IQ based on combining the verbal and nonverbal measures.

Labeling Effects. Another potentially serious criticism of IQ scores concerns the appropriateness of the IQ label. You take a test as a child, your IQ is derived by comparing your performance with that of other kids your age, and the score becomes part of your continuing academic "record." Once the IQ label is applied—you're smart, you're below average, and so on—expectations are generated in those who have access to your score. A number of studies have shown that intelligence labels influence how teachers interact with their students in the classroom. There is a kind of "rich get richer" and "poor get poorer" effect—the kids with the "smart" label are exposed to more educational opportunities and are treated with more respect. Things are held back from the "slow" kids, so they're less likely to be exposed to factors that might nurture academic growth (Oakes, 1985; Rosenthal & Jacobson, 1968).

FIGURE 10.5
Examples from the WAIS. The Wechsler Adult Intelligence Scale was designed to measure both verbal and nonverbal aspects of intellectual ability. Included here are samples of the various question types. (From Weiten, 1995)

Did the elementary school that you attended use a "tracking" system—that is, were children early on divided into different classes based on standardized test scores?

Within 24 hours of arrival at Ellis Island, immigrants were subjected to a variety of mental and physical examinations. Unfortunately, these exams were sometimes used to discriminate among population groups unfairly; at the time, administrators were simply not sensitive to how cultural factors could influence test performance.

The negative effects of labeling were particularly serious in the early decades of the 20th century, when intelligence tests were in their formative stages of development. Tests were widely administered—for example, to newly arriving immigrants and all Army recruits—but before the impact of cultural and educational factors on test performance were widely understood. As we'll discuss later, people can perform poorly on an intelligence test because the test has certain built-in biases with respect to language and cultural lifestyle. Imagine, for example, that as part of an intelligence test I ask you to identify the vegetable broccoli. Easy, but not if you were raised in a culture that did not include broccoli as part of its diet. In such a case you would probably get the question wrong, but it wouldn't say anything about your true intellectual ability.

Researchers were not very sensitive to these concerns when the early intelligence tests were developed. The result was that certain population groups, such as immigrants from southern and eastern Europe, generally performed poorly on these tests. Some psychologists even went so far as to label these immigrant groups "feeble minded" or "defective" based on their test performance. Immigration laws enacted in the 1920s even discriminated against poorly performing groups by reducing immigration quotas. In modern times, psychologists are more aware of test bias, but its impact on test performance remains controversial to this day.

Discovering the Sources of Intelligence: The Nature-Nurture Issue

We've seen that people differ, and we've considered some of the ways to measure these individual differences. We've also discussed methods for conceptualizing these differences theoretically—Lee may be smart, and Dale may be intellectually challenged, because they differ in amount of *g*, that single underlying attribute of mind. Perhaps Lee's internal neurons simply communicate faster, or Dale lacks the cognitive subroutine that allows for the mapping of higher-order relationships. But what accounts for these differences in the first place? Why is Lee's *g* higher or lower than Dale's? Why is Jefferson Tarpy able to generate and monitor effective global strategies for problem solution, but Larry Steinway can't? Is there anything that can be done about these differences, or are they fixed in stone?

There are two primary ways for us to explain how measured differences in intelligence arise. First, we can appeal to biological processes, particularly the internal *genetic code*—those strands of DNA that determine eye color, thickness of hair, and possibly *g*. According to this view, intellectual potential is established at conception through some particularly fortunate (or unfortunate) combinations of genes. Alternatively, we can reject an internal explanation and appeal to an external one, the *environment*. Variations in *g* might be attributable to one's particular past history—perhaps Lee was reinforced for intellectual pursuits or went to excellent schools; perhaps Dale was exposed to toxins as a child (such as lead paint). In this section, we'll frame this classic nature-nurture debate and consider the evidence relevant to each position. But first, we have a practical issue to consider—how stable is the IQ measure itself?

The Stability of IQ

One way to answer questions about the origins of intelligence is to ask whether IQ, once measured, changes significantly over a lifetime. If intelligence is mediated by something like a "fast brain," we might expect intellectual ability to change little over time, or at least remain stable throughout the course of normal adulthood. On the other hand, if intelligence is determined mainly by a nurturing environment, we would probably expect to find variability in the measured score: IQ might rise and fall with changes in experience or environmental setting. Neither of these arguments is airtight—for instance, your environment might remain constant over time, or the genetic code might express itself throughout your lifetime; it might also be the case that IQ is determined by early experience and remains fixed after a certain point in development. But examination of the stability of the IQ measure is a reasonable place to start the search.

When intelligence is measured in the standard way, through performance on a battery of tests, the stability of the measure depends on when the measuring process begins. Before the age of about 3 or 4, it's difficult to get an accurate assessment of intellectual ability. Infants can't talk or show sustained attention, so conventional testing procedures cannot be used. Investigators resort to indirect measures, such as recording whether babies choose to look at old or new pictures presented on a screen. There is some evidence that babies who quickly "habituate," or lose interest, in response to repeated presentations of the same picture, and who prefer to look at novel pictures when they're shown, score higher on intelligence tests later in childhood (Bornstein, 1989; McCall & Carriger, 1993). But in general, it's widely believed that reliable assessments of IQ cannot be obtained until somewhere between ages 4 and 7; from that point onward, IQ scores tend to predict performance on later IQ tests reasonably well (Honzik, Macfarlane, & Allen, 1948; Sameroff and others, 1993).

The most widely known investigation of the stability of *adult* intelligence is the Seattle Longitudinal Study, which has examined mental test performance for approximately 5000 adults ranging in age from 25 through 88 (Schaie, 1983, 1989, 1993). The subjects have been tested in seven-year cycles, dating back to 1956, using a battery of tests to assess such things as verbal fluency, inductive reasoning, and spatial ability. Schaie and his colleagues have found great stability in intellectual ability throughout adulthood. From age 25 to about age 60, there appears to be no uniform decline in general intellectual ability, as measured through the test battery (see Figure 10.6). After age 60, abilities begin to decline a bit, although the losses are not profound. There are also large individual differences—some people show excellent test performance in their 80s, whereas others do not.

 Elderly people are often said to possess "wisdom." In what ways do you think the label "wise" differs from the label "intelligent"?

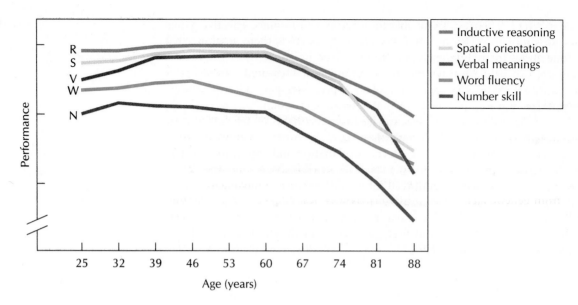

FIGURE 10.6
The Stability of Intellectual Ability. These data from the Seattle Longitudinal Study show how performance changes on a variety of mental tasks from age 25 to age 88. Notice that average performance is remarkably stable up to about age 60, at which point some declines are seen. (Data from Schaie, 1983)

It's always difficult to know how to interpret changes in IQ with age because many factors change concurrently with age. Elderly people are more likely to have physical problems, for example, that can affect performance. Declines in intelligence with age also appear to depend on the type of intellectual ability being measured. Earlier, we discussed the distinction between *fluid intelligence,* which taps basic reasoning and information processing skills, and *crystallized intelligence,* which taps acquired knowledge. The current thinking is that fluid intelligence may decline with age—perhaps because the biology of the brain changes—whereas crystallized intelligence remains constant or even increases (Horn, 1982). The brain may become a bit slower with age, but people continue to add knowledge and experiences that are invaluable in their efforts to solve the problems of everyday life.

The Genetic Argument

A number of the early pioneers in intelligence testing, including Galton, were strong advocates of inherited mental ability. After all, Galton argued, it's easy to demonstrate that intellectual skill runs through family lines (remember, his cousin was Charles Darwin, and his grandfather was another famous evolutionist, Erasmus Darwin). But family-tree arguments, used in isolation, are flawed. Environmental factors, such as social and educational opportunities, can explain why members of the same family might show similar skills. Growing up in a family that places value on intellectual pursuits determines to some extent what sort of behaviors will be rewarded in a child, or the particular type of role models that will be available. In fairness to Galton, he realized that both inherited and environmental factors are needed to explain mental ability fully—in fact, it was Galton who coined the term "nature versus nurture" (Galton, 1869, 1883).

To establish a genetic basis for any psychological or physical attribute, it is necessary to control for the effects of the environment. In principle, if two people are raised in exactly the same environment and receive exactly the same experiences, we can attribute any reliable differences in IQ to inherited factors (*nature*). In this case, we've held any nurturing effects of the environment constant, so any differences must be due to genetics. Alternatively, if two people are born with exactly the same genetic blueprint but end up with quite different intelligence scores, it must be the environment, not genes, that is responsible (*nurture*). We can't per-

The Bell Curve, *by Richard Herrnstein and Charles Murray, generated enormous controversy in 1994 for its strong assertion that population differences in IQ may be genetically based and therefore essentially immutable.*

form these kinds of experimental manipulations in the laboratory, for obvious reasons, but we can look for natural comparisons that are relevant. As we discussed in Chapter 3, psychologists often study *identical twins,* who share nearly complete genetic overlap, to tease apart the nature and nurture components of mind and behavior.

Twin Studies. In twin studies, researchers search for identical twins who have been raised together in the same household or who have been separated at birth through adoption (Bouchard & McGue, 1981; Bouchard and others, 1990). The effects of the environment are assumed to be similar for the twins raised together but quite different, at least on average, for twins raised apart. If intelligence arises primarily from genetic factors, we would expect identical twins to have very similar intelligence scores, regardless of the environments in which they have been raised. One way to measure similarity is in terms of a correlation. More specifically, how well can we predict the IQ of one twin given knowledge about the IQ of the other?

If genes are entirely responsible for intelligence, we would expect to get a strong positive correlation between IQ scores for identical twins. We wouldn't necessarily expect it to be exactly +1.00 because of measurement error or other uncontrolled factors. In reviewing the research literature on this issue, Bouchard and McGue (1981) found strong evidence for the genetic position: The IQ scores of identical twins are indeed quite similar, irrespective of the environment in which the twins have been reared. As shown in Figure 10.7, the IQ scores for twins reared together showed an average correlation of .86; when reared apart, the average correlation remained strongly positive at .72 (Bouchard & McGue, 1981).

Researchers who conduct twin studies are actually interested in a number of different comparisons. For instance, it's useful to compare intelligence scores for fraternal twins (who are genetically no more similar than normal siblings) and among unrelated people who have been reared together or apart. In general, the impressive finding is that the closer the overlap in genes, the more similar the resulting IQs. Notice, for example, that the average correlation for adopted siblings who have been reared together (.30) is much lower than the average correlation for identical twins reared apart (.72). Thus, similarity in environmental history is not as strong a predictor of intelligence as similarity in genetic background.

Do you think it would be possible to tease apart the relative contributions of nature and nurture to intelligence by studying animals in the laboratory?

FIGURE 10.7
Nature Versus Nurture. The horizontal bars show the mean correlation coefficients for pairs of people with differing amounts of genetic overlap and who have been reared in similar or different environments. For example, the top bar shows the average correlation for identical twins who have been reared together in the same environment. The bottom bar shows the correlation coefficient for adopted siblings reared together. Higher correlations mean that the measured IQ scores are more similar. (Data from Bouchard & McGue, 1981)

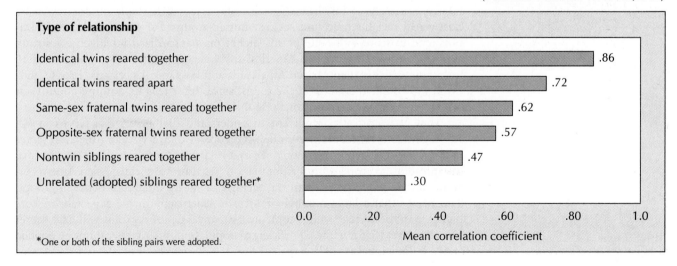

Type of relationship

Identical twins reared together	.86
Identical twins reared apart	.72
Same-sex fraternal twins reared together	.62
Opposite-sex fraternal twins reared together	.57
Nontwin siblings reared together	.47
Unrelated (adopted) siblings reared together*	.30

0.0   .20   .40   .60   .80   1.0
Mean correlation coefficient

*One or both of the sibling pairs were adopted.

Data like these suggest that genetic history plays an important role in intelligence, at least when intelligence is measured through conventional IQ testing.

Heritability. Intelligence researchers often use the concept of **heritability** to describe the influence of genetic factors on intelligence. Heritability is a mathematical index that represents the extent to which the IQ differences that are found in a particular population can be accounted for by genetic factors. It's expressed as a percentage, indicating the proportion of the total variability in intelligence found in a given group that is due to genes. Consequently, if the heritability of intelligence were 100%, that would mean that all differences in measured IQ among people in a given group could be explained by appealing to genetic factors. Most estimates of the heritability of intelligence, derived from twin studies, hover at around 50%, which means that approximately half of the variability in intelligence in a particular population is determined by genetic structure. Other researchers propose values even higher, closer to 70% (Bouchard et al., 1990).

It's important to understand that estimates of heritability apply only to groups, not to individuals. A heritability estimate of 70% does not mean that 70% of someone's intelligence is due to his or her genetic blueprint. To see why, imagine two groups of people with the same genetic histories. Group A maintains rigid control of the environment—everyone is treated exactly the same. Group B allows the environment to vary. If IQ scores are influenced by the environment in any way, we would expect the heritability values to be quite different for the two groups, even though the groups' genetic backgrounds are identical. Because the environment is held constant in group A, all of the variability in measured IQ will be due to genes. In group B, the heritability index will be lower because some of the differences in IQ will be due to environmental effects. Heritability tells us only that for a given group, a certain percentage of the differences in intelligence can be explained by genetic factors.

The Environmental Argument

There is little doubt that intelligence, as measured by standardized IQ tests, is influenced by genetic factors. But did you notice in Figure 10.7 that identical twins and siblings reared together have IQs that are more similar than do twins or siblings reared apart? This means that individual differences in intelligence cannot be explained completely through genetic background. The environment also plays an important role.

In this section, we'll consider some environmental influences on IQ by addressing a controversial topic in the study of intelligence: group differences in IQ. The majority of intelligence researchers agrees that stable differences in IQ exist across racial, ethnic, and socioeconomic groups. For example, Asian Americans tend to score 4 or 5 IQ points higher on standardized intelligence tests, on average, than white European Americans. White Americans, on average, score 10 to 15 points higher than African Americans and Hispanic Americans (Brody, 1992; Lynn, 1994). But the fact that these differences exist tells us nothing about their origin. How can we account for these differences?

First, it is critically important to understand that group differences in IQ, although stable, reflect *average* group differences. Not every Asian American scores high on an intelligence test, nor does every African American score low. In fact, the spread of IQ scores within a population (African Americans, Asian Americans, and so on) is much larger than the average, or mean, difference between groups. This means that a large number of African Americans can be expected to score higher than the average white score, just as many Asian Americans will have scores below the average for whites. The average population differences cannot be applied to single individuals.

Second, there are significant economic differences among racial/ethnic groups that make interpretation of the IQ differences difficult. For example, African Americans and Hispanic Americans are more likely to live at or below the poverty level in the United States. Associated with poverty, of course, are problems with nutrition, proper health care, and accessibility to adequate schools. African Americans and Hispanic Americans are also much more likely to suffer racial discrimination than whites. The impact of these factors on intelligence testing is not completely understood, although they almost certainly play an important role.

People may be born with a certain genetic potential, but the environment plays a key role in developing that potential. Most psychologists agree that the environment is partly—and perhaps entirely—responsible for documented differences in IQ across population groups.

African Americans, whites, and Hispanic Americans tend to live in very different and somewhat isolated worlds. As a consequence, it is extremely difficult to disentangle the effects of the environment from any genetic differences that might contribute to intelligence.

Third, there is evidence to suggest that test *biases* can contribute to population differences in IQ scores (Bernal, 1984). Racial/ethnic group differences depend, to a certain extent, on the type of intelligence test that is administered (Brody, 1992). Most traditional IQ tests of the type that we've discussed in this chapter are written, administered, and scored by white, middle-class psychologists. This raises the very real possibility that cultural biases might be contaminating some of the test questions. For example, if I ask you a question such as "Who wrote *Faust?*" (which once appeared on a Wechsler test), your ability to answer correctly will depend partly on whether your culture places value on exposure to such information. African American psychologist Robert L. Williams has shown that when an intelligence test is used that relies heavily on African American terms and expressions, white students who have had limited experience with African American culture perform poorly. Psychologists have worked hard to remove bias from standard intelligence and achievement tests (Raven, Court, & Raven, 1985), and, in some cases, the development of "culture fair" tests has reduced racial differences in measured ability. But significant differences usually remain even after culture-bound questions have been altered or removed. Consequently, bias is recognized as an important contributor to measured intelligence, but it's unlikely to be the sole determinant of group differences in IQ (Cole, 1981; Kaplan, 1985).

Fourth, a more direct test of environmental explanations of racial/ethnic differences comes from studies looking at the IQs of African American children who have been reared in white homes. If the average African American childhood experience leads to skills that do not transfer well to standard tests of intelligence (for whatever reason), then African American children raised in white, middle-class homes should be expected to produce higher IQ scores. In general, this assumption is supported by the data. Scarr and Weinberg (1976) investigated interracial adoptions in Minnesota and found that the average IQ for African American children reared in economically advantaged white households was significantly higher than the national African American mean score. This finding was confirmed again in later follow-up studies (Waldman, Weinberg, & Scarr, 1994; Weinberg, Scarr, & Waldman, 1992). You should not conclude from this finding that white, middle-

Do you think it's possible to eliminate cultural influences completely from a psychological test? Won't all intelligence tests remain culturally bound at least to some degree?

class households are somehow "better" than other households. The results simply imply that certain cultural experiences give one an "advantage" on the kinds of tests currently being used to assess intelligence.

The Interaction of Nature and Nurture

So what are we to conclude about the relative contributions of genetics and the environment to intelligence? Nature-nurture issues are notoriously difficult to resolve, and this is especially true in the politically sensitive area of intelligence. It's extremely difficult to control for the effects of either the environment or genetics. Consider the twin studies—how reasonable is it to assume that twins who have been "reared apart" have had unrelated environmental experiences? Are children who are adopted really representative of the racial or ethnic populations from which they have been drawn? It's difficult to answer questions like these, because neither the environment nor genetic structure can be manipulated directly in the laboratory (at least for humans).

The most reasonable position to take at the present time is that one's intelligence, like many other psychological attributes, is determined by a mixture of genes and environment. The genes that you inherit from your parents place upper and lower bounds on intellectual ability. Genes determine how your brain is wired, and possibly the speed of neural transmission, but the expression of your genetic material is strongly influenced by the environment.

Recall from Chapter 3 that geneticists use the term *genotype* to refer to the genetic message itself and *phenotype* to refer to the observable characteristics that actually result from genetic expression. An analogy of the genotype/phenotype relationship that is sometimes used by intelligence researchers compares the development of intelligence to the nurturing of flowering plants (Lewontin, 1976). Imagine that we have a packet of virtually identical seeds and we toss half into a pot containing fertile soil and half into a pot of barren soil (see Figure 10.8). The seeds tossed into the poor soil would undoubtedly grow, but their growth would

Suppose we broaden the concept of intelligence to include athletic and artistic ability. Would it bother you to think of these abilities as being influenced primarily by the genetic blueprint?

FIGURE 10.8
Between- and Within-Group Variation. In the plant analogy described in the text, all of the variation in plant height within a pot is due to genetics, but the overall height difference between the two pots is attributable to the environment (rich soil versus poor soil).

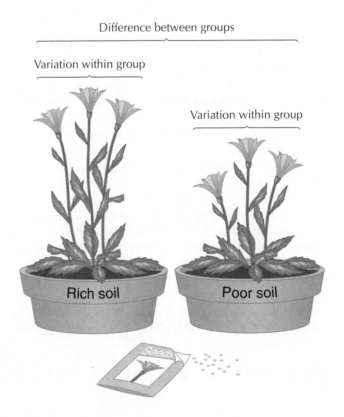

Difference between groups

Variation within group

Variation within group

Rich soil

Poor soil

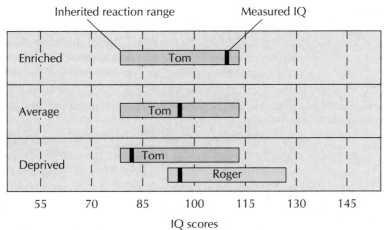

Quality of environment (for realizing intellectual potential)

Inherited reaction range   Measured IQ

Enriched   Tom

Average   Tom

Deprived   Tom

Roger

55   70   85   100   115   130   145

IQ scores

FIGURE 10.9
Reaction Range. Each person may be born with genes that set limits for intellectual potential (sometimes called a reaction range). In this case, Tom has inherited a capacity for obtaining an IQ anywhere between 80 and about 112. The IQ that Tom actually obtains (shown as the dark bar) is determined by the kind of environment in which he is reared. Notice that Roger inherits a greater IQ potential than Tom, but when Tom is raised in an enriched environment his IQ may actually turn out to be higher than Roger's.

be stunted relative to that of the group planted in the rich soil. Because these are virtually identical groups of seeds, containing similar distributions of genetic information, any differences in growth between the pots would be due entirely to the environment (the soil). So, too, with intelligence—two people can be born with similar genetic potential, but the degree to which their intellectual potential will "blossom" will depend critically on the environment.

Consider as well that within each handful of seeds there will be variations in genetic information. Some plants will grow larger than others, regardless of the soil in which they have been thrown. A similar kind of result would be expected for intelligence—variations in the genetic message will produce individual differences in IQ that cannot be adequately explained by environmental variables. In fact, after analyzing the differences within a pot, we might conclude that all of the differences are due to inherited factors. But even if the differences within a group are due to genes, the differences between groups would still be due to the environment (fertile or barren soil). This kind of insight might help account, in part, for the racial/ethnic differences in IQ that we discussed earlier. Even though genes may exert a strong influence within a population, between-population differences could still be determined primarily by the environment (Eysenck & Kamin, 1981; Lewontin, 1976).

One other feature of the interaction between nature and nurture is worth noting. Environmental experiences do not occur independently of inherited factors. It's a two-way street. The environment will partly determine how genetic information is expressed, but so, too, will genetic information determine experience. If you're born with three arms, because of some odd combination of inherited factors, then your interactions with the world will be quite different from those of a normal person. The fact that you have three arms will color your environment— it will determine how you are treated and the range of opportunities to which you are exposed. If you're born with "smart" genes, then early on you're likely to be exposed to opportunities that will help you realize your full intellectual potential; conversely, if you're born "slow," the environment is likely to shape you away from intellectually nurturing experiences (see Figure 10.9). Such is the way of life and of the world.

► SOLVING THE PROBLEMS: A SUMMARY

What is intelligence? We've seen in this chapter that the concept of intelligence arises primarily from the study of individual differences. People differ, and we can try to develop tests that measure these differences effectively. From an analysis of individual variability, psychologists have tried to develop theories of intellectual functioning: What kinds of mental processes underlie intelligent thought? We've seen that one way to characterize intelligence is in terms of the adaptability of behavior. What makes one species member intelligent, and another not, may be dictated by how well organisms adapt to rapidly changing environments and solve the problems of survival. From this perspective, the single nutcracker, in its successful search for a cache of seeds, fits the adaptive view of intelligence just as well as the cocky student who aces the SAT.

In this chapter our discussion revolved around three conceptual and practical problems that researchers interested in intelligence have attempted to resolve.

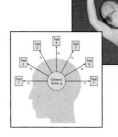

▶ **CONCEPTUALIZING INTELLIGENCE** Researchers have attempted to conceptualize intelligence in a number of ways. Proponents of psychometric approaches to intelligence map out fundamental aspects of the mind by analyzing performance on a battery of mental tests. They traditionally draw distinctions between a general factor of intelligence, *g*, which applies broadly, and specific factors, *s*, which tap particular separate abilities. The idea that intelligence needs to be broken down into several, or multiple, kinds of ability remains popular today, although researchers disagree as to how many or what types of intelligence need to be included.

Cognitive approaches to intelligence seek to discover the internal processes that account for intelligent behavior. There's some evidence to suggest that performance on traditional tests of mental ability might be related to the speed of processing among neurons in the brain. The multiple intelligences approach of Howard Gardner and the triarchic theory of Robert Sternberg both suggest that the concept of intelligence needs to be defined broadly. We cannot rely entirely on things such as academic ability to define intelligence—everyday intelligence and "street smarts" also enhance people's ability to adapt.

▶ **MEASURING INDIVIDUAL DIFFERENCES** Concepts such as intelligence really have little meaning outside of the study of individual differences—it's how the mental ability of Sam differs from the mental ability of Jennifer that makes the concept of intelligence meaningful. A good test of intelligence has three main characteristics: reliability, validity, and standardization. Understanding the concept of test validity is crucial because it holds the key to appreciating the widespread use of standardized measures such as IQ or tests such as the SAT. Researchers who study individual differences are often primarily interested in using measured differences to make predictions about future success. Will Jennifer perform well in school? Will Sam make it as a graduate student in psychology? As we've seen, the IQ test itself was originally developed to measure academic ability, not as some ultimate measure of mental capacity.

▶ **DISCOVERING THE SOURCES OF INTELLIGENCE** There are two primary ways to explain how measured differences in intelligence might arise: genetics and the environment. Twin studies provide convincing evidence that at least some kinds of mental ability are inherited, although how much remains controversial. However, the role of the environment in determining IQ—cultural background, economic status, and even built-in test biases—cannot be discounted. Intelligence, like many psychological attributes, grows out of an interaction between nature and nurture. People may be born with certain potential, but it's the environment that ultimately dictates where they sit in the final distribution of measured mental ability.

Terms to Remember

intelligence An internal capacity or ability that psychologists assume accounts for individual differences in mental test performance. The term is also used to describe the mental processes that underlie the ability to adapt to ever-changing environments.

CONCEPTUALIZING INTELLIGENCE

psychometrics The use of psychological tests to measure the mind and mental processes.

factor analysis A statistical procedure developed by Charles Spearman that groups together related items on tests by analyzing the correlations among test scores. It's often used by psychologists to determine underlying common "factors," or abilities.

g (general intelligence) According to Spearman, a general factor, derived from factor analysis, that underlies or contributes to performance on a variety of mental tests.

s (specific intelligence) According to Spearman, a specific factor, derived from factor analysis, that is unique to a particular kind of test.

fluid intelligence The natural ability to solve problems, reason, and remember; fluid intelligence is thought to be relatively uninfluenced by experience.

crystallized intelligence The knowledge and abilities acquired as a result of experience (as from schooling and cultural influences).

multiple intelligences The notion proposed by Howard Gardner that people possess a set of separate and independent "intelligences" ranging from musical to linguistic to interpersonal ability.

triarchic theory Robert Sternberg's theory of intelligence; it proposes three types of intelligence: analytic, creative, and practical.

MEASURING INDIVIDUAL DIFFERENCES

achievement tests Psychological tests that measure a person's current level of knowledge or competence in a particular subject.

aptitude tests Psychological tests that measure the ability to learn or acquire knowledge in a particular subject.

reliability A measure of the consistency of test results; reliable tests produce similar scores or indices from one administration to the next.

validity An assessment of how well a test measures what it is supposed to measure. *Content validity* assesses the degree to which the test samples broadly across the domain of interest; *predictive validity* assesses how well the test predicts some future criterion; *construct validity* assesses how well the test taps into a particular theoretical construct.

standardization Keeping the testing, scoring, and interpretation procedures similar across all administrations of a test.

intelligence quotient (IQ) Originally, mental age divided by chronological age and then multiplied by 100. More recently, defined in terms of deviation from the average score on an IQ test. *See* deviation IQ.

mental age The chronological age that best fits a child's level of performance on a test of mental ability. Mental age is typically calculated by comparing a child's test score with the average scores for different age groups.

deviation IQ An intelligence "score" that is derived from determining where an individual's performance sits in an age-based distribution of test scores.

mental retardation A label that is generally assigned to someone who scores below 70 on a standard IQ test.

gifted A label that is generally assigned to someone who scores above 130 on a standard IQ test.

DISCOVERING THE SOURCES OF INTELLIGENCE

heritability A mathematical index that represents the extent to which IQ differences in a particular population can be accounted for by genetic factors.

Right now, as you read the printed words on this page, somewhere in the world a test is being administered. More than likely, the test is designed to measure general ability—the ubiquitous factor *g*. Based on the test taker's performance, his or her *g* will be calculated and a crucial decision will be made. Perhaps it's a career path in law enforcement that's on the line, or maybe acceptance or rejection for a highly valued industrial job. Whether the test taker is aware of it or not, he or she sits squarely at a kind of crossroads in life: Performance on this single test will determine important aspects of the future.

Most psychologists recognize and champion the value of standardized tests of intelligence. Intelligence tests have proven to be excellent predictors of performance in many domains, from school to a wide variety of occupations (Estes, 1992). The general ability index *g* is known to be a reasonable predictor of future performance; in fact, it may be the best predictor that we have for overall job performance (see Jensen, 1993; Ree & Earles, 1992). But as you now know, psychologists are keenly aware of the fact that standard objective tests, such as the ones that measure *g*, are not complete remedies or cures for the problem of predicting future performance. General measures of intelligence still cannot account for all (or even most) of the differences typically found in job performance (Sternberg & Wagner, 1993). A person who scores well on a job-related test may indeed become a good employee, but so might a person who does not score well.

As we've discussed in this chapter, one problem with conventional tests is that they measure intelligence in a rather narrow way. General ability is defined in an "academic" sense; standardized intelligence tests are full of questions that are quite specific and well defined. One must have certain knowledge in order to perform well; there are right and wrong answers for each question. There's also usually only one path or method for solving the problem. But success on a

Successful managers understand the unspoken rules and strategies—so-called "tacit knowledge"—that are rarely, if ever, taught directly.

job typically requires knowledge that is not so cut and dried—there are unspoken rules and strategies that are rarely if ever taught formally. This kind of unspoken practical "know-how" is called *tacit* knowledge, and some psychologists believe that it will turn out to be an even better predictor of job performance than *g*.

Categorizing Tacit Knowledge

How can this kind of unspoken knowledge, which everyone in the workplace knows is important, be categorized and assessed? Wagner and Sternberg (1985) divide tacit knowledge into three categories. First, there is tacit knowledge about *managing self*—these are the unspoken rules that people use to judge the importance of tasks and that help them decide how a task should best be approached. Only individuals know the little things that motivate them to perform. Moreover, the individual's ability to tap into those features will undoubtedly predict, at least in part, his or her level of job performance. Second,

there is tacit knowledge about *managing others*—these are the unspoken rules about how to interact with and use the skills of co-workers. Effective managers know how to get the best out of their subordinates, how to make co-workers happy and more productive. Third, there is tacit knowledge about *managing career*—these are the little unwritten rules about how a reputation or career is established. If you're a college professor, should you concentrate on the quality of teaching, try to get grant money from the government, or publish a research article in a prestigious journal?

The important point about tacit knowledge is that it's rarely if ever assessed on standardized tests of intelligence. This kind of knowledge isn't written in books and it's not usually taught. It's the kind of knowledge that comes primarily from experience—from watching and analyzing the behavior of others. Furthermore, people clearly differ in their grasp of job-relevant tacit knowledge. Some managers understand the rules for maximizing the performance of their subordinates better than others do. If we could somehow measure tacit knowledge, it might turn out to be an excellent predictor of job performance.

Assessing Tacit Knowledge

If tacit knowledge is really tacit, meaning unspoken or not openly expressed, then how can it possibly be measured? The tack taken by Wagner and Sternberg (1985; Sternberg & Wagner, 1993) has been to develop brief descriptions, or scenarios, that describe certain problem-solving or decision-making situations. The scenarios are then given to people with different amounts of relevant experience, and each person is asked to rate the value of suggested solutions. Here's one of these scenarios:

You are responsible for selecting a contractor to renovate several large buildings. You have narrowed the choice to two contractors on the basis of their bids, and after further investigation, you are considering awarding the contract to Wilson & Sons Company. Rate the importance of the following pieces of information in making your decision to award the contract to Wilson & Sons:

_____ The company has provided letters from satisfied customers.

_____ The Better Business Bureau reports no major complaints about this company.

_____ Wilson & Sons has done good work for your company in the past.

_____ Wilson & Sons' bid was $2000 less than the other contractor's (approximate total cost of the renovation is $325,000).

_____ Former customers whom you have contacted strongly recommend Wilson & Sons for the job.

People have different ideas about the relative importance of each of these options. Wagner and Sternberg's (1985) critical comparisons are made between the ratings of successful managers—those with lots of work experience—and novices with little or no relevant work experience. It's common to assume that successful managers possess tacit knowledge and are able to use this information in their evaluations. The potential job applicant's answers are then compared to the expert performance and an index or profile of tacit knowledge is calculated.

It turns out that tacit knowledge, as measured by Wagner and Sternberg, bears little relation to general ability, as measured by g. There is almost never a significant correlation with IQ, for example. But measurements of tacit knowledge do a reasonably effective job of predicting job performance. Sternberg and Wagner (1993) have argued that their index correlates significantly with such things as salary, performance ratings, and the prestige of the business or institution where the participant is employed. Moreover, tacit knowledge

improves with work experience, which is what we should expect.

The idea that it's useful to develop and use multiple strategies to perform successfully is almost certain to be true. The adaptive mind soaks up knowledge where it can, and as we've seen in earlier chapters, modeling others is an important vehicle for guiding behavior. As it stands now, however, the concept of tacit knowledge, while intuitively plausible, remains slippery scientifically. Recent critics of Wagner and Sternberg's research have questioned whether tacit knowledge is really anything different from job knowledge (Schmidt & Hunter, 1993). It may not be some human ability, like g, that can be tapped by the appropriate test; instead, measurements of tacit knowledge may simply be indices of what has been learned on the job. Other critics have questioned the finding that tacit knowledge fails to correlate significantly with IQ (Jensen, 1993), and they wonder whether adding tacit knowledge really helps predict job performance over and above g. Few psychologists question the belief that intelligence is more than a single general ability, but whether tacit knowledge will ultimately be determined to be a separate component of intelligence remains uncertain.

11

You sense only rapid movement at first. A glint to your right and the cool feel of metal on your cheek. You exhale, gasping, as a bony arm wraps itself around your neck. "Welcome to your nightmare, my friend," a voice growls. "Your wallet, your watch, or your life." Inside, your sympathetic nervous system jumps into action—releasing epinephrine, targeting the critical organs of the body and the neural communication chains. Your mind, flooded with the arousal, struggles to understand and decide on the best response. But you see only jumbled images of the sidewalk and needle tracks dotting the arm hugging your neck. No focused clarity, no clear course of action appears to guide your response. In your mind, there is simply surprise, confusion, and the smothering grip of fear. . . .

Not a very pleasant scenario. Two people, reacting to circumstance, who are each in a highly activated state. But the interplay sets an interesting stage for the psychologist. The unfolding action strikes at the core of what psychology is about: understanding the causes and motivations of behavior. What factors underlie the initiation and direction of behavior? What causes the criminal to usurp the victim: Is it the reinforcing value of money? Is it the loss of control driven by the internal need for a "fix"? And what about the emotions that accompany the act—fear, excitement, despair? In what way does an emotion such as fear, with its often paralyzing consequences, enhance the functioning of the adaptive mind? Could it be that emotions themselves motivate and direct behavior? These are some of the topics we'll consider in this chapter, and we'll see how the adaptive mind and body have evolved to react quickly to environmental circumstances, thereby satisfying a variety of basic needs.

Motivation can be defined as the set of factors that *initiate* and *direct* behavior, usually toward some goal. If you're motivated, your behavior becomes activated and goal-directed. Hunger is a classic example of an internal condition or "state" that stimulates an organism to pursue food. The desire for a "fix" leads the junkie on a persistent and directed search to acquire the drug of salvation. As we saw in Chapter 7, people are also likely to become motivated if they've recently been rewarded for behaving in a particular way—they're likely to act in a similar way again to get the reward. **Emotions** are complex psychological events that are often associated with the initiation and direction of behavior. Emotions typically involve (1) a *physiological* reaction, usually arousal; (2) some kind of *expressive* reaction, such as a distinctive facial expression; and (3) some kind of *subjective experience,* such as the conscious feeling of being happy or sad.

Most psychologists are convinced that the concepts of motivation and emotion need to be closely linked. Both terms, in fact, derive from the Latin *movere,* meaning "to move." Many conditions that are motivating give rise as well to the experience of emotion. Consider the case in which your thirst motivates you to put change into a soda machine. If the money gets stuck, stalling the pursuit of your goal, frustration and anger are likely. Moreover, once aroused, the emotional experience affects your ability to direct your behavior successfully. If you continue to scream and kick the soda machine, it's unlikely that your goal—quenching your thirst—will be satisfied anytime soon. For reasons like these, it's difficult to discuss the topic of motivation without also considering emotion.

PREVIEWING THE ADAPTIVE PROBLEMS

To study motivation, we must ask questions about the fundamental *causes* of behavior (Mook, 1995). Obviously, then, the topic cuts a wide swath across psychology. Each of the preceding chapters is relevant in one way or another to the question of *why* behavior occurs, but we'll focus our discussion in this chapter on a set of specific adaptive problems that relate to motivation: What are the "factors" that activate behavior, and how do they interact to produce goal-directed actions? How do people satisfy the specific biological need for food and sustenance? What biological mechanisms promote sexual behavior, thereby assuring survival of the species? Finally, how are emotions expressed and experienced, and what functions do they serve?

ACTIVATING BEHAVIOR   Any organism seeking to survive in a changing environment must react quickly to its needs. It must anticipate future outcomes and act accordingly, *now,* with vigor and persistence. Much of the time people's actions are controlled by *internal* factors that "push" them in the direction of a goal. For example, if your body is deprived of food or water, a delicate internal balance is disrupted inside your body. A specific need is signaled, which you seek to satisfy in order to restore the internal balance.

At other times people seem to be motivated by *external* events, things in their environment that exert powerful "pulling" effects. The sight of an attractive person, or a recently sliced piece of chocolate cake, can be sufficient to initiate and direct your behavior. We discussed in Chapter 7 how external events often act as signals for reinforcement. People respond vigorously in a particular situation to enhance their pleasure or to avoid discomfort. We'll see in this chapter that internal and external factors usually interact to induce motivation; to analyze most goal-directed behaviors, we must consider both.

MEETING BIOLOGICAL NEEDS: HUNGER AND EATING   Food consumption is not a matter of personal choice—it's a requirement of living. Consequently, your adaptive mind needs foolproof methods for assuring that you eat at regular intervals. To understand how people's bodies maintain the proper levels of internal energy, we'll consider the relevant *internal* and *external* cues that activate and control eating. First, we'll discuss how the body monitors internal physiological states, using brain mechanisms to check up on levels of energy reserves (for example, the amount of sugar in the blood). Next, we'll discuss how external cues in the environment compel people to consume, and how these cues can influence the food selection process. Whether a person likes broccoli, rejects mushrooms, or happily consumes squid depends on a variety of factors, including what he or she has learned about these foods. Finally, we'll consider the physical and psychological determinants of weight control: What causes some to overeat themselves into obesity and others literally to starve themselves to death?

MEETING BIOLOGICAL NEEDS: SEXUAL BEHAVIOR   Although you may know someone who is "consumed" by sex, or at least has a reasonably intense sexual "appetite," sexual activity is not necessary for individual survival. In principle, people can live perfectly happy and productive lives without ever once engaging in sexual behavior or exploring their sexuality. But adequate sexual performance is needed for survival of the *species*. It's reasonable to assume, then, that there are internal cues, rooted in the genetic code or in active biological systems, that help motivate an interest in sex. We'll discuss some of the biological mechanisms that

There may be internal cues, rooted in the genetic code or in active biological systems, that help to motivate an interest in sexual behavior. Besides the pleasurable and reinforcing aspects of sex, sexual desire drives people to pursue a mate, thereby opening the door for companionship, protection, and love.

motivate sexual behavior, as well as some of the physiological characteristics of the human sexual response. Like hunger, sexual motivation is also greatly affected by external cues. People's sense of attractiveness, their willingness to engage in sex-related behaviors, their views on pornography, abortion, or sexual "normalcy"—each is influenced to a large extent by what they've been taught by significant role models in their culture.

▶ **EXPRESSING AND EXPERIENCING EMOTION** All psychologists agree that emotions have considerable adaptive significance. Consider an emotion like *anger.* Anger typically arises in response to an environmental event, usually the perceived misdeed of another, and the body enters a highly aroused state. The arousal activates behavior and leads to reactions that may substantially increase (or decrease) the likelihood of survival. Once the emotion gains hold, overt physical expressions arise, particularly in the form of easy-to-identify facial expressions. From an adaptive perspective, the sight of an angry person carries important signaling properties—others know to shy away and avoid interaction. As we'll see, emotions are easy to identify but difficult to define. In an effort to understand how people experience and express emotions, we'll look first at the question of whether basic emotions even exist. Then we'll examine the nature of emotional experiences—both the physiological arousal and the internal subjective experience. Finally, we'll examine some theories that have been offered to explain the origins of emotions.

Activating Behavior

Let's turn our attention to the first problem: What are the general factors that activate and control goal-directed behavior? Initially, psychologists considered the possibility that there might be a single source of motivation, grounded either in the internal workings of the body or in the external environment. It's possible, for example, that people are born with biological machinery that compels them to act in predetermined ways, like automatons, irrespective of what they learn from experience. But this idea is largely rejected by current psychologists, who believe instead that no single explanation of goal-directed behavior, based on either biological or environmental factors, is likely to be found. The reason is simple: Virtually all forms of behavior are determined by multiple causes. Factors both inside and outside the body—*internal* and *external* factors—contribute to motivation. In the following sections, we'll consider some examples of these influences.

Internal Factors: Instincts and Drive

For an organism to survive in its environment, it must do certain things. Breathing, eating, drinking—these are activities that need to be performed at regular intervals. It makes sense then to assume that the motivation to perform life-sustaining activities is built directly into the biological or genetic code. In nature, birds don't need to be taught to build nests in the springtime or to fly south in the winter; cats don't need to be taught to show interest in small, rapidly moving furry creatures. These are unlearned, characteristic patterns of responding—called **instincts**—that are controlled by specific triggering stimuli in the world. Instincts share properties with *reflexes,* which we discussed in Chapter 3, but "instincts" typically encompass more complex patterns of behavior than those covered by the simple reflexes.

The factors that are initiating and directing this bobcat's behavior include internal ones, such as depleted energy resources, and external ones, such as the sight of an attractive meal. As we'll see, internal and external factors often interact to produce motivated behavior.

The behavior of many animals is motivated, at least in part, by instincts—unlearned, characteristic patterns of responding that are controlled by specific triggering stimuli in the environment.

Human Instincts. It's widely accepted that instincts are important controlling forces in nonhuman species. But do instincts play any role in controlling human behavior? A number of early psychologists followed the lead of Charles Darwin in suggesting a major role for instincts in human motivation. Humans don't need to be taught to take care of their young, William James (1890) argued, or to cry as infants, to clean themselves when dirty, or even to play, love, imitate, or be curious. These are ingrained biological "musts" that are as natural to the human as nest building is to the bird.

But it turns out to be rather difficult to determine whether such behaviors are truly "instinctive" in humans. The mere fact that a behavior occurs with regularity does not mean it's *instinctive*—that is, unlearned and characteristic in its display. There is no way to open up the body and directly measure an instinct, so it's easy to fall into a trap of circular reasoning: People demonstrate some regular behavior, such as showing sympathy for a child in need, and the temptation is to propose a corresponding "sympathy" instinct (Holt, 1931). Over the years, psychologists argued about which behaviors should be appropriately labeled as instinctive. For example, William James (1890) suggested some 20 physical and 17 mental instincts in his writings; William McDougall (1908), on the other hand, was convinced of only 12 (he later changed his mind and upped the number to 17). For these and other reasons, instincts eventually fell out of favor as a widely applied explanation for goal-directed human behavior.

Drive. To replace instinct, psychologists turned to the concept of *drive*. A **drive** is a psychological state that arises in response to an internal physiological *need*, such as hunger or thirst. It's clear that the human body is designed to seek fairly stable and constant internal conditions. For example, it's important for the body to maintain an adequate internal supply of fluids, or a constant internal temperature. Psychologists use the term **homeostasis** to refer to the process through which the body maintains its steady state, much like the thermostat in a house maintains a constant internal temperature by turning the heat on or off (Cannon, 1929). Once a specific need is detected, "drive" serves a general activating function—drive energizes the organism, causing it to seek immediate reduction of the

Instincts produce behaviors that are rigid and inflexible, such as mating rituals of the types you may have seen in some animals. Can you think of any instances of human behavior that are rigid and characteristic in their display?

FIGURE 11.1

Homeostasis. It's adaptive for the body to maintain stable and constant internal conditions. If a person's internal temperature rises above or falls below an optimal level, he or she is driven to perform actions that will restore the "steady state."

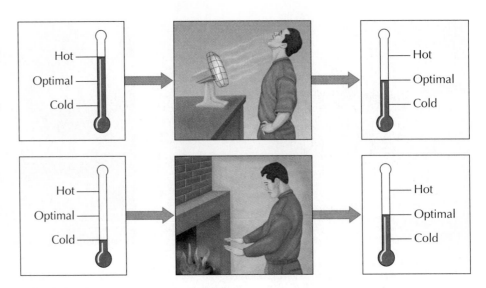

need. So if their water supply is depleted, people become "driven" to restore the appropriate balance. Similar processes are assumed to operate for hunger and for the maintenance of internal body temperature (see Figure 11.1).

Drive is a considerably more flexible concept than instinct. The organism seeks to reduce drive—to restore homeostatic balance—but it doesn't really matter *how* balance is restored. People can use what they learn from experience to help them act appropriately; they're not stuck with one fixed pattern of behavior that is triggered only by a restricted set of stimuli. You can think about drive as somewhat analogous to running the engine in a car. A properly running engine is necessary for the car to move, as drive is necessary to initiate goal-directed behavior, but it's not sufficient to get across town. Other factors, such as knowledge about the layout of the town, must be used in conjunction with the operating engine in order to move about. As we'll see shortly, it's also the case that the vigor or intensity with which an individual acts depends critically on the value, or *incentive,* of the goal. People are much more likely to motivate themselves to eat if they like the food, even though a wide variety of food options may satisfy the internal need. People sometimes even eat in the absence of an internal need, as in the case in which you have that second brownie just because it looks good.

External Factors: Incentive Motivation

Consequently, by itself, the concept of drive is insufficient to explain motivated behavior. Goal-directed behavior depends as well on what people learn from experience. External rewards, such as money or a good grade, exert powerful "pulling" and guiding effects on a person's actions. Generally, whether someone will be motivated to perform an action will depend on the value—positive or negative—of the incentive. For this reason, psychologists often use the term **incentive motivation** as a way of explaining goal-directed behavior. For example, Whitney is motivated to jog for an extra 5 minutes so that she can eat that extra brownie; conversely, Julie is motivated to avoid the kitchen because of the extra calories (and guilt) that she knows the brownie consumption will produce. Note that this type of motivation is quite different from drive—drive is an internal "push" that compels a person to action; incentives are external "pulls" that tempt people with the prospects of receiving powerful reinforcing or punishing consequences.

Of course, internal factors interact with external factors in a number of ways. Whether a person is thirsty, for example, probably affects the incentive value of water; water tastes better, and is more rewarding, when one has been deprived of it for a while (Blundell & Rogers, 1991; Bolles, 1972). Internal states of deprivation can also act as cues for responding. A person might learn to perform a certain type of action when he or she is thirsty or hungry (Hull, 1943); alternatively, a person might learn that hunger or thirst means that food or water will be especially rewarding (Davidson, 1993). It's important to remember that motivated behavior is virtually always jointly determined by internal and external factors.

Achievement Motivation

One example of motivated behavior that clearly depends on both internal and external factors is the striving for achievement. A number of psychologists have argued that each person, to varying degrees, has an internally driven need for achievement (Atkinson, 1957; McClelland and others, 1953; Murray, 1938). The **achievement motive** pushes people to seek success and significant accomplishment in their lives. Studies have demonstrated that people who rate high in achievement motivation tend to work harder and more persistently on tasks, and they tend to achieve more than those who rate low in achievement motivation (Atkinson & Raynor, 1974; Cooper, 1983).

But whether people will work hard on any particular task depends on (1) their expectations about whether their efforts will be successful, and (2) how much they value succeeding at the task (Atkinson, 1957). This means that individuals can have a high internal need for achievement but choose not to persist on a task either because they place no value on the task, or because they have no confidence in their ability to succeed. For example, young children who experience failure on mathematics problems early in life can develop a "helpless" attitude that prevents them from persisting and succeeding on mathematical tasks later in life (Smiley & Dweck, 1994). Conversely, children who perform well on such tasks gain confidence in their ability and appear motivated to take on similar tasks in the future (Wigfield, 1994).

Parents, teachers, and other significant role models play an important part in determining achievement motivation. If a child's parents value a task, it's likely

External rewards, such as this young girl's blue ribbon, can exert powerful pulling and guiding effects on people's actions.

Every society in the world sets standards for achievement—what skills are important and unimportant—and these standards influence what members of the society seek to achieve.

Children who experience failure on mathematical problems early in life can develop a "helpless" attitude that prevents them from persisting and succeeding in mathematics later in life.

that the child will value it as well and will appear more motivated to succeed (Eccles and others, 1983). Every society in the world establishes standards for achievement—what skills and tasks are deemed important and unimportant—and these standards influence what the members of the society seek to achieve, and perhaps the level of productivity of the society as a whole (McClelland, 1961). Many researchers believe that gender differences in achievement—such as the tendency for men to outperform women, on average, in mathematics—may be partly tied to such cultural factors. In the United States, for instance, the parents of sons have been found to place greater value on success in mathematics than the parents of daughters do (Parsons, Kaczala, & Meece, 1982). Consequently, the expectations and values of the parents help to determine the achievement motivation of the children.

Intrinsic Motivation

Sometimes people seem to engage in actions for which there is no obvious internal or external motivational source. A child spends hours carefully coloring a picture or playing with a doll; an adult becomes transfixed by a crossword puzzle or by a long walk on the beach. Certainly there is no biological *need* that drives coloring or walking. There's also no clear-cut external incentive: Nobody pays the child for coloring or the adult for finishing the crossword puzzle. Psychologists use the term **intrinsic motivation** to describe situations in which behavior appears to be entirely self-motivated. People engage in the action for its own sake, not because someone offers them a reward or because the action restores some internal homeostatic balance.

What convinced many researchers that intrinsic motivation deserves special status was a counterintuitive finding: It's possible to lower someone's interest in performing a task by applying external reward. In a classic study by Lepper, Greene, and Nisbett (1973), preschool children who were naturally interested in drawing were asked to draw either for its own sake or to win a "Good Player" certificate. Psychologically, we would expect the external reward to bolster drawing even more than normal—after all, drawing is now followed by a concrete positive consequence. But it didn't. The children in the reward condition showed less interest in drawing a week later. The reward apparently "killed" the behavior, making it less rewarding or interesting than it otherwise would have been.

Suppose you spend every Saturday morning volunteering at a local homeless shelter, preparing meals and helping to clean up. How do you think your attitude toward this activity would change if you began receiving a weekly paycheck for your time?

This study has been repeated with other rewards, as well as with activities other than drawing (see Deci & Ryan, 1985). The story is much the same: Externally supplied "rewards" can lower one's desire to perform a task. Once a person receives a reward for performing a task, he or she seems less likely to enjoy that task for its own sake in the future. Many sports fans complain that the external reward of money has ruined professional sports. Even baseball players sometimes lament that the game was more fun back in the sandlot, before millions of dollars entered into the motivational chain. How can a reward lead to a negative effect? One possibility is that people perceive external rewards to be insidious ways of controlling their behavior. Drawing loses its intrinsic value because it's now something that you must do to please me—by being given a reward, you're performing at my beck and call, rather than drawing simply because it pleases you (Rummel & Feinberg, 1988). Another way of stating this case is to argue that the so-called "reward" is not really a reward at all. When coupled with the loss of control, the consequence becomes a net negative.

Another possibility is that external reward leads to what has been called *overjustification:* Rather than assuming that you are self-motivated to perform a task because it is intrinsically reinforcing, you conclude that it is the external reward that is motivating you to perform the task (Bem, 1972; Deci & Ryan, 1985).

Do you think these two volunteers at a local food bank would feel better about their work if they were also paid for their activities?

Rewarding someone for performing a task in a sense "degrades" the intrinsic value that the task would normally deliver (that is, the baseball player begins to believe that it's the money that makes him play, rather than love for the game). Some researchers have even suggested that things like creativity should never be rewarded, lest the positive internal value of engaging in a creative act be destroyed (Amabile, 1983; Schwartz, 1990).

But not all psychologists are comfortable with these conclusions. External reward can enhance creativity under some circumstances, and the negative effects of reward on task motivation may occur only in restricted circumstances (see Dickinson, 1989; Eisenberger, 1992). For example, in the study by Lepper and colleagues, children did indeed choose to draw less frequently when they were rewarded for drawing, but this effect occurred only when the children *expected* the reward. When children were given an unexpected reward for drawing, they later spent more time drawing than a group who had received no reward. Therefore, the negative effect of reward on intrinsic motivation may be related to the expectation or *promise* of reward rather than to the reward itself (Cameron & Pierce, 1994).

Maslow's Hierarchy of Needs

Most general theories of motivation rest on a fulcrum of biological *need*. The body seeks to maintain a delicate internal balance (homeostasis), and if that balance is disrupted, the person is motivated to restore it. But as we've just seen, not all needs are biological in origin—such as the need for achievement (Murray, 1938). For this reason, some psychologists have tried to classify need and to determine whether some needs are more important than others.

Among the more influential of these classification systems is the **need hierarchy** introduced by the humanistic theorist Abraham Maslow. The essential component of Maslow's theory is the *prioritizing* of needs: Some needs, he argued, have special priority and must be satisfied before others can be addressed. Obviously, if people don't eat or drink water on a regular basis, they'll die. Maslow's theory is usually represented in the form of a pyramid, to emphasize the fact that human

FIGURE 11.2

A Hierarchy of Needs. Maslow proposed that human needs are prioritized: Some needs, such as physiological and safety needs, must be satisfied before others can be addressed. At the top of the pyramid sits the need for self-actualization, which represents people's natural desire to reach their true potential.

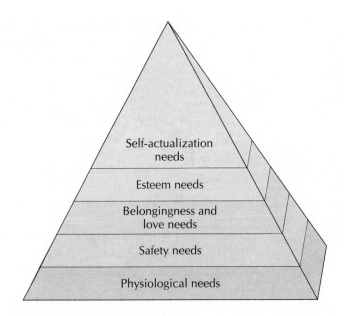

Try turning back to the chapter on development and thinking about the various personal "crises" that people confront as they age. Is there any way you can tie these crises to the needs that Maslow discusses in his hierarchy?

motivation rests on a foundation of biological and security "musts" (see Figure 11.2). It is only after satisfying the survival needs—such as hunger and thirst—that people can consider personal security and more social or spiritual needs, such as the need for love or self-esteem. At the top of the structure sits the need for self-actualization, which Maslow believed represented people's desire to reach their true potential as human beings.

The pyramid is an appropriate symbol for Maslow's system because it captures the upward thrust of human motivation. As a humanistic psychologist, Maslow believed that all people have a compelling need to grow, to better themselves as functioning individuals. In his own words: "A musician must make music, an artist must paint, a poet must write if he is ultimately to be at peace with himself" (Maslow, 1954). Maslow was strongly influenced by people who he felt had reached their fullest potential, such as Albert Einstein and Thomas Jefferson. He used their personality characteristics as a way of defining what it means to sit at the top of the pyramid—to be self-actualized. Some of these characteristics included spontaneity, openness to experience, and a high degree of ethical sensitivity (see Mook, 1995). We'll return to humanistic views on personality in Chapter 12.

Probably the most important feature of the Maslow hierarchy is the laddering of needs. Psychologists might disagree about the specific order that Maslow proposed—does the need to belong and be accepted really have higher priority than the need for self-esteem?—but the idea that humans have a wide diversity of needs and that those needs are prioritized has been enormously influential. It's important to understand that how people act is often controlled by unfilled needs that may have a high priority. Someone who has to worry about putting food on the table, and consequently steals from others on a regular basis, might appear deficient in moral or ethical values. But this isn't necessarily a permanent fixture of his or her personality—under different circumstances, with a full stomach, the person might be a leader in the promotion of ethical values.

Critics of Maslow's theory often point to its lack of scientific rigor. Because the various "needs" are not defined clearly, in a way that each can be individually measured, the proposals of the need hierarchy become essentially untestable (Wahba & Bridwell, 1976). But the theory continues to exert considerable influence on the way that psychologists think. For example, applied psychologists have extended Maslow's ideas to the workplace, to help employers better understand the behavior of their employees. Many employers now recognize that an employee's needs change depending on his or her position in the management hierarchy. When a person receives low pay or has poor job security, his or her work behavior is directed toward satisfying basic needs. Promotion may help satisfy the fundamental needs, but new, perhaps more demanding ones will quickly arise. Employers need to be sensitive to the particular needs that accompany each point in the management hierarchy (Muchinsky, 1993).

Meeting Biological Needs: Hunger and Eating

We've discussed some general sources of motivation, as well as the concept of need. Now we'll turn our attention to a vital motivational problem that must be dealt with every day: initiating and controlling eating behavior. Eating is a constant in everyone's life, but the reasons that people eat are considerably more complex than you might think. Ask any child to explain why we eat, and he or she will be likely to respond with something like, "Because we're hungry" or "Because my tummy hurts." An adult's response will appear more sophisticated, but it usually amounts to much the same thing: "We eat because our bodies need food, internal energy." This is true; eating is a biologically driven behavior. But eating is a psychologically driven behavior as well. Hunger can arise in the *absence* of physical need and, as any dieter knows, the physical need can be present but the will to *resist* can overcome the meeting of food with mouth.

Internal Factors

Researchers have spent decades attempting to understand the internal mechanisms that influence the initiation and control of eating. We now know, for example, that the body monitors itself, particularly its internal supply of resources, in a number of ways. For example, there is a connection between the volume and content of food in the stomach and the amount that neurons will fire in certain areas of the brain (Sharma and others, 1961). Psychologically, people report little, if any, hunger or interest in food when the stomach is distended (full), and hunger increases in a relatively direct way as the stomach empties (Sepple & Read, 1989).

Internal factors, such as the amount of food in the stomach or the amount of glucose in the blood, play an important role in making people feel "sated" after a meal.

Chemical Signals for Hunger. It's not just the contents of the stomach that are monitored. The body has several important suppliers of internal energy that it checks regularly. One critical substance is **glucose,** a kind of sugar that cells require for energy production. Receptors in the liver are thought to react to changes in the amount of glucose in the blood, or perhaps to how this sugar is being used by the cells, and to communicate appropriate signals upward to the brain (Mayer, 1953; Russek, 1971). When the amount of usable glucose falls below an optimal level, which usually occurs after some period of food deprivation, people start to feel hungry and seek out food. If blood glucose levels are high, a condition that arises after a meal, people lose interest in food. This link between blood sugar levels and hunger is not simply correlational: In the laboratory it is possible to increase or decrease how much an animal will eat by artificially manipulating the amount of glucose in its blood (Smith & Campfield, 1993).

Another key element that the body monitors is **insulin,** a hormone released by the pancreas. The body needs insulin to help pump the nutrients present in the blood into the cells, where they can be stored as fat or metabolized into needed energy. At the start of a meal, the brain sends signals to the pancreas to begin the production and release of this hormone, in preparation for the rise in blood sugar produced by the food. As insulin does its job, the levels of blood sugar go down and the person eventually feels hungry once again. It's probably a glucose-insulin interaction that is actually monitored internally, because both substances play pivotal roles in the metabolic, or energy-producing, process. If laboratory animals are given continuous injections of insulin, they tend to balloon in weight and grossly overeat—the insulin keeps the blood sugar level low, which signals the animal to start looking for something to eat.

Although glucose and insulin are believed to play key roles in motivating eating behavior, it's unlikely that any one single chemical (or even two) dictates when and whether a person will become hungry. Other internal stimuli, such as the overall level of body fat (Keesey & Powley, 1975), are undoubtedly also involved. Of course, ultimately the experience of hunger originates in the brain. It is the activation of brain structures that initiates and directs the search for food. We mentioned in Chapter 3 that structures in the limbic system are involved in the initiation and control of significant motivational and emotional behaviors. As we'll see momentarily, structures associated with the *hypothalamus* have long been thought to be of central importance in eating.

The Role of the Hypothalamus. It's been known for decades that if a particular portion of the **ventromedial hypothalamus** is lesioned (destroyed) in laboratory animals, a curious and dramatic transformation occurs. The animal appears to be in a prolonged state of hunger, characterized by a striking tendency to overeat. Once the brain lesion occurs, the appetite of these animals can seem insatiable. They become eating machines, and, if allowed, they can balloon up to several times their normal weight (Hetherington & Ranson, 1942). If this same area is stimulated electrically, rather than destroyed, the opposite pattern emerges. Stimulation causes the animal to lose all interest in food, even if there is a compelling need for nutrients in the body. At first glance, these data seemed to support the idea that the ventromedial hypothalamus functions as a kind of stop, or *satiety,* center in the brain. Activation of the region turns off hunger and eating when food intake has been sufficient to fulfill the body's energy needs. This would be an adaptive process because it would prevent someone from accumulating too many nutrients in the blood—more than the body can handle.

If activation of the ventromedial hypothalamus stops an animal from eating, researchers asked, then what starts the eating process? One logical candidate was the **lateral hypothalamus,** because this structure acts as a kind of mirror image of the ventromedial hypothalamus. Damage to the lateral hypothalamus can create an animal that typically starves itself, instead of eating voraciously; electrical stimulation of the same area induces immediate eating rather than starvation. This suggested that the lateral hypothalamus acts as a kind of eating "start up" center, whose activity is modulated by concurrent activity in the ventromedial hypothalamus. This division of labor in the brain paints a cohesive picture—two regions of the hypothalamus working together to initiate and control eating behavior.

Unfortunately, the cohesiveness of this picture has unraveled considerably in recent years. Although both regions of the hypothalamus undoubtedly help to control eating, researchers are uncertain about their precise roles. Part of the problem is that destruction of either area tends to affect the nervous system in a number of ways, so it's difficult to determine the exact causes of the eating changes. Lesions to the ventromedial hypothalamus, for example, may affect the secretion of insulin (Weingarten, Chang, & McDonald, 1985) or damage the effectiveness of various

If a particular portion of the ventromedial hypothalamus is destroyed, rats become eating machines and can balloon up to several times their normal weight.

other important pathways in the brain (Kirchgessner & Sclafani, 1988). Moreover, a closer examination of animals with lesions to the ventromedial hypothalamus revealed that they won't eat just anything, as the start-stop hypothesis would predict. Instead, they're somewhat picky and won't eat certain foods (Ferguson & Keesey, 1975).

Just as the brain monitors the levels of several internal "fuels" to determine the need for food, several important locations in the brain seem to control eating behavior. There is evidence that portions of the brainstem are critical in the initiation of eating (Grill & Kaplan, 1990), and the hippocampus may be involved as well. You may remember from Chapter 8 that we discussed an amnesiac called H.M. who was doomed to live in a kind of perpetual present—he could remember nothing of what happened to him moments before. It turns out that H.M., who has damage to his temporal lobes and hippocampus, also has trouble monitoring his need for food. He is sometimes convinced that he's hungry immediately after finishing a meal. He may have simply forgotten that he ate; but, as Davidson (1993) points out, he clearly is also unable to use internal signals from his body as cues for hunger or satiety. These data suggest an important role for the hippocampus in feeding behavior (see also Davidson & Jarrad, 1993).

External Factors

From an adaptive standpoint, it's important to stress the biological role that eating and food selection play in continuing one's existence. People can't let their internal energy sources fall too low; otherwise they wouldn't have an adaptive mind to consider. But it would be a mistake to think about hunger and eating as simply a means to satisfy a variety of internal energy needs. People often eat for reasons that are unrelated to restoring internal homeostatic balance. Haven't you ever eaten to reduce stress or simply to make yourself feel good? Haven't you ever eaten to promote social interaction, as in going out to dinner with friends? We all have. If you think about it, you'll realize that we even eat at times to make artistic, aesthetic, or moral judgments. For example, some individuals are vegetarians because they believe it's wrong to eat other animals.

Food, and particularly eating, is clearly reinforcing. It's fun to eat and to be around good food. Animals learn that certain kinds of food signal positive consequences, and these signals motivate them to act accordingly. If hungry rats are taught that a flashing light signals food, later on they'll start eating in the presence of the light even if they've been fully fed moments before (Weingarten, 1983). Waiters at fine restaurants push the dessert tray under your nose after a filling

One's cultural and ethnic background exerts a powerful effect on food selection. Would you be willing to consume the insect delicacies shown in the picture on the right?

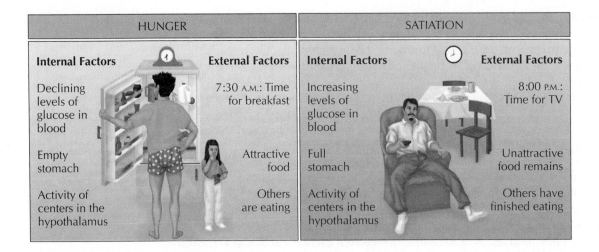

HUNGER		SATIATION	
Internal Factors	**External Factors**	**Internal Factors**	**External Factors**
Declining levels of glucose in blood	7:30 A.M.: Time for breakfast	Increasing levels of glucose in blood	8:00 P.M.: Time for TV
Empty stomach	Attractive food	Full stomach	Unattractive food remains
Activity of centers in the hypothalamus	Others are eating	Activity of centers in the hypothalamus	Others have finished eating

FIGURE 11.3
Factors Controlling Hunger.
Whether people will choose to start or stop eating depends on a variety of internal and external factors; only some of the factors controlling hunger are listed here.

meal because they know that the sight (or "presentation") of the sugar-filled array will be more likely to break down your reserve than just hearing about what's for dessert. Again, your choice of the New York cheesecake in the strawberry sauce is not driven by internal need. Your blood contains plenty of appropriate nutrients—the sight of the food, and its associations with past pleasures, acts as an external "pull," motivating your choice to consume.

Cultural and ethnic backgrounds also exert powerful influences on food selection. Most people who grow up in the United States would not willingly choose to eat dogs or sheep's eyes, but these "foods" are considered delicacies in some parts of the world. You might not think twice about eating pork or beef, unless you're an Orthodox Jew or a native of India. And it's not just the appearance of food, or where it comes from. People around the world often discriminate among who it is appropriate to eat with. For example, members of some social classes would never consider eating with those that they consider to be social "inferiors." People have established eating "habits," which develop in large part by modeling the behavior of others, and these learned habits underlie much of their decision making about food. For a general overview of the internal and external factors that control hunger, take a look at Figure 11.3.

Regulating Body Weight

What determines a person's everyday body weight? Why are some people thin and others obese? Not surprisingly, internal and external factors combine to regulate body weight. But some factors, such as genetic predispositions, exert a particularly powerful influence. When identical twins—those sharing the same genetic material—are fed identical diets, they tend to gain virtually the same amount of weight. But if two unrelated people are given matched diets, the differences in weight gain can be substantial (Bouchard, C., and others, 1990). Some people can appear to eat continuously and never gain weight; others balloon considerably after what seems to be only a small daily increase in caloric intake. In short, the amount of food that someone eats only partly determines his or her usual weight.

Can you think of any other factors, besides modeling, that might help determine eating habits? What about the availability of the food—when was the last time you saw sheep's eyes on the menu at your local restaurant?

Set Point. Some researchers believe that all people have a natural body weight, or **set point,** that more or less controls their tendency to gain or lose weight (Keesey & Powley, 1975). Most people show little variation in weight from year to year, presumably because their bodies manipulate the motivation to eat, as needed, to maintain the appropriate set point weight. When people go on a diet and dip below their natural weight, well over 90% of them eventually gain that weight back

(Martin, White, & Hulsey, 1991). Here again, the idea is that the body adjusts how much it eats, rebounding after a diet, to produce stability in body weight.

What determines an individual's particular set point? Probably genetic factors are responsible: Different people are born with different numbers of fat cells, and this number may constrain just how much weight someone can hope to gain or lose (Faust, 1984). Metabolic rate—how quickly one burns off calories—is another important internal factor; once again, it's determined, in part, by the person's genetic makeup.

At one time it was thought that overweight, or obese, people simply lacked sufficient willpower to resist overeating, especially when appealing food was in view (Schachter, 1971). Studies were conducted showing that overweight people are more likely to order a specific dish in a restaurant after a tasty description (Herman & Polivy, 1988). Overweight people are also more likely than nonobese people to report that food still tastes good after a filling meal. But to explain obesity by appealing to willpower, or to any one psychological factor, is simplistic and misleading. The roots of obesity lie in biology and psychology: metabolic rate, set point, number of fat cells, learned eating habits, cultural role models, level of stress—all contribute in one way or another to weight control (Rodin, 1981).

Eating Disorders

People's quest for the perfect body shape and weight is a multimillion-dollar industry whose influence stretches worldwide. As you know, society signals weight "ideals," often through advertising, and people's notions about attractiveness have become closely tied to meeting these standards (Jacobi & Cash, 1994). There are adaptive reasons why you might seek to emulate role models in your culture (see Chapter 7), but in the case of weight control you're traveling along a dangerous two-way street. On the one hand, if you're extremely overweight, you're more likely to suffer from health problems that may lead to an early death. Thus, it's useful to watch your weight by monitoring the nutritional value and volume of your meals. But the pursuit of *unrealistic* weight goals, ones that you can never hope to

Social standards concerning weight "ideals" have changed considerably over the years.

This young woman is suffering from anorexia nervosa, a condition characterized by an intense fear of being overweight.

reach because of ingrained biological predispositions, can lead to significant psychological problems. Unhappiness and depression are the all-too-often by-products of the failure to reach the "proper" ideal (Rodin, Schank, & Striegal-Moore, 1989).

Interestingly, people's assessments of their own weight, and its relation to these standards, are typically inaccurate. People often have distorted views of their own body image. For example, on average, women rate their own weight as higher than what they consider to be the ideal and most attractive weight. People also misrepresent what members of the opposite sex consider to be an ideal body weight (Fallon & Rozin, 1985). On average, women tend to think men prefer thinner women than men actually do; when men are asked about their own ideal weight, it tends to be heavier than what the average woman rates as most attractive. Not surprisingly, these mistaken beliefs help promote a negative body image. One of the consequences of a negative body image is increased susceptibility to eating disorders, such as *anorexia nervosa* and *bulimia nervosa.*

In a recent survey of eighth- and tenth-grade students, it was discovered that over 60% of the females and 28% of the males were in the midst of dieting (Hunnicutt & Newman, 1993). The concern—some would say obsession—with weight and dieting starts early in Western cultures, and for an unfortunate few the consequences can be life-threatening. In the condition called **anorexia nervosa,** an otherwise healthy person refuses to maintain a normal weight level, typically because she or he has an irrational fear of being overweight. In such cases, a person can literally be starving to death and still see an overweight person in the mirror. The condition affects mainly young women between the ages of 12 and 18 (perhaps as many as 1% of adolescent women) and it's been estimated that as many as 20% of those with the disorder will eventually die as a result, either from medical problems or from suicide (Ratnasuriya and others, 1991).

In the eating disorder known as **bulimia nervosa,** the principal symptom is *binge eating.* A binge is an episode in which a person consumes large quantities of food, often junk food, in a limited period of time. You might find a person suffering from bulimia locked in a room, surrounded by his or her favorite snacks, eating literally thousands of calories in a single sitting. The condition is marked by a lack of control—the person feels unable to stop the eating or to control the content of the food being consumed. A bingeing episode is often followed by *purging,* in which the person voluntarily vomits or uses laxatives in an effort to stop potential weight gain. Like anorexia, bulimia affects primarily women and is characterized by an obsessive desire to be thin. It, too, often has serious medical consequences.

Meeting Biological Needs: Sexual Behavior

It's difficult to think of a topic more ingrained in the history and practice of human culture, and psychology for that matter, than sex. Whereas your particular world may not revolve around sex, there's no denying that sex is a powerful motivator of people around the world. Every significant culture, regardless of where you look, has well-established rules and guidelines for the teaching and practice of behavior related to courtship, mating, and the sexual act. Just think for a moment about advertising, television, movies. Enough said.

But where exactly is the need? What problem is solved by the pursuit and completion of the sexual act? Is there some kind of internal sex "gauge" that monitors sexual deprivation and adjusts behavior accordingly? Are people compelled by bio-

For centuries, cultures around the world have maintained rules and guidelines for the teaching and practice of courtship, mating, and the sexual act. This Japanese woodblock print from 1821 was designed to stimulate and enhance the sexual experience.

logical forces to restore an internal erotic balance? People certainly won't die if their goal-directed sexual pursuits fail, as they would from an unsuccessful search for nutrients. At the same time, sexual motivation clearly has great value at the level of the species. Through reproduction, people pass on their genetic material to offspring and thereby help ensure continuation of the species. Think about it: If everyone suddenly lost his or her interest in sex, the human race would be doomed to elimination in a single generational cycle.

But sexual motivation has its advantages within a single lifetime, too. Besides the pleasurable and reinforcing aspects of sex, sexual desire drives people to pursue a mate, thereby opening the door for companionship, protection, and love. The search for an ideal mate is itself a problem to be solved by the adaptive mind. As we'll see, how that particular problem is handled is determined in part by people's conceptions of attractiveness. We'll first consider the human sexual response cycle; then we'll look at the internal and external factors that motivate sexual behavior; we'll conclude with a look at issues involved in mate selection.

The Sexual Response Cycle

Humans are capable of wide and imaginative varieties of lovemaking, but biologically the sexual response follows a standard four-component sequence (see Figure 11.4). According to researchers William Masters and Virginia Johnson (1966), who spent years studying the human sexual response in the laboratory, the response cycle begins with an **excitement phase.** Sexual excitement is characterized by changes in muscle tension, increased heart rate and blood pressure, and a rushing of blood into the genital organs. In men, the increased blood supply causes an erection in the penis; in women, the clitoris swells and the lining of the vaginal walls becomes lubricated.

The excitement phase then shifts into a **plateau phase,** during which sexual arousal continues to increase, at a slower rate, toward a "maximum" point. The penis becomes fully erect, and vaginal lubrication increases. Other changes begin that are appropriate to the reproductive process—the internal shape of the vagina changes in preparation for the receipt of the sperm-laden semen; the testes of men rise up in preparation for ejaculation. Sexual release is next, in the **orgasmic phase,**

Given the importance of the sexual act to the continued survival of the species, can you see why some theorists—including Sigmund Freud—placed such a special emphasis on sexual desire in their theories of behavior and mind?

FIGURE 11.4
The Sexual Response Cycle.
Biologically, the human sexual response is believed to follow a four-component sequence: (1) an initial *excitement phase,* during which arousal increases rapidly; (2) a *plateau phase,* in which arousal increases steadily but more slowly; (3) the *orgasmic phase,* during which sexual release occurs; and (4) a *resolution phase,* in which arousal falls back toward normal levels. For men, the resolution phase is characterized by a refractory period during which further stimulation fails to produce visible signs of arousal or orgasm. (Based on Masters & Johnson, 1966)

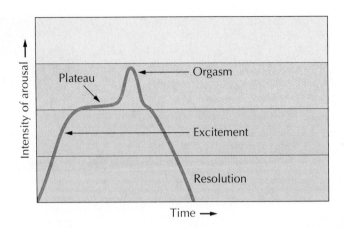

and occurs in the form of rhythmic contractions in the sex organs; in men, these rhythmic contractions are accompanied by ejaculation. The subjective experience of the orgasm is apparently quite similar for males and females, despite the obvious physiological differences. When asked to review written descriptions of the orgasmic experience, outside readers usually cannot tell whether a description was written by a man or a woman (Proctor, Wagner, & Butler, 1974).

The sexual response cycle is completed with a **resolution phase,** during which arousal returns to normal levels and, at least for men, there is a *refractory period* in which further stimulation fails to produce visible signs of arousal or orgasm. The length of the resolution phase is highly variable—it can last anywhere from a few minutes to several days—and no one is quite sure exactly what determines when it will end. Age and prior frequency of sexual release seem to be important factors, as well as the degree of emotional closeness with one's partner (Crooks & Baur, 1993).

Internal Factors

For most of the animal kingdom, including primates like orangutans and gorillas, sexual behavior is strongly under the control of chemical messengers (sex hormones) that regularly rise and fall in cycles. A female rat will assume a character-

Great Frigatebirds engaged in a stereotypic mating ritual.

istic posture—signaling receptivity to mounting and copulation by the male—but only during the time in her hormonal cycle when she is most likely to become impregnated. She'll adjust her posture to prepare for the weight of the male, she'll move her tail aside, and she'll even approach and nuzzle the male to assure his amorous attention (Carlson, 1991). But these behaviors are tightly locked to the presence of the appropriate hormones—estradiol and progesterone in the case of the female rat. If these hormones are absent, the female will show no interest in sex at all, choosing instead to display indifference or hostility toward the sexually active male. If these hormones are injected artificially, sexual receptivity can be promoted under conditions in which it would not normally occur (Lisk, 1978). In the case of the male rat as well, sexual behavior depends on the presence of the appropriate hormone—testosterone. If testosterone is absent, so, too, is the desire to procreate.

Humans also show regular cyclic variations in the hormones relevant to sex and reproduction. These sets of hormones—*estrogens* in women and *androgens* in men—play a critical role in physical development, affecting everything from the development of the sex organs to the wiring structure of the brain (see Chapter 3). But the initiation and control of adult sexual behavior does not appear to be simply a matter of mixing and matching the right internal chemicals. Human sexual behavior remains actively under an individual's control, although learned social and cultural factors exert an important influence. Instead of instinctive posturing and fixed courtship rituals, people in most human cultures largely choose when and where they engage in sex and the particular manner in which the sexual act is consummated.

This does not mean that hormones play no role in human sexual behavior. There is some evidence to suggest that a woman's peak of sexual desire occurs in the middle of her menstrual cycle, near the time of ovulation (Adams, Gold, & Burt, 1978; Harvey, 1987). There is also evidence that testosterone affects both male and female sexual desire. For example, when testosterone levels are reduced sharply—as occurs, for instance, following removal of the testes (medical castration) in men—there is often a loss of interest in sex. In fact, sex offenders are sometimes treated by administering drugs that block the action of testosterone. But neither males nor females are rigidly controlled by these hormones. Some castrated men continue to enjoy and seek out sexual encounters, even without hormone replacement therapy. Similarly, women continue to seek out and enjoy sexual relations after menopause, when the levels of female sex hormones decline.

External Factors

Rather than appealing to the flow of hormones, an alternative way to explain sexual desire is to appeal to the value, or incentive, of the sexual act. Clearly, there's something about the internal wiring of the brain that makes the sexual act itself immensely rewarding for most people. When someone attractive wanders by and acts as a signal for something pleasurable, we are "pulled," or motivated, as a consequence toward the object that may potentially lead to reinforcing sexual release.

Perhaps you won't resonate much to this kind of description of sexual desire. But there's no question that humans are regular recipients of a vast array of sexual signals in their environment, and these signals often successfully stimulate sexual desire. Both men and women are sexually aroused by explicit visual stimuli, although women, if questioned, are less likely to report the arousal (Kelley, 1985). If excitement is measured through physiological recording devices attached to sensitive genital regions, men and women tend to show comparable arousal responses to erotic pictures and movies (Rubinsky and others, 1987). The way people dress and wear their hair, the shapes of their bodies—all, of course, contribute to popular conceptions of attractiveness and desirability.

What people consider to be "attractive" is very much in the eye of the beholder; different societies often have unique cultural definitions of what constitutes attractiveness.

Touch is a particularly important external source of sexual arousal. Careful stimulation of certain regions of the body (known commonly as erogenous zones) is highly arousing for most people and may be one of the few completely natural, or unlearned, arousal sources (although other "erotic zones" may develop or be influenced by experience). In contrast, in many animals it is odor or smell that initiates sexual interest. In Chapter 5, we discussed chemicals called *pheromones* that are released by the females of many species during periods of receptivity. Although these odor-producing chemicals drive dogs, pigs, and other creatures into a sexual frenzy, there's little solid evidence that pheromones affect human sexual desire (Quadagno, 1987). Smells, and tastes as well, are sometimes reported as an important pleasurable part of the sexual experience, but learned associations rather than biological wiring probably underlie for these reports.

Mate Selection

The initiation of the sexual act is guided by one very important external source: a person's selection of and acceptance by an appropriate mate. Not surprisingly, what people consider to be "attractive" is strongly influenced by sociocultural factors. Societies have unique cultural definitions of attractiveness, their own rules for attracting a mate, and idiosyncratic views on what kinds of sexual behavior are considered appropriate. In some societies, for example, sexual activity is encouraged at very young ages—even 5- and 6-year-olds are allowed to engage in casual fondling of a willing partner's genitals. In other societies, sexual expression in childhood is strictly prohibited.

Sexual Scripts. According to researchers John Gagnon and William Simon, as people grow they acquire **sexual scripts**—learned programs that instruct them on how, why, and what to do in their interactions with sexual partners (Gagnon & Simon, 1973). These scripts may differ from one culture to the next, and they contribute to many of the idiosyncrasies seen in male and female sexual behavior. Among other things, sexual scripts affect the attitudes individuals hold toward the sexual act. Boys typically learn, for example, to associate sexual intimacy with genital fondling; girls are more likely to identify sexuality with romantic love. These scripts affect expectations and sometimes are responsible for miscommunication between the sexes. For instance, over half of teenage girls who engage in premarital sex expect to marry their partners, but this expectation is true for only 18% of the male partners (Coles & Stokes, 1985).

Despite the many differences that exist in the formation of sexual scripts, there are still fundamental similarities among peoples that may be rooted in the evolutionary history of the species. For example, in nearly every culture men are more likely than women to pursue what David Buss and David Schmitt call *short-term* sexual strategies—brief affairs or one-night stands. In interviews with college students, Buss and Schmitt (1993) found that most men had few qualms about the idea of having sexual intercourse with a woman they'd met only an hour before; for most women, the idea of such casual sex was a "virtual impossibility." Across all parts of the world, men seem to value attractiveness in a long-term mating partner and universally tend to prefer to mate with women who are on the average younger than themselves (Buss, 1989). Women, on the other hand, tend to place much greater value on a mating partner's financial prospects than men do— a pattern that again holds across the world (see Figure 11.5).

The fact that these differences are present in virtually every society strongly suggests that there may be ingrained adaptive reasons for these gender-based behaviors. Men might pursue multiple sexual partners in an effort to increase the likelihood of successful reproduction (Dawkins, 1986). Women might prefer to consider a man's economic means because the responsibility of rearing and nur-

In what ways do you think a person's physical "attractiveness" affects the way others think and act—that is, other than stimulating sexual desire? (We'll discuss this issue in some depth in Chapter 13, which deals with social psychology.)

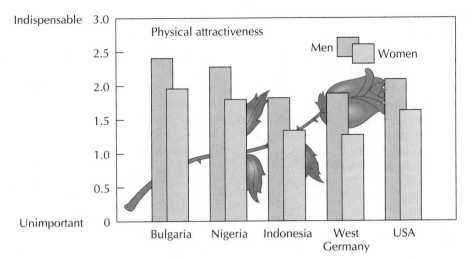

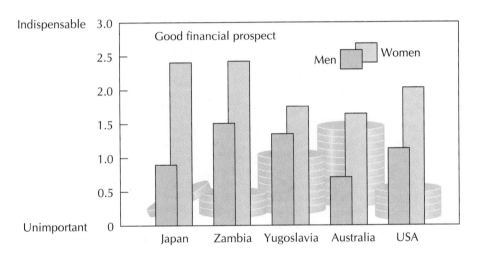

FIGURE 11.5
Cross-Cultural Mating Strategies. Men and women in different parts of the world were asked to rate how important physical attractiveness and financial prospects would be in a long-term marriage partner. On average, men rated physical attractiveness as a more important quality than women did, whereas women were more likely than men to consider a partner's financial prospects as important. (Data from Buss & Schmitt, 1993)

turing a child often falls on the woman's shoulders. According to Buss and Schmitt (1993), as well as a movement that grew out of the study of animal behavior called **sociobiology,** the sexual strategies of men and women are best understood from an evolutionary perspective. Men and women, thoughout evolutionary history, have faced unique and gender-specific reproductive problems; their attitudes and mating rituals undoubtedly have developed, in part, to help resolve these problems.

But remember, the patterns of behavior that we've been discussing are not "fixed" at birth for all women and men. As noted before, human sexual behavior shows considerable flexibility—the biological forces of nature influence but need not determine people's final behavior. Moreover, it's worth noting that some human sexual strategies could have developed early in the species' evolutionary history but may no longer be needed or even particularly effective. We'll return to the debate about the roles of biology versus the environment, specifically with respect to conceptions of attractiveness, later in Chapter 13.

Expressing and Experiencing Emotion

Let's return for a moment to the vignette that opened the chapter. The nightmare is replayed—control of your freedom and your life has been transferred to a malicious criminal seeking money and the thrill of violence. Your mind and body react

INSIDE THE PROBLEM: *Sexual Orientation*

When psychologists use the term **sexual orientation,** they are referring to whether a person is sexually and emotionally attracted to members of the same sex or the other sex. The term *homosexual* is applied when the attraction is predominantly to members of the same sex; *heterosexual* refers to the more typical other-sex attraction. Estimates of the number of people in the United States who fit the description of "homosexual" vary, ranging from 1–2% to perhaps as high as 10% (Rogers & Turner, 1991). Exact numbers are difficult to determine, partly because people are often reluctant to disclose intimate information about sexual preference. Moreover, in some respects sexual orientation is best seen as a continuum rather than as a category with fixed boundaries. People who are predominantly homosexual sometimes seek out heterosexual relationships, while many heterosexuals have had sexual experiences with members of the same sex.

But what accounts for a sexual and emotional preference for members of the same sex? If the "purpose" of sexual desire is to procreate—to assure continuation of the species—in what way can homosexuality be considered adaptive? There is no simple answer to

this question, although certainly same-sex relationships have many nurturing qualities that go well beyond sexual encounters. For many years psychologists were convinced that a homosexual orientation developed as the result of experience, particularly the experiences children have with their parents. Homosexuality was considered to be an abnormal condition that arose from dysfunctional home environments, usually as a consequence of having a domineering mother and a passive father. But this view is no longer widely accepted, primarily because a close examination of family histories revealed that the home environments of heterosexuals and homosexuals are actually quite similar (Bell, Weinberg, & Hammersmith, 1981).

Recent research suggests that sexual orientation may be at least partly determined by biological factors (Gladue, 1994). When researcher Simon LeVay (1991) compared the autopsied brains of homosexual and heterosexual men, he discovered that a cluster of neurons associated with the hypothalamus was consistently larger in heterosexual men. Exactly how or why this portion of the brain influences sexual orientation is unknown. There have also been reports

over the past several years pointing to a genetic locus for sexual orientation. For example, twin studies have revealed that if one identical twin is homosexual, there is an approximately 50% chance that the other twin will share the same sexual orientation; for fraternal twins or nontwin bothers and sisters, the likelihood that both will be homosexual is considerably lower (Bailey & Pillard, 1991; Bailey and others, 1993). In another recent study, a systematic analysis of the chromosomes of homosexual brothers suggested evidence for what the researchers believe might be a "gay gene" (Hamer and others, 1993).

It's simply too early to tell what all these data truly mean. The biological findings remain correlational—that is, we simply know that sexual orientation may be *associated* with certain brain structures or genetic markers—but correlational data do not allow us to determine the *cause* of sexual orientation. Moreover, it seems very unlikely that appeals to biological factors alone will solve the mysteries of sexual orientation (after all, 50% of identical twins of homosexuals do *not* share this orientation). The environment is certain to play an important role, but the nature of that role has yet to be determined.

---

rapidly: heart rate, blood pressure, and respiration rate all shoot upward. Your facial expression adopts a characteristic grimace, one that would reliably be recognized as fear in all of the known cultures of the world. Inside, your thought patterns are altered—you become immersed in the subjective experience of confusion, pain, and fear. Behaviorally, your body slumps downward, as you contemplate the possibility of struggle. You are in the midst of experiencing and expressing the most powerful of human capacities—*emotion.*

As we discussed at the beginning of this chapter, an emotion is a complex psychological event that involves a mixture of reactions: (1) a *physiological response* (usually arousal), (2) an *expressive reaction* (distinctive facial expression, body posture, or vocalization), and (3) some kind of *subjective experience* (internal thoughts and feelings). Each of these components, which are shown in Figure 11.6, can be measured or evaluated externally, although some, especially the subjective-cognitive reaction, are difficult to monitor reliably. Emotions are multidimensional entities—they're not just feelings inside people's heads. Emotions are biological, psychological, and even social reactions to significant events that arise in our environment.

But why experience emotions in the first place? The general belief among psychologists is that emotional reactions facilitate one's ability to adapt to rapidly changing environmental conditions. Emotions are powerful motivators of behavior—they help people prioritize their thoughts and orient themselves toward a particular problem solution. Physiological arousal, for instance, prepares the body for "fight or flight" and helps people to direct and sustain their reactions in the face of danger. Through expressive behaviors, such as the characteristic facial grimace of anger, people can instantly communicate their mental state to others and affect behavior accordingly. Emotions can even stimulate social behaviors. Individuals perform better and are more likely to help others when they feel happiness (Hoffman, 1986); people are also more likely to volunteer aid after doing something for which they feel "guilt" (Carlsmith & Gross, 1969).

Are There Basic Emotions?

The English language is full of words, literally hundreds in fact, that relate in one way or another to the expression and experience of emotion. But are there hundreds of emotions, or just a basic few? This is an important question, but one that is difficult to answer. To get a sense of the difficulty, try compiling your own list of emotional states. While you're at it, ask your friends and see how much you agree. Let's see: anger, fear, joy . . . how about interest, loathing, jealousy, or distraction? Psychologists have been compiling their own lists for decades, but no general consensus has been reached.

If forced to choose, most people (including emotion researchers) agree on about a half-dozen basic emotional states. Most lists include anger, fear, happiness, and sadness, for example (Ortony & Turner, 1990). Researchers who argue that such emotions are basic, or universal, believe that certain emotional displays, such as anger, increase the likelihood of survival. They also point to data showing that emotional experiences are highly similar across the world's cultures. All humans recognize expressions of anger, fear, sadness, and happiness, in part because these emotional states produce characteristic facial expressions. In classic research, Paul Ekman and his colleagues asked people to match photographs of grimacing, smiling, or otherwise provocative facial displays to a number of basic emotion labels. There was wide agreement on six fundamental emotions: happiness, surprise, fear, sadness, anger, and disgust combined with contempt (Ekman, 1992; Ekman & Friesen, 1986).

More important, it doesn't matter where you look in the world, everyone seems to agree. Regardless of the culture, people recognize that there are certain facial expressions that signal and reliably identify emotional states. For example, a furrowed brow and a square mouth with pursed lips signify a prototypical expression of anger worldwide (Boucher & Carlson, 1980; Ekman & Friesen, 1975). In one case, Ekman and Friesen (1975) even tested members of a rural, isolated culture in New Guinea. These people had no experience with Western culture, yet they correctly identified the emotions expressed on photographed Caucasian faces. Similarly, when U.S. college students were later shown photos of the New Guinea people acting out various emotions, they, too, were able to identify the emotions with a high degree of accuracy. Although there may be methodological problems with some of these cross-cultural studies—for example, it's not clear that the emotion labels mean the same thing across cultures (Russell, 1994)—most researchers are convinced that there is universal recognition of emotion from facial expressions (Ekman, 1994; Izard, 1994).

EMOTION
Body response (arousal)   Increased blood pressure, heart rate, muscle tension, respiration
Expressive reaction   Facial expression, acting out
Subjective experience   Feeling of happiness, anger, fear, etc.

FIGURE 11.6
The Components of Emotion.
Emotions are complex experiences involving (1) a *physiological response;* (2) an *expressive reaction;* and (3) some kind of *subjective experience.*

The facial expressions that signify emotion carry important signaling properties. Would you want to interact with this woman right now?

Different emotions are often associated with particular facial expressions. Can you identify the emotion expressed in each of these photos?

Have you ever heard actors talk about how, when playing emotional parts, they "become the role" and have trouble leaving the part at work? What might a psychologist tell the actor to help him or her understand why this happens?

The cross-cultural results suggest that the expression of emotion may have a biological or genetic origin. Babies show a wide range of emotional expressions at a very young age (Izard, 1994), and even babies who are born blind, or hearing-impaired and blind, show virtually the same facial expressions as sighted babies (Eibl-Eibesfeldt, 1973). It appears then that people may purse their lips and furrow their brow when they're mad because these tendencies are built directly into the genetic code, rather than having been learned. Some psychologists even believe that it is the muscular feedback from these innate facial expressions that underlies the emotional experience itself. According to the **facial-feedback hypothesis,** muscles in the face deliver signals to the brain that are then interpreted, depending on the pattern, as subjective emotional states (Tomkins, 1962). This hypothesis makes the unique prediction that if subjects are asked to mimic a particular facial posture, they should experience a corresponding change in emotionality. Indeed, forced smiling, frowning, or grimacing does appear to modulate emotional reports, although the effects may be small (Matsumoto, 1987). Some therapists even recommend that clients who are depressed literally force themselves to smile for a while when they are feeling depressed.

Babies show a wide range of emotional expressions at very young ages.

The Components of Emotion. Is the reliable recognition of facial expressions for fear, anger, or happiness sufficient evidence to allow us to conclude that these emotions are somehow more primary or basic than others? Some psychologists think not. Remember, many psychologists disagree about which emotions belong on the "basic" list. Does interest, wonder, or guilt belong? How about shame, contempt, or elation? Each of these terms has been identified as "basic" by at least one prominent emotion researcher. The problem is that humans are capable of an enormous variety of emotional experiences. Consider the differences between fear, terror, panic, distress, rage, and even anxiety. It is clearly appropriate to use these terms in some circumstances and not in others. How can we explain a complex emotion such as terror? If it's not a basic emotion, is it somehow manufactured in the brain by combining or blending more fundamental emotions like fear, surprise, and possibly anger?

Psychologists Andrew Ortony and Terence Turner (1990; Turner & Ortony, 1992) believe that it's simply not possible to explain the diversity and complexity of human emotional experiences by manipulating and combining a set of basic emotions. Rather than basic emotions, they argue, it's better to think of basic response "components" that are *shared* by a wide variety of emotional experiences. For example, the furrowed brow commonly seen in anger is not exclusive to anger but occurs as well when people are frustrated, puzzled, or even just working hard on a task. The furrowed brow may occur in any situation in which a person is somehow blocked from reaching a goal; its appearance, by itself, is not sufficient to infer that the person is angry.

It may help to think about the analogy of human language. There are hundreds of different languages across the world, and each follows certain universal rules (relating to sound and word combinations). But it doesn't make any sense to argue that some of these languages are more basic than others. Human languages are built up from basic components and share many features in common. But the components—the rules of sound and meaning—are not themselves languages (Ortony & Turner, 1990). Similarly, when people are in the grip of an emotion, they may experience many basic and universal things (such as a tendency to smile or frown, approach or avoid), but these are merely the components of emotion, not emotions themselves.

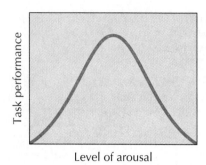

FIGURE 11.7
Arousal and Task Performance.
For a given task, performance tends
to be best at intermediate levels of
arousal. Too little or too much
arousal often leads to a decrease in
performance.

Earlier, we discussed the fact
that facial expressions are
extremely important parts of
the experience of emotions.
Do you think people make distinctive
and identifiable facial expressions
when they lie?

The Emotional Experience: Arousal

Psychologists may disagree about whether there are basic emotions, but everyone agrees that certain aspects of the emotional *experience* are basic and reliable. Virtually all emotions, for instance, lead to *physiological arousal.* Muscles tense, heart rate speeds up, and blood pressure and respiration rates skyrocket. These emotional "symptoms" arise from activity of the autonomic nervous system as it prepares the muscles and organs of the body for a "fight or flight" response. People usually experience emotions in situations that are significant for one reason or another—for instance, the headlights of the drunken driver swerve sharply into their path, or the sound of breaking glass from the basement window startles them awake. It's adaptive for the body to react quickly in such cases, and the rapid onset of physiological arousal serves that function well.

Arousal and Performance. The relationship between arousal and performance is not simple and direct—emotional arousal can have a negative side as well. Too much arousal can lead to a breakdown in behavioral, biological, or psychological functioning. Figure 11.7 depicts the general relationship that exists between level of arousal and task performance. Notice that the pattern looks like an arch or an inverted U. For a given task, as arousal levels increase from low to moderate levels, performance generally rises. Some people perform better under pressure—the track star runs a little faster or jumps a little higher. You may well perform better on a test if the test is particularly important. But too much pressure, which leads to too much arousal, leads to a sharp drop-off or breakdown in task functioning. Did you have trouble thinking when you took the SAT? Too much emotional pressure can create a level of arousal that hurts rather than helps normal mental functioning.

Understanding the relationship between arousal and performance has helped psychologists interpret behavior in a variety of situations. For example, you may remember from Chapter 8 that people who witness crimes are sometimes inaccurate in their later recollections. One factor that contributes to these inaccuracies is the high level of arousal generated when someone witnesses a crime. If someone is holding a gun to your head, your arousal levels are so high that you are incapable of normal cognitive processing. You are simply too aroused to process the details of the crime scene in a manner that will lead to effective remembering. Moreover, as we'll see in Chapter 13, the relationship between arousal and performance also helps us to understand how our behavior changes in the presence of other people—our performance is either facilitated or impaired when other people are around, perhaps because the presence of others changes our overall level of arousal.

The Polygraph Test. The link between emotions and arousal naturally led researchers to assume that arousal could be used as a reliable index of emotional experience. If you're experiencing an emotion, your body ought to show the characteristic patterns of physiological arousal. The lie detector, or **polygraph test,** is a good example of this kind of logic in action. The polygraph is not a mysterious and magical device that measures "truth"—there's no secret location in the brain, chest, or fingertips that sends up a red flag when a person is lying. The polygraph test simply measures mundane things like heart rate, blood pressure, breathing rate, and whether or not you're sweating. The assumption behind the test is that lying leads to greater emotionality, which can then be picked up through measurements of general physiological arousal.

In a polygraph test the critical comparisons are made between the arousal levels induced by what are called *relevant* and *control* questions. Testers understand that people might become aroused just from taking the test, whether they're lying or not, so testers are mainly interested in comparing how arousal levels change across different question types. During the test, you're typically asked a series of neutral questions to establish a kind of baseline arousal level ("What's your name?" and so on). In some cases, the tester may even ask you to lie on purpose—to answer with the wrong day of the week or with someone else's name—to get a record of how your body responds when you do, in fact, lie. Relevant questions are then asked about a specific event ("Did you change the bank records?"), and the examiner compares the amount of recorded arousal with the various baseline controls.

This woman is undergoing a polygraph test, which is based on the idea that lying leads to greater emotionality that can then be picked up through measurements of general physiological arousal.

But remember, "polygraph pens do no special dance when we are lying" (Lykken, 1981), so conclusions about truthfulness need to be interpreted with caution. There are two main problems. First, these tests are relatively easy to beat. If you can control your arousal responses—and many hardened criminals feel little, if any, guilt about their crimes—it's possible to pass the test even if you're lying. Clever criminals can also mask lying by increasing their level of arousal on control questions—perhaps by pinching themselves or biting their lip; if arousal levels on the control questions are high, the critical difference between the readings on relevant and control questions will be reduced. If arousal levels are similar across the different question types, the criminal is likely to pass the test.

The second problem with the polygraph test is that it can lead to a lot of "false positives." Innocent people are judged to be lying when, in fact, they are telling the truth. Estimates of the frequency of false positives vary from study to study, but they may go as high as 75% (Saxe, 1994). This is a significant problem. Consider that even if testers arrived at incorrect lying judgments only 5% of the time, that would still mean 50 out of 1000 people might be falsely accused of a crime. If the error rate were higher, say 50%, then perhaps 500 of those 1000 people would be falsely accused of a crime. For these reasons, the U.S. Congress passed the Employee Polygraph Protection Act of 1988, which bans the use of polygraph tests as a screening criterion for employment (although certain drug and security companies, and government agencies, are not covered by the ban). In addition, most courtrooms do not currently allow the results of polygraph tests to be used as evidence for guilt or innocence.

The Emotional Experience: Subjective Reactions

Experiencing an emotion involves much more than just a facial expression or a flood of physiological arousal. People's thoughts, their perceptions, the things they notice in the environment, even their motivation to perform certain tasks and not others—all change coincident with the onset of the emotional experience. But as we discussed before, it's difficult to gauge the internal experience accurately and reliably. After all, the emotional experience is, by definition, personal and subjective. We can ask someone to report what it feels like to be happy, sad, or scared, but the natural constraints of language restrict the answers we will receive. Some cultures don't even have a word in their language to describe the concept of an emotion. The Ifaluks of Micronesia, for example, have only the word *niferash*, which roughly translates as "our insides" (Lutz, 1982; Matsumoto, 1994).

It is possible to study the conditions that lead to the experiencing of emotions. For example, we can document situations that promote sadness, euphoria, or anger. In the case of anger, people have been asked to keep daily and weekly records and to note when everyday occurrences lead to mild or intense feelings of anger. Most people get angry at least several times a week (but to different degrees); some experience the emotion several times a day (Averill, 1983). These studies have documented a number of reasons for the anger reaction. If people are restrained in some way, physically or psychologically, they're likely to get mad (Reeve, 1992). Individuals also get angry when their expectations are violated. If

Despite what you might think, winning 6 million dollars in the lottery does not necessarily guarantee future happiness.

a person is counting on someone to act a certain way, or on a place or thing to deliver certain rewards, and these expectations are violated, that person will probably get mad. This is one of the reasons why people often get irritated at the ones they love. They tend to expect more from someone close; the consequences of these expectations, however, are that loved ones set themselves up for an angry encounter.

What Makes People Happy? The idea that emotional experiences arise from violations of expectations or beliefs also helps account, in part, for the experience of *happiness*. Despite what you might think, there is little, if any, relationship between observable characteristics such as age, sex, race, or income and the experience of happiness (Myers & Diener, 1995). Instead, people seem to gain or lose happiness as a result of the comparisons that they make—either with others (a well-known tendency called *social comparison*) or with things or experiences from their past. People set standards or baselines for satisfaction, and they're happy to the extent that these standards are maintained or surpassed. The trouble is that people's standards are constantly in flux—Eddie and Lucinda may be able to keep up with the Joneses next door, but there's always the Smiths down the street who just bought that new boat. Once people obtain one level of satisfaction, they form a new one and thereby immerse themselves in a spiral that never quite leads to utopian bliss.

Actually, many psychological judgments, not just emotions, arise from comparisons with some standard, or *adaptation level*. You may recall from Chapter 5 that whether people will hear one tone as louder than another depends on how loud the standard tone is to begin with. Human judgments are relative—there is no sense in which a tone is "loud," a light is "bright," or a person is "happy" or "sad" without answering the question "Relative to what?" The fact that the subjective experience of happiness is relative helps explain some seemingly inexplicable phenomena. Why is that couple who just won the multimillion-dollar lottery still bickering? Why is Ed, who recently succeeded in getting the most popular girl in class out on a date, now anxiously seeking the amorous attentions of someone else? How can that homeless man, with only scraps to eat and tattered clothes, wake up every morning with a smile on his face? Happiness is not an absolute Holy Grail that people can seek and sometimes find—it's an elusive and fickle condition that can disappear as soon as it appears.

Theories of Emotion: Body to Mind

We've seen that emotions are complex, multidimensional phenomena. People subjectively experience happiness or sadness, but they also experience important changes in their body and on their face. Questions about how these various components interact have perplexed emotion researchers for decades. For example, what exactly causes the bodily reaction? Is physiological arousal a by-product of the internal subjective experience, or is someone happy or sad because his or her body has been induced to react in a particular way?

There are a number of possible explanations (for an overview, see Figure 11.8). The most natural argument is that the subjective experience drives the physiological reaction. People tremble, gasp, and increase their heart rate because some event has caused them to become afraid. They detect the grasp of an arm around their neck, they feel fear, and their body reacts with physiological arousal. Surprisingly, this straightforward "theory" of emotion has been essentially rejected by emotion

FIGURE 11.8
Four Views of Emotion. The *commonsense* view, largely rejected by psychologists, assumes that an environmental stimulus creates a subjective experience (fear), which in turn leads to a physiological reaction (arousal). The *James-Lange theory* proposes instead that the body reaction drives the subjective experience. In the *Cannon-Bard theory,* the body reaction and the subjective experience are assumed to be largely independent processes. In *two-factor theory,* it is the cognitive interpretation and labeling of the body response that drives the subjective experience.

Theory	Stimulus	Response		Report
Common sense		Fear → Subjective experience → Body response (arousal)		"My heart is pounding because I feel afraid."
James-Lange		Body response (arousal) → Fear Subjective experience		"I feel afraid because my heart is pounding."
Cannon-Bard		Body response (arousal) / Fear Subjective experience		"The dog makes me feel afraid and my heart pound."
Two-factor		Body response (arousal) → Interpretation → Fear Subjective experience		"My pounding heart means I'm afraid because I interpret the situation as dangerous."

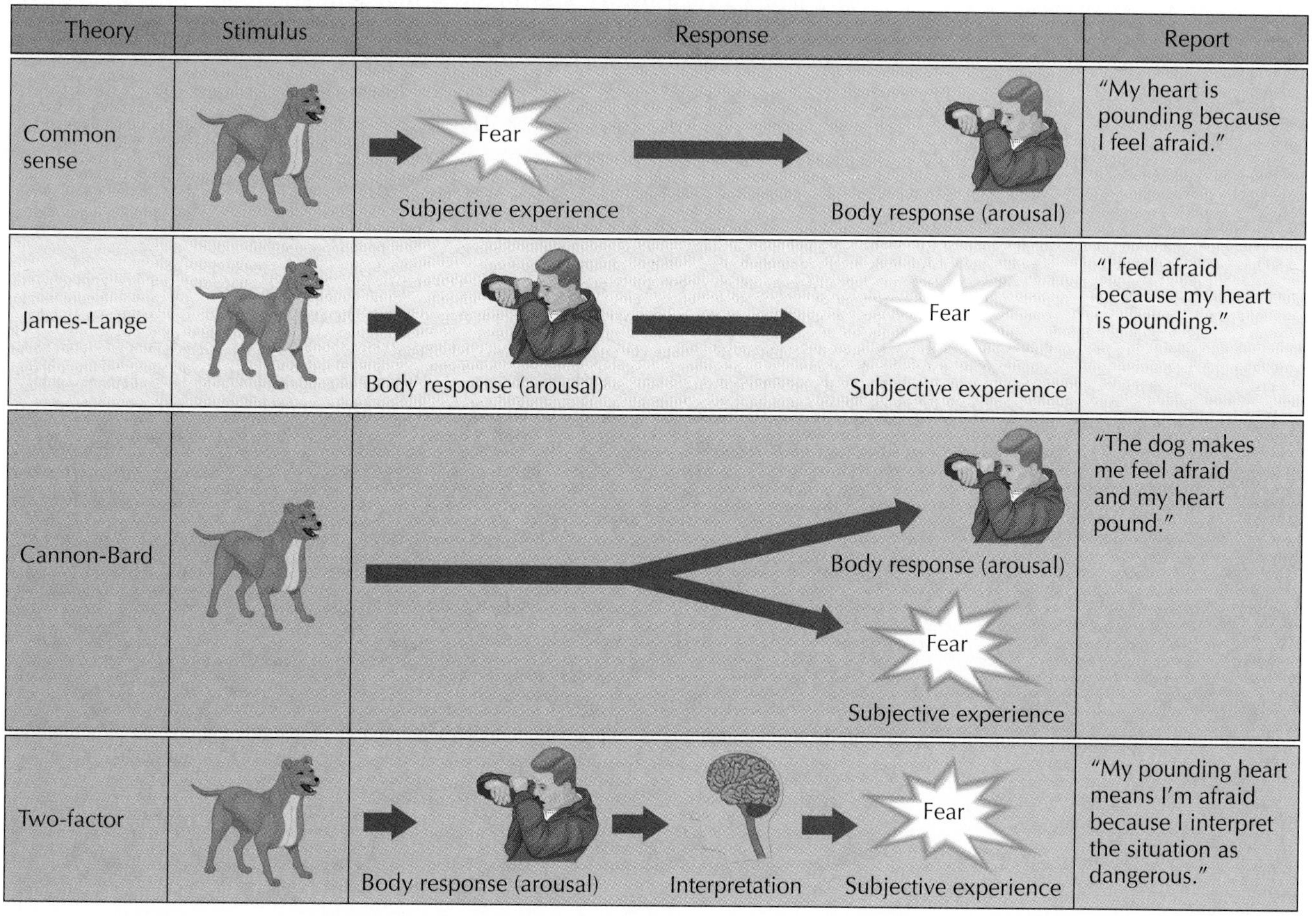

researchers for over a century. William James (1890) saw the commonsense view as backward. In his own words: "the more rationale statement is that we feel sorry because we cry, angry because we strike, afraid because we tremble, and not that we cry, strike, or tremble because we are sorry, angry, or fearful" (p. 1066). Although James did not deny that one's "interpretation" of the situation is also important (Ellsworth, 1994; James, 1894), he believed that the body reaction occurs before the subjective experience of emotion, rather than the other way around.

The James-Lange Theory. The idea that the body reaction drives the subjective experience of emotion became known as the **James-Lange theory** of emotion. Lange is coupled with James because Danish physiologist Carl Lange proposed a similar idea at roughly the same time as James. Why reject the commonsense approach in favor of such a counterintuitive view? Actually, neither James nor Lange presented much evidence in support of this account (other than personal impressions). But some significant predictions can be derived from the view. For instance, imagine that we could somehow reduce or eliminate significant body reactions. The James-Lange theory predicts that we should lose the corresponding experience of emotion. To test this idea, a number of interviews have been conducted with people suffering from spinal cord injuries. Because of nerve damage, these people have either lost feeling in major portions of their bodies or at least have reduced sensory feedback. In support of the James-Lange view, some paraplegics report a corresponding drop-off in the intensity of their emotional experience (for example, anger loses its "heat") (Hohmann, 1966). But the general finding is that strong emotional feelings remain intact despite the loss of body feedback (Lowe & Carroll, 1985).

The James-Lange theory also predicts that unique physical changes should accompany each of the different emotional experiences. That is, a particular body response must produce anger, happiness, fear, and so on. But as we noted before, the dominant physiological correlate of an emotion is *arousal.* And heart rate changes, sweaty palms, and increased breathing rate seem to be characteristic of virtually all emotions rather than just a select few. Think about how your body feels just before an important exam. Do you notice any similarities with the feelings that you get before an important and long-awaited date? Would you describe the emotions as similar?

Recently, however, sophisticated measuring devices are enabling researchers to record small, previously undetectable changes in body reactions. These new data may eventually help us to distinguish one emotional state from another by appealing only to physiological indices (Lang, 1994; Levenson, 1992). It turns out that anger, fear, and sadness, for example, may lead to greater heart rate acceleration than an emotion such as disgust; there is also apparently a greater increase in finger temperature during fear than during anger (Levenson, 1992). Establishing definitive links between emotional states and physiological responses would be an important step for emotion researchers, although perhaps not an unexpected one. After all, anger and happiness certainly are experienced differently and therefore must ultimately reflect some differences in brain activity.

The Cannon-Bard Theory. It didn't take too long before critics of the James-Lange theory of emotion began to emerge. Physiologist Walter Cannon mounted an influential attack in the 1920s (Cannon, 1927). Cannon recognized that the body reacts in essentially the same way across emotional experiences. He also argued that the conscious experience of emotion has a rapid onset—people feel fear immediately after seeing an attacking dog—but the physiological reactions that arise from activity of the autonomic nervous system have a relatively slow onset time (glands need to be activated, hormones need to be released into the bloodstream, and so on). Cannon felt that the subjective experience of emotion and the associated body reactions are independent processes. Emotions and arousal may occur together, but one doesn't cause the other. Cannon's view was later modified somewhat by Philip Bard, so this approach is now generally known as the **Cannon-Bard theory** of emotion.

Two-Factor Theory. You've now been exposed to three different accounts of the relationship between body and mind: (1) people experience emotions subjectively, which then leads to body reactions such as arousal (the commonsense view); (2) the body generates a characteristic internal reaction, which then produces the appropriate emotional experience (James-Lange); (3) body reactions and subjective experiences occur together, but independently (Cannon-Bard). None of these views remains popular among modern emotion researchers.

The major problem with this trio of emotion theories is that they fail to take into account the "cognitive" side of emotion. To understand exactly what this means, we need to consider a rather complex study that was conducted in the early 1960s by psychologists Stanley Schachter and Jerome Singer (see Figure 11.9). College students were recruited to participate in an experiment testing the effects of

FIGURE 11.9
The Schachter and Singer Experiment. Volunteer subjects were injected with a drug that produced physiological arousal symptoms. Half the subjects were informed about the drug's effects; the other half were not. When placed in a room with either a euphoric or an angry accomplice, only the uninformed subjects adopted the mood of the accomplice. Presumably, the informed subjects "interpreted" their arousal symptoms as due to the drug, whereas the uninformed subjects "interpreted" the arousal symptoms as an emotional experience.

vitamin injections on vision. Unknown to the subjects, the vitamin cover story was actually a ploy—rather than vitamins, participants were injected with either a dose of epinephrine (which produces physiological arousal symptoms) or a dose of saline (which produces no effects). A second manipulated variable was subject expectation: Half the subjects in each of the injection groups were told to expect arousal symptoms—it's a side effect of the vitamins, you see—and the other half were told to expect no reaction of any kind.

Now let's consider what effect these conditions might be expected to have on emotional reactions. Suppose you're sitting in a room, waiting for further instructions from the experimenter, when suddenly your heart begins to race and your palms begin to sweat. According to James-Lange, this arousal should translate into some kind of emotional experience; you might, for example, expect to become scared or irritated. But what Schachter and Singer (1962) found was that the experience of emotion was determined virtually entirely by expectation. Those subjects who were told to anticipate arousal from the injection showed little emotional reaction to the arousal when it occurred. Only when the arousal was unexpected did subjects begin to report robust experiences of emotion.

Even more interesting, Schachter and Singer were able partly to determine the qualitative aspects of the emotion when it occurred. Joining the subject in the waiting room was a "disguised" member of the experimental team, introduced as another participant in the experiment. Unknown to the real subject, the accomplice was instructed to act in a fashion that was either playful and euphoric or angry and disagreeable. In later assessments of mood, Schachter and Singer found that aroused but uninformed subjects tended to adopt the mood of the accomplice. If the accomplice was playful, the subjects reported feeling happy; if the accomplice was angry, the subjects reported feeling irritation.

These results led to the proposal of what is known as the **two-factor theory** of emotion. In two-factor theory, autonomic arousal is still a critical determinant of the emotional experience (factor 1). But equally important is the *cognitive appraisal* or *interpretation* of that arousal when it occurs (factor 2). An intense body reaction may be necessary for the full experience of an emotion, but it's not sufficient. It's how individuals *interpret* the arousal that dictates their subjective emotion. You're scared when faced with the out-of-control bakery truck because your body is aroused, but also because your mind understands that the source of the reaction is dangerous. You *label* the arousal and thereby determine the emotion that is experienced.

Like the other psychological theories of emotion, two-factor theory has generated its share of criticism. Some researchers have failed to replicate certain of the Schachter-Singer results (Reisenzein, 1983). Other researchers have pointed out that some of the original findings deemed important failed to reach acceptable levels of statistical significance (Marshall & Zimbardo, 1979). However, it is possible to draw several tentative conclusions. First, it's reasonably clear that bodily arousal contributes to the experience of emotion. Second, the situation in which the arousal occurs, and people's expectations about the source of the arousal, contribute to the emotional experience. Third, rather than saying that the body reaction creates the emotion, or vice versa, it's better to conclude that emotions arise from *interactions* among several sources: the stimulus event that precipitates the reaction, autonomic changes in arousal, and the expectation-based cognitive labels applied to everything involved.

 If expectations play an important role in determining whether an emotion will be experienced, do you think it's possible that some cultures will be more likely to show emotion than others?

► SOLVING THE PROBLEMS: A SUMMARY

It is the function of the adaptive mind to initiate, direct, and control behavior. Motivation, and its intimate companion, emotion, are vehicles that enable people to accomplish these things—to react to sudden changes in the environment, to maintain their internal energy needs, and even to prolong the species. There are certain things that human beings simply *must* do—consume food, drink liquids, maintain a constant internal temperature—and psychologists have struggled for decades to discover appropriate ways to describe the mechanisms that ensure that people accomplish these ends.

▸ **ACTIVATING BEHAVIOR** As we've seen, it's best to describe motivation as dependent on an interplay between internal and external factors. Much of the time behavior is controlled by internal factors that compel organisms in the direction of a goal. The body is constantly monitoring internal energy levels, and once a disruption in the "homeostatic balance" is detected, the organism feels hunger or thirst and seeks to restore the appropriate balance. In these cases, it's likely that motivated behavior arises directly as a consequence of the genetic code and requires no direct experiences with the environment.

But even something as biologically significant as eating or drinking cannot be explained by appealing just to innate internal factors. All forms of motivated behavior are influenced by external factors as well. External rewards, or incentives, exert powerful "pulling" and guiding effects on human actions. Understanding motivation then becomes a matter of specifying how these *external* factors interact with *internal* factors to activate and control behavior. One way in which internal and external factors interact is described by Maslow's notion of a need hierarchy. The essential component of Maslow's theory is the prioritizing of need: Some needs, especially those critical to survival, must be satisfied before others, such as the need for self-actualization, can be pursued.

▸ **MEETING BIOLOGICAL NEEDS: HUNGER AND EATING** What are the internal and external sources that initiate and control eating? Internally, the body monitors everything from the amount and content of food in the stomach to the level of glucose in the blood in order to determine its energy needs. If the level of glucose falls below a certain level, for example, one starts to feel hungry and seeks out food. Although researchers are uncertain about its precise role in controlling eating, the hypothalamus is currently thought to play an important role in initiating and controlling eating. But people also eat for reasons that appear unrelated to restoring homeostatic balance. Food, and particularly eating, is clearly reinforcing. As we've seen, people are much more likely to motivate themselves to eat if they like the food—the vigor or intensity with which they respond depends critically on the value, or incentive, of the food. A number of factors, both genetic (such as having a "set point") and environmental, play a role in regulating body weight. Eating disorders such as anorexia nervosa and bulimia nervosa tend to have psychological origins related to body image and to the need for (or lack of) control.

▸ **MEETING BIOLOGICAL NEEDS: SEXUAL BEHAVIOR** What underlies the strong motivation that all species have to pursue sexual activity? Sexual activity is adaptive for a species because it increases the likelihood that the species will continue. But on an individual level, sex is also reinforcing, and sexual desire compels individuals to pursue a mate, thereby opening the door for companionship, protection, and love. The sexual response itself consists of four main phases (excitement, plateau, orgasmic, and resolution). Hormones appear to play much less of a role in controlling sexual desire in humans when compared with other animals. Different cultures have different views of attractiveness and different codes of conduct for sex-

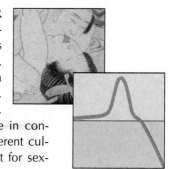

ual activity. Many psychologists believe that people acquire "sexual scripts" that instruct them on how, why, and what to do in their interactions with potential sexual partners.

▶ **EXPRESSING AND EXPERIENCING EMOTION** Emotions typically involve a mixture of reactions, including a physiological response (arousal), a characteristic expressive reaction (such as a distinctive facial expression), and some kind of subjective experience (such as the feeling of happiness or sadness). The physical expression of an emotion allows people to communicate their behavioral intent to others. The internal components—arousal, for example—prepare individuals for action. Thoughts become prioritized, and muscles are ready to respond. Emotions are therefore powerful adaptive tools: They not only increase the likelihood of survival, but also, for many, make life itself worth living. The internal subjective experience of emotion is often relative—whether people feel happy, for example, seems to depend on the comparisons they make with others and with their past experiences. Although a number of theories have tried to explain the relation between physiological arousal and the experience of emotion, most psychologists believe that the experience of emotion depends partly on the presence of a body response—general arousal—and partly on the cognitive appraisals one makes about the origin of arousal when it occurs.

Terms to Remember

motivation The set of factors that initiate and direct behavior, usually toward some goal.

emotions Psychological events involving (1) a physiological reaction, usually arousal; (2) some kind of expressive reaction, such as a distinctive facial expression; and (3) some kind of subjective experience, such as the conscious feeling of being happy or sad.

ACTIVATING BEHAVIOR

instincts Unlearned characteristic patterns of responding that are controlled by specific triggering stimuli in the world; they are not thought to be an important factor in explaining goal-directed behavior in humans.

drive A psychological state that arises in response to an internal physiological need, such as hunger or thirst.

homeostasis The process through which the body maintains a steady state, such as a constant internal temperature or an adequate amount of fluids.

incentive motivation External factors in the environment—such as money, an attractive person, or tasty food—that exert "pulling" effects on people's actions.

achievement motive An internal drive or need for achievement that is possessed by all individuals to varying degrees. Whether people will work for success on any given task depends on (1) their expectations about whether they will be successful, and (2) how much they value succeeding at the task.

intrinsic motivation Goal-directed behavior that seems to be entirely self-motivated.

need hierarchy The idea popularized by Maslow that human needs are prioritized in a hierarchy. Some needs, especially physiological ones, must be satisfied before others, such as the need for achievement or self-actualization, can be pursued.

MEETING BIOLOGICAL NEEDS: HUNGER AND EATING

glucose A kind of sugar that cells require for energy production.

insulin A hormone released by the pancreas that helps pump nutrients in the blood into the cells, where they can be stored as fat or metabolized into needed energy.

ventromedial hypothalamus A portion of the hypothalamus that, when lesioned, produces an animal that typically overeats and gains large amounts of weight. Once thought to be a kind of stop eating, or satiety, center in the brain; its role in eating behavior is currently unknown.

lateral hypothalamus A portion of the hypothalamus that, when lesioned, creates an animal that is reluctant to eat; like the ventromedial hypothalamus, it probably plays some role in eating behavior, but the precise role is unknown.

set point A natural body weight, perhaps produced by genetic factors, that the body seeks to maintain. When body weight falls below the set point, one is motivated to eat; when weight exceeds the set point, one feels less motivated to eat.

anorexia nervosa An eating disorder diagnosed when an otherwise healthy person refuses to maintain a normal weight level because of an intense fear of being overweight.

bulimia nervosa An eating disorder in which the principal symptom is binge eating (consuming large quantities of food) followed by purging, in which the person voluntarily vomits or uses laxatives to prevent weight gain.

MEETING BIOLOGICAL NEEDS: SEXUAL BEHAVIOR

excitement phase The first component of the human sexual response cycle, as described by Masters and Johnson. It's characterized by changes in muscle tension, increased heart rate and blood pressure, and a rushing of blood into the genital organs; in men, the penis becomes erect; in women, the vaginal walls become lubricated.

plateau phase The second stage in the human sexual response cycle. Arousal continues to increase, although at a slower rate, toward a preorgasm "maximum" point.

orgasmic phase The third stage in the human sexual response cycle. It's characterized by rhythmic contractions in the sex organs; in men, ejaculation occurs. There is also the subjective experience of pleasure that appears to be similar for men and women.

resolution phase The fourth and final stage in the human sexual response cycle. Arousal returns to normal levels. For men, there is a refractory period during which further stimulation fails to produce visible signs of arousal.

sexual scripts Learned cognitive programs that instruct individuals on how, why, and what to do in their interactions with sexual partners; the nature of sexual scripts may vary from one culture to the next.

sociobiology A theory proposing that social behavior should be understood from an evolutionary/genetic perspective.

sexual orientation A person's sexual and emotional attraction to members of the same sex or the other sex; homosexuality, heterosexuality, and bisexuality are all sexual orientations.

EXPRESSING AND EXPERIENCING EMOTION

facial-feedback hypothesis The proposal that muscles in the face deliver signals to the brain that are then interpreted, depending on the pattern, as a subjective emotional state.

polygraph test A device that measures various indices of physiological arousal in an effort to determine whether someone is telling a lie. The logic behind the test is that lying leads to greater emotionality, which can be picked up through such measures of arousal as heart rate, blood pressure, breathing rate, and sweating.

James-Lange theory A theory of emotion that argues that body reactions precede and drive the subjective experience of emotions.

Cannon-Bard theory A theory of emotion that argues that body reactions and subjective experiences occur together, but independently.

two-factor theory A theory of emotion that argues that the cognitive interpretation, or appraisal, of a body reaction drives the subjective experience of emotion.

You arrive home late, tired and slightly irritated after a hard day of work. You flip on the lights in your bathroom and glance downward at your red and gold toothbrush, still lying face up on the side of the tile sink. There, nestled in the slightly frayed bristles, lies a cockroach. Reluctant to move, the insect waves its feelers at you—a perverted sort of greeting. The mirror captures your reaction: You wrinkle your nose and your mouth drops open in a characteristic gape. Internally, arousal coupled with nausea rise up as your mind plots the exact form of its soon-to-be expressive behavior. What you are experiencing, of course, is a highly adaptive, often food-related emotion known as *disgust*.

If there is a core group of basic emotions, disgust, a marked aversion toward something distasteful (literally meaning "bad taste"), is a likely candidate for inclusion. It's easy to appreciate why this emotion is an important tool for the adaptive mind, especially as a mechanism to ensure that people select and reject the appropriate foods. The facial expression that typically accompanies disgust is itself an adaptive reaction to a potentially harmful substance: Wrinkling the nose

closes off the air passages, cutting off any offending odor; the gaping expression "causes the contents of the mouth to dribble out" (Rozin & Fallon, 1987).

But in recent years, researchers have come to recognize that there is a psychology to the emotion of disgust that extends beyond its role in food rejection. The study of disgust is revealing important things about how humans perceive objects in their world, as well as insights into people's ingrained beliefs about how objects and humans are destined to interact. The study of disgust may even provide a kind of model for the acquisition of values and culture (Rozin & Fallon, 1987).

To illustrate, consider this question: What are the odds that you're going to use that toothbrush again? Suppose I were to drop it into boiling water for a requisite period to ensure sterilization. Would you use it now? Probably not by choice. In one study by Paul Rozin and his colleagues, a dead but sterilized cockroach was dropped into a glass of juice and offered to thirsty subjects. Not surprisingly, subjects showed little interest in drinking the juice, even though they knew the roach had been sterilized (Rozin and others, 1986). Most people would be reluctant to consume

their favorite soup if they witness the bowl being stirred by a never-used comb or fly swatter (Rozin & Fallon, 1987).

What accounts for these effects? According to some researchers, humans are likely to succumb to what has been called *sympathetic magic* (Frazer, 1890/1959; Mauss, 1902/1972; Rozin & Fallon, 1987). People believe that when two objects come in contact, they acquire "like" properties. The juice acquires some of the disgusting properties of the cockroach, perhaps through a process akin to contagion. The soup becomes associated with flies, even though one knows that the fly swatter has never come into contact with a fly. Objects apparently need only be associated with other disgusting objects to elicit an emotional reaction. These are not conscious rational processes at work here, although they may be thought processes that are fundamental and common to all people (Rozin & Fallon, 1987). (It may also be that classical conditioning is involved—some kind of higher-order association may be formed between the juice, for example, and an object that elicits disgust [see Chapter 7]).

Types of Disgust

Paul Rozin and his colleagues have identified four broad categories of "disgust elicitors"—those things that seem to generate the emotion reliably. Objects such as roaches and flies are examples of *core disgust elicitors*. These are objects that are potentially capable of contaminating food. People shy away, presumably, for adaptive reasons that are related to survival. More generally, people tend to become disgusted by anything that reminds them of their animal origins. *Animal-reminder disgust elicitors* make people come to grips with a sense of "animalness," which Rozin believes is threatening to their sense of mortality. Therefore, people tend to be disgusted by death, poor hygiene, or any bizarre form of sexual behavior.

Social interactions can also lead to disgust. *Sociomoral disgust* is the emotional reaction to people and events

Would you brush your teeth with this toothbrush?

that are distasteful because of one's sense of morality. Aren't you disgusted by acts of violence—murder, rape, or abuse? Do you cringe when you imagine an act of violence in your mind's eye? *Interpersonal disgust* arises when people come into contact with someone of undesirable or unsavory origins. Would you wear a sweatshirt that had previously been worn by Jeffrey Dahmer— that gruesome serial killer who included human flesh as part of his diet? Does simply the thought disgust you? Many social and interpersonal disgust elicitors are importantly culture-bound. For example, certain people in Hindu India are reluctant to eat food that has been handled by a person of a lower caste, whereas such contact is unlikely to elicit disgust in individuals in other parts of the world (Rozin & Fallon, 1987).

The Development of Disgust

Although the experience of disgust appears to be universal—appearing cross-culturally—the emotion in all of its various forms does not appear to be intact at birth. If children under age 4 are presented with what adults would consider to be a disgusting odor (feces or synthetic sweat), they tend not to be bothered, or they may even react positively (Stein, Ottenberg, & Roulet, 1958). Children under age 2, as any parent knows, are happy to put just about anything into their mouths, even "disgusting" objects. In one study, it was found that 62% of tested children under age 2 would put imitation dog feces in their mouth; 31% would mouth a whole, sterilized grasshopper (Rozin and others, 1986). Children simply have no conception that these objects are potentially harmful and thus must learn what not to put in their mouths.

It also apparently takes a while for the idea of object contamination to become ingrained in people's minds. You won't brush your teeth with a toothbrush that once housed a cockroach, but a 7-year-old might. Children of this age typically report that a drink has been returned to normal after a disgusting object has been removed (Fallon, Rozin, & Pliner, 1984). In several studies, children under the age of 7 have shown a willingness to drink a beverage after simply removing an object like a fly—they're even willing to drink something if a tiny bit of a disgusting object sits in the bottom of the glass (see Rozin, 1990, for a review). Notions about contagion and contamination clearly develop with experience and may even require the attainment of a certain developmental stage.

It's somehow fitting that we end this chapter with a discussion of *disgust*. As a food-related emotion, it fits snugly into the topic of motivation, as well as into the theme of the adaptive mind. People need to be activated and driven to pursue food; otherwise they would die. But what people eat is as important as when and whether they eat. It's necessary for all species to develop appropriate methods of food selection. An emotion such as disgust, with its accompanying physical and facial expressions, serves a protective function: It prevents consumption, and it helps communicate to others that an inappropriate food is present. Through witnessing the reactions of others (especially parents), children learn the dos and don'ts of food consumption and thereby increase their likelihood of survival.

"Human action can be modified to a certain extent, but human nature cannot be changed."

Abraham Lincoln

It is the curse of humankind, reasoned Dr. Henry Jekyll, that within every human spirit lies not one but truly two persons. On the one hand is the moral and intellectual side, capable of uplifting achievement; on the other, the dark side resides—the unrepentant seeker of pleasure. If only these two natures could be housed in separate identities, Jekyll speculated, the unjust could walk free, relieved of the strict sensibilities of its bothersome twin. The moral arm could seek knowledge and truth without succumbing to the evil tendencies of the flesh. As the smoking ebullition in the glass subsided, he raised the glass to his lips and drank. . . .

In *The Strange Case of Dr. Jekyll and Mr. Hyde,* Robert Louis Stevenson personifies a dual nature of human personality through the characters of Jekyll and Hyde. Actually one and the same man, Dr. Jekyll transforms himself into the insidious Mr. Hyde, the personification of evil, by drinking a potion composed of salts and other wholesale chemicals. If you read the novel, you will see that the results are disastrous for them "both," but the thesis is a fascinating one for the psychologist to consider. How reasonable is it to assume that behavior is controlled by enduring fixed psychological characteristics or traits? This may seem like a given to you, but the issue is actually quite controversial among psychologists. Moreover, assuming these traits exist, is it fair to describe them as "good" or "evil"—are humans, like Luke Skywalker in *Star Wars,* actively engaged in an unrelenting battle against the dark side of their nature? As we'll see in this chapter, some psychologists have argued that there are indeed multiple sides to human nature, and these sides are engaged in a kind of constant internal battle.

Our topic in this chapter is **personality,** which can be defined as the distinguishing pattern of psychological characteristics—thinking, feeling, and behaving—that differentiates us from others and leads us to act consistently across situations. At its core, the study of personality, like the study of intelligence, is first and foremost the study of individual differences (Cronbach, 1957). People seem to differ in enduring ways: Rowena is outgoing, confident, and friendly; Roger is shy in social settings and has an annoying proclivity toward lying. In a very real sense, personality **traits,** or predispositions to respond in a certain way, define people. Traits make people unique, identifiable, and generally predictable across time. Potentially, we can use them to explain why Rowena and Roger remain stable and consistent in their actions across diverse situations.

One of the tasks facing those who study personality is to determine whether any single instance of behavior, such as the helping behavior shown by this man, represents an enduring trait of the individual—something that applies in lots of situations.

▶ PREVIEWING THE CONCEPTUAL AND PRACTICAL PROBLEMS

It's difficult to treat a topic such as personality as a simple solution to an adaptive problem, like eating or communicating internally. Personality is something that psychologists infer from behavior in order to explain individual differences and to help predict how people might act in a given context. Of course, consistency in behavior and thought from one situation to the next is likely to have considerable adaptive value. It's useful to maintain at least some stable tendencies in one's behavioral and cognitive repertoire, especially if those tendencies lead to actions that are successful. Many researchers believe that people possess traits such as fearfulness or aggressiveness because those traits motivate them to act in ways that increase the likelihood of survival (Buss, 1988).

Do all people have a "dark side" to their personality, waiting to be expressed by the right environmental conditions? Is it possible that mass murderer Henry Lee Lucas, shown here in prison along with photographs of his victims, was simply born with the wrong kind of genes?

Our focus in this chapter will be on how psychologists have attempted to resolve the conceptual and practical problems central to the study of personality. What is the proper way to conceptualize and measure the traits that make individuals both consistent and unique? How and why do these traits develop—what factors in development lead to stable and consistent behavior? Finally, do people really act consistently across a wide variety of situations, and, if so, what kind of evidence can reliably demonstrate this fact?

▶ **CONCEPTUALIZING AND MEASURING PERSONALITY** To gain insight into the concept of personality, it's necessary to consider the whole person. This means that psychologists cannot simply note the actions of the individual in a restricted situation, or even in several situations. We need to define and measure the *enduring* aspects of behavior—those things that distinguish one person from another consistently across time. To use the analogy of one personality researcher, the proper focus should be on "not one time at bat in baseball but the season's hitting average, not an evening's flirtation or adventure but marriage or an enduring relationship" (Buss, A. H., 1989). Unfortunately, there is no simple way of addressing this problem. We'll consider several approaches in this section. Some researchers, for example, try to identify the building blocks of human personality by studying selected individuals in great detail. Others analyze the performance of large groups of individuals, usually through paper-and-pencil questionnaires, and glean the structure of personality from sophisticated analyses of the responses. We'll also consider some of the more widely used practical personality assessment techniques in this section. How do prospective employers or clinical practitioners arrive at quick and reliable assessments of an individual's personality traits?

▶ **DETERMINING HOW PERSONALITY DEVELOPS** It's one thing to identify and measure what appear to be a person's enduring traits, but quite another to understand their origin. Where do personality traits come from, and what accounts for the individual variability? Why does Roger have that nasty proclivity to lie, and why does sweet Rowena always see the sunny side of a rotten situation? It is here, in the study of personality development, that we find some of the most ambitious and best-known attempts at psychological theory. One classic example is the *psychodynamic* approach to personality, which emphasizes deeply rooted unconscious processes and conflicts. We'll outline this perspective, which began with the ideas of Sigmund Freud, and we'll see how psychodynamic theories have changed and evolved with time. Next, we'll turn our attention to *humanistic* approaches to understanding personality. Humanistic theorists, including Carl Rogers and Abraham Maslow, reject the pessimistic determinism of Freud and emphasize free will and choice instead. To a humanist, people actively construct their own enduring qualities, based on their sense of self and their beliefs about the world. Finally, we'll discuss several *cognitive/behavioral* approaches to personality. Here the emphasis will be primarily on the environment and how it shapes people's actions. It is the external world, coupled with people's interpretations of that world, that creates consistencies in human behavior.

▶ **RESOLVING THE PERSON-SITUATION DEBATE**   Virtually all types of human behavior are influenced by the environment. All major theories of personality assume that the environment shapes behavior; where they differ is in the degree to which the environment is important and in the mechanisms through which the environment exerts its influence. But since personality consists of those traits that remain the same across diverse contexts, we are faced with a kind of theoretical puzzle. In essence, personality represents a psychological characteristic that should be largely independent of the environment. Remember, people are supposed to act the same regardless of the situation. Is behavior really as consistent across situations as many people, including psychologists, assume? In the final section of the chapter, we'll discuss the evidence—and controversy—that bears on this issue.

Conceptualizing and Measuring Personality

It's not necessary to have a well-developed theory about the origins of personality to identify and measure differences among people. In fact, it could be argued that we need some bormal way of classifying individual differences before we can know what it is that needs to be explained. **Trait theories** are formal systems for assessing how people differ, particularly in their predispositions to respond in certain ways across situations. As a general rule, trait theories use a *psychometric approach*—that is, they seek to identify stable individual differences by analyzing the performances of large groups of people on a series of rating tests or questionnaires.

If you open up any dictionary, you'll find thousands of words that fit the everyday definition of a personality trait. In fact, it's been estimated that approximately 1 out of every 22 words in the English language describes some kind of trait disposition (Allport & Odbert, 1936). One goal of the trait theorist is to try to reduce these thousands of descriptive terms into a smaller set of more "basic" terms—to find a kind of common denominator among groups of terms. For example, when you describe someone with words like *kind*, *trusting*, and *warm*, you might really be tapping into some more general disposition of the person, such as *agreeableness* or *pleasantness* (Goldberg, 1993). The researcher attempts to identify the "basic" traits from among the thousands of personality descriptors that are common in the language.

The Factor Analytic Approach

One way to approach the problem is to use the statistical technique of *factor analysis*. As we discussed in Chapter 10, factor analysis is a mathematical procedure that is used to analyze correlations among test responses. The goal is to identify a set of "factors" that in combination do a reasonable job of predicting test performance. To see how this works in the case of personality, imagine that we ask a large group of people to rate themselves on 100 personality characteristics. For example: "On a scale of 1 to 7, how well do you think the term *brooding* is characteristic of you?" If each person provides 100 rating responses, we will undoubtedly see lots of individual differences. Some people will see themselves as brooders, others won't; some people will score high on aggressiveness and competitiveness; others will classify themselves as passive and shy.

But the real question of interest centers on how the trait ratings correlate with one another. Do people who rate themselves as, say, *kind* also tend to rate themselves as *warm* and *trusting*? More specifically, can we predict someone's rating on one trait given that we know their rating on some other trait? If we can, then it may be reasonable to assume that some higher-level personality disposition, such as *pleasantness,* is being tapped by the more specific personality descriptors. This is the logic behind factor analysis—discover the common denominators for personality by noting which terms "cluster" statistically in a group. Once these factors are identified, they should in principle help predict someone's behavior, or at least explain why an individual acts consistently from one situation to the next.

Source Traits and Superfactors. Psychologists have applied the factor analytic technique to many different kinds of personality data. For practical reasons, it's most common for researchers to rely on ratings of personality descriptors, such as *kind* or *warm,* which people give about themselves or others. Psychologist Raymond Cattell, for example, was able to use rating data of this sort to identify 16 basic personality factors from a set of traits that originally numbered in the thousands (Cattell, Eber, & Tatsuoka, 1970). Cattell's 16 factors, which he called "source traits," are listed in Figure 12.1. Notice that each factor is represented as a dimension marked by an opposing pole: reserved-outgoing, trusting-suspicious, humble-assertive, and so on. Any particular individual is assumed to have a unique personality "profile," reflecting his or her standing on each of the dimensions.

FIGURE 12.1

A Personality Profile. Shown here is a sample personality profile as measured by Cattell's 16 Personality Factor test. Notice that an individual's "personality" is defined by his or her standing on each of the 16 trait dimensions. (From Cattell, 1973)

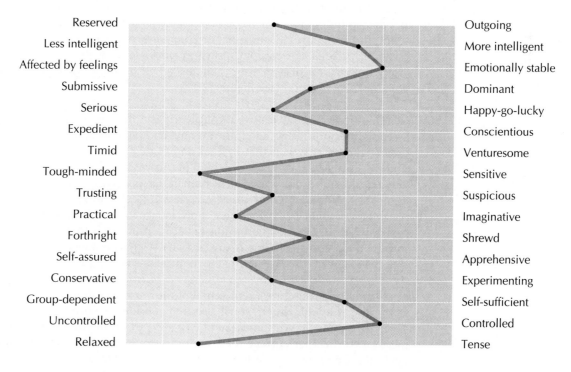

Neuroticism

1. Does your mood often go up and down?
2. Do you often feel "fed up"?
3. Are you an irritable person?

Extroversion

1. Do you like mixing with people?
2. Do you like going out a lot?
3. Would you call yourself happy-go-lucky?

Psychoticism

1. Do you enjoy cooperating with others?
2. Do you try not to be rude to people?
3. Do good manners and cleanliness matter to you?

But the exact set of factors that are "discovered" by the researcher depends partly on how the mathematical technique of factor analysis is applied. Whereas Cattell reported 16 primary factors (along with some additional secondary or second-order factors), Hans Eysenck has argued that the rudiments of personality can be better described by appealing to only 3 factors: (1) the dimension of *extroversion*, which refers roughly to how outgoing and sociable someone is; (2) the dimension of *neuroticism*, which captures a person's degree of anxiety, worry, or moodiness; and (3) the dimension of *psychoticism*, which represents a person's tendencies to be insensitive, uncaring, or cruel toward others (Eysenck, 1970, 1991). Particular personality descriptors, such as *touchy* or *lively*, are presumed to reflect some combination of a person's standing on each of the three primary dimensions, or "superfactors" (see Figure 12.2).

The Big Five. How can we reconcile the fact that researchers like Cattell and Eysenck differ so strongly about the number and types of basic personality dimensions? A simple answer is that Eysenck and Cattell are merely operating at different levels of analysis: Eysenck, with his 3 primary dimensions, is interested in mapping out the more global aspects of human personality, whereas Cattell's analytic techniques paint a more fine-tuned description (see Feist, 1994). But increasingly, researchers seem to be settling on a more intermediate solution: It is now widely believed that the best solution to the factoring problem is to propose 5 basic personality dimensions (McCrae & Costa, 1985; Wiggins & Pincus, 1992).

The so-called **Big Five** personality dimensions (see Figure 12.3) include *extroversion, agreeableness, conscientiousness, neuroticism,* and *openness.* Notice that *extroversion* and *neuroticism* represent 2 of the 3 primary dimensions suggested by Eysenck; if you look closely, you'll also find considerable overlap with the factors suggested by Cattell. Why 5 instead of 3 or 16? Part of the reason is technical, having to do with what current researchers believe is the most appropriate way to apply the factor analytic technique (see Digman, 1990 or Goldberg, 1993). But

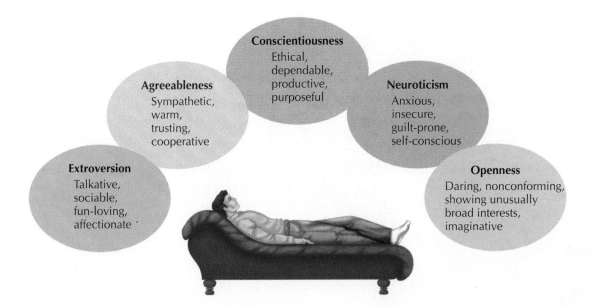

FIGURE 12.3
The Big Five. Many psychologists now believe that personality is best analyzed in terms of five fundamental personality dimensions: extroversion, agreeableness, conscientiousness, neuroticism, and openness.

there are other reasons. For example, a number of cross-cultural studies have analyzed trait ratings collected from people around the world. Regardless of the language used—and different languages can have quite different personality descriptors—there still appear to be 5 basic dimensions that best explain the ratings (Digman, 1990). There are currently some disagreements about the proper labels for these basic dimensions, but most trait theorists agree that virtually all personality terms used in human language will correlate with, or be accounted for by, at least one of these 5 dimensions.

Allport's Trait Theory

Like the factor analysts, psychologist Gordon Allport (1897–1967) was convinced that all people possess certain underlying personality traits, or "predispositions to respond." But he was less convinced that the building blocks of personality could be gleaned from massive statistical analyses of group responses. Allport believed that personality, in essence, is a measure of one's "uniqueness" as an individual. So, the proper focus should be on individuals, he argued, not groups. His approach, which he called *idiographic* (which means "relating to the individual"), was to study particular individuals in great detail. An advantage of this kind of "case study" approach is that consistencies in behavior across an entire lifetime can actually be recorded.

One of Allport's main contributions was his general classification scheme for identifying personality traits (Allport, 1937). Allport believed, for example, that some people could be described in terms of what he called cardinal traits. **Cardinal traits** are the ruling passions that dominate an individual's life. If you spend your life huddled in a mountain monastery, rejecting all worldly possessions, your passion "to serve god" would likely satisfy Allport's description of a cardinal trait. Perhaps you know someone whose every thought or action seems to revolve around the pursuit of wealth, fame, or power. People with cardinal traits do not represent the average—these people are driven and highly focused; every action appears to be motivated by some particular goal. Notice that we cannot really capture something like a cardinal trait by applying a technique such as factor analysis, because cardinal traits are uniquely defined by the individual rather than the group.

When comparing the relative merits of the idiographic approach versus the factor analytic approach, you might think back to some of our discussions in Chapter 2. Can you remember the advantages and disadvantages of using case studies, which examine single individuals, versus surveys, which use the responses from large groups of individuals?

Cardinal traits are the ruling passions that dominate a person's life, such as a compelling need to help others at the expense of personal comfort.

Allport believed that cardinal traits are rare. Most people have personalities that are controlled by several dispositions or enduring qualities, which Allport labeled as **central traits.** These are the five to ten descriptive terms that you would probably use to describe someone you know. Rowena? She's outgoing and friendly, very trustworthy, sentimental at times, and honest to the core. In addition to central traits, Allport suggested that everyone has **secondary traits,** which are less obvious because they may not always appear in an individual's behavior. For example, Rowena might also have a secondary trait of "testiness" that shows up only when she goes on an extended diet. Personality characteristics, therefore, can appropriately be described in terms of *levels* ranging from dominant (cardinal) to representative (central) to occasional (secondary).

Personality Tests

Most trait theories of the type that we've been discussing were developed to uncover the fundamental dimensions of human personality. Trait researchers have tried to find the essential factors, or building blocks, that in combination produce distinguishing patterns of psychological characteristics. But there are practical reasons why it's important to measure personality traits—reasons that are unrelated to general psychological theory. Suppose you are the personnel director at a large nuclear power plant. You need to hire responsible people to run the plant, people who have the right stuff to handle potentially dangerous materials in an emergency. You wouldn't want to hire someone like Roger, with his proclivity for lying and his tendency to act compulsively under pressure. How do you make the proper determination for a given individual? You can choose from two main categories of personality tests: *self-report inventories* and *projective tests.*

Self-Report Inventories. **Self-report inventories** use a paper-and-pencil format to identify personality characteristics. People are asked to answer groups of questions about how they typically think, act, and feel. Their responses, or *self-reports,* are scored objectively, and the results are then compared to test "averages" that have been compiled from the performances of thousands of other test takers. As a general rule, self-report inventories are easy to administer, and they paint a reasonably reliable picture of how someone differs from the average. Roger, for instance, would probably raise red flags on a number of measures; his answers are likely to show some disregard for social customs (compared to the average) and a marked tendency toward impulsiveness. If you were the personnel director, you could easily make your hiring—or more accurately, "no hire"—decision based on the test results.

Many kinds of self-report inventories are currently employed by professionals. Some tests are based on popular trait theories. For example, to assess "normal" personality traits one can administer the **16 Personality Factor,** which is an

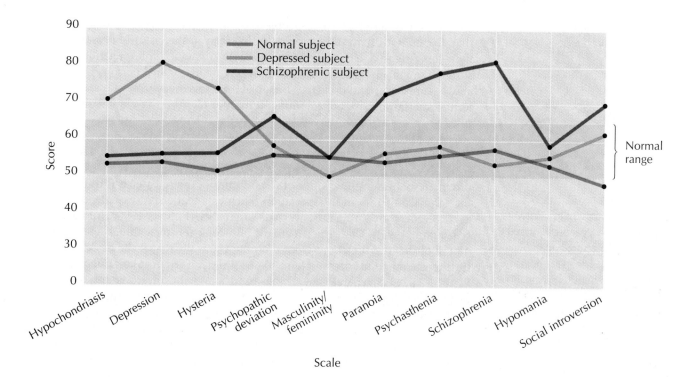

FIGURE 12.4
MMPI Profiles. The MMPI is often used to help psychologists diagnose psychological disorders. A client's scores on the various clinical scales can be compared to average scores from people who are not suffering from psychological problems, as well as from people who have been diagnosed with particular psychological problems (such as depression or schizophrenia). (Adapted from Weiten, 1995)

187-item questionnaire designed to measure the 16 primary personality factors identified by Cattell (Cattell, Eber, & Tatsuoka, 1970). Alternatively, there is the **NEO-PI-R,** which is designed to measure a person's standing on the Big Five personality traits identified in Figure 12.3 (NEO-PI-R stands for Neuroticism Extroversion Openness-Personality Inventory–Revised). However, the most widely used self-report inventory is the **Minnesota Multiphasic Personality Inventory (MMPI),** although this test is used primarily as a tool for identifying psychological disorders. The MMPI requires test takers to answer hundreds of true-false questions about themselves (e.g., "I never get angry"), and it's now available in several revised forms (see Butcher, 1995). An individual's answers are expressed in terms of a personality profile that describes his or her scores on various subscales (see Figure 12.4).

As mentioned, the MMPI is typically used as a technique for diagnosing psychological disorders. A person's responses are compared to those of average test takers but also to the responses of individuals with known psychological problems. There are records, for example, of how people who suffer from such disorders as paranoia (irrational beliefs of persecution) are likely to answer certain questions. The test responses of someone like Roger can then be compared with the average "paranoia" personality profile to see if he fits the bill. Comparisons of this sort are useful in diagnosing problems and in making judgments about how appropriate an individual might be for a high-risk form of employment.

Projective Personality Tests. As an alternative to standardized personality tests like the NEO-PI-R, psychologists sometimes use projective personality tests. In a **projective test,** a person is asked to interpret an unstructured or ambiguous stimulus for the test administrator. The underlying idea is that people will "project" their thoughts and true feelings into the stimulus interpretation, thereby revealing elements of their personality. For example, take a look at the inkblot shown in Figure 12.5, which is similar to the kind of unstructured stimulus used on the *Rorschach test.* Clearly, you argue, this stimulus exemplifies the fundamental decay of human society. The image symbolizes the need for aggressive action

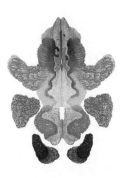

FIGURE 12.5
Projective Tests. In projective personality tests, people are asked to interpret unstructured or ambiguous stimuli. Their answers are presumed to provide insight into personality. What do you see hidden in this inkblot—the fundamental decay of human society? (From Kalat, 1996)

on the part of all responsible people—we must rise up and defeat the tyranny that, like an out-of-control cancer, is eating away at the virtue and values of common folk. Right? Well . . . Can you see how someone's interpretation of such a stimulus might provide insight into aspects of his or her personality? If Roger always sees snakes and decaying dragons in the images, whereas Rowena sees butterflies and flowers, it's not too difficult to infer that they have quite different personality characteristics.

One of the advantages of projective tests is that they allow a person to respond freely, in a manner that is less restrictive than the requirements imposed by self-report inventories. Psychologists have tried to develop reliable standards for interpreting responses in these kinds of tests. Typically, the researcher is trained to look for common themes in interpretation (such as a tendency to see death, decay, or aggressiveness) or for qualities such as originality (Edberg, 1990; Hurt, Reznikoff, & Clarkin, 1995). The clinician might also look for such things as the realistic nature of the interpretation: Does the response really match the perceptual structure of the stimulus? If you claim to see a dragon in an inkblot like the one in Figure 12.5, your general view of the world may slant toward fantasy rather than reality. The degree to which you seek help in your interpretation may also be instructive. For example, individuals who constantly seek guidance from the clinician before giving an answer are likely to be classified as dependent.

None of the personality assessment procedures that we've discussed is perfect, neither self-report inventories nor projective tests, and each has been subject to criticism (see Beutler & Berren, 1995). For example, the scoring procedures for projective tests still tend to be somewhat unreliable; it's not uncommon for administrators to arrive at quite different interpretations of the same subject's responses. Questions about the validity of the interpretations have also been raised: Do these tests really measure the key features of personality? Critics of self-report inventories such as the MMPI have complained that subjects sometimes deliberately bias their responses in ways to make themselves look positive. Other critics have questioned the test's true ability to predict job performance, or have suggested that the test and its applications may invade the privacy of the individual. Even with these criticisms, however, both categories of personality test remain extremely popular. Changes in test construction as well as more rigorous scoring criteria are regularly introduced in an effort to answer the critics (Edberg, 1990).

Determining How Personality Develops

Do you see any connection between the interpretation of projective test responses and the interpretation of a client's dreams? Do you think we could use dream interpretation as a way of inferring elements of someone's personality?

Largely through the efforts of the trait theorists, it is now possible to obtain an objective measure of general personality. We can describe the personality traits of Roger or Rowena—perhaps their standing on the Big Five—and there is a good chance that our measurements will be reasonably accurate and reliable. But description is not the same as explanation. We may know that Rowena has a bright and sunny disposition, but the trait theories provide little insight into the origin of those characteristics. This is the problem to which we now turn: determining how personality develops. Why do Roger and Rowena differ? What mechanisms in the mind produce and maintain those differences?

In this section, we'll consider three quite different approaches to understanding personality development. Each asserts that individual uniqueness arises from the operation of general psychological principles. People are not unique or consistent in their behavior by accident or chance; rather, processes are at work inside our head, or in the external environment, that shape and mold our actions. In each case, personality is conceived of as a by-product of general adaptive principles that help initiate and control behavior in widely diverse contexts.

The Psychodynamic Approach of Freud

Consider the following scenario. You're a practicing clinician and your latest patient, 18-year-old Katharina, complains of persistent physical problems. "I'm often overcome with a frightful choking feeling," she insists. "I have trouble catching my breath, my head begins to spin, and I truly think I must be about to die." Extensive examinations have revealed no physical cause; the attacks appear suddenly without warning and seem unrelated to activity or general health. Katharina herself provides no insight: "There's nothing in my head when the attacks begin; my mind is a blank." The only additional information that you have about Katharina is her reluctance to involve herself with members of the opposite sex and her persistent dream in which she appears as a young child pursued from room to room by a shadowy figure.

Think about this case study for a moment. Can you draw any general conclusions about the operating characteristics of Katharina's mind from an analysis of her symptoms? The case itself is typical of the kinds of clinical problems that Sigmund Freud (1856–1939) faced in the late 19th century. As we noted in Chapter 1, Freud was a medical doctor by training. He established a private practice in Vienna, where he specialized in neurology, a branch of medicine concerned with disorders of the nervous system. He routinely encountered patients like Katharina, who showed severe physical problems without any identifiable physical cause. Such cases (they were known in that time as *hysterics*) were to form the basis for Freud's highly influential **psychodynamic theory** of personality and mind, as well as for his method of treatment known as *psychoanalysis*.

Sigmund Freud is shown here in 1891, at a time when he was becoming increasingly convinced that certain physical problems may have psychological origins.

The Structure of Mind. Freud believed that the human mind could be partitioned into three major structural parts: the conscious, the preconscious, and the unconscious. The contents of awareness—those things that occupy the focus of one's current attention—make up the **conscious mind.** As you read the words on this page and think about Freud's theory, you are engaging and using the processes of this conscious mind. In contrast, the **preconscious mind** contains all of the inactive but potentially accessible thoughts and memories—those things that people could easily recall, if they desired, but are simply not thinking about at the moment. Consider the word *aardvark*—it's unlikely that you were thinking about this word moments ago; but as I draw your attention to the word, it changes from a preconscious to a conscious state. Finally, there is the **unconscious mind,** which houses all the memories, urges, and conflicts that Freud believed are beyond awareness. He was convinced that the contents of the unconscious mind exert powerful and long-lasting influences on behavior, but they remain hidden and unavailable to conscious introspection.

Think back to our discussion of memory in Chapter 8. Do the modern memory concepts of "short-term memory" and "long-term memory" remind you of any part of Freud's view of the mind?

From Freud's perspective, Katharina's panicky behavior is undoubtedly controlled by forces that lie beyond her conscious access. She has no idea why she suffers sporadic panic attacks; in fact, in all likelihood she will be startled to discover that the cause of her problems is psychological rather than physical. Freud saw such lack of awareness as strong confirmation that psychological forces originate unconsciously. He believed that the unconscious mind acts as a kind of mental prison, housing forbidden thoughts and feelings that are normally kept at bay by the psychological forces that make up personality. Although they rarely, if ever, reach a conscious state, Freud was convinced that these committed "inmates" of the unconscious will reveal themselves to the attentive observer—but only indirectly or symbolically through dreams or occasional "slips of the tongue."

Consider Katharina's repetitive dream of being chased through her house by a shadowy figure. She can remember the details of the dream—her appearance as a young child, perhaps the color and shapes of the rooms—but her conscious memory of the dream, in the Freudian view, is in all likelihood superficial and misleading. The remembered elements of the dream, or its *manifest content,* represent what is merely a symbolic and disguised version of the dream's true unconscious meaning, or *latent content.* As you may recall from our discussion in Chapter 6, dreams to Freud represented a mental mechanism for wish fulfillment; dreams are simply one way that the mind attempts to gratify desires or deal with forbidden conflicts that are normally deeply entrenched in the unconscious. In Katharina's case, the pursuing shadowy figure may well have arisen from a traumatic childhood experience—perhaps an unwelcome sexual advance by a relative—or even from her own unconscious desire for a forbidden sexual experience. Katharina is not aware of the reason because it's unconscious, but it continues to influence her behavior and haunt her dreams. Freud relied heavily on dream interpretation as a technique for mapping out the contents of the unconscious mind. Dreams, Freud argued, represent a "royal road to the unconscious" (Freud, 1900/1990).

The Structure of Personality. Freud also proposed a tripartite (three-part) theory for the structure of personality (see Figure 12.6). Regularities in behavior result from interactions among the motivating forces of what he called the *id, ego,* and *superego.* As a student of neurology, Freud was committed to the idea that much of human behavior is influenced by biological forces. He believed that people are born with powerful instinctual drives, particularly related to sex and aggression, that motivate and control many of their actions. Among Freud's more radical ideas was his proposal that even children possess strong, though unconscious, sexual urges. As we'll discuss later, he believed that the way children deal with their burgeoning sexuality importantly influences their psychological development.

Freud used the term **id** to represent the portion of personality that is governed by inborn drives (translated from the Latin, *id* means "it"). As a component of personality, the id seeks immediate satisfaction of innate urges, without concern for the morals and customs of society. It obeys what Freud called the *pleasure principle*—the relentless pursuit of pleasure through the satisfaction of animalistic urges. Ironically, from an adaptive standpoint, it is this dark side of personality—the unrepentant seeker of pleasure—that guarantees survival of the species by motivating a desire for sexual intercourse.

FIGURE 12.6
Freud's View of Personality.
Freud believed that people's personalities are influenced by three forces: (1) the *id*—the unconscious and unrepentant seeker of pleasure; (2) the *superego*—the "moral" seeker of ideal behavior; and (3) the *ego*—the executive that acts in accordance with reality. Just as most of an iceberg's structure lies beneath the water, much of personality structure operates at an unconscious level.

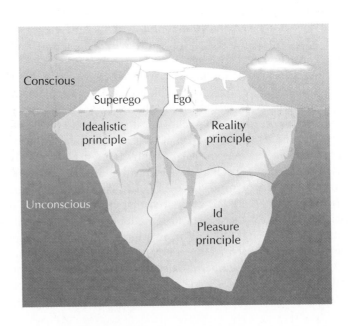

But Freud also recognized that humans are more than just irrational sexual machines. He suggested that the forces of the id are appropriately balanced by a moral or provincial arm of personality. The **superego** represents the tendency in people to act in an ideal fashion—to act in accordance with the moral customs defined by parents and culture. The superego is acquired from experience and it acts, in part, as a conscience; it makes people feel good when they act the way they should and feel guilty when their behavior strays from accepted standards. Like the id, however, the superego is essentially irrational in its concerns—it seeks only moral perfection. Left to its own devices, the superego would undercut or block satisfaction of the more basic urges, even though those urges may help the individual satisfy fundamental survival needs. The superego follows an *idealistic principle:* Always act in a proper and ideal fashion as defined by parents and culture.

Sitting between the forces of the id and superego, and acting as a mediator, is the ego. The **ego,** which derives from the Latin word for "I," serves an executive role in Freud's conception of personality. The ego induces people to act with reason and deliberation and helps them conform to the requirements of the external world. Freud suggested that the ego obeys a *reality principle;* it monitors the real world looking for appropriate outlets for the id's needs, but it also listens intently to the moralistic preachings of the superego. The ego's goal is compromise among three demanding masters: the external world, the id, and the superego. Freud liked to call up the image of a horseback rider to describe the ego's function (Freud, 1923; Gay, 1988). The rider valiantly attempts to control the horse, which represents the id, by making the animal conform to the requirements of the environmental terrain (keeping on the path, avoiding trees, and so on). But the horse is clearly stronger than the rider, and reigning in the animal is a taxing and often not very successful enterprise. At various times the horse veers from the appropriate path, acting to satisfy its own impulses, occasionally placing both rider and itself in danger. Meanwhile, swarming angrily overhead is a collection of bees, the superego, who really don't approve of the ride in the first place. To the superego, satisfying the animalistic urges of the id cannot be considered ideal behavior (especially in Freud's Victorian era), so it's best if the animal remains locked up and out of sight in the stable.

Mechanisms of Defense: The Ego's Arsenal. Human personality arises from the battlefield—the continuing confrontations among the id, ego, and superego. According to Freud, individuals are usually unaware of the conflict because the battlefield is located in the unconscious mind. They consciously experience only the side effects of the battle. For example, the experience of *anxiety* (an unpleasant feeling of dread) arises in part from confrontations between the ego and the id or superego (of course, anxiety can also come from dangers in the real world). But the ego does not enter the battle unarmed. Freud believed that the ego has at its disposal a variety of **defense mechanisms,** which are unconscious processes that can ward off the anxiety that comes from confrontation with the id.

The most important weapon in the ego's arsenal is **repression,** a process that actively keeps anxiety-producing thoughts and feelings buried in the unconscious. When a primitive urge from the id rears its ugly head, or a traumatic experience from childhood threatens to surface, the ego actively represses the thought or feeling. The urge is blocked out, jammed down into the dark recesses of the unconscious. Freud was convinced that people are particularly likely to repress sexual thoughts or experiences because society at large condemns their expression. Unrestricted sexual activity is typically frowned on by parents and society—this was particularly true in Freud's time—so sexual thoughts and feelings need to be actively confronted by the reality-driven ego. In contrast, people have few repressed thoughts or memories about eating or drinking, although both are instinctual urges, because these behaviors tend to violate few, if any, societal norms.

What do you think are the adaptive qualities of the superego? What would happen to the human species if the superego always motivated and controlled behavior?

Freud believed that people sometimes deal with unacceptable feelings by attributing them to others, through a process called projection. *The anger shown in this photo, Freud might argue, could be actually symbolic of some deeper conflict that the woman on the left is "projecting" onto the woman on the right.*

Once repressed, however, blocked memories or the ever-present urges of the id continue to exert their influence. The id must eventually express itself, so slamming the door to awareness will never be completely successful. The urges or conflicts will only seek release or expression in other ways, possibly in a disguised form. Returning to the example of Katharina, in her case the repressed memories of a sexual assault, or perhaps her unconscious wishes for a forbidden sexual encounter, have surfaced in a physical form. The disabling panic attacks and recurring dreams are symbolic of her unconscious conflicts. To Freud, every behavior or thought, no matter how trivial or incidental, potentially bears the mark of the unconscious. Like the patch on a leaky hose, repression may hide outward appearances, but it cannot stop the fact that beneath the covering there is an ever-active flow.

Repression is really a kind of self deception—the mind "deals" with the anxiety-producing impulse by acting as if it isn't there. Similar kinds of self-deception occur with the other defense mechanisms Freud proposed. For example, through a process called **projection,** people deal with unacceptable feelings or wishes by attributing them to others. A person harboring strong sexual feelings toward a married neighbor—an impulse likely to engender considerable guilt—might "project" his or her feelings onto the neighbor. It is the neighbor who harbors the desire, certainly not I. **Reaction formation** occurs when people transform an anxiety-producing wish into a kind of opposite—they actually behave in a way that counters the way they truly feel. For example, a mother who secretly resents the birth of her daughter and unconsciously wishes her dead might smother the child with exaggerated care and affection; the unconscious anti-Semite, who wishes the degradation of all Jews, might become an active and tireless volunteer for organizations championing Jewish rights. Notice that in each of these cases, the unconscious conflict receives attention, but the attention is disguised in a self-deceptive way.

Once again, the point of the self-deception is to reduce the experience of anxiety. Defense mechanisms enable the ego to deal indirectly with unacceptable psychological thoughts and feelings. Suppose you are an extremely aggressive person who unconsciously would love to hurt others. According to Freud, you might use

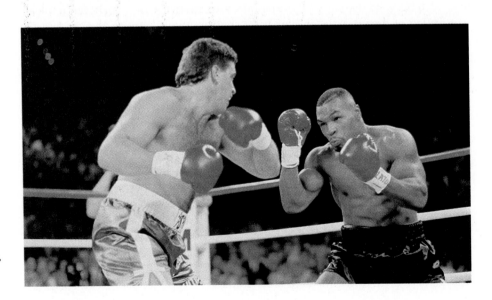

Through sublimation, unacceptable impulses, such as a desire to hurt others, are channeled into socially acceptable activities.

the defense mechanism of **sublimation,** in which unacceptable impulses are channeled into socially acceptable activity, to deal with the potential anxiety. Perhaps you will choose a career in professional football, or become an aggressive member of the local police force. Here, the aggressive impulse will be satisfied, but in an indirect and socially acceptable manner.

The Development of Personality. Psychodynamic theory conceives of the unconscious as a bubbling cauldron of hidden conflicts, repressed memories, and biological urges striving for release. In the case of the biological urges, their origin is relatively clear—people are born with instinctual drives for self-preservation and sex. But where do the other conflicts come from? Why are people tormented by repressed memories that arise directly from life's experiences? Freud believed that individuals travel through stages of psychosexual development in their childhood (Freud, 1905/1962). How children deal with their emerging sexuality importantly affects the way they think and feel when they reach adulthood.

Each developmental stage is associated with a particularly sensitive body region of pleasure or sexual gratification, which Freud called an *erogenous zone.* In the first year or so of life—during the **oral stage**—pleasure is derived primarily from sucking and from placing things in the mouth (such as the mother's breast). The adaptive significance of this first stage is clear—gaining pleasure through sucking increases the probability that one will get the nourishment one needs for survival. In the second year of life, the focus of pleasure shifts to the anus. During this **anal stage,** pleasure arises from the process of defecation, the passing of feces. From ages 3 through 5, in the **phallic stage,** the genital regions of the body receive the focus of attention. The child obtains intense gratification from self-stimulation of the sexual organs.

Freud believed that children move through these stages for primarily biological reasons. All organisms, including humans, need to learn how to gain nourishment, control the elimination of waste, and satisfy the sexual drive. But these stages can have important and long-lasting implications for personality development because it's possible to become stalled, or fixated, at a particular stage. By *fixation,* Freud meant that a person will continue to act in ways that are appropriate for a particular stage, seeking pleasure in stage-dependent ways, even after he or she has physically matured and gone beyond that stage. There are two primary ways in which the fixation process can occur: first, if the child gains excess gratification from a stage or, second, if the child becomes excessively frustrated. It is the second of these two situations that has received the most attention.

Notice that the oral and anal stages, for example, are associated with the potentially traumatic experiences of weaning and toilet training. Freud placed enormous emphasis on these experiences because a child can become easily frustrated during either event. Individuals who are fixated in the oral stage, Freud believed, continue to derive pleasure from oral activities into adulthood. They become excessive smokers, or overeaters, or people who bite their nails. Fixation at the anal stage might lead to excessive neatness or messiness. The pleasure-seeking activities in these instances are symbolic, of course; compulsive room cleaning might be a symbolic attempt at the gratification a child sometimes receives from the retention of feces. Regardless, Freud would place the origin of such adult behaviors in events that occurred during the first few years of childhood.

Freud's interpretation of the events that surround the phallic stage of psychosexual development was particularly controversial. He was convinced that small children have intense but unconscious sexual urges that become focused during this stage. Such a view was considered outrageous in his time, because the prevailing opinion was that prepubescent children are uninfluenced by the sexual drive. Freud argued that small children not only have erotic tendencies but that they tend to direct those sexual feelings toward the opposite-sex parent. For exam-

Freud believed that people can become "fixated" at a particular psychosexual stage if activities associated with that stage, such as toilet training during the anal stage, are particularly traumatic or frustrating.

Most people reject or deny that they ever harbored sexual feelings toward their opposite-sex parent. If you were Freud, how would you explain these denials?

ple, boys become erotically attracted to their mother, a condition Freud called the *Oedipus complex* (after the Greek tragedy of Oedipus, who unknowingly killed his father and married his mother); girls identify with their father in what has been called the *Electra complex* (after the mythical Greek Electra, who hated and conspired to murder her mother). Desire for the opposite-sex parent creates enormous unconscious conflicts in the developing child that need to be resolved. Freud believed that many adult sexual or relationship problems can be traced back to a failure to resolve these conflicts adequately.

After the age of 5 or 6, boys and girls enter a kind of psychosexual lull—called the **latency period**—during which their sexual feelings are largely suppressed. During this period children direct their attention to social concerns, such as developing solid friendships. Finally, coincident with the onset of puberty, one enters the **genital stage.** Here, sexuality reawakens, but in what Freud considered to be a more direct and appropriate fashion. Erotic tendencies now tend to be directed toward members of the opposite sex.

The Rise of the Neo-Freudians. Freud's intense emphasis on the role of sexuality in personality development was received with skepticism by many, even from those who were firmly committed to his general approach. One of the first to split from Freud's inner circle of disciples was Alfred Adler (1870–1937). Adler disagreed strongly with Freud about the role of early psychosexual experience. He felt that the important determinant of personality development was not childhood trauma but rather how individuals come to deal with a basic sense of *inferiority.* To Adler, personality arises from people's attempts to overcome or compensate for fundamental feelings of inadequacy. Adler was responsible for coining the popular term *inferiority complex,* a concept that he argued underlies and motivates a great deal of human behavior. It is the human's natural drive for superiority that explains motivation, not sexual gratification as envisioned by Freud (Adler, 1927).

Adler was not the only dissenting voice. Others who had been early advocates of Freud's theory began to break away and offer new and revised forms of the theory (hence the term *neo,* or "new" Freudians). One of the biggest personal blows to Freud was the departure of his disciple Carl Jung (1875–1961), whom at one point Freud had picked as his intellectual heir. Jung, like Adler, was dissatisfied with Freud's narrow reliance on sexuality as the dominant source of human motivation. Jung believed instead in the idea of a "general life force," which he adopted from his extensive study of Eastern religions and mythology. This general life force was sexual in part but included other basic sources of motivation as well, such as the need for creativity (Jung, 1923). Among Jung's more influential ideas was his concept of the **collective unconscious.** Jung believed that each person has a shared unconscious, in addition to the personal unconscious described by Freud, that is filled with mystical symbols and universal images that have accumulated over the lifetime of the human species. These symbols are inherited—passed from one generation to the next—and tend to represent enduring concepts (or *archetypes*), such as God, Mother, earth, and water. Actually, the idea that all humans share certain concepts buried deep in a collective unconscious can also be found in the writings of Freud, but Jung expanded on the idea and assigned it a central focus.

Another blow to Freud was the dissenting voice of Karen Horney (1885–1952), one of the first women to learn and practice psychodynamic theory. Although Horney agreed with Freud's basic approach, she rebelled against what she felt was Freud's male-dominated views of sexuality. Freud had argued in his writ-

Carl Jung, shown here, believed that all people share a collective unconscious filled with mystical symbols and universal images.

ings that women are fundamentally dissatisfied with their sex—they suffer from what he called *penis envy*—a view that Horney found unsatisfactory in many ways. She boldly confronted Freud, both personally and in her writings, and offered revised forms of psychodynamic theory that treated women in a more balanced way (Horney, 1967). One of her more lasting theoretical contributions was her insistence that a link exists between the irrational beliefs people hold about themselves and their psychological problems (Horney, 1945). As we'll see in Chapters 14 and 15, this idea continues to be influential in the conceptualization and treatment of psychological disorders.

Karen Horney, pictured here, rebelled against what she felt was Freud's male-dominated views on sexuality.

Current Evaluations of Psychodynamic Theory. Few psychological theories have carried the impact of Freud's. Many of the terms and concepts he introduced—particularly the ideas of unconscious influences and psychological defense mechanisms such as repression—remain solidly entrenched in modern language and beliefs. You were probably familiar with such Freudian terms as *repression, id, ego,* and *projection* before you opened this psychology text. Moreover, the suggestion that personality is determined in part by the manner in which people learn to satisfy basic biological processes, as well as deal effectively with the demands of society and the outside world, is still a very modern and widely accepted idea (Buss, 1991; Revelle, 1995). But psychodynamic theory, as envisioned by Freud, has been steadily losing its influence over the past several decades, for a number of reasons.

Part of the problem is that many of the ideas that Freud proposed lack scientific rigor; he never articulated such concepts as the id, superego, and ego with ringing precision. As a result, it's been difficult, if not impossible, to subject them to proper scientific testing. Consider the concept of repression, which Freud believed to be the bedrock of psychodynamic theory. If repressed memories are hidden behind the veil of the unconscious, expressing themselves only in masked and largely symbolic ways, can we ever be sure that that we have correctly identified and interpreted the source and content of these unconscious influences? Most of the evidence for repression has come from clinical case studies, from individuals who are probably not representative of the general population. Psychologists have been unable to study repression in the laboratory either, because of ethical concerns or because it's unclear what conditions need to be met for repression to occur. Moreover, there are many examples, for instance, of people who have undergone traumatic events in their childhood yet remain psychologically healthy (Loftus, 1993).

Besides the problems of testability and lack of scientific rigor, Freud's theory is often criticized for its biases against women. There is no question that Freud viewed women as the weaker sex psychologically. As mentioned earlier, he painted women as individuals unsatisfied with their gender, who need to come to grips with the fact that they lack a penis. Freud also had a tendency to refuse to believe women's testimonials of rape or childhood sexual abuse—he saw these accounts as symbolic expressions of unconscious conflicts, rather than as actual events. Many modern psychologists consider these positions, along with Freud's general male-oriented approach, to be unrealistic and even distasteful (Masson, 1984; Vitz, 1988).

Do you see why it would be unethical to conduct research on repression with humans? What about with animals? Do you think it would be wise or ethical to create "traumatic experiences" in animals?

Humanistic Approaches to Personality

There is another reason why many psychologists have been dissatisfied with Freud's psychodynamic approach: It paints a dark and dismal view of human nature. In describing the origins of personality, Freud himself often used the apt metaphor of the battlefield, where irrational forces are continuously engaged in a struggle for control over the largely unknowing conscious mind. According to the psychodynamic perspective, human actions are motivated primarily by the need to satisfy animalistic urges related to sex and aggression; people's conscious awareness of why they act is deemed to be misleading and symbolic, representative of conflicts created during toilet training or during the trauma of being weaned from the mother's nipple.

Humanistic psychology is largely a reaction against this pessimistic view of the human spirit. For humanists, the metaphor shifts from battlefields and conflict to fertile ground and supportive striving for growth and potential. It is not the collective animal and its urges that is stressed in explaining personality, it is the *human* with his or her unparalleled capacity for self-awareness, choice, responsibility, and growth. Humanistic psychologists believe that ultimately individuals can control their own behavioral destiny—they can consciously rise above whatever animalistic urges might be coded into their genetic structure. Humans are built and designed for personal growth, to seek their fullest potential, to "self-actualize"—to become all they are capable of becoming.

To a humanist, individual differences in behavior arise from several sources. First, every human being is considered to be naturally *unique,* and a proper analysis of personality requires acceptance of this fact. People are more than the sum of a set of predictable parts—everyone is a unique and individual *whole.* Second, although the environment does not play a pivotal role in humanistic theories, the environment can thwart or nurture the natural growth process. Like plants, people will grow best in fertile and supportive environments; barren environments cannot stop the growth process, but they can prevent the individual from realizing his or her own true potential (Rogers, 1963). Third, and perhaps most important, personal actions are governed by the individual's unique view of the world—his or her interpretation of reality. People's subjective experience of the environment—their *phenomenological experience*—guides and motivates their actions. Notice that the emphasis is on conscious mental processes. Individuals are assumed to be responsible for their own actions, although sometimes our subjective experience of reality is not a very accurate reflection of the world as it really is. We'll consider the views of two prominent humanistic psychologists in this section: Carl Rogers and Abraham Maslow.

Carl Rogers and the Self. To humanist Carl Rogers (1902–1987), the essence of personality is wrapped up in the concept of the "self" or, more specifically, in what he referred to as the *self-concept.* He defined the **self-concept** as an organized set of perceptions about one's abilities and characteristics—it amounts to that keen sense of oneself, what it means to be "I" or "me." This self-concept arises primarily as a product of social interactions, Rogers believed, particularly the interactions that individuals have with their parents, friends, and other significant role models throughout their lifetime. The people around us mold and shape our self-image through their ongoing evaluations of our actions.

People rely on the judgments of others to tell them what they truly are and can hope to become, Rogers argued, because everyone has an ingrained need for **positive regard.** People value what others think of them and consistently seek others' approval, love, and companionship. Unfortunately, in real life **conditions of worth** tend to be attached to the approval of others. For instance, let's suppose that you come from a family that values education and intellectual pursuits. You, however, couldn't care less about such things—your interests are in popular music and athletics. To gain acceptance from your parents, you may well deny or distort your true feelings and modify your self-concept to bring it more in line with what your parents believe: "I'm not someone who cares about a trivial activity like sports, I'm someone who cares intensely about the pursuit of knowledge."

But herein lies a major problem, Rogers argued. The self-concept that individuals work so hard to form inevitably conflicts with what they truly feel from

Carl Rogers proposed that people have an ingrained need for positive regard—we value what others think of us and consistently seek their approval and companionship.

experience. You may decide to spend the evening reading the philosophical musings of Immanuel Kant, but you'll probably find your mind drifting and your feelings of self-worth diminishing. Rogers called this condition **incongruence,** which he defined as a discrepancy between the image people hold of themselves—their self-concept—and the sum of all their experiences. Incongruence leads to the experience of anxiety and ultimately forms the basis for a variety of psychological problems. True psychological health, Rogers suggested, comes when the self-concept is *congruent* (agrees) with a person's true feelings and experiences—that is, when individuals' opinions and beliefs about themselves accurately reflect their everyday experiences. We'll have more to say about what Rogers felt was the appropriate therapeutic solution to conditions of incongruence in Chapter 15. To anticipate the discussion just a bit, Rogers was convinced that the therapist's proper role is to be nonjudgmental—to accept the feelings and actions of the client unconditionally. By eliminating the *conditions of worth,* the idea is to help the client develop a self-concept that is more congruent with reality.

With respect to personality and its development, Rogers saw the key to understanding regularities in behavior as lying largely in the self-concept. People will tend to behave in ways that support their vision of themselves. Personality is defined by consistent behavior across situations; people tend to act consistently, Rogers believed, simply because their actions consistently mirror the established self-concept. Individuals act in ways that support rather than contradict their beliefs about themselves. More often than not, people will actively seek to protect their self-image. Given a choice, you might consistently choose to read philosophy rather than watch television because it's consistent with your vision of *you.* If you choose television, you would need to reconsider who you really are, which is the sort of confrontation that people will tend to avoid.

Think about how good it can make you feel to talk to a really close friend. From the perspective of Rogers's theory, why do you think this is the case?

Abraham Maslow and Self-Actualization. Although Carl Rogers was committed to the role played by the self-concept, he also believed strongly in the potential for personal growth. Individuals may act defensively and seek to protect a relatively rigid self-concept, but at their core they are all creative people who have the power to fulfill their personal potential. This idea that everyone has a basic need for **self-actualization**—the need to move forward toward the realization of potential—also plays a pivotal role in Abraham Maslow's view of personality.

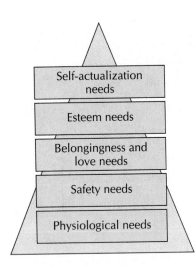

FIGURE 12.7
Maslow's Hierarchy of Needs.
Maslow proposed that an individual's observable personality characteristics will reflect where he or she is positioned in the hierarchy of needs. Someone who must worry constantly about biological or safety needs will act differently from someone who is seeking to satisfy needs at the highest levels of the pyramid.

You may remember that we encountered Maslow's views once before, in Chapter 11, when we discussed motivation. Maslow believed that human motivation is grounded in the satisfaction of *need*. There are certain things that humans *must* do, such as obtain food and water and protect themselves from danger, before the full expression of their potential can be realized. As we saw in Chapter 11, one of Maslow's main contributions was his proposal of the *need hierarchy,* shown in Figure 12.7, which expresses the order or priority with which needs must be satisfied. For example, notice that safety and survival needs sit below the need for love and belonging in the need hierarchy. It is unlikely that people will appear to the world as spiritual, loving individuals if they are constantly worrying about their next meal or whether they will be eaten by an approaching predator. It is only after the basic needs are satisfied—those related to survival—that the more spiritual side of the personality can be developed.

A particular individual's personality characteristics will reflect where he or she is positioned in the hierarchy of needs. Maslow was convinced that all people are inherently good; a person may consistently act unkind, defensive, or aggressive, but these personality traits arise from the failure to satisfy basic needs—they will never be fundamental to the human spirit. To back up this claim, Maslow pointed to the behavior of individuals who he felt had progressed through the entire hierarchy. The characteristics of human personality, he argued, turn out to be highly consistent across individuals at the highest levels of the hierarchy. People who are self-actualizing show none of the darker personality traits exhibited by those locked in at lower levels; they tend to be positive, creative, accepting individuals.

Maslow's conclusions were based largely on the study of particular individuals, people whom he knew and admired. He also noted the personality traits of individuals who had reached the pinnacle of success, such as Albert Einstein, Abraham Lincoln, and Eleanor Roosevelt. All self-actualizing people, he argued, share certain personality traits. They tend to be accepting of themselves and others, to be self-motivated and problem oriented, and to have a strong ethical sense and hold democratic values. Self-actualizing people also often undergo what Maslow called "peak experiences"—emotional, often religious, experiences in which one's place in a unified universe becomes clear and meaningful. Notice that these are all quite positive traits; self-actualizing people tend to be at peace with themselves and with the world that surrounds them.

A Critique of the Humanistic Approach. There is no question that the humanistic approach, with its optimistic emphasis on positive growth, has exerted considerable influence in psychology. Concepts such as the *self* are now receiving a great deal of attention among researchers (see the Adaptive Mind section at the close of this chapter), and, as we'll see in Chapter 15, humanistic approaches to psychotherapy are popular and widely applied. The humanistic approach provides a nice balance to the pessimism of Freud. Rather than ignoring the conscious influences on behavior, humanists champion personal choice and responsibility. Take a trip to your local bookstore and check the shelves devoted to psychology—you're going to find that many of the books emphasize the control *you* can exert over your own behavior. This is one indication of the humanists' widespread impact, especially in tapping the general population's interest in psychology.

But as contributors to scientific psychology, humanistic psychologists are often criticized. Many of the fundamental concepts that we've discussed, such as the potential for growth and self-actualizing tendencies, are vague and difficult to pin down. It's also not clear where these tendencies come from and under which conditions they will fully express themselves. Remember, too, that the humanists place important emphasis on personal, subjective experience. This means that researchers must often rely on self-reports by individuals to generate data, and we cannot always be sure that these reports are reliable and accurate representations of internal psychological processes. So in addition to problems of conceptual vagueness, humanism lacks adequate testability.

The humanistic approach to personality is also criticized for adopting too optimistic a view of human nature. In part, the arguments of humanists like Rogers and Maslow are reactions against the pessimism of Freud. But like Freud, humanistic theorists have adopted a rather extreme view of human nature, albeit one that is the opposite of Freud's. People are basically good, unless constrained in some way by social "conditions of worth," and are driven to pursue lofty goals. Thus, we have the dark view exposed by Freud (people are all driven by unconscious animalistic urges) countered by the extremely optimistic convictions of the humanists. Many psychologists believe that it's probably better to adopt a more balanced approach: People are neither inherently good nor evil; they sometimes act in self-interested ways that may appear animalistic, but these actions are often adaptive and increase one's likelihood of survival. At the same time, too much emphasis on unconscious genetic or biological motives is itself misleading—humans undoubtedly exercise considerable conscious control over their behavior.

Cognitive-Behavioral Approaches to Personality

One particularly important characteristic of both the psychodynamic and humanistic approaches to personality is their emphasis on built-in determinants of behavior. People are born with animalistic urges that must be satisfied, or they greet the world naturally good with a compelling need for personal growth. The environment plays a critical role in determining one's final "personality," but the role is essentially secondary—personal experiences and cultural norms merely constrain or enhance the full expression of natural needs.

But what about the possibility that people simply *learn* to act in consistent ways that differentiate them from others? Isn't it possible that Roger's nasty proclivity toward lying and Rowena's outgoing and sunny disposition arise entirely from experience? Maybe Roger stole candy when he was 4 and was rewarded by not being caught; maybe Rowena learned at an early age that smiles are often met with smiles and that a good deed can be returned in kind. According to **cognitive-behavioral theories** of personality, human experience, not human nature, is the primary determinant of personality growth and development. The *behavioral* side of the approach emphasizes the actual experiences delivered by the environment; the *cognitive* side emphasizes how interpretations and expectations about the events people experience play a significant role in determining what they learn.

The Environment's Role: Rewards, Punishments, and Models.
An exclusively behavioral approach to personality development would propose that it is the outside world, alone, that drives people's actions. As we discussed in Chapter 1, behaviorists believe that the only proper province for psychologists is the analysis of *observable* behavior; the research goal is to understand how observable behavior changes systematically after the application of rewards and punishments. Personality, then, might really be nothing more than the collective responses that people have learned to produce in various situations. As with all other animals, if their behavior is rewarded in a particular situation, individuals will be more likely to perform that behavior again the next time they encounter the same situation.

There are three main ways that people could acquire situation-specific response tendencies (see Chapter 7). First, through *classical conditioning,* individuals learn that certain kinds of events signal other events. Imagine that as a small child little Albert is frightened in the presence of a white furry rat; he develops a specific fear, or phobia, of small furry animals that continues on into adulthood.

His behavior is consistent and regular over time—he panics at the sight of anything small and furry—due in large part to this early childhood experience. Second, through *instrumental conditioning,* people learn about the consequences of their behavior. If they are rewarded in some context for acting aggressively, they will tend to act aggressively in the future. If individuals are repeatedly put down at parties for acting outgoing, they will learn to be withdrawn and to avoid social situations. Here it is the environment alone—one's past history of rewards and punishments—that is shaping behavior.

The third way that regularities in behavior can develop is through observational learning, or *modeling.* People observe the behavior of others around them—especially role models—and imitate the models' behavior. As we discussed in Chapter 7, it's adaptive for organisms to mimic the behavior of others, because in this way they can learn appropriate behavior without directly experiencing the consequences of an inappropriate action. Rhesus monkeys, for example, learn to show fear in the presence of snakes through modeling their parents' behavior, not from directly experiencing the negative consequences of a bite (Mineka, 1987). According to **social learning theory,** many important personality traits come from copying the behavior of others, especially when the behavior of the model regularly leads to positive, reinforcing outcomes (Bandura, 1986; Mischel, 1968).

The Role of the Mind: Expectations and Cognitions.

But very few psychologists actually believe that the environment *alone* determines personality growth. The reason is that the psychological effect of most experiences—positive or negative—depends crucially on the expectations and beliefs that a person holds about the experience. For example, suppose we ask two groups of people to perform a relatively difficult task, such as predicting sequences of numbers. We tell one of the groups that performance on the task is based on skill, and the other group is told that success or failure is due entirely to chance. (Unknown to the participants, we actually rig the procedure so that people in both groups will succeed and fail the same number of times.) What we'll find in such a situation is that task effort, as well as the amount that is learned, depends on how much control a person thinks he or she has over the outcome. That is, people who believe that their performance is skill-based work harder and learn more from the task (Rotter, Liverant, & Crowne, 1961).

The important point here is that the groups perform differently even though everyone receives exactly the same number of rewards and punishments. So it is not the literal distribution of rewards and punishments that matters; one's *beliefs* about the origins of those consequences are equally important. Some psychologists have suggested that people acquire enduring personality traits based on their perceived **locus of control**—how much control they feel they can actually exert over their environment (Rotter, 1966). People who are oriented externally, known as *externals,* perceive little connection between their own actions and the occurrence of rewards; such people tend to see themselves as powerless and generally have low levels of self-esteem (Lefcourt, 1982). On the other hand, internally oriented individuals *(internals)* view the world as fundamentally responsive to their actions; they feel confident that they can control the occurrence of rewards and punishment. Internally oriented people display high levels of self-confidence and tend to score higher than externally oriented individuals on a variety of academic and social indices (see Ryckman, 1993).

The concept of locus of control is related to another psychological concept, **self-efficacy** (Bandura, 1986, 1993). Whereas locus of control refers to people's beliefs about how much control they can exert over the environment, self-efficacy is defined as the beliefs that people hold about their own ability. For example, Albert might be convinced that people can control their environment but feel that he personally lacks the skill. In this case, he would be rated as low in self-efficacy,

Carla receives an A in her psychology class but attributes it to the fact that her instructor is easy. Does she have an internal or external locus of control, and how confident do you think she is in her own abilities?

The way people act and feel often depends on how much control they think they have over their environment. Externals, who perceive little connection between their own actions and the occurrence of rewards, tend to see themselves as powerless and possess low levels of self-esteem.

with an internal locus of control. On the other hand, he might be extremely confident in his basic abilities (high self-efficacy) but believe that he can do little to control the things around him (external locus of control). Often a person's degree of self-efficacy is related to particular situations or tasks. You might believe strongly in your ability to excel academically but lack any measure of confidence in your social skills.

Concepts such as locus of control and self-efficacy are important because they indicate that what people learn from the environment depends on more than just the delivery of rewards and punishments. Expectations and beliefs about the world and one's abilities influence the types of tasks one will choose to engage in, as well as the effectiveness of rewards and punishments. If you're convinced you have little or no ability in social settings—your self-efficacy is low—you will either tend to avoid going to parties or act nervous and uncomfortable if you do go. If you feel you have no chance of succeeding in your psychology course because the teaching assistant doesn't like you—that is, you've adopted an external locus of control—your motivation to work hard is likely to be low. Note that in these cases your internal beliefs end up affecting your overt behavior (avoidance of parties or class), which in turn affects the likelihood that you will either receive or be exposed to potential rewards. Psychologist Albert Bandura (1986) has referred to this relationship between beliefs, overt behavior, and the environment as one of **reciprocal determinism:** beliefs, behavior, and the environment interact to shape what is learned from experience (see Figure 12.8).

Critiques of the Cognitive-Behavioral Approach. All psychologists recognize that behavior is importantly influenced by what one learns from the environment. Thus, the idea that at least some personality traits might be learned is not considered controversial. Furthermore, the idea that cognitive factors are involved in learning, in the form of expectations and beliefs, has also gained relatively wide acceptance. Critics of the cognitive-behavioral approach simply argue that it is insufficient as a general account of personality development (Feist, 1994; Ryckman, 1993). Cognitive-behavioral theory, for example, tends to neglect the individual as a *whole,* choosing instead to concentrate on how people have learned to respond in particular situations. The approach has been criticized as well for fail-

FIGURE 12.8
Reciprocal Determinism.
Bandura proposed that personality is shaped by complex interactions among expectations and beliefs, behavior, and the rewards and punishments delivered by the environment. In this case, the expectation of failure in class (personal/cognitive factors) affects studying (behavior), which in turn affects the likelihood of success on the test (environment). Note that the arrows point both ways, suggesting that these factors can interact in a complex manner.

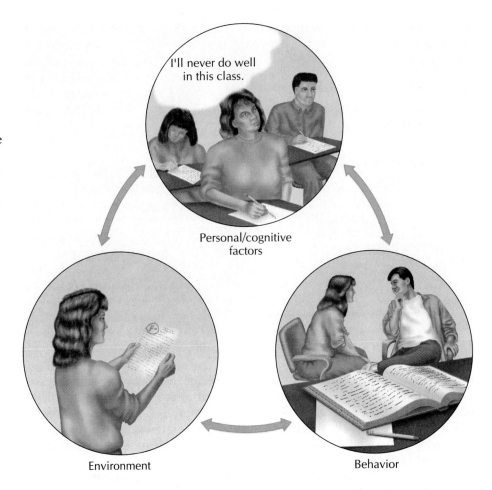

Personal/cognitive
factors

Environment

Behavior

ing to emphasize adequately the role of biological and genetic factors in development. Perhaps ingrained drives and urges are not the primary determinants of personality, but biological ancestry cannot be ignored completely. By choosing to focus primarily on the environment, the cognitive-behaviorists sometimes ignore potentially important motivational factors that are controlled largely by biological processes.

Resolving the Person-Situation Debate

In some sense, the cognitive-behavioral approach characterizes the individual in a piecemeal fashion. According to this perspective, behavior is primarily the product of the environment, and as a result, people might be expected to behave somewhat inconsistently from one situation to the next. If you are rewarded for acting bold and aggressive when negotiating a deal (such as buying a car), you will almost certainly act bold and aggressive in such situations in the future. But if similar actions lead to rejection in the classroom or in social situations, you might very well turn meek and mild in those situations in the future. If you think about it, don't you know people who seem to change their behavior at the drop of a hat, acting one way in one situation and quite differently in another?

However, this kind of reasoning really strikes at the core of what personality is all about. Remember, personality is defined in terms of enduring qualities—distinguishing patterns of characteristics that differentiate us from others and lead us to act *consistently* from one situation to the next. Throughout this chapter, we've assumed that such qualities exist and that they can be measured and interpreted through the application of psychological principles. But the assumption of cross-situational consistency in behavior has been challenged by some prominent psychologists, notably Walter Mischel, and the issue has come to be known as the **person-situation debate.**

The Person-Situation Debate

The argument is really a simple one. If people possess unique and enduring personality traits, we should be able to predict their behavior from one situation to the next. If we believe Roger to be dishonest, perhaps because we witnessed him peering over Rowena's shoulder during a history test, we expect him to be dishonest in the future. We predict that he will pocket a fallen wallet, or at least take the money that Rowena left lying on the counter. Put more technically, measurements of overt behavior should *correlate* across situations; that is, given that we know the likelihood of someone performing a trait-related action in Situation A, we should be able to predict the likelihood of the person performing an action related to the same trait in Situation B.

Unfortunately, as Walter Mischel (1968) pointed out in a highly influential review of the research literature, there is little evidence for this assumption (see also Peterson, 1968). If we look carefully at studies reporting correlations between measures of behavior that tap a particular kind of personality trait (such as honesty), the correlations are virtually always low. Whereas a correlation of 1.00 implies perfect behavioral consistency across situations, Mischel found that actual correlations rarely exceeded 0.30 and were usually quite a bit lower (see also Kenrick & Funder, 1988; Ross & Nisbett, 1991). To say the least, Mischel's conclusions were quite controversial; in fact, they rocked the foundation of personality theory, because without consistency in behavior, the psychological construct of personality has little meaning.

Actually, very few psychologists (including Mischel) ended up rejecting personality altogether as a viable psychological construct. Although people may not always act consistently *across* diverse situations, they do tend to act consistently *within* a situation. For example, in a famous study by Hartshorne and May (1928), the honesty of schoolchildren was tested by placing them in situations in which they could act dishonestly without much likelihood of being caught (money was left on a table; cheating on a test was possible, and so on). Little evidence of cross-situational consistency was found, but the children did tend to act the same way in a similar situation. For instance, kids who cheated on a test were not necessarily more likely to steal money, but they were more likely to cheat on a test again if given the chance. In short, people do act consistently from one situation to the next, as long as the situations are similar (Mischel & Peake, 1982; Mischel & Shoda, 1995). This is exactly the type of finding that you would expect if people are simply learning specific kinds of actions in particular circumstances. So the evidence for within but not across situational consistency is often used to support cognitive-behavioral approaches to personality development.

Other psychologists have pointed out that low cross-situational correlations, by themselves, can be misleading. Data of the type reported by Hartshorne and May and others (see Mischel, 1968) have been based primarily on the observation of single individual behaviors (did the child steal the money on the table?) rather than on collections of behaviors. To get an accurate estimate of a true personality trait, we should probably collect lots of observations, not just one; single observations tend to be unreliable and not necessarily representative of true behavior

(Epstein, 1979). One reason that reliable personality traits are measured by the paper-and-pencil tests of the trait theorists (see our earlier discussion) might be because the collected ratings are based on a long history of watching oneself or others behave (Ross & Nisbett, 1991).

Moreover, the tendency to act consistently or haphazardly across different situations may itself be a kind of personality trait. There is some evidence to suggest that people differ in the extent to which they engage in chameleon-like **self-monitoring** (Snyder, 1974, 1987). People who are high self-monitors attend closely to the situation at hand and change their behavior to best fit their needs. These are people who are likely to alter their behavior, and even their stated opinions and beliefs, simply to please someone with whom they are currently interacting. People who are low self-monitors are less likely to change their actions or beliefs and therefore are more likely to show consistency in their behavior across diverse situations (Gangestad & Snyder, 1985).

Currently, most psychologists resolve the person-situation debate by simply assuming that it is necessary to take both the person and the situation into account. It is unlikely that either alone, the person or the situation, is going to explain behavior or allow us to predict consistency. People *interact* with situations, and the expression of enduring qualities or traits will depend partly on what's required by current needs. Personality traits will tend to reveal themselves primarily in situations in which they are relevant (Kenrick and others, 1990) and may not otherwise (see the accompanying Inside the Problem). Similarly, given the right situational demands, individuals can act in ways that may appear to violate their basic nature. We'll return to this issue, and provide some compelling illustrations of the power of the situation, when we take up the general topic of social psychology in Chapter 13.

Genetic Factors in Personality

There is another kind of evidence that can be used to confirm personality as an important and valid characteristic of the adaptive mind. In recent years, evidence has accumulated suggesting that there may be ingrained *genetic* reasons why individuals display unique and enduring traits. People may be born with certain genetic predispositions—perhaps their brains are wired in a certain way—that compel them to act in an idiosyncratic and regular fashion throughout their lifetime. Certainly it is not unusual for family members to show similar personality traits, although experience could play an important role in producing these similarities. At the same time, as we all know, siblings (brothers/sisters) can show strikingly different personality traits, even though they have been raised under what seem to be highly similar environmental conditions. Observations like these appear to indicate that more may be at work in determining personality than the environment.

As in the study of intelligence, most of the evidence for genetic factors in personality comes from twin studies. Identical twins, who share virtually the same genetic structure, are compared with fraternal twins, who share some but not complete genetic overlap, under circumstances in which the twins have been reared together or apart. Perhaps you've seen reports in the popular media of identical twins who were separated at birth but ended up sharing many of the same personality traits. There is the case of identical twins Oscar and Frank—one raised as a Nazi in Czechoslovakia and the other as a Jew in Trinidad. When they were reunited in 1979, it was discovered that they shared numerous odd but regular behaviors. For example, they both had a habit of sneezing deliberately in elevators to surprise people, and they both liked to flush toilets before and after use.

Successful politicians are often high self-monitors, which means they attend closely to the situation and change their behavior accordingly.

We've seen that the consistency of behavior across situations depends on an interaction between the characteristics of the person and the specifics of the situation. Personality "traits" may only reveal themselves in contexts in which those traits are relevant, and not otherwise. Such a conclusion implies, however, that the traditional trait approach—which seeks to find personality characteristics that cut across situations—may be limited in some important ways. It may not be possible to talk about someone's personality "traits" without also considering the particular tasks or problems that the person is currently trying to solve.

According to psychologist Nancy Cantor and her colleagues, rather than thinking about personality as something that a person "has," we should think about personality as something that a person "does" (Cantor, 1990; Cantor & Harlow, 1994). Each person approaches life with a unique set of goals, or personal strivings. Individuals differ in the things that are important to them and in their own personal agenda for accomplishment. Roger may be concerned with accumulating wealth and fame; Rowena may be seeking to master her interpersonal skills, whether to meet new people or to help others. To solve these problems, or "life tasks," individuals use strategies or characteristic ways of responding that help them meet the challenges that arise (Cantor & Harlow, 1994). The strategies they adopt may cause them to act consistently, but only to the extent that the goal is met, or the problem resolved.

The important point to remember is that we cannot understand a person's "personality" without considering these strategies for solving life tasks. Cantor and her colleagues have found that students in academic settings often adopt quite different strategies to cope with the

How students cope with the problem of performing well in school depends on the type of "life task" strategy that they adopt.

same task, such as performing well in school. Some students adopt "pessimistic" strategies, in which they ignore past accomplishments and consistently report low expectations for success on assignments and exams; pessimists spend an inordinate amount of time thinking and worrying about their academic performance. Other students are optimists, which means they set high expectations for themselves and try not to worry or dwell on negative thoughts. But surprisingly, Cantor has found that these two types of students often perform equally well on exams. They simply have different strategies for meeting the same end. The pessimists are able to confront their anxieties effectively by dwelling on the possibility of failure, whereas the optimists prepare better by accentuating the positive. The pessimists and the optimists seem to have different "personalities," but those special charac-

teristics may have arisen simply as a result of the strategies they've adopted to solve a particular life task.

Two final points. First, this view of personality predicts that if someone's personal "life tasks" change, he or she may well adopt new strategies that will affect how he or she behaves. Thus, an individual's personal actions could appear to change, or be inconsistent, across situations, but only because he or she is trying to solve a different kind of problem. Second, this "problem-solving" description of personality also predicts that individuals from different cultures or social groups may appear to possess unique personality traits. As the problems of a culture change, so, too, should the strategies that its people adopt. We'll have more to say about the relationship between culture and the individual in Chapter 13.

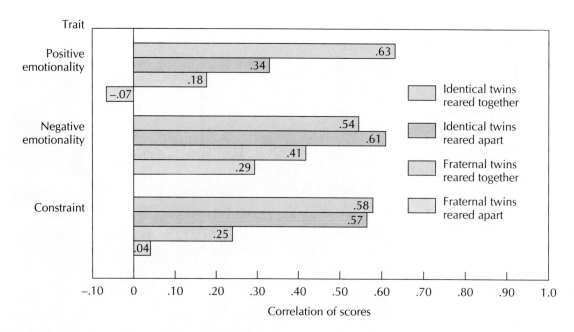

FIGURE 12.9

The Genetics of Personality. Are identical twins more likely to share basic personality traits than fraternal twins? Does the rearing environment matter? These average correlations from the Tellegen and colleagues (1988) study reveal consistent differences between identical and fraternal twins, irrespective of the rearing environment, suggesting that genetics plays a role in determining personality. The environment also had a significant effect in some cases, but overall it appeared to play a less important role. (Adapted from Tellegren et al., 1988)

However, reports like these do not make a convincing scientific case (Horgan, 1993). Coincidences are possible, and there are indications that some of the more famous reunited twins may have had ulterior motives for manufacturing shared idiosyncrasies (for example, Oscar and his brother eventually sold the rights to their "story" in Hollywood). More compelling evidence comes from group studies, in which the personality characteristics of large numbers of twins are systematically analyzed. In one such study (Tellegen et al., 1988), 217 pairs of identical twins who had been reared together and 44 pairs of twins who had been reared apart were compared with 114 pairs of fraternal twins reared together and 27 pairs reared apart. Each of the participants was administered the MMPI, which, as we discussed earlier, is a widely used questionnaire designed to measure a variety of personality traits.

Some of the results of this study are shown in Figure 12.9, for several of the personality traits measured by the MMPI. Of main interest is the similarity between members of a twin pair, expressed in terms of correlation coefficients. In other words, for a trait such as aggressiveness or positive emotionality, can we predict the score that one twin will receive on the MMPI if we know the score of the other twin? Correlations that are close to 1.00 suggest that members of a twin pair share many of the same personality traits. As the figure indicates, identical twins tend to show higher correlations than fraternal twins, regardless of whether they have been reared in the same or different environments. Twins who share the same genes but have been reared in different households tend to have more similar personality traits than fraternal twins who have been reared together.

Data like these have convinced many psychologists that at least some enduring psychological traits have their origins in genetic predispositions present at birth. Of course, as we discussed in the chapter on intelligence, the expression of genetic tendencies depends on the nurturing conditions (the environment): Nature interacts with nurture in determining a person's final physical and psychological makeup. Therefore, although genes may play a critical role in determining how personality develops, environmental factors cannot be neglected.

◣ SOLVING THE PROBLEMS: A SUMMARY

There is little question in most people's minds about the status of a concept like personality—anyone will tell you that people differ in enduring ways. All individuals have behavioral quirks that differentiate them from others, and people at least give the impression of acting relatively consistently across situations. If asked, people have little trouble making judgments about the personality of others. We quickly and without hesitation identify Rowena as friendly and outgoing and Roger as nasty and generally no good. Moreover, as discussed at the outset of this chapter, it makes adaptive sense for people to act consistently, especially when particular actions help them to survive and live productive lives. Thus, personality is clearly an important and useful feature of the adaptive mind.

To psychologists, however, the study of personality has proven to be a difficult and elusive enterprise. Historically, researchers have disagreed about how to best approach the topic. As we've seen, questions have even been raised about the validity of the concept itself—how useful is a concept such as personality in describing individual differences in behavior? (Remember, similar issues were raised about the study of intelligence.) Still, the vast majority of psychologists agree that the concept of personality is needed to describe the full range of human psychological functioning. Personality is indeed something to be studied, and understanding it is a conceptual as well as practical problem to be solved by the psychological community.

▶ CONCEPTUALIZING AND MEASURING PERSONALITY

Trait theories are formal systems for measuring and identifying personality characteristics, such as emotional stability or extroversion. Currently, the trait theorists seem to agree that there are five basic personality dimensions—the so-called Big Five (extroversion, agreeableness, conscientiousness, neuroticism, and openness)—that accurately and reliably describe a person's unique and consistent attributes. Psychometric techniques such as factor analysis, along with the development of personality tests such as the NEO-PI-R and the MMPI, have proven useful in advancing theory and in applying what we've learned about personality to practical settings. For example, the MMPI is sometimes used in business settings as part of the decision-making process for hiring new employees.

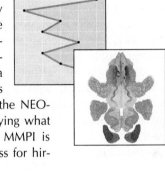

▶ DETERMINING HOW PERSONALITY DEVELOPS
Identifying stable personality traits, however, leaves unanswered the general question of how those traits originate. Noted psychologists have developed several "grand" theories of personality development, including the psychodynamic approach of Freud, the humanistic perspective of Rogers and Maslow, and the cognitive-behavioral approach of Bandura, Mischel, and others. These theoretical frameworks propose very different mechanisms for personality development and offer quite different conceptions of basic human nature. The pessimism of Freud, with his emphasis on battling unconscious biological urges, is counterbalanced by the optimism of the humanists. To the cognitive-behaviorists, the environment and beliefs about controlling that environment underlie the consistent actions that define personality. Each of these perspectives has been enormously influential in the past and remains so today.

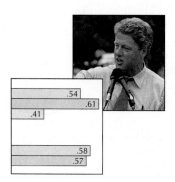

> **RESOLVING THE PERSON-SITUATION DEBATE** The concept of personality demands at least some consistency in behavior across situations. But some evidence suggests that cross-situational consistency in behavior may be low. In light of the person-situation debate, a proper analysis of behavior requires consideration of the interaction between the person and the situation. We must also keep in mind the contribution of genetics to personality stability—twin studies indicate that there may be a genetic component to enduring behavior.

Terms to Remember

personality The distinguishing pattern of psychological characteristics—thinking, feeling, and behaving—that differentiates us from others and leads us to act consistently across situations.

trait A stable predisposition to act or behave in a certain way.

CONCEPTUALIZING AND MEASURING PERSONALITY

trait theories Formal systems for assessing how people differ, particularly in their predispositions to respond in certain ways across situations. Most trait theories rely on psychometric tests to identify stable individual differences among people.

Big Five The five dimensions of personality—extroversion, agreeableness, conscientiousness, neuroticism, and openness—that have been isolated through the application of factor analysis; it is widely believed that virtually all personality terms in language can be accounted for by appealing to one or more of these basic dimensions.

cardinal traits Allport's term to describe personality traits that dominate an individual's life, such as a passion to serve others or to accumulate wealth.

central traits Allport's term to describe the five to ten descriptive traits that you would use to describe someone you know—friendly, trustworthy, and so on.

secondary traits The less obvious characteristics of an individual's personality that do not always appear in his or her behavior, such as testiness when on a diet.

self-report inventories Personality tests in which people answer groups of questions about how they typically think, act, and feel; their responses, or self-reports, are then compared to average responses compiled from large groups of prior test takers.

16 Personality Factor A self-report inventory developed by Cattell and colleagues to measure normal personality traits.

NEO-PI-R A self-report inventory developed to measure the Big Five personality dimensions.

Minnesota Multiphasic Personality Inventory (MMPI) A widely used self-report inventory for assessing personality traits and for diagnosing psychological problems.

projective test A type of personality test in which individuals are asked to interpret unstructured or ambiguous stimuli; the idea is that subjects will "project" their true thoughts and feelings into the interpretation, thereby revealing elements of their personality.

DETERMINING HOW PERSONALITY DEVELOPS

psychodynamic theory An approach to personality development based largely on the ideas of Sigmund Freud and holding that much of behavior is governed by unconscious forces.

conscious mind The contents of awareness—those things that occupy the focus of one's current attention.

preconscious mind The part of the mind that contains all of the inactive but potentially accessible thoughts and memories.

unconscious mind The part of the mind that Freud believed housed all the memories, urges, and conflicts that are truly beyond awareness.

id In Freud's theory, the portion of personality that is governed by inborn instinctual drives, particularly those related to sex and aggression.

superego In Freud's theory, the portion of personality that motivates people to act in an ideal fashion, in accordance with the moral customs defined by parents and culture.

ego In Freud's theory, the portion of personality that induces people to act with reason and deliberation and helps them conform to the requirements of the external world.

defense mechanisms According to Freud, unconscious processes that the ego uses to ward off the anxiety that comes from confrontation, usually with the demands of the id.

repression A defense mechanism used to bury anxiety-producing thoughts and feelings in the unconscious.

projection A defense mechanism in which unacceptable feelings or wishes are dealt with by attributing them to others.

reaction formation A defense mechanism used to transform an anxiety-producing wish into a kind of opposite—people behave in a way that counters the way they truly feel.

sublimation A defense mechanism used to channel unacceptable impulses into socially acceptable activities.

oral stage The first stage in Freud's conception of psychosexual development, occurring in the first year of life; in this stage, pleasure is derived primarily from sucking and placing things in the mouth.

anal stage Freud's second stage of psychosexual development, occurring in the second year of life; pleasure is derived from the process of defecation.

phallic stage Freud's third stage of psychosexual development, lasting from about age 3 to age 5; pleasure is gained from self-stimulation of the sexual organs.

latency period Freud's period of psychosexual development, from age 5 to puberty, during which the child's sexual feelings are largely suppressed.

genital stage Freud's final stage of psychosexual development, during which one develops mature sexual relationships with members of the opposite sex.

collective unconscious The notion proposed by Carl Jung that certain kinds of universal symbols and ideas are present in the unconscious of all people.

humanistic psychology An approach to personality that focuses on people's unique capacity for choice, responsibility, and growth.

self-concept An organized set of perceptions that one holds about one's abilities and characteristics.

positive regard The idea that individuals value what others think of them and constantly seek others' approval, love, and companionship.

conditions of worth The expectations or standards that people believe others place on them.

incongruence A discrepancy between the image people hold of themselves—their self-concept—and the sum of all their experiences.

self-actualization The ingrained desire to reach one's true potential as a human being.

cognitive-behaviorial theories An approach to personality that suggests it is human experiences, and interpretations of those experiences, that determine personality growth and development.

social learning theory The idea that most important personality traits come from modeling, or copying, the behavior of others.

locus of control The amount of control that a person feels he or she has over the environment.

self-efficacy The beliefs that we hold about our own ability to perform a task or accomplish a goal.

reciprocal determinism The idea that beliefs, behavior, and the environment interact to shape what is learned from experience.

RESOLVING THE PERSON-SITUATION DEBATE

person-situation debate A controversial debate centering on whether people really do behave consistently across situations.

self-monitoring The degree to which a person monitors a situation closely and changes his or her behavior accordingly; people who are high self-monitors may not behave consistently across situations.

By consuming his mysterious potion of salts and other wholesale chemicals, Dr. Henry Jekyll was able to quite literally get in touch with the dark side of his nature. Hyde emerged as a new personality, one with unique characteristics that were certainly different from Jekyll's, and actions that were consistent across situations. If psychologists could have administered a personality test like the MMPI to Jekyll before and after his transformation, they would undoubtedly have detected very different personality profiles for pre-potion Jekyll and after-potion Hyde. To the author of the novel, these multiple personalities were not created by the potion itself; rather, the chemical mixture simply helped a hidden side of Jekyll's nature gain physical as well as psychological control of the body.

Compelling fiction, to be sure. Certainly no such potion exists, and the idea that people could instantaneously transform their bodies into a different form defies what is currently known about biological systems. But the idea that individuals are in some sense many different kinds of people—that each person may have multiple internal "selves"—is actually an enduring idea in the history of psychology, dating back at least to the 19th century and the work of William James (Kihlstrom & Cantor, 1984; Linville & Carlston, 1994; Wyer & Srull, 1989). As we'll see in Chapter 14, there is even a rare psychological disorder, called dissociative identity disorder, in which people can show rapid transitions among relatively complete and different personalities—perhaps changing from a shy and retiring introvert to an outgoing and provocative extrovert.

The concept of personality itself is intimately tied to the concept of the self, which we defined earlier as an organized set of perceptions about one's abilities and characteristics. To get some idea of what it means to have multiple selves, consider the different roles that you regularly play in your life. Don't you think and act in particular ways in your role as a son or daughter, student, worker, employee, lover, and friend? Consider the consistency of your actions in these situations. There are certainly things that you would never say in your role as a student or employee; you also have relatively well-defined expectations about your abilities as a lover or friend that you would never expect to transfer to your "student self" or "worker self." It turns out that these different senses of self importantly determine not only how people act, but the kinds of things they pay attention to, what inferences they draw about things, and what they remember (Greenwald & Pratkanis, 1984; Kihlstrom & Cantor, 1984; Markus & Nurius, 1986).

Self-Schemas

Psychologists refer to these multiple senses of self as *self-schemas*. Self-schemas are organized knowledge packages that people carry around in their heads to help them interpret the present, reconstruct the past, and motivate and guide their actions (Markus, 1977). Each of the various identities that individuals may have—daughter, father, boss, worker, wife, husband, woman, man—is thought to be associated with a particular self-schema that guides how environmental situations are interpreted and dictates what behaviors will emerge (Linville & Carlston, 1994). If people are asked to make predictions or judgments about trait words that are consistent or inconsistent with one of their self-schemas (independent, cooperative, and so on), they react quicker and are more confident about words that are consistent with the schema. For example, if you think of yourself as an "independent person," you react more quickly to a word such as *individualistic* than to a word such as *cooperative* (Markus, 1977). You will also be able to retrieve more examples of behavior that are consistent with one of your "identities," and you will show some resistance to evidence that is contrary to your self-schema (Linville & Carlston, 1994).

There is even evidence to suggest that people carry around identities that are locked in the past, as well as possible selves that may occur in the future. Perhaps you still have an identity from several years ago of an "irresponsible self," before you got your act together and seriously committed yourself to your studies. You almost certainly have identities from childhood—the "child self"—that remain inactive most of the time but may emerge during holiday visits home. You even have relatively well-defined self-schemas about how you are likely to act in the future. For example, Markus and Nurius (1986) asked college students to rate whether certain descriptions fit them now or might fit them in the future. These descriptions could involve such things as general abilities (cooking well), lifestyle possibilities (having an active social life), even future occupations (Supreme Court justice or janitor). The results indicated that people were quite likely to view themselves in terms of well-defined *possible* selves. Whereas fewer than half the respondents viewed themselves as someone who traveled widely, for example, well over 90% saw this as a viable future identity. (By the way, you are much more likely to see yourself as a media personality or as an owner of a successful business than as a janitor or a prison guard.)

The Adaptive Value

From the perspective of the adaptive mind, what's the value of these multiple past, present, and future selves? Does the act of compartmentalizing one's identities in any way help solve problems or increase the likelihood of successful adaptive behavior? Most psychologists believe so. First, well-defined self-schemas can help a person understand his or her own behavior. Each separate identity provides an interpretative framework that allows us to understand past, present, and even future actions. Remember, we've already seen how these schemas can affect the way people process information and remem-

People commonly adopt different roles, and employ unique "self-schemas," in the various situations of life.

ber things. Second, self-schemas may play a critical role in regulating actions. People's particular beliefs about themselves can promote consistent actions—if Rowena knows the proper set of behaviors for a "good student" identity, this knowledge can guide and motivate her to act in ways that are consistent with the schema.

Finally, the establishment of multiple selves in the form of self-schemas may actually provide people with a kind of psychological self-protection. People who report having a complex and diverse sense of self tend to respond more effectively in diverse contexts, and they seem to display lower levels of stress (Linville, 1985, 1987). For example, if you define yourself entirely in terms of one self-identity—such as fabulous athlete or great student—then if you blow the game or flunk the course, you have little to fall back on. If you see yourself as wearing many hats, as being many possible and present people, then you're more likely to display flexibility in adapting to changing environments. Indeed, psychologist Patricia Linville (1987) has shown that people with multiple senses of self are less likely to show depression or prolonged mood swings after failing to perform success-fully in some desired task or activity.

Social Psychology

13

It's the annual Christmas party for Everville Industries. Al Hobart has worked at the company for a year and a half now, and he's itching for a promotion to the advertising department. To his left stands the head of advertising, Mr. Barker, along with several of Hobart's equally ambitious co-workers. The topic of conversation is the company's recent disastrous marketing campaign, spearheaded by Barker, whose shortcomings are recognized by everyone in the group save one—Barker himself.

"It just goes to show you," spouts Barker confidently, "you can never underestimate the ignorance of the people. It was a brilliantly conceived but unappreciated plan."

"Absolutely," offers Ms. Adler, "a brilliant plan."

"People are just stupid," employee Jones remarks. "They wouldn't know a good marketing campaign if it came up and bit them on the cheek."

I'm working with jerks, the little voice inside Hobart's head chimes. These people have no values—no sense of personal integrity. Everyone knows that campaign was terrible.

"And what about you, Hobart," Barker says, eyes pointing directly at Al's. "What do you think?"

"Brilliant plan, sir," Hobart says, hesitating only slightly; "the work of genius. . . ."

Put on your psychological thinking cap for a moment, and let's analyze Hobart's behavior. From this brief exchange, can you draw any conclusions about what kind of person he is? What does your psychological training up to this point tell you? He clearly violated his own beliefs and outwardly conformed to the opinions expressed by the ambitious people around him. He also drew some rather nasty conclusions about his colleagues, concluding that they were jerks for shamelessly agreeing with the misguided boss. Do you think Hobart will now apply those same negative personality traits to himself? Do you suppose he might have acted differently if the head of advertising had been absent, or if the job promotion had already been his? Now, stop for a moment and think about how *you* might have acted in this situation. Would you have conformed to the opinions of others? Would you, like Hobart, have left the conversation thinking your co-workers suffered from fundamental personality flaws?

Throughout this text, we've stressed that most behaviors, as well as internal thoughts and feelings, are importantly shaped by the immediate context. Not only do people behave differently in different situations, but they think differently as well. Hobart's example is relatively harmless, but other situations can have more far-reaching and disturbing consequences. Suppose, for example, that Mr. Barker was not simply the head of the advertising department but a commanding officer in the military, and the locale was an Asian nation at war. The topic of conversation? Not a marketing campaign, but rather Barker's decision to execute all of the inhabitants, including women and children, of a just-captured village. How would you react now? Would you still conform to the opinions of your superior?

It's adaptive to monitor the environment closely and to change one's behavior accordingly. But the "environment" can consist of much more than just impersonal things such as the temperature of the room or the amount of money received for performing a task. The mere presence of other people, as well as their behaviors, can be among the most powerful and pervasive of environmental influences. Our behaviors and thoughts change in characteristic ways when we are in the presence of other people, and it's to this social aspect of psychology that we now turn our attention.

Interpreting the behavior of others	Behaving in the presence of others	Establishing relations with others

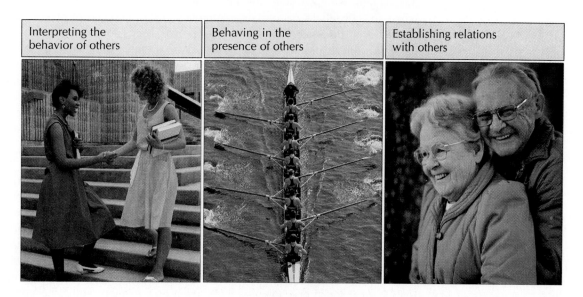

FIGURE 13.1
Summarizing the Adaptive Problems. In this chapter we address three main adaptive problems studied by social psychologists.

PREVIEWING THE ADAPTIVE PROBLEMS

Social psychology is the discipline that studies how people think about, influence, and relate to other people. Social psychologists study such phenomena as persuasion, interpersonal attraction, attitude formation and change, and the behavior of groups. In keeping with the theme of the adaptive mind, we'll tackle the topics of social psychology from the perspective of three important adaptive problems: How do individuals interpret the behavior of others? How do they alter and adjust their behavior when others are present? Finally, how do people establish relations with others, especially interpersonal relations that help guarantee individual survival as well as the survival of the species? These three adaptive problems are summarized in Figure 13.1.

INTERPRETING THE BEHAVIOR OF OTHERS As social animals, living in a social world, people are constantly seeking to interpret the behavior of others. They form impressions of their friends, teachers, and the countless other people that they meet on the street or in the workplace. People concoct theories about *why* individuals behave the way they do, using what psychologists refer to as the attribution process. Added to the mix are the numerous attitudes and beliefs that individuals hold. As we'll see, attitudes importantly shape one's reactions to the presence of others. Generally, impressions, attributions, and attitudes are useful because they establish behavioral guidelines that help people act in the most adaptive way in the presence of particular individuals or groups. At the same time, the interpretations that people draw about others can be wrong and they can lead to actions that are regrettable. In this section, we'll discuss how impressions and attitudes are formed, how they can be changed, and some of the psychological factors that influence the attribution process.

BEHAVING IN THE PRESENCE OF OTHERS Regardless of the interpretations that people give to the actions of others, individual behavior is strongly influenced by the social context. A person's behavior changes when others are present, and the result of social influence can be either positive or negative. To begin this section, we'll consider the phenomenon of social facilitation, which occurs when an individual's performance improves in the presence of others. Then we'll counter with discussions of social interference, social loafing, and the sometimes paralyzing effects of interacting in groups. Also on the agenda are the topics of conformity and obedience. We'll expand our psychological analysis of Hobart's behavior and extend it to a broader range of situations. What are the factors that determine when people will yield to the demands of others, and what implications do these factors have for the structure of society? Do people behave merely at the whims of those authority figures surrounding them, or do they have final control over their own behavior?

▶ **ESTABLISHING RELATIONS WITH OTHERS** It's certainly adaptive to interpret the behavior of others and to change behavior accordingly in their presence. But among the most important social actions that people engage in are the relationships that they establish with others. Without attraction and romantic love, it's unlikely that the human species would survive; it's not just mating that people need—they rely on the relationships within the family as well as the social structures within society to help protect and nurture themselves and their offspring. We'll discuss what social psychologists think about how relations with others are formed. We'll include an extended treatment of the topics of romantic love and attraction. What determines when someone will be attracted to another, and what are the psychological factors that determine love?

Interpreting the Behavior of Others: Social Cognition

We begin our treatment of social psychology with a discussion of how people *think about* other people—how impressions of others are formed, how causes are attributed to behavior, and what mechanisms underlie the formation of attitudes about people and things. Social psychologists typically group these topics together under the rubric of **social cognition,** which can be defined as the study of how people use cognitive processes, such as perception, memory, and thought, to help make sense of other people as well as themselves. First up is the topic of person perception, which deals specifically with how people form impressions of others.

Person Perception: How Do Individuals Form Impressions of Others?

When we first discussed the topic of perception in Chapter 5, we focused on the processes used to interpret elementary sensations into meaningful wholes. In that chapter we stressed that perception is driven by a combination of *bottom-up processing*—the actual physical sensations received by the sensory equipment—and *top-down processing*, which takes into account people's expectations and beliefs about the world. People do not simply see what's "out there" in the physical world; their perceptions of objects are also influenced by their *expectations* of what's "out there."

A similar kind of analysis applies to the perception of people. When you encounter a person for the first time, your initial impressions are typically influenced by physical factors—attractiveness, facial expression, skin color, clothing—and by your meaningful interpretations of those physical attributes. If you see a sloppily dressed, unshaven man weaving down the street toward you, you are likely to form a negative first impression, partly because past experiences may have taught you to avoid people who fit this description. You could be wrong, of course, but in the face of limited information, it's usually adaptive to predict what the consequences of an interaction might be like.

One of the most powerful determinants of a first impression is the *physical attractiveness* of the person. A number of studies have shown that when people first look at a physically attractive person, they naturally assume that he or she is more intelligent, better adjusted, and more socially aware than someone with only average looks (Eagly and others, 1991; Feingold, 1992). "Judging a book by its cover" is not always an effective long-term strategy for impression formation (Feingold, 1992), and not all first impressions about attractive people are positive, but it can be a viable short-term strategy. If the approaching person appears attractive and well kept, at least you know that he or she adheres to some of the accepted standards and norms of the culture (Damhorst, 1990). Think about it. If you were in trouble and needed help, whom would you approach—someone with poor personal hygiene and tattered clothes, or someone neat, clean, and well dressed?

The important point to remember is that when people form a *first* impression of another, they use the information that is available. Physical appearance is always likely to be noticed, along with the person's facial expression and even the way he or she may be walking or sitting. These raw materials are combined with the observer's background knowledge to generate an expectation about what an encounter with that person might be like.

The physical appearance of this individual is likely to activate a "social schema" that will direct and guide your behavior. Social schemas are generally adaptive, but they can lead to inappropriate conclusions or actions under some circumstances.

Social Schemas. Psychologists are convinced that much of the background knowledge people use in social situations is derived from cognitive representations called *schemas*. We've discussed schemas at several places in this book, particularly in the chapter on memory. Schemas are general knowledge structures that are stored in memory, such as one's knowledge about how houses are constructed or about what it's like to go to a restaurant or the doctor's office. Schemas are used not only to help people reconstruct what happened to them in the past but also to help them organize and interpret ongoing experience. A schema can represent just about anything—a person, a place, or a thing. When schemas are about social experiences or people, they are commonly called **social schemas** (Fiske, 1993).

Returning to the unshaven, sloppily dressed man on the street, your initial impression is likely to be negative because his tattered appearance activates a common social schema about people. An unkempt appearance is associated with negative social characteristics—such as laziness or even criminal behavior—and his weaving gait signals possible drunkenness as well. All these things lead you to categorize the man as "trouble" and make it less likely that you will either ask him for help or give help to him if he requests it (Benson and others, 1980). Both the man's physical appearance and his behavior feed into your existing social schema about seedy characters and, once he has been categorized, the schema directs you to alter your behavior accordingly.

Overall, schemas are extremely useful features of the adaptive mind. They help people direct their actions in uncertain situations. But schemas can have unintended side effects. For example, the weaving man might not be a criminal or an undesirable person—he might be ill or in need of help—yet your social schema leads you to assume otherwise. In some cases, social schemas even have a **self-fulfilling prophecy effect,** which occurs when your expectations about someone's actions induce that person to behave in the expected way (Merton, 1948). If you expect someone to be unreliable and generally seedy, and you act in accordance with your expectations (such as snubbing or avoiding the person), the chances that he or she will assume that role in the future may actually increase.

Let's consider an experiment demonstrating the self-fulfilling prophecy effect. In a study by Mark Snyder and colleagues (1977), undergraduate men were asked to talk to undergraduate women, whom they had never met, on the telephone. Prior to the conversation, the men were shown a photograph of their prospective telephone "partner." The partner appeared as either physically attractive or unattractive. In reality, the photos were of women from another college; they were not

Do you think the social schemas that were activated in the telephone experiment were different for the men and the women? If so, in what way?

really photos of the women participating in the study. The intention of the experimenters was simply to lead the men to *believe* they were talking to a woman who was attractive or unattractive. As for the women, they were not given a photo of their partner, nor were they told that the man had been biased to think of them in a particular way. All of the telephone calls were taped, and social aspects of the men's and women's conversational styles were then rated by judges who were unaware of the men's assignment group.

Not surprisingly, if the men thought they were talking to an attractive female, their conversational styles tended to be rated as friendly and positive—more so than if their partner had been depicted as unattractive. But the important finding of the study focused on the women. It turned out that the women's conversational styles also differed, depending on whether or not the man they were talking to thought they were attractive. The women who were presumed by their partners to be attractive were rated by the judges as more friendly, open and poised, and generally more pleasant than the women depicted as unattractive. Remember, these women had no idea that their male partners had preformed opinions about their attractiveness. Apparently, the friendly, positive conversational styles of the men were able to elicit similar qualities from the women. This is the self-fulfilling prophecy effect—the expectations that people have toward someone, along with their resultant actions, can lead that individual to act in the expected way (see Figure 13.2).

Stereotypes. One kind of commonly used social schema is a **stereotype,** which consists of the beliefs held about the personal traits and behaviors of individuals belonging to groups. People form stereotypes about all kinds of social groups, from insurance agents to college professors, but the three most common stereotypes are based on gender, race, and age (Fiske, 1993). Most people carry around a collection of beliefs and expectations about men and women, for example, and these expectations importantly influence behavior: Men are typically seen as strong, dominant, and aggressive; women are typically seen as sensitive, warm, and dependent (Deaux & Lewis, 1984).

Stereotypes are useful cognitive tools, but they can lead to rigid interpretations of people. For example, stereotypes can cause people to overgeneralize and place too much emphasis on the differences that exist *between* groups (for instance,

Teachers need to be careful not to let stereotypes based on gender and race influence their expectations about children's success in school.

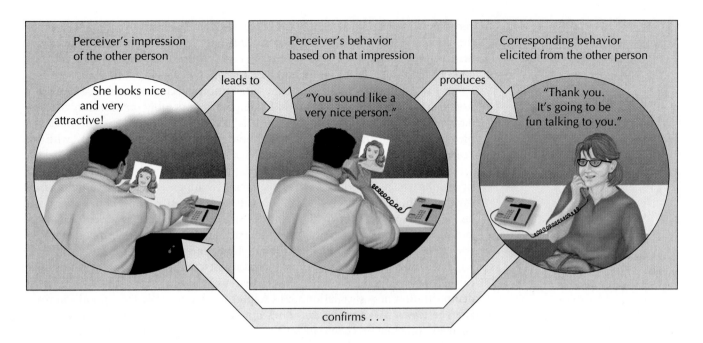

| Perceiver's impression of the other person | Perceiver's behavior based on that impression | Corresponding behavior elicited from the other person |

"She looks nice and very attractive!"   *leads to*   "You sound like a very nice person."   *produces*   "Thank you. It's going to be fun talking to you."

confirms . . .

FIGURE 13.2
The Self-Fulfilling Prophecy Effect. The impressions held about a person by others can affect how that person behaves, leading him or her to act in the expected way. In the study by Snyder and colleagues, if a male subject thought he was talking to an attractive female, his conversational style was rated as more friendly and positive—but so, too, was the conversational style of his female telephone partner.

between men and women), and too little emphasis on the differences that exist *within* groups. Not all women are dependent, nor are all men strong. Furthermore, when negative or extreme beliefs are held about a group, stereotypes increase the likelihood of *prejudice* and discriminatory behavior. Individuals can be excluded from jobs, or even criminally assaulted, just because of negative beliefs engendered by their skin color or sexual preference.

Recent research suggests that it is sometimes possible to reduce the prejudicial feelings that arise from stereotypes through repeated exposure to *individuals* in the stereotyped group. For instance, one study found that as the amount of social contact between heterosexuals and homosexuals increased, negative feelings decreased (Whitely, 1990). But a number of crucial elements are at work in the maintenance of stereotypic beliefs, and whether beliefs will change depends on such factors as the nature of the social interactions and the representativeness of the contacted individuals to their stereotyped group. Moreover, the contact needs to be widespread and repeated; otherwise, people will attempt to "defend" their stereotypic views by explaining away individual contacts as unrepresentative of the group (Weber & Crocker, 1993).

Stereotypes are not necessarily *accurate* representations of people, nor can they be expected to apply to all individuals within a group. But as general "rules of thumb," researchers assume that stereotypes do have adaptive value. They help people carve their social worlds into meaningful chunks, thereby providing a sense of direction about how to act when encountering new people (Oakes & Turner, 1990). Furthermore, not all of the components of stereotypes are inaccurate, nor are they necessarily negative (Eagly & Johnson, 1990). Stereotyping occurs in every culture of the world, and it simply represents yet another instance of how the adaptive mind organizes and categorizes the world.

Attribution Theory: Attributing Causes to Behavior

It's natural for us to try to interpret the behavior of others. A wife tries to understand why her husband sits channel surfing in front of the television during their anniversary dinner; a student tries to understand why the teacher responds to his plaintive appeal for a grade change with a gruff "I didn't give you the grade, you earned the grade." When people assign causes to behaviors, psychologists refer to the inferences that are made as **attributions;** attribution theories are concerned primarily with the psychological processes that underlie these inferences of cause and effect (Heider, 1944; Jones & Davis, 1965).

Let's consider an example of the attribution process at work. Suppose you notice that the mood of your friend Ira improves noticeably on Monday, Wednesday, and Friday afternoons, after he returns from lunch. He smiles a lot, exchanges pleasantries, and offers advice freely. These behaviors contrast sharply with his normal gruff manner and generally sour disposition. What accounts for the behavior change? According to the *covariation model of attribution* (Kelley, 1967), the first thing you'll look for is some factor that happens at the same time as, or *covaries* with, the behavior change. You will try to identify an event or some other factor that is present when the behavior change occurs and is absent when the behavior change does not occur. In this particular example, it turns out that Ira goes to his aerobic exercise class between 12:00 and 1:00 on those three days.

But covariation by itself is not a sufficient condition for the attribution of causality, for much the same reason that we cannot infer causality from the demonstration of a correlation (see Chapter 2). Just because Ira's mood improves after he leaves his exercise class does not mean that exercise is the cause of the change—other factors could be involved. According to the covariation model, people rely on three additional pieces of information to help them make the appropriate inference: *consistency, distinctiveness,* and *consensus.* When assessing *consistency,* people try to determine whether the change occurs regularly when the causal event is present—does Ira's mood consistently improve after exercise class? *Distinctiveness* provides an indication of whether the change occurs uniquely in the presence of the event—does Ira's mood improve after lunch only if he's been exercising? Finally, people look for *consensus,* which tells them whether other individuals show similar reactions when they are exposed to the same causal event—is elevation of mood a common reaction to exercising?

The Locus of Causality. These three factors—consistency, distinctiveness, and consensus—work in combination to help people form an attribution. In the particular example we've been considering, it's likely that people will assume it's the *external* event—the exercise class—that is the cause of Ira's mood change. People tend to make an **external attribution,** which appeals to external causes, when the behavior in question is high in consistency, distinctiveness, and consensus. In the case of Ira's pleasant demeanor, it's highly consistent (it happens every Monday, Wednesday, and Friday afternoon); it's occurrence is distinctive (it occurs only after exercise class); and there is a high level of consensus (exercise tends to make lots of people happy).

But what if no single event or situation in the environment can be used to explain someone's behavior? For example, suppose Ira consistently smiles and acts pleasant in the afternoon, but he also smiles during the mornings and on days he has skipped the exercise class. Under these conditions, it's doubtful that people will appeal to the environment to explain his behavior; instead, they'll be likely to make an **internal attribution,** which means they'll attribute his pleasant behavior to some *internal* personality trait or disposition: "Ira just has a great personality; he's a friendly, pleasant guy." Internal attributions are common when the consistency of a behavior is high but its distinctiveness and consensus are low. If Ira is pleasant all the time, his postlunch behavior lacks distinctiveness, and people will be unlikely to appeal to some lunch activity to explain his behavior. Similarly, if the consensus is low—suppose exercise rarely improves mood for most people—people will again resist attributing his pleasantries to this particular event (see Figure 13.3).

Suppose you're forced to make an attribution quickly, without much time for thought. Do you think quickly formed attributions are more likely to be internal or external? Why?

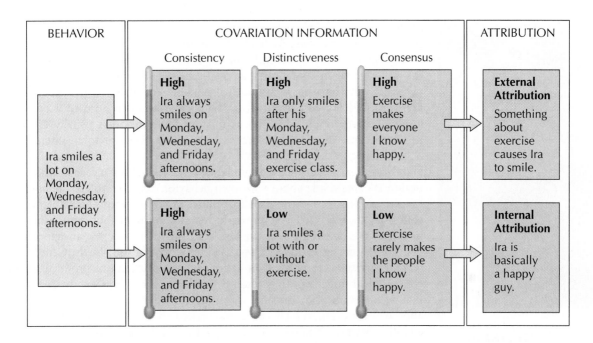

BEHAVIOR	COVARIATION INFORMATION			ATTRIBUTION
	Consistency	Distinctiveness	Consensus	
Ira smiles a lot on Monday, Wednesday, and Friday afternoons.	**High** Ira always smiles on Monday, Wednesday, and Friday afternoons.	**High** Ira only smiles after his Monday, Wednesday, and Friday exercise class.	**High** Exercise makes everyone I know happy.	**External Attribution** Something about exercise causes Ira to smile.
	High Ira always smiles on Monday, Wednesday, and Friday afternoons.	**Low** Ira smiles a lot with or without exercise.	**Low** Exercise rarely makes the people I know happy.	**Internal Attribution** Ira is basically a happy guy.

FIGURE 13.3
The Covariation Model of Attribution. When people make internal attributions, they "attribute" behavior to internal personality characteristics; external attributions "attribute" behavior to factors in the environment. In Kelley's attribution model, whether an internal or external attribution will be made about a particular behavior depends on *consistency, distinctiveness,* and *consensus.* Generally, behaviors that are consistent, that are highly distinctive, and that lead to consensus are attributed to the environment, whereas consistent behaviors that are not distinctive and show little consensus are attributed to internal characteristics.

Attribution Biases. Although our discussion thus far suggests that people are quite logical and rational when forming attributions, this characterization is a bit misleading. Social psychologists have discovered that it's common for people to take "shortcuts" in the attribution process, probably because they're often required to make attribution judgments quickly, and it's effortful and time-consuming to consider all potential factors logically (Gilbert, 1989; Trope & Liberman, 1993). What happens, however, is that these shortcuts tend to produce consistent biases and errors in the judgment process. One of the most pervasive of these biases is the **fundamental attribution error**: When people seek to interpret someone else's behavior, they tend to overestimate the influence of internal personal factors and underestimate the role of external situational factors (Jones, 1990; Ross, 1977).

For instance, Jones and Harris (1967) had college students read essays expressing either positive or negative opinions about Fidel Castro's communist regime in Cuba (at the time—the mid-1960s—Castro's Cuba was a "hot" topic of discussion). Before reading the essays, one group of students was told that the person writing the essay had been allowed to write freely and choose the position adopted in the text. A second group was told that the writer had no choice and had been forced to adopt a particular pro or con position. Afterward, the students in both groups were asked to speculate about the writer's true opinion on the topic. Thinking logically, you might assume that if the writer had been given a choice, then the essay position probably reflected his or her true opinion on Castro. Alternatively, if the writer was simply following directions, it would be difficult to tell. To the surprise of the experimenters, however, the students tended to believe that the essay *always* reflected the writer's true opinion, even when the students knew that the essay writer had been forced to adopt a particular position. This represents the fundamental attribution error at work: People tend to attribute an individual's activities to internal personal factors, even when there are strong situational explanations for the behavior (Jones, 1990).

Now consider another example: You're driving down the street, at a perfectly respectable speed, when you glance in your rearview mirror and see a pickup truck bearing down on your bumper. You speed up a bit, only to find the truck mirroring your every move. Being tailgated like this is a relatively common experience. But what kind of attribution do you typically make about the driver? Do you

People often think that popular game show hosts, such as Alex Trebek, are extremely knowledgeable individuals. What attribution processes might underlie such an inference?

attribute the behavior to the person or to the situation? If you're like most people, your first response is likely to be an internal attribution—you naturally assume that the driver behind you has some severe personality flaw; put simply, the driver is a jerk. You ignore the possibility that situational factors might be compelling the driver to drive fast. Isn't it possible, for instance, that the driver is late for work or has a sick child in the backseat who is in need of a doctor? These kinds of attributions, which focus on the situation, don't usually enter people's minds, because our first tendency is to attribute behavior to an internal personal characteristic.

But let's switch gears for a moment. Now think about a case in which the attribution is being made about your own behavior. Suppose you're the one doing the tailgating. It's extremely unlikely that under these conditions you'll blame your tailgating on the fact that you're a jerk; instead, your attribution will be situation-based. You're tailgating, you explain, because you're late for an appointment, or because the driver in front of you is simply driving too slowly. Generally, people will take internal credit for their actions when those actions produce positive outcomes—such as attributing a solid A on the psychology test to hard work and intelligence—but they'll blame the situation when their behaviors are questionable or lead to failure. This tendency, called the **self-serving bias,** is considered adaptive because it allows people to bolster and maintain their self-esteem and project a sense of self-importance and confidence to the world (Snyder, 1989).

The biases that social psychologists have discovered in the attribution process have important implications, not just for an individual's own life but for society as well. The tailgating example is relatively harmless, but think about a situation in which the focus of analysis is on welfare or homelessness. Because of attribution biases, people might naturally attribute, for example, being on welfare or losing a job to laziness, incompetence, or some other negative internal trait. But in many cases an individual ends up on welfare or out of work because of situational factors, perhaps because of some catastrophic life event. Attribution biases may have considerable adaptive value—because they allow people to make quick decisions about the causes of behavior—but they do have a downside; they can lead to misleading or even incorrect conclusions.

How people interpret "risky" behavior on the highway depends on who is doing the driving. When someone else commits the risky move, people are likely to attribute it to an internal personality characteristic of the driver; when we're the ones doing the driving, it is likely to be the environment that receives the blame.

Attitudes and Attitude Change

The final topic that we'll consider in our discussion of social cognition is the study of attitudes and attitude change. An **attitude** is simply a positive or negative evaluation or belief that people hold about something, which in turn may affect their behavior. Like the other forms of social cognition that we've discussed, attitudes are beneficial for a number of reasons. When they guide behavior, attitudes help people remain consistent in their actions and help them make use of their knowledge about an individual or situation. Attitudes also play an important role in people's perception and interpretation of the world. They help individuals focus their attention on information relevant to their beliefs, particularly information that can help confirm their existing beliefs. As a result, attitudes serve a kind of defensive function, protecting people's basic beliefs about themselves as well as about others (Fazio, 1986).

Typically, social psychologists divide attitudes into three main components: a *cognitive* component, an *affective* component, and a *behavioral* component (Olson & Zanna, 1993). The cognitive component arises from what people know or believe about the object of their attitude; the affective component is made up of the feelings that the object engenders; and the behavioral component is a predisposition to act toward the object in a particular way.

To see how these three components work together, let's suppose that you've formed an unfavorable attitude toward your landlord. Your attitude rests on a foundation of facts and beliefs about behavior. You know, for instance, that the landlord has raised your rent three times in the last year, that he enters your apartment without first asking permission, and that he won't let you keep your declawed pet cat Kepler without a huge pet deposit. These facts and beliefs form the cognitive component of your attitude. Accompanying these facts are your emotional reactions, which make up the affective component—when you see or think about your landlord, you get angry and slightly sick to your stomach. Finally, the behavioral component of your attitude predisposes you to act in certain ways. You may spend every Sunday reading the classified ads looking for a new apartment, and you may constantly complain about your landlord to anyone who'll listen. It's these three factors in combination—cognitive, affective, and behavioral—that compose what psychologists mean by an "attitude" (see Figure 13.4).

Notice that the behavioral component of the attitude is described as a *predisposition* to act. This is an important point to remember, because attitudes do not always directly affect behavior. As you know, people sometimes act in ways that are inconsistent with their attitudes (Ajzen & Fishbein, 1977). When directly confronting your landlord, for instance, you may be all smiles even though underneath you're steaming. Attitudes do not always connect with behavior because behavior is usually determined by multiple factors—especially external factors such as the situation. In some situations it is simply unwise to express true feelings, such as when dealing with the landlord. In other situations, people act quickly and mindlessly without considering the true meaning or ramifications of their behavior (Langer, 1989). For example, people often sign petitions for activities they may not completely believe in, or buy products that they don't really want, simply because they're in a hurry and don't want to be bothered further. For an attitude to guide behavior, it needs to come to mind—that is, it needs to be accessible—and it should be appropriate or relevant to the situation (Pratkanis & Greenwald, 1989).

Attitude Formation. Where do attitudes come from, and how are they acquired? There are many routes to attitude formation. People use their everyday experiences as grist for many of their ideas and beliefs. It's also the case that how individuals interpret those experiences depends partly on their inborn intellectual

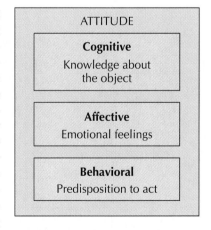

FIGURE 13.4
The Three Components of Attitudes. Social psychologists typically divide attitudes into three main components: cognitive, affective, and behavioral.

Don't you think it's likely that all humans have an inborn attitude, or preference, for pleasurable things over painful things? No one needs to learn to dislike stepping on a rusty nail.

and personality traits (Tesser, 1993). Even something as simple as *mere exposure* can be sufficient to change one's feelings about an object. In classic work by Robert Zajonc (1968), subjects were shown photographs of undergraduate men taken from a school yearbook. Some of the photos were shown only once or twice; others were shown up to 25 times. Following exposure, everyone was asked to give an estimate of how much they liked each of the men shown. The results revealed that the more often a photo had been presented, the more the subjects claimed to "like" the person shown. It is not clear exactly how to interpret this finding, in part because people's ratings change on a whole host of dimensions following exposure (Mandler, Nakamura, & Van Zandt, 1987). But it demonstrates how easily attitudes can be affected.

Experience is generally agreed to be the single most important factor affecting attitude formation. A great deal of evidence suggests that attitudes can be conditioned, through experiences of the type discussed in Chapter 7. Events that occur outside of one's control can acquire signaling properties, through *classical conditioning,* and then serve as an initial foundation for an attitude. Advertisers commonly try to manipulate how people feel toward consumer products by pairing the product with something pleasurable, such as an attractive model or a successful athlete. Through *instrumental conditioning,* attitudes are influenced by the rewards and punishments people receive for their actions. Certainly if you express a tentative opinion on a subject—"We've got too much big government in this country"—and this opinion is reinforced by people whom you respect, you're likely to express this same attitude again. Instrumental conditioning teaches people about the consequences of their behavior, and direct experience of this sort plays a significant role in attitude formation.

Finally, much of what individuals acquire from experience is the result of *observational learning.* People model significant others—parents, peers, teachers, and so on—when it comes to attitudes as well as to behavior. The political convictions of most people, for example, turn out to mirror quite closely the political attitudes of their parents (McGuire, 1985). People use their peers, too, as a reference comparison group for judging the acceptability of their behaviors and beliefs. All you need to do is take a random sample of the behavior of teenagers in the local mall to see how important modeling behavior can be. Everything from language to musical taste to hairstyle to shoe type is replicated from one teen to the next. Ask yourself: How differently do you think and act from the people in your immediate circle of friends? Modeling may not be the only reason why people in a peer group often act and think in a similar way, but its influence is often profound.

Persuasion and Attitude Change. For decades, social psychologists have been interested not only in how attitudes are formed initially but also in how attitudes can be changed. We live in a world that is constantly trying to convince us of something. We are bombarded daily by dozens of persuasive messages from sources in business, politics, religion, and the arts. For obvious reasons, psychologists have sought to determine the important ingredients of persuasion: What are the factors that determine the likelihood that you'll be convinced to buy a particular product or support a particular political campaign? According to one popular theory of attitude change, known as the **elaboration likelihood model,** there are two primary routes to persuasion, one that is central and one that is peripheral (Petty & Cacioppo, 1986).

The *central route* to persuasion is the most obvious and familiar one. It operates in those situations in which people are motivated and are inclined to process an incoming persuasive communication with care and attention; they'll listen carefully to the arguments of the message, then judge those arguments according to their merits. Suppose you've recently changed your views on the topic of abortion

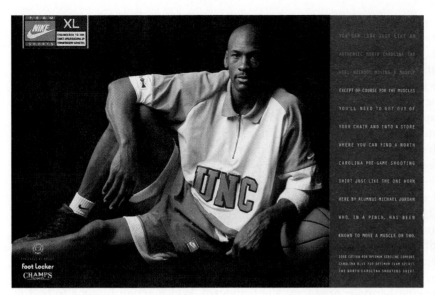

In situations in which a person's level of involvement or commitment to a message is low, advertisers tend to capitalize on the peripheral route to persuasion by using celebrity endorsers or humor in the persuasive message.

after listening to a persuasive speaker at your school. If you carefully weighed the quality and strength of the arguments and then changed your attitude accordingly, you've been convinced via the central route. Not surprisingly, attitude changes that result from this kind of central processing tend to be stable and long-lasting (Olson & Zanna, 1993).

The *peripheral route* to persuasion operates when people are either unable to process the message systematically or are unmotivated to do so. When people's level of involvement in or commitment to the message is low, their attitudes are much more susceptible to change from superficial cues. In such a situation, one might be influenced by the physical appearance of the communicator or by the superficial content of the message (such as its humor). Advertisers typically capitalize on the peripheral route to persuasion because most of the time people don't process advertisements on television or in magazines with a high level of involvement. Viewers are likely to judge a product on the basis of its celebrity endorser rather than on the strength of the ad's intellectual arguments. When our motivation to process the message is low, we also tend to rely on processing shortcuts (*heuristics*) to form opinions (Chaiken, Liberman, & Eagly, 1989). For instance, you might adopt a favorable attitude toward an expensive product because you believe that "better products are more expensive," or you might buy the product endorsed by Michael Jordan because "Michael wouldn't endorse something that isn't quality."

Actions and Attitudes. People can also use their own behavior to help frame their attitudes toward things. In a highly influential study of attitude change conducted by Festinger and Carlsmith (1959), male college students were asked to perform some incredibly boring tasks, such as placing sewing spools onto a tray, during an hour session. At the end of the hour, some of the participants (the experimental group) were given a bogus cover story. They were told that one purpose of the study was to examine the effects of motivation on task performance. The next subject, the researcher explained, needed to be told that the experiment was actually filled with interesting and enjoyable tasks. Would they mind going into the adjacent waiting room and telling him that the experiment was interesting and enjoyable? To provide an incentive, the experimenter offered some of the participants a monetary reward of $1 and others, a reward of $20.

Next time you watch television, notice which ads rely on logical arguments and which ads rely on humor or celebrity endorsement. Do you see any relationship between the type of ad and the likelihood of central processing at the point of purchase?

The point of the offer was to induce the members of the experimental group to act in a way that contradicted their true feelings, or attitudes, about the experiment. The task was clearly boring, so they were essentially asked to lie for either a small or a large reward. Festinger and Carlsmith were interested in what effect this behavior would have on subjects' attitudes about the experiment. After accepting the offer, and trying to convince the next subject, the students' attitudes about the experimental tasks were assessed through an interview. The researchers found that attitudes about the experimental tasks did indeed change—they became more positive relative to the attitudes of the members of the control group, who had not been asked to lie. Moreover, the positive shift was larger for subjects receiving $1 as opposed to $20. The more subjects were paid to act inconsistently with their true feelings, the less likely their attitudes were to change (see Figure 13.5).

These results may seem perplexing. You would probably have predicted that the students receiving $20 would show the greatest attitude change—after all, wouldn't a large reward have a greater reinforcing effect on counterattitudinal behavior? The answer, according to Festinger's (1957) theory of **cognitive dissonance,** lies in the amount of tension—or what he called *dissonance*—that the inconsistent behavior produces. Think about it. Which action is going to lead to greater internal turmoil and angst: lying to receive $1, or lying to receive $20? Most people can easily justify a simple white lie when offered a reasonable amount of money, especially when asked by an authority figure (remember as well that $20 was worth a lot more in the 1950s than it is now). But to lie for a measly $1 is tough to justify—unless, of course, one can justify the action by changing one's initial attitude about the task. According to cognitive dissonance theory, if the discrepancy between what a person believes and how the person acts is great, he or she will either (1) change the behavior, or (2) change the beliefs.

Since cognitive dissonance theory was first introduced in the 1950s, hundreds of follow-up studies have been conducted (Aronson, 1992). Most have confirmed Festinger and Carlsmith's basic finding. When people are induced to act in ways that are inconsistent with their attitudes, those attitudes often change as a consequence. But not all psychologists are convinced that some kind of internal tension, or dissonance, drives this process. The concept of cognitive "dissonance" is rather vague and not easy to measure directly. Psychologists have also had some difficulty predicting when dissonance will occur and, if it's present, how people will choose to reduce it (Joule, 1986). For these reasons, alternative explanations of attitude change have emerged.

FIGURE 13.5
Cognitive Dissonance. Festinger proposed that attitudes change when a discrepancy exists between what a person believes and how he or she acts. People who lied about the boring experimental task for a measly $1 later claimed to enjoy the task more than did people who lied for $20 or who were not asked to lie. Presumably, it was tough to justify lying for a small amount of money, which created a lot of cognitive dissonance, so the subjects in the $1 condition simply changed their original attitude about the task. (Data from Festinger & Carlsmith, 1959)

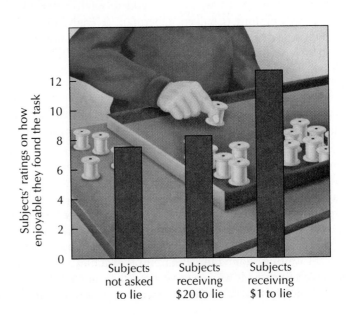

FIGURE 13.6
Self-Perception Theory. Some psychologists believe that people form attitudes, at least in part, by observing their own behavior. If I regularly eat hamburgers, then my attitude about hamburgers must be positive.

Among the various alternatives to dissonance theory is psychologist Daryl Bem's (1967, 1972) **self-perception theory.** The idea behind self-perception theory is that people are active processors of their own behavior. Individuals learn from their behavior and use their actions as a basis for inferring their internal beliefs. For example, if I sit down and practice the piano for 2 hours a day, it must be the case that I like music and think I have at least a modicum of musical talent. If I regularly stop for hamburgers and fries for lunch, it must be the case that I like fast food. The basis for the attitude is self-perception—behavior is observed, and attitudes follow from the behavior (see Figure 13.6).

Many experimental findings support these ideas. Let's consider one classic example. Using what has come to be known as the *foot-in-the-door technique,* Jonathan Freedman and Scott Fraser (1966) convinced a group of California householders to sign a petition expressing support for safe driving. Several weeks later, the researchers returned with a request that the householders now place a large and quite ugly "Drive Safely" billboard in their yards. The petition signers were three times more likely to comply with this new request than a control group of people who did not initially sign a petition. What's the interpretation? The signing of the original petition triggered *self-perception,* which then helped shape the attitude: If I signed the petition, then I must be a strong advocate for safe driving. Of course, there are boundary conditions for these effects—people do not always simply match their attitudes to their behaviors—but monitoring one's own behavior is clearly an important ingredient of attitude formation and change.

 How might you also use cognitive dissonance theory to explain the foot-in-the-door technique?

Behaving in the Presence of Others: Social Influence

We now turn our attention to the topic of **social influence**: How is the behavior of the individual affected by the presence of others? Obviously, by the term *others,* social psychologists are referring to the general social context, but "others" can have a variety of meanings in practice. Our behavior might change as a consequence of interacting with a single individual, perhaps an authority figure such as our boss or an intimate friend, or by the collective behavior of individuals in a group. Moreover, the "influence" that is seen can manifest itself as a change in performance or as a change in attitudes and beliefs. Think back to the ambitious underling, Al Hobart, whom we met in the chapter opening. His behavior certainly changed in the presence of others; he violated his beliefs and conformed to the opinions of his colleagues and his self-serving boss.

Social Influences on Task Performance

One of the simplest and most widely documented examples of social influence can be found in the phenomenon of social facilitation. **Social facilitation** is the *enhancement* in performance that is sometimes found when an individual performs in the presence of others. To demonstrate social facilitation, we need to compare someone's task performance in two conditions: when performing alone, and when performing in the presence of other people. If performance improves when other people are around, we've demonstrated social facilitation. In an early investigation of this effect, Norman Triplett (1898) discovered that adolescents

would wind in a fishing line faster when working in pairs than when working alone. Task performance *improved* in the presence of others, which is the defining characteristic of social facilitation.

Social facilitation is a widespread phenomenon, occurring in many kinds of social environments and for many kinds of tasks. Motorists drive through intersections faster when another car is traveling in the lane beside them (Towler, 1986); people run faster when others are present (Worringham & Messick, 1983); people even eat more when dining out with friends than when eating alone (Clendenen, Herman, & Polivy, 1994). In fact, the effect is not even restricted to humans—ants will excavate dirt more quickly to build their nests when other ants are present (Chen, 1937); hungry chickens will peck food more when other chickens observe passively though a clear plastic wall (Tolman, 1968); cockroaches will even run faster down an alleyway when a "spectator" roach watches from a small plastic enclosure (Zajonc, Heingartner, & Herman, 1969).

But there is another side to the coin. It's easy to think of examples of how people have "risen to the occasion" and excelled when an audience was present, but the opposite can be the case as well. Sometimes performing in a crowd impairs performance—the person "chokes," and this tendency is referred to as **social interference.** Talented Angela, who finally performs Bach's Invention No. 1 perfectly in her last practice session, finds her fingers fumbling helplessly during the piano recital. Confident Eddie, who thought he had learned his lines to perfection, finds that on opening night he's standing embarrassingly silent on center stage. Psychologists believe that *task difficulty* is one important factor that

Demonstrating the phenomenon of social facilitation, people tend to eat more when they're in the presence of others.

determines whether the presence of others will help or hinder performance. If the task is relatively easy, the presence of others will spur the person on, and we'll see social facilitation; if the task is new or difficult, the presence of others can have an inhibitory effect, and we'll find social interference. (It's worth noting that social psychologists typically use the term *social facilitation* to refer to both increases and decreases in performance when others are present; for our purposes, we'll draw a distinction between social *facilitation* and social *interference* to make the concepts easier to understand.)

When tasks are difficult, performing in the presence of others can lead to social interference; what seemed easy in practice becomes a nightmare during the recital.

According to psychologist Robert Zajonc (1965), we can explain the relationship between task difficulty and social influence by appealing to how an audience's presence influences *arousal*. When others are watching, Zajonc argued, it's reasonable to assume that the performer's general level of arousal increases. Arousal, in turn, naturally biases the performer toward engaging in "dominant," or well-learned, responses. If the task is a relatively easy one, such as running or solving simple math problems, then such "well-learned" responses are apt to be useful and enhance performance. But when tasks are difficult, performers are likely to need new responses that are less practiced or well learned. For difficult tasks then, performance is likely to be impaired because the high arousal levels will bias the person toward responses that are not very useful. Thus, the influence that others have on performance is explained by appealing to the relationship between general arousal and its effects on task performance.

Social Influences on Altruism: The Bystander Effect

In addition to task performance, the presence of other people can dramatically influence whether people will choose to be *altruistic*—that is, to show unselfish concern for the welfare of others. Think about the last time that you were driving on the highway and noticed some poor individual standing alongside his or her disabled car by the side of the road. Did you stop and help? Did you at least get off at the nearest exit and telephone the police or highway patrol? If you're like most people, you probably did nothing. In all likelihood, you failed to accept responsibility for helping—you left that job for someone else.

The problem is more serious than you might think. In March of 1964, while walking home from work at 3:30 in the morning, Catherine "Kitty" Genovese was stalked and then brutally attacked by a knife-wielding assailant outside her apartment building in Queens, New York. "Oh my god, he stabbed me!" Kitty screamed. "I'm dying! I'm dying!" Inside the apartment building, awakened by the screams, some 38 of her neighbors sat silently listening as the attacker finished the job. Kitty was stabbed repeatedly before she eventually died—in fact, the attacker actually left and came back to rape her and finish the job. No one in the apartment build-

When you drive by someone who is in need of assistance, do you stop and help? Do you at least get off at the nearest exit and telephone the police or highway patrol?

ing came to her aid or called the police until approximately 30 minutes after the first attack. Did they simply not want to get involved in a situation like this, or was some other, more general psychological process at work?

Most social psychologists are convinced that the behavior of these Queens apartment dwellers is neither atypical nor representative of general apathy. Instead, the reluctance to get involved—to help others—can be explained by appealing once again to the powerful role of social context. People tend not to lend a hand, or get involved, because the presence of others leads to **diffusion of responsibility**—they believe that others have already done something to help or will soon get involved. If people know that others are present in the situation, and certainly many occupants of the apartment building heard the terrible screams, they allow their sense of responsibility to *diffuse,* or spread out widely among the other people presumed to be present. It is this diffusion of responsibility that social psychologists believe underlies the **bystander effect**: the reluctance to come to someone's aid when other people are present (Darley & Latané, 1968).

It's actually possible to study these kinds of effects in the laboratory. Consider the following scenario. You've volunteered to participate in a psychology experiment that involves groups of students discussing the problems of college life. To minimize embarrassment, you're allowed to sit in a small cubicle where you can communicate with the others via an intercom system. Before the experiment begins, you're told that one, two, or five other people will be participating. The session begins and suddenly one of the group members, who had previously mentioned being subject to epileptic seizures, begins to have a seizure. Over the intercom, his voice begins to garble—"Somebody-er-er-help-er-uh-uh-uh"—followed by silence. What do you do? Do you get up and help, or sit where you are?

In the actual version of this experiment, of course, no one actually had a seizure; the incident was manufactured by the experimenters to observe the bystander effect. There was also only one real subject in the experiment—the "others" were simply voices recorded on tape. The researchers found that the likelihood that the real subject would offer some kind of help to the imaginary seizure victim depended on how many other people the subject believed to be present. When the subject was convinced that only one other person was participating in the group, he or she almost immediately rose to intervene. But when it was presumed that four others (in addition to the seizure victim) were present, personal responsibility apparently diffused, and only 62% of the subjects offered aid (Darley & Latané, 1968).

The bystander effect is a disturbing but powerful example of social influence. The basic demonstration of diffusion of responsibility has been replicated many times in numerous social settings that extend beyond the laboratory (Latané & Nida, 1981). As a general rule, the more witnesses there are, the less likely it will be that any one will step forward to offer aid. There are exceptions to the rule—for instance, people are more likely to help if they have recently observed others being helpful—but diffusion of responsibility remains the rule rather than the exception. The tendency to diffuse responsibility doesn't mean that people are bad or selfish; it simply provides yet another indication of how behavior can be strongly influenced by social factors in the environment. Our behavior changes when we are in the presence of others, and while the forces that produce the bystander effect may not make us feel good about ourselves, this behavior may be adaptive. Stopping to help someone in need could place one in danger—there may be a definite cost to helping behavior—and diffusion of responsibility is one way of reducing the potential cost.

The Power of the Group: Caving in to Social Pressure

The power that the social context exerts on human behavior is especially apparent when individuals act as members of a well-defined group. Behavior is shaped not only by the characteristics of the group—its size and the unanimity of its members—but even by the mere fact that one is *in* a group. In one study, volunteer subjects were instructed to clap and cheer as loudly as possible while blindfolded and listening to noise over headphones. Just before they began the task, the participants were informed that they would be clapping either with a group of other subjects or alone by themselves. When the volunteers believed they were part of a clapping group, their individual output dropped considerably. This tendency to put out less effort when working in a group, compared to when working alone, is known generally as **social loafing** (Latané, Williams, & Harkins, 1979).

Social loafing is a complex phenomenon, like many of the phenomena we've discussed in this chapter. Whether it occurs in a particular context will depend on numerous factors, including the importance of the task and the cohesiveness of the group. But many social psychologists believe that an underlying connection exists between social loafing and the bystander effect. Bibb Latané (1981) has argued that both effects result from diffusion of responsibility. In the bystander effect, people suspect that others either will or have become involved; in social loafing, people assume that others will carry the load. In both cases, the fact that individuals are simply one of many makes them feel less accountable for their behavior. They fail to step up and take full responsibility, or to work to their fullest capabilities, because the responsibility can be diffused or spread to the other members of the group.

In what way is the phenomenon of social loafing similar to and different from the phenomenon of social interference?

Conformity. Participation as a member of a group has much more than a passive effect on behavior. Groups exert *active* influences on members' behaviors and opinions that extend well beyond simple diffusion of responsibility. Whether people recognize it or not, when they participate in a group setting they open themselves to social pressures that promote **conformity,** which means that their opinions, feelings, and behaviors will start to move toward the group norm. People have a tendency to comply, or go along, with the wishes of the group even though they may not always be aware that they are doing so. Studies investigating issues of conformity and compliance to group norms are among the oldest and best known of all social psychology experiments.

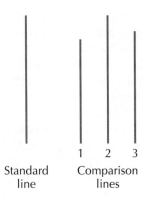

Standard line

Comparison lines

1   2   3

FIGURE 13.7

The Asch Study of Conformity.
Do you think you would have any trouble choosing the correct comparison line in this task? Asch found that people often conformed to the group opinion. The photo shown here is taken from one of Asch's actual experiments.

Notice that when people conform, they act in a way that is inconsistent with their beliefs. Based on our earlier discussion of attitude change, what effect do you think conforming might have on subjects' attitudes or beliefs about themselves or about the experiment?

In one of the classic studies of conformity, psychologist Solomon Asch (1951, 1955) rigged the following experimental setup. Subjects were asked to participate in a simple perception experiment that required them to make judgments about line length. Two cards were shown, one displaying a standard line of a particular length, and the other showing three comparison lines of differing lengths. The subject was required to state aloud which of the three comparison lines was the same length as the standard line (see Figure 13.7). The task was really quite simple—there was no question as to what the correct answer should be. The catch was that this was a group experiment, and the other members of the group were really confederates of the experimenter—they were not, in fact, volunteers, but rather were there to put social pressure on the true participant.

The confederate "subjects" were instructed to lie on a certain number of the trials. They were told to give a response, aloud, that was clearly wrong (such as picking comparison line 1 as the correct answer). Asch's main concern was how often these incorrect answers would affect the answers of the real subject. Imagine yourself in this situation—you know the answer is line 2, but four of your fellow subjects have already given 1 as a response. Do you conform to the opinions of your peers, even though doing so conflicts with what you know to be true? The results were not particularly encouraging for those who champion individualism. Asch found that in approximately 75% of the sessions, subjects complied on at least one of the trials, and the overall rate of conformity was around 37%. Although peer pressure wasn't always effective in altering the behavior of the subjects—in fact, only 5% of the subjects conformed on every trial—it was a powerful influence. In describing his results, Asch (1955) put it this way: "That reasonably intelligent and well-meaning young people are willing to call white black is a matter of concern" (p. 34).

As you might imagine, the Asch experiments had quite an impact on the psychological community. Over the ensuing decades, similar experiments were conducted on dozens of occasions, not only in the United States but also in many other countries around the world. Generally, Asch's results have held up well, although a number of variables affect the likelihood that conformity will occur. Asch himself found, for example, that the rate of compliance dropped dramatically when one of the confederates dissented from the majority and gave the correct answer. It was also discovered that the size of the group is not as important as you might think. Conformity increases as the size of the pressure group gets larger, but it levels off relatively quickly. The pressure to conform does not increase directly with group size; after a certain point, usually when the majority group contains three to five members, adding even more pressure has a diminishing effect (Tanford & Penrod, 1984). Finally, feelings about the status of the group as a whole also matter; if individuals have little or no respect for the other members of the group, they're less likely to conform. Conformity is particularly likely when pres-

Group polarization occurs when the group's majority opinion becomes stronger and more extreme with time. What's the likelihood that the members of this group of protesters will adopt more tolerant views on abortion in the future?

sure comes from an **in-group**—that is, a group of individuals with whom one shares features in common or with whom one identifies (Abrams and others, 1990).

Why do people conform to the majority opinion? One possibility is *normative social influence*—people generally seek approval in social settings and try to avoid rejection, so they act in accordance with social customs and "norms." Clearly, voicing a dissenting opinion increases the risk of rejection by the group, so the individual chooses to conform. But it may also be the case that people use the majority group opinion as a source of information, which is commonly referred to as *informational social influence.* If four or five people around you are convinced that comparison line 1 is the correct answer, perhaps your perception of the stimulus is flawed in some way. Perhaps your angle of sight is misleading, or your memory for the comparison lines is wrong. Consequently, you use the opinions of the others in the group as information or evidence about what has really been presented.

Group Behavior. As we've just seen, members of an in-group can exert considerable pressure on one another to conform to the standards or norms of the group. One of the consequences of these internal pressures is that groups tend to take on behavioral characteristics of their own. For example, when members of an in-group arrive at a consensus of opinion, there is a tendency for the group's opinion to polarize. **Group polarization** occurs when the group's dominant point of view—which is usually determined by the initial views of the majority—becomes stronger and even more extreme with time. If you join a local action group dedicated to exposing corporate corruption and the group tends to believe initially that corporate corruption is a significant and rising problem, it's likely that over time you and the rest of the members of the group will become even more convinced of that position (Moscovici & Zavalloni, 1969; Myers, 1982).

The trend toward consensus and polarization of opinion is also influenced by what psychologist Irving Janis has labeled **groupthink**: Members of a group become so interested in seeking a consensus of opinion that they start to ignore and even suppress dissenting views. Janis (1982, 1989) found evidence for groupthink when he looked at how well-established in-groups arrived at decisions, particularly policy decisions by members of the government. He and others have analyzed a number of watershed events in U.S. policymaking, including the decision to escalate the war in Vietnam, the decision by President John F. Kennedy to invade Cuba in 1961, and even the decision by NASA to launch the ill-fated *Challenger* Space Shuttle. In an alarming number of cases, it was discovered that group members systematically sought consensus at the expense of critical analysis. Group members often acted as if they were trying to convince themselves of the correctness of their position. When alternative views were expressed, those views were either suppressed or dismissed. The management at NASA had clear evidence that freezing launch temperatures might pose a problem for *Challenger,* but the managers chose to ignore that evidence in the interest of going forward with the mission. The result of groupthink is general closed-mindedness and an overestimation of the uniformity of opinion.

Can either groupthink or group polarization be avoided? According to Janis (1982), it is possible to counteract these negative effects of social context by following certain prescriptions. For instance, it helps to have a leader who acts impartial, one who does not quickly endorse a particular position. One or more members of the group can also be assigned a kind of "devil's advocate" role in which they are expected and encouraged to represent a dissenting position. Perhaps most important, however, is the simple recognition by the group that social influences such as groupthink are real phenomena that affect behavior, irrespective of group members' intelligence or commitment to the truth.

The Power of Authority: Obedience

Up to this point in our discussion of social influence, we've concentrated on how behavior is affected by the presence of "others," where the others have simply been any individuals who happen to be present in the social context. But in many cases it does matter *who* these others happen to be—on what roles these people play in one's life. Think back once again to Al Hobart, who opened the chapter. Do you think he would have agreed so readily with his co-workers if the head of advertising had not been standing there, drink in hand, listening intently to his opinions? To what degree was Hobart's behavior changed because it was someone in a

Obedience to authority reached shocking levels in 1978 when followers of Reverend Jim Jones chose, under his direct orders, to commit mass suicide by drinking Kool-Aid laced with cyanide.

position of authority who had asked him his opinion? The question of how behavior changes in the presence of authority is a crucial one, and its study has produced some of the most intriguing and controversial empirical studies in the history of social psychology.

Psychologists use the term **obedience** to refer to the form of compliance that occurs when people respond to the orders of an authority figure. You're of course aware of the fact that during World War II, millions of Jewish men, women, and children were systematically executed by scores of German soldiers working under orders from Nazi officials. In a rural area of Guyana, South America, in 1978, hundreds of converts to the religious teachings of Reverend Jim Jones chose, under his direct orders, to commit mass suicide. Most people find it extremely difficult to understand such events and consider them to be social aberrations committed by people far different from themselves. Admittedly, you might toe the line in front of your boss, and do and say things that you don't really believe, but murder innocent people? Drink Kool-Aid laced with cyanide? Never.

The Milgram Experiment. In what is perhaps the most controversial social psychology experiment ever conducted, psychologist Stanley Milgram set out to determine just how resistant the average person really is to the demands of authority. He placed an advertisement in a local newspaper recruiting men for what was billed as a study looking at the effects of punishment on learning. The participants were told that for a small fee, they would be asked to play one of two roles in the experiment: either a *learner,* which required memorizing and then recalling lists of word pairs, or a *teacher,* whose task it would be to administer an electric shock to the learner whenever he made any recall errors. Each session required two subjects, one teacher and one learner, and the assignment of condition was decided by drawing slips of paper out of a hat.

But things were not exactly what they appeared to be. In fact, in every case the "true" volunteer, the one who had actually responded to the ad, was picked to be the teacher. The "learner" was a *confederate* of the experimenter, someone who was fully informed about the true nature of the study. Although it was rigged to look like he was receiving shocks throughout the session, he never actually did. The idea was to get the confederate to make learning errors and then to assess how willing the teacher would be to administer the shock, under the authority of a hovering and demanding experimenter.

To begin the setup, the unwitting teacher watched as the "learner" was led away to an adjacent room and hooked up to a shock-administering apparatus. Back in the original room, the teacher was then placed in front of an imposing-looking electrical shock generator, which contained some 30 different switches. It was explained that each switch was able to generate a particular level of shock intensity, ranging from 15 volts (Slight Shock), through 150 volts (Strong Shock), and finally up to 450 volts (labeled simply XXX). With the experimenter standing

These three photos were taken during one of Milgram's early experiments on obedience to authority. The first photo shows the shock generator used during the experiment; the second photo shows the "learner," who was actually a confederate of the experimenter, being hooked up to the shocking apparatus; the third photo shows the "teacher" sitting in front of the shock generator, in the presence of the demanding experimenter.

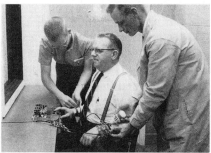

by his side, the teacher was instructed to begin reading and then testing the learner's memory for the words, via intercom, and to administer a shock whenever the learner failed to call out the correct answer. Moreover, in order see how the degree of punishment influenced learning, the teacher was instructed to increase the voltage level of the shock, by moving to a new switch, with each new mistake.

Remember, no one was actually shocked in this experiment; the "learner" was *in* on the experiment, and he was told to make mistakes consistently throughout the session. To add to the "cover," he was also instructed to respond vocally and actively to the shocks, via the intercom, whenever they were delivered. At first, when the shock levels were low, there wasn't much response. But as the prearranged mistakes continued—which, of course, necessitated the teacher to continue increasing the voltage of the shock—loud protests began to come over the intercom. By the time the mistake-prone learner was receiving 150-volt "shocks," he was demanding to be released from the experiment. By around 300 volts, he was screaming in agony in response to each delivered shock and pounding on the wall; after the 330-volt level, the shocks yielded no response at all—simply silence.

Listening to these disturbing pleas for help did not, of course, make the average "teacher" very comfortable. In fact, most quickly expressed concern over the consequences of the shocking and wanted to discontinue the experiment. But the teacher's concerns were met with resistance from the authoritative experimenter, who demanded that the shocks go on. "Please continue," the experimenter responded. "You have no other choice, you must go on." What would you do in this situation? You're participating in an experiment, which is being conducted in the name of science, but the task requires you to inflict quite a bit of pain and suffering on someone else. Do you blindly go forward, delivering shocks in compliance with the requests of the authority figure, or do you quit and give the experimenter a piece of your mind? Of course, this was exactly the question of interest to Milgram—how obedient would people be to unreasonable requests by an authority figure?

Interestingly, before the experiment actually began, Milgram asked a number of people, including professionals, to predict how much shock subjects would be willing to deliver in his task. Most predicted that obedience would be low; the estimates were that only a few people in a thousand would deliver shocks up to 450 volts and that most subjects would defy the experimenter after discomfort was expressed by the learner. In reality, the results were far different. Milgram found that 65% of the 40 subjects who participated were willing to deliver shocks up to 450 volts, and no subject quit before the pounding on the wall started. This means that 26 of the 40 subjects went all the way to the final switch—the one with the ominous XXX label—despite the agonizing pleas from the learner. This remarkable finding rocked the psychological community and initiated a great deal of subsequent research, as well as a firestorm of controversy.

Milgram's (1963) experiment was controversial for two main reasons. First, the manner in which it was conducted raised some serious *ethical* questions. The subjects in his study were misled from the beginning and became severely distressed during their participation. Milgram observed a number of indications of distress during the experiment—the "teachers" sometimes groaned, bit their lips, trembled, stuttered, and even broke into a sweat. Many critics feel that this kind of psychological manipulation—even though it was done to advance knowledge—cannot be justified (Baumrind, 1964; Schlenker & Forsyth, 1977). In response, Milgram (1974) argued that his subjects were thoroughly debriefed at the end of the experiment—they were told in detail about the true nature of the experiment—and were generally glad they had participated. Follow-up questionnaires sent to the subjects months later revealed that only a handful felt negative about the experiment.

The other major question raised about the experiment concerned the procedure itself. Some critics argued that perhaps the participants had seen through the cover and were simply trying to please the experimenter; others argued that the results, although interesting, had no general applicability beyond the laboratory. Subjects must have assumed that things were okay, these critics reasoned; otherwise no one would have believed that an experiment of this type could be conducted. In retort, Milgram again pointed out that his subjects tended to get extremely distressed in the setting, which suggests that they could not have figured out the hoax and were acting in accordance with their true feelings.

In the three-plus decades since Milgram's original experiment was conducted, his general procedure has been repeated a number of times, in many countries around the world (see Blass, 1991; Meeus & Raaijmakers, 1987). Few psychologists today question the validity of his basic findings, although it's clear that the degree of compliance that people will show to authority depends on many factors. For example, the Milgram experiment was conducted at a prestigious university (Yale); when the same study was conducted in a less prestigious setting—a rundown office building—compliance dropped (although it remained alarmingly high). People were also less likely to comply if the authority figure left the room after explaining the experiment or if the person giving the orders looked "ordinary" rather than official or scientific (Milgram, 1974). Thus, obedience to authority is not absolute—it depends on the characteristics of the situation as well as on the characteristics of the person giving the orders.

Can you think of any reasons why it might be adaptive for people to respond so readily to the demands of an authority figure?

Establishing Relations with Others

We have defined social psychology as the discipline that studies how people think about, influence, and relate to other people. Our first two adaptive "problems" have dealt with social thought and social influence. We now turn our attention to the third and final component: How do people establish and maintain *relations* with others? People are not merely objects to be interpreted, or forces that exert influences on behavior. For most individuals, it is the personal relationships they establish with the people around them that are paramount in their lives. People depend on their interactions with friends, lovers, and family not only for protection and sustenance but also to help give their lives meaning.

We've actually encountered the topic of social relations several times in earlier chapters. In Chapter 4, for example, when we discussed social development we dealt in detail with the topic of *attachment*. But in that case, we were concerned with how people use social bonds to help solve the problems that arise during development. Infants are born with limited motor skills and somewhat immature perceptual systems; consequently, they need to establish strong bonds with their caregivers in order to survive. In Chapter 11, when we discussed motivation and emotion, we saw how people use facial expressions to communicate their emotions to others and how people are motivated to secure sexual partners. Again, the emphasis was placed on the adaptive value of the relationship rather than on understanding the role that the social context plays in the process. In this section, we'll consider some of the factors that influence interpersonal attraction, which often forms the basis for relationship development, and then we'll discuss how psychologists have attempted to tackle the mysterious subject of love.

Interpersonal Attraction: Determinants of Liking and Loving

If you had to list all the things you look for in a friend, what would they be? Understanding? a sense of humor? intelligence? What if the word *husband, wife,* or *lover* were substituted for *friend*—would the characteristics on your list change?

INSIDE ▷ THE PROBLEM: *Culture and the Individual*

We've discussed how the thoughts and actions of individuals change when they're in the presence of others, particularly groups. The group can exert a powerful influence on members' judgments, leading to conformity, groupthink, and obedience to authority. In some cases, people may find themselves succumbing to the group's demands at the expense of their own personal convictions. Remember Al Hobart and the questions we posed at the opening to this chapter? Have the preceding sections in this chapter changed your mind about how you might act in such a situation?

But is the tendency to conform, or to sacrifice one's individual desires for the collective, necessarily bad? Is conformity or obedience a sign of weakness, or is it a sign of strength? The answer depends partly on the culture in which people are raised. In most Western cultures, such as the United States, people are taught from a very young age to adopt an *independent* view of the self; that is, people are rewarded for viewing themselves as unique individuals, with special and distinctive qualities. American children, for example, are likely to be told things like "the squeaky wheel gets the grease." Be someone different, be an individual with unique qualities—these are the things that count. Although Western cultures certainly value acts of charity or unselfish devotion to others, such acts are typically viewed as reflecting distinctive personal qualities—qualities that make someone stand out as an admirable *individual.*

In some Asian cultures, children are encouraged to adopt an "interdependent" view of self; that is, they are taught to view themselves primarily as members of a group with common goals rather than as individuals striving to be different.

In many non-Western cultures, particularly Asian cultures, people adopt a very different, *interdependent* view of the self (Markus & Kitayama, 1991, 1994). In Japan, for example, children are taught to think of themselves from the perspective of the collective—as members of a group with common goals—rather than as individuals striving to be different. In Japan, children are told, "The nail that stands out gets pounded down." Such cultural differences are reflected in people's inner thoughts and feelings. When asked to write self-descriptions, Asians are likely to list personal qualities that they share with others ("I come from Kyoto") and to think they are more similar to others than others are to them. Westerners, in contrast, tend to describe themselves as dissimilar to others, and they use individ-ualistic characteristics ("I'm very talented on the flute") to describe themselves (Trafimow, Triandis, & Goto, 1991). The majority of Westerners also tend to think of themselves as above average in intelligence and leadership ability, which is a trend rarely seen among Asians (Markus & Kitayama, 1991).

What do such findings mean? They should reinforce in your mind the idea that cultural factors cannot be ignored in the interpretation and study of behavior and mind. People's thoughts and actions often arise from their efforts to adapt successfully to their individual environments. As cultural demands on the individual vary, so too will the resulting behaviors that are seen.

Might you add wealth, security, or attractiveness? If you actually ask people to create such a list—and psychologists have done so on a number of occasions—most people have no trouble coming up with a "wish list" of characteristics for "friend" or "marriage partner of my dreams." But how important do these well-thought-out and carefully chosen factors turn out to be? Do people really form friendships, or choose marriage partners, based on some relationship "equation" that sums desirable and undesirable attributes in a logical and rational way?

One of the most important lessons of this textbook, and certainly of this chapter, is that human behavior is strongly influenced by external forces in the environment. People act the way they do partly because of conscious, internally driven processes, but also because the environment shapes and constrains the behaviors that are possible. In the case of interpersonal attraction, it turns out that the environment often plays a major role in determining whom one chooses to spend time with, as well as whom one considers to be attractive. As was pointed out earlier in this chapter, even mere exposure to something can be sufficient to increase its likability (Zajonc, 1968). People like things that are familiar, even when that familiarity has been induced by simple repetition in the environment.

Proximity. In a classic study conducted nearly 50 years ago, psychologist Leon Festinger and his colleagues (1950) analyzed the friendships that formed among students living in an apartment complex near the Massachusetts Institute of Technology. The apartment building was an excellent testing ground for the study because as students, the occupants were unlikely to have known each other prior to moving into the building, and they were assigned to particular apartments on essentially a random basis. Festinger and his colleagues found that they could predict the likelihood of a friendship forming by simply noting the *proximity*—defined in terms of the closeness of living quarters—between two people in the building. When the students were asked to list their three closest friends, two-thirds of the time they named students who lived in their same apartment complex. Moreover, when a fellow apartment dweller was listed as a friend, two-thirds of the time he or she lived on the same floor as the respondent. Clearly, the choice of friends is strongly influenced by where one lives. People tend to end up with friends who live nearby.

Of course, it isn't really proximity by itself that leads to liking and loving. When somebody lives close by, you see him or her a lot, and it may be the increased exposure that promotes the attraction. We've already seen that increased exposure leads to an increase in rated likability, but it also provides the opportunity for interaction. When you consistently interact with someone, mutual feelings of connectedness and belonging tend to follow (Cantor & Malley, 1991). You tend to see each other as members of the same "in-group"—that is, as individuals who share features in common. In fact, you don't even have to interact physically with someone for increased liking to occur. Psychologists John Darley and Ellen Berscheid (1967) found that even the anticipation of an interaction with someone that you don't already know can cause you to rate that person as more attractive.

Our friends often turn out to be people who live nearby, demonstrating a role for "proximity" in interpersonal attraction.

Birds of a feather do tend to flock together—more often than not, we form lasting relationships with people who are similar to ourselves.

Similarity. Proximity promotes interaction, and interaction sets the occasion for the discovery of similarities. More often than not, people tend to like and form relationships with others who are *similar* to them. Friends and intimate partners typically resemble each other in age, social status, education level, race, religious beliefs, political attitudes, intelligence, and even physical attractiveness. People may report preferring physically attractive mates, but most end up marrying someone who is approximately equal to them in degree of physical attractiveness (Feingold, 1988, 1990). So, if you believe in the idea that "opposites attract," think again—in reality, it is the birds of a feather that tend consistently to flock together.

Although few psychologists question the finding that similarities attract, there are disagreements about how best to interpret this finding. The fact that correlations exist among the physical and attitudinal dimensions of friends and lovers doesn't provide any insight into *why* these similarities exist. As we discussed in Chapter 2, correlations do not imply causality. One possibility is that we like others who share our beliefs and attitudes because they *validate* those beliefs, which further helps convince us that our beliefs are the right ones (Byrne, 1971; Laprelle and others, 1990). Another possibility is that we spend time with others like ourselves because we *dislike* people who hold different views (Rosenbaum, 1986). It's not so much that we want to spend time with those who resemble us, it's that we don't want to spend time with those we despise.

A third possibility is that personal and intellectual characteristics shape the environment in such a way as to limit the range of possible candidates for a relationship. Part of the reason that partners in romantic relationships tend to be matched in level of physical attractiveness may be that they are unable to attract mates who are more attractive; or, it could be that society dictates that they reject those who are less attractive. Socioeconomic class also tends to limit people's options. If you are poor and live in a poor section of town, your interactions are likely to be with individuals who are members of the same socioeconomic class. Generally, people who live in the same neighborhood, attend the same church, or go off to the same university already share many features in common, and it is from this pool that people typically find their companions.

Think about your own experiences in relationships. Have you ever felt peer pressure to find a partner who meets a well-defined set of standards?

Reciprocity. There is also a role in the dynamics of interpersonal attraction for **reciprocity,** or people's tendency to return in kind the feelings that are shown toward them. If someone doesn't like you and displays hostility at every turn, you usually have similar negative feelings toward him or her. If someone likes you, or even if you simply think the person likes you, then you tend to like that person back (Curtis & Miller, 1986; Kelley, 1983). In a study by Curtis and Miller (1986), participants were asked to have a conversation with someone who they believed had been told either positive or negative information about them (actually, the conversation partner hadn't been told anything). If the subjects believed they were talking to someone who perceived them in a positive light, they tended to be friendlier and more open in their conversation—they acted as if they liked their partner more.

Reciprocity helps lead to interpersonal attraction, because it is self-fulfilling and because people who like you tend to be reinforcing and accepting of your actions. But it doesn't always work. If you feel that the positive actions of another are motivated for some selfish reason—as part of a con job or to get something such as a promotion—then your reaction will typically be negative (Jones, 1964). Ingratiation, in which a person consciously tries to win the affections of another for some ulterior motive, is likely to backfire as a strategy if it is discovered.

The Psychology of Romantic Love

When psychologists study a topic such as *interpersonal attraction,* it's likely to be seen as an interesting and important research endeavor by most casual observers. But when psychologists turn to the study of "love," as you might imagine, the reactions are often far different. How, you ask, can someone understand, define, or attempt to measure something like love? Love is a topic to be tackled by the poet or the artist, not the questionnaire-laden social psychologist. Perhaps, but as you'll soon see, that hasn't stopped psychologists from trying.

Defining Love. Love is generally recognized to be a complex psychological state that comes in a variety of forms. There is the love that exists between parent and child, between lovers, between husband and wife, even between friends. In each case, when it's measured through a questionnaire, the relationship is typically characterized by the giving and receiving of support, a kind of mutual understanding, and intense personal satisfaction (Fehr & Russell, 1991; Sternberg & Grajek, 1984). Although there may be fundamental similarities in how love is experienced, the amount of love that is reported depends on the type of relationship studied. Women, for example, might report *loving* their lover more than a best friend, but *liking* their best friend more; men, on the other hand, report liking *and* loving their lover more than they report these feelings for their friends (Sternberg, 1986).

When the relationship between two individuals is romantic, it is popular to distinguish further between passionate love and companionate love. **Passionate love** is an intense emotional state in which the individual is enveloped by a powerful longing to be with the other person (Hatfield, 1988). For many people, passionate love resembles a ride on a kind of emotional roller coaster—they experience intense joy if the feelings are reciprocated, and intense pain and despair if their feelings are unrequited. **Companionate love** tends to be less emotional and intense, but its feelings of trust and warmth can be more enduring. Whereas passionate love leads to intense arousal, companionate love leads to self-disclosure—we are willing to reveal our innermost secrets because the relationship sits on a bedrock of trust. It is, of course, possible for both passionate love and companionate love to be present in the same relationship, but this is not always the case.

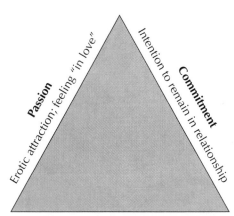

Passion

Erotic attraction: feeling "in love"

Commitment

Intention to remain in relationship

Confiding in others and sharing feelings
Intimacy

Passion	Intimacy	Commitment	Type of love that results
+	−	−	Infatuated love
−	+	−	Liking (friendship)
−	−	+	Empty love
+	+	−	Romantic love
−	+	+	Companionate love
+	−	+	Fatuous love

FIGURE 13.8
The Triangular View of Love.
Robert Sternberg has proposed that there are many kinds of love, each defined by the degree of *passion*, *intimacy*, and *commitment* present in the relationship. For example, "infatuation" is a kind of love with lots of passion but little intimacy or commitment, whereas "empty love" has commitment but little passion or intimacy. (Based on Sternberg, 1986)

 If you had to write out a prescription for a successful marriage, what ratings on each of the dimensions of the triangle—intimacy, passion, and commitment—would you personally recommend?

The Triangular View of Love. Psychologist Robert Sternberg (1986, 1988) has argued for what he calls a triangular view of love. He sees love as triangular because it is composed of three major dimensions—*intimacy, passion,* and *commitment*—that vary in relation to one another (see Figure 13.8). Intimacy is the emotional component that brings closeness, connectedness, and warmth to a relationship. Passion is the motivational component that underlies arousal, physical attraction, and sexual behavior. Commitment is the decision-making arm of love—how willing are the partners to stick with the relationship in times of trouble? All forms of love can be seen as some combination of these three components. For example, according to Sternberg (1986), romantic love is marked by a combination of intimacy and passion (but it may lack the commitment), companionate love is high in intimacy and commitment (but without passion), and "empty" love occurs when there is commitment but little or no passion or intimacy.

In addition to using his triangle as a vehicle for defining love, Sternberg has followed other researchers in attempting to map out how the components of love change over time (see Berscheid, 1985; Hatfield & Rapson, 1993). What patterns have been found? Do couples gain intimacy? lose passion? become increasingly willing to commit? It is impossible to predict for any particular relationship, but the theory proposes some general trends. On the average, for example, the passion component of love builds early and rapidly in a relationship—it can even be experienced almost immediately on meeting another—but it's difficult to sustain for long periods. Commitment, on the other hand, is slow to develop but can be quite long-lasting. Intimacy, too, is unlikely to be found early in a relationship (there is too much uncertainty), but it grows and maintains itself in most successful relationships. The components of love are conceived therefore as fluid, changing over time in ways that reflect the successes and failures of the interactions between the partners.

► SOLVING THE PROBLEMS: A SUMMARY

Throughout this text, we've repeatedly stressed the idea that humans neither develop nor live in a vacuum. People's actions, thoughts, and feelings arise out of their interactions with ever-changing environments. Among the most powerful components of the environments that people face are *social* ones—their thoughts and actions are strongly influenced by others around them. Social psychology is the discipline that studies how people think about, influence, and relate to others. In this chapter, we tackled the topic areas of social psychology from the perspective of three major adaptive problems.

▶ **INTERPRETING THE BEHAVIOR OF OTHERS** As individuals move through the social world, it's extremely adaptive for them to use their cognitive processes to help make sense of others around them. People form initial impressions of others by using the information they have available—such as the physical appearance of the person—and by relying on preexisting knowledge structures, called social schemas, to help them interpret that information. Schemas are useful features of the adaptive mind because they enable people to direct their actions in uncertain situations. But schemas can also lead to stereotypes—beliefs about individuals belonging to groups—which, although useful in many ways, can produce prejudice.

An important part of the overall interpretation process is people's attributions—how they infer the causes of another's behavior. When searching for reasons *why* others act the way they do, people look for factors that covary with the behavior and they assess the consistency of the behavior, its distinctiveness, and whether or not there is consensus among people. Whether one places the locus of causality in the external environment or within the person depends on how these factors of consistency, distinctiveness, and consensus work together. There are also some basic attribution biases—such as the fundamental attribution error—that help shape the attributions people make.

Attitudes, which are positive or negative evaluations, are typically separated into three components: a cognitive component, an affective component, and a behavioral component. Attitude formation is influenced by a number of factors, but direct experience plays a major role. One popular theory of attitude change is the elaboration likelihood model, which proposes that there are central and peripheral routes to persuasion. It's clear from a number of research studies that when people are induced to act in ways that are inconsistent with their existing attitudes, their attitudes often change as a result.

▶ **BEHAVING IN THE PRESENCE OF OTHERS** Psychologists use the term *social influence* to refer to how behavior is affected by other people in one's environment. Sometimes social influence can produce positive effects, as in social facilitation, and sometimes the presence of others hinders performance, as in social interference. The relationship between arousal and performance might explain some of these patterns. The presence of other people can have an arousing effect, and depending on whether the task is easy or hard, performance will be facilitated or impaired. The presence of other people can also affect one's willingness to deliver aid to people in need. The bystander effect demonstrates that individuals are generally reluctant to come to someone's aid when other people are present. One interpretation of this effect appeals to diffusion of responsibility: The individual believes that others have already done something to help or will soon get involved.

Behavior is also strongly influenced by the social pressures of groups and of authority. Participation as a member of a well-defined group can make people conform, which means that their opinions and behaviors will tend to move toward the group norm. Conformity operates on the group level as well. It is common for groups to polarize, which means that the group's dominant point of view tends to become stronger and more extreme with the passage of time. If the phenomenon of "groupthink" is present, members have become so interested in seeking a consensus of opinion that dissenting views start to be ignored or suppressed. Milgram's famous experiment on obedience to authority demonstrated that people can be induced by an authority figure to engage in behavior that they would not engage in otherwise.

The degree of compliance depends on the characteristics of the situation and on the characteristics of the person giving the orders.

▶ **ESTABLISHING RELATIONS WITH OTHERS** Often the most meaningful things in people's lives are the social relations they establish with others. Among the factors that influence liking and loving are familiarity, proximity, similarity, and reciprocity. People are more likely to be attracted to someone they know, who lives nearby, who is similar to themselves, and who likes them back. Psychologists have also attempted to understand love, which is typically defined in terms of multiple components—such as intimacy, passion, and commitment—acting together. Whether a person ends up in a relationship based on passionate love or companionate love depends on the relative amounts of each of these three components in the relationship.

Terms to Remember

social psychology The discipline that studies how people think about, influence, and relate to other people.

INTERPRETING THE BEHAVIOR OF OTHERS: SOCIAL COGNITION

social cognition The study of how people use cognitive processes—such as perception, memory, thought, and emotion—to help them make sense of other people as well as themselves.

social schemas General knowledge structures, stored in long-term memory, that relate to social experiences or people.

self-fulfilling prophecy effect A condition in which people's expectations about the actions of another person actually lead that person to behave in the expected way.

stereotypes The collection of beliefs held about the personal traits and behaviors of individuals belonging to a particular group; common stereotypes include those based on gender, race, and age.

attributions The inference processes people use to assign cause and effect to behavior.

external attribution Attributing the cause of a person's behavior to an external event or situation in the environment.

internal attribution Attributing the cause of a person's behavior to an internal personality trait or disposition.

fundamental attribution error The fact that people seeking to interpret someone else's behavior tend to overestimate the influence of internal personal factors and underestimate the role of situational factors.

self-serving bias The tendency to make internal attributions about one's own behavior when the outcome is positive and to blame the situation when one's behavior leads to something negative.

attitude A positive or negative evaluation or belief held about something, which in turn may affect one's behavior; attitudes are typically broken down into cognitive, affective, and behavioral components.

elaboration likelihood model A model proposing two primary routes to persuasion and attitude change: a *central* route, which operates when people are motivated and focusing their attention on the message, and a *peripheral* route, which operates when people are either unmotivated to process the message or are unable to do so.

cognitive dissonance The tension produced when people act in a way that is inconsistent with their attitudes; attitude change may occur as a result of attempting to reduce cognitive dissonance.

self-perception theory The idea that people use observations of their own behavior as a basis for inferring their internal beliefs.

BEHAVING IN THE PRESENCE OF OTHERS: SOCIAL INFLUENCE

social influence The study of how the behaviors and thoughts of individuals are affected by the presence of others.

social facilitation The enhancement in performance that is sometimes found when an individual performs in the presence of others.

social interference The impairment in performance that is sometimes found when an individual performs in the presence of others.

diffusion of responsibility The idea that when people know, or think, that others are present in a situation, they allow their sense of responsibility for action to diffuse, or spread out widely, among those who are present.

bystander effect The reluctance to come to the aid of a person in need when other people are present.

social loafing The tendency to put out less effort when working in a group compared to when working alone.

conformity The tendency to comply, or go along, with the wishes of the group; when people conform, their opinions, feelings, and behaviors generally start to move toward the group norm.

in-group A group of individuals with whom one shares features in common, or with whom one identifies.

group polarization The tendency for a group's dominant point of view to become stronger and more extreme with time.

groupthink The tendency for members of a group to become so interested in seeking a consensus of opinion that they start to ignore and even suppress dissenting views.

obedience The form of compliance that occurs when people respond to the orders of an authority figure.

ESTABLISHING RELATIONS WITH OTHERS

reciprocity The tendency for people to return in kind the feelings that are shown toward them.

passionate love An intense emotional state characterized by a powerful longing to be with a specific person; passionate love is marked by a combination of intimacy and passion, but commitment may be lacking.

companionate love A kind of emotional attachment characterized by feelings of trust and companionship; companionate love is marked by a combination of intimacy and commitment, but passion may be lacking.

For most people, few things are as alluring as the sight of an attractive face. Beauty is a powerful motivator of behavior, which is confirmed by the fact that many millions of dollars are spent annually on cosmetics and other beauty aids. The concept of attractiveness is important to the psychologist because people's physical appearance often helps shape how their behavior will be interpreted, and thereby how they will be treated by others. As we've discussed in this chapter, people commonly rely on social schemas to form impressions, and there is considerable evidence to suggest that they use physical attractiveness as a basis for generating expectations about others (Eagly and others, 1991). Just think about the words of the 19th-century German poet Johann Schiller: "Physical beauty is the sign of an interior beauty, a spiritual and moral beauty." Schiller's insight is certainly not lost on modern advertisers who, as we know, rely heavily on the power of an attractive face to help sell their clients' products.

But what exactly is it that makes a face physically beautiful? What are the qualities that determine whether someone's looks are considered desirable? One way to think about this problem is from the perspective of evolutionary theory. If the purpose of attraction is to snare an "ideal" mate, then preferably it should be someone with a high reproductive capacity or someone who is able to provide protection for his or her children and compete successfully for needed resources. This kind of reasoning predicts that people should be attracted to opposite-sex members who are youthful, vigorous, and healthy looking, because these qualities increase the likelihood of successful reproduction and child-rearing (Alley & Cunningham, 1991; Buss, 1989; Buss & Schmitt, 1993).

Another prediction of the evolutionary perspective is that features of attractiveness should cut across cultural boundaries. If attractiveness is grounded somewhere deep in our genetic ancestry, then it shouldn't matter much where individuals are reared and what experi-

ences they have; in general, there should be worldwide agreement about what constitutes attractiveness. Notice that this conclusion contrasts sharply with the generally accepted idea that "beauty is in the eye of the beholder," but it's supported, at least in part, by empirical research. A number of studies have found that when ratings of attractiveness are compared cross-culturally, attractive faces share a number of basic structural features (Bernstein, Lin, & McClelland, 1982; McArthur & Berry, 1987). It has also been discovered that babies as young as 3 months prefer to look at pictures of faces that adults have rated as attractive over faces that have been rated as unattractive (Langlois and others, 1987). It's unlikely that we can appeal to experience—that is, sustained exposure to some culturally based definition of beauty—to account for this preference.

Attractive Faces Are Average
Recent research by psychologists Judith Langlois and Lori Roggman (1990; Langlois, Roggman, & Musselman, 1994)

The faces shown in each row are composites created by averaging either two individual faces (far left), 8 faces (middle photos in each row), or 32 faces (far right). The stimuli were created using the averaging process employed by Langlois and Roggman. (Courtesy Judith Langlois)

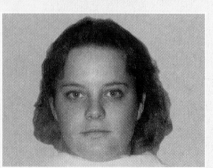
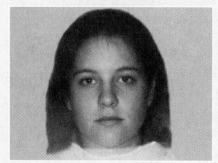
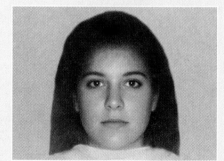

suggests that the universality of attractiveness may be partly due to the fact that people are programmed to prefer faces that are "average" representations of faces in the population. By average, Langlois and Roggman do not necessarily mean common, typical, or frequently occurring faces. Instead, they mean prototypical faces—that is, faces that are good representations of the category "faces." Back in Chapter 9, we defined category prototypes as the best or most representative members of a category—a robin, for example, is probably close to the prototype for the category *bird*. According to Langlois and Roggman, attractive faces are those that are particularly *facelike*, or representative of the category of faces.

They based their conclusions on research in which subjects were asked to rate the attractiveness of "average faces" that were generated electronically on a computer. To create these faces, hundreds of individual black-and-white photographs, composed of either male or female Caucasians, Asians, and Hispanics, were first scanned by a computer and then digitized into matrices of individual "gray values." Each of these gray values corresponded to a shade of gray sitting at a particular small location on the scanned face. A whole face was represented by many thousands of these gray values, as they are in a typical newspaper photo or video display. As you probably know, any image that you see in a newspaper or on a video monitor is actually a configuration of many rows and columns of individual

intensity dots or pixels. When viewed as a whole, the dots blend together to form a familiar image on the page or screen.

The unique feature of the Langlois and Roggman research was that people were sometimes shown faces that were generated by averaging the gray values across a large collection of individual faces. An individual dot in one of these *composite* faces was set by averaging the values of all the dots at the same relative location in the face "pool." The result was a kind of blended face that did not look exactly like any one of the individual faces but rather represented a kind of "prototype" face in the population. Volunteer participants were asked to rate these faces for attractiveness, along with the individual faces that had been used to form the composite. The surprising result was that people generally rated the composite faces as more attractive than the individual faces.

Why would people prefer faces that are prototypical? Langlois and Roggman offer several speculative reasons. One possibility is that prototypical faces are easy to identify and classify as human faces. Classifying something as a face may not seem like much of task for adults, but it could well be for the newborn infant. It is critical for infants to be able to recognize a looming visual configuration as a face, because they are dependent on their social interactions with people for survival. Yet the visual acuity of the newborn is limited, so faces that are particularly "facelike" may make this critical classification process easier. Another possibility is that people are

programmed biologically to prefer prototypical faces because individuals with average features may be less likely to harbor potentially harmful genetic mutations. Generally, it is the average or normal characteristics that tend to be preferred over extreme ones in a population.

The Subjective Component
Despite the evidence for universality in how people conceive of attractiveness, most psychologists recognize that there is a strong subjective component to the perception of beauty as well. Standards of beauty have changed over time in most cultures of the world. In Western societies, for instance, our icon of beauty, the fashion model, has ranged from a "curvaceous bustiness" at one point to slender tomboyishness at the next (Silverstein and others, 1986). It's also the case that features considered attractive in one culture—pierced noses, liposuctioned thighs, elongated ear lobes—are considered abhorrent in another. Perceptions of attractiveness and beauty also clearly change with experience. People rate those they know and like as more attractive, and if they've just been shown a picture of a strikingly attractive person, their ratings of average-looking people go down (Kenrick, Gutierres, & Goldberg, 1989). Beauty is not entirely in the eye of the beholder, as the research of Langlois and Roggman (1990) indicates, but there is indeed a measurable subjective component that cannot be ignored.

Psychological Disorders

14

Though this be madness, yet there be method in't.

William Shakespeare
Hamlet

You shouldn't really be reading this book, you know. In fact, put it down—now. The author's intentions are not pure . . . he doesn't have your best interest in mind. He wants to convince you that you have no true control over your life. To him, you are nothing more than a mindless automaton shaped by the whims of changing environments; you are the product of forces outside of your control—biological drives, toilet-training habits, unbalanced mixtures of neurotransmitters in your brain.

But you and I are more than that—we are more than the product of brain biochemistry or dirty little habits. We have inner control over our lives. You and I are in touch with the essence of the inner one, although, perhaps, it is only I who recognizes this fact at the moment. I've stopped you because it's time to prepare ourselves now . . . the first of the tribe arrived weeks ago . . . he's here, inside my head, and he's telling me the real truth. There's nothing to fear . . . we're still in control . . . it will be our choice, not theirs, to submit. And when we do, the truth about the conspiracy will be revealed to all. . . .

Imagine being on the receiving end of such a conversation. What would be your reaction? At best, I suspect you'd categorize this person as odd; more likely, you'd label him as definitely disturbed. There are features to his line of thought that are distorted, and he is more than a bit paranoid. But does he suffer from a *true* psychological disorder needing treatment, or is he simply eccentric? How can we tell? What are the criteria that psychologists use to define and describe psychological disorders and abnormal behavior? Is distorted thinking merely a personal choice, to be respected and endured, or is it something more akin to strep throat or a bladder infection—something that we should make a concerted effort to treat and cure?

Over the next two chapters, we'll turn our attention to the classification and treatment of psychological disorders. Obviously, before treating a psychological problem, it needs to be determined that there is indeed a problem that needs to be treated. Making this determination is more difficult than you might think. Let's suppose you arrive home tonight and find your roommate awake but slumped in a corner with his cap pulled down over his eyes. You ask him to explain, but he tells you to mind your own business. Later that night, you hear sobbing and crying coming from behind his locked bedroom door. His bizarre behavior continues for the next two days. He refuses to respond to questions, he stops going to class, and he refuses to eat or clean himself. He's suffering from a psychological disorder, right? Perhaps, but what if I tell you that his father and mother were just killed in an automobile accident? What would your reaction be now? Would you conclude that he is psychologically disturbed, or is he simply showing an intense but normal grief reaction?

PREVIEWING THE CONCEPTUAL AND PRACTICAL PROBLEMS

To help you understand what psychologists mean when they talk about psychological or mental disorders, our discussion will revolve around three basic conceptual and practical problems: What is the proper way to conceptualize and define abnormal behavior? How can experts classify the various psychological disorders that reliably produce abnormal behavior? Finally, what are the underlying causes of psychological disorders?

CONCEPTUALIZING ABNORMALITY The behavior of individuals who suffer from psychological problems is typically considered to be "abnormal." Indeed, the terms *abnormal* and *abnormal behavior* are often used as roughly equivalent to the term *psychological disorder*. But over the years, psychologists have struggled with how best to define the concept of abnormality. When individuals act abnormally, their behavior tends to be unusual or dysfunctional, and they often appear to be suffering from considerable personal distress. But for reasons that we'll discuss in the first section of the chapter, none of these criteria alone is sufficient to capture the concept. Most conceptualizations of abnormality rely on multiple criteria.

Further, should abnormal behavior be viewed as reflective of a "disease" in the physical body that needs to be "treated" like any other medical problem? Some mental health professionals believe it should, but others think it's inappropriate to view psychological problems as "illnesses"; instead, most forms of abnormal behavior may be better seen as adjustment problems, or problems in living. We'll discuss these arguments, in part, because they'll help you understand how disorders are classified in terms of the "medical model." Finally, we'll consider some of the consequences of labeling someone as abnormal. Once the diagnosis is made, the label "abnormal" can affect how people react to the labeled individual, often with negative and unproductive consequences.

CLASSIFYING PSYCHOLOGICAL DISORDERS Even if psychologists can reach agreement about the proper way to define abnormality, they still need a means for naming and classifying the underlying disorders that lead to abnormal behavior. Psychologists and psychiatrists have worked hard to develop a rigorous system for the diagnosis and classification of psychological disorders. We'll consider the current system, which is detailed in the *Diagnostic and Statistical Manual of Mental Disorders* (4th ed.), and we'll see how it is used to diagnose a variety of mental problems. There are many kinds of known psychological disorders—ranging from anxiety disorders to depression to schizophrenia—and each is classified on the basis of a relatively fixed set of criteria. Although it is a common belief among the general public that psychological disorders are idiosyncratic—which means that they arise in different ways for different individuals—we'll see that most disorders actually produce symptoms that are fairly reliable; they occur consistently across diagnosed individuals.

UNDERSTANDING PSYCHOLOGICAL DISORDERS In the final section of the chapter, we'll discuss how researchers attempt to understand the causes of psychological disorders. What causes an anxiety disorder, a mood disorder such as depression, or schizophrenia? Do psychological disorders reflect some kind of mental breakdown, or are they simply adaptive reactions of the mind to stress? If it's a breakdown, is the locus of the breakdown biological or environmental? When someone is depressed, for example, is it because of a problem with the chemistry of the brain? Or has the afflicted individual learned to act in depressed ways either through modeling the behavior of others or because acting depressed has received some reinforcement? We'll consider the major theoretical tools that psychologists use to explain abnormal behavior. Not surprisingly, the answer to many psychological problems lies in an interaction between biological, cognitive, and environmental factors.

Although it looks as if this person is suffering from a psychological disorder, she might be showing a normal grief reaction, such as to the death of a relative or friend.

Conceptualizing Abnormality: What Is Abnormal Behavior?

When you encounter someone who babbles on about how voices in his or her head are busy plotting a conspiracy, it's not difficult for you to categorize this behavior as abnormal; clearly, this person is in trouble and in need of some professional help. But as we've seen, sharp dividing lines do not always exist between normal and abnormal behavior. Sometimes behavior that appears abnormal can turn out to be a reasonable reaction to a stressful event, such as the roommate's reaction to the death of his parents. It's also the case that a behavior that seems abnormal in one culture can appear to be perfectly normal in another. Entering a trance state and experiencing visual hallucinations is considered abnormal in Western cultures, but in other cultures it may not be (Bentall, 1990).

Even within a culture, conceptions of abnormality can change over time. For many years homosexuality was considered deviant and abnormal by the psychological community. But this view of homosexuality is rejected by most psychologists today. Fifty years ago, a strong dependence on tobacco would not have raised many eyebrows, but today such a dependence might be classified as a substance-related disorder by many professionals. As times change, so do conceptions of what are "appropriate" and "inappropriate" actions. For these reasons, psychologists are justifiably cautious when it comes to applying the label of abnormality. Behavior usually needs to match a set of criteria before it can be labeled as abnormal.

> Suppose a 70-year-old entered college and started acting exactly the same way as a 20-year-old sophomore. Would you consider his or her behavior to be "abnormal"?

Characteristics of Abnormal Behavior

Over the years, researchers have proposed and discussed a variety of defining criteria for the concept of abnormality. In each case, as you'll see, the proposed criteria capture some of the important features of what is agreed to be "abnormal behavior," but not others.

 Statistical Deviance. One relatively straightforward way to define abnormal behavior is in terms of **statistical deviance,** or infrequency. For any given behavior, such as arguing with your neighbors or hearing voices, there is a certain probability that the behavior will occur in society at large. Most people have argued with their neighbors at one time or another, but few actually converse with dis-

Entering a trance state is likely to be classified as "abnormal behavior" in Western cultures, but in other cultures it may not be.

embodied voices. According to the concept of statistical deviance, a behavior is abnormal if it occurs infrequently among the members of a population. As you've learned elsewhere in this text, it's not unusual for psychologists to classify behavior on the basis of statistical frequency. For example, terms such as *gifted* and *mentally retarded* are defined with respect to statistical frequencies. So it should come as no surprise that statistical frequencies have been used to define abnormality.

But statistical deviance—that is, something that is extreme or different from the average—cannot be used as the sole criterion for labeling a behavior as abnormal. It's easy to come up with a list of behaviors or abilities that are statistically infrequent but are not abnormal in a psychological sense. For example, Michael Jordan and Shaquille O'Neal have skills on the basketball court that are extreme, and thereby statistically deviant, but to be a great athlete does not make one abnormal. Similarly, only a handful of individuals have reached the intellectual heights of Albert Einstein or Isaac Newton, but superior intelligence is not abnormal in the usual psychological sense of the word. An additional problem with the concept of statistical deviance is the establishment of a criterion point: Just how infrequent or unusual does a behavior need to be to be characterized as abnormal? No answer to this question is likely to be widely accepted by psychologists.

Michael Jordan's behavior on a basketball court is certainly "statistically deviant," but it's not something that we would want to classify as "abnormal" in a psychological sense.

Cultural Deviance. Another possible criterion is **cultural deviance,** which compares behavior to existing cultural norms. In this case, a behavior is abnormal if it violates the accepted standards of society. In most cultures, for example, it is not considered normal or acceptable to walk to class in the nude or to engage in sexual relations with children. These behaviors break the established rules of our culture, and if you engage in either it's likely that people will think you have a serious problem.

But once again, cultural deviance, by itself, fails as a sufficient criterion. Many criminals violate the established norms of society—stealing cars or embezzling money, for example. Such behavior might be abnormal by both statistical and cultural standards, but that doesn't mean all criminals suffer from psychological disorders. There are also many individuals who suffer from legitimate psychological problems, such as anxiety or depression, who never violate any law or established standard of society. Finally, as we discussed previously, behaviors that are abnormal in one culture may be considered normal in another. There are cultures in the world, for instance, where nakedness in public breaks no established cultural rules. People who suffer from psychological disorders may indeed violate cultural norms in some instances, but often they do not.

Emotional Distress. A third characteristic of many kinds of abnormal behavior is the presence of personal or **emotional distress.** People who suffer from psychological disorders, especially of the type that we'll be considering in this chapter, often experience great despair and unhappiness. They feel hopeless, lost, and alienated from others. In fact, it is the emotional distress that usually leads them to seek professional help for their problem. But as you can probably guess, not all disorders make people unhappy. There are individuals, for example, who have little contact with reality but seem perfectly content in their fantasy world. Likewise, there are many distressed people in the world—for example, those who have recently lost a loved one or a job—who would not be classified as abnormal by the psychological community.

Dysfunction. A final criterion for abnormality assesses the general adaptiveness of the individual's behavior. Is there a breakdown in normal functioning—a **dysfunction**—that prevents the individual from successfully following adaptive strategies? People who suffer from psychological disorders are often unable to function well in typical daily activities—they may not eat properly, clean themselves, or be able to hold a job. Their ability to think properly may be impaired,

Suppose you're a U.S. fighter pilot shot down over enemy lines. Don't you think it would be adaptive to think that everyone around you is out to get you?

To identify abnormal behavior, mental health professionals often look for a breakdown in global functioning: How well can the individual function in typical daily activities?

which affects their ability to adapt successfully in their environment. As we'll see later, the assessment of global functioning—defined as the ability to adapt in social, personal, and occupational environments—plays a large role in the diagnosis and treatment of psychological disorders.

Summarizing the Criteria. We've seen that abnormal behavior can be behavior that is statistically or culturally deviant, it can involve personal or emotional distress, and it can signal impairment or dysfunction. Normal behavior, then, could be any behavior that is relatively common, does not cause personal distress, or generally leads to adaptive consequences. However, psychologists will usually refuse to label any behavior as normal or abnormal unless it satisfies several of these criteria rather than just one. Crying hysterically for hours at a time may be a normal grief reaction, or it may signal a serious disorder. Even a behavior that seems to be clearly abnormal—such as a paranoid delusion that people are out to get you—might be adaptive in some environments. To paraphrase comedian Woody Allen, paranoids can have enemies, too.

It's also important to remember that "abnormal" and "normal" are not fixed and rigid categories that define people. Each of us can relate in one way or another to the criteria of abnormality that we've just discussed. We all know people who have occasionally acted unusually, suffered from emotional distress, or failed to follow an adaptive strategy. Many psychological disorders are characterized by behaviors or feelings that are merely exaggerations of "normal" ones, such as anxiety, feelings of sadness, or concerns about one's health. Consequently, it's better to think about normal and abnormal behavior as endpoints on a *continuum*, rather than as nonoverlapping categories (see Figure 14.1). (For a discussion of the legal concept of *insanity,* which differs from the concept of a psychological disorder, see the accompanying Inside the Problem section.)

The Medical Model: Conceptualizing Abnormality as a Disease

To understand fully how psychologists conceptualize abnormality, we must briefly address another issue: When abnormality is present, is it appropriate to think of the individual as suffering from a physical problem—that is, something that is broken or not working properly in the body—or is abnormality better seen as a failure to adjust appropriately to the environment? We'll discuss the possible causes of psychological disorders in detail later in the chapter, but to understand how disorders are typically classified, it helps to have some familiarity with what is known generally as the *medical model.* According to the **medical model,** abnormal behav-

FIGURE 14.1
The Normal-to-Abnormal Continuum. "Abnormal" and "normal" are not fixed and rigid categories that define people—they are better seen as endpoints on a continuum. To a certain degree, everyone has acted unusually, suffered from emotional distress, or failed to follow an adaptive strategy.

Normal	Criteria	Abnormal
Common	Statistical deviance	Rare
Acceptable	Cultural deviance	Unacceptable
Low	Emotional distress	High
Adaptive	Dysfunction	Maladaptive

As we've just discussed, it's not easy to find an acceptable definition for abnormal behavior. Behavior can mean different things depending on the context in which it occurs—something that is abnormal in one situation may be quite normal in another. Someone can act in a way that is deviant from statistical or cultural norms, yet still seem normal to most observers. Still, regardless of where you travel in the world, some kinds of behavior will always be recognized as abnormal: Consider, for example, the behavior of serial killer Jeffrey Dahmer, who admitted butchering, cannibalizing, and having sex with the dead bodies of over a dozen young men and boys. Everyone, including the mental health professionals who examined Dahmer, was in agreement—this was a man who was suffering from some serious psychological problems.

But did you know that from a legal standpoint, Jeffrey Dahmer was judged by a jury to be perfectly sane? Despite the best efforts of his legal team to have him declared mentally unfit, and thus not responsible for his crimes, Dahmer was found legally sane. He stood trial and was convicted of his crimes (later, while serving his life sentence, he was brutally murdered himself by a fellow inmate). Are you wondering how this could be possible? The answer lies in the fact that *insanity* is a *legal* concept rather than a *psychological* one. Although its definition varies somewhat from state to state, **insanity** is usually defined in terms of the defendant's thought processes *at the time of the crime*: A criminal is insane, and therefore not guilty by reason of insanity, if, because of a "mental disease," he or she fails to appreciate or understand that certain actions are "wrong" in a legal or moral sense (Ogloff, Roberts, & Roesch, 1993). Dahmer was judged capable of understanding the wrongfulness of his actions; that is, the jury determined that he was fully aware of the fact that his actions were wrong. As a result, he failed the insanity test, even though he was clearly suffering from serious psychological problems.

From a legal standpoint, Jeffrey Dahmer (shown in the middle) was considered sane because he was judged capable of understanding the wrongfulness of his actions.

The concept of legal insanity has generated considerable controversy over the years. But the controversy has not usually come from cases like Dahmer's, in which someone with a disorder has been declared legally sane. Instead, the brunt of the concern has been over instances of acquittal—in which someone who obviously committed a crime has been judged not guilty by reason of insanity. A case in point is the landmark trial of Daniel M'Naghten in 1843. Driven by "voices from God," M'Naghten set out to kill the British prime minister, Sir Robert Peel, but ended up killing Peel's secretary instead. The court acquitted M'Naghten, for reasons of insanity, because "the party accused was labouring under such a defect of reason, from disease of the mind, as not to know the nature and quality of the act he was doing . . ." (*Regina v. M'Naghten,* 1843). This particular ruling was strongly criticized by the public, even though M'Naghten spent the rest of his life in a mental hospital. But it remains important because the so-called M'Naghten rule for insanity—which focuses on what the criminal understands at the time of the crime—is still the foundation for most current standards of insanity.

The last few decades have seen a number of widely publicized uses of the insanity defense in the United States.

John Hinckley, Jr., who attempted to assassinate President Ronald Reagan in 1981, was declared not guilty by reason of insanity. You probably also remember that Lorena Bobbitt was held not legally responsible for cutting off her husband's penis. In both these cases the jury's verdict led to considerable public debate. In fact, even before these cases, there was growing concern—and even cynicism—in many public sectors about the insanity defense. But the public tends to overestimate how often it is actually used in criminal felony cases, as well as how often the insanity defense leads to acquittal (Pasewark & Seidenzahl, 1979). In reality, the insanity defense is used in less than 1% of all felony cases, and it's successful only 26% of the time (Silver, Cirincione, & Steadman, 1994).

Thus, the insanity defense is not a widely used legal loophole, despite the impressions of the general public. Moreover, most mental health professionals support the idea that people with serious psychological disorders are sometimes incapable of judging the appropriateness of their actions. As this chapter will illustrate, psychological disorders can lead to distorted views of the world—affected individuals not only act in a way that is abnormal, but their very thoughts, beliefs, and perceptions of the world can be wildly distorted as well.

ior is symptomatic of an underlying *disease* that can be *cured* with the appropriate therapy. Mental *illness* is "caused" by something, and it can be "fixed" if the appropriate therapy or treatment is applied.

This conception of abnormality has been quite influential. As you already know, there are good reasons to believe that behavior is strongly influenced by biological factors, such as an oversupply or undersupply of neurotransmitters in the brain. In addition, biomedical therapies, such as the administration of psychoactive drugs, are often effective in treating certain kinds of psychological problems. As we'll see shortly, it's also the case that many psychological disorders can be reliably classified in terms of measurable *symptoms*. Depression, for example, is characterized by one or more of the following: sad mood, diminished interest in pleasure, difficulty in sleeping, feelings of worthlessness, and so on. The medical influence pervades the very language that psychologists use—they talk about mental health, mental illness, or psychopathology in much the same way that a physician would describe a medical condition.

But is the medical model an appropriate way to view abnormality? Some researchers have argued that it's misguided to draw direct comparisons between physical illness and psychological problems (Szasz, 1961, 1990). Both strep throat and depression are associated with a set of reliable symptoms. But whereas we have clear evidence that the physical problem—strep throat—is caused by something foreign to the body (bacteria), at this point the causal agent of depression has not been firmly established. In addition, people often seek treatment for psychological problems that are perhaps more accurately described as "problems in living." How these adjustment problems are interpreted also seems to depend on the particular social or cultural context, which is not true for most medical conditions. We pointed out earlier that some kinds of bizarre behavior typed as abnormal in one culture can be considered normal in another. On the other hand, strep throat produces fever and pain in swallowing regardless of the cultural environment that one happens to be in.

Problems Associated with Labeling

Critics of the medical model also express concern about **diagnostic labeling effects.** Labeling a psychological problem as an illness or a disorder tends to attach a stigma to the person that can be difficult to overcome (Scheff, 1984). A number of studies have demonstrated that the label "mental patient" leads people to interpret someone's behavior in a far different light than they would otherwise. In one study, professional therapists watched a videotape of a man describing his personal adjustment problems (Langer & Abelson, 1974). If, prior to viewing the tape, the therapists were told that the man was a mental patient, they rated his adjustment problems more negatively than did other therapists who were supplied the label "job applicant" (see Figure 14.2). People's expectations, as we've stressed in previous chapters, importantly influence how they interpret new information.

The Rosenhan Study. In one particularly influential study of labeling effects, David Rosenhan, along with seven other co-investigators, arrived separately at several psychiatric hospitals in the early 1970s with the complaint that they were hearing voices (Rosenhan, 1973). Actually, the participants were all perfectly normal. They simply adopted the role of "pseudopatient"—they feigned, or faked, a disorder—in order to assess how an initial diagnosis of abnormality might color subsequent treatment. On arrival, they reported to the psychiatric staff that they were hearing a disembodied voice in their head, a voice that repeated things like "empty," "hollow," and "thud." They were all admitted to hospitals, and virtually all received the diagnosis of schizophrenia (schizophrenia, as we'll see later, is a condition characterized by serious disturbances in thought and emotion).

What effect do you think acceptance of the medical model has on the availability of treatment options? Might it lead to an overemphasis on physical types of treatments for psychological problems?

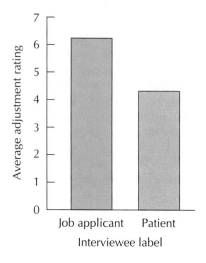

FIGURE 14.2
Labeling Effects. In a study by Langer and Abelson (1974), therapists were asked to provide adjustment ratings for people labeled as either "patient" or "job applicant." The interviewees were judged to be better adjusted when the therapists thought them to be job applicants rather than patients. (Data from Langer & Abelson, 1974)

The purpose of the study was to see how an initial diagnosis of "schizophrenia" would affect how they were subsequently treated. From the point of admission, none of the pseudopatients continued to act in any abnormal way. In all interactions with the hospital staff and with the other patients after admission, they acted normally and gave no indications that they were suffering from a disorder. Despite their apparent "sanity," however, none of the staff ever recognized them as pseudopatients; indeed, the written hospital reports revealed that the staff members sometimes interpreted normal behaviors as symptomatic of a disorder. It was the real patients, in fact, who felt that the researchers somehow did not "belong"; several actually voiced their suspicions, claiming "You're not crazy. You're a journalist or a professor" (these comments were partly made in reaction to the fact that the pseudopatients tended to spend time taking notes). Once the pseudopatients had been admitted and labeled as "abnormal," their behaviors were seen by the staff through the "lens" of expectations, and normal, sane behavior was never recognized as such. On average, the pseudopatients remained in the hospital for 19 days—the stays ranged from under a week to almost two months—and on release all were given the diagnosis of schizophrenia "in remission" (which means not currently active).

The Rosenhan study is important because it suggests that diagnostic labels can become self-fulfilling prophecies. Once individuals are diagnosed, they are apt to be treated as if they are suffering from a disorder, and this treatment may (1) make it difficult to recognize normal behavior when it occurs, and (2) actually increase the likelihood that the person will act in an abnormal way. If the people in your environment expect you to act abnormally, you may very well start to act in a way that is consistent with those expectations (see Chapter 13).

Since its publication in 1973, the Rosenhan study has been widely analyzed in psychological circles. Its lessons about the hazards of labeling are clear. But at the same time, two points about the study are worth noting. First, you should appreciate that the admission of the pseudopatients by the hospital staff, as well as the subsequent diagnoses, were reasonable given the patients' reported symptoms. The diagnosis of a psychological disorder is often dependent on what the patient reports, and the trained professionals in this case had no reason to assume that the patients were lying or manufacturing symptoms. Second, it's possible and even reasonable to dispute the claim that the attending staff failed to recognize that the pseudopatients were acting normally. After all, they were released with the label "in remission," so the staff must have recognized that they were no longer acting in an abnormal way (Spitzer, 1975).

Do you think it was ethical for Rosenhan and his colleagues to "trick" the hospital staff? Did the research "ends" justify the means?

Most mental health professionals are careful about rigidly applying "labels" to clients during therapy; diagnostic labels can sometimes become self-fulfilling prophecies.

Classifying Psychological Disorders: The DSM-IV and Selected Clinical Syndromes

Even if we reject the idea that psychological disorders are *caused* by physical disease or impairment, it is still possible to use a medical analogy to help classify the various kinds of abnormal behavior. That is, specific psychological disorders can be treated as analogous to physical disorders in that each can be diagnosed in terms of a set of defining criteria or symptoms. This is basically the approach used by the framers of the widely used *Diagnostic and Statistical Manual of Mental Disorders,* which is published by the American Psychiatric Association. From this point forward, we'll refer to this manual by its more commonly used acronym: **DSM-IV** (the "IV" simply designates that the classification system is currently in its fourth edition). The purpose of the DSM-IV is to provide clinicians with a well-defined classification system, based on objective and measurable criteria, so that reliable diagnoses of psychological disorders can be produced worldwide (Maser, Kaelber, & Weise, 1991; Spitzer and others, 1994). The DSM-IV is intended only for the purposes of diagnosis and classification; it does not provide any reference to appropriate therapies for its various listed disorders.

How does the classification system work? The DSM-IV is composed of five major rating dimensions, or *axes* (see Figure 14.3). We'll focus our attention mainly on the first axis, which defines the major clinical syndromes (such as depression and schizophrenia), but all five help frame the complete diagnostic process. The clinician uses the criteria outlined in Axis I (Clinical Syndromes) and Axis II (Personality Disorders) to classify and label any abnormal behavior that may be present. Axis III allows the clinician to record any medical conditions that the individual may be experiencing. It's important for the clinician to know a person's medical history because some medical conditions (such as Alzheimer's disease) can contribute to abnormal behavior. Axis IV rates any environmental or psychosocial problems that may be present in the individual's life. For example, is the client going through a difficult divorce, or has he or she recently been fired?

FIGURE 14.3

The Five Axes of the DSM-IV Diagnostic System. The DSM-IV is composed of five major rating dimensions, or *axes*. Information collected from each axis is integrated into final diagnosis and treatment decisions. For example, it's important to know whether a person diagnosed with a disorder identified on Axis I or II is also suffering from an existing medical condition (Axis III) or whether he or she has been exposed recently to a significant psychosocial or environmental problem (Axis IV). Finally, the psychologist will use the person's ability to function well in everyday settings in considering the appropriate treatment (Axis V). (From DSM-IV, APA, 1994)

Axis I: Clinical Disorders and Other Conditions That May Be a Focus of Clinical Attention	Axis II: Personality Disorders and Mental Retardation	Axis III: General Medical Conditions	Axis IV: Psychosocial and Environmental Problems
Examples: Substance-related disorders Schizophrenia and other psychotic disorders Mood disorders Anxiety disorders Somatoform disorders Dissociative disorders Sexual and gender identity disorders Eating disorders Sleep disorders	**Examples:** Paranoid personality disorder Schizotypal personality disorder Antisocial personality disorder Borderline personality disorder Narcissistic personality disorder Dependent personality disorder	**Examples:** Infectious and parasitic diseases Endocrine, nutritional, and metabolic diseases and immunity disorders Diseases of the nervous system and sense organs Diseases of the circulatory system Diseases of the respiratory system Diseases of the digestive system Diseases of the genitourinary system Congenital anomalies	**Examples:** Problems with primary support group Problems related to the social environment Educational problems Occupational problems Housing problems Economic problems

Finally, on Axis V the clinician codes the individual's current level of adaptive or global functioning. Is the client able to function adequately in social, personal, and occupational settings?

The clinician uses this "multiaxial" classification system to get the widest possible assessment of the individual's current psychological status. It matters to the clinician how someone is functioning in daily life, for example, because the degree of global functioning may determine the kind of treatment program that will be most effective. If the person is so severely impaired that he or she cannot hold a job, go to school, or even keep clean, it may be necessary to initiate a period of hospitalization. Our discussion will focus primarily on the diagnostic criteria that are used to classify the most common psychological disorders, as depicted on Axis I. We'll consider the major clinical syndromes and then end the section with a brief discussion of Axis II–based personality disorders. But remember, labeling or categorizing the disorder is only part of the diagnostic process—the remaining axes also play an important role in the diagnosis. Figure 14.4 summarizes some of the syndromes that we'll be discussing, as well as the incidence of each in the population at large.

Anxiety Disorders: Fear and Apprehension

Although it may be difficult to understand the paranoid delusions of the severely disordered, it is not difficult to understand the apprehension, worry, and fear that characterize *anxiety*. Most people understand anxiety because it's often an important part of their everyday experience. We become anxious when we meet someone new, when awaiting the beginning of an exam, or when an out-of-control car swerves dangerously close to our path. Moreover, even though it typically leads to negative emotional and body sensations, anxiety is basically an *adaptive* human response. The physical changes that accompany anxiety prepare the body to take action—to fight or flee—and thereby increase the likelihood of survival.

But there is a dark side to anxiety. When it becomes too persistent and intense, it interferes with the ability to function. **Anxiety disorders** are diagnosed when

Axis V:
Global Assessment of Functioning (GAF) Scale

Code	Examples of symptoms:
100	Superior functioning in a wide range of activities
90	Absent or minimal symptoms, good functioning in all areas
80	Symptoms transient and expectable reactions to psychosocial stressors
70	Mild symptoms or impairment in social, occupational, or school functioning, but general functioning is pretty good
60	Moderate symptoms or impairment in social, occupational, or school functioning
50	Serious symptoms or impairment in social, occupational, or school functioning
40	Major impairment in work or school, family relations, judgment, thinking, mood; some communication impairment
30	Influenced by delusions or hallucinations, serious impairment in communication or judgment
20	Some danger of severely hurting self or others, gross impairment in communication, sporadic personal hygiene
10	Persistent danger of severely hurting self or others

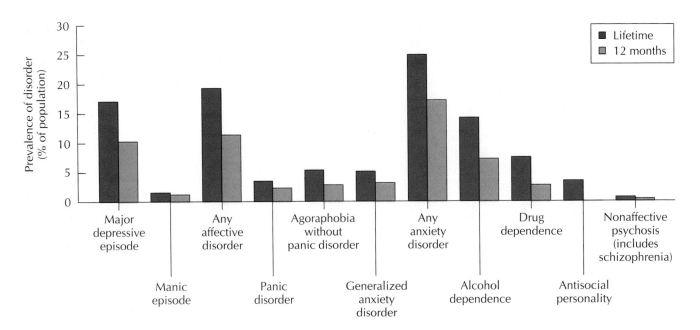

FIGURE 14.4

Prevalence Rates for Various Psychological Disorders. Each bar shows the percentage of individuals in a large sample (over 8000 participants) who reported suffering from the listed psychological disorder during the last 12 months or at some point in their lifetime. Note: A given individual might have reported suffering from more than one of these disorders concurrently. (Data from Kessler and others, 1994)

one's apprehension and worry become so extreme that overall behavior is impaired in some way. For example, if you consistently fail on exams because you cannot collect your thoughts, or if you refuse to leave the house because you're convinced you will experience a frightening "panic attack," you're likely to be suffering from an anxiety disorder. Anxiety disorders actually comprise a class of maladies, and each member of the class is defined by its own set of DSM-IV diagnostic criteria. There is a certain amount of overlap among the criteria for each of the classified anxiety disorders, and a single individual can suffer from more than one at the same time. We'll concentrate on some common ones in this section: *generalized anxiety disorder, panic disorder, obsessive-compulsive disorder,* and *specific phobias.*

Generalized Anxiety Disorder. The defining characteristic of **generalized anxiety disorder** is excessive and chronic worrying that lasts for a period of at least 6 months. The anxiety is "free-floating," as Freud described it, and cannot be attributed to any single identifiable source. Individuals who suffer from this problem worry *in general* (which is captured in the name *generalized* anxiety disorder), and they fret incessantly about any number of minor things (Sanderson & Barlow, 1990). More important, the worrying that occurs is unrealistic—it's not directly related to the likelihood that a feared event will actually occur (Brown, Barlow, & Liebowitz, 1994).

Further, because anxiety is associated with activity of the autonomic nervous system, generalized anxiety disorder tends to be accompanied by a range of physical symptoms, including high pulse and respiration rates, chronic diarrhea, a need to urinate frequently, and chronic digestive problems. Someone burdened with generalized anxiety disorder is likely to have trouble sleeping and becomes easily irritated. These kinds of symptoms are relatively easy to understand—after all, these individuals are living in a world of perpetual fear; the worst, they assume, is always about to happen.

Panic Disorder. Generalized anxiety is marked by chronic, unfocused worrying. In **panic disorder,** the individual suffers from recurrent episodes or "attacks" of extremely intense fear or dread (Craske & Barlow, 1993). A *panic attack* is a sudden and unexpected event, and it can make the sufferer feel as if he or she is about to die (or, sometimes, go crazy). Panic attacks are brief, but they produce high levels of anxiety and, as a result, are accompanied by a collection of physical symptoms: a pounding heart, shortness of breath, sweating, nausea, chest pains, and so on. These symptoms can be devastating experiences, and they often cause the affected individual to show persistent concern about the possibility of having additional attacks (Barlow, 1988). It's worth noting that a single isolated panic attack is not sufficient for diagnosis of a panic disorder; the attacks need to occur repeatedly and unexpectedly.

Panic disorder is sometimes associated with an additional complication, called *agoraphobia,* that arises when people obsess about the possibility that further panic attacks will occur. **Agoraphobia**—which translates from the Greek as "fear of the marketplace"—can cause an individual to restrict his or her normal activities in an extreme

People who suffer from agoraphobia are often reluctant to leave the house; they're afraid that once outside they will experience a panic attack and be rendered helpless.

way. People who suffer from agoraphobia often stay away from crowded or public places, such as shopping malls or restaurants, because they're afraid they will experience a panic attack and be rendered helpless. In extreme cases, individuals with agoraphobia might actually refuse to leave their house; home, they reason, is the only really "safe place" where they have others who can help if needed. For obvious reasons, panic disorder with accompanying agoraphobia can significantly reduce a person's ability to function successfully in the world.

Obsessive-Compulsive Disorder. In **obsessive-compulsive disorder,** anxiety manifests itself through persistent, uncontrollable thoughts, called *obsessions,* or by the presence of a compelling need to perform one or more actions repeatedly, which is called a *compulsion.* Compulsions are related to obsessions in the sense that the repetitive action is usually performed in response to some kind of obsessive thought (Riggs & Foa, 1993). Have you ever had part of a song or jingle ramble incessantly through your head—one that keeps repeating despite your best efforts to stop it? This is somewhat analogous to an obsession, although in obsessive-compulsive disorder the obsessions tend to focus on fears (such as being contaminated by germs), doubts (such as forgetting to turn off the stove), and impulses (such as hurting oneself or another) (Jenike, Baer, & Minichiello, 1986; Salkovskis, 1985).

A person suffering from obsessive-compulsive disorder may feel the need to engage in a repetitive activity, such as compulsively lining up pencils, to reduce anxiety or to avoid thinking inappropriate thoughts.

Compulsions consist of such actions as cleaning or checking, or actions that prevent some inappropriate impulse from occurring. For example, someone might repeat the alphabet aloud over and over in an effort to divert his or her thinking away from a frightening or inappropriate aggressive or sexual impulse. (Stepping over cracks in the sidewalk to prevent maternal harm is an innocuous kind of compulsion that almost everyone has experienced.) In extreme cases, the compulsions are so repetitive and ritualistic that they essentially prevent the sufferer from leading anything resembling a normal life. Some people become housebound, relentlessly cleaning rooms; others feel irresistibly compelled to leave work 10 to 15 times a day to check and make sure the gas wasn't left on in the stove. Interestingly, in the majority of such cases the suffering individuals understand that their actions are irrational and of little adaptive value (Stern & Cobb, 1978). The disorder simply compels the action.

Specific Phobic Disorder. The defining feature of a **specific phobic disorder** is a highly focused fear of a specific object or situation—such as a bug, a snake, flying, heights, an animal, a closed place, or a storm. Like the other anxiety dis-

FIGURE 14.5
Prevalence Rates for Various Specific Phobias. Each bar shows the percentage of people in a large sample who reported suffering from a particular kind of specific phobia. (Data from Agras, Sylvester, & Oliveau, 1969)

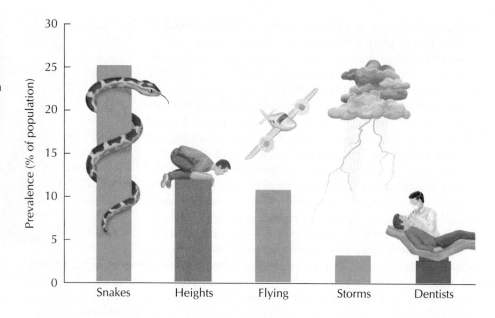

orders we've discussed, specific phobias are irrational, which means that the level of anxiety the object or situation produces is in no way justified by reality. Elevators do fall, snakes can bite, planes do crash—but these events are not likely to happen on a daily basis. Many people show mild forms of phobic reactions—and, again, in some cases the object of the anxiety might indeed be dangerous (some snakes do kill)—but in specific phobic disorder the fear and distress can be severely disabling. To avoid the anxiety-producing object or situation, individuals with a specific phobic disorder might significantly disrupt their normal routines; they might avoid going to work or school or traveling to anywhere different in the slight chance that they will encounter the object of their fear.

Specific phobias typically revolve around one of four classes of fear-inducing objects or situations: (1) animals (insects, snakes, dogs, etc.), (2) natural environments (storms, heights, water, etc.), (3) blood-injection-injury (the sight of blood or even the thought of an injection), and (4) specific situations (fears associated with public transportation or closed-in places). These four categories capture the majority of phobic reactions, although there are others—such as fear of choking or fear of costumed characters—that do not fit easily into these established categories. For an indication of the incidence of various specific phobias among the general population, see Figure 14.5.

Somatoform Disorders: Body and Mind

A common phenomenon, called the "medical student syndrome," often plagues medical students as they first learn about the various diseases of the body. The students find that the symptoms described in class, or in the text, are increasingly familiar and personal. A deep pain that appears suddenly in the night is interpreted as a signal for the final stages of pancreatic cancer; that darkening blemish on the forehead becomes the rare form of skin cancer that often accompanies AIDS. In almost every case, the student is perfectly healthy, but the mind plays its tricks and the student fears the worst.

Do you think the "medical student syndrome" also applies to beginning psychology students? Do you find yourself suddenly suffering from a variety of psychological "disorders"?

Mental health professionals classify psychological problems that focus on the physical body as **somatoform disorders** (*soma* means "body"). Obviously, like medical students, most people have experienced imagined illnesses at some point in their lives. But when the preoccupation with bodily functions or symptoms is excessive and is not grounded in any physical reality, a true psychological disorder may be indicated. The DSM-IV lists a number of basic somatoform disorders; we'll focus briefly on three: *hypochondriasis, somatization disorder,* and *conversion disorder.*

Hypochondriasis. The main diagnostic criterion for **hypochondriasis** is a persistent preoccupation with the idea that one has developed a serious disease, based on what turns out to be a misinterpretation of normal bodily reactions. The pain in the side, the slight case of indigestion, the occasional irregular heartbeat—these are interpreted as symptomatic of a serious medical condition. Moreover, unlike the situation for the normal medical student, these preoccupations persist for months and often cause significant distress and impaired functioning. Hypochondriasis is typically associated with excessive anxiety and, in fact, may be strongly related to the types of anxiety disorders we discussed earlier.

Somatization Disorder. **Somatization disorder** is related to hypochondriasis and, in fact, mental health professionals sometimes have a difficult time distinguishing between the two. Both involve the persistent complaint of symptoms with no identifiable physical cause, but in somatization disorder it is the *symptoms* that receive the focus of attention rather than the existence of an underlying disease. In both cases, the person searches endlessly for doctors who will confirm his or her symptoms, but usually with little or no success (because there is no real physical problem). The major difference between hypochondriasis and somatization disorder seems to be that in hypochondriasis the anxiety arises because of a presumed underlying disease, whereas in somatization disorder the presence of the symptoms themselves causes the anxiety. People with somatization disorder are not typically afraid of dying from a serious disease; rather, they are looking for someone to understand and sympathize with their countless physical problems.

A person suffering from hypochondriasis is prone to misinterpreting normal body reactions as symptomatic of a serious disease.

Conversion Disorder. In **conversion disorder,** unlike the other two somatoform disorders we've considered, there appears to be real physical or neurological impairment. Someone suffering from a conversion disorder might report being blind, or paralyzed, or seemingly unable to speak. These are not feigned symptoms; that is, these problems are not intentionally produced by the individual to gain sympathy or attention. These are real problems, although no physical cause can be discovered.

Obviously, in such cases there is always the possibility that a true neurological or other physical problem does exist; physical problems are indeed sometimes misdiagnosed as conversion disorders (Fishbain & Goldberg, 1991; Slater & Glithero, 1965). But when the reported problems disappear after an effective psychological intervention, a psychological origin is indicated. You may remember from our discussion of personality in Chapter 12 that Sigmund Freud often used his psychoanalytic techniques to treat patients with conversion disorders (although the problem was known as *hysteria* in his day). In fact, the term *conversion,* as used here, originates from psychodynamic theory and the proposal that unconscious conflicts have been "converted" into a physical form.

Dissociative Disorders: Disruptions of Identity or Awareness

Some of the more colorful types of psychological disorders, at least as envisioned by Hollywood or the popular press, come from a class of problems called dissociative disorders. **Dissociative disorders** are characterized by the separation, or *dissociation,* of conscious awareness from previous thoughts or memories. People who are affected by one of these disorders lose memory for some specific aspect of their life, or even their entire sense of identity. The theme of the confused amnesiac, searching for his or her identity among myriad ambiguous clues, has been

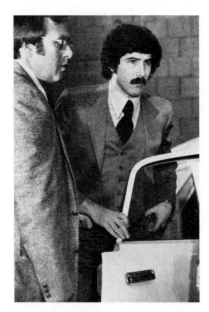

Kenneth Bianchi, known as the Hillside Strangler, claimed that he could not be held responsible for the rape and murder of a number of California women because he was suffering from dissociative identity disorder. The evidence presented at trial suggested that Bianchi was "faking" the disorder, and he was later convicted and sentenced to life imprisonment.

explored repeatedly in Hollywood films throughout the years. We'll focus our attention on three types of dissociative disorder: *dissociative amnesia, dissociative fugue,* and *dissociative identity disorder.*

Dissociative Amnesia. In Chapter 8, when we tackled remembering and forgetting, we discussed various kinds of *amnesia,* or the inability to remember or retain personal experiences. It was noted that amnesia could arise from either physical factors (such as brain damage) or psychological factors (such as traumatic stress). In **dissociative amnesia,** which is assumed to be psychological in origin, the person is unable to remember important personal information. The amnesia can be quite general, as in the failure to remember one's identity or family history, or it can be localized, such as the failure to remember a specific traumatic life experience. In dissociative amnesia, the forgetting can last for hours or for years. It often disappears as mysteriously as it arises.

Dissociative Fugue. In **dissociative fugue,** there is also a loss of personal identity—people forget who they are—but it's accompanied by an escape or flight from the home environment (*fugue* literally means "flight"). Imagine leaving for work or school, as usual, only to "awaken" some time later in a different city or state. Sometimes the fugue state can last months or even years; some individuals experiencing this disorder have even adopted different identities in their new locale. Recovery can be sudden and often complete, but affected individuals will typically claim that they have no knowledge of their activities during the "blackout" period.

Dissociative Identity Disorder. In what is perhaps the most baffling of all dissociative disorders, **dissociative identity disorder,** a person alternates among what appear to be two or more distinct identities or personality states (hence the alternative name, *multiple personality disorder*). Some cases of this disorder have been widely publicized, and movies have even been made about them. Perhaps you're familiar with Sybil Dorsett, who was diagnosed with 16 personalities (Schreiber, 1973); she was portrayed by Sally Field in the television movie *Sybil.* Another well-known case is "Eve," who alternated among three personality types (Thigpen & Cleckley, 1957); she was portrayed by Joanne Woodward in the film *The Three Faces of Eve.*

In dissociative identity disorder, the unique personalities or identities appear to take control of the affected individual's thoughts and actions, one personality at a time. More important, the personality in control will profess to have only limited awareness of the other personality "inhabitants." It is for this reason that the disorder is classified as *dissociative*—there is a separation of current conscious awareness from prior thoughts and memories. Dozens of different identities may be involved, including both males and females, and a given identity will tend to have unique physical attributes, such as a distinct tone of voice, facial expression, handwriting style, or behavioral habit (Putnam and others, 1986).

Dissociative identity disorder is recognized as a legitimate disorder in the DSM-IV, but not all mental health professionals are comfortable with this designation (Fahy, 1988). Controversy often surrounds the diagnosis, for a number of reasons. First, this disorder often co-occurs with other psychological problems (such as depression and somatization disorder), so it's quite difficult to pinpoint the ultimate cause of any particular symptom (Ross and others, 1990). Second, although each of the observed "personalities" may be distinguished on the basis of personality tests or physiological indices, we still cannot be completely sure about the true origins of these differences—other factors, such as mood or arousal differences, may partly account for the distinct performance patterns (Fahy, 1988; Lilienfeld, 1994).

Third, several studies have shown that it's relatively easy to "fake" or simulate multiple personalities (Spanos, Weeks, & Bertrand, 1985). This raises the possibility that people with dissociative identity disorder may actually be "role playing" in some fashion, perhaps in a way comparable to those who have been hypnotized. As you might recall from Chapter 6, many psychologists question whether hypnosis really represents some kind of dissociated "state"; instead, hypnotized people often seem eager to please the hypnotist by acting in accordance with a hypnotized "role." This is not necessarily a conscious choice made by those who have been hypnotized; instead, it may represent a kind of unconscious or involuntary compliance (Lynn, Rhue, & Weekes, 1990). Some researchers are convinced that dissociative identity disorder is best interpreted as a kind of self-hypnosis that arises partly to please the therapist. There has been an unusually rapid rise in the number of cases of dissociative identity disorder, as the disorder has been publicized in the media, which lends support to the "role playing" hypothesis.

Despite the controversy, dissociative identity disorder was retained as a diagnostic disorder in the DSM-IV, which was published in 1994. It does seem clear that not all aspects of the disorder can be consciously "faked" (Kluft, 1991). Highly specific physiological differences have been reported across personalities—such as differences in visual acuity or eye muscle balance (Miller, 1989)—and it seems unlikely that such things could be easily contrived (see Figure 14.6). There also appear to be certain similarities in the past histories of affected individuals that have convinced many of the validity of the diagnosis. For example, in a recent study of 97 cases, 95% of the individuals were found to have suffered some form of abuse, usually sexual or physical, most often during childhood (Ross and others, 1990). The diagnosis of dissociative identity disorder remains controversial, but it is currently considered to be a legitimate disorder by the psychological community at large.

Disorders of Mood: Depression and Mania

From time to time, everyone experiences depression, that overwhelming feeling that things are completely hopeless and sad. For most, thankfully, the experience is brief; moreover, most people can usually account for their depressed mood by pointing to a particular experience or event in their lives: They failed the test; their beloved pet died; their once-trusted romantic partner now prefers the affections of another. But when an extreme mood swing is not short-lived and is accompanied by other symptoms, such as a prolonged loss of appetite and a negative self-concept, a mood disorder may be present. **Mood disorders**—which are defined as prolonged and disabling disruptions in emotional state—come in two main varieties: (1) *depressive disorders,* in which the person suffers primarily from depression, and (2) *bipolar disorders,* which are characterized by mood *swings* between extreme highs, called manic states, and the lows of depression. We'll consider each of these types of disorders separately.

Depressive Disorders. The DSM-IV lists some specific criteria for the diagnosis of depressive disorders, which are among the most common of all psychological disorders. For something to qualify as a **major depressive episode,** for instance, the person must show five or more of the following types of symptoms for a period of at least two weeks: (1) depressed mood for most of the day, (2) loss of interest in normal daily activities, (3) a significant change in weight (either a loss or a gain), (4) difficulty sleeping, or a desire to sleep all the time, (5) a change in activity level (either extreme restlessness or lethargy), (6) daily fatigue or loss of energy, (7) a negative self-concept, including feelings of worthlessness or excessive guilt, (8) trouble concentrating or in making decisions, and (9) suicidal thoughts.

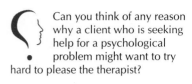

Can you think of any reason why a client who is seeking help for a psychological problem might want to try hard to please the therapist?

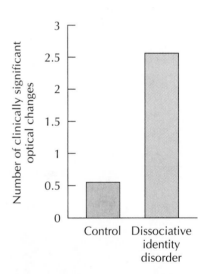

FIGURE 14.6

Optical Changes Across Personalities. In a study by Miller (1989), individuals diagnosed with dissociative identity disorder were asked to undergo ophthalmological (eye) exams while "inhabited" by each of three different personalities. Significant differences were found in optical functioning across personalities, more so than occurred for normal control subjects who were asked to "fake" different personalities during each exam. (Data from Miller, 1989)

When a person enters a major depressive episode, the world is seen through a kind of dark filter. The person feels extremely sad and is full of self-doubt, and the environment seems overwhelming, imposing, and full of obstacles that cannot be overcome (Young, Beck, & Weinberger, 1993). This "worldview" of the depressed individual is a particularly grim aspect of the disorder—to the depressed individual, the future seems hopeless with little or no possibility of a reprieve. Moreover, the accompanying negative self-image appears to the affected person to be solidly grounded in reality; depressed individuals are absolutely convinced about the "truth" of their hopelessness, which tragically leads some to consider suicide as their only outlet.

It is important to understand that major depression is more than just feeling sad. Affected individuals literally view and interpret the world differently when they are depressed, which tends to feed back and confirm their negative self-concept. Normal activities are interpreted as indicating some dire consequence (for example, if a friend fails to call, it must mean the friend no longer likes me). As we'll see in the next chapter, often one of the goals of therapy in treating depression is to change depressed individuals' thought patterns—to make them see the world in a more realistic way.

Mental health professionals distinguish among several types of depressive disorders, based partly on the length and severity of the depressive episode. For example, a major depressive episode can be classified as *recurrent,* which means that it has occurred more than once in an individual's lifetime (but separated by a period of at least two months). There is also a condition called *dysthymic disorder,* in which the depressive symptoms tend to be milder and less disruptive but more chronic. Most major depressive episodes end after a period of weeks or months, and the person returns to normal, but people affected by dysthymic disorder show a relatively continuous depressed mood for a period of at least two years. A major depressive episode can even occur at the same time as dysthymic disorder, in which case the condition is referred to as *double depression* (Keller & Shapiro, 1982).

Biopolar Disorders. When depression is manifested as *unipolar,* the depressive episode typically runs its course and the person returns to a normal state. The depression may occur again, but the disorder is marked by a mood shift in only one direction—toward the negative. In a **bipolar disorder,** the person experiences disordered mood shifts in two directions: traversing from the depths of depression (a major depressive episode) to a hyperactive, euphoric condition called a **manic state.** When individuals are in a manic state, they become hyperactive, talkative, and goal-directed, and they often have a decreased need for sleep. These attributes may seem to be positive and desirable, but they are balanced by tendencies toward grandiosity, distractibility, and an increased likelihood of engaging in activities that have a high potential for disaster. In a manic state, a person might attempt a remarkable feat—such as scaling the Statue of Liberty—or perhaps will go on a sudden spending spree, cashing in all his or her savings. People who are in a manic state report feeling great—at times as if they're experiencing one continuous sexual orgasm—but their thinking is far from normal or rational. Their speech can appear disrupted because they shift rapidly from one fleeting thought to another.

To be classified as a manic episode in the DSM-IV, this abnormally elevated state of euphoria must persist for at least a week, although it can last for months. Like a depressive episode, the manic state typically goes away, even without treatment, and the person either returns to normal or roller-coasters into another depressive episode. People who suffer from bipolar disorders live lives of extreme highs and lows; not surprisingly, their ability to function normally in society is often severely impaired. Moreover, tragically, it's been estimated that as many as 19% of individuals who are affected with bipolar disorders end up successfully

During depressive disorders, the world is seen through a kind of dark filter and the suffering individual can adopt a sense of hopelessness about the future.

committing suicide, usually during one of their episodes of depression (Jamison, 1986). (For a discussion of the possible connection between bipolar disorders and creativity, see the Adaptive Mind section that closes this chapter.)

Schizophrenia: When Thought Processes Go Awry

For most of the psychological disorders that we've considered so far, you probably experienced at least a glimmer of recognition. Everyone can identify with anxiety, the occasional obsessive thought, or even a slight case of depression. It's only when these tendencies become *excessive* and interfere with normal functioning that someone is likely to be diagnosed as suffering from an actual psychological disorder. But in the case of **schizophrenia,** which translates literally as "split mind," the psychological changes that occur can be so profound that the affected individual is thrust into a world that bears little resemblance to everyday experience. The person with schizophrenia lives in an internal world marked by thought processes that have gone awry; delusions, hallucinations, and generally disordered thinking become the norm.

Schizophrenia is actually a group or class of disorders. There are different subtypes of schizophrenia, defined by different DSM-IV criteria, but each case is characterized by some kind of fundamental disturbance in thought processes, emotion, or behavior. Schizophrenia is a bit unusual compared to the other disorders that we've considered because of its diversity of expression; whereas everyone who suffers from an anxiety disorder feels apprehensive, or in depression feels sad, each of the symptoms of schizophrenia need not be shared by all affected individuals. Schizophrenia is a complex disorder that is expressed in a variety of complex ways—no single symptom must be present for the diagnosis to be applied.

It is important to understand that schizophrenia is not the same thing as a dissociative identity disorder, despite the translation of schizophrenia as "split mind." Schizophrenia is generally characterized by faulty thought processes and inappropriate emotions, not by a dissociation among distinct personality types. In fact, when the Swiss psychiatrist Eugen Bleuler (1908) originally introduced the term *schizophrenia,* he was referring primarily to the fact that affected individuals have trouble holding onto a consistent line of thought. Their thinking is disorganized; their thought lines and associations seem to split apart and move forward in inconsistent ways. Both schizophrenia and dissociative identity disorder are serious psychological problems, but they fall into completely different categories in the DSM-IV.

Diagnostic Symptoms. There are two main types of symptoms in schizophrenia: *positive symptoms* and *negative symptoms*. Positive symptoms usually involve some kind of overt expression of abnormal behavior, such as a delusion or a hallucination; negative symptoms consist of deficits in behavior, such as an inability to express emotion. The DSM-IV requires that two or more characteristic symptoms be present for the diagnosis of schizophrenia, but a particular individual may have only positive symptoms or a combination of both positive and negative symptoms. As with the other disorders we've considered, these symptoms need to last for a significant period of time, they must cause social or job distress, and they cannot be due to the effects of a general medical condition or to the use of a drug or medication.

Let's consider some of the major positive symptoms of schizophrenia in more detail. As noted earlier, one of the main problems in schizophrenia is distorted or disorganized thinking. People with schizophrenia often suffer from *delusions,* which are thoughts with inappropriate content. If someone sitting next to you in class leaned over and claimed to be Elvis in disguise, or Jesus Christ, or Adolf Hitler, the content of his or her thoughts would clearly be inappropriate or

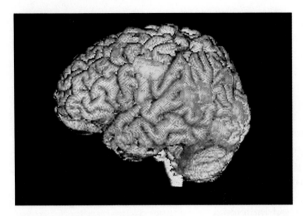

Shown here are areas of the brain that appear to be selectively activated during auditory and visual hallucinations. The highlighted areas were captured through the use of a PET scanning procedure, during which a young man who was suffering from schizophrenia was asked to press a button, initiating the scan, every time he experienced a hallucination.

deviant—this individual would be suffering from a delusion. People suffering from schizophrenia sometimes hold a *delusion of grandeur,* which is a belief that they are more famous or important than they actually are, or a *delusion of persecution,* which is a belief that others are conspiring or plotting against them in some way.

It is also not unusual for a person with schizophrenia to report distorted perceptions of the world. For them, objects can seem to change their shape or size; distances can be perceived in ways that are discrepant from reality. Frequently, these *hallucinations*—which are perceptions that have no basis in external stimulation—are auditory. People with schizophrenia claim to hear disembodied voices in their heads, giving them commands or commenting on the quality of their activities ("You're an idiot," "You should stay away from that person," and so on). Some researchers believe that these "voices" may originate from the same areas of the brain that control language production. It may be the case that people with schizophrenia are actually "listening" to their inner voice (see Chapter 8) but fail to recognize the voice as their own. Instead, they falsely attribute the source of the voice to something external (Cleghorn and others, 1992; McGuire, Shah, & Murray, 1993).

Two other "positive" symptoms of schizophrenia that may be present are *disorganized speech* and *catatonia.* Sometimes the speech patterns of a person with schizophrenia appear quite jumbled and incoherent; the affected individual jumps repeatedly from one disconnected topic to another ("I went to the beach today where the moon pulls the rabbit out of the hat. I'm the world's greatest cook, but that's because volcanic magma heats the glaciers and makes the water and the sand.") It's as if the mind has lost its internal editor—ideas or thoughts arise and lead immediately to other ideas or thoughts that are only loosely related. In addition to displaying these overt speech problems, someone with schizophrenia can behave in ways that are quite disorganized and bizarre. The person might engage in repetitive activities, such as swirling his or her arms repeatedly, or will appear to laugh or cry at inappropriate times. When *catatonia* is present, the affected person will sometimes adopt a peculiar stance or position and remain immobile for hours; or, they may wildly and suddenly change position for no apparent reason.

Negative symptoms of schizophrenia are expressed in terms of the elimination or reduction of normal behavior. For example, it's quite common for people with schizophrenia to display *flat affect,* which means that they show little or no emotional reaction to events. Show someone with flat affect an extremely funny movie or a tragic, heart-rending photo, and the person is unlikely to crack a smile or shed a tear. People with schizophrenia also often refuse to engage in the most basic and important of everyday activities. They may refuse to wash or clean themselves, eat, or dress themselves. Activities that are pleasurable to most people become unpleasurable or uninteresting to some individuals with schizophrenia.

For obvious reasons, people with schizophrenia are often unable to cope successfully at school or at work. In many cases, their behavior becomes so maladaptive that hospitalization is required. As you'll see later in the chapter, there are reasons to believe that people with schizophrenia may be suffering from a kind of "broken" brain—fundamental neurological problems may underlie the bizarre thinking and behaviors that plague people affected with the disorder.

When catatonia is present as a positive symptom of schizophrenia, the affected person might adopt a peculiar stance or position and remain immobile for hours.

Personality Disorders

All of the psychological disorders we've considered up to now are described on Axis I of the DSM-IV (Clinical Syndromes). Axis II describes **personality disorders,** which are essentially chronic or enduring patterns of behavior that lead to significant impairments in social functioning. People with personality disorders have a tendency to act repeatedly in an inflexible and maladaptive way. They may show a pervasive distrust of others, as in **paranoid personality disorder,** or they may show an excessive and persistent need to be taken care of by others, as in **dependent personality disorder.** One of the best-known examples of a personality disorder, occurring mainly in males, is the **antisocial personality disorder.** People with this type of "disorder" show little if any respect for social customs or norms. They act as if they have no conscience—they lie, cheat, or steal at the drop of a hat and show no remorse for their actions if caught. Someone with antisocial personality disorder is likely to have no qualms about committing criminal acts, even murder. Many end up with long criminal records and spend significant periods of time in jail.

What is it about personality disorders that requires them to be placed on their own classification axis? Do personality disorders have characteristics that fundamentally distinguish them from the major clinical syndromes described on Axis I? Most mental health professionals believe that personality disorders are unique primarily because they tend to be more *ingrained* and *inflexible* than the major clinical syndromes outlined on Axis I (Barlow & Durand, 1995). These are not problems that typically appear and disappear over time, which is the case with many psychological disorders. These "problems" arise from someone's basic personality and, as a result, tend to continue throughout adulthood and are quite resistant to therapeutic intervention. They are placed on a separate axis in the DSM-IV in part to force the clinician to consider the possibility that it is a personality characteristic, rather than a major clinical syndrome, that is contributing to the appearance of abnormal behavior.

Because personality "disorders" are thought to arise from the individual's personality, some mental health professionals have argued that it's wrong to think of them as *disorders* in the same sense as something like a specific phobia or depression (Gunderson, 1992; Trull & McCrae, 1994). In Chapter 12, which dealt with the topic of personality, we discussed the idea that personality can be defined in terms of what are called the Big Five personality dimensions (McCrae & Costa, 1985). Some researchers have argued it is better to think about people with personality disorders as simply extreme or deviant on one or more of these five dimensions—extroversion, agreeableness, conscientiousness, neuroticism, and openness (Clark & Livesley, 1994). For example, the dimension of *agreeableness* measures how kind, warm, and trusting an individual is. It's possible that people classified with a paranoid personality disorder may simply lie near an extreme pole on the agreeableness scale—they trust almost no one. At present, questions are still being raised about the proper way to think about personality disorders, and the matter is in no way resolved.

Understanding Psychological Disorders: Biological, Cognitive, or Environmental?

The DSM-IV classification system is designed to provide a reliable way for mental health professionals to diagnose psychological problems. The word *reliable* in this case refers to whether professional clinicians will tend to arrive at the same or similar diagnoses for individuals presenting a given set of symptoms. In general, the DSM system is considered to be quite reliable, although agreement is higher for some diagnostic categories than for others. But it is important to remember that the DSM-IV is only a classification system—it does not indicate anything about the root cause, or *etiology,* of the underlying disorder. What factors, alone or in combination, conspire to produce a major clinical syndrome such as depression, anxiety, or schizophrenia? The answer, in a nutshell, is that we don't know for sure. But most current explanations, as well as most approaches to therapy, appeal to *biological, cognitive,* or *environmental* factors.

Biological Factors: Is It in the Brain or Genes?

Over the past several decades, there have been significant advances in our understanding of the brain and its functions. Most researchers are now convinced that at least some kinds of abnormal behavior arise directly from brain dysfunction. The disordered thoughts and perceptions of someone with schizophrenia, for example, may be partly attributable to a "broken" or at least a malfunctioning brain. What is the evidence? Biological appeals are typically supported by two kinds of findings. First, it's been discovered that abnormal brain chemistry or abnormal brain structures accompany some kinds of mental disorders. Second, through the close study of family histories, it has been determined that a number of psychological disorders may have a powerful genetic component—psychological disorders tend to run in families in ways that cannot be easily explained by environmental histories. We discussed some of these findings in Chapter 3; we'll review and expand on that discussion here.

Malfunctioning Brains. As you may recall from Chapter 3, schizophrenia has been linked to an excess supply of the neurotransmitter *dopamine* (Seeman and others, 1976; Snyder, 1976), or possibly to an interaction between dopamine and the neurotransmitter *serotonin* (Kahn and others, 1993). Support for a neurochemical basis for schizophrenia has come primarily from studying how different drugs affect the disorder. Among the most effective treatments for schizophrenia are medications that act as dopamine *antagonists,* which means they reduce or block dopamine use in the brain (Gershon & Reider, 1992). It's also the case that drugs that increase the level of dopamine in the brain can sometimes produce side effects that resemble the symptoms found in schizophrenia (Braff & Huey, 1988; Davidson and others, 1987). Abnormal dopamine levels may not act as the sole cause of schizophrenia—for example, not all people with schizophrenia are helped by dopamine-reducing medications—but evidence that problems in brain neurochemistry are at least partly responsible continues to mount.

Neurotransmitter imbalances may also contribute to mood disorders, such as manic states and depression. Once again, most of the effective medications for these problems act by altering the actions of neurotransmitters in the brain. Fluoxetine (more commonly known by its brand name, *Prozac*) is one of the most commonly prescribed treatments for depression; it acts by slowing the reuptake of *serotonin,* thereby prolonging the neurotransmitter's effectiveness. More generally, depression and mania have been linked to a group of neurotransmitters called *monoamines,* which include serotonin, norepinephrine, and dopamine. Researchers currently believe that these neurotransmitters are involved in the regulation of mood, although the specifics have yet to be worked out. It's unlikely that mood disorders are caused by an inadequate supply of any one of these neurotransmitters. Instead, a decrease in one may have multi-

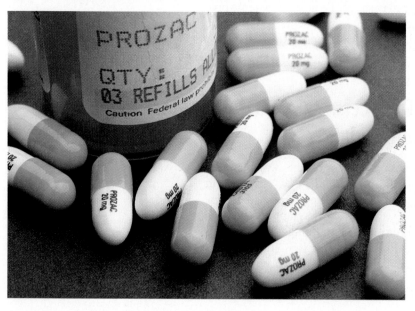

Some psychological disorders, such as depression, can be effectively treated by administering drugs that correct neurotransmitter imbalances in the brain.

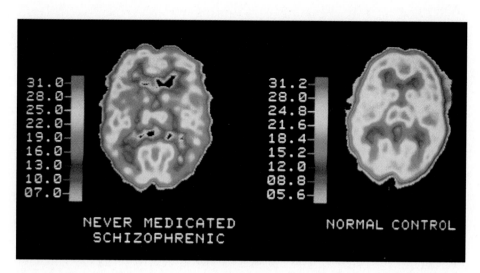

NEVER MEDICATED
SCHIZOPHRENIC

NORMAL CONTROL

People who suffer from disorders such as schizophrenia may possess malfunctioning brains. These two PET scans, taken from a person diagnosed with schizophrenia (left) and one without the disorder (right), show dramatic differences in brain activity levels. The blue and purple colors in the scans show areas of relatively low brain activity.

ple effects on the others. A decrease in serotonin, for instance, may "permit" the levels of other neurotransmitters in the brain to vary more widely; these more complex interactions probably conspire in some way to alter mood abnormally (Goodwin & Jamison, 1990).

In addition to neurochemical problems, such as imbalances in neurotransmitters, there may also be structural problems in the brains of people suffering from serious psychological problems. In the case of schizophrenia, anatomical and brain-imaging studies have revealed that people with schizophrenia tend to have larger *ventricles,* which are the liquid-filled cavities in the brain. (For reasons that are not yet clear, increased ventricle size tends to be more likely in men who suffer from schizophrenia.) Larger ventricles are associated with the loss, or shrinkage, of brain tissue, and this factor may help explain some instances of schizophrenia (Pahl, Swayze, & Andreasen, 1990). There is also evidence that level of activity in the frontal areas of the brain may be abnormally low in schizophrenia patients (Berman & Weinberger, 1990). Although it's not clear why these activity levels are low, decreased brain activity in certain prefrontal regions may directly or indirectly alter the neural pathways associated with the neurotransmitter dopamine (Davis and others, 1991).

These data are convincing, but it's important to remember that not all people with schizophrenia show these kinds of neurological problems; not all people with schizophrenia have larger ventricles or show lower frontal lobe activity. Moreover, not all people who have been diagnosed with depression respond to drug therapies that alter the levels or actions of monoamines. So we're left with a somewhat cloudy picture. There's little doubt that psychological disorders are sometimes associated with observable abnormalities in brain chemistry or function. But whether these factors are the true *cause* of disorders such as schizophrenia or depression, or simply one cause, or occur somehow as a consequence of having the disorder, is not currently known. For example, larger ventricle size is observed more often in people who have suffered from schizophrenia for a long time, so it's conceivable that the structural abnormality is partly a consequence of the disorder or even of its treatment.

Genetic Contributions. Increasingly, researchers are concluding that individuals may inherit predispositions toward abnormality. For example, the odds that any particular individual in the population will develop schizophrenia are roughly 1 in 100. But if you have a brother, sister, or parent with the disorder, the odds increase dramatically, perhaps to 1 in 10. If you have an identical twin—someone who has essentially the same genetic blueprint as you do—and your twin has been

FIGURE 14.7
The "Genetics" of Schizophrenia.
Each bar shows the risk of developing schizophrenia when one or more "relatives" have been diagnosed with the disorder. For example, if one identical twin is diagnosed with schizophrenia, there is a roughly 50% risk that the other will also develop the disorder. In general, the closer the individual is related genetically to the person with schizophrenia, the more likely he or she is to develop the disorder. (Based on Gottesman, 1991)

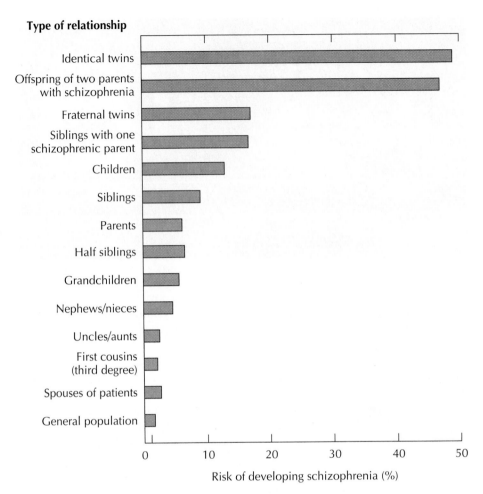

Type of relationship

Risk of developing schizophrenia (%)

diagnosed with schizophrenia, the odds that you will develop the disorder during your lifetime jump to about 1 in 2 (Gottesman, 1991) (see Figure 14.7). Notice that the disorder cannot be explained entirely by appealing to genetic factors—otherwise, identical twins would always share the disorder—but these data suggest that genetics probably plays a significant role.

As you know from our many discussions of the nature-nurture issue throughout this book, it is not easy to separate inherited characteristics from those acquired through experience. Just because there is a family history of a disorder does not mean that the cause is genetic; family members are typically raised in similar environments, so experience could account for the shared psychological problems. In the case of schizophrenia, however, even when children are adopted and raised apart from their biological parents, there still appears to be a familial link. Adopted children who have biological parents with schizophrenia have an increased likelihood of being diagnosed with schizophrenia themselves, even if they've had little or no contact with the parents (Tienari, 1992).

A similar pattern emerges with mood disorders. Depression and bipolar disorder tend to run in families, and the *concordance rate,* which measures the likelihood of sharing a disorder, is quite high between identical twins. A number of studies have shown that if one twin is diagnosed with depression, there is a 50% or greater chance that the other twin will also be diagnosed with depression; the concordance rate may be even higher for bipolar disorders (Gershon, 1990). It is also the case that adoptees with biological parents who suffer from a mood disorder are themselves more likely to suffer from a mood disorder. It is the biological history rather than the environmental history that, on average, predicts the chances of becoming affected by the disorder (Wender and others, 1986).

Genetic factors help predict the likelihood that someone will suffer from certain psychological disorders, but genetic factors are not sufficient to explain abnormal behavior. Having an identical twin with schizophrenia or bipolar disorder does not guarantee that you will have a similar problem. Your genetic code may predispose you to a disorder—it may "set the stage"—but other environmental factors will need to be present for the disorder to actually develop. Anxiety disorders, for example, may be likely to occur in people who are born with sensitive "temperaments," but experience will determine whether a full-blown disorder actually develops. To repeat a common theme, it is the *interaction* between nature and nurture that is important.

Cognitive Factors: Thinking Maladaptive Thoughts

If you look closely into the mind of someone suffering from a psychological disorder, you will often find fixed and disordered styles of thinking. People who are afflicted with anxiety disorders, somatoform disorders, or just about any of the other disorders we've discussed, typically believe things about themselves or about the world that have little or no basis in reality. Robert, who is depressed, is convinced that he lacks ability and drive, even though he is a successful banker. Jill, who suffers from agoraphobia, refuses to leave her house because she's convinced that something terrible will happen outside, even though she can think of no real reason for this belief.

Many psychologists feel that such faulty beliefs may be more than just symptoms of an underlying disorder—they may contribute to, or even cause, the disorder itself. To see how this might work, suppose that I am able to convince you, by feeding you false but convincing reports, that evil extraterrestrials have landed in a nearby city. Your anxiety level would certainly shoot up, and there's little question that your behavior would change. You might not leave your house, and you might, in fact, end up spending a lot of your time huddled under a table in your basement. This is abnormal behavior, but it might be rational given that the underlying cause of the behavior—the belief that the world may end soon—is true. Many people with psychological disorders act the way they do because they have incorrect beliefs. If you're absolutely convinced that you're no good and can never succeed at anything, it's not surprising that you withdraw from social situations and fail to secure steady employment.

Maladaptive Attributions. Psychologists use the term *attribution* to refer to the processes involved in assigning causality to a behavior (see Chapter 13). When you fail at something, such as a test or a new job, you attribute the failure to a cause, such as your own incompetence or the lousy teacher. It turns out that people who have psychological disorders, particularly depression, have relatively distinctive and predictable attributional or explanatory styles. Unfortunately, the attributions that these people make are often maladaptive, which means that they lead to behaviors that are abnormal or unproductive.

As Figure 14.8 shows, when something bad happens to a person prone to depression, he or she is apt to explain its occurrence in terms of *internal* ("I'm to blame rather than the situation"), *stable* (long-lasting), and *global* (widespread) attributions (Abramson, Metalsky, & Alloy, 1989). Let's suppose that you fail a test at school. If you're depressed, you will probably attribute that failure to some personal inadequacy (internal) that is likely to be long-lasting (stable) and that will probably apply in lots of situations other than school (global). People who are not prone to depression tend to have more flexible explanatory styles. They might attribute the fact that they failed to some *external* source ("I've got a rotten

FIGURE 14.8
Maladaptive Thoughts in Depression. Depressed individuals tend to explain failure, such as an F on a test, in terms of internal, stable, and global attributions.

Some kinds of fears may be learned, perhaps as a consequence of an early traumatic experience.

teacher") and consider the failure to be *unstable* ("I had a bad day"), and they probably will make a *specific* rather than global attribution. Nondepressed people have less of a tendency to overgeneralize from a situation at school to other areas of life.

What produces these different explanatory styles? It's difficult to know whether people who make maladaptive attributions do so because they are depressed, or whether it is the depression that creates the unfortunate explanatory style. Some researchers have argued that prolonged experience with failure may be one contributing factor. According to the **learned helplessness** theory of depression (Seligman, 1975), if people repeatedly fail while attempting to control their environment, they acquire a general sense of helplessness. They give up and become passive, which, the theory proposes, leads to depression. Still, it's unlikely that we can account for all forms of depression by appealing simply to repeated failure. Experience with failure may be a necessary condition for acquiring depression, but it is not a sufficient condition. Many people fail repeatedly, yet show no tendencies toward depression.

Moreover, it isn't really the failure that leads to depression but rather the individual's attributions about the failure. Instead of learning to be helpless, it is really the sense of *hopelessness*—the belief that things cannot become better because of internal, stable, and global factors—that is more likely to produce depression. Whether this sense of hopelessness can be explained by appealing to experience alone or to some interaction between experience and biological/genetic predispositions remains to be seen.

Environmental Factors: Do People Learn to Act Abnormally?

All theories of psychological disorders ultimately appeal either directly or indirectly to environmental factors. Even if a researcher believes that a disorder such as schizophrenia is primarily caused by a genetically induced "broken brain," it is still necessary to explain why identical twins don't always share the disorder. Experience clearly plays a pivotal role. Similarly, the irrational beliefs and explanatory styles that characterize depression must be "learned" somewhere, although two people with the same experiences may not always end up with the same set of beliefs. Once again, experience is the bedrock on which the psychological interpretation is built.

A number of mental health professionals feel that certain kinds of psychological disorders may be essentially *learned*. People can learn to act and think abnormally in perhaps the same way they might learn how to bake a cake, make friends, or avoid talking in class. Experts with this view of abnormality propose that learning principles of the type that we discussed in Chapter 7 help explain why psychological disorders develop and how they can be best treated. A specific phobia, for example, could be acquired through *classical conditioning;* individuals might learn to associate a particular stimulus or event with another event that makes them afraid. Alternatively, an individual might learn to act abnormally, through *instrumental conditioning,* because he or she has been reinforced for those actions. Acting in a strange way thus becomes more likely than it was before.

Learning theorists often stress the role of *modeling,* or observational learning, in the etiology of psychological disorders. As we discussed in Chapter 7, there are reasons to believe that specific phobias might sometimes be acquired through modeling. Some of the best evidence has come from animal studies, in which it is possible to control how the fear reaction is initially acquired. Rhesus monkeys who are raised in the wild show an extremely strong fear response to snakes; monkeys who have been reared in the laboratory will show a similar reaction, but only if they've witnessed other monkeys reacting fearfully when snakes are introduced into the cage. This research has made it clear that it is not necessary for the animal to directly experience something negative, such as getting attacked and bitten by the snake; the animal can acquire its fear simply by watching other monkeys act afraid (Cook & Mineka, 1989). Modeling in this case makes adaptive sense because appropriate actions can be learned without directly experiencing negative consequences.

Some psychologists believe that children can acquire phobias by modeling the fears of significant role models. If someone has a father who is afraid of heights, for example, there is an increased chance that the child, too, will be afraid of heights.

The monkey data are important because they show how modeling can lead to the acquisition of a strong fear response. Obviously, for monkeys in the wild it's quite adaptive to be afraid of snakes. For humans, we know that modeling is also a powerful way to learn, but the evidence that modeling underlies specific phobias—which, after all, are essentially irrational fears—is still largely indirect at this point. We know that many people with specific phobias cannot remember having a traumatic experience with the object of their fear (Rachman, 1990). It's also the case that specific phobias tend to run in families—if your father was afraid of heights, for instance, there's an increased chance that you, too, will be afraid of heights (Fyer and others, 1990). This kind of evidence is consistent with a modeling account of specific phobias (although it does not preclude alternative accounts). From our adaptive perspective, it's interesting to note that modeling, which is essentially an adaptive process, might under certain conditions lead people to acquire behaviors that are not very adaptive.

As with the biological, genetic, and cognitive factors that we've considered, it's unlikely that learning principles alone will be able to account for the genesis of psychological disorders. People probably can't "learn" to be schizophrenic, for example, although stressful events in the environment may play an important role in precipitating this disorder. Even with phobias, which may be largely learning-based, it is probably necessary to be predisposed to anxiety for a full-blown phobia to develop (Barlow, 1988). Experience plays a significant role in the etiology of most psychological disorders, but it does not act alone. Behavior, both normal and abnormal, is virtually always produced by multiple causes.

Do you suffer from any kind of specific phobia? Can you trace the fear to a particular experience in your life? Does anyone else in your family share the same fear?

SOLVING THE PROBLEMS: A SUMMARY

In this chapter, we've considered what happens when a person's thoughts and actions become disordered. Most mental health professionals believe it's possible and useful to distinguish between "normal" and "abnormal" behavior. In addition, as we've seen, a relatively precise and rigorous classification system exists for the diagnosis and labeling of psychological disorders when they occur. But what are the implications for our general theme of the adaptive mind? It hardly seems adaptive to suffer from a psychological disorder—in fact, lack of adaptiveness is often used as a criterion for the identification of a behavior as abnormal.

It's important to keep in mind that so-called "abnormal" behaviors are often simply extreme versions of behaviors that otherwise have adaptive qualities. Anxiety, for instance, is an adaptive body response that prepares people for action and helps keep them vigilant about their surroundings. It becomes a problem only in its extreme form, when it is prolonged and chronic enough to impair normal functioning. Sigmund Freud believed that certain kinds of psychologically based amnesias are adaptive because they prevent traumatic memories from intruding into conscious awareness. Thus, to paraphrase William Shakespeare, there may indeed be a bit of method in madness. On the other hand, it's also reasonable to propose that psychological disorders may represent a kind of breakdown in the system. Schizophrenia, in particular, may arise from faulty brain functioning—the system ceases to be adaptive because it no longer has the capacity to function properly.

▶ **CONCEPTUALIZING ABNORMALITY** Conceptualizing *abnormal* behavior turns out to be a rather difficult thing to do. A number of criteria have been proposed, including the notions of statistical and cultural deviance. By the term *deviance*, psychologists typically mean behavior that is essentially unusual in some way, either in terms of its statistical likelihood or with respect to the accepted norms of the culture. Abnormality can also be defined in terms of emotional distress or dysfunction. None of these criteria alone is sufficient to capture the concept. Instead, the concept of abnormality is usually defined in terms of some combination of these factors.

Currently, many mental health professionals conceive of abnormal behavior in terms of a medical model. According to this view, psychological disorders are best described as "illnesses" that can be "fixed" through appropriate treatment. There are pros and cons to this approach, and it should not be taken too literally. Physical illnesses often have clearly identifiable causes, but this is seldom true for psychological disorders. Also of concern are the effects of diagnostic labeling of disorders: Diagnostic labels can sometimes become self-fulfilling prophecies, which can make it harder for a suffering person to recover.

▶ **CLASSIFYING PSYCHOLOGICAL DISORDERS** Once we recognize that a behavior is abnormal, is there a reliable way to classify the underlying problem? Mental health professionals tend to rely on the DSM-IV, which lists objective criteria for the diagnosis of psychological disorders. The DSM-IV is composed of five major rating dimensions, or axes, which are used to record the presence of clinical or personality disorders, existing medical conditions, environmental problems, and the ability of the individual to function globally. In this chapter we focused our attention on Axis I, which lists the major clinical syndromes.

Anxiety disorders are diagnosed when a person's apprehension and worry become so extreme that behavior is impaired. Generalized anxiety disorder is characterized by chronic worrying that cannot be attributed to any obvious source. Obsessive-compulsive disorders are characterized by the presence of persistent, uncontrollable thoughts, called *obsessions,* or by compelling needs to perform actions repetitively, called *compulsions.* Specific phobias are highly focused fears of specific objects or events.

In somatoform disorders, the focus of an individual's disorder revolves around the body: The person might have a persistent preoccupation with the possibility that he or she has a serious disease (hypochondriasis), or the individual might appear to suffer from an actual physical problem that has no identifiable physical cause (conversion disorder).

In dissociative disorders, the person appears to separate, or dissociate, previous thoughts and memories from current conscious awareness. These disorders include dissociative amnesia, dissociative fugue states, and the more controversial dissociative identity disorder, in which the person appears to have two or more distinct personalities.

Mood disorders typically come in two forms: depressive disorder, in which the affected individual is mired in depression, and bipolar disorder, in which the individual alternates between the highs of mania and the lows of depression. The final clinical syndrome that we discussed, schizophrenia, is characterized by distorted thoughts and perceptions. The positive symptoms of schizophrenia include delusions, hallucinations, and disorganized speech and behavior. The negative symptoms include flat affect, which means that the person shows little or no emotional reactions to events. Personality disorders are listed in Axis II because they tend to be more ingrained and inflexible than the major clinical syndromes described on Axis I.

▶ **UNDERSTANDING PSYCHOLOGICAL DISORDERS** What are the primary causes of the psychological disorders classified in the DSM-IV? Mental health professionals currently believe that the root cause, or etiology, of most disorders lies in a combination of biological, cognitive, and environmental factors. Some disorders may result from broken or abnormal brains. There is evidence to support the idea that some psychological problems arise from neurotransmitter problems in the brain or perhaps from structural problems in brain anatomy. Many psychological disorders also appear to have a genetic basis—individuals may inherit a predisposition for a particular kind of problem.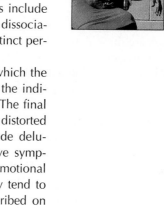

Psychological disorders are also typically characterized by maladaptive thinking, and it has been suggested that maladaptive beliefs and attributions contribute to the appearance of abnormal behavior. Depressed individuals, for example, tend to attribute negative events to internal, stable, and global causes; these attributions are often associated with a sense of hopelessness, or the faulty belief that things cannot get better. Finally, all theories of psychological disorders rely in one form or another on the environment. The environment clearly plays a role in the expression of biological or genetic predispositions, and past history is a critical determinant of the kinds of attributions that people make. Some psychological problems may arise almost entirely from environmental influences. It is possible that people learn to act abnormally, either through conditioning or through modeling the behavior of significant people around them.

Terms to Remember

CONCEPTUALIZING ABNORMALITY: WHAT IS ABNORMAL BEHAVIOR?

statistical deviance A criterion of abnormality stating that a behavior is abnormal if it occurs infrequently among the members of a population.

cultural deviance A criterion of abnormality stating that a behavior is abnormal if it violates the rules or accepted standards of society.

emotional distress A criterion of abnormality stating that abnormal behaviors are those that lead to personal distress or emotional upset.

dysfunction A breakdown in normal functioning; abnormal behaviors are those that prevent one from pursuing adaptive strategies.

insanity A legal term usually defined as the inability to understand that certain actions are wrong, in a legal or moral sense, at the time of a crime.

medical model The view that abnormal behavior is symptomatic of an underlying "disease" that can be "cured" with the appropriate therapy.

diagnostic labeling effects The fact that labels for psychological problems can become self-fulfilling prophecies; the label may make it difficult to recognize normal behavior when it occurs, and it may actually increase the likelihood that a person will act in an abnormal way.

CLASSIFYING PSYCHOLOGICAL DISORDERS: THE DSM-IV AND SELECTED CLINICAL SYNDROMES

DSM-IV *The Diagnostic and Statistical Manual of Mental Disorders* (4th ed.), which is used for the diagnosis and classification of psychological disorders. The DSM-IV is composed of five major rating dimensions, or *axes*.

anxiety disorders A class of disorders marked by excessive apprehension and worry that in turn impairs normal functioning.

generalized anxiety disorder Excessive worrying, or "free-floating" anxiety, that lasts for at least six months and that cannot be attributed to any single identifiable source.

panic disorder A condition marked by recurrent discrete episodes or "attacks" of extremely intense fear or dread.

agoraphobia An anxiety disorder that causes an individual to restrict his or her normal activities; someone suffering from agoraphobia tends to avoid public places out of fear that a panic attack will occur.

obsessive-compulsive disorder An anxiety disorder that manifests itself through persistent and uncontrollable thoughts, called *obsessions*, or by the compelling need to perform repetitive acts, called *compulsions*.

specific phobic disorder A highly focused fear of a specific object or situation.

somatoform disorders Psychological disorders that focus on the physical body.

hypochondriasis A long-lasting preoccupation with the idea that one has developed a serious disease, based on what turns out to be a misinterpretation of normal body reactions.

somatization disorder A long-lasting preoccupation with body symptoms that have no identifiable physical cause.

conversion disorder The presence of real physical problems, such as blindness or paralysis, that seem to have no identifiable physical cause.

dissociative disorders A class of disorders characterized by the separation, or dissociation, of conscious awareness from previous thoughts or memories.

dissociative amnesia A psychological disorder characterized by an inability to remember important personal information.

dissociative fugue A loss of personal identity that is often accompanied by a flight from home.

dissociative identity disorder A condition in which an individual alternates among what appear to be two or more distinct identities or personalities (also known as *multiple personality disorder*).

mood disorders Prolonged and disabling disruptions in emotional state.

major depressive episode A type of mood disorder characterized by depressed mood and other symptoms.

bipolar disorder A type of mood disorder in which the person experiences disordered mood shifts in two directions—from depression to a manic state.

manic state A disordered state in which the person becomes hyperactive, talkative, and has a decreased need for sleep; a person in a manic state may engage in activities that are self-destructive or dangerous.

schizophrenia A class of disorders characterized by fundamental disturbances in thought processes, emotion, or behavior.

personality disorders Chronic or enduring patterns of behavior that lead to significant impairments in social functioning.

paranoid personality disorder A personality disorder characterized by pervasive distrust of others.

dependent personality disorder A personality disorder characterized by an excessive and persistent need to be taken care of by others.

antisocial personality disorder A personality disorder characterized by little, if any, respect for social laws, customs, or norms.

UNDERSTANDING PSYCHOLOGICAL DISORDERS: BIOLOGICAL, COGNITIVE, OR ENVIRONMENTAL?

learned helplessness A general sense of helplessness that is acquired when people repeatedly fail in their attempts to control their environment; learned helplessness may play a role in depression.

It is a common belief that inside the hearts and minds of truly creative people lies an element of madness. The poet, covered by a dark shroud of depression, finds divine insight that is born, it seems, only from suffering. The scientific genius, who appears eccentric and disorganized to most, solves a universal problem by weaving together wholly disconnected ideas into a common thread of understanding. For thousands of years, it's been suggested that there is something to madness, perhaps the "untroubled surrender to momentary fancies and moods," that "sets free powers which otherwise are constrained" (Kraepelin, 1921).

But is there scientific evidence to back up these claims? Is there a factual basis for the belief that psychological disorders such as mania and depression contribute to creativity and genius? Currently, two lines of evidence have been offered to support the connection. First, a number of investigators have discovered a correlation between highly creative individuals and the appearance of psychological problems (Andreasen, 1987; Jamison and others, 1980). The data suggest that creative people are more likely, on average, to be troubled by a psychological disorder. Second, if we analyze the behaviors and thought processes of people who claim to be in the midst of a highly creative and productive period, we find a resemblance to the conditions present in the manic state of a bipolar disorder (Jamison, 1989). Let's consider this evidence in a bit more detail.

The Evidence Favoring a Connection

If we take a journey through history and consider the psychological "health" of prominent individuals, it's not difficult to find examples of psychological problems. In this century alone, there have been at least five Pulitzer Prize–winning poets (including Sylvia Plath) who have committed suicide in the midst of depression. So, too, have a number of fiction writers (Ernest Hemingway). It is now recognized that Abraham Lincoln,

Teddy Roosevelt, and Winston Churchill all probably suffered from bipolar disorder, marked by swings between manic states and depression.

Such examples are intriguing, but they don't constitute solid scientific evidence. More systematic data have come from studies in which pools of highly creative and "average" people are matched on a number of dimensions and the incidence rate of psychological problems is then compared. In one such study, Nancy Andreasen (1987) compared the psychiatric diagnoses of 30 creative writing faculty at the University of Iowa Writers' Workshop (a highly regarded creative writing program) with those of 30 "control" individuals who were matched to the writers on age, sex, and educational status. Andreasen discovered that the writers had a substantially higher rate of psychological disorders than the controls—in fact, 43% of the writers were found to have experienced the symptoms of a bipolar disorder at some point in their lives. This was the case for only 10% of the controls. Andreasen also found a higher prevalence of mental problems among the writers' first-degree relatives (parents and siblings).

In a somewhat different approach on the issue, Kay Redfield Jamison (1989) looked to see whether similarities might exist between creative states and the characteristics of manic states. She interviewed 47 famous British writers and artists—all had won at least one prestigious literary or artistic prize—and asked them to describe their moods, thoughts, and actions during spurts of creative activity. She found striking similarities between their answers and the symptoms found in manic states; virtually all of the subjects reported experiencing creative states characterized by a decreased need for sleep, increases in energy, enthusiasm, self-confidence, speed and fluency of thoughts, as well as an elevated mood and sense of well-being. Moreover, when Jamison asked the subjects how important these extremes in mood and thoughts were to the

creation of their work, 90% of the participants stated that the moods and feelings were integral, necessary, or very important (Jamison, 1989).

Correlations and Causality

Some interpretive problems serve as drawbacks to the studies we've just considered. Most important, these studies simply demonstrate what appear to be correlations between some of the characteristics of mood disorders and creativity: Creative individuals are more likely to have mood disorders, and the thoughts and feelings that accompany creative periods share properties with the symptoms of mood disorders. But this kind of evidence does not indicate whether the psychological disorder is really *causing* the creative activity. Other factors might be involved.

For example, one possibility is that when creative individuals are in a manic state, they simply do more work because of their high energy levels. This increase in output can make it look like the mania is enhancing creativity, even though it is the *quantity* rather than the *quality* of the work that is really changing. Suppose that you're capable of writing one really good poem for every 10 attempts that

The composer Robert Schumann (1810–1856).

you make. If normally you make 10 attempts in a month, you will end up with one excellent result. Now suppose you enter a manic state, which increases your output to 30 poems in a month. Even if the mania doesn't affect the quality of your work one bit, it will still look as if you have tripled the number of "great" works that you have produced. Madness and creativity may co-occur, but one is not directly causing the other.

To examine the possibility that it may be the quantity rather than the quality of output that is affected by a mood disorder, psychologist Robert Weisberg (1994) conducted a detailed case study of the composer Robert Schumann (1810–1856). Schumann is believed to have suffered from bipolar disorder; throughout his life, he repeatedly entered either manic or depressive states, and he eventually starved himself to death in an institution at age 46. Schumann is an excellent case to study because there are medical records, as well as other data, that pinpoint, on a year-by-year basis, which kind of mood state he was in. Weisberg found a clear relationship between Schumann's mood state and his productivity as a composer: For the years that he was primarily in a state of depression, he completed, on average, fewer than 3 compositions per year. On the other hand, his output during "manic" years was a little over 12 compositions per year (see Figure 14.9).

But were the compositions from his "manic" years of high quality? To find out, Weisberg (1994) determined the number of times Schumann's compositions had been recorded professionally over the years. If a composition is recorded often by professionals, Weisberg argued, it's reasonable to conclude that

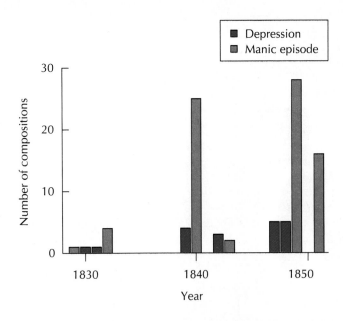

FIGURE 14.9
Musical Productivity and Mood State. The graph shows the number of musical compositions written by Robert Schumann during years in which his mood state was characterized primarily as manic (red) or depressed (blue). (Based on Weisberg, 1994)

the piece is of high quality. Weisberg found that when the quality of Schumann's compositions—defined as the average number of recordings available for each composition in a particular year—was compared across manic and depressive years, no significant differences emerged. Although Schumann composed more during his manic periods, he was not more likely to produce works of extremely high quality. In this particular case, then, madness affected the quantity of creative output but not the quality.

Determining whether there really is a causal relationship between certain kinds of psychological problems and

genius or creativity is a difficult thing to do. Obviously, psychologists cannot conduct a well-controlled experiment (inducing madness in one randomly sampled group of creative people and normalcy in another), so they are typically forced to rely on correlational studies or on anecdotes as the basis for their opinions. Weisberg's research, with its careful and objective separation of quality from quantity, suggests that the anecdotal evidence may be wrong or misleading, at least for people suffering from bipolar disorders. The link between madness and creativity may turn out to be quite tenuous, despite centuries of belief to the contrary.

Therapy

15

We are all born mad. Some remain so.

Samuel Beckett

People who suffer from serious psychological disorders often have trouble leading normal lives. They can't hold a job or make friends; they may even have trouble carrying on a coherent conversation. It's essential, then, for such individuals to seek out and receive **psychotherapy,** or treatment to deal with their mental, emotional, or behavioral problems. But even those with less severe disturbances can benefit from the right kind of therapy. Ralph, for example, turns down the job of national sales manager because he is afraid of flying; Julie spends most of her time alone in her apartment because she's convinced she'll embarrass herself in social settings. Treatment options are available to tackle such "problems in living," and the result can be a substantial improvement in the quality of life.

As we'll see in this chapter, mental health professionals have a variety of tools at their disposal to help people regain their ability to function well in their surroundings. The particular tool used by the therapist depends on a number of factors, including the specific type of psychological disorder being treated and the personality of the person seeking treatment. There are also a variety of ways that a treatment can be administered. Some individuals respond well to one-on-one encounters with a therapist; other individuals thrive best in group settings. As we discussed in Chapter 1, good therapists are often *eclectic,* meaning that they tailor the treatment option to meet the needs of the particular client. This commitment to "eclecticism" does not necessarily require the therapist to abandon his or her theoretical orientation (Lazarus & Messer, 1991), but it does require the recognition that a method that proves effective for one person can turn out to be quite ineffective for another.

PREVIEWING THE CONCEPTUAL AND PRACTICAL PROBLEMS

As we saw in Chapter 14, when psychologists seek to understand the cause of a psychological disorder, they usually appeal to biological, cognitive, or environmental factors. Abnormal behavior can arise from brain dysfunction, irrational beliefs and attributions, environmental experiences, or a combination of these factors. Most forms of psychotherapy are specifically designed to address the following questions: How can the therapist specifically treat the body, the mind, or the environment? As you'll soon see, these three factors create a convenient way of classifying the various forms of treatment available to the therapist (see Figure 15.1). We'll end the chapter by considering how mental health professionals evaluate the effectiveness of therapy and how individuals can best go about choosing a therapist.

TREATING THE BODY Virtually all psychologists acknowledge that there is a close link between biology and behavior. Abnormal functioning in the brain is thought to contribute to a number of psychological disorders. Schizophrenia, for example, might be traceable in part to imbalances in neurotransmitters; depression and mania have been linked to the activities of neurotransmitters as well. To address these kinds of problems, it makes sense to consider treating the body itself. One option might be to administer a drug designed to restore the proper balance of neurotransmitters in the brain; another option might be surgery to "fix" the damage that exists in a particular region of the brain, or even the use of electric "shock" treatment. We'll review some of the major *biomedical therapies* currently available, and we'll consider the advantages and disadvantages of each.

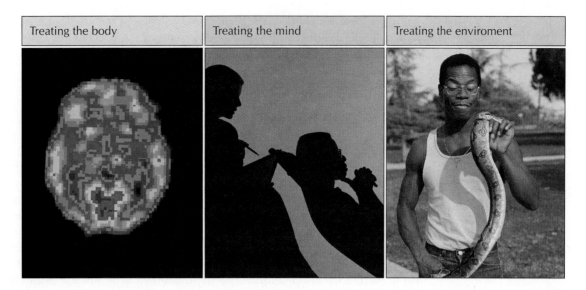

| Treating the body | Treating the mind | Treating the enviroment |

FIGURE 15.1
Previewing the Problems.
Psychologists face three main conceptual and practical problems as they seek to administer and evaluate therapy.

▶ **TREATING THE MIND** When most people think of psychotherapy, they probably imagine someone lying on a couch talking about dreams and early childhood experiences. Although this stereotypical image is accurate in some respects, you'll see in our discussion of *insight therapies* that many therapists have abandoned the couch, as well as the emphasis on dreams and early experiences. What remains is the idea that self-knowledge, or insight, about one's thought processes can be an effective tool for solving psychological problems. Psychological disorders are often associated with abnormal thoughts and beliefs, and many psychologists are convinced that if they can change those thoughts and beliefs, the disorder will be effectively treated. We'll consider the major insight therapies in this section of the chapter, including Freud's classic psychoanalysis, some more contemporary versions of psychodynamic therapies, and the "thought-changing" techniques of modern cognitive therapy. Finally, we'll look at how humanistic psychologists use insight to nurture and treat the human spirit.

▶ **TREATING THE ENVIRONMENT** In Chapter 14, we also discussed the idea that certain kinds of psychological disorders can be learned. People might learn to think and act in maladaptive ways in much the same way that they acquire other thoughts and actions—through the experiences of instrumental conditioning, classical conditioning, or by modeling the actions of others. The idea behind *behavioral therapies* is to use basic learning principles to change "maladaptive" behavior patterns into "adaptive" behavior patterns. For example, if experience has taught a person to associate high places with disabling fear, it might be possible to alter the association either through extinction or by "counterconditioning" relaxation to replace the fear. In other cases, a person might be reinforced for acting in an adaptive fashion and punished for acting in a maladaptive way. We'll examine the major behavioral therapies currently in use, and we'll specify the kinds of psychological disorders that behavioral theories seem best equipped to handle.

▶ **EVALUATING AND CHOOSING PSYCHOTHERAPY** In the final section of the chapter, we'll focus on how mental health professionals evaluate the effectiveness of psychotherapy. Do all forms of therapy "work," or are some more effective than others? Therapy can be a costly and time-consuming process, so it's important to evaluate the advantages and disadvantages of the intervention. A number of studies have been conducted comparing people who have undergone therapy with those left untreated. Although the balance of the studies clearly demonstrate the effectiveness of psychotherapy, some of the findings may surprise you. We'll also consider the factors that should be taken into account when choosing a therapist.

Treating the Body: Biomedical Therapies

The 20th century can claim no special monopoly on abnormal behavior. Modern psychologists may have rigorous classification systems for diagnosing and labeling disordered behavior, but people have shown the classic symptoms of psychological disorders since the beginning of recorded history. For just as long, people have speculated about what causes abnormal behavior and have offered "remedies" for its treatment. At one time it was popular to appeal to supernatural forces: People who exhibited bizarre or deviant behavior, it was believed, must be "possessed" by one or more evil spirits or demons. The "cure," if we can call it that, was to punish or torture the affected individual in an effort to drive out the evil inhabitants.

But not all serious thinkers adopted such views. In fact, over 2000 years ago, Hippocrates (469–377 B.C.) and his followers suggested that psychological disorders should be treated as manifestations of the body. People get depressed or exhibit manic states, they argued, for much the same reason that people fall victim to the common cold—the body and brain, and hence the mind, are affected by some kind of "disease." Hippocrates even went so far as to recommend changes in diet and exercise as a way of treating depression, a course of action that many modern therapists would consider appropriate today.

This idea that at least some mental problems can be treated as "illnesses" was placed on firmer scientific ground in the 19th and early 20th centuries as scientists began to establish links between known physical problems and the symptoms of psychological disorders. For example, by the end of the 19th century it was recognized that the venereal disease *syphilis* was responsible not only for a steady deterioration in physical health (and eventually death) but also for the appearance of paranoia and hallucinations. Establishing that a link existed between syphilis and psychological "symptoms" was an important step in the eventual development of biologically based therapies. Later "cures" for the disease were created by injecting sufferers with the blood of malaria patients in an effort to induce a high fever that would "burn out" the syphilis bacteria; today, of course, doctors use antibiotics to treat syphilis.

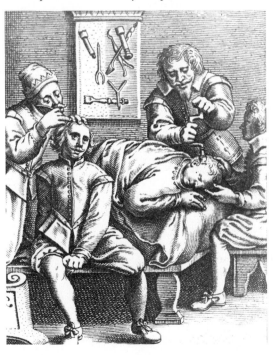

This engraving from 1598 demonstrates an early form of "therapy" for psychological disorders—drilling holes in the head to promote the release of evil spirits.

In this section of the chapter, we'll consider several modern biological approaches to the treatment of psychological disorders. **Biomedical therapies** use physiological interventions in an effort to reduce or eliminate the symptoms that arise from psychological disorders. By far the most popular approach is treatment with drugs, and we'll consider this approach first, but other biomedical therapies are available, including electroconvulsive therapy and psychosurgery.

Drug Therapies

The psychological community began to recognize the remarkable potential of drug therapy in the early 1950s when two French psychiatrists, Jean Delay and Pierre Deniker, reported success in treating the positive symptoms of schizophrenia with a drug called *chlorpromazine* (often sold under the brand name Thorazine). Patients who suffered from severe delusions and hallucinations showed considerable improvement after prolonged use of the drug. Since that time, dozens of other drugs have proven successful in treating a wide variety of psychological disorders. In fact, there are now specific medications available to treat most of the disorders that we considered in Chapter 14—everything from obsessive-compulsive disorder to depression. Unfortunately, these drugs do not work for all people affected with mental illness and, as we'll see, some drugs have disturbing side effects. But they have helped thousands of people, and in many ways they have revolutionized the mental health profession.

One noticeable by-product of medications such as chlorpromazine has been a sharp reduction in the number of patients who require extended stays in mental hospitals or institutions. Prior to the 1950s, hundreds of thousands of people were institutionalized, often for many years, because their symptoms were simply too severe to allow them to cope successfully in everyday settings. Partly through the administration of drugs, it has become possible to control the severity of these symptoms, allowing individuals to be treated outside of a hospital or institution. The results have been dramatic: By 1983, the number of people institutionalized for psychological problems had dropped to less than 150,000 from over 600,000 in the 1950s (Kiesler & Sibulkin, 1987). Other factors have contributed to the decline as well—improvements in alternative forms of therapy (including behavioral and cognitive), as well as cutbacks in the levels of funding needed to maintain high levels of care.

Antipsychotic Drugs. Medications that reduce the severity of the positive symptoms of schizophrenia—delusions, hallucinations, disorganized speech—are commonly called **antipsychotic drugs.** Chlorpromazine is an example of such a drug, but a number of others are also currently in use. The majority of these antipsychotic drugs are believed to act on the neurotransmitter *dopamine* in the brain. As we discussed in Chapter 14, some researchers believe that schizophrenia is caused, at least in part, by excess supplies of dopamine. Chlorpromazine acts as a dopamine *antagonist,* meaning that it blocks or slows down the use of dopamine in the brain (Gershon & Reider, 1992) (see Figure 15.2). The fact that dopamine

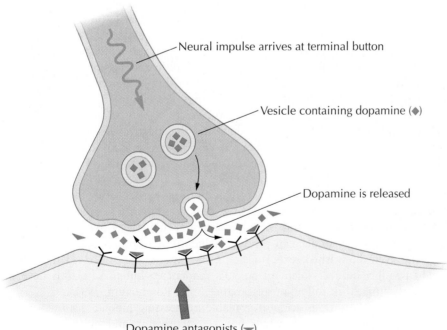

- Neural impulse arrives at terminal button
- Vesicle containing dopamine (♦)
- Dopamine is released

Dopamine antagonists (↽)
prevent dopamine from binding
to membrane receptors (Υ)

FIGURE 15.2
Dopamine Antagonists. Some antipsychotic medications act as antagonists, which means they block or slow down the action of neurotransmitters in the brain. Here, a dopamine antagonist is binding with the receptor membrane, blocking the neurotransmitter.

Just because the administration of dopamine antagonists reduces the severity of the symptoms of schizophrenia does not mean that too much dopamine *causes* schizophrenia. Why not? (Hint: Do correlations imply causality?)

antagonists work so well in reducing the severity of positive symptoms is usually taken to be strong support for the dopamine hypothesis of schizophrenia (Barlow & Durand, 1995).

But dopamine antagonists do not work for all sufferers of schizophrenia. Moreover, these drugs tend to work almost exclusively on positive symptoms. The negative symptoms of schizophrenia, such as the sharp decline in the normal expression of emotions, are not affected very much by the administration of antipsychotic medications. Antipsychotic drugs can also produce unwanted and persistent side effects in some patients, including drowsiness, difficulties in concentrating, blurry vision, and movement disorders (Windgassen, 1992). One particularly serious side effect is a condition called *tardive dyskinesia,* which produces disabling involuntary movements of the tongue, jaw, mouth, and face that can sometimes be permanent (Kane and others, 1986). These side effects act as a two-edged sword: Not only are they extremely uncomfortable for the patient, but they also increase the chances that the patient will stop taking the medication. Without the medication, of course, it's likely that the positive symptoms of the disorder will reemerge.

In the past decade, a new medication, called *clozapine* (brand name Clozaril), has been introduced that seems to work well for patients who do not respond to the more traditional dopamine antagonists (Kane & Marder, 1993). Clozapine does not produce movement side effects such as tardive dyskinesia, although medical complications are still a concern. From a research standpoint, the effectiveness of clozapine is noteworthy because it apparently does not work by simply regulating the amount of dopamine in the brain. It is currently believed that clozapine may affect a number of neurotransmitters, including both dopamine and serotonin (Potter & Manji, 1993). This suggests that dopamine alone, as we noted in Chapter 14, cannot account entirely for schizophrenic disorders.

Antidepressant Drugs. The 1950s also witnessed the emergence of medications for treating manic states and depression. Mood disorders have been linked to several neurotransmitters, including norepinephrine and serotonin. **Antidepressant drugs,** like the antipsychotic drugs, act by modulating the availability or effectiveness of these kinds of neurotransmitters. The group of antidepressants called *tricyclics,* for example, alter mood by acting primarily on norepinephrine; tricyclics apparently allow norepinephrine to linger in synapses longer than normal, which eventually modulates its effectiveness. The antidepressant fluoxetine—known commercially as Prozac—comes from a different class of antidepressants. Prozac acts primarily on serotonin, again by blocking its "reuptake" into the neuron, thereby allowing it to linger in the synapse (see Figure 15.3).

At present, researchers still do not know exactly how or why these medications affect mood, outside of the fact that they alter the effectiveness of neurotransmitters. Fortunately, it's clear that they do work quite well for many individuals affected with depression. It's been estimated that sustained use of antidepressants successfully controls depression in over 50% of all depressed patients (Depression Guideline Panel, 1993). On the down side, it typically takes several weeks for these medications to begin working (the time periods may differ across the different types of antidepressants), and there are potential side effects that must be monitored. Prozac, for example, can produce agitation or restlessness, difficulty sleeping, and even diminished sexual desire. Early reports also suggested that Prozac might possibly induce violent or suicidal tendencies, but these claims have not been substantiated in follow-up research (Fava & Rosenbaum, 1991).

Effective medications are also available for treating bipolar disorders, which are characterized by mood swings between depression and hyperactive manic states. Bipolar disorders are usually treated by administering a common salt called *lithium carbonate.* Lithium is more effective for bipolar disorder than the antide-

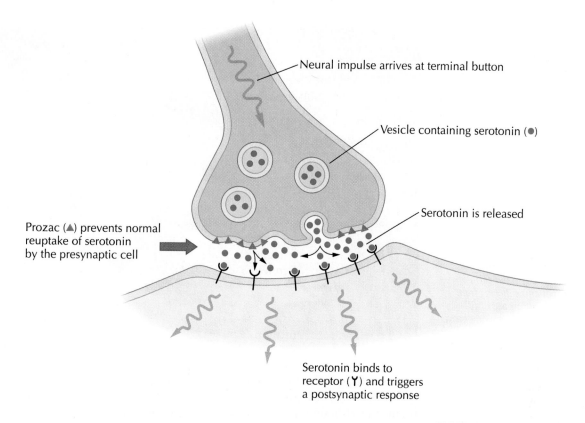

Neural impulse arrives at terminal button

Vesicle containing serotonin (●)

Serotonin is released

Prozac (▲) prevents normal reuptake of serotonin by the presynaptic cell

Serotonin binds to receptor (Y) and triggers a postsynaptic response

FIGURE 15.3
Reuptake Blockers. Some kinds of antidepressant medications block the reabsorption of neurotransmitters, which allows those neurotransmitters to linger longer in the synapse and continue to activate receptor neurons. Prozac is in the class of antidepressants that block the reabsorption of serotonin.

pressants because it works well on the manic state; it puts affected individuals on a more "even keel" and helps to prevent the reoccurrence of future manic episodes. But it, too, needs to be monitored closely because lithium use can lead to a variety of medical complications.

Antianxiety Drugs. Among the most common drugs prescribed for the treatment of psychological problems are **antianxiety drugs,** known more generally as *tranquilizers.* Tranquilizers come from a class of chemicals called *benzodiazepines*—Valium and Xanax are popular trade names—and they are used primarily to reduce tension and anxiety. It's been estimated that 10–20% of adults in the Western world were "popping" tranquilizers in the mid-1970s (Greenblatt & Shader, 1978), which gives you some idea of their widespread use. In recent years, tranquilizer use has been on the decline, primarily because mental health professionals recognize a downside to their sustained use.

Most benzodiazepines appear to work on an inhibitory neurotransmitter in the brain called gamma-aminobutyric acid (GABA). The effectiveness of GABA increases after taking the drug, which leads to a lowering of excitation in affected neurons (Lickey & Gordon, 1991). Potential side effects include drowsiness, impaired motor coordination, and possible psychological dependence (Rickels and others, 1990). Tranquilizers can act as a kind of psychological "crutch" after sustained use, so the majority of clinicians now recommend that they be used primarily as a short-term remedy for anxiety rather than as a long-term "cure."

Electroconvulsive Therapy

We turn our attention now to a quite different, and very controversial, biomedical therapy: "shock" treatment. At face value, few psychological therapies seem as uncivilized as the idea of strapping someone down on a table and passing 100 or

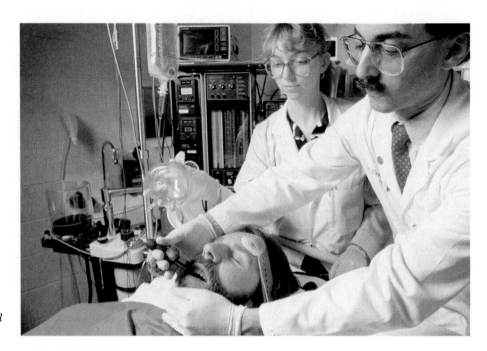

ECT, as currently administered, is a reasonably safe and effective form of treatment for patients suffering from severe depression, but its use is still considered controversial by many mental health professionals.

so volts of electricity into his or her brain. As you know, the language of the nervous system is partly electrical in nature. If electric shock is administered to the brain, a brief brain seizure will occur that produces, among other things, convulsions and loss of consciousness. When **electroconvulsive therapy (ECT)** was first introduced in the 1930s, it was a terrifying and hazardous procedure; patients suffered serious side effects that included the occasional broken bone from the convulsions. Thankfully, modern applications of ECT are much less physically traumatic; the patient is given a light anesthetic and medications that relax the muscles so that injuries will not occur.

Many mental health professionals believe that ECT, as currently administered, is a reasonably safe and effective form of treatment for patients who are suffering from severe depression. It is used almost exclusively for depression (it is ineffective for most other psychological problems), although many professionals consider it to be a kind of treatment of "last resort." It is used in cases in which people have shown little or no response to conventional antidepressant drugs or other "talk" therapies. Controlled research studies have found that ECT is successful some 50–70% of the time in lessening the symptoms of depression in patients who have not otherwise responded to treatment (Prudic, Sackeim, & Devanand, 1990; Weiner & Coffey, 1988). Typically, these studies involve direct comparisons between depressed patients who receive ECT and patients who undergo the same procedural preparations but don't actually receive the shock.

Despite the demonstrated effectiveness of ECT as a treatment for severe depression, there are several reasons why the procedure remains controversial. First, no one is certain exactly why the treatment works. It's possible that shocking the brain affects the release of neurotransmitters or changes some structural feature of the brain, but at present there is no definitive answer as to why the procedure changes mood (Kapur & Mann, 1993). Second, ECT produces side effects, particularly confusion and a loss of memory for events surrounding the treatment (Breggin, 1991). These side effects are usually temporary, and they're not serious for most patients, but they remain a concern. Third, some researchers worry about the possibility that ECT might cause permanent brain damage. Effective ECT usually requires repeated administrations of the shock over several weeks, and it's not known what long-term effects these treatments have on the brain.

Imagine you are treating a severely depressed patient who is clearly suicidal. Remember, drug therapies often take weeks to work. Would you consider ECT for such a patient? How about an elderly patient who refuses to eat, just wants to die, and cannot be given medications because of side effects?

Is ECT worth the risks? The answer depends mainly on the needs of the particular patient. If you are someone who is deeply depressed and no other treatment options have provided you any relief, ECT might literally be a lifesaver. Many clinicians believe that if it comes down to a desperate choice between ending your life and suffering some confusion and long-lasting memory loss, trying ECT is certainly worth the risk.

Psychosurgery

We've made the case that a direct connection exists between biological problems in the brain and the emergence of some psychological disorders. Some people who are afflicted with schizophrenia, for example, show structural abnormalities in the brain. It makes sense, then, to consider the possibility of direct intervention, through brain surgery, to fix these problems permanently. Certainly if your appendix or your gall bladder were infected and the diseased organ was creating a whole host of physical symptoms, you wouldn't think twice about calling the local surgeon. Wouldn't it be nice if we could adopt a similar approach for psychological problems?

Actually, the use of **psychosurgery**—surgery that destroys or alters tissue in the brain in an effort to affect behavior—has been around for decades. In the 1930s, a surgical procedure called the *prefrontal lobotomy* was pioneered by a Portuguese physician named Egas Moniz (and later in the United States by Walter Freeman and James Watts). The operation involved a crude separation of the frontal lobes from the rest of the brain. The intent of the surgery was to sever various connections in the brain's circuitry, in the hope that it might produce calming tendencies in disturbed patients. The procedure was widely used for several decades, and, in fact, Moniz was awarded the Nobel Prize for his work in 1949. But prefrontal lobotomies eventually fell into disrepute. Many patients were killed by the procedure, and it produced serious cognitive deficits in many of the patients who underwent the surgery. They lost their ability to plan and coordinate actions, capabilities associated with activity in the frontal lobes.

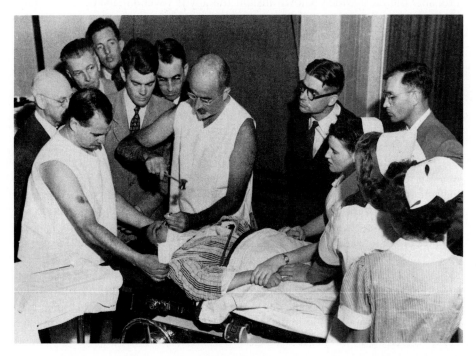

Dr. Walter Freeman is shown here in 1949 performing psychosurgery on a patient suffering from a psychological disorder. He is inserting an instrument under the patient's upper eyelid in order to sever certain neural connections in the brain and thereby relieve symptoms of the disorder. Operations of this type are no longer performed.

Psychosurgery is still used as a way of treating problems that have failed to respond to conventional forms of therapy, but its use is exceedingly rare. One modern form of psychosurgery, called a *cingulotomy,* is sometimes used to treat obsessive-compulsive disorder and severe forms of depression (Jenike et al., 1991). It's a surgery that destroys a small portion of tissue in the limbic system of the brain. As with ECT, however, physicians really have no idea why this procedure works, nor can they explain why it works in some patients but not in others. It's another treatment of last resort that has proven effective for some but has not gained wide acceptance among the general psychological community.

Treating the Mind: Insight Therapies

The minds of individuals afflicted with psychological disorders are often filled with faulty beliefs about the world and about themselves. Many clinical psychologists and psychiatrists are convinced that the key to effective therapy lies in confronting these maladaptive thoughts and beliefs directly through what are called insight therapies. **Insight therapies** are designed to give clients self-knowledge, or *insight,* into the contents of their thought processes, usually through extensive one-on-one verbal interactions with the therapist. The hope is that with insight the individual will adopt a more realistic, adaptive view of the world, and behavior will change accordingly.

There are many forms of insight therapy available for use by mental health professionals. We'll consider three in this section: *psychoanalysis, cognitive therapies,* and *humanistic approaches.* Most of the other insight therapies are related in one form or another to these three main approaches. The common thread that ties them all together is the belief that cognitive or mental insight can produce significant changes in one's psychological condition. The therapies differ in terms of what kinds of beliefs or memories are considered of vital importance and in how the client's "insight" can best be obtained.

Psychoanalysis: Resolving Unconscious Conflicts

Probably the most widely known insight therapy is **psychoanalysis,** which traces back to the work of Sigmund Freud. As you may recall, we discussed Freud's theory rather extensively in Chapter 12. Freud placed enormous emphasis on the concept of the *unconscious mind.* He believed that all people have a kind of hidden reservoir in their minds that is filled with memories, primitive urges, and conflicts that are well beyond conscious awareness. One cannot directly think about the urges and memories stored in this unconscious mind, but they affect behavior nonetheless. Through the help of a therapist trained in psychoanalysis, Freud believed, these hidden impulses and memories can be brought to the surface of awareness, freeing the patient from his or her disordered thoughts and behavior.

Freud based his theory primarily on case studies of individuals he encountered in his private practice. He routinely treated patients with troubling psychological problems, and he discovered that he could sometimes help these people by inducing them to recall and relive traumatic experiences they had apparently forgotten, or "repressed." The emotionally significant experiences of childhood were of particular interest to Freud, because he believed it is during childhood that individuals progress through a number of psychologically "fragile" stages of psychosexual development (see Chapter 12). Traumatic experiences are, by definition, anxiety-provoking and therefore difficult for the young mind to deal with, so they are buried in the unconscious. Although no longer consciously available, these experiences continue to dominate and color behavior in ways that are completely beyond the person's awareness.

The Tools of Excavation. The goal of psychoanalysis is to help the patient uncover, and thereby relive, these unconscious conflicts. Obviously, because the patient is unaware of the conflicts, the therapist needs certain tools to gain access to the contents of the unconscious mind. Freud liked to compare psychoanalysis to "the technique of excavating a buried city," but instead of picks and shovels, his tools of excavation were the uncensored expressions and feelings of his patients. Freud relied heavily on a technique called **free association,** in which patients were asked to relax on a couch and freely express whatever thoughts and feelings happened to come into their minds. To the untrained eye, the result was a series of meaningless and unrelated streams of thought, but to Freud, these free associations represented symbolic clues to the contents of the unconscious.

Freud's other important therapeutic tool was patient dreams. Through **dream analysis,** he felt the therapist was handed a "royal road to the unconscious." As we discussed in Chapter 6, Freud was convinced that dreams are partly a psychological mechanism for wish fulfillment, a way to satisfy hidden desires that are too anxiety-provoking to be allowed to come to consciousness directly. The storyline of dreams, he believed, is largely symbolic—there is a hidden meaning to dreams, a *latent content,* that reveals the unconscious. Freud therefore encouraged his patients to describe their dreams, so he could acquire further clues in his search for hidden psychological truth.

Resistance and Transference. In classical psychoanalysis, the therapist seeks to understand the contents of the unconscious, but it is really the patient who needs the insight. The therapist cannot simply relay the hidden meanings that are uncovered—explanation is not enough. Instead, the patient needs to face the emotional conflicts directly and relive them, and the therapist can only act as a kind of "learned" guide. But the journey toward "insight" is not an easy one, and the therapist usually needs to maneuver around a number of roadblocks. For example, patients typically go through periods in which they are quite uncooperative. They show **resistance,** which Freud felt was an unconsciously motivated attempt to subvert or hinder the therapy (see Figure 15.4).

Why would people try to block their own therapy? Because the hidden conflicts that the therapist is working hard to uncover are anxiety-provoking, and the patient will use defense mechanisms to reduce the anxiety. As Freud (1912/1964) put it, "Resistance accompanies the treatment at every step; every single association, every act of the patient's . . . represents a compromise between the forces aiming at cure and those opposing it" (p. 140). The resistance can express itself in a variety of ways; the patient might become inattentive, claim to forget dreams, skip therapy sessions, or argue with the directions suggested by the therapist.

Overcoming patient resistance is a major challenge for the therapist. Freud believed that a turning point of sorts comes when the patient begins to show a type of resistance called transference. **Transference** occurs when the patient starts to express thoughts or feelings toward the therapist that are actually representative of the way the patient feels about other significant people in his or her life. The patient "transfers" feelings of love, hate, or dependence onto a substitute figure, the therapist. Depending on the repressed feelings being tapped, the patient might turn the therapist into an object of passionate love or into a hated and despised individual (see Figure 15.4).

Transference is a significant event in analysis because it means that the patient's hidden memories and conflicts are bubbling up close to the surface of

What do you think Freud would have thought about the value of biomedical therapy? Would he have supported or rejected the idea of treating psychological disorders through medications, shock treatments, or psychosurgery?

FIGURE 15.4
Resistance and Transference.
(top) According to Freud, during therapy people typically go through periods in which they are uncooperative—skipping a session, arriving late, or arguing with the therapist. Freud believed that such actions, which he called *resistance,* were unconsciously motivated attempts to subvert the therapeutic process. (bottom) Through *transference,* Freud believed that people "transfer" unconscious feelings, such as love or hate, toward significant others in their lives, onto the therapist.

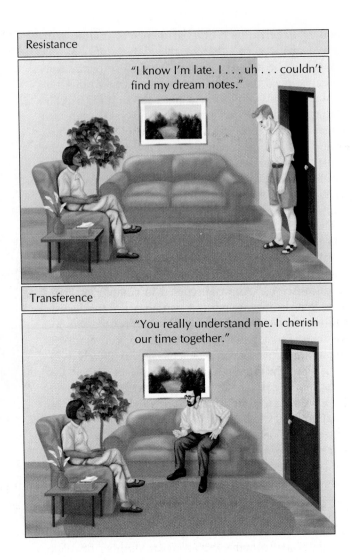

consciousness. The patient is fully aware of the strong feelings he or she is experiencing—although the "object" of those feelings is inappropriate—and this gives the therapist an opportunity to help the patient work through what those feelings might mean. The patient is no longer in denial of powerful emotional urges—they're right there on the surface, ready to be dealt with. At the same time, it's important for the therapist to recognize that the patient's feelings at this point are symbolic. It's not uncommon for the patient to express feelings of strong sexual desire for the therapist, for example, and it would be inappropriate and unethical for the therapist to take them as literal truth.

Current Directions. Classical psychoanalysis, as practiced by Freud and his contemporaries, is a tedious and time-consuming process. It can take years for the analyst to excavate the secrets of the unconscious, and the patient needs to be "prepared" to accept the insights when they are delivered. Remember, the patient is setting up roadblocks throughout the process. So this kind of therapy is certainly far from a quick fix. It's not only time-consuming but also expensive.

For these reasons, modern practitioners of psychoanalysis often streamline the therapeutic process. So-called "brief" forms of psychoanalysis encourage the therapist to take a more active role in the analytic process (Horvath & Luborsky, 1993).

Rather than waiting for patients to find "insight" themselves in response to subtle nudgings, the analyst is much more willing to offer interpretations in the early stages of therapy. Rather than waiting for transference to occur on its own, the analyst might actually encourage role playing in an attempt to get the patient to deal with deep-seated feelings. So, rather than requiring years of analysis, progress can occur in weeks or months.

Besides increasing the speed of treatment, modern versions of psychoanalysis are often tailored to meet the needs of the particular patient. No attempt is made to excavate and reconstruct the patient's entire personality; instead, the analyst focuses on selective defense mechanisms or conflicts that are more pertinent to the individual's particular symptoms (Luborsky, Barber, & Crits-Cristoph, 1990). There is also often a greater emphasis placed on improving the patient's interpersonal and social skills and less of an emphasis is placed on sexual and aggressive drives. Because these forms of treatment differ from classical psychoanalysis, they usually go by the more general term *psychodynamic therapy.*

Cognitive Therapies: Changing Maladaptive Beliefs

According to Freud's theory, a person's conscious thoughts, beliefs, and feelings are of primary importance only because they provide clues to the inner workings of the unconscious mind. **Cognitive therapies,** in contrast, place a much greater emphasis on the conscious beliefs themselves, rather than on what those beliefs may mean symbolically. Cognitive therapists assume that irrational beliefs and negative thoughts are primarily responsible for psychological disorders. If one can change the negative thoughts and beliefs, the psychological disorder will be changed as well.

Let's take depression as an example. People who are depressed usually think in a very unproductive way. They view themselves as essentially worthless and unlovable, and they see little chance that things will change for the better in the future. Thinking in such a negative way clouds the way normal events are interpreted; everyday experiences are passed through a kind of negative "filter." The result is that depressed people often jump to irrational conclusions. For instance, a depressed woman whose husband arrives home slightly late from work might be immediately convinced that her husband is having an affair. The depressed student who fails the test might see the F as confirmation of a dull and stupid mind.

Cognitive therapists believe that it is not direct experience, such as failure on a test, that actually produces depression. Think about it. It is not particularly difficult to fail a test—just stop going to class or refrain from studying. The F by itself doesn't logically mean much. You can fail a test for many reasons, and most of these reasons have nothing to do with your intrinsic worth as a human being. But in the mind of a depressed person, the event (failing the test) is accompanied by an irrational belief ("I'm incredibly stupid"), and it is this belief that leads to negative emotional consequences (feeling sad and depressed). Thus, it is the *interpretation* of the event, not the event itself, that leads to problems (Beck, 1991; Ellis, 1962, 1993) (see Figure 15.5 on page 539).

Rational-Emotive Therapy. The goal of cognitive therapy, then, is to get rid of these irrational beliefs. But how can irrational beliefs be changed? One technique is to challenge the beliefs directly, through active and aggressive confrontation. In **rational-emotive therapy,** developed by Albert Ellis, the therapist acts as a kind of cross-examiner, verbally assaulting the client's irrational thought processes. Here's an excerpt from an exchange between a therapist practicing rational-emotive therapy and a client showing signs of depressed thinking (from Walen, DiGuiseppe, & Dryden, 1992, pp. 204–205):

Albert Ellis, shown here, developed Rational-Emotive Therapy to help people eliminate their irrational thoughts and beliefs.

Therapist: You really believe that you're an utterly worthless person. By definition, that means that you're doing things poorly. Can you prove to me that that's correct?

Client: But I've failed at so many things.

Therapist: Just how many?

Client: I've lost my job, my wife is threatening to leave me, I don't get along with my kids—my whole life's a mess!

Therapist: Well, let me make two points. First of all, that's not every aspect of your life. Second, you seem to take total responsibility for all of those events, rather than only partial responsibility.

Client: But even if I'm not totally responsible, I'm still a failure.

Therapist: No. You've failed at those things. There are other things you haven't failed at.

Client: Like what?

Therapist: You still manage to get up every morning, you keep up appearances, you manage your finances well considering your economic plight—there's lots of things you do well.

Client: But they don't count!

Therapist: They don't count to you right now because you're overly concerned with negative issues, but they certainly *do* count. There are lots of people who don't do those things well. Are *they* failures?

Client: No, but . . .

Therapist: You know, Jack, you're one of the most conceited people I've ever met!

Client: What do you mean? I've just been telling you how lousy I am!

Therapist: The fact that you hold two different standards tells me how conceited you are. You hold much higher standards for yourself than for anyone else, which implies that you think you're much better than others. It's okay for those lowly slobs to have problems, but not a terrific person like you. Isn't that contradictory to your notion that you're worthless?

Client: Hmmmmm.

Therapist: How about instead of rating yourself as worthless, you just accept the failings that you do have and try your best to improve them?

Client: That sounds sensible.

Therapist: Let's take one of those problem areas now and see how we can improve things . . .

Notice that the core component of rational-emotive therapy is the therapist's attack on the rationality of the client's beliefs. The therapist points out the irrationality of the client's thought processes, often in a confrontational manner, in the hope that his or her beliefs will ultimately be rejected and their emotional consequences lessened. The creator of rational-emotive therapy, Albert Ellis (1962), has identified what he believes to be some of the major types of irrational beliefs

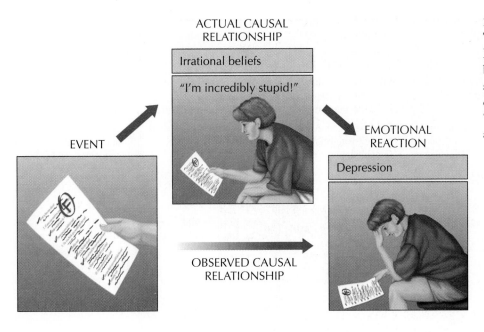

ACTUAL CAUSAL
RELATIONSHIP

Irrational beliefs

"I'm incredibly stupid!"

EVENT

EMOTIONAL
REACTION

Depression

OBSERVED CAUSAL
RELATIONSHIP

FIGURE 15.5
The Cognitive View of Depression. Cognitive therapists believe that it is not direct experience, such as failing a test, that leads to depression. Instead, the depression is "caused" by one's internal thoughts and beliefs about the event.

that affect people who seek treatment for psychological disorders. The therapist tries initially to pinpoint which of these beliefs characterize a particular client's thought processes, so they can be changed accordingly. Here are a few examples from Ellis's list:

1. I must be loved and approved of by every significant person in my life, and if I'm not, it's awful.
2. It's awful when things are not the way I'd like them to be.
3. I should be very anxious about events that are uncertain or potentially dangerous.
4. I am not worthwhile unless I am thoroughly competent, adequate, and achieving at all times, or at least most of the time in at least one major area.
5. I need someone stronger than myself on whom to depend or rely.

What makes these beliefs irrational is their inflexibility and absoluteness. I *must* be loved and approved; I *must* be thoroughly competent; I *need* someone stronger than myself. The client firmly believes that things must be a particular way or something awful or catastrophic will happen. Ellis has used the term *musterbation* to refer to this kind of irrational thinking. Anytime you find yourself thinking that something *must* be a particular way, you're guilty of musterbation.

Where do you think irrational ideas like these come from? Is it possible that people are taught to think in these absolute and inflexible ways by their parents, role models, or the general culture at large?

Beck's Cognitive Therapy. Although all forms of cognitive therapy focus on changing irrational thought processes, not all treatments are as direct and harsh as rational-emotive therapy. The rational-emotive therapist will essentially lecture—and in some instances even belittle—the client in an effort to attack faulty beliefs. Other cognitive therapies, such as the treatment procedures pioneered by Aaron Beck, take a more subtle tack. Rather than directly confronting clients with their irrational beliefs, Beck suggests it is more therapeutic for clients to identify negative forms of thinking themselves. The therapist acts as an adviser, or co-investigator, helping clients discover their own unique kinds of faulty beliefs.

In a sense, clients who undergo Beck's cognitive therapy are asked to become psychological "detectives." Part of the therapy involves extensive record keeping or "homework." Between therapeutic sessions, Beck asks his clients to record their automatic (or knee-jerk) thoughts and emotions in a notebook as they experience

	Situation	Emotion(s)	Automatic thought(s)	Rational response	Outcome
	Describe: 1. Actual event leading to unpleasant emotion, or 2. Stream of thoughts, daydream or recollection, leading to unpleasant emotion.	1. Specify sad/anxious/angry, etc. 2. Rate degree of emotion, 1–100.	1. Write automatic thought(s) that preceded emotion(s). 2. Rate belief in automatic thought(s), 0–100%.	1. Write rational response to automatic thought(s). 2. Rate belief in rational response, 0–100%.	1. Rerate belief in automatic thought(s), 0–100%. 2. Specify and rate subsequent emotions, 0–100.
Date					
7/15	Audre didn't return my phone call.	Anxious – 75 Sad – 55 Angry – 40	People don't like talking to me – 75% I'm incompetent 65%	She's out walking the dog so she hasn't had the time to call back. 70%	1. 35% 15% 2. Relieved – 35

Explanation: When you experience an unpleasant emotion, note the situation that seemed to stimulate the emotion. (If the emotion occured while you were thinking, daydreaming, etc., please note this.) Then note the automatic thought associated with the emotion. Record the degree to which you believe this thought: 0% = not at all, 100% = completely. In rating degree of emotion: 1 = a trace, 100 = the most intense possible.

FIGURE 15.6

"Homework" from a Cognitive Therapist. During cognitive therapy, people are often asked to record their automatic (knee-jerk) thoughts and emotions in a notebook. Notice that the daily log requires the person to construct a rational response to the situation and then rerate his or her emotional reaction. (Adapted from Beck & Young, 1985)

various situations during the day. Clients are then asked to write rational responses to those thoughts and emotions, as if they were scientists evaluating data. Is the thought justified by the actual event? What's the evidence for and against the conclusions that I reached? The therapist hopes clients will eventually discover the contradictions and irrationality in their thinking and realign their beliefs accordingly (see Figure 15.6).

Humanistic Therapies: Treating the Human Spirit

In cognitive therapy, the goal is for clients to gain understanding or "insight" into their faulty and irrational ways of thinking. In classical psychoanalysis, the focus of the insight is on the patient's hidden conflicts and desires. In the final type of insight-based treatment that we'll consider—**humanistic therapy**—the purpose of therapy is to help the client gain insight into his or her own fundamental *self-worth* and *value* as a human. Therapy is a process of discovering one's own unique potential, one's ingrained capacity to grow and better oneself as a human being.

Humanistic therapists believe that all people are capable of controlling their own behavior—individuals can "fix" their own problems—because everyone ultimately has free will. The problem is that people sometimes lose sight of their potential because they are concerned about what others think of them and their actions. People let others control how they think and feel. It is the therapist's job to help clients rediscover their natural self-worth—to help them get back "in touch" with their own true feelings, desires, and needs—by acting as a confidant and friend.

Client-Centered Therapy. Humanistic therapies resemble cognitive therapies in their emphasis on conscious thought processes. But the intention of humanistic therapy is not to criticize or correct irrational thinking; quite the contrary, it's to be totally supportive in all respects. The therapist's proper role is to be non-judgmental, which means the client should be accepted unconditionally. According to humanistic therapists such as Carl Rogers, the most effective form of therapy is **client-centered**—it is the client, not the therapist, who ultimately holds the key to psychological health and happiness.

We discussed the theoretical ideas of humanistic psychologists, especially Carl Rogers, in some detail in Chapter 12. Rogers was convinced that most psychological problems originate from *incongruence,* which he defined as the discrepancy between people's self-concept and the reality of their everyday experiences. People often hold an inaccurate view of themselves and their abilities, Rogers argued, because of an ingrained need for *positive regard*—they seek the approval, love, and companionship of significant others (such as their parents). But these significant others tend to attach *conditions of worth* to their approval: They demand that one think and act in ways that may not be consistent with one's true inner feelings. The road to improvement lies in providing a warm and supportive environment—without conditions of worth—that will encourage clients to accept themselves as they truly are.

In client-centered therapy, there are three essential core qualities that the therapist seeks to provide to the client: *genuineness, unconditional positive regard,* and *empathy.* As the client's confidant, the therapist must be completely genuine—he or she must act without phoniness, and express true feelings in an open and honest way. The second quality, unconditional positive regard, means that the therapist cannot place conditions of worth on the client. The therapist must be totally accepting and respectful of the client at all times, even if the client thinks and acts in a way that seems irrational or inappropriate. Remember, humanists believe that all people are essentially good—they simply need to be placed in an environment that will nurture their innate tendencies toward positive growth.

The third quality, empathy, is achieved when the therapist is able to truly understand and accept what the client is feeling—to see things from the client's perspective. Through empathy, the therapist acquires the capacity to reflect those feelings back in a way that helps the client gain insight into himself or herself. Consider the following interaction between Carl Rogers and one of his clients, a woman coming to grips with deep feelings of betrayal and hurt that she's tried to cover up (from Rogers, 1961, p. 94):

Client: I never did really know. But it's—you know, it's almost a physical thing. It's—it's sort of as though I were looking within myself at all kinds of—nerve endings and bits of things that have been sort of mashed.

Rogers: As though some of the most delicate aspects of you physically almost have been crushed or hurt.

Client: Yes. And you know, I do get the feeling, "Oh, you poor thing." (Pause)

Rogers: Just can't help but feel very deeply sorry for the person that is you.

Client: I don't think I feel sorry for the whole person; it's a certain aspect of the thing.

Rogers: Sorry to see the hurt.

Client: Yeah.

Notice that Rogers reflects back the feelings of the client in a completely non-judgmental fashion. He is seeking to understand and empathize with her feelings, thereby validating their existence and helping her to work through them. Notice as well that it is the client, not the therapist, who is doing the analyzing. Client-centered therapy is founded on the idea that it is the clients who understand what truly hurts them psychologically, and it is the clients who have the best sense of how to proceed with therapy. All the therapist can do is provide the right kind of supportive environment and help clients recognize their own self-worth and trust their own instincts.

Think about the interactions you've had with a really close friend. Do you see any similarities between these interactions and the client-centered therapy approach of Carl Rogers?

Other Humanistic Approaches. Client-centered therapy is the most popular form of humanistic therapy, but it is not the only one. *Gestalt therapy,* developed by Fritz Perls (1969; Perls, Hefferline, & Goodman, 1951), also places the burden of treatment in the hands of a "naturally good" client, but the approach is far less gentle and nondirective than client-centered therapy. In Gestalt therapy, clients are actively encouraged—even forced—to express their feelings openly. The emphasis is on the "here and now," and the therapist uses a variety of techniques to get the client to open up. For example, in the "empty chair" technique, clients are asked to project their feelings onto an empty chair in the room and then, literally, "talk" to the feelings. The idea is that only through fully understanding and overtly expressing oneself as a "whole" person (the word *gestalt* roughly translates from the German as *whole*), can a person hope to take responsibility for those feelings and change them for the better.

There is another group of humanistic treatments known collectively as *existential therapies* (Yalom, 1980). Existential therapists believe that psychological problems originate from the anxieties created by personal choices, such as whether to stay in school, get married, or quit a job. These fundamental choices—choices that relate to one's daily "existence" as a human being—are often difficult to face, and individuals may choose not to deal with them directly. Existential therapists encourage their clients to accept responsibility for these decisions, but in a supportive environment that encourages positive growth.

Treating the Environment: Behavioral Therapies

Traditional insight therapists address psychological problems by delving into the minds of their clients in search of hidden conflicts, faulty beliefs, or damaged self-worth. But there are alternative approaches to therapy that essentially leave the mind alone. **Behavioral therapies** treat *behavior* rather than thoughts or memories. Behavioral therapies are designed to change unwanted or maladaptive behavior through the application of basic learning principles.

As we discussed in Chapter 14, many psychologists are convinced that at least some psychological problems can be *learned,* or acquired as a result of experience. Afraid of snakes? It's possible you had a frightening experience at some point in your life—you may have been bitten by a snake—and this experience caused you to associate snakes with a negative emotional experience. It's not that the snake is symbolic of some hidden sexual conflict—you just learned that when snakes are around you can be bitten; snakes, as a result, have become "signals" for something bad.

If you believe that a psychological problem has essentially been learned, it doesn't make a lot of sense to spend months or years searching for a hidden "reason" for the problem. It's better to learn something new, by rewarding more productive actions, or to try to counteract the negative associations you've formed. We'll consider several behavioral approaches, beginning with an effective technique for treating phobias that is based on the principles of *classical conditioning.*

It's also the case that avoidance of the feared object, such as snakes, is reinforcing, too. Isn't it true that every time you stay away from a snake you avoid being bitten?

Conditioning Techniques

In Chapter 7, we discussed how dogs and people learn about the signaling properties of events. In Pavlov's classic experiments, dogs learned that one event, called the *conditioned stimulus,* signaled the occurrence of a second event, called the *unconditioned stimulus.* After pairing the conditioned stimulus and the unconditioned stimulus together in time, Pavlov found that his dogs responded to the conditioned "signal" in a way that anticipated the arrival of the unconditioned stimulus. For example, if a bell (the conditioned stimulus) was repeatedly presented just prior to food (the unconditioned stimulus), the dogs would begin to drool (the conditioned response) to the bell in anticipation of the food. Pavlov also showed that this conditioned response, the drooling, was sensitive to how well the conditioned stimulus predicted the occurrence of the unconditioned stimulus: If the bell was rung repeatedly after conditioning but the food was no longer presented, the dog eventually stopped drooling to the bell (a procedure Pavlov called *extinction*).

Now let's consider the case of a specific phobia, such as fear of snakes. Specific phobias are highly focused fears of objects or situations. When the feared object or situation is present, it produces an intense anxiety reaction. In the 1920s, psychologist Mary Cover Jones proposed that intense fear reactions like these can be treated as if they are classically conditioned responses. A snake produces fear because some kind of earlier experience has taught you to associate snakes with something fearful. Perhaps while standing near one as a child, your brother or sister screamed in terror, thereby scaring you. Jones's analysis suggested a treatment: It might be possible to eliminate phobias by teaching a new association between the feared object and something pleasurable. As she reported in 1924, she was able to use this logic to treat a little boy's fear of rabbits. She fed the boy some tasty food in the presence of the rabbit, which extinguished the association between the rabbit and an earlier negative experience and replaced it with a more pleasurable association (Jones, 1924).

This child's fear of the water might have been acquired as a result of an earlier frightening experience.

Systematic Desensitization. The treatment pioneered by Mary Cover Jones was later refined by psychiatrist Joseph Wolpe into a technique known as **systematic desensitization** (Wolpe, 1958, 1982). As with Jones's approach, systematic desensitization uses *counterconditioning* as a way of reducing the fear and anxiety that has become associated with a particular object or event. The therapist attempts to replace the negative association with something relaxing and pleasurable. It's a gradual process that involves three major steps:

1. The therapist helps the client construct an *anxiety hierarchy,* which is an ordered list of situations that lead to fearful reactions. The client is asked to imagine a series of anxiety-provoking situations, beginning with the least fear-arousing situation and ending with the feared situation itself.

2. The therapist spends time teaching the client ways to induce deep muscle relaxation. A state of deep relaxation is inconsistent with the experience of anxiety—you can't be afraid and relaxed at the same time.

3. With the help of the therapist, the client then attempts to work through the anxiety hierarchy, forming an image of each of the scenes, while maintaining the state of relaxation. The idea is to pair the images of fearful situations with the pleasurable state of relaxation so as to extinguish the old negative association and replace it with something relaxing.

Let's imagine you have a deep, irrational fear of flying in an airplane. Treatment starts by having you concoct a list of flying-related situations that are increasingly frightful. Next, you would receive lessons in how to relax yourself fully. Finally, you would begin working through your hierarchy. Perhaps you might start by simply imagining a picture of an airplane. If you can remain relaxed under these conditions, the therapist will direct you to move up the hierarchy to the next most stressful situation—perhaps imagining the airplane actually taking off. Gradually, over time, you will learn to relax in increasingly more stressful situations, even to the point where you can imagine yourself strapped in the seat as the plane rolls down the runway. The key to the technique is to maintain the relaxation. If

Psychologist Mary Cover Jones, shown here, proposed that intense fear reactions, such as those seen in phobias, could be treated as if they were classically conditioned responses.

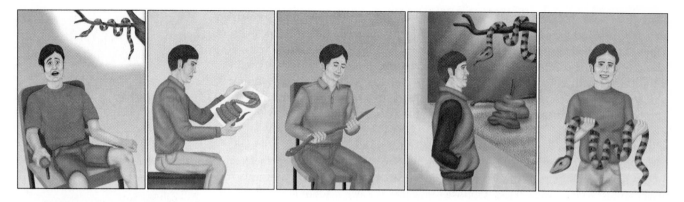

FIGURE 15.7

Systematic Desensitization. After learning relaxation techniques, the client works slowly through his or her anxiety hierarchy. At first he simply imagines the feared object while relaxed. Eventually he reaches a point in which the relaxation response can be maintained while actually experiencing the fearful situation.

you can stay relaxed—which is incompatible with fear and anxiety—the fearful association with planes should extinguish and be replaced by an association that is neutral or positive. Eventually, when you move to a real situation, the learning will generalize and you will no longer be afraid to fly in a plane. This type of therapy is summarized in Figure 15.7 using another type of specific phobia—fear of snakes.

Aversion Therapy. Systematic desensitization attempts to eliminate unpleasant associations by replacing them with pleasant ones. In **aversion therapy,** the therapist tries to replace a pleasant reaction to a harmful stimulus with something unpleasant, such as making the client feel bad rather than good after smoking a cigarette or having a drink of alcohol. Once again, the idea is to use counterconditioning, but the intent is to make the target situation something to be avoided rather than approached.

In the case of alcohol dependency, it's possible to give people a drug (Antabuse) that causes them to be become nauseated and vomit if a drink is consumed. The drug interacts with the ingested alcohol, causing extreme discomfort. Under these conditions, the person who is drinking learns a new association that helps combat the alcohol dependency—drinking leads to an unpleasant feeling. A similar technique can be used for smoking. There are drugs containing chemicals

In aversion therapy, the intention is to replace positive associations with negative ones, such as making an individual feel bad rather than good after smoking a cigarette.

that leave an extremely bad taste in one's mouth after smoking. The old association connecting pleasure with smoking is replaced by a new association connecting smoking with a terrible taste.

Aversion therapy can be quite effective, as long as the client takes the aversive drug for a sufficient period of time. The problem is that people who undergo this therapy are often reluctant to continue the treatment unless they're kept under close supervision. If the client stops the treatment and returns to normal drinking or smoking, the newly learned negative association will extinguish and be replaced by the old, positive association. Ethical concerns have also been raised about this form of treatment. Although those who participate do so voluntarily, they are often people who are desperately seeking a solution to their problems. Because the treatment directly induces extremely unpleasant experiences, many therapists are convinced that it should be used only as a treatment of last resort.

Applying Rewards and Punishments

As we discussed in Chapter 7, it is possible to change behavior by teaching people about the direct consequences of their behavior. People can be shaped, through the application of rewards and punishments, away from unproductive behaviors and toward more productive actions. Although aversion therapy involves elements of "punishment"—the act of drinking is followed by an extremely unpleasant consequence—its goal is mainly to replace prior pleasant emotional associations with unpleasant ones. Behavioral therapies that use rewards and punishments are designed to modify specific unwanted *behaviors* by teaching people about the consequences of their actions.

> Do you recall (from Chapter 7) the procedure called "shaping," which involves the reinforcement of successive approximations to a desired behavior? In what ways is shaping similar to and different from the technique of systematic desensitization?

Token Economies. The delivery of contingent reward has proven to be particularly effective in institutional settings. When people are confined to mental hospitals or other kinds of institutions, it is usually because they cannot cope successfully without constant supervision. If people cannot take proper care of themselves—if they don't wash properly, eat proper foods, or protect themselves from harm—they need a structured environment around them. In institutional settings, therapists have found that setting up **token economies**—in which patients are rewarded for behaving appropriately—can be quite effective in teaching patients how to cope with the realities of everyday life (Ayllon & Azrin, 1968; Lindsley & Skinner, 1954; Paul & Lentz, 1977).

In a token economy, institutionalized patients are rewarded with small tokens (such as poker chips) whenever they engage in an appropriate activity. Certain rules are established and explained to the patient, which determine when tokens are handed out (or taken away). For example, if Bob, who is suffering from schizophrenia, takes his medication without complaint, he is given a plastic token. Sally might receive tokens for getting out of bed in the morning, washing her hair, and brushing her teeth. The tokens can later be exchanged for certain privileges, such as being able to watch a video or stay in a private room. Similarly, if a patient acts in an inappropriate manner, the therapist might choose to take tokens away, as a form of punishment. This technique is called a token *economy* because it represents a voluntary exchange of goods and services—the patient exchanges appropriate behavior for the privileges that tokens provide.

Token economies are highly successful in helping patients develop the skills they'll need to function well inside and outside of the institution. Not only do the everyday "maintenance" activities of the patients improve, but token rewards can be used as well to shape social behavior and even vocational skills (for a closer look, see the accompanying Inside the Problem). Token economies have also been used in classroom settings to reward children for showing appropriate individual and group behavior (Kazdin, 1982).

▶ INSIDE THE PROBLEM: *Social Skills Training in Schizophrenia*

Serious psychological disorders can have a devastating impact on a person's ability to function successfully in virtually all environments, especially social ones. In schizophrenia, for example, social or occupational dysfunction is one of the defining characteristics of the disorder. Patients with schizophrenia tend to isolate themselves from others, and, when they do interact socially, they typically act in odd or peculiar ways.

Consider the conversational speech of David, a 25-year-old with schizophrenia, during an interaction with his therapist (Barlow & Durand, 1995):

> **Therapist:** I was sorry to hear that your Uncle Bill died a few years ago. How are you feeling about him these days?
>
> **David:** Yes, he died. He was sick and now he's gone. He likes to fish with me, down at the river. He's going to take me hunting. I have guns. I can shoot you and you'd be dead in a minute.

In the words of his therapist, David's conversational speech "resembled a ball rolling down a rocky hill. Like an accelerating object, his speech gained momentum the longer he went on, and as if bouncing off obstacles, the topics almost always went in unpredictable

directions" (Barlow & Durand, 1995, p. 556).

In such cases, therapists face a practical problem: How can they improve the social skills of the person with the disorder? This is a particularly important concern in schizophrenia, which is often difficult to treat. Even with effective medications, many patients suffer "relapses" of symptoms (Liberman, Kopelowicz, & Young, 1994), and some symptoms of the disorder, including social withdrawal and "flat affect," are not affected by conventional psychoactive drugs. For these reasons, therapists sometimes turn to *social skills training,* which is a form of behavioral therapy that uses modeling and reinforcement to shape appropriate adjustment skills (McFall, 1976; Wong and others, 1993).

Social skills training usually consists of a series of steps. To teach conversational skills, for example, the therapist might begin with a discussion of appropriate verbal responses in a conversation, followed by a videotaped demonstration. The patient is then asked to "role play" an actual conversation, and the therapist provides either corrective feedback or positive reinforcement.

"Homework" might then be assigned, in which the patient is encouraged to practice his or her skills outside of the training session, preferably in new situations. If the training is conducted in an institutional setting, such as a mental hospital, the therapist is careful to monitor the patient's subsequent interactions so that appropriate reinforcement can be delivered.

Social skills training usually takes place over many sessions, and it's often combined with other forms of treatment (such as psychoactive drugs or some form of insight therapy). Reviews of the research literature indicate that the application of these simple learning principles—positive reinforcement and modeling—can lead to significant improvements in social functioning, and in the quality of life for individuals affected with psychological disorders (Benton & Schroeder, 1990). You should understand that one of the most important goals of any therapy is to improve global functioning; at times focusing on specific symptoms—even something as simple as knowing how to answer a casual question in an appropriate way—can make an enormous difference in the life of a troubled individual.

Punishment. Token economies tend to be based primarily on the application of reward as a way of changing unwanted behaviors. But as we've seen, punishment can also be an effective way to teach people about the consequences of their behavior. And, indeed, there are instances in which therapists feel that following a behavior with an aversive stimulus (sometimes even a shock) or removing something pleasant is justified. Consider someone who is extremely self-destructive—perhaps a disturbed child who continually bangs his or her head against the wall. Under these conditions, the safe delivery of an aversive event has been shown to reduce these self-destructive behaviors, thereby preventing serious injury (Lovaas, 1987; Lovaas and others, 1973).

But punishment is rarely used as the sole kind of behavioral intervention, for several reasons. First, punishment has side effects—for example, it can damage the working relationship between the therapist and the client. Second, punishment, by itself, only teaches someone what *not to do*; it doesn't teach someone the appropriate way to act. Third, punishing someone who is in the grips of a psychological disorder raises ethical concerns. We cannot be sure the person on the receiving end of the aversive event approves of the treatment, even though the therapist may be convinced it is in the client's best interest.

Evaluating and Choosing Psychotherapy

When people make the decision to enter therapy, they do so because they're in need of help. Ralph is unable to advance his career in sales because of his extreme fear of flying; Julie lives a life of quiet desperation, mostly alone in her room, because she suffers from a social phobia. We've now examined the major types of therapy that are available, but we've said little about their relative effectiveness. How well does psychotherapy actually work? Are all forms of therapy equally effective, or do some forms of therapy work better than others?

Assessing the effectiveness of any therapy requires carefully controlled research. As we discussed in Chapter 2, just because a manipulation changes someone's behavior does not mean that it was the manipulation that caused the change. Someone might enter therapy and leave improved some time later, but the change could have occurred for reasons unrelated to the actual treatment. Perhaps the person simply improved spontaneously over time. Most people who get the flu improve over time—even if they never see a doctor—and it could be that the same kind of thing happens with psychological disorders. A control group—in which no treatment is given—is needed to be sure that it was indeed the therapy that was responsible for the improvement. Fortunately, a number of such controlled research studies have been conducted.

Clinical Evaluation Research

Let's begin by considering a well-known example of a clinical evaluation study (Sloane et al., 1975). In this study, conducted at a Philadelphia psychiatric clinic in the mid-1970s, men and women who were seeking treatment primarily for anxiety disorders were assigned at random to one of three treatment conditions. One group of patients was assigned to therapists experienced in the practice of *psychodynamic* techniques (the analysis of unconscious conflicts and memories); a second group was assigned to experienced *behavioral* therapists (using systematic desensitization and other learning-based techniques); a third group—the *control* group—was placed on a "waiting list" and received no immediate treatment. After four months, an independent team of therapists, who were unaware of the treatment assignments, was called in to evaluate the progress of the patients in each of the three groups.

The results were somewhat surprising. The good news is that the therapies clearly worked. As shown in Figure 15.8, the people who were given either the psychodynamic or the behavioral therapy showed significantly more improvement after four months than the people who were left on the waiting list (although it's interesting to note that the waiting list people "improved" as well). But there were no significant differences between the two treatment conditions—the behavioral approach worked just as well as the psychodynamic approach. Even more surprising was the finding that eight months later, at a year-end follow-up assessment, the patients in the control group had essentially "caught up" with the treatment patients—they had improved enough to be comparable to the patients in the other two groups. Thus, the treatments worked, but it seems that their primary effect was simply to speed up natural improvement.

> Researchers who conduct clinical evaluation studies are often faced with a dilemma: Is it ethical to assign patients who are seeking help for their problems to a no-treatment control?

Meta-analysis. The Philadelphia study is important because it represents a kind of "model" of how evaluation research should be conducted—random assignment to groups, the use of a no-treatment control, and an independent assessment procedure (Wolpe, 1975). Since that study was first reported, hundreds of other studies have been conducted (although not all have included the same rigorous control procedures). Rather than picking and choosing from among these

FIGURE 15.8
Evaluating Forms of Treatment.
In the study by Sloane and colleagues (1975), men and women seeking treatment for anxiety disorders were randomly assigned to (1) behavior therapy, (2) psychodynamic therapy, or (3) a control "waiting list." After four months, the people receiving therapy showed significantly less severe symptoms than people in the control group, but there were no significant differences between types of therapy (behavior versus psychodynamic). (Data from Sloane et al., 1975)

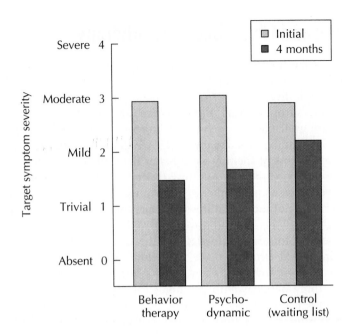

studies, mental health professionals often rely on a technique called **meta-analysis** to help them draw conclusions about this research. In a meta-analysis, many different studies are compared statistically on some common evaluation measure. The comparison standard is usually something called an "effect size," which is essentially a standardized measure of the difference between treatment and control conditions.

In one of the first extensive meta-analytic studies, Smith and colleagues analyzed the results of 475 research studies designed to evaluate one or more forms of psychotherapy (Smith & Glass, 1977; Smith, Glass, & Miller, 1980). Although the individual studies covered a wide range of psychological problems and therapeutic techniques, in each case it was possible to compare a treatment condition to some kind of control condition (usually an untreated group). Smith and colleagues reached two major conclusions from their meta-analysis of the data. *First,* there was a consistent and large treatment advantage (see Figure 15.9). People who experienced some kind of active psychotherapy were better off, on average, than roughly 80% of the people who were left untreated. *Second,* when the various kinds of psychotherapy were compared, few, if any, differences were found. It really didn't matter whether the patient was receiving an insight therapy or a behavioral therapy—all produced the same amount of improvement.

There have been hundreds of other attempts to meta-analyze evaluation studies. Some have sought to exercise more control over the research quality of the studies included (Lipsey & Wilson, 1993); others have attempted to extend the areas of examination to such things as client characteristics, experience of the therapist, or length of the treatment (Lambert & Bergin, 1994). In general, the finding have been, once again, that therapy works and that the effects of therapy are long-lasting. For example, one recent review of meta-analysis studies, which examined some 302 published meta-analyses, found that only 6 produced negative effect sizes (which means that patients undergoing therapy actually got worse than untreated controls), and the vast majority were overwhelmingly positive (Lipsey & Wilson, 1993).

Controversies. There is widespread agreement among professionals that psychotherapy works, but clinical evaluation studies remain the subject of debate. For example, what should constitute the proper evaluation "control"? Let's return to

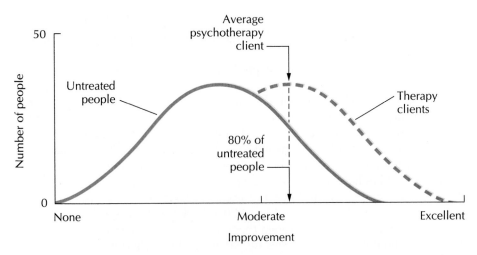

FIGURE 15.9
The Effectiveness of Psychotherapy. In the meta-analysis by Smith and colleagues (1980), which assessed hundreds of clinical evaluation studies, people who experienced some form of active psychotherapy were better off, on average, than roughly 80% of the people who were left untreated. (Data from Smith, Glass, & Miller, 1980)

the Philadelphia experiment in which two treatment groups (psychodynamic and behavioral) were compared with a group containing people who were left on a waiting list. Remember, the control patients actually got considerably better over time, to a point in which, after a year, they had improved to the same levels as the treatment groups. Psychologists call this kind of improvement in the absence of treatment **spontaneous remission,** and it's been estimated that psychological disorders may improve on their own as much as 30% or more of the time (Eysenck, 1952; Lambert & Bergin, 1994).

But did the people who were left on the waiting list in the Philadelphia experiment really receive no treatment? This turns out to be a difficult question to answer—it depends on how you define "treatment." Although these people received no formal psychotherapy, they were given initial psychological tests and were called frequently and given support. Their simple involvement in the study, along with the expectation that they would be receiving some help, may itself have acted as a kind of therapy. Similar problems are commonly found with many "placebo" controls, in which clients are given attention and support but not formal therapy. Many critics have argued that these no-treatment conditions actually involve factors—such as social support—that are common to most forms of therapy (Horvath, 1988). We'll return to this issue in the next section.

The reported finding that all types of psychotherapy are equally effective has also proven to be controversial. It's probably reasonable to assume that certain treatments work best for certain kinds of problems. For example, cognitive therapies may be particularly effective for treating depression (Robinson, Berman, & Neimeyer, 1990), and behavioral therapies may be ideal for combating anxiety disorders such as specific phobias (Bowers & Clum, 1988). But even if the treatment is matched to the problem, there are also "client variables" that can influence the effectiveness of the therapy. Not all people have the desire or capacity to respond to rational, verbal arguments of the type used by some cognitive therapists, or to the probing questions of the psychoanalyst. It is very difficult, as a result, to conduct an evaluation study that properly takes all of these factors into account.

Common Factors Across Psychotherapies

Clinical researchers have also considered the possibility that there may be common, "nonspecific" factors shared by all therapies, regardless of surface differences. Although the various therapies that we've considered seem to be very different, and they're clearly driven by very different assumptions about human psychology, they do share features in common (Grencavage & Norcross, 1990; Rosenzweig,

1936). Michael Lambert and Allen Bergin (1994) have suggested that these common factors can be grouped into three main categories: *support factors, learning factors,* and *action factors.*

First, virtually all therapies that produce positive outcomes provide tangible *support* for the client. People who enter therapy find themselves face to face with someone who is willing to accept and understand their problems. Both the therapist and the client have a common goal, which is to help the client get better. Regardless of their particular theoretical orientation—psychodynamic, cognitive, behavioral, or humanistic—effective therapists are clearly interested in listening to and reassuring their clients and in developing a positive, trusting relationship. A number of studies have found a strong correlation between the amount of "empathy" that the therapist establishes with the client and the effectiveness of the treatment (Lafferty, Beutler, & Crago, 1991; Miller, Taylor, & West, 1980).

Second, when people go through therapy, they *learn* things about themselves. They learn about their thought processes, or about their behavior, or about important factors in their past that might be contributing to current discomforts. Effective therapists often act as mirrors, reflecting back a client's beliefs and actions in ways that provide critical insight. Regardless of the method of treatment, effective therapists also give feedback about how various experiences relate to one another. They point out connections among experiences—how people might behave and think similarly across different situations. People are often helped because they're given a reason or a rationale for their problems.

Finally, all forms of therapy ultimately provide people with a set of specific suggestions for *action.* Troubled clients might be asked to face their fears, take risks, or directly test irrational beliefs. They might be given specific strategies for coping with anxiety, or training in how to relax. Irrespective of the particular suggestions, just providing clients with a tangible course of action may be sufficient to give them *hope* and allow them to feel in control of their problem.

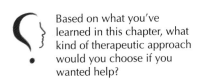

Based on what you've learned in this chapter, what kind of therapeutic approach would you choose if you wanted help?

Choosing a Therapist

At some point in your life, you might find yourself in need of a psychotherapist. Perhaps you'll experience a simple "problem in living," or maybe something more serious. What should you do? Given our discussion about the relative effectiveness of the various treatment options, it might seem natural to conclude that it doesn't make much difference whom you choose. But remember, one of the best predictors of treatment success is the amount of "empathy" between the client and the therapist. As a result, it's critical for you to find someone whom you trust and with whom you feel comfortable interacting. The level of trust that you feel with the therapist is very important; don't be afraid to shop around a bit to find the right person.

Currently, most psychotherapists describe themselves as being *eclectic* in their orientation. This means they are willing to pick and choose from among treatment options to find the techniques that work best for the individual client. It used to be the case that therapists would align themselves with a particular approach or "school"—such as psychoanalysis or behavior therapy—but in a recent survey of 800 therapists, 68% of those responding described their orientation as eclectic (Jensen, Bergin, & Greaves, 1990). You can expect most therapists to be flexible in their approach, and if one form of treatment is not yielding results—or if you feel uncomfortable with the approach—you can expect the therapist to be open to trying something different. Effective therapy requires open communication, and the therapist is dependent on your feedback as a client throughout the treatment process.

Cultural barriers sometimes make it difficult for members of ethnic minorities to benefit from mental health resources. It's essential for a therapist to be sensitive to a client's cultural background and general "world view."

Cultural Factors. Mental health professionals also now recognize that cultural factors are important in both the diagnosis and the treatment of psychological disorders (Sue & Zane, 1987; Tseng & McDermott, 1975). For many years, cultural barriers have made it difficult for members of ethnic minorities to use and benefit from mental health resources. Language differences between the client and the therapist clearly undermine effective communication, as do differences between the therapist's and the client's "worldview." To take a case in point, many Asians feel uncomfortable with open self-disclosure and the expression of emotions. As a result, it's unlikely that many Asians will benefit from Western therapists who encourage "letting it all hang out" (Sue, Zane, & Young, 1994).

Does this mean you should always seek a therapist with a cultural background identical to your own? Not necessarily. For one thing, there is still a shortage of therapists from ethnic minorities in the United States (Mays & Albee, 1992). This means that finding a cultural "match" may be difficult. Moreover, with the increased exposure to cultural influences, many therapists are now making concerted efforts to become "culturally sensitive." In fact, special training programs are now available to help therapists break down some of the barriers that exist for clients from diverse cultural backgrounds. By gaining knowledge about a variety of customs and lifestyles, as well as by working directly with culturally diverse clients, therapists hope to remove barriers to effective empathy.

SOLVING THE PROBLEMS: A SUMMARY

In this chapter, we've discussed the various tools that therapists have at their disposal to treat psychological disorders. In each case, the overarching goal of the therapist is to find a way to improve his or her client's ability to function successfully in the world. As we've seen, most forms of therapy are designed to address one or more of the three basic factors thought to contribute to psychological disorders: biological factors, cognitive factors, and environmental factors.

TREATING THE BODY Therapies that use physiological interventions to treat the symptoms of psychological problems are called *biomedical therapies*. The idea that psychological disorders might be treated as "illnesses," in the same way that physicians might treat the common cold, has a long history in human thought. The most popular form of biomedical therapy is drug therapy, in which certain medications are given to affect thought and mood by altering the actions of neurotransmitters in the brain. Antipsychotic drugs, for example, reduce the symptoms of schizophrenia by acting as antagonists to the neurotransmitter dopamine in the brain. The antidepressant drug Prozac acts on the neurotransmitter serotonin, and antianxiety drugs—tranquilizers—are believed to act on inhibitory neurotransmitters in the brain.

In the event that drug therapies fail, mental health professionals sometimes turn to other forms of biomedical intervention, particularly electroconvulsive therapy (ECT) and psychosurgery. Shock therapy is used to treat severe forms of depression, but usually only if more conventional forms of treatment have failed. No one is completely sure how or why the administration of electric shock affects mood, but there's wide agreement that ECT works for many patients. Even more controversial than ECT is the use of psychosurgery, in which some portion of the brain is destroyed or altered in an attempt to eliminate the symptoms of a mental disorder. The infamous prefrontal lobotomies of yesteryear are no longer conducted (partly because they produced unacceptable side effects), but some kinds of surgical intervention in the brain are still used.

TREATING THE MIND In insight therapy, the psychotherapist attempts to treat psychological problems by helping clients gain insight, or self-knowledge, into the contents of their thought processes. Usually, this insight is obtained through prolonged verbal, one-on-one, interactions between the therapist and the client. Perhaps the best-known form of insight therapy is Freudian *psychoanalysis*. The goal of psychoanalysis is to help the client uncover and relive conflicts that have been hidden in the unconscious mind. The psychoanalyst uses such techniques as free association and dream analysis to help probe the contents of the unconscious. As hidden conflicts begin to surface during the course of therapy, the client will typically show what Freud called resistance—an attempt to hinder the progress of therapy—and transference, in which the client "transfers" feelings about others onto the therapist.

Cognitive therapists believe that psychological problems arise primarily from irrational beliefs and thought processes. The therapist attempts to change the client's negative beliefs and thoughts by actively attacking them in verbal exchanges. The therapist points out the irrationality of negative thoughts, using evidence where possible, in the hope that the client will reject the beliefs, thereby lessening their emotional consequences. *Humanistic therapies* have a quite different goal. Here, the idea is to help clients gain insight into their own self-worth and value as humans. It is the client, not the therapist, who holds the key to self-improvement. Humanistic therapists view therapy as a process of discovering one's natural tendencies toward growth and free will. In client-centered therapy, the therapist tries to provide an approving and nonjudgmental environment, thereby allowing the client to better recognize and trust his or her own true instincts.

TREATING THE ENVIRONMENT *Behavioral therapies* are designed to treat overt behavior rather than inner thought processes. Behavioral therapists assume that many kinds of psychological problems have been learned and can be treated through the application of learning principles. With many counterconditioning techniques, for example, the therapist attempts to replace learned associations that are negative with new, pleasurable associations. Thus, in systematic desensitization, specific phobias are treated by having the subject (1) construct an anxiety hierarchy of fear-inducing situations, (2) learn relaxation techniques, and (3) work through the anxiety hierarchy, imagining each of the scenes, while maintaining a feeling of relaxation. Pairing the feared object with relaxation is intended to extinguish the old, negative association and replace it with something pleasurable. Other behavioral therapies make use of rewards and punishments to change behavior. In token economies, patients are rewarded with small tokens whenever they engage in normal or appropriate behaviors. The tokens can then be exchanged later for more tangible rewards or privileges.

▶ **EVALUATING AND CHOOSING PSYCHOTHERAPY** Evaluating any form of psychotherapy requires controlled research in which treatment groups are compared with appropriate control conditions. Hundreds of such studies have been conducted, and meta-analyses of their results typically reach two main conclusions. First, people who receive psychotherapy do significantly better than those left untreated. Second, there are few, if any, advantages for one type of psychotherapy over another.

One reason that most forms of treatment are equally effective may be that there are common factors that cut across all psychotherapies. These common factors can be grouped into three main categories: support, learning, and action. All therapists provide some kind of support for their client, and therapist empathy has been shown to be important to outcome success. All forms of therapy also help clients learn about themselves and their behavior, and clients are provided specific prescriptions for action or behavior change. In choosing a therapist, it's critical that you find someone whom you trust and with whom you feel comfortable interacting. Cultural factors are also important, because for therapy to work, the therapist needs to be sensitive to the client's cultural worldview.

Terms to Remember

psychotherapy Treatment designed to help people deal with mental, emotional, or behavioral problems.

TREATING THE BODY: BIOMEDICAL THERAPIES

biomedical therapies Biologically based treatments for reducing or eliminating the symptoms of psychological disorders; they include drug therapies, "shock" treatments, and, in some cases, psychosurgery.

antipsychotic drugs Medications that reduce the positive symptoms of schizophrenia; the majority act on the neurotransmitter dopamine.

antidepressant drugs Medications that modulate the availability or effectiveness of the neurotransmitters implicated in mood disorders; Prozac, for example, increases the action of the neurotransmitter serotonin.

antianxiety drugs Medications that reduce tension and

anxiety. Many work on the inhibitory neurotransmitter GABA.

electroconvulsive therapy (ECT) A treatment used primarily for depression in which a brief electric current is delivered to the brain.

psychosurgery Surgery that destroy or alters tissues in the brain in an effort to affect behavior.

TREATING THE MIND: INSIGHT THERAPIES

insight therapies Treatments designed to give clients self-knowledge, or insight, into the contents of their thought processes, usually through one-on-one interactions with a therapist.

psychoanalysis Freud's method of treatment that attempts to bring hidden impulses and memories, which are locked in the unconscious, to the surface of awareness, thereby freeing the patient from his or her disordered thoughts and behaviors.

free association A technique used in psychoanalysis to explore the contents of the unconscious; patients are asked to relax and freely express whatever thoughts and feelings happen to come into their minds.

dream analysis A technique used in psychoanalysis; Freud believed that dreams are symbolic and contain important information about the unconscious.

resistance In psychoanalysis, a patient's unconsciously motivated attempts to subvert or hinder the process of therapy.

transference In psychoanalysis, the patient's expression of thoughts or feelings toward the therapist that are actually representative of the way the patient feels about other significant people in his or her life.

cognitive therapies Treatments designed to remove irrational beliefs and negative thoughts that are presumed to be responsible for psychological disorders.

rational-emotive therapy A form of cognitive therapy, developed by Albert Ellis, in which the therapist acts as a kind of cross-examiner, verbally assaulting the client's irrational thought processes.

humanistic therapy Treatments designed to help clients gain insight into their fundamental self-worth and value as human beings; therapy is a process of discovering one's own unique potential.

client-centered therapy A form of humanistic therapy, developed by Carl Rogers, proposing that it is the client, not the therapist, who holds the key to psychological health and happiness; the therapist's role is to provide genuineness, unconditional positive regard, and empathy.

TREATING THE ENVIRONMENT: BEHAVIORAL THERAPIES

behavioral therapies Treatments designed to change behavior through the use of established learning techniques.

systematic desensitization A technique that uses counterconditioning and extinction to reduce the fear and anxiety that have become associated to a particular object or event. It's a multistep process that attempts to replace the negative learned association with something relaxing.

aversion therapy A treatment for replacing a positive reaction to a harmful stimulus, such as alcohol, with something negative, such as feeling nauseous.

token economies A type of behavioral therapy in which patients are rewarded with small tokens when they act in an appropriate way; the tokens can then be exchanged for certain privileges.

EVALUATING AND CHOOSING PSYCHOTHERAPY

meta-analysis A statistical technique used to compare findings across many different research studies; comparisons are based on some common evaluation measure, such as the difference between treatment and control conditions.

spontaneous remission Improvement in a psychological disorder without treatment—that is, simply as a function of the passage of time.

Eileen remembered nothing for a very long time. In the 20 years since the incident had occurred—the murder of 8-year-old Susan Kay Nason—Eileen had lived a normal life, married with two children, unencumbered by any persistent or lingering thoughts about the unsolved death of her childhood friend. But on a January afternoon, 20 years later, as she looked into the eyes of her own 5-year old daughter, a door began to open in her mind, and the memories returned. At first, it was simply the look of betrayal in Susan's eyes; later, it was the realization that her father, George Franklin, had committed the brutal crime and that she, Eileen, had been present during the whole incident. Aided by her therapist, Eileen was eventually able to recover rich and detailed images of her father sexually assaulting Susan and then crushing her skull with a rock. Based primarily on his daughter's testimony, George Franklin was eventually tried and convicted of murder.

Although dramatic cases like this one are relatively rare, the idea that people carry around forgotten memories of traumatic events is popular among some practicing psychotherapists. Often these memories are assumed to involve some form of child abuse, particularly single or repeated instances of sexual abuse. As you know from our earlier discussions, Sigmund Freud believed that traumatic events, especially in childhood, are actively *repressed*— buried in the unconscious—as a way of defending against anxiety. Although no longer accessible to conscious awareness, these memories continue to exert a hidden influence on everything from the development of personality, to thoughts and feelings, to overt behaviors. For some therapists, it is essential that these buried memories of abuse resurface—to be "relived"—in order to achieve "a sense of wholeness, to help the client recapture lost parts of herself" (Courtois, 1992).

But within the scientific community, the notion of repressed memories is considerably more controversial. The focus of the controversy is not on the reality of childhood abuse, nor on its potential impact on the psychological health of the abuse "survivor." All mental health professionals recognize that child abuse is an enormous problem and that its psychological effects can be long-lasting (Kutchinsky, 1992). Rather, the issue is cases like Eileen's, in which dormant memories of trauma are suddenly "recovered" during the course of therapy and are then used to explain the appearance of psychological problems. Given what is known about the reconstructive nature of memory and its fallibility, the critics argue, it's important to question the accuracy of the recollections. In the absence of corroborating evidence, how do we know that the client is really recovering accurate memories of childhood? Could it be that these early memories of abuse are simply fabrications induced by well-meaning therapists? Is there any scientific evidence to support Freud's concept of repression?

The Nature of the Evidence
Surprisingly, little scientific evidence exists to support the idea of repression. As we discussed in Chapter 8, there are many reasons why people forget, and the fact that someone fails to remember something traumatic from his or her past does not mean that an active process of repression is involved. Repression is not something that can easily be studied in the laboratory—it would be unethical to induce traumatic episodes—which may partly explain why evidence for the concept is sparse. Most of the pertinent data have come from case studies, collected by therapists, or from surveys conducted with people who are currently undergoing some form of therapy. Let's consider some examples of this kind of evidence, along with some alternative interpretations.

In one widely cited study, 475 adults who were undergoing psychotherapy were asked about their memories of childhood sexual abuse. Each of these participants had reported an incident of abuse during childhood, and each was asked the following specific question: "During the period of time when the first forced sexual encounter happened and your 18th birthday, was there ever a time when you could not remember the forced sexual experience?" (Briere & Conte, 1993). Fifty-nine percent of the people who answered the question responded "yes," suggesting that the memories had been pushed out of consciousness for at least some period of time. In another study supporting the same conclusion, Williams (1992) asked 100 women who had been medically treated for sexual abuse as children—the abuse was documented by hospital and other records—whether they remembered the incident 17 years later. Thirty-eight percent of those responding reported no memory for the abuse, again providing support for the concept of repression.

But as memory researcher Elizabeth Loftus and her colleagues have pointed out, it is possible to explain results like these without appealing to repression (Loftus, 1993; Loftus, Polonsky, & Fullilove, 1994). First, as we've noted, just because something is forgotten does not mean that it is being actively repressed. There are many reasons why people forget. Second, in the Briere and Conte (1993) study, it's possible that the participants interpreted the critical memory question in a way that simply made it look as if they had repressed the event. For example, because memories of abuse are extremely unpleasant, perhaps the participants simply tried hard not to think about the incident and therefore reported they were able to push it out of their minds. Third, it's rare for people to remember any event that occurred very early in childhood (before the age of 4 or 5), so some instances of what appear to be repression could actually be due to a more widely documented phenomenon—childhood amnesia (Usher & Neisser, 1993).

Finally, it's important to stress that many "repressed" memories are recovered only during the course of

therapy. It's possible, therefore, that therapists may sometimes indirectly influence what their clients remember. As noted before, some therapists are convinced that repressed memories of abuse are at the heart of psychological disorders. If you believe that dissociative identity disorder, for example, is the result of childhood abuse, then as a therapist it's reasonable for you to explore the early childhood history of your client, perhaps with the expectation of finding abuse. Unfortunately, decades of memory research have shown that what people "remember" is often influenced by expectations—people reconstruct what they think must have happened to them previously, and these reconstructions can often be inaccurate. No one is suggesting that therapists are purposely implanting false memories

into their clients, but it can happen as an unintentional by-product of the therapeutic process.

Do Repressed Memories Exist?
The failure to find solid scientific evidence for the concept of repression does not mean that traumatic events are never forgotten. As Freud noted, a process of repression might be adaptive in the sense that it can prevent or reduce anxiety. It may also be the case that "forgotten" events continue to exert indirect influences on behavior in ways that bypass awareness. But the data do suggest that memories, whether "recovered" in therapy or simply in the normal course of everyday activities, should not be taken at face value. It is adaptive for people to use prior knowledge, as well as current expecta-

tions, to help them remember—but perhaps at the cost that those individuals may sometimes remember things that didn't actually happen.

Of course, from the client's perspective, the accuracy of the memory is often of secondary importance. The pain that is associated with recovered memories is real, even if the memories themselves are not. Moreover, in attempting to nurture empathy and closeness with their client, many therapists feel it would be inappropriate for them to act as "detectives" and directly challenge the client's beliefs. However, the critics argue that verification does become an issue when others are involved. Is it reasonable to convict someone of a serious crime when the only available evidence comes from recovered memories?

The False Memory Syndrome Foundation was established in 1992 to help individuals who may have been falsely accused of abuse on the basis of "recovered" memories.

Currently, there are many abuse "survivors," armed with an arsenal of recovered memories, who have sought confrontation with their alleged abusers. In response to the recent rise in such accusations, the False Memory Syndrome Foundation was established in 1992. This foundation provides support and legal advice for parents and others who have been suddenly, and perhaps falsely, accused of abuse based on memories recovered during therapy. Once again, memories of abuse should not be dismissed out of hand—such memories may indeed be accurate. But given the problems associated with verifying memories of the distant past, considerable effort should be given to collecting additional objective evidence to confirm the abuse.

16

Push, push, push. It hits you from all sides—school, work, relationships, family. Although we may not be able to claim exclusive rights to the "age of stress," we certainly live in a time of increased expectation. Everybody expects something from us, and they seem to want it now. Your teachers expect the subject matter to be learned, the paper written; your boss expects overtime, in addition to your regular hours; your parents expect that weekly phone call, delivered in a pleasant and friendly tone. Is it any wonder that you can't seem to shake that cold, or that you feel the need to leave the antacid tablets by your bedside at night?

The idea that a close relationship exists between your psychological state and the physical reactions of your body should, by now, be firmly implanted in your mind. The mind and the body interact, and the interaction works in two directions. As we've discussed, disruptions in the delicate balance of neurotransmitters in the brain can contribute significantly to psychological problems such as schizophrenia and depression. At the same time, beliefs, expectations, and reactions to the environment modulate when and how those neurotransmitters are manufactured and used in the brain. In this chapter, we'll see that the mind-to-body connection affects not only the way people think, feel, and react; it affects their overall state of health as well.

Our focus in this chapter is the general topic of **health psychology.** Health psychology is part of a broad movement, known as *behavioral medicine*, that seeks to understand how biological, psychological, environmental, and cultural factors are involved in the promotion of physical health and the prevention of illness. Not surprisingly, health psychologists are particularly interested in the psychological and environmental contributions (Adler & Matthews, 1994). They tend to ask questions such as: Are there particular personality characteristics that determine who becomes sick or who will recover from an illness once it is acquired? Can the same theories that have been used successfully to diagnose and treat psychological disorders be applied to the promotion of physical health? Is it possible to identify the kinds of working environments that lead to illness or promote recovery? Are there specific strategies, or lifestyle choices, that reduce the likelihood of getting sick?

PREVIEWING THE ADAPTIVE PROBLEMS

Much of our discussion in this chapter will deal with the topic of psychological stress and its effects on health. Stress is essentially an adaptive reaction that people make to events in their world, but prolonged exposure to stressful environments can have a negative long-term impact on health. How and why does the body produce stress, and how is it experienced? How does the body react when the exposure to stressful situations is prolonged? What strategies can people use to reduce and cope with stress? Finally, what are the general factors and lifestyle choices that people can make to promote physical and psychological health?

EXPERIENCING STRESS Everyone has an intuitive sense of what *stress* is, but the term can actually be defined in a variety of ways. We'll discuss some of the meanings of the term, as well as the various components of the stress response. It's popular to conceive of stress not as a single reaction, such as a sudden release of

We live in a time of increased expectation—everyone seems to want something from us, and they seem to want it now.

Prolonged exposure to stress can lead to physical as well as psychological problems.

activating hormones, but rather as an extended response that occurs over time. Next, we'll turn our attention to some of the situations that produce stress. It turns out that the experience of stress is affected by both external and internal factors. External factors include such things as getting fired from your job, a breakup in a relationship, or the death of a loved one. Internal factors include personality traits and general styles of thinking. Whether you'll experience an event as stressful depends on who you are and how you think. Not all people react to environmental events in the same way—what's stressful to one person may be a walk in the park to another.

▶ **REACTING TO PROLONGED STRESS** What are the long-term consequences of prolonged exposure to stressful situations? The human body is usually ably equipped to deal with unexpected trauma by activating those portions that are needed to respond to the emergency. But if the threat continues for an extended period of time, the body's defenses can begin to break down. We'll consider some of the physical consequences of prolonged exposure to stress, including the role that stress plays in the immune system. But reactions to prolonged stress are not simply physical—there are psychological consequences as well. High levels of stress can impair one's ability to perform tasks, they can affect one's general level of motivation, and they can even lead to serious psychological problems.

▶ **REDUCING AND COPING WITH STRESS** Given that prolonged exposure to stress can have negative long-term consequences, psychologists have developed specific methods of treatment for reducing and controlling stress. A number of techniques are available for managing stress, and we'll consider some of them in this section. One approach is to deal with the physical stress response itself. People can learn relaxation techniques, combined perhaps with specific physiological monitoring called *biofeedback*. Social support is also important—people who are involved in supportive social relationships seem better able to cope with demanding situations. People can also be taught to recognize and avoid situations that produce stress, or to reappraise just how much of a threat the stressful situation actually represents.

▶ **LIVING A HEALTHFUL LIFESTYLE** Finally, we'll close the chapter with a discussion of some general lifestyle issues. Whether you will remain healthy throughout your life depends importantly on the lifestyle habits you choose. Obviously, if you choose to engage in risky behaviors—such as smoking, failing to get adequate nutrition, or practicing unsafe sex—then you increase your likelihood of illness or death. Health psychologists have joined with other professionals, including physicians, to offer prescriptions for a healthful lifestyle. We'll discuss some of these recommendations along with their foundations in psychological theory.

Experiencing Stress: Stressors and the Stress Response

"Stress" is one of those concepts that is easy to identify but difficult to define precisely. Part of the problem is that the term can be used in a variety of ways. For example, people frequently describe stress as if it was an actual *stimulus* (such as an event or a person) that places a demand on them or threatens their well-being ("That final next week is placing me under a lot of stress"). On the other hand, people are just as likely to describe stress as a physical *response* or reaction that they feel ("I'm really stressed out"). To complicate matters even further, as we'll see later, whether people feel stress depends on how they interpret the situation they're in (Lazarus, 1966, 1991). Consequently, some researchers describe stress as an internal psychological *process* through which external events are interpreted as threatening or demanding.

For our purposes, we'll define **stress** as the physical and psychological reaction that people have to demanding situations, and we'll refer to the demanding or threatening situations that produce stress as **stressors.** This means that the jack-knifed tractor trailer that blocks your speedy route home from school is a stressor, whereas your fuming physical and emotional reaction to such a situation is stress. First, we'll consider some of the physical and psychological characteristics of stress, then we'll examine the external and internal factors that create stress.

The Stress Response

If you're like most people, you probably think of stress as a bad thing. Certainly when you're "stressed out," you tend to feel lousy, and there's no question that extended exposure to stressful situations can have long-term negative consequences. But it's important to understand that stress is in many ways an adaptive reaction. When you're in a threatening situation, or when someone is placing demands on you, it's important that your body become "activated" so you can respond to the threat in the most appropriate way. The experience of stress does exactly that, at least initially—it activates you.

The early stages of the stress response are clearly adaptive because they help organisms initiate a "fight-or-flight" response.

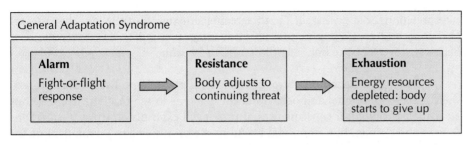

FIGURE 16.1
**The General Adaptation
Syndrome.** Hans Selye proposed
that the body reacts to threat or
demand in three stages, or phases: (1)
an *alarm reaction* that corresponds to
the fight-or-flight response; (2) a
resistance phase, during which the
body adjusts its reaction in an effort
to cope with a threat that is still
present; and (3) *exhaustion,* which
occurs when the body's energy reserves become so taxed and depleted
that the body starts to give up.

Physiological Reactions. In the 1930s, a physician named Hans Selye introduced an influential model of the stress reaction that he called the **general adaptation syndrome (GAS)** (Selye, 1936, 1952, 1974). Selye was convinced that our
reaction to stressful situations is general and nonspecific, by which he meant that
people are biologically programmed to respond to most threats in the same way.
He was initially led to this idea as a medical student, when he was struck by the
similarities that he saw among his patients. Across wildly diverse illnesses and
injuries, his patients seemed to share a "syndrome of just being sick" that suggested
to Selye that the body was reacting to each threatening situation in a very general
way (no matter what the illness or the injury). Later, working in the laboratory
with rats, he was able to confirm his hypothesis under controlled experimental
conditions. Rats subjected to a variety of quite different kinds of threat—cold,
heat, shock, restraint—produced a quite similar pattern of responses.

Selye's concept of the GAS proposes that the body reacts to threat or demand
in three stages, or phases (see Figure 16.1). The first phase, the *alarm reaction,* corresponds to the adaptive fight-or-flight response that we've discussed in previous
chapters (Cannon, 1932). The body becomes energized, through activation of the
sympathetic division of the autonomic nervous system, and hormones are released
by the glands of the endocrine system. Heart rate and respiration rate increase, as
does blood flow to the muscles; each of these actions helps prepare the body for
immediate defensive or evasive action. The alarm reaction enables one to get out
of life-threatening jams, but it is extremely intense and cannot be sustained for
long periods without serious negative consequences (even death).

If the threat continues but is not serious enough to demand a continued alarm
reaction, the body enters a *resistance* phase. During this phase, the body adjusts its
physiological reaction in an effort to reduce, or cope with, the still-present threat.
Arousal levels remain higher than normal, but the body is capable of replenishing
at least some of its resources. During the resistance phase, people are able to function reasonably well, but they are particularly susceptible to other stressors in the
environment and may begin to suffer from health problems, or what Selye called
"diseases of adaptation."

Finally, if the person is unable to find a way to neutralize the threat, the body
eventually enters the *exhaustion phase* of the GAS. The body simply cannot continue to maintain a high state of readiness for extended periods of time. Eventually, energy reserves become so taxed and depleted that the body starts to give up.
During this period, resistance declines to the point at which the stress reaction
becomes more and more maladaptive. Death, or some kind of irreversible damage, becomes a real possibility.

Selye's notion of the GAS remained influential over the years. But today, many
researchers believe that the body's reaction to threat may not be as general and
nonspecific as Selye suggested. Different stressors may well produce somewhat different patterns of response in the body (Krantz & Manuck, 1984; Mason, 1975).
Moreover, as we'll see momentarily, the stress reaction depends on the cognitive

interpretation, or appraisal, of the threatening situation. But the idea that stress is best conceived as a complex process of adaptation is still widely accepted, as is Selye's discovery of the link between stress and health.

Psychological Reactions. Stress is not just a physiological reaction to threat; there are also emotional and behavioral components to the reaction. We will consider the psychological consequences of prolonged exposure to stressful situations later in the chapter, but emotional reactions are an important component of the stress response regardless of when or how long it occurs. *Fear* is a common reaction to threat, as is *anger*. Stressful situations can also lead to feelings of *sadness, dejection,* or even *grief* (Lazarus, 1991). Notice that this diverse set of emotional reactions is another piece of evidence suggesting that the stress reaction is not completely general and nonspecific—people are capable of responding emotionally to different stressors in quite different ways.

The psychological experience of stress does not even have to be negative. Stress can have significant short-term and long-term psychological benefits. For example, one study that examined the psychological characteristics of people who suffered from frequent illness found them to be more understanding (empathetic) of others and more tolerant of uncertainty (Haan, 1977). Stressful situations require people to use their skills and to interact with the environment. As individuals deal with stress they often learn useful things about themselves and about their abilities (Haan, 1993). Moreover, individuals who can successfully resolve a stressful situation gain confidence in their abilities. Laboratory work has even found that rats who are allowed to escape from shock, thereby reducing stress, show better immune system functioning than rats who receive no shock (Laudenslager and others, 1983).

Remember, just because two things occur together, such as the frequency of physical illness and empathy, does not mean that one causes the other. What would you need to do to determine whether physical illness truly causes more empathy?

Cognitive Appraisal

Many psychologists are convinced that stress is closely related to the concept of emotion (Lazarus, 1993). The reason is that the experience of stress is critically influenced by the way that people perceive or *appraise* the situation that they're in. To feel stress, it's necessary to (1) perceive there is some kind of demand or threat present, and (2) come to the conclusion that you may not have adequate resources available to deal with that threat. If you have a black belt in the martial arts, then the sudden appearance of an unarmed thug is not likely to cause much stress—the threat is there, but you have adequate defensive resources should you need to use them.

This idea that the experience of stress depends on the **cognitive appraisal** of the situation is reminiscent of what we know about the experience of emotions. As you may remember from Chapter 11, the same general physiological reaction can lead to different subjective emotional experiences, depending on how one interprets the arousal experienced. The same is true for stress. Identical environmental events can lead to two quite different stress reactions, depending on how the event is interpreted. Consider an upcoming exam: everyone in the class receives the same test, but not everyone will feel the same amount of stress. Those people who are prepared for the exam—the people like you who read the chapter—are likely to feel less stress. Again, you are perceiving the threat, but you have adequate resources to deal with it (see Figure 16.2). The converse is true as well—dangerous situations must be perceived as dangerous in order for a stress response to be produced. A small child does not necessarily understand that a loaded gun is dangerous and so may feel no stress while handling it.

A great deal of evidence confirms the role of cognitive appraisal in the experience of stress. In one study that looked at elementary school children, urine samples were taken from the children on both normal school days and on days when

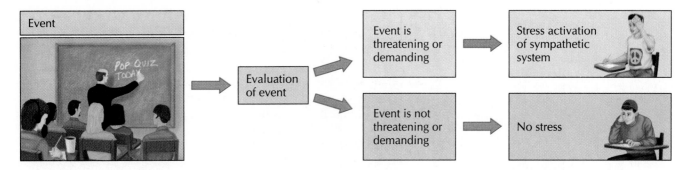

FIGURE 16.2
Cognitive Appraisal. As with emotion, whether an event will create stress depends on how that event is interpreted. A stress reaction is more likely to occur if you feel you have inadequate resources to deal with the potential threat.

they were about to take standardized achievement tests. The point of the urine sample was to measure the amount of cortisol, an important stress hormone, that each child produced (notice that the researchers provided an operational definition of stress in terms of the amount of hormone measured). Not surprisingly, more cortisol was found on test days, suggesting a higher level of stress, but the increase in stress depended on the child's previously recorded overall intelligence score. The children with higher intelligence scores showed less of a stress reaction on test days, presumably because they considered the test to be less of a threat (Tennes & Kreye, 1985).

External Sources of Stress

The fact that the stress reaction depends on one's appraisal of the situation means that it will never be possible to compile an exhaustive list of life's stressors. We can never predict how everyone will react to an environmental event, even though it may seem clearly stressful to the majority. But it is possible to catalogue external situations, or life events, that induce stress reactions in *most* individuals. We'll consider three major classes of external stressors in this section: significant life events, daily hassles, and other factors in the environment.

Significant Life Events. Certain events in people's lives are virtually guaranteed to produce stress. We can all agree that something such as the death of a loved one or getting fired from a job is likely to lead to an extended stress reaction in most people. On a larger scale, catastrophes and natural disasters—such as wars or earthquakes—unquestionably produce stress that is prolonged and widespread. In each of these cases, studies have established clear relationships between such events and subsequent physical and psychological problems (Goldberger & Breznitz, 1993). To cite just one example, in the seven months following the 1980 volcanic eruption of Mount Saint Helens in Washington State, one nearby town reported a more than 30% increase in the number of hospital emergency room visits, compared to a comparable period in the year prior to the eruption (Adams & Adams, 1984) (see Figure 16.3). These visits were *not* for injuries directly caused by the eruption but rather for general health problems that may have been created or enhanced by the experience of stress.

Over the years, researchers have tried to compile lists of external life stressors. The best-known example is the Social Readjustment Rating Scale, which was put together by researchers Thomas Holmes and Richard Rahe (1967). Holmes and Rahe interviewed thousands of people who were suffering from health problems and then tried to determine whether there were certain kinds of events that preceded the onset of the health problems. The results are shown in Table 16.1 on page 567. This table lists the various significant life events mentioned by the people who were interviewed, ranked in terms of "life change units" (roughly representing the amount of adjustment that the event caused in the person's life).

Try listing and ranking the life events that cause, or have caused, you the most stress. Are your rank orderings comparable to the ones listed in Table 16.1?

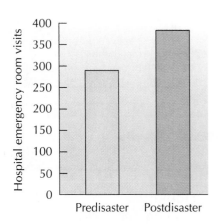

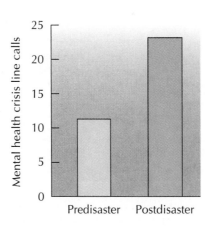

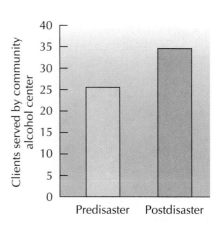

FIGURE 16.3
Reacting to a Natural Disaster.
In the seven months following the volcanic eruption of Mount Saint Helens in 1980, the residents of Othello, Washington, showed dramatic increases, on average, in a variety of stress-related behaviors. The data shown here present the mean monthly hospital emergency room visits, mental health crisis line calls, and number of clients served by a community alcohol center for comparable time periods before and after the disaster. (Data from Adams & Adams, 1984)

Even positive significant life events, such as Christmas, can lead to stress reactions.

There are two interesting things to notice about the results shown in the table. First, most of these life events are associated with some kind of *change* in a person's day-to-day activities. Thus, it may be that the disruption caused by the event is just as important as the event itself in eliciting the stress reaction. People get stressed, in part, because something happens that requires them to alter their ways or lifestyle. Second, notice that many of the events listed in the table are actually quite *positive*. For example, marriage and retirement make the top ten. Even vacations and Christmas make the list. This is not really too surprising if you think about it, because each is associated with some kind of temporary or long-lasting change or disruption of normal routines.

The results listed in Table 16.1 are over 30 years old, but they continue to be used by researchers as a vehicle for predicting the likelihood of stress. Dozens of research studies have shown that there are significant correlations between the rankings shown in the table and various measures of stress, including physical and psychological problems (Derogatis & Coons, 1993; Miller, 1993). However, not all experts are satisfied with the methods that have been used to compile such lists (Brett and others, 1990; Cleary, 1980; Schroeder & Costa, 1984), and clearly change, by itself, will not automatically lead to stress reactions in all individuals. So you cannot automatically assume that if one of these events happens to you, you will feel stress. Remember, it's how you appraise the event that is really important, along with your assessment of whether you have adequate resources to deal with the life change when it occurs.

Daily Hassles. Psychologists also recognize that it is not just the big events that cause problems. The little things, the daily irritations and hassles of life, also contribute significantly to the experience of stress. Think about how you feel when you're stuck in a long checkout line at the market, when someone's tailgating you on the freeway, or when you're hungry and you've waited a half-hour or more for your order at a restaurant. Some psychologists believe the cumulative effect of these "daily hassles" may actually be more important in creating stress than the kinds of life events that we just considered (Lazarus & Folkman, 1984; Miller, 1993). Kanner and others (1981) have developed what they call a Hassles Scale, and it seems to predict, on average, the likelihood of physical and mental health problems. The more "hassles" you experience in your daily life, the more likely you'll experience health problems. Included on the scale are such things as concern about one's weight and physical appearance, home maintenance, and worries about misplacing or losing something.

TABLE 16.1
Social Readjustment Rating Scale

Rank	Life Event	Point Value		Rank	Life Event	Point Value
1	Death of spouse	100		22	Change in responsibilities at work	29
2	Divorce	73		23	Son or daughter leaving home	29
3	Marital separation	65		24	Trouble with in-laws	29
4	Jail term	63		25	Outstanding personal achievement	28
5	Death of close family member	63		26	Wife begins or stops work	26
6	Personal injury or illness	53		27	Begin or end school	26
7	Marriage	50		28	Change in living conditions	25
8	Fired at work	47		29	Revision of personal habits	24
9	Marital reconciliation	45		30	Trouble with boss	23
10	Retirement	45		31	Change in work hours or conditions	20
11	Change in health of family member	44		32	Change in residence	20
12	Pregnancy	40		33	Change in schools	20
13	Sex difficulties	39		34	Change in recreation	19
14	Gain of new family member	39		35	Change in church activities	19
15	Business readjustment	39		36	Change in social activities	18
16	Change in financial state	38		37	Mortgage or loan less than $10,000	17
17	Death of close friend	37		38	Change in sleeping habits	16
18	Change to different line of work	36		39	Change in number of family get-togethers	15
19	Change in number of arguments with spouse	35		40	Change in eating habits	15
20	Mortgage over $10,000	31		41	Vacation	13
21	Foreclosure of mortgage or loan	30		42	Christmas	12
				43	Minor violations of the law	11

Source: Holmes & Rahe, 1967.

Other Environmental Factors. People are also subjected to stress by their environment. *Noise* is a good example. Think about how difficult it is to study when someone is talking loudly nearby, or how irritated you get when you're roused from sleep by the whirring, clanging sounds of the morning garbage truck. Chronic exposure to noise interferes with everyday activities, and it's been linked with the appearance of such stress-related disorders as ulcers, high blood pressure (Nagar & Panady, 1987), and with a general decline in the perceived quality of life (Evans, Hygge, & Bullinger, 1995). Apparently, it's not the loudness of the noise that really matters; people are bothered most by noises that are new, intermittent, or unpredictable (Graig, 1993).

Another environmental factor that has been linked to stress is *crowding.* The more people who live or work around you, the more likely you'll experience a stress reaction (Weiss & Baum, 1987). Living in a crowded environment, on average, makes people more susceptible to health problems and increases the likelihood that they'll become aggressive. People who live in high-rise apartment buildings, filled with tenants, are more likely to behave aggressively than those who live in apartment buildings with fewer floors (Bell and others, 1990). The effects of crowding on health and aggression have also been studied extensively in prison settings—again, inmates who live in crowded environments suffer more health problems and are more likely to act aggressively than inmates housed in less crowded environments (Paulus, 1988).

The daily hassles of life, such as getting stuck in a long line at the store, may be among the most important contributors to stress.

Results like the ones we're discussing apply only to the average case. Suppose you discovered a group of people living in a crowded and noisy environment who show little or no stress reaction. How would you interpret your findings?

Crowding and noise are two examples of environmental stressors, but there are many others. There is, in fact, an entire specialty in psychology—called **environmental psychology**—devoted to the study of environmental effects on behavior and health. Environmental psychologists have shown particular interest in the psychology of urban living, because living in a large city is likely to expose one to a variety of environmental stressors (particularly noise and crowding). In general, people succumb to stress when they're forced to live in situations in which there is excessive stimulation, movement is constrained, or resources are limited (Graig, 1993).

Internal Sources of Stress

As you are now aware, no single event, or set of living conditions, will automatically lead to stress in everyone. Stress is very much in the eye of the beholder, which means we need to know something about the internal characteristics of the individual before we can predict whether he or she will experience stress. Stress arises out of an interaction between individual people and events in the world—neither alone is sufficient to predict the reaction. But what exactly are these internal characteristics? We'll consider three in this section: perceived control, explanatory or attributional style, and personality characteristics.

Perceived Control. To experience stress, you need to perceive a threat or some kind of demand, and you need to feel you lack the resources to deal effectively with that threat. This second part of the appraisal process, the assessment of resources, is influenced by a psychological construct called **perceived control,** which is the amount of influence you feel you have over the situation and your reaction to it. It turns out that perceived control significantly affects the amount of stress you will experience. If you perceive a demand or threat and you think you have no control over the situation, your body is likely to react with arousal and the release of stress hormones. If the situation continues for a prolonged period, negative physical and psychological consequences are likely to result.

There are lots of examples, both scientific and anecdotal, that support the link between perceived control and stress. Early in the manned space program, for instance, the Mercury astronauts insisted that manual controls and windows be placed in the orbiting space capsule. Although not necessary from an engineering standpoint, doing so gave the astronauts a "sense of control" over their environment, which reduced their stress. In laboratory studies, animals who are exposed to shocks that they can turn off by turning a wheel are less likely to develop ulcers than animals who receive the same amount of shock but cannot control it (Weiss, 1977).

Explanatory Style. The results of the cognitive appraisal process, and therefore susceptibility to stress, are also influenced by one's general style of thinking. At several points in the text, we've discussed the importance of the process of *attribution,* which refers to how individuals arrive at conclusions about cause and effect. People offer different kinds of explanations for the positive and negative events that occur in their world. For example, someone with an *internal, stable,* and *global* explanatory style is likely to attribute a negative event to some long-lasting personal inadequacy that applies in lots of situations: "My spouse left me because I'm witless; I've always been witless, and I can never hope to convince anyone otherwise."

We've seen elsewhere that a person's explanatory style contributes to psychological disorders such as depression (see Chapter 14). Perhaps not surprisingly, explanatory style has also been linked to physical health and susceptibility to stress. People who consistently make internal, stable, and global attributions for negative events have been found to suffer from increased stress-related health problems in midlife as well as later in life (Kamen-Siegel and others, 1991; Peterson, Seligman, & Vaillant, 1988). In one particularly intriguing study, Peterson and Seligman (1987) analyzed the explanatory styles of 94 members of the Baseball Hall of Fame who had played at some point between 1900 and 1950. Many of these players were dead at the time of the study, so the researchers had to glean the players' explanatory styles from stories and quotations in old newspapers. The players with the negative explanatory styles were found, on average, to have lived shorter lives.

Personality Characteristics. Both perceived control and explanatory style are related more generally to personality. Previously, we defined *personality* as the set of unique psychological characteristics that differentiate us from others and lead us to act consistently across situations. Explanatory style may be linked to a personality characteristic such as *optimism*—the belief that good things will happen—which some psychologists have argued is a relatively enduring trait that changes little over a lifetime (Scheier & Carver, 1993). "Optimism scales" have been developed and used to look for a connection between personality and health. In one study, optimism was assessed on the day before a group of men underwent coronary bypass surgery. The optimists reacted physiologically to the surgery in ways that lowered the risk of heart attack; they also recovered more quickly after the surgery (Scheier and others, 1989). An optimistic view of life therefore appears to reduce stress and its associated health risks.

The most widely recognized personality characteristics that have been linked to stress-related health disorders, particularly coronary heart disease, are the famous **Type A** and **Type B** behavior patterns. You're familiar with the Type A personality: hard driving, ambitious, easily annoyed, and impatient. Those with a Type A personality seem to be immersed in a sea of perpetual self-imposed stress; they're too busy to notice or enjoy the things around them because they're engaged in a relentless pursuit of success. Type B personality types are essentially people who lack the Type A attributes—they put themselves under less pressure and appear more relaxed.

Type A personality types seem to be immersed in a sea of perpetual stress, and they're significantly more likely to develop coronary heart problems than Type B personality types.

Do you think Type A personalities are more likely to perceive a threat, to feel inadequately equipped to deal with a threat, or both?

The connection between Type A behavior patterns and heart disease was first noted by cardiologists Meyer Friedman and Ray Rosenman (1974). Friedman and Rosenman were interested in explaining why only some people with known risk factors for heart disease—such as smoking, obesity, inactivity, and so on—actually develop heart problems. People can appear to have identical risk profiles but end up healthy in one instance and disease-prone in another. Friedman and Rosenman proposed that the solution lies in the connection between personality and stress. People who are psychologically prone to stress—Type A personalities—will prove more susceptible to diseases of the heart.

Over the past several decades, a number of very ambitious studies have been conducted to explore the health consequences of Type A behavior patterns. Thousands of individuals have participated in these studies, and they have been studied over long periods of time. Generally, the results have supported the proposals of Friedman and Rosenman: People who are classified as Type A personality types are at least twice as likely to develop coronary heart problems as Type B personality types (Lyness, 1993). But not all studies have found this result, and there have even been studies showing the opposite pattern (Ragland & Brand, 1988).

Recent work suggests that a more complete answer may lie in further analyzing the Type A behavior pattern or personality, which turns out to be quite complex. To be classified as a Type A personality requires that a person be rated on a number of dimensions—competitiveness, ambition, hostility, and so on—and not all of these attributes are equally important. Some researchers believe it is hostility, anger, or the expression of anger that is most responsible for producing subsequent coronary artery disease (Adler & Matthews, 1994). Others have stressed the need to consider cultural factors—some societies encourage competition and others do not (Thoresen & Powell, 1992). At this point, it's widely believed that personality characteristics do affect susceptibility to stress and disease (Friedman, Hawley, & Tucker, 1994), but we probably can't just draw a sharp line between Type A and Type B personality types and hope to explain all the data.

Reacting to Prolonged Stress: Physical and Psychological Effects

There is a definite connection between prolonged exposure to stress and physical and psychological health. Stress is an adaptive reaction to threat—it helps people to fight or flee. But when it is prolonged, when one is not able to reduce or eliminate the perceived threat, the mind and body start to break down. If the stress reaction is extreme enough, the breakdown can be sudden and may even result in death; in most cases, however, the effects are gradual and manifest themselves slowly through a growing list of physical and psychological problems. In this section of the chapter, we'll consider the nature of these breakdowns and how and why they occur.

Physical Consequences of Stress

Stress has been implicated in a wide variety of health problems. Besides ulcers and heart disease, it has been linked to everything from the common cold to chronic back pain, multiple sclerosis, and even cancer. Most of the scientific evidence is correlational, which means a statistical relationship has been found between the incidence of a health problem such as heart disease and some measurement of stress. Large numbers of people are interviewed, and health histories as well as stress levels are measured. The net result is that we can predict whether someone, on average, will have an increased likelihood of developing a particular kind of health problem by knowing the amount of stress they experience on a regular basis. But this does not tell us whether a causal relationship exists between stress and illness. To determine that, we must turn to experimental research.

It's difficult to conduct experimental research on the relationship between stress and health for obvious ethical reasons. Ethically, we can't randomly divide people into groups, subject some of them to high levels of stress, and then monitor the later consequences of that manipulation on health. But experimental studies have been conducted on groups of people who have been previously identified as having either a high or low level of stress in their lives. In one study (Cohen, Tyrrell, & Smith, 1993), high- and low-stress people were given nasal drops that either contained or did not contain a common cold virus. It was a double-blind study, so neither the participants nor the researchers were aware during the course of the study who was getting the actual virus and who was not. Afterward, when the subject assignments were "decoded," it was found that the high-stress people who received the virus were the ones most likely to show cold symptoms. Living a stressful life apparently lowers one's ability to fight off disease.

Prolonged stress may compromise the functioning of the immune system, decreasing the ability of the body to fight off disease.

The Immune Response. To understand *why* stress increases susceptibility to illness, you need to understand something about the human immune system. The human body has a complex defense system, called the *immune system,* that is constantly on the lookout for foreign substances, such as viruses or bacteria. The primary weapons of the immune system are **lymphocytes,** which are specialized white blood cells that have the job of attacking and destroying most of these foreign invaders. Stress can lower the immune response by either decreasing the number of lymphocytes in the bloodstream or by somehow suppressing the response of the lymphocytes to foreign substances that have invaded the body. The underlying mechanisms that produce these changes have not been completely determined, although the prolonged release of stress hormones into the bloodstream probably plays a significant role (Stein & Miller, 1993).

Several investigations have shown that stressful life events directly affect the immune response. Medical students, on average, have fewer lymphocytes in their blood during a period of final exams compared to levels found before exams (Kiecolt-Glaser et al., 1984); they are also more likely to get sick during exams. People who have recently had a spouse or loved one die also show a suppressed immune response. One investigative team tracked the immune response in men married to women with advanced breast cancer. Samples of the men's blood were taken during a period of months preceding and following their wife's death. On average, the existing lymphocytes in blood samples drawn *after* the wives had died showed a weaker response to foreign substances (Schleifer and others, 1983).

The fact that stress weakens the immune system has led researchers to wonder about the effects of stress on more chronic illnesses, such as cancer. In the laboratory, it's been shown that stress can increase the growth rate of cancerous tumors in rats, although the particular type of tumor apparently matters (Justice, 1985). There have also been reports that cancer patients who are optimistic, or who are given therapy to help reduce anxiety and depression, survive longer than patients who are hopeless or depressed (Andersen, 1992; Spiegel and others, 1989). Stress may affect not only the body's ability to fight cancer but also the likelihood that cancer cells will form in the first place (Schneiderman and others, 1992).

At present, however, most researchers remain cautious about the link between psychology, the immune system, and cancer. Not all studies have found associations between psychological factors and cancer (Adler & Matthews, 1994), and the fact that data linking cancer to stress have come primarily from correlational studies means that it is difficult to draw conclusions about cause and effect. For example, it's possible that "stressful" people, on average, have a greater risk of acquiring cancer because they tend to engage in unhealthful behaviors—such as smoking—as a way of dealing with the stress. It may also be the case that people who are optimistic about their survival from cancer tend to comply more with the recommendations of their doctors. So, although there may be a statistical association between stress and cancer, that does not necessarily mean that stress is causing cancer by compromising the functioning of the immune system.

Cardiovascular Disease. Health psychologists have also intensively studied the well-documented relationship between stress and cardiovascular disease (problems connected with the heart and blood vessels). We discussed the connection between Type A behavior and heart problems earlier, but we left the mechanisms through which stress undermines cardiovascular health unspecified. The two most important risk factors in heart disease are (1) high cholesterol levels in the blood and (2) high blood pressure. Prolonged exposure to stress increases exposure to both of these risk factors.

Increased blood pressure, a natural by-product of the stress response, is generally helpful over the short term (as part of the fight-or-flight response). But if the elevated pressure continues, it causes wear and tear on the blood vessels in the body, which can lead to cardiovascular disease as well as to kidney problems. Stress can also directly affect the level of cholesterol in the blood. For example, when college students are anticipating an upcoming exam, samples of their blood show higher levels of cholesterol (Van Doornen & Van Blokland, 1987). People who display Type A behavior patterns have also been found, on average, to have higher levels of blood cholesterol. One possibility is that when people sense threat, the body directs the blood flow to the muscles and away from internal organs, such as the liver, that remove fat and cholesterol from the blood.

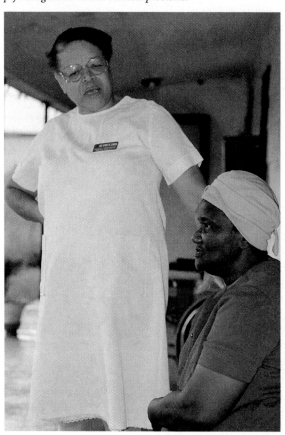

Many psychologists believe that stressful life events play a role in the onset of psychological as well as medical problems.

Psychological Consequences of Stress

Think about how you feel when you're "stressed out." That recurring cold or that sour stomach seems like it'll never go away. But the mental and emotional changes can be just as profound. You feel anxious, out of control, emotionally drained, and, after a while, possibly even sad and depressed. Stress is not a pleasant experience, and if the stress reaction is intense enough, or if it continues long enough, serious psychological problems can result.

Most psychologists are convinced that stressful life events play a significant role in the onset of many psychological disorders. If you interview people who have suffered from major depression or a bipolar disorder, you will find that most have experienced some kind of major stressor just before or early into the depressive episode—they got fired from their job, they moved to a new town, they're mired in a nasty divorce, and so on (Barlow & Durand, 1995). Stress has also been implicated in the onset of schizophrenia. Several studies have shown that stressful life events tend to immediately precede schizophrenic episodes (Brown & Birley, 1968; Ventura and others, 1989).

But importantly, not all people who experience intense stress go on to develop serious psychological problems. In fact, the *majority* of people who experience a traumatic life stressor do not subsequently develop psychological disorders. Psychologists assume that the person must have some kind of vulnerability, perhaps rooted in the genetic code, before stress will lead to an extreme disorder, such as major depression or schizophrenia. Similar arguments apply to anxiety disorders, such as posttraumatic stress disorder, which we discuss briefly below.

Posttraumatic Stress Disorder. You're familiar with the scenario: Soldier returns home from war, shell shocked, suffering from sleepless nights and flashbacks of traumatic episodes in battle. Hollywood has exploited this image, to the point where the "unstable Vietnam vet" has become an unfortunate part of our collective sense of the Vietnam experience. In reality, the vast majority of soldiers who returned from Vietnam or the Gulf War have experienced no long-term psychological problems. At the same time, even though the percentages are small, psychologists do recognize that exposure to extreme stress can produce a serious psychological condition known as **posttraumatic stress disorder.** This disorder is not limited to battle veterans; it can occur in any individual who has undergone a traumatic episode, such as a physical attack, rape, or a natural disaster (Foa & Riggs, 1995).

In the DSM-IV, posttraumatic stress disorder is classified as an anxiety disorder, and the diagnosis is made if the following three types of symptoms occur for a period lasting longer than one month:

1. *Flashbacks.* When a flashback occurs, the person relives the traumatic event in some way. These flashbacks can take the form of persistent thoughts or images of the traumatic scene, and they can even involve vivid hallucinations; the affected person seems at times to be reexperiencing the event—fighting the battle anew or fending off the attacker.

2. *Avoidance of stimuli associated with the trauma.* People with posttraumatic stress disorder actively try to avoid anything that reminds them of the event. This avoidance behavior can lead to significant disruptions in normal social functioning, as the affected person turns away from friends and loved ones who in some way remind them of the trauma.

3. *Chronic arousal symptoms.* These symptoms can include sleep problems, irritability or outbursts of anger, and difficulties in concentrating.

Can you think of any way that the onset of a psychological disorder, such as depression, might actually be an adaptive reaction to prolonged stress? Could one's behavior change in a way that reduces stress and its wear and tear on the body?

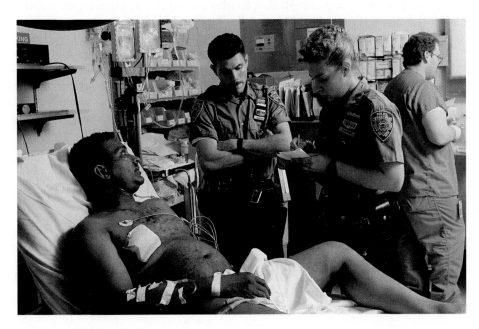

Posttraumatic stress disorder can occur when an individual experiences some kind of traumatic episode, such as a physical attack.

Obviously, posttraumatic stress disorder is a disabling condition, not only for the individuals who are directly affected but also for family and friends. The cause of the disorder is clear—traumatic stress—but the reason that only some people who experience trauma develop posttraumatic stress disorder remains a mystery. There is evidence that the intensity of the trauma may be important. For example, Vietnam veterans who were in heavy combat were significantly more likely to develop posttraumatic stress disorder than those serving in noncombat roles (Goldberg and others, 1990). But, once again, this does not explain why the disorder remains relatively rare even among people who have experienced extreme trauma. As is the case for most psychological disorders, the likelihood that posttraumatic stress disorder will develop undoubtedly depends on a complex mix of biological and environmental factors.

Burnout. Stress does not need to be extreme to produce unpleasant psychological consequences. In the 1970s, the term **burnout** was introduced by psychologists to describe a syndrome that develops in certain people who are exposed to stressful situations that are demanding but not necessarily traumatic (Freudenberger, 1974; Maslach, 1976). Although the term *burnout* has become a household word, to psychologists it refers to "a state of physical, emotional, and mental exhaustion caused by long-term involvement in emotionally demanding situations" (Pines & Aronson, 1988). When burnout occurs, affected individuals essentially lose their spirit—they become emotionally drained, they feel used up, and they lose their sense of personal accomplishment (Maslach & Jackson, 1981).

As with posttraumatic stress disorder, stress is a necessary but not a sufficient condition for producing burnout. Not everyone who has a demanding and stressful job becomes burned out. Burnout seems to occur only in idealistic individuals—people who have entered their careers with a high sense of motivation and commitment. In the words of psychologist Ayala Pines (1993), "You cannot burn out unless you were 'on fire' initially." Because burnout tends to occur only in highly motivated individuals, it can have a high cost for organizations as well as for the individual. People who suffer from burnout lose their edge on the job—they become disillusioned with their work, are frequently absent from the job, and usually are at increased risk for a host of physical problems.

Why does burnout occur? The underlying cause may well be related to a loss of meaning in life (Pines, 1993). People who are subject to burnout are usually those who think of their work as a kind of "calling." They use success on the job as a way of validating their existence. They identify so closely with their work that when failure happens, their entire lives lose meaning. Failure is much more likely when the job is demanding and taxes the individual's resources, which is probably the reason why stress is typically associated with the syndrome. If the overall stress levels can be reduced, perhaps by providing a better support system within the work environment, burnout is much less likely to occur (Maslach, 1982; Pines & Aronson, 1988).

Reducing and Coping with Stress: Techniques of Stress Management

Because stress is associated with so many physical and psychological problems, it is obviously in people's best interest to develop techniques for reducing stress. Unfortunately, stressors are often outside of the individual's direct control—you cannot prevent the tornado that skirts the neighborhood trailer park, or the death of a valued friend from accident or illness. But techniques are available for coping with stressors when they're present. **Coping** is a term that psychologists use to describe efforts to manage conditions of threat or demand that tax one's resources (Lazarus, 1993).

There are a variety of effective coping strategies that you can use. For example, you can attempt to control the stressor directly in some way, thereby reducing its ability to induce stress. Or, you can focus your attention on reducing the emotional reaction that the stressor produces. In this section, we'll consider three coping strategies for controlling or reducing stress: (1) learning relaxation techniques, (2) forming effective social support systems, and (3) learning to reappraise the environment in a less threatening way.

Relaxation Techniques

By definition, the stress response is incompatible with relaxation. You cannot be prepared to fight or flee if your body is calm, relaxed, and free from arousal-inducing stress hormones. Studies have shown that high-stress individuals can reduce the physically threatening components of the stress reaction—such as high blood pressure—by simply practicing a regimen of relaxation techniques. You may remember that we discussed in Chapter 15 how relaxation can be used effectively in the treatment of anxiety disorders; similar relaxation techniques have proven effective in reducing long-term stress reactions (Stoyva & Carlson, 1993).

Several types of relaxation procedures are available to help manage stress. In *progressive muscle relaxation,* you're taught to concentrate on specific muscle groups in the body, to note whether there is any tension, and then to try to relax those specific groups (Jacobson, 1938). Often in progressive relaxation, you learn to address muscle groups in sequence. For example, you might begin with the muscle groups in the neck, move to the shoulders, and so on, first tensing and then relaxing each group. In this way you learn to pay attention to how muscles in your body feel when tense or relaxed. In *autogenic relaxation,* you're taught to focus on directing blood flow toward tense muscle groups, "warming" and relaxing each group (Linden, 1990).

Relaxation techniques such as these are sometimes accompanied by *meditation* training. We discussed some of the benefits of meditation in Chapter 6. Meditation essentially involves learning how to relax, using techniques similar to progressive muscle relaxation. But you're also taught some time-tested mental "exercises," such as repeating a string of words or sounds over and over again in your head. The mental repetition focuses awareness and helps prevent potentially distracting or stress-producing thoughts from interfering with the relaxation response. (For instance, if you're concentrating on repeating the phrase "I'm at one with the universe," you cannot simultaneously be worrying about whether the relaxation technique is working.) Daily meditation sessions clearly help people deal with stress-related arousal (Eppley, Abrams, & Shear, 1989).

Biofeedback. The goal of relaxation training is to lower components of the stress response, such as blood pressure, heart rate, and muscle tension. If stress-related headaches, for example, are caused by tension in the muscles of the head and scalp, then people should be able to reduce or eliminate the pain by relaxing these specific muscle groups. Some researchers have suggested it helps matters by giving people feedback—*biofeedback*—about the effectiveness of their relaxation efforts. When biofeedback is used, you're hooked up to monitoring equipment that provides a continuous reading of your physiological state. In the case of tension headaches, the feedback would be about the tension levels in the muscles of the head; for blood pressure or heart rate, you would be able to read your blood pressure and heart rate directly from appropriate monitoring equipment.

FIGURE 16.4

Biofeedback, Perceived Control, and Stress. In the study by Andrasik & Holroyd (1980), subjects in three groups were led to believe that they could *lower* the amount of muscle tension in their foreheads through biofeedback. Actually, the subjects learned to increase, decrease, or keep the tension levels the same. Yet all three groups showed significant improvement in headache symptoms, irrespective of condition. Apparently, the mere fact that the subjects believed they were lowering the tension levels was sufficient to produce improvement. Also shown are the data for control subjects who received no biofeedback. (Data from Andrasik & Holroyd, 1980)

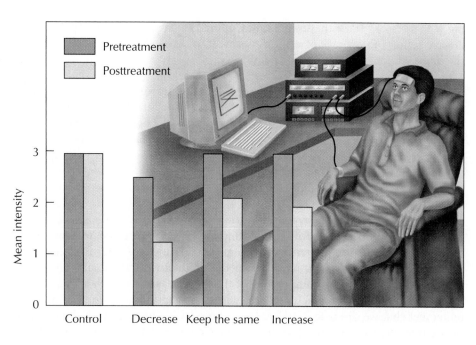

You might consider returning to the Adaptive Mind section of Chapter 6 and reading about the effectiveness of subliminal perception. Do you see any connection between those techniques and the biofeedback techniques described here?

Not surprisingly, biofeedback works. When people are given information about how well their relaxation efforts are succeeding, compared with control subjects who are given no feedback, it's clearly easier to control the relevant physiological response (Blanchard, 1992). But researchers are still debating exactly *why* biofeedback produces its beneficial effects. One possibility is that it may simply be the feeling of *control* that biofeedback provides that leads to reductions in the stress response.

For instance, in one study on tension headaches, three groups of subjects were given a feedback signal that they were led to believe indicated a successful lowering of muscle tension in their foreheads. Actually, unknown to the subjects, the signal had three different meanings: In one group, it appeared only when subjects successfully *increased* the amount of tension in their foreheads; in a second group, the signal appeared whenever the amount of tension decreased; in a third group, it appeared when tension levels remained the same. Remarkably, despite the misleading feedback in two of the groups, everyone reported headache improvement (see Figure 16.4). Apparently, feeling that you have some control over your body can be sufficient to lower stress-induced pain (Andrasik & Holroyd, 1980). This finding does not mean that biofeedback is an ineffective way to treat stress. Whether you will experience a stress response depends on a cognitive appraisal of your resources. If you feel you have the ability to control the threat or demand, even if that control is illusory, you're less likely to experience stress.

Social Support

Although it may seem like a cliché, having a good friend or loved one to lean on during a time of stress really does matter. Psychologists use the term **social support** to refer to the resources that individuals receive from other people or groups, often in the form of comfort, caring, or help. There is a great deal of evidence to suggest that social support can improve one's psychological and physical health (Cohen & Wills, 1985). People with well-established social support systems are less likely to suffer a second heart attack (Case and others, 1992), are more likely to survive life-threatening cancer (Colon and others, 1991), and are less likely to consider suicide if they're infected with HIV (Schneider and others, 1991). Other studies have established that social support plays a role in lowering the likelihood of such psychological problems as depression and in speeding recovery (McLeod, Kessler, & Landis, 1992).

Social support probably helps reduce stress for many reasons (Sarason, Sarason, & Pierce, 1994). Once again, the evidence tends to be correlational (researchers cannot manipulate the amount of support someone receives, for ethical reasons), so firm cause-and-effect relationships have proven difficult to establish. One possibility is that social contacts help people maintain a healthful lifestyle. Friends and family push you out the door for your morning jog, force you to take your medications, or encourage you to visit the doctor regularly. Family and friends also bolster your confidence in times of stress, so you're more likely to feel that you have the necessary resources to cope with the demand. In a time of loss, such as immediately after the death of a spouse, social support lowers the likelihood that a grieving person will engage in unhealthful behaviors, such as drinking (Jennison, 1992).

It's also the case that simply having someone to talk things over with helps people cope with stress. James Pennebaker (1990) has conducted a number of studies in which college students were encouraged to talk or write about upsetting events in their lives (everything from a divorce in the family to fears about the future). When compared to "control" students, who were asked to talk or write about trivial things, the students who opened up showed improved immune functioning and were less likely to visit the college health center over the next several months. Pennebaker has found similar benefits for people who lived through natural disasters (such as earthquakes) or were part of the Holocaust. Opening up, talking about things, and confiding in others really seemed to help these people cope.

On the other hand, psychologists recognize that social support can have a negative side as well. For example, if you've come to depend on another for support and that support is no longer delivered, your ability to cope can be compromised. Social support can also reduce self-reliance in some people, which may produce psychological distress and hurt their ability to cope. It's been found that whether people respond favorably to social support and the receipt of aid, or consider it to be a meddling nuisance, depends to some extent on how much control they feel they have over their own actions and the outcomes of their actions (Hobfoll, Shoham, & Ritter, 1991).

Do you think it's possible that those who are healthier tend to elicit more support than those who are sick? Might this account partly for the correlation?

There is a good deal of evidence suggesting that social support can improve one's physical and psychological health.

INSIDE ▸ THE PROBLEM: *Pet Support*

Having a loved one or a good friend to talk to about your problems makes a difference, and that friend doesn't even need to be human. The companionship of pets—dogs, cats, even birds—has repeatedly been found to be an effective form of social support. Heart attack victims who own pets, for example, are more likely to survive the first year after the attack than non-pet owners are. Correlational studies among the elderly have found that pet ownership is inversely related to the severity of psychological problems: People who are attached to their pets are less likely to show the symptoms of depression (Garrity and others, 1989). Ownership of a dog, in particular, is an excellent predictor of whether or not an elderly person will feel the need to visit a doctor (Siegel, 1990).

There's some evidence to suggest that having a pet around may even be a more effective buffer against stress than having a human companion. In an experiment conducted by Karen Allen and her colleagues (1991), female dog lovers agreed to have several physiological

reactions monitored while they tried to solve relatively difficult math problems. Prior to starting the task, the women were randomly divided into three groups. In one group, the women were allowed to have their dog with them in the room while completing the math task. In a second group, no dogs were allowed but each woman was allowed the presence of a close human friend. In the third group, no social support was present during the testing.

A variety of physiological reactions were measured, including heart rate and blood pressure. Not surprisingly, solving difficult math problems led directly to stress-related arousal—heart rate increased, as did blood pressure. But the amount of reactivity depended on the group: The women who were allowed to have their dog with them showed the lowest arousal effects compared to the women in the other two groups (see Figure 16.5). The presence of the pet apparently acted as an effective buffer against stress. The surprise finding of the study was that having a close human friend sit nearby while solving the math

Pets serve as effective buffers against stress for many individuals.

problems actually led to the highest relative stress reaction.

Does this mean that pets are more therapeutic than friends or loved ones?

Reappraising the Situation

When thinking about how to cope with stress, it's important to remember that the origin of the stress reaction is essentially psychological. In most instances, it is not the sudden life event or the daily hassle that leads people to experience stress—it's their *interpretation* of that event that really matters. Even the death of a spouse or the occurrence of a natural disaster, cruel as it may seem, will create significant stress only if the event is appraised in a negative way. Imagine if your spouse were suffering from an incurable disease, one that produced extreme and persistent pain. Under these conditions, death could be seen as a kind of blessing.

Remember, too, that many instances of stress are caused by the little things, the daily hassles of life. Getting stuck in traffic, or in the wrong line at the supermarket, makes people feel stressed only because they have a tendency to "catastrophize" the situation: "This is absolutely awful . . . I can't stand waiting here any longer . . . I'm going to get home late and my family will be mad." It's not the delay that creates the stress, it's the things people tell themselves about the delay that cause the problems. As a result, many psychologists feel that stress can be managed effectively through logical reanalysis and positive reappraisal. If people can interpret the hassle in a more logical and positive manner, they can reduce or eliminate the stress reaction.

⟨ Can you see any link between the recommendations of these stress management programs and the techniques used in the cognitive therapies, such as rational-emotive therapy, that we discussed in Chapter 15?

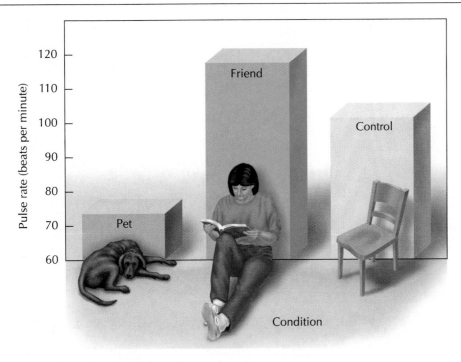

FIGURE 16.5

Pets as Stress Moderators. In the study by Allen and colleagues (1991), having a pet present during a stressful task significantly lowered the stress reaction, measured here in terms of pulse rate, compared to a condition in which a friend was present or a control condition in which neither a friend nor a pet was present. (Data from Allen et al., 1991)

For some people in some situations, the answer may well be "Yes." Allen and her colleagues argued that pets are often effective buffers against stress because they are essentially nonevaluative. Pets don't make value judgments about their caretakers. Your dog or cat doesn't care one bit about how well you're doing on some math task, but your close human friend might. A friend's expectations can place added pressure on you as you perform an already stressful task. A woman who participated in the study by Allen and colleagues put it this way: "Pets never withhold their love, they never get angry and leave, and they never go out looking for new owners." Another woman offered the following: "Whereas husbands may come and go, and children may grow up and leave home, a 'dog is forever.'" The opinions of these women may not be shared by everyone, nor do you need to hold these strong views to appreciate the value of pet companionship. The data indicate that pets can be an important part of an individual's social network and as such can help him or her cope with stress.

Stress management techniques that rely on cognitive reappraisal take a variety of forms. For instance, you can be taught to focus on certain aspects of the situation that distract you from catastrophizing. If you're stuck in the wrong checkout line, rather than concentrating on how you "must" get home on time, pick up one of the tabloids and read about the latest sighting of Elvis. Alternatively, try using your past experiences to reappraise the consequences: "Let's see, this certainly is not the first time I've been stuck in a checkout line, and my family and friends still think I'm okay." Another approach would be to analyze the situation logically and derive alternatives for the future: "Every time I come to the market at 5:30, right after work, I get stuck in a line—maybe if I wait and go after dinner, there will be less of a wait."

Some stress management programs recommend that clients keep daily records of the specific situations that have led to stress, as well as the specific symptoms and thoughts that arose (an example is shown in Figure 16.6). The value of a stress record is that it allows the client to recognize any unrealistic thoughts or conclusions on the spot, because they need to be written in the record. With time, clients get a pretty good idea of the situations that lead to the highest stress, and they gain insight into the thought processes that underlie their reaction. As each unrealistic thought is recognized, the client can work at reappraising the situation and confronting any negative attitudes or beliefs (Barlow & Rapee, 1991).

Daily Stress Record
(sample)

Week of _____

	8	Extreme stress
	7	
	6	Much stress
	5	
	4	Moderate stress
	3	
	2	Mild stress
	1	
	0	No stress

Date	(1) Starting time	(2) Ending time	(3) Highest stress (0-8)	(4) Triggers	(5) Symptoms	(6) Thoughts
1–5	10:00 am	11:00 am	7	Sales meeting	Sweating, headache	My figures are bad.
1–7	5:15 pm	5:35 pm	6	Traffic jam	Tension, impatience	I'll never get home.
1–8	12:30 pm	12:32 pm	3	Lost keys	Tension	I can't find my keys.
1–9	3:30 pm	4:30 pm	4	Waiting for guests	Sweating, nausea	Are they lost?

FIGURE 16.6
A Daily Stress Record. Stress management programs often recommend that clients keep daily records of situations that lead to stress, along with the specific symptoms and thoughts that arise. (From Barlow & Rapee, 1991)

Living a Healthful Lifestyle

One of the challenges of the health psychology movement is to devise a comprehensive and workable framework for health promotion (Winett, 1995). In a recent review of the literature, researchers Nancy Adler and Karen Matthews (1994) summed up the goals of the health psychologist by asking three essential questions: "First, who becomes sick and why? Second, among the sick, who recovers and why? Third, how can illness be prevented or recovery be promoted?" Such questions are appropriately addressed to a psychologist because, as we've seen, a close and intimate connection exists among mind, behavior, and health.

In offering "prescriptions" for healthful lifestyles, psychologists recognize that not all risk factors can be controlled. Men, for example, have a much greater risk of developing heart disease than women, and the elderly are at a greater risk of developing a whole host of health-related problems. Obviously, people have no control over heredity and they can't help the fact that they grow old. But as I'm sure you're aware, there are lifestyle choices that can make a difference.

Get Fit: The Value of Aerobic Exercise

Exercise is an excellent example of an activity that can have a substantial positive impact on physical and psychological health, especially if the exercise is sustained and aerobic. **Aerobic exercise** consists of high-intensity activities that increase both heart rate and oxygen consumption, such as fast walking, running, dancing,

Regular exercise is an important ingredient in living a healthful lifestyle.

rowing, swimming, and so on. As you probably know, regular aerobic exercise improves cardiovascular fitness over the long term and, on average, increases the chances that one will live longer (Belloc & Breslow, 1972; Blair and others, 1989).

Psychologically, regular exercise improves mood and makes people more resistant to the effects of stressors (Stoyva & Carlson, 1993). Much of the evidence is correlational (studies have shown statistical relationships between the regularity of exercise and reported mental health), but controlled experimental studies have reached the same conclusion. For example, in a study by McCann and Holmes (1984), volunteer female college students who were suffering from mild depression were asked to (1) engage in a regular program of aerobic exercise, (2) learn relaxation techniques, or (3) do nothing. After 10 weeks the aerobic exercise group showed the largest improvement in mood. In another experimental study looking at stress resistance, men were randomly assigned to exercise conditions that involved either aerobic activity or nonaerobic strength-and-flexibility training. After 12 weeks of training, the men in the aerobic group showed lower blood pressure and heart rate when they were exposed to situations involving mental stress (Blumenthal and others, 1988).

But researchers have yet to understand fully how or why exercise improves psychological health and functioning. Over the short term, vigorous exercise increases the amount of oxygen that reaches the brain, which undoubtedly improves cognitive functioning, and sustained exercise may alter mood-inducing neurotransmitters in the brain (Sheridan & Radmacher, 1992). It is also clearly the case that aerobic exercise, as it improves cardiovascular health, will lessen the physiological effects of the stress reaction. But there may also be placebo-like effects involved: People who choose to exercise regularly are convinced that they're going to get better, and they subsequently rate themselves as more psychologically healthy than they may in fact be (Pierce and others, 1993).

Don't Smoke: Tobacco and Health

Virtually everyone knows that smoking or the oral ingestion (chewing) of tobacco is bad for one's health. There is no shortage of correlational and experimental studies available to document this fact. Few researchers question, for example, that

Tobacco companies often attempt to associate their products with healthy, vigorous lifestyles.

smoking contributes annually to hundreds of thousands of deaths in the United States alone, from associated heart disease, cancer, stroke, and emphysema. And it's not just the smokers who are affected—the babies of women who smoke during pregnancy tend to have lower birth weights and are at increased risk for birth defects; even people who are simply exposed to smoke secondhand may suffer from subsequent health problems (Byrd, 1992). So why, given that it is so damaging to their health, do people smoke?

First, despite what you might have heard on television (especially from tobacco company executives), smoking is recognized to be *addictive* by the vast majority of mainstream researchers in the health-related sciences. Many people who smoke regularly become dependent on their daily dosage, and when they try to quit, they suffer physical and psychological withdrawal symptoms. The DSM-IV lists criteria for a diagnosis of "nicotine withdrawal" that include insomnia, irritability, difficulty concentrating, and increased appetite or weight gain. The symptoms of withdrawal can be severe enough to cause a significant disruption in normal everyday functioning. This conclusion, of course, comes as no surprise to anyone who has ever tried to quit smoking after prolonged use.

The reinforcing effects of cigarette smoking can be explained by appealing to chemical reactions in the brain as well as to factors in the culture at large. Within the brain, it takes only seconds for nicotine—the active agent in cigarette smoke—to stimulate the central nervous system, elevating heart rate, blood pressure, and mood. Many smokers report that cigarettes not only improve mood but help alleviate anxiety and stress. At the same time, tobacco companies launch advertising campaigns designed to make smoking appear desirable. Tobacco use is identified with role models—often thin, vigorous and healthy types on horseback or frolicking on the beach—or is associated with independence and nonconformity. Unfortunately, these types of advertising campaigns are often particularly effective for those in adolescence, which is the time when most smokers begin their habit.

You've probably heard the saying that the best way to stop smoking is never to start. It's undoubtedly true, because once started, tobacco use is a difficult habit to break. The psychological and physical withdrawal symptoms associated with tobacco use make quitting extraordinarily difficult. A variety of smoking cessation techniques have been developed that rely on psychological principles, but they tend to be effective only over the short term. For example, some programs use learning principles to "punish" tobacco use and encourage users to replace positive associations with negative ones. These programs often prove effective initially, but in the long run the vast majority of smokers return to the habit (Schelling, 1992). In the words of Mark Twain: "To cease smoking is the easiest thing I ever did; I ought to know because I've done it a thousand times."

But the news is not all bad. There has been a significant drop in the percentage of people who smoke in the United States and Canada, especially over the past two or three decades. In the mid-1960s, for example, a little over 40% of people in the United States smoked; by 1990, that percentage had dropped to about 25%. More and more people are quitting—although often only after many relapses. Perhaps more significantly, large numbers of people are choosing never to start.

Eat Right: The Value of Proper Nutrition

In Chapter 11 we dealt with the adaptive problem of how to motivate eating behavior. Obviously, to maintain proper functioning of body and mind, people need to consume the necessary amounts of food. In our earlier discussion of eating, we didn't pay too much attention to the *quality* of the food that people consume; instead, our concern was mainly with the internal and external factors that underlie the *motivation* to eat. But proper nutrition is vitally important in maintaining a healthful body and mind, and health psychologists are engaged in a vigorous campaign to improve people's dietary habits.

The dietary habits of most North Americans leave much to be desired. Our diet tends to be too high in calories, fat, cholesterol, sugar, protein, and salt (Sheridan & Radmacher, 1992). High-fat diets have been linked to heart disease, stroke, and several kinds of cancer, as well as to obesity. Diets that are high in cholesterol contribute to heart disease because the cholesterol can lodge in the walls of arteries, leading to a hardening and narrowing that restricts blood flow. Of course, not everyone who maintains a diet high in fat or cholesterol will develop these problems (because genetic predispositions are also a factor) but there's no question that many people eat themselves into an early grave.

Given the overwhelming amount of evidence linking diet to health, why don't people eat better? For many people, it's not the amount of food they eat but their choice of food that creates the problems. Consider the following: A potato that is baked has 0.5% of its calories as fat; when that same potato is french fried, it has 42% of its calories as fat (Winikoff, 1983). Everyone has a handy list of reasons for choosing to stop for fast food, including the fact that it tastes good. But from a nutritional standpoint, fast foods tend to come up short because they're packed with fat and sodium. The best advice is to eat a variety of foods and to avoid foods with too much fat, cholesterol, sugar, and sodium. This is not a new message for you, I'm sure, but remember: You're now much more sophisticated about the psychological factors that influence your choice of foods (see Chapter 11). So think before you eat—it might make a difference.

Do you think there's a connection between age and the likelihood of living a healthful lifestyle? If so, why do you think this is the case?

Fast food may be tasty and easy to acquire, but it comes up short from a nutritional perspective.

Avoid Risky Behavior: Protect Yourself from Disease

Choosing a healthful lifestyle requires having the right kind of information about how to prevent health-impairing habits. Health psychologists often distinguish among three main types of prevention programs (Winett, 1995):

1. *Primary prevention* is designed to educate the public as a whole in ways to reduce or eliminate a problem before it starts. Teaching children about the potential hazards of smoking or drug use is an example of primary prevention.
2. *Secondary prevention* involves the early identification of risk factors in specific population groups, such as checking for HIV infection in intravenous drug users or looking for early signs of disease through screening.
3. *Tertiary prevention* seeks to handle and contain an illness or habit once it has been acquired.

All three types of prevention programs are needed, but stopping an illness or habit before it starts—primary prevention—obviously has greater long-term significance.

AIDS. Living in the age of **AIDS** (acquired immune deficiency syndrome) dramatically underscores the need for primary prevention programs. As you probably know, AIDS is an infectious disease that involves a gradual weakening and disabling of the immune system. AIDS is "acquired," meaning that it's not a by-product of the genetic code, and it's thought to develop as a result of infection with the *human immunodeficiency virus* (HIV). HIV does its damage by attacking cells in the immune system, which leaves the body unable to fight off "opportunistic" infections that would otherwise be controlled. The disease AIDS is diagnosed in the latter stages of HIV infection when the immune system has been sufficiently compromised.

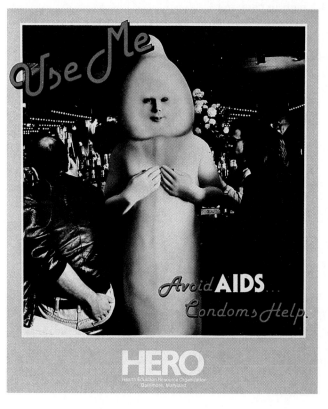

Primary prevention is crucial in battling the AIDS epidemic.

Because infection with HIV, as far as we know, ultimately leads to AIDS and death, it's crucial that all three types of prevention programs be initiated, with special emphasis on primary prevention. Fortunately, infection with HIV is preventable when the proper steps are taken to control its transmission. HIV is transmitted through contact with bodily fluids, particularly blood and semen. The virus is found in saliva, urine, and tears, but the amount is so small that infection through casual contact—even kissing—is extremely unlikely. The most likely means of transmission is through sexual contact or the sharing of intravenous needles with someone infected with the virus. The use of latex condoms during sexual activity dramatically reduces the chances of infection.

Although AIDS and HIV infection are medical conditions, psychologists have two important roles to play. First, the only effective way to control widespread HIV transmission is to prevent risk-taking behavior. The public needs to be educated about how HIV spreads, and the many misconceptions that currently exist need to be countered. For example, there are still people who are convinced that AIDS is just a homosexual problem, despite the fact that the disease can be—and is being—readily transmitted through heterosexual contact. Indeed, in most parts of the world unprotected heterosexual contact is primarily responsible for spreading the virus. The other key role that psychologists are playing in the AIDS epidemic is a therapeutic one. Once infected, people with HIV are subjected to an overwhelming amount of stress. Not only are these individuals faced with the prospects of an early death, but they must face the stigma that often accompanies the disease. Psychologists are actively involved in the establishment of treatment programs that can help AIDS patients cope with their disease (Chesney, 1993).

▶ SOLVING THE PROBLEMS: A SUMMARY

The close relationship that exists between thoughts and emotions and the physical reactions of the body means that understanding and promoting physical health requires some attention to psychological factors. As mentioned at the beginning of the chapter, health psychology is part of a broader movement, called behavioral medicine, that is seeking to understand the medical consequences of the interaction between body and mind. Health psychologists, in particular, are interested in the psychological and environmental factors—everything from personality characteristics to the work environment—that both produce illness and affect the likelihood of recovery.

EXPERIENCING STRESS Stress has historically been a somewhat tough concept to define. It can be conceived of as a stimulus, as a response, or as a process through which external events are interpreted as threatening or demanding. We chose to treat stress as the physical and psychological reaction that is shown in response to demanding situations. The stress response is often treated as an extended reaction that occurs in phases. According to the general adaptation syndrome proposed by Hans Selye, the body initially reacts to threat with a highly adaptive fight-or-flight response; if the threat continues, the body goes through resistance and exhaustion phases that make it vulnerable to disease.

People's reactions are critically influenced by the way they perceive or appraise a situation. To experience stress, it's necessary to both perceive a threat and feel that you lack the necessary resources to deal with it effectively. This means that identical environmental events can lead to quite different stress reactions, depending on how the situation is interpreted. Overall, however, it is possible to identify some common sources of stress. External sources of stress include significant life events, daily hassles, and environmental factors such as noise and crowding. Internal sources of stress include perceived control—how much influence people feel they have over the situation—as well as explanatory style.

Certain personality characteristics have been linked to stress. Type A individuals—those who are hard driving, ambitious, and impatient—appear to be at increased risk for subsequent heart disease. The Type A behavior pattern is complex, however, and researchers are in the process of trying to determine which of the many components of this personality "type" contribute most to the onset of disease.

REACTING TO PROLONGED STRESS Stress is an adaptive reaction to threat, but if the threat is extended over time, both body and mind can start to break down. Stress has been implicated in a wide variety of health problems, ranging from heart disease to the common cold. A number of studies have shown that prolonged stress can affect immune functioning, which is the body's method for fighting off disease. Stress can compromise the immune response by either lowering the number of specialized white blood cells (lymphocytes) or by somehow suppressing the response of those lymphocytes to foreign substances that have invaded the body.

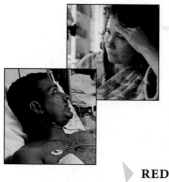

Two chronic psychological consequences of prolonged stress are posttraumatic stress disorder and burnout. Posttraumatic stress disorder results from exposure to extreme trauma, such as that experienced during battle or as a result of a physical assault such as rape. The symptoms of the disorder include flashbacks in which the traumatic event is reexperienced, avoidance of stimuli associated with the trauma, and chronic arousal problems. Burnout is a term that psychologists use to describe a state of physical, emotional, and mental exhaustion that sometimes develops after prolonged stress.

▶ **REDUCING AND COPING WITH STRESS** The term *coping* describes efforts to manage conditions of threat or demand that tax one's resources. Effective coping techniques include relaxation training, the use of social support, and reappraisal. The stress response is incompatible with relaxation, and relaxation training can help lower components of the stress response (such as blood pressure and heart rate). In progressive relaxation training, the client is taught to concentrate on specific muscle groups in the body, note whether they seem tense, and then relax those specific groups. Sometimes it's useful to provide biofeedback as well.

Additional evidence indicates that social support—the resources received from other people—can also help individuals cope effectively with stress. Friends and family help people maintain a healthful lifestyle, boost confidence, or simply provide an avenue for individuals to open up and express their feelings. Talking about things and confiding in others really seem to help people deal with stress. Finally, because stress depends on how people interpret the threatening or demanding situation, it can often be managed effectively through cognitive reappraisal. People can be taught to reinterpret significant life events or daily hassles in a less stressful way. Some stress management programs encourage clients to keep daily stress records. By identifying the kinds of situations that create stress, as well as the negative thoughts those situations induce, people become better prepared to reinterpret those situations and thoughts in a more adaptive manner.

▶ **LIVING A HEALTHFUL LIFESTYLE** Aerobic exercise is one example of an activity that can have a substantial effect on physical and psychological health. Regular exercise improves mood and makes people more resistant to the effects of stressors. Another lifestyle choice that directly affects physical health is the decision not to smoke. Smoking and other tobacco use contribute to hundreds of thousands of deaths annually in the United States alone, from associated heart disease, cancer, stroke, and emphysema. Tobacco use stimulates activity in the central nervous system, which is immediately reinforcing, but prolonged use leads to addiction or dependence that can be difficult to overcome.

Proper nutrition is another important ingredient in maintaining a healthy body and mind. The North American diet tends to be too high in calories, fat, cholesterol, sugar, protein, and salt. Poor dietary habits can lead to significant long-term health problems. Finally, maintaining a healthful lifestyle includes avoiding risky behaviors and preventing disease. For example, psychologists are playing an important role in the AIDS epidemic by educating the public about risky behavior, and through the establishment of treatment programs they are helping AIDS patients cope with the psychological effects of the disease.

Terms to Remember

health psychology The study of how biological, psychological, environmental, and cultural factors are involved in physical health and the prevention of illness.

EXPERIENCING STRESS:
STRESSORS AND THE STRESS RESPONSE

stress People's physical and psychological reactions to demanding situations.

stressors The demanding or threatening situations that produce stress.

general adaptation syndrome (GAS) Hans Selye's model of stress as a general, nonspecific reaction that occurs in three phases: alarm reaction, resistance, and exhaustion.

cognitive appraisal The idea that in order to feel stress one needs to perceive a threat and come to the conclusion that one may not have adequate resources to deal with the threat.

environmental psychology A specialty area in psychology devoted to the study of environmental effects on behavior and health, such as the effects of crowding or noise.

perceived control The amount of influence you feel you have over a situation and your reaction to it.

Type A An enduring pattern of behavior linked to stress-related health disorders; it is characterized by being hard driving, ambitious, easily annoyed, and impatient.

Type B People who lack the Type A traits—they put themselves under less pressure and appear more relaxed.

REACTING TO PROLONGED STRESS:
PHYSICAL AND PSYCHOLOGICAL EFFECTS

lymphocytes Specialized white blood cells that have the job of attacking foreign substances, such as viruses and bacteria.

posttraumatic stress disorder A trauma-based anxiety disorder characterized by flashbacks, avoidance of stimuli associated with the traumatic event, and chronic arousal symptoms.

burnout A state of physical, emotional, and mental exhaustion created by long-term involvement in an emotionally demanding situation.

REDUCING AND COPING WITH STRESS:
TECHNIQUES OF STRESS MANAGEMENT

coping Efforts to manage or master conditions of threat or demand that tax one's resources.

biofeedback Specific physiological feedback that people are given about the effectiveness of their relaxation efforts.

social support The resources that individuals receive from other people or groups, often in the form of comfort, caring, or help.

LIVING A HEALTHFUL LIFESTYLE

aerobic exercise High-intensity activities that increase both heart rate and oxygen consumption, such as running and swimming.

AIDS Acquired immune deficiency syndrome, a disease that gradually weakens and disables the immune system.

It's easy to see the adaptive value of the basic stress response. When faced with a threat, such as the sudden appearance of a stranger with a gun, people need to mobilize and direct their resources in preparation for the fight-or-flight response. The brain directs the release of hormones that energize the body—heart and respiration rate increase, blood begins to flow to the muscles, the pupils in the eyes even dilate for better distance vision. In response to the threat, people prepare themselves for immediate defensive or evasive action. But what about the link between stress and the immune response? We've seen that one of the by-products of stress is *suppression* of the immune response. If prolonged, this suppression can lead to long-lasting negative health consequences. How, then, can suppression of the immune response be considered adaptive?

We can answer this question, in part, by considering the many components of the overall immune response. As you know, the immune system is the body's defense system; it defends people not only against disease but also against injury. If the body is cut or damaged in some way, part of the immune response is to promote swelling or inflammation around the injured site. Swelling helps prevent the spread of disease-producing organisms and is an important part of the tissue repair process. But this healing process takes energy resources from the body. In a time of threat, it's probably better that these resources be directed toward the muscles. When you have a desperate need to fight or flee, it may well be quite adaptive to delay the healing process by temporarily suppressing the immune response (Maier, Watkins, & Fleshner, 1994).

Another component of the immune response, called the *acute response phase,* produces general defensive reactions that affect the entire body. For example, when there is a widespread infection in the body, part of the acute response phase is the production of fever. Fever is an adaptive part of the

immune response because the increased temperature in the body slows the spread of foreign substances, accelerates healing, and increases the rate at which immune cells are produced. But fever dramatically taxes the body's resources: a 1-degree increase in body temperature may require as much as a 7–13% increase in energy production. So when the body is faced with a threat, one demanding a fight-or-flight reaction, it's actually adaptive to delay or suppress the immune response.

Anticipating the Threat Through Conditioning

In Chapter 7, we discussed the adaptive value of conditioning. Through classical conditioning, for example, people learn about the signaling properties of events, which makes it possible to predict when significant events will occur. If you're walking home alone late at night and see a shadowy figure emerge from an alleyway, you feel stress because you've learned that those kinds of situations can signal something threatening. The ability to anticipate the threat, and energize your body accordingly, makes it more likely that you'll be able to defend yourself if the need does arise.

It turns out that the body's immune response can also be affected by conditioning. Signals that predict the appearance of a significant threat lead not only to stress-related arousal but also to conditioned suppression of the immune response. This kind of conditioning of the immune response was first demonstrated by Robert Ader and Nicholas Cohen (1975) in a series of experiments using rats. Actually, a bit of accidental discovery was involved in the original research. Robert Ader started out simply to investigate how rats learn to avoid certain tastes that signal gastrointestinal upset. In his experiments, thirsty rats were first allowed to drink water sweetened with saccharin and then were injected with a drug, called cyclophosphamide (CY), that made them sick. Because of the experience, not surprisingly, the rats were somewhat reluctant

to consume any more of this sweetened water. But to Ader's surprise, they also began to die at a significantly increased rate.

Ader and Cohen (1975) surmised that the increased death rate might be due to a learned suppression of the immune response. Reexposure to the saccharin-flavored water during testing could have caused the rats to suppress their immune systems, in anticipation of more illness, which then increased their susceptibility to disease-producing organisms in the environment. Ader and Cohen based their reasoning on the fact that the drug CY, in addition to producing gastrointestinal upset, also acts as an immunosuppressant (something that suppresses the immune system). They hypothesized that the pairing of the saccharin with the CY injection resulted in suppression of the immune system as a conditioned response. To test their reasoning, they designed an experiment like the one shown in Figure 16.7.

The experiment actually contained a number of groups of rats, but we'll concentrate on only three: a conditioned group, a nonconditioned group, and a placebo control. On the first day of the experiment, the rats in the *conditioned* group were given saccharin-flavored water and a short time later were injected with the immunosuppressant CY. The *nonconditioned* group was also injected with CY, but after drinking plain water. The *placebo* control animals drank water, like the nonconditioned group, but were injected with distilled water (which produces neither illness nor immune suppression) instead of CY. After allowing the animals two days to recover, on the fourth day two things happened: (1) All animals were injected with a foreign substance—sheep red blood cells—which under normal conditions should produce a strong immune system reaction, and (2) the animals in the conditioned and nonconditioned groups were given saccharin to drink.

Ader and Cohen (1975) were primarily interested in the following question: What kind of immune response

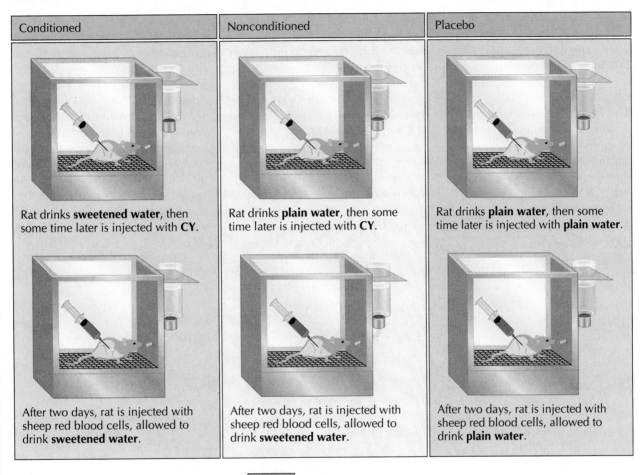

Conditioned	Nonconditioned	Placebo
Rat drinks **sweetened water**, then some time later is injected with **CY**.	Rat drinks **plain water**, then some time later is injected with **CY**.	Rat drinks **plain water**, then some time later is injected with **plain water**.
After two days, rat is injected with sheep red blood cells, allowed to drink **sweetened water**.	After two days, rat is injected with sheep red blood cells, allowed to drink **sweetened water**.	After two days, rat is injected with sheep red blood cells, allowed to drink **plain water**.

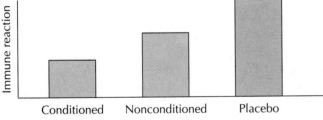

FIGURE 16.7

Learned Suppression of the Immune Response. Ader and Cohen (1975) discovered that environmental stimuli, such as saccharin-flavored water, could acquire the ability to suppress the immune reactions of rats. After drinking sweetened water that had earlier been paired with an illness-producing drug, rats in the conditioned group showed less of an immune reaction to injected sheep red blood cells than did rats in a nonconditioned or placebo group.

will the different groups of rats show to the sheep red blood cells? If the animals in the conditioned group learned to associate the saccharin with CY, because they were paired together, then drinking saccharin on the fourth day should have suppressed their immune systems as a kind of conditioned response. But no such suppression should have occurred in the other two groups, as these animals never received a pairing of saccharin with CY. To measure the strength of the immune response, blood was taken from each of the animals and analyzed. As expected, the rats in both the placebo and nonconditioned groups showed a strong immune reaction to the sheep cells, although the reaction in the

placebo animals was slightly stronger (remember, the placebo animals were never injected with the CY). The critical finding was that the conditioned animals, who had received a pairing of saccharin with the CY, showed significantly lower immune reactions than either of the other two groups. Drinking saccharin on the fourth day, even though it was not followed again by CY, was apparently sufficient to lower the immune reaction. Through learning, the saccharin had acquired the properties of an immunosuppressant.

Practical Applications

The finding that previously neutral stimuli, such as saccharin, can acquire the properties of immunosuppressants has some potentially important practical applications. In certain medical procedures, such as organ transplants, it is sometimes useful to suppress the immune system temporarily to delay organ rejection. But immunosuppressant drugs are usually quite toxic to the body, so it might be possible to use conditioned immunosuppressants, which are not naturally toxic, to reduce the immune response in a safer way (Grochowitz and others, 1991).

Conditioning of the immune response has also proven relevant to cancer treatments such as chemotherapy. Cancer patients undergo chemotherapy to inhibit the rapid replication and spread of cancer cells. But chemotherapy also produces a suppression of the immune system (in fact, the drug CY is often used in chemotherapy). Researchers have discovered that people who receive these drugs sometimes develop conditioned immune suppression responses to the place where the chemotherapy is administered. Simply arriving at the hospital has been found to suppress the immune system, presumably because an association has formed between the hospital and receiving the chemotherapy drugs (Bøvjberg and others, 1990).

Glossary

absolute threshold The level of intensity that lifts a stimulus over the threshold of conscious awareness; it's usually defined as the intensity level at which people can detect the presence of the stimulus 50% of the time.

accommodation The process through which people change or modify existing schemata to "accommodate" new experiences when they occur; also, in vision, the process through which the lens changes its shape temporarily in order to help focus light on the retina.

acetylcholine A neurotransmitter that plays several roles in the central and peripheral nervous systems, including the excitation of muscle contractions.

achievement motive An internal drive or need for achievement that is possessed by all individuals to varying degrees. Whether people will work for success on any given task depends on (1) their expectations about whether they will be successful, and (2) how much they value succeeding at the task.

achievement tests Psychological tests that measure a person's current level of knowledge or competence in a particular subject.

action potential The "all-or-none" electrical signal that travels down a neuron's axon.

activation-synthesis hypothesis The idea that dreams represent the brain's attempt to make sense out of the random patterns of neural activity during sleep.

adaptation. *See* sensory adaptation

adaptive mind A term referring to the fact that people use their brains in purposive ways, adjusting their thoughts and actions, often in a flexible and strategic manner, to meet the needs of new conditions as they arise.

aerobic exercise High-intensity activities that increase both heart rate and oxygen consumption, such as running and swimming.

agoraphobia An anxiety disorder that causes an individual to restrict his or her normal activities; someone suffering from agoraphobia tends to avoid public places out of fear that a panic attack will occur.

AIDS Acquired immune deficiency syndrome, a disease that gradually weakens and disables the immune system.

algorithms Step-by-step rules or procedures that, if applied correctly, guarantee a problem solution.

alpha waves The pattern of brain activity observed in someone who is in a relaxed state.

amnesia Forgetting that is caused by physical problems in the brain, such as those induced by injury or disease.

anal stage Freud's second stage of psychosexual development, occurring in the second year of life; in this stage, pleasure is derived from the processes of defecation.

analogies. *See* searching for analogies

anorexia nervosa An eating disorder diagnosed when an otherwise healthy person refuses to maintain a normal weight level because of an intense fear of being overweight.

antianxiety drugs Medications that reduce tension and anxiety. Many work on the inhibitory neurotransmitter GABA.

antidepressant drugs Medications that modulate the availability or effectiveness of the neurotransmitters implicated in mood disorders. Prozac, for example, increases the action of the neurotransmitter serotonin.

antipsychotic drugs Medications that reduce the positive symptoms of schizophrenia; the majority act on the neurotransmitter dopamine.

antisocial personality disorder A personality disorder characterized by little, if any, respect for social laws, customs, or norms.

anxiety disorders A class of disorders marked by excessive apprehension and worry that in turn impairs normal functioning.

applied psychologists Psychologists who attempt to extend the principles of scientific psychology to practical, everyday problems in the world. Applied psychologists might work in schools, helping students or teachers perform well, or in industry, helping to improve employee morale or training.

aptitude tests Psychological tests that measure the ability to learn or acquire knowledge in a particular subject.

assimilation The process through which people fit—or assimilate—new experiences into existing schemata.

attachments Strong emotional ties formed to one or more intimate companions.

attention The internal processes that people use to set priorities for mental functioning.

attention-deficit disorder A psychological condition, occurring most often in children, marked by difficulties in concentrating or in sustaining attention for extended periods.

attitude A positive or negative evaluation or belief held about something, which in turn may affect one's behavior; attitudes are typically broken down into cognitive, affective, and behavioral components.

attributions The inference processes people use to assign cause and effect to behavior.

automaticity Fast and effortless processing that requires little or no focused attention.

autonomic system The collection of nerves that control the more automatic needs of the body, such as heart rate, digestion, blood pressure, and so on; part of the peripheral nervous system.

availability heuristic The tendency to base estimates on the ease with which examples come to mind. For example, if you've just heard about a plane crash, your estimates of the likelihood of plane crashes increases because "plane crashes" easily come to mind.

aversion therapy A treatment for replacing a positive reaction to a harmful stimulus, such as alcohol, with something negative, such as feeling nauseous.

axon The long tail-like part of a neuron that serves as the cell's transmitter device.

basic-level categories The levels in a category hierarchy that provide the most useful and predictive information; the "basic level" usually resides at an intermediate level in a category hierarchy.

basilar membrane A flexible membrane running through the cochlea that, through its movement, displaces the auditory receptor cells, called hair cells.

behavior Overt actions such as moving, talking, gesturing, and so on; can also refer to the activities of cells, as measured through physiological recording devices, and to thoughts and feelings, as measured through oral and written expression.

behavioral therapies Treatments designed to change behavior, through the use of established learning techniques, rather than to change thoughts, beliefs, or memories.

behaviorism A school of psychology holding that the proper subject matter of psychology is overt behavior, and the situations that lead to changes in behavior, rather than immediate conscious experience.

Big Five The five dimensions of personality—extroversion, agreeableness, conscientiousness, neuroticism, and openness—that have been isolated through the application of factor analysis; it is widely believed that virtually all personality terms in language can be accounted for by appealing to one of these basic dimensions.

binocular disparity The spatial differences between the images in the two eyes; it's thought to provide an important cue for depth perception.

biofeedback Specific physiological feedback that people are given about the effectiveness of their relaxation efforts.

biological clocks Brain structures that schedule rhythmic variations in bodily functions by triggering them at the appropriate times.

biomedical therapies Biologically based treatments for reducing or eliminating the symptoms of psychological disorders; they include drug therapies, "shock" treatments, and in some cases, psychosurgery.

bipolar disorder A type of mood disorder in which the person experiences disordered mood shifts in two directions—from depression to a manic state.

blind spot The point where the optic nerve leaves the back of the eye.

brightness The aspect of the visual experience that changes with light intensity; in general, as the intensity of light increases, so does its perceived brightness.

bulimia nervosa An eating disorder in which the principal symptom is binge eating (consuming large quantities of food) followed by purging, in which the person voluntarily vomits or uses laxatives to prevent weight gain.

burnout A state of physical, emotional, and mental exhaustion created by long-term involvement in an emotionally demanding situation.

bystander effect The reluctance to come to the aid of a person in need when other people are present.

Cannon-Bard theory A theory of emotion that argues that body reactions and subjective experiences occur together, but independently.

cardinal traits Allport's term to describe personality traits that dominate an individual's life, such as a passion to serve others or to accumulate wealth.

case study A descriptive research technique in which the research effort is focused on a single case, usually an individual.

catalepsy A hypnotically induced behavior characterized by an ability to hold one or more limbs of the body in a rigid position for long periods without tiring.

category A class of objects (people, places, or things) that most people agree belong together.

category exemplars Specific examples of category members that are stored in long-term memory.

central nervous system The brain and the spinal cord.

central traits Allport's term to describe the five to ten traits that you would use to describe someone you know—friendly, trustworthy, and so on.

cerebellum A hindbrain structure at the base of the brain that is involved in the coordination of complex motor skills.

cerebral cortex The outer layer of the brain, considered to be the seat of higher mental processes.

chemoreceptors Receptor cells that react to invisible molecules scattered about in the air or dissolved in liquids, leading to the senses of smell and taste.

chunking A short-term memory strategy that involves rearranging incoming information into meaningful or familiar patterns.

circadian rhythms Biological activities that rise and fall in accordance with a 24-hour cycle.

classical conditioning A set of procedures, initially developed by Pavlov, used to investigate how organisms learn about the signaling properties of events. Classical conditioning leads to the learning of relations between events—conditioned and unconditioned stimuli—that occur outside of one's control.

client-centered therapy A form of humanistic therapy, developed by Carl Rogers, proposing that it is the client, not the therapist, who holds the key to psychological health and happiness; the therapist's role is to provide genuineness, unconditional positive regard, and empathy.

clinical psychologists Professional psychologists who specialize in the diagnosis and treatment of psychological problems; clinical psychologists often work in clinics or private practice delivering human services such as psychotherapy or counseling.

cochlea The bony, snail-shaped sound processer in the inner ear, where sounds get translated into nerve impulses.

cocktail party effect The ability to focus on one auditory message, such as a friend's conversation at a party, and ignore others; the term also refers to the tendency to notice whether one's name suddenly appears in a message one has been actively ignoring.

cognitive appraisal The idea that in order to feel stress, one needs to perceive a threat and come to the conclusion that one may not have adequate resources to deal with the threat.

cognitive-behavioral theories An approach to personality that suggests it is human experiences, and interpretations of those experiences, that determine personality growth and development.

cognitive dissonance The tension produced when people act in a way that is inconsistent with their attitudes; attitude change may occur as a result of attempting to reduce cognitive dissonance.

cognitive revolution The shift away from strict behaviorism, begun in the 1950s, characterized by renewed interest in fundamental problems of consciousness and internal mental processes.

cognitive therapies Treatments designed to remove irrational beliefs and negative thoughts that are presumed to be responsible for psychological disorders.

cold fibers Neurons that respond to a cooling of the skin by increasing the production of neural impulses.

collective unconscious The notion proposed by Carl Jung that certain kinds of universal symbols and ideas are present in the unconscious minds of all people.

companionate love A kind of emotional attachment characterized by feelings of trust and companionship; companionate love is marked by a combination of intimacy and commitment, but passion may be lacking.

computerized tomography scan (CT scan) The use of highly focused beams of X rays to construct detailed anatomical maps of the living brain.

concrete operational period Piaget's third stage of cognitive development, lasting from about ages 7 to 11. Children acquire the capacity to perform a number of mental operations, but still lack the ability for abstract reasoning.

conditioned inhibition Learning that an event signals the absence of the unconditioned stimulus.

conditioned response (CR) The acquired response that is produced to the conditioned stimulus in anticipation of the arrival of the unconditioned stimulus. Often, the conditioned response resembles the unconditioned response, although not always.

conditioned stimulus (CS) A neutral stimulus (one that does not produce the unconditioned response prior to training) that is paired with the unconditioned stimulus during classical conditioning.

conditions of worth The expectations or standards that people believe others place on them.

cones Receptor cells in the central portion of the retina that transduce light energy into neural messages; they operate best when light levels are high, and they are primarily responsible for the ability to sense color.

confidentiality The principle that all personal information obtained from a participant in research or therapy should not be revealed without the individual's permission.

conformity The tendency to comply, or go along, with the wishes of the group. When people conform, their opinions, feelings, and behaviors generally start to move toward the group norm.

confounding variable An uncontrolled variable that varies systematically with the independent variable.

conscious mind The contents of awareness—those things that occupy the focus of one's current attention.

consciousness The subjective awareness of internal and external events.

conservation The ability to recognize that the physical properties of an object remain the same despite superficial changes in the object's appearance.

constancy. *See* perceptual constancy

construct validity. *See* validity

content validity. *See* validity

conventional level In Kohlberg's theory of moral development, the stage in which actions are judged to be right or wrong, based on whether they maintain or disrupt the social order.

conversion disorder The presence of real physical problems, such as blindness or paralysis, that seem to have no identifiable physical cause.

coping Efforts to manage or master conditions of threat or demand that tax one's resources.

cornea The transparent and protective outer covering of the eye.

corpus callosum The collection of nerve fibers that connect the two cerebral hemispheres and allow information to pass from one side to the other.

correlation A statistic that indicates whether two variables are related, or vary together in a systematic way; correlation coefficients vary from -1.00 to $+1.00$.

cross-sectional design A research design in which people of different ages are compared at the same time.

crystallized intelligence The knowledge and abilities acquired as a result of experience (as from schooling and cultural influences).

CT scan. *See* computerized tomography scan

cue-dependent forgetting The idea that forgetting is caused by a failure to access the appropriate retrieval cue.

cued recall A testing condition in which subjects are given an explicit retrieval cue to help them remember.

cultural deviance A criterion of abnormality stating that a behavior is abnormal if it violates the rules or accepted standards of society.

dark adaptation The process through which the eyes adjust to dim light.

debriefing At the conclusion of an experimental session, informing the participants about the general purpose of the experiment, including any deception that was involved.

decay The idea that memories are forgotten or lost spontaneously with the passage of time.

decision making The thought processes involved in evaluating and choosing from among a set of alternatives; it usually involves some kind of risk.

deep structure The underlying representation of meaning in a sentence.

defense mechanisms According to Freud, unconscious processes that the ego uses to ward off the anxiety that comes from confrontation, usually with the demands of the id.

defining features The set of features that are necessary to make objects acceptable members of a category (for example, to be a "bird," the object must have wings and feathers, must fly, and so on).

delta activity The pattern of brain activity observed in stage 3 and stage 4 sleep; it's characterized by synchronized slow waves. Also called slow-wave sleep.

dementia Physically based losses in mental functioning.

dendrites The branchlike fibers that extend outward from a neuron and receive information from other neurons.

dependent personality disorder A personality disorder characterized by an excessive and persistent need to be taken care of by others.

dependent variable The behavior that is measured or observed in an experiment.

depolarization The change in a neuron's electrical potential from negative toward zero; depolarization usually occurs when positive ions flow into the cell as a result of neural communication.

depressants A class of drugs that slow or depress the ongoing activity of the central nervous system.

descriptive research The tactics and methods that underlie the direct observation and description of behavior.

descriptive statistics Mathematical techniques that help researchers describe their data.

development The age-related physical, intellectual, social, and personal changes that occur throughout an individual's lifetime.

deviation IQ An intelligence "score" that is derived from determining where an individual's performance sits in an age-based distribution of test scores.

diagnostic labeling effects The fact that labels for psychological problems can become self-fulfilling prophecies; the label may make it difficult to recognize normal behavior when it occurs, and it may actually increase the likelihood that a person will act in an abnormal way.

dichotic listening A technique in which different auditory messages are presented separately and simultaneously to each ear. Usually the subject's task is to shadow, or repeat aloud, one of the messages while ignoring the other.

difference threshold The smallest difference in the magnitude of two stimuli that an observer can detect.

diffusion of responsibility The idea that when people know, or think, that others are present in a situation, they allow their sense of responsibility for action to diffuse, or spread out widely, among those who are present.

discrimination. *See* stimulus discrimination

discriminative stimulus The stimulus situation that "sets the occasion" for a response to be followed by reinforcement or punishment.

dissociative amnesia A psychological disorder characterized by an inability to remember important personal information.

dissociative disorders A class of disorders characterized by the separation, or dissociation, of conscious awareness from previous thoughts or memories.

dissociative fugue A loss of personal identity that is often accompanied by a flight from home.

dissociative identity disorder A condition in which an individual alternates among what appear to be two or more distinct identities or personalities. Also known as *multiple personality disorder.*

distinctiveness A term used to refer to how well initial encoding processes have differentiated the to-be-remembered information from other things in memory.

distributed practice Spacing the repetitions of to-be-remembered information over time.

dopamine A neurotransmitter that often leads to inhibitory effects; decreased levels have been linked to Parkinson's disease, and increased levels have been linked to schizophrenia.

double-blind study An experimental design in which neither the participants nor the research observers are aware of who has been assigned to the experimental and control groups; it's used to control for both subject and experimenter expectancies.

dream analysis A technique used in psychoanalysis; Freud believed that dreams are symbolic and contain important information about the unconscious.

drive A psychological state that arises in response to an internal physiological need, such as hunger or thirst.

drug dependency A condition in which an individual experiences a physical or a psychological need for continued use of a drug.

DSM-IV The *Diagnostic and Statistical Manual of Mental Disorders* (4th ed.), which is used for the diagnosis and classification of psychological disorders. The DSM-IV is composed of five major rating dimensions, or *axes.*

dysfunction A breakdown in normal functioning; abnormal behaviors are those that prevent one from pursuing adaptive strategies.

echoic memory The system that produces and stores auditory memories.

eclectic approach The position adopted by many psychologists that it's useful to select or adopt information from many sources—one need not rely entirely on any single perspective or school of thought.

EEG. *See* electroencephalograph

ego In Freud's theory, the portion of personality that induces people to act with reason and deliberation and helps them conform to the requirements of the external world.

elaboration An encoding process that involves the formation of connections between to-be-remembered input and other information in memory.

elaboration likelihood model A model proposing two primary routes to persuasion and attitude change: a *central* route, which operates when people are motivated and focusing their attention on the message, and a *peripheral* route, which operates when people are either unmotivated to process the message or are unable to do so.

electroconvulsive therapy (ECT) A treatment used primarily for depression in which a brief electric current is delivered to the brain.

electroencephalograph (EEG) A device used to monitor the gross electrical activity of the brain.

embryonic period The period of prenatal development lasting from implantation to the end of the eighth week; during this period the human develops from an unrecognizable mass of cells to a somewhat familiar creature.

emotional distress A criterion of abnormality stating that abnormal behaviors are those that lead to personal distress or emotional upset.

emotions Psychological events involving (1) a physiological reaction, usually arousal; (2) some kind of expressive reaction, such as a distinctive facial expression; and (3) some kind of subjective experience, such as the conscious feeling of being happy or sad.

empiricism The idea that knowledge arises directly from experience.

encoding The processes that determine and control the acquisition of memories.

encoding specificity principle The idea that specific encoding processes determine which retrieval cues will be effective in aiding later memory.

endocrine system A network of glands that uses the bloodstream, rather than neurons, to send chemical messages that regulate growth and other internal functions.

endorphins Morphine-like chemicals that act as the brain's natural pain-killers.

environmental psychology A specialty area in psychology devoted to the study of environmental effects on behavior and health, such as the effects of crowding or noise.

episodic memory Memories for particular events, or episodes, that happened to one personally, such as remembering what one ate for breakfast this morning, or where one went on vacation last year.

excitement phase The first component of the human sexual response cycle, as described by Masters and Johnson. It's characterized by changes in muscle tension, increased heart rate and blood pressure, and a rushing of blood into the genital organs. In men, the penis becomes erect; in women, the vaginal walls become lubricated.

experimental research A technique in which the investigator actively manipulates or alters some aspect of the environment (defined broadly) in order to observe the effect of the manipulation on behavior.

explicit memory Conscious, willful remembering.

external attribution Attributing the cause of a person's behavior to an external event or situation in the environment.

external validity The extent to which the results of an observation generalize to other situations, or are representative of real life.

extinction Presenting a conditioned stimulus repeatedly without the unconditioned stimulus, resulting in a loss in responding.

facial-feedback hypothesis The proposal that muscles in the face deliver signals to the brain that are then interpreted, depending on the pattern, as a subjective emotional state.

factor analysis A statistical procedure developed by Charles Spearman that groups together related items on tests by analyzing the correlations among test scores. It's often used by psychologists to determine underlying common "factors," or abilities.

family resemblance The core features that category members share; a given member of the category may have some, but not necessarily all, of these features.

feature detectors Cells in the visual cortex that respond to very specific visual events, such as bars of light at particular orientations.

fetal period The period of prenatal development lasting from the ninth week until birth, during which the fetus develops functioning organ systems and increases are seen in body size and in the size and complexity of brain tissue.

fixed-interval schedule A schedule in which the reinforcement is delivered for the first response that occurs following a fixed interval of time.

fixed-ratio schedule A schedule in which the number of responses required for reinforcement doesn't change from trial to trial.

flashbulb memories Rich memory records of the circumstances surrounding emotionally significant and surprising events.

flavor A psychological term used to describe the gustatory experience. Flavor is influenced by taste, smell, and the visual appearance of food, as well as by expectations about the food's quality.

fluid intelligence The natural ability to solve problems, reason, and remember; fluid intelligence is thought to be relatively uninfluenced by experience.

forebrain The outer portion of the brain, including the cerebral cortex and the structures of the limbic system.

forgetting The loss in accessibility of previously stored material.

formal operational period Piaget's last stage of cognitive development; thought processes become adultlike, and the individual gains mastery over abstract thinking.

fovea The "central pit" area in the retina where the cone receptors are located.

framing The way in which the alternatives in a decision-making situation are structured.

free association A technique used in psychoanalysis to explore the contents of the unconscious; patients are asked to relax and freely express whatever thoughts and feelings happen to come into their minds.

free recall A testing condition in which a person is asked to remember information without explicit retrieval cues.

frequency principle The idea that pitch perception is determined partly by the frequency of neural impulses traveling up the auditory pathway.

frontal lobe One of four anatomical regions of each hemisphere of the cerebral cortex, located on the top front of the brain; it contains the motor cortex and may be involved in higher-level thought processes.

functional fixedness The tendency to see objects, and their functions, in certain fixed and typical ways.

functionalism An early school of psychology that suggested the proper route to understanding immediate conscious experience and behavior lies in analyzing their function and purpose.

fundamental attribution error The fact that people seeking to interpret someone else's behavior tend to overestimate the influence of internal personal factors and underestimate the role of situational factors.

g (general intelligence) According to Spearman, a general factor, derived from factor analysis, that underlies or contributes to performance on a variety of mental tests.

gate-control theory The idea that neural impulses generated by pain receptors can be blocked, or gated, in the spinal cord by signals produced in the brain.

gender roles Specific patterns of behavior that are consistent with how society dictates males and females should act.

gender schemas The organized sets of beliefs and perceptions held about men and women.

general adaptation syndrome (GAS) Hans Selye's model of stress as a general, nonspecific reaction that occurs in three phases: alarm reaction, resistance, and exhaustion.

generalizations. *See* stimulus generalization

generalized anxiety disorder Excessive worrying, or "free-floating" anxiety, that lasts for at least six months and that cannot be attributed to any single identifiable source.

genes Segments of chromosomes that contain instructions for influencing and creating particular hereditary characteristics.

genital stage Freud's final stage of psychosexual development, during which one develops mature sexual relationships with members of the opposite sex.

genotype The actual genetic information inherited from one's parents.

germinal period The period in prenatal development from conception to implantation of the fertilized egg in the wall of the uterus.

Gestalt principles of organization The organizing principles of perception proposed by the Gestalt psychologists. These principles include the laws of proximity, similarity, closure, continuation, and common fate.

gifted A label that is generally assigned to someone who scores above 130 on a standard IQ test.

glial cells Cells in the nervous system that do not transmit or receive information but that perform a variety of functions, such as removing waste, filling in empty space, or helping neurons to communicate efficiently.

glucose A kind of sugar that cells require for energy production.

grammar The rules of language that allow the communicator to combine arbitrary symbols to convey meaning; grammar includes the rules of phonology, syntax, and semantics.

group polarization The tendency for a group's dominant point of view to become stronger and more extreme with time.

groupthink The tendency for members of a group to become so interested in seeking consensus of opinion that they start to ignore and even suppress dissenting views.

gustation The sense of taste.

habituation The decline in responsiveness to an event that has become familiar through repeated exposure.

hallucinogens A class of drugs that tend to disrupt normal mental and emotional functioning, including distorting perception and altering reality.

health psychology The study of how biological, psychological, environmental, and cultural factors are involved in physical health and the prevention of illness.

heritability A mathematical index that represents the extent to which IQ differences in a particular population can be accounted for by genetic factors.

heuristics "Rules of thumb" that people use to solve problems; heuristics can usually be applied quickly, but they do not guarantee that a solution will be found.

hindbrain A "primitive" part of the brain that sits at the juncture point where the brain and spinal cord merge. Structures in the hindbrain, including the medulla, pons, and reticular formation, act as the basic life-support system for the body.

homeostasis The process through which the body maintains a steady-state, such as a constant internal temperature or an adequate amount of fluids.

hormones Chemicals released into the blood by the various endocrine glands to help control a variety of internal regulatory functions.

hue The dimension of light that produces color; hue is typically determined by the wavelength of light reflecting from an object.

humanistic psychology A movement in psychology that emerged largely as a reaction against the pessimism of Freud. Humanistic psychologists focus on people's unique capacity for choice, responsibility, and growth.

humanistic therapy Treatments designed to help clients gain insight into their fundamental self-worth and value as human beings; therapy is a process of discovering one's own unique potential.

hyperpolarization An increase in the negative electrical potential of a neuron, reducing the chances of the cell generating an action potential.

hypersomnia A chronic condition marked by excessive sleepiness.

hypnosis A form of social interaction that produces a heightened state of suggestibility in a willing participant.

hypnotic dissociation A hypnotically induced "splitting" of consciousness, during which multiple forms of awareness coexist.

hypnotic hypermnesia The supposed enhancement in memory that occurs under hypnosis; there is little, if any, evidence to support the existence of this effect.

hypochondriasis A long-lasting preoccupation with the idea that one has developed a serious disease, based on what turns out to be a misinterpretation of normal body reactions.

hypothalamus A forebrain structure thought to play a role in the regulation of various motivational activities, including eating, drinking, and sexual behavior.

iconic memory The system that produces and stores visual sensory memories.

id In Freud's theory, the portion of personality that is governed by inborn instinctual drives, particularly those related to sex and aggression.

identity. *See* personal identity

ill-defined problem Problems, such as the search for "happiness," that have no clearly stated goals, no clear starting point, and no specific mechanisms for evaluating progress.

illusions. *See* perceptual illusions

implicit memory Remembering that occurs in the absence of conscious awareness or willful intent.

incentive motivation External factors in the environment—such as money, an attractive person, or tasty food—that exert "pulling" effects on people's actions.

incongruence A discrepancy between the image people hold of themselves—their self-concept—and the sum of all their experiences.

independent variable The aspect of the environment that is manipulated in an experiment. It must consist of at least two conditions.

inferential statistics Mathematical techniques that help researchers decide whether recorded behaviors are representative of a population or whether differences among observations can be attributed to chance.

informed consent The principle that before consenting to participate in research, people should be fully informed about any significant factors that could affect their willingness to participate.

in-group A group of individuals with whom one shares features in common, or with whom one identifies.

insanity A legal term usually defined as the inability to understand that certain actions are wrong, in a legal or moral sense, at the time of a crime.

insight therapies Treatments designed to give clients self-knowledge, or insight into the contents of their thought processes, usually through one-on-one interactions with a therapist.

insomnia A chronic condition marked by difficulties in initiating or maintaining sleep, lasting for a period of at least one month.

instincts Unlearned characteristic patterns of responding that are controlled by specific triggering stimuli in the world; they are not thought to be an important factor in explaining goal-directed behavior in humans.

instrumental conditioning A procedure for studying how organisms learn about the consequences of their own voluntary actions; they learn that their behaviors are instrumental in producing rewards and punishments. Also called *operant conditioning.*

insulin A hormone released by the pancreas that helps pump nutrients in the blood into the cells, where they can be stored as fat or metabolized into needed energy.

intelligence An internal capacity or ability that psychologists assume accounts for individual differences in mental test performance. The term is also used to describe the mental processes that underlie the ability to adapt to ever-changing environments.

intelligence quotient (IQ) Originally, mental age divided by chronological age and then multiplied by 100. More recently, defined in terms of deviation from the average score on an IQ test. *See also* deviation IQ

interference. *See* proactive interference; retroactive interference

internal attribution Attributing the cause of a person's behavior to an internal personality trait or disposition.

internal validity The extent to which an experiment has effectively controlled for confounding variables; internally valid experiments allow for the determination of causality.

interneurons Neurons that make no direct contact with the world, but rather, convey information from one neuron or processing site to another.

intrinsic motivation Goal-directed behavior that seems to be entirely self-motivated.

introspection. *See* systematic introspection

iris The ring of colored tissue surrounding the pupil.

James-Lange theory A theory of emotion that argues that body reactions precede and drive the subjective experience of emotions.

kinesthesia In perception, the ability to sense the position and movement of one's body parts.

latency period Freud's period of psychosexual development, from age 5 to puberty, during which the child's sexual feelings are largely suppressed.

latent content According to Freud, the true psychological meaning of dream symbols, which represent hidden wishes and desires that are too disturbing to be expressed directly.

lateral hypothalamus A portion of the hypothalamus that, when lesioned, creates an animal that is reluctant to eat; it probably plays some role in eating behavior, but the precise role is unknown.

law of effect The idea that if a response in a particular situation is followed by a satisfying or pleasant consequence, it will be strengthened; if a response in a particular situation is followed by an unsatisfying or unpleasant consequence, it will be weakened.

learned helplessness A general sense of helplessness that is acquired when people repeatedly fail in their attempts to control their environment; learned helplessness may play a role in depression.

learning A relatively permanent change in behavior, or potential to respond, that results from experience.

lens A flexible piece of tissue that helps focus light toward the back of the eye.

light The small part of the electromagnetic spectrum that is processed by the visual system. Light is typically classified in terms of *wavelength* (the physical distance from one energy cycle to the next) and *intensity* (the amount of light falling on an object).

limbic system A system of structures thought to be involved in motivational and emotional behaviors (the amygdala) and memory (the hippocampus).

linguistic relativity hypothesis The proposal that language determines the characteristics and content of thought.

locus of control The amount of control that a person feels he or she has over the environment.

long-term memory The system used to maintain information for extended periods of time.

longitudinal design A research design in which the same people are studied or tested repeatedly over time.

lymphocytes Specialized white blood cells that have the job of attacking foreign substances, such as viruses or bacteria.

magnetic resonance imaging (MRI) A device that uses magnetic fields and radio-wave pulses to construct detailed, three-dimensional images of the brain; "functional" MRIs can be used to map changes in blood oxygen use as a function of task activity.

major depressive episode A type of mood disorder characterized by depressed mood and other symptoms.

manic state A disordered state in which the person becomes hyperactive, talkative, and has a decreased need for sleep; a person in a manic state may engage in activities that are self-destructive or dangerous.

manifest content According to Freud, the actual symbols and events experienced in a dream.

materialist identity theory The philosophical position purporting that the mind arises entirely from the physical properties of the brain.

mean The arithmetic average of a set of scores.

means-end analysis A problem-solving heuristic that involves devising actions, or means, that reduce the distance between the current starting point and the desired end (the goal state).

median The middle point in an ordered set of scores; half of the scores fall at or below the median score, and half fall at or above the median score.

medical model The view that abnormal behavior is symptomatic of an underlying "disease" that can be "cured" with the appropriate therapy.

meditation A technique for self-induced manipulation of awareness, often used for the purpose of relaxation and self-reflection.

memory The capacity to preserve and recover information.

memory span The number of items that can be recalled from short-term memory in their proper presentation order on half of the tested memory trials.

menopause The period during which a woman's menstrual cycle slows down and finally stops.

mental age The chronological age that best fits a child's level of performance on a test of mental ability. Mental age is typically calculated by comparing a child's test score with the average scores for different age groups.

mental retardation A label that is generally assigned to someone who scores below 70 on a standard IQ test.

mental sets The tendency to rely on well-established habits of perception and thought when attempting to solve problems.

meta-analysis A statistical technique used to compare findings across many different research studies; comparisons are based on some common evaluation measure, such as the difference between treatment and control conditions.

midbrain The middle portion of the brain, containing such structures as the tectum, superior colliculus, and inferior colliculus; midbrain structures serve as neural relay stations and may help coordinate reactions to sensory events.

middle ear The portion between the eardrum and the cochlea containing three small bones (the malleus, incus, and stapes) that help to intensify and prepare the sound vibrations for passage into the inner ear.

mind The contents and processes of subjective experience: sensations, thoughts, and emotions.

Minnesota Multiphasic Personality Inventory (MMPI) A widely used self-report inventory for assessing personality traits and for diagnosing psychological problems.

mnemonic devices Special mental tricks that help people think about material in ways that improve later memory. Most mnemonic devices require the use of visual imagery.

mode The most frequently occurring score in a set or distribution of scores.

modeling The natural tendency to imitate the behavior of significant others in one's surroundings.

mood disorders Prolonged and disabling disruptions in emotional state.

morality The ability to distinguish between appropriate and inappropriate actions; a child's sense of morality may be tied to his or her level of cognitive development.

morphemes The smallest units in a language that carry meaning.

motivation The set of factors that initiate and direct behavior, usually toward some goal.

motor neurons Neurons that carry information away from the central nervous system to the muscles and glands that directly produce behavioral responses.

MRI. *See* magnetic resonance imaging

multiple intelligences The notion proposed by Howard Gardner that people possess a set of separate and independent "intelligences" ranging from musical to linguistic to interpersonal ability.

multiple personality disorder. *See* dissociative identity disorder

nativism The idea that certain kinds of knowledge and ideas are innate—present at birth.

naturalistic observation A research technique that involves recording only naturally occurring behavior, as opposed to behavior produced in the laboratory.

need hierarchy The idea popularized by Maslow that human needs are prioritized in a hierarchy. Some needs, especially physiological ones, must be satisfied before others, such as the need for achievement or self-actualization, can be pursued.

negative punishment An event that, when *removed* after a response, lowers the likelihood of that response occurring again.

negative reinforcement An event that, when *removed* after a response, increases the likelihood of that response occurring again.

NEO-PI-R A self-report inventory developed to measure the Big Five personality dimensions.

nerves Bundles of axons that make up neural "transmission cables."

neurons The cells in the nervous system that receive and transmit information by generating an electrochemical signal; neurons are the basic building blocks of the nervous system.

neuroscience An interdisciplinary field of study directed at understanding the brain and its relation to behavior.

neurotransmitters Chemical messengers that relay information from one neuron to the next. They are released from the terminal buttons into the synapse, where they interact chemically with the cell membrane of the next neuron; the result is either an excitatory or an inhibitory message.

night terrors A condition in which the sleeper, usually a child, awakens suddenly in an extreme state of panic; not thought to be associated with dreaming.

nightmares Frightening and anxiety-arousing dreams that occur primarily during the REM stage of sleep.

obedience The form of compliance that occurs when people respond to the orders of an authority figure.

object permanence The ability to recognize that objects still exist when they're no longer in sight.

observation. *See* naturalistic observation

observational learning Learning that occurs as a result of observing the experiences of others. Also called *social learning.*

obsessive-compulsive disorder An anxiety disorder that manifests itself through persistent and uncontrollable thoughts, called *obsessions*, or by the compelling need to perform repetitive acts, called *compulsions.*

occipital lobe One of four anatomical regions of each hemisphere of the cerebral cortex, located at the back of the brain; visual processing is controlled here.

olfaction The sense of smell.

operant conditioning. *See* instrumental conditioning

operational definition Defining concepts in terms of how those concepts are measured.

opiates A class of drugs that reduce anxiety, lower sensitivity to pain, and elevate mood; opiates often act to depress nervous system activity.

opponent-process theory A theory of color vision proposing that cells in the visual pathway increase their activation levels to one color and decrease their activation levels to another color—for example, positive to red and negative to green.

oral stage The first stage in Freud's conception of psychosexual development, occurring in the first year of life; in this stage pleasure is derived primarily from sucking and placing things in the mouth.

orgasmic phase The third stage in the human sexual response cycle. It's characterized by rhythmic contractions in the sex organs; in men, ejaculation occurs. There is also the subjective experience of pleasure that appears to be similar for men and women.

orienting response An inborn tendency to shift one's focus of attention toward a novel or surprising event.

pacinian corpuscles A type of sensory receptor in the skin that responds most actively to pressure.

pain An adaptive response by the body to any stimulus intense enough to cause tissue damage.

panic disorder A condition marked by recurrent discrete episodes or "attacks" of extremely intense fear or dread.

paranoid personality disorder A personality disorder characterized by pervasive distrust of others.

parietal lobe One of four anatomical regions of each hemisphere of the cerebral cortex, located roughly on the top middle portion of the brain; it contains the somatosensory cortex, which controls the sense of touch.

passionate love An intense emotional state characterized by a powerful longing to be with a specific person; passionate love is marked by a combination of intimacy and passion, but commitment may be lacking.

perceived control The amount of influence you feel you have over a situation and your reaction to it.

perception The collection of processes used to arrive at a meaningful "interpretation" of sensations; through perception, the simple components of an experience are organized into a recognizable form.

perceptual constancy Perceiving the properties of an object to remain the same, even though the physical properties of the sensory message are changing.

perceptual illusions Inappropriate interpretations of physical reality. Perceptual illusions often occur as a result of the brain's using otherwise adaptive organizing principles.

peripheral nervous system The network of nerves that link the central nervous system with the rest of the body.

personal identity A sense of who one is as an individual and how well one stacks up against one's peers. Erik Erikson's theory postulates that personal identity is shaped by a series of personal crises that each person confronts at characteristic stages of development.

personality The distinguishing pattern of psychological characteristics—thinking, feeling, and behaving—that differentiates individuals from others and leads them to act consistently across situations.

personality disorders Chronic or enduring patterns of behavior that lead to significant impairments in social functioning.

person-situation debate A controversial debate centering on whether people really do behave consistently across situations.

PET. *See* positron emission tomography

phallic stage Freud's third stage of psychosexual development, lasting from about age 3 to age 5; in this stage, pleasure is gained from self-stimulation of the sexual organs.

phenotype A person's observable characteristics, such as red hair. The phenotype is controlled mainly by the genotype, but it can also be influenced by the environment.

phonemes The smallest significant sound units in speech.

phonology Rules governing how sounds should be combined to make words in a language.

pinna The external flap of tissue normally referred to as the "ear"; it helps capture sounds.

pitch The psychological experience that results from the auditory processing of a particular frequency of sound.

pituitary gland A kind of "master gland" in the body that controls the release of hormones in response to signals from the hypothalamus.

placebo An inactive, or inert, substance that resembles an experimental substance.

place theory The idea that the location of auditory receptor cells activated by movement of the basilar membrane underlies the perception of pitch.

plateau phase The second stage in the human sexual response cycle. Arousal continues to increase, although at a slower rate, toward a preorgasm "maximum" point.

polygraph test A device that measures various indices of physiological arousal in an effort to determine whether someone is telling a lie. The logic behind the test is that lying leads to greater emotionality, which can be picked up through such measures of arousal as heart rate, blood pressure, breathing rate, and sweating.

positron emission tomography (PET) A method for measuring how radioactive substances are absorbed in the brain; it can be used to detect how different tasks activate different areas of the brain.

positive punishment An event that, when *presented* after a response, lowers the likelihood of that response occurring again.

positive regard The idea that individuals value what others think of them and constantly seek others' approval, love, and companionship.

positive reinforcement An event that, when *presented* after a response, increases the likelihood of that response occurring again.

postconventional level Kohlberg's highest level of moral development, in which moral actions are judged on the basis of personal codes of ethics that are general and abstract and that may not agree with societal norms.

posttraumatic stress disorder A trauma-based anxiety disorder characterized by flashbacks, avoidance of stimuli associated with the traumatic event, and chronic arousal symptoms.

pragmatics The practical knowledge used to comprehend the intentions of a speaker and to produce an effective response.

preconscious mind The part of the mind that contains all of the inactive but potentially accessible thoughts and memories.

preconventional level In Kohlberg's theory, the lowest level of moral development, in which decisions about right and wrong are made primarily in terms of external consequences.

predictive validity. *See* validity

preoperational period Piaget's second stage of cognitive development, lasting from ages 2 to about 7; children begin to think symbolically, but often lack the ability to perform mental operations such as conservation.

primacy effect The better memory seen for items near the beginning of a memorized list.

proactive interference A process in which old memories interfere with the establishment and recovery of new memories.

procedural memory Knowledge about how to do things, such as riding a bike or swinging a golf club.

projection A defense mechanism in which unacceptable feelings or wishes are dealt with by attributing them to others.

projective tests A type of personality test in which individuals are asked to interpret unstructured or ambiguous stimuli; the idea is that subjects will "project" their true thoughts and feelings into the interpretation, thereby revealing elements of their personality.

prototype The best or most representative member of a category (such as robin for the category "bird").

psychiatrists Medical doctors who specialize in the diagnosis and treatment of psychological problems. Unlike psychologists, psychiatrists are licensed to prescribe drugs.

psychoactive drugs Drugs that affect behavior and mental processes through alterations of conscious awareness.

psychoanalysis Freud's theory of mind and his method of treatment that attempts to bring hidden impulses and memories, which are locked in the unconscious, to the surface of awareness, thereby freeing the patient from his or her disordered thoughts and behaviors.

psychodynamic theory An approach to personality development based largely on the ideas of Sigmund Freud and holding that much of behavior is governed by unconscious forces.

psychology The scientific study of behavior and mind.

psychometrics The use of psychological tests to measure the mind and mental processes.

psychophysics A field of psychology in which researchers search for ways to map the transition from the physical stimulus to the psychological experience of that stimulus.

psychosurgery Surgery that destroys or alters tissues in the brain in an effort to affect behavior.

psychotherapy Treatment designed to help people deal with mental, emotional, or behavioral problems.

puberty The period during which a person reaches sexual maturity and is potentially capable of producing offspring.

punishment Consequences that decrease the likelihood of responding in a similar way again. *See also* negative punishment; positive punishment.

pupil The "hole" in the center of the eye that allows light to enter; the size of the pupil changes with light intensity.

random assignment A technique ensuring that each participant in an experiment has an equal chance of being assigned to any of the conditions in the experiment.

random sampling A procedure for selecting a representative subset of a target population; the procedure guarantees that everyone in the population has an equal likelihood of being selected for the sample.

range The difference between the largest and smallest scores in a distribution.

rational-emotive therapy A form of cognitive therapy, developed by Albert Ellis, in which the therapist acts as a kind of cross-examiner, verbally assaulting the client's irrational thought processes.

reaction formation A defense mechanism used to transform an anxiety-producing wish into a kind of opposite—people behave in a way that counters the way they truly feel.

reactivity The extent to which an individual's behavior is changed as a consequence of being observed; the behavior becomes essentially a reaction to the process of being observed.

recency effect The better memory seen for items near the end of a memorized list.

receptive field For a given neuron in the visual system, that portion of the retina that, when stimulated, causes the activity of the neuron to change.

reciprocal determinism The idea that beliefs, behavior, and the environment interact to shape what is learned from experience.

reciprocity The tendency for people to return in kind the feelings that are shown toward them.

recognition by components The idea proposed by Biederman that people recognize objects perceptually via smaller components called *geons*.

reflexes Largely automatic body reactions—such as the knee jerk—that are controlled primarily by spinal cord pathways.

refractory period The period of time following an action potential, during which more action potentials cannot be generated.

rehearsal A strategic process that helps to maintain short-term memories indefinitely through the use of internal repetition.

reinforcement Response consequences that increase the likelihood of responding in a similar way again. *See also* negative reinforcement; positive reinforcement; schedules of reinforcement

reliability A measure of the consistency of test results; reliable tests produce similar scores or indices from one administration to the next.

REM A stage of sleep characterized by rapid eye movements and low-amplitude, irregular EEG patterns similar to those found in the waking brain. REM is typically associated with dreaming.

REM rebound The tendency to increase the proportion of time spent in REM sleep after a period of REM deprivation.

representativeness heuristic The tendency to make decisions based on an alternative's similarity, or representativeness, in relation to an ideal. For example, people decide whether a sequence is "random" based on how irregular the sequence looks.

repression A defense mechanism that individuals use, unknowingly, to push anxiety-producing thoughts, memories, and feelings out of conscious awareness.

research psychologists Psychologists who conduct experiments or collect observations in an attempt to discover the basic principles of behavior and mind. Research psychologists often work in academic settings or in private laboratories to advance the understanding of both basic and applied issues in psychology.

resistance In psychoanalysis, the patient's unconsciously motivated attempts to subvert or hinder the process of therapy.

resolution phase The fourth and final stage in the human sexual response cycle. Arousal returns to normal levels, and for men there is a refractory period, during which further stimulation fails to produce visible signs of arousal.

resting potential The tiny electrical charge in place between the inside and outside of the resting neuron.

retina The thin layer of tissue that covers the back of the eye and that contains the light-sensitive receptor cells for vision.

retrieval The processes that determine and control how memories are recovered and translated into performance.

retroactive interference A process in which the formation of new memories hurts the recovery of old memories.

rods Receptor cells, located mainly around the sides of the retina, that transduce light energy into neural messages; these visual receptors are highly sensitive and are active in dim light.

s (**specific intelligence**) According to Spearman, a specific factor, derived from factor analysis, that is unique to a particular kind of test.

sampling. *See* random sampling

schedules of reinforcement A rule that an experimenter uses to determine when particular responses will be reinforced. Schedules may be fixed or variable, ratio or interval.

schema An organized knowledge structure in long-term memory.

schemata Mental models of the world that people use to guide and interpret their experiences.

schizophrenia A class of disorders characterized by fundamental disturbances in thought processes, emotion, or behavior.

scientific method An investigative method that generates empirical knowledge—that is, knowledge derived from systematic observations of the world. It involves generating a hypothesis on the basis of observed regularities, then testing the hypothesis with further observations.

searching for analogies A problem-solving heuristic that involves trying to find a connection between the current problem and some previous problem one has solved successfully.

secondary traits The less obvious characteristics of an individual's personality that do not always appear in his or her behavior, such as testiness when on a diet.

second-order conditioning A procedure in which an established conditioned stimulus is used to condition a second neutral stimulus.

self-actualization The ingrained desire to reach one's true potential as a human being.

self-concept An organized set of perceptions that one holds about one's abilities and characteristics.

self-efficacy The beliefs that people hold about their own ability to perform a task or accomplish a goal.

self-fulfilling prophecy effect A condition in which people's expectations about the actions of another person actually lead that person to behave in the expected way.

self-monitoring The degree to which a person monitors a situation closely and changes his or her behavior accordingly; people who are high self-monitors may not behave consistently across situations.

self-perception theory The idea that people use observations of their own behavior as a basis for inferring their internal beliefs.

self-report inventories Personality tests in which people answer groups of questions about how they typically think, act, and feel; their responses, or self-reports, are then compared to average responses compiled from large groups of prior test takers.

self-serving bias The tendency to make internal attributions about one's own behavior when the outcome is positive, and to blame the situation when one's behavior leads to something negative.

semantic memory Knowledge about the world, stored as facts that make little or no reference to one's personal experiences.

semantics The rules used in language to communicate meaning.

semicircular canals A receptor system attached to the inner ear that responds to movement and acceleration and to changes in upright posture.

sensations The elementary features, or building blocks, of an experience, such as a pattern of light and dark, a bitter taste, or a change in temperature.

sensitization An increase in the tendency to respond to an event that has been repeated; sensitization is more likely when a repeated stimulus is intense.

sensorimotor period Piaget's first stage of cognitive development, lasting from birth to about 2 years of age; schemata revolve around sensory and motor abilities.

sensory adaptation The tendency of sensory systems to reduce sensitivity to a stimulus source that remains constant.

sensory memory The capacity to preserve and recover sensory information in a relatively pure, unanalyzed form; sensory memories are usually accurate representations of externally presented information and last on the order of seconds.

sensory neurons Neurons that make initial contact with the environment and carry the message inward toward the spinal cord and brain.

serotonin A neurotransmitter that has been linked to sleep, dreaming, and general arousal and may also be involved in some psychological disorders, such as depression and schizophrenia.

set point A natural body weight, perhaps produced by genetic factors, that the body seeks to maintain. When body weight falls below the set point, one is motivated to eat; when weight exceeds the set point, one feels less motivated to eat.

sexual orientation A person's sexual and emotional attraction to members of the same sex or the other sex. Homosexuality, heterosexuality, and bisexuality are all sexual orientations.

sexual scripts Learned cognitive programs that instruct individuals on how, why, and what to do in their interactions with sexual partners; the nature of sexual scripts may vary from one culture to the next.

shaping A procedure in which reinforcement is delivered for successive approximations of the desired response.

short-term memory A limited-capacity "working memory" system that holds information, after it has been analyzed, for periods usually lasting less than a minute or two. Short-term memory is the system used to temporarily store, think about, and reason with information.

signal detection A technique that can be used to determine the ability of someone to detect the presence of a stimulus.

single-blind study An experimental design in which the participants do not know to which of the conditions they have been assigned (e.g., experimental versus control); it's used to control for subject expectancies.

16 Personality Factor A self-report inventory developed by Cattell and colleagues to measure normal personality traits.

sleepwalking A condition in which the sleeper rises during sleep and wanders about; not thought to be associated with dreaming.

social cognition The study of how people use cognitive processes—such as perception, memory, thought, and emotion—to help them make sense of other people as well as themselves.

social facilitation The enhancement in performance that is sometimes found when an individual performs in the presence of others.

social influence The study of how the behaviors and thoughts of individuals are affected by the presence of others.

social interference The impairment in performance that is sometimes found when an individual performs in the presence of others.

social learning. *See* observational learning

social learning theory The idea that most important personality traits come from modeling, or copying, the behavior of others.

social loafing The tendency to put out less effort when working in a group compared to when working alone.

social psychology The discipline that studies how people think about, influence, and relate to other people.

social schemas General knowledge structures, stored in long-term memory, that relate to social experiences or people.

social support The resources that individuals receive from other people or groups, often in the form of comfort, caring, or help.

sociobiology A theory proposing that social behavior should be understood from an evolutionary/genetic perspective.

soma The cell body of a neuron.

somatic system The collection of nerves that transmits information toward the brain and connects to the skeletal muscles in order to initiate movement; part of the peripheral nervous system.

somatization disorder A long-lasting preoccupation with body symptoms that have no identifiable physical cause.

somatoform disorders Psychological disorders that focus on the physical body.

sound The physical message delivered to the auditory system; it's mechanical energy that requires a medium such as air or water in order to move.

sound localization The ability to determine where a sound is coming from in space; sound localization relies on several cues that involve comparisons between the messages received by the two ears.

specific phobic disorder A highly focused fear of a specific object or situation.

spontaneous recovery The recovery of an extinguished conditioned response after a period of nonexposure to the conditioned stimulus.

spontaneous remission Improvement in a psychological disorder without treatment—that is, simply as a function of the passage of time.

standard deviation An indication of how much individual scores differ or vary from the mean in a set of scores.

standardization Keeping the testing, scoring, and interpretation procedures similar across all administrations of a test.

statistical deviance A criterion of abnormality stating that a behavior is abnormal if it occurs infrequently among the members of a population.

stereotypes The collection of beliefs held about the personal traits and behaviors of individuals belonging to a particular group; common stereotypes include those based on gender, race, and age.

stimulants A class of drugs that increase central nervous system activity, enhancing neural transmission.

stimulus discrimination Responding differently to a new stimulus than one responds to an established conditioned stimulus.

stimulus generalization Responding to a new stimulus in a way similar to the response produced by an established conditioned stimulus.

storage The processes that determine and control how memories are stored and maintained over time.

strange-situation test Gradually subjecting a child to a stressful situation and observing his or her behavior toward the parent or caregiver. This test is used to classify children according to type of attachment—e.g., secure, resistant, or avoidant.

stress People's physical and psychological reactions to demanding situations.

stressors The demanding or threatening situations that produce stress.

structuralism An early school of psychology that argued for understanding the structure of immediate conscious experience by breaking it down into its basic constituent parts, much like a chemist might try to understand a chemical compound.

sublimation A defense mechanism used to channel unacceptable impulses into socially acceptable activities.

superego In Freud's theory, the portion of personality that motivates people to act in an ideal fashion, in accordance with the moral customs defined by parents and culture.

surface structure The literal ordering of words in a sentence.

survey A descriptive research technique designed to gather limited amounts of information from many people, usually by administering some kind of questionnaire.

synapse The junction, or small gap, between neurons, typically between the terminal buttons of one neuron and the dendrite or cell body of another neuron.

syntax Rules governing how words should be combined to form sentences.

systematic desensitization A technique that uses counterconditioning and extinction to reduce the fear and anxiety that has become associated to a particular object or event. It's a multistep process that attempts to replace the negative learned association with something relaxing.

systematic introspection An investigative technique used to study the mind that requires subjects to look inward and provide rigorous descriptions of their own subjective experiences.

taste buds The receptor cells on the tongue involved in taste.

temporal lobe One of four anatomical regions of each hemisphere of the cerebral cortex, located roughly on the sides of the brain; it's involved in certain aspects of speech and language perception.

teratogens Environmental agents—such as disease organisms—that can potentially damage the developing embryo or fetus.

terminal buttons The tiny swellings at the end of a neuron's axon that contain chemicals important to neural transmission.

thalamus A relay station in the forebrain thought to be an important gathering point for input from the senses.

theta waves The pattern of brain activity observed in stage 1 sleep.

thinking The processes that underlie the mental manipulation of knowledge, usually in an attempt to reach a goal or solve a problem.

threshold. *See* absolute threshold; difference threshold

token economies A type of behavioral therapy in which patients are rewarded with small tokens when they act in an appropriate way; the tokens can then be exchanged for certain privileges.

tolerance An adaptation that the body makes to compensate for the continued use of a drug, such that increasing amounts of the drug are needed to produce the same physical and behavioral effects.

trait A stable predisposition to act or behave in a certain way.

trait theories Formal systems for assessing how people differ, particularly in their predispositions to respond in certain ways across situations. Most trait theories rely on psychometric tests to identify stable individual differences among people.

transduction The process by which external messages are translated into the internal language of the brain.

transfer-appropriate processing The idea that the likelihood of correct information retrieval is increased if a person uses the same kind of mental processes during testing that he or she used during encoding.

transference In psychoanalysis, the patient's expression of thoughts or feelings toward the therapist that are actually representative of the way the patient feels about other significant people in his or her life.

triarchic theory Robert Sternberg's theory of intelligence; it proposes three types of intelligence: analytic, creative, and practical.

trichromatic theory A theory of color vision proposing that color information is extracted by comparing the relative activations of three different types of cone receptors.

two-factor theory A theory of emotion that argues that the cognitive interpretation, or appraisal, of a body reaction drives the subjective experience of emotion.

tympanic membrane The "eardrum," which responds to incoming sound waves by vibrating.

Type A An enduring pattern of behavior linked to stress-related health disorders; it is characterized by being hard driving, ambitious, easily annoyed, and impatient.

Type B People who lack the Type A traits—they put themselves under less pressure and appear more relaxed.

unconditioned response (UR) The observable response that is produced automatically, prior to training, on presentation of an unconditioned stimulus.

unconditioned stimulus (US) A stimulus that automatically produces—or elicits—an observable response prior to any training.

unconscious mind The part of the mind that Freud believed housed all the memories, urges, and conflicts that are truly beyond awareness.

validity An assessment of how well a test measures what it is supposed to measure. *Content validity* assesses the degree to which the test samples broadly across the domain of interest. *Predictive validity* assesses how well the test predicts some future criterion. *Construct validity* assesses how well the test taps into a particular theoretical construct.

variability A measure of how much the scores in a distribution of scores differ from one another.

variable-interval schedule A reinforcement schedule in which the allotted time before a response will yield reinforcement changes from trial to trial.

variable-ratio schedule A reinforcement schedule in which a certain number of responses is required for reinforcement, but the number of required responses typically changes from trial to trial.

variables. *See* confounding variable; dependent variable; independent variable

ventromedial hypothalamus A portion of the hypothalamus that, when lesioned, produces an animal that typically overeats and gains large amounts of weight. Once thought to be a kind of stop eating, or satiety, center in the brain, its role in eating behavior is currently unknown.

vestibular sacs The receptor system thought to be primarily responsible for the sense of balance.

visual acuity The ability to process fine detail in vision.

visual imagery The processes used to construct an internal visual image, perhaps using the same brain mechanisms used to perceive events in the physical world.

visual neglect A complex disorder of attention characterized by a tendency to ignore things that appear on one side of the body, usually the right side.

warm fibers Neurons that respond vigorously when the temperature of the skin increases.

Weber's law The principle stating that the ability to notice a difference in the magnitude of two stimuli is a constant proportion of the size of the standard stimulus. Psychologically, the more intense a stimulus is to begin with, the more intense it will need to become for one to notice a change.

well-defined problem A problem with a well-stated goal, a clear starting point, and a relatively easy way to tell when a solution has been obtained.

withdrawal Clear and measurable physical reactions, such as sweating, vomiting, changes in heart rate, or tremors, that occur when a person stops taking certain drugs after continued use.

working backward A problem-solving heuristic that involves starting at the goal state and moving backward toward the starting point in order to see how the goal state can be reached.

zygote The fertilized human egg, containing 23 chromosomes from the father and 23 chromosomes from the mother, which pair up to form the master genetic blueprint.

References

Abel, E. L. (1981). Behavioral teratology of alcohol. *Psychological Bulletin, 90,* 564–581.

Abrams, D., Wetherell, M., Cochrane, S., Hogg, M. A., & Turner, J. C. (1990). Knowing what to think by knowing who you are: Self-categorization and the nature of norm formation, conformity, and group polarization. *British Journal of Social Psychology, 29,* 97–119.

Abramson, L. Y., Metalsky, G. I., & Alloy, L. B. (1989). Hopelessness depression: A theory-based subtype of depression. *Psychological Review, 96,* 358–372.

Achenbach, T. M. (1992). Developmental psychopathology. In M. H. Bornstein & M. E. Lamb (Eds.), *Devlopmental psychology: An advanced textbook.* Hillsdale, NJ: Erlbaum.

Adair, R., Bauchner, H., Phillip, B., Levenson, S., & Zuckerman, B. (1991). Night waking during infancy: Role of parent presence at bedtime. *Pediatrics, 87,* 500–504.

Adams, D. B., Gold, A. R., & Burt, A. D. (1978). Rise in female-initiated sexual activity at ovulation and its suppression by oral contraceptives. *New England Journal of Medicine, 299,* 1145–1150.

Adams, P. R., & Adams, G. R. (1984). Mount Saint Helens's ash-fall: Evidence for a disaster stress reaction. *American Psychologist, 39,* 252–260.

Ader, R., & Cohen, N. (1975). Behaviorally conditioned immunosuppression. *Psychosomatic Medicine, 37,* 333–340.

Adler, A. (1927). *Understanding human nature.* New York: Greenberg.

Adler, N., & Matthews, K. (1994). Health psychology: Why do some people get sick and some stay healthy? *Annual Review of Psychology, 45,* 229–259.

Aggleton, J. P. (1993). The contribution of the amygdala to normal and abnormal emotional states. *Trends in Neuroscience, 16,* 328–333.

Agras, W. S., Sylvester, D., & Oliveau, D. (1969). The epidemiology of common fears and phobia. *Comprehensive Psychiatry, 10,* 151–156.

Ainsworth, M. D. S. (1979). Attachment as related to mother-infant interactions. In J. S. Rosenblatt, R. A. Hinde, C. Beer, & M. Busnel (Eds.), *Advances in the study of behavior* (Vol. 9). New York: Academic Press.

Ainsworth, M. D. S., Blehar, M., Waters, E., & Wall, S. (1978). *Patterns of attachment.* Hillsdale, NJ: Erlbaum.

Ainsworth, M. D. S., & Wittig, B. A. (1969). Attachment and exploratory behavior of one-year-olds in a strange situation. In B. M. Foss (Ed.), *Determinants of infant behaviour* (Vol. 4). London: Methuen.

Ajzen, I., & Fishbein, M. (1977). Attitude-behavior relations: A theoretical analysis and review of empirical research. *Psychological Bulletin, 84,* 888–918.

Albert, M. S., & Moss, M. B. (1992). The assessment of memory disorders in patients with Alzheimer's disease. In L. R. Squire & N. Butters (Eds.), *Neuropsychology of memory* (2nd ed.). New York: Guilford.

Allen, K. M., Blascovich, J., Tomaka, J., & Kelsey, R. M. (1991). Presence of human friends and pet dogs as moderators of autonomic responses to stress in women. *Journal of Personality and Social Psychology, 61,* 582–589.

Alley, T. R., & Cunningham, M. R. (1991). Average faces are attractive, but very attractive faces are not average. *Psychological Science, 2,* 123–125.

Allison, J. (1989). The nature of reinforcement. In S. B. Klein & R. R. Mowrer (Eds.), *Contemporary learning theories: Instrumental conditioning and the impact of biological constraints on learning.* Hillsdale, NJ: Erlbaum.

Allison, T., & Cicchetti, D. V. (1976). Sleep in mammals: Ecological and constitutional correlates. *Science, 194,* 732–734.

Allport, A. (1989). Visual attention. In M. I. Posner (Ed.), *Foundation of cognitive science.* Cambridge, MA: MIT Press.

Allport, G. W. (1937). *Personality: A psychological interpretation.* New York: Holt.

Allport, G. W., & Odbert, H. H. (1936). Trait-names: A psycho-lexical study. *Psychological Monographs, 47*(1, Whole No. 211).

Amabile, T. M. (1983). *The social psychology of creativity.* New York: Springer-Verlag.

American Psychological Association. (1992). Ethical principles of psychologists and code of conduct. *American Psychologist, 47,* 1597–1611.

American Psychological Association. (1993). *Profile of all APA members: 1993.* Washington, DC: Author.

Anastasi, A. (1985). Psychological testing: Basic concepts and common misconceptions. *G. Stanley Hall Lecture Series, 5,* 87–120.

Andersen, B. L. (1992). Psychological interventions for cancer patients to enhance quality of life. *Journal of Consulting and Clinical Psychology, 60,* 552–568.

Anderson, J. R. (1990a). *The adaptive character of thought.* Hillsdale, NJ: Erlbaum.

Anderson, J. R. (1990b). *Cognitive psychology and its implications* (3rd ed.). New York: Freeman.

Anderson, J. R., & Schooler, L. J. (1991). Reflections of the environment in memory. *Psychological Science, 2,* 396–408.

Andersson, B. E. (1992). Effects of day-care on cognitive and socio-emotional competence of thirteen-year-old Swedish school-children. *Child Development, 63,* 20–36.

Andrasik, F., & Holroyd, K. A. (1980). A test of specific and nonspecific effects in the biofeedback treatment of tension headache. *Journal of Consulting and Clinical Psychology, 48,* 575–586.

Andreasen, N. C. (1987). Creativity and mental illness: Prevalence rates in writers and their first-degree relatives. *American Journal of Psychiatry, 144,* 1288–1292.

Angell, J. R. (1903). The relations of structural and functional psychology to philosophy. *Philosophical Review, 12,* 203.

Apgar, V., & Beck, J. (1974). *Is my baby all right?* New York: Pocket Books.

Araoz, D. L. (1982). *Hypnosis and sex therapy.* New York: Brunner/Mazel.

Aronson, E. (1992). The return of the repressed: Dissonance theory makes a comeback. *Psychological Inquiry, 3,* 303–311.

Asch, S. E. (1951). Effects of group pressure on the modification and distortion of judgments. In H. Guetzkow (Ed.), *Groups, leadership, and men.* Pittsburgh, PA: Carnegie Press.

Asch, S. E. (1955, May). Opinions and social pressures. *Scientific American, 193,* 31–35.

Aschoff, J., & Wever, R. (1981). The circadian system of man. In J. Aschoff (Ed.), *Handbook of behavioral neurobiology: Vol. 4. Biological rhythms.* New York: Plenum.

Aserinsky, E., & Kleitman, N. (1955). Two types of ocular motility occurring in sleep. *Journal of Applied Physiology, 8,* 1–10.

Atkinson, J. W. (1957). Motivational determinants of risk- taking behavior. *Psychological Review, 64,* 359–372.

Atkinson, J. W., & Raynor, J. O. (Eds.). (1974). *Motivation and achievement.* Washington, DC: Winston.

Atkinson, R. C., & Shiffrin, R. M. (1968). Human memory: A proposed system and its control processes. In K. Spence & J. Spence (Eds.), *The psychology of learning and motivation* (Vol. 2). New York: Academic Press.

Atkinson, R. C., & Shiffrin, R. M. (1971, August). The control of short-term memory. *Scientific American, 225,* 82–90.

Averbach, E., & Coriell, A. S. (1961). Short-term memory in vision. *Bell System Technical Journal, 40,* 309–328.

Averill, J. R. (1983). Studies on anger and aggression: Implications for theories of emotion. *American Psychologist, 38,* 1145–1160.

Ayllon, T., & Azrin, N. H. (1968). *The token economy: A motivational system for therapy and rehabilitation.* New York: Appleton-Century-Crofts.

Baddeley, A. D. (1992). Working memory. *Science, 255,* 556–559.

Baddeley, A. D., & Lieberman, K. (1980). Spatial working memory. In R. Nickerson (Ed.), *Attention and performance VIII.* Hillsdale, NJ: Erlbaum.

Baddeley, A. D., Thomson, N., & Buchanan, M. (1975). Word length and the structure of short-term memory. *Journal of Verbal Learning and Verbal Behavior, 14,* 575–589.

Bahrick, H. P. (1984). Semantic memory content in permastore: 50 years of memory for Spanish learned in school. *Journal of Experimental Psychology: General, 113,* 1–29.

Bahrick, H. P., & Hall, L. K. (1991). Lifetime maintenance of high school mathematics content. *Journal of Experimental Psychology: General, 120,* 20–33.

Bailey, J. M., & Pillard, R. C. (1991). A genetic study of male sexual orientation. *Archives of General Psychiatry, 48,* 1089–1096.

Bailey, J. M., Pillard, R. C., Neale, M. C. I., & Agyei, Y. (1993). Heritable factors influence sexual orientation in women. *Archives of General Psychiatry, 50,* 217–223.

Baillargeon, R. (1994). How do infants learn about the physical world? *Psychological Science, 5,* 133–140.

Baker, T. B., & Tiffany, S. T. (1985). Morphine tolerance as habituation. *Psychological Review, 92,* 78–108.

Ballard, P. A., Tetrud, J. W., & Langston, J. W. (1985). Permanent human parkinsonism due to 1-methyl-4-phenyl-1,2,3,6-tetrahydropyridine (MPTP). *Neurology, 35,* 949–956.

Baltes, P. B. (1987). Theoretical propositions of life-span developmental psychology: On the dynamics between growth and decline. *Developmental Psychology, 23,* 611–626.

Baltes, P. B., Reese, H. W., & Lipsitt, L. P. (1980). Life-span developmental psychology. *Annual Review of Psychology, 31,* 65–110.

Bandura, A. (1986). *Social foundations of thought and action.* Englewood Cliffs, NJ: Prentice Hall.

Bandura, A. (1993). Perceived self-efficacy in cognitive development and functioning. *Educational Psychologist, 28,* 117–148.

Bandura, A., Ross, D., & Ross, S. A. (1963). Imitation of film-mediated aggressive models. *Journal of Abnormal and Social Psychology, 66,* 3–11.

Banks, M. S., & Salapatek, P. (1983). Infant visual perception. In M. M. Haith & J. J. Campos (Eds.), *Handbook of child psychology.* New York: Wiley.

Banks, M. S., & Shannon, E. (1993). Spatial and chromatic visual efficiency in human neonates. In C. E. Granrud (Ed.), *Visual perception and cognition in infancy.* Hillsdale, NJ: Erlbaum.

Barber, T. X. (1976). *Pitfalls in human research: Ten pivotal points.* New York: Pergamon.

Barber, T. X., Spanos, N. P., & Chaves, J. (1974). *Hypnosis, imagination, and human potentialities.* New York: Pergamon.

Bargones, J. Y., & Werner, L. A. (1994). Adults listen selectively; infants do not. *Psychological Science, 5,* 170–174.

Barkley, R. A. (1981). *Hyperactive children: A handbook for diagnosis and treatment.* New York: Guilford.

Barlow, D. H. (1988). *Anxiety and its disorders: The nature and treatment of anxiety and panic.* New York: Guilford.

Barlow, D. H., & Durand, V. M. (1995). *Abnormal psychology: An integrative approach.* Pacific Grove, CA: Brooks/Cole.

Barlow, D. H., & Rapee, R. M. (1991). *Mastering stress: A lifestyle approach.* Dallas, TX: American Health.

Bartlett, F. C. (1932). *Remembering.* Cambridge: Cambridge University Press.

Bastien, C., & Campbell, K. (1992). The evoked K-complex: All or none phenomenon? *Sleep, 15,* 236–245.

Baumrind, D. (1964). Some thoughts on the ethics of research: After reading Milgram's "Behavioral study of obedience." *American Psychologist, 19,* 421–423.

Baumrind, D. (1985). Research using intentional deception: Ethical issues revisited. *American Psychologist, 40,* 165–174.

Beck, A. T. (1991). Cognitive therapy: A 30-year retrospective. *American Psychologist, 46,* 368–375.

Beck, A. T., & Young, J. E. (1985). Depression. In D. H. Barlow (Ed.), *Clinical handbook of psychological disorders.* New York: Guilford.

Békésy, G. von (1960). *Experiments in hearing.* New York: McGraw-Hill.

Bell, A. P., Weinberg, M. S., & Hammersmith, S. K. (1981). *Sexual preference: Its development in men and women.* Bloomington: Indiana University Press.

Bell, P. A., Fisher, J. D., Baum, A., & Greene, T. E. (1990). *Environmental psychology* (3rd ed.). Fort Worth, TX: Holt, Rinehart and Winston.

Belloc, H. B., & Breslow, L. (1972). Relationship of physical health status and health practice. *Preventive Medicine, 1,* 409–421.

Belsky, J. (1988). The "effects" of infant daycare reconsidered. *Early Childhood Research Quarterly, 3,* 235–272.

Bem, D. J. (1967). Self-perception: An alternative interpretation of cognitive dissonance phenomena. *Psychological Review, 74,* 183–200.

Bem, D. J. (1972). Self-perception theory. In L. Berkowitz (Ed.), *Advances in experimental social psychology* (Vol. 6). New York: Academic Press.

Bem, S. L. (1981). Gender schema theory: A cognitive account of sex-typing. *Psychological Review, 88,* 354–364.

Benes, F. M. (1989). Myelination of cortical-hippocampal relays during late adolescence. *Schizophrenia Bulletin, 15,* 585–593.

Benson, H. (1975). *The relaxation response.* New York: Morrow.

Benson, P. L., Dehority, J., Garman, L., Hanson, E., Hochschwender, M., Lebod, C., Rohr, R., & Sullivan, J. (1980). Intrapersonal correlates of nonspontaneous helping behavior. *Journal of Social Psychology, 110,* 87–95.

Bentall, R. P. (1990). The illusion of reality: A review and integration of psychological research on hallucinations. *Psychological Bulletin, 107,* 82–95.

Benton, M. K., & Schroeder, H. E. (1990). Social skills training with schizophrenics: A meta-analytic evaluation. *Journal of Consulting and Clinical Psychology, 58,* 741–747.

Berkeley, D., & Humphreys, P. (1982). Structuring decision problems and the "bias heuristic." *Acta Psychologica, 50,* 201–252.

Berman, K. F., & Weinberger, D. R. (1990). Lateralization of cortical function during cognitive tasks: Regional cerebral blood flow studies of normal individuals and patients with schizophrenia. *Journal of Neurology, Neurosurgery, and Psychiatry, 53,* 150–160.

Bernal, E. M. (1984). Bias in mental testing: Evidence for an alternative to the heredity-environment controversy. In C. R. Reynolds & R. T. Brown (Eds.), *Perspectives on bias in mental testing.* New York: Plenum.

Bernstein, I. H., Lin, T., & McClelland, P. (1982). Cross- vs. within-racial judgments of attractiveness. *Perception & Psychophysics, 32,* 495–503.

Bernstein, I. L. (1978). Learned taste aversions in children receiving chemotherapy. *Science, 200,* 1302–1303.

Berscheid, E. (1985). Interpersonal attraction. In G. Lindzey & E. Aronson (Eds.), *Handbook of social psychology* (Vol. 2). New York: Random House.

Bertenthal, B. I., Campos, J. J., & Kermoian, R. (1994). An epigenetic perspective on the development of self-produced locomotion and its consequences. *Current Directions in Psychological Science, 3,* 140–145.

Best, J. B. (1989). *Cognitive psychology* (2nd ed.). St. Paul, MN: West Publishing.

Beutler, L. E., & Berren, M. R. (Eds.). (1995). *Integrative assessment of adult personality.* New York: Guilford.

Beyth-Marom, R., & Lichtenstein, S. (1984). *An elementary approach to thinking under uncertainty.* Hillsdale, NJ: Erlbaum.

Biederman, I. (1987). Recognition-by-components: A theory of human image understanding. *Psychological Review, 94,* 115–147.

Biederman, I. (1990). Higher-level vision. In D. H. Osherson, S. M. Kosslyn, & J. M. Hollerbach (Eds.), *An invitation to cognitive science: Visual cognition and action* (Vol. 2). Cambridge, MA: MIT Press.

Bigelow, H. J. (1850). Dr. Harlow's case of recovery from the passage of an iron bar through the head. *American Journal of Medical Science, 20,* 13–22.

Binder, J. R., Rao, S. M., Hammeke, T. A., & Yetkin, F. Z. (1994). Functional magnetic resonance imaging of human auditory cortex. *Annals of Neurology, 35,* 662–672.

Binet, A., & Simon, T. (1916; reprinted 1973). *The development of intelligence in children.* New York: Arno Press.

Bisiach, E. (1992). Understanding consciousness: Clues from unilateral neglect and related disorders. In A. D. Milner & M. D. Rugg (Eds.), *The neuropsychology of consciousness.* London: Academic Press.

Bisiach, E., & Rusconi, M. L. (1990). Break-down of perceptual awareness in unilateral neglect. *Cortex, 26,* 643–649.

Black, J. E., Isaacs, K. R., & Greenough, W. T. (1991). Usual vs. successful aging: Some notes on experiential factors. *Neurobiology of Aging, 12,* 325–328.

Blair, S. N., Kohl, H. W., Paffenbarger, R. S., Clark, K. H., & Gibbons, L. W. (1989). Physical fitness and all-cause mortality: A prospective study of healthy men and women. *Journal of the American Medical Association, 262,* 2395–2401.

Blanchard, E. B. (1992). Psychological treatment of benign headache disorders. *Journal of Consulting and Clinical Psychology, 60,* 537–551.

Blass, T. (1991). Understanding behavior in the Milgram obedience experiment: The role of personality, situations, and their interactions. *Journal of Personality and Social Psychology, 60,* 398–413.

Bleuler, E. (1908). Die prognose der Dementia praecox (Schizophreniegruppe). *Allgemeine Zeitschrift fur Psychiatrie, 65,* 436–464.

Blumenthal, J. A., Emery, C. F., Walsh, M. A., Cox, D. R., Kuhn, C. M., Williams, R. B., & Williams, R. S. (1988). Exercise training in healthy Type A middle-aged men: Effects on behavioral and cardiovascular responses. *Psychosomatic Medicine, 50,* 418–433.

Blundell, J. E., & Rogers, P. J. (1991). Hunger, hedonics, and the control of satiation and satiety. In M. I. Friedman, M. G. Tordoff, & M. R. Kare (Eds.), *Chemical senses* (Vol. 4). New York: Marcel Dekker.

Bolanowski, S. J., Jr. (1989). Four channels mediate vibrotaction: Facts, models, and implications. *Journal of the Acoustical Society of America, 85,* S62.

Bolles, R. C. (1972). Reinforcement, expectancy, and learning. *Psychological Review, 79,* 394–409.

Bolles, R. C. (1993). *The story of psychology: A thematic history.* Pacific Grove, CA: Brooks/Cole.

Boomer, D. S. (1965). Hesitation and grammatical encoding. *Language and Speech, 8,* 145–158.

Bootzin, R. R., Manber, R., Perlis, M. L., Salvio, M., & Wyatt, J. K. (1993). Sleep disorders and the elderly. In P. B. Sutker & H. F. Adams (Eds.), *Comprehensive handbook of psychopathology* (2nd ed.). New York: Plenum.

Boring, E. G. (1950). *A history of experimental psychology* (2nd ed.). New York: Appleton-Century-Crofts.

Bornstein, M. H. (1989). Stability in early mental development: From attention and information processing in infancy to language and cognition in childhood. In M. H. Bornstein & N. A. Krasnegor (Eds.), *Stability and continuity in mental development: Behavioral and biological perspectives.* Hillsdale, NJ: Erlbaum.

Bornstein, M. H. (1992). Perception across the life span. In M. H. Bornstein & M. E. Lamb (Eds.), *Developmental psychology: An advanced textbook* (3rd ed.). Hillsdale, NJ: Erlbaum.

Bornstein, M. H., Kessen, W., & Weiskopf, S. (1976). Color vision and hue categorization in young human infants. *Journal of Experimental Psychology: Human Perception and Performance, 2,* 115–129.

Bortz, W. M. (1990). The trajectory of dying: Functional status in the last year of life. *Journal of the American Geriatrics Society, 38,* 146–150.

Bouchard, C., Tremblay, A., Despres, J., Nadeau, A., Lupien, P. J., Theriault, G., Dussault, J., Moorjani, S., Pinault, S., & Fournier, G. (1990). The response to long-term overfeeding in identical twins. *New England Journal of Medicine, 322,* 1477–1487.

Bouchard, T. J., Jr., Lykken, D. T., McGue, M., Segal, N. L., & Tellegean, A. (1990). Sources of human psychological differences: The Minnesota study of twins reared apart. *Science, 250,* 223–228.

Bouchard, T. J., Jr., & McGue, M. (1981). Familial studies of intelligence: A review. *Science, 212,* 1055–1059.

Boucher, J. D., & Carlson, G. E. (1980). Recognition of facial expression in three cultures. *Journal of Cross-Cultural Psychology, 11,* 263–280.

Bouton, M. E. (1991). Context and retrieval in extinction and in other examples of interference in simple associative learning. In L. Dachowski & C. F. Flaherty (Eds.), *Current topics in animal learning.* Hillsdale, NJ: Erlbaum.

Bøvjberg, D. H., Redd, W. H., Maier, L. A., Holland, J. C., Lesko, L. M., Niedzwiecki, D., Rubin, S. E., & Hakes, T. B. (1990). Anticipatory immune suppression in women receiving cyclic chemotherapy for ovarian cancer. *Journal of Consulting and Clinical Psychology, 58,* 153–157.

Bower, T. G. R. (1982). *Development in infancy* (2nd ed.). San Francisco: Freeman.

Bowers, T., & Clum, G. (1988). Relative contributions of specific and nonspecific treatment effects: Meta-analysis of placebo-controlled behavior therapy research. *Psychological Bulletin, 103,* 315–323.

Bowlby, J. (1969). *Attachment and loss: Vol. 1. Attachment.* New York: Basic Books.

Bowlby, J. (1988). *A secure base: Parent-child attachment and healthy human development.* New York: Basic Books.

Bowmaker, J. K., & Dartnall, H. J. A. (1980). Visual pigments of rods and cones in a human retina. *Journal of Physiology, 298,* 501–511.

Boynton, R. M. (1979). *Human color vision.* New York: Holt, Rinehart & Winston.

Braff, D. L., & Huey, L. (1988). Methylphenidate-induced information processing dysfunction in non-schizophrenic patients. *Archives of General Psychiatry, 45,* 827–832.

Bransford, J. D., & Stein, B. S. (1993). *The ideal problem solver* (2nd ed.). New York: Freeman.

Breggin, P. R. (1991). *Toxic psychiatry.* New York: St. Martin's.

Bregman, A. S. (1990). *Auditory scene analysis.* Cambridge, MA: Bradford/MIT Press.

Breland, K., & Breland, M. (1961). The misbehavior of organisms. *American Psychologist, 16,* 681–684.

Brett, J. F., Brief, A. P., Burke, M. J., George, J. M., & Webster, J. (1990). Negative affectivity and the reporting of stressful life events. *Health Psychology, 9,* 57–68.

Briere, J., & Conte, J. (1993). Self-reported amnesia for abuse in adults molested as children. *Journal of Traumatic Stress, 6,* 21–31.

Broad, W., & Wade, N. (1982). *Betrayers of the truth.* New York: Simon & Schuster.

Broadbent, D. E. (1952). Failures of attention in selective listening. *Journal of Experimental Psychology, 44,* 428–433.

Broadbent, D. E. (1958). *Perception and communication.* London: Pergamon Press.

Broberg, D. J., & Bernstein, I. L. (1987). Candy as a scapegoat in the prevention of food aversions in children receiving chemotherapy. *Cancer, 60,* 2344–2347.

Broca, P. (1861). Remarques sur le siege de la faculte du langage articule, suivies d'une observation d'aphemie (perte de la parole). *Bulletin de la Societé Anatomique* (Paris), *36,* 330–357.

Brody, N. (1992). *Intelligence* (2nd ed.). San Diego, CA: Academic Press.

Bromley, D. B. (1986). *The case-study method in psychology and related disciplines.* Chichester, England: Wiley.

Brown, A. D., & Murphy, D. R. (1989). Cryptomnesia: Delineating inadvertent plagiarism. *Journal of Experimental Psychology: Learning, Memory, & Cognition, 15,* 432–442.

Brown, G. W., & Birley, J. L. T. (1968). Crisis and life change and the onset of schizophrenia. *Journal of Health and Social Behavior, 9,* 203–214.

Brown, R., & Kulick, J. (1977). Flashbulb memories. *Cognition, 5,* 73–99.

Brown, T. A., Barlow, D. H., & Liebowitz, M. R. (1994). The empirical basis of generalized anxiety disorder. *American Journal of Psychiatry, 151,* 1272–1280.

Bruce, D. (1985). The how and why of ecological memory. *Journal of Experimental Psychology: General, 114,* 78–90.

Buck, L., & Axel, A. (1991). A novel multigene family may encode odorant receptors: A molecular basis for odor recognition. *Cell, 65,* 175–187.

Buell, S. J., & Coleman, P. D. (1979). Dendritic growth in the aged human brain and failure of growth in senile dementia. *Science, 206,* 854–856.

Buss, A. H. (1988). *Personality: Evolutionary heritage and human distinctivness.* Hillsdale, NJ: Erlbaum.

Buss, A. H. (1989). Personality as traits. *American Psychologist, 44,* 1378–1388.

Buss, D. M. (1989). Sex differences in human preferences: Evolutionary hypotheses tested in 37 cultures. *Behavioral and Brain Sciences, 12,* 1–49.

Buss, D. M. (1991). Evolutionary personality psychology. *Annual Review of Psychology, 42,* 459–491.

Buss, D. M., & Schmitt, D. P. (1993). Sexual strategies theory: An evolutionary perspective on human mating. *Psychological Review, 100,* 204–232.

Butcher, J. N. (1995). Interpretation of the MMPI-2. In L. E. Beutler & M. R. Berren (Eds.), *Integrative assessment of adult personality.* New York: Guilford.

Butler, R. W., Rorsman, I., Hill, J. M., & Tuma, R. (1993). The effects of frontal brain impairment on fluency: Simple and complex paradigms. *Neuropsychology, 7,* 519–529.

Byrd, J. C. (1992). Environmental tobacco smoke: Medical and legal issues. *Medical Clinics of North America, 76,* 377–398.

Byrne, D. (1971). *The attraction paradigm.* New York: Academic Press.

Cameron, J., & Pierce, W. D. (1994). Reinforcement, reward, and intrinsic motivation: A meta-analysis. *Review of Educational Research, 64,* 363–423.

Campbell, D. T., & Stanley, J. C. (1966). *Experimental and quasi-experimental designs for research.* Chicago: Rand McNally.

Campos, J. J., Langer, A., & Krowitz, A. (1970). Cardiac responses on the visual cliff in prelocomotor human infants. *Science, 170,* 196–197.

Cannell, C. G., & Kahn, R. L. (1968). Interviewing. In G. Lindzey and E. Aronson (Eds.), *Handbook of social psychology: Research methods* (Vol. 2). Reading, MA: Addison-Wesley.

Cannon, W. B. (1927). The James-Lange theory of emotions: A critical examination and an alternative theory. *American Journal of Psychology, 39,* 106–124.

Cannon, W. B. (1929). *Bodily changes in pain, hunger, fear, and rage.* New York: Appleton.

Cannon, W. B. (1932). *The wisdom of the body.* New York: Norton.

Cantor, N. (1990). From thought to behavior: "Having" and "doing" in the study of personality and cognition. *American Psychologist, 45,* 735–750.

Cantor, N., & Harlow, R. E. (1994). Personality, strategic behavior, and daily-life problem solving. *Current Directions in Psychological Science, 3,* 169–172.

Cantor, N., & Malley, J. (1991). Life tasks, personal needs, and close relationships. In G. Fletcher & F. Fincham (Eds.), *Cognition in close relationships.* Hillsdale, NJ: Erlbaum.

Carlsmith, J. M., & Gross, A. E. (1969). Some effects of guilt on compliance. *Journal of Personality and Social Psychology, 11,* 240–244.

Carlson, N. R. (1991). *Physiology of behavior* (4th ed.). Boston: Allyn & Bacon.

Carrasco, M., & Ridout, J. B. (1993). Olfactory perception and olfactory imagery: A multidimensional analysis. *Journal of Experimental Psychology: Human Perception and Performance, 19,* 287–301.

Cartwright, R. (1991). Dreams that work: The relation of dream incorporation to adaptation to stressful events. *Dreaming, 1,* 2–9.

Case, R. B., Moss, A. J., Case, N., McDermott, M., & Eberly, S. (1992). Living alone after myocardial infarction: Impact on prognosis. *Journal of American Medical Association, 267,* 515–519.

Cattell, R. B. (1963). Theory of fluid and crystallized intelligence: A critical experiment. *Journal of Educational Psychology, 54,* 1–22.

Cattell, R. B. (1973, July). A 16PF profile. *Psychology Today,* 40–46.

Cattell, R. B., Eber, H. W., & Tatsuoka, M. M. (1970). *Handbook of the 16 personality factor questionnaire (16PF).* Champaign, IL: Institute for Personality and Ability Testing.

Caudill, M., & Butler, C. (1990). *Naturally intelligent systems.* Cambridge, MA: MIT Press.

Caughy, M. O., DiPietro, J. A., & Strobino, D. M. (1994). Day-care participation as a protective factor in the cognitive development of low-income children. *Child Development, 65,* 457–471.

Cavanaugh, J. C. (1993). *Adult development and aging* (2nd ed.). Pacific Grove, CA: Brooks/Cole.

Ceci, S. J. (1991). How much does schooling influence intellectual development and its cognitive components? A reassessment of the evidence. *Developmental Psychology, 27,* 703–722.

Cermak, L. S. (1982). The long and the short of it in amnesia. In L. S. Cermak (Ed.), *Human memory and amnesia.* Hillsdale, NJ: Erlbaum.

Chaiken, S., Liberman, A., & Eagly, A. H. (1989). Heuristic and systematic information processing: Within and beyond the persuasion context. In J. S. Uleman & J. A. Bargh (Eds.), *Unintended thought.* New York: Guilford.

Chase, W. G., & Simon, H. A. (1973). The mind's eye in chess. In W. G. Chase (Ed.), *Visual information processing.* New York: Academic Press.

Chen, S. C. (1937). Social modification of the activity of ants in nest-building. *Physiological Zoology, 10,* 420–436.

Cherry, E. C. (1953). Some experiments on the recognition of speech with one and with two ears. *Journal of the Acoustical Society of America, 25,* 975–979.

Chesney, M. A. (1993). Health psychology in the 21st century: Acquired immunodeficiency syndrome as a harbinger of things to come. *Health Psychology, 12,* 259–268.

Chomsky, N. (1957). *Syntactic structures.* The Hague: Mouton.

Chomsky, N. (1986). *Knowledge of language: Its nature, origins, and use.* New York: Praeger.

Chumlea, W. C. (1982). Physical growth in adolescence. In B. J. Wolman (Ed.), *Handbook of developmental psychology.* Englewood Cliffs, NJ: Prentice-Hall.

Clarke, L. A., & Livesley, W. J. (1994). Two approaches to identifying the dimensions of personality disorder: Convergence on the five-factor model. In P. T. Costa, Jr. & T. A. Widiger (Eds.), *Personality disorders and the five-factor model of personality.* Washington, DC: American Psychological Association.

Clarke-Stewart, A. K. (1989). Infant day care: Maligned or malignant? *American Psychologist, 44,* 266–273.

Cleary, P. J. (1980). A checklist for life event research. *Journal of Psychosomatic Research, 24,* 199–207.

Cleghorn, J. M., Franco, S., Szechtman, B., Kaplan, R., Szechtman, H., Brown, G. M., Nahmias, C., & Garnett, E. S. (1992). Toward a brain map of auditory hallucinations. *American Journal of Psychiatry, 149,* 1062–1069.

Clendenen, V. I., Herman, C. P., & Polivy, J. (1994). Social facilitation of eating among friends and strangers. *Appetite, 23,* 1–13.

Cohen, J. D., & Servan-Schreiber, D. (1992). Context, cortex, and dopamine: A connectionist approach to behavior and biology in schizophrenia. *Psychological Review, 99,* 45–77.

Cohen, S., Tyrrell, D. A., & Smith, D. A. (1993). Negative life events, perceived stress, negative affect, and susceptibility to the common cold. *Journal of Personality and Social Psychology, 64,* 131–140.

Cohen, S., & Wills, T. A. (1985). Stress, social support, and the buffering hypothesis. *Psychological Bulletin, 98,* 310–357.

Coile, D. C., & Miller, N. E. (1984). How radical animal activists try to mislead humane people. *American Psychologist, 39,* 700–701.

Cole, M. (1992). Culture in development. In M. H. Bornstein & M. E. Lamb (Eds.), *Developmental psychology: An advanced textbook.* Hillsdale, NJ: Erlbaum.

Cole, N. S. (1981). Bias in testing. *American Psychologist, 36,* 1067–1077.

Coleman, L., & Kay, P. (1981). Prototype semantics: The English word *lie. Language, 57,* 26–44.

Coleman, P. (1993). Overview of substance abuse. *Primary Care, 20,* 1–18.

Coleman, P. D., & Flood, D. G. (1987). Neuron numbers and dendritic extent in normal aging and Alzheimer's disease. *Neurobiology of Aging, 8,* 521–545.

Coles, R., & Stokes, G. (1985). *Sex and the American teenager.* New York: Harper & Row.

Colon, E. A., Callies, A. L., Popkin, M. K., & McGlave, P. B. (1991). Depressed mood and other variables related to bone marrow transplantation survival in acute leukemia. *Psychosomatics, 32,* 420–425.

Colwill, R. M., & Rescorla, R. A. (1986). Associative structures in instrumental learning. In G. H. Bower (Ed.), *The psychology of learning and motivation* (Vol. 20, pp. 55–104). Orlando, FL: Academic Press.

Commons, M. L., Sinnott, J. D., Richards, F. A., & Armon, C. (Eds.). (1989). *Adult development: Vol. 1. Comparisons and applications of adolescent and adult developmental models.* New York: Praeger.

Compas, B. E., Hinden, B. R., & Gerhardt, C. A. (1995). Adolescent development: Pathways and processes of risk and resilience. *Annual Review of Psychology, 46,* 265–293.

Conrad, R. (1964). Acoustic confusion in immediate memory. *British Journal of Psychology, 55,* 75–84.

Conway, M. A., Anderson, S. J., Larsen, S. F., Donnelly, C. M., McDaniel, M. A., McClelland, A. G. R., Rawles, R. E., & Logie, R. H. (1994). The formation of flashbulb memories. *Memory & Cognition, 22,* 326–343.

Cook, M., & Mineka, S. (1989). Observational conditioning of fear to fear-relevant versus fear-irrelevant stimuli in rhesus monkeys. *Journal of Abnormal Psychology, 98,* 448–459.

Cook, T. D., & Campbell, D. T. (1979). *Quasi-experimentation: Design and analysis for field settings.* Chicago: Rand McNally.

Cooper, W. H. (1983). An achievement motivation nomological network. *Journal of Personality and Social Psychology, 44,* 841–861.

Corballis, M. C. (1991). *The lopsided ape: Evolution of the generative mind.* New York: Oxford University Press.

Coren, S., Porac, C., & Theodor, L. H. (1987). Set and subjective contour. In S. Petry & G. E. Meyer (Eds.), *The perception of illusory contours.* New York: Springer-Verlag.

Coren, S., Ward, L. M., & Enns, J. T. (1994). *Sensation and perception* (4th ed.). Fort Worth, TX: Harcourt Brace.

Corina, D. P., Vaid, J., & Bellugi, U. (1992). The linguistic basis of left hemisphere specialization. *Science, 255,* 1258–1260.

Courtois, C. A. (1992). The memory retrieval process in incest survivor therapy. *Journal of Child Sexual Abuse, 1,* 15–30.

Cowan, G., & Hoffman, C. D. (1986). Gender stereotyping in young children: Evidence to support a concept-learning approach. *Sex Roles, 14,* 211–224.

Cowan, N. (1995). *Attention and memory: An integrated framework.* New York: Oxford University Press.

Cowan, N., Lichty, W., & Grove, T. R. (1990). Properties of memory for unattended spoken syllables. *Journal of Experimental Psychology: Learning, Memory, & Cognition, 16,* 258–269.

Cox, M. J., Owen, M. T., Henderson, V. K., & Margand, N. A. (1992). Prediction of infant-father and infant-mother attachment. *Developmental Psychology, 28,* 474–483.

Craig, J. C. (1985). Attending to two fingers: Two hands are better than one. *Perception & Psychophysics, 38,* 496–511.

Craig, K. D. (1978). Social disclosure, coactive peer companions, and social modeling determinants of pain communications. *Canadian Journal of Behavioural Science, 10,* 91–104.

Craik, F. I. M. (1994). Memory changes in normal aging. *Current Directions in Psychological Science, 5,* 155–158.

Craik, F. I. M., & Jacoby, L. L. (1979). Elaboration and distinctiveness in episodic memory. In L. Nilsson (Ed.), *Perspectives on memory research: Essays in honor of Upsala University's 500th anniversary.* Hillsdale, NJ: Erlbaum.

Craik, F. I. M., & Lockhart, R. S. (1972). Levels of processing: A framework for memory research. *Journal of Verbal Learning and Verbal Behavior, 11,* 671–684.

Craik, F. I. M., & McDowd, J. M. (1987). Age differences in recall and recognition. *Journal of Experimental Psychology: Learning, Memory, & Cognition, 13,* 474–479.

Craik, F. I. M., & Tulving, E. (1975). Depth of processing and the retention of words in episodic memory. *Journal of Experimental Psychology: General, 104,* 268–294.

Craske, M. G., & Barlow, D. H. (1993). Panic disorder and agoraphobia. In D. H. Barlow (Ed.), *Clinical handbook of psychological disorders* (2nd ed.). New York: Guilford.

Cronbach, L. J. (1957). The two disciplines of scientific psychology. *American Psychologist, 12,* 671–684.

Crooks, R., & Baur, K. (1993). *Our sexuality* (5th ed.). Redwood City, CA: Benjamin Cummings.

Crowder, R. G. (1976). *Principles of learning and memory.* Hillsdale, NJ: Erlbaum.

Crowder, R. G., & Neath, I. (1991). The microscope metaphor in human memory. In W. E. Hockley & S. Lewandowsky (Eds.), *Relating theory and data: Essays on human memory in honor of Bennet B. Murdock.* Hillsdale, NJ: Erlbaum.

Crutcher, R. J. (1994) Telling what we know: The use of verbal report methodologies in psychological research. *Psychological Science, 5,* 241–244.

Curtis, R. C., & Miller, K. (1986). Believing another likes or dislikes you: Behaviors making the beliefs come true. *Journal of Personality and Social Psychology, 51,* 284–290.

Czeisler, C. A., Kronauer, R. E., Allen, J. S., Duffy, J. F., Jewett, M. E., Brown, E. N., & Ronda, J. M. (1989). Bright light induction of strong (Type 0) resetting of the human circadian pacemaker. *Science, 244,* 1328–1333.

Damhorst, M. L. (1990). In search of a common thread: Classification of information communicated through dress. *Clothing and Textiles Research Journal, 8,* 1–12.

Damon, W., & Hart, D. (1992). Self-understanding and its role in social and moral development. In M. H. Bornstein & M. E. Lamb (Eds.), *Developmental psychology: An advanced textbook.* Hillsdale, NJ: Erlbaum.

Darley, J. M., & Berscheid, E. (1967). Increased liking as a result of the anticipation of personal contact. *Human Relations, 20,* 29–39.

Darley, J. M., & Latané, B. (1968). Bystander intervention in emergencies: Diffusion of responsibilities. *Journal of Personality and Social Psychology, 8,* 377–383.

Darwin, C. (1859). *On the origin of species.* London: Murray.

Darwin, C. (1871). *Descent of Man.* London: Murray.

Davidson, M., Keefe, R. S. E., Mohs, R. C., Siever, L. J., Losonczy, M. F., Horvath, T. B., & Davis, K. L. (1987). L-dopa challenge and relapse in schizophrenia. *American Journal of Psychiatry, 144,* 934–938.

Davidson, T. L. (1993). The nature and function of interoceptive signals to feed: Toward integration of physiological and learning perspectives. *Psychological Review, 100,* 640–657.

Davidson, T. L., & Jarrard, L. E. (1993). A role for hippocampus in the utilization of hunger signals. *Behavioral and Neural Biology, 59,* 167–171.

Davies, G. M., & Thomson, D. M. (Eds.). (1988). *Memory in context: Context in memory.* Chichester, England: Wiley.

Davis, K. L., Kahn, R. S., Ko, G., & Davidson, M. (1991). Dopamine in schizophrenia: A review and reconceptualization. *American Journal of Psychiatry, 148,* 1474–1486.

Dawkins, R. (1986). Wealth, polygyny, and reproductive success. *Behavioral and Brain Sciences, 9,* 190–191.

Day, N. L., & Richardson, G. A. (1994). Comparative teratogenicity of alcohol and other drugs. *Alcohol Health and Research World, 18,* 42–48.

Deaux, K., & Lewis, L. L. (1984). The structure of gender stereotypes: Interrelationships among components and gender label. *Journal of Personality and Social Psychology, 46,* 991–1004.

de Boysson-Bardies, B., Sagat, L., & Durand, C. (1984). Discernable differences in the babbling of infants according to target language. *Journal of Child Language, 11,* 1–16.

DeCasper, A. J., & Fifer, W. P. (1980). Of human bonding: Newborns prefer their mothers' voices. *Science, 208,* 1174–1176.

DeCasper, A. J., & Spence, M. J. (1986). Prenatal maternal speech influences newborns' perception of speech sounds. *Infant Behavior and Development, 9,* 133–150.

Deci, E. L., & Ryan, R. M. (1985). *Intrinsic motivation and self-determination in human behavior.* New York: Plenum.

de Lacoste-Utamsing, C., & Holloway, R. L. (1982). Sexual dimorphism in the human corpus callosum. *Science, 216,* 1431–1432.

Dement, W., & Kleitman, N. (1957). The relation of eye movements during sleep to dream activity: An objective method for the study of dreaming. *Journal of Experimental Psychology, 53,* 339–346.

Dennis, W., & Dennis, M. G. (1940). The effect of cradling practices upon the onset of walking in Hopi children. *Journal of Genetic Psychology, 56,* 77–86.

Depression Guideline Panel. (1993). *Depression in primary care: Vol. 1. Detection and diagnosis.* Rockville, MD: U.S. Department of Health and Human Services.

Derogatis, L. R., & Coons, H. L. (1993). Self-report measures of stress. In L. Goldberger & S. Breznitz (Eds.), *Handbook of stress: Theoretical and clinical aspects* (2nd ed.). New York: Free Press.

DeValois, R. L., & DeValois, K. K. (1980). Spatial vision. *Annual Review of Psychology, 31,* 309–341.

Dewey, J. (1896). The reflex arc concept in psychology. *Psychological Review, 3,* 357–370.

Dickinson, A. (1989). The detrimental effects of extrinsic reinforcement on "intrinsic motivation." *The Behavior Analyst, 12,* 1–15.

Dickinson, A., & Charnock, D. J. (1985). Contingency effects with a constant probability of instrumental reinforcement. *Quarterly Journal of Experimental Psychology, 37B,* 397–416.

Digman, J. M. (1990). Personality structure: Emergence of the five-factor model. *Annual Review of Psychology, 41,* 417–440.

Dinges, D. F., Whitehouse, W. G., Orne, E. C., & Powell, J. W. (1992). Evaluating hypnotic memory enhancement (hypermnesia and reminiscence) using multitrial forced recall. *Journal of Experimental Psychology: Learning, Memory, and Cognition, 18,* 1139–1147.

Domjan, M. (1993). *Domjan and Burkhards' The principles of learning and behavior.* Pacific Grove, CA: Brooks/Cole.

Domjan, M., & Purdy, J. E. (1995). Animal research in psychology: More than meets the eye of the general psychology student. *American Psychologist, 50,* 496–503.

Donlon, T. F. (Ed.). (1984). *The College Board technical handbook for the Scholastic Aptitude Test and achievment tests.* New York: College Entrance Examination Board.

Dooley, D., Catalano, R., Mishra, S., & Sexner, S. (1992). Earthquake preparedness: Predictors in a community survey. *Journal of Applied Social Psychology, 22,* 451–470.

Druckman, D., & Bjork, R. A. (1991). *In the mind's eye: Enhancing human performance.* Washington, DC: National Academy Press.

Druckman, D., & Swets, J. A. (Eds.). (1988). *Enhancing human performance: Issues, theories, and techniques.* Washington DC: National Academy Press.

Duncker, K. (1945). On problem solving. *Psychological Monographs, 58*(5, Whole No. 270).

Dupont, P., Orban, G. A., De-Bruyn, B., & Verbruggen, A. (1994). Many areas in the human brain respond to visual motion. *Journal of Neurophysiology, 72,* 1420–1424.

Durie, D. J. (1981). Sleep in animals. In D. Wheatley (Ed.), *Psychopharmacology of sleep.* New York: Raven Press.

Eagly, A. H., Ashmore, R. D., Makhijani, M. G., & Longo, L. C. (1991). What is beautiful is good, but . . . : A meta-analytic review of research on the physical attractiveness stereotype. *Psychological Bulletin, 110,* 109–128.

Eagly, A. H., & Johnson, B. T. (1990). Gender and leadership style: A meta-analysis. *Psychological Bulletin, 108,* 233–256.

Ebbinghaus, H. (1885/1964). *Memory: A contribution to experimental psychology.* New York: Dover.

Eccles, J., Adler, T. F., Futterman, R., Goff, S. B., Kaczala, C. M., Meece, J., & Midgley, C. (1983). Expectancies, values, and academic behaviors. In J. T. Spence (Ed.), *Achievement and achievement motives.* San Francisco: Freeman.

Edberg, P. (1990). Rorschach assessment. In A. Goldstein & M. Hersen (Eds.), *Handbook of personality assessment.* New York: Pergamon.

Edelman, G. M. (1987). *Neural Darwinism.* New York: Basic Books.

Egan, D., & Schwartz, B. (1979). Chunking in recall of symbolic drawings. *Memory & Cognition, 7,* 149–158.

Eibl-Eibesfeldt, I. (1973). The expressive behavior of the deaf-and-born-blind. In M. von Cranach & I. Vine (Eds.), *Social communication and movement.* San Diego: Academic Press.

Eichenbaum, H., Otto, T., & Cohen, N. J. (1994). Two functional components of the hippocampal memory system. *Behavioral and Brain Sciences, 17,* 449–517.

Einhorn, H. J., & Hogarth, R. M. (1981). Behavioral decision theory: Processes of judgment and choice. *Annual Review of Psychology, 32,* 53–88.

Eisenberger, R. (1992). Learned industriousness. *Psychological Review, 99,* 248–267.

Ekman, P. (1992). Are there basic emotions? *Psychological Review, 99,* 350–353.

Ekman, P. (1994). Strong evidence for universals in facial expressions: A reply to Russell's mistaken critique. *Psychological Bulletin, 115,* 268–287.

Ekman, P., & Friesen, W. V. (1975). *Unmasking the face.* Englewood Cliffs, NJ: Prentice-Hall.

Ekman, P., & Friesen, W. V. (1986). A new pan-cultural facial expression of emotion. *Motivation and Emotion, 10,* 159–168.

Elicker, J., Englund, M., & Sroufe, L. A. (1992). Predicting peer competence and peer relationships in childhood from early parent-child relationships. In R. D. Parke & G. W. Ladd (Eds.), *Family-peer relationships: Modes of linkage.* Hillsdale, NJ: Erlbaum.

Ellis, A. (1962). *Reason and emotion in psychotherapy.* Secaucus, NJ: Prentice-Hall.

Ellis, A. (1993). Fundamentals of rational-emotive therapy for the 1990s. In W. Dryden & L. K. Hill (Eds.), *Innovations in rational-emotive therapy.* Newbury Park, CA: Sage.

Ellis, H. C., & Hunt, R. R. (1993). *Fundamentals of cognitive psychology* (5th ed.). Madison, WA: Brown & Benchmark.

Ellis, W. D. (1938). *A source book of gestalt psychology.* London: Routledge & Kegan Paul.

Ellman, S. J., Spielman, A. J., Luck, D., Steiner, S. S., & Halperin, R. (1991). REM deprivation: A review. In S. J. Ellman & J. S. Antrobus (Eds.), *The mind in sleep* (2nd ed.). New York: Wiley.

Ellsworth, P. C. (1994). William James and emotion: Is a century of fame worth a century of misunderstanding? *Psychological Review, 101,* 222–229.

Elmes, D. G., Kantowitz, B. H., & Roediger, H. L., III. (1995). *Research methods in psychology* (5th ed.). St. Paul: West Publishing.

Engel, S. A., Rumelhart, D. E., Wandell, B. A., & Lee, A. T. (1994). MRI of human visual cortex. *Nature, 369,* 525.

Eppley, K., Abrams, A., & Shear, J. (1989). The differential effects of relaxation techniques on trait anxiety: A meta-analysis. *Journal of Clinical Psychology, 45,* 957–974.

Epstein, S. (1979). The stability of behavior: On predicting most of the people much of the time. *Journal of Personality and Social Psychology, 37,* 1097–1126.

Erickson, M. H. (1964). A hypnotic technique for resistant patients. *American Journal of Clinical Hypnosis, 7,* 8–32.

Ericsson, K. A., & Simon, H. A. (1993). *Verbal reports as data* (Rev. ed.). Cambridge, MA: MIT Press.

Erikson, E. (1963). *Childhood and society.* New York: Norton.

Erikson, E. (1968). *Identity: Youth and crisis.* New York: Norton.

Erikson, E. (1982). *The life cycle completed: Review.* New York: Norton.

Estes, W. K. (1992). Postscript on ability tests, testing, and public policy. *Psychological Science, 3,* 278.

Evans, E. F. (1982). Functions of the auditory system. In H. B. Barlow & J. D. Mollon (Eds.), *The senses.* Cambridge: Cambridge University Press.

Evans, G. W., Hygge, S., & Bullinger, M. (1995). Chronic noise and psychological stress. *Psychological Science, 6,* 333–338.

Eysenck, H. J. (1952). The effects of psychotherapy: An evaluation. *Journal of Consulting Psychology, 16*, 319–324.

Eysenck, H. J. (1970). *The structure of human personality* (3rd ed.). London: Methuen.

Eysenck, H. J. (1991). Dimensions of personality: 16, 5, or 3?—Criteria for a taxonomic paradigm. *Personality and Individual Differences, 12*, 773–790.

Eysenck, H. J., & Eysenck, S. B. G. (1975). *Manual of the Eysenck Personality Questionnaire.* San Diego: EdITS.

Eysenck, H. J., & Kamin, L. (1981). *The intelligence controversy: H. J. Eysenck vs. Leon Kamin.* New York: Wiley.

Fackelmann, K. A. (1993). Marijuana and the brain. *Science News, 143*, 88–94.

Fahy, T. A. (1988). The diagnosis of multiple personality: A critical review. *British Journal of Psychiatry, 153*, 597–606.

Fallon, A. E., & Rozin, P. (1985). Sex differences in perceptions of desirable body shape. *Journal of Abnormal Psychology, 94*, 102–105.

Fallon, A. E., Rozin, P., & Pliner, P. (1984). The child's conception of food: The development of food rejections with special reference to disgust and contamination sensitivity. *Child Development, 55*, 566–575.

Fantz, R. L. (1961, May). The origin of form perception. *Scientific American, 204*, 66–72.

Farah, M. J. (1988). Is visual imagery really visual? Overlooked evidence for neuropsychology. *Psychological Review, 95*, 307–317.

Faust, I. M. (1984). Role of the fat cell in energy balance physiology. In A. J. Stunkard & E. Stellar (Eds.), *Eating and its disorders.* New York: Raven.

Fava, M., & Rosenbaum, J. F. (1991). Suicide and fluoxetine: Is there a relationship? *Journal of Clinical Psychiatry, 52*, 108–111.

Fazio, R. H. (1986). How do attitudes guide behavior? In R. M. Sorrentino & E. T. Higgins (Eds.), *Handbook of motivation and cognition: Foundations of social behavior* (Vol. 1). New York: Guilford.

Fehr, B., & Russell, J. A. (1991). The concept of love: Viewed from a prototype perspective. *Journal of Personality and Social Psychology, 60*, 425–438.

Feingold, A. (1988). Matching for attractiveness in romantic partners and same-sex friends: A meta-analysis and theoretical critique. *Psychological Bulletin, 104*, 226–235.

Feingold, A. (1990). Gender differences in effects of physical attractiveness on romantic attraction: A comparison across five research paradigms. *Journal of Personality and Social Psychology, 59*, 981–993.

Feingold, A. (1992). Good-looking people are not what we think. *Psychological Bulletin, 111*, 304–341.

Feist, J. (1994). *Theories of personality* (3rd ed.). Fort Worth, TX: Harcourt Brace.

Ferguson, N. B. L., & Keesey, R. E. (1975). Effect of a quinine-adulterated diet upon body weight maintenance in male rats with ventromedial lesions. *Journal of Comparative and Physiological Psychology, 89*, 478–488.

Ferster, C. B., & Skinner, B. F. (1957). *Schedules of reinforcement.* New York: Appleton-Century-Crofts.

Festinger, L. (1957). *A theory of cognitive dissonance.* Stanford, CA: Stanford University Press.

Festinger, L., & Carlsmith, J. M. (1959). Cognitive consequences of forced compliance. *Journal of Abnormal and Social Psychology, 58*, 203–210.

Festinger, L., Riecken, H. W., & Schacter, S. (1956). *When prophecy fails.* Minneapolis: University of Minnesota Press.

Festinger, L., Schachter, S., & Black, K. (1950). *Social pressures in informal groups: A study of human factors in housing.* New York: Harper.

Fischbach, G. D. (1992, September). Mind and brain. *Scientific American, 267*, 48–57.

Fishbain, D. A., & Goldberg, M. (1991). The misdiagnosis of conversion disorder in a psychiatric emergency service. *General Hospital Psychiatry, 13*, 177–181.

Fiske, S. T. (1993). Social cognition and social perception. *Annual Review of Psychology, 44*, 155–194.

Fiss, H. (1991). Experimental strategies for the study of the function of dreaming. In S. J. Ellman & J. S. Antrobus (Eds.), *The mind in sleep* (2nd ed.). New York: Wiley.

Flavel, J. H. (1971). Stage-related properties of cognitive development. *Cognitive Psychology, 2*, 421–453.

Flavel, J. H., Miller, P. A., & Miller, S. A. (1993). *Cognitive development* (3rd ed.). Englewood Cliffs, NJ: Prentice-Hall.

Fleishman, E. A., & Parker, J. F., Jr. (1962). Factors in the retention and relearning of perceptual motor skill. *Journal of Experimental Psychology, 64*, 215–226.

Foa, E. B., & Riggs, D. S. (1995). Posttraumatic stress disorder following assault: Theoretical considerations and empirical findings. *Current Directions in Psychological Science, 4*, 61–65.

Fodor, J. A., & Pylyshyn, Z. W. (1981). How direct is visual perception? Some reflections on Gibson's "ecological approach." *Cognition, 9*, 139–196.

Fong, G. T., Krantz, D. H., & Nisbett, R. E. (1986). The effects of statistical training on thinking about everyday problems. *Cognitive Psychology, 18*, 253–292.

Fong, G. T., & Nisbett, R. E. (1991). Immediate and delayed transfer of training effects in statistical reasoning. *Journal of Experimental Psychology: General, 120*, 34–45.

Frazer, J. G. (1890/1959). *The new golden bough: A study in magic and religion* (abridged ed., T. H. Gaster, Ed.). New York: Macmillan.

Freedman, J. L. (1988). Television violence and aggression: What the evidence shows. In S. Oskamp (Ed.), *Television as a social issue* (Vol. 8). Beverly Hills, CA: Sage.

Freedman, J. L., & Fraser, S. C. (1966). Compliance without pressure: The foot-in-the-door technique. *Journal of Personality and Social Psychology, 4*, 195–202.

Freud, S. (1900/1990). *The interpretation of dreams.* New York: Basic Books.

Freud, S. (1905/1962). *Three contributions to the theory of sexuality.* New York: Dutton.

Freud, S. (1910). The origin and development of psychoanalysis. *American Journal of Psychology, 21*, 181–218.

Freud, S. (1912/1964). The dynamics of transference. In J. Strachey (Trans. & Ed.), *The standard edition of the complete works of Sigmund Freud* (Vol. 12). London: Hogarth Press.

Freud, S. (1923). *The ego and the id.* New York: Norton.

Freud, S. (1940). *An outline of psychoanalysis.* New York: Norton.

Freudenberger, H. J. (1974). Staff burnout. *Journal of Social Issues, 30*, 159–165.

Friedman, H. S., Hawley, P. H., & Tucker, J. S. (1994). Personality, health, and longevity. *Current Directions in Psychological Science, 3*, 37–41.

Friedman, M., & Rosenman, R. F. (1974). *Type A behavior and your heart.* New York: Knopf.

Friedrich-Cofer, L., & Huston, A. C. (1986). Television violence and aggression: The debate continues. *Psychological Bulletin, 100*, 364–371.

Fukuda, T., Kanada, K., & Saito, S. (1990). An ergonomic evaluation of lens accommodation related to visual circumstances. *Ergonomics, 33,* 811–831.

Fyer, A. J., Mannuzza, S., Gallops, M. S., Martin, L. Y., Aaronson, C., Gorman, J. M., Liebowitz, M. R., & Klein, D. F. (1990). Familial transmission of simple phobias and fears: A preliminary report. *Archives of General Psychiatry, 47,* 252–256.

Gagnon, J., & Simon, W. (1973). *Sexual conduct: The social sources of human sexuality.* Chicago: Aldine.

Galef, B. G., Jr. (1985). Social learning in wild Norway rats. In T. D. Johnston & A. T. Pietrewicz (Eds.), *Issues in the ecological study of learning.* Hillsdale, NJ: Erlbaum.

Galton, F. (1869). *Hereditary genius: An inquiry into its laws and consequences.* New York: Appleton.

Galton, F. (1883). *Inquiries into human faculty and development.* London: Macmillan.

Gandelman, R. (1992). *Psychobiology of behavior development.* New York: Oxford University Press.

Gandevia, S. C., McCloskey, D. I., & Burke, D. (1992). Kinaesthetic signals and muscle contraction. *Trends in Neurosciences, 15,* 62–65.

Gangestad, S. W., & Snyder, M. (1985). On the nature of self-monitoring: An examination of latent causal structure. In P. Shaver (Ed.), *Review of personality and social psychology* (Vol. 6). Beverly Hills, CA: Sage.

Garcia, J., & Koelling, R. A. (1966). Relation of cue to consequence in avoidance learning. *Psychonomic Science, 4,* 123–124.

Gardner, E. B., & Costanzo, R. H. (1981). Properties of kinesthetic neurons in somatosensory cortex of awake monkeys. *Brain Research, 214,* 301–319.

Gardner, H. (1983). *Frames of mind: The theory of multiple intelligences.* New York: Basic Books.

Gardner, H. (1993). *Multiple intelligences: The theory in practice.* New York: Basic Books.

Gardner, R. A., & Gardner, B. T. (1969). Teaching sign language to a chimpanzee. *Science, 165,* 664–672.

Gardner, R. A., Gardner, B. T., & Van Cantfort, T. E. (Eds.). (1989). *Teaching sign language to chimpanzees.* Albany, NY: SUNY Press.

Garrity, T. F., Stallones, L., Marx, M. B., & Johnson, T. P. (1989). Pet ownership and attachment as supportive factors in the health of the elderly. *Anthrozoos, 3,* 35–44.

Gay, P. (1988). *Freud: A life for our times.* New York: Anchor Books.

Gazzaniga, M. (1967, August). The split brain in man. *Scientific American, 217,* 24–29.

Gazzaniga, M. S. (1970). *The bisected brain.* New York: Appleton-Century-Crofts.

Gazzaniga, M. S., Bogen, J. E., & Sperry, R. W. (1965). Observations on visual perception after disconnection of the cerebral hemispheres in man. *Brain, 88,* 221–236.

Gazzaniga, M. S., & LeDoux, J. E. (1978). *The integrated mind.* New York: Plenum.

Geiselman, R. E., Fisher, R. P., MacKinnon, D. P., & Holland, H. L. (1985). Eyewitness memory enhancement in the police interview: Cognitive retrieval mnemonics versus hypnosis. *Journal of Applied Psychology, 70,* 401–412.

Gelman, S. A., & Markman, E. M. (1986). Categories and induction in young children. *Cognition, 23,* 183–209.

Gerbner, G., & Gross, L. (1976). Living with television: The violence profile. *Journal of Communications, 26,* 172–199.

Gershon, E. S. (1990). Genetics. In F. K. Goodwin & K. R. Jamison (Eds.), *Manic-depressive illness.* New York: Oxford University Press.

Gershon, E. S., & Reider, R. O. (1992, April). Major disorders of mind and brain. *Scientific American, 267,* 126–133.

Gibbs, R. W. (1979). Contextual effects in understanding indirect requests. *Discourse Processes, 2,* 1–10.

Gibson, E. J., & Walk, R. D. (1960, April). The "visual cliff." *Scientific American, 202,* 64–71.

Gibson, J. J. (1966). *The senses considered as perceptual systems.* Boston: Houghton Mifflin.

Gibson, J. J. (1979). *The ecological approach to visual perception.* Boston: Houghton Mifflin.

Gick, M. L., & McGarry, S. J. (1992). Learning from mistakes: Inducing analogous solution failures to a source problem produces later successes in analogical transfer. *Journal of Experimental Psychology: Learning, Memory, & Cognition, 18,* 623–639.

Giguere, C., & Abel, S. M. (1993). Sound localization: Effects of reverberation time, speaker array, stimulus frequency, and stimulus rise/decay. *Journal of Acoustical Society of America, 94,* 769–776.

Gilbert, D. T. (1989). Thinking lightly about others: Automatic components of the social inference process. In J. S. Uleman & J. A. Bargh (Eds.), *Unintended thought.* New York: Guilford.

Gilligan, C. (1982). *In a different voice: Psychological theory and women's development.* Cambridge, MA: Harvard University Press.

Gillin, J. C. (1993). Clinical sleep-wake disorders in psychiatric practice: Dyssomnias. In D. L. Dunner (Ed.), *Current psychiatric therapy.* Philadelphia: Saunders.

Gladue, B. A. (1994). The biopsychology of sexual orientation. *Current Directions in Psychological Research, 3,* 150–154.

Glaser, B. G., & Strauss, A. L. (1968). *Time for dying.* Chicago: Aldine.

Gleitman, H. (1996). *Basic psychology.* New York: Norton.

Glenberg, A. M., & Fernandez, A. (1989). Evidence for auditory temporal distinctiveness: Modality effects in order and frequency judgments. *Journal of Experimental Psychology: Learning, Memory, & Cognition, 14,* 728–737.

Goldberg, J., True, W. R., Eisen, S. A., & Henderson, W. G. (1990). A twin study of the effects of the Vietnam War on posttraumatic stress disorder. *Journal of the American Medical Association, 263,* 1227–1232.

Goldberg, L. R. (1993). The structure of phenotypic personality traits. *American Psychologist, 48,* 26–34.

Goldberger, L., & Breznitz, S. (Eds.). (1993). *Handbook of stress: Theoretical and clinical aspects.* New York: Free Press.

Goldstein, B. (1994). *Psychology.* Pacific Grove, CA: Brooks/Cole.

Golub, S. (1992). *Periods: From menarche to menopause.* Newbury Park, CA: Sage.

Goodall, J. (1990). *Through a window: My thirty years with the chimpanzees of Gombe.* Boston: Houghton Mifflin.

Goodenough, D. R. (1991). Dream recall: History and current status of the field. In S. J. Ellman & J. S. Antrobus (Eds.), *The mind in sleep* (2nd ed.). New York: Wiley.

Goodwin, K. F., & Jamison, K. R. (1990). *Manic depressive illness.* New York: Oxford University Press.

Gopnick, A. (1982). Words and plans: Early language and the development of intelligent action. *Journal of Child Language, 9,* 303–318.

Gopnick, A. (1993). How we know our minds: The illusion of first-person knowledge in intentionality. *Behavioral and Brain Sciences, 16,* 1–14.

Gottesman, I. I. (1991). *Schizophrenia genesis: The origins of madness.* New York: Freeman.

Gould, R. L. (1978). *Transformations: Growth and change in adult life.* New York: Simon & Schuster.

Graf, P., Mandler, G., & Haden, P. E. (1982). Simulating amnesic symptoms in normal subjects. *Science, 218,* 1243–1244.

Graf, P., & Schacter, D. L. (1985). Implicit and explicit memory for new associations in normal and amnesic subjects. *Journal of Experimental Psychology: Learning, Memory, & Cognition, 11,* 501–518.

Graffen, N. F., Ray, W. J., & Lundy, R. (1995). EEG concomitants of hypnosis and hypnotic susceptibility. *Journal of Abnormal Psychology, 104,* 123–131.

Graig, E. (1993). Stress as a consequence of the urban physical environment. In L. Goldberger & S. Breznitz (Eds.), *Handbook of stress: Theoretical and clinical aspects* (2nd ed.). New York: Free Press.

Granrud, C. E. (Ed.) (1993). *Visual perception and cognition in infancy.* Hillsdale, NJ: Erlbaum.

Granvold, D. K. (Ed.). (1994) *Cognitive and behavioral treatment: Methods and applications.* Pacific Grove, CA: Brooks/Cole.

Greenblatt, D. J., & Shader, R. I. (1978). Pharmacotherapy of anxiety with benzodiazepines and beta-adrenergic blockers. In M. Lipton, A. DiMascio, & F. Killiam (Eds.), *Psychopharmacology: A generation of progress.* New York: Raven.

Greene, R. L. (1992). *Human memory: Paradigms and paradoxes.* Hillsdale, NJ: Erlbaum.

Greenough, W. T., Black, J. E., & Wallace, C. S. (1987). Experience and brain development. *Child Development, 58,* 539–559.

Greenwald, A. G., & Pratkanis, A. R. (1984). The self. In R. S. Wyer & T. K. Srull (Eds.), *Handbook of social cognition* (Vol. 3). Hillsdale, NJ: Erlbaum.

Greenwald, A. G., Schuh, E. S., & Klinger, M. R. (1995). Activation of marginally perceptible ("subliminal") stimuli: Dissociation of unconscious from conscious cognition. *Journal of Experimental Psychology: General, 124,* 22–42.

Greenwald, A. G., Spangenberg, E. R., Pratkanis, A. R., & Eskenazi, J. (1991). Double-blind tests of subliminal self-help audiotapes. *Psychological Science, 2,* 119–122.

Grencavage, L. M., & Norcross, J. C. (1990). Where are the common factors? *Professional Psychology: Research and Practice, 21,* 372–378.

Grice, H. P. (1975). Logic and conversation. In P. Cole & J. L. Morgan (Eds.), *Syntax and semantics: Vol. 3. Speech acts.* New York: Seminar Press.

Grill, H. J., & Kaplan, J. M. (1990). Caudal brainstem participates in the distributed neural control of feeding. In E. M. Stricker (Ed.), *Handbook of behavioral neurobiology* (Vol. 10). New York: Plenum.

Grochowitz, P. M., Schedlowski, M., Husband, A. J., King, M. G., Hibberd, A. D., & Bowen, K. M. (1991). Behavioral conditioning prolongs heart allograft survival in rats. *Brain, Behavior, and Immunity, 5,* 349–356.

Grossberg, S., & Rudd, M. E. (1992). Cortical dynamics of visual motion perception: Short-range and long-range apparent motion. *Psychological Review, 99,* 78–121.

Groves, P. M., & Thompson, R. F. (1970). Habituation: A dual-process theory. *Psychological Review, 77,* 419–450.

Gruneberg, M. M., Sykes, R. N., & Gillett, E. (1994). The facilitating effects of mnemonic strategies on two learning tasks in learning disabled adults. *Neuropsychological Rehabilitation, 4,* 241–254.

Gulick, W. L., Gescheider, G. A., & Frisina, R. D. (1989). *Hearing: Physiological acoustics, neural coding, and psychoacoustics.* New York: Oxford University Press.

Gunderson, J. G. (1992). Diagnostic controversies. In A. Tasman & M. B. Riba (Eds.), *Review of psychiatry* (Vol. 11). Washington, DC: American Psychiatric Press.

Gurman, E. B. (1994). Debriefing for all concerned: Ethical treatment of human subjects. *Psychological Science, 5,* 139.

Haan, N. (Ed.). (1977). *Coping and defending: Processes of self-environment organization.* New York: Academic Press.

Haan, N. (1993). The assessment of coping, defense, and stress. In L. Goldberger & S. Brezitz (Eds.), *Handbook of stress: Theoretical and clinical aspects* (2nd ed.). New York: Free Press.

Hamer, D. H., Hu, S., Magnuson, V. L., Hu, N., & Pattatucci, A. M. L. (1993). A linkage between DNA markers on the X chromosome and male sexual orientation. *Science, 261,* 321–327.

Hansen, C. H. (1989). Priming sex-role stereotypic event schemas with rock music videos: Effects on impression favorability, trait inferences, and recall of a subsequent male-female interaction. *Basic and Applied Social Psychology, 10,* 371–391.

Hanson, V. L. (1990). Recall of order information by deaf signers: Phonetic coding in temporal order recall. *Memory & Cognition, 18,* 604–610.

Harlow, H. F., Harlow, M. K., & Meyer, D. R. (1971). From thought to therapy: Lessons from a primate laboratory. *American Scientist, 59,* 538–549.

Harlow, H. F., & Zimmerman, R. R. (1959). Affectional responses in the infant monkey. *Science, 130,* 421–432.

Harmon, T. M., Hynan, M. T., & Tyre, T. E. (1990). Improved obstetric outcomes using hypnotic analgesia and skill mastery combined with childbirth education. *Journal of Consulting and Clinical Psychology, 58,* 525–530.

Hartshorne, H., & May, A. (1928). *Studies in the nature of character: Vol. 1. Studies in deceit.* New York: Macmillan.

Harvey, S. (1987). Female sexual behavior: Fluctuations during the menstrual cycle. *Journal of Psychosomatic Research, 31,* 101–110.

Hasher, L., Stolzfus, E. R., Zacks, R. T., & Rypma, B. (1991). Age and inhibition. *Journal of Experimental Psychology: Learning, Memory, & Cognition, 17,* 163–169.

Hasher, L., & Zacks, R. R. (1979). Automatic and effortful processes in memory. *Journal of Experimental Psychology: General, 108,* 356–388.

Hastie, R. (1991). A review from a high place: The field of judgment and decision making as revealed in its current textbooks. *Psychological Science, 2,* 135–138.

Hatfield, E. (1988). Passionate and companionate love. In R. J. Sternberg & M. L. Barnes (Eds.), *The psychology of love.* New Haven, CT: Yale University Press.

Hatfield, E., & Rapson, R. L. (1993). *Love, sex, and intimacy.* New York: HarperCollins.

Hauri, P. (1982). The sleep disorders. Kalamazoo, MI: Upjohn.

Hayes, C. (1952). *The ape in our house.* London: Gollacz.

Hayes, K. J., & Hayes, C. (1951). The intellectual development of a home-raised chimpanzee. *Proceedings of the American Philosophical Society, 95,* 105–109.

Hearold, S. (1986). A synthesis of 1043 effects of television on social behavior. In G. Comstock (Ed.), *Public communication and behavior.* New York: Academic Press.

Hearst, E., & Franklin, S. R. (1977). Positive and negative relations between a signal and food: Approach-withdrawal behavior to the signal. *Journal of Experimental Psychology: Animal Behavior Processes, 3,* 37–52.

Hebb, D. O. (1949). The organization of behaviour. New York: Wiley-Interscience.

Heider, E. (1972). Universals of color naming and memory. *Journal of Experimental Psychology, 93,* 10–20.

Heider, F. (1944). Social perception and phenomenal causality. *Psychological Review, 51,* 358–374.

Heiman, G. A. (1995). *Research methods in psychology.* Boston: Houghton Mifflin.

Hellige, J. B. (1990). Hemispheric asymmetry. *Annual Review of Psychology, 41,* 55–80.

Hellige, J. B. (1993). Unity of thought and action: Varieties of interaction between the left and right cerebral hemispheres. *Current Directions in Psychological Science, 2,* 21–25.

Henley, N. M. (1989). Molehill or mountain? What we know and don't know about sex bias in language. In M. Crawford & M. Gentry (Eds.), *Gender and thought: Psychological perspectives.* New York: Springer-Verlag.

Herman, C. P., & Polivy, J. (1988). Studies of eating in normal dieters. In B. T. Walsh (Ed.), *Eating behavior in eating disorders.* Washington, DC: American Psychiatric Press.

Herrmann, D., Raybeck, D., & Gutman, D. (1993). *Improving student memory.* Seattle, WA: Hogrefe & Huber.

Hetherington, A. W., & Ranson, S. W. (1942). The relation of various hypothalamic lesions to adiposity in the rat. *Journal of Comparative Neurology, 76,* 475–499.

Higbee, K. L. (1988). *Your memory* (2nd ed.). Englewood Cliffs, NJ: Prentice-Hall.

Hilgard, E. R. (1965). *Hypnotic susceptibility.* New York: Harcourt, Brace, & World.

Hilgard, E. R. (1986). *Divided consciousness: Multiple controls in human thought and action* (Rev. ed.). New York: Wiley.

Hilgard, E. R. (1987). *Psychology in America: An historical survey.* New York: Harcourt Brace Jovanovich.

Hilgard, E. R. (1992). Dissociation and theories of hypnosis. In E. Fromm & M. Nash (Eds.), *Contemporary hypnosis research.* New York: Guilford.

Hines, M. (1982). Prenatal gonadal hormones and sex differences in human behavior. *Psychological Bulletin, 92,* 56–80.

Hintzman, D. L. (1986). "Schema abstraction" in a multiple-trace memory model. *Psychological Review, 93,* 411–428.

Hitch, G. J., & Halliday, M. S. (1983). Working memory in children. *Philosophical Transactions of the Royal Society London B, 302,* 325–340.

Hobfoll, S. E., Shoham, S. B., & Ritter, C. (1991). Women's satisfaction with social support and their receipt of aid. *Journal of Personality and Social Psychology, 61,* 332–341.

Hobson, J. A (1988). *The dreaming brain.* New York: Basic Books.

Hobson, J. A., & McCarley, R. W. (1977). The brain as a dream state generator: An activation-synthesis hypothesis of the dream process. *American Journal of Psychiatry, 134,* 1335–1348.

Hodges, J., & Tizard, B. (1989). IQ and behavioral adjustment of ex-institutional adolescents. *Journal of Child Psychology and Psychiatry, 30,* 53–75.

Hoffman, M. L. (1986). Affect, cognition, motivation. In R. M. Sorrentino & E. T. Higgins (Eds.), *Handbook of motivation and cognition: Foundations of social behavior.* New York: Guilford.

Hohmann, G. W. (1966). Some effects of spinal cord lesions on experienced emotional feelings. *Psychophysiology, 3,* 143–156.

Holland, P. C. (1977). Conditioned stimulus as a determinant of the form of the Pavlovian conditioned response. *Journal of Experimental Psychology: Animal Behavior Processes, 3,* 77–104.

Holland, P. C., & Rescorla, R. A. (1975). The effects of two ways of devaluing the unconditioned stimulus after first- and second-order appetitive conditioning. *Journal of Experimental Psychology: Animal Behavior Processes, 1,* 355–363.

Holmes, D. S. (1976). Debriefing after psychological experiments: I. Effectiveness of postdeception dehoaxing. *American Psychologist, 31,* 858–867.

Holmes, D. S. (1987). The influence of meditation versus rest on physiological arousal: A second examination. In M. A. West (Ed.), *The psychology of meditation.* Oxford: Clarendon Press.

Holmes, T. H., & Rahe, R. H. (1967). The Social Readjustment Rating Scale. *Journal of Psychosomatic Research, 11,* 213–218.

Holt, E. B. (1931). *Animal drive and the learning process: An essay toward radical empiricism.* New York: Holt.

Homa, D. (1984). On the nature of categories. In G. H. Bower (Ed.), *The psychology of learning and motivation* (Vol. 18). Orlando, FL: Academic Press.

Honzik, M. P., Macfarlane, J. W., & Allen, L. (1948). The stability of mental test performance between two and eighteen years. *Journal of Experimental Education, 17,* 309–324.

Hooker, W. D., & Jones, F. T. (1987). Increased susceptibility to memory intrusions and the Stroop interference effect during acute marijuana intoxication. *Psychopharmacology, 91,* 20–24.

Hopkins, B. (1991). Facilitating early motor development: An intracultural study of West Indian mothers and their infants living in Britain. In J. K. Nugent, B. M. Lester, & T. B. Brazelton (Eds.), *The cultural context of infancy: Vol. 2. Multicultural and interdisciplinary approaches to parent-infant relations.* Norwood, NJ: Ablex.

Horgan, J. (1993, June). Eugenics revisited. *Scientific American, 268,* 123–131.

Horgan, J. (1994, July). Can science explain consciousness? *Scientific American, 271,* 88–94.

Horn, J. L. (1982). The aging of human abilities. In J. Wolman (Ed.), *Handbook of developmental psychology.* Englewood Cliffs, NJ: Prentice-Hall.

Horn, J. L. (1985). Remodeling old models of intelligence. In B. B. Wolman (Ed.), *Handbook of intelligence.* New York: Wiley.

Horn, J. L., & Cattell, R. B. (1966). Refinement and test of the theory of fluid and crystallized ability intelligences. *Journal of Educational Psychology, 57,* 253–270.

Horne, J. A. (1988). *Why we sleep: The functions of sleep in humans and other mammals.* Oxford: Oxford University Press.

Horne, J. A., & Minard, A. (1985). Sleep and sleepiness following a behaviourally "active" day. *Ergonomics, 28,* 567–575.

Horney, K. (1945). *Our inner conflicts: A constructive theory of neurosis.* New York: Norton.

Horney, K. (1967). *Feminine psychology.* New York: Norton.

Horvath, A. O., & Luborsky, L. (1993). The role of the therapeutic alliance in psychotherapy. *Journal of Consulting and Clinical Psychology, 61,* 561–573.

Horvath, P. (1988). Placebos and common factors in two decades of psychotherapy research. *Psychological Bulletin 104,* 214–225.

Houle, M., McGrath, P. A., Moran, G., & Garrett, O. J. (1988). The efficacy of hypnosis- and relaxation-induced analgesia on two dimensions of pain for cold pressor and electrical tooth pulp stimulation. *Pain, 33,* 241–251.

Hubbel, J. C. (1990, January). Animal rights war on medicine. *Reader's Digest,* 70–76.

Hubel, D. H., & Wiesel, T. N. (1962). Receptive fields, binocular interaction, and functional architecture in the cat's visual cortex. *Journal of Physiology, 160,* 106–154.

Hubel, D. H., & Wiesel, T. N. (1979, September). Brain mechanisms and vision. *Scientific American, 241,* 150–162.

Hull, C. L. (1943). *Principles of behavior.* New York: Appleton-Century.

Hull, J. G., & Bond, C. F., Jr. (1986). Social and behavioral consequences of alcohol consumption and expectancy: A meta-analysis. *Psychological Bulletin, 99,* 347–360.

Hunnicutt, C. P., & Newman, I. A. (1993). Adolescent dieting practices and nutrition knowledge. *Health Values, 17,* 35–40.

Hunt, E. (1985). The correlates of intelligence. In D. K. Detterman (Ed.), *Current topics in human intelligence* (Vol. 1). Norwood, NJ: Ablex.

Hunt, E., & Agnoli, F. (1991). The Whorfian hypothesis: A cognitive psychology perspective. *Psychological Review, 98,* 377–389.

Hunt, R. R., & Einstein, G. O. (1981). Relational and item-specific information in memory. *Journal of Verbal Learning and Verbal Behavior, 20,* 497–514.

Hunt, R. R., & McDaniel, M. A. (1993). The enigma of organization and distinctiveness. *Journal of Memory and Language, 32,* 421–445.

Hurt, S. W., Reznikoff, M., & Clarkin, J. F. (1995). The Rorschach. In L. E. Beutler & M. R. Berren (Eds.), *Integrative assessment of adult personality.* New York: Guilford.

Hyde, J. S., & Lin, M. C. (1988). Gender differences in verbal ability: A developmental meta-analysis. *Psychological Bulletin, 104,* 53–69.

Izard, C. E. (1994). Innate and universal facial expressions: Evidence from developmental and cross-cultural research. *Psychological Bulletin, 115,* 288–299.

Jacobi, L., & Cash, T. F. (1994). In pursuit of the perfect appearance: Discrepancies among self-ideal percepts of multiple physical attributes. *Journal of Applied Social Psychology, 24,* 379–396.

Jacobson, E. (1938). *Progressive relaxation.* Chicago: University of Chicago Press.

Jacobson, J. L., & Jacobson, S. W. (1994). Prenatal alcohol exposure and neurobehavioral development: Where is the threshold? *Alcohol Health and Research World, 18,* 30–36.

Jacoby, L. L., & Witherspoon, D. (1982). Remembering without awareness. *Canadian Journal of Psychology, 36,* 300–324.

Jacoby, L. L., Woloshyn, V., & Kelley, C. M. (1989). Becoming famous without being recognized: Unconscious influences of memory produced by dividing attention. *Journal of Experimental Psychology: General, 118,* 115–125.

James, W. (1884). Some omissions of introspective psychology. *Mind, 9,* 1–26.

James, W. (1890). *The principles of psychology.* New York: Holt. (Reprinted Cambridge, MA: Harvard University Press, 1983).

James, W. (1894). The physical basis of emotion. *Psychological Review, 1,* 516–529.

Jamison, K. R. (1986). Suicide and bipolar disorders. *Annals of the New York Academy of Science, 487,* 301–315.

Jamison, K. R. (1989). Mood disorders and patterns of creativity in British writers and artists. *Psychiatry, 52,* 125–134.

Jamison, K. R., Gerner, R. H., Hammen, C., & Padesky, C. (1980). Clouds and silver linings: Positive experiences associated with primary affective disorders. *American Journal of Psychiatry, 137,* 198–202.

Janis, I. L. (1982). *Victims of groupthink* (2nd ed.). Boston: Houghton Mifflin.

Janis, I. L. (1989). *Crucial decisions: Leadership in policymaking and crisis management.* New York: Free Press.

Jarrad, L. E. (1993). On the role of the hippocampus in learning and memory in the rat. *Behavioral and Neural Biology, 60,* 9–26.

Jasper, J. H., & Tessier, J. (1969). Acetylcholine liberation from cerebral cortex during paradoxical (REM) sleep. *Science, 172,* 601–602.

Jaynes, J. (1976). *The origin of consciousness in the breakdown of the bicameral mind.* Boston: Houghton Mifflin.

Jenike, M. A., Baer, L., Ballantine, T., & Maetuga, R. L. (1991). Cingulotomy for refractory obsessive-compulsive disorder: A long-term follow-up of 33 cases. *Archives of General Psychiatry, 48,* 548–557.

Jenike, M. A., Baer, L., & Minichiello, W. E. (Eds.). (1986). *Obsessive-compulsive disorders: Theory and management.* Littleton, MA: PSG Publishing.

Jenkins, H. M., Barrera, F. J., Ireland, C., & Woodside, B. (1978). Signal-centered action patterns of dogs in appetitive classical conditioning. *Learning and Motivation, 9,* 272–296.

Jenkins, J. G., & Dallenbach, K. M. (1924). Obliviscence during sleep and waking. *American Journal of Psychology, 35,* 605–612.

Jenner, P. (1990). Parkinson's disease: Clues to the cause of cell death in the substantia nigra. *Seminars in the Neurosciences, 2,* 117–126.

Jennison, K. M. (1992). The impact of stressful life events and social support on drinking among older adults: A general population survey. *International Journal of Aging and Human Development, 35,* 99–123.

Jensen, A. R. (1992). Commentary: Vehicles of *g. Psychological Science, 3,* 275–278.

Jensen, A. R. (1993). Why is reaction time correlated with psychometric *g? Current Directions in Psychological Science, 2,* 53–56.

Jensen, A. R., & Weng, L. (1994). What is a good *g? Intelligence, 18,* 231–258.

Jensen, J. P., Bergin, A. E., & Greaves, D. W. (1990). The meaning of eclecticism: New survey and analysis of components. *Professional Psychology: Research and Practice, 21,* 124–130.

John, E. R., Prichep, L. S., Fridman, J., & Easton, P. (1988). Neurometrics: Computer-assisted differential diagnosis of brain dysfunction. *Science, 239,* 162–169.

Johnson, C. H., & Hastings, J. W. (1986). The elusive mechanism of the circadian clock. *American Scientist, 74,* 29–36.

Johnson, L. M., & Morris, E. K. (1987). Public information on research with nonhumans. *American Psychologist, 42,* 103–104.

Johnson, M. H., Dziurawiec, S., Ellis, H., & Morton, J. (1991). Newborns' preferential tracking of face-like stimuli and its subsequent decline. *Cognition, 40,* 1-19.

Johnson, R. C., McClearn, C. G., Yuen, S., Nagoshi, C. T., Ahern, F. M., & Cole, R. E. (1985). Galton's data a century later. *American Psychologist, 40,* 875–892.

Jones, E. E. (1964). *Ingratiation.* New York: Appleton-Century-Crofts.

Jones, E. E. (1990). *Interpersonal perception.* New York: Freeman.

Jones, E. E., & Davis, K. E. (1965). A theory of correspondent inferences: From acts to dispositions. In L. Berkowitz (Ed.), *Advances in experimental social psychology* (Vol. 2). New York: Academic Press.

Jones, E. E., & Harris, V. A. (1967). The attribution of attitudes. *Journal of Experimental Social Psychology, 3*, 1–24.

Jones, E. R., & Childers, R. L. (1993). *Contemporary college physics* (2nd ed.). Reading, MA: Addison-Wesley.

Jones, G. V., & Martin, M. (1992). Misremembering a familiar object: Mnemonic illusions, not drawing bias. *Memory & Cognition, 20,* 211–213.

Jones, L. A. (1988). Motor illusions: What do they reveal about proprioception? *Psychological Bulletin, 103,* 72–86.

Jones, M. C. (1924). A laboratory study of fear: The case of Peter. *Pedagogical Seminary, 31,* 308–315.

Jones, R. T. (1971). Tetrahydrocannabinol and the marijuana-induced social "high" or the effects on the mind of marijuana. In A. J. Singer (Ed.), Marijuana: Chemistry, pharmacology, and patterns of social use. *Annals of the New York Academy of Sciences, 191,* 155–165.

Jou, J., Shanteau, J., & Harris, R. J. (1996). An information processing view of framing effects: The role of causal schemas in decision making. *Memory & Cognition, 24,* 1–15.

Joule, R. V. (1986). Twenty-five on: Yet another version of cognitive dissonance theory? *European Journal of Social Psychology, 16,* 65–78.

Jung, C. G. (1923). *Psychological types.* New York: Pantheon Books.

Justice, A. (1985). Review of the effects of stress on cancer in laboratory animals: Importance of time stress application and type of tumor. *Psychological Bulletin, 98,* 108–138.

Kahn, R. S., Davidson, M., Knott, P., Stern, R. G., Apter, S., & Davis, K. L. (1993). Effect of neuroleptic medication on cerebrospinal fluid monoamine metabolite concentrations in schizophrenia: Serotonin-dopamine interactions as a target for treatment. *Archives of General Psychiatry, 50,* 599–605.

Kahneman, D. (1973). *Attention and effort.* Englewood Cliffs, NJ: Prentice-Hall.

Kahneman, D., Slovic, P., & Tversky, A. (Eds.). (1982). *Judgment under uncertainty: Heuristics and biases.* Cambridge: Cambridge University Press.

Kail, R. (1991). Developmental change in speed of processing during childhood and adolescence. *Psychological Bulletin, 109,* 490–501.

Kail, R., & Salthouse, T. A. (1994). Processing speed as a mental capacity. *Acta Psychologica, 86,* 199–225.

Kalat, J. W. (1992). *Biological psychology* (4th ed.). Belmont, CA: Wadsworth.

Kalat, J. W. (1996). *Introduction to psychology* (4th ed.). Pacific Grove, CA: Brooks/Cole.

Kaler, S. R., & Freeman, B. J. (1994). Analysis of environmental deprivation: Cognitive and social development in Romanian orphans. *Journal of Child Psychology and Psychiatry, 35,* 769–781.

Kales, A., & Kales, J. D. (1984). *Evaluation and treatment of insomnia.* New York: Oxford.

Kamen-Siegel, L., Rodin, J., Seligman, M. E. P., & Dwyer, J. (1991). Explanatory style and cell-mediated immunity in elderly men and women. *Health Psychology, 10,* 229–235.

Kamil, A. C., & Balda, R. P. (1990). Differential memory for different cache sites by Clark's nutcrackers (*Nucifraga columbiana*). *Journal of Experimental Psychology: Animal Behavior Processes, 16,* 162–168.

Kamin, L. J. (1968). "Attention-like" processes in classical conditioning. In M. R. Jones (Ed.), *Miami symposium on the prediction of behavior: Aversive stimulation.* Miami: University of Miami Press.

Kandel, E. R. (1991). Cellular mechanisms of learning and the biological basis of individuality. In E. R. Kandel, J. H. Schwartz, & T. M. Jessel (Eds.), *Principles of neural science* (3rd ed.). New York: Elsevier.

Kandel, E. R., & Schwartz, J. H. (1982). Molecular biology of learning: Modulation of transmitter release. *Science, 218,* 433–443.

Kanner, A. D., Coyne, J. C., Schaefer, C., & Lazarus, R. S. (1981). Comparison of two modes of stress measurment: Daily hassles and uplifts versus major life events. *Journal of Behavioral Medicine, 4,* 1–39.

Kane, J. M., & Marder, S. R. (1993). Psychopharmacologic treatment of schizophrenia. *Schizophrenia Bulletin, 19,* 287–302.

Kane, J. M., Woerner, M., Weinhoold, P., Wegner, J., Kinon, B., & Bernstein, M. (1986). Incidence of tardive dyskinesia: Five-year data from a prospective study. *Psychopharmacology Bulletin, 20,* 387–389.

Kaplan, R. M. (1985). The controversy related to the use of psychological tests. In B. B. Wolman (Ed.), *Handbook of intelligence: Theories, measurements, and applications.* New York: Wiley.

Kapur, S., & Mann, J. J. (1993). Antidepressant action and the neurobiologic effects of ECT: Human studies. In C. E. Coffey (Ed.), *The clinical science of electroconvulsive therapy.* Washington, DC: American Psychiatric Press.

Karni, A., Tanne, D., Rubenstein, B. S., Askenasy, J., & Sagi, D. (1994). Dependence on REM sleep of overnight improvement of a perceptual skill. *Science, 265,* 679–682.

Kauer, J. S. (1987). Coding in the olfactory system. In T. E. Finger & W. L. Silver (Eds.), *Neurobiology of taste and smell.* New York: Wiley.

Kausler, D. H. (1994). *Learning and memory in normal aging.* San Diego, CA: Academic Press.

Kazdin, A. E. (1982). The token economy: A decade later. *Journal of Applied Behavior Analysis, 15,* 431–445.

Keesey, R. E., & Powley, T. L. (1975). Hypothalamic regulation of body weight. *American Scientist, 63,* 558–565.

Keller, M. B., & Shapiro, R. W. (1982). Double depression: Superimposition of acute depressive episodes on chronic depressive disorders. *American Journal of Psychiatry, 139,* 438–442.

Kelley, H. H. (1967). Attribution theory in social interaction. In E. E. Jones, D. E. Kanouse, H. H. Kelley, R. E. Nisbett, S. Valins, & B. Weiner (Eds.), *Attribution: Perceiving the causes of behavior.* Morristown, NJ: General Learning Press.

Kelley, H. H. (1983). Love and commitment. In H. H. Kelley, E. Berscheid, A. Christensen, J. H. Harvey, T. L. Huston, G. Levinger, E. McClintock, L. A. Peplau, & D. R. Peterson (Eds.), *Close relationships.* New York: Freeman.

Kelley, K. (1985). Sex, sex guilt, and authoritarianism: Differences in responses to explicit heterosexual and masturbatory slides. *Journal of Sex Research, 21,* 68–85.

Kellogg, W. N., & Kellogg, L. A. (1933). *The ape and the child.* New York: McGraw-Hill.

Kelly, D. D. (1991). Sleep and dreaming. In E. R. Kandel, J. H. Schwartz, & T. M. Jessell (Eds.), *Principles of neural science* (3rd ed.). New York: Elsevier.

Kenrick, D. T., & Funder, D. C. (1988). Profiting from controversy: Lessons of the person-situation debate. *American Psychologist, 43,* 23–34.

Kenrick, D. T., Gutierres, S. E., & Goldberg, L. (1989). Influence of erotica on judgments of strangers and mates. *Journal of Experimental Social Psychology, 25,* 159–167.

Kenrick, D. T., McCreath, H. E., Govern, J., King, R., & Bordin, J. (1990). Person-environment intersections: Everyday settings and common trait dimensions. *Journal of Personality and Social Psychology, 58,* 685–698.

Keppel, G., & Underwood, B. J. (1962). Proactive inhibition in short-term retention of single items. *Journal of Verbal Learning and Verbal Behavior, 1,* 153–161.

Kerkhoff, G., Munssinger, U., & Meier, E. K. (1994). Neurovisual rehabilitation in cerebral blindness. *Archives of Neurology, 51,* 474–481.

Kessler, R. C., McGonagle, K. A., Shanyang, Z., Nelson, C. B., Hughes, M., Eshleman, S., Wittchen, H., & Kendler, K. S. (1994). Lifetime and 12-month prevalence of DSM-III-R psychiatric disorders in the United States. *Archives of General Psychiatry, 51,* 8–19.

Key, W. B. (1973) *Subliminal seduction.* Englewood Cliffs, NJ: Prentice-Hall.

Kiecolt-Glaser, J. K., Garner, W., Speicher, C., Penn, G. M., Holliday, J., & Glaser, R. (1984). Psychosocial modifiers of immunocompetence in medical students. *Psychosomatic Medicine, 46,* 7–17.

Kiesler, C. A., & Sibulkin, A. E. (1987). *Mental hospitalization: Myths and facts about a national crisis.* Beverly Hills, CA: Sage.

Kihlstrom, J. (1985). Hypnosis. *Annual Review of Psychology, 36,* 385–418.

Kihlstrom, J., & Cantor, N. (1984). Mental representations of the self. In L. Berkowitz (Ed.), *Advances in experimental social psychology* (Vol. 17). New York: Academic Press.

Kihlstrom, J., & McConkey, K. M. (1990). William James and hypnosis: A centennial reflection. *Psychological Science, 1,* 174–178.

Kimble, G. A. (1993). A modest proposal for a minor revolution in the language of psychology. *Psychological Science, 4,* 253–255.

Kimelberg, H. K., & Norenberg, M. D. (1989, April). Astrocytes. *Scientific American, 260,* 66–76.

Kimura, D. (1992, September). Sex differences in the brain. *Scientific American, 267,* 118–125.

Kimura, D., & Hampson, E. (1994). Cognitive pattern in men and women is influenced by fluctuations in sex hormones. *Current Directions in Psychological Science, 3,* 57–61.

Kirchgessner, A. L., & Sclafani, A. (1988). PVN-hindbrain pathway involved in the hypothalamic hyperphagia-obesity syndrome. *Physiology and Behavior, 42,* 517–528.

Klatzky, R. L. (1984). *Memory and awareness: An information-processing perspective.* New York: Freeman.

Klatzky, R. L., Lederman, S. J., & Metzger, V. A. (1985). Identifying objects by touch: An "expert system." *Perception & Psychophysics, 37,* 299–302.

Kline, P. (1991). *Intelligence: The psychometric view.* New York: Routledge, Chapman, & Hall.

Kluft, R. P. (1991). Multiple personality disorder. In A. Tasman & S. M. Goldfinger (Eds.), *Review of psychiatry* (Vol. 10). Washington, DC: American Psychiatric Press.

Kohlberg, L. (1963). The development of children's orientations toward a moral order: I. Sequence in the development of moral thought. *Vita Humana, 6,* 11–33.

Kohlberg, L. (1969). Stage and sequence: The cognitive-developmental approach to socialization. In D. A. Goslin (Ed.), *Handbook of socialization theory and research.* Chicago: Rand McNally.

Kohlberg, L. (1986). *The psychology of moral development.* New York: Harper & Row.

Kolb, B., & Whishaw, I. Q. (1990). *Fundamentals of human neuropsychology* (3rd ed.). New York: Freeman.

Konarski, E. A., Jr. (1985). The use of response deprivation to increase the academic performance of EMR students. *The Behavior Therapist, 8,* 61.

Kosslyn, S. M. (1983). *Ghosts in the mind's machine: Creating and using images in the brain.* New York: Horizon.

Kosslyn, S. M., Alpert, N. M., Thompson, W. L., & Maljkovic, V. (1993). Visual mental imagery activates topographically organized visual cortex: PET investigations. *Journal of Cognitive Neuroscience, 5,* 263–287.

Kosslyn, S. M., Ball, T. M., & Reiser, B. J. (1978). Visual images preserve metric spatial information: Evidence from studies of image scanning. *Journal of Experimental Psychology: Human Perception and Performance, 4,* 47–60.

Kosslyn, S. M., & Koenig, O. (1992). *Wet mind: The new cognitive neuroscience.* New York: Free Press.

Kraepelin, E. (1921). *Manic-depressive insanity and paranoia.* London: Churchill Livingstone.

Kramer, P. D. (1993). *Listening to Prozac.* New York: Viking.

Krantz, D. S., & Manuck, S. B. (1984). Acute psychophysiologic reactivity and risk of cardiovascular disease: A review and methodologic critique. *Psychological Bulletin, 96,* 435–464.

Krause, N., & Liang, J. (1993). Stress, social support, and psychological distress among the Chinese elderly. *Journals of Gerontology, 48,* 282–291.

Kübler-Ross, E. (1969). *On death and dying.* New York: Macmillan.

Kübler-Ross, E. (1974). *Questions and answers on death and dying.* New York: Macmillan.

Kuhn, D. (1992). Cognitive development. In M. H. Bornstein & M. E. Lamb (Eds.), *Developmental psychology: An advanced textbook.* Hillsdale, NJ: Erlbaum.

Kutchinsky, B. (1992). The child sexual abuse panic. *Nordisk Sexoligi, 10,* 30–42.

Labouvie-Vief, G., Hakim-Larson, J., & Hobart, C. J. (1987). Age, ego level, and the life-span development of coping and defense processes. *Psychology and Aging, 2,* 286–293.

Labov, W. (1973). The boundaries of words and their meanings. In C. J. N. Bailey & R. W. Shiny (Eds.), *New ways of analyzing variation in English* (Vol. 1). Washington, DC: Georgetown University Press.

Lackner, J. R., & DiZio, P. (1991). Decreased susceptibility to motion sickness during exposure to visual inversion in microgravity. *Aviation, Space, and Environmental Medicine, 62,* 206–211.

Ladd, G. T. (1892). Contributions to the psychology of visual dreams. *Mind, 1,* 299–304.

Lafferty, P., Beutler, L. E., & Crago, M. (1991). Differences between more or less effective psychotherapists: A study of select therapist variables. *Journal of Consulting and Clinical Psychology, 57,* 76–80.

Lamb, M. E., Ketterlinus, R. D., & Fracasso, M. P. (1992). Parent-child relationships. In M. H. Bornstein & M. E. Lamb (Eds.), *Developmental psychology: An advanced textbook.* Hillsdale, NJ: Erlbaum.

Lamb, M. E., & Sternberg, K. L. (1990). Do we really know how day care affects children? *Journal of Applied Developmental Psychology, 11,* 351–379.

Lambert, M. J., & Bergin, A. E. (1994). The effectiveness of psychotherapy. In A. E. Bergin & S. L. Garfield (Eds.), *Handbook of psychotherapy and behavior change* (4th ed.). New York: Wiley.

Lancet, D., Gross-Isseroff, R., Margalit, T., & Seidemann, E. (1993). Olfaction: From signal transduction and termination to human genome mapping. *Chemical Senses, 18,* 217–225.

Landauer, T. K. (1962). Rate of implicit speech. *Perceptual and Motor Skills, 15,* 646.

Lang, P. J. (1994). The varieties of emotional experience: A meditation on James-Lange theory. *Psychological Review, 101,* 211–221.

Langer, E. J. (1989). *Mindfulness*. Cambridge, MA: Addison-Wesley.

Langer, E. J., & Abelson, R. P. (1974). A patient by any other name . . . : Clinician group differences in labeling bias. *Journal of Consulting and Clinical Psychology, 42*, 4–9.

Langlois, J. H., & Roggman, L. A. (1990). Attractive faces are only average. *Psychological Science, 1*, 115–121.

Langlois, J. H., Roggman, L. A., Casey, R. J., Ritter, J. M., Rieser-Danner, L. A., & Jenkins, V. Y. (1987). Infant preferences for attractive faces: Rudiments of a stereotype? *Developmental Psychology, 23*, 363–369.

Langlois, J. H., Roggman, L. A., & Musselman, L. (1994). What is average and what is not average about attractive faces? *Psychological Science, 5*, 214–220.

Laprelle, J., Hoyle, R. H., Insko, C. A., & Bernthal, P. (1990). Interpersonal attraction and descriptions of the traits of others: Ideal similarity, self similarity, and liking. *Journal of Research in Personality, 24*, 216–240.

Latané, B. (1981). The psychology of social impact. *American Psychologist, 36*, 343–356.

Latané, B., & Nida, S. A. (1981). Ten years of research on group size and helping. *Psychological Bulletin, 89*, 308–324.

Latané, B., Williams, K., & Harkins, S. (1979). Many hands make light the work: The causes and consequences of social loafing. *Journal of Personality and Social Psychology, 37*, 822–832.

Laudenslager, M. L., Ryan, S. M., Drugen, R. L., Hyson, R. L., & Maier, S. F. (1983). Coping and immunosuppression: Inescapable but not escapable shock suppresses lymphocyte proliferation. *Science, 221*, 568–570.

Lazarus, A. A., & Messer, S. B. (1991). Does chaos prevail? An exchange on technical eclecticism and assimilative integration. *Journal of Psychotherapy Integration, 1*, 143–158.

Lazarus, R. S. (1966). *Psychological stress and the coping process*. New York: McGraw-Hill.

Lazarus, R. S. (1991). *Emotion and adaptation*. New York: Oxford University Press.

Lazarus, R. S. (1993). Why we should think of stress as a subset of emotion. In L. Goldberger & S. Breznitz (Eds.), *Handbook of stress: Theoretical and clinical aspects* (2nd ed.). New York: Free Press.

Lazarus, R. S., & Folkman, S. (1984). *Stress, appraisal and coping*. New York: Springer.

Lefcourt, H. M. (1982). *Locus of control: Current trends in theory and research*. Waterloo, Ontario: University of Waterloo.

Leibowitz, H. W. (1971). Sensory, learned, and cognitive mechanisms of size perception. *Annals of the New York Academy of Sciences, 188*, 47–62.

Lenneberg, E. H. (1967). *Biological foundations of language*. New York: Wiley.

Lepper, M. R., Greene, D., & Nisbett, R. E. (1973). Undermining children's intrinsic interest with external reward: A test of the "overjustification" hypothesis. *Journal of Personality and Social Psychology, 28*, 129–137.

Lerman, H. G. (1986). From Freud to feminist personality theory: Getting here from there. *Psychology of Women Quarterly, 10*, 1–18.

LeVay, S. (1991). A difference in hypothalamic structure between heterosexual and homosexual men. *Science, 253*, 1034–1037.

Levenson, R. W. (1992). Autonomic nervous system differences among emotions. *Psychological Science, 3*, 23–27.

Levine, D. N., Warach, J., & Farah, M. J. (1985). Two visual systems in mental imagery: Dissociation of "what" and "where" in imagery disorders due to bilateral posterior cerebral lesions. *Neurology, 35*, 1010–1018.

Levine, G., & Parkinson, S. (1994). *Experimental methods in psychology*. Hillsdale, NJ: Erlbaum.

Levinson, D. J., Darow, C. N., Klein, E. B., Levinson, M. H., & McKee, B. (1978). *The seasons of a man's life*. New York: Knopf.

Lewontin, R. (1976). Race and intelligence. In N. J. Block & G. Dworkin (Eds.), *The IQ controversy: Critical readings*. New York: Pantheon.

Liberman, R. P., Kopelowicz, A., & Young, A. S. (1994). Biobehavioral treatment and rehabilitation of schizophrenia. *Behavior Therapy, 25*, 89–107.

Lickey, M. E., & Gordon, B. (1991). *Medicine and mental illness: The use of drugs in psychiatry*. New York: Freeman.

Liebert, R. M., & Liebert, L. L. (1995). *Science and behavior: An introduction to methods of psychological research* (4th ed.). Englewood Cliffs, NJ: Prentice-Hall.

Lilienfeld, S. O. (1994). Conceptual problems in the assessment of psychopathy. *Clinical Psychology Review, 14*, 17–38.

Linde, L., & Bergstrom, M. (1992). The effect of one night without sleep on problem solving and immediate recall. *Psychological Research, 54*, 127–136.

Linden, W. (1990). *Autogenic training: A clinical guide*. New York: Guilford.

Lindsley, O. R., & Skinner, B. F. (1954). A method for the experimental analysis of psychotic patients. *American Psychologist, 9*, 419–420.

Lindvall, O., Rehncrona, S., Brundin, P., Gustavii, B., Åstedt, B., Widner, H., Lindholm, T., Björklund, A., Leenders, K. L., Rothwell, J. C., Frackowiak, R., Marsden, D., Johnels, B., Steg, G., Freedman, R., Hoffer, B. J., Seiger, A., Bygdeman, M., Strömberg, I., & Olsen, L. (1989). Human fetal dopamine neurons grafted into the striatum in two patients with severe Parkinson's disease. *Archives of Neurology, 46*, 615–631.

Linton, M. (1975). Memory for real-world events. In D. A. Norman & D. E. Rumelhart (Eds.), *Explorations in cognition*. San Francisco: Freeman.

Linville, P. (1985). Self-complexity and affective extremity: Don't put all your eggs in one cognitive basket. *Social Cognition, 3*, 94–120.

Linville, P. (1987). Self-complexity as a cognitive buffer against stress-related illness and depression. *Journal of Personality and Social Psychology, 52*, 663–676.

Linville, P., & Carlston, D. E. (1994). Social cognition of the self. In P. G. Devine, D. L. Hamilton, & T. M. Ostrom (Eds.), *Social cognition: Its impact on social psychology*. New York: Academic Press.

Lipsey, M. W., & Wilson, D. B. (1993). The efficacy of psychological, educational, and behavioral treatment: Confirmation from meta-analysis. *American Psychologist, 48*, 1181–1209.

Lisk, R. D. (1978). The regulation of sexual "heat." In J. B. Hutchinson (Ed.), *Biological determinants of sexual behaviour*. New York: Wiley.

Livingstone, M., & Hubel, D. H. (1988). Segregation of form, color, movement, and depth: Anatomy, physiology, and perception. *Science, 240*, 740–749.

Loftus, E. L. (1979). *Eyewitness testimony*. Cambridge, MA: Harvard University Press.

Loftus, E. L. (1991). *Witness for the defense*. New York: St. Martin's.

Loftus, E. L. (1993). The reality of repressed memories. *American Psychologist, 48*, 518–537.

Loftus, E. L., & Loftus, G. R. (1980). On the permanence of stored information in the brain. *American Psychologist, 35,* 409–420.

Loftus, E. L., & Palmer, J. C. (1974). Reconstruction of automobile destruction: An example of the interaction between language and memory. *Journal of Verbal Learning and Verbal Behavior, 13,* 585–589.

Loftus, E. L., Polonsky, S., & Fullilove, M. T. (1994). Memories of childhood sexual abuse. *Psychology of Women Quarterly, 18,* 67–84.

Logan, G. D. (1988). Toward an instance theory of automatization. *Psychological Review, 95,* 492–527.

Logan, G. D. (1991). Automaticity and memory. In W. E. Hockley & S. Lewandowsky (Eds.), *Relating theory and data: Essays on human memory in honor of Bennet B. Murdock.* Hillsdale, NJ: Erlbaum.

Lorenz, K. Z. (1958, December). The evolution of behavior. *Scientific American, 199,* 67–78.

Lovaas, O. I. (1987). Behavioral treatment and normal educational and intellectual functioning in young autistic children. *Journal of Consulting and Clinical Psychology, 55,* 3–9.

Lovaas, O. I., Koegel, R., Simmons, J. Q., & Long, J. S. (1973). Some generalization and follow-up measures on autistic children in behavior therapy. *Journal of Applied Behavior Analysis, 6,* 131–166.

Lovdal, L. T. (1989). Sex role messages in television commercials: An update. *Sex Roles, 21,* 715–724.

Lowe, J., & Carroll, D. (1985). The effects of spinal cord injury on the intensity of emotional experience. *British Journal of Clinical Psychology, 24,* 135–136.

Luborsky, L., Barber, J. P., & Crits-Cristoph, P. (1990). Theory-based research for understanding the process of dynamic psychotherapy. *Journal of Consulting and Clinical Psychology, 58,* 281–287.

Luria, A. R. (1968). *The mind of a mnemonist.* New York: Basic Books.

Lutz, C. (1982). The domain of emotion words in Ifaluk. *American Ethnologist, 9,* 113–128.

Lykken, D. T. (1981). *A tremor in the blood: Uses and abuses of the lie detector.* New York: McGraw-Hill.

Lyness, S. A. (1993). Predictors of differences between Type A and Type B individuals in heart rate and blood pressure reactivity. *Psychological Bulletin, 114,* 266–295.

Lynn, R. (1994). Some reinterpretations of the Minnesota transracial adoption study. *Intelligence, 19,* 21–27.

Lynn, S. J., Rhue, J. W., & Weekes, J. R. (1990). Hypnotic involuntariness: A social cognitive analysis. *Psychological Review, 97,* 169–184.

Mackay, D. G. (1983). Prescriptive grammar and the pronoun problem. In B. Thorne, C. Kramarae, & N. Henley (Eds.), *Language, gender, and society.* Rowley, MA: Newbury House.

Maier, N. R. F. (1931). Reasoning in humans II: The solution to a problem and its appearance in consciousness. *Journal of Comparative Psychology, 12,* 181–194.

Maier, N. R. F., & Burke, R. J. (1967). Response availability as a factor in the problem-solving performance of males and females. *Journal of Personality and Social Psychology, 5,* 304–310.

Maier, S. F., Watkins, L. R., & Fleshner, M. (1994). Psychoneuroimmunology: The interface between behavior, brain, and immunity. *American Psychologist, 49,* 1004–1017.

Malt, B. C., & Smith, E. E. (1984). Correlated properties in natural categories. *Journal of Verbal Learning and Verbal Behavior, 23,* 250–269.

Mandler, G., Nakamura, Y., & Van Zandt, B. J. S. (1987). Nonspecific effects of stimuli that cannot be recognized. *Journal of Experimental Psychology: Learning, Memory, & Cognition, 13,* 646–648.

Mandler, J. M. (1992). How to build a baby: II. Conceptual primitives. *Psychological Review, 99,* 587–604.

Mann, T. (1994). Informed consent for psychological research: Do subjects comprehend consent forms and understand their legal rights? *Psychological Science, 5,* 140–143.

Marcia, J. E. (1966). Development and validation of ego identity status. *Journal of Personality and Social Psychology, 3,* 551–558.

Marcus, D. E., & Overton, W. F. (1978). The development of cognitive gender constancy and sex-role preferences. *Child Development, 49,* 434–444.

Markus, H. (1977). Self-schemata and processing information about the self. *Journal of Personality and Social Psychology, 35,* 63–78.

Markus, H., & Kitayama, S. (1991). Culture and the self: Implications for cognition, emotion, and motivation. *Psychological Review, 98,* 224–253.

Markus, H., & Kitayama, S. (1994). A collective fear of the collective: Implications for selves and theories of selves. *Personality and Social Psychology Bulletin, 20,* 568–579.

Markus, H., & Nurius, P. (1986). Possible selves. *American Psychologist, 41,* 954–969.

Marshall, G. D., & Zimbardo, P. G. (1979). Affective consequences of inadequately explained physiological arousal. *Journal of Personality and Social Psychology, 37,* 970–988.

Marshall, J. C., & Halligan, P. W. (1988). Blindsight and insight in visuo-spatial neglect. *Nature, 336,* 766–767.

Marson, L., & McKenna, K. E. (1994). Stimulation of the hypothalamus initiates the urethrogenital reflex in male rats. *Brain Research, 638,* 103–108.

Martin, K. M., & Aggleton, J. P. (1993). Contextual effects on the ability of divers to use decompression tables. *Applied Cognitive Psychology, 7,* 311–316.

Martin, P., & Bateson, P. (1993). *Measuring behavior: An introductory guide* (2nd ed.). Cambridge: Cambridge University Press.

Martin, R. J., White, B. D., & Hulsey, M. G. (1991). The regulation of body weight. *American Scientist, 79,* 528–541.

Marx, M. H., & Cronan-Hillix, W. A. (1987). *Systems and theories in psychology.* New York: McGraw-Hill.

Maser, J. D., Kaelber, C., & Weise, R. E. (1991). International use and attitudes toward DSM-III and DSM-III-R: Growing consensus in psychiatric classification. *Journal of Abnormal Psychology, 100,* 271–279.

Mash, D. C., Flynn, D. D., & Potter, L. T. (1985). Loss of M2 muscarine receptors in the cerebral cortex in Alzheimer's disease and experimental cholinergic denervation. *Science, 228,* 1115–1117.

Maslach, C. (1976). Burned out. *Human Behavior, 5,* 16–22.

Maslach, C. (1982). *Burnout—The cost of caring.* Englewood Cliffs, NJ: Prentice-Hall.

Maslach, C., & Jackson, S. E. (1981). The measurement of experienced burnout. *Journal of Occupational Behavior, 2,* 99–113.

Maslow, A. H. (1954). *Motivation and personality.* New York: Harper.

Mason, J. R., & Reidinger, R. F. (1982). Observational learning of aversions in red-winged blackbirds (*Agelaius phoeniceus*). *Auk, 99,* 548–554.

Mason, J. W. (1975). A historical view of the stress field. *Journal of Human Stress, 1,* 22–36.

Masson, J. (1984). *The assault on truth: Freud's suppression of the seduction theory.* New York: Farrar, Straus, & Giroux.

Masters, W. H., & Johnson, V. E. (1966). *Human sexual response.* Boston: Little, Brown.

Matlin, M. W., & Foley, H. J. (1992). *Sensation and perception.* Needham Heights, MA: Allyn & Bacon.

Matsumoto, D. (1987). The role of facial response in the experience of emotion: More methodological problems and a meta-analysis. *Journal of Personality and Social Psychology, 52,* 769–774.

Matsumoto, D. (1994). *People: Psychology from a cultural perspective.* Pacific Grove, CA: Brooks/Cole.

Matthews, K. A. (1992). Myths and realities of the menopause. *Psychosomatic Medicine, 54,* 1–9.

Matzel, L. D., Held, F. P., & Miller, R. R. (1988). Information and expression of simultaneous and backward associations: Implications for contiguity theory. *Learning and Motivation, 9,* 317–344.

Mauss, M. (1902/1972). *A general theory of magic* (R. Brain, Trans.). New York: Norton.

Mayer, D. J. (1953). Glucostatic mechanism of regulation of food intake. *New England Journal of Medicine, 249,* 13–16.

Mays, V. M., & Albee, G. W. (1992). Psychotherapy and ethnic minorities. In D. K. Freedheim (Ed.), *History of Psychotherapy: A century of change.* Washington, DC: American Psychological Association.

McArthur, L. Z., & Berry, D. S. (1987). Cross-cultural agreement in perceptions of babyfaced adults. *Journal of Cross-Cultural Psychology, 18,* 165–192.

McCall, M. (1994). Decision theory and the sale of alcohol. *Journal of Applied Social Psychology, 24,* 1593–1611.

McCall, R. B., & Carriger, M. S. (1993). A meta-analysis of infant habituation and recognition memory performance as predictors of later IQ. *Child Development, 64,* 57–79.

McCann, I. L., & Holmes, D. S. (1984). Influence of aerobic exercise on depression. *Journal of Personality and Social Psychology, 46,* 1142–1147.

McClelland, D. C. (1961). *The achieving society.* Princeton, NJ: Von Nostrand.

McClelland, D. C., Atkinson, J. W., Clark, R. A., & Lowell, E. W. (1953). *The achievement motive.* New York: Appleton-Century-Crofts.

McClelland, J. L., & Elman, J. L. (1986). The TRACE model of speech perception. *Cognitive Psychology, 18,* 1–86.

McCloskey, M., & Cohen, N. J. (1989). Catastrophic interference in connectionist networks: The sequential learning problem. In G. H. Bower (Ed.), *The psychology of learning and motivation.* New York: Academic Press.

McCrae, R. R., & Costa, P. T., Jr. (1985). Updating Norman's "adequate taxonomy": Intelligence and personality dimensions in natural language and in questionnaires. *Journal of Personality and Social Psychology, 49,* 710–721.

McCrae, R. R., & Costa, P. T., Jr. (1990). *Personality in adulthood.* New York: Guilford.

McDermott, K. B., & Roediger, H. L., III. (1994). Effects of imagery on perceptual implicit memory tests. *Journal of Experimental Psychology: Learning, Memory, & Cognition, 20,* 1379–1390.

McDougall, W. (1908). *An introduction to social psychology.* London: Methuen.

McFall, R. M. (1976). Behavioral training: A skill-acquisition approach to clinical problems. In J. T. Spence, R. C. Carson, & J. W. Thibaut (Eds.), *Behavioral approaches to therapy.* Morristown, NJ: General Learning Press.

McGhee, P. E., & Frueh, T. (1980). Television viewing and the learning of sex-role stereotypes. *Sex Roles, 6,* 179–188.

McGuire, P. K., Shah, G. M. S., & Murray, R. M. (1993). Increased blood flow in Broca's area during auditory hallucinations. *Lancet, 342,* 703–706.

McGuire, W. J. (1985). Attitudes and attitude change. In G. Lindzey & E. Aronson (Eds.), *Handbook of social psychology* (Vol. 2). New York: Random House.

McIntosh, A. R., Grady, C. L., Ungerleider, L. G., & Haxby, J. V. (1994). Network analysis of cortical visual pathways mapped with PET. *Journal of Neuroscience, 14,* 655–666.

McKenna, S. P., & Glendon, A. I. (1985). Occupational first aid training: Decay in cardiopulmonary resuscitation (CPR) skills. *Journal of Occupational Psychology, 58,* 109–117.

McKinlay, S. M., Brambilla, D. J., & Posner, J. G. (1992). The normal menopause transition. *Maturitas, 14,* 103–115.

McLeod, J. D., Kessler, R. C., & Landis, K. R. (1992). Speed of recovery from major depressive episodes in a community sample of married men and women. *Journal of Abnormal Psychology, 101,* 277–286.

McNeil, B. J., Pauker, S. G., Cox, H. C., Jr., & Tversky, A. (1982). On the elicitation of preferences for alternative therapies. *New England Journal of Medicine, 306,* 1259–1262.

Medin, D. L. (1989). Concepts and conceptual structure. *American Psychologist, 44,* 1469–1481.

Medin, D. L., Goldstone, R. L., & Gentner, D. (1993). Respects for similarity. *Psychological Review, 100,* 254–278.

Medin, D. L., & Ross, B. H. (1992). *Cognitive psychology.* Fort Worth: Harcourt Brace Jovanovich.

Medin, D. L., & Shaffer, M. M. (1978). A context theory of classification learning. *Psychological Review, 85,* 207–238.

Meeus, W. H. J., & Raaijmakers, Q. A. W. (1987). Administrative obedience as a social phenomenon. In W. Doise & S. Moscovici (Eds.), *Current issues in European social psychology* (Vol. 2). Cambridge, England: Cambridge University Press.

Meisel, A., & Roth, L. H. (1983). Toward an informed discussion of informed consent: A review and critique of the empirical studies. *Arizona Law Review, 25,* 265–346.

Melamed, B. G., & Siegel, L. J. (1975). Reduction of anxiety in children facing hospitalization and surgery by use of filmed modeling. *Journal of Consulting and Clinical Psychology, 43,* 511–521.

Melzack, R. (1973). *The puzzle of pain.* New York: Basic Books.

Melzack, R., & Wall, P. D. (1965). Pain mechanisms: A new theory. *Science, 150,* 971–979.

Melzack, R., & Wall, P. D. (1982). *The challenge of pain.* Harmondsworth: Penguin.

Merikle, P. M. (1988). Subliminal auditory messages: An evaluation. *Psychology & Marketing, 5,* 355–372.

Merikle, P. M., & Skanes, H. E. (1992). Subliminal self-help audiotapes: A search for placebo effects. *Journal of Applied Psychology, 77,* 772–776.

Merton, R. (1948). The self-fulfilling prophecy. *Antioch Review, 8,* 193–210.

Mesulam, M. M. (1987). Neglect (selective inattention). In G. Adelman (Ed.), *Encyclopedia of neuroscience* (Vol. 2). Boston: Birkhauser.

Milgram, S. (1963). Behavioral study of obedience. *Journal of Abnormal and Social Psychology, 67,* 371–378.

Milgram, S. (1974). *Obedience to authority.* New York: Harper & Row.

Miller, D. B. (1977). Roles of naturalistic observation in comparative psychology. *American Psychologist, 32,* 211–219.

Miller, G. A. (1956). The magical number seven plus or minus two: Some limits on our capacity for processing information. *Psychological Review, 63,* 81–97.

Miller, G. A., Galanter, E., & Pribram, K. H. (1960). *Plans and the structure of behavior.* New York: Holt.

Miller, L. L., & Branconnier, R. J. (1983). Cannabis: Effects on memory and the cholinergic limbic system. *Psychological Bulletin, 93,* 441–456.

Miller, N. E. (1985). The value of behavioral research on animals. *American Psychologist, 40,* 423–440.

Miller, N. E. (1991). Commentary on Ulrich: Need to check truthfulness of statements by opponents of animal research. *Psychological Science, 2,* 422–424.

Miller, S. D. (1989). Optical differences in cases of multiple personality disorder. *Journal of Nervous and Mental Disease, 177,* 480–486.

Miller, T. W. (1993). The assessment of stressful life events. In L. Goldberger & S. Breznitz (Eds.), *Handbook of stress: Theoretical and clinical aspects* (2nd ed.). New York: Free Press.

Miller, W. R., Taylor, C. A., & West, J. C. (1980). Focused versus broad-spectrum behavior therapy for problem drinkers. *Journal of Consulting and Clinical Psychology, 48,* 590–601.

Millsaps, C. L., Azrin, R. L., & Mittenberg, W. (1994). Neuropsychological effects of chronic cannabis use on the memory and intelligence of adolescents. *Journal of Child and Adolescent Substance Abuse, 3,* 47–55.

Milner, A. D., & Rugg, M. D. (Eds.). (1992). *The neuropsychology of consciousness.* London: Academic Press.

Milner, B. (1966). Amnesia following operation on the temporal lobes. In C. W. M. Whitty & O. L. Zangwill (Eds.), *Amnesia.* London: Butterworths.

Mineka, S. (1987). A primate model of phobic fears. In H. Eysenck & I. Martin (Eds.), *Theoretical foundations of behavior therapy.* New York: Plenum.

Mischel, W. (1968). *Personality and assessment.* New York: Wiley.

Mischel, W., & Peake, P. K. (1982). Beyond déjà vu in the search for cross-situational consistency. *Psychological Review, 89,* 730–755.

Mischel, W., & Shoda, Y. (1995). A cognitive-affective system theory of personality: Reconceptualizing situations, dispositions, dynamics, and invariance in personality structure. *Psychological Review, 102,* 246–268.

Mook, D. G. (1995). *Motivation: The organization of action* (2nd ed.). New York: Norton.

Moray, N. (1959). Attention in dichotic listening: Affective cues and the influence of instructions. *Quarterly Journal of Experimental Psychology, 11,* 56–60.

Morelli, G. A., Rogoff, B., Oppenheim, D., & Goldsmith, D. (1992). Cultural variations in infants' sleeping arrangements: Questions of independence. *Developmental Psychology, 28,* 604–613.

Moret, V., Forster, A., Laverriere, M. C., & Lambert, H. (1991). Mechanism of analgesia induced by hypnosis and acupuncture: Is there a difference? *Pain, 45,* 135–140.

Moscovici, S., & Zavalloni, M. (1969). The group as a polarizer of attitudes. *Journal of Personality and Social Psychology, 12,* 125–135.

Moskowitz, H. (1985). Marihuana and driving. *Accident Analysis and Prevention, 17,* 323–345.

Mozel, M. M., Smith, B., Smith, P., Sullivan, R., & Swender, P. (1969). Nasal chemoreception in flavor identification. *Archives of Otolaryngology, 90,* 367–373.

Muchinsky, P. M. (1993). *Psychology applied to work.* Pacific Grove, CA: Brooks/Cole.

Murdock, B. B., Jr. (1960). The distinctiveness of stimuli. *Psychological Review, 67,* 16–31.

Murray, H. A. (1938). *Explorations in personality.* New York: Oxford University Press.

Muter, P. (1980). Very rapid forgetting. *Memory & Cognition, 8,* 174–179.

Myers, D. G. (1982). Polarizing effects of social interaction. In H. Brandstatter, J. H. Davis, & G. Stocker-Kreichgauer (Eds.), *Group decision making.* New York: Academic Press.

Myers, D. G., & Diener, E. (1995). Who is happy? *Psychological Science, 6,* 10–19.

Myers, D. G., & Ridl, J. (1979, August). Can we all be better than average? *Psychology Today,* pp. 89–98.

Nagar, D., & Panady, J. (1987). Affect and performance on cognitive tasks as a function of crowding and noise. *Journal of Applied Social Psychology, 17,* 147–157.

Nairne, J. S. (1990). A feature model of immediate memory. *Memory & Cognition, 18,* 251–269.

Nairne, J. S. (1996). Short-term/working memory. In E. L. Bjork & R. A. Bjork (Eds.), *Handbook of perception and cognition* (Vol 10: Memory). New York: Academic Press.

Nairne, J. S., & Rescorla, R. A. (1981). Second-order conditioning with diffuse auditory reinforcers in the pigeon. *Learning and Motivation, 12,* 65–91.

Naveh-Benjamin, M., & Ayres, T. J. (1986). Digit span, reading rate, and linguistic relativity. *Quarterly Journal of Experimental Psychology, 38A,* 739–751.

Neath, I. (1993). Distinctiveness and serial position effects in recognition. *Memory & Cognition, 21,* 689–698.

Neisser, U. (1967). *Cognitive psychology.* New York: Appleton-Century-Crofts.

Neisser, U. (1978). Memory: What are the important questions? In M. M. Gruneberg, P. E. Morris, & R. N. Sykes (Eds.), *Practical aspects of memory.* London: Academic Press.

Neisser, U., & Harsch, N. (1992). Phantom flashbulbs: False recollections of hearing the news about Challenger. In E. Winograd & U. Neisser (Eds.), *Affect and accuracy in recall: Studies of "flashbulb memories."* Cambridge: Cambridge University Press.

Nelson, K. (1973). Structure and strategy in learning to talk. *Monographs of the Society for Research in Child Development, 38*(Serial No. 149).

Newell, A., & Simon, H. A. (1972). *Human problem solving.* Englewood Cliffs, NJ: Prentice-Hall.

Nickerson, R. S., & Adams, M. J. (1979). Long-term memory for a common object. *Cognitive Psychology, 11,* 287–307.

Nicolaus, L. K., & Nellis, D. W. (1987). The first evaluation of the use of conditioned taste aversion to control predation by mongooses upon eggs. *Applied Animal Behaviour Science, 17,* 329–346.

Nobel, K. D., Robinson, N. M., & Gunderson, S. A. (1993). All rivers lead to the sea: A follow-up study of gifted young adults. *Roeper Review, 15,* 124–130.

Norman, D. A. (1988). *The psychology of everyday things.* New York: Basic Books.

Nosofsky, R. M. (1986). Attention, similarity, and the identification-categorization relationship. *Journal of Experimental Psychology: General, 115,* 39–57.

Novick, L. R. (1988). Analogical transfer, problem similarity, and expertise. *Journal of Experimental Psychology: Learning, Memory, & Cognition, 14,* 510–520.

Nowakowski, R. S. (1987). Basic concepts of CNS development. *Child Development, 58,* 568–595.

Oakes, J. (1985). *Keeping track: How schools structure inequality.* New Haven, CT: Yale University Press.

Oakes, P. J., & Turner, J. C. (1990). Is limited information processing capacity the cause of social stereotyping? *European Review of Social Psychology, 1,* 112–135.

Offer, D., & Schonert-Reichl, K. A. (1992). Debunking the myths of adolescence. *Journal of the American Academy of Child and Adolescent Psychiatry, 31,* 1003–1013.

Ogden, J. A., & Corkin, S. (1991). Memories of HM. In W. C. Abraham, M. C. Corballis, & K. G. White (Eds.), *Memory mechanisms: A tribute to G. V. Goddard.* Hillsdale, NJ: Erlbaum.

Ogloff, J. R. P., Roberts, C. F., & Roesch, R. (1993). The insanity defense: Legal standards and clinical assessment. *Applied & Preventive Psychology, 2,* 163–178.

Olds, J. (1958). Satiation effects in self-stimulation of the brain. *Journal of Comparative and Physiological Psychology, 51,* 675–678.

Oller, D. K., & Eilers, R. E. (1988). The role of audition in infant babbling. *Child Development, 59,* 441–449.

Olson, J. M., & Zanna, M. P. (1993). Attitudes and attitude change. *Annual Review of Psychology, 44,* 117–154.

O'Mahony, M. (1978). Smell illusions and suggestion: Reports of smells contingent on tones played on television and radio. *Chemical Senses and Flavor, 3,* 183–187.

Orne, M. T. (1959). The nature of hypnosis: Artifact and essence. *Journal of Abnormal and Social Psychology, 58,* 277–299.

Orne, M. T. (1969). Demand characteristics and the concept of quasi-controls. In R. Rosenthal & R. L. Rosnow (Eds.*), Artifact in behavioral research.* New York: Academic Press.

Ortony, A., & Turner, T. J. (1990). What's basic about basic emotions? *Psychological Review, 97,* 315–331.

Pahl, J. J., Swayze, V. W., & Andreasen, N. C. (1990). Diagnostic advances in anatomical and functional brain imaging in schizophrenia. In A. Kales, C. N. Stefanis, & J. A. Talbott (Eds.), *Recent advances in schizophrenia.* New York: Springer-Verlag.

Paivio, A. (1971). *Imagery and verbal processes.* New York: Holt, Rinehart & Winston.

Parkes, J. D., & Block, C. (1989). Genetic factors in sleep disorders. *Journal of Neurology, Neurosurgery, and Psychiatry, 52,* 101–108.

Parkin, A. J. (1993). *Memory: Phenomena, experiment, and theory.* Oxford, England: Blackwell.

Parmelee, A. H., & Sigman, M. D. (1983). Perinatal brain development and behavior. In M. M. Haith & J. J. Campos (Eds.), *Handbook of child psychology: Vol. 2. Infancy and developmental psychobiology.* New York: Wiley.

Parsons, J. E., Kaczala, C., & Meece, J. L. (1982). Socialization of achievement attitudes and beliefs: Classroom influences. *Child Development, 53,* 322–339.

Pasewark, R. A., & Seidenzahl, D. (1979). Opinions concerning the insanity plea and criminality among mental patients. *Bulletin of the American Academy of Psychiatry and Law, 7,* 199–202.

Pashler, H. (1992). Attentional limitations in doing two tasks at the same time. *Current Directions in Psychological Science, 1,* 44–48.

Paul, G. L., & Lentz, R. J. (1977). *Psychosocial treatment of chronic mental patients: Milieu versus social learning programs.* Cambridge, MA: Harvard University Press.

Paulus, P. B. (1988). *Prison crowding: A psychological perspective.* New York: Springer.

Payne, J. W. (1994). Thinking aloud: Insights into information processing. *Psychological Science, 5,* 241–248.

Pedersen, D. M., & Wheeler, J. (1983). The Müller-Lyer illusion among Navajos. *Journal of Social Psychology, 121,* 3–6.

Penfield, W., & Perot, P. (1963). The brain's record of auditory and visual experience. *Brain, 86,* 595–696.

Pennebaker, J. W. (1990). *Opening up: The healing power of confiding in others.* New York: Morrow.

Penney, C. G. (1989). Modality effects and the structure of short-term verbal memory. *Memory & Cognition, 17,* 398–422.

Perls, F. S. (1969). *Gestalt therapy verbatim.* Moab, UT: Real People Press.

Perls, F. S., Hefferline, R. F., & Goodman, P. (1951). *Gestalt therapy.* New York: Julian.

Perner, J., Leekam, S., & Wimmer, H. (1987). Three-year-olds' difficulty understanding false belief: Cognitive limitation, lack of knowledge or pragmatic misunderstanding. *British Journal of Developmental Psychology, 5,* 125–137.

Perrett, D. I., & Mistlin, A. M. (1987). Visual neurones responsive to faces. *Trends in Neuroscience, 10,* 358–364.

Perry, W. (1970). *Forms of intellectual and ethical development in the college years.* New York: Holt, Rinehart & Winston.

Pert, C. B., & Snyder, S. H. (1973). The opiate receptor: Demonstration in nervous tissue. *Science, 179,* 1011–1014.

Peterson, A. C. (1988). Adolescent development. *Annual Review of Psychology, 39,* 583–607.

Peterson, C., & Seligman, M. E. P. (1987). Explanatory style and illness. *Journal of Personality, 55,* 237–265.

Peterson, C., Seligman, M. E. P., & Vaillant, G. E. (1988). Pessimistic explanatory style is a risk factor for physical illness: A thirty-five-year longitudinal study. *Journal of Personality and Social Psychology, 55,* 23–27.

Peterson, D. R. (1968). *The clinical study of social behavior.* New York: Appleton-Century-Crofts.

Peterson, L. R., & Peterson, M. J. (1959). Short-term retention of individual items. *Journal of Experimental Psychology, 58,* 193–198.

Petty, R. E., & Cacioppo, J. T. (1986). *Communication and persuasion: Central and peripheral routes to attitude change.* New York: Springer-Verlag.

Pfaff, D. W., & Sakuma, Y. (1979). Deficit in the lordosis reflex of female rats caused by lesions in the ventromedial nucleus of the hypothalamus. *Journal of Physiology, 288,* 203–210.

Piaget, J. (1929). *The child's conception of the world.* New York: Harcourt Brace.

Piaget, J. (1952). *The origins of intelligence in children.* New York: International Universities Press.

Piaget, J. (1970). Piaget's theory. In P. H. Mussen (Ed.), *Carmichael's manual of child psychology* (Vol. 1). New York: Wiley.

Pickles, J. O. (1988). *An introduction to the physiology of hearing* (2nd ed.). London: Academic Press.

Pierce, T. W., Madden, D. J., Siegel, W. C., & Blumenthal, J. A. (1993). Effects of aerobic exercise on cognitive and psychosocial functioning in patients with mild hypertension. *Health Psychology, 12,* 286–291.

Pinel, J. P. J., & Treit, D. (1979). Conditioned defensive burying in rats: Availability of burying materials. *Animal Learning & Behavior, 7,* 392–396.

Pines, A. (1993). Burnout. In L. Goldberger & S. Breznitz (Eds.), *Handbook of stress: Theoretical and clinical aspects* (2nd ed.). New York: Free Press.

Pines, A., & Aronson, E. (1988). *Career burnout: Causes and cures* (2nd ed.). New York: Free Press.

Plous, S. (1991). An attitude survey of animal rights activists. *Psychological Science, 2,* 194–196.

Porter, R. H., Makin, J. W., Davis, L. B., & Christensen, K. M. (1992). Breast-fed infants respond to olfactory clues from their own mother and unfamiliar lactating females. *Infant Behavior and Development, 15,* 85–93.

Posner, M. I. (1993). Interaction of arousal and selection in the posterior attention network. In A. Baddeley & L. Weiskrantz (Eds.), *Attention: Selection, awareness, and control. A tribute to Donald Broadbent.* Oxford, England: Clarendon Press.

Posner, M. I., & Keele, S. W. (1970). Retention of abstract ideas. *Journal of Experimental Psychology, 83,* 304–308.

Posner, M. I., & Rothbart, M. K. (1992). Attentional mechanisms and conscious experience. In A. D. Milner & M. D. Rugg (Eds.), *The neuropsychology of consciousness.* London: Academic Press.

Potter, W. Z., & Manji, H. K. (1993). Are monamine metabolites in cerebral spinal fluid worth measuring? *Archives of General Psychiatry, 50,* 653–656.

Pratkanis, A. R., & Greenwald, A. G. (1989). A sociocognitive model of attitude structure and function. *Advances in Experimental Social Psychology, 22,* 245–285.

Pratt, G. J., Wood, D., & Alman, B. M. (1988). *A clinical hypnosis primer.* New York: Wiley.

Preilowski, B. (1975). Bilateral motor interaction: Perceptual-motor performance of partial and complete split-brain patients. In K. J. Zülch, O. Creutzfeldt, & G. C. Galbraith (Eds.), *Cerebral localization.* New York: Springer-Verlag.

Premack, D. (1962). Reversibility of the reinforcement relation. *Science, 136,* 255–257.

Premack, D. (1976). *Intelligence in ape and man.* Hillsdale, NJ: Erlbaum.

Proctor, F., Wagner, N., & Butler, J. (1974). The differentiation of male and female orgasm: An experimental study. In N. Wagner (Ed.), *Perspectives on human sexuality.* New York: Behavioral Publications.

Proctor, R. W., & Van Zandt, T. (1994). *Human factors in simple and complex designs.* Boston: Allyn & Bacon.

Provence, S. A., & Lipton, R. C. (1962). *Infants in institutions.* New York: International Universities Press.

Prud'homme, M. J. L., Cohen, D., & Kalaska, J. F. (1994). Tactile activity in primate somatosensory cortex during active arm movements: Cytoarchitectonic distribution. *Journal of Neurophysiology, 71,* 173–181.

Prudic, J., Sackeim, H. A., & Devanand, D. P. (1990). Medication resistance and clinical response to electroconvulsive therapy. *Psychiatry Research, 31,* 287–296.

Putnam, F. W., Guroff, J. J., Silberman, E. K., Barban, L., & Post, R. M. (1986). The clinical phenomenology of multiple personality disorder: Review of 100 recent cases. *Journal of Clinical Psychiatry, 47,* 285–293.

Quadagno, D. M. (1987). Pheromones and human sexuality. *Medical Aspects of Human Sexuality, 21,* 149–154.

Quirion, R. (1993). Cholinergic markers in Alzheimer's disease and the autoregulation of acetylcholine release. *Journal of Psychiatry and Neuroscience, 18,* 226–234.

Rachman, S. J. (1990). *Fear and courage.* New York: Freeman.

Ragland, D. R., & Brand, R. J. (1988). Type A behavior and mortality from coronary heart disease. *The New England Journal of Medicine, 318,* 65–69.

Raichle, M. E. (1994, April). Visualizing the mind. *Scientific American, 270,* 58–64.

Rakic, P. (1991). Plasticity of cortical development. In S. E. Brauth, W. S. Hall, & R. J. Dooling (Eds.), *Plasticity of development.* Cambridge, MA: Bradford/MIT Press.

Ralph, M. R., Foster, R. G., Davis, F. C., & Menaker, M. (1990). Transplanted suprachiasmatic nucleus determines circadian period. *Science, 247,* 975–978.

Ramachandran, V. S. (1992). Filling in gaps in perception: I. *Current Directions in Psychological Science, 1,* 199–205.

Ratcliff, R. (1990). Connectionist models of recognition memory: Constraints imposed by learning and forgetting functions. *Psychological Review, 97,* 285–308.

Ratnasuriya, R. H., Eisler, I., Szmuhter, G. I., & Russell, G. F. (1991). Anorexia nervosa: Outcome and prognostic factors after 20 years. *British Journal of Psychiatry, 158,* 495–502.

Raugh, M. R., & Atkinson, R. C. (1975). A mnemonic method for learning a second-language vocabulary. *Journal of Educational Psychology, 67,* 1–16.

Raven, J. C., Court, J. H., & Raven, J.(1985). *A manual for Raven's progressive matrices and vocabulary scales.* London: H. K. Lewis.

Ree, M. J., & Earles, J. A. (1992). Intelligence is the best predictor of job performance. *Current Directions in Psychological Science, 1,* 86–89.

Reed, T. E., & Jensen, A. R. (1992). Conduction velocity in a brain nerve pathway correlates with intelligence. *Intelligence, 16,* 259–272.

Reeve, J. (1992). *Understanding motivation and emotion.* Fort Worth, TX: Harcourt Brace Jovanovich.

Reisenzein, R. (1983). The Schachter theory of emotion: Two decades later. *Psychological Bulletin, 94,* 239–264.

Rescorla, R. A. (1968). Probability of shock in the presence and absence of CS in fear conditioning. *Journal of Comparative and Physiological Psychology, 66,* 1–5.

Rescorla, R. A. (1988). Pavlovian conditioning: It's not what you think it is. *American Psychologist, 43,* 151-160.

Rescorla, R. A. (1992). Hierarchical associative relations in Pavlovian conditioning and instrumental training. *Current Directions in Psychological Science, 1,* 66–70.

Resnick, S. M., Berenbaum, S. A., Gottesman, I. I., & Bouchard, T. J. (1986). Early hormonal influences on cognitive functioning in congenital adrenal hyperplasia. *Developmental Psychology, 22,* 191–198.

Revelle, W. (1995). Personality processes. *Annual Review of Psychology, 46,* 295–328.

Revusky, S. H., & Garcia, J. (1970). Learned associations over long delays. In G. H. Bower & J. T. Spence (Eds.), *The psychology of learning and motivation* (Vol. 4). New York: Academic Press.

Richards, F. A., & Commons, M. L. (1990). Postformal cognitive-developmental theory and research: A review of its current status. In C. N. Alexander & E. J. Langer (Eds.), *Higher stages of human development: Perspectives on adult growth.* New York: Oxford University Press.

Richman, A. L., Miller, P. M., & LeVine, R. A. (1992). Cultural and educational variations in maternal responsiveness. *Developmental Psychology, 28,* 614–621.

Rickels, K., Schweizer, E., Case, W. G., & Greenblatt, D. J. (1990). Long-term therapeutic use of benzodiazepines. I. Effects of abrupt discontinuation. *Archives of General Psychiatry, 47,* 899–907.

Riegel, K. F. (1976). The dialectics of human development. *American Psychologist, 31,* 689–700.

Riggs, D. A., & Foa, E. B. (1993). Obsessive-compulsive disorder. In D. H. Barlow (Ed.), *Clinical handbook of psychological disorders* (2nd ed.). New York: Guilford.

Rips, L. J. (1989). Similarity, typicality, and categorization. In S. Vosniadou & A. Ortony (Eds.), *Similarity and analogical reasoning.* Cambridge, England: Cambridge University Press.

Rips, L. J., & Conrad, F. G. (1989). Folk psychology of mental activities. *Psychological Review, 96,* 187–207.

Roberts, C. J., & Lowe, C. R. (1975). Where have all the conceptions gone? *Lancet, 1,* 498–499.

Robinson, J. O., Rosen, M., Revill, S. I., David, H., & Rus, G. A. D. (1980). Self-administered intravenous and intramuscular pethidine. *Anaesthesia, 35,* 763–770.

Robinson, L. A., Berman, J. S., & Neimeyer, R. A. (1990). Psychotherapy for the treatment of depression: A comprehensive review of controlled outcome research. *Psychological Bulletin, 100,* 30–49.

Rodin, J. (1981). Current status of the internal-external hypothesis for obesity: What went wrong? *American Psychologist, 36,* 361–372.

Rodin, J., Schank, D., & Striegal-Moore, R. H. (1989). Psychological features of obesity. *Medical Clinics of North America, 73,* 47–66.

Roediger, H. L., III, & McDermott, K. B. (1993). Implicit memory in normal human subjects. In F. Boller & J. Grafman (Eds.), *Handbook of neuropsychology* (Vol. 8). Amsterdam: Elsevier.

Roediger, H. L., III, Weldon, M. S., Stadler, M. L., & Riegler, G. L. (1992). Direct comparison of two implicit memory tests: Word fragment and word stem completion. *Journal of Experimental Psychology: Learning, Memory, & Cognition, 18,* 1251–1269.

Rogers, C. R. (1951). *Client-centered therapy.* Boston: Houghton Mifflin.

Rogers, C. R. (1961). *On becoming a person: A therapist's view of psychotherapy.* Boston: Houghton Mifflin.

Rogers, C. R. (1963). The actualizing tendency in relation to "motives" and to consciousness. In M. R. Jones (Ed.), *Nebraska symposium on motivation.* Lincoln: University of Nebraska.

Rogers, S. M., & Turner, C. F. (1991). Male-male sexual contact in the U.S.A.: Findings from five sample surveys, 1970–1990. *Journal of Sex Research, 28,* 491–519.

Roggman, L. A., Langlois, J. H., Hubbs-Tait, L., & Rieser-Danner, L. A. (1994). Infant day-care, attachment, and the "file drawer problem." *Child Development, 65,* 1429–1443.

Roitblat, H. L., & von Ferson, L. (1992). Comparitive cognition: Representations and processes in learning and memory. *Annual Review of Psychology, 43,* 671–710.

Rosch, E., & Mervis, C. B. (1975). Family resemblances: Studies in the internal structure of categories. *Cognitive Psychology, 7,* 573–605.

Rosch, E., Mervis, C. B., Gray, W. D., Johnson, D. M., & Bayes-Braem, P. (1976). Basic objects in natural categories. *Cognitive Psychology, 8,* 382–439.

Rosen, D. L., & Singh, S. (1992). An investigation of subliminal embed effect on multiple measures of advertising effectiveness. *Psychology & Marketing, 9,* 157–173.

Rosenbaum, M. E. (1986). The repulsion hypothesis: On the nondevelopment of relationships. *Journal of Personality and Social Psychology, 51,* 1156–1166.

Rosenhan, D. L. (1973). On being sane in insane places. *Science, 179,* 250–258.

Rosenthal, R. (1966). *Experimenter effects in behavioral research.* New York: Appleton-Century-Crofts.

Rosenthal, R. (1994). Science and ethics in conducting, analyzing, and reporting psychological research. *Psychological Science, 5,* 127–134.

Rosenthal, R., & Jacobson, L. (1968). *Pygmalion in the classroom: Teachers' expectations and pupils' intellectual development.* New York: Holt, Rinehart & Winston.

Rosenthal R., & Rosnow, R. L. (Eds.). (1969). *Artifact in behavioral research.* New York: Academic Press.

Rosenthal, R., & Rosnow, R. L. (1975). *The volunteer subject.* New York: Wiley.

Rosenthal, R., & Rosnow, R. L. (1991). *Essentials of behavioral research: Methods and data analysis* (2nd ed.). New York: McGraw-Hill.

Rosenzweig, M. R. (1984). Experience, memory, and the brain. *American Psychologist, 39,* 365–376.

Rosenzweig, S. (1936). Some implicit common factors in diverse methods of psychotherapy. *American Journal of Orthopsychiatry, 6,* 422–425.

Rosnow, R. L., & Rosenthal, R. (1993). *Beginning behavioral research: A conceptual primer.* New York: Macmillan.

Ross, C. A., Miller, S. D., Reagor, P., Bjornson, L., Fraser, G. A., & Anderson, G. (1990). Structured interview data on 102 cases of multiple personality disorder from four centers. *American Journal of Psychiatry, 147,* 596–601.

Ross, L. (1977). The intuitive psychologist and his shortcomings: Distortions in the attribution process. In L. Berkowitz (Ed.), *Advances in experimental social psychology* (Vol. 10). New York: Academic Press.

Ross, L., & Nisbett, R. E. (1991). *The person and the situation: Perspectives of social psychology.* New York: McGraw-Hill.

Rothlind, J., Posner, M. I., & Schaughency, E. (1991). Lateralized control of eye movements in attention deficit hyperactivity disorder. *Journal of Cognitive Neuroscience, 3,* 377–381.

Rotter, J. B. (1966). Generalized expectancies for internal versus external locus of control of reinforcement. *Psychological Monographs, 80*(Whole No. 609).

Rotter, J. B., Liverant, S., & Crowne, D. P. (1961). The growth and extinction of expectancies in change controlled and skilled tasks. *Journal of Psychology, 52,* 161–177.

Rovee-Collier, C. (1993). The capacity for long-term memory in infancy. *Current Directions in Psychological Science, 2,* 130–135.

Rozin, P. (1990). Development in the food domain. *Developmental Psychology, 26,* 555–562.

Rozin, P., & Fallon, A. E. (1987). A perspective on disgust. *Psychological Review, 94,* 23–41.

Rozin, P., Hammer, L., Oster, H., Horowitz, T., & Marmara, V. (1986). The child's conception of food: Development of categories of accepted and rejected substances. *Journal of Nutrition Education, 18,* 75–81.

Rubinsky, H., Eckerman, D., Rubinsky, E., & Hoover, C. (1987). Early-phase physiological response patterns to psychosexual stimuli: Comparisons of male and female patterns. *Archives of Sexual Behavior, 16,* 45–55.

Ruble, D. N., Balaban, T., & Cooper, J. (1981). Gender constancy and the effects of sex-typed televised toy commercials. *Child Development, 52,* 667–673.

Rumbaugh, D. M. (Ed.). (1977). *Language learning by a chimpanzee: The Lana project.* New York: Academic Press.

Rumelhart, D. E., & McClelland, J. L. (Eds.). (1986). *Parallel distributed processing: Explorations in the microstructure of cognition* (Vol. 1). Cambridge, MA: MIT Press.

Rummel, A., & Feinberg, R. (1988). Cognitive evaluation theory: A meta-analytic review of the literature. *Social Behavior and Personality, 16,* 147–164.

Russek, M. (1971). Hepatic receptors and the neurophysiological mechanisms controlling feeding behavior. In S. Ehrenpreis (Ed.), *Neuroscience research.* New York: Academic Press.

Russell, J. A. (1994). Is there universal recognition of emotion from facial expression? A review of the cross-cultural studies. *Psychological Bulletin, 115,* 102–141.

Ryckman, R. M. (1993). *Theories of personality* (5th ed.). Pacific Grove, CA: Brooks/Cole.

Sakai, F., Stirling Meyer, J., Karacan, I., Yamaguchi, F., & Yamamoto, M. (1979). Narcolepsy: Regional cerebral blood flow during sleep and wakefulness. *Neurology, 29,* 61–67.

Salkovskis, P. M. (1985). Obsessional compulsive problems: A cognitive behavioral analysis. *Behaviour Research and Therapy, 23,* 571–577.

Salthouse, T. A. (1994). The nature of the influence of speed on adult age differences in cognition. *Developmental Psychology, 30,* 240–259.

Sameroff, A. J., Seifer, R., Baldwin, A., & Baldwin, C. (1993). Stability of intelligence from preschool to adolescence: The influence of social and family risk factors. *Child Development, 64,* 80–97.

Sanders, R. J. (1989). Sentence comprehension following agenesis of the corpus callosum. *Brain and Language, 37,* 59–72.

Sanderson, W. C., & Barlow, D. H. (1990). A description of patients diagnosed with a DSM-II-R anxiety disorder. *Journal of Nervous and Mental Disease, 178,* 588–591.

Sanson, A., & di-Muccio, C. (1993). The influence of aggressive and neutral cartoons and toys on the behaviour of preschool children. *Australian Psychologist, 28,* 93–99.

Sarason, I. G., Sarason, B. R., & Pierce, G. R. (1994). Social support: Global and relationship-based levels of analysis. *Journal of Social and Personal Relationships, 11,* 295–312.

Sarbin, T. R., & Coe, W. C. (1972). *Hypnosis: A social psychological analysis of influence communication.* New York: Holt, Rinehart & Winston.

Saron, C. D., & Davidson, R. J. (1989). Visual evoked potential measures of interhemispheric transfer times in humans. *Behavioral Neuroscience, 103,* 1115–1138.

Savage-Rumbaugh, E., McDonald, D., Sevcik, R., Hopkins, W., & Rupert, E. (1986). Spontaneous symbol acquisition and communicative use by pygmie chimpanzees. *Journal of Experimental Psychology: General, 115,* 211–235.

Saxe, L. (1994). Detection of deception: Polygraph and integrity tests. *Current Directions in Psychological Science, 3,* 69–72.

Scarr, S., & Weinberg, R. A. (1976). IQ test performance of black children adopted by white families. *American Psychologist, 31,* 726–739.

Schachter, S. (1971). *Emotion, obesity, and crime.* New York: Academic Press.

Schachter, S., & Singer, J. E. (1962). Cognitive, social, and physiological determinants of emotional state. *Psychological Review, 69,* 379–399.

Schaie, K. W. (1983). The Seattle Longitudinal Study: A twenty-one-year exploration of psychometric intelligence in adulthood. In K. W. Schaie (Ed.), *Longitudinal studies of adult psychological development.* New York: Guilford.

Schaie, K. W. (1989). The hazards of cognitive aging. *Gerontologist, 29,* 484–493.

Schaie, K. W. (1993). The Seattle longitudinal studies of adult intelligence. *Current Directions in Psychological Science, 2,* 171–175.

Schedlowski, M., Fluge, T., Richter, S., & Tewes, U. (1995). b-Endorphin, but not substance-P, is increased by acute stress in humans. *Psychoneuroendocrinology, 20,* 103–110.

Scheff, T. J. (1984). *Being mentally ill: A sociological theory.* New York: Aldine.

Scheier, M. F., & Carver, C. S. (1993). On the power of positive thinking: The benefits of being optimistic. *Current Directions in Psychological Science, 2,* 26–30.

Scheier, M. F., Matthews, K. A., Owens, J. F., Magovern, G. J., Sr., Lefebvre, R. C., Abbott, R. A., & Carver, C. S. (1989). Dispositional optimism and recovery from coronary artery bypass surgery: The beneficial effects on physical and psychological well-being. *Journal of Personality and Social Psychology, 57,* 1024–1040.

Schelling, T. C. (1992). Addictive drugs: The cigarette experience. *Science, 255,* 430–433.

Schleifer, S. J., Keller, S. E., Meyerson, A. T., Raskin, M. J., Davis, K. L., & Stein, M. (1983). Suppression of lymphocyte stimulation following bereavement. *Journal of the American Medical Association, 250,* 374.

Schlenker, B. R., & Forsyth, D. R. (1977). On the ethics of psychological research. *Journal of Experimental Social Psychology, 13,* 369–396.

Schmidt, F. L., & Hunter, J. E. (1993). Tacit knowledge, practical intelligence, general mental ability, and job knowledge. *Current Directions in Psychological Science, 2,* 8–9.

Schnapf, J. L., & Baylor, D. A. (1987, April). How photoreceptor cells respond to light. *Scientific American, 256,* 40–47.

Schneider, J. S., Sun, Z. Q., & Roeltgen, D. P. (1994). Effects of dopamine agonists on delayed response performance in chronic low-dose MPTP-treated monkeys. *Pharmacology, Biochemistry, and Behavior, 48,* 235–240.

Schneider, S. G., Taylor, S. E., Hammen, C., Kemeny, M. E., & Dudley, J. (1991). Factors influencing suicide intent in gay and bisexual suicide ideators: Differing models for men with and without human immunodeficiency virus. *Journal of Personality and Social Psychology, 61,* 776–788.

Schneiderman, N., Antoni, M. H., Ironson, G., Laperriere, A., & Fletcher, M. A. (1992). Applied psychological science and HIV-1 spectrum disease. *Applied and Preventive Psychology, 1,* 67–82.

Schreiber, F. (1973). *Sybil.* New York: Warner Books.

Schroeder, D. H., & Costa, P. T. (1984). Influence of life event stress on physical illness: Substantive effects or methodological flaws? *Journal of Personality and Social Psychology, 46,* 853–863.

Schwartz, B. (1990). The creation and destruction of value. *American Psychologist, 45,* 7–15.

Schweickert, R., Guentert, L., & Hersberger, L. (1990). Phonological similarity, pronunication rate, and memory span. *Psychological Science, 1,* 74–77.

Sclafani, A. (1994). Eating rates in normal and hypothalamic hyperphagic rats. *Physiology and Behavior, 55,* 489–494.

Scott, T. R., Plata-Salamn, C. R., & Smith-Swintosky, V. L. (1994). Gustatory neural coding in the monkey cortex: The quality of saltiness. *Journal of Neurophysiology, 71,* 1692–1701.

Sebrechts, M. M., Marsh, R. L., & Seamon, J. G. (1989). Secondary memory and very rapid forgetting. *Memory & Cognition, 17,* 693–700.

Seeman, P., Lee, T., Chau Wong, M., & Wong, K. (1976). Antipsychotic drug doses and neuroleptic/dopamine receptors. *Nature, 261,* 717–719.

Segall, M. H., Dasen, P. R., Berry, J. W., & Poortinga, Y. (1990). *Human behavior in global perspective.* New York: Pergamon.

Sekular, R., & Blake, R. (1990). *Perception* (2nd ed.). New York: McGraw-Hill.

Seligman, M. E. P. (1975). *Helplessness: On depression, development, and death.* San Francisco: Freeman.

Selkoe, D. J. (1992, September). Aging brain, aging mind. *Scientific American, 267,* 135–142.

Selye, H. (1936). A syndrome produced by diverse nocuous agents. *Nature, 138,* 32.

Selye, H. (1952). *The story of the adaptation syndrome.* Montreal: Acta.

Selye, H. (1974). *Stress without distress.* Philadelphia: Lippincott.

Sepple, C. P., & Read, N. W. (1989). Gastrointestinal correlates of the development of hunger in man. *Appetite, 13,* 183–191.

Shaffer, D. R. (1993). *Developmental psychology: Childhood and adolescence* (3rd ed.). Pacific Grove, CA: Brooks/Cole.

Shapiro, A. K. (1960). A contribution to a history of the placebo effect. *Behavioral Science, 5,* 109–135.

Shapley, R. (1990). Visual sensitivity and parallel retinocortical channels. *Annual Review of Psychology, 41,* 635–658.

Shapley, R., & Kaplan, E. (1989). Responses of magnocellular LGN neurons and M retinal ganglion cells to drifting heterochromatic gratings. *Investigative Ophthalmology and Visual Science, 30,* 323.

Sharma, K. N., Anand, B. K., Due, S., & Singh, B. (1961). Role of stomach in regulation of activities of hypothalamic feeding centers. *American Journal of Physiology, 201,* 593–598.

Shaywitz, S. E., Fletcher, J. M., & Shaywitz, B. A. (1994). Issues in the definition and classifiction of attention deficit disorder. *Topics in Language Disorders, 14,* 1–25.

Shepard, R. N. (1990). *Mind sights.* New York: W. H. Freeman.

Sheridan, C. L., & Radmacher, S. A. (1992). *Health psychology: Challenging the biomedical model.* New York: Wiley.

Shields, S. A. (1975). Functionalism, Darwinism, and the psychology of women: A study in social myth. *American Psychologist, 30,* 739–754.

Shiffrin, R. M., & Schneider, W. (1977). Controlled and automatic human information processing II: Perceptual learning, automatic attending, and a general theory. *Psychological Review, 84,* 127–190.

Shirley, M. M. (1933). *The first two years: A study of 25 babies. Vol. 1: Postural and locomotor development.* Minneapolis: University of Minnesota Press.

Shweder, R. A., Mahapatra, M., & Miller, J. G. (1990). Culture and moral development. In J. W. Stigler, R. A. Shweder, & G. Herdt (Eds.), *Cultural psychology.* New York: Cambridge University Press.

Siegel, J. M. (1983). A behavioral approach to the analysis of reticular formation unit activity. In T. E. Robinson (Ed.), *Behavioral approaches to brain research.* New York: Oxford University Press.

Siegel, J. M. (1990). Stressful life events and use of physician services among the elderly: The moderating role of pet ownership. *Journal of Personality and Social Psychology, 58,* 1081–1086.

Siegel, S. (1983). Classical conditioning, drug tolerance, and drug dependence. In Y. Israel, F. B. Glaser, R. E. Popham, W. Schmidt, & R. G. Smart (Eds.), *Research advances in alcohol and drug problems* (Vol. 7). New York: Plenum.

Siegel, S. (1989). Pharmacological conditioning and drug effects. In A. J. Goudie & M. W. Emmett-Oglesby (Eds.), *Psychoactive drugs: Tolerance and sensitization.* Clifton, NJ: Humana Press.

Siegler, R. S. (1994). Cognitive variability: A key to understanding cognitive development. *Psychological Science, 3,* 1–5.

Sigelman, C. K., & Shaffer, D. R. (1995). *Life-span human development* (2nd ed.). Pacific Grove, CA: Brooks/Cole.

Sigmundson, H. K. (1994). Pharmacotherapy of schizophrenia: A review. *Canadian Journal of Psychiatry, 39,* 570–575.

Silver, E., Cirincione, C., & Steadman, H. J. (1994). Demythologizing inaccurate perceptions of the insanity defense. *Law and Human Behavior, 18,* 63–70.

Silverstein, B., Perdue, L., Peterson, B., & Kelly, E. (1986). The role of the mass media in promoting a thin standard of bodily attractiveness for women. *Sex Roles, 14,* 519–532.

Simmons, J. M., & Gallistel, C. R. (1994). Saturation of subjective reward magnitude as a function of current and pulse frequency. *Behavioral Neuroscience, 108,* 151–160.

Simon, H. A. (1969). *The sciences of the artificial.* Cambridge, MA: MIT Press.

Simon, H. A. (1992). What is an "explanation" of behavior? *Psychological Science, 3,* 150–161.

Siqueland, E. R., & DeLucia, C. A. (1969). Visual reinforcement of nonnutritive sucking in human infants. *Science, 165,* 1144–1146.

Sivian, L. S., & White, S. D. (1933). On minimum audible sound fields. *Journal of Acoustical Society of America, 4,* 288–321.

Skinner, B. F. (1938). *The behavior of organisms: An experimental analysis.* New York: Appleton-Century.

Skinner, B. F. (1948). "Superstition" in the pigeon. *Journal of Experimental Psychology, 38,* 168–172.

Skinner, B. F. (1956). A case history in scientific method. *American Psychologist, 11,* 221–233.

Skinner, B. F. (1969). *Contingencies of reinforcement: A theoretical analysis.* New York: Appleton-Century-Crofts.

Slater, E., & Glithero, E. (1965). A follow-up of patients diagnosed as suffering from hysteria. *Journal of Psychosomatic Research, 9,* 9–13.

Sloane, R. B., Staples, F. R., Cristol, A. H., Yorkston, N. J., & Whipple, K. (1975). *Psychotherapy versus behavior therapy.* Cambridge, MA: Harvard University Press.

Slovic, P., Fischoff, B., & Lichtenstein, S. (1982). Facts versus fears: Understanding perceived risk. In D. Kahneman, P. Slovic, & A. Tversky (Eds.), *Judgment under uncertainty: Heuristics and biases.* Cambridge, England: Cambridge University Press.

Smiley, P. A., & Dweck, C. S. (1994). Individual differences in achievement goals among young children. *Child Development, 65,* 1723–1743.

Smith, E. E. (1989). Concepts and induction. In M. Posner (Ed.), *Foundations of cognitive science.* Cambridge, MA: MIT Press.

Smith, E. R., & Mackie, D. M. (1995). *Social psychology.* New York: Worth.

Smith, F. J., & Campfield, L. A. (1993). Meal initiation occurs after experimental induction of transient declines in blood glucose. *American Journal of Physiology, 265,* R1423–R1429.

Smith, M. L., & Glass, G. V. (1977). Meta-analysis of psychotherapy outcome studies. *American Psychologist, 32,* 752–760.

Smith, M. L., Glass, G. V., & Miller, T. I. (1980). *The benefits of psychotherapy.* Baltimore, MD: Johns Hopkins University Press.

Snyder, C. R. (1989). Reality negotiation: From excuses to hope and beyond. Self-illusions: When are they adaptive? [Special issue] *Journal of Social and Clinical Psychology, 8,* 130–157.

Snyder, F. (1967). In quest of dreaming. In H. A. Witkin & H. B. Lewis (Eds.), *Experimental studies of dreaming.* New York: Random House.

Snyder, M. (1974). The self-monitoring of expressive behavior. *Journal of Personality and Social Psychology, 30,* 526–537.

Snyder, M. (1987). *Public appearances/Private realities: The psychology of self-monitoring.* New York: Freeman.

Snyder, M., Tanke, E. D., & Berscheid, E. (1977). Social perception and interpersonal behavior: On the self-fulfilling nature of social stereotypes. *Journal of Personality and Social Psychology, 35,* 656–666.

Snyder, S. H. (1976). The dopamine hypothesis of schizophrenia: Focus on the dopamine receptor. *American Journal of Psychiatry, 133,* 197–202.

Snyder, S. H., & D'Amato, R. J. (1986). MPTP: A neurotoxin relevant to the pathology of Parkinson's disease. *Neurology, 36,* 250–258.

Spanos, N. P. (1982). Hypnotic behavior: A cognitive, social psychological perspective. *Research Communications in Psychology, Psychiatry, and Behavior, 7,* 199–213.

Spanos, N. P. (1986). Hypnotic behavior: A social psychological interpretation of amnesia, analgesia, and "trance logic." *The Behavioral and Brain Sciences, 9,* 449–502.

Spanos, N. P., Weeks, J. R., & Bertrand, L. D. (1985). Multiple personality: A social psychological perspective. *Journal of Abnormal Psychology, 92,* 362–376.

Sparks, D. L. (1988). Neural cartography: Sensory and motor maps in the mammalian superior colliculus. *Brain, Behavior, and Evolution, 31,* 49–56.

Spearman, C. (1904). "General intelligence," objectively determined and measured. *American Journal of Psychology, 15,* 201–293.

Spelke, E. S. (1991). Physical knowledge in infancy: Reflections on Piaget's theory. In S. Carey & R. Gelman (Eds.), *The epigenesis of mind: Essays on biology and cognition.* Hillsdale, NJ: Erlbaum.

Spelke, E. S., Breinlinger, K, Macomber, J., & Jacobson, K. (1992). Origins of knowledge. *Psychological Review, 99,* 605–632.

Sperling, G. (1960). The information available in brief visual presentations. *Psychological Monographs, 74*(Whole No. 48).

Spiegel, D., Bloom, J. R., Kramer, H. C., & Gotheil, E. (1989). Effect of psychosocial treatment on survival of patients with metastatic breast cancer. *Lancet, 14,* 888–891.

Spitz, R. A. (1945). Hospitalism: An inquiry into the genesis of psychiatric conditions in early childhood. *Psychoanalytic Study of the Child, 1,* 53–74.

Spitzer, R. L. (1975). On pseudoscience in science, logic in remission, and psychiatric diagnosis: A critique of Rosenhan's "On being sane in insane places." *Journal of Abnormal Psychology, 84,* 442–452.

Spitzer, R. L., Gibbon, M., Skodol, A. E., Williams, J. B., & First, M. B. (Eds.). (1994). *DSM-IV Casebook.* Washingtin, DC: American Psychiatric Press.

Sponheim, S. R., Clementz, B. A., Iacono, W. G., & Beiser, M. (1994). Resting EEG in first episode and chronic schizophrenia. *Psychophysiology, 31,* 37–43.

Springer, S. P., & Deutsch, G. (1989). *Left brain, right brain.* (3rd ed.). New York: Freeman.

Squire, L. R. (1992). Memory and the hippocampus: A synthesis of findings with rats, monkeys, and humans. *Psychological Review, 99,* 195–231.

Squire, L. R., Ojemann, J. G., Miezin, F. M., Petersen, S. E., Videen, T. O., & Raichle, M. E. (1992). Activation of the hippocampus in normal humans: A functional anatomical study of memory. *Proceedings of the National Academy of Sciences, 89,* 1837–1841.

Staddon, J. E. R., & Simmelhag, V. L. (1971). The "superstition" experiment: A reexamination of its implications for the principles of adaptive behavior. *Psychological Review, 78,* 3–43.

Steblay, N. M., & Bothwell, R. K. (1994). Evidence for hypnotically refreshed testimony: The view from the laboratory. *Law and Human Behavior, 18,* 635–651.

Steele, C. M., & Josephs, R. A. (1990). Alcohol myopia: Its prized and dangerous effects. *American Psychologist, 45,* 921–933.

Stein, M., & Miller, A. H. (1993). Stress, the immune system, and health and illness. In L. Goldberger & S. Breznitz (Eds.), *Handbook of stress: Theoretical and clinical aspects* (2nd ed.). New York: Free Press.

Stein, M., Ottenberg, P., & Roulet, N. (1958). A study of the development of olfactory preferences. *American Medical Association Archives of Neurology & Psychiatry, 80,* 264–266.

Steiner, J. E. (1977). Facial expressions of the neonate infant indicating the hedonics of food-related chemical stimuli. In J. M. Weiffenbach (Ed.), *Taste and development.* Bethesda, MD: Department of Health, Education, and Welfare.

Stern, R. S., & Cobb, J. P. (1978). Phenomenology of obsessive-compulsive neurosis. *British Journal of Psychiatry, 132,* 233–234.

Sternberg, R. J. (1977). *Intelligence, information processing, and analogical reasoning.* Hillsdale, NJ: Erlbaum.

Sternberg, R. J. (1985). *Beyond IQ: A triarchic theory of human intelligence.* New York: Cambridge University Press.

Sternberg, R. J. (1986). A triangular theory of love. *Psychological Review, 93,* 119–135.

Sternberg, R. J. (1988a). Triangulating love. In R. J. Sternberg & M. L. Barnes (Eds.), *The psychology of love.* New Haven, CT: Yale University Press.

Sternberg, R. J. (1988b). *The triarchic theory of mind: A new theory of human intelligence.* New York: Viking Press.

Sternberg, R. J., & Gardner, M. K. (1983). Unities in inductive reasoning. *Journal of Experimental Psychology: General, 112,* 80–116.

Sternberg, R. J., & Grajek, S. (1984). The nature of love. *Journal of Personality and Social Psychology, 47,* 312–329.

Sternberg, R. J., & Wagner, R. K. (1993). The g-ocentric view of intelligence and job performance is wrong. *Current Directions in Psychological Science, 2,* 1–5.

Stevens, S. S. (1939). Psychology and the science of science. *Psychological Bulletin, 36,* 221–263.

St.-Jean, R., McInnis, K., Campbell-Mayne, L., & Swainson, P. (1994). Hypnotic underestimation of time: The busy beaver. *Journal of Abnormal Psychology, 103,* 565–569.

Stoyva, J. M., & Carlson, J. G. (1993). A coping/rest model of relaxation and stress management. In L. Goldberger & S. Breznitz (Eds.), *Handbook of stress: Theoretical and clincial aspects* (2nd ed.). New York: Free Press.

Strassman, R. J. (1992). Human hallucinogen interactions with drugs affecting serotonergic neurotransmission. *Neuropsychopharamacology, 7,* 241–243.

Streissguth, A. P., Randels, S. P., & Smith, D. F. (1991). A test-retest study of intelligence in patients with fetal alcohol syndrome: Implications for care. *Journal of the American Academy of Child and Adolescent, 30,* 584–587.

Sue, S., & Zane, N. (1987). The role of culture and cultural techniques in psychotherapy: A critique and reformulation. *American Psychologist, 42,* 37–45.

Sue, S., Zane, N., & Young, K. (1994). Research on psychotherapy with culturally diverse populations. In A. E. Bergin & S. L. Garfield (Eds.), *Handbook of psychotherapy and behavior change* (4th ed.). New York: Wiley.

Sussman, J. R., & Levitt, B. (1989). *Before you conceive: The complete pregnancy guide.* New York: Bantam Books.

Suzdak, P. D., Glowa, J. R., Crawley, J. N., Schwartz, R. D., Skolnick, P., & Paul, S. M. (1986). A selective imidazobenzodiazepine antagonist of ethanol in the rat. *Science, 234,* 1243–1247.

Szasz, T. (1961). *The myth of mental illness: Foundations of a theory of personal conduct.* New York: Hoeber-Harper.

Szasz, T. (1990). Law and psychiatry: The problems that will not go away. *The Journal of Mind and Behavior, 11,* 557–564.

Tanford, S., & Penrod, S. (1984). Social influence model: A formal integration of research on majority and minority influence processes. *Psychological Bulletin, 95,* 189–225.

Tanner, J. M. (1990). *Foetus into man: Physical growth from conception to maturity* (Rev. ed.). Cambridge, MA: Harvard University Press.

Taylor, F. K. (1965). Cryptomnesia and plagiarism. *British Journal of Psychiatry, 111,* 1111–1118.

Taylor, F. W. (1911). *Principles of scientific management.* New York: Harper.

Teeter, J. H., & Brand, J. G. (1987). Peripheral mechanisms of gustation: Physiology and biochemistry. In T. E. Finger & W. L. Silver (Eds.), *Neurobiology of taste and smell.* New York: Wiley.

Tellegen, A., Lykken, D. T., Bouchard, T. J., Jr., Wilcox, K. J., Segal, N. L., & Rich, S. (1988). Personality similarity in twins reared apart and together. *Journal of Personality and Social Psychology, 54,* 1031–1039.

Tennes, K., & Kreye, M. (1985). Children's adrenocortical responses to classroom activities and tests in elementary school. *Psychosomatic Medicine, 47,* 451–460.

Terman, L. M. (1925). *Mental and physical traits of a thousand gifted children.* Stanford, CA: Stanford University Press.

Terman, L. M. (1954). The discovery and encouragement of exceptional talent. *American Psychologist, 9,* 221–238.

Terman, L. M., & Ogden, M. (1947). *Genetic studies of genius. Vol. 5. The gifted child grows up.* Stanford, CA: Stanford University Press.

Tesser, A. (1993). The importance of heritability in psychological research: The case of attitudes. *Psychological Review, 100,* 129–142.

Thibos, L. N., Bradley, A., Still, D. L., & Zhang, X. (1990). Theory and measurement of ocular chromatic aberration. *Vision Research, 30,* 33–49.

Thigpen, C. H., & Cleckley, H. A. (1957). *Three faces of Eve.* New York: McGraw-Hill.

Thomas, A., & Chess, S. (1977). *Temperament and development.* New York: Bruner/Mazel.

Thompson, S. K. (1975). Gender labels and early sex-role development. *Child Development, 46,* 339–347.

Thomsen, P. H. (1994). Obsessive-compulsive disorder in children and adolescents: A review of the literature. *European Child and Adolescent Psychiatry, 3,* 138–158.

Thoresen, C. E., & Powell, L. H. (1992). Type A behavior pattern: New perspectives on theory, assessment and intervention. *Journal of Consulting and Clinical Psychology, 60,* 595–604.

Thorndike, E. L. (1898). Animal intelligence: An experimental study of the associative processes in animals. *Psychological Review, Monograph Supplements, 2*(Serial No. 8).

Thorndike, E. L. (1911). *Animal intelligence: Experimental studies.* New York: Macmillan.

Thorndike, E. L. (1914). *The psychology of learning.* New York: Teacher's College.

Thurstone, L. L. (1938). *Primary mental abilities.* Chicago: University of Chicago Press.

Tienari, P. (1992). Implications of adoption studies on schizophrenia. *British Journal of Psychiatry, 161,* 52–58.

Tiffany, S. T. (1990). A cognitive model of drug urges and drug-use behavior: Role of automatic and nonautomatic processes. *Psychological Review, 97,* 147–168.

Timberlake, W. (1980). A molar equilibrium theory of learned performance. In G. H. Bower (Ed.), *The psychology of learning and motivation* (Vol. 14). New York: Academic Press.

Timberlake, W., & Silva, F. J. (1994). Observation of behavior, inference of function, and the study of learning. *Psychonomic Bulletin and Review, 1,* 73–88.

Tinbergen, N. (1951). *The study of instinct.* London: Oxford University Press.

Titchener, E. B. (1899). Structural and functional psychology. *Philosophical Review, 8,* 290–299.

Tolman, C. W. (1968). The role of the companion in social facilitation of animal behavior. In E. C. Simmel, R. A. Hoppe, & G. A. Milton (Eds.), *Social facilitation and imitative behavior.* Boston: Allyn & Bacon.

Tomkins, S. S. (1962). *Affect, imagery, and consciousness* (Vol. 1). New York: Springer.

Tomlinson-Keasey, C., & Little, T. D. (1990). Predicting educational attainment, occupational achievement, intellectual skill, and personal adjustment among gifted men and women. *Journal of Educational Psychology, 82,* 442–455.

Towler, G. (1986). From zero to one hundred: Coaction in a natural setting. *Perceptual and Motor Skills, 62,* 377–378.

Trafimow, D., Triandis, H. C., & Goto, S. G. (1991). Some tests of the distinction between the private self and the collective self. *Journal of Personality and Social Psychology, 60,* 649–655.

Treisman, A. (1960). Contextual cues in selective listening. *Quarterly Journal of Experimental Psychology, 12,* 242–248.

Triplett, N. (1898). The dynamogenic factors in pacemaking and competition. *American Journal of Psychology, 9,* 507–533.

Trope, Y., & Liberman, A. (1993). The use of trait conceptions to identify other people's behavior and to draw inferences about their personalities. *Personality and Social Psychology Bulletin, 19,* 553–562.

Trull, T. J., & McCrae, R. R. (1994). A five-factor perspective on personality disorder research. In P. T. Costa, Jr. & T. A. Widiger (Eds.), *Personality disorders and the five-factor model of personality.* Washington, DC: American Psychological Association.

Tseng, W., & McDermott, J. F. (1975). Psychotherapy: Historical roots, universal elements, and cultural variations. *American Journal of Psychiatry, 132,* 378–384.

Tulving, E. (1983). *Elements of episodic memory.* Oxford, England: Oxford University Press.

Tulving, E., & Pearlstone, Z. (1966). Availability versus accessibility of information in memory for words. *Journal of Verbal Learning and Verbal Behavior, 5,* 381–391.

Tulving, E., & Thomson, D. M. (1973). Encoding specificity and retrieval processes in episodic memory. *Psychological Review, 80,* 352–373.

Turner, T. J., & Ortony, A. (1992). Basic emotions: Can conflicting criteria converge? *Psychological Review, 99,* 566–571.

Tversky, A., & Kahneman, D. (1973). On the psychology of prediction. *Psychological Review, 80,* 237–251.

Tversky, A., & Kahneman, D. (1974). Decision making under uncertainty: Heuristics and biases. *Science, 185,* 1124–1131.

Tversky, A., & Kahneman, D. (1983). Extensional versus intuitive reasoning: The conjunction fallacy in probability judgment. *Psychological Review, 90,* 293–315.

Ulrich, R. E. (1991). Commentary: Animal rights, animal wrongs and the question of balance. *Psychological Science, 2,* 197–201.

Usher, J. A., & Neisser, U. (1993). Childhood amnesia and the beginnings of memory for four early life events. *Journal of Experimental Psychology: General, 122,* 155–165.

Van Doornen, L. J., & Van Blokland, R. (1987). Serum-cholesterol: Sex-specific psychological correlates during rest and stress. *Journal of Psychosomatic Research, 31*, 239–249.

van Ijzendoorn, M. H., & Kroonenberg, P. M. (1988). Cross-cultural patterns of attachment: A meta-analysis of the strange situation. *Child Development, 59*, 147–156.

Ventura, J., Nuechterlein, K. H., Lukoff, D., & Hardesty, J. P. (1989). A prospective study of stressful life events and schizophrenia relapse. *Journal of Abnormal Behavior, 98*, 407–411.

Vernon, P. E. (1983). Speed of information processing and general intelligence. *Intelligence, 7*, 53–70.

Vernon, P. E., & Mori, M. (1992). Intelligence, reaction times, and peripheral nerve conduction velocity. *Intelligence, 16*, 273–288.

Vitz, P. C. (1988). *Sigmund Freud's Christian unconscious.* New York: Guilford.

Vogel, G. W., Buffenstein, A., Minter, K., & Hennessey, A. (1990). Drug effects on REM sleep and on endogenous depression. *Neuroscience and Biobehavioral Reviews, 14*, 49–63.

Vokey, J. R., & Read, J. D. (1985). Subliminal messages: Between the media and the devil. *American Psychologist, 40*, 1231–1239.

von Frisch, K. (1967). *The dance language and orientation of bees.* Cambridge, MA: Belknap Press.

Vygotsky, L. S. (1978). *Mind in society: The development of higher psychological processes.* Cambridge MA: Harvard University Press.

Wagenaar, W. A. (1986). My memory: A study of autobiographical memory over six years. *Cognitive Psychology, 18*, 225–252.

Wagner, A. R. (1981). SOP: A model of automatic memory processing in animal behavior. In N. E. Spear & R. R. Miller (Eds.), *Information processing in animals: Memory mechanisms.* Hillsdale, NJ: Erlbaum.

Wagner, R. K., & Sternberg, R. J. (1985). Practical intelligence in real-world pursuits: The role of tacit knowledge. *Journal of Personality and Social Psychology, 49*, 436–458.

Wahba, M. A., & Bridwell, L. G. (1976). Maslow reconsidered: A review of research on the need hierarchy theory. *Organizational Behavior and Human Performance, 15*, 212–240.

Waldman, I. D., Weinberg, R. A., & Scarr, S. (1994). Racial-group differences in IQ in the Minnesota Transracial Adoption Study: A reply to Levin and Lynn. *Intelligence, 19*, 29–44.

Walen, S. T., DiGuiseppe, R., & Dryden, W. (1992). *A practitioner's guide to rational-emotive therapy.* New York: Oxford University Press.

Walker, L. J. (1989). A longitudinal study of moral reasoning. *Child Development, 60*, 157–166.

Walters, J. M., & Gardner, H. (1986). The theory of multiple intelligences: Some issues and answers. In R. J. Sternberg & R. K. Wagner (Eds.), *Practical intelligence: Nature and origins of competence in the everyday world.* New York: Cambridge University Press.

Walton, G. E., & Bower, T. G. R. (1993). Newborns form "prototypes" in less than 1 minute. *Psychological Science, 4*, 203–205.

Wasow, T. (1989). Grammatical theory. In M. I. Posner (Ed.), *Foundations of cognitive science.* Cambridge, MA: MIT Press.

Waters, E., Wippman, J., & Sroufe, L. A. (1979). Attachment, positive affect, and competence in the peer group: Two studies in construct validation. *Child Development, 50*, 821–829.

Watson, J. B. (1913). Psychology as a behaviorist views it. *Psychological Review, 20*, 158–177.

Watson, J. B. (1919). *Psychology from the standpoint of a behaviorist.* Philadelphia: Lippincott.

Watson, J. B., & Rayner, R. (1920). Conditioned emotional reactions. *Journal of Experimental Psychology, 3*, 1–14.

Webb, E. J., Campbell, D. T., Schwartz, R. D., Sechrist, L., & Grove, J. B. (1981). *Nonreactive research in the social sciences.* Boston: Houghton Mifflin.

Webb, W. B. (1981). The return of consciousness. *G. Stanley Hall Lecture Series, 1*, 129–152.

Weber, R., & Crocker, J. (1993). Cognitive processes in the revision of stereotypic beliefs. *Journal of Personality and Social Psychology, 45*, 961–977.

Weinberg, R. A., Scarr, S., & Waldman, I. D. (1992). The Minnesota Transracial Adoption Study: A follow-up of IQ test performance at adolescence. *Intelligence, 16*, 117–135.

Weiner, R. D., & Coffey, C. E. (1988). Indications for use of electroconvulsive therapy. In A. J. Frances & R. E. Hales (Eds.), *Review of Psychiatry* (Vol. 7). Washington, DC: American Psychiatric Press.

Weingarten, H. P. (1983). Conditioned cues elicit feeding in sated rats: A role for learning in meal initiation. *Science, 220*, 431–433.

Weingarten, H. P., Chang, P. K., & McDonald, T. J. (1985). Comparison of the metabolic and behavioral disturbances following paraventricular and ventro-medial-hypothalamic lesions. *Brain Research Bulletin, 14*, 551–559.

Weinstein, L. N., Schwartz, D. G., & Arkin, A. M. (1991). Qualitative aspects of sleep mentation. In S. J. Ellman & J. S. Antrobus (Eds.), *The mind in sleep* (2nd ed.). New York: Wiley.

Weir, W. (1984, October). Another look at subliminal "facts." *Advertising Age,* 46.

Weisberg, H. F., Krosnick, J. A., & Bowen, B. D. (1989). *An introduction to survey research and data analysis* (2nd ed.). Glenview, IL: Scott, Foresman.

Weisberg, R. W. (1994). Genius and madness? A quasi-experimental test of the hypothesis that manic-depression increases creativity. *Psychological Science, 5*, 361–367.

Weiskrantz, L. (1992). Introduction: Dissociated issues. In A. D. Milner & M. D. Rugg (Eds.), *The neuropsychology of consciousness.* London: Academic Press.

Weiss, J. M. (1977). Psychological and behavioral influences on gastrointestinal lesions in animal models. In J. D. Maser & M. E. P. Seligman (Eds.), *Psychopathology: Experimental models.* San Francisco: Freeman.

Weiss, L., & Baum, A. (1987). Physiological aspects of environment-behavior relationships. In E. Zube & G. Morre (Eds.), *Advances in environmental psychology* (Vol. 1). New York: Plenum.

Weiten, W. (1995). *Psychology: Themes and variations* (3rd ed.). Pacific Grove, CA: Brooks/Cole.

Weldon, M. S., & Roediger, H. M., III. (1987). Altering retrieval demands reverses the picture superiority effect. *Memory & Cognition, 15*, 269–280.

Wellman, H. M., & Estes, D. (1986). Early understanding of mental entities: A reexamination of childhood realism. *Child Development, 57*, 910–923.

Wender, P. H., Kety, S. S., Rosenthal, D., Schlusinger, F., Ortmann, J., & Lunde, I. (1986). Psychiatric disorders in the biological and adoptive families of adopted individuals with affective disorders. *Archives of General Psychiatry, 43*, 923–929.

Wernicke, C. (1874). *Der Aphasische Symptomenkomplex.* Breslau, Poland: Cohn & Weigert.

Wertheimer, M. (1987). *A brief history of psychology* (3rd ed.). New York: Holt, Rinehart & Winston.

Wertsch, J. V., & Tulviste, P. (1992). L. S. Vygotsky and contemporary developmental psychology. *Developmental Psychology, 28*, 548–557.

Wever, E. G. (1949). *Theory of hearing.* New York: Wiley.

Whitbourne, S. K. (1985). *The aging body.* New York: Springer.

Whitbourne, S. K., Zuschlag, M. K., Elliot, L. B., & Waterman, A. S. (1992). Psychosocial development in adulthood: A 22-year sequential study. *Journal of Personality and Social Psychology, 63,* 260–271.

White, L., Tursky, B., & Schwartz, G. E. (1985). *Placebo: Theory, research, and mechanisms.* New York: Guilford.

Whitely, B. E., Jr. (1990). The relationship of heterosexuals' attributions for the causes of homosexuality to attitudes toward lesbians and gay men. *Personality and Social Psychology Bulletin, 16,* 367–377.

Whorf, B. L. (1956). *Language, thought, and reality: Selected writings of Benjamin Lee Whorf.* New York: Wiley.

Wigfield, A. (1994). Expectancy-value theory of achievement motivation: A developmental perspective. *Educational Psychology Review, 6,* 49–78.

Wiggins, J. S., & Pincus, A. L. (1992). Personality: Structure and assessment. *Annual Review of Psychology, 43,* 473–504.

Williams, D. A., Overmier, J. B., & LoLordo, V. M. (1992). A reevaluation of Rescorla's early dictums about Pavlovian conditioned inhibition. *Psychological Bulletin, 111,* 275–290.

Williams, L. M. (1992). Adult memories of childhood abuse: Preliminary findings from a longitudinal study. *The Advisor, 5,* 19–20.

Willingham, W. W., Lewis, C., Morgan, R., & Ramsit, L. (1990). *Predicting college grades: An analysis of institutional trends over two decades.* Princeton, NJ: Educational Testing Service.

Wilson, E. O. (1963, May). Pheromones. *Scientific American, 208,* 100–114.

Windgassen, K. (1992). Treatment with neuroleptics: The patient's perspective. *Acta Psychiatrica Scandinavica, 86,* 405–410.

Winett, R. A. (1995). A framework for health promotion and disease prevention programs. *American Psychologist, 50,* 341–350.

Winikoff, B. (1983). Nutritional patterns, social choices, and health. In D. Mechanic (Ed.), *Handbook of health, health care, and the health professions.* New York: Free Press.

Wise, R. A., & Bozarth, M. A. (1987). A psychomotor theory of addiction. *Psychological Review, 94,* 469–492.

Wise, R. A., & Rompre, P. P. (1989). Brain dopamine and reward. *Annual Review of Psychology, 40,* 191–225.

Wissler, C. (1901). The correlation of mental and physical tests. *Psychological Review, Monograph Supplement 3*(No. 6).

Witelson, S. F. (1992). Cognitive neuroanatomy: A new era. *Neurology, 42,* 709–713.

Wixted, J. T., & Ebbesen, E. B. (1991). On the form of forgetting. *Psychological Science, 2,* 409–415.

Wollberg, Z., & Newman, J. D. (1972). Auditory cortex of squirrel monkey: Response patterns of single cells to species-specific vocalizations. *Science, 175,* 212–214.

Wolpe, J. (1958). *Psychotherapy by reciprocal inhibition.* Stanford, CA: Stanford University Press.

Wolpe, J. (1975). Forward. In B. Sloane, F. Staples, A. Cristol, N. Yorkston, & K. Whipple (Eds.), *Psychotherapy versus behavior therapy.* Cambridge, MA: Harvard University Press.

Wolpe, J. (1982). *The practice of behavior therapy.* New York: Pergamon.

Wong, S. E., Martinez-Diaz, J. A., Massel, H. K., Edelstein, B. A., Wiegand, W., Bowen, L., & Liberman, R. P. (1993). Conversational skills training with schizophrenic inpatients: A study of generalization across settings and conversants. *Behavior Therapy, 24,* 285–304.

Worringham, C. J., & Messick, D. M. (1983). Social facilitation of running: An unobtrusive study. *Journal of Social Psychology, 121,* 23–29.

Wright, A. A. (1990). Memory processing by pigeons, monkeys, and people. In G. H. Bower (Ed.), *The psychology of learning and motivation* (Vol. 24). New York: Academic Press.

Wright, A. A., Santiago, H. C., Sands, S. F., Kendrick, D. F., & Cook, R. G. (1985). Memory processing of serial lists by pigeons, monkeys, and people. *Science, 229,* 287–289.

Wundt, W. (1896). *Outlines of psychology.* C. M. Judd (Trans.). New York: Stechart.

Wyer, R. S., Jr., & Srull, T. K. (1989). *Memory and cognition in its social context.* Hillsdale, NJ: Erlbaum.

Yalom, I. D. (1980). *Existential psychotherapy.* New York: Basic Books.

Yamamoto, T., Yuyama, N., & Kawamura, Y. (1981). Central processing of taste perception. In Y. Katsuki, R. Norgren, & M. Sato (Eds.), *Brain mechanisms of sensation.* New York: Wiley.

Yapko, M. D. (1994). Suggestibility and repressed memories of abuse: A survey of psychotherapists' beliefs. *American Journal of Clinical Hypnosis, 36,* 163–179.

Yates, F. A. (1966). *The art of memory.* Chicago: University of Chicago Press.

Yeomans, J. M., & Irwin, D. E. (1985). Stimulus duration and partial report performance. *Perception & Psychophysics, 37,* 163–169.

Young, J. E., Beck, A. T., & Weinberger, A. (1993). Depression. In D. H. Barlow (Ed.), *Clinical handbook of psychological disorders* (2nd ed.). New York: Guilford.

Zacks, R. T., & Hasher, L. (1994). Directed ignoring: Inhibitory regulation of working memory. In D. Dagenbach & T. H. Carr (Eds.), *Inhibitory processes in attention, memory, and language.* San Diego, CA: Academic Press.

Zahorik, D. M., Houpt, K. A., & Swartzman-Andert, J. (1990). Taste-aversion learning in three species of ruminants. *Applied Animal Behaviour Science, 26,* 27–39.

Zajonc, R. B. (1965). Social facilitation. *Science, 149,* 269–274.

Zajonc, R. B. (1968). Attitudinal effects of mere exposure. *Journal of Personality and Social Psychology, 9,* Monograph Supplement, No. 2, part 2.

Zajonc, R. B., Heingartner, A., & Herman, E. M. (1969). Social enhancement and impairment of performance in the cockroach. *Journal of Personality and Social Psychology, 13,* 83–92.

Zametkin, A. J., Nordahl, T., Gross, M., King, A. C., Semple, W. E., Rumsey, J., Hamburger, S., & Cohen, R. M. (1990). Cerebral glucose metabolism in adults with hyperactivity of childhood onset. *New England Journal of Medicine, 323,* 1361–1366.

Zeki, S. (1992, September). The visual image in mind and brain. *Scientific American, 267,* 68–76.

Zelazo, P. R., Zelazo, N. A., & Kolb, S. (1972). "Walking" in the newborn. *Science, 176,* 314–315.

Zigler, E. F., & Stevenson, M. F. (1993). *Children in a changing world* (2nd ed.). Pacific Grove, CA: Brooks/Cole.

Zotterman, Y. (1959). Thermal sensations. In J. Fields, H. W. Magoun, & V. E. Hall (Eds.), *Handbook of physiology: Section I. Neurophysiology, 1,* 431–458. Washington, DC: Physiological Society.

Name Index

Subject Index

Credits

Chapter 1

13: Figure 1.4 from *The Story of Psychology*, by R. C. Bolles, p. 277. Copyright ©1993 Brooks/Cole Publishing Co.

Chapter 3

95: Figure from *Introduction to Psychology*, Fourth Edition, by J. Kalat, p. 117, Brooks/Cole Publishing Company, 1996.

Chapter 4

117: Figure 4.3 adapted from *Life-Span Human Development*, by C. K. Sigelman and D. R. Shaffer, p. 92. Copyright ©1995 Brooks/Cole Publishing Co. **127:** Figure 4.9 graph adapted from *Cognition, 40*, by M. H. Johnson, S. Dziurawiec, H. Ellis, and J. Morton, "Newborns' Preferential Tracking of Face-Like Stimuli and Its Subsequent Decline," pp. 1–19, 1991, with kind permission of Elsevier Science–NL, Sara Burgerhartstraat 25, 1055 KV Amsterdam, The Netherlands.

Chapter 5

175: Figure 5.15 from "Higher-Level Vision," by I. Biederman. In D. H. Osherson, S. M. Kosslyn, & J. M. Hollerback (Eds.), *An Invitation to Cognitive Science: Visual Cognition and Action*, Vol. *2*, p. 135. Copyright ©1990 MIT Press. Reprinted by permission. **179:** Figure 5.19 (b) from *Mind Sights*, by R. N. Shepard. Copyright ©1990 by Roger N. Shepard. Reprinted by permission of W. H. Freeman & Company.

Chapter 6

216: Figure 6.5 from *Current Concepts: The Sleep Disorders*, by P. Hauri, 1982, The Upjohn Company, Kalamazoo, Michigan. Reprinted by permission.

Chapter 7

241: Figure 7.1 graphs reprinted with permission from "Memory Processing of Serial Lists by Pigeons, Monkeys and People," by A. A. Wright, H. C. Santiago, S. F. Sands, D. F. Kendrick, and R. G. Cook, 1985, *Science, 229*, pp. 287–289. Copyright ©1985 American Association for the Advancement of Science.

Chapter 8

294: Figure 8.10 from "Long-Term Memory for a Common Object," by R. S. Nickerson and M. J. Adams, 1979, *Cognitive Psychology, 11*, pp. 287–307. Used by permission of Academic Press and the author.

Chapter 9

329: Figure 9.5 from *Psychology*, by B. Goldstein, p. 324, Brooks/Cole Publishing Company, 1994.

Chapter 10

359: Figure 10.3 adapted from "Conduction Velocity in a Brain Nerve Pathway Correlates with Intelligence," by T. E. Reed and A. R. Jensen, 1992, *Intelligence, 16*, pp. 259–272. Copyright ©1992 Ablex Publishing Corp. Reprinted by permission. **369:** Figure 10.5 from *Psychology: Themes and Variations*, Third Edition, by W. Weiten, p. 343, Brooks/Cole Publishing Company, 1995. **381:** Excerpt from "The G-ocentric View of Intelligence and Job Performance Is Wrong," by R. J. Sternberg and R. K. Wagner, 1993, *Current Directions in Psychological Science, 2*, pp. 1–5. Copyright ©1993 Cambridge University Press. Reprinted by permission of Cambridge University Press.

Chapter 12

425: Figure 12.1 from "A 16PF Profile," by R. B. Cattell, 1973, *Psychology Today*, July 1973, pp. 40–46. Copyright ©1973 Sussex Publishers, Inc. Reprinted with permission from Psychology Today Magazine. **429:** Figure 12.4 adapted from *Psychology: Themes & Variations*, Third Edition, by W. Weiten, p. 509, Brooks/Cole Publishing Company, 1995. **448:** Figure 12.9 adapted from "Personality Similarity in Twins Reared Apart and Together," by A. Tellegen, D. T. Lykken, T. J. Bouchard, Jr., K. J. Wilcox, N. L. Segal, and S. Rich, 1988, *Journal of Personality and Social Psychology, 54*(6), 1031–1039. Copyright ©1988 by the American Psychological Association. Adapted by permission of the author.

Chapter 14

500, 501: Figure 14.3 reprinted with permission from the American Psychiatric Association *Diagnostic and Statistical Manual of Mental Disorders*, Fourth Edition. Washington D.C., American Psychiatric Association, 1994.

Chapter 15

540: Figure 15.6 adapted from "Depression," by A. T. Beck and J. E. Young. In D. H. Barlow (Ed.), *Clinical Handbook of Psychological Disorders: A Step by Step Treatment Manual*, pp. 667–668. Copyright ©1985 Guilford Press. Reprinted by permission.

Chapter 16

567: Table 16.1 reprinted by permission of the publisher from "The Social Readjustment Rating Scale," by T. H. Holmes and R. H. Rahe in *Journal of Psychosomatic Research*, 11, pp. 213–218. Copyright 1967 by Elsevier Science Inc. **580:** Figure 16.6 from Barlow, D. H., Rapee, R. M., *Daily Stress Record, Mastering Stress: A Lifestyle Approach*, 1991, p. 12. Reproduced with permission of American Health Publishing Company, Dallas, Texas. All rights reserved. For ordering information call 1-800-736-7323.

PHOTO CREDITS

Chapter 1

2–3: © M. C. Escher/Cordon Art and the M. C. Escher Foundation. **4:** (far left) © John Livzey; (near left) © John Livzey; (near right) © John Livzey; (far right) © John Livzey; (inset) © Alfred Pasieka/ Science Photo Library. **8:** (left) © Richard Hutchings/ Photo Researchers; (center) © Tom McCarthy/Rainbow; (right) © Science Photo Library/ Photo Researchers. **10:** (left) © Gale Zucker/Stock Boston; (center) © Dan McCoy/Rainbow; (right) © Hank Morgan/Rainbow. **12:** Descartes: "Tractatus de Homine," 1677. **14:** (top left) © Stephen Krasmann/Photo Researchers; (top right) © Art Wolfe/Tony Stone; (bottom left) © Charles Addams/The New Yorker Magazine. **15:** Archives of the History of American Psychology, University of Akron, OH. **16:** (top) The Bettmann Archive; (bottom) Courtesy Wellesley College Archives/ © Notman. **17:** Archives of the History of American Psychology, University of Akron, Ohio. **18:** © Nina Leen/Life Magazine. **19:** (top) The Bettmann Archive; (bottom) Michael Rougier/Life Magazine/ © Time Warner Inc. **21:** © Dan McCoy/Rainbow. **27:** (all) © John Livzey.

Chapter 2

28–29: © Peter Menzel/ Stock Boston. **32:** © Paul Conklin/ Photo Edit. **33:** © Joel Gordon. **34:** © Laura Dwight. **36:** © Dan McCoy/ Rainbow. **38:** © John Livzey. **39:** © Laura Dwight. **43:** (left) © David Woo/Stock Boston; (right) © Bob Daemmrich/Stock Boston. **44:** (left) © A. Sieveking/Petit Format; (right) © David M. Grossman. **46:** © Monkmeyer/Byron. **51:** © Tony Freeman/ Photo Edit. **52:** © Monkmeyer/ Goldberg. **56:** © Brad Markel /Liaison International. **57:** © Rafael Macia/ Photo Researchers.

Chapter 3

64–65: © John Eastcott/YVA Momatiuk/The Image Works. **68:** © John Livzey. **69:** © CNRI/Science Photo Library. **76:** © The Bettmann Archive. **77:** © John Livzey. **78:** © M. Granitsas/ The Image Works. **81:** © Dan McCoy/ Rainbow. **83:** © Catherine Pouedras/Science Photo Library. **84:** (top) © Richard T. Nowitz/Photo Researchers; (bottom) CEA/ORSAY/CNRI/ Science Photo Library. **85:** (top) Courtesy of Siemens Medical Systems; (bottom) © Scott Camazine/Photo Researchers. **87:** © Hank Morgan/Rainbow. **90:** Courtesy of Warren Museum, Harvard Medical School. **93:** © John Livzey. **99:** © Peter Cade/Tony Stone Images. **100:** © Monkmeyer/Rogers.

657

Chapter 4

110–111: © David A. Wagner/Phototake NYC. 113: (left) © Garry Watson/Science Photo Library; (center) © Laura Dwight; (right) © Monkmeyer/Smith. 114: © Dan McCoy/Rainbow. 116: (top far left) © Petit Format/Nestle/Science Source; (top near left) © Petit Format/Nestle/Science Source; (top near right) © James Stevenson/Science Photo Library; (top far right) © Petit Format/Nestle/Science Scource; (bottom left) Courtesy of American Cancer Society. 117: (left) © 1994 George Steinmetz; (right) © Monkmeyer Press/Pollak. 120: (top left) © Victor Englebert/Photo Researchers; (top right) © John Livzey; (bottom left) © B. Daemmrich/The Image Works. 121: (top) © Bob Daemmrich/Stock Boston; (bottom) © Bob Daemmrich/Stock Boston. 123: (all) Courtesy Dr. Dorothy G. Flood/University of Rochester Medical Center. 126: Courtesy Dr. Carolyn Rovee-Collier. 128: (top left) © John Livzey; (top center) © John Livzey; (top right) © John Livzey; (bottom left) © by Enrico Ferorelli. 129: © Bill Anderson/Monkmeyer Press Photo Service. 131: (top) © Charles Gupton/Stock Boston; (bottom left) © Monkmeyer/Goodman; (bottom right) © Monkmeyer Press/Goodman. 134: © David Young-Wolff /Photo Edit. 136: (top) © Sid Lathan/Photo Researchers; (bottom) © Catherine Karnow/Woodfin Camp. 137: © Kevin Horan/Stock Boston. 139: © Laura Dwight. 140: (left) © Martin Rogers/Stock Boston; (right) © Martin Rogers/Woodfin Camp. 141: © T. Stoddart/Katz '91/Woodfin Camp. 142: © Bob Daemmrich/Stock Boston. 143: UPI/ Bettmann Newsphotos. 144: © Dana Schuerholz/Impact Visuals. 145: © Bob Daemmrich/ Tony Stone Images. 146: © John Livzey. 148: (top) © Myrleen Cate/Tony Stone Images; (bottom) © Lawrence Migdale/Stock Boston. 149: © Joel Gordon. 154: (top) © Dorothy Littell/Stock Boston; (bottom) © Laura Dwight.

Chapter 5

156–157: © Bev Doolittle, "Woodland Encounter"–Greenwich Workshop. 162: (all) © Enrico Ferorelli. 163: (top) © Stephen Frisch/ Stock Boston; (bottom) © Omikron/ Photo Researchers. 167: Fritz Goro/Life Magazine/ © Time, Inc. 1971. 168: (top) D. F. Benson/ Archives of Neurology/American Medical Association; (bottom) Courtesy of Dr. Patrick Dupont Ph.D. 169: (top) © Gary Conner/Photo Edit; (bottom) Fritz Goro/ © Time/Warner, Inc. 173: © Bev Doolittle, "The Forest Has Eyes"–The Greenwich Workshop. 176: (left) © Denis Waugh/Tony Stone Images; (center) © Maggie Leonard/ Rainbow; (right) © John Elk III/Stock Boston. 178: © Richard Nowitz/Phototake, NYC. 182: © Enrico Ferorelli. 183: © Bob Daemmrich/Stock Boston. 185: © Richard Pasley/Stock Boston. 186: © Martin Rogers/Stock Boston. 187: © Peter Menzel/Stock Boston. 189: (top) © Jery Wachter/Photo Researchers; (bottom) © Chad Slattery/Tony Stone Images. 190: © Renee Lynn/Photo Researchers. 191: © Omikron/ Photo Researchers. 192: © F. Pedrick/The Image Works. 195: (left) © Stefan May/Tony Stone Images. 197: © John Elk III/Stock Boston; (right) © M. Bernsau/The Image Works.

Chapter 6

202–203: © Galen Rowell/Peter Arnold. 204: © Catherine Pouedras/Science Photo Library. 205: © Thompson & Thompson/Tony Stone Images. 206: (far left) © Coco McCoy/Rainbow; (near left) © Enrico Ferorelli; (near right) © Monkmeyer/Hiller; (far right) © David Attie/Phototake. 208: © Alan Carey/The Image Works. 209: © David Harvey/Woodfin Camp. 211: © Richard Hutchings/Photo Edit. 215: © David Grossman. 218: © Mike Mazzaschi/Stock Boston. 222: © Al Cook/Stock Boston. 224: (left) © Hank Morgan/Rainbow; (right) © M. Antman/The Image Works. 226: © M. Farrell/The Image Works. 228: © Jean-Loup Charmet/Science Photo Library. 230: © Bob Daemmrich/Stock Boston. 233: © Coco McCoy/Rainbow. 236: American Association of Advertising Agencies.

Chapter 7

238–239: © Richard Hutchings/Photo Researchers. 243: (left) © Chad Hutchings/Photo Researchers; (center) © Stephen J. Krasemann/ Photo Researchers; (right) © Anthony Wood/Stock Boston. 244: © Allan Roberts. 246: Sovfoto. 251: © Simon Fraser/Royal Victoria Infirmary/Newcastle/Science Scource. 254: Courtesy of Professor Benjamin Harris. 262: (top left) © Bob Daemmrich/Stock Boston; (top right) © Michael P. Gadomski/Photo Researchers; (bottom left) Phyllis Picardi/Stock Boston; (bottom right) © Willie L. Hill Jr./Stock Boston. 264: Courtesy Doctors Robert and Marian Breland Bailey. 265: © Stephen Green/Focus On Sports. 267: (top left) © Gerard Vandystadt/Photo Researchers; (top right) © C. J. Allen/Stock Boston; (bottom left) Tom McCarthy Photos/Rainbow; (bottom right) © John Livzey. 269: © Bob Daemmrich Photos/Stock Boston. 270: © Richard Hutchings/Photo Researchers.

Chapter 8

276–277: © Monkmeyer/Forsyth. 280: © Lien/Nibauer/Liaison International. 281: © M. Douglas/The Image Works. 283: © Joel Gordon. 287: (left) © Leonard Lessin/Peter Arnold; (right) © Leonard Lessin/Peter Arnold. 288: © Leanna Rathkelly/Tony Stone Images. 289: (left) © Eastcott/The Image Works; (center) © Will & Deni McIntyre/Photo Researchers; (right) © Jeff Isaac Greenberg/Photo Researchers. 291: © J. Pat Carter/Gamma Liaison Network. 297: (top) © Monkmeyer/Conklin; (bottom) © K. Harrison/ The Image Works. 299: © Esbin-Anderson/The Image Works. 303: © Tony Freeman/Photo Edit. 304: Bettmann Archive. 307: © B. Bachmann/The Image Works. 309: © Mazziotta et al /Science Photo Library.

Chapter 9

314–315: © Paul Avis/Liaison International. 317: (far left) © Charles Gupton/Stock Boston; (near left) © P. McCarten/Photo Edit; (near right) © Robert Brenner/Photo Edit; (far right) © Bryce Flynn/Stock Boston. 318: © Yoav Levy/ Phototake. 319: © Martin Rogers/Stock Boston. 320: © Scott Camazine/Photo Researchers. 324: (left) © Laura Dwight; (right) © David Young-Wolff/Photo Edit. 326: (left) © Susan Kuklin/Photo Researchers; (right) © Enrico Ferorelli. 327: © Jeff Greenberg/Rainbow. 328: ©

Alex Bartel/Science Photo Library. 329: © Dan McCoy/Rainbow. 332: (left) © Tim Davis/Photo Researchers; (center) © Tom & Pat Leeson/Photo Researchers; (right) © Eric Neurath/Stock Boston. 333: (left) © Blair Seitz/Photo Researchers; (right) © Monkmeyer/ Brady. 338: © Robert Brenner/Photo Edit. 341: © Cary Wolinsky/Stock Boston. 344: UPI/Bettmann.

Chapter 10

350–351: © Bill Gallery/Stock Boston. 352: UPI/Corbis/Bettmann. 353: (left) © Paul Merideth; (right) © Tom Ulrich/Tony Stone Images. 355: (all) Archives of the History of American Psychology. 356: © J. Crawford/The Image Works. 361: (left) © Bonnie Kamin/Photo Edit; (right) © Michael Abramson/Gamma Liaison. 365: © Bob Daemmrich/Stock Boston. 366: Archives of the History of American Psychology. 370: Archives of the History of American Psychology. 372: © Leonard Lessin/Peter Arnold. 375: © Porter Gifford/Gamma Liaison. 380: © Michael Rosenfeld/Tony Stone Images.

Chapter 11

382–383: © Dan McCoy/Rainbow. 386: (left) © Jean F. Stoick/Peter Arnold; (right) © Capital Features/The Image Works. 389: (top) © David Young-Wolff/Photo Edit; (bottom left) © Mike Yamashita/Woodfin Camp; (bottom right) © Bill Binzen/Rainbow. 390: © Jeff Greenberg/Rainbow. 393: © John Livzey. 394: © Richard Howard. 395: (left) © Richard Pasley/Stock Boston; (right) © Xinhua/Gamma Liaison. 397: (left) © David Young-Wolff/Photo Edit; (right) Courtesy Meyers Photo-Art. 398: © Tony Freeman/Photo Edit. 399: Bridgeman/Art Resource, NY. 400: © Sid Bahrt/ Photo Researchers. 402: (left) © Enrico Ferorelli; (right) © Alon Reininger/Woodfin Camp. 405: © David Woo/Stock Boston. 406: (top left) © Crandall/The Image Works; (top center) © Tom McCarthy/Photo Edit; (top right) © Dan McCoy/Rainbow; (bottom left) © Bob Daemmrich/Stock Boston; (bottom center) © R. Lord/The Image Works; (bottom right) © Lawrence Migdale/Stock Boston. 407: © Monkmeyer/Merrim. 409: © Srulik Haramaty/Phototake. 410: Reuters/Bettmann. 416: © Lawrence Migdale/Stock Boston. 418: © John Livzey.

Chapter 12

420–421: Paramount/Courtesy Kobal. 422: © Bob Daemmrich/The Image Works. 423: © Enrico Ferorelli. 428: © Betty Press/Woodfin Camp. 431: Archiv/Photo Researchers. 434: (top) © David Young-Wolff/Photo Edit; (bottom) © David Waite/Gamma Liaison. 435: © Erika Stone/Peter Arnold. 436: © Karsh/Woodfin Camp. 437: © Corbis/Bettmann. 439: © Bruce Ayres/Tony Stone. 443: © David XimenoTejada/Tony Stone. 446: © Bob Daemmrich/The Image Works. 447: © Christopher Morrow/Stock Boston. 453: (all) © Tony Freeman/Photo Edit.

Chapter 13

454–455: © Willie L. Hill, Jr./Stock Boston. 457: (left) © W. Hill, Jr./The Image Works; (center) © Corporal F. Stuart Westmorland/ Photo Researchers; (right) © Joel Gordon. 459:

© Matthew McVay/Tony Stone Images. **460:** © Lawrence Migdale/Stock Boston. **464:** (top) Courtesy of Columbia Tristar Television; (bottom) © Bill Gallery/Stock Boston. **467:** (left) Courtesy Nike Inc.; (right) © Don Smetzer/Tony Stone Images. **470:** © Bob Daemmrich/Stock Boston. **471:** © Johnny Crawford/The Image Works. **472:** © Monkmeyer/Schaefer. **474:** William Vandivert/Scientific American. **475:** © Jack Kurtz/Impact Visuals. **476:** © Washington Post-Frank Johnston/Woodfin Camp. **477:** (all) Stanley Milgram, 1965 "Obedience"/Penn State University. **480:** © Dominique Buisson/Photo Researchers. **481:** © Richard Pasley/Stock Boston. **482:** © Stewart Cohen/Tony Stone. **488:** (all) Courtesy Dr. Judith Langlois.

Chapter 14

490–491: © Monkmeyer/Goldberg. **493:** © Ex-Rouchon/Photo Researchers. **494:** © C. Fishman/Woodfin Camp. **495:** UPI/Corbis/Bettmann. **496:** © R. Kent Bailey/Tony Stone. **497:** Reuters/Corbis-Bettmann. **499:** © David Harry

Stewart/Tony Stone. **503:** (top) © Bob Daemmrich/The Image Works; (bottom) © Cathlyn Melloan/Tony Stone. **505:** © Bard Wrisley/Liaison International. **506:** UPI/Bettmann. **508:** © Bruce Ayres/Tony Stone Images. **510:** (top) Wellcome Dept. of Cognitive Neurology/Science Photo Library; (bottom) © Monkmeyer Press/Grunnitus. **512:** © Paul S. Howell/Liaison International. **513:** © Dr. R. Haier/Peter Arnold. **516:** © Martin Rogers/Stock Boston. **517:** © Monkmeyer/Kopstein. **522:** The Bettmann Archive.

Chapter 15

524–525: © Will & Deni McIntyre/Science Source. **527:** (left) © Hank Morgan/Science Source; (center) © Will & Deni McIntyre/Photo Researchers; (right) © Michael Newman/Photo Edit. **528:** The Bettmann Archive. **532:** © Will & Deni McIntyre/Photo Researchers. **533:** UPI/Corbis-Bettmann. **535:** The Bettmann Archive. **538:** Courtesy of The Institute for Rational-Emotive Therapy. **543:** (top) © Peter

Southwick/Stock Boston; (bottom) Archives of the History of Amlerican Psychology University of Akron. **544:** © Lester Sloan/Woodfin Camp. **551:** © Michael Newman/Photo Edit. **556:** Courtesy False Memory Syndrome Foundation.

Chapter 16

558–559: © Ed Pritchard/Tony Stone. **561:** (left) © Michael Newman/Photo Edit; (right) © Steven Peters/Tony Stone. **562:** © S. Purdy Matthews/Tony Stone Images. **566:** © Julie Marcotte/Tony Stone. **567:** © Rhoda Sidney/Stock Boston. **569:** © Monkmeyer/Collins. **571:** © D. Ermakoff/The Image Works. **572:** © William Cochrane/Impact Visuals. **573:** © Joel Gordon. **577:** © Lawrence Migdale/Tony Stone Images. **578:** © Seth Resnick/Liaison International. **581:** © Alon Reininger-Contact Press Images/Woodfin Camp. **582:** © Peter Menzel/Stock Boston. **583:** © Dan McCoy/Rainbow. **584:** © Jacques Chenet/Woodfin Camp. **585:** © Steven Peters/Tony Stone.

O THE OWNER OF THIS BOOK:

I hope that you have enjoyed *Psychology: The Adaptive Mind* as much as I enjoyed writing it. I would like to know as much about your experience as you would care to offer. Only through your comments and those of others can I learn how to make this a better text for future readers.

School:_____ Your instructor's name: _____

1. What did you like most about *Psychology: The Adaptive Mind*?: _____

_____

_____

_____

2. Do you have any recommendations for ways to improve the next edition of this text?

_____

_____

_____

3. In the space below or in a separate letter, please write any other comments you have about this book. (For example, were any chapters or concepts particularly difficult?) I'd be delighted to hear from you!

_____

_____

_____

_____

_____

_____

_____

_____

_____

_____

Optional:

Your name

May Brooks/Cole quote you, either in promotion for *Psychology: The Adaptive Mind* or in future publishing ventures?

Yes ☐   No ☐

Thanks!